D0252869

Opera

THE ROUGH GUIDE

Other Rough Guides music reference titles:

The Rough Guide to World Music
The Rough Guide to Jazz
The Rough Guide to Classical Music
The Rough Guide to Rock
The Rough Guide to Reggae

Credits

Editor: Jonathan Buckley
Proofreading: Margaret Doyle and Kate Berens
Design and image scanning: Henry Iles and Ben Rudder
Typesetting: Judy Pang
Production: Susanne Hillen

Author's acknowledgements

So many people contributed in some way to this book that it would be impossible to thank them all. However, most deserving of gratitude is Jonathan Buckley, without whose friendship, encouragement and wisdom the Rough Guide to Opera would never have seen the light of day. Thanks are also due to Joe Staines, Matthew Rye, Simon Broughton, Philip Tebbs, Nick Kimberley, Angelo Villani, Robert Wilson of Tower Records, Ivor Morgan of the Stockhausen Society, David and Ruth Summerfield, Mandy Little, Brian and Kath Watterson, and all those at Rough Guides who played a role in the creation of the book. Finally, I want to thank three special people for their support throughout its gestation: Keith Burstein, for his tireless friendship; my mother Bette, for her endless optimism and good humour; and Jill Watt, who first opened my eyes and ears to the joys of opera, and to whom this book is dedicated.

Editor's acknowledgements

The editor would like to thank the crucial Rough Guide staff and associates: Vanessa Kelly (picture research), Susanne Hillen (production), Henry Iles (design), Margaret Doyle and Kate Berens (proofreading), Joe Staines (editorial assistance) and Judy Pang (typesetting). Thanks also to all those who responsed to our never-ending requests for CDs, especially Victoria Bevan at Harmonia Mundi, Lucy Maxwell-Stewart at Deutsche Grammophon, Sophie Beck at Decca, Erica Worth at EMI, Pat Zaiger at Target, Celia Ballantine at Hyperion, Alf Goodrich at Nimbus, John Jones at Collins, Paul Westcott at Chandos, Mike Cox at Discovery, Karen Pitchford at Koch and Harriet Capaldi at Warner.

Publishing details

Published April 1997 by Rough Guides Ltd, 1 Mercer St, London WC2H 9QJ. Reprinted in September 1997.
Distributed by the Penguin Group:
Penguin Books Ltd, 27 Wrights Lane, London W8 5TZ
Penguin Books USA Inc., Hudson Street, New York 10014, USA
Penguin Books Australia Ltd, 487 Maroondah Highway, PO Box 257, Ringwood, Victoria 3134, Australia
Penguin Books Canada Ltd, 10 Alcorn Avenue, Toronto, Ontario, Canada M4V 1E4
Penguin Books (NZ) Ltd, 182–190 Wairau Road, Auckland 10, New Zealand

Typeset in Bodoni and Gill Sans to an original design by Henry Iles.
Printed in the UK by The Bath Press, Bath.

688pp.

A catalogue record for this book is available from the British Library.
ISBN 1-85828-138-5

Opera

THE ROUGH GUIDE

Written by
Matthew Boyden

With contributions from
Joe Staines, Matthew Rye, Simon Broughton,
Philip Tebbs and Nick Kimberley

Edited by
Jonathan Buckley

THE ROUGH GUIDES

CONTENTS

Chapter Five – Verdi, Wagner and their contemporaries

Chapter Six – Opera in Transition: The Generation of Puccini, Massenet and Debussy

Chapter Seven – The Era of Modernism

Chapter Eight – Opera since World War II

INTRODUCTION

The combination of music and drama is a thrillingly potent mix, but opera remains off-putting for too many people. Partly this is due to the social exclusivity cultivated by many opera houses, especially in the English-speaking world, but the sheer diversity of the music is also a factor. Thousands of operas have been written since Monteverdi and his colleagues pioneered the genre some four hundred years ago, and though many of these are no longer performed, the repertoire can still seem daunting. Opera-house schedules place late-Renaissance pageants alongside Italian melodramas or modern psychodramas, and the situation is even more perplexing when you look at the CD catalogue, where you'll find more than two hundred complete recordings of Verdi's operas, for example, and around thirty of *La traviata* alone. Whether you're new to opera or are already familiar with many of its masterpieces, **THE ROUGH GUIDE TO OPERA** is the essential guide through this mass of music, providing concise biographies of all the significant composers, incisive discussions of their major works, and definitive surveys of the recordings. On top of all that, it features a rundown of the world's best opera houses – after all, recordings are just a substitute for the real thing, and contrary to the popular image, live opera is not the preserve of the wealthy.

The entire history of opera is covered here, from its beginnings in late-Renaissance Italy to the latest exciting work from contemporary names such as John Adams and Judith Weir. Mozart, Wagner, Verdi, Puccini, Strauss and all the other greats are discussed in depth, as are lesser-known figures from Auber to Zimmerman. Of course, a completely comprehensive guide to opera, even one that restricted itself to opera on CD, would be impossibly unwieldy, so we've excluded some figures we regard as being peripheral, and we've been selective with the output of many composers, concentrating on what we think are the key operas. Gaetano Donizetti, for example, wrote more than seventy operas, but we've concentrated on the half-dozen you're likeliest to encounter either on disc or on stage. Similarly, we pick up Wagner's career with *The Flying Dutchman*, because it's this opera, his fourth, that marks the beginning of the work that makes him the most influential musician in the history of the genre. To this tally of the top rank we've added some composers who have been unfairly neglected, such as Zemlinsky, Busoni and Schreker, some operas that should be better known, such as Cavalli's *La Calisto*, plus a few masterpieces from the world of operetta, the half-sister of opera.

When it comes to CDs the situation requires far greater selectivity, for the CD era has brought with it a welter of new opera releases – though the bulk of these are re-issues of old recordings, with so-called "historic" items (which generally means pre-stereo) now being something of a boom area. There are two reasons for this glut of re-processed music. In the first place, with classical music rarely shifting units except when an event like the "Three Tenors" circus catches the attention of the TV cameras, few record companies can afford regularly to make a new studio recording of an opera. Most new opera sets are taped at a live performance and then digitally tidied up by the engineering virtuosos, which is a far cheaper process than getting soloists, orchestra and conductor into the studios for a long haul. The economics of opera are also relevant to the second point, which is that the older recordings are often better. More than ever before, opera – both live and recorded – is a celebrity business, and whenever a label does invest in a studio session, it's almost obliged to reduce the risk by building the set round stars who are in high demand all over the world. So you get a situation in which jet-setting singers and conductors might be appearing in London one night, Paris the next, then turning up in a New York studio for a few days to record something with people they hadn't met until the morning of the first session. Sometimes this system produces exciting results, but often it doesn't, and it's increasingly rare to find new recordings that have the sense of cohesion that was commonplace when record labels used to sign up an entire company to make recordings with a core cast and a single conductor.

And there's one other factor to take into account – the dearth of great singers for some types of opera. In the 1950s there were plenty of tenors capable of producing a memorable Otello; since the 1970s one singer has had a virtual monopoly of the role – Placido Domingo. The same problem affects Wagner singing: listen to a *Ring* cycle recorded back in the 1960s and you'll hear amazingly strong and passionate performances right through the cast; pick up a recent set, and you'll find weaknesses even in the major parts. However, the situation isn't as grim as some fogeyish critics like to make out. There are some fabulous young singers on the circuit, such as Angela Gheorghiu and Cecilia Bartoli, while conductors such as John Eliot Gardiner and Daniel Barenboim have shown time and again that every generation can find something fresh in the music that has lasted. On top of that, an upsurge of interest in early opera has been fuelled by ear-opening interpretations from a rising number of specialist groups and labels, and there are more top-flight Mozart singers at work today than at any time since the 1950s. Challenging new work is being written, and several opera producers are capable of putting on a show that's as exciting as anything in modern theatre. With a wealth of material old and new to explore, there has never been a better time to get into opera, and *The Rough Guide to Opera* is the book to take with you on your exploration.

How this book works

Because an understanding of the evolution of opera is important to an appreciation of the individual composers, this book is structured **chronologically**. Each chapter begins with an introduction that gives a broad overview of the period covered in the following pages, and picks out the key composers, each of whom is discussed in detail. Within each chapter the composers are arranged in chronological order as far as possible, though composers of the same nationality have been grouped together whenever that makes the story clearer – it would muddy the waters, for example, to split the section on Mikhail Glinka, the founding figure of Russian opera, from those on Mussorgsky, Tchaikovsky and their ilk, just because strict chronology demanded it.

The discussion of each **individual composer** begins with an introduction that gives the biographical essentials and the context, as well as picking out the **major works**. Each of these operas then gets a detailed section to itself, beginning with the dates of its composition and premiere, the name of the librettist, and a **synopsis**. After that comes a plain-speaking and entertaining discussion of the work, followed by our **CD recommendations**. For operas that are well-represented on disc, we have headed our CD listings with a **Recordings Overview**, which gives a brief survey of the alternatives to our selection and alerts you to excellent recordings that are currently out of print but may soon re-appear. In some instances we've also pointed out the existence of great live performances that are sporadically available on some small labels. (Every decent classical music store stocks a selection of these semi-legitimate – and often poor-quality – recordings, but finding them is a fairly hit-and-miss affair.) Our detailed recommendations are sometimes ranked in order of preference, but with opera it's not often the case that one recording stands head and shoulders above the competition – on some sets the singing might be the main attraction, while a rival performance features a more exciting orchestra. Anyway, no performance can be described as definitive, which is one reason why, wherever possible, we have recommended more than one set. Another reason is that the catalogue is in a state of perpetual flux, with sets disappearing from the lists then re-emerging a few years later, re-packaged and re-priced. Nearly every CD in this guide is available both in Europe and in North America, though not even the biggest stores will have all our recommendations in stock. In most cases you'll have to order your selection, either through your store, or a mail-order specialist, or through the Internet.

The CD **listings** conform to a regular format: soloists first, then chorus and orchestra, then conductor, with the record company, serial number and number of discs in parenthesis. (The serial number is generally the same in North America and Europe, except that the -2 suffix is usually dropped in North America.) Each listing is preceded by a symbol indicating the price range, as in the following listings for Verdi's *Il trovatore*:

Bergonzi, Stella, Cossotto, Bastianini; La Scala Chorus and Orchestra; Serafin (Deutsche Grammophon 445 451-2GX2; 2 CDs) = under £7 or $8 per disc

Bonisolli, Price, Cappuccilli, Obraztsova; Berlin Chorus; Berlin Philharmonic Orchestra; Karajan (EMI CMS7 69311-2; 2 CDs) = £7–10 or $8–13 per disc

Corelli, Tucci, Merrill, Simionato; Rome Opera Chorus and Orchestra; Schippers (EMI CMS7 63640-2; 2 CDs) = over £10 or $13 per disc

New recordings nearly always come out in the top price category. The majority of re-issues and historic recordings emerge as mid-price boxes, with documentation that is often less complete than first time round, though the essential component – the libretto – is nearly always included, both in the original language and in English translation if necessary. With budget-price re-issues, however, you often have to settle for a detailed synopsis only, though a few companies manage to cram a libretto into the package.

At the end of the book you'll find **directories of singers and conductors**, explaining who is best at what kind of music, and recommending a selection of recital and highlight discs. There's also a full **glossary** of opera-related terms, and a **directory of opera houses** across Europe, North America, Australia and New Zealand, with tips on the sort of repertoire in which they specialize and details on how to get hold of tickets – we've even included opera-house sites on the World Wide Web. *The Rough Guide to Opera* is not just the definitive buyer's guide to opera on CD, it's a guide for those who want to experience the most overwhelming form of drama in the flesh.

1

THE BIRTH OF OPERA

MONTEVERDI TO PURCELL

THE BIRTH OF OPERA

MONTEVERDI TO PURCELL

The major impetus behind the emergence of opera came from a series of largely theoretical discussions about the nature of Greek tragedy, conducted by the Camerata, a society of Florentine poets and musicians who met from about 1580. The Camerata sought to recreate what they supposed to be the musico-dramatic tradition of ancient Greece, but were hampered in their enterprise by knowing almost nothing of the substance, character and performance of Greek dramatic music: the only surviving example – a fragment from a chorus of Euripides' *Orestes* – was discovered after the first European operatic experiments. Opera's pioneers derived their inspiration from literary sources, primarily Aristotle, whose *Poetics* – itself written over a century after the works of Sophocles and Euripides – confirmed that music had played a significant role in the performance of tragedy: "Tragedy, then, is an imitation of some action that is important, entire and of a proper magnitude – by language rendered pleasurable. . . language that has the embellishments of rhythm, melody and metre . . . in some parts metre alone is employed, in others, melody."

So Greek tragedy was performed in a declamatory manner that resembled a semi-musical form of speech. That, at least, was the conclusion of the Florentine scholar Girolamo Mei, a regular correspondent with the two leading members of the Camerata: Count Giovanni Bardi, at whose house the Camerata met, and the musical theorist Vincenzo Galilei, father of the great astronomer. Hitherto, the predominant style of sixteenth-century vocal music had been polyphony, in which several independent lines of music were combined to create a rich and complex layer of overlapping sounds. Such music, Galilei argued, was inadequate to convey the meaning of the words being sung: and word-setting had become the major aesthetic issue for composers during the Renaissance. Madrigal composers, in particular, had become ever more inventive in the musical colouring of words, employing devices like a falling note to convey a sigh, or a clash of notes to suggest anguish. Indeed some composers saw a dramatic potential in the madrigal, and in madrigal cycles such as *L'Amfiparnaso* (The Slopes of Parnassus), written by Orazio Vecchi and performed in 1594, songs were presented in a sequence that made up a simple narrative. Galilei, however, felt that the ornate musical word-painting employed by the madrigalists was ridiculous. What he advocated was a type of monody – that is, a single line of music – in which the natural rhythms of speech were suggested and the words clearly enunciated.

The first significant composer to fully develop these ideas was Jacopo Peri (1561–1633), whose *Dafne*, written to a text by Ottavio Rinuccini and first performed in 1594, is generally regarded as the very first opera. Only fragments of *Dafne* have survived, but Peri's next collaboration with Rinuccini, *L'Euridice*, has fared better. In this work Peri was employing a new musical style of declamation, halfway between speech and song, in which the voice was accompanied by a bass instrument that often employed one sustained note until reaching a moment in the text that needed emphasis, at which point the note would change. The new style of singing was called "*stile rappresentivo*" or recitative; the accompaniment was called the continuo.

L'Euridice was written for the celebrations surrounding the marriage of Maria de' Medici and Henri IV of France in 1600, and festivities such as these played a crucial role in the evolution of the new genre. Eleven years earlier, Peri had contributed to the enormously lavish entertainments, devised by Bardi, in honour of another Medici wedding, that of the Grand Duke Ferdinando to Christine of Lorraine. On that occasion Peri provided music for one of the *intermedi* accompanying the comedy *La pellegrina* (The Pilgrim). *Intermedi* were musical interludes performed between the acts of a play, involving dance, song and often spectacular scenic effects, and early opera owed more to these diverting episodes than it did to madrigal cycles, even if – even at their most atmospheric – *intermedi* were essentially stylized allegorical tableaux rather than real dramatic narratives.

The use of music and drama in Christian worship was another influential feature of the culture within which opera was born. In the middle ages liturgical dramas such as the famous *Ludus Danielis* (Play of Daniel) had developed from dialogues inserted into the Easter Mass into fully staged, sung dramas. Such performances were a way of helping to make religious ideas and stories more vital and accessible, and by the middle of the sixteenth century the need for a more direct type of music making within the Catholic Church became increasingly urgent as the Protestant Reformation swept through Europe. Like Galilei, the Church authorities felt that polyphony was too abstract and rarefied a musical language to win hearts and minds, and at the same time as opera was emerging in Florence so too was a form of sacred music-drama called oratorio, named after the type of chapel, or oratory, in which it was performed. In 1600 Emilio de Cavalieri (1550–1602), the artistic supervisor of the Medici wedding celebrations of 1589, staged his own composition, *La rappresentatione di Anima et di Corpo* (The Portrayal of the Soul and the Body), at the Oratory of Santa Maria in Valicella in Rome: the world's first oratorio, it employed the same new recitative style as Peri had used in *L'Euridice*.

Opera's first undisputed masterpiece was staged at the Gonzaga ducal palace in Mantua in 1607. With *Orfeo* **Claudio Monteverdi** took the experiments of Peri and Cavalieri and transformed them into a convincingly dramatic whole. Borrowing ideas from the Camerata and the more ornate and dramatic tradition of Venetian sacred music, Monteverdi was the first to humanize his characters, loosening the narrow formality of the Florentine proto-operas. Meanwhile, in Rome, opera was following a slightly different course. In 1632 a lavish private opera house opened in the Palazzo Barberini with the performance of Stefano Landi's *Il Sant'Alessio* (Saint Alexis), the first opera to use an historical subject. Landi's music employed a fluid recitative style, but there were also several choruses, a dramatic dance (*un ballo*) at the end of each act, and most significantly an orchestral prelude (*sinfonie*) to each act – a forerunner of the operatic overture.

In 1637 the first ever public opera house, the Teatro San Cassiano, was opened in Venice, following a successful performance by a Roman opera group in nearby Padua. Monteverdi, whose early works had been lavish court entertainments, now began producing operas of a more dynamic, less esoteric nature: for his final opera, *L'incoronazione di Poppea* (The Coronation of Poppea), he abandoned the world of classical allegory in favour of a steamy, close-up view of aristocratic corruption in ancient Rome. Venice became Europe's main centre for opera, where it quickly developed into a genuinely popular art form. Plots became increasingly complicated and full of comic intrigue; the drama was divided into three acts, rather than five, to give it greater clarity; and more songs were included, to satisfy popular taste. These developments are evident in the work of Monteverdi's pupil **Pier Francesco Cavalli**, who, after his master's death in 1643, took over as the leading Venetian opera composer. In his hands the separation of recitative from song gradually became more distinct than in Monteverdi, paving the way for the great set-piece aria.

Largely through the agency of Italian touring companies, opera spread fairly rapidly throughout Europe, reaching Spain and Germany by 1627. In France it was not so readily received but when it did finally take root in the 1670s, it established its own traditions under the leadership of the composer **Jean-Baptiste Lully**. One reason for the delay was the supremacy of dance at the court of Louis XIV, where dances were more opulent and sophisticated than anywhere else in Europe – indeed the King's nickname of "Le Roi Soleil" derived from a performance in which he danced the role of Apollo. Italian opera did make occasional, ill-starred appearances in Paris: the expense of Luigi Rossi's *Orfeo* nearly led to riots in 1647, and fifteen years later Cavalli's *L'Ercole amante* took so long to reach completion and was so indifferently received (Lully's dance interludes were preferred) that its composer vowed to give up writing for the stage.

The decisive moment for French opera came in 1669 when the composer Robert Cambert (c.1627–77) and the poet Pierre Perrin received royal permission to set up the Académie Royale de Musique, which they inaugurated with *Pomone* in 1671. It was a spectacular success but unfortunately Perrin was soon in debt, at which point Lully, with typical opportunism, secured the opera patent for himself and consolidated his position as France's musical dictator. With his librettist, the tragedian Philippe Quinault, he produced sixteen operas, or *tragédies lyriques* as they were known, over the next fifteen years. Thus Lully virtually invented French opera, fusing the courtly ballet with the conventions of classical French tragedy into one enormous spectacle in which the setting, the scenic effects and the choreography were all as important as the music, and everything served to glorify the King.

Lully's virtual monopoly of French theatre music ended with his death in 1687, an event that opened the door to a far more talented composer, **Marc-Antoine Charpentier**. France's leading composer of sacred music, Charpentier also worked with the playwright Molière, in succession to Lully, and supplied the music for his most successful work *Le malade imaginaire* (The Hypochondriac). Even more significant were his sacred opera, *David et Jonathas*, written for a Jesuit college in 1687, and his one complete public opera, *Médée*, a work of far greater musical and emotional daring than anything by Lully, and arguably the finest of all seventeenth-century French operas.

As French opera grew out of the ballet, so English opera grew out of the masque, a form of allegorical court entertainment related to the French *ballet de cour*. The masque reached its apogee during the reigns of James I and Charles I, in the increasingly spectacular collaborations of the writer Ben Jonson and the architect and designer Inigo Jones. Only one court masque has survived in its entirety: James Shirley's *Cupid and Death*, with music by Christopher Gibbons and Matthew Locke. By a peculiar irony this was performed during the Interregnum (in 1653 and 1659), when the Puritans closed down all the theatres and banned public entertainments. Private musical entertainments of a morally improving nature were still permitted, however, and in 1656 William D'Avenant staged what is generally regarded as the very first English opera, *The Siege of Rhodes*, with music (now lost) by a variety of composers.

When Charles II was restored to the English throne in 1660, the ban on theatres was immediately lifted, two companies were licensed, and women were permitted to appear on the stage. Charles had developed a taste for French music while in exile, and in 1666 he employed Louis Grabu, a pupil of Cambert, as Master of the King's Music – much to the irritation of English composers. Grabu's collaboration with John Dryden, *Albion and Albanius*, turned out to be another false start in the attempt to establish opera in England. Commissioned in 1683, it had to be postponed when Charles II died, and when it was finally produced in 1685 its run was cut short by the panic caused by Monmouth's rebellion.

Opportunities for native-born composers to write operas were so scarce that in 1683 **John Blow** and Nicholas Staggins petitioned the King to allow them to set up "an Academy or Opera of musick for performing . . . therein their musicall compositions". Nothing seems to have come of it, but around the same time Blow composed his *Venus and Adonis*, which was performed first at court and later at a girls' school in Chelsea run by the leading dancing master of the day, Josias Priest. Priest's school was also the site of a performance in around 1689 of the only English operatic masterpiece of the period, *Dido and Aeneas* by **Henry Purcell**. But the lack of any known public performance of either of these works seems to indicate an almost total absence of public enthusiasm for operatic productions in England. What the English theatre-going public did have a taste for was the curious hybrid form known as semi-opera: essentially a play, with musical elements from the court masque inserted at the end of each act. Such pieces were produced by the actor-manager Thomas Betterton, first with the composer Matthew Locke (his *Psyché* was an adaptation of a Lully-Molière collaboration), and then, to even greater success, with Henry Purcell. When Purcell died in 1695, any hope that his efforts might have led towards the establishment of a national opera was gone. Less than ten years after his death the *Spectator* lamented: "At present, our Notions of Musick are so very uncertain, that we do not know what it is we like, only, in general, we are transported with anything that is not English: so if it be of a foreign Growth, let it be Italian, French or High-Dutch, it is the same thing. In short, our English Musick is quite rooted out, and nothing yet planted in its stead."

CLAUDIO MONTEVERDI

b. CREMONA, ITALY, MAY 15, 1567; d. VENICE, NOVEMBER 29, 1643.

Claudio Monteverdi has the strongest claim to be called the founder of opera. His works represent the culmination of an age of experiment, and through his efforts the monotonous nature of Florentine music-drama gave way to a dramatic experience in which musical resources were fully deployed in the service of a theatrical text. Only three of his nineteen stage works have survived, but their power and imagination make them the only early operas to have firmly established a place in the modern repertory.

Monteverdi was born in Cremona in northern Italy, the son of a pharmacist-physician. After studying with Marc'Antonio Ingegneri, the *maestro di cappella* at Cremona's cathedral, he joined the ducal court at Mantua in around 1590 and was employed there for over twenty years. This was a highly cultivated if somewhat claustrophobic working environment: Duke Vincenzo I was tyrannical, demanding and often late in paying his employees their derisory salaries, and Monteverdi frequently felt unappreciated. The Gonzagas were not one of Italy's most powerful families but they lived in great style, employing several important artists, including, at this time, the painter Rubens and, as their *maestro di cappella*, Giaches de Wert – one of the most expressively audacious madrigalists of the day, and a powerful influence on his young colleague.

Monteverdi is known to have travelled with the duke in Hungary and the Netherlands, and it is quite likely that he was in Florence in 1600 and attended the performance of Peri's *Euridice*. Seven years later, at the instigation of the duke's eldest son, Francesco, he composed his first opera, *Orfeo*, to a libretto by the court secretary Alessandro Striggio. In the same year the death of his wife, Claudia, a court singer whom he had married in 1599, sent Monteverdi into a profound depression. He returned to his father in Cremona but was summoned back to Mantua in 1608 to write a new opera, *Arianna*, and a dance-work with singing, *Il ballo delle ingrate*, both for the wedding of Francesco Gonzaga. *Arianna* was a huge success, but unlike *Orfeo* the music was never published, and only a fragment of it, the highly influential "Lament of Arianna", has survived. Monteverdi's unhappiness at court may have prompted him to write one of his greatest works, the *Vespers* of 1610, as a kind of calling-card signalling his availability. Dedicated to the Pope, the work is a compendium of his talents as a composer of church music, and it reveals, as do his operas, a willingness to mix different types of music within the one work: monody, madrigal-like choruses, florid ornamentation and echo effects are all combined into a highly varied and dramatic whole.

In 1612 Vincenzo Gonzaga died and his son Francesco – the new duke – dismissed Monteverdi, apparently without any notice. Once again he returned to Cremona before unexpectedly being offered the post of *maestro di cappella* at St Mark's in Venice, a position that made him the chief musician of the Venetian Republic and a person of honour with a salary commensurate to his ability. Initially administration took up much of his time, as did the task of raising the standard of the St Mark's choir, and after a while Monteverdi began to find the strain of his official position too demanding. Thus he began to employ assistants, including Cavalli, thereby freeing himself for other kinds of music. One of his most significant secular works from this period was *Il combattimento di Tancredi et Clorinda*, a dramatic scene in one act that was first performed at the Palazzo Mocenigo in 1624. Monteverdi took as its text a section from Tasso's chivalric epic *Gerusalemme liberata*, telling of a duel between a Christian knight and a Saracen woman disguised as a man. To recount the story more vividly, he employed a new, highly graphic and emotional musical language, the *stile concitato* or "agitated style", in which, for example, the sound of trotting hoofs and the clashing of swords was conveyed through imitative musical sounds. The premiere is said to have reduced its audience to tears.

Monteverdi continued to get commissions from the court at Mantua but he was less

LEBRECHT COLLECTION

Stozzi's portrait of Claudio Monteverdi

inclined to carry them out. A letter to Striggio about one proposed project indicates his priorities: "I have noticed that the interlocutors are winds. . . how can I, by such means, move the passions? Arianna moved us because she was a woman and Orpheus because he was a man, not a wind." By the late 1620s he had become less active as a composer, and in 1630 a large number of his operas were lost when Mantua was sacked by Austrian troops. Later the same year disaster struck again when Venice was ravaged by the plague, reducing its population by almost a third. Shortly after this Monteverdi took holy orders, and his final years might have passed away quietly but for the opening of the first public opera house, the Teatro San Cassiano, in Venice in 1637. His enthusiasm for opera was rekindled, perhaps at the instigation of Cavalli, who was closely involved in the running of the San Cassiano. During the remaining six years of his life he worked regularly for the stage, revising *Arianna* and composing several new works, of which only two, *Ulisse* and *Poppea*, have survived.

Orfeo

Orpheus

Composed 1607.
First performed February 24, 1607.
Libretto by Alessandro Striggio, after Rinuccini and Ovid.

Synopsis

Prologue

The spirit of music invites the audience to listen to the story of Orpheus (Orfeo), whose music could tame wild animals and conquer the underworld.

Act I

In the fields of Thrace the marriage of Orpheus and Eurydice (Euridice) is being celebrated. Orpheus sings a song of love and praise. The nymphs and shepherds share in his joy as they accompany him to the temple.

Act II

Orpheus sings to the woods but his mood of celebration is ended by the arrival of Sylvia, who tells him of Eurydice's death from a snake bite. He is overcome with grief but resolves to bring Eurydice back from Hades.

Act III

Orpheus is led by Hope (Speranza) to the gates of Hell, where she leaves him. At the River Styx he sings to the boatman Charon ("Possente spirto, e formidabil nume" – Powerful spirit, formidable god), who pities him but does not let him cross. After more singing from Orpheus, Charon falls into a deep sleep. Orpheus takes the oars and crosses the river.

Act IV

In Hades, Proserpine (Prosperina), who has heard Orpheus's music, begs her husband Pluto to allow him to return to earth with Eurydice. Pluto agrees on condition that Orpheus leads her out of the underworld without once looking back. On their journey home, Orpheus begins to doubt that Eurydice is behind him and, hearing a sound, he turns back and Eurydice vanishes before his eyes. Orpheus continues alone, accompanied by the lamentations of the chorus.

Act V

In the fields of Thrace, Orpheus pours forth his grief but is answered only by Echo. He vows to renounce women. His father, Apollo, descends from the skies in order to console him. Together they ascend to the heavens, where Orpheus will once again see Eurydice in the sun and the stars.

𝄞 *L'Orfeo, Favola in Musica* – Orpheus, a Legend in Music – was commissioned by the Accademia degl'Invaghiti, an aristocratic intellectual society of which both Striggio and Francesco Gonzaga were members, and was almost certainly performed in the Palazzo Ducale in Mantua, once on February 24, 1607, and again a week later. The myth of Orpheus and Eurydice had already proved a favourite for operatic treatment and remained popular long after: its simple narrative and strong emotions are perfect for a genre that deals in extremes, and, of course, the protagonist embodies the tranformational power of music. Furthermore, in Renaissance neo-Platonist philosophy the figure of Orpheus – who undergoes a kind of resurrection – was also identified with Christ, thus giving the tale an extra allegorical dimension. But although this opera may function on an esoteric level, its greatest strength is the directness of the story-telling and the humanity of its drama.

Both Monteverdi and Striggio were well acquainted with Peri and Rinuccini's interpretation of the myth, the influence of which is clear in the verse-based arias and declamatory recitative. And Striggio, like Rinuccini, changes the story from a harrowing tragedy into a reassuring pastoral – a poetic genre which had recently been given a new lease of life by the success of Guarini's poem *Il Pastor Fido* (The Faithful Shepherd). Whereas the ancient myth of Orpheus ends with his being torn to pieces by frenzied women, this version ends happily, though that doesn't seem to have been Striggio's original intention: in the libretto, published before the performance so that the audience could follow the words, he followed the myth exactly. For some reason, perhaps to satisfy courtly taste, a more reconciliatory ending was preferred.

In *Orfeo* Monteverdi follows Florentine precedent in making music the servant of the text. What makes him different from his forebears is the sheer inventiveness with which he pursues this end. Recitative is the dominant form of vocalizing, but it takes on many different guises, its flexibility deriving from the fact that the accompaniment is always subservient to the voice, which moves freely over the bass line. The aria, as a clearly distinct vocal style, is not apparent in *Orfeo* as it is in Monteverdi's later operas. Even the pivotal moment of the opera, "Possente spirto", when Orpheus employs all his musical skill in order to enter Hades, is hardly melodic in a modern sense – you would be hard pressed to sing along even after repeated hearings. Rather, what you hear is wonderfully ornamented declamation, almost certainly written with Mantua's star vocalist, Francesco Rasi, in mind. Ironically, Orpheus's singing works only because it sends Charon to sleep, a possible comment on inattentive Mantuan courtiers.

The strongest melodies in *Orfeo* are found in the *ritornelli*, the short instrumental passages that punctuate the drama, appearing before and after songs, and even between their verses. Their name indicates the fact that they return, and, indeed, the opening *ritornello*, which re-occurs at the end of Act II and at the beginning of Act V, takes on an almost emblematic function, signifying both the world of mortals and the healing power of music. At Mantua, Monteverdi had a richly supplied orchestra at his disposal and in *Orfeo*, the only one of his opera scores to be published, he often specifies which combination of instruments he requires: many of these choices seem to have been dictated by the practicalities of performance, but there is a clear distinction between the underworld, represented by darkly sonorous trombones, and the world of the living, which is scored mainly for strings.

However you look at *Orfeo*, it is an astonishing achievement for an art form still in its infancy, which makes it all the more surprising that for the planned celebrations for Francesco Gonzaga's wedding, scheduled for the following year, it was not Monteverdi who was asked to write a new opera, but a now-forgotten colleague of Peri, Marco da Gagliano.

RECORDINGS OVERVIEW

After its first run of performances, *Orfeo* went unperformed for almost three hundred years until 1904, when it was rediscovered by the composer Vincent d'Indy. The first complete recording was made in 1939 by Ferruccio Calusio for EMI/Angel; a more scholarly approach was evident in a recording by Discophiles Français in 1950, and five years later the first "period instrument" recording was made by Archiv. The real breakthrough came in 1968 with Harnoncourt's recording for Teldec, a decidedly unsentimental, "period" approach with lively speeds, a dry instrumental sound and skilfully executed ornamentation. Since then there have been at least nine more recordings, making *Orfeo* by far the most recorded of Monteverdi's operas. None of them has been ideal, largely because the title role is so packed with tricky ornamentation – notably the typically Monteverdian single-note *trillo caprino* or bleat, a vocal device in which a single note is rapidly reiterated. The somewhat unfocused Orfeo in René Jacobs' 1995 recording, for example, is the principal reason that this characteristically vivacious reading cannot be rated with the ones listed below. One of the role's most technically adept interpreters, Nigel Rogers, has recorded it twice: for Archiv in 1973 and for EMI in 1984. The first recording is marred by some rather ponderous instrumental playing, while the second goes to the other extreme, denuding the textures to the point of vulnerability. Even so, both are worth hearing for Rogers' virtuosic rendition of "Possente spirto" – an astonishing performance, if not a particularly moving one.

Ainsley, Gooding, Bott; New London Consort; Pickett.
(L'Oiseau Lyre 433 545-2; 2 CDs).

From the sparkling attack of the opening Toccata it is clear that this is going to be a highly spirited account. Pickett played the recorder on EMI's 1984 recording, a set that this one resembles in its preference for light textures, but far excels in the warmth of its playing. Pickett's sleevenotes give detailed reasoning about his choice of instrumental combinations, and the result communicates both the intimacy of the drama and its idyllic freshness. The dilemmas and emotions of the protagonists seem real and immediate, not simply because of convincing characterization but also because the instrumental colouring does so much to create a context for the action. Orpheus himself is a complex and self-absorbed character, qualities that are convincingly conveyed by John Mark Ainsley's finely judged performance, which more than any other communicates a real sense of Orpheus's power as a musician. Some of the supporting roles are markedly Anglo-Saxon in their vocal style (it is extraordinary that there are no Italian recordings of any Monteverdi operas), but Julia Gooding's delicate Euridice makes an ideal foil to Ainsley's more dynamic singing, and Catherine Bott subtly distinguishes her multiple roles of Music, the Messenger and Prosperina.

Kosma, Hansmann, Berberian; Vienna Concentus Musicus; Harnoncourt.
(Teldec 2292-42494-2; 2 CDs).

The earliest of Harnoncourt's two recordings has, in many ways, held up well over the years. Typically for this conductor, the approach is idiosyncratic and lively, with some particularly robust playing, as evident immediately in the opera's brilliant, fanfare-like Toccata – an opening that must have stunned its first audience. Things move along at a fair pace, with Harnoncourt treating the opening *ritornelli* very much as jaunty, courtly dances. There is also some unusually energetic and expressive singing from the choruses, notably in "Ahi, caso acerbo" (Ah, bitter occurrence), when Euridice's death is announced. Overall Harnoncourt's refusal to let authenticity undermine dramatic vitality is refreshing, but where it falls down is in his choice of soloists, which include both early-music specialists and more conventional operatic performers. By far the most satisfying singers are the versatile Cathy Berberian, doubling as the Messenger and Hope, and the ubiquitous Nigel Rogers in the relatively minor roles of second shepherd and first spirit. Rotraud Hansmann as Euridice and Music is fine, if a little predictable in her phrasing, but the gamble that doesn't come off is the choice of Lajos Kosma for the role of Orfeo, who alternates between bold declamation and Neapolitan crooning. "Possente spirto" – the real test for all who try this role – just fails to convince, and is marred by a very audible edit just after it begins. Too often Kosma sounds like a singer who would far rather be in an opera written about two hundred years later.

Il ritorno d'Ulisse in patria

The Return of Ulysses to his Homeland

Composed 1640.
First performed February 1640.
Libretto by Giacomo Badoaro, after Homer.

Synopsis

Prologue

Human Frailty recognizes its subservience to the power of Time, Fortune and Love.

Act I

In the palace of Ulysses (Ulisse) on the island of Ithaca, Penelope, Ulysses' wife, awaits his return from the Trojan wars, lamenting his absence to her nurse Eurycleia. Two lovers, Melantho (Melanto) and Eurymachus (Eurimaco), extol the joys of love. Ulysses is returned to Ithaca by Phaeacian sailors, whose ship turns to stone as soon as they have disembarked him; Ulysses wakens on the beach and is greeted by the goddess Minerva, disguised as a shepherd, who tells him that he has arrived home. He bathes in a sacred fountain and emerges as an old beggar in order to deceive his wife's suitors. Eumaeus (Eumete), a faithful swineherd, greets the disguised Ulysses, who tells him of his master's imminent return.

Act II

Eumaeus welcomes Ulysses' son Telemachus (Telemaco), who has returned with the help of Minerva, and introduces the boy to the old beggar. A ray of light reveals the beggar's true identity, and father and son are reunited. At the palace Penelope is seen resisting the advances of the suitors, who are unnerved to hear of Telemachus's return. Minerva offers Ulysses a plan for removing the suitors while Telemachus tells his mother of his recent travels. Ulysses appears, disguised once more as the old beggar, and is taunted by one of the suitors. After a fight, Penelope insists that Ulysses be welcomed and proclaims that she will marry whoever is able to string her husband's great bow. The suitors fail, leaving Ulysses to prepare the weapon, which he turns upon them.

Act III

Despite the massacre of the suitors, Penelope is not convinced that the old beggar is in fact her husband, and not even Telemachus can persuade her of the truth. Minerva and Juno plead with Jove on Ulysses' behalf and, after various proofs are given by Eurycleia and Ulysses, Penelope and her husband are reunited.

𝄞 *Il ritorno d'Ulisse in patria* was the first opera to be written by Monteverdi specifically for the public opera houses of Venice: it opened at the Teatro Santi Giovanni e Paolo early in 1640. Based on the last ten books of Homer's *Odyssey*, *Il ritorno* looks back to the classical world and courtly elegance of *Orfeo*, and yet it inhabits a far more rugged landscape than its pastoral predecessor, one peopled by somewhat more complex characters, albeit still at the mercy of the Gods. Like Orpheus, Ulysses is a hero who strives to be reunited with his wife, but he is a warrior not an artist, and his struggles are more physical than metaphysical. But Monteverdi's librettist, the Venetian patrician Giacomo Badoaro, by opening the opera with the trauma of Penelope's twenty-year abandonment, provides an ambivalent view of Ulysses' heroics. Badoaro also supplies the opera with elements that were already popular with Venetian audiences, like the special scenic effects of the Phaeacian's ship turning to stone, and the comic incidental characters, like the glutton Irus.

Monteverdi's musical response to this text was to an extent governed by his change of circumstances. He no longer had the splendid facilities of Mantua to call on, but instead had to work with a small pit orchestra that typically comprised about five strings, two theorbos (large lutes) and two harpsichords. (The two surviving manscripts are both incomplete and neither of them indicates specific scoring, tempi or dynamics, and so these decisions are largely at the discretion of the conductor.) The instrumental *ritornelli* that were such an integral part of *Orfeo* have all but gone, and the choruses are greatly reduced. Instead there is much more emphasis on the exposed voice, either solo or in duets and trios: the final love duet between Penelope and Ulysses, with which the opera ends, was the prototype for a standard item of Venetian opera. Recitative still dominates and is used in several of the opera's most

A VENETIAN NIGHT AT THE OPERA

Gaze down from the cheap seats at many of the world's great opera houses and you'll see a fair number of people who would appear to be less interested in the music than in the company they are keeping. This situation is not new – and at least today's high-society clientele generally go quiet when the lights go down. In seventeenth-century Venice, as elsewhere in Europe at that time, a night at the opera was a social function above all, with the customers talking and walking throughout the performance, at times drowning out the sound of the singers and players. The focus of the action was not so much the stage as the boxes, where the city's shakers and movers gathered to conduct their business. As one eyewitness recorded, the opera box "became simply another room in a rambling mansion, the obvious means of cramming as many people into a confined space, yet preserving the amenities of a civilised social life. . . . The French ambassador assured a friend that it is necessary for all diplomats to attend the opera regularly because there it was possible to discover the secrets which would be concealed from them in the ordinary course of events." Those of less exalted status were forced to stand on the ground-floor level, a stifling space in which the music-lovers had to contend with a contingent of fops whose primary concern was the presence of other similarly dedicated narcissists. Here, as in the boxes, a symphony of gossiping supplied an almost constant accompaniment to the evening's entertainment.

It's remarkable that anyone was able to treat the opera as just so much background music, for the impresarios of Venice lavished as much money on their shows as any Broadway producer. What follows is a description of Manelli's *Andromeda*, staged in Venice's first public opera house, San Cassiano, in 1637, within a year of its opening.

"The scene was entirely sea. In the distance was the view of water and rocks. So contrived that its naturalness (although feigned) moved the spectators to doubt whether they were in a theatre or on a real sea shore. The scene was quite dark except for the light given by a few stars which disappeared one after another, giving place to Aurora who came to make the Prologue. She was dressed entirely in cloth of silver with a shining star on her brow, and appeared inside a very beautiful cloud which sometimes grew large and sometimes small. . . . Then Juno came out on a golden car drawn by her peacocks, blazing in a coat of cloth of gold with a superb variety of jewels on her head or in her crown. . . . One saw the scene change from a seascape to a wood so natural that it carried our eyes to the life to real snowy heights, real flowering countryside, a regal spreading wood and unfeigned melting of water. . . . The scene turned in a moment from the wood to the seascape. Neptune appeared and Mercury came out to meet him in a wonderful machine. Neptune was on a great silver shell, drawn by four sea-horses and a sky-blue mantle covered him. . . . to the tune of a sweet melody of instruments Astrea appeared in the sky and Venus in the sea: one in a silver cloud and the other in her shell drawn by swans. . . .The scene changed to a woodland and Andromeda came out with her train. Six of her ladies, for joy of killing a boar, did a light and wonderful ballet with such varied and different weaving of paces that truly one was able to call it a leaping labyrinth. . . . The palace disappeared and we saw the scene entirely of sea with Andromeda bound to a rock. The sea monster came out. The animal was made of such beautiful cunning that, although not real, he put people in terror. Except for the act of tearing to pieces and devouring he did everything as if alive and breathing. Perseus arrived on Pegasus, and with three blows of a lance and five with a rapier he overthrew the monster and killed it. . . . The sky opened and one saw Jove and Juno in glory and other divinities. This great machine descended to the ground to the accompaniment of a concerto of voices and instruments truly from heaven. The two heroes, joined to each other, it conducted to the sky."

There's an element of press-release mentality to this account, but the extravagance it evokes was not uncommon at the time. Indeed, many of Venice's sixteen opera houses, linked as they were to individual factions of patronage, were able to spend mad sums of money on presenting with extraordinary flair what were frequently poorly prepared and direly sung works of music.

powerful moments, like Penelope's Act I monologue and her presentation of Ulysses' bow to the suitors ("Ecco l'arco d'Ulisse") in Act III. Arias are much more clearly defined than before and although Penelope has just one ("Illustratevi o cieli"), at the end of Act III, it is surely the emotional highpoint of the opera, possessing a poignancy unmatched by anything in *Orfeo*.

With *Il ritorno d'Ulisse* Monteverdi rose magnificently to the challenge of writing for a relatively uninitiated audience: the convoluted plot, with its vivid episodes and use of disguise, make the opera an unprecedently theatrical event, and – more importantly – the allegorical elements of his earlier work have given way to palpably human relationships.

RECORDINGS OVERVIEW

Ulisse is the least recorded of Monteverdi's operas, with just four sets having been issued since the first, now very dated performance from Vox in 1964. Two of these were lively and invigorating recordings from Harnoncourt, one made in 1971 and the other in 1981, of which the earlier is available on CD – it's reviewed below, along with the contrasting interpretation from René Jacobs. Raymond Leppard's Glyndebourne productions of early Italian opera did so much to re-establish them in the repertoire, but his 1979 recording of *Ulisse* for CBS can't be recommended: his habit of filling out Monteverdi's sparse scoring with an anachronistically large string section is at its least convincing here, although Frederica von Stade makes a powerful and moving Penelope.

Prégardien, Fink, Högman, Hunt; Concerto Vocale; Jacobs.
(Harmonia Mundi HMC 901 427.29; 3 CDs).

Ulisse is a more epic work than *Orfeo* and would seem to demand a more "operatic" performing style. Under the direction of René Jacobs, it gets just such a reading here. As with most of his opera recordings, this one derives from a stage production, and a lot of his musical decisions are a result of theatrical expedients. In a defensive sleevenote essay, Jacobs justifies his deployment of a rich variety of instruments (it sounds better) and the plugging of musical gaps with other music (it gives the work more coherence, and it was done in Monteverdi's day). The result is more successful than otherwise, with some wonderfully sensuous sounds emerging out of the instrumental combinations in the opening sinfonia. This is a very much darker and fuller sound-world than that created by Harnoncourt, and the singers are correspondingly more expressive. Bernarda Fink's Penelope borders on the neurotic, but the commitment of her performance pays off in the sheer cumulative intensity of the final scene, when Ulysses (a sweet-toned but rather young-sounding Prégardien) tries to convince her of his identity and she is torn between the desire to believe and her sense of honour. The recording's one drawback is an occasional loss of energy and spontaneity.

Hansmann, Lerer, Eliasson; Concentus Musicus Wien; Harnoncourt.
(Teldec 2292-42496-2; 3 CDs).

The lack of a published score means that performances of *Ulisse* vary much more drastically than is the case with *Orfeo*. Harnoncourt could not be more different from Jacobs: true to the conditions in Monteverdi's Venice, he employs a fairly small orchestra, and the performance is directed as if the audience were close enough to the action to warrant restraint. This works well at the beginning of the opera – Penelope's long lament has a certain gravity for not being more overtly expressive – but the emotional temperature never really rises, with the result that by the end of the opera, when Penelope and Ulysses are finally united, you have long since given up caring about Norma Lerer's etiolated Penelope and Sven Olof Eliasson's woolly and unfocused Ulysses. More enjoyable are the comic roles: with Irus's parody lament being rendered very broadly (but very musically) by Murray Dickie, and the secondary lovers, Melantho and Eurymachus, proving rather more compelling than Ulysses and Penelope.

L'incoronazione di Poppea

The Coronation of Poppea

Composed 1643.
First performed autumn 1643.
Libretto by Giovanni Francesco Busenello, after Tacitus and Suetonius.

Synopsis

Prologue

Fortune, Virtue and Cupid argue over who is the most powerful. Cupid claims his superiority will be proved by the ensuing story.

Act I

At Poppea's Palace, Otho (Ottone), who loves Poppea, discovers that she is sleeping with the Emperor Nero (Nerone). The guards on duty complain of Nero and Poppea's adulterous behaviour. The two lovers enter and bid each other a fond farewell; Arnalta, Poppea's nurse, warns her to be careful. At the Emperor's palace, Nero's wife Octavia (Ottavia) is filled with despair by her husband's actions ("Disprezzata regina"). The philosopher Seneca arrives and tries to console her. The goddess Pallas Athene warns Seneca of his impending death, which he stoically welcomes. Nero arrives and informs Seneca that he wishes to divorce Octavia: Seneca tries to dissuade him. Nero's anger is calmed by Poppea, who suggests that Seneca be killed. Otho attempts a reconciliation with Poppea but she scorns his advances. He thinks of killing her, but instead turns his attention to Drusilla, who has long been in love with him. Otho swears his love to Drusilla but he still loves Poppea.

Act II

Seneca is told that he must die. Ignoring the pleas of his friends, he orders them to prepare the bath in which he will kill himself. Nero and the poet Lucan celebrate Seneca's death. Octavia tells Otho that he must disguise himself as a woman and kill Poppea. Drusilla agrees to lend him some of her clothes. Otho attempts to murder Poppea as she sleeps but is stopped by Cupid. The awakened Poppea thinks the fleeing Otho is Drusilla. Cupid sings of his success.

Act III

Drusilla celebrates the expected death of Poppea but is arrested for attempted murder and is sentenced to death. She protests her innocence but when Otho begins to confess his guilt she changes her story and both admit the plot. Nero banishes them, along with Octavia, whose complicity he has discovered. Nero tells Poppea that she will be crowned Empress the same day. Octavia makes her final, grief-stricken appearance, and Arnalta triumphs in her mistress's success. Poppea is crowned Empress and as the opera ends Nero and Poppea sing of their love.

Monteverdi's last opera is the first Venetian opera to be located in the realm of history rather than that of mythology (although divine intervention continues to take place), and it inhabits a comprehensively different world from that of *Orfeo* or *Ulisse*: a world of sensuality and depravity, in which power is exercised without responsibility and lust triumphs over reason. It is also the most complex of Monteverdi's operas, with a cast of more than twenty characters (including several comic roles), all of whom are affected by Poppea's unrelenting ambition and Nero's infatuation with her. Busenello's libretto is outstanding, but his motive for seeming to celebrate immorality has often been discussed. His intellectual background – he was a member of the libertine Accademia degli Incogniti – was of a decidedly free-thinking nature, and his main source for *Poppea* was the historian Tacitus, whose writings, it has been suggested, provided the Venetian intelligentsia with a model for the presentation of the reality behind the masks of the great and beautiful. Few of the original audience would have been unaware that Poppea was kicked to death by Nero while pregnant with his child: a fact that makes the meltingly beautiful love duet that closes the opera grimly ironic.

The music for *Poppea* is more lyrical and contains more arias than Monteverdi's previous operas, but the narrative is still carried along by recitative. One of the great moments of the work is Octavia's first appearance when she sings the lament "Disprezzata regina", a recitative pushed to the limits of expressiveness, in which changes of mood are indicated by changes of speed, and the use of rests between repeated phrases adds to the dramatic naturalism. Unsurprisingly the most sensuous lyricism occurs in the scenes between Nero and Poppea, with their final love duet "Pur ti miro" justly celebrated as one of the supreme moments of seventeenth-century opera. Unfortunately the music is almost certainly not by Monteverdi nor the words by Busenello: Benedetto Ferrari, a contemporary of Cavalli, is usually credited with both, while other sections of the opera, the opening sinfonia for example, have been attributed to Cavalli himself. This is a measure of the freedom with which impresarios treated operas, but it doesn't alter the fact that *Poppea* is the greatest achievement of Venetian opera, and the nearest it gets to the early ideal of a play enhanced by music. From here on music starts to assert itself as the dominant partner in opera's collaborative equation – increasingly to the detriment of clear meaning, if not of emotional impact.

RECORDINGS OVERVIEW

Like *Ulisse*, *Poppea* was a late starter in the studio, and it was not recorded until 1963, when Rudolf Ewerhart conducted a heavily cut edition for Vox. The following year EMI recorded Pritchard and the Glyndebourne company in another drastically edited version. The first complete recording was prepared and conducted by Nikolaus Harnoncourt in 1974, and this remains the benchmark. Mysteriously, Richard Hickox's fine performance for Virgin was deleted within a few years of its release: it deserves to be brought back into the catalogue, not least for Arleen Augér's Poppea and the Nero of Della Jones. The casting of Nero is a major issue for conductors, since the balance of voices can drastically alter the thrust of the work. Originally the role would have been sung by a castrato, but it is now usually performed by a mezzo-soprano, occasionally by a tenor, and sometimes even by a counter-tenor.

Donath, Söderström, Berberian, Lucciardi; Vienna Concentus Musicus; Harnoncourt.
(Teldec 2292-42547-2; 4 CDs).

This recording has one major drawback, and that is the expense of four full-price CDs, but the performance is worth it, especially for the quality of the soloists. As with his *Orfeo*, Harnoncourt goes for big voices in the main roles, and this time, with one exception, it works triumphantly. Elizabeth Söderström and Helen Donath make a well-matched Nero and Poppea, brilliantly conveying the obsessive nature of their love. Cathy Berberian shines as a particularly involved Octavia, a psychological portrait of great subtlety and depth which brings out the conflicting impulses of duty and the desire to be avenged. Only Giancarlo Luccardi lets the side down, his clotted tone and unwieldy approach conveying nothing of Seneca's calm nobility. The instrumentation is slight but effective, and Harnoncourt balances his forces well to produce one of his finest opera recordings.

McNair, Von Otter, Hanchard, Chance; English Baroque Soloists; Gardiner.
(Archiv 447 088-2; 3Ds).

If theatricality is what you want, this is the pick of the bunch – recorded live in 1993, it has unsurpassed vitality and immediacy. Using the Naples manuscript of Poppea, with new ritonelli from musicologist Peter Holman, Gardiner conducts an orchestra that's smaller than on the rival sets, pushing the voices into sharp relief. Sylvia McNair is a very sexy Poppea and Diana Hanchard is an imperiously hard Nero, but Octavia and Otho practically steal the show, as is so often the case. Anne Sofie von Otter is especially moving in her long farewell to the city and her friends.

Borst, Laurens, Larmore, Schopper; Concerto Vocale; Jacobs.
(Harmonia Mundi HMC 90 1330/2; 3 CDs).

Jacobs prepared his own edition of the score, in which he made a number of textual transpositions and some cuts. He also interpolates a number of sinfonias by Monteverdi's contemporaries during scene changes or character entrances. The end result is a performance that's less grand than Harnoncourt's but of great charm and drama, in which the cast succeed, as no other, in bringing an improvisatory touch to the recitatives. Guillemette Laurens' level-headed Nero is an interesting contrast to Söderström's burning intensity, while Danielle Borst's enthusiastic Poppea comes across as more of a bimbo than a machiavel, making the work seem

less claustrophobic than is customary and lending the final duet a sweetness and nonchalance that was probably more effective on stage. The outstanding performance is Jennifer Larmore's Octavia, not as twitchy as Berberian but no less dignified. Though not as overwhelming an experience as Harnoncourt's performance, this one has a vigour and an intimacy that are highly refreshing.

PIER FRANCESCO CAVALLI

b. CREMA, ITALY, FEBRUARY 14, 1602; d. VENICE, JANUARY 14, 1676.

By the middle of the seventeenth century the Venetian mania for opera was already at its height, with sixteen opera houses in operation to satisfy public demand. Cavalli, a pupil of Monteverdi, was quick to exploit the situation: in 1639 he signed a contract with the Teatro San Cassiano which involved him in running the company as well as composing for it, a position that must have made him acutely sensitive to the needs of his audience. Cavalli was the first composer to set out to produce an accessible, repeatable operatic formula, and though he's not of the same stature as Monteverdi, his best works have a vitality and a dramatic atmosphere that makes them effortlessly accessible and enjoyable.

Cavalli's first teacher was his father, Giovanni Battista Caletti, the maestro di cappella of Crema cathedral. In 1616 Cavalli was taken to Venice by the governor of Crema, Federico Cavalli, whose name he adopted. Before his involvement in the theatre, Cavalli gradually rose through the ranks at St Mark's, beginning as a fifteen-year-old singer, becoming second organist in 1639, and first organist six years later. As in the case of Monteverdi, working at St Mark's was not regarded as being incompatible with writing for the theatre, although by the time Cavalli finally attained the ultimate

CASTRATI

The castrato came into being at around the same time as opera. Throughout the Middle Ages the Church had upheld Saint Paul's injunction to "Let your women keep silence in the churches" by using children and falsettists (counter-tenors) for choral music. It's not known exactly when their ranks were joined by castrated adult males, but they seem to have become commonplace by the middle of the sixteenth century, though the earliest castrati whose names have survived were Pietro Folignato and Girolamo Rossini, who were drafted into the Sistine Chapel choir in 1599.

If medical assistance could not be afforded, the child's mother usually conducted the operation, which was recorded by the French lawyer Charles d'Ancillon, who wrote one of the first books about castration. The testicles were removed by "putting the patient into a bath of warm water, to soften and supple the parts, and make them more tractable. Then the jugular veins were pressed, making the party so stupid and insensible that he fell into a kind of apoplexy." The knife was warmed before the cut was made, and opium was sometimes administered to calm the victim, despite the fact that this palliative was more likely to kill the child. Castration of one's offspring was technically punishable by death or excommunication, but the Church was prepared to believe the stories of childhood mishap – an attack by a dog, a kick from a horse, or, most common of all, a bite from a wild pig – that virtually every castrated soprano offered to explain his mutilation. Powerless to reverse the dreadful deed, choirmasters took the view that the unfortunate child might as well be put to good use. These uses were initially exclusively church-bound, and a top-class castrato could earn good money if he agreed to remain faithful to one diocese. Such was the allure of the potential income that by the end of the sixteenth century some four thousand children were being castrated annually in Italy alone, according to one estimate, and the number may well have been as great in Spain. The Church was soon full to overflowing with male sopranos, and supply would have far outstripped demand had Peri's *Euridice* not revealed the opportunities for stardom in the new genre of opera. From 1600 until the time of Mozart, the castrato was an essential component of opera, and in their eighteenth-century heyday the castrati commanded astronomical fees – it was not rare for a star castrato to be paid one hundred times more than the best-paid orchestral player.

But only a tiny number of castrated children ever found fame or fortune – after all, losing your testicles was no more guaranteed to make you a great singer than buying a paint-box was certain to make you a great painter. Other consequences of amputation were more predictable: the castrato could expect to develop uncommonly thick hair on his head but remain bald everywhere else; he was certain to suffer from obesity and grow rapidly upwards, often reaching far greater than average height (the ludicrously mannered poses of many castrati were adopted to counter their ill-formed gait); his face would be inclined to a crimson corpulence; and his chest would become abnormally developed – hence the freakish breath control demonstrated by the successful castrati, who were able to hold a single line of music for up to two minutes.

Another aspect of the adult castrato's life remains controversial. Marriage for castrati was banned by both Catholics and Protestants, but many of them seem to have been singularly popular as consorts for both sexes. Modern endocrinology suggests that the sexual activities of the castrati could not have involved the use of their undeveloped genitals, so there remains some doubt as to what exactly they got up to. But there is no doubt that some retained their sexual drive while presenting no risk of conception, and enjoyed a thriving parallel career as high-class prostitutes.

position of maestro di cappella in 1668, his career as an opera composer was largely over.

From Monteverdi Cavalli had learned a lyrical tenderness which he was to maintain throughout his career. But opera was now subject to the vagaries of public taste, and its emphasis changed regularly throughout the seventeenth century. To keep costs down, impresarios reduced the size of the orchestra and the role of the chorus, thus placing ever increasing emphasis on the solo singer. At the same time music was ceasing to be the servant of the libretto as it had been for both the Camerata and for Monteverdi. Cavalli's early operas are still dominated by recitative but this was supplemented by a more lyrical form known as arioso, which stood halfway between recitative and aria, and increasingly by arias themselves. Songs, or arias, were initially employed sparingly in Venetian opera, as episodes of contemplation or emotional outpouring outside of the dramatic narrative – this is how they are used in Monteverdi and in Cavalli's earlier works. But by the 1660s opera had become aria-crammed at the expense of narrative integrity, and although Cavalli succumbed to the public's craze for arias, he didn't go far enough to prevent two of his later works from being rejected by anxious impresarios.

Cavalli's most important librettist was the poet Giovanni Faustini, who was also the impresario of San Cassiano. The ten operas they produced together are among the most artistically successful of Cavalli's output, if not necessarily the most popular during his lifetime. The typical Cavalli-Faustini opera abandoned mythology for invention (*La Calisto* is the exception to this rule), combined comic and tragic elements, and usually involved two pairs of noble lovers having to overcome cruel hardships and complex emotional entanglements before perfect happiness can be attained. It's a world not dissimilar from that of Shakespeare's comedies, and one that encompassed a wide range of human emotions, giving Cavalli plenty of opportunities to display his skill at conveying pathos.

At the time of Faustini's death in 1651, the new trend was for semi-historical plots, exemplified by the work of Nicolò Minato, with whom Cavalli wrote three operas, the most successful of which was *Xerse* in 1654. By 1660 Cavalli's fame was so great that he was invited to Paris by Cardinal Mazarin to write an opera, *L'Ercole amante*, for the wedding of Louis XIV to Maria Teresa of Austria. He reluctantly accepted. It was an enormously lavish production, with ballet interludes written by Lully, but the premiere was delayed until 1662 by a series of disasters (his *Xerse* was performed as a stopgap), and it was received with little enthusiasm. Dejected by this failure, Cavalli entered semi-retirement until 1668, when he was persuaded to return to work. By now his style was outdated and the fickle Venetian public largely ignored him, but he retained his position at St Mark's until his death, by which time he had amassed a considerable fortune and a substantial number of opera scores (including works by Monteverdi).

Giasone

Jason

Composed 1649.
First performed 1649.
Libretto by Giacinto Andrea Cicognini.

Synopsis

Prologue

Apollo and Cupid debate the outcome of the drama that is about to unfold. Apollo champions Medea as a wife for Jason, while Cupid supports the cause of Hypsipyle.

Act I

Hercules (Ercole) has persuaded Jason (Giasone) to abandon his betrothed, Hypsipyle (Isifile), and continue his quest for the Golden Fleece. Jason finds himself on Colchis, where he becomes the lover of the Queen Medea without realizing her identity. Medea returns Jason's love and rejects her betrothed Aegeus (Egeo). Orestes (Oreste), a friend of Hypsipyle, tries unsuccessfully to cross-examine Demo, the stuttering servant of Aegeus. Medea and Jason meet and, to his delight, she identifies herself as his lover and the mother of his two children. Employing her supernatural powers, Medea invokes Pluto ("Dell'antro magico") to assist Jason in his quest.

Act II

Hypsipyle waits for news of Jason. On learning of Jason's love for Medea, she resolves to go to Colchis. Meanwhile Jason captures the Golden Fleece, after killing the monsters who guard it. On the journey home the Gods wreck Jason's and Medea's ship and bring them to Hypsipyle's island home in order to ensure Jason's marriage to her. When she appears, Jason denies all knowledge of her and claims she is mad.

Act III

Jason is persuaded to kill Hypsipyle by the jealous Medea, and orders Besso, one of his guards, to carry out the murder. But the plan goes wrong and Besso throws Medea into the sea instead of Hypsipyle. She is saved by Aegeus and is forced to acknowledge his fidelity as he swears revenge on Jason. As Jason sleeps, Aegeus attempts to kill him but is stopped by Hypsipyle. Seeing Hypsipyle alive, Jason is told by Besso of the death of Medea. Medea appears, accompanied by Aegeus, and encourages Jason to return to Hypsipyle but he refuses. However, Hypsipyle's lament ("Infelice, che ascolto") wins him back and the opera ends in joyful reconciliation.

𝄞 *Giasone* became one of the most popular operas of the seventeenth century, spreading the new genre throughout Italy and Europe, but it is difficult to see quite why it was such a huge success while *La Calisto* was a comparative failure. Both have mythological plots (after Orpheus, Medea must be the most overworked of mythological tales in opera), but Cicognini takes even greater liberties with his source (the *Argonautica* of Apollonius) than Faustini does with his, adding a wealth of comic types, including Demo the stuttering servant and Delfa the old nurse of Medea, and giving the story a happy ending. Cicognini cleverly integrates the different elements of his bewilderingly complex plot, so that the romantic intrigues of the comic characters run in parallel to those of the supposedly noble principals. In general the quality of Cicognini's verse is higher than Faustini's, although the humour can be crude, reflecting how quickly operatic scenarios had moved away from the overriding sense of decorum that prevailed in Monteverdi's stage works.

Giasone marks the point in the development of Cavalli's operatic style when recitative and aria become quite clearly separated, with the former being employed for moving the action along, while the latter is reserved for moments of reflection or decision, often in the manner of a soliloquy. A fine example of Cavalli's aria style comes with the opera's most dramatic moment, at the end of Act I: for Medea's incantation to the spirits of the underworld, Cavalli employs a simple, repeated chordal accompaniment over which Medea's powerful arpeggios build to a frightening climax. In marked distinction, the rather insipid Hypsipyle gets to sing mostly recitative and arioso, albeit of a quite passionate nature; her biggest moment is the lament in Act III, which begins as an aria over four descending notes in the bass, but develops into recitative as it becomes more impassioned. For the comic roles Cavalli uses a less mellifluous style, setting the text syllabically for Delfa's aria in Act I, and again, to great comic effect, for Demo's patter song in the same act.

Mellon, Dubosc, Banditelli, Chance, Fagotto; Concerto Vocale; Jacobs. (Harmonia Mundi HMC40 1282/4; 3 CDs).

This recording, issued in 1988, has recently been deleted but it would be well worth trying to track down a copy. As with his Monteverdi recordings, Jacobs produces a marvellously theatrical performance. The Concerto Vocale, with its light but generous timbre, is a wonderfully fluent force under Jacobs' direction – a former singer himself, he is an outstanding handler of singers, allowing them a great deal of scope to express themselves. Employing the original vocal registers, Michael Chance (alto) and Gloria Banditelli (contralto) present fluid and passionate portrayals of Jason and Medea, but Catherine Dubosc's soprano is not so well cast as the wronged Hypsipyle, and the gravity of her lament is only barely suggested. Gianpaolo Fagotto's Demo, however, is a treat, making much of his character's stuttering patter-song, and Dominique Visse (a Jacobs regular) makes an hilarious Delfa. Jacobs has made some cuts to the score (and one self-penned addition), but this does not detract from the character and energy of the performance.

La Calisto

Callisto

Composed 1651.
First performed November 1651.
Libretto by Giovanni Faustini, after Ovid.

Synopsis

Prologue

Nature and Eternity celebrate those mortals who have climbed the path to immortality. Destiny insists that the name of Callisto (Calisto) be added to the list.

Act I

Jove (Giove) and Mercury (Mercurio) are visiting Arcadia. Jove sees the nymph Callisto, a follower of Diana, the virgin goddess of the hunt, and attempts to seduce her. She resists his advances, but finally succumbs when he disguises himself as Diana. Meanwhile the real Diana, because of her vow of chastity, cannot return the love of the beautiful shepherd boy Endymion (Endimione). Diana is supported by one of her nymphs, the elderly Lymphea (Linfea), who secretly yearns for a husband but spurns the advances of a young satyr.

Act II

On Mount Lycaeus Endymion sings to the moon, the symbol of Diana. As he sleeps Diana covers him with kisses. He awakes and they sing of their love. Jove's infidelity is discovered by his wife Juno, while Diana's secret is found out by Pan, the god of the forest, who has long desired her. Endymion is persecuted by Pan and his satyrs.

Act III

The Furies turn Callisto into a bear at the command of the outraged Juno. Jove sadly confesses all to Callisto: she must live the rest of her life as a bear but eventually he will raise her to the stars. Diana rescues Endymion and they agree that kissing will be the extent of their love-making. Jove, Mercury and Callisto celebrate Callisto's ascension to the heavens.

Though not a success on its premiere at the Teatro San Apollinare, *La Calisto* is today the most frequently performed of all Cavalli's operas. Even so, it deserves to be better known: its excellent libretto – Faustini's ninth for Cavalli – combines two stories from Ovid's *Metamorphoses* and turns them into something that at times resembles a *Carry On* film, with much sexual innuendo, cross-dressing and furtive coupling. In doing this Faustini was simply forcing classical legend, which was no longer very popular on the stage, into the shape of the comedy of sexual intrigue, which was. Cavalli matches his librettist for inventiveness, employing different types of music for different characters: sensual sweetness for Callisto ("the words are sweet but the tune is lewd" is how Mercury describes one of her arias); opulent lyricism for Diana and her lover Endymion, heard at its most beautiful in Endymion's song to the moon, "Lucidissima face"; and punchy arioso recitatives for Pan and his satyrs, which effectively suggest a completely alien culture (analogous to the conventional representation of servants).

As in *Giasone*, much of the dramatic momentum and wit of the piece is created by changes of pace and switches of musical style. In the scene when the satyrs, having captured Endymion, are threatening to kill him, his plaintive arioso entreaties are met with a lyrical, rustic serenade, "Miserabile", sung by his tormentors – a particularly black piece of irony. The popularity of the love duet with Venetian audiences was such that Jove and Callisto are given two, the first an extraordinarily rhapsodic exchange of short phrases, very close in feeling to the end of *Poppea*.

Faustini died during the run of this opera, which may explain its mysterious lack of success. And with Faustini gone, Cavalli's later operas – though still full of beautiful music – failed to combine their miscellaneous dramatic elements quite as successfully as *Calisto* and *Giasone*.

Bayo, Lippi, Pushee, Mantovani; Concerto Vocale; Jacobs.
(Harmonia Mundi HMC 901515.17; 3 CDs).

As in his previous recordings of seventeenth-century opera, Jacobs has no qualms about filling out the textures (though not to the extent of Leppard) and adding instrumental music by other composers when it seems appropriate. On this recording it works to perfection, and Jacobs reveals *La Calisto* as a dramatic masterpiece. Each separate domain of the opera – the Gods, the mortals and the satyrs – is clearly defined, and the casting is strong in every role. As Jove, Marcello Lippi is a *tour de force*: using his natural voice, a warm baritone, when playing Jove himself, and a comical but not unpleasant falsetto when disguised as Diana. Maria Bayo's Callisto is appropriately languorous and sweet-toned, and Graham Pushee's Endymion is close in timbre to James Bowman but rather sparer in tone. Perhaps the one small disappointment is Alessandra Mantovani as Diana, whose hard tone and slight wobble mean that her scenes with Endymion, though good, are not as enjoyable as they should be. Even so, this is one of the very best recordings that Jacobs has made.

Baker, Bowman, Cotrubas, Trama; Glyndebourne Festival Chorus; London Philharmonic Orchestra; Leppard.
(Decca 436 216-2; 2 CDs).

Much of the credit for the Cavalli revival can be ascribed to Raymond Leppard, who from the late 1960s edited and directed a number of his operas at Glyndebourne and elsewhere. Far from being grateful, many musicologists regard his editions, which are heavily cut and use highly romanticized orchestration, as bordering on the criminal. Do not let that put you off. This recording, made in 1972, is well worth hearing, above all for the sublime combination of James Bowman (Endymion) and Janet Baker (Diana), both in their vocal prime. Their scene together at the start of Act II contains some wonderful singing that is absolutely in keeping with the suppressed eroticism of Cavalli's music. It's true that, at times, the lushness of the string sound is closer to *fin de siècle* Vienna than seventeenth-century Venice, but it perfectly matches the full-blooded approach of the singers.

JEAN-BAPTISTE LULLY

b. FLORENCE, NOVEMBER 28, 1632; d. PARIS, MARCH 22, 1687.

Few men have dominated any artistic milieu to the extent that Lully dominated the French music scene during the reign of Louis XIV. Through his friendship with the King and some unscrupulous wheeler-dealing, he managed to achieve almost complete control of the musical life of Paris and Versailles. Between 1672 and 1687 he was the sole composer of French opera, and thus was entirely responsible for forging a national operatic style: a style that was rooted in formal and grandiose court spectacle, yet at the same time was concerned to convey the language of his libretti in as clear and direct a fashion as possible.

MARY EVANS

The mighty Jean-Baptiste Lully

Lully was born an Italian but went to France at the age of fourteen as a servant to a cousin of Louis XIV. Though an outstanding violinist, he first attracted attention as a dancer and a mime, performing alongside the young King in a piece called *Le Ballet de la nuit* in 1653 (the King played the part of Apollo). In the same year he joined the royal household as Composer of the King's Instrumental Music, and over the ensuing decade he composed several *ballets de cour* – spectacular court entertainments in which elaborate and varied dances were interspersed with vocal music and burlesque scenes. In 1664 Lully began his successful collaboration with the playwright Molière, in a new genre, the *comédie-ballets*, devised by Molière to rejuvenate the *ballet de cour*. The *comédie-ballet* combined a spoken text with dance interludes that were inserted between each act, an arrangement in which music and text had equal weight. In their last work together, *Le Bourgeois Gentilhomme*, the two elements were very closely integrated, but Lully seems not to have been interested in taking the plunge into opera, apparently thinking that it was an essentially Italian genre and unsuited to the entirely different demands of the French language. The success of *Pomone* by Cambert and Perrin in 1671 persuaded him to change his mind.

Lully's burgeoning musical empire received its crowning glory in 1672 with his purchase of the exclusive right to produce opera, following the financial collapse of Cambert and Perrin's venture. The first theatre of Lully's Académie de Musique was a converted tennis court, but with Molière's death in 1672 he moved rent-free into the theatre of the Palais Royal. For the next fifteen years Lully produced an opera per year, mostly to libretti by the tragedian Phillipe Quinault. Their success and Lully's unrivalled power – he even forbade music in the marionette theatre – made him many enemies. One resentful entrepreneur, Henri Guichard, allegedly tried to poison him by putting arsenic in his snuff. More damaging were reports of Lully's taste for young boys, which reached the ears of the King, who threatened to make an example of him. His death was a bizarre mixture of grandeur and farce: conducting his own *Te Deum*, composed to celebrate the King's recovery from illness, he jabbed one of his toes with the stick he was using to beat time. A gangrenous abscess developed but he refused amputation and died – an immensely wealthy man – some two months later.

During the reign of Louis XIV, French art existed almost exclusively for the glorification of the monarch. Lully's music was therefore primarily an instrument of flattery, illuminating the transcendental magnificence of "Le Roi Soleil". The King himself possessed little musical talent, but frequently dictated the subject and style of operatic commissions. Most of Quinault's plots were presented as allegories of the royal character, ennobling aspects of the human condition "personified" by Louis. Five acts long, they were introduced by sycophantic prologues that highlighted recent events in the King's life, and invariably had nothing to do with the ensuing drama. The vicissitudes of love were presented in the form of well-known mythological or chivalric plots. Comic scenes were unusual, but supernatural elements regularly occurred, providing wonderful opportunities for elaborate scenic effects.

Two important innovations were developed by Lully. The first involved the creation of a type of fluid recitative which was more melodious and varied than the Italian model. Supposedly derived from the declamatory style of actors performing the verse tragedies of Racine and Corneille, Lully's recitative placed the poetic language very much in the foreground and helped to move the narrative along. Arias, or airs as they were called in France, were barely distinguishable from recitative. The second innovation was the introduction of what became known as the French overture: an introductory piece of instrumental music in two sections: the first slow and stately, the second more animated and usually fugal. Nearly every subsequent French opera until the nineteenth century included an overture that followed this format.

Unlike his counterparts in the Venetian opera, Lully had considerable funds for staging his works, for the magnanimity and splendour of the absolutist monarch was reflected not just in the subject matter of the opera but in the production values too. (Extravagance was not a uniquely French quality – in Vienna, for example, a spectacular 1668 staging of Cesti's *Il Pomo d'Oro* lasted eight hours and contained no fewer than twenty-three scene changes.) The profligate resources at his disposal did not prevent Lully from imposing an incredibly tight discipline in the production of his operas. Neither the instrumentalists nor the singers were permitted to improvise any ornamentation, for everything was controlled by Lully in the cause of his own notions of dramatic unity. The dances, a highly popular element of the opera, became more closely integrated into the proceedings, and from *Atys* (Attis) onwards all subplots were abandoned, along with comedy and burlesque. The result is a resolutely serious form of music-drama, which often, to modern perceptions, collapses into banality and pomposity. Lully is nowadays rarely produced outside of France, but at their best his works have a formal integrity and stately elegance that can be deeply satisfying if rarely overwhelming.

Atys

Attis

Composed 1676.
First performed January 10, 1676.
Libretto by Philippe Quinault, after Ovid.

Synopsis

Prologue

Time, in his palace, promises fame to the glorious hero (Louis XIV). Flora joins the celebrations. Melpomene, the tragic muse, is united with Flora in order for the drama of Attis (Atys) to unfold.

Act I

In the land of Phrygia, Attis awaits the arrival of the earth goddess Cybele (Cybèle). Sangaride, due to be married to King Celaenus (Célénus), sings of her unrequited love for Attis. Seeing her distress, Attis confesses that he too loves her. Cybele descends in her chariot.

Act II

Attis and Celaenus cannot decide which of them will be the High Priest for Cybele. Cybele also loves Attis and selects him to be High Priest, confessing that it was for him and not Celaenus's marriage that she descended to earth.

Act III

At the instigation of Cybele, Attis falls into a dream-filled sleep in which he hears songs of love but also warnings of danger should he deceive the gods. He wakes to find Cybele at his side ready to comfort him. Sangaride begs Attis to prevent her marriage to Celaenus, and he promises to support her. Cybele, suspecting their love, laments her fate.

Act IV

Sangaride thinks that Attis no longer loves her, but he reassures her and they celebrate their love. As the High Priest of Cybele, Attis calls off the wedding of Sangaride and Celaenus.

Act V

Cybele and Celaenus plot revenge against the lovers. The goddess places Attis under a spell and, in his delusion, he murders Sangaride, thinking her to be a monster. After regaining his reason, Attis tries to take his own life, and Cybele turns him into a pine tree. She laments the loss of her one true love, and the opera ends in desolation.

Atys, the fourth collaboration between Lully and Quinault, was first performed before King Louis at Saint-Germain-en-Laye and quickly established a reputation as the King's favourite opera, enjoying several revivals. The story, derived from Ovid, is a tragedy of unrequited love and Divine discontent, and is one of the few of Lully's works that ends in disaster for all the protagonists. But Cybele, the goddess at the centre of the drama, is not a malevolent figure, even though she is the direct cause of the final suffering: rather she is a figure of human dimensions, racked by inner conflict and doubt.

There is much fine recitative in this opera, notably Atys's avowal of love for Sangaride in Act I, but perhaps the most striking aspect of the work is Lully's atmospheric and descriptive orchestral music. Famously, Act III contains a divertissement on the subject of Sleep, which begins with a gently soothing passage for recorders and strings, then develops into a series of solos and ensembles for Sleep and his followers. Pleasant dreams then appear and inform Attis of Cybele's love for him; they are followed by baleful dreams who warn Attis not to resist the goddess, in a chorus of rapidly repeated chords. Lully frequently employs the chorus like that of a Greek tragedy, commenting on events as they unfold. This is typified by the moment when Attis stabs Sangaride: the chorus tries to warn him of what he is about to do, but fails to save him from his error, passing their final judgement –"Atys lui-même fait perir ce qu'il aime" (Atys, you have killed the one you love) – with music of grave and moving solemnity.

Mellon, de Mey, Laurens, Rime; Les Arts Florissants; Christie.
(Harmonia Mundi HMC90 1257-9; 3 CDs).

There is no doubt that Lully's *tragédies lyriques* are an acquired taste. There is plenty of beautiful music, and the stories are engagingly extreme, but the stately decorum and formality preclude much sense of danger and excitement. But if anyone can make a persuasive case for this music, William Christie can: his characteristically bright and colourful approach is memorably employed throughout this typically convincing Les Arts Florissants recording. The ensemble's strong and earthy timbre may occasionally lack tenderness but this recording is full of personality, and Christie's flexible, spontaneous direction is marvellously imaginative. The casting is exceptional: Guy de Mey's effortless tenor brings beauty and substance to the mercurial character of Attis, Agnès Mellon's well-nourished soprano is perfectly suited to Sangaride's equable disposition, and the chorus sings with polish and refinement.

Armide

Armida

Composed 1686.
First performed January 15, 1686.
Libretto by Philippe Quinault, after Tasso.

Synopsis

Prologue

Wisdom and Glory discuss their rivalry: in wartime Glory is supreme, but in peacetime Wisdom rules.

Act I

In a square in Damascus the sorceress Armida (Armide) receives praise for having beguiled and captured a band of crusaders. However, she has been eluded by Rinaldo (Renaud), the most formidable of the crusaders, who is resistant to her charms. Her uncle, Hidraoth, King of Damascus, begs that she turn from war to love, but she swears that she will only marry the conqueror of Rinaldo. News arrives that Rinaldo has freed the captured crusaders.

Act II

In nearby countryside Rinaldo is enchanted by demons sent by Armida and Hidraoth, and he sings of the beauty of his surroundings. Armida is determined to kill Rinaldo, but on seeing him she is filled with love. Demons transport them both to a desert.

Act III

Armida recognizes that Rinaldo's love for her is reliant upon magic. She summons Hatred to help expunge her love, but then relents.

Act IV

Two knights are sent to find Rinaldo. They are armed with magic weapons which enable them to overcome monsters and resist the spirits sent to seduce them.

Act V

In Armida's enchanted palace, Rinaldo and Armida sing of their love. She leaves him, surrounded by pleasures, but the two knights arrive and release him from her charms. Armida returns and fruitlessly implores Rinaldo to stay. Left alone, Armida rages with mounting desperation before summoning demons to destroy her palace.

Armide, the last of Lully's *tragèdies lyriques*, is generally reckoned to be his greatest dramatic achievement. Quinault's libretto is based on episodes from Tasso's *Gerusalemme liberata*, a chivalric verse epic that was extremely popular with composers at the time – indeed, the story of Rinaldo and Armida had been set several times before Lully's version. *Armide* has much in common with *Atys*: both contain extraordinary *sommeil* scenes, in which the hero is lulled into a deep sleep in order to be beguiled, and both contain a female protagonist with supernatural powers who is rejected by the object of her desire, thus precipitating her fury. But the character of Armida is a more rounded one than Cybele, with far greater psychological depth. The role was first performed by Marie Le Rochois, one of Lully's regular singers, who created a sensation with her very first entry and whose final desperate arioso – a *tour de force* of emotional abandon – produced a profound effect on its first audience. The Lully-Quinault recitative reaches its peak in this opera, and the internal conflict expressed by Armida as she attempts to kill the sleeping Rinaldo was regarded by eighteenth-century writers, including Rameau, as the absolute model of the form. The opera's ending was unique among Lully's works in that, although it contained a spectacular *coup de thèatre* in the destruction of Armida's palace, its closing moments were intimate and tragic – despite the fact that Rinaldo has escaped the sorceress's clutches.

Laurens, Crook, Gens, Rime, Deletré, Ragon; La Chapelle Royale; Collegium Vocale; Herreweghe.
(Harmonia Mundi HMC901456.57; 2 CDs).

No recording of a Lully opera can represent anything like the totality of the proceedings, but this elegant and persuasive performance goes a long way to making Lully's music seem dramatically feasible on its own. There is a great deal of contrast and variety here, ranging from the sprightly rhythms of the ever-present dance music to the meltingly beautiful prelude at the beginning of the third scene of Act II. Herreweghe, whose reputation is as a choral conductor, is well served by his soloists, with the forceful Guillemette Laurens brilliant at conveying the ambivalent emotions of Armida, nowhere more powerfully than in her final scene, which wavers between rage and despair. Howard Crook's Rinaldo is necessarily a rather bloodless characterization, but he has an unerringly elegant sense of the music's line.

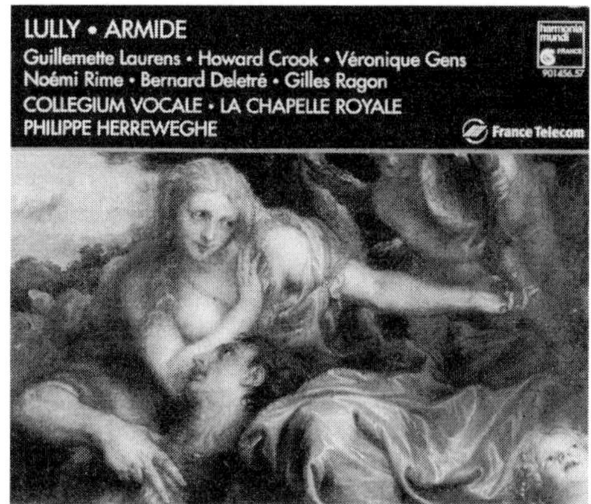

LULLY • ARMIDE
Guillemette Laurens • Howard Crook • Véronique Gens
Noémi Rime • Bernard Deletré • Gilles Ragon
COLLEGIUM VOCALE • LA CHAPELLE ROYALE
PHILIPPE HERREWEGHE
France Telecom

MARC-ANTOINE CHARPENTIER

b. PARIS, some time between 1645 and 1650; d. PARIS, FEBRUARY 24, 1704.

Lully's domination of musical life at the court of Louis XIV was such that he could thwart the career of anybody he saw as a rival. One such person was Charpentier, who in the course of a long life, spent mostly in Paris, failed to win even the smallest court appointment, despite his widely recognized skill as a composer. Even so, his career was hardly one of abject failure, and in the field of sacred music he produced an extremely varied but consistently brilliant body of work. His training took place in Italy and, whereas Lully gradually expunged the Italian elements from his style, Charpentier succeeded in reconciling an Italianate expressiveness with the simpler and more formal language of French music.

Little is certain about Charpentier's early life. He was born in Paris and is known to have been in Rome in the mid-1660s, where he studied with the leading oratorio composer Carissimi, whose music was famous for its ability to stir the emotions. Back in Paris he served a series of aristocratic patrons, beginning around 1675 with the Duchess of Guise, a woman noted for her piety and for the magnificence of her musical establishment, which Charpentier directed and sang in as a counter-tenor. For the Duchess, Charpentier wrote several musical dramas, including the short one-act works *Actéon* and *Les arts florissants*. These escaped the vigilance of Lully simply because they were private entertainments, performed at the Hôtel de Guise in the mid-1680s.

Before joining the household of the Duchess of Guise, Charpentier had begun working with Molière, whose association with Lully had ended in 1672. Charpentier composed music for two of Molière's *comédie-ballets*, including his greatest success *La malade imaginaire* (The Hypochondriac), in which the verbal dexterity of the text is wonderfully served by the wit of the music. Charpentier continued to work for the Comédie-Française after Molière's death in 1673, producing music for some twenty-six works over the next twelve years, despite Lully's ever more restrictive rules on the use of musicians in the theatre.

In the 1680s he was on the fringes of the court, serving the dauphin as music director and acting as teacher to the Duke of Chartres, but illness intervened when he seemed close to an appointment at the Royal Chapel. It was also in the 1680s that Charpentier gained the position of composer and *mâitre de musique* of the main Jesuit church of St Louis, a position described by the lexicographer Sébastien de Brossard as "among the most brilliant in French musical life". For the leading Jesuit college of Louis-le-Grand, Charpentier wrote two sacred operas, *Celse Martyr* (now lost) and *David et Jonathas*. These were fully staged works in the manner of a Lullian *tragédie lyrique* but, not surprisingly, with rather less dance music. *David et Jonathas* was performed in 1688 as an *intermède* to the spoken play *Saul*, telling the same story from a different perspective. Charpentier stayed at St Louis until 1698, when he took up a similar position at Saint-Chapelle du Palais, an ecclesiastical appointment second only to the directorship of the Royal Chapel at Versailles in importance and prestige.

Charpentier's only secular opera, *Médée*, was first performed at the Académie Royale de Musique in December 1693. A critical but not a popular success, it ran only for ten performances, despite winning the approval of the King. Although it followed the conventional Lullian pattern, audiences may have been disturbed by the way the emotional complexity of the plot was underlined by far richer and more vivid harmonies than they were accustomed to with Lully. Sébastien de Brossard thought *Médée* was "the one opera without exception in which one can learn the things most essential to good composition" and believed that its unenthusiastic reception was due to "a cabal of the envious and ignorant". *Médée* was published the next year, and given a further performance at Lille in 1700; thereafter it more or less disappeared from sight, waiting until relatively recent times for proper re-assessment and revival.

Médée

Medea

Composed 1693.
First performed December 4, 1693.
Libretto by Thomas Corneille.

Synopsis

Prologue

Various rustics sing the praises of Louis XIV and call down Glory, Victory and the goddess of war. Victory tells how she resides in France because of the country's wise ruler who desires to bring peace to the world.

Act I

The sorceress Medea (Médée) and her husband Jason are in Corinth, under siege from the Thessalians for plotting against their King. Creon (Créon), King of Corinth, has allied himself with Orontes (Oronte), Prince of Argos, by promising him that he can marry Creon's daughter Creusa (Créuse). Medea rightly suspects Jason of loving Creusa.

Act II

Medea is asked to leave Corinth by Creon, since his people fear her presence. Creon proceeds to encourage the love between Jason and his daughter.

Act III

Medea warns Orontes about Jason and Creusa who, it emerges, are to marry with Creon's blessing. Medea infuses with poison the robe she has promised to give to Creusa.

Act IV

Creusa enters wearing the robe but the poison has not yet taken effect. Medea tells Orontes that the marriage between Jason and Creusa will not take place. She warns Creon that unless his daughter marries Orontes, she will never leave Corinth. Creon attempts to arrest her but Medea turn his guards against each other and invokes her magic powers to drive the King mad.

Act V

Creusa begs Medea to restore her father's sanity. Medea agrees but the news arrives that Creon has killed Orontes and then himself. Creusa seeks vengeance, but Medea makes the poison in her robe begin to work. Upon finding the princess dying, Jason swears revenge, but is mocked by Medea who tells him that she has killed their children. The opera ends with Medea's destruction of the palace.

In many ways the first audience of *Médée* must have felt that they were on familiar territory. Here was a *tragédie lyrique* about a sorceress who creates havoc when scorned, with Lully's star singer, Marie Le Rochois, in the title role, and his chief designer Jean Berain providing the scenery and costumes. But Charpentier was not Lully's disciple, he was Lully's rival and, despite their outward similarities, there are marked differences between *Médée* and a work like *Armide*. First of all Thomas Corneille's treatment of the classical story, unlike his brother Pierre's famous play, starts with Jason and Medea's life in Corinth, just as Medea starts to suspect her husband of infidelity. This has been criticized for producing an undramatic first two acts, but it allows the characters to be built up through small, detailed touches, and the momentum slowly gathers pace before the maelstrom of evil at the end of Act III.

Medea's story is one of the great crimes of passion, and Charpentier responds to the narrative's wide range of emotions with an extraordinary variety of orchestral colour, vividly suggesting the various shifts of mood and feeling. There is much use of chromaticism and dissonance for underlining, a markedly Italianate effect which is positively shocking after the buttoned-up charm of Lully, and it was almost certainly this indecorous expressiveness that incurred the wrath of the still influential supporters of Lully.

Hunt, Deletré, Zanetti, Padmore; Les Arts Florissants; Christie.
(Erato 4509-96558-2; 3 CDs).

The serious revival of interest in Charpentier is largely due to the advocacy of the American conductor William Christie, who has such affection for Charpentier's opera that he's recorded it twice, with different companies. In 1985, with Harmonia Mundi, he produced a polished if over-careful account of an incomplete score, which was followed nine years later by this more complete version for Erato. This time round, the spice and colouring are especially pronounced, illuminating textures and cross-rhythms that the earlier recording failed to capture. Lorraine Hunt's soprano is light but she uses her voice with great intelligence to convey Medea's disintegration from devoted wife and mother to murdering avenger. The scene in Act V in which she justifies to herself the killing of her children is brilliantly judged and genuinely chilling. Mark Padmore's Jason is sweet-toned and direct and his voice combines well with the superb Creusa of Monique Zanetti, notably in her death scene; there are moments, though, when you feel that Jason, for all the character's weakness and vacillation, ought to be a little more forceful. The orchestral playing is outstanding, and overall the sound is extremely well balanced.

JOHN BLOW

b. NEWARK, ENGLAND, probably 1649; d. LONDON, OCTOBER 1, 1708.

John Blow's importance as a composer has been largely eclipsed by the genius of his younger contemporary and sometime pupil, Henry Purcell. This situation is compounded by the fact that Blow's one opera, *Venus and Adonis*, was only rediscovered in 1902, by which time Purcell's near-contemporary work, *Dido and Aeneas* – which had been largely modelled on Blow's work – was firmly established as an English classic. The inevitable comparisons between the two operas have consistently favoured Purcell, but *Venus and Adonis* is very much more than an historical curiosity: it contains much striking and original word-setting and an extremely moving denouement, of which Venus's lament and the subsequent chorus form a memorable climax.

Although he wrote other secular works, including incidental music for the theatre, it is as a composer of sacred music that Blow is best known. Today his most frequently performed work is almost certainly the Latin anthem *Salvator Mundi*, a strongly atmospheric work full of harsh and disturbing dissonances. Blow's career was inextricably bound up with both church and court, beginning in the early 1660s when he became one of the Children of the Chapel Royal (a chorister in the King's private chapel at St James's Palace) under the tutelage of Captain Henry Cooke. This was very much a musical hothouse, in which Blow's contemporary, the precocious Pelham Humfrey, shone as the brightest talent. Humfrey was to be granted a scholarship for foreign travel, thus providing an important link between his English colleagues and the latest musical developments in France and Italy.

In 1667 Blow was presented to the diarist Samuel Pepys, with whose son he performed unaccompanied songs. Betraying more than a hint of jealousy, Pepys noted that although the young Blow was gifted with "extraordinary skill", his voice would "make a man mad, so bad it was". The following year, at the early age of nineteen, he was appointed organist at Westminster Abbey, a post he held until 1679, when he was succeeded by Henry Purcell. Despite Pepys's poor opinion of his voice, he became a Gentleman of the Chapel Royal in 1674 and later the same year he succeeded the recently deceased Pelham Humfrey as both Master of the Children of the Chapel Royal and Composer-in-Ordinary for Voices at Court, positions he was to hold for the remaining 34 years of his life.

As Master of the Children of the Chapel Royal, Blow was responsible for both the general as well as the musical education of the boys under his care. Among these was Henry Purcell, who continued under Blow's instruction even after he had left the Chapel Royal. Both men seem to have benefited from their long association: Blow's later songs seem consciously modelled on those of his younger colleague, and one of his most eloquent works is his setting of Dryden's *Ode on the Death of Mr Henry Purcell.* If Blow was a less profound composer than Purcell, he was often a more startling one, and both the *Ode* and *Venus and Adonis* are full of quirky and unpredictable shifts in harmony.

Venus and Adonis was first performed at court, possibly in Oxford, in the presence of King Charles II. The exact date is uncertain, but the part of Venus is known to have been played by the actress Mary Davies, one of the King's discarded mistresses, while that of Cupid was performed by their illegitimate daughter, Lady Mary Tudor. The Children of the Chapel Royal appeared as the little Cupids. The rather cynical and licentious nature of the text (in the Prologue Cupid associates constancy with ugliness) can be read as a celebration of Charles II's hedonistic court or, conversely, as a gently satirical rebuke and a reminder to Charles of his responsibilities. Perhaps the fact that Lady Mary Tudor was granted an annuity of £1500 in 1683 is not a coincidence. One year later, in April, *Venus and Adonis* was given another performance at the girls' school in Chelsea run by the dancing master Josias Priest, with Priest's daughter taking the part of Adonis. There is no evidence that the opera was ever shown to a wider public.

Venus and Adonis

First performed c. 1682.
Libretto by unknown writer (possibly by Aphra Behn), after Ovid.

Synopsis

Prologue

Cupid, accompanied by a group of shepherds, sings of the power of Love.

Act I

Venus and Adonis are seen embracing on a couch. The sound of a hunt is heard, and Venus eventually persuades the reluctant Adonis to join in the boar-chase.

Act II

Venus and Cupid discuss the arts of love and teach a group of infant Cupids how to spell. After a dance, the Graces enter and perform a suite of dances during which the Cupids adorn Venus.

Act III

Venus is distraught as Adonis is brought in, mortally wounded by the boar. She implores the Gods to have pity on her, but Adonis dies. The Cupids sing a chorus of mourning.

Subtitled "A Masque for the Entertainment of the King", *Venus and Adonis* is in fact the first through-composed opera (ie without spoken dialogue) to be performed in English. It is a short work (less than an hour) with few arias or big moments, but it possesses a dramatic effectiveness largely through the stark contrast between the sensuousness of the opening scene and the anguish of its ending. The odd deviation of the libretto from its source, whereby Venus persuades Adonis to join the hunt (in Ovid's *Metamorphoses* she begs him not to), makes the denouement all the more poignant in that the goddess's grief at his death is combined with guilt at being the cause of it.

In its style and construction *Venus and Adonis* shows a certain indebtedness to the Lullian *tragédie lyrique*, particularly in its French overture and in the use of dances to punctuate the drama. Even so, its harmonies and counterpoint are determinedly English, as are the melodies, which boast an earthiness and immediacy that distinguish them from any other national school. The influence of *Venus and Adonis* on Purcell's *Dido and Aeneas* is very striking and is perhaps at its most obvious in the opera's most powerful moment when Venus's stately lament, "With solemn pomp", gives way to the elegaic chorus, "Mourn for thy servant".

Argenta, Varcoe, Dawson; London Baroque; Medlam.
(Harmonia Mundi 1901276; 1 CD).

Venus and Adonis is not the easiest work to bring off, and of the three recordings that have made it onto CD the one directed by Charles Medlam in 1987 is the most satisfying. Using light forces and an intimate ambience, Medlam finds exactly the right balance between playfulness, passion and courtly artifice. Nancy Argenta and Stephen Varcoe give strong and committed performances in the title roles without ever overplaying them. The moment in the last act when Venus plaintively calls Adonis's name, echoing a similar but more enraptured moment in the first act, is particularly moving, as is the restrained account of the wonderful closing chorus "Mourn for thy servant".

HENRY PURCELL

b. LONDON, probably 1659; d. LONDON, NOVEMBER 21, 1695.

In the history of opera, Henry Purcell is often presented as one of the great might-have-beens: though he was famed, in the words of a contemporary, for "having a peculiar Genius to express the Energy of English Words", his career coincided with a period in which opera repeatedly failed to establish itself in England. Had he lived just fifteen years more he would have experienced the London opera mania that was to bring the young Handel such extraordinary success. Instead Purcell wrote just one short operatic masterpiece, *Dido and Aeneas*, and four semi-operas that tend to be treated as cumbersome, and largely unperformable, historical freaks. Fortunately, the tercentenary of his death brought a spate of recordings and performances that at last revealed the whole range of his genius and brought some of his great theatre works from out of the shadow of *Dido and Aeneas*.

ROYAL COLLEGE OF MUSIC

Henry Purcell

Music was the Purcell family business. His father, also named Henry, and his uncle Thomas were both musicians at the court of Charles II, and his brother Daniel was a composer and organist. Unsurprisingly the young Henry had very close connections with the leading English musicians of the day: first as one of the twelve Children of the Chapel Royal, and later as a student with Matthew Locke, whom he succeeded as court composer for the violins in 1677, and with John Blow, whom he succeeded as organist of Westminster Abbey in 1679. Purcell spent all of his life in the environs of Westminster, and his principal places of work – Whitehall Palace, the Chapel Royal at St James's, and Westminster Abbey – were all within walking distance of his home. From 1680 he travelled further afield, supplementing his official income by writing music for the Dorset Garden Theatre in the City of London. His theatrical activities intensified in 1689, the probable year of *Dido and Aeneas*, after William and Mary cut down on musical activities at court.

In 1690 both Purcell and Priest were engaged by Thomas Betterton, the great actor-manager, to work on his adaptation of Fletcher and Massinger's play *The History of Dioclesian*. Though Purcell had written a substantial amount of incidental music for Betterton, this was his first semi-opera. Staged at the Dorset Garden Theatre, it was an enormous success and led to three more: *King Arthur* in 1691, *The Fairy Queen* in 1692, and *The Indian Queen* in 1694–95, completed on Purcell's death by his brother Daniel. Of these three *The Fairy Queen* was the most ambitious, costing an extraordinary £3000, much of it presumably spent on the machinery needed to effect the spectacular transformation scenes that Betterton required. Despite the fact that "the Court and the Town were wonderfully satisfied with it", the show lost money – the only semi-opera to do so.

Like his French contemporary Charpentier, Purcell synthesized certain aspects of the French style – the two-part overture, rhythmically defined dances, and declamatory vocalizing – with the more lyrical and expressive style of the Italians. However, what makes his musical language unique is the way these elements are suffused by a sense of national identity, typified by heavy chromaticism, elaborate counterpoint, extended melody and, above all, emotional immediacy.

Dido and Aeneas

Composed 1689.
First performed possibly April 1689.
Libretto by Nahum Tate, after Virgil.

Synopsis

Act I

Dido, Queen of Carthage, is unable to declare her love for the Trojan prince Aeneas, a guest at her court; he is soon to resume his journey in search of a site for a new city to replace Troy. Her confidante Belinda and her courtiers persuade Dido to speak her love and the act ends with general rejoicing.

Act II

In a cave, a sorceress and her witches plot the downfall of Dido and Carthage. They decide to conjure up a storm and force the lovers to take refuge in their cave, where an elf, disguised as Mercury, will remind Aeneas of his duties. Meanwhile, Dido and Aeneas, having spent the night together, are being entertained in a grove by Belinda and a courtier. A storm arises and they are separated; Aeneas enters the witches' cave and is commanded by the false Mercury to leave Carthage.

Act III

At the quayside Aeneas's men are preparing to leave. The witches gloat over their victory and sing of their delight. Back at court, Dido has been informed of her lover's planned departure and seeks Belinda's counsel. The Queen confronts Aeneas, silences his excuses and dismisses him. After her lament ("When I am laid in earth"), Dido kills herself. Cupids mourn her, scattering roses on her tomb.

The first known performance of Purcell's *Dido and Aeneas* was at the same girls' school in Chelsea where Blow's *Venus and Adonis* had received its second performance. Run by the dancing master Josias Priest, this was no ordinary school but one with strong connections to both the court and the London stage. The date of the Chelsea performance is unknown but an epilogue, written by the poet Thomas D'Urfey, refers to the girls as "Protestant and English nuns", thus pointing to a performance after the accession of William and Mary in 1689. The music, however, suggests a rather earlier date so perhaps, like *Venus and Adonis*, it had already been performed at court. Nahum Tate, who adapted his own play *Brutus of Alba* for the libretto, has been ridiculed as a talentless hack ever since Alexander Pope lambasted him in the *Dunciad*. In fact he provides an admirably condensed version of the story, and he follows the rules (set down by Dryden) for verses that are to be set to music: namely that they be short, with frequent stops, repeated lines, and the avoidance of too many consonants.

Dido and Aeneas, perhaps more than any other of his works, displays Purcell's remarkable skill as a setter of words. This is particularly evident in his recitatives, in which emotional nuance is communicated by an arioso vocalizing of extraordinary subtlety. It can be heard in Dido's recitative "Thy hand, Belinda", which immediately precedes her famous lament, "When I am laid in earth". The recitative is highly chromatic – that is it uses notes foreign to the key that it is in – with the voice moving in a series of small intervals on the syllable "dar" of the word "darkness". The effect is like someone feeling their way in the dark step by step, or, in Dido's case, coming to a true realization of the enormity of her imminent death. The opera is full of such telling details, with the lament having pride of place. This episode has almost talismanic status in English music, and its fame is justified: indeed the single-note repetition of the words "Remember me" must be one of the most agonized and vulnerable moments in the whole of opera.

Aeneas, by comparison with Dido, is psychologically underdeveloped, a characteristic he shares with several operatic heroes. His lack of substance is a far cry from Virgil's noble warrior but it makes Dido's misjudgement of him, and the tragedy that ensues, all the more stark. Equally unlike Virgil is the introduction of malevolent witches as the agents of Dido's destruction (in the *Aeneid* Aeneas is reminded of his duty by the real Mercury). In Tate's restructuring of the story, the witches function as a kind of negative image of Dido and her court, and in fact it is not unknown for Dido and the Sorceress to be played by the same singer.

The supernatural had an extremely strong hold over the seventeenth-century imagination, and the Sorceress embodies a powerful tradition, to which Lully's *Armide* and Charpentier's *Médée* both belong.

RECORDINGS OVERVIEW

Dido's brevity has contributed to its popularity with record companies. For many years it was regarded as a star vehicle for a leading soprano or mezzo, and this is reflected in the casting of the earlier recordings. The first complete recordings were made by Decca in 1935, with Nancy Evans, and by HMV a little later, with Joan Hammond. No further recordings of any significance were made until 1952 when Kirsten Flagstad, who had performed the role of Dido at the Mermaid Theatre in London, made a recording for EMI. This was an immensely powerful reading which reigned supreme until 1961, the year that Janet Baker made her supreme recording, conducted by the Baroque music scholar Anthony Lewis. "Celebrity" recordings have continued to appear – notably with Victoria de los Angeles in 1965 and Jessye Norman in 1986 – but since the early 1980s the trend has been towards the recreation of a more authentic Baroque sound. Of the numerous "authentic" *Dido* sets, the one listed below is the one to listen to first.

Baker, Herincx, Clark, Sinclair; St Anthony Singers; English Chamber Orchestra; Lewis.
(Decca 425 720-2DM; 1 CD).

Vocally, this remains the most gratifying recording of Purcell's opera. As epitomized by the closing lament, Janet Baker's attention to the music's emotional substance has never been equalled: there is a nobility and a fragility about her interpretation that is extraordinarily affecting. Anthony Lewis's direction of the solidly inauthentic ECO is reliable and frequently lively, and Baker is ably supported by Raimond Herincx's baritone Aeneas and Patricia Clark's Belinda. Some will find the over-characterized Sorceress of Monica Sinclair irritating, although it is less peculiar than many. But it is for Janet Baker's performance that this analogue recording is to be recommended – but do not confuse this 1961 production with her disappointing 1975 performance.

Von Otter, Varcoe, Dawson, Rogers; English Concert Choir and Orchestra; Pinnock.
(Archiv 427-624-2AH; 1 CD).

Trevor Pinnock's 1989 account, with Anne Sofie von Otter, is the best recent recording. The English Concert are a fresh and flexible outfit, and under Pinnock's direction they are especially good at registering the mood changes of this work, from public joy to private grief. Anne Sofie von Otter is a remarkably well-judged Dido, elegant and poised, possessing real gravitas. Her performance of the opening aria, with the cello continuo more forward than usual, is particularly affecting in its simplicity and directness. She is well supported by Lynn Dawson's bright-toned Belinda, but Stephen

DEUTSCHE GRAMMOPHON

Anne-Sofie von Otter

Varcoe's Aeneas is solid rather than inspiring, and Nigel Rogers' doubling of the Sailor and the Sorceress is irritatingly arch. But where this performance loses out to the Lewis recording is in its failure to convey a sense of theatre. This is largely due to Pinnock's pacing: every choice of tempo seems valid individually, but in succession the incidents seem too unvaried.

The Fairy Queen

Composed 1691; revised 1693.
First performed May 2, 1692.
Libretto anonymous (possibly Thomas Betterton), from Shakespeare.

Synopsis

Act I

By order of Duke Theseus, Demetrius must marry Hermia, even though he actually loves Helena. At the same time Hermia is in love with Lysander. The four lovers escape from the town. In a forest nearby, a group of tradesmen are rehearsing a play to celebrate the wedding. Titania (the Fairy Queen) has argued with Oberon (the Fairy King) over an Indian boy. In a masque Titania's retinue of fairies entertains her with music before teasing a drunken poet who has entered the forest.

Act II

Oberon and Puck (his right-hand fairy) prepare a love potion distilled from a flower. In the second masque Titania's fairies sing to her, before she is lulled to sleep by Night, Mystery and Secrecy. Puck then administers the love potion to Titania and to the lovers.

Act III

Lysander and Demetrius are now both in love with Hermia. The tradesmen rehearse and one of them, Bottom, is turned into an ass by Puck. Titania awakes and falls in love with him. She entertains him with a masque of love in which two rustics, Coridon and Mopsa, flirt with each other.

Act IV

Oberon restores the true lovers back to each other, Bottom returns to human form, and Titania is released from her enchantment. Oberon and Titania's reconciliation (and his birthday) are celebrated in a masque of the seasons.

Act V

Duke Theseus discovers the lovers and agrees to them marrying as they wish. Oberon and Titania appear. In the final masque – a celebration of the state of matrimony – the goddess Juno blesses the lovers, and a Chinese entertainment takes place, followed by a monkey dance, before Hymen, the god of marriage, draws the proceedings to a close.

Like the Broadway musical, the semi-opera was a calculatedly populist extravaganza that mixed singing, dancing, and speech with spectacular scenic effects. Unlike the musical, it did not integrate its musical moments with its spoken ones but inserted them, at the end of each act, in the form of a masque – a self-contained entertainment, using separate performers, that neither helped the narrative progress nor developed the characters. The problem for modern productions, and recordings, is that if the play text is abandoned (none are especially good), you are left with five relatively incoherent scenes, but each containing a wealth of music of the highest quality.

The quality of the music is especially high in *The Fairy Queen*, the text of which was fairly closely based on Shakespeare's *A Midsummer Night's Dream* but was modernized by an unknown author (probably Betterton) to suit contemporary taste. Without setting one word of Shakespeare, Purcell manages to convey the essential qualities of the source play: its mystery, its anarchic humour, its sexiness. There is an astonishing variety of music, from the spine-tingling air "Hush no more", with its eloquent silences, to the knockabout comedy of the "Dialogue between Coridon and Mopsa" adapted in the 1693 revision of the work for a counter-tenor who specialized in comic drag roles. There is also a range of theatrical musical devices, such as the echo effect in "May the God of Wit inspire" the recorders imitating birdsong in the prelude to Act II. This last piece uses a ground bass, a form that occurs frequently in *The Fairy Queen*, most famously in Act V's "O let me weep", added in the 1693 revision to cover a scene change, and markedly similar to the lament in *Dido and Aeneas*.

Argenta, Dawson, Corréas, Deletré, Desrochers, Gens, Piau, Daniels, Randle; Les Arts Florissants; Christie. (Harmonia Mundi HMC 1308.09; 2 CDs).

This is music-making of great vividness and immediacy, and it stands out from its eight rival recordings precisely for that reason. Despite the problematic lack of any real narrative in the masques, Christie refuses to treat them merely like a collection of songs, but instead – through well-judged speeds and lively characterization – turns them into a theatrical event. This is equally true of the plentiful dance music, which sounds spring-heeled and lively – in other words, like real dances. His approach is consistently un-precious and inventive, and he has no qualms about brightening up orchestral textures with, for instance, percussion in the dances and some tremolando strings for the marvellously sombre winter aria in the masque of the seasons. The singing is wonderfully fresh and committed, with Christie employing a mix of mainly English and French singers. The pronunciation of some of the latter crew is occasionally a bit odd, but this is such a bizarre and magical work that it merely adds a kind of exotic charm.

2

BAROQUE OPERA

VIVALDI TO HANDEL

BAROQUE OPERA

VIVALDI TO HANDEL

Cavalli's *Giasone* was the most popular opera of the seventeenth century, but it was not without its critics. Writing in 1700, Giovanni Maria Crescimbeni attacked its libretto for, among other things, mixing comedy and tragedy, a hybrid that resulted in "the complete ruin of the rules of poetry . . . which, forced to serve music, lost its purity, and became filled with idiocies". Crescimbeni was not alone in feeling that Italian opera had become a degraded spectacle: many poets and intellectuals shared this view, and it was their attempts to rationalize the libretto that formed the basis of the reforms that produced **opera seria** – the dominant operatic genre for most of the eighteenth century.

Of all these poet-reformers, the most significant were Apostolo Zeno and Pietro Trapassi. Zeno re-established the five-act format, used plots from ancient history, limited the characters to no more than six, and banished the comic sub-plot. The far more gifted Trapassi – better known as Metastasio – added further refinements, and such was his influence that his name became synonymous with opera seria. In compliance with Metastasio's theories, the aria came to comprise two stanzas of contrasting feelings, and was placed at the end of a scene, where it could summarize the emotional situation and motivate the character's exit from the stage. His impact upon the subject and structure of the plot was equally marked. A typical Metastasian libretto revolved around a conflict between love and duty, and would usually involve some kind of amatory mismatch, to which a case of mistaken identity added further complexity. This was not greatly dissimilar from previous plots: the difference lies in the refinement of the verse; the absence of comedy; and the moral seriousness of the conclusion, where all was resolved not by some supernatural *deus ex machina* but by the exemplary conduct and magnanimity of an enlightened ruler. The success of Metastasio's sixty or so libretti was phenomenal: it has been estimated that almost one thousand operas written in the eighteenth century were settings of his work.

But the evolution of opera seria was not simply a question of changes to the libretto. Both Zeno and Metastasio were responding to musical developments that had appeared in Italian opera towards the end of the seventeenth century, and were exemplified by the work of Alessandro Scarlatti (1660–1725), the most successful composer working in Italy at the turn of the century. Scarlatti was born in Rome, but from 1684 to 1702 and from 1709 until his death he served as *maestro di cappella* to the Spanish viceroy in Naples, which had become an operatic centre to rival Venice. Whether Scarlatti founded a specifically Neapolitan school of opera is arguable, but his many operas helped to consolidate a number of musical conventions that would become staple elements of opera seria. The most important of these was the da capo aria, an aria which was divided into three distinct sections, the second of which acted as a contrast – both musically and poetically – to the first, while the third section was simply a repetition of the first but with ornamentation added by the singer. There was also a consolidation of the changes in recitative, of which there were now two main types: *recitativo secco* (dry recitative), in which the notes followed the speech patterns and which was accompanied by the continuo alone, and *recitativo accompagnato*, which was more lyrical and with a full orchestral accompaniment. Other developments to be found in Scarlatti's operas include the "Italian" overture in three sections (the outer ones fast, the middle one slow) and a richer harmonic language combined with greater orchestral colour (*Tigrane* is the first opera to use French horns). Unfortunately Scarlatti's work has so resolutely resisted revival that even his two most highly regarded works, *Mitridate Eupatore* and *Tigrane*, are unavailable on record.

The clear-cut separation of the aria from recitative was linked with the spectacular rise in artistic status of individual singers. By 1700 many people went to the opera primarily to see star performers displaying their skills, often blatantly in competition with each other. The principal parts were written for high voices: the leading male role would be sung by a castrato, while the principal female role was usually assigned to a soprano (tenors and basses being mainly employed for comic roles). Improvised ornamentation of an aria by a principal singer – castrati were especially renowned for their vocal agility – became increasingly elaborate, sometimes to the point of absurdity. Naples, with its plethora of music academies, was particularly renowned as a breeding ground for brilliant singers: the leading Neapolitan opera composer after Scarlatti, Nicola Porpora (1686–1768), was also one of the most renowned singing teachers in Europe, training two of the most successful castrati, Farinelli and Caffarelli.

Naples' hegemony among Italian operatic centres meant that its composers and its principal singers were highly sought after, even in so proudly independent a city as Venice. But one Venetian who held his own in his native city, albeit briefly, was **Antonio Vivaldi**, a composer better known for his instrumental works but who from 1713 devoted much of his energy to opera. Vivaldi was not as progressive a composer as Scarlatti, though he set a number of Metastasian texts, but his operas are full of wonderfully rich music, which is gradually being investigated by both performers and recording companies. Venice's major contribution in the early years of the century was in the field of comedy. As opera seria became established, the problem arose of what to do with those comic elements that had been an integral part of opera – not to mention those singers who specialized in comedy. The solution was the creation of the Intermezzo, a miniature comic opera, presented between the acts of a longer work. Generally featuring just two or three characters occupying a world of domestic strife and intrigue, the intermezzi originated in Venice, where Pietro Pariati became the most celebrated exponent, producing libretti for composers like Tomaso Albinoni (1671–1751). Pariati's most famous work, *Pimpinone*, was set by Albinoni in 1708 and again by Telemann in 1725.

In Naples the popularity of the intermezzi was paralleled by a vogue for full-length comic operas in dialect, staged at the Teatro dei Fiorentini. Scarlatti contributed one example of the new genre, *Il trionfo dell'onore* (The Triumph of Honour), in 1718 but the best-known example, recently revived at La Scala, is **Pergolesi**'s *Lo frate 'nnamorato* (The Enamoured Brother) of 1732. It was also Pergolesi who composed the one intermezzo that is still regularly performed, *La serva padrona* (The Maid Turned

Mistress), a work written to be performed between the acts of his now forgotten opera seria *Il prigoniero superbo* (The Proud Prisoner).

But it was at Venice in the 1740s, through the highly successful collaborations between the playwright Carlo Goldoni and the composer Baldassare Galuppi, that comic opera, or **opera buffa**, really became established as a genre to rival opera seria, with characters of somewhat greater depth than the stock types of the intermezzi. Goldoni's most important contribution to the genre, however, was the incident-packed ensembles that acted as "finales" to the first two acts of his operas and which enabled composers to provide "action" music in the shape of quartets, quintets or sextets. Goldoni and Galuppi's most successful collaboration, *Il filosofo di campagna* (The Country Philosopher), 1754, was one of the most popular of all eighteenth-century operas; it remains unrecorded, however.

As the new century began in France, the spectre of Lully still hung like a fog over operatic life, stifling the kind of rapid development that was occurring in Italy. The Lullian *tragédie lyrique* was still the supreme form of music-theatre, but an alternative did exist in the form of a lighter genre called the **opéra-ballet**, which consisted of three or four acts, combining singing and dancing, and loosely connected by a picturesque theme. The milieu was contemporary and exotic rather than ancient and mythological, and the genre was likened by the playwright Cahusac to the delicate paintings of Watteau. It was largely the creation of the composer **André Campra**, who enjoyed great success in 1710 with his opéra-ballet *Les fêtes vénitiennes* (The Venetian Festivities), but he also wrote the outstanding *tragédies lyriques* of the period, including *Idoménée*. A progressive composer, Campra endeavoured to reconcile the native idiom of the *tragédies lyriques* with certain Italianate elements, like the da capo aria – an ambition that was enough to win the enmity of the more conservative critics, since the debate over the relative merits of the two national styles still raged furiously, largely in the form of endless pamphlets on the subject.

The composer who more than any other revitalized the Lullian tradition was **Jean-Philippe Rameau**, whose first opera, *Hippolyte et Aricie*, composed when he was fifty years old, astonished its audiences with the vividness and daring of its musical language. Some found it crude and offensive; others, including Campra, hailed it as the music of the future; and factional disputes duly broke out between his supporters, the Ramistes, and his critics, the Lullistes. In fact Rameau stuck fairly closely to the Lullian formula, with mostly classical subjects presented in a prologue and five acts, with an abundance of dance interludes. On the other hand, the treatment of the stories was much more human and rather less geared to celebrating monarchical *gloire*. The music was not there to serve the words – Rameau's librettists are generally inferior to Quinault – but rather to bring them dramatically to life, and Rameau's pictorial writing has an inventiveness and richness of instrumental colouring that far transcends its models. Rameau's theatre music is not confined to *tragédies lyriques*, of which there are four; he also raised the opéra-ballet to new heights, notably with *Les Indes galantes*, and wrote one *comédie lyrique*, *Platée*. By the time of his death, Rameau's reputation was supreme, but like Lully he is not a composer who has travelled successfully, and performances outside of France are infrequent, despite a number of outstanding recordings in recent years.

In Germany, the work of Metastasio fuelled the highly prolific Johann Adolf Hasse (1699–1783), a Dresden-based composer who set all of the poet's libretti except one. Hasse was Italian-trained, possibly under Scarlatti, and was married to the greatest mezzo-soprano of the age, Faustina Bordoni (see p.59). More than any other composer, Hasse came to exemplify Metastasian opera seria, with its emphasis on fast-moving recitative and formulaic arias with which to display the prowess of a virtuosic performer, but he is yet another important opera composer whose work remains almost completely unrecorded. His contemporary **Georg-Philipp Telemann** has fared marginally better than Hasse, even though fewer than half of his forty or so operas have survived, most of them dating from his directorship of the Hamburg Opera. Telemann was largely self-taught, and his surviving works show an eclectic range of styles and a genuine originality – especially in the directness of his musical language, which is akin to German folksong. He seems to have specialized in comedy, both sophisticated and slapstick, and his best-known work is a version of the intermezzo *Pimpinone*, an opera that shows an awareness of the new Italian buffa style and predates Pergolesi's similar *La serva padrona* by some eight years. Several of Telemann's operas combine languages, with Italian in the arias and German for the recitatives, a precedent established by his Hamburg predecessor Reinhard Keiser (1674–1739). Keiser coined the term Singspiel (Song-play) for his works, a term that was later applied to the comic or sentimental operas with spoken dialogue: the form became popular in Germany slightly later in the century, and was to reach a peak with Mozart.

The greatest of all composers of opera seria, **George Frideric Handel**, began his operatic career in Hamburg, but his real successes were achieved away from the operatic mainstream, in England. Beginning in 1711 with *Rinaldo* and ending in 1741 with *Deidamia*, Handel produced thirty-five operas for the London stage, before declining interest in the genre and ill health forced him to turn his attention to oratorio. Opera seria in London was not a court-sponsored activity, as it was virtually everywhere else, but rather a commercial one involving rival companies. Despite this commercial pressure, Handel did not transform the conventions of the genre so much as invest them – especially the da capo arias – with new emotional conviction and psychological insight. Handel's operas possess both tenderness and contrapuntal vigour, which perhaps explains why they alone, out of all the thousands of Baroque operas, have been regularly and effectively revived during the last fifty years.

The pretensions and potential idiocies of opera seria were rapidly seized upon by critics wherever it was performed. In England, Joseph Addison, writing in the *Spectator* in 1711, scoffed at the castrato Nicolini for being "exposed to a tempest in robes of ermine, and sailing in an open boat upon a sea of pasteboard". Audiences, Addison went on to say, "have often been reproached by writers for the coarseness of their taste; but our present grievance does not seem to be the want of a good taste, but of common sense". The most swingeing attack on the Italian opera in London appeared in 1728: **John Gay**'s *The Beggar's Opera* parodied the more absurd operatic conventions while, at the same time, portraying the government of the day as a bunch of crooks. Gay's text was original but the music was borrowed, mixing folksongs with arias by such composers as Purcell and Handel (with whom Gay once collaborated), much in the manner of the French vaudeville. It was a huge success, and although it did not completely kill off the Italian opera, it did create a whole new genre – the ballad opera – that was enormously popular in England and an important influence on the Singspiel of Germany.

ANTONIO VIVALDI

B. VENICE, MARCH 4, 1678; D. VIENNA, JULY 28, 1741.

Though first and foremost a composer of instrumental music, Vivaldi devoted a large proportion of his career to the composition and production of opera: sixteen of his forty-odd works in the genre have survived, although none has become established in the modern repertory.

His initial studies were with his father, a violinist who worked at both St Mark's and the Venetian theatres, and then with Giovanni Legrenzi, the *maestro di cappella* at St Mark's and one of Venice's leading opera composers. In 1703 Vivaldi became a priest, but he stopped celebrating Mass almost immediately on the grounds of ill-health, though his condition never seems to have impeded his frequently arduous travels as a composer. In the same year as his ordination Vivaldi entered the service of the Pio Ospedale della Pietà – the most distinguished of several orphanages for girls, in which musical education and performance reached the very highest standards. For the best part of a decade Vivaldi taught the children and composed for the Pietà's choir and orchestra (which was renowned throughout Europe), but in 1713 he was granted leave of absence to supervise the production of his first opera, *Ottone in villa*, in Vicenza. His Venetian debut followed in 1714 with *Orlando finto pazzo*, and for the next five years he devoted his energies to opera, both as a composer and as the manager of the Sant'Angelo and San Moisè theatres.

After that came a two-year sojourn in Mantua and the creation of a further three operas, then in 1720 a move back to Venice, where he discovered that fashion had shifted and that the operatic style which he practised had come under satirical attack. In particular Benedetto Marcello's *Il teatro alla moda* (The Fashionable Theatre) poured scorn on all those who diminished the genre by using it to fulfil their own vain ambitions. Vivaldi (thinly disguised in the book as Aldiviva) responded by taking up several offers from outside Venice, including two spells in Rome, but he returned to Venice in 1725 where he was once again appointed impresario of the Teatro Sant'Angelo. From this period stems his close association with Anna Girò, a young soprano (but not a great one, according to Goldoni) who often took the principal roles in operas staged at Sant'Angelo. Throughout the 1730s Vivaldi travelled all over Italy, accompanied by Anna Girò and her sister Paolina, producing his operas in frequently inadequate conditions. Touring did not stop him composing, but his later works were unfashionable and his orchestral writing, though attractive, was conceived as nothing more than support for an ever more florid vocal manner. In 1738 he was forbidden from entering Ferrara by the archbishop because of his questionable relationship with Anna Girò and, more importantly, because of his refusal to say Mass. He returned to Venice where he heard of the failure of his opera *Siroe* in Ferrara – according to Vivaldi because of alterations introduced by the harpsichordist. In reality, however, Vivaldi's operas were now dated and even the Venetian public began to lose interest. It was for this reason that, in August 1740, he left Venice for Vienna, arriving in June the following year. He died a pauper within a month of arriving, and, like Mozart, was buried in a communal grave – though in Vivaldi's case the location is known.

In all his dramatic work, Vivaldi placed the weight of his talent upon the accompaniment rather than the voices, and vivid characterization is not the strong point of his operas. They are overpopulated with one-dimensional stock figures such as the amorous hero, the vengeful widow and the blustering tyrant, and the plots are similarly predictable, revolving around palace intrigues, the conflict between Love and Duty and, most frequently, Revenge. Indeed, the plots are often established before the curtain rises, thanks to prefatory expositions on who does what to whom, and why. Most of Vivaldi's opera scores are equally routine: vocal expression is kept to a minimum, his arias are brief, there are few ensembles, and almost no choruses. There are some highlights – when the need arises for the expression of more than one character simultaneously he introduces them one after the other, until the three or four singers are indulging in quite intricate counterpoint. Unfortunately, such effects are all too rare and clearly demanded more time than Vivaldi could afford.

In operatic terms, Vivaldi was born thirty years too late. Had his instrumentally dominated style emerged at the same time as the Neapolitans, such as Alessandro Scarlatti, he might have fared better with an audience obsessed with vocal ensemble, instrumental detail, the da capo aria and fussy, intricate harmony. The grand manner of his near-contemporary Handel is beyond the conservative Vivaldi and, for a composer of such extraordinary gifts, his operas are disappointingly uneven in quality. There are some exceptions to this rule, though, most notably *Orlando*, otherwise known as *Orlando Furioso*.

Orlando

Composed 1727.
First performed autumn 1727.
Libretto by Grazio Braccioli, after Ariosto.

Synopsis

Act I

The action takes place on the island ruled by the enchantress Alcina. The knight Orlando loves Angelica, although she still loves Medoro, who is missing. Suddenly Angelica sees Medoro's ship bearing down on the rocks and she calls on Alcina for help. Alcina saves Medoro and brings him safely ashore, just as Orlando arrives. He is jealous of Medoro but Alcina persuades him he is Angelica's brother.

Act II

Alcina bewitches a new arrival, the knight Ruggiero. His wife Bradamante is astonished to find him lying in the enchantress's arms and horrified when he fails to recognize her. Bradamante manages to break the spell but then spurns him. Another knight, Astolfo, arrives on the island and is duly bewitched, while Bradamante and Ruggiero are reunited. Angelica and Medoro trick Orlando into one of Alcina's magic traps, allowing them to marry. He is freed from the spell but upon discovering Angelica and Medoro's mutual expressions of love carved into a tree he is driven insane with rage. Ruggiero and Astolfo vow revenge against Alcina although it is against Angelica that Orlando wants vengeance.

Act III

The deranged Orlando enters Alcina's temple and, thinking it to be Angelica, he tries to embrace the statue of Merlin, which is the repository of Alcina's magic. To reach the statue he has to do battle with the invincible guard Arontes. Triumphant, he pulls the statue to the ground, breaking the enchantress's spell. Alcina's reign is at an end and Orlando wakes to forgive Angelica and Medoro.

Vivaldi had a hand in three different operas based on the tale of Orlando. In 1713, while impresario at Sant'Angelo, he presented – and added a few numbers to – a setting of a Grazio Braccioli libretto, *Orlando Furioso*, by the little-known composer Giovanni Ristori. The work proved enormously popular, receiving over forty consecutive performances. Exactly a year later Vivaldi produced his own companion piece, *Orlando finto pazzo*, but this was enormously unpopular and Vivaldi withdrew it almost immediately. Thirteen years later, he produced a new setting of Braccioli's text, calling it *Orlando*.

Vivaldi's *Orlando* is not exactly a mainstream opera, but it is something of a gold mine, albeit one in which the nuggets are buried beneath a mighty weight of debris. Several factors mark out *Orlando* as the most successful Vivaldi opera. The extensive recitative is excellent and some of the arioso passages are extremely well organized, with some fine instrumental accompaniments. Orlando himself gets two monologues which might be over-long but still contain the finest of Vivaldi's vocal music – both occur in Act II, the first when Orlando is freed from Alcina's spell ("Nel profundo cieco mondo"), the second when he finds Angelica and Medoro's names carved on a tree. There's another aria of great beauty in Act II: Ruggiero's song of love ("Sol da te, mio dolce amore"), which is also of historical interest for its complex flute part – the first known use of the instrument as an operatic obbligato. The effect is both hauntingly lyrical and dazzlingly impressive – some passages contain 48 notes to a bar.

Horne, De Los Angeles, Valentini, Kozma; Amici della Polifonia; Solisti Veneti; Scimone.
(Erato 2292-45147-2; 3 CDs).

Marilyn Horne and Victoria De Los Angeles bring much to this opera. Horne's Orlando is a weighty portrayal, but her dark and powerful tone is leavened by typically unhurried articulation, and she brings great presence to the two second-act arias, languishing in the extended melodies. De Los Angeles, as Angelica, has a limpid and unfussy tone that serves as a foil to Horne's pressured vitality. Scimone's heavily cut score reduces the overall length by almost an hour (the full version lasts four), but with only fifteen arias left in place the set is rather dominated by its recitatives. On the other hand, the bright sound and feisty orchestral playing go some way towards relieving the tedium.

FERRI, SIFACE AND FARINELLI

The annals of the great castrati begin with **Baldassare Ferri** (1610–80), whose talents are detailed in Giovanni Bontempi's *History of Music* (1695): "After an incredibly long, sustained and lovely passage beyond the lung capacity of any singer, he would, without taking breath, go into a very long and lovely trill and then into still another passage, more brilliant and beautiful than the first, and all this while remaining still as a statue, without any movement of the brow, the mouth or the body. To sing a descending chromatic scale, trilling on each note, from the high G and A to the same notes in the lower octave, a feat impossible for any other singer, was child's play for Ferri; for again, without taking a breath, he would continue onto other trills, passages and artistic wonders." Ferri's stupendous skills made him the first idolized singer: there are reports of his carriage being strewn with flowers and of the Florentine people greeting his arrival in a line that stretched three miles beyond the city walls.

Giovanni Francesco Grossi (1653–97) was the first castrato to give himself a "nom de chant" – he styled himself **Siface**, from the role in Cavalli's opera *Scipione Africano*, which made him a household name. But he is famous less for his singing than for his private life. After achieving great success at the court of Queen Mary of England (where Henry Purcell wrote a short keyboard work in his honour), he became the lover of Countess Elena Forni, the wife of a Modenese aristocrat. Their exploits were notoriously audible and were widely reported. Word got back to her family, who then dispatched the poor woman to a convent, but this was not enough to put an end to their affair. When Siface's boasting again alerted the family, they decided the time for half-measures was past: the great Siface was found face down in a river, with his throat – once the wonder of Europe – cut out.

The most famous castrato of all was Carlo Broschi – otherwise known as **Farinelli** (1705–82). Born in Este, to a wealthy family (which was very unusual for a castrato), he received his "warm bath" shortly after his seventh birthday, and studied music with his father Salvatore and his brother Riccardo, who later composed some of the singer's most ornate showpieces. He made his opera debut in 1720, moved to Rome, and within five years was being acclaimed as "the acknowledged monarch of European singing". After touring much of the continent, Farinelli moved to London in 1724, and there amassed a huge fortune, which he carefully saved. An even greater fortune was soon to be his: in 1737 he was invited to sing for the eccentric, terminally miserable Philip V in Madrid. After the second song the king offered him anything within his power: Farinelli asked him to wash, shave and dress in fresh clothes – delighting the queen and greatly improving the humour of a monarch notorious for his appalling standard of hygiene. Philip was so taken by Farinelli that he offered him a huge salary if he would agree to sing for him every night. Farinelli agreed, and for the next twenty-five years he sang the same four songs every night, in addition to keeping the king engaged in conversation from midnight until 5am. He remained in Spain after Philip's death, working as a producer of opera for Ferdinand VI and then Charles III, with whom he eventually fell out over matters of foreign policy. In 1759 he retired to an enormous villa in Bologna (the building stands to this day), where he was visited by, among others, Gluck, Mozart, Casanova, and Emperor Joseph II.

Of the hundreds of tributes to Farinelli's gifts, perhaps the most revealing is Charles Burney's account of the singer's contest with a member of the orchestra of Rome's opera house. "There was a struggle every night between Farinelli and a famous player on the trumpet in a song accompanied by that instrument; this, at first, seemed amicable and merely sportive, till the audience began to interest themselves in the contest, and to take different sides. After severally swelling a note in which each manifested the power of his lungs and tried to rival the other in brilliancy and force . . . Farinelli, with a smile on his countenance, showing he had only been sporting with him all that time, broke out all at once in the same breath, with fresh vigour, and not only swelled and shook the note, but ran the most rapid and difficult division and was at last silenced only by the acclamations of the audience. From this period may be dated that superiority which he ever maintained over all his contemporaries."

GIOVANNI PERGOLESI

b. IESI, ITALY, JANUARY 4, 1710; d. POZZUOLI, MARCH 16, 1736.

Pergolesi was dogged by ill health and lived for a mere twenty-six years. He strove, without conspicuous success, to achieve fame as a composer of opera seria, but was more popular for his comic works, one of which – *La serva padrona* – achieved such notoriety during the Querelle des Bouffons (see p.49) that his posthumous reputation became greatly inflated and music by others was regularly ascribed to him by unscrupulous publishers.

Pergolesi's working life was spent in Naples, where an operatic style had evolved which emphasized the beauty and virtuosity of the solo voice at the expense of dramatic unity. Sponsored by the Marquis Cardolo Pianetti, he moved to the city at an early age to study at the Conservatorio dei Poveri di Gesù with the up-and-coming opera composer Leonardo Vinci (1696–1730). Pergolesi's first opera seria, *Salustia* (1732), was a failure, but in the same year *Lo frate 'nnamorato*, a comedy in Neapolitan dialect, was enthusiastically received and showed clearly where his real talents lay. In the following year he produced a more successful opera seria, *Il prigionier superbo* (The Proud Prisoner), but this work is now famous simply for the fact that *La serva padrona* was performed between its acts. This pattern was repeated in 1734 when the opera seria *Adriano in Siria* (a setting of Metastasio) was enlivened by the intermezzo *Livietta e Tracollo*.

In spite of public opinion, Pergolesi continued to apply himself to opera seria, producing one more setting of Metastasio, *L'Olimpiade* (1735), before teaming up once again with Gennar'antonio Federico, the brilliant librettist of *Lo frate* and *La serva padrona*, for a full-length comedy called *Il Flaminio* (1735). This was his final work for the theatre. By now illness (probably tuberculosis) forced him to leave the unhealthy air of Naples for a monastery at neighbouring Pozzuoli. According to legend he died having just completed his *Stabat Mater*, his greatest and most emotionally direct work, which like *La serva padrona* was to take on an almost talismanic significance in the second half of the eighteenth century.

HULTON DEUTSCH

Giovanni Pergolesi

La serva padrona

The Maid Turned Mistress

Composed 1733.
First performed August 28, 1733.
Libretto by Gennar'antonio Federico.

Synopsis

Part I

Uberto complains about his maidservant Serpina, who is late bringing him his chocolate and has become a dictator in his home. He tells his servant Vespone to find him a wife who will do what she is told. Serpina overhears and offers herself but Uberto is adamant that it should be anybody but her.

Part II

Serpina persuades Vespone to join her in tricking the master into marrying her. She tells Uberto of her plans to marry Captain Tempest and when he asks to meet her suitor she introduces a disguised Vespone. Serpina tells him of the silent Captain's wish for a dowry. If he does not receive the money he will insist that Uberto marry her in his place. Valuing money above peace and quiet, Uberto agrees to marry Serpina and when Vespone reveals himself, Uberto realizes that he has loved Serpina all along.

La serva padrona more than deserves its reputation as one of the century's most accomplished comic operas, but, as with the majority of intermezzi, its melodic beauty is outweighed by the lengthy recitative – in short, to modern ears it can be a finely crafted bore. Within the 45-minute span there are just two proper arias (one by each of the principles – Vespone is silent) and one duet, the remainder being made up of a brief overture, arioso and recitative. On the other hand, the orchestral writing (for two violins, one viola and a cello – in other words a string quartet) is cheerful, the pace of the action is swift, the accompaniments typically unobtrusive and the two parts are separated by no more than a brief pause.

The characterization is simple but vivid and the players' primary emotions are neatly established through direct and tuneful vocal writing. Serpina's "Stizzoso, mio Stizzoso" establishes her as a demanding shrew, and neatly sets the scene for her Part II aria "A Serpina penserete" in which she proves, through music of almost introverted beauty, that she is not so bad after all. This heralds Uberto's "indecision" aria "Son imbrogliato io già", in which he begins to crack under the pressure; and the opera ends with a wonderful ensemble in which Uberto finally confesses his love and Serpina celebrates her victory, cruelly hinting that Uberto has not, after all, made the right decision.

RECORDINGS OVERVIEW

There have been fifteen recordings of *La serva padrona*, but only two are currently available on CD, and one of these is difficult to track down. The best versions were made in the mid-1950s, when Ferdinand Leitner produced a scintillating and fanciful account for Archiv and Renato Fasano made an excellent set for Ricordi with a youthful Renata Scotto enjoying herself as Serpina. RCA released a fine recording in 1962 with Anna Moffo as a genuinely coloratura heroine, but in the absence of this trio, go for the perfectly satisfactory version reviewed below.

Poulenard, Cantor; Ensemble Baroque de Nice; Bezzina.
(Pierre Verany PV 795111; 1 CD).

This is not a perfect recording but it is certainly a very energetic and engaging one, and in fact the slightly rough-and-ready quality of the Ensemble Baroque de Nice helps to recreate the theatricality and spontaneity that must have informed the original Italian touring companies' performances. The recitatives are delivered with a panache that prevents them from clogging up the momentum – a fault of several other recordings. The two soloists are well cast and work well together: Philippe Cantor's Uberto is suitably gruff and bothered but without resorting to bluster, and Isabelle Poulenard as the scheming Serpina cleverly conveys the character's waspish and insidious charm, while always in complete control of the often difficult passagework. Bezzina's busy but unfussy direction keeps the whole thing scampering along with considerable élan; occasionally his tempi border on the madcap – Uberto's aria "Sempre in contrasti" is an extreme example – but he keeps the adrenaline flowing.

Farkas, Gregor; Capella Savaria; Németh.
(Hungaroton HCD 12846-2; 1 CD).

This elusive recording is a delightful introduction to Pergolesi's intermezzo, with excellent buffo characterizations from the bass József Gregor and the soubrette Katalin Farkas. Gyula Németh's direction is light and engagingly articulated, and the Capella Savaria provide suitably flexible support. The digital recording is clear and intelligently engineered.

ANDRÉ CAMPRA

b. AIX-EN-PROVENCE, FRANCE, DECEMBER 4, 1660; d. VERSAILLES, JUNE 29, 1744.

André Campra was the most important French opera composer between Lully and Rameau. Like many of his French Baroque contemporaries, he sought to reconcile aspects of the Italian style (such as the da capo aria) with that of the French – in his own words, to mix French "délicatesse" with Italian "vivacité".

He began his career as a church musician but from quite early on this seems to have been compromised by his penchant for the stage – in 1681, while at the church of St Sauveur in Aix, he was officially reproved for his involvement in theatrical performances. The fact that he was studying for the priesthood may have had something to do with it, but the incident didn't prevent him becoming a chaplain in the same year. After a number of appointments in southern France, including *maître de musique* at Ste Trophime in Arles and at St Etienne in Toulouse, in 1694 he was appointed *maître de musique* at the cathedral of Notre Dame in Paris. His first known theatre works date from his arrival in Paris, but in order to protect his position he published them anonymously or under his younger brother's name. Not until 1700 did he give up his job at Notre Dame and publish the *tragédie lyrique Hésione* under his own name.

Campra went on to write nine *tragédies lyriques*, all of which were revived during the eighteenth century, but historically his most significant contribution to French theatre was the creation of the opéra-ballet. This was a typically French combination of dance and song that replaced the serious and exemplary world of mythology and chivalry (found in *tragédie lyrique*) with a frivolous and hedonistic fantasy world, much like that of Watteau's *fêtes galantes*. The first example of the new genre, *L'Europe galante*, was staged in 1697, and its reception encouraged Campra to leave Notre Dame. His success as a theatre composer began to diminish from 1718, the year of his last opéra-ballet, *Les âges*, and two years later he began once more to compose for the church, sharing the position of *sous-maître de musique* at the chapel royal between 1723 and 1735.

Idoménée

Idomeneus

Composed 1711.
First performed January 12, 1712.
Libretto by Antoine Danchet after Crébillon.

Synopsis

Prologue

A group of winds beg Aeolus (Eole), the god of the winds, to release them from the rocks to which they are chained. Venus arrives and requests the winds to blow up a storm in order to punish King Idomeneus (Idoménée) of Crete for his defeat of the Trojans. On their release the winds hurry away to carry out her wishes.

Act I

On the island of Crete, in the royal palace, the captive Trojan princess Ilione reveals her love for Idamantes (Idamante), the son of Idomeneus. Idamantes enters and tells her that he has decided to free her Trojan companions because of the love that he feels for her. Amid the rejoicing, news arrives that Idomeneus is lost at sea. The Greek Elektra (Electre), who is staying at the palace, also loves Idamante and expresses her jealousy and her desire for revenge.

Act II

During a violent storm off the Cretan coast, Neptune rises from the sea and calms the storm. Safe on shore, Idomeneus confesses that he has vowed to Neptune that he will sacrifice the first person that he meets, but that turns out to be his son Idamantes whom he warns to keep away from him. The frustrated Elektra calls on Venus to destroy the love of Ilione and Idamantes. Venus calls on Jealousy to poison Idomeneus's feelings for his son.

Act III

In the harbour of Cydonia, Idomeneus is troubled by his jealous feelings towards his son. He decides that Idamantes should accompany Elektra on her journey back to Argos. When Ilione enters, Idomeneus accuses her of loving his son. Elektra rejoices in her imminent departure with Idamantes, but before they can leave there is another storm and the sea god Proteus (Protée) appears, demanding that Idomeneus keep his vow or a monster will attack Crete.

Act IV

Ilione is initially pleased at the suffering caused by the monster but fears for the safety of Idamantes. Idamantes enters full of grief and wishing to die. Ilione confesses her love for him and tells him that his father loves her also. Idomeneus enters and begs Idamantes to leave, before praying to Neptune to cease his anger. News arrives that Idamantes has slain the monster. Idomeneus gives up his pursuit of Ilione and relinquishes the throne to his son.

Act V

Elektra is incensed by the happy outcome and swears to invoke Neptune's rage once again. Idomeneus is about to lead his son to the throne when a terrible noise is heard and Nemesis, the goddess of Vengeance, appears from the underworld. Idomeneus goes mad and kills his son. When his sanity returns and he realizes what he has done, he tries to kill himself but Ilione tells him that his punishment will be to live.

The theme of Idomeneus – a father obliged to sacrifice a child – is a particularly compelling one, with direct parallels in the Old Testament stories of Jeptha, and of Abraham and Isaac. Antoine Danchet, who was Campra's main collaborator, based his libretto on Crébillon's highly successful play of 1705 in which the myth of Idomeneus had already been elaborated by a rivalry between father and son for the love of Ilione. To this, Danchet adds the further complication of Elektra's jealous love of Idamantes, which acts as a catalyst to the story's tragic outcome.

The opera follows the conventions of the Lullian *tragédie lyrique* with the welcome exception of having a prologue that has a direct bearing on the opera's story rather than the usual paean to royal *gloire*. In fact the prologue gives a clear indication of the variety of musical riches that are about to enfold. Campra's approach is much more dynamic and dramatically convincing than Lully's, in two respects in particular. First, his orchestral writing is much more colourful and descriptive, with particular types of music associated with particular characters or situations. Thus in the prologue the desperate entreaties of the winds are accompanied by music of extreme agitation while Aeolus's interruptions are slow, forceful and majestic. Second, Campra employs the chorus with far more dramatic effect: they are no longer mere commentators on the drama but active participants. The offstage chorus of shipwrecked people at the beginning of Act II is the most frequently quoted example (the idea was later used by Rameau in his opera *Zoroastre*), but just as powerful is the wonderful combination of soloist and chorus in Act IV, when Idomeneus prays to Neptune to be merciful. Equally impressive is the way Campra invests the declamatory passages with vigour and passion, particularly in the extended dialogues that recur in the work. The first meeting of Idamantes and Idomeneus was singled out by the *Mercure de France* as one of the high points of the opera, and its effectiveness stems largely from the way Campra uses changes of harmony and pace to signify increasing emotional disquiet.

Overall this is a remarkable dramatic achievement – even the extended divertissements and wonderfully elegant dance music are carefully integrated into the logic of the action. On the strength of this work alone, Campra deserves to be far better known, even more so if you consider that his finest work is found in the opéra-ballets, none of which is currently available on CD.

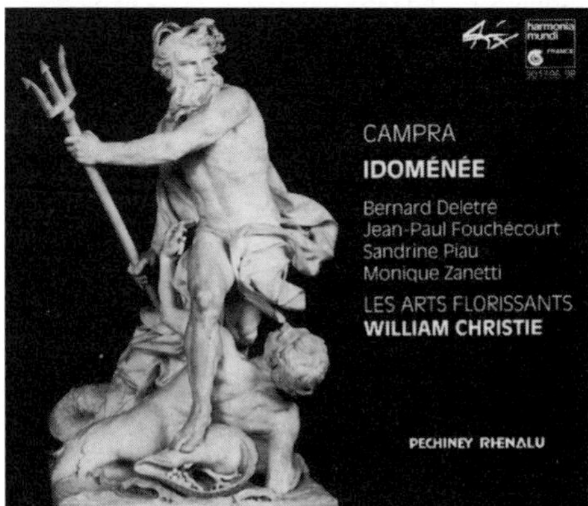

harmonia mundi
CAMPRA
IDOMÉNÉE
Bernard Deletré
Jean-Paul Fouchécourt
Sandrine Piau
Monique Zanetti
LES ARTS FLORISSANTS
WILLIAM CHRISTIE
PECHINEY RHENALU

Deletré, Fouchécourt, Piau, Zanetti; Les Arts Florissants; Christie.
(Harmonia Mundi HMC 901396.98; 3 CDs).

This may be a venture into one of the obscurer corners of French Baroque music but Christie and Les Arts Florissants pull out all the stops to produce one of their very finest achievements. The cast includes many Christie regulars, yet this set seems almost perfectly cast without any obvious weak links. Ironically, given her malevolent intent, some of the most lyrical moments are given to Elektra (notably the Handelian aria "Que mes plaisirs" in Act III), a role to which Sandrine Piau brings a wonderful clarity and intensity. Equally impressive is the harder-toned Monique Zanetti in the more stoical role of Ilione. The many recitative-style sections to this work are especially well handled: there is no attempt to rush them out of the way, but instead the dramatic purpose of each scene is allowed to unfold at a rate dictated by the emotional content.

JEAN-PHILIPPE RAMEAU

b. DIJON, FRANCE, SEPTEMBER 25, 1683; d. PARIS, SEPTEMBER 12, 1764.

LEBRECHT COLLECTION

Jean-Philippe Rameau

In Voltaire's words: "After Lully, all other musicians . . . simply imitated him until Rameau came." Rameau's operas did not make a conspicuous break with tradition: their subjects remained myth-bound and involved displays of theatrical opulence, incorporating choruses and ballets. But aspects of his style caused great controversy, notably his predilection for complex counterpoint, his theatrical use of harmony, his lyrical vocal manner and, most important, his move towards a smoother manner of construction. The most lasting of his innovations, however, was his cultivation of a highly expressive form of recitative, accompanied by a chromatic and colourful orchestral presence. The effect electrified French theatres and it remained his most lasting gift to Gluck. Remarkably, Rameau did not compose the first of his operas until 1733, when he was already fifty years old. His success had been a long time in coming partly because he had spent the first forty years of his life in the provinces, and partly because what reputation he had made was as a music theorist, an occupation generally thought incompatible with the business of composing. In spite of his academic background his music does not sound especially cerebral – indeed the very opposite is true.

He was born the seventh of eleven children. His father was the organist of the cathedral of Dijon, a post to which Jean-Philippe succeeded in 1709. His early career was spent largely as an organist at a series of French cathedrals, including Clermont-Ferrand, where in 1722 he published his famous *Traité de l'harmonie* (Treatise on Harmony), in which he examined the origins of harmony and the relationships between chords. The following year he left for Paris but achieved only modest success writing light theatrical works and teaching the harpsichord, before being taken up by one of the city's greatest patrons, the financier La Riche de la Pouplinière. One of the wealthiest men in France, La Pouplinière was prodigal in his expenditure on art and maintained a private chapel with an orchestra of fourteen players at his château at Passy near Paris. Patron and composer became great friends: from 1731 until 1753 Rameau was the music director at Passy, and it was La Pouplinière who provided the money and contacts that launched Rameau's late-flourishing operatic career.

Strange though it might now seem, his operas stirred controversy at the outset. The concentrated drama of *Hippolyte et Aricie* unnerved the conservative establishment, for whom Lully's well-mannered style was the benchmark, and it was not long before the Paris Opéra was riven by factionalism. In one corner stood the Ramistes, champions of the vivid theatrics of Rameau, and in the other stood the Lullistes, urging a return to order and decorum. The conflict raged, on and off, for twenty years, during which time Rameau became increasingly popular – so popular that he became a cornerstone of the establishment against which he had once rebelled. Indeed by 1752, when he became embroiled in the so-called Querelle des Bouffons (see p.49), Rameau was being attacked as the establishment's foremost representative. He continued working into his seventies, producing *Les Boréades* in his eightieth year, but even before his death he was being dismissed as a fossil. With Gluck's arrival in Paris, Rameau was more or less forgotten.

Hippolyte et Aricie

Hippolytus and Aricia

Composed 1733.
First performed October 1, 1733.
Libretto by Simon-Joseph Pellegrin, after Racine.

Synopsis

Prologue

Diana (Diane) is persuaded by Jupiter to permit her chaste forest-dwellers to follow Cupid on one day of the year. But she vows to protect Hippolytus (Hippolyte) and Aricia (Aricie).

Act I

Aricia is the last descendant of Pallas, the enemy of King Theseus (Thesee), and she must take a vow of chastity in the temple of Diana. Before the ceremony takes place, she and Hippolytus, Theseus's son, reveal to each other their mutual love and ask Diana for assistance. Phaedra (Phèdre), Theseus's wife, arrives to make sure that the vow has taken place. She is enraged when she discovers Aricia's disobedience and orders the sacking of the temple; but Diana descends to prevent it and tells the lovers that she will protect them. The news that Theseus has descended into Hades (the world of the dead) means that Phaedra can now express her love for her stepson Hippolytus.

Act II

Theseus, though believed dead, is wandering Hades looking for his comrade Peirithous, who has tried to abduct Prosperina, Pluto's wife. Theseus is tried at the court of Pluto as Peirithous's accomplice. He asks his father Neptune for help, and Mercury descends to intercede for him. Before he leaves the underworld, however, the Fates predict that he will find Hell in his own home.

Act III

In Theseus's palace, Hippolytus pledges his support to Phaedra, but she mistakes this for love and offers him the throne and herself. Hippolytus responds by telling her that he loves Aricia, and in her rage Phaedra attempts to snatch his sword and kill herself; as they wrestle for the weapon, Theseus appears. Remembering the Fates' prophesy, he assumes the worst and calls on his father to punish Hippolytus.

Act IV

Hippolytus and Aricia flee to Diana's sacred grove and decide to share a life of exile. Suddenly a sea monster appears and Hippolytus is carried off. Phaedra arrives, hears what has happened, and is filled with remorse.

Act V

Phaedra has killed herself but before dying she tells Theseus the truth. Stricken, he is about to throw himself into the sea when Neptune intervenes to reveal that Hippolytus is alive. However, because of his readiness to believe in his son's guilt, Theseus is condemned never to see him again. Meanwhile Diana attempts to console the distraught Aricia by promising her a husband. Hippolytus enters and the two lovers are reunited.

𝄞 Rameau's first opera, *Hippolyte et Aricie*, diverted a river through the stables of French musical life. Here a heightened dramatic awareness and emotional sensibility were applied to a classical myth in which characterization was unprecedentedly real. Aricia, who had played only a minor role in Racine's *Phèdre* – Pellegrin's source – was now the drama's pivotal influence, while Hippolytus's heroic qualities were displaced by romantic inclinations that, for many, were almost too human. Rameau's Phaedra is far more likely to excite sympathy than Racine's, and the part of Theseus was also greatly enhanced – his scene in Hades was interpolated so that Rameau could indulge in some rich character development and some even richer pictorialism. Theseus leaves the stage a grander and less distant figure than had traditionally been the case.

Trouncing convention, Rameau's score illuminates each character as a developing person. Phaedra is initially presented through stringent harmony and arid melody, her character cold and repellent; but with her confession of guilt Rameau's music ripens – the swelling orchestration, the opulent melody and the interjections of a horrified crowd giving her a new magnitude. "Here lies the god of Harmony" read one of Rameau's epitaphs, and *Hippolyte* abounds with vivid orchestral writing – the storm in Act I and the boiling waters of Act III (comparable in violence to the earthquake in *Les Indes galantes*) are among the most gripping episodes in French Baroque opera.

Gens, Fouchécourt, Fink, Smythe; Les Musiciens du Louvre; Minkowski
(Archiv 445 853-2; 3 CDs).

From the opening bars it is easy to hear why the original audience would have found this work so shocking: it has a contrapuntal complexity that still sounds daring, and the impression of a restlessly active imagination at work is emphasized by Minkowski's forceful interpretation. For the protagonists Minkowski uses two Harmonia Mundi regulars: Veronique Gens makes a touchingly convincing Aricie and Jean-Paul Fouchécourt a strong Hippolyte, although his performance is markedly less committed than in Campra's *Idoménée*. Both at times seem a little cowed by their orchestral support, and Bernarda Fink as Phèdre is the only singer who really establishes a real sense of a developed characterization. Archiv's engineers create a rather marked distance between the singers and the listener, an effect that is probably closer to a live performance but which on CD is a little uninvolving – especially if you're used to the more close-up ambience of Harmonia Mundi.

Les Indes galantes

The Amorous Indies

Composed 1735.
First performed August 23, 1735.
Libretto by Louis Fuzelier.

Synopsis

Prologue

The youth of four European nations abandon the pleasures of the palace of Hebe to follow Bellona, the goddess of war. Cupid descends and sends his minions away to the furthest corners of the Indies to seek and create followers of Love.

Entrée I: The generous Turk

The young French girl Emile has been captured and sold as a slave to the Pasha Osman. He falls in love with her, but she cannot forget Valère, a French sailor. Valère's ship runs aground, and he is captured and brought before the Pasha. Osman recognizes him as the one who liberated him from slavery and then releases him and Emile.

Entrée II: The Incas of Peru

In the Peruvian desert the Incas are preparing their Festival of the Sun in the shadow of a volcano. A Spanish officer, Don Carlos, and a Peruvian girl, Phani, have fallen in love but the High Priest Huascar disapproves and causes the volcano to erupt, claiming it as a sign of the Sun God's displeasure. Don Carlos, wise to the deception, escapes with Phani, leaving Huascar to bring the volcano down upon his own head.

Entrée III: The Flowers, a Persian festival

Tacmas, a young Persian prince, and his confidant Ali have fallen in love with each other's slaves: Tacmas with Zaïre and Ali with Fatima. On the day of the flower festival all four meet, but with Tacmas disguised as a woman and Fatima as a man there is much confusion. When it emerges that each of the slaves loves the other's master, a swap is engineered and the new couples enjoy the festival.

Entrée IV: The Savages

In an American forest, Adario, the commander of a defeated tribe of Indians, is preparing to celebrate peace with the victorious Europeans. He is in love with Zima, the chief's daughter, who is also desired by the Spaniard, Don Alvar, and the Frenchman, Damon. However, claiming that the Spaniard is too jealous a lover and the Frenchman too indifferent a one, Zima chooses Adario. The festivities culminate in a dance of the pipe of peace.

After the dramatic excess of *Hippolyte* Rameau turned to the lighter vein of opéra-ballet. The four dramas, each set in an exotic location, presented the composer with an irrestible challenge to his pictorial skills, a challenge to which he rose with consummate panache, from the volcano in Entrée I to the Indian dances of Entrée IV. However, there's more to *Les Indes galantes* than the conventional special effects of opéra-ballet, for the romances at the heart of Fuzelier's consistently witty libretto gave Rameau an opportunity to cover the full emotional range from *opera-lyrique* to *tragédie en musique*. Unlike most examples of the genre, this opéra-ballet is populated by living personalities – even the Sun God turns out to be a jealous oaf.

The array of ballets, choruses and airs is traditional enough, but Rameau's fluency – with each episode running smoothly into the next – is astounding, and its coherence made *Les Indes galantes* one of Rameau's most widely praised creations (Berlioz was a later admirer). The variety of its dance forms, from complex chaconnes to simple minuets, and of its choruses, from laments to the "Brillant Soleil" of Entrée II, makes this opera endlessly entertaining, while Fuzelier's ethnic caricatures illuminate the ways in which non-European culture was perceived during the *ancien régime*. Not all the noble savages are derived from secondhand sources: the final entrée contains a reworking of Rameau's work for harpsichord "Les sauvages", which was inspired by the appearance of two native Americans in Paris in 1725.

McFadden, Corréas, Poulenard, Rivenq; Arts Florissants Chorus, Arts Florissants Orchestra; Christie.
(Harmonia Mundi HMC90 1367-9; 3 CDs).

This is a superb recording. William Christie brings out the music's vitality and its architecture, and his team of soloists – all of whom had worked together on a stage production of the opera at the Aix-en-Provence festival in 1991 – are equally alert to its qualities. They are clearly at ease with Christie's rapid tempi, and there

THE QUERELLE DES BOUFFONS

Rameau's music was not the only challenge to the Lullian tradition – another was posed by the *comédies en vaudeville* that were held at Paris's great annual fairs of Saint-Laurent and Saint-Germain. These earthy and largely satirical entertainments took the form of spoken plays combined with well-known popular songs to which new words had been added – not unlike England's ballad operas, as perfected by John Gay (see p.63). Unfortunately the Opéra and the Comédie-Française – frequent targets of vaudevillian parody – did everything in their power to enforce their own privileges and suppress the activities of the fairground players. Even when the various vaudevillian companies were merged in 1715 to form an official Théâtre de L'Opéra-Comique, it was still consistently undermined by the spoiling tactics of the other companies. The new company began to come into its own from 1743, under the management of Jean Monnet, who surrounded himself with the brilliant talent of, among others, the painter Boucher (as set designer) and the librettist Charles-Simon Favart.

It was during Monnet's management in 1752 that the *Querelle des Bouffons* blew up. The most heated row during almost a century of debate about the relative merits of French and Italian operatic styles, the *Querelle* was sparked by a performance of Pergolesi's *La serva padrona* by Bambini's troupe of Italian comic actors (the "bouffons"). Battle lines were drawn up: the French tradition was defended by Rameau, while the progressive position – arguing that opera buffa offered a way of revitalizing the stolid conventions of *tragédie lyrique* – was advocated by the *philosophes*, in particular Jean-Jacques Rousseau, whose *Lettre sur la musique française* was the most sustained intellectual critique of French opera ever published. Even the court became embroiled: indeed, the *Querelle* was known in some circles as the *Guerre des Coins* (War of the Corners), as it became common for supporters of serious opera to group around the king's box at the Opéra, while supporters of comic opera gathered about the queen.

Bambini's troupe left Paris in 1754 and the debate ground to a halt with neither side triumphant. At the Opéra the *tragédie lyrique* continued as the dominant genre for the next twenty years, but opera buffa had made its impact on French comic opera, even if it failed to win Italian opera a permanent foothold in France. Rousseau himself wrote a rather naive Italian-style opera in French, *Le Devin du Village* (The Village Soothsayer), while Monnet commissioned an opera buffa in French, *Les Troqueurs*, from an unknown Italian composer who in fact turned out to be a Frenchman, Antoine Dauvergne. *Les Troqueurs* was extremely popular – even Rameau was said to admire it – and it established a pattern of Italianate comic works, with recitative replacing spoken dialogue, that was successfully built on by composers like Duni, Philidor and Gretry. As for the perennial France-versus-Italy argument, it was to re-emerge with increased fervour in the Gluck/Piccini conflict of 1777 (see p.71).

are some marvellous comic touches from Nicolas Rivenq as Osman and Bernard Delétré as Huascar. The orchestra and chorus are excellent as well, only rarely sacrificing dramatic fluency and character to detail and precision.

Castor et Pollux

Composed 1737; revised 1754.
First performed October 24, 1737.
Libretto by Pierre-Joseph Justin Bernard.

Synopsis (revised version)

Act I

Pollux is to marry Telaira (Télaïre), even though she is in love with his twin brother Castor, who in turn loves her. Castor bids her farewell, preferring exile to hopeless love. Pollux overhears Castor and Telaira, and he tells them of his decision to allow Castor to marry Telaira, because he cannot bear to witness the unhappiness of the two people he loves most. The Spartans sing in praise of the happy couple and of Pollux's generosity, but then the twins' rival Linceus attacks the palace in his lust for Telaira. In the ensuing battle Castor is killed; the chorus calls on Pollux to avenge his brother.

Act II

Pollux is persuaded by Telaira to ask his father Jupiter to bring the dead Castor back to life. Jupiter reluctantly agrees to Pollux's wish but in return he must take his brother's place in Hades. Pollux agrees.

Act III

Encouraged by Telaira and aided by Mercury, Pollux defeats the demons barring his way to the underworld.

Act IV

Castor wanders Elysium, alone and unhappy. He misses Telaira but forgets everything when his brother arrives. He refuses to accept Pollux's sacrifice but agrees to return to earth for a single day.

Act V

Castor and Telaira are reunited, but she is distraught when he tells her he must leave again. Moved by the brothers' love for each other, Jupiter restores Pollux to life and grants them both immortality and a place in the firmament.

With *Castor et Pollux* Rameau and his librettist produced an opera that complied with the enduring demand for mythological subjects, but characteristically added a twist. Plenty of operas had ennobled the love between a man and a woman, but *Castor et Pollux* raised filial love to a position of comparable glory. Many were initially repelled by the presentation of the passionate companionship of two men – irrespective of their brotherhood – but the opera was championed as Rameau's greatest when it was revived in 1754. Its reception second time round was doubtless helped by Rameau's extensive revisions: the prologue was removed, a new and brief scene-setting first act was written, the third and fourth acts were fused (to retain the conventional five-act format) and a large amount of recitative was cut. In addition, the descriptive instrumental passages and heavily contrapuntal dances were rewritten for the much-inflated orchestra that Rameau had at his disposal second time round. The resulting opera is much better constructed, and this is the version most often played.

Castor et Pollux is dominated by the former's tenor and the latter's high bass. Initially their writing appears a little narrow, but as the action develops and their behaviour becomes more and more selfless, the music grows in expressivity, reaching its climax when the brothers are united, to music of Gluck-like magnitude. Castor's famously haunting soliloquy "Séjour de l'eternelle paix" is a profoundly moving example of Rameau's elegiac vocal style, a style coloured by an Italianate coloratura.

Jeffes, Huttenlocher, Smith, Buchan; English Bach Festival Chorus and Orchestra; Farncombe.
(Erato 4509-95311-2; 3 CDs).

Recorded in 1982, Charles Farncombe's performance of the 1754 *Castor et Pollux* is unquestionably the best sung, with Peter Jeffes's tenor and Philipe Huttenlocher's ever-resourceful baritone (low enough to tackle the role) bringing some bewitching tones to their intelligent, emotive interpretations. Jeffes's singing of "Séjour de l'eternelle paix" is particularly unforgettable. The female cast are equally impressive and although the EBCO lacks the personality of more recent ensembles, they play with spirit, clearly relishing the Act III descent into the underworld and the final chaconne. Excellent, resonant sound.

Platée

Plataea

Composed 1745.
First performed March 31, 1745.
Libretto by Adrien-Joseph Le Valois d'Orville, after Autreau.

Synopsis

Prologue

The Birth of Comedy: Thespis plots with Momus (god of ridicule), Thalie (muse of comedy) and Love to teach mortals and gods a lesson.

Act I

King Cithaeron (Cithéron) plots with Mercury to cure Juno of her jealousy. Jupiter, her husband, is to woo the grotesque, swamp-dwelling nymph Plataea (Platée).

Act II

As part of his courtship Jupiter changes shape into a donkey, a cloud and other forms, before finally appearing in his own shape, accompanied by lightning. As the seduction continues he orders a divertissement in Plataea's honour, led by Momus and La Folie, attended by their servants dressed as babies and Greek philosophers.

Act III

News of the affair has reached Juno and she arrives, disguised, at the wedding. Heavily disguised to hide her identity, Plataea is delivered by frog-drawn chariot to her wedding; Momus arrives as L'Amour, with an outsized bow and quiver. Jupiter is about to recite his marriage vows when Juno swoops down and tears off Plataea's mask. Juno's jealousy is thus shown to be absurd; ridiculed by the entire cast, Plataea returns to her marsh.

𝄞 It's hard to imagine why such an opera that is largely an exercise in humiliation was commissioned for the wedding of the dauphin to the famously unattractive Spanish princess Maria Theresa at Versailles in 1745. Perhaps because comedy was never exactly central to the French operatic tradition it came as a welcome surprise, no matter the unfortunate personal references. To be fair, the opera's cruelty is more acute in synopsis than on stage, and Rameau does direct one's sympathies towards the nymph, but nonetheless it can't have been a comfortable experience for the dauphin's bride.

On one level, *Platée* is a parody of serious opera, in which Rameau ridicules the stilted gestures, language and music of Lullian drama: the exaggerated vocal acrobatics will seem ludicrous even if you don't know what they are lampooning. The music descends into delicious farce with Plataea's marriage ceremony, in which Momus, pretending to be Love, is accompanied by outrageous glissandi to mimic his gifts of tears and sighs, and the celebrants dance to a "plus noble" chaconne that is anything but noble. In addition to this arsenal of satire, Rameau employs some delightful naturalistic effects in the imitation of Plataea's swamp friends (the frogs, cuckoos etc) and Jupiter's various animal incarnations. Not everything is intended to amuse (Plataea's rejection is really unpleasant), but so sweet and ingenuous is Rameau's melody and so beguiling are the ensembles that only rarely do you feel ill-disposed to Jupiter's subterfuge.

Ragon, Smith, de Mey, le Texier; Ensemble Vocale Françoise Herr, Musiciens du Louvre; Minkowski.
(Erato 2292-45028-2; 2 CDs).

With such an eminent cast, it is a shame that Mark Minkowski should have chosen to place such store by exaggerated gestures and exclamations – they are intended to draw your attention to the comedy, but much of the comedy is self-evident. However, Gilles Ragon's Plataea and Guy de Mey's Mercury are marvellous and Vincent Le Texier's Jupiter is both eloquent and amusing. The Musiciens du Louvre are one of the drier authentic bands, and Minkowski might have sweetened the tone, but they are attentive to detail and produce clear and expressive support.

GEORG-PHILIPP TELEMANN

b. MAGDEBURG, GERMANY, MARCH 14, 1681; d. HAMBURG, JUNE 25, 1767.

Telemann was the most prolific composer of his day and during the first half of the eighteenth century was universally regarded as Germany's greatest composer. Two hundred years later, history has judged Telemann an overproductive also-ran, vastly inferior to his friend and colleague J.S. Bach. As an opera composer, however, Telemann has nothing to fear from the comparison, for Bach wrote not a single opera.

Telemann was born at Magdeburg into an affluent, middle-class family. Both his father and his brother were clergymen, and despite showing musical aptitude from an early age – his first opera, *Sigismunde*, was written at the age of twelve – he was intended for a similarly respectable career. In 1701 he went to the University of Leipzig to study law, but once his musical talents were discovered by others, including the mayor, he was persuaded to follow his true vocation. He founded the Collegium Musicum, a student music society that gave public concerts, became organist of the Neue Kirche, then director of Leipzig Opera, and achieved such dominance of the city's musical life that its ostensible music director, Kuhnau, started to complain. Telemann left Leipzig in 1705, and after positions at Sorau, Eisenach and Frankfurt he was invited by the city of Hamburg to be cantor of the Johanneum (the grammar school) and to be responsible for the music at the city's five principal churches. He arrived in Hamburg in 1721, and the following year was also appointed director of the celebrated Hamburg Opera, a position that he held until its closure in 1738.

Hamburg was a commercially thriving city-state, and its opera house, the Theatre am Gänsemarkt, was the leading civic company in Germany as well as the main centre for opera sung in German. Its success with its middle-class audience had been established at the beginning of the century by Reinhard Keiser (1674–1739), whose pragmatic and eclectic approach bypassed the reforms of Metastasio and provided a precedent for Telemann. At Hamburg there were no qualms about mixing musical styles, comedy and tragedy, or indeed the German and Italian language (the latter was preferred for the great display arias).

Telemann continued the Hamburg tradition, even before his appointment as director: for example, *Der geduldige Socrates* (The Patient Socrates), performed at the Gänsemarkt theatre in 1721, mixes the comic and the contemplative, sometimes in the same scene. Telemann's orchestral writing also bears the imprint of Hamburg's more adventurous approach, and he is among the first to look to the orchestra as a source of character, rather than just accompaniment, frequently using it as a means towards a dramatic end. Moreover, he followed Keiser in regularly introducing folk music into his operas, a populist ploy that varied the means of delineating character – and looked forward to the folkloric aspects of German Romantic music. Unfortunately, any analysis of Telemann's work as an opera composer is inhibited by the scarcity of manuscripts. Few of his forty or so opera scores have survived and his operatic reputation is carried by a single work, *Pimpinone*, an intermezzo (or *zwischenspiel*) first performed during Telemann's adaptation of his friend Handel's opera *Tamerlano*.

Pimpinone

Composed 1725.
First performed September 27, 1725.
Libretto by Pietro Pariati, translated and adapted by Johann Praetorius.

Synopsis

Part I

Vespetta, a chambermaid, is looking for a rich husband. She meets Pimpinone, a rich and gullible merchant who is looking for a serving girl. Won over by her good looks and her flattery, he decides to employ her.

Part II

Vespetta threatens to leave Pimpinone's employ because of the hard work and the gossip about their relationship. Pimpinone offers to marry her, and she agrees on condition that she receives a large dowry.

Part III

Vespetta is now married but unhappy: she wants to go out and have a good time. Pimpinone threatens to beat her but she is unafraid and threatens him back. Vespetta points out that the terms of the marriage stipulate that she gets the dowry if they divorce. Pimpinone submits to her will.

Telemann was the most Teutonic of composers, but his only opera to have survived the passing of time is a decidedly Italianate comedy. *Pimpinone* was immensely popular in its day, and Telemann's swift and highly entertaining music, together with its brevity (just over an hour), have ensured its continuing performance. *Pimpinone* develops devices that were to become standard comic effects until well into the next century, such as rapid "babblings" on a single note, the frequent repetition of fragmentary motifs, unexpected instrumental interjections, and sudden changes in vocal register, colour and mood ("interrupted flow" was to become something of a Rossini trademark). In classic opera buffa style, the melodies are light, the vocal writing bounces along, and the characters are homely and sympathetic. On top of this Telemann tapped into a rich vein of folk music that had exercised only cursory interest for Hamburg composers such as Keiser. In this respect, he can be seen as a nationalist composer before his time.

All this suggests that Telemann might well have been one of the most innovative composers of his period, but conclusive evidence of his achievement is lacking. Telemann composed a sequel, *Die amours der Vespetta*, in 1727, but the score has never been found.

Baird, Ostendorf; Baroque Orchestra of St Luke's; Palmer.
(Newport Classic NCD 60117; 1 CD).

This is the only recording of *Pimpinone* currently available, but it is difficult to recommend. The fault lies largely with conductor Rudolph Palmer, who takes everything at the same flat-footed pace and robs the music of all dramatic contrast. The two soloists are enthusiastic but inadequate: Julianne Baird's Vespetta lacks the requisite sparkle and attack and tries to compensate by hamming it up. As Pimpinone, John Ostendorf (who wrote the excellent sleeve-notes) is better but the woolliness of the orchestral playing holds him back. For a comedy this is a singularly depressing experience, best avoided by all but the insatiably curious.

GEORGE FRIDERIC HANDEL

b. HALLE AN DER SALLE, GERMANY, FEBRUARY 23, 1685; d. LONDON, APRIL 14, 1759.

Handel was one of the greatest composers of the eighteenth century, yet his operas – to which he devoted most of his creative life – have never commanded as much enthusiasm as his oratorios and instrumental works. Handel was rarely an innovator: he accepted most of the conventions he inherited, the majority of his subjects are taken from the stock library of history, myth and romantic legend, and his characterizations are too often unremarkable. Furthermore, his vocal writing is frequently formulaic, and his scores – often composed under impossible conditions – are often repetitious. Yet for all that, Handel's operas contain some of the most gorgeous music of the eighteenth century, and it's impossible to understand the operatic culture of the period without some knowledge of his output.

Handel's first and keenest influence was the composer Reinhard Keiser, director of the opera house in Hamburg, the city to which Handel moved in 1703, a year after the death of his father. Handel played violin and harpsichord in Keiser's orchestra, and in 1705–06 Keiser helped stage Handel's first four operas, *Almira*, *Nero*, *Florindo* and *Doro*. Only the first of these has survived, but it's clear from *Almira* that Handel was, at best, imitating Keiser's well-established models: its libretto is a mixture of German and Italian, as was common in Hamburg, and the score betrays an obvious debt to Italian music. Handel's taste for Italian Baroque can be traced back to 1698, when he took a trip to the Berlin court and came into contact with the composers Attilio Ariosti and Giovanni Bononcini. His Italianate leanings were further encouraged in 1705, when Prince Ferdinando de' Medici, son of the Grand Duke of Tuscany, visited Hamburg and urged Handel to continue his studies of Italian music.

So enthused was the composer that, the following year, he left Hamburg for Florence (where he was introduced to Alessandro and Domenico Scarlatti), Rome and Florence, where his opera *Vincer se stesso è la maggior vittoria* – also known as *Rodrigo* – was staged. Like *Almira*, the opera followed the Keiser/Hamburg template and achieved little success, but his breakthrough came in the winter of 1709 when, moving to Venice, he produced the greatest of his "Italian" operas, *Agrippina*. On the strength of this triumph, Handel gained employment the following year with the Elector of Hanover, who immediately gave the composer a year's leave to visit England. Handel arrived to find himself the flavour of the moment, as some of his music had found its way into a popular show at the Haymarket, and he set out to consolidate his popularity by exploiting the fashion for opera seria. In just two weeks he composed *Rinaldo*, a work which, with its grand orchestra and flamboyant staging, achieved instant success, doing much to cement the prominence of Italian opera in England. It's a sign of its status that some of *Rinaldo*'s music found its way into Gay's *Beggar's Opera*.

In 1711, his year in London having expired, Handel reluctantly returned to Hanover, but in 1712 the Elector took the uncommonly generous step of granting his errant composer another leave of absence – on condition that he return within a reasonable time. Arriving back in England, Handel saw his most recent opera, *Il pastor fido*, produced at the Haymarket, but neither this nor *Tesseo* realized anything like the popularity of *Rinaldo*. Handel had to look to the aristocracy for patronage, and in 1713 Queen Anne granted him the annual encouragement of a £200 pension. The next year Anne died and Handel's Hanoverian patron – who had long been expecting his protégé back in Germany – became King George I, placing Handel in a highly embarrassing situation. Although he was temporarily in disgrace for having disobeyed his benefactor, Handel was now free to remain

HULTON DEUTSCH

The youthful Mr Handel

in England, where for the next two decades he dominated the country's operatic culture.

The next four years saw the composition of only one opera (*Amadigi di Gaula*), but in 1720 he was introduced to the Royal Academy of Music, a group of high-society amateurs who, recognizing the financial demands of opera production, aimed to raise the necessary funds through subscription. Handel was made music director of the Academy, and for its second production he composed *Radamisto*, which turned out to be his first unmitigated success since *Agrippina*. Notwithstanding his rivalry with Bononcini, who for a while was the more popular of the two, Handel concentrated on his operas, and between 1721 and 1726 he wrote what are now held to be his masterpieces in the genre – *Floridante*, *Ottone*, *Giulio Cesare* and *Tamerlano*.

Then in 1728 the Royal Academy collapsed, partly because Handel and his colleagues had submitted to the fashion for celebrity singers. Nobody doubted that singers such as the sopranos Francesca Cuzzoni and Faustina Bordoni were Europe's finest, but their fees ate heavily into the Academy's profits, the stars were impossible to control, and the rivalry between Cuzzoni and Bordoni became more important than the music they were singing. However, the death blow was dealt by John Gay, whose *Beggar's Opera* torpedoed traditional Italianate opera in England. The contrivances and downright idiocies endemic to opera seria were lampooned and eclipsed by the irreverent and unpretentious genre of the ballad opera, and even though Handel composed two new works for the Academy, the company failed to make it into the new year.

Two years later *The Beggar's Opera* had begun to tire a city in which almost everyone able to understand it had done so, and Handel decided to have another go. He approached a number of the defunct Academy's wealthier survivors, making a fresh start at the King's Theatre, but his new works were not well received and a solitary attempt at comedy was utterly disastrous. Similarly weak were Handel's attempts at reviving past hits, and with the advent of a rival company, the Opera of the Nobility, the pressure to succeed became enormous. Opera of the Nobility acquired the services of a number of the Academy's former celebrities and, in the greatest coup of all, they secured the London debut of the most famous castrato of the day, Carlo Broschi, known as Farinelli (see p.41). Handel responded by moving to Covent Garden, where he engaged the dancer Maria Sallé for a lavish production of his spectacular *Ariodante*, following this up with *Alcina* – again with Sallé. The contest lost Handel a fortune, and in 1732 a revival of one of his early oratorios, *Esther*, suggested to Handel that his future lay outside the theatre, a notion confirmed by the reception of another oratorio, *Deborah*, in 1733.

Handel nonetheless went on to compose a further eight operas, but none met with any favour – indeed at least three of them (including *Serse*) might be counted among his greatest commercial though not artistic catastrophes. By 1741 he was forced to recognize that the public no longer wanted his operas, and they disappeared from the repertoire for some two hundred years. Handel was saved by the massive successes of his dramatic oratorios *Messiah* and *Samson*, the monumental power and beauty of which ensured that, at his death, he was mourned a national hero.

Agrippina

Composed 1709.
First performed January 1710.
Libretto by Vincenzo Grimani.

Synopsis

Act I

Agrippina plots with her son Nero (Nerone) to ensure that he succeeds her husband, the Roman emperor Claudius (Claudio). It is announced that the emperor has drowned and Agrippina arranges for her son's coronation, but in fact Claudius has been saved by Otto (Ottone) and the ceremony is abandoned. In gratitude, Claudius pronounces that Otto will succeed him. Otto tells Poppea that he loves her, while Agrippina hints to Poppea that Otto agreed to give her to Claudius in return for the crown.

Act II

Poppea successfully sets Claudius against Otto while Agrippina convinces her husband that Otto has betrayed him and that he should, therefore, name Nero as his successor.

Act III

Poppea explains to Claudius that whereas she once thought Otto had betrayed him it was in fact Nero, whom she then reveals hiding behind a curtain in her room. Claudius dismisses his stepson, who informs his mother of Poppea's treachery. Agrippina confronts Claudius, berates him for succumbing to Poppea's influence, and claims that Otto loves Poppea, thereby forcing Claudius to summon all three. He orders Nero to marry Poppea and leaves the succession with Otto, but requests that he might forgo the crown for Poppea's hand in marriage. Claudius agrees, and blesses Poppea and Otto's marriage.

At the age of just twenty-four, Handel here showed himself fully able to assimilate the elegant art of Italian masters such as Scarlatti into what was, essentially, a German framework. According to Handel's biographer John Manwaring, *Agrippina*'s first performance greatly impressed the audience – "never had they known till then all the powers of harmony and modulation so closely arrayed, and forcibly combined". The hero-worshipping Manwaring noted that "the theatre at almost every pause, resounded with shouts of Viva il caro Sassone" (Long live the dear Saxon), and many others recorded an overwhelmingly positive response to an opera that commenced with a French-style two-part overture (with a thrilling allegro) and contained no fewer than forty arias, thirty-one of which were accompanied by full orchestra – another departure from tradition.

Like a number of his contemporaries, Handel spiced his score with episodes of tone painting and musical illustration – most obviously Claudius's "Cade il mondo" in Act II, with its fearful plunge through two octaves to a low bass D. Claudius and Nero are given some delightful melodies, especially during the final act's "comic" resolutions, and if the anti-heroic libretto sometimes sits uncomfortably with the events depicted, Vincenzo Grimani at least supplied Handel with a highly engaging cast of characters (notably Agrippina herself), whose musical embodiment is the finest the composer ever devised.

Bradshaw, Hill, Saffer, Isherwood; Capella Savaria; McGegan.
(Harmonia Mundi HMU 907063-5; 3CDs).

McGegan's recording of *Agrippina* is the only one presently available, but it would be highly recommendable in any field. The sessions took place during McGegan's production of the opera during the 1991 Göttingen Festival, and the buzz of live performance evidently carried over into the studio. Sally Bradshaw's Agrippina is a little anonymous but her sound is beautiful, while Wendy Hill's Nero is excellent fun, as is Lisa Saffer's sexy Poppea. Nicholas Isherwood, a powerful, ringing bass, is successful in animating some of Handel's more melodramatic effects. McGegan adopts provocative tempi and is also a passionate punctuator, spitting accents into Handel's fluid lines – a habit that can be irritating. All in all, this is an entertaining realization and worth every penny.

Rinaldo

Composed 1710–11; revised 1731.
First performed February 24, 1711.
Libretto by Giacomo Rossi, after Tasso.

Synopsis

Act I

In a Christian camp outside Jerusalem, Rinaldo reminds Goffredo that, if he takes the city, he is to marry Goffredo's daughter Almirena. Armida, sorceress and queen of Damascus, descends from the skies and tells her pagan lover Argante that they must destroy Rinaldo if they are to survive. She kidnaps Almirena, after which Goffredo and Eustazio suggest Rinaldo seeks help from a hermit.

Act II

Goffredo, Eustazio and Rinaldo are looking for the hermit, but then a spirit, claiming to be sent by Almirena, lures Rinaldo away. In Armida's enchanted garden, Argante reveals his affection for Almirena and offers to break the spell, but she repulses him. Rinaldo arrives and is infuriated when the victorious Armida offers him her own love. She transforms herself into Almirena but Rinaldo is wise to the deception; Armida bemoans her rejection. Argante enters and, in order to disguise her true feelings, Armida again takes Almirena's shape, a ploy which makes Argante reveal his true feelings, thus leading to the end of their partnership. Armida seeks revenge.

Act III

With the help of magical "fatal wands" supplied by the hermit, Goffredo and Eustazio burst in on Armida's garden just as the witch moves to stab Almirena. The Christians prevail, the lovers are reunited, the pagans are defeated in battle, and Argante and Armida are captured. Armida realizes the error of her ways and professes the Christian faith with Argante.

Rinaldo was Handel's first London opera and it could not have made more of an impact. The widely circulated story that Handel had completed the opera in only fourteen days (it is littered with arias and passages from earlier works, which would have speeded things up) made the composer's name a thing of wonder, and come the first night the Haymarket Theatre was on the point of hysteria. The production lived up to the hype, for Aaron Hill's designs made complete use of the Haymarket's recently modernized stage machinery in order to set the musical virtuosity of *Rinaldo*'s Italian singers within the sort of extravagant scenic effects associated with the English masque tradition. The results were, by all accounts, unprecedented. During the garden scene, where Rinaldo and Almirena are accompanied by singing birds, live doves were released from the stage while Handel's twittering flutes imitated their flight. The *Spectator* of March 6, 1711, summed up the show: "The opera of *Rinaldo* is filled with Thunder and Lightning, Illuminations and Fireworks."

The characterization in *Rinaldo* might be weak – especially Armida herself – but Handel's music has the power to glorify the trivial by painting it as, in his own words "a manifestation of the eternal". The arias in this opera are not concerned with the delineation of personality or the propulsion of the action but with the encapsulation of a mood or emotion, and in this they succeed brilliantly.

Rinaldo's arias are particularly varied and contain some of his most perfect melodies: Charles Burney thought "Cara sposa" from Act I to be "by many degrees the most pathetic song, and with the richest accompaniment, which had been then heard in England". Similarly moving are such wonders as "Lascia ch'io pianga", the Christian March and, in particular, Armida's recitative "Dunque i lacci d'un volto" and aria "Vò far guerra" – the opera's most elaborate vocal firework display.

Horne, Gasdia, Palacio, Weidinger; La Fenice Orchestra; Fisher.
(Nuova Era 6813-4; 2 CDs).

Marilyn Horne is celebrated for her performances of Rossini's more flamboyant mezzo-soprano roles, but she has made a unique contribution to the survival of Handel's operas. Taped live in Venice in 1989, this *Rinaldo* will shock those with a taste for "authentic" recreation, and the score is heavily cut, but the singing, especially Horne's in the title role, makes this set a delight. Full-bodied, agile and expressive, she makes a formidable hero and only rarely does her widening vibrato (she made her debut 35 years earlier!) disrupt Handel's linear purity. The remaining cast lack Horne's mettle but Cecilia Gasdia's account of Almirena's "Lascia ch'io pianga" is a performance to die for, and Christine Weidinger indulges in some elegant, unforced coloratura as Armida. A stale orchestra and John Fisher's faceless conducting detract from the vocal achievements, but even so Horne's imperious presence makes this a first choice until Malgoire's CBS recording is released on CD.

Giulio Cesare

Julius Caesar

Composed 1723–24.
First performed February 20, 1724.
Libretto by Nicola Francesco Haym.

Synopsis

Act I

Egypt welcomes Caesar (Cesare), who has come to do battle with Pompey (Pompeo). On behalf of Ptolemy (Tolomeo), ruler of Egypt, Achilla brings gifts to Caesar, including Pompey's severed head – to Caesar's disgust. Cornelia (Pompey's wife) attempts suicide and her son Sextus (Sesto) swears to avenge his father. Cleopatra, equally disgusted, looks to ally herself with Caesar against her brother Ptolemy. Achilla boasts to Ptolemy that he will kill the Roman emperor – in return for Cornelia. Sextus challenges Ptolemy to a duel but the Egyptian has the boy arrested and has his mother assigned to garden duties. Achilla offers himself to Cornelia in return for her freedom. She spurns him.

Act II

Disguised as "Lidia", Cleopatra plans to seduce Caesar. Meanwhile Cornelia, feverishly pursued by Achilla and Ptolemy, again attempts suicide but is restrained by her son. Caesar and "Lidia" meet in a garden, where their increasingly friendly chat is interrupted by news that Caesar has been betrayed and that people are seeking his death. "Lidia" discloses her true identity and tries to calm the situation, but she fails and begs Caesar to flee. The emperor refuses and moves to confront his aggressors. In another garden, Ptolemy confirms his desire for Cornelia and narrowly avoids being assassinated by Sextus, who is foiled by Achilla. Ptolemy, after fighting Achilla over Cornelia, leaves for battle with the Romans. Sextus is prevented from killing himself by his mother.

Act III

Achilla betrays Ptolemy by placing his soldiers at Cleopatra's disposal. Ptolemy takes his sister prisoner, but just as Cleopatra is bidding farewell to her friends, Caesar arrives to save her. Meanwhile Ptolemy is advancing upon Cornelia, whose son promptly enters to kill her assailant. In Alexandria, Caesar and Cleopatra acknowledge Cornelia and Sextus as friends and proclaim their love for each other. The opera ends with a celebration of peace.

Giulio Cesare is a Promethean creation, conceived on a lavish scale – it lasts just under three and a half hours on record, and a staged performance would have taken longer than Wagner's *Parsifal*. Haym's immensely complicated libretto is drawn from a variety of literary sources yet retains its dramatic cohesion to a greater extent than anything Handel had previously worked with – a fact for which the composer should probably take much credit, as the libretto was almost certainly written with his involvement. Handel's music matches the drama's scale, but principal amongst the score's qualities is its concentration on solo arias. The role of Cleopatra (first sung by Cuzzoni) is one of Handel's greatest creations for the female voice, and her Act II recitative and aria "Se pietà di me non sento", in which she laments her fate, yearns for revenge and longs for the love of Caesar, is especially wonderful – with a melody of effortless conviction, this is the opera's most emotive episode. The accompanied recitative is also notable for its startling number of modulations. The title role is a weak element in Haym's text, leaving it entirely to the music to bring Caesar's idealized nobility and courage to life, but *Giulio Cesare* marks a pinnacle of Handel's period at the Royal Academy. In the opinion of many, it is his greatest opera.

RECORDINGS OVERVIEW

Giulio Cesare is the most frequently revived and the most recorded of Handel's operas. The earliest set was conducted in 1952 by Hans Swarovsky, who cut the score in half, leaving little more than a series of poorly related excerpts. The first complete recording came from Deutsche Grammophon in 1969, under Karl Richter's direction: Tatiana Troyanos made an incredibly nimble Cleopatra, but her singing was outweighed by poor contributions from Schreier and Fischer-Dieskau, and by Richter's inelegant conducting. Those more interested in singing than authenticity might want to sample Orfeo's live 1965 recording, for the cast includes Lucia Popp, Walter Berry, Christa Ludwig and Fritz Wunderlich.

Lamore, Schlick, Ragin, Rorholm; Cologne Concerto; Jacobs.
(Harmonia Mundi HMC 90 1385-7; 4 CDs).

Unsurprisingly, René Jacobs has turned out to be the first to produce an ideal recording of Handel's *Cesare*. Basing his studies on Handel's own 1724 edition of the opera, Jacobs has got rid of inaccuracies perpetuated by old editions and recordings, and his faithful attention to vocal registers has resulted in a fitting balance of voices. Dorothy Lamore is more at home with Rossini than Handel, but her artfully masculine presence is engagingly resourceful. Barbara Schlick is sensitive as Cleopatra and Derek Lee Ragin is an enjoyably ominous counter-tenor Ptolemy, reaching stratospheric heights without strain. Jacobs' fluid, almost romantic, attention to line avoids the ear-flinching harshness common to many "authentic" conductors – indeed, the recording's great theatricality stems largely from his expressively relaxed tempi. Beautifully recorded, and supplemented by an excellent booklet.

Masterson, Jones, Baker, Walker, Bowman, Tomlinson; English National Opera Chorus, English National Opera Orchestra; Mackerras.
(EMI CMS7 69760-2; 3 CDs).

EMI's *Giulio Cesare* was recorded in the studio soon after the ENO production in 1984. It is, therefore, in English; but the translation is good and the stylish Mackerras has an astonishing cast at his disposal. Unsurprisingly, Janet Baker is not the mezzo she was but her experience and perception shine throughout her performance of the title role. The rich and dark quality of her voice is mirrored by the similarly placed mezzos of Della Jones as Sextus and Sarah Walker as Cornelia, but the effect is glorious, if a little decadent. Valerie Masterson's Cleopatra is dignified and elegant and her clear, high-lying soprano is ideally suited to the metamorphic emotions of "Se pietà di me non sento". Tomlinson is ever reliable as Achilla, revealing unexpected agility, but Bowman's androgynous counter-tenor Ptolemy is neither attractive nor especially characterful.

Tamerlano

Tamburlaine

Composed July 1724.
First performed October 31, 1724.
Libretto by Nicola Francesco Haym.

Synopsis

Act I

The despot Tamburlaine (Tamerlano) has imprisoned the Ottoman emperor Bajazet, with whose daughter, Asteria, he has fallen in love (despite his engagement to Irene, princess of Trebizond). Bajazet attempts suicide but is reminded by Andronicus (Andronico), a Greek prince and Tamburlaine's ally, that his death would leave his daughter an orphan. Unknown to Tamburlaine, Andronicus and Asteria are in love. Tamburlaine, in need of Andronicus's help in breaking down Bajazet, offers the prince Irene's hand in marriage. Andronicus is horrified at the suggestion and so Tamburlaine agrees to release the emperor on the condition that he be allowed to marry his daughter. Bajazet refuses. Meanwhile, Asteria accuses Andronicus of siding with Tamburlaine in return for Irene's hand and her kingdom, and renounces her love. Irene arrives to find she is to marry not Tamburlaine but his aide Andronicus.

Act II

Andronicus persuades Irene to disguise herself and plead her cause to Tamburlaine. This she does, and

FRANCESCA CUZZONI

Opera's first prima donna was **Francesca Cuzzoni** (1698–1770), a singer of legendary abilities – and a legendary pain in the neck.

In the summer of 1722 Handel began to realize that he would need more than a successful opera to restore his good name with audiences at His Majesty's Theatre. He resolved to find a star, and was informed that a Parma soprano by the name of Cuzzoni had made a sensational Venetian debut in 1719. Handel duly offered her an annual salary of £2000 if she would come to London. She accepted but failed to turn up. Handel therefore dispatched his harpsichordist, Sardoni, to go and fetch her for the following season. On the journey home Sardoni and Cuzzoni fell in love and married.

When Handel first set eyes on the woman, however, he was sorely disappointed. According to Horace Walpole, Cuzzoni was not merely "short and squat with a cross face", she was "not a good actress, dressed ill, and was silly and fantastical". Her first rehearsal with Handel became the stuff of legend. The composer had written the role of Teofane, in *Ottone*, expressly for his new songbird, but when he presented her with the words and music of "False imagine" – an aria of which he was very proud – she refused outright to sing it. Handel rounded on Cuzzoni: "I well know that you are truly a She-Devil: but I will have you know that I am Beelzebub, chief of the Devils", he yelled, and swore that he would throw her out of the window if she did not do as she was asked. Cuzzoni had met her match and began to sing, revealing to the composer the "most beautiful voice" he had ever heard. Cuzzoni went on to create several further roles for Handel – including Cleopatra (*Giulio Cesare*) and Asteria (*Tamerlano*) – and he tolerated her tantrums for as long as audiences were willing to pay for them.

Three years after Cuzzoni's debut in London, rumours began to circulate of a voice that was even more beautiful than Cuzzoni's. This voice belonged to **Faustina Bordoni** (1700–81), known to all simply by her first name. The two prima donnas soon hated each other, continuing a feud that reached its climax on June 6, 1727, when both appeared in an opera at the Haymarket. According to the *British Journal* of June 10: "On Tuesday night last, a great disturbance happened at the opera, occasioned by the partisans of the two celebrated rival ladies, Cuzzoni and Faustina. The contention at first was only carried on by hissing on one side and clapping on the other; but proceeded at length to catcalls and other great indecencies." The *Journal* chose not to mention that the fans were only taking their cue from the singers themselves, who began by merely jostling each other but ended up flying at each other like cats, with much pulling of hair and scratching at eyes. The curtain was brought down and the theatre descended into a riot, with furniture being passionately exchanged between rival boxes.

Notwithstanding the attentions of Faustina, Cuzzoni remained a dominant force until the 1740s, when her career took a bitter turn. On September 7, 1741, the *London Daily Post* reported that "the famous singer Mrs C-z-ni is under sentence of death, to be beheaded, for poisoning her husband." She survived to make a final visit to the English capital in 1749, where on May 18 she hired the Haymarket Theatre for a concert aimed at those concerned about her "pressing debts". The concert was a disaster, and she escaped debtor's prison only through the intervention of the Prince of Wales. Cuzzoni fled to Holland and another prison, but was released after agreeing to sing at the local theatre every night for free. She managed to escape to Bologna, where the once-great soprano lived out her final years making buttons.

she is joined by Asteria who admits that she loves Andronicus. Tamburlaine decides to take Asteria as his wife, claiming that if she fails to please him he can always turn to Irene. Bajazet is appalled to hear that his daughter is to join Tamburlaine on his throne. Andronicus swears death to himself and Tamburlaine if Asteria marries him, not realizing that Asteria plans to murder the monster herself. Her father enters the throne room, determined to prevent the marriage; after various complications Bajazet demands his daughter step down in favour of Irene or he will kill himself. She eventually does as she is asked, and both father and daughter are sentenced to death.

Act III

Tamburlaine commands Andronicus to inform Asteria that she is still welcome at his side, but she professes her love for Andronicus. Asteria attempts to poison Tamburlaine, but Irene warns Tamburlaine, who then demands Asteria and her father drink first from the poisoned cup. As she brings the cup to her mouth, Andronicus knocks it to the floor. Asteria is sent into slavery, Tamburlaine takes Irene as his wife and Bajazet dies by his own hand. Andronicus's attempted suicide is prevented by Tamburlaine, who magnanimously concedes that too much blood has already been shed. He allows Asteria freedom to marry Andronicus.

The wicked Tamburlaine had stimulated a number of composers before Handel, but he seems to have taken his cue from the play by poet laureate Nicholas Rowe, which at that time was performed every November in London to coincide with the anniversary of Guy Fawkes' plot. With both eyes on the box office, Handel and the Academy decided to turn the legend into an opera and approached Nicola Haym, whose commercial acumen was legendary, for a libretto. Haym came up with the sort of plot Gay had in mind when he wrote his *Beggar's Opera*, packed with complications and implausibilities, but librettist and composer ensured success by playing the celebrity card again. At the first performance Tamburlaine was created by the castrato Senesino, while Bajazet became a vehicle for the "widely praised" tenor voice of Francesco Borosini. Opera seria had, till then, presented no leading opportunities for tenors.

Asteria is the most interesting role, however. Throughout the first two acts she is cold and unyielding, as one might expect, with a suitably detached musical presence; but from the beginning of the final act she begins to grow in stature and finally, in a lament of profound resignation, sings the opera's most affecting aria, "Cor di padre". The other central characters are too inconsistent to engender much sympathy – Tamburlaine's conversion from the path of evil, allowing the opera to end happily, is especially preposterous. Handel was clearly reluctant to allow the drama a complete change of direction: the chorus following Bajazet's death, as Tamburlaine gives Asteria to Andronicus and agrees to marry Irene himself, is scored in a minor key, thereby undercutting the text.

Ragin, Argenta, Robson, Chance; English Baroque Soloists; Gardiner. (Erato 4509-997722-2; 3 CDs).

Gardiner has done more for Handel's oratorios than any other conductor since the 1920s but he has shown markedly less enthusiasm for the operas: to date, *Tamerlano* is his only undertaking. This set was taped live and its atmosphere is a primary attraction, along with the thrilling singing of the two countertenors Derek Lee Ragin (Tamburlaine) and Michael Chance (Andronicus). Nancy Argenta's Asteria is initially a little winsome but with "Cor di padre" she blossoms into a glorious presence. Gardiner's pacing is sometimes eccentric, and the English Baroque Soloists produce an uncharacteristically mean sound, but the direction, balance and texture of the ensembles is exciting, and the set as a whole makes a lasting impression.

Alcina

Composed 1735.
First performed April 16, 1735.
Libretto by Antonio Fanzaglia, after Ariosto.

Synopsis

Act I

Blinded by love, the sorceress Alcina has taken Ruggiero captive. His betrothed, Bradamante – accompanied by her guardian Melisso – arrives on the enchanted island to win him back, disguised as Bradamante's brother Ricciardo. They are met by Alcina's sister, Morgana, who takes great interest in "Ricciardo". Alcina's general Oronte warns Ruggiero that, with "Ricciardo" on the island, he is likely to suffer the same fate as all the enchantress's previous lovers and find himself turned into a tree or a stream. Eventually Bradamante is forced to reveal her true identity to Ruggiero, but he merely believes this to be another of Alcina's tricks.

Act II

Melisso, disguised as Ruggiero's tutor Atlante, gives him a magic ring that restores him to his senses. Alcina prepares to turn "Ricciardo" into a beast but she is stopped by her sister, who believes that he may love her. Bradamante's nephew Oberto has now arrived, looking for his long-lost father Astolfo; Alcina tells him that they shall soon be reunited. Meanwhile, Morgana is heartbroken to discover "Ricciardo" and Ruggiero together, and Alcina is distraught to find that her magic is useless against the magic ring and that she is unable to detain Ruggiero.

Act III

In a palace courtyard Morgana and Oronte are reunited in their love for each other. Ruggiero and Bradamante are preparing to leave by ship, but Bradamante refuses to leave until Alcina's spells are lifted and her past victims (presently in the form of streams, animals and rocks) are returned to life. Ruggiero discovers the urn in which Alcina's magic is contained, smashes it, and so releases all her men from their enchantments. Among them is Astolfo. Father and son embrace, and the opera ends with a chorus and dance.

At the close of the 1733–34 season on July 6, the King's Theatre was let to the Opera of the Nobility and Handel moved to Rich's Theatre in Covent Garden, which had opened in December the previous year. Battle then commenced. The Nobility announced the engagement of the castrato Farinelli and presented him to the London public on October 29, creating a sensation and filling every seat. Having fallen out with the castrato Senesino, Handel decided to engage the services not of a celebrity vocalist but a celebrity dancer – the French ballerina Marie Sallé. His season consisted mainly of revisions of his own work (many with dances added to accommodate Sallé) and the first production of a new opera, *Ariodante*. With the freakishly gifted Farinelli making all the headlines, on April 16 Handel presented another new opera, *Alcina*, which brought him the greatest success of the season, running for eighteen successive nights. However, the success was not unallayed. Sallé, dancing the part of Cupid, was of ever diminishing value to the composer, and for later performances she was forced to resort to a revealing costume – but this created the wrong sort of sensation. Once the season was over, Handel rid himself of the ballerina and she never again stepped foot in England. Once the dust had settled it was clear that, although *Alcina* had been popular with the public, the season as a whole had been a disaster.

Alcina showed how quickly fashion passed. No sooner had *The Beggar's Opera* flitted across the London stage than Handel was back with an entirely traditional and irrational plot (Alcina is effectively defeated before the final act), replete with numerous unnecessary roles, spectacular scenic effects and excuses for plenty of instrumental picture-painting. The rich musical fabric of *Alcina* is dominated by its arias. As Burney wrote – "if any one of Handel's works should be brought on the stage without a change or mixture of its airs, this would well sustain a revival". The most famous of these airs is Ruggiero's "Verdi prati"; rejected by the castrato Carestini for its lack of brilliance, this extended but deceptively simple melody imparts Ruggiero's intense regret at the imminent decay of the landscape around him, a mood then magically intensified by Alcina's attempt to prevent Ruggiero from leaving. Alcina herself is a reasonably rounded creation, passing through various stages of degeneration before singing her final aria, "Mi restano le lagrime", an eloquent lament that makes you almost despair at the mechanical nonsense with which Handel ends the opera.

Augér, Jones, Kwella, Tomlinson; City of London Baroque Sinfonia; Hickox. (EMI CDS7 49771-2; 3 CDs).

This is one of two recordings of *Alcina* in the catalogue – the other is conducted by Richard Bonynge and is notable for the beauty of Joan Sutherland's singing, though barely a word can be understood amid her gorgeous flutterings and swoopings. Hickox's version is superior chiefly because it generates far more momentum: like most good studio recordings of opera, it was taped shortly after a stage production, and Hickox's handling of pace, mood and colour are excellent. The cast can't match the stellar qualities of the Bonynge set, but Arleen Augér is a sweet-toned Alcina, playing down the coloratura displays to concentrate on the less immodest writing, and in terms of dramatic integrity this account is unrivalled.

Serse

Xerxes

Composed 1738.
First performed 1738.
Libretto by Bononcini, after Stampiglia.

Synopsis

Act I

Xerxes (Serse), King of Persia, is sitting beneath a tree enjoying its shade when his brother Arsamene arrives, looking for Romilda, with whom he is in love. Romilda's distant voice attracts Xerxes but Arsamene warns him that she is of low birth and thus unworthy of his attentions. Despite this, Xerxes requests his brother to arrange a meeting, causing Arsamene considerable distress. When Arsamene relays his brother's intentions to Romilda, her sister Atalanta – who is attracted to Arsamene – hears what she believes to be the good news. Xerxes attempts to coerce Romilda into marriage and Arsamene intervenes, provoking the king into banishing him. Romilda refuses to marry Xerxes, however. Xerxes' betrothed Amastre arrives, disguised as a man, to hear Xerxes' plans for Romilda. Arsamene sends a note to Romilda expressing his love, but she is doubtful of his constancy and warns her sister to keep away from him.

Act II

Atalanta intercepts Arsamene's letter to Romilda and shows it to Xerxes, telling him that it had been written to her. Serse, determined to see his brother marry Atalanta, shows Romilda the letter as proof of Arsamene's faithlessness, but not even this is enough to convince her to marry Xerxes. He tries to force himself upon her but Amastre (still in disguise) intercedes, offering to support her against the emperor.

Act III

Atalanta, confronted by Romilda, claims she pretended to be the subject of Arsamene's letter in order to shield Romilda from Xerxes. When Xerxes makes yet another move towards Romilda she announces that she needs the permission of Ariodate, her father, before any talk of marriage. Xerxes duly informs Ariodate that his daughter is to marry into royalty, gaining his immediate agreement – Ariodate thinking that the suitor is Arsamene. Romilda and Arsamene, attended by Ariodate, get married, which prompts Xerxes to order Ariodate's arrest. Xerxes then receives a letter from his betrothed in which she threatens suicide, to which he responds by giving Arsamene a sword and commanding him to kill his new wife. Amastre seizes the sword and turns it on Xerxes. Duly repentant, Xerxes blesses his brother's marriage.

Come the 1737–38 season Handel was at last rid of the competition from the Opera of the Nobility (which had given its last performance in June 1737), but he could afford no more failures. With creditors banging on the door and threatening him with debtor's prison, he had to secure at least one profit-making success. The season's launch was interrupted by the death of Queen Caroline, wife of George II, on November 20, and Handel had to wait until January 3 before presenting the first of the season's new operas, *Faramondo*. Audience reactions to this barely comprehensible work did not bode well, and a satirical musical called *The Dragon of Wantley* was ridiculing Italian opera in similar style to *The Beggar's Opera*. Handel persevered and rushed out *Serse* in April. It failed, perhaps because its tale of high-born romantic intrigue is rather over-extended, at more than three hours long.

Yet *Serse* is well worth sampling, not least because it features one of the most beautiful arias in all opera – "Ombra mai fu", otherwise known as "Handel's Largo". This delightful melody, sung by Xerxes in praise of a tree (a hint of self-parody from Handel), is far from being an isolated highlight. Indeed *Serse* is a well-varied creation, encompassing full-scale bravura da capo arias, such as Xerxes' "Più che penso" and "Crude furie", and some adroit theatrical conceits, notably the Act II "Gran pena è gelosia" in which Xerxes and Amastre sing their private but interconnected thoughts at opposite ends of the stage, each believing the other to be absent. The comic touches are rarely subtle, and the plot occasionally tries the audience's patience, but *Serse* has a lot of stage potential, to which various opera companies have been attracted in recent years – indeed, thanks to English National Opera's sprightly production, *Serse* is probably the best known of all Handel's operas in Britain at the moment.

RECORDINGS OVERVIEW

There have been only two studio recordings of *Serse*, and neither is currently available. The earlier, taped by Westminster in 1965, featured a strong but unlikely cast, with Lucia Popp as Xerxes and Margaret Forrester as Amastre. Its rival, Malgoire's 1979 recording for CBS, also featured some unlikely Handelians, including Barbara Hendricks and Cheryl Studer. The latter is a quasi-authentic performance but is dry and characterless; the former is dated but preferable. For those with a taste for great tenor singing, Fritz Wunderlich's 1960s live performance of *Serse*, in German, with the soprano role transposed down, is exceptional; the score is heavily cut, the casting is otherwise weak and the sound is poor, but for Wunderlich's contribution alone it is worth tracking down – it's occasionally available on tiny specialist labels.

JOHN GAY

b. DEVON, SEPTEMBER 1685; d. LONDON, DECEMBER 4, 1732.

England's hopes of an indigenous operatic culture – independent of the Italians, French and Germans – died with Henry Purcell. However, England's enthusiasm for Italian opera at the end of the seventeenth and beginning of the eighteenth centuries produced an interesting reaction: unable to compete with Italy, the English resorted to ridicule and created a satirical genre known as ballad opera. The best-known and least dreadful example of this bastard form is John Gay's *Beggar's Opera*. A poet, playwright and general wit, Gay was a friend of both Pope and Handel (for whom he wrote the libretto to *Acis and Galatea*) and a successful theatre manager – shortly before his death he built the first of Covent Garden's three theatres. Musical talent, however, was not among his accomplishments: he created the genre of ballad opera by piecing together some popular tunes (including music from Handel's *Rinaldo*), engaging a composer named John Christopher Pepusch to provide a structure and overtures, and then threading the whole thing together with his own comic dialogue.

The idea for *The Beggar's Opera* is thought to have come via Jonathan Swift who, in 1715, wrote to Gay that "a Newgate Pastoral might make an odd, pretty sort of thing". The next phase in the gestation came in 1724, when highwayman Jack Shepherd was hanged at Newgate prison, and the crook who had informed against him, Jonathan Wild, was stabbed to death in court. In celebration of these thrilling events

LEBRECHT COLLECTION

Hogarth's caricature of The Beggar's Opera

Gay penned "Newgate's Garland", and three years later he set to work on his *Beggar's Opera*, completing the compilation of the three acts and sixty-nine airs shortly before the first performance on January 29, 1728.

It was an enormous success, giving rise to the quip that *The Beggar's Opera* "made Rich Gay and Gay Rich" – Rich being the manager of the Lincoln's Inn theatre where the piece was performed. Indeed its impact was such that when Gay produced a sequel titled *Polly* in 1729, the targets of the first work's satire felt so threatened that they succeeded in getting it banned. (*Polly* remained unproduced until 1777 – forty-five years after Gay's death.) *The Beggar's Opera* had been performed sixty-two times by the season's end and had dealt a body blow to conventional opera, then dominated by Handel. As one Mrs Pendarves wrote shortly after the first performance: "Yesterday I was at the rehearsal of the new opera composed by Handel; I like it extremely, but the taste of the town is so depraved, that nothing will be approved of but the burlesque. *The Beggar's Opera* entirely triumphs over the Italian one." The English appetite for bawdy, tuneful and accessible entertainments like *The Beggar's Opera* was in time exhausted, but the future did not look bright for highbrow opera in 1728, and the success of *The Beggar's Opera* was enough to divert Handel from Italian opera to English oratorios.

The Beggar's Opera

First performed January 29, 1728.
Music arranged by John Christopher Pepusch.
Libretto by John Gay.

Synopsis

Act I

After an introduction in which a Beggar and a Player ask for their work to be "allowed an Opera in all its forms", there is an overture which leads into the first scene in the house of Peachum, a common criminal. He is going through his accounts when, in discussion with his wife, the subject of murder is touched upon. This leads to talk of the highwayman Macheath, with whom Mrs Peachum suspects their daughter, Polly, is involved. Polly confesses that she does indeed love the robber, but promises to maintain her virginity. When it emerges that Polly and Macheath have married, Peachum and his wife try and fail to make her see reason. Macheath arrives, and Polly persuades him to make good his escape.

Act II

In a tavern Macheath and his gang are planning ahead. Peachum enters with the constabulary, who arrest Macheath and take him to Newgate, where he is placed in the care of Mr Lockit, whose daughter he once seduced. He agrees to marry her if she will help him escape. They go in search of the prison chaplain. Meanwhile Peachum and Lockit cannot agree on how to divide the reward money and so begin to fight, until "mutual interest" returns them to their senses. Macheath and Lucy return to encounter Polly, who is prepared to follow her husband to death. The two women battle it out until Peachum pulls his daughter free. Macheath and Lucy leave together.

Act III

Lockit is seen berating his daughter while Macheath is seen meeting his gang. He is recognized and reported to Peachum. Lucy poisons Polly's drink but when Macheath is brought back to prison, she drops her glass. The final scene is set in Macheath's cell where, awaiting death, he is confronted by four women – each carrying a child. "This is too much", cries Macheath. Agreeing, the Player beseeches the Beggar not to allow Macheath's hanging and to end the work happily. Uniting Macheath and Polly, the Beggar concludes his opera with an exuberant chorus and dance.

The broad, essentially English satire of *The Beggar's Opera* has many targets, one of its principal objects of derision being the fashionable opera of the day: "I have a Prison-scene, which the ladies always reckon charmingly pathetic. . . . I hope I may be forgiven, that I have not made my Opera throughout unnatural, like those in vogue, for I have no recitative." Gay also took time to caricature visiting Italian personalities such as the rival prima donnas Faustina and Cuzzoni (satirized in the rivalry of Polly and Lucy), and to pour scorn upon those in authority (notably the Prime Minister Sir Robert Walpole, the model for Lockit). The force of some of this ridicule has of course been lost as its victims recede into history, but Gay's subversive wit still packs a punch in the modern world, as demonstrated by Bertold Brecht's and Kurt Weill's production of *Die Dreigroschenoper*, an adaptation of *The Beggar's Opera* produced two hundred years after the first performance of Gay's masterpiece.

Above all, however, *The Beggar's Opera* survives as one of the funniest entertainments ever created for the English stage, with much of the humour deriving from the honesty and directness with which the low-life world is depicted and the way criminality is presented as having its own skewed morality. Gay is also brilliant at making his hard-hitting words jar ironically with the original sentiment of the song, as when Purcell's tenderly sensuous "If love's a sweet passion" from *The Fairy Queen* is transformed into Lucy's description of her deflowerment, or when the march from Handel's *Rinaldo* is performed by a gang of tavern cutpurses about to set out on a job. Most modern productions of *The Beggar's Opera* treat it as a romp in fancy dress, but even with its happy ending (in itself ridiculing the convention), it is a profoundly cynical work which suggests that most people are motivated by greed and selfishness and that everybody has a price. The work's nihilism is oddly undepressing, however, largely because of the sheer panache with which Gay's characters pursue their wickedness.

Mills, Thompson, Dawson, Walker, Hoskins; Broadside Band; Barlow.
(Hyperion CDA 66591; 2 CDs).

Because there is no definitive text of *The Beggar's Opera*, conductors usually make their own arrangements for recording purposes. Of these, Jeremy Barlow's is one of the best: his instrumental accompaniments are simple and broadly eighteenth century in style, he directs the work with passion and wit, and the cast is ideal. Bob Hoskins's Beggar is overacted enough to compensate for the lack of visual stimulus, while Sarah Walker's Mrs Peachum is all bloomers and indignation – though she makes Adrian Thompson's Macheath sound pallid by comparison. Unlike some, Barlow leaves Gay's text unedited, which is entirely reasonable, as the songs are all but meaningless without the intervening dialogue, and the spoken episodes do nothing to disrupt this engagingly fluid production. Benjamin Britten's arrangement of *The Beggar's Opera* might be the best known, but this one is truest to the spirit of the original.

3

THE REFORMATION OF OPERA

GLUCK TO MOZART

THE REFORMATION OF OPERA

GLUCK TO MOZART

In cultural as in political terms, the second half of the eighteenth century was the twilight of the *ancien régime*. In the period between the death of Handel and the death of Mozart, opera underwent radical changes, as florid and stately presentations of the lives of monarchs and heroes gave way to creations in which the emotional complexities of everyday life provided the focus of attention. The prophet of this reformation was **Christoph Willibald Gluck**, whose work belongs with the novels of Samuel Richardson and the writings of Jean-Jacques Rousseau in the history of the modern European sensibility. Gluck and his favoured librettist Ranieri da Calzabigi strove to free opera of the stilted affectations of the Baroque era, to tap a seam of more instinctive feeling and to appeal to the experience of an increasingly middle-class audience. The two most famous of Gluck's collaborations with Calzabigi – *Orfeo ed Euridice* and *Alceste* – are populated by characters who superficially resemble the mythical stereotypes of the previous era, but with the crucial difference that their behaviour is entirely human and empathetic. Charles Burney caught the essence of the change after visiting Vienna in 1772. "Metastasio and Hasse may be said to be at the head of one of the principal sects; and Calzabigi and Gluck of another", he noted. "The first, regarding all progress as quackery, adhere to the ancient form of the musical drama . . . whereas Gluck's genius seems more calculated for exciting terror in painting difficult situations, occasioned by complicated misery and the tempestuous fury of unbridled passions." As an indication of his priorities, Gluck assigned the first performance of *Alceste* not to an opera seria company, but to a troupe of buffa players, wanting to secure the services of actors who could sing rather than singers who may or may not have been able to act.

Buffa theatre played a major role in the opera revolution of the late eighteenth century. While most of the larger, city-based theatres persisted with productions of opera seria, opera buffa flourished in the smaller theatres, whose facilities precluded the elaborate settings and overpaid singers required by operatic tragedy. Instead, they performed light and accessible comic works by the likes of Logroscino, Vinci, Piccini (see p.71), and, most important, **Giovanni Paisiello** and **Domenico Cimarosa**. The former's elegant operas were pivotal to the elevation of buffa from light entertainment into a form as respectable as opera seria, while Cimarosa enlarged upon Paisiello's achievement in a manner that anticipated the fizzing lyricism of Rossini and Donizetti, two of the dominant figures in the succeeding Italian generation.

At the centre of opera buffa's development was the work of Venetian dramatist Carlo Goldoni (1707–93), the Metastasio of opera buffa. Generally credited as the first specialist of the comic libretto, Goldoni adapted the basic outline of the intermezzo, creating tales of commonplace characters in everyday situations and spicing the action with a repertoire of what became standard theatrical devices, such as characters in disguise and ensemble finales. Furthermore, he developed a dramatic form called the *dramma giocoso*, in which elements of opera seria were fused with the knockabout humour of opera buffa.

The most famous settings of Goldoni's work were by a German composer, **Joseph Haydn**, whose long service for the Esterházy family produced some of the finest comic opera of the late eighteenth century. Although Haydn's operas are musically not of the same stature as his symphonies and quartets, they provide an ideal point of reference by which to judge what makes the operas of **Wolfgang Amadée Mozart** so remarkable. Mozart is the most popular opera composer of them all – five of his works feature on the list of the ten operas most frequently performed worldwide. He brought an unprecented and unsurpassed tunefulness, wit, vivacity and drama to every species of opera, and transformed every category in which he worked. Thus the quintessentially German genre of the Singspiel, once an assembly of folkish musical numbers separated by comic dialogue, gained an Italianate élan through Mozart's *Die Entführung aus dem Serail* and his last opera, *Die Zauberflöte*. Similarly, he brought the *dramma giocoso* to its highest point with *Don Giovanni*, reversing the customary polarities of that hybrid genre – *Don Giovanni* is a tragedy leavened with humorous episodes rather than a comedy tempered with seriousness. And with *Le Nozze di Figaro* he wrote what is quite simply the most perfect comic opera ever written.

Mozart redirected European opera by composing music-dramas in which the drama comes first and foremost from the music. With Gluck, the composer had served the poet, taking the libretto's lead; Mozart, by contrast, wrote operas in which each episode, personality and relationship was defined primarily by the music. Indeed, in their embodiment of the notion that the musical component of opera should connote its own spectrum of meanings, rather than functioning as the scaffolding of the text, the operas of Mozart and his much-maligned contemporary, **Antonio Salieri**, can be seen as harbingers of the Romantic age.

CHRISTOPH WILLIBALD GLUCK

b. ERASBACH, GERMANY, JULY 2, 1714; d. VIENNA, NOVEMBER 15, 1787.

In Gluck's operas the creative stagnation typified by Handel gives way to a new emphasis on emotional truth, directly comparable to that embodied by Rousseau's theories of "naturalness". Central to Gluck's artistic credo, as articulated in the preface to his opera *Alceste*(1767), was the idea that opera should be less regulated and more organic – that the arias, recitatives, ensembles and choruses should serve the drama, instead of being received components around which the opera was contructed. The distinction between recitative and aria remained, but the distinction lost its sharpness as recitative became considerably longer and more elaborate, and was increasingly accompanied by the full orchestra. Individual scenes now blended into each other to create an unprecedented continuity. The unification of dramatic and musical interests also had lasting implications for singers. Gluck was the first composer to deny his singers any opportunity to indulge in mere display and to insist that they immerse themselves in their theatrical as well as their musical characterizations. Gluck's reforms were the antithesis of the cult of the celebrity.

Gluck was born into a family of Bohemian foresters who quickly recognized the boy's precocious talents and sent him to Prague for study. In 1736, after four years, he moved to Vienna where he spent some time as a chamber musician in the employment of Prince Ferdinand Lobkowitz (father of Beethoven's patron); the following year Gluck was in Milan, where he took lessons from Sammartini, under whose guidance he composed his first opera, *Artaserse*. By 1745 he had composed a further seven operas, but although their fluid melodic lines and compulsive energy are peculiar to Gluck, none of them prefigures the revolutionary principles for which his later work is famous.

In 1745 he moved to London where he presented two ineffectual operas – it was during this visit that he met Handel, who passed the infamous judgement "he knows no more of counterpoint than Waltz, my cook". The following year he left England for a four-year tour of Europe, at the end of which he settled in

GLUCK VERSUS PICCINI

During the 1770s, when Gluck's *Alceste* and *Iphigénie en Aulide* began to shatter box-office records at the Opéra, there arose in Paris a fractious division between champions of the German invader and defenders of the Italian comic tradition which Gluck's reformations threatened. Lacking a strong advocate, the Italian faction sent a delegation to Rome, to enlist the aid of Nicolò Piccini (1728–1800), a composer with limited abilities but considerable prominence, versatility and wealth. Piccini wrote around one hundred operas, many of them in the Neapolitan buffa style of Paisiello and Cimarosa, and it was in this capacity that he was thrown into the Parisian limelight when he arrived in the city with his troupe of Italian singers. He was championed by the French dramatist and critic Jean François Marmontel, an infamous troublemaker, who brought the situation to boiling point in 1777 when he published his inflammatory *Essai sur les révolutions de la musique*, promoting Piccini as the operatic ideal and Gluck as an incompetent.

While Gluck and Piccini strove to maintain their detachment from a call to arms that neither man had wanted, the aesthetic dispute degenerated into fisticuffs. Opera performances in Paris were beset by outbreaks of violence, as fighting broke out in the Conservatoire, the Opéra and the Opéra-Comique. Marmontel, the director of the Opéra, sought to drive the rivalry to a new height by arranging for both Gluck and Piccini to set Quinault's *Roland*; but when Gluck discovered that Piccini had been working on *Roland* for some weeks he withdrew, setting *Armide* instead. Marmontel next arranged for both composers to set *Iphigénie en Tauride*, the consequence of which was the virtual eclipse of the old guard. Piccini remained in France for a while, moved to Naples and ended his life with another conflict – he was killed in a duel at the age of seventy-two. His music did not survive him and not until 1942, when Richard Strauss set his *Capriccio* in Paris at the time of the Gluck-Piccini war, did Piccini's operas (which are quoted throughout by Strauss) again receive an airing.

The last word should be left to Benjamin Franklin, his country's representative in France during the fracas, which he satirized as follows: "We had been shown numberless skeletons of a kind of little fly, called an ephemera, whose successive generations, we were told, were bred and expired within the day. I happened to see a living company of them on a leaf, who appeared to be engaged in conversation . . . they were disputing warmly on the merit of two foreign musicians . . . in which dispute they spent their time, seemingly as regardless of the shortness of life as if they had been sure of living a month. Happy people! you live certainly under a wise, just and mild government, since you have no public grievances to complain of, nor any subject of contention but the perfections and imperfections of foreign music."

Vienna. In December 1752 he was appointed Kapellmeister to the Prince of Saxe-Hildburghausen, a position that effectively enabled him to take control of Viennese musical life. Working often to contracts from Giacomo Durazzo, the manager of Vienna's state theatres, Gluck composed a series of French-style comic operas that brought an inundation of commissions. It was not long before Gluck began working in collaboration with librettists he had chosen himself, rather than accepting completed texts as part of a contract – a crucial development in the history of the genre.

His collaboration with the poet Ranieri Calzabigi brought about radical reforms in the composition and production of opera, as typified by *Orfeo ed Euridice* (1762), a work whose dramatic orchestration and overall sense of direction were enthrallingly original. Composed five years later, also to a libretto by Calzabigi, *Alceste* furthered the development of Gluck's mission to "restrict music to its true office of serving poetry by means of expression and by following the situation of the story" and "to strive for a beautiful simplicity". However, *Alceste* was not immediately the success it would later become, and in 1770 Gluck left Vienna.

In order to fulfil the Opéra's commission for *Iphigénie en Aulide*, Gluck next settled in Paris, remaining there for three years. The production of this latest work was a sensation, as were his revisions of *Orfeo* and *Alceste*, but his fame provoked passionate jealousies, notably among the supporters of Nicolò Piccini (see box on p.71), whom the Opéra's director commissioned to set *Iphigénie en Tauride*, a libretto on which Gluck was already working. Piccini's version was fairly successful (despite the leading lady's serious intoxication); Gluck's – with its unprecedentedly integrated fusion of dance, drama, choruses and solos – was a triumph. In 1779 Gluck retired to Vienna where he lived in regal splendour; he died after ignoring his doctor's orders not to drink alcohol after dinner.

Late in life, Gluck sent an open letter to the French press in which he said that when composing *Armide*, he had striven to be "more painter and poet than musician". In that phrase lies the essence of Gluck's forward-looking art. Without exaggeration it could be said that Wagner's music dramas were the apotheosis of everything to which Gluck and Calzabigi had aspired when they wrote their introduction to *Alceste* in 1767.

Orfeo ed Euridice

Orpheus and Eurydice

Composed Vienna 1762; Paris 1774.
First performed October 5, 1762; August 2, 1774.
Libretto by Ranieri Calzabigi; Pierre Louis Moline.

Synopsis – Viennese version

Act I

Orpheus stands before Eurydice's tomb, lost in grief. Coming to his senses, he resolves to rescue his lover from Hades. Amor (Love) comforts him, telling him that with love anything can be overcome. However, she imposes conditions. When leading Eurydice from Hell, he must let go of her hand and not look upon her until they have reached the earth's surface again.

Act II

Orpheus approaches Hades, where the Furies sing of Cerberus, the three-headed guard dog of Hell. The beauty of his singing finally elicits their compassion and they allow him safe passage. He arrives in Elysium (during which, in the 1774 version, is heard the famous Dance of the Blessed Spirits) and sings of the beauty that surrounds him but also of its emptiness, as he cannot find Eurydice. She is brought to him blindfolded and they prepare to leave.

Act III

On a path leading out of Hades, Eurydice reproaches Orpheus for what she takes to be his coldness and suggests that death would have been preferable. Unable to bear her laments, Orpheus turns to look at her, and Eurydice dies. Orpheus is prevented from killing himself by Love who, bringing Eurydice back to life, reunites the lovers. The opera ends with a chorus in praise of Love.

Gluck composed *Orfeo* twice: in 1762 for Vienna (in Italian) and again in 1774 for Paris (in French, as *Orphée et Euridice*). This was no mere revision. The Viennese version lasted an hour and forty minutes, the title role was scored for castrato, and dramatic fluency was its main aim and achievement. The Paris version was considerably longer, the title role was written for a soprano (for whom, somewhat regressively, Gluck composed a showpiece aria to end Act I), and it included two new ballets, the Dance of Furies and the Dance of the Blessed Spirits, a famous flute showpiece. These concessions to Parisian taste, delightful though

ZOË DOMINIC

Janet Baker leads the way as Orfeo

they are, dissipated the emotional gravity and dramatic cohesion of the original score, and it's the first *Orfeo* that became the starting block for subsequent composers, most notably Mozart.

A comparison between the opening of Gluck's *Orfeo* and Monteverdi's treatment of the same episode perfectly illustrates how much opera had changed in the intervening century and a half. Where Monteverdi's hero informs the audience of his unhappiness, and the orchestra as it were verifies his emotion through a poignant accompaniment, Gluck dramatizes Orpheus's condition: his heart-rending cries of "Eurydice" punctuate a funereal lament sung by a chorus of nymphs surrounding Eurydice's tomb, a passage which leads into the transformation of the hero's misery into an exquisite song of resignation, "Chiamo il mio ben cosi". The tale is the same but Gluck's music presents a more fully realized mental state, in which emotions are complex and variable.

The eruptions of emotion that occur throughout *Orfeo* gain potency from the poise with which they are expressed. Denuded of all ornament, Gluck's vocal writing possesses a simple beauty that reaches its highest pitch in Orpheus's "Che faro senza Euridice?" (What shall I do without Eurydice?), an outpouring of grief comparable to the closing lament of Purcell's *Dido and Aeneas*. Gluck's recitative is no less fascinating. Calzabigi taught him how to make greater dramatic use of a convention that previously had too often dragged the action to a standstill – here the recitative is a fluid element, accompanied by music that remains uninterrupted. Choruses are sumptuous and are allocated sparingly throughout the whole, while the ballet interludes – notably the Dance of the Furies – reveal an exceptional choreographic imagination.

Orfeo may not be Gluck and Calzabigi's greatest work but it is probably their most exhilarating, and the joy with which Gluck immersed himself in his poet's work is mirrored throughout the score. As the composer wrote many years later: "If my music has had some success, I think it is my duty to recognize that I am beholden for it to him. . . . However much talent a composer may have, he will never produce any but mediocre music if the poet does not awaken in him that enthusiasm without which the productions of all the arts are but feeble and drooping."

RECORDINGS OVERVIEW

Gluck's *Orfeo* has been recorded more than twenty times, using various editions of the Paris and Vienna versions, and considering the cast-lists of many of these it is incredible that only four or five are worth owning. EMI's first recording starred Kathleen Ferrier in one of the two roles she sang on stage before her tragically early death in 1953; this 1951 broadcast captures her sumptuous contralto in imposing form, but the score is heavily cut and she is poorly supported by an inferior cast and a conductor who seems desperate to get the performance over and done with. RCA's first attempt offered the heavenly line-up of Peters, Della Casa and Stevens, all weighed down by the conducting of Pierre Monteux; EMI's third version paraded the talents of Annelise Rothenberger and Grace Bumbry; and Decca's first featured the potentially utopian trio of Donath, Lorengar and Horne, all smashed into line by the ever-sensitive Georg Solti. With very few exceptions, notably the two listed below, the only recordings to do justice to this magnificent opera were made after 1982, the date of Sigiswald Kuijken's pioneering authentic recreation.

Ragin, McNair, Sieden; Monteverdi Choir; English Baroque Soloists; Gardiner.
(Philips 434 093-2PH2; 2 CDs).

John Eliot Gardiner has conducted two recordings of different texts of *Orfeo*, and both are superb. This digital set of the Viennese version features Derek Lee Ragin's counter-tenor and Sylvia McNair's soprano, an ideal couple if ever there were one. McNair, one of the outstanding lyrical talents of our time, is especially impressive, giving an effortless portrayal of Eurydice. Directed by the ever-flexible Gardiner, this performance is wonderfully fresh and benefits from well-spaced recording and full documentation.

Von Otter, Hendricks, Fournier; Monteverdi Choir; Lyon Opera Orchestra; Gardiner.
(EMI CDS7 49834-2; 2 CDs).

For his stab at the French *Orfeo* Gardiner turned to Berlioz's edition of the score, which is a sort of hybrid of the two versions, with a chorus from *Echo et Narcisse* tacked on to the finale. (Berlioz also cut the Dance of the Furies, which Gardiner reinstates.) Gluck's proto-romantic gestures, emphasized by Berlioz's rehashed instrumentation, are nicely brought out by Gardiner, whose orchestra plays with varying degrees of urgency and repose. However, the recording's prime attraction is Sofie von Otter's beguiling mezzo-soprano, here at its most youthful; she brings a disciplined suffering to her portrayal of Orpheus. Barbara Hendricks' high-lying soprano works well with von Otter, and Fournier makes an attractive if rather too sexy Amor.

Verrett, Moffo, Raskin; Rome Polyphonic Chorus; Virtuosi di Roma; Fasano.
(RCA GD 87896; 2 CDs).

The little-known Renato Fasano follows the 1889 Ricordi edition of the score, which is the Vienna text plus the Paris dance numbers, but omitting Orpheus's "Addio, o mei sospiri" – which is a bit odd, as it would have been a perfect vehicle for Shirley Verrett. Obviously Verrett is much weightier in her approach than a counter-tenor such as Ragin, but her use of vocal colour and her variations of attack balance out her matronly style. Moffo is a little unsure in the lower registers but, like Verrett, the beauty of her projection and the character of her portrayal are full compensation. Judith Raskin is a solid Amor and Fasano keeps the music dancing throughout. Well recorded for 1963.

Simionato, Jurinac, Sciutti; Vienna State Opera Chorus; Vienna Philharmonic; Karajan.
(Deutsche Grammophon 439 101-2GX2; 2 CDs).

Karajan's passionately un-authentic account of the Vienna *Orfeo*, recorded live at the Salzburg Festival in 1959, is notable primarily for its singing and, in particular, the one-in-a-million union of Simionato and Jurinac. With Sciutti making a touching if lightweight Amor, this is a must for sopranophiles.

Simoneau, Danco, Alarie; Lamoureux Orchestra; Rosbaud.
(Philips 434 784-2PM2; 2 CDs).

Like the Karajan recording above, Rosbaud's *Orphée* is interesting primarily for its singing or, in this case, singer. Despite transposing some of the higher passages, Léopold Simoneau's tenor Orpheus is a revelation, phrasing with a golden, polished tone that was as unique in 1956 as it is today. This is perhaps the most perfect of his regrettably few recordings. The French soprano Suzanne Danco brings a strong personality and crisp enunciation to the part of Eurydice, but her vibrato is irritating and she seems uneasy with the music. Rosbaud, a conductor celebrated primarily for his work on modern music, makes an excellent impression here and provides good support, relaxing noticeably when accompanying Simoneau.

Alceste

Alcestis

Composed Vienna 1767; Paris 1775.
First performed December 26, 1767; April 23, 1776.
Libretto by Ranieri Calzabigi; Marie Francois Leblanc du Roullet; both after Euripides.

Synopsis – Viennese version

Act I

Admetus (Admète), king of Thebes, is dying. Apollo's oracle announces that Admetus can live if someone takes his place. Alcestis (Alceste), the king's wife, offers herself to the underworld.

Act II

Alcestis asks the gods if she can see her husband one more time. The city celebrates as the king returns to health, but no-one can understand why Alcestis weeps. The truth slowly emerges and she bids farewell to life.

Act III

Admetus implores his wife to renounce her pact but she remains true to her word and dies. After yet more mourning Apollo is forced to revoke his oracle's pact and restores Alcestis to life, reuniting her with her husband.

Like *Orfeo*, *Alceste* was derived from ancient Greek sources and was composed twice, first for Vienna in Italian, then for Paris in French. As with Orpheus, there are substantial differences between the two versions, but both are built on a larger scale than *Orfeo*, while spurning the comedy that Lully milked from the same material in favour of the intensely serious drama of the two main protagonists. Its concentration on the inner life of its empathetic characters makes *Alceste* the most important of the "reform operas" – and of course it was in the preface to this opera that Gluck and Calzabigi laid out their dramatic manifesto. Revealingly, *Alceste* was initially labelled a "tragedia per musica" by its creator, and was first played by a troupe of opera buffa performers rather than by opera seria singers, for what Gluck wanted was a well-acted music-drama, not the sort of semi-animated vocal recital that opera seria artists tended to produce. And for the first time ever in a grand Italian opera, Gluck dispensed with castrati, a decision partly based on the absence of singers of the calibre of Farinelli, but equally attributable to the fact that whereas *Orfeo* concerned itself with supernatural characters, *Alceste* revolved around the traumas of "real" people.

Gluck himself admitted that the more grandiose Vienna version, with its heavy choruses, was prone to tedium. The Paris revision, though longer by some thirty minutes and encumbered by the introduction of the character of Hercules, is swifter moving, chiefly because Gluck cut back on the chorus work and removed all the arias assigned to the secondary characters. He also introduced new ballets and a finely wrought aria for Alceste in Act I, as well as modifying the instrumental divertissements in line with suggestions made by Rousseau, who had written an unfavourable review of the Viennese production. Ultimately, the revision is considerably more theatrical, and this second version of *Alceste* can be seen as the distant ancestor of Romantic opera and Wagner's music-dramas – even if, jealous and bloody-minded, Wagner sneered that "the famous revolution of Gluck . . . really consisted only in the revolt of the composer against the arbitrariness of the singer".

Gedda, Norman, Krause, Gambill; Bavarian Radio Chorus and Symphony Orchestra; Baudo.
(Orfeo CO27823F; 3 CDs).

This live recording of the Paris *Alceste* features a cast of spectacular singers. The problem is that the singers are perhaps a bit too large-scale for this music: Jessye Norman is especially overwhelming, and her huge and glowing voice washes over much of the diction. The conductor, Serge Baudo, doesn't have much of a grip on proceedings, as if in awe of his leading lady, and this reading misses much of the opera's dramatic intensity. For all that, it all sounds very beautiful.

Flagstad, Jobin, Clark, Young; Jones Singers & Orchestra; Jones.
(Decca 436 234-2DMO3; 3 CDs).

Flagstad was approaching the end of her career when John Culshaw took her into the studio to record the Viennese (Italian-language) *Alceste* in 1956. It might be argued that her voice was too big for the title role but she had sung Gluck early in her career (before turning exclusively to Wagner) and she brings a rare nobility and presence to this recording. Raoul Jobin copes well as Admetus, and the session band strolls along in good spirits, even if neither the musicians nor their conductor are in the same class as the soprano. Good early stereo.

Iphigénie en Aulide

Iphigenia on Aulis

Composed 1771–73.
First performed April 19, 1774.
Libretto by Marie François Leblanc du Roullet, after Racine and Euripides.

Synopsis

Act I

Returning to Troy, the Greeks are stranded on Aulis (Aulide) by high winds. Artemis demands a sacrifice if she is to calm the weather. Agamemnon, unsure of what to do, summons Iphigenia (Iphigénie) for what she believes will be her marriage to Achilles. Eventually she arrives with her mother, Clytemnestra, whom Agamemnon tells that Achilles has changed his mind about the marriage.

Act II

Arcas reveals the truth to Iphigenia, who takes the news surprisingly well. Achilles promises to defend her and confronts Agamemnon who, after ordering the sacrifice, relents.

Act III

The soldiers, furious at being made to wait, begin to demand blood. Despite her lover's protestations and her mother's lamentations, Iphigenia is willing to die for her father. As she awaits her death Achilles bursts in and, threatening to kill Calchas, the King's advisor, prevents the sacrifice. At this moment the sacrificial pyre is mysteriously ignited and the weather calms, to allow Agamemnon and his army safe passage home.

Gluck's first French work, *Iphigénie en Aulide* was written in part to secure his reputation in Europe's cultural capital, and also with a view to establishing a musical school through which he might disseminate his operatic reformation. His move to the Paris Opéra certainly brought about enormous changes. Acting had never been high on the list of the Opéra's priorities, but when Gluck arrived he insisted that not only must the principals acquire acting skills but the chorus must as well, and he had to "carry himself like a military man" in order to achieve his objectives. In hindsight, it seems odd that the cast was unable to recognize that *Iphigénie en Aulide* had been written to be acted as well as sung, because the action is constructed as a sequence of interconnecting and rapid dramatic tableaux, rather than a series of juxtaposed and almost static images. It is hardly surprising that both Wagner and Mahler invested considerable efforts into reviving this landmark opera.

The orchestration of *Iphigénie en Aulide* is less detailed than in the Calzabigi operas (he was aware of the Parisian orchestra's weaknesses), but the fervent overture is the finest he ever wrote, and throughout the opera the rhythms are more animated and the vocal declamation is better defined than in previous operas, with clearer, crisper accompaniments. (A fine example is Agamemnon's monologue at the end of Act II, where the supple accompaniment mirrors his anguish over whether to stand by his country or by his daughter.) The musical sequences linking arias to choruses are punchier, less florid and more coherent as well. Indeed, the work as a whole possesses an extraordinary cogency, as Charles Burney remarked when Gluck played the opera to him – "it is seldom that a single air . . . can be taken out of its niche, and sung singly, with much effect; the whole is a chain, of which a detached link is but of small importance". There is one moment, however, that stands out from all the rest: Iphigenia's farewell at the end of Act III, "Adieu! conservez dans votre âme", an aria that Ernest Newman described as "one of the most perfect emotional utterances of the eighteenth century".

Dawson, van Dam, von Otter, Aler; Monteverdi Choir; Lyon Opera Orchestra; Gardiner.
(Erato 2292-45003-2; 2 CDs).

Gardiner's is the only recording of *Iphigénie en Aulide* and is likely to remain so for some years. The cast is unsurpassable, with José van Dam darkly impressive as Agamemnon, Lynne Dawson deeply moving as Iphigenia, von Otter vibrant as Clytemnestra and John Aler heroically naive as Achilles. The theatrical attack from soloists, orchestra and especially the chorus is electrifying, and Gardiner's urgent tempi convey much of the vitality of the stage production that preceded it. A little detail is lost by the modern instruments but this is a small price to pay for such dynamic music-making.

Armide

Armida

Composed 1776.
First performed September 23, 1777.
Libretto by Philippe Quinault, after Tasso.

Synopsis

Act I

The pagan sorceress Armida (Armide) has seduced a large number of Godfrey's Christian knights on the crusade. She claims to hate Rinaldo (Renaud) but he is pure and, as such, beyond her reach. Despite her claims of hatred, she is in love with him.

Act II

Armida lures Rinaldo to a secret garden and there prepares to kill him; but she cannot and, submitting to her feelings, carries him to her enchanted palace.

Act III

Armida reveals the depth of her feelings for Rinaldo but she cannot allow them to interfere with her task and she summons Hate to rid her of her passions; but she rejects it before her love is affected.

Act IV

Two knights come to rescue Rinaldo.

Act V

After a short love scene (the only time Rinaldo and Armida address each other) the knights shame their hero into returning with them. Furious, the sorceress destroys her palace.

Gluck's use of Quinault's libretto represented a shift in ideals. He took the text of Lully's last opera almost in its original form, simply removing the Prologue and adding one or two lines to Act III. In a sense this tactic was an assault on the archaisms of French opera, for Gluck was showing how a modern composer could revitalize the five-act formulas of seventeenth-century drama, but he was nonetheless abandoning a concept that had been central to his reforms – the creative liaison between writer and composer. And even Gluck couldn't put flesh on all the bones of Quinault's text, for it simply did not possess the dramatic economy of the libretti produced by Calzabigi. Nonetheless, the opera has its qualities – and it was, after all, one of Gluck's greatest successes. The idyllic and sensuous colour of the score looks towards Romantic opera, and there are moments of quasi-nineteenth-century passion, not least the Act V love duet between Armida and Rinaldo. There's enough decent music here to warrant exploration, but there's no CD available at the moment. With luck EMI will re-release Richard Hickox's 1983 recording with the City of London Sinfonia.

OPERA AS PUPPET THEATRE

The problem of how to sing while acting in a manner that might be taken for natural behaviour is a perennial difficulty for modern opera producers. It was a problem unknown to Handel and his contemporaries, however, for the role of the opera singer prior to the age of Gluck was simply to sing the music and perhaps make a few appropriate gestures. The conventions that Gluck had to overturn may be judged from the directorial instructions of Pietro Metastasio, a figure now chiefly remembered as a theorist and librettist. The following plan was written in February 1748 and shows the positions he expected the six characters to adopt and maintain in every performance of the first act of his *Demofoönte*.

STAGE RIGHT	CENTRE	STAGE LEFT
	Scene I	
Matusio		Dircea
	Scene II	
Dircea		Timante
	Scene III	
Adrasto	Demofoönte	Timante
	Scene IV	
	Timante	
	Scene V	
Creusa		Cherinto
	Scene VI	
Creusa	Timante	Cherinto

Regardless of how impassioned their script might be, the singers stood their ground and launched their voices at each other or the audience. And it would appear that the vast majority of operas prior to the advent of Gluck and Mozart were played in this way, presenting a drama with all the mobility of a hedgerow in a breeze. It's remarkable that, less than a century later, Richard Wagner was annotating every other bar of his scores with detailed directions to his actor-singers, to ensure that every potential of the stage was fully exploited.

Iphigénie en Tauride

Iphigenia on Tauris

Composed Paris 1778; Vienna 1781.
First performed May 18, 1779; October 23, 1781.
Libretto by Nicholas-François Guillard, after Claude Guimond de la Touche and Euripides; Johann Baptist von Alxinger, after Guillard.

Synopsis – Paris Version

Act I

Around the temple of Artemis on the island of Tauris a storm is raging, through which can be heard the voices of Iphigenia (Iphigénie) and her priestesses asking for the protection of the gods. They oblige, calming the weather, but Iphigenia is tormented by dreams of the death of her parents (Agamemnon and Clytemnestra) and of the murder of her brother (Orestes) by herself. She prays to Artemis. Thoas, king of Scythia, is fearful when two strangers appear on the island, and he demands their sacrifice to appease the gods.

Act II

The strangers turn out to be Pylades (Pylade) and Orestes (Oreste), who has been hounded by the Furies for killing his mother and is seeking atonement by recovering Tauris's statue of Artemis, which has been desecrated by human sacrifice. Orestes, separated from Pylades, falls to a fit in which the Furies and the ghost of his mother torment him. Iphigenia arrives to question him; he tells her that Agamemnon has been murdered by Clytemnestra, that their son in revenge has murdered his mother, and that he now is dead. Iphigenia laments her fate.

Act III

Struck now by Orestes' resemblance to her brother, Iphigenia tries to save him from Thoas by asking him to take a letter to Elektra, her sister. Orestes refuses to abandon Pylades, who consents to leave the island, planning to return with a rescue party.

Act IV

As Iphigenia prepares for the sacrifice of Orestes, she and her brother recognize each other, but Thoas enters, baying for blood. In the nick of time, Pylades returns with his crew and kills Thoas. Artemis descends to ensure that her statue is no longer profaned by human blood.

Boasting the finest libretto that Gluck ever set, *Iphigénie en Tauride* comes as close as possible to the complete realization of the composer's ideal. More sensual, expressive and taut than any other Gluck creation, it was adored by Berlioz and by Richard Strauss – the latter went so far as to prepare a performing edition in which he "modernized" some of the harmony, changed the finales of the first and last acts and introduced ballet music from *Orfeo* and *Armide*. The opening is one of Gluck's most wondrous innovations: there is no overture but rather a brief scene-setting prelude, evoking a rising storm, out of which grows the voice of Iphigenia and the commencement of the first scene. This dramatic seamlessness, typical of the entire piece, must have left contemporary audiences dazzled.

Gluck's application of instrumentation as a psychological device is as astounding as the opera's structural perfection. Perhaps the best-known example comes during Act II, when Gluck uses trombones to signify the Furies and then, in a remarkable twist, introduces throbbing semiquavers on one note, stressed every first beat, to indicate that Orestes might not ever free himself from guilt. But of course the orchestra is used for more than local effect: the score is, in fact, almost symphonic in its richness, and the shifts between recitative, aria and chorus are eased by a stream of constantly inventive instrumental music. With its enthralling sense of unstoppable momentum, *Iphigénie en Tauride* is the Gluck opera that most closely prefigures the masterworks of the nineteenth century.

Montague, Aler, Allen, Argenta; Monteverdi Choir; Lyon Opera Orchestra; Gardiner.
(Philips 416 148-2PH2; 2 CDs).

This recording of the Paris version is one of John Eliot Gardiner's finest sets. His grasp of the score's architecture, the tensile strength of his tempi and the vivid punctuation of his rhythms make this as headily theatrical as any Gluck opera recording. His customary attention to detail, heightening instrumental clarity to a point just short of pedantry, gives the orchestral counterpoint unprecedented power. The cast respond well to Gardiner's direction, and the momentum of the ensemble is consistently impressive – though the voices are rather light, with the exception of Thomas Allen's Orestes. Perfect sound, and a good booklet too.

JOSEPH HAYDN

b. ROHRAU, GERMANY, MARCH 31, 1732; d. VIENNA, MAY 31, 1809.

Opera is the one field of musical activity in which history has judged Haydn a failure, yet opera consumed an enormous amount of his time, almost from the start of his career. He first came into contact with opera in 1752, when he met the actor and theatre manager Joseph von Kurz, who commissioned him to provide music for the comedy *Der krumme Teufel*. In 1761 he moved to Eisenstadt, the country home of Prince Paul Anton Esterházy, where he wrote his first four complete operas. (Like *Der krumme Teufel*, all four have been lost.) That same year Esterházy made Haydn his court *Kapellmeister* and the composer remained exclusively in that family's employment for the next thirty years, composing all but one of his twenty-eight operas for their entertainment. Unlike Mozart, whose relationship with his patrons was turbulent, Haydn lived happily within the confines of his master's world and benefited enormously both from his seclusion and from having a permanent orchestra and theatre with which to work. As he later remarked:

LEBRECHT COLLECTION

The dapper Papa Joe Haydn

"There was no-one there to confuse me, so I was forced to become original."

When Prince Paul's brother Nikolaus inherited the family title in 1762, the Eisenstadt court relocated to Esterháza, a vast summer palace forty miles south of Vienna. There Haydn had at his disposal what was probably Europe's best-equipped theatre, in which Haydn oversaw performances of operas by himself and numerous other composers, doing much to raise the expectations of performing standards throughout Europe. At its peak, the theatre employed some twenty-five singers, administrators and stage hands, as well as the full-time orchestra of twenty, and as a non-Italian house of Italian opera, it was rivalled only by London's Covent Garden. Between 1780 and 1790, the year Nikolaus died, more than one thousand performances of more than one hundred operas were given at Esterháza, and in 1786 alone the year's tally included eight premieres.

After Nikolaus's death Haydn and his court musicians were dismissed but, as a sign of the family's respect for his loyalty, they continued paying his salary and allowed him to keep his *Kapellmeister* title. Out of work, he moved to Vienna where he received an invitation from the impresario J.P. Salomon to visit England. There, as part of his contract, he composed an opera for a travelling company but because George III refused to grant a license for its performance, the four completed acts of *L'anima del filosofo'* (a version of the Orpheus myth) were never performed. It was to be Haydn's last opera.

So the story of Haydn and opera is the story of Haydn and the Esterházy family. Between 1762 and 1783 he composed sixteen operas, all of them in Italian and the vast majority of them comic, which might seem odd in view of the fact that he started his Eisenstadt career with *Acide*, a sober opera seria. However, it would appear that he was much affected by the comic works of Cimarosa, Paisiello and Piccini, among others (a number of which he staged at Esterháza), and the prince was clearly happier with such fare. It is possible that Haydn's proclivity for tragedy was frustrated by his patron, and that the palace's preference for light opera contributed to his early retirement from opera composition in 1783 – seven years before his patron's death. It is surely significant that his only post-Esterházy opera, *L'anima del filosofo*, was to have ended with the death of Eurydice.

Haydn's reputation as an opera composer will probably always be overshadowed by the coruscating figure of Mozart. Haydn's operas are blithely tuneful but only rarely are the tunes memorable; his characterization is sometimes witty but lacks psychological incisiveness; his pacing is often heavy and uneven; and, with no house-poet with whom to work, Haydn was required to use secondhand and frequently mediocre libretti.

However, when compared to the work of his Italian contemporaries, Haydn's operas take on a more positive aspect. He was first and foremost an instrumental composer and the accompaniments in many of his operas impart a shine to the dull vocal writing. Haydn's harmony might not always be suitable to the situation, but it is highly original and suggests a subversive desire to remain true to himself. His recitative isn't terribly interesting, but in his two opera serie it reflects a knowledge of Gluck's reforms, as does his development of finales out of small but seamlessly linked sections – and some of his ensemble endings are positively exciting. In brief, Haydn's operas may not be as arresting as his symphonies and string quartets – of which he is one of history's greatest masters – but they do provide cheerful, undemanding entertainment. That was, after all, his intention.

L'infedeltà delusa

Infidelity Outwitted

Composed 1773.
First performed July 26, 1773.
Libretto by Marco Coltellini and Carl Friberth.

Synopsis

Act I

In his country house, Filippo and his neighbour Nencio are arranging the marriage of the former's daughter, Sandrina, to the latter. Although she loves Nanni she pretends to accede to her father's wishes. When Sandrina tells Nanni the news he is hurt and frightened, just as Nanni's sister Vespina fears losing Nencio, whom she loves. Nencio serenades Sandrina, threatening to take her by force if necessary; furious, Sandrina spurns him, and Vespina emerges to slap his face.

Act II

Disguised as an old woman, Vespina tells Filippo that she is looking for her daughter's husband, Nencio. Leaving Filippo and Sandrina horrified, she dons another disguise, goes to Nencio as the emissary of a Marquis and tells him that the Marquis wishes to marry Filippo's daughter. Nencio confronts Filippo just as "the Marquis" (Vespina again) arrives to explain that because Sandrina is of lowly status she will be marrying one of his servants rather than the Marquis himself. Nanni, disguised as the servant, marries Sandrina. Filippo is forced to accept the outcome when the truth is revealed, and the opera ends with a double celebration as Nencio and Vespina are married.

L'infedeltà delusa was very well received by Nikolaus Esterházy, and it reflected glory on the prince just over a month after its premiere, when the Empress Maria Theresa, paying her only visit to the summer palace, was inspired to remark, "If I want to hear good opera, I go to Esterháza." Yet for all its immediate success the opera fell from the repertoire almost immediately after the empress's departure, and it remained shelved until the 1960s.

Haydn subtitled *L'infedeltà delusa* a "Burletta per musica" (musical jest), an indication that the comedy is even frothier than the usual buffa routine. Nonetheless there are a number of more substantial episodes (notably the face-slapping in Act I), and the character of Vespina stands out amid the two-dimensional cast. There's also the novelty value of having the father-figure sung by a tenor, which is explained by the fact that librettist Carl Friberth was also a tenor. However, the opera's appeal is essentially instrumental, and it is Haydn's ever-inventive manipulation of orchestral forces that holds the attention.

Mathis, Hendricks, Ahnsjö, Baldin, Devlin; Lausanne Chamber Orchestra; Dorati.
(Philips 432 413-2PH2; 2 CDs).

This is marginally the best of the three recordings that have been made of *L'infedeltà delusa*, chiefly thanks to the performances of Edith Mathis and Barbara Hendricks as Vespina and Sandrina. Mathis's voice is essentially light but she manages to create a variety of faces as the old woman, the servant, the Marquis and the notary. The modern-instrument orchestra is moulded with elegance and enthusiasm by Dorati and the pacing is sprightly. The booklet documentation is excellent.

L'incontro improvviso

The Unforeseen Encounter

Composed 1775.
First performed August 29, 1775.
Libretto adapted by Carl Friberth from Dancourt's libretto for Gluck's opera of the same name.

Synopsis

Act I

Forced from his homeland by his brother, Prince Ali has found shelter with the King of Persia. He and the King's daughter Rezia are in love – though they know she has been promised to another. They escape by ship, are captured by pirates and are separated.

Act II

Ali arrives in Cairo where Rezia is now in the Sultan's harem. Ali receives a request for an anonymous assignation, which he reluctantly accepts, though he takes the precaution of taking his servant Osmin along. Ali is offered a beautiful slave but turns her away, whereupon Rezia (who is behind this test of his virtue) emerges to hug Ali with joy, reassuring him that she has so far managed to avoid the Sultan's bed.

Act III

The lovers are captured before they can flee. Just as their heads are about to be removed, the Sultan has a change of heart and agrees to their marriage.

Like Mozart's *Die Entführung*, which has a similar plot outline and was composed just seven years later, *L'incontro improvviso* is a product of a European vogue for all things Turkish. In music the chief manifestation of this vogue was so-called Janissary music, a derivation of Turkish marching music. The Janissary band was a percussion unit, featuring a triangle, cymbals, bass drum, kettle drum and a crescent, a pole covered with tiny bells that was banged on the ground to mark time (known throughout Europe as a "Jingling Johnny"). For most western composers, Janissary music simply provided a dash of exotic colour; Haydn's opera is intriguing in that it works the material into the plot – in Act I there is a captivating episode in which the dervishes try to teach Osmin their "strange" music.

However, despite a sprinkling of comic incidents, *L'incontro* is an over-long and gracelessly constructed piece. Parts of it, especially during the first act, can seem interminable, and, unlike Gluck, Haydn was simply not capable of maintaining tortuous dialogue. (Attention spans were obviously greater in the eighteenth century – the premiere of this three-hour opera was followed, on the same day, by performances of two German plays and a marionette version of *Alceste*). The vocal writing, divided into forty-seven separate numbers, is pleasant if unimaginative, with the notable exception of the ensembles – with its long, high-lying and sensuous melodies, the Act I trio "Mi sembra un sogno" is especially touching. Moments such as this, together with Haydn's ever-dependable instrumental accompaniments, constitute the opera's attraction.

Ahnsjö, Zoghby, Marshall, Jones, Luxon; Lausanne Chamber Orchestra; Dorati.
(Philips 432 416-2PH3; 3 CDs).

Dorati's account of *L'incontro improvviso* manages to conjure a musical fluidity which masks the weak dramatic architecture of the piece, and his cast is excellent if a little mannered at times. Ahnsjö's high tenor is mellow yet exciting as Ali – he hits a stratospheric E flat with ease. Della Jones and Margaret Marshall are delightful slaves and Domenico Trimarchi is a suitably clownish Osmin. However, it is Linda Zoghby's Rezia who steals the show – yet for some reason her glass-bell soprano can only be heard here and in one other Dorati/Haydn set.

Il mondo della luna

The World on the Moon

Composed 1777.
First performed August 3, 1777.
Libretto by Carlo Goldoni.

Synopsis

Act I

The astrologer Ecclitico and a group of his students manage to convince the sour Bonafede that a better life awaits him on the moon. In come the knight Ernesto and his servant Cecco. It transpires that Ernesto and Ecclitico are in love with Bonafede's daughters, Flamina and Clarice, while Cecco loves their maid Lisetta. The couples are determined to marry but they must have Bonafede's blessing. They persuade the irascible old man to drink a sleeping potion, which they say will send him to the moon. He says goodbye, causing his daughters to believe he is dying; but they are calmed by a forged will in which they are left substantial sums of money.

Act II

Ecclitico has disguised his garden as the moon. Bonafede wakes to prepare for his meeting with the emperor of the moon (Cecco disguised). He then tries to seduce his daughter's maid but she rejects him, as she is preparing to be crowned queen of the lunatics. He eventually agrees to his daughters' marriages.

Act III

They reveal the charade and beg Bonafede's forgiveness. Bonafede gives his blessing to the triple wedding, Ecclitico announces his retirement from astrology and the entire cast celebrate the good fortune brought by the world on the moon.

To an extent *Il mondo della luna* is deeply conventional, in that it follows the typical construction of a *dramma giocoso*. Created by Carlo Goldoni (this opera's librettist), this derivation of opera buffa features three sets of stock characters: the *parti buffe* or comic players (here Bonafede, Lisetta and Cecco); the *parti serie* or serious players (Flamina and Ernesto); and the *parti di mezzo carattere* or serio-comic players (Clarice and Ecclitico). Haydn's contribution to the genre, though not matching the subversive brilliance of Mozart's *Don Giovanni* (see p.95), is lifted out of the formulaic rut by the wit of the music, which defines the characters by allocating an individual style to each. The potency of the vocal writing, the adroitness of the pacing and the radiance of the orchestral score (with frequent instrumental interludes) make this whimsical farce Haydn's finest opera.

Il mondo della luna is the only one of Haydn's operas that can bear comparison with Mozart's comedies, and Haydn himself was evidently pleased with what he'd done: the overture became the first movement of the 63rd Symphony, one of Ernesto's arias appeared in the *Missa Cellensis* and other episodes crop up in the six trios for two violins and cello of 1784. Yet for some reason *Il mondo della luna* was poorly received at its first performance, and it seems that no contemporary performances took place outside Esterháza.

Trimarchi, Alva, von Stade, Augér, Mathis, Rolfe Johnson; Lausanne Chamber Orchestra; Dorati.
(Philips 432 420-2PH3; 3 CDs).

This 1977 recording of Haydn's best opera received the best of Philips' budget. The singing is tremendous throughout, the sound is magnificent and the comic timing might actually make you laugh. Such starry casting for such a peripheral opera would be unimaginable today.

GIOVANNI PAISIELLO

b. ROCCAFORZATA, ITALY, MAY 9, 1740; d. NAPLES, JUNE 5, 1816.

Paisiello deserves to be better known, for he was one of the principal influences behind the transformation of opera buffa from light entertainment into vital theatre, and alongside Cimarosa he represents the high point of that genre prior to Mozart. He wrote the first of his eighty or so operas in 1764, just a year after completing his formal studies. Two years later he accepted a court appointment from Empress Catherine II in St Petersburg, and for the remainder of his life he lived at the mercy of fickle patronage: in 1784 he moved to Naples and King Ferdinand IV, in 1802 to Paris and Napoleon, then back to Naples and King Joseph (Napoleon's brother) in 1806, and finally back to Ferdinand IV in 1815. Paisiello composed the majority of his operas for Naples but his best-known work, *Il barbiere di Siviglia*, was written for St Petersburg, and was so popular that when Rossini asked permission to set the same libretto, Paisiello promptly gave his blessing, so sure was he that the young composer could not possibly trump him. However, although Paisiello's supporters successfully ruined the premiere, Rossini's opera soon became a fantastic success, contributing heavily towards the decline of the older composer's critical valuation.

Il barbiere di Siviglia

The Barber of Seville

Composed 1782.
First performed September 26, 1782.
Libretto by anonymous writer, after Beaumarchais.

Synopsis

Act I

The wandering barber Figaro meets Count Almaviva, who, disguised as a student, is wooing Bartolo's ward, Rosina. Bartolo is jealously protective, as he would like to marry her himself. Rosina drops a note from her balcony to the Count, who gives his name as Lindoro.

Act II

Rosina is told of Lindoro's love by the barber Figaro, whom she gives a letter to take to her suitor. Now disguised as a soldier, the Count arrives to take his billet at Bartolo's house. He tries to hand Rosina a letter but Bartolo catches them at it and demands to see the note. Rosina manages to exchange it for another, less inflammatory note.

Act III

Now disguised as Alonso, a pupil of the music master Don Basilio, Count Almaviva meets Rosina (who assumes he is Lindoro) and gives her a music lesson. Don Basilio arrives, knowing nothing of his new pupil, and is paid to leave immediately. Bartolo, while being shaved by Figaro, overhears the lovers planning to elope and interrupts their clandestine discussion.

Act IV

Don Basilio reveals the Count's subterfuge to Bartolo, who then informs Rosina that Alonso is an impostor, perhaps an agent for the Count. Bartolo, triumphant, leaves to find the guard, but Figaro and the Count then arrive, and Bartolo arrives to find Rosina and the Count have married. The guard departs, refusing to arrest the Count.

𝄞 Paisiello chose this subject chiefly because his patron in Russia was a noted admirer of Beaumarchais' writings, and whoever wrote the libretto took pains to retain the comedy's pivotal elements. This fidelity to the text was not entirely sensible, for in order to match the music to the drama, Paisiello was obliged to disperse his arias and ensembles unevenly through the opera. Thus, for example, Figaro is forced to sing all his finest numbers before the end of the second act. But there are some excellently crafted comic episodes, the music is a constant stream of good-natured invention, the arias are assured, and Paisiello writes some fine exchanges between the Count and Rosina. Nowadays Paisiello's opera seems little more than an intriguing historical perspective on Rossini's remarkable undertaking, but Mozart and da Ponte were clearly taken by it – after seeing it staged in Vienna in 1783, they were inspired to create *Le nozze di Figaro*, the sequel to the story of the Barber of Seville.

Gáti, Laki, Gregor, Gulyás; Hungarian State Opera; Fischer.
(Hungaroton HCD 12525-6; 2 CDs).

Adám Fischer's recording of *Il Barbiere* has been deleted but, as it is the only one ever made, it may well re-emerge soon. Like so many other Hungarian State Opera recordings, the production has a dramatic unity that compensates for any weakness in the vocal contributions. István Gáti's Figaro is engagingly camp, Krisztina Laki's Rosina is cautious but beautifully rounded, and though Dénes Gulyás's Almaviva is somewhat thin and nasal, his characterization might serve as a model for many a bigger name.

DOMENICO CIMAROSA

b. AVERSA, ITALY, DECEMBER 17, 1749; d. VENICE, JANUARY 11, 1801.

Cimarosa, the most famous opera buffa composer of the late eighteenth century, holds a unique record. Leopold II was so taken by *Il matrimonio segreto* that, after treating the cast to dinner, he had the entire three-hour comedy repeated – making Cimarosa's masterpiece the only opera ever to be encored at its first performance. As prolific as Paisiello, Cimarosa also spent some time in St Petersburg as court composer to Catherine II, but unlike Paisiello he floated precariously on the edges of patronage, and he hated his stay in Russia – almost as vehemently as Russia hated him.

He originally studied with Pietro Gallo in Naples but was later adopted by the better-known Piccini. His first operas were staged in Naples (again like Paisiello), then in 1787 he moved to St Petersburg, whence, after his contract expired in 1791, he beat a swift retreat to Vienna. There Leopold II appointed him *Kapellmeister* in place of Salieri; three months later Cimarosa composed *Il matrimonio segreto*.

With Mozart dead and Paisiello retired, Cimarosa revelled in his pre-eminence, but his good fortune was short-lived. Only three weeks after the premiere of *Il matrimonio segreto* Leopold died, leaving Cimarosa without a patron. He returned to Italy and found work as organist to yet another of Paisiello's ex-patrons, Ferdinand IV of Naples. Naples remained a stable base until 1799, when the composer's involvement in libertarian politics led to his arrest and a death sentence. After four months in prison his conviction was reduced to exile and he moved to Venice, where, within the year, he died – some say of stomach cancer, others of poison.

Cimarosa's tunefulness and spontaneity are typical of the finest opera buffa, but as with Paisiello, his work has suffered through comparison with Mozart's infinitely more profound comic operas. But it's as well to remember that profundity was not an Italian operatic ideal, and Cimarosa succeeded brilliantly in what he set out to do, devising light and witty pieces with a charm and melodic fluidity that prefigures the world of Donizetti and bel canto.

Il matrimonio segreto

The Secret Marriage

Composed 1792.
First performed February 7, 1792.
Libretto by Giovanni Bertati, after Colman and Garrick.

Synopsis

Act I

Geronimo, a wealthy and deaf Bolognese merchant, has two daughters, Elisetta and Carolina, and a sister, Fidalma, who runs the house. Fidalma loves Paolino without realizing that he has been secretly married to Carolina. Elisetta is to marry Count Robinson but when he arrives, he falls in love with her sister. Carolina fails to dissuade him. Geronimo remains oblivious.

Act II

Geronimo agrees to the Count's marriage to Carolina. Paolino is distraught and approaches Fidalma for help. She interprets his pleas as a proposal, causing Paolino to faint into her arms. Naturally, Carolina enters to see Fidalma cradling the young man and she is only just won round by her husband's protestations of love. The Count, endeavouring to distance Elisetta from him, behaves appallingly. Carolina and Paolino try to run off together, but are caught by Elisetta who, assuming the man to be her Count, summons the others. The plot is then unravelled, Geronimo blesses the marriage of Paolino and Carolina, and the Count agrees to honour his obligation to Elisetta.

Il matrimonio segreto was performed 67 times during its first run, has been translated into a dozen languages, and earned the praise of no less a judge than Giuseppe Verdi, who regarded it as a "true musical comedy, which has everything an opera buffa should". Nowadays it is very rarely staged or recorded: modern audiences find it over-extended, and its considerable debt to Mozart is now clearer than it would have been at the time. In its defence it should be pointed out that it does have a number of memorably fizzy arias, especially those for Carolina and Paolino, as well as a series of notable ensembles, in particular the comedy duet between Geronimo and the Count in the last act and the opera's ensemble finale. But, like most buffa operas, *Il matrimonio segreto* loses a lot of its impact on record, and it should only really be considered if you've developed a passionate fascination with the genre.

Augér, Varady, Fischer-Dieskau, Hamari, Davies; English Chamber Orchestra; Barenboim.
(Deutsche Grammophon 437 696-2GX3; 3 CDs).

Barenboim has made a name for himself conducting some of the grandest music ever written, notably Wagner, and his work with earlier, lighter music is frequently neglected. One of his finest achievements is this recording of *Il matrimonio segreto*, a set on which the singing is so gorgeous that it makes you forget the fatuous dialogue and the tedious recitatives. Husband-and-wife team Fischer-Dieskau and Varady play their hearts out as Geronimo and Elisetta, while Arleen Augér's duets with Varady are among the most beautiful examples of buffa singing on record. The recording sounded good on its release in 1975; after its transfer onto CD it sounds even better.

ANTONIO SALIERI

b. LEGNAGO, ITALY, AUGUST 18, 1750; d. VIENNA, MAY 7, 1825.

Salieri's name might well have been forgotten long ago were it not for the persistence of the absurd notion that he murdered Mozart. This fantasy, first dramatized by Pushkin and then turned into an opera by both Rimsky-Korsakov and Lortzing, has achieved the weight of fact thanks to Peter Schaeffer's wilfully dishonest play *Amadeus* and the Oscar-winning movie that was made of it. In reality, Salieri fully acknowledged and was reconciled to the superiority of the freakish genius who was born six years after him and died over a quarter of a century before him. And Salieri's neglect owes almost as much to Beethoven's popularity as it does to Mozart's. In 1791, the year of Mozart's death, Beethoven was just getting into his stride, and by the time Salieri's life came to an end, just a couple of years before Beethoven's, the musical culture of Europe was moving into the era of Romanticism. Salieri's efficient classicism stood little chance of survival.

As a fifteen-year-old, he travelled to Vienna where he was introduced to Emperor Joseph II, Metastasio and Gluck. Each had a decisive effect on Salieri. Joseph II employed him as a chamber musician, Metastasio taught him how to write for the operatic voice and Gluck became his patron, although at no point did he give him instruction. In 1774 he was promoted to Court Composer, directing Italian opera for the emperor, and four years later he took over Vienna's most powerful musical post, that of imperial *Kapellmeister*. Salieri remained in the capital for the rest of his life, but he was enthusiastically received right across the continent. His *L'Europa riconosciuta* was a hit at La Scala in 1778, but his greatest success came in Paris in 1784 with the staging of *Les Danaïdes*, in the wake of which Salieri was hailed in various quarters as Gluck's successor.

It's not a claim that bears any examination. Salieri wrote operas in most genres, including opera seria, opera buffa and Singspiel, and he set the libretti of a number of impressive writers, including da Ponte and Beaumarchais. But he never achieved either the memorability or the psychological acuity of Mozart's operas with the same librettists, and he was unable to adapt to the musical changes happening around him – his premature retirement from stage-work in 1804 might be taken as an acknowledgement of his constitutional inflexibility. Though Salieri is an interesting historical figure (after all, he taught Beethoven, Schubert and Liszt, among others), only a couple of his operas justify a trip to the CD shop.

Les Danaïdes

Composed 1784.
First performed April 26, 1784.
Libretto by François Bailly de Roullet and Louis Théodore Baron de Tschudy, after Calzabigi.

Synopsis

Act I

Danaus and his fifty daughters, the Danaïdes, vow loyalty to their enemy Aegyptus, Danaus's brother. Aegyptus dies and is succeeded by his eldest son, Lynceus (Lyncée). He and his brothers each agree to marry one of the Danaïdes; Danaus instructs his daughters to take revenge by killing their husbands.

Act II

Lynceus's wife Hypermnestra (Hypermnestre) is alone in refusing to obey her father's order, even after Danaus confronts her with the prophecy that he will be murdered himself if she fails to satisfy his lust for vengeance.

Act III

After the wedding ceremony Hypermnestra manages to escape with Lynceus, just as his brothers are being killed.

Act IV

Danaus is enraged when news of Lynceus's escape reaches him but he is distracted from his anger when Lynceus storms the city, killing all the Danaïdes except Hypermnestra and burning the palace to the ground.

Act V

The Danaïdes are sent to Hades where their father is seen chained to a rock, his entrails being torn from him by a vulture. The Furies promise an eternity of suffering.

Calzabigi originally wrote the libretto of *Les Danaïdes* for Gluck but the aged composer was unable to write the music in time to meet the Opéra's schedule and so asked Salieri to take it over. This he was happy to do, but Salieri was so in awe of Gluck's "light and genius" that he insisted that their names appear together on the libretto. Though flattered, Gluck was not foolish enough to risk too close an association with Salieri's work and diplomatically informed the press: "The music of *Danaïdes* is completely by Salieri, my only part in it having been to make suggestions which he willingly accepted." Audiences primed by the operas of Gluck took well to Salieri's swiftly moving drama, with its bold proto-romantic gestures and stomach-churning finale: the premiere at the Paris Opéra was an immediate success, and the work remained in the repertoire for a considerable period.

While the grand marches, choruses and ballets of *Les Danaïdes* are well marshalled, with some fine setting of recitative dialogue, it is in the vocal writing that the die-hard classicist seemed most at ease – in this respect, as with the effortlessly spun melodies and simple orchestrations, Salieri's opera is most closely comparable to the music of his pupil Schubert. The bass role of Danaus is one of the few written at this time for the lowest of the male voices, and though he has his moments of tedium this confused and desperate character has some memorably noble music. Hypermnestra's soprano, which dominates the opera in a manner that anticipates the soprano-centred opera of Cherubini and Spontini, is technically well written, but, typical of the opera as a whole, Salieri seemed incapable of developing the basic material beyond the formulas inherited from Gluck. In the final analysis Salieri lacked the inventive spark of Gluck and Mozart, but the fine soprano role, the tremendously grim finale, and the brevity of *Les Danaïdes* (ten minutes under two hours) have ensured that the opera has made it onto CD.

Marshall, Kavrakos, Giménez, Bartha; Stuttgart Radio Chorus and Orchestra; Gelmetti.
(EMI CDS7 54073-2; 2 CDs).

This set was recorded in 1990 as a vehicle for the soprano Margaret Marshall, whose sparkling performance is the recording's primary appeal, although the young and sophisticated lyric tenor of Raúl Giménez (Lynceus) is another strong attraction. Dimitri Kavrakos lacks spite as Danaus and Gelmetti's tempi tend to be inconsistent, but the playing is crisp and the Stuttgart chorus sings with gusto and precision. An interesting document, with enjoyable highlights.

Falstaff

Composed 1798.
First performed January 3, 1799.
Libretto by Carlo Prospero Defranceschi, after Shakespeare.

Synopsis

Act I

Sir John Falstaff brags that he intends to seduce Meg and Alice, the wives of Page and Ford. He sends identical letters to both women, who then decide to teach him a lesson. Falstaff's assignation with Alice is interrupted by Ford, and he is pitched into the Thames.

Act II

Falstaff is invited to meet Alice again in Windsor Forest where he is given a sound trouncing by the insulted wives, dressed as goblins and fairies. The chaos is resolved as masks are removed, and Falstaff admits the error of his ways.

Shakespeare's plays have been exploited by opera composers more often than any other writer's, and *The Merry Wives of Windsor* has attracted more than its fair share of attention. Adam, Verdi and Vaughan Williams, among others, have followed where Salieri led. Strangely for the time, Salieri and Defranceschi stayed fairly close to the original, cutting back on a few of the work's less essential characters and adding only one scene, a witty episode in which Mistress Ford visits Falstaff disguised as a German maid.

Falstaff is one of Salieri's last operas and his most successful comic creation, with some charming music, funny dialogue and highly sympathetic characterization. The architecture of the piece – dozens of arias bridged by brisk recitative, leading towards grand finales – is designed to keep the action flowing, and the pace scarcely flags during the three-hour span. There's no great musical development, such as you'd get from Mozart, but it's a good-humoured and tuneful knockabout, with a few highlights along the way, including the military overture, Falstaff's strutting Act I aria, the technically brilliant "laughter" trio in Act II and the ensemble finale to Act III.

Gregor, Zempléni, Gulyás, Gáti; Salieri Chamber Choir and Orchestra; Pál.
(Hungaroton HCD 12789-91; 3 CDs).

The Hungaroton recording is not widely distributed but it is well worth trying to get hold of. Tamás Pál keeps things moving at an almost exhausting pace, and the Hungarian State Opera are at their collective best, supporting a cast that clearly enjoys singing together. Gregor is splendid as the swaggering Falstaff and Dénes Gulyás's highly attractive tenor voice brings much to the potentially innocuous role of Master Ford. The rest of the cast is unremarkable but Pál's direction keeps your attention even when the singing is below par. Good sound, poor booklet.

WOLFGANG AMADÉE MOZART

b. SALZBURG, JANUARY 27, 1756; d. VIENNA, DECEMBER 5, 1791.

Mozart's operas are the apotheosis of the ideal towards which Gluck and his successors were striving: the elevation of a text, through its synthesis with music, into a form of drama possessing a unique resonance and complexity. His handling of operatic structure is without equal, as you'd perhaps expect of the only prolific composer to produce as many great symphonies as stage works, but what makes the initial impact is the emotional power of Mozart's music. Whatever the material he was given to set, he could create music that enriched and diversified its meaning, applying an amazing mastery of the orchestra's resources. Referring to the composition of Belmonte's aria in *Die Entführung aus dem Serail*, Mozart wrote: "Would you like to know how I have expressed it – and even indicated his throbbing heart? By the two violins playing octaves. . . . You feel the trembling – the faltering – you see how his throbbing breast begins to swell; this I have expressed by a crescendo. You hear the whispering and the sighing – which I have indicated by the first violins with mutes and a flute playing unison." This attention to detail is characteristic of all Mozart's operatic masterpieces, as is the composer's unerring ability to find musical gestures so entirely appropriate to the situation that no effort appears to have been involved in their creation.

HULTON DEUTSCH

One of the less idealized portraits of Mozart

The idea of naturalness is crucial to Mozart, who took the conventions and formulas of eighteenth-century opera and adapted them to the creation of rounded individuals. Even the most exalted protagonists, like Count Almaviva in *Le nozze di Figaro* or Sarastro in *Die Zauberflöte*, are living, breathing, fallible characters, rather than the intermittently animated mannequins who populate many eighteenth-century operas. Later opera composers, most notably Wagner, plumbed psychological states that were unknown to Mozart, but none has ever shown a more profound comprehension of the emotional entanglements of human society, and none has matched Mozart's uncanny gift for capturing a many-shaded mood in just a few notes of music. The rejection of high-flown libretti was an essential part of Mozart's enterprise, as was the elimination of the castrato, for the idea of fat, middle-aged, flute-voiced singers trying to portray amorous young males was incompatible with verisimilitude. It is these dramatic properties as much as the musical glory of Mozart's operas that separate them from everything that had gone before.

Mozart was a frighteningly precocious child. He composed his first three operas before he was twelve years old, and they were no mere whimsies – the second of them, *La finta semplice*, was a two-and-a-half-hour three-act marathon. In 1770, aged fourteen, he was commissioned by the ducal theatre of Milan to compose *Mitridate, re di Ponto*, an opera seria lasting nearly four hours – stretched to six hours for the first performance, thanks to interpolated ballets and arias. It was a great success, running for twenty-two consecutive performances, and it secured some handsomely paid employment for the young composer, who wrote three more operas for Milan. But he soon began to tire of the prevailing Italian style, and in 1775, having completed an opera for the Bavarian Elector in Munich, Mozart accepted a commission from the archbishop of Salzburg, who wanted an opera to celebrate a visit from the Archduke Maximilian Franz: it was the start of a long and fractious relationship.

Two years later, having failed to secure a suitable court appointment, Mozart left Salzburg with his mother, visiting Munich, Augsburg and Mannheim (where they heard the famous orchestra) before arriving in Paris in 1778. However, Mozart was now twenty-two years old and the former boy wonder proved of little interest to a city in which the rivalry between Gluck and Piccini was keeping the cognoscenti enthralled (see p.71). His increasing depression deepened after his mother's death in July and, unable to find a lucrative job in Paris, he returned to Salzburg, where he worked for two years as a court and cathedral organist, thus resuming his uneasy alliance with the archbishop. Deliverance arrived in the form of the Bavarian Elector, who in 1780 gave Mozart another opera commission. The outcome was the composer's first great stage work, *Idomeneo*, produced in Munich on January 29, 1781 – shortly before Mozart and the archbishop finally lost patience with each other. After one final confrontation Mozart resigned and moved to Vienna, where in August 1782 he married Constanze Weber.

Vienna suited Mozart. Almost immediately he embarked upon what was to prove not just the most productive period of his short life, but one of the greatest unbroken periods of composition in the history of music. Virtually all of Mozart's well-known piano concertos, quartets, symphonies and operas were created in this final decade. *Die Entführung aus dem Serail*, commissioned by Joseph II and premiered a few days after Mozart's wedding, resoundingly proved that his genius had evaporated with his youth. This was followed by a series of stage projects that were abandoned because of their appalling libretti, but in 1785 he began setting a libretto by an Italian poet named Lorenzo da Ponte. Thought by many to be Mozart's operatic masterpiece (indeed many hold it to be the most perfect of all operas), *Le nozze di Figaro* heralded two further miraculous works of music-theatre with libretti from da Ponte: *Don Giovanni* (1787) and *Così fan tutte* (1790). This astonishing trio of operas would have been sufficient to secure Mozart's reputation as the century's supreme opera composer but in 1791, three months before his death, he completed two more operas, *Die Zauberflöte* and *La Clemenza di Tito*. In December, his weak health worsened by the pressure of his workload, Mozart died, leaving unfinished his magnificent *Requiem*. The night before his death, Mozart fell into a delirium during which he thought himself present at the Wiednertheater, at that night's performance of *Die Zauberflöte*. He whispered to his wife what are thought to have been his last words: "Silence! Silence! Now Hofer [the first Queen of the Night] is taking her high B-flat" – and, indeed, at that very moment, his sister-in-law was singing the Queen of the Night's second aria, "Die Hölle Rache". He was buried, alongside a number of nameless corpses, in a communal grave, the location of which has never been identified.

Mozart was born at exactly the right time: the classical orchestra had grown rapidly in size and range; singers had learned to accept the need for a modicum of acting ability; and opera had become a highly popular art form, rather than an adjunct of aristocratic life. Mozart made the most of these opportunities, and while audiences may not always have appreciated the subtle musical and theatrical detail, they were aware that they were witnessing the appearance of something that was beyond the scope of his contemporaries. Reinventing the perennial themes of love, hatred, loyalty and revenge, Mozart's operas had the universality, and have demonstrated the durability, of Shakespeare's plays. As Aaron Copland once wrote: "It is the happy balance between flight and control, between sensibility and self-discipline, simplicity and sophistication of style that is his particular province. . . . Mozart tapped once again the source from which all music flows, expressing himself with a spontaneity and refinement and breathtaking rightness that has never since been duplicated."

Idomeneo

Idomeneus

Composed 1780–81.
First performed January 29, 1781.
Libretto by Abbé Giambattista Varesco, after Antoine Danchet and André Campra.

Synopsis

Act I

King Idomeneus (Idomeneo) has sent prisoners from Troy back to Crete, including Ilia, King Priam's daughter. Unknown to Idomeneus, Ilia and Idamantes (Idamante), Idomeneus's son, are in love, and Idamantes is also loved by Elektra (Elletra). Idomeneus is set to return to Crete, at which point the prisoners will be granted amnesty, but a storm forces him to offer to Neptune a sacrifice of the first living thing he meets as he steps ashore. This turns out to be his son.

Act II

Idomeneus tries to avoid his obligation to Neptune by sending Idamantes to Argos as an escort for Elektra, but Neptune raises a terrible storm out of which appears a monster which then begins to tear the island apart. The people realize that someone has offended the gods, and Idomeneus confesses.

Act III

Idamantes prepares to battle with the monster. Before doing so he tells Ilia that he loves her. The jealous Elektra bursts in with Idomeneus, who then tells of his vow to Neptune. Idamantes kills the monster then offers himself in fulfilment of his father's promise to Neptune. The voice of Neptune intervenes, sparing Idamantes' life but demanding that Idomeneus abdicate. Idamantes duly takes the throne, with Ilia at his side.

Mozart began this three-and-a-half-hour opera (which originally included a ballet that extended the running time by thirty minutes) in October 1780 and completed the score in January the following year, despite having to work on various unrelated projects simultaneously. Preparation for the first performance was marred by difficulties with his soloists, chiefly the 67-year-old tenor Anton Raaf, who obliged Mozart to devote a huge amount of time to rewriting the arias for the title role. He was further hampered by the flabby construction of the libretto and the need to compose for a castrato, and yet, though the first run extended to just three performances, *Idomeneo* was well received. Even Mozart was happy, despite his dissatisfaction with Raaf and the castrato singing the role of Idamante, whom he referred to as "the two worst actors any stage has ever borne".

There is much that is old-fashioned in *Idomeneo*: arias are strictly segregated by passages of recitative (in later works the recitative flows into the arias); one of the principals is scored for a male soprano; and there are a number of coloratura arias that invite the soloist to improvise. Indeed *Idomeneo* is one of Mozart's few surviving "singer's operas", conceived for celebrities who were out to impress, and there are relatively few ensembles.

Yet this is the first operatic score to reveal Mozart's powers at full strength, for at every turn the music enhances the dramatic strengths and camouflages the limitations of his libretto. (Commenting on the third act, Mozart said to his father that "it seems naive to think that everybody hurries off [after the Oracle has spoken) just to leave Elektra alone."[Through the subtle manipulation of thematic material, such as a prominent falling interval, or a particular trill, or a certain instrumental combination, Mozart reminded his audience of events that had previously occurred or generated an anticipation of what was to happen, thereby oiling the creaking archaisms of his text.

To ensure that every nuance of the score came through, he turned to the Mannheim orchestra, Europe's finest body of players, but even they found the score a strain. Mozart's father wrote that "every musician needs astonishing continuous concentration", which was a shock for players accustomed to ambling accompaniments that left them with time to snooze or at least take a breather. Each part now had a role to play: solo parts are prominent (especially in the woodwind), the string ensembles are required to play music as difficult as much of the stuff written for contemporary soloists, and the brass and percussion are applied to great scenic effect. There are spectacular orchestral episodes in *Idomeneo*, such as the Act II storm and the Oracle scene in Act III, and they are not just a sideshow – rather, they are placed in positions of pivotal dramatic importance. The juxtaposition of this rich orchestral music and the florid, old-fashioned vocal writing is primarily what distinguishes *Idomeneo* from the now forgotten works of Jommelli, Traetta and Sarti – all big names in their day. This was not Mozart's last opera seria, but it is perhaps the most advanced.

RECORDINGS OVERVIEW

Idomeneo has not been well served on record. The Haydn Society issued a fumbling account of a vigorously edited score in 1950, and some memorable excerpts were recorded at Glyndebourne in 1951, with Fritz Busch conducting, but the first serious attempt came in 1956, when EMI engaged John Pritchard, the Glyndebourne Festival and a fabulous cast that included Jurinac and Simoneau. Were it available on CD, this would be a strong contender for first choice, as indeed would the expressive account recorded twelve years later for Philips by Colin Davis, the first conductor to dare to offer a rival to the Pritchard set. Conspicuous later efforts include Karl Böhm's vocally sumptuous but unincisive account for Deutsche Grammophon in 1977, Harnoncourt's pioneering "period instrument" recreation four years later, and another recording from Pritchard in 1983, with Pavarotti tackling the title role too late. None of these can be recommended in front of John Eliot Gardiner's version.

JIM FOUR/DGG

John Eliot Gardiner

Rolfe Johnson, von Otter, McNair, Martinpelto; Monteverdi Choir and Orchestra; Gardiner.
(Deutsche Grammophon Archiv 431 674 2; 3 CDs).

Presented as the first recording to use all the surviving music Mozart composed for Munich in 1781, Gardiner's live recording of *Idomeneo* is no dessicated exercise in musico-archaeology. It might impress rather than move, but this is an intoxicatingly beautiful account. The Ilia of Sylvia McNair makes a heavenly sound, while Anthony Rolfe Johnson's Idomeneus outclasses all others except Simoneau, applying his powerful voice with intelligence and sensitivity. Gardiner's conducting is characteristically springy, the choruses are magnificent, if a little crisp, and the wind and brass fart and burp their way through Mozart's colourful score with great enthusiasm. Excellent recording quality.

Die Entführung aus dem Serail

The Escape from the Harem

Composed 1781–82.
First performed July 16, 1782.
Libretto by Gottlieb Stephanie the Younger, after Bretzner and André.

Synopsis

Act I

Pedrillo, Constanze and her servant Blonde are being held captive by Pasha Selim. Belmonte, Pedrillo's master and Constanze's long-lost lover, comes looking for her. In the palace garden he meets Osmin, one of the Pasha's stewards, who initially refuses to talk to him but then flies into a rage when mention is made of Pedrillo's name. Osmin leaves, and Belmonte and Pedrillo meet. Pedrillo plots to introduce his master to the Pasha as an architect. The Pasha arrives with great ceremony, accompanied by Constanze, whom he begs in vain to give him her love. Pedrillo introduces Belmonte to the Pasha.

Act II

Osmin tries to woo Blonde (who is in love with Pedrillo), but as "a free-born Englishwoman" she demands her right to choose. Constanze is resigned to death, rather than betray her love for Belmonte. Pedrillo informs Blonde of his escape plan and removes Osmin from the equation by getting him drunk. The four lovers are reunited.

Act III

Osmin foils the escape attempt and drags the thwarted fugitives before the Pasha. It transpires that Belmonte is the son of the man who forced the Pasha into exile; but rather than revenge himself against the young man, the Pasha shows magnanimity and allows all four their freedom.

Mozart's move to Vienna coincided with the accession of Joseph II, one of whose earliest and most significant cultural initiatives was the establishment of a German opera company, the National-Singspiel. Naturally enough, Mozart

was invited to provide a Singspiel for the company, and he came up with *Die Entführung*, one of the more interesting manifestations of the current predilection for Turkish themes. The subject of damsels endangered by exotic infidels might be unoriginal, but *Die Entführung* is one of Mozart's most straightforward and snappy creations, packing a lot of entertainment into just two hours.

The charm of *Die Entführung* is more consistent than its musical style. Hero and heroine have big Italianate arias to sing, the servants are given folksongs, Pedrillo has a ballad in Act III that was added as something of a last-minute gesture, and the Pasha is a spoken role with limited theatrical opportunities. The rhythm of the piece is also not as fluid as that of most of the later masterpieces: true to the conventions of Singspiel, the action is principally related through spoken dialogue, to which the arias and duets serve as commentary. For all that, each of the cast (except the Pasha, a spoken role) get to sing exquisite and typically Mozartian melodies, even if, due to the less flexible construction of German poetry, the phrases are shorter and less ornate than those Mozart could apply to da Ponte's texts. Similarly beguiling is the orientalist atmosphere that Mozart imparts to the proceedings through the use of jangling Janissary music (see p.81) and strange quasi-middle-eastern modulations, while the punchy rhythms of the overture, ceremonial episodes and grand choruses add an extra dash of excitement. With its resourceful lovers, bumbling adversary, compassionate despot and gloriously uplifting denouement, *Die Entführung* is an irresistible eighteenth-century vaudeville.

RECORDINGS OVERVIEW

Josef Krips set a very high standard in 1950 when he became the first conductor to make a "complete" recording of this opera – ie, an edited version of the full opera rather than an assembly of highlights. The roster of conductors who have subsequently tackled *Die Entführung* includes some impressive names, such as Colin Davis, Harnoncourt, Gardiner, Solti and Christopher Hogwood, and Krips himself had a second stab at it, producing a set that was notable more for its cast than for its conducting. The four accounts listed below are the pick of a crowded field.

Köth, Schädle, Wunderlich, Lenz; Bavarian State Opera Chorus; Bavarian Radio Symphony Orchestra; Jochum.
(Deutsche Grammophon 439 708-2; 2 CDs).

Jochum's recording of *Die Entführung* was the first entirely without cuts, but at the time of its release this fact made less of a stir than the performance of one member of its cast, the tenor Fritz Wunderlich. In 1965 – the year before his death – he was arguably the world's most famous German tenor and this recording amply proves why. His generous, open-throated voice phrases Belmonte's high-lying music in lines of seamless beauty, and his performance of "Hier soll ich dich denn sehen", right after the overture, all but steals the show. (Something similar happens in his recording of *Die Zauberflöte* with Böhm – see p.104.) The remaining cast members have technical shortcomings but their enthusiasm makes up for it, and Jochum conducts with just the right mixture of warmth and theatricality. The sound might be a little close and prone to distortion, but this is one of the greatest Mozart recordings in the catalogue.

Augér, Grist, Schreier, Neukirch, Moll; Leipzig Radio Chorus; Dresden Staatskapelle; Böhm.
(Deutsche Grammophon 429 868-2; 2 CDs).

Böhm's cycle of Mozart operas for Deutsche Grammophon was made with the pick of the world's talent, and his 1973 *Die Entführung* is outstanding even by the standards he set in that cycle. Augér is an exquisite Constanze, Kurt Moll's bumptious Osmin is the most winning interpretation on record, and Schreier – whose voice would not have seemed ideal for Belmonte – is surprisingly confident in the role, taking the upper reaches with great surety. Böhm was something of a magician when in front of the Dresden Staatskapelle (an orchestra he first conducted in the 1930s), and the sense of communication between conductor, musicians and singers makes this an example of operatic ensemble at its finest.

Studer, Szmytka, Streit, Missenhardt; Vienna State Opera Chorus; Vienna Symphony Orchestra; Weill.
(Sony S2K 48053; 2 CDs).

Looking at the cast list you might think this recording was a vehicle for the mercurial talents of Cheryl Studer, but the cast is generally very fine: Elzbieta Szmytka has a particularly interesting, characterful voice, and Kurt Streit's Belmonte is immensely likable. Günter Missenhardt, as Osmin, is the only disappointment – an attractive voice but a one-dimensional actor. As for Studer, she is magnificent, tackling even the most delicate passages with extraordinary ease. Weil, clearly enjoying himself, maintains quick tempi, generates some lovely tone from the VSO and keeps the texture light.

Lipp, Loose, Ludwig, Klein; Vienna State Opera Chorus; Vienna Philharmonic Orchestra; Krips.
(Decca 443 530-2; 2 CDs).

The first of Krips' recordings of *Die Entführung* is a splendid achievement. Although he takes a somewhat laissez-faire attitude towards Mozart's tempi, with some markings wholly ignored, it is clear by the end of Belmonte's Act I aria that he is a master of the lyrical rather than the dramatic aspect of this opera. Above all, he follows his singers, allowing them the sort of freedom that modern conductors are too quick to deny, and the Vienna Philharmonic – at the time the world's finest Mozart orchestra – respond impeccably to his direction. Lipp is a gorgeous Constanze, and Emmy Loose copes well with Blonde's awkwardly lying music. Peter Klein's feeble Pedrillo and the thin sound quality are the only minus points.

Le nozze di Figaro

The Marriage of Figaro

Composed 1785–86.
First performed May 1, 1786.
Libretto by Lorenzo da Ponte, after Beaumarchais.

Synopsis

Act I

Figaro and Susanna, Count Almaviva's servants, are preparing for their imminent wedding, when Susanna reveals that she is being pursued by the Count. Meanwhile Bartolo and Marcellina are trying to hold Figaro to a promise he made to marry Marcellina if he failed to pay back a loan to Bartolo. The page Cherubino tells Susanna of his love for the Countess, just as the Count arrives. Cherubino hides and overhears Almaviva's attempted seduction of Susanna. Don Basilio's arrival forces the Count into hiding as well which, in turn, forces Cherubino to move from his hiding place. The indiscreet Basilio talks of the Count's love for Susanna and of Cherubino's love for the Countess. The Count then emerges from hiding, precipitating a scene that ends with Cherubino being packed off by the Count to join the army.

Act II

The Countess, distressed by her husband's philandering, plots with Susanna to humiliate the Count: Susanna will write to the Count agreeing to a rendezvous, but they will send Cherubino (who is still skulking round the palace) in her place, dressed in women's clothes. As Cherubino is being disguised, the Count arrives, and Cherubino is pushed into an adjoining room. The Count, hearing noises, leaves to fetch tools with which to break open the door. In the meantime Cherubino leaps out of the window while Susanna takes his place. When the Count returns and finds Susanna in the room, he is forced to apologize for having doubted his wife.

Act III

Figaro stalls Marcellina by telling her that he is of noble birth and cannot marry without his parents' consent. He reveals a birthmark on his arm, whereupon Marcellina realizes that she and Bartolo have found their long-lost son. They embrace just as Susanna enters; she is furious but once the situation is explained she joins in the celebration. After the Countess has dictated the note that Susanna is to pass to the Count, a double wedding follows – Susanna and Figaro being joined by Marcellina and Bartolo.

Act IV

Figaro encounters Barbarina, the gardener's daughter, who inadvertently reveals that Susanna has received a message from the Count. Figaro assumes the worst, and decides to catch his errant wife when she arrives for her tryst in the garden. The Countess and Susanna appear in each other's clothes (Susanna has now taken Cherubino's place in the subterfuge) and much mistaken identity ensues in the darkness (Cherubino is there to meet Barbarina too). Eventually Figaro realizes his wife is faithful and the Count realizes he has been tricked. He begs for his wife's forgiveness, and receives it.

Die Entführung had demonstrated Mozart's mastery of German music-theatre; *Le nozze di Figaro* proved that his talent was equally well suited to Italian opera, which by 1785 was back in vogue in Vienna. Its source material was a scandalously sexual and politically explosive play that had been banned in France in 1784, and banned again in Vienna later that year. As he never tired of telling people, it was Lorenzo da Ponte who convinced Emperor Joseph II that Mozart could tackle an Italian opera and satisfied Joseph's demands that "anything that might offend good taste or public decency" would be removed from Beaumarchais' text. In the event, the sexual intrigue remained in place, but the political subversion was toned down – thus, for example, an outburst from Figaro against social injustice was converted into a rant against the fickleness of women. Da Ponte and Mozart also excised a number of scenes and minor characters, but they added a dimension that had been missing in Beaumarchais. Stendhal summed up the process when he wrote that Mozart "has transformed into real passions the superficial inclinations which amuse the easy-going inhabitants" of the Beaumarchais play.

The Count, Countess, Figaro, Susanna and Cherubino ultimately trace their genealogy back to the stereotypes of opera buffa, but it's a distant kinship. Mozart's protagonists possess real substance, thanks to the composer's uncanny ability to devise melodies and orchestral accompaniments that lift even the plainest verbal utterance into the realm of poetic complexity. For a superb example, listen to the Countess's aria at the start of Act II, "Porgi amor, qualche ristoro" (God of love, grant me some remedy): the words do little more than establish the Countess's misery, but Mozart's music conjures such depths of yearning and desolation that in the space of a couple of minutes the opera acquires a wholly new emotional dimension. Act I could have been taken as a well-crafted knockabout, but from this point onwards there is the shadow of tragedy behind the farce.

You could pick examples of Mozart's astounding eloquence and economy of gesture from any scene in *Figaro*, a work in which the basic musical ingredients used by other buffa composers, such as Paisiello or Cimarosa, are transformed into a seamless unity. Da Ponte's tailor-made libretto enabled Mozart to break down the divisions that traditionally separated arias, ensembles and recitative, and at every turn some change in tempo, key or setting resolves one episode while preparing the way for a new one. Nowhere during the three hours of this masterpiece is there any weak or inessential music, nor any point at which the momentum flags. Listen to it just once and you'll understand why, two hundred years after its first performance, it remains the most frequently performed opera in the world.

MICHAEL KELLY, FIGARO'S UNSUNG HERO

The roles of Basilio and Curzio in *Le nozze di Figaro* were both first performed by the Irish tenor Michael Kelly, a good friend of Mozart's. Kelly left another mark on musical history in the form of his *Reminiscences*, as self-aggrandizing a memoir as any ever written by a singer – and they are not a notably reticent species. The book was first published in 1826, by which time only da Ponte was left alive to challenge the singer's claims, which he duly did: "The jests and the romantic nonsense which you wrote, or had written for you, in your ridiculous book are so worthless that it is a waste of time for a man of any sense to give himself the trouble of denying them." Da Ponte's fury was perhaps not unrelated to the fact that he was writing his memoirs at the time, and didn't much appreciate being pipped to the post by Kelly, though there's no denying that Kelly was a far from reliable witness. At a distance from events, however, it's impossible not to enjoy Kelly's shameless self-promotion, as typified by his account of the premiere of Figaro.

"In the sestetto, in the second act (which was Mozart's favourite piece of the whole opera), I had a very conspicuous part, as the Stuttering Judge [Basilio]. All through the piece I was to stutter; but in the sestetto, Mozart requested I would not, for if I did I should spoil the music. I told him, that although it might appear very presumptuous in a lad like me to differ with him on this point, I did, and was sure the way I intended to introduce the stuttering would not interfere with the other parts, but produce an effect . . . and I added . . . that unless I was allowed to perform the part as I wished, I would not perform it at all. Mozart at last consented that I should have my own way, but doubted the success of the experiment.

Crowded houses proved that nothing ever on stage produced a more powerful effect; the audience was convulsed with laughter, in which Mozart himself joined. The Emperor repeatedly cried out 'Bravo!' and the piece was loudly applauded and encored. When the opera was over, Mozart came on the stage to me, and shaking me by both hands, said, 'Bravo! young man, I feel obliged to you; and acknowledge you to have been in the right, and myself in the wrong.'"

RECORDINGS OVERVIEW

Having received twenty-five studio recordings since the first in 1935, *Figaro* is the most recorded of Mozart's operas, but the three sets listed below are at the head of the pack. Not listed here is the first of Karl Böhm's three *Figaro* recordings, which was taped in 1938 from a Stuttgart broadcast and is only available on Preiser, a small and mysterious import label. It is poorly recorded and heavily cut, but it captures a truly great occasion, with one of the greatest Mozart casts ever captured on record. It's a must for anyone with a passion for *Figaro*, and *Figaro* is an opera a lot of people get passionate about. Two other readings are also worth a listen: Vittorio Gui's 1955 Glyndebourne recording for EMI (a bargain-price two-disc set), which is heavily cut but features superb singing from Jurinac, Sciutti, Stevens and Cuénod; and Böhm's second studio *Figaro*, taped in 1956 by Philips (three mid-price discs), with an engagingly homogeneous Viennese cast and another splendid Countess from Jurinac.

Siepi, Gueden, Poell, della Casa, Danco, Rössl-Majdan, Corena, Dickie; Vienna State Opera Chorus; Vienna Philharmonic Orchestra; Kleiber.
(Decca 417 315-2DM3; 3 CDs).

Stendhal called *Figaro* a "sublime mixture of wit and melancholy, which has no equal", and Erich Kleiber's 1955 sessions came as close as possible to achieving a perfect balance of both qualities. Kleiber is at once theatrical and lyrical, applying a sense of pace that has never been rivalled, and as an accompanist he is preternaturally sensitive to the individual qualities of his singers. And these singers are beyond praise. Cesare Siepi as Figaro and Hilde Gueden as Susanna give performances that make all subsequent portrayals appear in some way flawed. Lisa della Casa's Countess perhaps depends too much on the beauty of her voice, while conversely Suzanne Danco's Cherubino is possibly too characterful, but these are trivial reservations about a sublime recording of a sublime opera.

Taddei, Waechter, Moffo, Schwarzkopf, Cossotto; Philharmonia Chorus and Orchestra; Giulini.
(EMI CMS7 63266-2; 2 CDs).

Although it was taped only four years after the Kleiber sessions, EMI's fifth (!) *Figaro* featured a new generation of singers, marshalled by a conductor who was then relatively new to studio recording. Judged by the criterion of vocal beauty alone, this is the finest *Figaro* ever made in a studio. Schwarzkopf is free of the fey, self-conscious flutterings to which she was prone later on – proud yet sensitive and vulnerable, she revels in Mozart's extended lyricism. Moffo is a self-assured Susanna and an excellent foil to Schwarzkopf, even if she lacks the mischievousness of, for example, Graziella Sciutti (Susanna for Gui in 1955). Cossotto's impulsive Cherubino is a little too full-voiced, but her taste for da Ponte's language and comedy are peerless. To cap it all, Eberhard Waechter all but steals the show as an especially lusty Almaviva. The only ways in which this set falls short of the Kleiber recording is that it uses a cut score and Giulini is sometimes a little fastidious and humourless, but this is of little consequence when there is so much to enjoy.

Ramey, Popp, Allen, Te Kanawa, von Stade, Moll, Tear, Langridge; London Opera Chorus; London Philharmonic Orchestra; Solti.
(Decca 410 150-2DH3; 3 CDs).

Recorded in 1981, this was the first digital *Figaro*. It is also Solti's finest operatic recording to date – graceful, refined and tender (not qualities readily associated with the Hungarian dynamo). Ramey's ringing bass is a little emphatic for Figaro and Lucia Popp is vocally not at her best as Susanna, but Kurt Moll's Bartolo and Jane Berbié's Marcellina are fine, while Frederica von Stade indulges her lyrical gifts to the full in the role of Cherubino. The highlight, though, is Kiri Te Kanawa's Countess. Her voice was especially rich in 1981, but there's more to her performance than just radiant sound – there is a freshness and spontaneity to this portrayal that has scarcely ever been matched. This *Figaro* is perhaps Dame Kiri's greatest moment on record.

Don Giovanni

Composed 1787.
First performed October 29, 1787.
Libretto by Lorenzo da Ponte, after Bertati.

Synopsis

Act I

Leporello awaits his master Don Giovanni, who is up to no good in the house of Donna Anna. She cries for help and her father, the Commendatore, runs to her assistance. In the ensuing fight Don Giovanni kills the Commendatore; Donna Anna and her betrothed, Don Ottavio, vow revenge. Donna Elvira, recently jilted by Don Giovanni, arrives in search of the Don; he makes good his escape by leaving Leporello to read out his "book of conquests", in which the names of the Don's 2065 lovers are recorded.

Don Giovanni comes across a peasant wedding and promptly begins to charm the bride, Zerlina, but Elvira arrives and alerts her to the Don's intentions. Donna Anna and Don Ottavio then arrive, and as the Don takes his leave of them Anna identifies him as the man who had tried to rape her.

At a party held by Don Giovanni, Zerlina reassures her lover Masetto of her affections, but she begins to weaken in the Don's presence. Wearing masks, Anna, Elvira and Ottavio arrive at the ball, which is interrupted by Zerlina's scream. She stumbles onto the stage, the Don attempts to blame Leporello for the attack, and Anna, Elvira and Ottavio unmask themselves to publicly denounce the Don.

Act II

Don Giovanni exchanges his costume with Leporello and serenades Elvira's maid as soon as Elvira has left with Leporello, believing him to be the remorseful Don. Masetto arrives with a gang of men who are intent on punishing the Don; the Don, pretending to be Leporello, tells Masetto how to find the murderer, then beats Masetto half to death. The Don and his servant meet in a graveyard, where the statue of the Commendatore addresses them; the Don flippantly invites him to supper. The statue duly arrives and demands the Don's repentance; unbending, Don Giovanni is finally dragged screaming into hell. Elvira, Ottavio, Anna and Leporello address the audience with the moral: "Evildoers always come to an evil end."

𝄞 *Le nozze di Figaro* was premiered in Vienna but it was received with greater enthusiasm in Prague, where it was staged by the Bondini company. Invited to pay a visit to the city, Mozart arrived in Prague on January 11, 1787 and stayed for four weeks, during which time he conducted a performance of *Figaro*, gave the first performance of a new symphony and agreed, with little hesitation, to accept a commission from Bondini for a new opera, to be produced the following autumn. Upon returning to Vienna he teamed up again with da Ponte, and the two of them decided that the subject of their new work would be the legend of the Stone Guest or, as it is more commonly known, the story of Don Juan. Various cities – notably Seville – claim the real Don Juan as a native son, but the hell-bound womanizer seems to have sprung into being from the imagination of Tirso de Molina (1571–1641), author of the play *El Burlador de Sevilla*. Later writers added their contributions to the legend: Molière created his own version of the Don (introducing the character of Donna Elvira for the first time), and in 1736 Carlo Goldoni wrote the first play in which the anti-hero's name features in the title. However, da Ponte quarried most of his material from a second-rate libretto by one Giovanni Bertati, a text originally set to music in 1787 by Giuseppe Gazzaniga. Taking advice from the the world's most notorious real-life seducer, Giovanni Giacomo Casanova, da Ponte made a silk purse from Bertati's sow's ear, creating one of the most powerful operatic characters of all time.

The title page classifies *Don Giovanni* as a *dramma giocoso*, which would place it in the same serio-comic category as Haydn's *L'incontro improvviso* and *Il mondo della luna* (see pp.81–82). There are indeed comic elements to *Don Giovanni*: viewed from a certain angle, it's pure opera buffa in its tale of a bad master and his bumbling attendant, crashing into crises from which they have to extricate themselves by hook or by crook. That perennial device of opera buffa, the disguise, is central to *Don Giovanni* as it is to *Figaro*. But the comedy in *Don Giovanni*, even when it's unqualified, is but a contrasting episode to make the licentiousness, violence and cruelty of the Don's career appear yet darker. Lightheartedness in *Don Giovanni* never lasts long. For example, in the terrible denouement of the banquet scene, Mozart throws in a jaunty quotation from *Figaro*, a delightfully witty touch, but within a couple of minutes the Don's fatal struggle with the Commendatore has begun. And the upbeat epilogue, in which the survivors gloat over the Don's demise and look forward to their new lives, isn't a sufficient counterbalance to the rest of the opera, a work that establishes the precariousness of morality as convincingly as any essay by Freud. It's hardly surprising that when *Don Giovanni* was first performed in the Austrian capital, the emperor remarked to the composer, "It is too difficult for the singers and too tough for the teeth of the Viennese." (The reply was "Give them time to chew on it.")

Mozart wrote of *Don Giovanni*: "Whenever I sit at the piano with my new opera, I have to stop, for it stirs my emotions too deeply." It is indeed a relentlessly immediate work: every scene boasts at least one powerful aria or ensemble, and each character is vividly delineated by his or her own musical style, from the feverish, vengeance-filled Donna Anna to the foppish Ottavio. Beneath this multidimensional melody lies a tightly screwed orchestral score, a score characterized by an unusually percussive timbre and frequent aggressive instrumental interjections – all underlining the urgency of the drama (it takes place over just 24 hours) and its deadly seriousness. And underlying every moment of the opera is the Manichaean clash of the Don and the Commendatore: from the dread-filled opening of the overture the action is moving implacably towards their final confrontation, a course charted through the recurrence of the chords and tonalities with which they are associated.

DON GIOVANNI'S LAST-DITCH OVERTURE

Listening to the opening of *Don Giovanni*, you'd never guess that this amazing piece of music was the ultimate rushed job. With the last rehearsal completed, Mozart was reminded that he had yet to write an overture for the opera. Mozart and his wife drew up an emergency plan: to keep him working through the night, she would sit beside him, ply him with punch to keep his morale up, and read him folk tales to keep him alert. And so, as Constanze recited the stories of Aladdin's Lamp and Cinderella, Mozart began to create the overture to *Don Giovanni*. Eventually, however, weariness overcame him, and he curled up on the sofa, asking Constanze to wake him in one hour. Doubtless owing to the punch he'd drunk, Mozart slept more soundly than he'd anticipated, and Constanze left him for an extra hour. Mozart woke at five o'clock with more than half the piece left to write, and yet two hours later the fully orchestrated overture was in the hands of the copyists – and it took them longer to transcribe the manuscript for the orchestra members than it had taken Mozart to write it in the first place. And so it was that, as the opera house filled to capacity behind them, the musicians were handed their parts with the ink still wet on the paper, and then commenced to play an overture they had never seen before.

The dominant figure is of course the Don himself, even though he has just two brief solos in the course of the entire opera. One of opera's true monsters, the Don is the more terrible for being an irresistible monster: the seductive beauty of his serenade to Elvira's maid, the superhuman energy of his "champagne aria", and the ambiguous passions he inspires in the women he encounters, all prompt the suspicion that Mozart was a covert member of the devil's party. Though chillingly adept at playing on the weaknesses of his prey, whether she be a coquettish country girl like Zerlina or a wary aristocrat like Donna Elvira, the Don explodes into animalistic violence when thwarted – by the opera's close he has committed (or at least attempted) two rapes, murdered one man and badly wounded another. Yet for all his barbarity the balance of sympathy is never tipped conclusively against the Don (the opera would fall apart if it did), and in his final moments he achieves something of the dark nobility of the fallen Lucifer: ignoring the terror-struck interjections of Leporello, the Don defies the Commendatore's implacable demands for repentance, even as the voices of the damned rise to summon him to hell. There is still no scene in all opera that is more intense and shocking.

RECORDINGS OVERVIEW

There have been more than thirty studio recordings of *Don Giovanni* and probably as many live versions. The first complete set, taped at Glyndebourne in 1936 with the exiled Fritz Busch overseeing a first-rate cast, is still well worth hearing (it's on EMI), as is the mono recording conducted by Krips for Decca in 1955. The roll-call of conductors who have subsequently had a go at the *Don* makes impressive reading – Fricsay, Leinsdorf, Klemperer, Böhm, Davis, Karajan and Solti have all made at least one recording of it, and every couple of years a new version hits the record shops. Nonetheless, with the exception of John Eliot Gardiner's recent interpretation, the middle-century heavyweights listed below are still the ones to attend to first.

Waechter, Sutherland, Schwarzkopf, Sciutti, Alva, Taddei, Cappuccilli, Frick; Philharmonia Chorus and Orchestra; Giulini.
(EMI CDS7 47260-8; 3 CDs).

Don Giovanni is Mozart's most melodramatic opera and Giulini's is the most melodramatic recording, full of exaggerated colour and generally fast-paced. Waechter's Don is the nastiest on record – he employs his huge voice with stinging, compulsive clarity. Taddei's multifaceted Leporello can appear both repulsive and lovable within the space of ten bars, while the women – especially Sutherland's Donna Anna and Sciutti's Zerlina – are magnificent. This kaleidoscopic and viscerally exciting vision of *Don Giovanni* is an obvious first choice if you're coming fresh to the music.

Gilfry, Silvestrelli, Orgonasova, Prégardien, D'Arcangelo; Monteverdi Choir; English Baroque Soloists; Gardiner.
(Archiv 445 870-2; 3 CDs).

This 1994 live period-instrument performance is astoundingly dramatic: the tempi are fast but flexible, with minute fluctuations creating an unnerving feeling of

SILVIA LELLI MASOTTI/DGG

Rodney Gilfry – the Don on Gardiner's outstanding Don Giovanni

tension, while the attention to dynamic expression, rhythmic detail and orchestral colour is stupendous. The two final scenes are taken very quickly – compared to Klemperer they almost take off – but everything fits as if it could be no other way. Gardiner's cast work brilliantly together, and some of the men are outstanding: Ildebrando d'Arcangelo is a scene-stealing Leporello, Andrea Silvestrelli is a Commendatore nobody would pick an argument with, and Christoph Prégardien's tenor Ottavio is the most beautiful on record since Leopold Simoneau. The sound is clear and bass-rich. All in all, this is the best recent *Don* by a long way.

Siepi, Grümmer, della Casa, Streich, Simoneau, Corena, Berry, Frick; Vienna State Opera Chorus; Vienna Philharmonic Orchestra; Mitropoulos.
(Sony SM3K 64263; 3 CDs).

Recorded live at the Salzburg Festival in 1956, this is the best-sung *Don Giovanni* on disc. Mitropoulos has enough self-confidence (and sense) to allow his special cast a lot of freedom and there are times when he, like the audience, seems to do no more than sit back and marvel. Though lacking the urgency of Furtwängler's performance with the same orchestra, this is a performance of unearthly beauty and an essential part of any collection of opera on CD.

Siepi, Grümmer, Schwarzkopf, Dermota, Edelmann, Berry, Ernster; Vienna State Opera Chorus; Vienna Philharmonic Orchestra; Furtwängler.
(EMI CHS7 63860-2; 3 CDs).

Moulded by Furtwängler's colossal musical intellect, this fatalistic reading of *Don Giovanni* is positively Wagnerian in its darkness and is definitely not for anyone new to the opera. The tempi are so slow that in any other conductor's hands the performance would have ground to a halt, but Furtwängler's grasp of overall structure is so firm and his use of accent, punctuation, dynamics and phrasing are so instinctive, that this conception of the opera burns itself into the memory. The cast is close to perfection. The mono sound is poor (this set was recorded live at the 1954 Salzburg Festival), but if you listen to this performance after getting to know the opera, you'll understand why it commands such reverence.

Così fan tutte

Women Are Like That

Composed 1789.
First performed January 26, 1789.
Libretto by Lorenzo da Ponte.

Synopsis

Act I

Ferrando and Guglielmo are convinced of the fidelity of Fiordiligi and Dorabella, the two sisters to whom they are betrothed. Don Alfonso, on the other hand, claims all women are fickle and wagers that he can prove it. The young men agree to take Alfonso's test, and he tells the sisters that their husbands-to-be have been enlisted into the army. Once the men have departed, the sisters' maid Despina is persuaded by

Alfonso to introduce two young Albanian friends (Ferrando and Guglielmo in disguise) to Fiordiligi and Dorabella. Each "stranger" then begins to court the other's fiancée, and they begin to make progress after pretending to take poison. Despina disguises herself as a doctor and successfully cures the Albanians.

Act II
When Ferrando learns that Dorabella has yielded to Guglielmo, he becomes yet more determined to win Fiordiligi's heart. Eventually, she too succumbs and a double wedding is planned – with Despina, again in disguise, as the notary. Just as the army is heard returning, the Albanian newlyweds disappear and Ferrando and Guglielmo appear in their place. Producing the marriage contract, they remonstrate with the sisters, who soon confess their deceit. After paying Alfonso his wager, Ferrando and Guglielmo forgive Fiordiligi and Dorabella.

Così fan tutte was composed just eight years after Pierre Choderlos de Laclos published *Les liaisons dangereuses*. These two works have more in common than just the period of their creation: both dramatize the erosion of codes of correct behaviour by the force of sexuality, and both are informed by a distinctly modern spirit of ironic self-awareness. Both, furthermore, have suffered from a scandalous reputation.

As with *Figaro*, little is known about the birth of *Così fan tutte* but it was probably commissioned after the Viennese revival of *Figaro* in August 1789. Mozart completed the music in under four months, and on January 21 he directed rehearsals at the Burgtheater in the presence of Haydn – who unfortunately left no record of his thoughts. After just five performances the death of Joseph II interrupted the opening run; five more shows were given during the summer, but *Così* received a lukewarm reception and dropped out of the repertoire. Its supposed immorality caused problems for a lot of people. Beethoven, ever a believer in love as a transcendent value, found it impossible to stomach *Così*, and the eminent English conductor Sir Michael Costa spoke for many when, finding it "incomprehensible that Mozart should have accepted such a poorly judged, sniggering little play", he declared that the "adulterous machinations of the four so-called lovers has no place on the operatic stage". In the latter part of the nineteenth century *Così* at last began to re-establish itself, and by the 1940s attitudes had changed so much that another English conductor, Sir Thomas Beecham, far from being troubled by Mozart's moral turpitude, could write: "In *Così fan tutte* the dying eighteenth century casts a backward glance over a period outstanding in European life for grace and charm." Certainly there is a vein of elegiac classicism about *Così*, but earlier critics were not entirely missing the point when they protested that this piece left a bitter taste in the mouth. Nobody comes away from a performance of *Così* thinking that a rosy future lies ahead of the protagonists.

The "test of faith" is a theme that can be traced back to Ovid, but for once, da Ponte's libretto was not directly derived from anyone else's work. His text has little of the textual subtlety or suppleness of *Don Giovanni* or *Figaro* – its strengths lie in the restraint of its language and the symmetry of its construction, and Mozart clearly relished working such a carefully balanced text, for he produced the most perfect ensemble opera ever written. This is not to say there are no arias or big tunes in *Così* (the three women and three men each have an aria in each act), but above all else this work demands six singers who can play their roles as part of something greater than themselves – if any one role dominates, *Così* doesn't work.

At times the ensembles explicitly make a point of their structural perfection – for example, "Alla bella Despinetta", in Act I, is an overt parody of the formality of opera seria. More typically, however, the music achieves a sublime union of poised eloquence and deep emotion. A fine example is Act I's "Soave sia il vento", a trio for the sisters and the roguish Alfonso: while the gentle string accompaniment imitates the breezes to which the women refer in their mournfully melodic farewell, the music and Alfonso's commentary are tinged with satisfaction at the way his plot is running. One of the most beautiful things Mozart ever composed, this ensemble is a consummate demonstration of his alchemical ability to make something extraordinary out of quite superficial utterances.

The precision of the plotting and of the ensembles is mirrored in the musical fabric of the opera as a whole. Beneath the surface of dazzling tunes lies a complex structure in which harmony, tonality and deployment of instruments all contribute to the cohesion of the opera. You might not consciously perceive it, but Mozart's inspired use of thematic references, snatches of melody and orchestration (prominent bassoon for buffa, horn for seria) links the opera's episodes and ideas like a daisy-chain. Analysis reveals *Così* to be one of Mozart's most remarkable creations, but you don't need to be a musician to be amazed by the finale, in which the opera's disparate musical components are – like the lovers themselves – brought together in a conclusion that seems completely natural.

RECORDINGS OVERVIEW

The problem with *Così* is that you need to find singers able to play the work as an ensemble opera and yet also create distinctly individual characterizations. A cast that has performed the opera on stage over an extended period is likeliest to succeed in the recording studio, as is proved by two of the sets recommended below.

Once again, the first complete recording came from Busch, when EMI taped his 1935 Glyndebourne production, and this remained the only version until 1952. Two years later Karajan's first recording, for EMI, set new standards, which were then smartly trumped the following year by Karl Böhm, who made a second superb recording in the following decade (see below). In 1963 Eugen Jochum made one of the most satisfying recordings of the score for Deutsche Grammophon, but sadly this has yet to make its way onto CD. A number of unexceptional readings followed, from Leinsdorf, Suitner, Solti, Davis and Klemperer, and after that the majority of readings are little more than rapidly assembled collections of names. Haitink's Glyndebourne performance is the only recent contender.

Schwarzkopf, Ludwig, Steffek, Kraus, Taddei, Berry; Philharmonia Chorus and Orchestra; Böhm.
(EMI CMS7 69330-2; 3 CDs).

This 1962 performance of *Così*, complete but for one of Ferrando's arias, has no equal. Schwarzkopf, as Fiordiligi, gives a fine display of character singing, and her silvery voice makes an ideal contrast with Christa Ludwig's darker, more mature sound. Prior to this recording none of the men had sung their roles before, but all three give inimitable portrayals, with Kraus especially delightful as Ferrando. Giuseppe Taddei is a weighty, haughty Guglielmo and Walter Berry has a marvellous time as Alfonso. There is only one weakness to this performance and that is the orchestra, which plays with too much English reserve.

della Casa, Ludwig, Loose, Dermota, Schöffler; Vienna State Opera Chorus; Vienna Philharmonic Orchestra; Böhm.
(Decca 417 185-2DM02; 2 CDs).

Böhm's first *Così* is more heavily cut than the above version, but this 1955 recording is stilll a landmark achievement. The tempi are generally spacious and the orchestral phrasing is wonderfully vocal, but above all else this recording transmits an unrivalled feeling of intimacy, for Böhm was working with an orchestra and a cast that had worked on this opera together for some time. Ludwig's bright and youthful mezzo is outstanding (despite suffering the brunt of the editing), Della Casa intelligently constrains her sumptuous tone to the needs of Fiordiligi's character, and in ensemble the women's voices are radiant. The male voices are warm and neatly articulated, and the early stereo is sweet for its time. An essential experience.

Vaness, Ziegler, Watson, Aler, Duessing; Glyndebourne Festival Chorus; London Philharmonic Orchestra; Haitink.
(EMI CDS7 47727-8; 3 CDs).

Haitink's 1986 *Così* lacks the vocal riches available to Böhm but there is nonetheless a great deal to enjoy here. Always a modest conductor, Haitink revels in the community spirit of Peter Hall's Glyndebourne production, and the absence of celebrity singers allows the cast room to breathe. Vaness tends to make you conscious of the skill with which she tackles Fiordiligi's music, but it's a likable performance that works well with Delores Ziegler's Dorabella. Ultimately, there are no surprises here, but taken as a whole it's a purposeful experience that does service, first and foremost, to *Così fan tutte*. The recording is exemplary digital stereo.

La Clemenza di Tito

The Clemency of Titus

Composed 1791.
First performed September 6, 1791.
Libretto by Caterino Tommaso Mazzolà, after Metastasio.

Synopsis

Act I

The emperor Titus (Tito), who was to have married Vitellia, has fallen in love with the Jewish princess Berenice. Vitellia persuades Sextus (Sesto), who loves her, to join a plot to assassinate the emperor. Titus announces that he has decided to banish Berenice and instead marry Servilia, Sextus's sister. When Servilia tells Titus that she loves Annius (Annio), he renounces her in favour of Vitellia, but Vitellia is unaware of this change of plan, and Sextus is dispatched to set fire to the Capitol and murder Titus. Sextus reports that he has stabbed Titus, and the Roman people sing a lament for their dead emperor.

Act II

Annius tells Sextus that the murdered man was not Titus, and manages to stop his friend from fleeing, telling him that others have been implicated. Publius (Publio) arrests Sextus, who refuses to reveal Vitellia's complicity. Titus, wishing to be remembered for his clemency, tears up the death sentence, but only after Sextus has been taken away to the arena. As the lions are brought in Vitellia decides to confess, but Titus is again forgiving and announces his intention to devote himself to the good of Rome.

Mozart dropped *Die Zauberflöte* midway through its composition and set to work on *La Clemenza di Tito*, principally because he needed the money – the Mozarts had recently had another child and Constanze's visits to the spa at Baden were eating into their resources. The commission, given in July 1791, was for an opera to be performed in Prague that September, as part of the ceremonies to celebrate the coronation of Leopold II of Bohemia. Having already accepted a request from an anonymous client for a Requiem Mass, Mozart cut as many corners as he could: he agreed to set an existing libretto (something he had not done in nearly a decade), and passed over the recitative and a number of arias to his pupil Süssmayr, who would later complete the *Requiem*. Mozart's first biographer, Niemetschek, suggested that Mozart began the score on August 25, in the coach taking him and his wife and newborn child to the first performance in Prague. If this was the case, then Mozart wrote *La Clemenza* in just twelve days, for it was finished by the afternoon of September 5 – the day before the premiere. Mozart conducted the first performance at the Nationaltheater, where it received a lukewarm reception.

The conditions of its creation were not conducive to greatness, and *La Clemenza* is a rather unengaged piece, with a feeble plot (Titus considers marriage to three different women in the course of a single day) and minimal dramatic tension. On the other hand, opera seria was primarily about the melodic skill of the composer, and *La Clemenza* is nothing if not melodic, and within the constraints of the genre Mozart did succeed in creating some psychological depth, most notably in the character of Vitellia. Passionate, fearful and tender, she is by far the most developed of the protagonists, and her music, which takes her from a low A to a high D, is among the most lucid in eighteenth-century dramatic opera – even if the role is brief.

Sextus's mezzo, Annius's soprano, Titus's tenor and Publius's bass all have at least one solo (albeit generally short), but the opera's most striking episode is the finale of the first act, in which Mozart combines on-stage soloists with off-stage chorus. Vitellia, desperate to know if Titus is dead, attempts to remain in control while the other protagonists scurry about the stage like frightened animals, the chorus sings of its horror at the conflagration on the Capitol, and the orchestra accentuates the atmosphere of frenzied agitation. Yet even this marvel of contrapuntal invention cannot disguise the fact that, with *Die Zauberflöte* waiting to be completed, Mozart was a man with only half his mind on the job.

RECORDINGS OVERVIEW

The low esteem in which *La Clemenza* is held is reflected by the existence of only seven complete recordings. However, only the very first set – recorded by a cast of unknowns in 1950 – does not boast a gathering of world-class Mozart singers and conductors. The first major production was conducted by Istvàn Kertész in 1967, for Decca, with the likes of Popp, Berganza and Fassbaender, but it used a cut score and lacks the sweep for which the recordings listed below are notable. Colin Davis's 1976 recording for Philips is also superbly cast (with Baker, Popp again, Minton, Burrows and von Stade), but in 1979 Karl Böhm gave a masterly reading that remains, alongside the more recent Gardiner effort, a clear first choice, despite later competition from Harnoncourt, Hogwood and Muti.

Varady, McNair, von Otter, Robbin, Rolfe Johnson; Monteverdi Choir; English Baroque Soloists; Gardiner.
(Archiv 431 806-2AH2; 2 CDs).

Gardiner's period-instrument *Tito* is the work of a conductor who evidently finds nothing arid about this opera seria – it's fast, crisply punctuated and totally animated. The cast cannot be faulted: Anthony Rolfe Johnson makes the title role as multidimensional as anyone could; Sylvia McNair is an especially beguiling Servilia; and Julia Varady's Vitellia is pungently dramatic. Recorded during live semi-staged performances, this is a wholly convincing account.

Varady, Mathis, Berganza, Schiml, Schreier; Leipzig Radio Chorus; Dresden State Orchestra; Böhm.
(Deutsche Grammophon 429 878-2GX2; 2 CDs).

Böhm was an old man when he conducted this set in 1979, but this is a spirited reading, warmer than the Gardiner version if not as biting. Julia Varady's intense Vitellia, perfectly cast against the fragile Servilia of Edith Mathis, is one of her finest moments on record, while Berganza's dark-toned Sextus is a very expressive interpretation. Peter Schreier is thin and ungainly in comparison to Rolfe Johnson, but on the whole this good-natured account is a strong alternative to the more rigorous Gardiner.

Die Zauberflöte

The Magic Flute

Composed 1791.
First performed September 30, 1791.
Libretto by Emanuel Schikaneder.

Synopsis

Act I

The Prince Tamino is rescued from a serpent by the Three Ladies of the Queen of the Night, but the bird-catcher Papageno claims victory over the monster. As punishment for his lie, the Ladies padlock his mouth. They give Papageno a painting of the Queen's abducted daughter Pamina; falling in love with her image, he sets out to rescue her. The Queen promises that, if he succeeds, she will agree to their marriage. Accompanied by Papageno and protected by a magic flute and bells, they journey to Sarastro's palace, where Pamina is being held. Papageno's blundering arrival inadvertently saves Pamina from being attacked by Monostatos, a moor in the service of Sarastro. Papageno and Pamina leave in search of Tamino, who has arrived at a temple whose priest informs him that it is the Queen and not Sarastro who is evil. Papageno and Pamina are confronted by Monostatos and his slaves but, using the bells, they manage to escape. Pamina and Tamino finally meet, and immediately fall in love.

Act II

Tamino and Papageno are told they have to undergo a series of trials if they are to be accepted into the brotherhood of the temple, the first being a period of silence. While Pamina is asleep Monostatos again approaches, but is warded off by the Queen, who gives her daughter a dagger and tells her that she can only regain her power if Sarastro is killed. Monostatos is once more forcing himself on Pamina when Sarastro enters. He knows of the Queen's plans but reminds Monostatos that the brotherhood is bound by love. Papageno is given a fleeting glimpse of his ideal mate, Papagena, but is warned that he will be denied her if he fails in his trials. Pamina is taken to Tamino, and together they undergo trials by fire and water. Aided by the magic flute they pass through safely, and Papageno is united with Papagena, despite his failure to maintain silence. The Queen, the Three Ladies and Monostatos are engulfed by a clap of thunder and the remainder of the cast celebrate the victory of light over darkness.

LEBRECHT COLLECTION

Schinkel's design for the Temple in an 1816 production of The Magic Flute

Die Zauberflöte is the strangest of Mozart's operas. On the one hand it's a beguiling story of lovers in jeopardy, as transparent and enjoyable as any pantomime; on the other, it's an opaque allegory that has occasioned more interpretative speculation than any opera outside the canon of Richard Wagner.

The bizarre libretto was written by Emanuel Schikaneder, an actor-singer-impresario who knew Mozart through their membership of the same Masonic lodge (the one Haydn had belonged to). It was primarily because of this Masonic connection that Mozart agreed to help Schikaneder secure the success at his Theater auf der Wieden that he needed to escape financial ruin. Both men agreed that a Singspiel would best suit his company of singing actors and that Schikaneder should set Liebeskind's "Lulu oder Die Zauberflöte", a fairy tale that had been published in 1786 (at least three other Viennese theatres were then making a killing out of fairy-tale operas). Schikaneder's libretto, like its source, was set in Egypt, a magic land of handsome princes, demonic queens, evil abductors, serpents and supernatural occurrences. It was also the land to which Masonry traced it origins.

The Masons of Mozart's Vienna saw themselves as a philosophical association persecuted by the Habsburg state and by the Catholic Church. Bearing this in mind, *Die Zauberflöte* takes on a new complexion: the seemingly benevolent but deranged Queen of the Night might be Maria Theresa, whose attitude to the Masons was distinctly variable; the thuggish Monostatos might represent the Church; the wise Sarastro might be the Viennese scientist Ignaz von Born, a prominent member of Mozart's Masonic lodge. In addition to these specific correlations, the remaining characters could embody aspects of Masonic idealism: thus Papageno and Papagena are simple children of nature, in counterpoint to Pamina and Tamino, a more refined couple who achieve union through spiritual perfection. The recurrence of the mystical number three similarly suggests a Masonic subtext: for example, the overture's dominant key is E flat, which has three flats, and it opens with three chords which are later repeated at the entrance of the Three Ladies and the Three Boys. Tamino is subjected to three trials, overseen by three priests, and the trials which he and Papageno undergo are clearly reminiscent of Masonic ritual. And yet, for all these parallels, neither the composer nor the librettist ever wrote anything on which a definitive analysis could be based, and even Jacques Chailly (father of conductor Riccardo), who wrote a three-hundred-page study entitled *The Magic Flute Unveiled*, was obliged to admit that his and every other thesis was reliant to some extent on guesswork.

Ultimately, though, the esoteric meaning of *Die Zauberflöte* is less important than the overt subject matter, which is conveyed through a consistently entertaining mix of popular tunes, high-art arias, solemn Gluck-like drama and bel canto display. As with Mozart's previous great Singspiel, *Die Entführung*, the style veers rapidly from one extreme to the other, ranging from exalted opera seria (The Queen of the Night and Sarastro) to knockabout opera buffa (Papageno) in the space of a few minutes. And within that range lie some of the finest vocal music Mozart ever produced, from heartfelt love songs (Tamino's love-at-first-glimpse outpouring, "Dies Bildnis"), to outrageously silly exchanges (Papageno's duet with Papagena, in which they sing "Pa-pa-pa-pa" some 48 times) and hair-raising coloratura dementia (the Queen of the Night's murderous, and murderously difficult "Die Hölle Rache"). The burlesque sometimes overwhelms the high purpose (that is what the audience wanted, after all), but when Mozart transmutes the sexual love of Tamino and Pamina into a spiritual ideal, *Die Zauberflöte* can be seen as an opera that simultaneously subsumes the conventions of Baroque opera and paves the way for the ecstatic music-drama of *Tristan und Isolde*.

RECORDINGS OVERVIEW

The first studio recording of *Die Zauberflöte* was made by Thomas Beecham in 1938 with the Berlin Philharmonic, a wonderfully old-fashioned and intimate performance that is now available on a superbly transferred CD set from Nimbus; were the later competition not so stiff, this would feature on our shortlist. Neither Beecham nor Karajan (1950 for EMI) included any dialogue, nor did Böhm in his first recording of the opera, a vocally excellent session taped in 1955 and available on Decca (budget price). The first conductor to include the essential spoken text was Fricsay, for Deutsche Grammophon in 1955, but this is just about the only merit of that recording, apart from a nimble Queen of the Night. After the Böhm and Klemperer recordings recommended below, there followed versions from such as Solti, Karajan again (for Deutsche Grammophon), Haitink, Davis, Levine, Mackerras, Harnoncourt (with narrative instead of dialogue!) and Norrington. Some of these are at least passable, some show very little sympathy for the music, and none surpasses the standards established by the mid-Sixties.

Lear, Peters, Wunderlich, Fischer-Dieskau, Crass, Hotter, Lenz, Otto, Hillebrecht; Berlin RIAS Chamber Choir, Berlin Philharmonic Orchestra; Böhm.
(Deutsche Grammophon 429 877-2GX3; 3 CDs).

Böhm's later *Zauberflöte* has some distinct advantages over his earlier version – it includes much of the dialogue (but thankfully not all of it) and the stereo is both fresher and better balanced. True, the Berlin Philharmonic doesn't quite match the verve of the Vienna Philharmonic and the cast lacks the sense of unity that was crucial to the earlier set, but there is some stupendous singing here, especially from the men. Wunderlich's Tamino is honeyed, lithe and uniquely beguiling, Franz Crass is the most convincing Sarastro on record, Friedrich Lenz is a characterful Monostatos, and Fischer-Dieskau's Papageno is one of his great successes as an operatic singer. On top of this, Roberta Peters is an electrifyingly powerful Queen of the Night – indeed, Evelyn Lear's workaday Pamina is the only real weakness. A bonus is the inclusion of a complete, rather quirky recording of Mozart's *Der Schauspieldirektor*, a one-act, three-voice "comedy with music", composed in 1785.

Mannion, Kitchen, Blochwitz, Scharinger; Les Arts Florissants; Christie.
(Erato 0630-12705-2; 2 CDs).

This 1996 recording is an absolute triumph. Christie's identification with the opera's mercurial character is absolute, and his period-instrument orchestra brings unusual warmth and colour to their playing, reflecting at every turn the animation of the soloists. The singers are generally fine, firm in texture and elegant in phrasing, although Hans Peter Blochwitz is an uncertain Tamino, Linda Kitchen's soprano is a little grand for Papagena and Natalie Dessay is a better musician than technician as the Queen of the Night. However, all three are very much in the spirit of the performance and, with even the slight parts perfectly cast (the Three Boys are the best on record), this is a highlight among recent Mozart recordings.

Janowitz, Popp, Gedda, Berry, Frick, Crass, Unger, Pütz, Schwarzkopf, Ludwig, Höffgen; Philharmonia Chorus and Orchestra; Klemperer.
(EMI CDS5 55173-2; 2 CDs).

Claims that the high-minded Klemperer was unsuited to the playful elements of Mozart's penultimate opera were sharply disproved when, in 1962, he produced and conducted *Zauberflöte* at Covent Garden. Many of the cast intact were in the EMI studio later the same year for what was to become Klemperer's finest achievement as a conductor of opera. Even at the time his tempi seemed slow, but the delicacy, wit, balance and momentum of his conducting make this a vital experience, informed by the authority of a lifetime's experience. As for the singing, it would be difficult to imagine anything better: Janowitz's Pamina is sublime, Popp's Queen of the Night is sensational, Berry is a vibrant Papageno, and the three ladies are sung by the amazing trio of Schwarzkopf, Ludwig and Höffgen. If only Klemperer hadn't omitted all the dialogue.

Greindl, Ludwig, Lipp, Seefried, Oravez; Vienna Philharmonic Orchestra; Furtwängler.
(Music and Arts CD-882; 3 CDs).

Where many conductors stress the pantomimic elements of *Zauberflöte*, Wilhelm Furtwängler treated it as philosophy, as this remarkable recording from the 1949 Salzburg Festival shows. His tempi are generally slow but they are never ponderous, as he moves through the work with a flexibility and gentleness that keeps the music light and theatrical. From the first chords of the overture, Furtwängler projects a vision of this opera as a single two-and-half-hour span, and his cast respond perfectly to his direction. The recording is adequately transferred and the accompanying highlights from a 1951 Salzburg recording show how radically Furtwängler's thoughts on the work changed in just two years. A wonderful if expensive document.

4

THE AGE OF ROMANTICISM

CHERUBINI TO BEL CANTO OPERA

THE AGE OF ROMANTICISM

CHERUBINI TO BEL CANTO OPERA

Romanticism is not so much a precise concept as a swarm of ideas that coalesce in combinations that vary from country to country and from artist to artist. As in its art and literature, certain notions can be said to be prevalent in the opera of the Romantic age: the beauty and terror of Nature; the power and ubiquity of supernatural forces; the purity of the rural life; the concepts of liberty and fraternity; the artist's mission, as the philosopher Schlegel expressed it, "to give life to that within". But as with all great cultural epochs, the Age of Romanticism has as many histories as it has historians.

In any account of the subject, however, the French Revolution looms large, and the cataclysm of 1789 is as valid a point as any from which to begin an overview of Romantic opera. As you would expect, the profound social changes of the Revolution were reflected in the music of the period: composers now perceived the opera house in terms of its appeal to the People, and their themes embodied the ideologies of post-aristocratic France. Composers such as the now-obscure André-Ernest-Modeste Grétry produced a stream of patriotic and uplifting dramas, many of them focusing on the rescue of an innocent from the forces of oppression. In terms of box-office success, the genre of the "rescue opera" reached its peak with *Lodoïska*, by the Paris-based **Luigi Cherubini**, but judged in terms of quality the apogee was reached not in France but in Germany, with *Fidelio* by **Ludwig van Beethoven** – the first composer to whom the label "Romantic" was applied.

Beethoven's *Fidelio* is the only opera he ever completed, and it cannot be said to have inspired any major emulators. Yet it is among the century's most important operas, as it stands as opera's most powerful embodiment of the idealism of the new democratic age. The novelty of *Fidelio* lies in its ideas rather than in its musical fabric, for in its general structure it looks back to the classic order of Mozart. The giganticism that could be taken to be a defining aspect of Romantic opera was again a product of France, where Grand Opéra (as it became known in the 1840s), was fathered by the likes of Cherubini and **Luigi Spontini** – both of them Italian composers who spent much of their lives in France. The typical Grand Opéra composer took an episode from history (or a literary reworking of history), padded it out to five-act length, inserted a few ballet sequences (often serving no dramaturgical purpose), and created plenty of opportunities for cast-of-dozens choruses and lavish scenographic effects. This genre, the enduring influence of which can be seen in works as dissimilar as Verdi's *Aida* and Wagner's *Götterdämmerung*, was further developed by **Daniel Auber**, the first French-born composer of Grand Opéra, and reached its intemperate maturity with the collaborative efforts of the poet Eugène Scribe and the composer **Giacomo Meyerbeer**. In their hands

Grand Opéra became a form in which discretion was tantamount to treason. For example, for the premiere of Meyerbeer's *Le Prophète*, one scene was accompanied by a twenty-two-piece on-stage band, the Opéra's stage was lit by electric light for the first time, and the effect of a frozen lake was achieved by having the cast slide about on roller skates. Yet between these eye-popping scenes Meyerbeer threaded some exquisitely beautiful music. In its combination of high melodrama and tuneful melancholy, Meyerbeer's masterpiece, *Les Huguenots*, is one of the finest examples of pure Grand Opéra, alongside *La juive* (The Jewess), the peak of **Jacques Halévy**'s output.

The gargantuan productions of Meyerbeer and his ilk didn't entirely monopolize the French stage, for the lighter side of French opera was maintained by the tunefully effervescent work of **François-Adrien Boïeldieu** whose *La dame blanche*, was among the most popular French works of the century. But large-scale thinking was more typical of the time, and no-one thought bigger than **Hector Berlioz**, the only composer to rival the self-obsession of Wagner. Berlioz produced a small number of operas, each different from the rest, but each characterized by wild harmonies and fantastic orchestration. A thorn in the side of the establishment, he battled all his life to get the opera houses to stage his madly ambitious productions, the most colossal of which, *Les Troyens*, might be seen as an eccentric offshoot of the Grand Opéra tradition.

Back in Germany, Beethoven was of course the great figurehead of Romantic culture, but the formulation of a distinctively German form of Romantic opera was largely the work of other composers. Outstanding among these were the polytalented **E.T.A. Hoffmann**, whose *Undine* drew much of its strength from its use of Germanic folksong, **Louis Spohr**, in whose *Faust* you can trace the ancestry of Wagner's music dramas, and – above all – **Carl Maria von Weber**, whose *Der Freischütz* is the quintessential German Romantic opera, with its melding of the bucolic and the supernatural. After Weber there's something of a lull in the story of German opera, with only two composers, **Heinrich Marschner** and **Albert Lortzing**, doing anything to further Weber's experiments prior to the emergence of Richard Wagner, though **Friedrich von Flotow** forms a substantial footnote, as his one lasting success, *Martha*, is notable for its assimilation of Italianate melody into German opera.

In Italy, the composer responsible for the revitalization of the occupied country's musical culture was **Gioacchino Rossini**, who rapidly developed a flexibly formulaic style of composition that virtually invited imitators. Equally adept as the creator of comedies (most famously *Il barbiere di Siviglia*) and grandiose melodramas (*Guillaume Tell*), Rossini exercised a profound influence right across Europe, but at home he was especially important to the art of bel canto ("beautiful song"), the seminal genre of Italian Romanticism. Along with Rossini, the two composers with whom bel canto is most closely associated are **Gaetano Donizetti** and **Vincenzo Bellini**, both of whom wrote highly dramatic operas in which the bulk of the emotional freight was carried by the vocal line – whereas in German opera the orchestra was emerging as the dominant partner. At its weakest, bel canto amounted to little more than floridly pretty music applied to a weak plot and inane libretto, but although the hugely prolific Donizetti was culpable of spinning a fair amount of musical candy-floss in his operas, the same could not be said of Bellini, who often applied himself assiduously to the setting of the texts he used.

Though British poets and writers were preeminent in the Romantic era, the country's composers were peripheral, to say the least. The lone success was **Michael Balfe**, who applied his ballad-writing skill to some of the daftest libretti ever set to music – but, to slightly misquote Novalis, music heals the wounds inflicted by reason.

LUIGI CHERUBINI

b. FLORENCE, SEPTEMBER 8, 1760; d. PARIS, MARCH 15, 1842.

The French Revolution was the single most significant political factor in the creation of the Romantic imagination, and yet the major figure in French musical life during the years of the Revolution was the Italian-born Luigi Cherubini, a classicist who had little time for the self-indulgences of the Romantics. He was, nonetheless, a model of technique for those with less disciplined inclinations.

Cherubini's first compositions were pieces of sacred music but he soon gravitated towards the stage, and by the time he moved to Paris in 1788 he had composed some fourteen operas. He arrived to find the Gluck/Piccini controversy in full flow (see p.71) and was drawn towards the reforming tendencies of Gluck. In 1789, after one notable failure, Cherubini opened a theatre in Paris, intending to promote Italian opera buffa, but with the Revolution in full flow it was immediately necessary to change direction. The vogue was for earthquakes, shipwrecks, volcanoes, and tales of the deliverance of the innocent – a genre known as "rescue opera", or "pièce à sauvetage". The vehicle commonly adopted by composers for these rescue dramas was the "opéra comique", a term that had once signified the French equivalent of opera buffa, but by this period meant something entirely different – operas with spoken dialogue had become the speciality of the Paris Opéra-Comique theatre, and it was through this connection that opéra comique came to signify such a mix. The first critically influential rescue opera was Cherubini's *Lodoïska* – the longest-running French opera of the 1790s.

Though Cherubini's musical technique was solidly classicist, the ideology of *Lodoïska* was proto-Romantic, as was the Alpine setting of his opera *Eliza*, produced in 1794. Three years later he turned to classical myth and the dread-filled tale of *Médée*, a work comparable to the revolutionary Neoclassicism of painters such as Jacques-Louis David, and in 1800 he produced another highly popular work, *Les deux journées*, in which he promoted the joys of post-revolutionary political and social reason. Nothing composed after 1800 brought him anything like the success of these four works: fashion was changing at a blistering pace, with Beethoven and Spontini taking ever greater risks, and Cherubini was unable to keep up. After *Les Abencérages* in 1813, Cherubini retired from the stage for twenty years and devoted himself to education and church music. His final opera, *Ali-Baba*, was an unequivocal failure, forcing him to recognize that his time had long been over.

Cherubini had little impact on his homeland or his adoptive country, but in Germany and Austria he was revered as one of the greatest composers of his time. Beethoven pronounced him his only equal, Weber referred to him as an inspiration and Wagner thought him a "master of his craft", according him greater prestige than Gluck. All three were drawn to Cherubini's fresh handling of the orchestra, his theatrical treatment of ensemble, his realistic portrayal of character, his evocations of nature, and (most importantly for Beethoven), his high moral tone, in which good and evil were as black and white as in a 1950s Western. Cherubini may have been unsympathetic towards Beethoven and utterly baffled by his nemesis Berlioz, but he was nonetheless a forefather of Romantic opera.

Lodoïska

Composed 1790.
First performed July 18, 1791.
Libretto by Claude-François Fillette Loraux.

Synopsis

Act I

The Tartar king Titzikan is planning an attack on the evil Dourlinski. One of his men advises him to ambush Dourlinski when he leaves his castle, but the king is adamant that victory should come through open battle. The Polish Count Floreski and his equerry Varbel arrive on their quest to find Floreski's beloved, Lodoïska, who has been abducted by Dourlinski. After a skirmish Floreski and Titzikan swear an oath of loyalty. Having discovered that Lodoïska is imprisoned in Dourlinski's castle, Floreski and Varbel decide to disguise themselves as Lodoïska's brothers.

Act II

The "brothers" are not allowed to see their sister, who has been moved to the castle's most secret chamber. Varbel discovers that the wine they are being offered by their host is poisoned; Floreski manages to swap his and Varbel's glasses with those of Dourlinski's agents. When the tyrant bursts in Floreski reveals his true identity. He and Varbel are taken prisoner.

Act III

Lodoïska begs Dourlinski to allow Floreski to go free and offers her life in place of his. Though Dourlinski is desperate to marry her she decides to accept death with Floreski instead. Suddenly shots are heard and it is announced that the castle is under siege. Titzikan bursts in; Floreski rescues Lodoïska, and Dourlinski is doomed.

Lodoïska received two hundred performances during its initial run, but in the long view its greatest significance is that this tale of overthrown tyranny cemented Beethoven's decision to write his own operatic celebration of the republican ethos. However, where Beethoven's *Fidelio* is an entirely serious work, Cherubini categorized *Lodoïska* as a "comédie héroïque", and the impact is weakened by the inclusion of a comic character, Varbel. His cowardice and buffoonery provide some excellent fun – not least during the glass-swapping – but you can't help wishing that Cherubini had spun a tighter dramatic thread and pared down the thick sentimentality while he was at it.

The opera is nonetheless a substantial creation, tightly plotted and with most of the weight being taken not by the solo voices but by the orchestra and ensembles. Particularly impressive are the choruses and the drawn-out finales – some of which are constructed of several movements, each in a different key. Cherubini's rhythmic inventiveness is another attractive feature: during the Act I duet, for example, he makes nice use of a polonaise, and the remainder of the score abounds with highly contrasting, constantly changing patterns. Dourlinski is an enjoyably nasty proto-Pizzaro, and resemblances to *Fidelio* are compounded by the positively symphonic texture of the writing, even if *Lodoïska*'s melodies are less memorable.

Devia, Pedaci, Lombardo, Moser; La Scala Chorus and Orchestra; Muti. (Sony S2K47290; 2 CDs).

Riccardo Muti, a lifelong advocate of Cherubini's music, resurrected *Lodoïska* at La Scala in 1991 in celebration of the opera's bicentenary. The move was widely criticized at the time, as many thought that neither the opera nor its composer merited even passing scrutiny, but the production – and this recording – were passionately received. *Lodoïska* is a lot less successful on record than in the theatre, but Muti's pacing is swift and his singers are committed.

Médée

Medea

Composed 1797.
First performed March 13, 1797.
Libretto by François Benoit Hoffmann, after Corneille.

Synopsis

Act I

King Creon's daughter Dirce (Dircé) is to marry Jason, who stole the Golden Fleece with the help of the sorceress Medea (Médée). Medea, who has abandoned her family and borne Jason two children, appears before Jason and demands his return. He rejects her, provoking a curse of revenge.

Act II

Creon banishes Medea from his city but she persuades him to allow her one more day with her children. In an act of reconciliation she gives her servant Neris two gifts to take to Dirce – a cloak and diadem, both given to her by Apollo.

Act III

Outside the Temple of Apollo, Medea embraces her children for the last time. As she does so screaming can be heard from within the palace – Dirce has been poisoned by the cloak, and the people want vengeance. Neris, Medea and her children hide in the temple, but almost immediately Neris emerges, horror-struck. Following her is Medea, carrying the blood-stained knife with which she has butchered her children. The Temple bursts into flames and Medea and her Furies disappear.

Of all the works inspired by Gluck's reform operas, the worthiest successor is *Médée*, despite the fact that in the original version of Cherubini's masterpiece the dramatic flow was broken by spoken dialogue. (It was revised in 1855 by Franz Lachner, who turned it into an Italian opera, with sung recitative.) Gluck's influence is clear in the structure of *Médée*, which basically comprises a succession of dramatically potent small forms. Yet, though Cherubini was a classicist at heart, *Médée* is a forward-looking opera in one crucial respect – in its concentration on a single central character it anticipates the grand tragedies of the later nineteenth and early twentieth centuries, such as Verdi's *Aida*, Puccini's *Tosca* and Strauss's *Elektra*. The fearsomely difficult high-soprano title role was made famous by its creator, Julie-Angélique Scio, whose early death was said to have been partly attributable to the stress of the part. In the 1950s Maria Callas tackled *Médée* with equal glory but with no appreciable damage to herself.

The range and bravura of the title role tend to obscure the opera's other qualities – not the least of which is the symphonic fluidity of the rich, multi-voiced orchestration, a fluidity enhanced through the skilful use of recurring motifs. The texture of the orchestral part seemed too dense to many of Cherubini's contemporaries – indeed Napoleon complained that there was "too much accompaniment". But to ears accustomed to the multiweave music of Richard Wagner or Richard Strauss, the layering of *Médée* seems positively fat-free.

RECORDINGS OVERVIEW

Médée has been recorded complete only three times (each, unfortunately, in the Italian version), but this neglect should be ascribed to the difficulty of the title role rather than to the opera's quality. Two of these recordings featured sopranos famous for their stamina: Maria Callas, in 1957, and Gwyneth Jones (Deutsche Grammophon), exactly ten years later. Another ten years passed before the third reading (Hungaroton), this time with Sylvia Sass taking the name role. The Callas and Sass sets are available on CD (though the latter is hard to find), along with various bootlegs of Callas singing the role live. The one you're likeliest to come across is that conducted by Vittorio Gui in Florence in 1953, released on Arkadia; the sound quality is poor, but Callas's performance is scorchingly intense.

Callas, Picchi, Scotto, Modesti; La Scala Chorus and Orchestra; Serafin. (EMI CMS7 63625-2; 2 CDs).

This recording is very good, if not the masterpiece many would have you believe. Callas was justifiably celebrated as Medea, but her performance in the Milanese studios was a pale reflection of her impact on the stage. The barbaric splendour of her declamation is undeniably impressive, but her top notes are thin, her vibrato unstable and self-conscious, and her tone vulnerable. And for once she is not helped by Serafin, who seems positively withdrawn, directing a sloppy and uninspired La Scala. The tenor Mirto Picchi is a solid Jason and the youthful Renato Scotto makes a delightful impression as Glauce (Dircé in Italian).

LUDWIG VAN BEETHOVEN

b. BONN, GERMANY, DECEMBER 15, 1770; d. VIENNA, MARCH 26, 1827.

The composer who wrote his only opera three times, provided it with two titles and four overtures and once grumbled that he found it easier to rework an old composition than begin a new one, was clearly not born to the opera house. *Fidelio* is Beethoven's sole contribution to the genre, perhaps because he found the experience of its composition too draining: it took ten years to bring to a form he thought "worthy of my name", for its subject – a wrongfully imprisoned man saved from execution by his brave and determined wife – required the translation into music of his most profound philosophical beliefs, forcing him to the very limits of what music-theatre could express. For most of his life Beethoven sought to encapsulate in music his faith in humanity as a transcendant value and his belief that good will ultimately triumph over evil. More than anything else he wrote, *Fidelio* is Beethoven's credo.

Typical nineteenth-century image of Beethoven the brooding Romantic hero

Beethoven first came into contact with opera when, as a young man, he played the viola for Bonn's new opera company. For four seasons from 1788 he performed operas by Cimarosa, Paisiello, Gluck and Mozart, but he did not attempt to write an opera himself until 1804 – some sixteen years later. The catalyst was a production of Cherubini's *Lodoïska* (see p.109) mounted in Vienna in 1802 by Schikaneder, Mozart's collaborator on *Die Zauberflöte*. The first French "rescue opera" to reach Vienna, Cherubini's masterpiece inspired Beethoven to attempt to make something of a Schikaneder libretto, which he soon abandoned in favour of "an old French libretto" – Jean Nicholas Bouilly's *Léonore, ou L'amour conjugal*. Using a translation by the Austrian poet Joseph Sonnleithner, Beethoven began work on his rescue opera, initially entitled *Leonore*, in 1804, and continued well into the following year. Prefaced by the second of its four overtures, the three-act *Fidelio* was premiered at Vienna's Theater an der Weiden on November 20, 1805, and became one of the composer's most celebrated failures. The theatre was half empty and scattered with uniformed French officers

(Napoleon's troops had occupied the city), and Beethoven's unconventional music was not well received – one member of the audience summarized the opera as "a miserable mixture of low manner and romantic situations". Shocked by the hostility, Beethoven completely revised the score, cutting one of the acts and replacing the overture; but the new version, first performed in March 1806, was only slightly less unpopular. Eight years later, Beethoven returned to his opera and after another extensive revision he produced a final, two-act *Fidelio*. Performed at the Kärntnertheater, this *Fidelio* was a success, perhaps because, in the words of Joseph August Röckel (who sang Florestan), it was played to "a select public".

Thereafter Beethoven considered numerous opera projects, including a work based on *Macbeth* (abandoned because the librettist, Heinrich Joseph von Collin, thought the play "too gloomy") and a lyrical opera to be titled *Bacchus*. At regular intervals he approached George Friedrich Treitschke – his collaborator on the last rewrite of *Fidelio* – with various ideas, including operas to be titled *The Ruins of Babylon* and *Romulus*. Most ambitiously, he wrestled with a setting of both parts of Goethe's *Faust*, a project on which he began work in 1809 and was working shortly before his death. He intended it to be "a work that would be the greatest achievement of my art", but it got no further than sketches.

Fidelio

Composed 1804–05; revised 1806, 1814.
First performed November 20, 1805; March 26, 1806; May 23, 1814.
Libretto by Joseph Sonnleithner and Georg Friedrich Treitschke, after Bouilly.

Synopsis

Act I

Florestan, a political prisoner, is incarcerated in Seville. Disguised as a boy named Fidelio, Florestan's wife Leonore gets herself employed by the jailer, Rocco, whose daughter Marzelline then falls in love with the newcomer – to the anger of her lover Jacquino. Fidelio begs to be allowed to work in the cells; Rocco agrees but he must first ask the governor, Pizarro. Rocco cautions her that there is one cell which she can never enter.

Pizarro arrives and is given a letter in which he is warned that the minister, Don Fernando, intends to visit the prison, as he has heard rumours of cruelty there. Alarmed that he might be caught out, Pizarro tells Rocco that he is going to kill Florestan and demands that the jailer prepare a grave. Fidelio manages to persuade Rocco to allow the prisoners into the light, but Florestan is not among them. Furious that the prisoners have been let out, Pizarro orders them back into their cells.

Act II

Florestan, starved and chained to a wall in his cell, begins to suffer hallucinations. He has a vision of an angel with Leonore's face, leading him from his life of suffering; rising to follow her, he falls to the ground unconscious. Rocco and Fidelio enter Florestan's cell, and even though his face is hidden, Fidelio swears to help the prisoner, no matter who he is. Florestan is woken and he and Leonore recognize each other. When Pizarro enters, Leonore draws a pistol, holding the governor at bay while Don Fernando can be heard arriving. Pizarro is arrested, the prisoners are released, and Don Fernando addresses the people. Justice and love have triumphed over tyranny and hatred. The opera ends in praise of the woman who risked her life to save her husband.

By some criteria *Fidelio* might not be rated a great opera. It is true that its Singspiel-like construction, with separate "numbers" isolated by spoken dialogue, isn't conducive to theatrical flow. The plot is scarcely a masterpiece of dramaturgy either, and though the dauntless character of Leonore is a radical departure from tradition (she is opera's first proto-feminist), the rest of the cast is conventional enough: Florestan is a production-line hero, and Pizarro is as melodramatic a villain as any in opera. What makes *Fidelio* wonderful are the uncompromising seriousness of its celebration of love within marriage and Beethoven's fanatical care in making every bar of music contribute to his theme.

The Act I quartet is a perfect example of Beethoven's genius. Not one of the four protagonists – Marzelline, Jacquino, Leonore and Rocco – says anything of any great eloquence, but Beethoven's canonic music, its gentle pulse building to a swell, transmutes the scene: by the end of the quartet you are left aching with sympathy. The monumental Prisoners' Chorus, in which the briefly liberated men whisper "We shall be free, we shall find rest" as they emerge into the light, is painfully mov-

BEETHOVEN DROPPED FROM THE PREMIERE

The soprano Wilhelmine Schröder-Devrient (1804–60) began her association with Beethoven's *Fidelio* at the age of seventeen, and throughout her life she continued to perform the part in her distinctively intemperate style: she was prone, for example, to deliver her challenge to Pizarro – "Noch einen schritt und du bist todt" (One more step and you are dead) – as a scream that was nowhere near the written note. In her defence she could point out that she was well placed to know what effect Beethoven wanted, having been rehearsed by the composer himself. Here she describes his typical rehearsal technique.

"Waving his baton to and fro with violent movements, a puzzled expression on his face and celestial inspiration in his eyes, he stood among the playing musicians and did not hear a note! When, in his opinion, a passage was to be played piano, he would creep almost under the music-stand; when he wanted forte, he would leap upwards with the most curious gestures and utter the strangest sounds. With every number our anxiety grew, and it seemed to me that I was watching one of Hoffmann's weird figures emerge before me. It was inevitable that the deaf composer caused the most complete confusion among the singers and orchestra and everyone got quite out of time, so that no-one knew any longer where they were. But Beethoven observed nothing of all that, and so we somehow managed to finish the rehearsal, with which he seemed to be quite satisfied, for he laid aside the baton with a cheerful smile. It was unthinkable, however, that he should be entrusted with the performance, and Kappellmeister Umlauf had to take the heart-breaking task of telling him that the opera could not be put on with him conducting."

Upon receiving the news, according to another source, Beethoven "sprang over the barrier into the stalls and said only, 'Let us go out quickly.' Without stopping, he ran towards his lodgings in the Pfarrgasse in the suburb of Leimgrube. Once inside the door, he threw himself down on the sofa, covered his face with his hands and stayed in that position until we sat down to the table. He made no sound during the meal; his whole body was a picture of the deepest depression and despondency."

ing, while Florestan's ten-minute soliloquy at the beginning of Act II, "Gott, welch' Dunkel hier" (God, what darkness is here), is one of the most heart-wrenching of all tenor arias and has become something of a showpiece. The ecstatic love duet between Florestan and Leonore borders on the religious, and in the final chorus of the opera you sense that Beethoven saw more of God in this music than in any of his liturgical settings. Indeed, Wilhelm Furtwängler summed up this opera perfectly when he remarked: "*Fidelio* is, in truth, a Mass rather than an opera."

Finally, a note on the overtures. Of the four, those known as *Fidelio* and *Leonore No. 3* are the finest. The brief, rhythmically pungent *Fidelio* overture anticipates the preludes of Wagner's masterpieces, and Wagner himself thought it the work's greatest moment, believing that the sentiments expressed in these first seven minutes were only "weakly and repellently" repeated in the rest of the opera. *Leonore No. 3* poses awkward problems. It is a Promethean composition, maniacally driven and, at nearly a quarter of an hour long, disproportionately weighty. Since the middle of the nineteenth century, when Otto Nicolai (see p.149) first interpolated this overture between the dungeon scene and the finale, it has become common practice to use it as a prelude to the final scene. In dramatic terms, this is even less successful, for the addition of some fifteen minutes of symphonic grandeur brings the action to a grinding halt. On recordings that include *Leonore No. 3*, it appears either in the second act or as an appendix, so you can choose whether to drop it into the action or enjoy one of the nineteenth century's finest orchestral showpieces in isolation.

RECORDINGS OVERVIEW

The recordings listed below are the ones to investigate first, but the catalogue also features a few sets that should be heard by connoisseurs of this inexhaustible opera. The first studio *Fidelio*, conducted by Karl Böhm in 1943, is available on the Preiser label;

the mono sound is lousy and the opera is badly cut, but the casting is sensational, with Hilde Konetzni as Leonore and Torsten Ralf as Florestan. Karajan's reading for EMI has fine performances from Vickers and Dernesch as husband and wife, though the over-aggressive conductor fails to make the most of them. Bernard Haitink's performance for Philips is exceptional for its atmosphere (it was taped in Dresden just after the Berlin Wall came down) and a glorious Leonore from Jessye Norman. On the other hand, there are some recordings to avoid: Bernstein's crude 1978 recording, Dohnányi's bland 1992 performance for Decca, and Toscanini's brutal reading, taken from NBC broadcasts made in 1944.

Flagstad, Patzak, Schöffler, Greindl, Schwarzkopf, Dermota; Vienna State Opera Chorus; Vienna Philharmonic Orchestra; Furtwängler.
(EMI CHS7 64901-2; 2 CDs).

There are two recordings boasting Furtwängler's name: an EMI studio session of 1952, and this one, taped at the Salzburg Festival two years earlier. The sound is far from perfect, but this recording has the sort of atmosphere that a studio session can never generate, and if your first concern is the music rather than the reproduction quality, this has to be your first choice. Slow and fearsomely weighty, Furtwängler's tempi make terrible demands on his singers and yet they all rise to the challenge. Flagstad is a massive-voiced and deeply heartfelt Leonore, and it's to Julius Patzak's great credit that he doesn't seem spineless alongside her (he gives a particularly powerful reading of "Gott, welch' Dunkel hier"). Schwarzkopf's Marzelline is sensual and beautifully sung, Anton Dermota is an elegant Jacquino and Schöffler's Rocco is so theatrical that Greindl's Pizarro appears almost pale by comparison. The chorus is magnificent and Furtwängler's reading of *Leonore No. 3* (inserted before the finale) is tremendously exciting. This is one of the very finest opera recordings available.

Ludwig, Vickers, Berry, Frick, Hallstein, Unger; Philharmonia Chorus and Orchestra; Klemperer.
(EMI CDS5 55170-2; 2 CDs).

Taped the same year as his stage production at Covent Garden, Klemperer's intense, slow-moving *Fidelio* is the best studio recording. Christa Ludwig's mezzo brings a Flagstad-like warmth to Leonore but her tone is firmer and her presence is more in keeping with the scale of the performance. Vickers, one of the true heroic tenors of the 1960s, never allows his strength to dominate the characterization. Walter Berry is the best-sung and vilest Pizarro on disc, while Frick's Rocco is warm and uniquely likable. The Philharmonia Chorus makes no more than a reliable contribution but the orchestra responds with character and precision. Klemperer does not, as he sometimes did in the theatre, include *Leonore No. 3*, but, considering the speed at which he was prone to take the overture during the early 1960s, its deletion was probably the only way to prevent the opera from spilling over onto a third CD.

Jones, King, Adam, Talvela, Schreier, Crass, Mathis; Leipzig Radio Chorus, Dresden Opera Chorus; Dresden Staatskapelle; Böhm.
(Deutsche Grammophon 445 448-2; 2 CDs).

According to his memoirs, *Fidelio* was Karl Böhm's favourite opera and he made a point of conducting it on special occasions. One such was the bicentenary of Beethoven's birth, when Böhm was the grand age of seventy-three. This performance is that of a man half his age, and includes a blistering *Leonore No. 3*. In complete contrast to Furtwängler and Klemperer, Böhm's reading is vivid but rigidly disciplined, which is a good thing as far as Gwyneth Jones is concerned – this performance is one of her most appealing, as her voice had yet to adopt the vicious wobble that affected her performances of Wagner. James King is a hair-raisingly powerful Florestan, and Theo Adam (Pizarro), Martti Talvela (Fernando), and Franz Crass (Rocco) are all equally convincing – Schreier's pedestrian Jacquino is the only real vocal weakness.

Margiono, Seiffert, Polgár, Leiferkus, Skovhus, Bonney, van der Walt; Arnold Schoenberg Choir; Chamber Orchestra of Europe; Harnoncourt.
(Teldec 4509-94560-2; 2 CDs).

This account opens well, with bright percussion, fruity brass and lightly placed strings, but the overture's momentum is then undermined by a conductor who seems to be trying just a little too hard to make an impression. Nonetheless this is the best *Fidelio* of recent years, with a high-quality cast. Peter Seiffert (Florestan), a nicely balanced tenor, shines during his duet with the large-voiced Charlotte Margiono, who brings real fire to the role of Leonore. The well-drilled Schoenberg Choir confirms its high standing as one of the world's finest choruses, and Teldec's engineers have captured much detail that goes unnoticed on the older recordings.

LUIGI SPONTINI

b. MAIOLATI, ITALY, NOVEMBER 15, 1774; d. MAIOLATI, JANUARY 24, 1851.

Spontini was a fastidious craftsman who took great care over the formal structure of his operas, and yet he has a good claim to be regarded as the father of Grand Opéra, a genre not noted for its orderliness. An acknowledged inspiration for Berlioz and Wagner, Spontini was a master of orchestral special effects, and in his lavish stagings he paved the way for the no-holds-barred extravaganzas of Meyerbeer.

He began his career composing light Neapolitan operas but when he arrived in Paris in 1802 he changed his style into something more suited to the heroics of opéra comique. Supported by Napoleon's wife Joséphine, he composed three works for Paris, the second of which, *Milton*, was a great success. One of *Milton*'s librettists, Étienne de Jouy, approached the composer with a view to setting one of his libretti, *La Vestale*, which he had unsuccessfully offered to Boïeldieu, Cherubini and Méhul. Spontini welcomed the challenge and in 1807 *La Vestale* opened at the Paris Opéra, securing his fame and fortune overnight. Simple in design but hypnotically eloquent, it was succeeded by more grandiose efforts such as *Fernand Cortéz* and *Olympie*, operas that clearly reflect the obesity of Napoleon's vanity and ambition. *Cortéz*, in particular, was a graphic affair, requiring a cavalry charge and the burning and sinking of the Spanish fleet.

In 1819, after *Olympie* had failed in Paris, Spontini moved to Berlin, where Frederick William III engaged him for the Berlin Court Opera. While his revisions of *Olympie* were highly successful, his new operas were not, and the argumentative and inflexible composer was forever at odds with the theatre's management. In 1821 he saw the beginning of his end, when Weber's *Der Freischütz* was given its first performance at the Court Opera. The premiere divided the city into two factions: the court and its supporters, who favoured Spontini, and the opera-going public, who favoured Weber's exhilarating supernaturalism. Spontini did his best to compete but his German operas were disastrous and in 1829 he did the decent thing and left for Paris. He did, however, make sporadic returns to Berlin where, on one famous occasion, he conducted a production of *La Vestale* prepared by the young Richard Wagner, who was much impressed by the Italian's music and by his conducting – the mainstay of his last twenty years.

One of Spontini's more notable qualities was his adventurousness with the orchestra. Determined to make the orchestra express much that had previously been left to those on stage, he radically increased the size of his orchestra, tried out new combinations and placings of instruments, and experimented with off-stage bands, thus becoming one of the first to create the theatrical illusion of space and distance. His inflated orchestra of course required much louder voices, and Spontini was one of the first to demand a tenor who was heroic both in style and execution. His melodically beautiful and dramatically thrilling tenor roles are beyond all but the most powerful voices – Franco Corelli in the 1950s was perhaps the last singer to be comfortable with their scale, range and length.

La Vestale

The Vestal Virgin

Composed 1805.
First performed December 15, 1807.
Libretto by Étienne de Jouy and A.M. Dieulafoy.

Synopsis

Act I

Although she is in love with Licinius, a Roman general, Julia has been forced by her father into becoming a princess of Vesta – which requires her to retain her chastity. In spite of her vows, Julia still longs for Licinius and when she is required to place the crown of victory upon his head, she makes it known that it is her responsibility to guard the temple flame at night.

Act II

Licinius goes to Julia at the temple where, in their passion, they allow the sacred flame to go out. Licinius escapes, Julia is sentenced to death but refuses to reveal who was with her in the temple.

Act III

Licinius begs the Pope to grant Julia a pardon but his pleas are rejected, even after he has confessed his involvement. Julia is about to be buried alive when a lightning bolt smashes into the altar and relights the torch: Vesta has forgiven Julia, and she and Licinius are reunited.

During rehearsals *La Vestale* was condemned by the Opéra's management as "bizarre, defective and noisy", and it was only after the personal intervention of Joséphine that the first performance went ahead, in the face of hostility from a vocal faction determined to rid French music of Italian influence. By the end of the performance, however, the opera was hailed as a masterpiece.

Many years later, Berlioz wrote of *La Vestale*: "It has been said that Spontini derived from Gluck. As regards dramatic inspiration, character portrayal, accuracy and vehemence of expression, this is true. But as regards melodic and harmonic style, scoring and musical colouring, Spontini proceeds from himself alone. His music has an individual look which it is impossible to mistake." That just about sums it up. There's a reticence and formality to the score that's offset by features that look forward to the melodrama of high Romanticism, such as the languid melodies and massive choruses. Anticipating Bellini's orchestral manner, Spontini set many of the more dramatic vocal lines over repeated instrumental patterns that focus attention onto the voice and away from the orchestra. Unlike *Medée* (the only contemporaneous "French opera" of comparable power), *La Vestale* is a melodically sumptuous opera, abounding with solos and ensembles. Dialogue is snappily handled, with some rapid, sparkling exchanges, and the dramatic recitative is tight and exciting.

The finales are also inventive, with their Rossini-like crescendi (the second act was described by Berlioz as one huge crescendo), and the conclusion of the last act is especially electrifying, ending with a stretta (an ever-quickening pulse) which looks forward not just to Meyerbeer but to Donizetti and Verdi as well. Ceremonial marches, triumphal processions and temple rites provide the pomp that was to be central to any Grand Opéra, and Spontini maintains dramatic tension through sudden, unexpected shifts of pace and mood, a customary device of the Romantic era.

Huffstodt, Moore, Raftery, Kavrakos; La Scala Chorus and Orchestra; Muti. (Sony S3K66 357; 3 CDs).

Karen Huffstodt is not ideal in the title role – she tends to force the tone in moments of high tension, and the voice begins to tire in the final act – but she is far preferable to her only rival on disc, Rosalind Plowright (on Orfeo). The tenor Anthony Michaels Moore is a splendid Licinius, light in texture but perfectly declaimed and very theatrical, while Dimitri Kavrakos is really into the role of the Pontiff, producing a rush of dark, expressive sound. Muti is in his element, driving La Scala's chorus and orchestra with irresistible conviction.

FRANÇOIS-ADRIEN BOÏELDIEU

b. ROUEN, FRANCE, DECEMBER 16, 1775; d. JARCY, OCTOBER 8, 1834.

Amidst the mass of foreign musicians working in Paris during the early nineteenth century, there was one successful native composer – François-Adrien Boïeldieu.

Impressed by the music of his compatriots Grétry, Méhul and Dalayrac, Boïeldieu composed his first opera in 1793. Only two years later he made the inevitable move to Paris and soon established himself as a composer of light opéra comique. In 1803 he made a surprising move to St Petersburg, where he directed opera at the court of Tsar Alexander I and composed an opera every year. He returned to Paris eight years later and went on to achieve enormous successes with *Jean de Paris*, *Le nouveau seigneur de village* and *La dame blanche*, the last of which was performed over a thousand times at the Paris Opéra between 1825 and 1865. Boïeldieu prospered until 1830 when, suffering from an illness contracted in Russia, he was deemed unfit for work and relieved of his duties as court composer and professor of composition at the Académie des Beaux-Arts.

Boïeldieu had an almost perfect technical command of his medium and was as comfortable with high comedy as with exotic drama. His music is never profound and is often repetitious, but he was one of the creators of a distinctively French nineteenth-century sound – characterized by clarity, refinement, restraint, simplicity and exquisite orchestral colour. His treatment of language is exceptional, as is the inventiveness of his orchestrations, which Berlioz and Wagner both admired – indeed, the "Bridal March" in the latter's *Lohengrin* is suspiciously similar to a chorus in Boïeldieu's *Les deux nuits*. Of all his operas, *La dame blanche* is the one that best exemplifies all these qualities, and it suffers from none of the monotony to which he was otherwise prone.

La dame blanche

The White Lady

Composed 1825.
First performed December 10, 1825.
Libretto by Eugène Scribe, after Walter Scott.

Synopsis

Act I

George Brown, returning to Scotland from war, is fascinated by Avenel castle, which, he has been told, is haunted by a kindly ghost known as the White Lady. Dickson, an estate tenant, is summoned by the Lady but he is unwilling to meet her. Brown agrees to go in his place.

Act II

It transpires that the castle and its estate are to be auctioned, in the absence of any heir to the late Count of Avenel. Gaveston, a steward to the Count, is intent on taking possession of the estate, despite the protests of his ward, Anna. Brown meets the White Lady, who asks him to outbid Gaveston at the auction. She will provide the money.

Act III

It turns out that the White Lady is Anna (who has found a treasure chest in the castle) and that Brown is the heir to the Avenel estate. He takes the castle as his home and Anna as his wife.

Rossini settled in Paris in 1823 and promptly became a national icon. His operas commanded the biggest audiences, and French composers were virtually obliged to ape the Rossini style if they wanted to make money. Boïeldieu himself was an admirer, but with reservations. "I believe that one can write very good music by imitating Mozart, Haydn, Cimarosa etc; but one is only a cheap mimic if one imitates Rossini. Why? Because Mozart, Haydn and Cimarosa etc. always speak to the heart, the spirit; they always speak the language of sentiment and reason. But Rossini . . . ."

Boïeldieu put himself under pressure to offer an alternative, and this he did with *La dame blanche*, which within weeks of its opening was being played across Europe. Distinctively French in its refined, light orchestration, *La dame blanche* has a tunefulness that betrays its creator's method of composition – Boïeldieu could only write his melodies by singing them. Whether a lament or a ballad, each of the opera's set-pieces is instantly appealing, with a sense of line like that later to be found in Gounod. Brown, a tenor role, has some particularly charming airs, such as the touching Act III romance, in which he tries to pick up the tune of the folk ballad "Robin Adair", which is being sung by the chorus. Emotional depth might not be Boïeldieu's strong suit (the "French" operas of Cherubini and Spontini are certainly meatier), and his feeling for dramatic structure was not profound: you find yourself wondering where all the climaxes have got to, then four come along at once. However, graceful sentiment rather than high passion was what Boïeldieu was aiming for, and in the deliciously moonstruck world of *La dame blanche* he achieved it.

Legros, Louvay, Sénéchal, Doniat, Berbié; Paris Symphony Chorus and Orchestra; Stoll.
(Accord 22086-2; 2 CDs).

Sadly, this is the only recording of *La dame blanche*. The veteran character-tenor Michael Sénéchal copes well as Brown, and if Françoise Louvay is a little quivery at times, that's no bad thing in the role of Anna. However, Pierre Stoll's direction is limp-wristed, and he has a flabby sense of rhythm and a predilection for exaggerated rubato. The Paris Symphony appear bored out of their minds. Boïeldieu's opera is much more entertaining than this recording.

DANIEL-FRANÇOIS-ESPRIT AUBER

b. CAEN, FRANCE, JANUARY 29, 1782; d. PARIS, MAY 13, 1871.

Auber was born five years before Mozart composed *Don Giovanni* and died twelve years after Wagner composed *Tristan und Isolde*. He thus witnessed a period in which opera underwent extraordinary changes, yet Auber's work bears few marks of the revolution through which he lived. On the other hand, one of his comic operas has continued to be popular, and one of his creations exercised a powerful influence over Meyerbeer and Grand Opéra in general.

After unsuccessful forays into opéra comique (inspired largely by studies with Cherubini), Auber retired from composition in 1814; after his father's bankruptcy he returned to work, and in 1819 he set three libretti handed down to him by Cherubini. The first failed but the second two did not, and they led Auber into a collaboration with Eugène Scribe that thrived until the writer's death in 1861. Two of Scribe's "Auber" libretti – *Gustave III* and *Manon Lescaut* – were later adopted by Verdi and Puccini respectively.

During the 1820s Auber came increasingly under the influence of Italian opera, and Rossini in particular, and his next three operas were conceived in imitation of Italian fashion. In 1824 he made a consciously patriotic return to the French style (nonetheless preserving some of Rossini's musical "tricks") with his self-styled "opéra française" *Léocadie*, and the following year he composed *Le maçon*, his first internationally successful collaboration with Scribe. In 1828 the Académie Royale de Musique commissioned Auber and Scribe to compose *La muette de Portici*, an opera that, with its use of local Neapolitan colour, huge crowd scenes, history-based plot, bold orchestration and immodest stage effects, inaugurated the era of Grand Opéra. Returning to the comic mode to which he was best suited, Auber then produced *Fra Diavolo*, the epitome of his synthesis of Italian and French models, combining piquant Gallic orchestral mannerisms with Latin structural vitality and melodiousness. He continued to compose comic operas until his death, when he was mourned as one of France's greatest composers.

Rossini judged Auber a "Piccolo musico, ma grande musicista" (a small musician but a great maker of music) while Wagner, who initially championed Auber's early work, famously damned him as a "barber who lathers but does not shave". It's true that there's not much steel in Auber's operas: as with so much nineteenth-century French music, charm is everything. Yet, while Auber's music is unlikely to touch the heart, its wispy textures, elegant phrasing and charming tunes place his work among the most successful examples of light opéra comique.

Fra Diavolo

Father Diavolo

Composed 1829.
First performed January 28, 1830.
Libretto by Eugène Scribe.

Synopsis

Act I

Although she is in love with a poor soldier, Lorenzo, Zerline is to marry the wealthy commoner, Francesco. Lord and Lady Cockburn arrive at the inn owned by Zerline's father Mathéo, having been robbed on the way. Lady Pamela is still wearing her diamonds, which the bandit Fra Diavolo – disguised as the Marquis of San Marco – rips from her neck. Lorenzo, who has been given the task of capturing Fra Diavolo, manages to find some of the Cockburns' possessions and is rewarded with enough money for him to marry Zerline.

Act II

Still in disguise, Fra Diavolo enters Zerline's bedroom (in order to steal yet more from the Cockburns' adjoining room), where he is confronted by Lorenzo, who assumes he is a rival for his lover's affections.

Act III

Fra Diavolo and his bumbling henchmen Giacomo and Beppo are trapped. Fra Diavolo is murdered and Zerline and Lorenzo are married.

For much of this century *Fra Diavolo* has surfaced only in fragmentary form, through frequent recordings of its virtuoso arias for tenor (Fra Diavolo) and soprano (Zerline). Its neglect is partly due to the absence of capable singers: the title role is extremely taxing in its range (not since Nicolai Gedda's prime has a tenor been able to do it justice), and Zerline similarly requires an unusually wide emotional and vocal palette. Even the comic characters Giacomo and Beppo demand outstanding actor-singers if they are to come alive. (Incidentally, these idiot bandits provided the inspiration for Laurel and Hardy's film *Fra Diavolo*, made in 1933.)

Possessing something of the momentum of a Rossini opera, this work has an abundance of memorable – if overdecorated – tunes, many of them with splendidly clunky, rumbustious accompaniments. It is for the vocal writing that *Fra Diavolo* survives: Lord and Lady Cockburn's duet and the subsequent quintet (in Act I) positively groan with melody, and Fra Diavolo's recitative and aria in Act III contain some of the most thrilling tenor writing in all French opera (someone like Gedda can even make it moving). The work is orchestrally less interesting (in Auber's words "counterpoint makes the symphony live but it kills the opera") but the choruses are excellent fun – again, frequently reflecting the irresistible influence of Rossini.

Gedda, Mesplé, Dran, Berbié, Corazza, Trempont, Hamel; Laforge Choral Ensemble, Monte Carlo Philharmonic Orchestra; Soustrot.
(EMI CDS7 54810-2; 2 CDs).

When this set was taped in 1983, Nicolai Gedda was some twenty years past his peak, but he was still able to reach the high notes demanded by Fra Diavolo, and his feel for line and phrasing brings unusual elegance even to Auber's most sugary music. Mady Mesplé, as Zerline, also turns in a remarkable performance: from the beauty of her coloratura you'd think she were in her twenties rather than her fifties. Jane Berbié, born the same year as Mesplé, is an excellent Lady Cockburn, and her ever-characterful mezzo sits well next to the Lord Cockburn of Remy Corazza. Trempont and Hamel are a suitably ludicrous but always musical Giacomo and Beppo.

Le Domino Noir

The Black Domino

Composed 1837.
First performed December 2, 1837.
Libretto by Eugène Scribe.

Synopsis

Act I

Horace, a young Spanish nobleman, remembers how, twelve months earlier at one of the Queen's masked balls, he fell in love with a young woman whose identity he never discovered. He is attending the annual ball in the hope of meeting her again. She duly arrives, again masked and again accompanied by the same female companion. They are Angèle, a cousin of the Queen, and Brigitte, both novice nuns. Angèle is attending the ball as her last venture into society while Brigitte has decided to renounce her vows and marry. At eleven, Horace's friend Count Juliano tricks Brigitte into believing that it is midnight – when the convent gates are closed – and she rushes from the ball, allowing Horace and Angèle some time together. However, when Angèle hears the clock strike twelve she too rushes from the ball.

Act II

Juliano's rooms. The Count is expecting guests (including Horace) when Angèle, locked out of the convent, raps at the door and begs his housekeeper Jacinthe to give her shelter for the night. Angèle realizes that she is bound to encounter Horace and is frightened that he will discover that she is a novice, but Jacinthe, who is expecting her niece Inésille, dresses Angèle in her niece's clothes and introduces her as Inésille to the guests. Horace nonetheless realizes who it is, but he is too stunned to believe his eyes. Jacinthe summons her admirer Perez (the convent porter) and ensures that Angèle is given the keys to return to the convent.

Act III

Through a series of bizarre coincidences Angèle is freed from her vows, leaving her free to marry Horace.

The Black Domino – named after the nun's habit – was a remarkably popular opera, receiving more than twelve hundred performances between its premiere and 1910. Auber's biographer Charles Malherbe described the work as "a celebrated piece where, for lightness, elegance and wit the words combine to produce a masterpiece of its genre, one of the most successful types of opéra comique". Scribe's libretto, with its translucent characterization and rococo sub-plotting, might be the flimsiest raft on which to build an opera, but Auber's music has an irresistible snappiness, and the Offenbach-like energy of the exchanges is compelling – especially during the scene in which Angèle plays Jacinthe's niece Inésille, a subtlely drawn picture of naive country innocence. The patter songs (reminiscent of Rossini), sparkling coloratura and decadent waltzes are beguilingly slick, and a touch of astringency comes from Auber's attitude towards religion. Touches like the chorus of gossipy nuns in Act III ("Ah, quel malheur") and the parodic sacred cadences and prayers earned the affection of Berlioz, whose *Le Damnation de Faust* could be read in part as a tribute to Auber's mockery.

Jo, Vernet, Ford, Power, Bastin; London Voices; English Chamber Orchestra; Bonynge.
(Decca 440 646-2; 2 CDs).

There would be little commercial logic to releasing a recording of *Le Domino Noir* without a coloratura soprano of outstanding abilities. Sumi Jo is just such a soprano. A student of the tenor Carlo Bergonzi, she has a sweet tone and a firecracker technique that punches out the high notes required by Angèle. Richard Bonynge, husband of Joan Sutherland, has plenty of experience with coloratura sopranos, and the strictness of his direction brings many dividends in pacing and momentum. The remaining cast are satisfactory and the production values are high, with good accompaniments from the ECO and excellent sound. With the spoken dialogue heavily cut, the opera lasts under an hour and a half, but Bonynge has included a filler: the ballet music from Auber's *Gustave III*.

GIACOMO MEYERBEER

b. VOGELSDORF, GERMANY, SEPTEMBER 5, 1791; d. PARIS, MAY 2, 1864.

During the first half of the nineteenth century French opera was dominated by non-French talent. Berlioz, characteristically forthright in opinions, blamed one man above all others for this cultural "occupation" – Giacomo Meyerbeer, a composer whose influence upon managers, artists, critics and audiences had put a stranglehold on the Paris Opéra. According to Berlioz, Meyerbeer had turned the Opéra into an institution "madly in love with mediocrity", and posterity has tended to concur. The very qualities that ensured Meyerbeer's success during his lifetime are those for which he is now condemned. The Parisian public wanted grand Romanticism and Meyerbeer gave it to them, in huge melodramas that required armies of musicians and stagings so opulent that what the audience saw was frequently more important than what they heard.

Born in Germany of Jewish descent, Meyerbeer began as a piano virtuoso but, nursing an ambition to write opera, he also produced a number of oratorio-like dramas, each of which proved disastrous. Salieri advised him to study in Venice and within a few months of arriving, in 1816, he had composed six "Italian" operas and was being compared to Rossini. However, this change of direction did him no favours in an increasingly nationalistic Germany, and though Weber produced some of Meyerbeer's operas, he did so while complaining of their composer's "Italian aberration". The massive Venetian success of *Il crociato in Egitto* in 1824 encouraged Meyerbeer to take the work to Paris, and the following year it opened to the sort of lunatic fuss that would not be seen again until the appearance of Paganini six years later. With this single work Meyerbeer was established as the dominating influence in French Grand Opéra, a position strengthened by *Robert le Diable*, *Les Huguenots* and a string of other money-minting successes.

His influence was not entirely due to his music. Meyerbeer possessed enormous inher-

ROYAL COLLEGE OF MUSIC

Giacomo Meyerbeer – the wealthiest composer of his time

ited wealth, and many of France's critics, managers and musicians came to him for loans, a situation that assured him of praise. In one instance, however, Meyerbeer's largesse produced the opposite result. He helped Wagner produce his first two operas by loaning him a regular monthly retainer, but after he heard of Wagner's racially motivated resentment of his patronage, Meyerbeer withdrew his support. Wagner then turned upon Meyerbeer, who became one of the principal targets for his vicious anti-Semitism, and the two remained bitter enemies until Meyerbeer's death in 1864. Ironically, Wagner's early music is heavily indebted to Meyerbeer: in particular, *Rienzi* is little more than a grand imitation of Meyerbeer's style, in which he does his best to trump the elder composer's massive choruses, set-pieces and Gothic settings.

In box-office terms, Meyerbeer was the most successful composer of Grand Opéra, thanks to a remarkable ability to respond swiftly and precisely to public demand. As the Russian composer Dargomyzhsky bitterly remarked: "As I listened to the music, I could not find a single inspired idea. Meyerbeer's skill and intelligence are incredible, but neither skill nor intelligence can stimulate the human heart. The greatest craftsman is still not a poet." However, Meyerbeer's operas do contain some unusually entertaining music. *Le Prophète*, *Les Huguenots* and *L'Africaine* have worked in concert and on record, which is more than can be said for the majority of Grand Opéra composers, whose scores collapse when left unsupported by the paraphernalia of the stage. His style is tuneful and frequently luscious, his orchestration is often inventive, his finest characters offer a lot of potential for interpretation, and his writing for the voice is as accomplished as any produced in the nineteenth century. It's true that all these qualities are united only in *Les Huguenots* and that the rest are bloated to the point of immovability, but Meyerbeer's operas are central to the history of the genre, representing a link between the early Romanticism of Spohr, Hoffmann and Cherubini and the late Romanticism of Verdi, Wagner and Strauss.

Les Huguenots

Composed 1832–36.
First performed February 29, 1836.
Libretto by Eugène Scribe and Emile Deschamps.

Synopsis

Act I

The action is set in France in 1572, during the civil war between the Calvinist Huguenots and the Catholic majority. In an act of reconciliation, the Catholic Comte de Nevers has invited a Huguenot nobleman, Raoul, to a banquet. Raoul tells how he rescued a mysterious lady, with whom he is now in love. The Comte is called away from the banquet; looking through a window into the garden, Raoul sees that he is talking to the mysterious lady. She is Valentine, the daughter of the Catholic leader St Bris, and is engaged, against her wishes, to the Comte – though Raoul does not know any of this.

Act II

The King's sister Marguérite de Valois plans to bring peace to the factions by getting Raoul to marry Valentine, a proposal to which Raoul willingly agrees. Various Huguenot and Catholic nobles swear their friendship on this happy occasion but when Raoul is introduced to Valentine, he recognizes her as the woman he took to be the Comte's mistress and rejects the proposed union.

Act III

Valentine is about to marry Nevers. Raoul challenges St Bris to a duel, and St Bris and Nevers plot to ambush him. Valentine, who still loves Raoul, has overheard her father's scheme and sends a warning. The duel is averted by the arrival of Marguérite. St Bris is horrified to learn that it was his daughter who warned Raoul of their trap, and Marguérite explains to Raoul the situation between Nevers and Valentine.

Act IV

Nevers and Valentine are married. After visiting her for "the last time", Raoul resolves to kill himself but, as he is leaving, St Bris, Nevers and their followers arrive. Valentine hides Raoul, and her father reveals his plan to massacre the Huguenots later that night. Nevers demurs at the dishonourable scheme; Raoul leaves to warn his colleagues.

Act V

During the battle, Raoul is joined by Valentine who tells him of her husband's death, her renunciation of Catholicism, and her desire to marry him. Raoul is wounded and nearing death as they are challenged by Catholic soldiers. St Bris orders them to open fire and Valentine is fatally wounded. As the lovers die, St Bris realizes the gravity of his actions. Marguérite arrives but can do nothing to prevent the escalating barbarity.

Schumann wrote of *Les Huguenots*: "I am no moralist, but it enrages a good Protestant to hear his dearest chorale shrilled out on the boards, to see the bloodiest drama in the whole history of his religion degraded to the level of an annual farce. The work exemplifies commonness, distortion, unnaturalness, immorality and unmusicality." A lot of people find it hard to take Meyerbeer's maximum-volume, cast-of-thousands approach to the St Bartholomew's Day Massacre, but *Les Huguenots* has to be seen in the context of its time, and when you compare it with other examples of Grand Opéra, *Les Huguenots* appears

GRAND OPÉRA – NOTHING SUCCEEDS LIKE EXCESS

The majority of Meyerbeer's most flamboyant premieres were given at the Paris Opéra, then housed in the Salle de la rue Peletier, the first theatre to use gaslight in place of oil. Seating fractionally under 2000, the theatre was huge for its time, and thanks to the triumvirate of Meyerbeer and designers Louis Daguerre (the pioneer of photography) and Pierre-Luc-Charles Cicéri, it became a centre of theatrical experiment – especially during its "golden decade" (1839–49), when Louis Véron was its manager.

Wagner famously denounced Meyerbeer's works as "effects without causes", but effects were what the ticket-buying public wanted, and the Paris Opéra had the personnel to supply them. Berlioz defined the Opéra's "full-strength" as a "chorus of 120, with 28 violins and double-wind" – in other words, around 220 performers if you combine orchestra and chorus. On top of that, there was an on-stage band of about fifteen musicians, a dance troupe averaging about thirty bodies, about twenty actors to be placed at certain points about the stage to add to the "vitality of the dramatic impression", and, of course, a complement of soloists. Add a conductor, and the final tally was a cast of 300, putting on a show that virtually no other theatre could afford to produce. (As Bedrich Smetana discovered, budget productions of Grand Opéra were a contradiction in terms: "How can we possibly play opera in a house as small as ours? In *Les Huguenots* the armies barely number eight on each side.")

Thanks to the skills of Cicéri and Daguerre, the Opéra's army of performers contrived to sack cities, sink ships and generally "recreate the trauma of conflict". The pressure to trump the previous extravaganza was a constant source of stress, as Meyerbeer acknowledged when, shortly before the premiere of *Les Huguenots*, he wrote to his wife Minna of "the public's incredible expectations of magnificence". But so huge were the fees being paid to soloists like Malibran and Nourrit (each of whom could command the same sum for a night's work as the entire orchestra) that to ignore the public's taste was tantamount to commercial suicide. Meyerbeer above all he was an astute businessman, and though he struggled to retain some portion of his artistic integrity he knew the battle was lost. His penultimate triumph, *Le prophète*, was to be the ultimate crowd-pleaser.

This opera was a piece of unremarkable music made remarkable by its staging. For one thing, Daguerre and Cicéri produced a mighty set that was lit by electricity, its first use in theatrical history. Changing landscapes were conjured up through vast moving backcloths, ingenious lighting effects and mechanical clouds that covered then revealed the sun and moon, while perspectival tricks gave the crowd scenes some sense of depth and movement. One onlooker described how the opera's first tableau, which depicted a public square, was suddenly transformed into "part of the cathedral . . . without noise or oscillation". Yet greater wonders occurred during the first scene of the third act, set in the "frozen landscape before the gates of Münster". Cicéri had instructed the dancers in the use of roller-skates (invented in 1790) for this scene, and as the stage filled with dozens of skaters gliding about to Meyerbeer's music, the galleries went berserk. (Local merchants quickly caught on and did a roaring trade in "Prophet Skates".) But not even this could have prepared the audience for the final scene, in which Daguerre and Cicéri blew up the stage, satisfying the librettist's demand for "the destruction, by explosion, of the Prophet, his mother and all those about them".

almost naturalistic. As for its musical qualities, they bear comparison with many of the finest works of the nineteenth century.

Les Huguenots rarely appears in the opera house nowadays because it makes enormous demands on the theatre's budget, orchestra and singers. The tenor part of Raoul is so arduous that not since Franco Corelli's prime has a singer been able to handle the role properly, and the remaining six principals are only slightly less difficult – the best is the minimum requirement for a staging of *Les Huguenots*. The opera's four-hour length doesn't work in its favour either (Berlioz thought there was "enough in it for ten operas"), and the plot is unnecessarily complicated by

Scribe's libretto, which takes liberties with history, but Meyerbeer's score is the most inventive of his career. During its preparation, he became the first major composer to carry out research into music history as part of the process of composition. To establish the appropriate tone he spent a long time studying sixteenth-century manuscripts in the national library, and he even made room for traditional Jewish music – an odd addition considering the resolutely Christian subject matter.

There is a lot of fine music in the course of this epic production, with grand choruses, thrilling climaxes and high notes all round, but five episodes stand out: Raoul's astonishing Act I romance, with its heart-stopping high C; Marguérite's Act II aria "O beau pays de la Touraine"; her seventeen-minute Act II duet with Raoul, which is as affecting as anything by Puccini (the only composer to rival Meyerbeer's skill at playing to the gallery); and two moments in the dramatic tour de force of Act IV: the duet between Raoul and Valentine and the "benediction of the daggers".

RECORDINGS OVERVIEW

In 1962 La Scala mounted a production of *Les Huguenots* essentially as a vehicle for the great baritenor Franco Corelli. It was recorded live and various labels have released highlights of what is one of the most impressive examples of tenor singing ever taped. Should it be released complete, this performance is an automatic first choice. In the interim, the choice is between the following pair, the only commercial recordings of this prohibitively expensive opera.

Raphael, Pollet, Borst, Martinovich, Leech, Ghiuselev; Montpellier Opera Chorus; Montpellier Philharmonic Orchestra; Diederich.
(Erato 2292-45027-2; 4 CDs).

Both available recordings suffer from serious flaws, but this set, recorded live at the 1988 Montpellier Festival, is the more theatrical performance. Some of the singing is desperately unsatisfactory, but there are exceptions. Françoise Pollet (Valentine) shows an ability to apply her gloriously large voice with great delicacy and has an excellent sense of line. Richard Leech (Raoul) is a light tenor and has little sympathy for the style of the writing, but at least he can sing the notes, and his duet with Pollet makes a lasting impression – purely in matters of tone, these two are better than Arroyo and Vrenios on the Decca set. Diederich is little known outside France but he has a commanding view of the score as a whole and, unlike Bonynge, he exercises discipline over his singers. The recording is clear and fresh.

Sutherland, Arroyo, Tourangeau, Vrenios, Bacquier, Ghiuselev, Cossa, Te Kanawa, Augér; Ambrosian Opera Chorus; New Philharmonia Orchestra; Bonynge.
(Decca 430 549-2DM4; 4 CDs).

This 1969 recording was a labour of love for conductor Richard Bonynge and his wife Joan Sutherland. However, neither is ideally suited to the music: Bonynge's vague grasp of the opera's dramatic architecture and its subtle changes in pace and temperament lead to lengthy periods of tedium. Sutherland's Marguerite is a mighty display of technique, and there are enjoyable cameos from the young Kiri Te Kanawa and Arleen Augér. The remaining names contribute little, and Vrenios is a remarkably feeble Raoul.

JACQUES FRANÇOIS HALÉVY

b. PARIS, MAY 27, 1799; d. NICE, MARCH 17, 1862.

Halévy has become a one-work-wonder, known solely for writing *La juive*, one of the few Grand Opéras to have survived into the twentieth century. His reputation doesn't do him justice, for of all the composers who committed themselves to the unsubtle, high-cost genre of Grand Opéra, he was rivalled only by Meyerbeer in skill and success.

Born to a Jewish family (his original name was Fromental Elias Levy), Halévy studied in Paris with Cherubini, among others, and in 1819, while at the Conservatoire, he won the Prix de Rome. After some failures and years of determined study, he achieved fame in 1828 with *Clari*, an opera written for the extraordinary talents of soprano Maria Malibran. Seven years later he joined forces with Eugène Scribe and together they produced Halévy's masterpiece, *La juive*. Its success was enormous – it reached both England and the United States within ten years of the premiere – and it inspired high praise from Berlioz, who admired the orchestration, and Wagner, who commended its "pathos of high lyric tragedy". Halévy continued to compose for the theatre well into the 1850s, but became increasingly devoted to the Conservatoire, where he taught Saint-Saëns, Gounod and Bizet, the last of whom married Halévy's daughter on June 3, 1869.

Halévy spent much of his life in awe of Meyerbeer, whose talents he thought superior to his own, but Halévy's aims were considerably higher than Meyerbeer's and his musical style reflects a more serious intent. He was criticized by his peers for producing music that was too learned for the Opéra's audiences and, for all their tunefulness, his Grand Opéras do suffer from a monotonous earnestness. However, his ability to muster large-scale forces, together with his interest in character motivation and his inventive writing for the voice, have secured Halévy – or rather *La juive* – a secure position in the roster of nineteenth-century opera.

La juive

The Jewess

Composed 1834–35.
First performed February 23, 1835.
Libretto by Eugène Scribe.

Synopsis

Act I

Constance, 1414. Samuel (Prince Leopold in disguise) works for the Jewish goldsmith Eléazar, with whose daughter, Rachel, he has fallen in love. Ruggiero, the town provost, orders a day's festivities in honour of the Emperor's visit; hearing Eléazar at work in his shop, he orders him and his daughter to be dragged out. Eléazar's life is saved only after Cardinal Brogni hears the commotion and urges understanding. Believing Samuel to be Jewish, Rachel invites him to celebrate Passover, but before he can say anything a crowd rushes through the square. Eléazar and his daughter are set upon by the mob, to be saved this time by Samuel, who is recognized as Leopold by a sergeant in the Emperor's army.

Act II

During the Passover meal, Samuel refuses the unleavened bread and confesses that he is a Christian. Eléazar is prevented from killing him by Rachel, then insists they marry. Everyone is shocked when Samuel tells her that this is impossible, for reasons he does not explain.

Act III

Eléazar and Rachel deliver a gold chain to Prince Leopold's wife Eudoxie, and duly discover that her husband is none other than Samuel. In her fury Rachel denounces Leopold for having consorted with a Jewess, namely herself; then Brogni, abandoning his former tolerance, condemns Rachel, her father and Leopold.

Act IV

Leopold is saved from execution after Rachel declares that he did not have an illicit relationship with her, but she and Eléazar refuse to deny their religion and so remain condemned.

Act V

Father and daughter are led to the scaffold. Eléazar reminds the Cardinal that it was a Jew who rescued his daughter from his burning house many years before, and as Rachel is thrown into a boiling cauldron Eléazar reveals that he was the rescuer. The Cardinal has murdered his own daughter.

The strength of this opera is Eléazar, one of the greatest tenor roles in the repertoire. Halévy originally intended to make Eléazar a bass part, which certainly would have suited the maturity and nobility of this character, but the composer was so taken by the tenor Albert Nourrit that he created Eléazar with his abilities in mind. Nourrit is said to have helped write Eléazar's music and it has even been suggested that he wrote the opera's most powerful aria, "Rachel, quand du Seigneur". The role is less demanding than Meyerbeer's Raoul (see p.123), but the characterization – pivoting on Eléazar's battle between devotion to his god and love for his daughter (whose life he saved by accepting Christianity) – is of a complexity that was rare in Grand Opéra.

The dramatic development, beginning with an intense overture in which "Christian" and "Jewish" themes are thrust against each other, is typical of Halévy, in that each successive episode is designed to create an ever-greater shock until the tragedy reaches its graphic, whiplash finale. This tension is maintained through the continuing antagonism between Christians and Jews, an antagonism that reaches fever pitch at the end of Act IV, when the Christians bay for the death of Eléazar and Rachel. *La juive* carries the traditional Grand Opéra baggage of vast ensembles and ballets, but if well performed it can stir you like no other Grand Opéra.

Carreras, Varady, Anderson, Furlanetto; Ambrosian Opera Chorus; Philharmonia Orchestra; de Almeida. (Philips 420 190-2PH3; 3 CDs).

In 1986, when Philips taped the majority of this three-hour recording, José Carreras was undergoing treatment for leukemia. In a remarkable gesture of good faith Philips went ahead with the rest of the cast, shelving the tapes until, three years later, Carreras was able to overdub his part. Philips released the recording in honour of the Spanish tenor's return to health, and that's the way this set should be treated – as a tribute to Carreras's courage and the beauty his voice formerly possessed. His once sweet and agile voice is here strained, with unwieldy vibrato and choked high notes, leaving Julia Varady's Rachel to dominate with her burnished, tender soprano. As Eudoxie, June Anderson's coloratura is light and flamboyant, providing an appealing foil to Varady's darker voice, while Furlanetto is a powerfully moving Cardinal. Considering the circumstances, the sound is surprisingly good and the Philharmonia play with passion and detail.

HECTOR BERLIOZ

b. LA CÔTE SAINT-ANDRÉ, FRANCE, DECEMBER 11, 1803; d. PARIS, MARCH 8, 1869.

Of all Romantic composers Hector Berlioz was the one who put most work into being Romantic. "My life to me is a deeply interesting romance", he declared, and with one eye to the scrutiny of posterity, he turned his life into a Byronic epic, recording it in one of the most entertaining and unreliable autobiographies ever published. In all his music, he measured himself against the titanic shadow of Beethoven, though his operas owed little if anything to the philosophical drama of *Fidelio*. Rather, they sprang from the extravaganzas of Meyerbeer, Spontini and Cherubini, whose explorations of the resources of the stage and orchestra offered him a springboard from which to launch his own creations. Yet Berlioz was both a more serious and a more discriminating musician than his contemporaries in France. He revered Gluck for his emphasis on dramatic structure, and unlike Meyerbeer, Spontini and Cherubini, whose music is often loud and little else, Berlioz possessed an infallible ear for texture, colour and detail. Even his grandest opera – *Les Troyens* – is marked by a miniaturist's attention to the musical fabric.

He was born near Grenoble to a family opposed to music as anything other than a means of domestic entertainment. Unlike most other musical giants, he learned neither the piano nor the violin as a child (both were forbidden by his father, a surgeon), though he later developed an enthusiasm for the flute and guitar. Notwithstanding his lack of practical musical ability and his father's hostility towards the arts in general, he began composing in 1819. His father derided his son's efforts and insisted that he pursue medicine as a career. Reliant upon his parental allowance, he did as he was told and enrolled at the Paris medical school. Student medical life did not suit the oversensitive Berlioz and in 1822 he began to take serious music lessons. Four years later he took the step his parents had dreaded – he abandoned medical school and entered the Conservatoire, where he developed at a bewildering speed, thanks in part to his lack of pianistic ability. Saved by his father "from the tyranny of keyboard habits, so dangerous to thought, and from the lure of conventional sonorities", Berlioz within a matter of weeks had realized that the orchestra was his true métier.

LEBRECHT COLLECTION

Contemporary cartoon of Berlioz

In 1827 he experienced one of many life-changing events when he went to see a performance of *Hamlet*. Even though he spoke no English, the play struck him "like a thunderbolt", as did the beauty of the leading lady, Harriet Smithson. It was to be the start of a lifelong addiction to Shakespeare and an equally intense, if less durable, passion for the questionably talented Miss Smithson, whom he married in 1833. As the *British Court Journal* reported: "Miss Smithson was married last week in Paris to Derlioz [sic], the musical composer. We trust this marriage will ensure the happiness of an amiable young woman, as well as secure us against her reappearance on the English boards."

In 1831 Berlioz read the autobiography of the great Renaissance sculptor and braggart Benvenuto Cellini, and – recognizing a spiritual kinship – he determined to set his life as an opera. In 1836 he offered a two-act work to the Opéra-Comique but this was rejected and so he revised his proposal for the Opéra who, against all the odds, accepted. *Cellini* was a highly publicized failure, and though Berlioz and his small band of admirers believed he was born to the stage, it was transparently obvious even to the composer that no-one wanted him to write another opera. He therefore produced *La Damnation de Faust*, which was written for performance as an "opéra de concert" – that is, for the concert hall rather than the stage (although it has since been staged more often than any of his "real" operas). As *Faust* was a relative success, Berlioz decided to have another go at composing a full-blown opera. It could not have been more full-blown: *Les Troyens*, at nearly five hours, is the grandest French opera ever written, and it was never performed complete during its creator's lifetime. The management of the Théâtre-Lyrique forced him to divide the opera into two parts, *La prise de Troie* and *Les Troyens à Carthage*. Berlioz heard the second part performed in 1863, with heavy cuts, and although it survived for twenty-one nights it was hardly the success that the composer had envisaged.

Les Troyens took Berlioz two years to complete and the effort nearly killed him, but within another two years he had begun an opera based on Shakespeare's *Much Ado about Nothing*. Described by its composer as a "caprice written with the point of a needle", *Béatrice et Benedict* was first performed in Baden-Baden and didn't reach Paris until 1890, when the Opéra-Comique mounted a somewhat perfunctory staging. It has never found a solid place in any theatre's repertoire, a situation that owes more to the meagre dramatic potential of the piece than to its music.

His last seven years were overshadowed by illness, despair and resentment at his country's inability or unwillingness to recognize his talent, and he died defeated and bitter. This critical alienation continued after his death, and even today he is too often dismissed as a megalomaniac whose self-mythologizing career is summarized by the *Symphonie Fantastique* and *Harold en Italie*. However, his greatest work is to be found in *Benvenuto Cellini*, *Faust*, and *Les Troyens*. Nobody would argue that these large-scale structures are perfect: their contruction is often uneven and clumsy; many episodes sound more like oratorio than theatre; and Berlioz relies too heavily on shock tactics. As Winton Dean wrote: "The series of adjacent blocks from which the operas are constructed frequently seem as if they have been conceived without reference to each other. When placed in succession they resemble . . . a window of exquisite stained glass incompletely leaded." Yet if judged on the merits of their parts, the operas of Berlioz are among the finest of the nineteenth century – his orchestration is the work of a magician, his melodies are frequently captivating, and many of his arias and ensembles are among the finest in French opera.

Benvenuto Cellini

Composed 1836–38; revised 1851–52.
First performed September 10, 1838; March 20, 1852.
Libretto by Léon de Wally and Auguste Barbier, after Cellini.

Synopsis

Act I

Rome, 1532. The papal treasurer Balducci is angry that Pope Clement II has commissioned Benvenuto Cellini – and not his future son-in-law Fieramosca – to make a statue of Perseus. His mood is not improved when Cellini and his friends sing a carnival song beneath his window. Cellini and Balducci's daughter Teresa plan to elope but they are heard plotting by Fieramosca. In Piazza Colonna Cellini and a crowd of metalworkers plot revenge against Balducci for the pathetic money being offered for *Perseus*. As they prepare to stage a satirical play opposite the Piazza, Fieramosca and Pompeo plan to foil Cellini's elopement with Teresa. The play is announced – *King Midas with the Ass's Ears* – and everyone gathers, including Balducci. The treasurer is outraged and a fight breaks out, during which Cellini kills Pompeo. He is being dragged to prison when the Sant'Angelo cannon announces the end of carnival. All the lights are put out and Cellini escapes.

Act II

In Cellini's studio Teresa prays for his safety. Suddenly he arrives and they are preparing to flee to Florence when Balducci and Fieramosca burst in. The ensuing argument is interrupted by the arrival of the pope, looking for his sculpture of Perseus. He grants absolution to Cellini on the condition that he completes the statue by the close of day. If not, he will hang. He works all day but is constantly frustrated by distractions – one of which is provided by Fieramosca, who challenges him to a duel. The metalworkers begin to tire but they are inspired when Fieramosca attempts to bribe them not to work. The pope arrives and demands that the casting begin, but there is not enough metal – so Cellini orders the melting of all his sculptures. The statue is cast, the pope blesses the sculptor and the opera ends in praise of the metalworkers.

As with every other significant development in Berlioz's career, the production of his first opera was a drama in itself. In its original form, as an opera with spoken dialogue, it was rejected by the Opéra-Comique, but after Berlioz inserted some recitative it

BERLIOZ VERSUS THE WORLD

Berlioz's memoirs are about as reliable as Cosima Wagner's recollections of her husband. They are, however, considerably more entertaining, being packed with accounts of his numerous triumphs and disasters (there's little in between) and of the plots hatched by his philistinic enemies. His description of the premiere of *Benvenuto Cellini* in September 1838 is typical.

"The director of the Opéra, Duponchel . . . consented to listen to a reading of the libretto of *Benvenuto*, and appeared to like it, for he went about saying that he was putting on the opera not because of the music, which he knew would be preposterous, but because of the book, which he found charming. Accordingly he had it out into rehearsal. I shall never forget the horror of those three months. . . . When we came to the orchestral rehearsals, the players, influenced by the surly manner of Haberneck [the conductor}, held aloof and treated me with reserve. They did their duty, however, which can hardly be said of Haberneck. . . . But by the time the final rehearsals were reached, they were openly enthusiastic about several numbers. . . . This reached the ears of Duponchel. I heard him one evening deriding the curious change: 'We are now told that Berlioz's music is charming. It seems our ridiculous orchestra is lauding it to the skies.' Some of them had, however, preserved their independence, like the two who discovered during the finale of the second act playing that well-known air "J'ai du bon tabac" instead of their own parts; they hoped it would ingratiate them with the conductor. I met the equal of this skullduggery on the stage. In the same finale, where the stage is darkened and represents the Piazza Colonna at night with an immense crowd in masks, the male dancers amused themselves by pinching the female dancers and, when they screamed, screaming too, to the discomfiture of the chorus, who were attempting to sing. When I indignantly appealed to the director to put an end to this insolent and undisciplined behaviour, Duponchel was nowhere to be found: he did not deign to attend rehearsals. Briefly, the performance took place. The Overture was extravagantly applauded; the rest was hissed with exemplary precision and energy."

was accepted by the Opéra, who lavished twenty-nine rehearsals and the world's most famous tenor – Gilbert Duprez – and France's most famous soprano – Julie Dorus-Gras – on its first production. But the first night was a fiasco: Duprez was in poor voice, and the audience booed and shouted throughout. After that the opera lay unperformed for fourteen years, but Berlioz was under no illusions as to its quality, writing in his memoirs: "I cannot help recognizing that it contains a variety of ideas, an energy and exuberance and a brilliance of colour such as I may perhaps never find again." Liszt revived it in Weimar, after premiering Wagner's *Lohengrin*, but Berlioz heavily edited the score for this performance, and it was in this truncated form that it was performed until Colin Davis rescued the Paris version for the first ever Covent Garden production in 1966.

Benvenuto Cellini is not just a portrait of a Renaissance art-hero – it's a passionate celebration of hot-blooded, life-affirming Italy as well. Superabundance rather than careful design is what makes it a thrilling creation, for unlike Wagner, whose colossal constructions are rigorously coherent, Berlioz was obsessed with cramming as much variety into his work as possible. The effect can be claustrophobic and exhausting, as the music piles on more harmonic, rhythmic and contrapuntal complexities than any ear can process immediately. The pacing is frenetic and the difficulties of the writing present daunting challenges to even the finest conductors. Indeed, virtuosity is a prerequisite for the entire cast. Cellini himself is an incredibly demanding high tenor role, Balducci's baritone necessitates an extremely accomplished character-actor, while the chorus scenes – especially during the carnival – are among the most elaborate ever written. Personifying the mercurial properties of the opera as a whole, the character of the pope, though no more than a cameo, is an extraordinary mixture of levity and gravity, of impatience and sympathy – rather like his creator.

Gedda, Bastin, Massard, Soyer, Lloyd, Herincx, Eda-Pierre; Royal Opera House Chorus; BBC Symphony Orchestra; Davis.
(Philips 416 955-2PH3; 3 CDs).

This, the only recording of *Cellini*, is conducted by a famed interpreter of his music, but Colin Davis's performance has an air of apology about it, smoothing down the rough edges, stressing the skill of Berlioz's orchestration to the detriment of raw power. However, his cast bring total commitment to the show: Nicolai Gedda makes a thrilling but sensitive hero. Jules Bastin's baritone is sensually rich as Balducci, and Roger Soyer's exuberant Pope Clement almost steals the show. The CD transfers are hissy, but otherwise satisfactory.

La Damnation de Faust

The Damnation of Faust

Composed 1845–46.
First performed December 6, 1846.
Text by Gérard de Nerval, Almire Gandonniere and the composer, after Goethe.

Synopsis

Part I

Faust sings of his never-ending solitude and of nature. Soldiers march past his house.

Part II

In his study Faust bemoans his continued isolation and the absence of joy in his life. He resolves to end his life but as he reaches for the poison the walls of his study part, to reveal the interior of a church. The congregation's singing comforts Faust, but then Mephistopheles appears and promises him all that he desires. They leave together, hungry for earthly experience. In Auerbach's cellar, where students and soldiers are revelling, Faust is granted a vision of Marguerite. The scene changes again to the banks of the Elbe, where Faust dreams of Marguerite.

Part III

Faust sings of his love for Marguerite; Mephistopheles mocks him before they enter her house. There follows a duet and, finally, a trio, during which the devil mocks Faust's love for Marguerite.

Part IV

Alone, Marguerite sings of her happiness, but when Faust deserts her she is desolated. In a mountain gorge Faust sings an invocation to nature before being carried off to his damnation. Marguerite is redeemed and, accompanied by angels, enters heaven.

Berlioz's masterpiece was not conceived as an opera, though it has effectively become one. Soon after the concert premiere Berlioz was prepared to rearrange *Faust* for the stage, but the Drury Lane theatre for which he was to carry out the revision was bankrupted after the failure of Balfe's *Maid of Honour*. Some years after Berlioz's death it became common practice to present *Faust* in costume and with sets, and it continues to appear as a dramatic production as frequently as it's played in concert.

Derived from Part One of Goethe's philosophical poem, *Faust* maintains the episodic structure of Goethe's text, which is bound together not by any narrative logic but by the thematic consistencies of its examination of isolation and the loss of hope. The action is provided primarily by the music, and each successive scene is a stupendous demonstration of musical pictorialism. The Ride to the Abyss, for example, is a thrilling tone-painting, violently evoking the precipitate gallop to hell, the jeering of the awaiting devils, and the terror of the doomed Faust. The gravity of Goethe's verse governs the dominant tone of the piece, but the emotional range of *Faust* is vast, encompassing the savage mockery of Mephistopheles's two-minute waltz "Devant le Maison", the raucous bonhomie of the tavern scene and the tear-prompting melancholy of Marguerite's "D'amour, l'ardente flamme". The title role is allotted three superb tenor arias, while Marguerite's mezzo-soprano and Mephistopheles's bass provide great musical and theatrical opportunities – indeed, Berlioz's devil is perhaps the most memorable of all diabolic musical characterizations. And the best way to enjoy the riches of *Faust* is as its creator composed it – as a work of pure music, devoid of visual distractions, which at best can only overemphasize what is already there in the score.

RECORDINGS OVERVIEW

Faust has been recorded many times and there are seven available CD recordings. Two are outstandingly good (see below) and two should be avoided: John Eliot Gardiner's performance is aridly fussy; and Eliahu Inbal's vapid reading for Denon is blighted by a truly ugly Marguerite from Maria Ewing. On the other hand, *Faust* addicts should sample Charles Munch's excellent 1950s performance for RCA, which boasts the incomparably touching Marguerite of Suzanne Danco, and Dutoit's Decca set, where Richard Leech is the star turn.

Verreau, Rubio, Roux, Mollet; FNR Maîtrisse, Brasseur Chorus; Lamoureux Orchestra; Markevitch. (Deutsche Grammophon 437 931-2GX2; 2 CDs).

This is the best *Faust* ever made. Markevitch is completely at home with Berlioz's unique mixture of the sacred and the profane, and the orchestral performance is wonderfully old-fashioned, with noisy percussion, austere brass and yielding strings. But it is the casting that makes this set so memorable. Richard Verreau – who seems to have made only one studio recording – is an extraordinarily moving Faust, with a slightly husky tone that conveys Faust's passion as expressively as his despair. Consuela Rubio also seems to have made only one recording, but she too is ideal, her light soprano bringing a rare fragility to the part of Marguerite. Michel Roux lacks the weight demanded by Mephistopheles, but he is a characterful singer and clearly enjoys himself. Good 1950s sound.

Gedda, Veasey, Bastin, van Allan; Ambrosian Singers; London Symphony Orchestra; Davis. (Philips 416 395-2PH2; 2 CDs).

Davis's 1973 recording has moments of unforgettable theatre – notably the Ride to the Abyss – but, again, he seems uneasy with many of the more purple passages. As with Markevitch, it is the singing that merits the highest praise. Gedda's yearning Faust is uniquely appealing in the hushed passages of "Merci doux crépescule" (in Marguerite's room) and thrilling during "Nature immense" (at the mountain gorge shortly before the ride to Hell), though his tone is thin compared to Verreau. Josephine Veasey is a dark, womanly Marguerite, and she makes much of Berlioz's aching melodies, while Jules Bastin is a riot as Mephistopheles, full of life, thick with menace but with an exquisite turn of phrase. Excellent recording quality.

Les Troyens

The Trojans

Composed 1856–58; revised 1859–60.
First performed November 4, 1863 (Acts III – V); December 6, 1890 (Acts I – II).
Libretto by the composer, after Virgil.

Synopsis

Part I: La prise de Troie (The taking of Troy)

Act I

The Greeks have deserted their camp outside Troy, leaving behind the wooden horse. The Trojan princess Cassandra (Cassandre), daughter of King Priam, predicts doom for her people but she is ignored, even by her lover Choroebus (Chorèbe), and the royal family and city luminaries celebrate their salvation. The ceremony is interrupted, first by the arrival of Hector's grieving widow Andromache (Andromaque) and her son Astyanax, and then by Aeneas (Énée), who brings news that the priest Laocoön has been killed by serpents after throwing a javelin at the wooden horse. The horse is then dragged to the city centre, as a gesture of appeasement to Athena.

Act II

Hector's ghost appears to Aeneas and tells him that Troy has fallen, and that Aeneas must flee with his son Ascanius (Ascagne) to establish a new city in Italy. Pantheus (Panthée) arrives and confirms the story of Troy's disaster and the death of Priam. Before Vesta's altar, Cassandra predicts that Aeneas will found a new Troy in Italy but declares she cannot face submission to the Greeks and stabs herself. Greek soldiers rush in and announce that Aeneas has escaped with the Trojan gold. The Trojan women commit suicide.

Part II: Les Troyens à Carthage (The Trojans at Carthage)

Act III

The palace of Dido (Didon) in Carthage. Dido and her sister Anna are informed that a foreign fleet has been blown to their shores. Dido grants them sanctuary. The Trojan chiefs, headed by Pantheus (and including a disguised Aeneas), explain Aeneas's mission to found a new Troy, but the peace and goodwill are shattered when Narbal, Dido's minister, bursts in with the news that the Numidian king Iarbas and his men have begun to attack Carthage. At this, Aeneas throws off his disguise and offers an alliance with the Queen. After leaving his son Ascanius to Dido's care, he rushes off to battle.

Act IV

Caught in a storm, Dido and Aeneas seek shelter in a cave, where they consummate their love. They celebrate their love again in Dido's gardens by the sea but they are disturbed by Mercury, who demands that Aeneas do his duty and establish his new city.

Act V

The sailor Hylas sings of home and Pantheus gathers the Trojans for departure. Aeneas is kept from returning to Dido by Trojan ghosts and just before they leave she arrives and denounces him. She asks the gods for vengeance and orders a funeral pyre to be built. As she mounts the fire she sees a vision of Rome.

Les Troyens may not be Berlioz's greatest opera, but it is his greatest achievement. According to his calculations, a complete performance (including a dinner interval) would last just short of six hours, but he never lived to see anything more than the last three acts. Critical opinion of the partial premiere was almost universally harsh, but there were some rogue voices, noticeably Pierre Scudo, who wrote "if he has failed, he has failed magnificently" – and Berlioz himself was overjoyed, writing "it aroused feelings in me I shall not attempt to describe". The first complete performance – conducted at Covent Garden by Colin Davis – was not given until May 3, 1969, when it was finally demonstrated that the opera contained considerably more high-quality music than the excerpts that had been periodically resurrected as orchestral showpieces, such as the Royal Hunt and Storm.

The idea for *Les Troyens* was the composer's own – he had been addicted to Virgil since childhood – but the motivation came from Liszt's lover, the Princess Sayn-Wittgenstein, who in 1855 told Berlioz of Wagner's plan for a cycle of four operas. Spurred by the German's ambitious project, Berlioz set to work on a Trojan libretto later the same year and in July 1856 he sent the princess a copy of the completed text. However, the similarities of date and scale are the limit of the resemblances between *Les Troyens* and the *Ring*. Whereas Wagner was moving towards a vast, fluid music-drama in which conventional notions of place and time were confounded, Berlioz wanted to return opera to the play-like structural rigour of the era of Gluck (his idol), albeit with an infusion of Romantic orchestral exuberance. And just like Gluck, Berlioz denies his soloists even the slightest opportunity for cheap-thrill display or ornamentation, no matter how intense the emotion.

This epic-scale opera is extremely difficult to produce, not least because of the frequent and drastic scene changes, and Berlioz himself virtually invited criticism of the opera's construction, for throughout his piano version of the score he makes numerous suggestions as to what might be cut for performance. However, the intensely lyrical and dazzlingly orchestrated music goes some way to draw attention away from the episodic structure, and a single theme (taken from the Trojan March at the end of Act III) occurs at key moments to lend cohesion when needed most. Characterization is subjugated to the concept of humanity as a component of the vast machinery of history, yet the vocal writing is consistently beautiful, especially for Dido (mezzo) and Aeneas (tenor) – indeed Dido's Lament is arguably the most emotive mezzo-soprano aria in all French opera. Like Wagner's *Ring*, *Les Troyens* is a demanding work, but it amply rewards the effort you put into it, and for the power of the melodies alone it is worth the expense of a recording.

RECORDINGS OVERVIEW

There have been just two complete recordings of *Les Troyens*: the set listed below and an account conducted by Charles Dutoit and released by Decca in 1994. Understandably, in view of the reputation of the previous recording and the ambitiousness of the undertaking, Dutoit's reading gained a lot of publicity, but it's a rudderless and mechanical performance, proving that an assemblage of singers does not necessarily constitute a cast (though the excellent Françoise Pollet does her best to salvage things).

Veasey, Vickers, Lindholm, Glossop; Royal Opera House Chorus and Orchestra; Davis.
(Philips 416 432-2PH4; 4 CDs).

This was the first complete recording of *Les Troyens*, made by much the same team as worked on the landmark Covent Garden production. Davis is in his element and he gives a passionate, convincing reading that imparts a theatrical unity to the whole span. The English orchestra and English-speaking cast are generally superb, but the absence of genuine French style is sometimes a problem. Jon Vickers, for example, is an unimprovably powerful and expressive Aeneas, yet at times he is simply incomprehensible; likewise Josephine Veasey is excellent as Dido, but French she is not. Nonetheless, this is a legendary production and decidedly preferable to the alternative.

Béatrice et Bénédict

Beatrice and Benedict

Composed 1860–62.
First performed August 9, 1862.
Libretto by the composer, after Shakespeare.

Synopsis

Act I

The town of Messina is celebrating the repulse of the besieging Moors. Hero, daughter of the governor of

Messina, sings of her love for Claudio, who then arrives with Bénédict. Béatrice and Bénédict proceed to mock each other. Don Pedro enters and the three men sing about how unenviable a status is marriage. Bénédict is adamant that he will die a bachelor and so Don Pedro plots with Claudio to trick Bénédict and Béatrice into loving one another. Bénédict overhears a conversation, lead by Don Pedro, in which it is revealed that Béatrice loves him. He is surprised but delighted. The same trick is played, by Ursule and Hero, on Béatrice.

Act II

After much deliberation and hesitation, Béatrice and Bénédict – alongside Hero and Claudio – find themselves in church being asked whether or not they are to be husband and wife. They are, and the opera ends with Bénédict acknowledging the power of love.

Like Verdi, Berlioz composed only one comic opera, derived it from a Shakespeare play and wrote it at the end of his life. He first considered "a lively opera" based on *Much Ado About Nothing* in 1833 – nearly thirty years before he actually came to write it – but did not set to work until he received a commission from a French impresario living in the German town of Baden-Baden. He approached the project as something of a vacation after the exertions of *Les Troyens*, and the music is lighter and more ingratiating than anything in the earlier operas.

Like its predecessors, *Béatrice et Bénédict* is weak in structure but powerful in content, its irritating omissions (Don John, Dogberry and Verges) and pointless additions (Somarone) being more than offset by its comic charm and delicious music. Though the action starts with an energetic overture (often played as a concert item) which packs in prefigurations of many of the subsequent arias and ensembles and concludes with an equally exuberant finale, *Béatrice et Bénédict* is characterized above all by chamber-music qualities of clarity and symmetry, refuting the cliché of Berlioz as a victim of musical elephantiasis. The beauty of the arias, the sparkle of the orchestration (particularly the fruity woodwind) and the pungent harmonies give a late-summer warmth to the proceedings, and though some people might object that Berlioz gives the title roles too dominating a presence, the gentleness and wit of his final opera should win over all but the flint-hearted.

Baker, Tear, Eda-Pierre, Watts, Allan, Bastin, Lloyd, van Allan; John Alldis Choir; London Symphony Orchestra; Davis. (Philips 416 952-2PH2; 2 CDs).

Colin Davis seems most comfortable with the lightest of Berlioz's stage works. His flowing and sensitive direction encourages elegant performances from Janet Baker (Béatrice) and Robert Tear (Bénédict), and they clearly enjoy the comedy – Baker especially. As Hero, Christiane Eda-Pierre is deliciously sensual, and the remaining cast are all of the highest quality. The LSO play with spirit and good attention to detail. Captured in rich sound, this is a fine account. Should you not be able to find it, the alternative is Daniel Barenboim's mid-price set on Deutsche Grammophon.

ERNST THEODOR AMADEUS HOFFMANN

b. KÖNIGSBERG, GERMANY, JANUARY 24, 1776; d. BERLIN, JUNE 25, 1822.

The reaction against Italian music that took hold of Germany during the early part of the nineteenth century had its roots in the writings and music of Carl Maria von Weber (see p.138) and E.T.A. Hoffmann, for whom Italian opera amounted to little more than a "frivolous diversion". In a famous review of Hoffmann's opera *Undine*, Weber wrote that it was "the opera Germans want, a self-contained work of art in which all elements, contributed by the related arts in collaboration, merge into one another and are absorbed in various ways so as to create a new world". In doing so, Weber drafted a credo that was to achieve its perfection with Wagner. Both Weber and Hoffmann championed this musico-dramatic synthesis as a specifically German achievement and each saw the other and himself as being central to the culture of Romanticism. Indeed for much of his life the multitalented Hoffmann – writer, composer, critic, painter – was regarded as the very embodiment of the intellectually unfettered Romantic ideal, and he was the first to apply the word Romantic to music, suggesting that music "is the most Romantic of all the arts – one might even say that it alone is purely Romantic".

Forced by his family into studying law, Hoffmann was appointed assistant judge at the high court in Posen on March 27, 1800, but music was always his passion. Moving to Warsaw, he completed his first opera, *Die lustigen Musikanten*, in 1804 and for the first time added "Amadeus" to his name, thus acknowledging his love of Mozart on the title page as well as throughout the score. Short of work and money, he left Poland in 1808 and after a short spell in Vienna moved to Bamberg, where he composed a number of unremarkable stage works. During this time he began to concentrate on criticism and fiction, writing the tales that were to become the basis of his lasting reputation, but in 1816 he completed an opera that played a decisive role in German Romantic music – *Undine*. However, Hoffmann failed to repeat *Undine*'s great success: his musical career foundered as Weber became the pre-eminent figure in German opera. In 1821 he and Weber fell out when Hoffmann translated Spontini's *Olympie* and pronounced that its virtues were of value to the German operatic school. It was a statement for which Weber never forgave him.

Hoffmann spent the last two years of his life fulfilling highly paid literary commissions. His only musical diversion was another opera, *Der Liebhaber nach dem Tode*, based on an idea suggested to him by Weber's librettist Helmina von Chezy; but the work was taken only to draft and it has subsequently been lost. After his early death his music was soon eclipsed by his stories, many of which were set to music, and he famously appeared as a protagonist in Offenbach's *Les contes d'Hoffmann* (see p.270).

Undine

Composed 1813–14; revised 1816.
First performed August 3, 1816.
Libretto by Frederich de la Motte Fouqué.

Synopsis

Act I

Undine, a water spirit and adopted daughter of a fisherman and his wife, loves Huldbrand of Ringstetten, a mortal whom she hopes to marry so that she can gain a soul. She is warned that she will die should Huldbrand betray her, but – in spite of the opposition of the chief spirit Küleborn – Undine and Huldbrand are married.

Act II

Undine and her new husband move to Ringstetten, where she is befriended by Berthalda, the adopted daughter of the Count and Countess. Berthalda discovers that her parents are the fisherman and his wife, and she runs from home. Huldbrand and Undine chase after her.

Act III

Huldbrand has become increasingly uneasy over his wife's continued association with the water spirits, and he eventually leaves her for Berthalda. At their wedding, Undine appears and regains Huldbrand: united in love, they die in each other's arms.

Although it's an enjoyable fantasy with much to commend it musically and theatrically, *Undine* is of interest principally as a precursor to Wagner's music dramas. Its epic, folkloric quality has obvious links with works such as *Lohengrin*, and the heady conjunction of love and death (termed *liebestod* by Hoffmann's friend Heilmann) clearly anticipates the world of *Tristan*, but the structural affinities are even more important. As Weber pointed out, Hoffmann's overriding concern was with dramatic continuity: the action of *Undine* unfolds swiftly and without breaks, with each number linked by motif or harmonic association, and no recitative or vocal decoration to get in the way. However, Hoffman's imagination frequently outran his technique, and the overall freedom and development of the basic material are of significantly greater interest than the material itself. Hoffmann's opera has some lovely qualities: Undine is a lively light soprano role, the depiction of nature – a major element in the opera – has the sparkle of Gluck or Cherubini, and the use of solo double-basses to signal the arrival of the Holy Man is a remarkably fresh stroke. But unlike Weber, Hoffmann was no tunesmith, and the short and declamatory melodies are unlikely to hold your attention unless you have a specialist interest in the era.

Laki, Hermann, Mekler, Ridderbusch; Berlin St Hedwig's Catholic Chorus; Berlin Radio Symphony Orchestra; Bader. (Schwann 310922; 3 CDs).

Taped in 1982, this is a difficult recording to trace but well worth the effort, primarily for bass Karl Ridderbusch's performance as Küleborn. Resonant in tone and very expressive, he makes a peculiarly human water spirit. Krisztina Laki makes an ideal Undine, light and wistful and yet capable of sudden changes in colour and character. Roland Hermann's baritone is perhaps a little grand for a character as impotent as Huldbrand but he is consistently impressive. Roland Bader gives a lively reading of the score – if only all opera conductors so patently enjoyed the job.

LOUIS SPOHR

b. BRUNSWICK, GERMANY, APRIL 5, 1784; d. KASSEL, OCTOBER 22, 1859.

Though remembered today for his chamber music, Louis (born Ludwig) Spohr was a talented and influential opera composer, several of whose works remained in repertoire throughout the nineteenth century. He was influential in another respect as well: even though he was unsympathetic to Weber's music and found late Beethoven incomprehensible, Spohr was the first prominent composer to back Richard Wagner, staging *Der fliegender Holländer* in 1843 and *Tannhäuser* in 1851.

His first works for the stage were routine operettas (one of which was nonetheless admired by Goethe), but then in 1813, when he set the Faust myth, Spohr revealed his true dramatic gifts. With its innovative use of chromaticism and leitmotif, *Faust* was greatly admired by Weber, the premiere's conductor, who wrote that "a few melodies, carefully and felicitously devised, weave through the whole work like delicate threads, holding it together". A landmark in the history of opera, *Faust* would perhaps have survived to the present day were it not for the competition from the better-known treatments composed by Berlioz and Gounod.

After abandoning work on a text upon hearing that Weber was working on the same drama (it became *Der Freischütz*), Spohr came up with *Zemire und Azore*, an adaption of a 1771 comédie ballet, then in 1823 produced his most successful opera, *Jessonda*, a regular feature of the German repertoire for the following seventy years. There followed further operas, including *Der Berggeist* (which anticipated the construction of *Der fliegende Holländer*) and *Pietro von Abano* (which took the daring step of dramatizing necrophilia), but by the mid-1840s he realized the times had outstripped his abilities and virtually retired from composition, devoting himself chiefly to producing. He died attempting to stage *Lohengrin*, an opera of which Spohr would have been incapable but which fulfilled everything to which he had devoted his life.

Faust

Composed 1813; revised 1852.
First performed September 1, 1816.
Libretto by Joseph Carl Bernard.

Synopsis

Act I

Faust has signed his soul to Mephistopheles but believes that he can still be saved if he uses his powers for good. However, his love for the virtuous Röschen is overtaken by his lust for Countess Kunigunde, whom Faust has rescued from the arms of the rogue knight Sir Gulf.

Act II

Faust visits the witches of Blocksberg and requests a potion to enable him to seduce the Countess. However, she marries Count Hugo, forcing Faust into drugging her at the wedding banquet. Her husband challenges Faust to a duel, and is killed.

Act III

As Faust nears the moment of damnation, Röschen drowns herself, and the opera ends with the necromancer being dragged to hell by Mephistopheles's demons.

Spohr and Goethe were generous in their praise of each other, and the high regard in which the composer held the writer's two-part *Faust* poem had much to do with his decision to base his own *Faust* on miscellaneous other versions of the legend. Subsequent efforts to set Goethe's intractable masterpiece have tended to reinforce the view that Spohr's humility was wise. Certainly Spohr's pioneering version of this quintessentially Romantic tale was a mighty achievement, and it became mightier still in its revised form. The first version, premiered in Prague (with Weber conducting) as a two-act opera with spoken dialogue, was regularly performed over the next twenty years, but by the late 1840s the impact of French Grand Opéra was being felt across the border. Thus, when Spohr was invited to provide a work for the 1852 London season, he revised *Faust* as a Grand Opéra, with a greatly expanded orchestral score and music for all the dialogue, greatly enhancing the work's fluency.

Even before its revision, *Faust* was remarkable for its imaginative use of leitmotif and for casting both protagonists as low voices (Faust as a baritone and Mephistopheles as a bass), breaking the convention in which the hero was scored as a tenor (even Wagner obeyed that rule). The music might be less involving than *Jessonda*, but it has some sweet melodies, combustive orchestration and enjoyably lush harmonies, and of course the plot is guaranteed never to pall.

Vier, von Jordis, Jennings, Bric, Eichwalder; Bielefeld Opera Chorus; Bielefeld Philharmonic Orchestra; Moull. (CPO 999 247-2; 2 CDs).

This recording of Spohr's revised version of *Faust* is marred by some bad singing, but at least the performance has character and the provincial ensemble doesn't lack enthusiasm. Moull seems to be enjoying himself – despite his cast – and the music is just about good enough to withstand the general humiliation.

Jessonda

Composed 1822–23.
First performed July 28, 1823.
Libretto by Eduard Gehe, after Antoine Lemierre.

Synopsis

Act I

Jessonda, the widow of the Raja of Goa, is to be burned at the stake, to follow her husband in death. The high priest Dandau sends Nadori to inform Jessonda of her fate, but the young Brahmin – smitten by Jessonda's sister Amazili – swears to save her from death. Meanwhile the Portuguese army approaches Goa.

Act II

Tristan, a Portuguese general, is mourning the mysterious loss of his beloved more than two years before. As Jessonda is brought to the stream for purification, Tristan recognizes her as his lover but, having sworn not to interfere with the ceremony, he is forced to watch her being taken away in preparation for her death.

Act III

Tristan is told by Nadori that the Indians have violated the truce by firing on his ships. A storm ensues, during which a colossal statue of Brahma is hit by lightning. Dandau interprets this as a sign that the gods are angry and decides to hurry the execution, but before Jessonda can be harmed Tristan and his army smash through the city walls. Tristan and Jessonda are united, as are Nadori and Amazili.

Jessonda is a thoroughgoing piece of Orientalist fantasy, complete with precisely prescribed Indian settings and copious musical allusions to the subcontinent. The current vogue for such exotica probably ensured a degree of success for the opera, but Spohr's music ensured the durability of its appeal – after the London premiere on June 18, 1840, one critic was moved to remark "it is a tissue of the most lovely melodies and delicious combinations of harmony we ever heard". Modern audiences might not be quite as enthusiastic about the Grand Opéra choruses, of which there are too many for an opera lasting under two and a half hours, nor about the inclusion of ballet music, which weakens the dramatic impact. However, it's still possible to be impressed by the score's vividly emotional harmonic language and by the treatment of recitative, which lets the music flow as in a mature Wagner opera. Above all, *Jessonda* is enjoyable for the figures of Tristan (another baritone hero) and Jessonda (a powerful dramatic soprano), two fine demonstrations of the composer's lyrical gifts. *Tannhäuser* it isn't, but this is a pleasant and mildly adventurous specimen of German Romanticism.

Varady, Behle, Moll, Moser, Fischer-Dieskau; Hamburg State Opera Chorus; Hamburg Philharmonic Orchestra; Albrecht.
(Orfeo C2409 12H; 2 CDs).

Kurt Albrecht is hardly known outside Germany but, as this performance amply demonstrates, he is among the most gifted operatic conductors of the present generation. The pacing and balance are superb, the control of orchestral sonority is remarkable, and the accentuation of orchestral and vocal line is wonderfully fluid. Julia Varady is in superb voice as the heroine, while Kurt Moll and Thomas Moser are impressive as Dandau and Nadori. The only weakness is Dietrich Fischer-Dieskau who, as Tristan, sounds tired – this was one of his last operatic recordings.

CARL MARIA VON WEBER

b. EUTIN, GERMANY, NOVEMBER 18, 1786; d. LONDON, JUNE 5, 1826.

If any one composer can be said to be the founder of German Romantic opera, it is Carl Maria von Weber, who was acknowledged as such not only by his contemporaries, such as Hoffmann and Marschner, but also by later figures, notably Wagner and Strauss. Mixing a quintessentially German brew of the folkloric and the supernatural, Weber produced in *Der Freischütz* (The Marksman) an opera of thrilling orchestral effects, great dramatic impetus and mythical resonance. Furthermore, with this and his other operas, Weber created a body of work that crystallized the German sense of national identity in much the same way as the music of Rossini gave voice to the Italian self-image.

Weber's father was a theatre director and his mother a singer-actress, and the boy's music lessons were frequently reliant upon the availability of a teacher in whichever town the family troupe was visiting. He benefited from the atten-

LEBRECHT COLLECTION

The ailing Weber contemplates his creations

tions of the piano virtuoso J.P. Heuschkel and the composer Michael Haydn (Joseph's brother), with whom he composed an apprentice opera, *Peter Schmoll*. The successful premiere of this charming if immature work in 1803 encouraged young Weber to move to Vienna, where he was adopted by the composer and theorist George Vogler. In 1804 Vogler saw to his pupil's appointment as *Kapellmeister* in Breslau, but Weber's efforts to place more emphasis on Mozart and contemporary French opera, and to reform the stage craft in the Breslau opera house, were continually frustrated by the conservative bosses and audience. After only two years he resigned – having come close to death after mistaking a glass of engraver's acid for Chianti.

Although the next three years were highly productive, he completed only one opera, *Abu Hassan*, and not until 1813 did he return to the theatre. Reluctantly Weber accepted the post of *Kapellmeister* at Prague's opera house, where again he found himself battling against managers intent on preventing him from modernizing the organization of the theatre and moving away from an Italian-based repertoire. Resignation and a three-month stay in Berlin followed, then in 1816 Weber accepted an appointment as Royal *Kapellmeister* in Dresden, where his superior, the infamously devious Francesco Morlacchi, did everything in his power to stop Weber from establishing a repertoire of German opera in tandem with the city's preferred Italian fare.

The next year he resumed work on an operatic project he had discarded earlier, and in 1821 *Der Freischütz* was completed. Within months *Der Freischütz* was being acclaimed throughout Europe as the composer's masterpiece and an epoch-making event, embodying a vision of opera as a form of absolute theatre that owed nothing to either the Italians or the French. Waved as a banner of national pride, *Der Freischütz* was the most performed German opera during the first half of the nineteenth century, and in present-day Germany it's still the most popular homegrown opera.

However, Weber's success made him careless. Weber based his next opera, *Euryanthe*, upon a hopelessly inept libretto. Despite a warm reception at the premiere in Vienna, it closed after only twenty performances, precipitating a twelve-month writer's block. Then in the spring of 1824 he was invited to write an opera for London and two years later, against his doctor's advice, he made the arduous journey to England for the premiere. He produced *Oberon* at Covent Garden in April 1826 and died on the day before his intended return to Germany. On June 21 he was buried in the Catholic Chapel in Moorfields, where his body remained until 1844, when Wagner and Meyerbeer arranged for its return to Dresden. He was reinterred to funeral music arranged from Weber's operas by Wagner, who was deeply affected by the occasion. Standing by the grave, he announced: "Behold, the Briton does you justice, the Frenchman admires you, but only the German can love you. You are his own, a bright day in his life, a drop of his blood, a particle of his heart."

Weber's achievements were many and varied: he was a notable critic and analyst of music; he reformed the way opera was staged in German theatres; he was a noted pianist; and he was one of the first great conductors – his control over intrumentalists and singers was legendary, and he did much to improve the quality of the orchestras he worked with. He produced a wide-ranging body of outstanding music, but above all he is celebrated as the founding figure of German Romantic opera. Had Weber lived beyond his fortieth year, the history of German music would doubtless have been greatly different; in the event, the reputation of German opera lived off the merits of a single work – *Der Freischütz*.

Der Freischütz

The Marksman

Composed 1817–21.
First performed June 18, 1821.
Libretto by Johann Friedrich Kind after Johann August Apel and Friedrich Laun.

Synopsis

Act I

In a Bohemian forest a party of peasants is celebrating Kilian's victory over the forester Max in a shooting competition. Max is distraught because he loves Agathe, daughter of Cuno, the head ranger, but cannot marry her unless he wins the shooting competition on the following day. Caspar, who has sold his soul to the evil spirit Samiel, suggests that Max follows his example. Cuno denounces the proposal but warns Max that if he fails the test he will not marry Agathe. Caspar offers to help Max win the contest and gives him his gun, with which Max shoots down a barely visible eagle with a magic bullet loaded by Caspar. Caspar then tells Max that seven more of these bullets are to be cast at midnight in the Wolf's Glen.

Act II

Unsettled by events, Agathe is comforted by her cousin, Ännchen. Max enters and tells them that he has to go to the Wolf's Glen to retrieve a stag he killed earlier in the day. In the Glen, Caspar summons Samiel on the stroke of midnight and they agree that Max should be substituted for Caspar in the diabolic pact. Max arrives and he and Caspar cast the seven bullets – the last of which, unknown to Max, is to go wherever Samiel wishes. Throughout the casting they are visited by increasingly terrible apparitions until, finally, Samiel appears and the two men fall senseless to the ground.

Act III

Max impresses everyone with his marksmanship in the contest, but then Prince Ottokar orders him to shoot a passing dove with his final bullet; though Agathe begs him not to (as she herself is the dove), Max shoots, and Agathe falls to the ground. However, Agathe has only fainted, and because Max was tempted to the Wolf's Glen by Caspar and did not act of his own free will, it is Caspar who must pay Samiel's fatal price. Max confesses his pact with Samiel and is forgiven by the Prince. The opera ends happily but inconclusively, with the audience left guessing as to whether or not Max and Agathe will marry.

After the first performance of *Der Freischütz* in 1821, Weber wrote in his diary: "Greater enthusiasm there cannot be, and I tremble to think of the future, for it is scarcely possible to rise higher than this." It was a prophetic observation, for *Der Freischütz* almost single-handedly overthrew the Italian monopoly of Germany's theatres, and not until the arrival of Wagner did Weber's masterpiece begin to lose its potency. Mixing the supernatural and the demonic with representations of earthy peasant life and unsullied Nature, *Der Freischütz* is a primer of German Romantic culture, and it was taken to heart by a nation that had yet to achieve its political identity in the wake of the Napoleonic era. Max's victory was viewed not merely as the triumph of good over evil – it was the triumph of the German spirit. Some thirty years before the Nazi era (when *Der Freischütz* once again became popular), the American critic Henry Krehbiel wrote: "There was never an opera, and there is no likelihood that there will ever be one, so intimately bound up with the loves, feelings, sentiments, emotions, superstitions, social customs and racial characteristics of a people."

Regardless of its power as a nationalist icon, *Der Freischütz* is a magnificent opera, as is apparent right from the overture (well known as a concert piece). Using different keys to portray contrasting emotions (C major for good, C minor for evil), the overture is innovative in being constructed almost entirely from material heard later in the opera, and Weber's deployment of the orchestra is amazingly inventive: with their diminished sevenths accompanied by low clarinets, tremolo strings and off-beat timpani, the mysterious last twelve bars of the overture are the very distillation of German Romanticism. The sense of dramatic cohesion is enhanced through Weber's use of leitmotif, a technique established at the outset when the overture announces material that will be heard later in the opera. Characters and key ideas are associated with certain motifs, some of them sung, many of them (notably the "Triumph" motif) expressed in connection with a particular instrument or harmony. Often these motifs can be found lurking beneath the melodic surface, creating a substratum on which the action rests – and foreshadowing the massive music-dramas of Wagner.

Weber's melodies are astounding in their number and quality (he was often referred to as the German Bellini), and his characterization is always well drawn: Agathe, Max and Caspar are finely rounded creations that offer endless dramatic possibilities for singer-actors. The choruses, specifically the quasi-rustic ones sung by the hunters and bridesmaids (who arrive mid Act III), are exceptionally rich and buoyant, while the dances, notably the march and waltz of Act I, remain equalled only by the dance music in Johann Strauss II's stage works. Yet one episode stands out above all the rest: the depiction of the Wolf's Glen is one of the most engrossing creations in all German opera, and the finest example of Romantic scene-painting before middle-period Wagner. Mysterious harmonies, monotone choruses, mixed spoken and sung dialogue, and sumptuous, multilayered orchestration contribute towards a genuinely intimidating evocation of unearthly powers.

RECORDINGS OVERVIEW

Der Freischütz is the most popular German opera from the era separating Beethoven from Wagner, but fewer than a dozen studio recordings have been made of it, and most of these omit or severely edit the dialogue. Of the readily available sets, the finest are Joseph Keilberth's (the first stereo recording) and Carlos Kleiber's. However, if you scour the stores you might come across a copy of Furtwängler's exhilarating performance at the 1954 Salzburg Festival – it is reissued from time to time, usually on shoestring European labels, often at a bargain price. Other than that, you might want to listen to Colin Davis's set, recorded in 1990, which is notable for a sonically spectacular reading of the Wolf's Glen scene, complete with an array of extra-musical sound effects; as an overall reading of the opera, though, it can't compete with the two below.

Grümmer, Schock, Otto, Kohn, Prey, Frick; Berlin Deutsche Opera Chorus; Berlin Philharmonic Orchestra; Keilberth.
(EMI CMS7 69342-2; 2 CDs).

Keilberth was one of the finest opera conductors of his or any generation, but he made only a handful of recordings. Of these, this 1958 *Freischütz* is arguably the best. Technically reckless but full of imagination, he warrants comparison with the mighty Furtwängler. Elizabeth Grümmer's flowing soprano is applied to an urgent, sensitive characterization of Agathe, while Lisa Otto makes a delicious Ännchen and Rudolph Schock is a powerful, earnest Max. The young Hermann Prey and the old Gottlob Frick are matchless in the subsidiary roles of Ottokar and the Hermit. The dialogue is included and the sound is orchestrally thin but vocally sumptuous.

Janowitz, Schreier, Mathis, Adam, Weikl, Crass, Vogel; Leipzig Radio Chorus; Staatskapelle Dresden; Kleiber.
(Deutsche Grammophon 415 432-2GH2; 2 CDs).

Carlos Kleiber's father, Erich, was a celebrated conductor of *Der Freischütz* but he never recorded the opera. It was therefore not entirely surprising that Carlos should have chosen *Freischütz* for his first opera recording. What was surprising, however, was his casting, and it is his singers (and the use of actors to speak the dialogue) that prevent this otherwise excellent performance from stealing a march on Keilberth. Gundula Janowitz's Agathe is beautiful but inconsequential (at times she could be singing her shopping list), and Schreier's Max is simply not up to the mark: his throaty tenor is strained above the stave, inaudible beneath. Theo Adam, a fierce Caspar, is the one outstanding solo singer, though

G. BRANDENSTEIN/DGG

The elusive Carlos Kleiber – perhaps the greatest living conductor

there are some splendid choruses. Kleiber's zealously detailed presentation of the orchestral score (magnificently played by the Dresden orchestra) is without equal, even if his obsession with clarity and texture leaves little room for spontaneity.

Euryanthe

Composed 1822–23.
First performed October 25, 1823.
Libretto by Helmine von Chézy.

Synopsis

Act I

In the hall of King Louis VI, Adolar sings of his love for his wife Euryanthe. Lysiart, vowing to prove her unfaithful, wagers his lands against Adolar's. The evil Eglantine, who loves Adolar, persuades Euryanthe to reveal the truth about the death of Adolar's sister, Emma. It emerges that she killed herself by taking poison from a ring.

Act II

Lysiart hears Eglantine admit to having stolen Emma's ring from her tomb and of her plan to use it as a weapon with which to destroy Euryanthe. In return for the ring, Lysiart offers to marry her so that Adolar's lands will be theirs. At court, Lysiart announces that he has won the wager: he produces Emma's ring – proving to Adolar that Euryanthe has shared "their" secret with another. Adolar, convinced that Euryanthe has been unfaithful, takes his wife into the desert to kill her.

Act III

High in the mountains Euryanthe saves her husband's life. Touched by her love, he cannot bring himself to harm her and so leaves her to wander the wastelands. She is found by the King and tells him of Eglantine and Lysiart's trickery. Adolar returns to his castle, where Lysiart and Eglantine are preparing to marry. The plot is revealed, Eglantine is stabbed by Lysiart, who is then led to the dungeons. Adolar and Euryanthe are reunited.

𝄞 *Euryanthe* was Weber's most ambitious opera and, judged purely by its music, it is his greatest. As a piece of theatre, however, it is one of the most complete disasters of the nineteenth century, for its nonsensical libretto is simply one of the worst efforts ever set by a first-rate composer. You can understand how the rehashed chivalric tale might have appealed to a composer keen to write a

Grand Opéra, but it is impossible to see how Weber could have tolerated the incompetence of Helmine von Chézy, who had to rewrite her text nine times – the last five attempts with the composer's direct assistance.

The libretto commits every dramatic blunder in the book, with essential characters dying before the curtain rises and living characters constantly acting contrary to their true natures in order to sustain the action. Yet for some reason this farrago inspired Weber to compose a score of astonishing beauty and theatrical intensity. He saw *Euryanthe* as an opportunity to correct what some critics had seen as the major flaw of *Der Freischütz*, namely that the work had been more Singspiel than opera and that the use of dialogue had slackened the drama. Weber intended *Euryanthe* to "create its effect by means of the combined effects of the sister arts", and if his ambitions were let down by Chézy's text, he nonetheless prefigured Wagner's *Gesamtkunstwerk* in the combination of an unbroken flow of music with thoroughly thought-out stagecraft.

On the whole, the solo contributions are less distinctive than in *Der Freischütz*, but the juxtaposition of two sopranos (Euryanthe and Eglantine) produces some extremely powerful sounds (as it did nearly a century later when Richard Strauss used the same combination in *Elektra*, *Der Rosenkavalier* and *Arabella*), and the tenor role of Adolar has some compulsive episodes of ardent, high-written declamation. Weber compensated for the dramatic weaknesses of the text by setting the vocal score above unusually fluent, multivoice orchestrations and the combination of chorus and orchestra, as in the first scene, is both beautiful and gripping. If the use of leitmotif is less innovative than in *Der Freischütz*, then the employment of key-associations to encapsulate character is a brilliant prototype for Wagner's elaborate systems. (There's an even more explicit link with Wagner – Telramund and Elsa, in *Lohengrin*, were clearly modelled on Lysiart and Eglantine.) Add to this some pungent local colour (the court scenes), bouyant melody (the May Song), vibrant folk-inspired chorus work (the Hunting Chorus), and atmospheric orchestrations (the music relating to Emma and her ring), and you have something that's as close to a silk purse as anyone could possibly have created out of the sow's ear of Helmine von Chézy's libretto.

Norman, Hunter, Gedda, Krause; Leipzig Radio Chorus, Staatskapelle Dresden; Janowski.
(Berlin Classics 001082BC; 3 CDs).

The singing on this excellent performance, originally taped in 1974 by EMI, goes a long way to overcoming the idiocies of Chézy's plot. Jessye Norman and Rita Hunter are two of the most powerful sopranos of their generation, and their contrasting voices – Norman's warm, Hunter's steely – make for some hair-raising listening. Tom Krause is in thrilling voice as the evil Lysiart but even he is overshadowed by Nicolai Gedda's impassioned Adolar, his lyric tenor reaching the silliest of heights with ease. Janowski conducts the ideal support for his singers, and the Dresden forces are luxurious as ever, particularly the chorus. The sound is excellent.

Oberon

Composed 1825–26.
First performed April 12, 1826.
Libretto by James Robinson Planché after Christoph Martin Wieland.

Synopsis

Act I
Having quarrelled over who is the more capricious, Man or Woman, Oberon and Titania have decided to part company until one or the other can find a faithful couple. With Puck's help and the use of a Magic Horn, Oberon sends Sir Huon and his squire Sherasmin to Baghdad to rescue the Caliph's daughter, Reiza.

Act II
Huon and Sherasmin successfully rescue Reiza and her maid Fatima (with whom Sherasmin falls in love) and leave the city by ship. All except Huon are captured and taken to Tunis by pirates.

Act III
Huon liberates his friends while Oberon, who has been reunited with Titania, transports the lovers back to Charlemagne's palace. The opera ends in universal rejoicing.

In almost every respect, *Oberon* was a giant step backwards for Weber. The rambling fantasy demands an absurd number of scene changes, introduces too many superfluous characters and is cluttered with non-singing actors, while the English libretto posed problems to which the non-English-speaking composer had no solutions. Weber wrote to his librettist in February 1825: "The intermixing of so many principal actors who do not sing, the omission of the music in the most important moments – all of these things deprive our *Oberon* the title of an Opera, and will make him unfit for all the other theatres in Europe." And so it has proved.

Weber's final work is notable only for the fairy-music heard at the beginning of Act I, the finales of Acts II and III and, in particular, the overture, which is the finest he ever wrote. The latter's horn call, muted strings and lively wind parts were all highly original and their import did not go unnoticed: Mendelssohn composed his *Overture to a Midsummer's Night Dream* only three months after the opening of *Oberon*.

Grobe, Nilsson, Domingo, Prey, Augér; Bavarian Radio Opera Chorus and Symphony Orchestra; Kubelik.
(Deutsche Grammophon 419 038-2GX2; 2 CDs).

Kubelik makes the most of *Oberon*'s strong points – he keeps things moving along nicely and his attention to orchestral texture is typically fastidious. But Nilsson and Domingo are not suited to Reiza and Huon – the former's soprano is simply too grand while Domingo has neither the required range nor the beauty of line. Perhaps he should have exchanged roles with Donald Grobe, who is a lightweight Oberon. Arleen Augér gives a delightful cameo as the Mermaid. Good sound and energetic playing from the BRSO.

HEINRICH MARSCHNER

b. ZITTAU, GERMANY, AUGUST 16, 1795; d. HANOVER, DECEMBER 14, 1861.

German opera suffered a bleak period between the death of Weber and the rise of Wagner, when the only composer to stake a valid claim to Weber's inheritance was Heinrich Marschner.

He found his voice with *Heinrich IV und d'Aubigné*, a work staged in 1820 by Weber. The two became friends after Marschner's move to Dresden in 1821, and Weber declared, "I will even go so far as to prophesy that such a passionate concern with dramatic truth combined with such a profoundly emotional nature will produce a dramatic composer worthy of our highest respect." However, Weber became threatened by Marschner's imitation of his style and resented the fact that the younger man was more interested in commercial gain than in the promotion of German national opera. Weber in the end ensured that Marschner did not succeed him as *Kapellmeister* in Dresden, so Marschner left the city and toured Germany with his third wife, the singer Marianne Wohlbrück, for whom he composed *Lucretia*, a ham-fisted attempt at Spontini-like Grand Opéra.

In 1827 he moved to Leipzig, collaborating with his brother-in-law on *Der Vampyr*, the most widely acclaimed and lucrative of his operas. In 1831 Marschner became a conductor at the Hoftheater in Hanover (where he was to spend the rest of his life), and two years later his opera *Hans Heiling* was produced in Berlin. *Der Vampyr* was his greatest success, but *Hans Heiling* was his creative peak: the rest of his career was marked by various imitative projects, including two Wagnerian music-dramas, *Kaiser Adolf von Nassau* and *Sangeskönig Hiarne*. Wagner himself dismissed the former as an "exercise in banality", and there's no denying the weakness of quality of Marschner's later work. Nonetheless, he is the strongest link between Weber and Wagner, and he deserves to be known for more than his influence upon *Der fliegende Holländer*.

Der Vampyr

The Vampire

Composed 1827–28.
First performed March 29, 1828.
Libretto by Wilhelm August Wohlbrück, after H.R. Ritter and J. Polidori.

Synopsis

Act I

The vampire Ruthven is told he can remain on earth if he sacrifices three virgins within the next 24 hours. He attacks and murders his first, Janthe, just as Berkley, her father, arrives with a search party. Ruthven is mortally wounded but Aubry revives him by dragging his body into the moonlight. Aubry is shocked when, having helped the killer, he discovers that Ruthven is to marry Malwina, Aubry's great love.

Act II

George and Emmy are celebrating their marriage when Ruthven arrives to take her as his second virgin. George fails to prevent the tragedy but he does manage to shoot the vampire as he flees. Ruthven lies in the moonlight and is once more revived. For his final victim he heads towards Malwina and their wedding. Aubry delays the ceremony and exposes Ruthven as the vampire. As the clock strikes twelve, Ruthven is killed by lightning.

The supernatural was a dominant strain in German culture in the early decades of the nineteenth century. Weber's *Freischütz* was the fourth operatic treatment of its subject within a few years, Mary Shelley's *Frankenstein*, first published in 1818, was translated into German the following year, and in 1822 a dramatization of John Polidori's *The Vampyre* was staged in Dresden – an event attended by Marschner. His opera based on this play duly became one of the century's most popular German operas.

Wagner was present at the premiere, and *Der Vampyr* provided a model for the younger composer when he came to write *Der fliegende Holländer* in 1843. Marschner's chromatic harmony, varied orchestration and vocal style (in which words or phrases are heightened in a manner approximating spoken German) must have made some impact on Wagner, but the primary link between the two lies in Marschner's treatment of the cursed protagonist and his pure female victims, and the way Marschner uses leitmotifs to link each section of the opera to form a continuous whole. Unlike Weber's operas, *Der Vampyr* is the work of a composer prepared to sacrifice melodic beauty to the needs of the drama – and that, after all, was central to Wagner's thought. The score contains enough highlights to justify a return to repertoire, a move to which the BBC made a contribution in 1992 when it broadcast an adaptation of the opera. There is no currently available recording.

Hans Heiling

Composed 1831–32.
First performed May 24, 1833.
Libretto by Philipp Edward Devrient, after a Bohemian legend.

Synopsis

Act I

After a prelude in which Hans Heiling leaves the safety of his mother's underworld (she is the Queen of the Earth Spirits) in order to be near Anna, Hans is upset by Anna's coldness towards him, while she in turn is frightened by Hans and the book of magic he has brought with him. Heiling agrees to burn the book but, later, when he sees Anna dancing with Konrad, he is driven to despair.

Act II

Alone in the forest Anna is confronted by Hans Heiling's mother who demands that she leave her son alone. Anna faints and is then found by Konrad, and the two declare their love for each other. Hans Heiling arrives and insists that Anna honour her promise to marry him. She refuses, whereupon he stabs Konrad and flees.

Act III

Hans appeals to the Earth Spirits for help but they refuse, telling him that Konrad is alive and soon to marry Anna. Hans rushes into the church bent on revenge but as he moves to attack Konrad his mother appears and reminds him of his promise to return home should his heart be broken. The congregation give thanks.

Marschner's finest opera was composed to a libretto originally written for Mendelssohn in 1827. Mendelssohn rejected it because of its obvious resemblance to the folkloric-supernatural worlds of *Der Freischütz* and *Undine*, but Marschner – eager to ride on Weber's coat-tails – was delighted by the similarities that had troubled Mendelssohn.

Though essentially a Singspiel, with simple, frequently folk-based tunes interpolated with spoken dialogue, *Hans Heiling* draws on a miscellany of influences. There are elements of Meyerbeer and Spontini in its expansive choruses and extended scenes, while the spirit world is evoked through ethereal music that's reminiscent of Mendelssohn's recently published *Midsummer Night's Dream* – the prelude is an especially mysterious, symphonic invention, anticipating Wagner's development of the form. Even more important, the work's through-composition marks a step towards Wagnerian music-drama: even when the music becomes tawdry or repetitious, Marschner maintains a compelling sense of propulsion through the use of motifs and key centres. If any evidence were required that Wagner took note of Marschner's operas then it is provided by the "announcement of death" motif in *Die Walküre*, the music of which is taken directly from "Sonst bist du verfallen", at the beginning of the second scene of Act II.

Mohr, Hajóssyová, Seniglova, Eklöf, Markus, Neshyba; Slovak Philharmonic Chorus and Orchestra; Körner.
(Marco Polo 8223306-7; 2 CDs).

Marco Polo have revived a lot of obscure, long-forgotten repertoire, and this is one of the label's most interesting projects. The performance is unlikely to win any awards for its playing or its singing, but there is a missionary zeal to Ewald Körner's conducting that more than compensates for the technical vagaries. The recorded sound is boxy and a little thin, but not distractingly so.

FRANZ SCHUBERT

b. HAMBURG, DECEMBER 6, 1791; d. COBURG, JANUARY 26, 1828.

Convinced that success in the opera house was a guaranteed way of gaining wider renown, Schubert devoted considerable energy to operatic composition, but the mechanics of music-drama constantly defeated him. The world's finest composer of song failed to write a first-rate opera, and of Schubert's sixteen completed works in the genre only three were performed during his lifetime and just one, *Fierrabras*, has achieved any posthumous celebrity.

Schubert's first operatic studies were encouraged by Salieri, who believed that a composer should "prove himself through his mastery of the dramatic arts". He completed his first stage work, *Des Teufels Lustschloss*, in 1813; clearly the work of a student, it was weighed down by an absurd plot and excessive reverence for Gluck, Mozart and Beethoven, but it did suggest something of the melodic facility that was to colour his later work. In 1815 Schubert began teaching at his father's school and during the next twelve months he produced four works for the stage – all of them, according to fashion, in the Singspiel style. It was not until 1819, when he had fallen under the spell of the baritone Johann Michael Vogl, that he completed another work for the theatre. Two operas from 1820, *Die Zwillingsbrüder* and *Die Zauberharfe*, were moderately successful, which perhaps reinforced Schubert's strange notion that the path to fame ran through the opera house. But of his last four operas only the incidental music to *Rosamunde* was performed during his lifetime and he died leaving his final opera, *Der Graf von Gleichen*, incomplete.

Fierrabras

Composed 1823.
First performed February 9, 1897.
Libretto by Joseph Kupelwieser.

Synopsis

Act I

Emma, daughter of King Karl, and Eginhard, a young knight, are in love with each other. Having just defeated the Moors in battle, Karl dispatches Roland with a message of peace, declaring all prisoners free to return to their homes. Among them is Fierrabras who, it emerges, also loves Emma. He sees Eginhard and Emma alone together and is wrongly imprisoned for attempting to abduct her.

Act II

Fierrabras's father Boland imprisons Eginhard and the peace delegation; Florinda, Fierrabras's sister, steals the keys and begins releasing them. However, only Eginhard chooses to leave, while the others, finding arms, barricade themselves into the tower.

Act III

Karl discovers his daughter's relationship with Eginhard and releases Fierrabras. Eginhard asks the king for his help in freeing the peace mission and, accompanied by Fierrabras, the troupe leave for Boland's castle. They arrive just as the knights are to be executed, and the opera ends with Emma and Eginhard and Roland and Florinda reunited. Fierrabras is accepted into the brotherhood of the Frankish knights.

Fierrabras was one of Schubert's rare operatic commissions. It came from the director of the Kärntnertheater who wanted a German opera for the 1822–23 season. Schubert offered two earlier operas but both were rejected for their "unsuitable" libretti and unfeasible stage requirements, so Schubert set to work on a new libretto, *Fierrabras*, which he completed within six months. It too was rejected and it remained unstaged until 1897, when a shortened version was produced in Karlsruhe.

As with all Schubert's stage works, the influences are never far from the surface – in particular, Schubert's use of recurrent motifs owes its prominence to the work of Weber and Hoffmann. But the borrowed stylistic traits are at least carefully assimilated and, though the inept plot could only really have worked had Schubert's dramatic grip been tighter, it is clear that he was working towards a smoother transition between scenes. As you'd expect with Schubert, the melodies are never less than pretty, and some are rather more than that. The duet for two sopranos and the four-part unaccompanied male chorus in Act II are particularly affecting, but the highlight is the romance between Eginhard and Emma at the end of Act I – this is the most touching episode in all Schubert's operas and one of the few passages to approach the level of his great songs.

Protschka, Mattila, Gambill, Hampson, Studer; Schoenberg Choir; Chamber Orchestra of Europe; Abbado. (Deutsche Grammophon 427 341-2GH2; 2 CDs).

In 1988 Claudio Abbado took the brave step of conducting *Fierrabras* in Vienna, a decision that proved to be remarkably well judged. Audiences and critics warmed to Abbado's vibrant reading, which was taped live by Deutsche Grammophon. Abbado throws himself at the score, generating a hum of vitality that does much to quicken the slack pacing of the plot. Josef Protschka, in the title role, and Robert Gambill, as Eginhard, respond well to Schubert's typically ripe phrase-lengths, while Cheryl Studer's light soprano is suitably placed for the role of Florinda and Karita Mattila is a seductive Emma. Good, atmospheric sound.

ALBERT LORTZING

b. BERLIN, OCTOBER 23, 1801; d. BERLIN, JANUARY 21, 1851.

Until quite recently Albert Lortzing was the most popular opera composer in Germany: in the 1958–59 season there were 1044 performances of his operas in 62 German theatres, which meant that only Verdi, Mozart and Puccini pulled in more fans. Since the 1960s, however, the audience for his safe and unsophisticated brand of comic opera has vanished. Today, though his *Zar und Zimmermann* is frequently performed in Germany, elsewhere he is remembered for a single romantic fantasy, *Undine*.

His abilities as composer, conductor, librettist, singer and actor were encouraged by his father, an actor with whom he spent most of his youth touring. One of the few composers to have matured without the benefits of organized tuition, he completed his first opera, *Ali Pascha*, in 1824, and then, after writing a string of Singspiels, committed himself to light-hearted, frequently sentimental comic operas. *Zar und Zimmerman*, premiered in Leipzig in 1837, made Lortzing a household name, and his reputation was enhanced by *Hans Sachs* (1840), a work that's now of interest only in relation to Wagner's *Die Meistersinger*.

By the early 1840s Lortzing was one of Germany's best-known composers, but Germany's erratic royalty system was not producing the financial rewards needed to support his large family. He found full-time work as Leipzig's *Kapellmeister* in 1844, but the appointment lasted less than a year and so in 1845 he looked to fantasy for salvation. The change of direction did not solve his problems: for all their qualities, *Undine* and *Rolands Knappen* didn't spark the same enthusiasm as his comic work. He moved to Vienna in 1846, became *Kapellmeister* at the Theatre an der Wien for an unhappy and brief period, and was eventually compelled to return to acting as a means of subsidizing his composition. Lortzing wrote his last opera, a one-act farce called *Die Opernprobe* (The Opera Rehearsal), for a lifeless and poverty-stricken theatre in Berlin.

Undine

Composed 1845.
First performed April 21, 1845.
Libretto by the composer, after the fairy tale.

Synopsis

Act I

The marriage of Hugo and Undine (adoptive daughter of a fisherman) is attended (in disguise) by Undine's real father, the Water Prince Kühleborn. He knows that Hugo should not have married Undine because he was promised to Berthalda, the daughter of Duke Heinrich; concerned for his daughter's wellbeing, Kühleborn follows the couple back to Hugo's home.

Act II

Undine reveals her true identity to Hugo. Berthalda seems unaffected by the news of Hugo's marriage and informs everyone of her engagement to the King of Naples. Kühleborn discloses that Berthalda is in fact the daughter of the fisherman and then discloses his own identity.

Act III

Undine warms to Berthalda and invites her to live with her and Hugo. Berthalda seduces Hugo, and Undine is carried back into the waters by Kühleborn.

Act IV

As Hugo prepares to marry Berthalda, Undine appears, filling the great hall with water. She drags Hugo into the depths, where Kühleborn forgives him – but only if he remains by his daughter's side in the palace of the water spirits.

Lortzing took his cue for *Undine* from the supernatural operas of Weber, Marschner and above all Hoffmann. Adapting the libretto of Hoffmann's *Undine*, which had been republished in 1843, Lortzing trimmed and tightened the text, in order to place more emphasis on the expressive range of his music, which in many respects resembles Hoffmann's, albeit in a more affluent guise. Folk-based melodies, descriptive orchestration (notably the water spirits' music of Act II), lush harmonies and recurring motifs are applied with a deft hand throughout the opera, and Lortzing shows himself adept at manipulating contrasting musical themes, such as lightness and darkness, water and earth. *Undine* is enlivened by unexpected theatrical irruptions – such as Undine's flooding of the hall in Act IV – but it would be misleading to make any great claims for the overall quality of the score. *Undine* is something of a stepping stone between the operas of Weber and the music-dramas of Wagner, and should be sampled only by those who want the complete picture.

Krause, Protschka, Hampe, Janssen; Cologne Radio Chorus and Symphony Orchestra; Eichhorn.
(Capriccio 60 017-2; 2 CDs).

This is a solid reading of Lortzing's opera, if nothing more than that. Monika Krause makes a passable impression as Undine, and Josef Protschka is easy on the ear as Hugo, though Christiane Hampe strains after seductiveness as Berthalda and John Janssen is unequipped to play the noble Kühleborn. Kurt Eichhorn, a reliable *Kapellmeister*, keeps the pace from dragging, and as with so many provincial opera recordings there is a sense of fraternity to the production that almost camouflages the obvious technical flaws.

OTTO NICOLAI

b. KÖNIGSBERG, GERMANY, JUNE 9, 1810; d. BERLIN, MAY 11, 1849.

"One must have German schooling, but Italian facility must be added to it", Otto Nicolai once remarked. "That is how Mozart came to be, and if I had his spirit I too could produce something good." The Italian-trained composer was not in thrall to the note-spinning of his Italian contemporaries: "I have more intellect than imagination, and therefore composing is more difficult for me than others," he wrote. "People such as Donizetti and the like write continuously without self-criticism." Nicolai was nonetheless one of the first German composers to concede that Italian lyricism had something to offer.

After a difficult childhood Nicolai ran away from home to Berlin where, with the support of a wealthy patron, he was accepted as a pupil by the song composer Carl Friedrich Zelter. In 1833, as organist to the Prussian Academy, he moved to Rome, where he immersed himself in a study of early Italian music. Soon, however, he was drawn towards the opera house, and in 1836 he began working on his first opera. Two years later he received his first commission, and *Enrico II* was given its first performance in Trieste in 1839. Hugely successful, it was followed by three further Italian operas which established Nicolai's reputation as a composer of lyric dramas in the mould struck by Bellini. In 1841 Nicolai was appointed *Kapellmeister* at the Hofoper in Vienna, where he stayed for six years, reworking his early operas and becoming one of the country's most renowned conductors. He founded the Vienna Philharmonic Orchestra in 1842 and created a sensation when he became the first to use Beethoven's *Leonore No. 3* overture as an orchestral interlude before the final act of *Fidelio* (see p.113).

While in Vienna he also composed what was to be his last opera, *Die lustigen Weiber von Windsor*, which the Hofoper turned down; Nicolai resigned his post and moved to Berlin, where, as *Kapellmeister* of the Court Opera, he gave the first performance. He died two months and two days later.

Die lustigen Weiber von Windsor

The Merry Wives of Windsor

Composed 1845–48.
First performed March 9, 1849.
Libretto by Hermann Salomon Mosenthal, after Shakespeare.

Synopsis

Act I

Sir John Falstaff sends identical love letters to Frau Fluth and Frau Reich. They plan revenge for the insult. Ensuring that her possessive husband knows of her plans, Fluth arranges to meet Falstaff. During their meeting Reich arrives, as arranged, to warn Fluth of her husband's arrival. They tumble Falstaff into a basket and prepare to throw it into the river.

Act II

At the inn, Falstaff is once again summoned by Fluth, while her disguised husband does his best to discover the identity of his wife's lover. Falstaff again meets with Fluth but when her husband arrives he has to escape dressed as a woman.

Act III

Fluth and Reich explain the situation to their husbands and discuss how best to punish the philandering Falstaff. They all meet in the park where, disguised, the couples torment the confused Sir John. Eventually, he admits his foolish behaviour and begs forgiveness.

Having failed to unearth a decent libretto despite announcing a competition to find one, Nicolai turned with some desperation to the plays of Shakespeare, though he believed only Mozart could do justice to the material. Yet *Die lustigen Weiber* turned out to be a comic masterpiece, full of witty ensembles, riotous finales and polished orchestrations. For its period it was unusually faithful to its source (Rossini's treatment of *Othello* was far less reverential – see p.161), but its most striking feature is its stylistic duality: the vocal melodies are pure bel canto, but the architecture of the opera (the location and pacing of ensembles, etc) is Germanic, as is Nicolai's use of folksong and the constant reference to the orchestral palette of *Der Freischütz*. Furthermore, Nicolai follows the Singspiel tradition of spoken dialogue, but brings to it a fluency, elegance and joyfulness that, while looking back to the inspirations of Mozart and Weber, anticipates the brilliance and abandon of Johann Strauss II and Franz Lehár.

RECORDINGS OVERVIEW

Of the three studio recordings of *Die lustigen Weiber* two are currently unavailable. Produced in 1963 by EMI, Robert Heger's performance is inspired in its conducting and superlative in its cast, which includes Fritz Wunderlich, Edith Mathis and Gottlob Frick. Bernhard Klee's recording, released by Deutsche Grammophon in 1976, bizarrely replaces dialogue with narration, but aside from this extraordinary revision, Klee and his singers (including Donath, Mathis, Moll and Weikl) present an idiosyncratic, purposeful vision of the opera. Should either of these sets emerge on CD, they would take precedence over the one below.

Donath, Sramek, Brendel, Schmidt, Ahnsjö, Ridderbusch; Bavarian Radio Chorus and Symphony Orchestra; Kubelik. (Decca 443 669-2; 2 CDs).

This recording, made in 1977, has two chief strengths: it includes the complete dialogue. However, most of the cast are well below par, and the situation is not aided by Kubelik's recklessly quick tempi, which place undue pressure on the singers. Almost bereft of humour, this is no more than a technically accurate sketch of what might have been.

FRIEDRICH VON FLOTOW

b. TEUTENDORF, GERMANY, APRIL 27, 1812; d. DARMSTADT, JANUARY 24, 1883.

Born into a highly cultured aristocratic German family, Friedrich von Flotow grew up to be something of a musical magpie character, developing a style in which German gravitas was lightened by gallic flair and Italianate tunefulness. His preference for easy-going melody at the expense of character and dramatic integrity led to some mediocre music, but it was a mediocrity for which audiences were willing to pay, and his most accomplished work, *Martha*, continues to exert its charms.

He studied at the Paris Conservatoire, where he was delighted by the operas (and company) of Cherubini, Rossini, Halévy, Donizetti, Auber and Offenbach. After the July Revolution of 1830 he moved back to Germany where he completed his first opera, *Pierre et Cathérine*, a drama about Peter the Great (like Lortzing's *Zar und Zimmermann*), but in 1835 he returned to Paris where, as a struggling unknown, his work was given only private performances. Not until 1839 did he make a name for himself, when he was asked to collaborate with Albert Grisar and Auguste Pilati on a three-act opera titled *La naufrage de la Méduse* (The Raft of Medusa), a work based on the same terrible shipwreck that Théodore Géricault had depicted in his headline-making painting of 1819. After Grisar pulled out Flotow became responsible for his third of the opera and within six months he and Pilati had completed what proved to be the latter's most successful work. In 1842 the manuscript was destroyed by fire and Flotow rewrote the entire work as *Die Matrosen*, with a new, four-act German libretto by Friedrich Riese. Its enormous popularity convinced Flotow that he had found his ideal theatrical partner in Riese but they collaborated on only two further works, *Alessandro Stradella* and *Martha*. The latter was the composer's most successful opera, thanks partly to the championship of the tenor Mario and the soprano Patti, and it typified Flotow's conflation of styles, fusing the rhythms of Auber and Offenbach, the orchestrations of Marschner and Lortzing, and the song-like qualities of Donizetti and Bellini. Flotow continued to compose, but *Martha* remained the one work readily associated with his name, a situation that has remained unchanged ever since.

Martha

Composed 1847.
First performed November 25, 1847.
Libretto by Friedrich Wilhelm Riese.

Synopsis

Act I

Lady Harriet, maid of honour to Queen Anne, has grown tired of life at court and is desperate to escape the affections of her cousin Lord Tristan. Eventually, accompanied by her maid Nancy (and the unwilling Tristan), she joins a group of girls on their way to Richmond Fair. Disguised as "Martha" and "Julia", Harriet and Nancy are hired by the farmers Plunkett and Lyonel.

Act II

Harriet and Nancy find working life too demanding and are rescued by Tristan, who has a carriage waiting – but not before Lyonel and Plunkett have fallen in love with them.

Act III

Out hunting with the Queen, Harriet is recognized by Plunkett and Lyonel; much to their frustration, she pretends not to know them.

Act IV

When it emerges that Lyonel is the son of the unfairly banished Earl of Derby, Lyonel takes his turn to rebuff Lady Harriet. She is stricken by her loss but Nancy and Plunkett organize another "Fair" outside the farmhouse, where Lyonel and Harriet meet once more and fall into each other's arms.

𝄞 With no dialogue to interrupt the succession of choruses, ensembles and arias, *Martha* floats its protagonists through the plot on a raft of pleasant melodies and gentle orchestrations. The opera's two best-known tunes, the "Last Rose of Summer" (stolen by Flotow from the traditional Irish song "The Grove of Blarney") and the ardent tenor aria "Ach so fromm", present show-stopping opportunities for gifted singers – which explains Mario and Patti's great interest in the work. The Act II "spinning" and "Gute Nacht" quartets are typical of Flotow's pretty style, and once in a while the music comes close to being emotionally engaging – the duet between Harriet and Lyonel in Act II is probably the most genuinely affecting episode.

Flotow knew when he was on to a good thing and the score is littered with repetition, but the opera's main problem is its language: *Martha*'s melodic style is essentially Italian, and it is in Italian translation that the music is best served. Within ten years of its premiere the opera was being sung in translation, as the lead roles were favoured by Italian singers trained in bel canto repertoire. Purists balk at this practice, which is now uncommon outside Italy, but the best-known highlight, "Ach so fromm", is now better known in its Italian version, "M'appari" – of which there are nearly thirty different interpretations currently available on CD.

RECORDINGS OVERVIEW

There have been three studio recordings of *Martha* and, remarkably, all three are available on CD, with EMI's 1968 version just ahead of the pack. Berlin Classics have released a very special live recording: taped at the Berlin Staatsoper in 1944, it captures one of the great German repertoire casts, including a superb Lyonel from Peter Anders, at its very best. The poor sound makes it a collector's item rather than a mainstream choice, but if you get a taste for the opera it is well worth owning.

Rothenberger, Gedda, Prey, Fassbaender; Bavarian State Opera Choir and Orchestra; Heger.
(EMI CMS 7 69339 2; 2 CDs).

This, the first German-language *Martha* and the first stereo recording of the opera, remains a solid first choice. Robert Heger and his compelling cast, which includes the superb quartet of Annelise Rothenberger, Nicolai Gedda, Hermann Prey and Brigitte Fassbaender, really bring Flotow's drama to life. Heger makes a number of cuts and his tempi are not exactly breakneck, but the warmth of the reading makes this the most convincing argument for a German-language *Martha*.

Rizzieri, Tassinari, Tagliavini, Tagliabue; Cetra Chorus; Italian (Turin) Radio Symphony Orchestra; Molinari-Pradelli.
(Fonit Cetra CDO 7; 2 CDs).

This live recording features some questionable singing and a lot of horrible playing, but the husband-and-wife team of Tagliavini and Tassinari as Lyonel and Nancy makes it irresistible. In his duets with Tassinari, the great tenor is in a class of his own, making the strongest possible case for the superiority of the Italian-language version of this opera.

GIOACCHINO ROSSINI

b. PÉSARO, ITALY, FEBRUARY 29, 1792; d. PARIS, NOVEMBER 13, 1868.

The world of Italian opera during much of the first half of the nineteenth century was dominated by one man – Gioacchino Rossini, the creator of nearly forty operas in less than two decades. Donizetti and Bellini – the other two great figures in Italian bel canto – worked in his shadow, and it was only when Verdi reached maturity in the late 1850s that Rossini was replaced at the centre of Italian operatic life. His impact upon the development of opera was immense: he was, for example, the first to do away with unaccompanied recitative, thus making the opera a continual musical fabric, and he was the first to write out all the embellishments for his singers, thereby leaving nothing to chance. But the key to his success was the sheer tunefulness of his music, a quality which seemed to cause him no effort – "Give me a

Gioacchino Rossini pictured during his comfortable semi-retirement

shopping list and I'll set it to music", he once remarked. Yet praise for Rossini was not universal. Berlioz spoke for many non-Italians when he raged against Rossini's conveyor-belt creations: "Rossini's melodic cynicism, his contempt for dramatic expression and good sense, his endless repetition of a single form of cadence, his eternal puerile crescendo and brutal bass drum, exasperated me to such a point that I was blind to the brilliant qualities of his genius, even in his masterpiece, the *Barber of Seville*, exquisitely scored though it is." Rossini's operas do indeed seem simple when compared to Mozart or Berlioz or Wagner. However, this simplicity is part of Rossini's strength. There is a directness and immediacy to his work that is missing from that of his Italian predecessors and contemporaries, whose plots seem ludicrously entangled alongside Rossini's and whose characters appear bloodless by comparison.

He was born to musical parents and by the time he was fourteen he had cultivated an excellent singing voice, mastered the basis of composition and was proficient on the harpsichord, piano, horn, violin and cello. Within three years of entering the Bologna conservatory in 1806 he had composed his first opera, and family contacts soon secured him commissions from various northern Italian theatres. By his twenty-first birthday he had composed ten complete operas,

BARBAIA THE IMPRESARIO

Domenico Barbaia (1778–1841) was one of Italy's wealthiest men and arguably the most influential opera promoter of the century – a remarkable achievement for someone who was, by his own admission, "barely educated". The first of a new breed of impresario, he was characterized by Bellini as a "shady, disreputable man", but he had a great eye for talent. According to the novelist Giuseppe Rovani, "he was a genius for making money, without paying attention to the means. . . . He was an inexorable usurer of composers, singers and dancers. He sniffed thus the odour of true merit, like a fox that, ever from afar, raising its muzzle in the air, catches the scent of a pullet."

Before moving into opera, he made his millions running Italy's largest gambling empire, founded upon the obsession for the recently invented game of roulette. In addition, he dreamed up the recipe for the delicacy known as Barbajada, a mixture of whipped cream, coffee and chocolate, which became a café-society favourite in northern Italy. In 1808, aged just thirty but already enormously wealthy, he obtained (through fantastically dishonest means) the licences of Naples' royal theatres, the San Carlo and the Fondo, and would later take over La Scala in Milan and the Kärntnertortheater in Vienna. In spite of his blunt manner and all-embracing lack of sophistication, he did more than anyone to launch the careers of Mercadante, Weber, Donizetti, Bellini, and, most importantly, Rossini – who was happy to admit Barbaia's "genius" for anticipating public taste, just as he was happy to take the impresario's mistress, the soprano Isabella Colbran, as his first wife.

An outstandingly mercenary man, Barbaia was perfectly happy to allow the opera-going gentry to take out long-term leases on seats in his theatre, regardless of how badly they behaved whenever they decided to turn up for a show. A contemporary writer recorded that at San Carlo each seat in the stalls "lifts up like the lid of a box, and has a lock to fasten it. There are in Naples enough gentlemen to hire by the year the first four rows next to the orchestra, who take the key of the chair home with them when the opera is finished, lifting up the seat and leaving it locked." As is prone to happen today, this meant that whenever a patron failed to show (and this happened more than not), a seat was left empty, a practice guaranteed to aggravate less wealthy lovers of opera. Rossini himself resented the practice but there was little he could do to remedy the situation. Indeed, he was made to jump through hoops as part of his contract with Barbaia, for apart from having to compose two operas a year (which included *Otello* and *La donna del lago*) he was forced to prepare other composers' music for performance as well as see to administration. As he later wrote, "If he had been able to, Barbaia would have put me in charge of the kitchen as well."

The kitchen was perhaps the fulcrum of Barbaia's world – it was said of him that the only two people with whom he was ever cordial were his housekeeper and his cook. But if his tastes were more earthy than aesthetic, there is no doubt that the European opera scene owed an enormous debt to his unflagging energy. And there is no better example of that energy than the aftermath of the fire that destroyed the San Carlo opera house in February, 1816. Surveying the wreckage, King Ferdinand remarked casually it would be wonderful if he could "attend the ballet" in the opera house on his next birthday, eleven months thence. Barbaia rose to the challenge, and just three hundred days later, thanks to his tireless fundraising, Naples had a new opera house. Described by Stendhal as "a symphony of gold and silver", it is still standing today.

many of them foreshadowing the wit and spirit of his later works, though they tended to be rather static and repetitious. Not until the composition of *La scala di seta* in 1812 and *Tancredi* in 1813 did Rossini appear to hit his stride. By the time he came to write *L'italiana in Algeri* it was clear that not only had he hit his stride, but he was well into it. For the next four years Rossini could do no wrong: he produced a string of brilliant comic operas, including *Il turco in Italia*, *Il barbiere di Siviglia*, *La Cenerentola* and *La gazza ladra* , all of which received performances right across Europe.

In 1817 Rossini moved to Naples, where he devoted most of his energy to serious opera, a genre to which he was rarely as well attuned as to comedy, though *Otello* and *Semiramide* must be counted among his greatest achievements. In 1824, aged only thirty-two, he moved to Paris, where he took up the directorship of the Théâtre-Italien and composed four works for the Opéra, the last of which, *Guillaume Tell*, caused a furore. Its scale and musical variety were unprecedented in French opera, and while some people found it overblown, most greeted it with enthusiasm, and the opulence and expansiveness of *Tell* – in its Italian translation as in the original French – had a profound impact on composers such as Bellini, Donizetti and Meyerbeer.

Yet Rossini composed no more operas. His decision to retire at the age of thirty-seven was due partly to the death of his mother, partly to his weakening health, and partly to the realization that his brand of opera was unlikely to thrive as it had done during the preceding twenty years. *Tell* had been a one-off attempt by Rossini to re-invent himself; but writing it had a taken a lot out of him and, as he knew, Meyerbeer and Donizetti found it much easier to devise works on a heroic scale. He wanted to bow out at the peak of his powers and the height of his popularity.

He remained in Paris as the director of the Théâtre-Italien until 1836, returned to Italy as director of the Bologna conservatory, then in 1855 was drawn back to Paris, where he became the country's pre-eminent musical pedagogue, holding court to just about every celebrated European composer and musician – including Wagner, of whom he approved, but for whose music he had little patience. Rossini died thirty-nine years after composing his last opera, and was buried in Père Lachaise, near Chopin, Cherubini and Bellini. The great soprano Adelina Patti, of whom Rossini had been extremely fond and who later recorded some of his music, sang at the funeral. In 1887 his body was disinterred and sent to Florence, where he was re-buried attended by a crowd of 6000.

The popularity of Rossini's operas had begun to wane as early as 1840, and within five years of his death all but a few had been forgotten. Towards the end of the century, however, they began a hesitant come-back, a revival that accelerated so quickly in the twentieth century that "Rossinian" is now as established a term as "Wagnerian". The former is effectively the antithesis of the latter, signifiying music that is instantly accessible, effortlessly entertaining and which brings a smile to the face; or anything with sparkle and fizz. D.H. Lawrence's assessment neatly sums up the appeal of Rossini: "I love Italian opera – it's so reckless. Damn Wagner, and his bellowings at Fate and death. . . . I like the Italians who run all on impulse, and don't care about their immortal souls, and don't worry about the ultimate."

La scala di seta

The Silken Ladder

Composed 1812.
First performed May 9, 1812.
Libretto by Giuseppe Foppa, after de Planard.

Synopsis

In defiance of her tutor Dormont, Giulia has married Dorvil, who climbs to her room each night on a silken ladder she lowers for him. Hearing that Dormont wants her to marry Dorvil's friend Blansac, Giulia determines to trick Blansac into falling in love with her cousin Lucilla. All goes to plan until Giulia's servant Germano hears her musing about a rendezvous – thinking Blansac is her lover, he congratulates him on his luck. Blansac is delighted at the prospect of an assignation with Giulia. Lucilla and Germano hide in Giulia's room, followed by Dorvil, until, at the stroke of midnight, Blansac finally appears. He is scared into hiding by the arrival of Dormont, who discovers each in their hiding places and demands to know what is going on Giulia then emerges to tell him of her marriage to Dorvil and, after Blansac agrees to marry Lucilla, Dormont gracefully resigns himself to the situation.

This one-act opera, the last of three Rossini wrote for the Teatro San Moisè in Venice, is an example of the Italian predilection for comedies of forbidden love: another such comedy, *Il matrimonio segreto* (see p.84), provided the model for *La scala di seta*, while *Don Pasquale* (see p.178) shows the continuing strength of the tradition in the mid-nineteenth century. With its carefully choreographed arrivals and discoveries, accompanied by the adroit use of screens, windows and closets, the libretto of *La scala di seta* also has strong affinities with the world of Beaumarchais and later French farceurs, and most of the characters are as one-dimensional as in any bedroom farce. Speed rather than depth is the essence of this opera's attraction, and it gets off to a cracking start: the overture (which was famous as a concert item even when the opera itself lay forgotten) is thrilling and a show-starter, establishing the sharp, repetitive rhythms that are a feature of most of the opera, right through to the frenetic denouement. Although there's little time for introspection, Giulia and Dorvil's cavatinas contain some touching melody, Germano is given music of dreamy resignation at the close, and Rossini makes clear his affection for the sozzled Germano (the opera's most substantial character), especially in his early duet with Giulia, "Io so c'hai buon core".

Corbelli, Ringholz, Vargas, de Carolis; English Chamber Orchestra; Viotti. (Claves CD50-9219-20; 2 CDs).

Claves assembled a young, enthusiastic cast for their 1992 recording of this operatic gem. Alessandro Corbelli is a delicious Germano, with just the right amount of bluster, and he is especially good in ensemble passages – especially with Teresa Ringholz's Giulia. Ramón Vargas is a superb Rossini tenor, his warm, easily floated voice making light work of Dorvil's high tessitura. The playing of the ECO is rather dry, but Viotti has a fine grasp of Rossinian style and his flexible pulse allows just the right balance of freedom and discipline.

Tancredi

Composed 1813.
First performed February 6, 1813.
Libretto by Gaetano Rossi, after Voltaire.

Synopsis

Act I

Syracuse, the eleventh century. After returning from exile in Sicily, Tancredi, in disguise, prevents Orbazzano from marrying Tancredi's lover Amenaide. The resentful Orbazzano intercepts a letter from Amenaide to Tancredi and produces it as evidence that she is in contact with the Saracen Solimar – the enemy of the Sicilians – and accuses her of treason. Amenaide is imprisoned, sentenced to death, rejected by Tancredi and disowned by her father, Argirio. Her only hope is the arrival of a champion who will fight for her honour.

Act II

Languishing in her cell, Amenaide determines to die with dignity and faithful to Tancredi. As Orbazzano is escorting her to the place of execution, the disguised Tancredi steps forward and challenges Orbazzano as Amenaide's champion – even though he believes she is guilty. He is victorious and leads the Sicilians to victory in battle. The dying Solimar assures Tancredi of Amenaide's innocence, and the opera ends in vindication and rejoicing.

Commissioned by Venice's main opera house, La Fenice, *Tancredi* is Rossini's first great opera seria. It's a work of bold strokes, which heroically overcomes the weaknesses of its libretto: whereas the original version of the story, Voltaire's *Tancrède*, has the lovers meeting just once, at the beginning, Gaetano Rossi's ham-fisted adaptation is punctuated by duets and ensembles that rob the tale of its underlying tension, which depends on the notion that Tancredi and Amenaide are unable to communicate with one another. Thanks to Rossini's glowing music, and despite the on-stage bickering between the lead singers (the curtain had to be brought down during Act II), the first production was a huge success, and its popularity was further consolidated by the gondoliers' adoption of the music to Tancredi's entrance aria "Di tanti palpiti" – this irritatingly memorable tune haunted the Venetian canals until the arrival, some years later, of Verdi's "La donna è mobile". Rossini prepared an alternative version for a production in Ferrara in 1833, but the public made it clear that they didn't much care for the new ending, in which Tancredi is mortally wounded and remains ignorant of Amenaide's innocence until moments before his death, and so Rossini created a fusion of the two editions, preserving some of the Ferrara revisions but reinstating the Venetian finale. It was in this form that the opera was performed until its disappearance in the 1840s, but modern revivals invariably revert to the first version.

Writing of *Tancredi*, the poet Giuseppe Carpani observed: "cantilena, and always cantilena, beautiful cantilena, new cantilena, magic cantilena, rare cantilena." Indeed, *Tancredi* boasts some of Rossini's most memorable melodies, with equal doses of soulful melancholy and acrobatic high jinks, contained within a structure that is surprisingly fluid, even though the numbers are separated by secco recitative. Momentum is created by the manipulation of contrast: each ensemble and quite a few of the arias move rapidly between different emotional states, with changes in key and harmony to accommodate the shifts. Rossini uses the old formula of the three-part number to dramatize complex states of mind, and he similarly makes maximum use of another retrogressive feature – assigning a female voice (a mezzo) to the male title role, a role whose difficulty goes a long way to explain why *Tancredi* fell out of the repertoire within ten years of the composer's retirement.

Horne, Cuberli, Palacio, Zaccaria; La Fenice Chorus and Orchestra; Weikert.
(Sony S3K39073; 3 CDs).

This performance, recorded live in 1983 in the theatre where *Tancredi* was premiered, really captures the spirit of the opera. Marilyn Horne, a celebrated Tancredi, was past her best when she made this recording, but her musicianship, dramatic perception and powerful declamation more than compensate for any technical fragility – she scales the extended heights of "Di tanti palpiti" through sheer force of character. Lella Cuberli's fresh-voiced coloratura is well suited to the florid demands of Amenaide, while Ernesto Palacio just about manages Argirio's high-lying role, though he is a wooden actor. Ralf Weikert could be more flexible, but he has a keen sense of momentum and a good ear for instrumental colour.

Podles, Jo, Olsen, Spagnoli, di Micco; Capella Brugensis; Collegium Instrumentale Brugense; Zedda.
(Naxos 8660037-8; 2 CDs).

This 1994 recording surprised many when it was released by the super-budget Naxos label. The production standards are exceptional and the casting, headed by the Polish mezzo Ewa Podles and the Korean coloratura soprano Sumi Jo, is world-class. The former is a proud and heady Tancredi, the latter is an electrifying Amenaide, while the American Rossini tenor Stanford Olsen is superlative as Argirio. The nimble period-instrument orchestra and small chorus are conducted with wit and spirit by the Rossini specialist Alberto Zedda, and the recorded sound is outstanding for the price.

L'italiana in Algeri

The Italian Girl in Algiers

Composed 1813.
First performed May 22, 1813.
Libretto by Angelo Anelli.

Synopsis

Act I

Mustafà, the Bey of Algiers, wants his wife Elvira to marry an Italian slave, Lindoro, so that he may take an Italian wife. Coincidentally, an Italian ship is reported wrecked off the coast. Two of its passengers, Isabella and her suitor Taddeo (whom she presents as her uncle), are taken prisoner. Isabella is looking for her lover – Lindoro. Mustafà asks Lindoro to accompany Elvira to Venice – which he accepts as a chance to escape – leaving the Bey free to entertain Isabella. She charms Mustafà and persuades him to give her Lindoro as a slave.

Act II

Isabella and Lindoro plan their escape. Lindoro tells the Bey that Isabella wants to make the Bey her "Pappatacci" – the title given to men who allow their women absolute freedom. Isabella prepares the ceremony, and makes the Bey swear to remain "deaf and blind" to all her enterprises. Lindoro and Isabella are accompanied by the other Italian captives to their waiting ship, which the Bey has been duped into thinking is part of the ceremony. Taddeo is left behind and realizes that they have been tricked, whereupon he alerts Mustafà; the Bey, wishing to remain true to the "Pappatacci", at first does nothing, but finally wakes to the deception, renounces Italian women and begs his wife for forgiveness.

Rossini composed *L'italiana in Algeri* as a favour to Cesare Gallo, the impresario of the crisis-laden Teatro San Benedetto in Venice. When the little-known Carlo Coccia failed to deliver a promised opera, Gallo turned to Rossini for help. With time short and Gallo increasingly hysterical, Rossini picked up a libretto that had already been set by Luigi Mosca in 1808, had it revised (it's not known by whom), and composed the two-and-a-quarter-hour score in just twenty-seven days, with Gallo standing behind him for much of the time. As Rossini later wrote to a friend, "Nothing primes inspiration more than necessity, whether it be the presence of a copyist waiting for your work or the prodding of an impresario tearing his hair. In my time, all the impresarios in Italy were bald at thirty." Rossini's creativity under duress was rewarded with rave notices: one reviewer noted that the opera was greeted with "deafening, continuous general applause", and judged that it was certain to "find a place among the finest works of genius and art". Stendhal was equally convinced and proclaimed *L'italiana* "perfection in the opera buffa style . . . as gay as our world is not".

The pacing of this opera is manic and the comedy thoroughly daft – as exemplified by the "sneezing" quintet (part of the Act II escape plan) and the Pappatacci coronation (almost certainly a parody of Masonic induction ceremonies) – but *L'italiana* carried a serious purpose. Italy had been an occupied nation since the coming of Napoleon (and would remain so after his fall), so Rossini's inclusion of a quote from the "Marseillaise" just before Isabella's inflammatory "Pensa alla patria" (Think of the homeland) was an unambiguously political gesture – indeed, the song found its way into music-boxes and barrel-organs and, prior to Verdi's "Ah, Pensiero" (from *Nabucco*), it was one of Italy's most popular anthems. The heroine Isabella, scornful of her captors and quicker witted than they, is a figure who would be at home in an opera seria setting, and her music is the opera's most serious and melancholic.

That said, the traditions of commedia dell'arte lie behind the opera's drastic changes of pace and mood, and in the characterization of the buffoonish Mustafà and idiotic Taddeo you can clearly detect the clownish personalities of Italian street theatre. Their music is full of traditional buffa silliness, including patter songs and wild intervals that leap out of the bass range for which both roles are scored. As for Lindoro, he's an off-the-peg sentimental tenor, but he does have one fine aria, once a favourite of lyric tenors. Richly varied, and populated by some of opera's most likable characters, *L'italiana in Algeri* is one of Rossini's most immediate works, embodying Leigh Hunt's description of Rossini's comedies as "the genius of sheer animal spirits".

RECORDINGS OVERVIEW

In addition to our first-choice recordings of *L'italiana*, two other sets merit a mention. Silvio Varviso's 1963 recording for Decca is marred by what may be Teresa Berganza's least convincing performance on record, but has a fine Lindoro from Luigi Alva – star of numerous Rossini recordings – and a superb Taddeo from Rolando Panerai. Claudio Abbado's 1987 recording for Deutsche Grammophon is very well sung, with outstanding work from Ruggero Raimondi, Agnes Baltsa and Frank Lopardo, but some lucklustre conducting weakens the impact.

Simionato, Sciutti, Valletti, Petri; La Scala Chorus and Orchestra; Giulini.
(EMI CHS 7 64041 2; 2 CDs).

Taped in the studio after a 1953 La Scala production in which Franco Zeffirelli made his operatic directing debut, this performance glows with confidence and good humour. Giulini shows an impeccable feel for shape and gets some sparkling energy out of the orchestra. The casting is a model of its kind, with Graziella Sciutti a spirited Elvira and Giulietta Simionato a graceful and deliciously sly Isabella. Cesare Valletti's Lindoro is firm but sensitive and Mario Petri and Marcello Cortis are ideal character-basses, hamming it up throughout. The score is heavily cut, and the mono sound will be a drawback for some, but this is a priceless recording.

Horne, Ramey, Battle, Palacio, Zaccaria; Prague Philharmonic Chorus; I Solisti Veneti; Scimone.
(Erato 2292-45404-2; 2 CDs).

The glories of this recording are almost exclusively vocal. Marilyn Horne's ringing, virtuosic display is alone in standing comparison to Simionato, while Kathleen Battle is less characterful than Sciutti but by far the more beautiful in tone. Samuel Ramey uses his magnificent bass with outstanding imagination and flair, though his Mustafà does make the Taddeo of Domenico Trimarchi sound commonplace. Scimone seems to spend much of the time with his head in the score and there are times when he ploughs on in defiance of his singers' nuances, but this is a beautiful-sounding performance.

Il turco in Italia

The Turk in Italy

Composed 1814.
First performed August 14, 1814.
Libretto by Felice Romani, after Mazzolà.

Synopsis

Act I

A Neapolitan gypsy camp, 1850. Having fled Turkey, Zaida is in mourning for her fiancé, Selim, whom she has left behind. The playwright Prosdocimo enters the camp in search of material for a new drama and is followed by Geronio, who is looking for a fortune-teller to advise him on how best to cure his wife, Fiorilla, of her flightiness. At the port Selim disembarks and almost immediately begins to flirt with Fiorilla, which angers her latest lover, Narciso. Selim prepares his ship for departure (with the intention of taking Fiorilla), but Zaida arrives and achieves a reconciliation with him. Then Narciso, Fiorilla and Geronio turn up, complicating the situation.

Act II

Geronio is approached by Selim, who suggests that he buy Fiorilla from him. Zaida and Fiorilla then invite Selim to choose between them, but Zaida recoils, regretting having invited such a cattle-market. Prosdocimo tells Geronio that the Turk intends to abduct his wife during the evening's masked ball. Zaida and Narciso sow confusion at the ball by dressing exactly like Fiorilla and Selim; when the dust settles, Selim and Zaida leave Italy together and Geronio and Fiorilla are reunited. Prosdocimo has the material he wanted.

Il turco in Italia was Rossini's first collaboration with Bellini's librettist Felice Romani (although he had set one of the poet's pre-existing texts the year before), and they appear to have enjoyed the experience. Romani understood the composer's love of pastiche and parody, providing him with a commedia dell'arte scenario that gave Rossini plenty of opportunity to mock traditions that he had helped cultivate in the first place. Prosdocimo, a one-man Greek chorus, makes the satire explicit. When he first encounters the gypsies, for example, he remarks with delight "Local colour!"; and when Selim is reunited with Zaida, Prosdocimo suggests that a chair be made ready since at this point the heroine normally faints – and when no-one falls to the ground he is greatly disappointed that the plot has deviated from the norm. Similarly ironic is the delightful Act I trio "Un marito scimunito", in which Geronio and Narciso dispute the comic roles they have been allotted by "the poet", with Rossini adding insult to injury by scoring the altercation as a piece of typical opera buffa patter.

Fiorilla is the only major solo role in an opera which derives much of its charm from its ensemble set pieces – in this respect, as in the subject of amorous errancy and reconciliation, *Il turco* resembles Mozart's *Così*. The rumbustious finale to Act I, the hilarious bass duet in which Geronio and Selim threaten each other, and the Act II quintet "Oh, guardate che accidente" are masterpieces of vitality and timing – the last, which occurs at the ball, where Geronio suffers from double vision, is especially clever, involving all the parties in a whirlwind of increasing panic. The Act II finale itself is something of a disappointment – probably written by another composer, it carries the inappropriately sober moral that everyone should be happy with their lot.

Alaimo, Jo, Fissore, Giménez; Ambrosian Opera Chorus; Academy of St Martin in the Fields; Marriner.
(Philips 434 128-2; 2 CDs).

This fine 1991 performance captured two stars in the making – Sumi Jo and Raúl Giménez. Jo's Fiorilla is perhaps too polite, lacking Callas's ball-breaking personality, but Giménez is a genuine lyric tenor and his timbre is beautifully placed for Rossini singing. The bass Simone Alaimo is a fine Selim and Susanne Mentzer gives a solid performance as the long-suffering Zaida. Conducting a bright and responsive orchestra, Marriner allies quick tempi with an unerring feel for ensemble. The digital recording is bright and realistically balanced.

Rossi-Lemeni, Callas, Calabrese, Stabile; La Scala Chorus, La Scala Orchestra; Gavazzeni.
(EMI CDS7 49344-2; 2 CDs).

Made in 1954, this is a heavily cut version of *Il turco*, but it's a classic nonetheless. Callas's dazzlingly temperamental performance shows a talent for light comedy that was not revealed as often as it should have been, and her timing and delicate phrasing are delightful. Rossi-Lemeni made very few recordings that did justice to him, but this was one of them, and his Selim is a lascivious charmer. Nicolai Gedda is a youthful Narciso, his light tenor navigating the difficult music with effortless grace; and the sixty-nine-year-old Mariano Stabile makes an unforgettable impression as Prosdocimo – one of the greatest character-baritones of the century, he is in shaky voice, but the experience of nearly half a century's operatic singing shines throughout.

Il barbiere di Siviglia

The Barber of Seville

Composed 1816.
First performed February 20, 1816.
Libretto by Cesare Sterbini, after Beaumarchais.

Synopsis

Act I

Passing himself off as a poor student called Lindoro, Count Almaviva is trying to seduce Rosina, the ward of the aged Doctor Bartolo, who would like to marry her himself. Figaro, the Count's barber and factotum, offers to help. Inside Bartolo's house, Rosina writes a letter to Lindoro. News is brought by the music master Don Basilio that Count Almaviva is in town, looking for Rosina. Basilio suggests a campaign of misinformation against the Count, and Bartolo asks for the marriage contract between himself and Rosina to be drawn up immediately. Disguising himself as a drunken soldier with an official order demanding lodging, Almaviva gains access to Bartolo's house, where he whispers to Rosina that he is really Lindoro. Bartolo and Don Basilio attempt to make him leave, but he refuses to budge and slips Rosina a letter, which she exchanges for a laundry list. The scene gets rowdy, soldiers arrive to find out what is happening, the Count finally leaves, and the act ends in confusion.

Act II

The Count returns to the house, this time disguised as the music teacher Don Alonso, who has been called in to replace the unwell Don Basilio. He soon gains the trust of Bartolo and, with his blessing, gives Rosina her lesson. While shaving Bartolo, Figaro steals a key that will enable the Count and Rosina to elope. Basilio makes an unexpected return but Almaviva bribes him into playing along with the plot. Even so, Bartolo is suspicious and tries to rush the marriage by sending Basilio to find a notary. Bartolo manages to persuade Rosina that Lindoro has been working for Almaviva, and that he does not really love her. So upset is Rosina that she confesses her plan to elope with the student that very night, but all is saved when Lindoro returns, reveals his true identity and proclaims his love. Things get worse when Basilio returns with the notary, but after more bribery he agrees to witness Rosina's marriage to the Count. Bartolo, returning to find Rosina married, is initially furious but soon calms down when he realizes he will not have to pay a dowry.

Rossini was a longtime admirer of Beaumarchais, and regarded his Figaro plays as ideal material for an opera. There was no point trying to improve on what Mozart and da Ponte had done with *The Marriage of Figaro*, but Rossini saw unexploited potential in the libretto for Paisiello's treatment of the *Barber* (see p.83), which recounted the early adventures of Figaro, Almaviva and many of the rest of the cast. When Rossini approached the elder composer for permission to set his libretto, Paisiello cheerfully gave his blessing, thinking it impossible that Rossini could produce anything more successful. The first performance of Rossini's version – titled *Almaviva, or The Useless Precaution*, to distinguish it from the earlier work – was played to an audience stuffed with Paisiello supporters, whose sole aim was to disrupt the upstart's new opera. "All the whistlers of Italy seemed to have given themselves for this performance", reported one observer, but by the second night the hecklers were silenced and Rossini's *Barber* was on the way to being hailed as the greatest of Italian comic operas.

Rossini is said to have composed the three-hour score in just two weeks, which seems unlikely even for a man of his prodigious skill. Yet it's known that the Teatro Argentina bullied him relentlessly to get the piece finished on time, and so pressing was the schedule that Rossini had to revise an older overture that he'd used twice already. "The public was completely satisfied", the composer reported, as indeed it was, for the *Barber* is remarkable for what Verdi characterized as an "abundance of true musical ideas". Tuneful, vivacious and inventive in its deployment of the orchestra, *Il barbiere* is a work of unbelievable energy, especially during the first act, in which nine of the most popular moments in all opera are packed into less than forty minutes of music.

This volcanic creativity is harnessed to a scrupulous attention to structure, which maximizes the impact of the frequent musical explosions. The most famous of these is Figaro's riotous Act I aria "Largo al factotum", a virtuosic demonstration of the so-called "Rossini crescendo", whereby tension and release are generated through the repetition of crisply articulated short phrases, which become louder and faster as the aria proceeds. The effect is unique to Rossini, and *Il barbiere* has a number of examples of it. There are moments of tranquillity too, usually centering on the lovers (eg Almaviva's "Ecco ridente" and their duet "Contro un cor"), though Rosina is for the most part a firecracker of a coloratura mezzo-soprano role. In short, Rossini's opera is a perfect fusion of the elegant wit of Beamarchais and the knockabout humour of commedia dell'arte.

RECORDINGS OVERVIEW

There have been many fine recordings of *Il barbiere* – a number of them in stereo – but their availability is erratic. Of those currently out of the catalogue, perhaps the most essential is Tullio Serafin's 1952 EMI recording with Victoria de los Angeles, Nicola Monti and the under-recorded Gino Bechi. Deutsche Grammophon's 1960 set, featuring Gianna d'Angelo's delicate Rosina and another Almaviva from Monti, is similarly invaluable but inaccessible. Of those that are available but flawed, de los Angeles's second recording for EMI (this time with Vittorio Gui conducting) suffers from a weak supporting cast, while Cecilia Bartoli's account of Rosina (on Decca) is a remarkable display of technique and stamina for a twenty-two-year-old, but misses the character's warmth and personality. Placido Domingo had a go at the baritone role of Figaro for Deutsche Grammophon in 1991, with Abbado in charge. Only the great tenor's truest fans need apply.

Callas, Gobbi, Alva, Ollendorff, Zaccaria; Philharmonia Chorus and Orchestra; Galliera.
(EMI CDS7 47634-8; 2 CDs).

This is one of Callas's most celebrated performances, and rightly so – she swoons and swoops her way through Rosina's music in a way that's entirely unique. As always, her partnership with Tito Gobbi is a joy, and he sings the role of Figaro with great expression and nuance. Luigi Alva, one of the rare breed of true Rossini tenors, recorded the role of Almaviva four times: this, his first, is arguably the best, with a delicious turn of phrase and some lovely floated head notes, all coloured with a finely judged portamento. The remaining cast is excellent and Galliera gives stylish, energetic direction. Magnificent stuff.

Berganza, Ausensi, Benelli, Corena, Ghiaurov; Naples Scarlatti Chorus and Orchestra; Varviso.
(Decca 417 164-2DM2; 2 CDs).

Berganza's two readings of Rosina (1964, 1971) are generally thought of as the best sung on record. This, the earlier version, is perhaps slightly the better: her warm and generous mezzo is ideal for the part and she tackles the coloratura with skill and finesse, dropping in a few high Cs for good measure. Her supporting cast is strong: Ugo Benelli gives a cultured portrayal of Almaviva, while Manuel Ausensi's wild Figaro introduces a devil-may-care frisson that's unrivalled even by Gobbi. Varviso's conducting is not the most exciting, but he has a fine ear for detail.

Otello

Othello

Composed 1816.
First performed December 4, 1816.
Libretto by Francesco Maria Berio di Salsa, after Shakespeare.

Synopsis

Act I

The victorious Othello returns to Venice where he is greeted by his servant Iago who, with Rodrigo, is plotting the Moor's destruction. Elmiro, Desdemona's father, intercepts a love letter from his daughter to Othello, thinking it is intended for Rodrigo. Desdemona loves Othello and does not realize that her father has offered her in marriage to Rodrigo. The wedding is planned and only at the last minute does she realize that she is to marry Rodrigo. Her horror is assuaged when Othello marches in and confirms that she is pledged to him.

Act II

Rodrigo begs Desdemona to reconsider but his situation takes a turn for the worse when Iago hands Desdemona's letter to Othello, who takes it to be addressed to Rodrigo. Othello fights a duel with Rodrigo and Elmiro damns his daughter.

Act III

The Senate has exiled Othello; Desdemona is desolate and prays for his return. While she sleeps he climbs through her window and, deaf to her cries of innocence, stabs her to death. The Doge, Elmiro and Rodrigo enter. Iago is killed trying to murder Rodrigo, but he confesses his intrigue before dying. Unaware that Desdemona is dead, Rodrigo withdraws his claim to Desdemona's hand, the Senate pardons Othello and Elmiro grants permission for Othello to marry his daughter. Othello stabs himself.

Rossini's *Otello* is the first known operatic setting of the play, though the relationship between Shakespeare's text and the words concocted by Francesco di Salsa is a distant one. Stendhal dismissed di Salsa as an "unmentionable literary hack", while Byron, having witnessed a performance in Venice, was beside himself with indignation: "They have been crucifying Othello into an opera – Music good but lugubrious – but as for the words! – all the real scenes with Iago are cut – & the greatest nonsense instead." But for all its failings as a piece of music-theatre, *Otello* contains some remarkable music, and it's notable that musicians have tended to be far more enthusiastic about it than have literary types. Meyerbeer commented, "what is so extraordinary is that its beauties are quite un-Rossini-like. First-rate declamation, continuously impassioned recitative, mysterious accompaniments full of local colour and, in particular, the style of the old romances brought to the highest perfection." Had Verdi – who thought Rossini's *Otello* a masterpiece – not produced his own miraculous version of the play in 1887, Rossini's work would probably not have drifted out of the repertoire.

Admittedly, Rossini's decision to cast all three male leads as tenors does lead to passages of textural monotony, but then again the combination of high male voices is often immensely effective – especially during Othello and Rodrigo's Act II confrontation, in which high Cs explode all over the place. Othello is a relent-

MALIBRAN'S DESDEMONA

The soprano Maria Malibran (1808–1836) was one of the greatest singers of all time – she was adored by Bellini, Donizetti, Lafayette, Hans Christian Andersen, Chopin and Paganini; Verdi thought her "sublime"; and Liszt was proud to admit that he had "sat at the feet of Maria Malibran". The daughter of the renowned tenor and singing teacher Manuel Garcia and the sister of the amazingly talented Pauline Viardot (who once sight-read the part of Isolde for Wagner – from Wagner's almost illegible manuscript), Malibran was famed throughout Europe, not just for her singing, but also for her wild lifestyle, her striking beauty, and lachrymose personality. Her early death put the seal on a Romantic legend.

One of her most celebrated roles was as Rossini's Desdemona, a part she learned when the Garcia family went to New York in 1826, becoming the first to introduce Italian opera to the United States. It took her just six days to memorize the three-hour opera, but as an eighteen year old of limited experience she was unable to capture the intense mixture of love and fear demanded by the Moor's wife. The final scene proved especially difficult and her father, who was playing her husband, went to great pains to illustrate how he thought the death should be played. His patience eventually snapped and grabbing his stage dagger he ran at the terrified girl screaming – "You will do it, my daughter, and if you fail in any way I will strike you dead." Come the opening night all went well until the penultimate scene, when her father walked onto the stage carrying a real and very large knife. Not realizing that he had simply mislaid the mock weapon, Malibran ran in terror and tried to climb the curtains in her desperation to get away; Garcia grabbed her by her hair and dragged her to the floor, where a fight ensued. Malibran bit her father's hand, he screamed, and the audience, believing the improvisation to be part of the show, roared for more.

Malibran swore never to play the role again, but it soon became her calling card, with her death scene usually singled out for praise. Not absolutely everyone was impressed, however. In April 1829 Felix Mendelssohn paid a visit to the King's Theatre in London to hear a performance of Rossini's *Otello*, and remained unmoved. "Mme Malibran is a young woman, beautiful and splendidly made, bewigged, full of fire and power, and at the same time coquettish; setting off her performance partly with clever embellishments of her own invention. . . . She acts beautifully, her attitudes are good, only it is unfortunate that she should so often exaggerate and so often border on the ridiculous and disagreeable. . . . After the second act came a long divertissement with gymnastics and absurdities . . . that went on till half-past eleven. I was half dead with weariness, but held out till a quarter to one, when Malibran was dispatched, gasping and screaming disgustingly. That was enough and I went home."

lessly passionate creature, whose demi-madness is characterized through unusually forceful music, anticipating the unhinged fury of Verdi's creation. Rodrigo is a similarly dramatic role, but the opera's chief glory is Desdemona, the one protagonist who is recognizable from Shakespeare. Initially a somewhat tepid presence (with the exception of her pain-filled Act I duet with Emilia, "Quanto son fieri palpiti"), she dominates the final act. The scene in which she is interrupted by a gondolier singing lines from Dante's *Inferno* is a harrowing experience, and, like the "Shepherd's Song" in Wagner's *Tristan*, it colours everything that follows – not least the dark, unresolved "Willow Song". This extended, minor-key lament, with its chromatic folk harmonies and ethereal orchestration for harp, strings and wind, concludes with some of Rossini's most intense writing for soprano, and the subsequent murder is remarkably unpleasant. Othello's suicide is oddly inconsequential, but this perfunctory episode does little to loosen the hold of the gripping finale.

Carreras, von Stade, Pastine, Fisichella, Ramey; Ambrosian Opera Chorus; Philharmonia Orchestra; López-Cobos.
(Philips 432 456-2PM2; 2 CDs).

José Carreras was in passionate voice when he recorded the role of Rossini's Othello, and his peculiarly husky timbre is well contrasted with the high tenor of Salvatore Fisichella as Rodrigo and Pastine's darker Iago. The combined effect is intoxicating and each delivers thrilling, committed portrayals. As Desdemona, von Stade gives a sublimely beautiful, emotional performance, as subtle and as varied as you could wish for. López-Cobos gives a well-paced reading.

La Cenerentola

Cinderella

Composed 1817.
First performed January 25, 1817.
Libretto by Jacopo Ferretti, after Perrault.

Synopsis

Act I

Clorinda and Thisbe (Tisbe), the daughters of Don Magnifico, are preening themselves as their stepsister Cinderella (Cenerentola) recalls the tale of a king who chooses a kind and simple bride. Prince Ramiro's tutor Alidoro enters, disguised as a beggar, and is treated to breakfast by Cinderella, thus angering her sisters. It is then announced that the Prince will be attending a ball where he will choose the most beautiful woman as his wife. Clorinda and Thisbe wake their father and tell him the good news. He tells them of his dream, in which he was a grandfather of kings, and everyone is thrilled. The disguised Prince Ramiro enters their house, and he and Cinderella (dressed in a ball gown) fall immediately in love. The Prince's servant Dandini, disguised as his master, is introduced to the stepsisters. Cinderella begs her stepfather to take her to the ball but he demands she stay at home.

With Alidoro's assistance Cinderella goes to the ball, where everyone is taken by the mysterious woman's beauty, while Clorinda and Thisbe are struck by her similarity to Cinderella.

Act II

Ramiro, touched by Cinderella's rejection of the "prince" Dandini, throws off his disguise and offers his hand in marriage; but she gives him a bracelet, the twin of one she is wearing, and tells him he must find out who she is before she will agree to marry him.

The sisters return to find Cinderella in her servant's attire and mock her for her similarity to the "mysterious lady". Alidoro ensures that the Prince's coach breaks down outside Don Magnifico's house; Ramiro recognizes Cinderella by her bracelet. They leave together and at the wedding banquet Cinderella publicly forgives her stepsisters now that her fortunes have changed for the better.

La Cenerentola was another last-minute commission, this time from Pietro Cartoni of Rome's Teatro Valle, who, having had a Rossini libretto banned by the church censors, was in dire need of an alternative. Two days before Christmas 1816, Cartoni summoned Rossini and the writer Jacopo Ferretti to his house, where they discussed "twenty or thirty" possible subjects for a melodrama. According to Ferretti, who kept a record of the evening, Rossini sat in bed trying to warm himself against the cold, while Cartoni slept. The conversation is said to have concluded:

Ferretti: Cinderella?

Rossini: Would you have the courage to write me a Cinderella?

Ferretti: Would you have the courage to set it to music?

Rossini: And the outline. . . ?

Ferretti: You can have the outline in the morning if I go without sleep tonight.

Rossini: Good night! (Wrapping himself in the bedclothes and falling like Homer's gods into a blessed sleep.)

The pressure of time meant that certain aspects of the opera, such as the recitative, had to be farmed off to other musicians, and, once again, the overture was reworked from an earlier opera. But for all the rush, the finished work was a masterpiece, turning Perrault's fairy tale into a touching story of the triumph of love over malice.

In outline, *La Cenerentola* might look like a conventional opera buffa, but there are shades of darkness in this opera. Dandini is a gleeful manipulator, while Don Magnifico is a thoroughly loathsome specimen – witness his announcement to Alidoro that the "third sister" is dead, a piece of nastiness accompanied by minor-key tonalities and brittle orchestrations that reveal Cinderella's disbelief at his callousness. The lovers are the most substantial characters, especially Cinderella, whose personality develops as the opera proceeds. When, for example, the naive and shy girl makes her first appearance in Act I, she is singing an inconsequential little tune that is very much in the buffa tradition; but when she emerges at the ball she stands tall and proud, delivering powerful, florid music that transforms her into a romantic heroine. For much of the work Ramiro is a routinely sensitive lyric tenor, but he leaps into another dimension whenever the moment requires – his famous Act II showstopper "Si, ritrovarla, io giuro" is a perfect example, with its ricochet intervals and barn-storming high

Cs. This duality of *La Cenerentola*, its oscillations between opera buffa and something altogether more ardent or serious, allied to Rossini's melodiousness and rhythmic vitality, makes it a uniquely engaging piece of entertainment.

RECORDINGS OVERVIEW

Cenerentola may not number among the top three Rossini operas in terms of audience appeal, but it was the second of his works to receive a commercial recording – by Cetra in 1949. However, the first all-round success (and the earliest of the available recordings) was Abbado's sparkling account with Berganza. Among more recent efforts, those starring Baltsa (Philips) and Bartoli (Decca) are both technically outstanding, but neither suggests the character's progress from waif to heroine as sensitively as Teresa Berganza.

Berganza, Alva, Capecchi, Montarsolo; Scottish Opera Chorus; London Symphony Orchestra; Abbado. (Deutsche Grammophon 423 861-2GH2; 2 CDs).

This fine performance followed a production at the 1970 Edinburgh Festival, and though it was taped in the studio, it has all the sparkle and immediacy of a live event, thanks largely to Teresa Berganza. At thirty-six, she was a little full-voiced for the young Cinderella, but her technical sureness, elegance and expressive range – the product of a decade of experience – are entrancing, and she makes a sensitive and determined heroine. Luigi Alva's tenor is nicely placed for Ramiro, with a smooth and tender legato and an impressive line in high notes. Renato Capecchi's Dandini is convincingly sly and, lacking the vocal agility of his youth, he makes much of his wide dynamics and detailed diction. The LSO players are in vintage form and they produce crisp, responsive support.

La gazza ladra

The Thieving Magpie

Composed 1817.
First performed May 31, 1817.
Libretto by Giovanni Gherardini, after Aubigny and Caigniez.

Synopsis

Act I

The farmer Fabrizio Vingradito would like his son Giannetto to marry their servant girl Ninetta, daughter of the famous soldier Fernando Villabella. Fortunately, the two are already in love. However, Giannetto's mother Lucia is opposed to any wedding, as she thinks Ninetta irresponsible. Ninetta is joined by a dishevelled, ragged man who turns out to be her father; he is on the run, having been imprisoned for trying to visit Ninetta against company orders. He gives Ninetta a silver fork and spoon to sell. Gottardo, the Mayor, arrives and attempts to seduce Ninetta, but he is interrupted by an urgent message which, as he is without his spectacles, he asks Ninetta to read aloud. It is an order to arrest her father, and so she changes the description of the fugitive. Meanwhile, a silver spoon has been stolen; Lucia accuses Ninetta of theft, and the girl is arrested for the crime. (Unknown to all, the family's pet magpie is the real thief.)

Act II

Ninetta is visited in prison by Giannetto and later by the Mayor, who offers her freedom in return for her love. At her trial, she is sentenced to death and Fernando's late arrival in court serves only to bring about his own arrest. As she is marched toward her execution the magpie's nest – and the stolen cutlery – are discovered atop the belltower but, as gunfire is heard in the distance, all seems lost. A joyful crowd proclaims Ninetta's safety and, as Fernando receives a royal pardon, all except the Mayor rejoice.

Based upon a true story (in which the girl was hanged), the libretto of *La gazza ladra* was originally offered to Paganini's teacher Fernando Paër, who turned it down. Rossini, however, immediately saw the opportunities of the finely crafted drama and took a lot of care over the composition, borrowing almost nothing from any previous work. The first performance, at La Scala, secured Rossini a much-needed Milanese following, but the days leading up to the premiere were extremely tense: "I composed the overture to *La gazza ladra* the day of its opening in the theatre itself, where I was imprisoned by the director and under the surveillance of four stagehands who were instructed to throw my original text out of the window, page by page, to the copyists below. In default of pages, they were ordered to throw me out."

The mood of *La gazza ladra* veers between the bucolic and the tragic, a contrast sketched in the famous overture, a piece of riotous jollity announced by a peremptory and rather ominous drum-roll. Sometimes the opera switches direction with shocking suddenness, most notably in the Mayor's mercurial displays of affection and cruelty. Another crucial feature of *La gazza ladra* is the inclusion of pathos-wringing stunts such as the funeral march and Ninetta's prayer, both of which look towards the excesses of Grand Opéra. Indeed, the pivotal relationship in this opera is not the one between Ninetta and Giannetto (as the love interest he is surprisingly lightweight), but the one between Ninetta and her father, a relationship that anticipates the full-on sentimentalism of *La juive* (see p.126), one of the cornerstones of the Grand Opéra repertoire.

Ricciarelli, Matteuzzi, Ramey, di Nissa; Prague Philharmonic Chorus; Turin Radio Symphony Orchestra; Gelmetti.
(Sony S3K45850; 3 CDs).

This live set is the only recording of *La gazza ladra*. Another is badly needed. Katia Ricciarelli is a justifiably celebrated dramatic soprano, but she is too loud and unsubtle for Ninetta, while William Matteuzzi struggles as Giannetto and is overtaxed by Gelmetti's hard and fast conducting. Samuel Ramey is surprisingly coarse and uncomfortable as Gottardo. Ferruccio Furlanetto makes a characterful impression as Fernando but it is not enough to redeem a recording in which the singers and chorus hardly ever seem at ease.

La donna del lago

The Lady of the Lake

Composed 1819.
First performed October 24, 1819.
Libretto by Andrea Leone Tottola, after Scott.

Synopsis

Act I

Dawn, on the shores of Lake Katrine. Ellen (Elena) crosses the lake from her cottage on the island, singing of her love for Malcolm, a highland clansman. She encounters Hubert (Uberto), King James V (Giacomo) in disguise, to whom she offers food and shelter in her cottage. She tells him that her father is his sworn enemy Douglas, and explains that, to seal an alliance, she is to marry Roderick (Rodrigo) – even though she loves another man. Hubert imagines that he is the lucky man and carries this hope with him when he leaves. Back at the cottage Malcolm enters and sings of his love for the absent Ellen. He is forced to hide when Ellen and her father return and argue over the wedding. When Douglas leaves, the lovers fall into each other's arms. Douglas then brings in Roderick, who begins to suspect. The men prepare for battle against the army of King James.

Act II

During the battle Hubert manages to find Ellen, to whom he wishes to declare his love. She confesses her love for Malcolm; wishing her happiness, Hubert offers her his ring and tells her that, should she ever find herself in trouble, she should take it to the king, who would then protect her. Roderick is killed, along with many of his clansmen, in their defeat at the hands of the king's army. Douglas rides to Stirling castle where he offers his life to the king, in return for the safety of his people. Ellen then arrives, asking to see the king so that she can beg for her father's life. When she realizes that Hubert and James are one and the same she is overjoyed – especially after he forgives Douglas and Malcolm. James marries the happy couple.

The swashbuckling tales of Sir Walter Scott were often mined for material by bel canto composers, and Rossini was the one who started the trend with this adaptation of Scott's poem (which Rossini read in a French translation). Donizetti and Bellini were both greatly impressed by the score, in which Rossini used Scottish dance rhythms, bardic harps and hunting horns to conjure the loch and mountain settings, and Stendhal rated it as the composer's most tuneful creation – indeed, Ellen and Malcolm's melancholic duet and the latter's two show-stopping tenor arias are among the most impressive items in the bel canto repertoire.

The heightened pathos, extended length and minor-key setting of many of the tunes in this opera strongly anticipate *Guillaume Tell*, as does the theme of liberation from foreign persecution – encapsulated by the stirring Chorus of the Bards at the end of the first act, a song swiftly adopted as a patriotic hymn. Apart from the seductive quality of the melodies (par for the course with Rossini), and the dashes of local colour, perhaps the most striking aspect of *La donna del lago* is Rossini's economic use of material to build tightly compacted, unbroken scenes. The opera opens with a fine example, with an introductory chorus followed by a grippingly beautiful love song from Ellen, a duet between Ellen and Hubert (based upon material taken from her aria) and a final chorus that also builds upon previously heard music.

Ricciarelli, Terrani, Gonzalez, Raffanti; Prague Philharmonic Chorus; Chamber Orchestra of Europe; Pollini.
(Sony S2K39311; 3 CDs).

Maurizio Pollini, famed as one of the greatest pianists of the century, has to date made just one recording as a conductor – and this 1983 set, recorded following a run at the Rossini Festival in Pésaro, is a very good job.

As in most of his work, the performance is well disciplined and admirably unsentimental, and his brisk tempi and the COE's wispish playing are ideal. Katia Ricciarelli's Ellen is a ravishing heroine, while Lucia Valentini Terrani's mezzo Malcolm provides just the right amount of gushing for the love interest. Dano Raffanti has a sensual, elegantly placed tenor and he manages Roderick's role with ease, but his opposite number, the tenor Dalmacio Gonzalez, is a thin and pinched Hubert. The recording is excellent.

Semiramide

Composed 1823.
First performed February 3, 1823.
Libretto by Gaetano Rossi, after Voltaire.

Synopsis

Act I

In the Babylonian Temple of Baal, the people await Semiramide's announcement of who will succeed her dead husband, King Nino. King Idreno of Indus and Prince Assur, Semiramide's accomplice in the murder of her husband, pay homage to her, but Semiramide is in love with the young soldier Arsace and wants to wait for his arrival in Babylon. When he fails to appear she begins the ceremony, but the sacred fire is extinguished by a storm, frightening everyone present. Arsace finally arrives, looking for Semiramide's daughter Azema, with whom he is in love. He brings with him a letter proving that Semiramide and Assur were responsible for Nino's death, which he gives to the high priest. In the Hanging Gardens, Arsace tries to tell Semiramide of his love for Azema, but she thinks it is she whom he loves. She then names Arsace king. Nino's ghost appears before the assembly and demands the blood of his murderers.

Act II

Assur confronts Semiramide and threatens to reveal her crime if she does not make him king. It is revealed to Arsace that Nino was his father – making Semiramide his mother – and so he accepts the responsibility of avenging the murder. When Arsace produces evidence of her crime she accepts the charge and offers herself up. Assur has a vision of Nino, falls to madness and vows to kill Arsace. He searches for him in Nino's tomb; Semiramide follows, hoping to save her son. In the darkness Assur strikes at Arsace but Semiramide steps betwen them and receives the fatal blow. Assur is arrested for the queen's murder while Arsace tries to kill himself. He is restrained, and accedes to the people's demand that he accept the crown of Babylon.

𝄞 For his last Italian opera Rossini again turned to Gaetano Rossi to make a libretto out of a Voltaire drama. Premiered to great acclaim almost exactly ten years after *Tancredi*, *Semiramide* differs completely in tone from its precursor – it ends in horror-struck desolation – but stylistically it bears more than a passing resemblance. Concentrating on creating a sense of epic power through the vocal score, Rossini anchored the action to three main ensembles (two in the first act and one in the second) but

ROSSINI AND THE HIRED SLEEPERS

Meyerbeer enjoyed a passionate but good-natured rivalry with Rossini. The latter's operas were always attended by two neatly attired gentlemen who were paid handsomely by Meyerbeer to sit in well-appointed box seats and fall asleep within the first fifteen minutes of the curtain's rising. They would remain audibly deep in slumber throughout the performance and would remain in their seats until the usher woke them to leave. Regular visitors to the opera were well acquainted with these "sommeilleurs de Meyerbeer", as of course was Rossini. For a performance of *Semiramide* Rossini sent two tickets to Meyerbeer with the note: "Please do me the favour of using these tickets yourself. The box is visible from all parts of the house. The chairs are comfortable. Shortly before the end of the performance I shall have you waked. Your true admirer, G. Rossini."

When the pair met a few days later, Meyerbeer asked after Rossini's health. "Shaky, cher maître, very shaky. My digestion, you know, my poor head. Alas! I'm afraid I am going downhill." As they moved on Rossini's companion asked, "How could you tell such lies? You have never known better health and yet you talk of going downhill." Rossini replied: "Ah well, why shouldn't I put it like that? It gives him such pleasure, and just a little hope."

made solo arias the dominant means of expression – and, reminiscent of *Tancredi*, these are predominantly classical in manner, with florid passage work a prevalent characteristic.

Some of the finest of these displays are given over to Semiramide herself, a dazzling coloratura role which Joan Sutherland revived at La Scala in 1962, but Rossini's fireworks are never mere display. For example, Semiramide's aria in the Hanging Gardens, "Bel raggio lusinghier", might in isolation be taken for an applause-milking virtuoso number, but its graphic expression of love is brilliantly modified as Arsace arrives, whereupon an atmosphere of suspicion and misunderstanding creeps into the music; this encounter just as fluently becomes a duet in which Semiramide's and Arsace's conflicting desires are intertwined. This emotional flexibility is used to startling effect during Assur's mad scene in Act II, where rapid key changes and the use of minor tonalities heighten the sense of inexorable doom as his vision-riddled mind crumbles in confusion. Listening to scenes like this, you understand what Verdi meant when he said that he could not have made such rapid progress as a dramatist without the inspiration of *Semiramide*.

Sutherland, Clark, Horne, Rouleau, Serge; Ambrosian Opera Chorus; London Symphony Orchestra; Bonynge.
(Decca 425 481-2DM3; 3 CDs).

Until 1993, when Cheryl Studer took a run at the fearsomely difficult title role (see below), this was the only recording of *Semiramide*. The opera was revived at La Scala in 1962 as a vehicle for Joan Sutherland, and her performance – recorded three years later – has assumed mythical status. She is at the peak of her vocal powers here, and although her reading of the murderous queen could have done with a little more menace, nobody could imagine a more lustrous tone. Marilyn Horne's Arsace is firm and disciplined, as spectacular as Sutherland but less self-conscious. By comparison, Joseph Rouleau's Assur is a pallid lad. Bonynge and the LSO produce solid support, although the conductor pays more attention to his singers than to Rossini's drama. The text has been heavily cut, but the editing makes little impact on this demonstration of world-class singing.

Studer, Larmore, Ramey, Lopardo; Ambrosian Opera Chorus; London Symphony Orchestra; Marin.
(Deutsche Grammophon 437 797-2GH3; 3 CDs).

This recording is more complete than the one above and reverses the polarities of the Sutherland-Horne effort. There the female voices dominated; here the men steal the show, with snarling Samuel Ramey and the elegant tenor Frank Lopardo giving splendid portrayals of Assur and Idreno. Cheryl Studer and Jennifer Larmore produce some attractive tones and variously competent fireworks, but their performances are meagre alongside the heroics of Ramey and Lopardo.

Le Comte Ory

Count Ory

Composed 1828.
First performed August 20, 1828.
Libretto by Eugène Scribe and Charles Gaspard Delestre-Poirson.

Synopsis

Act I

The men of the Castle de Formoutiers have gone on Crusade, leaving their women behind. The young and rakish Count Ory has his eye on the Countess Adèle – who is depressed at the absence of her brother – and disguises himself as a hermit, gifted with a knowledge of the ways of the heart. His friend Raimbaud generates interest in his talents and soon enough the Count's page Isolier approaches and asks how he might win the love of the Countess Adèle. Isolier announces a plan whereby he intends to sneak into the castle as a nun. Ory is impressed and determines to do exactly the same. The Countess's companion Ragonde advises her to seek the hermit's counsel. Adèle arrives and Ory advises her to fall in love, but when she hints at an affection for Isolier he warns her off anyone associated with the notorious Count Ory. When the hermit is suddenly unmasked, Ory has to conjure another scheme – quickly, as it is announced that the Crusaders are on their way home.

Act II

The women await the return of their husbands – glad that they have foiled Ory's plans; but they are disturbed by cries from below. It is a group of nuns (Ory and his friends in disguise) who claim they are being harassed by the licentious Count. Adèle lets them in and Sister Colette (Ory) thanks her profusely. Left to themselves, the nuns find the wine cellars, but Isolier manages to warn Adèle that Ory may well be in the building. Eventually, Adèle tricks the Count into making a fool of himself by embracing Isolier. Trumpets sound the return of the Crusaders, and the Count and his men are forced to beat a hasty retreat.

A real-life villain, Count Ory first appeared in fiction in an eighteenth-century ballad, which was later turned into a one-act play by Scribe and Delestre-Poirson in 1817. They offered the tale to Rossini, who requested a prefatory act to make the libretto long enough for a full evening's opera. Duly provided with the Hermit episode, Rossini set about one of the greatest acts of self-theft in operatic history, making up half of *Ory*'s score from *Il viaggio a Rheims*, an opera he had written three years before. Parisian audiences were used to such practices, but Rossini's stunt was too much for his librettists, who were so ashamed of what they had helped perpetrate that neither would allow his name to be printed on the libretto.

They shouldn't have been so precious, for Rossini's amazingly fluent and witty treatment of the text was a fitting swan-song to his career as a composer of comic opera. The drama abounds with manic situations and mad coincidences, set to music of typical verve and fluent pacing. The Count, a murderously high tenor role (sung at the premiere by Albert Nourrit – see p.174), dominates the opera right from his opening cavatina, "Que les destins prospères", a delightfully unctuous prelude in which he offers his services to anyone who might be looking for a husband. His duet with Isolier later in the same act has a vigour and good-natured charm that makes it difficult to deplore his chicanery. The high spot of the entire work – and one of the funniest episodes in all opera – occurs when Ory's "nuns" inveigle their way into the castle's wine cellars. Left to themselves they launch into a bawdy drinking song, but when Adèle and Ragonde make an appearance they turn the singalong into a sanctimonious prayer. The final trio, "A la faveur de cette nuit obscure", between Ory, Adèle and Isolier, is another sublime achievement, a Mozartian gem in which, despite the flurry of activity, each of the three is perfectly characterized through their melody. In the opinion of Berlioz, it was Rossini's "absolute masterpiece".

Oncina, Barabas, Sinclair, Roux; Glyndebourne Festival Chorus; Glyndebourne Festival Orchestra; Gui.
(EMI CMS7 64180-2; 2 CDs).

Recorded in 1956, this set did a lot to restore Rossini's reputation, for Gui's conducting is frothy and spontaneous, and his cast is almost perfect. Juan Oncina's tenor was among the most versatile of the time, and this recording shows why he was celebrated for his performances of Rossini's lusty Count. Sari Barabas and Monica Sinclair are superb as Adèle and Ragonde, while Michael Roux is in his element as the clowning Raimbaud. The "nun" scenes are hilarious, and this remains among the most infectious recordings ever made of a Rossini opera. The sound is mono and about fifteen minutes have been cut from the score.

Aler, Jo, Cachemaille, Quilico; Lyon Opera Chorus and Orchestra; Gardiner.
(Philips 422 406-2PH2; 2 CDs).

The advantages of this set are that it's not cut and it's in excellent digital sound. John Eliot Gardiner's speeds are quick, and the atmosphere is genial, but this performance just lacks a bit of character in comparison to the Gui version. John Aler's Ory is pretty if a little bland, but Sumi Jo's Adèle is a joy.

Guillaume Tell

William Tell

Composed 1829.
First performed August 3, 1829.
Libretto by Etienne de Jouy and Hippolyte Louis-Florent Blis, after Schiller.

Synopsis

Act I

Switzerland, 1307. Guillaume Tell leads the Swiss resistance against the Austrian overlords, led by Gessler. Tell is championed by Melcthal, patriarch of the village, and (hesitantly) by Melcthal's son Arnold, who is in love with the Austrian Princess Mathilde. An archery contest, in which Tell's son Jemmy is victorious, is interrupted by the arrival of Leuthold, who has killed an Austrian soldier who was trying to rape his daughter. Tell ferries him over the rapids and when the Austrians arrive the Swiss refuse to reveal the identity of the ferryman; the Austrians, led by Rodolphe, take Melcthal as a hostage and then loot the village.

Act II

Arnold and Mathilde proclaim their love but they are interrupted by Tell's arrival. He urges Mathilde to leave and then tells Arnold that his father has been executed. Arnold agrees to support a revolt, and there is a meeting of the three cantons to discuss the uprising.

Act III

Arnold and Mathilde, recognizing the futility of their relationship, agree to part. In the main square Gessler is demanding obedience, and he orders the Swiss to bow before his hat. When Tell refuses, Rodolphe recognizes him as the ferryman and has him arrested. Gessler challenges Tell to shoot an apple off the head of Jemmy, his son; he succeeds, then is arrested again and sent by Gessler to the castle of Küssnacht, on an island in the middle of Lake Lucerne. The Swiss people's outraged reaction to this is barely checked by the Austrian soldiers. Mathilde takes Jemmy into her care.

Act IV

On the lake's edge Arnold urges his compatriots to rise against the Austrians, then leads them into battle. Jemmy is reunited with his mother Hedwig by Mathilde and then lights a pyre, signalling the beginning of the uprising. Tell returns to the mainland and kills Gessler while Arnold captures the castle of Altdorf. The opera ends with a prayer of thanksgiving.

Schiller's *Wilhelm Tell* is virtually a compendium of Romantic themes: the scale of the action is heroic; its hero is a revolutionary who fights foreign occupation and represents the aspirations of the common people; the pastoral setting has the nostalgic mystique of the distant past; and Nature is upheld as the touchstone for all that is good. The homesick Rossini latched on to the play and boosted its impact with sublime music, packing the opera with tunes that were to be recycled as nationalist anthems and as barrel-organ favourites. But *Guillaume Tell* has never established itself in the repertoire, for reasons that are not hard to find: lasting nearly five hours in the theatre (Berlioz referred to *Tell*'s "mauvais quarts d'heures"), it requires vast scenic apparatus, a genius for a conductor and the finest tenor on earth (for the role of Arnold).

The first act is the weakest, with too many choruses and not enough arias, but even here there are some wonderful episodes, notably the overture. Opening with a gorgeous passage for five cellos – suggesting, in the words of Berlioz, "the calm of profound solitude, the solemn silence of nature when the elements and the human passions are at rest"– it develops into a blood-quickening gallop, a section made famous as the Lone Ranger theme tune.

Donizetti wrote that "God wrote the second act", and it does indeed contain some remarkable writing. Mathilde's "Sombre forêt" and Arnold's "Quand l'Helvetie" provide beautiful displays of bel canto melody, but it is the pacing that brings you to the edge of your seat, as the fervour mounts with the approach of the convention of three cantons, when the Swiss decide to throw off the Austrian yoke. With the exception of Tell's famous apple-shooting scene, the third act is dull (the opera's ballets, confined to acts two and three, are at best a drag) but the fourth is more than worth the wait. It opens with the opera's most celebrated aria, Arnold's passionate homage to his birthplace, "Asile hereditère", which leads into some of the opera's most intense drama, as Mathilde moves to centre stage. Her rescue of Jemmy and her conversion to the rebellion are set to wonderfully poignant music and her role in the trio "Je rends à votre amour" is highly touching. Following on from the somewhat perfunctory murder of Gessler, the atmosphere brightens and the skies clear: Arnold is overwhelmed by the beauty of the land before him (depicted with richly evocative music) and he leads the mighty hymn to Nature and freedom, "Tout change et grandit en ces lieux", with which Rossini ended his grandest opera and his career as an opera composer.

Bacquier, Caballé, Gedda, Mesplé, Howell; Ambrosian Opera Chorus; Royal Philharmonic Orchestra; Gardelli.
(EMI CMS 769951-2; 4 CDs).

Taped in 1973, this is the only recording of *Tell* in the language for which it was written. Gardelli directs a brisk, lucid performance of the mighty score and he encourages some animated playing from the RPO. The Ambrosian Chorus's French diction is poor, and it was odd to cast a Spanish soprano, Caballé, as Mathilde. However, the two male leads are both French-speakers and are in excellent form. Gedda was getting on by 1973 and some of the high notes are strained, but he is an elegant, ever-refined presence. Gabriel Bacquier is a rich, well-defined Tell, and the supporting cast all give their very best. The stereo is clean and the price irresistible.

Milnes, Freni, Pavarotti, Ghiaurov, Tomlinson, Jones; Ambrosian Opera Chorus; National Philharmonic Orchestra; Chailly.
(Decca 417 154-2DH4; 4 CDs).

Purists disapprove of *Guillaume Tell* in Italian, but you could argue that the language's open vowels and smoother lines serve the music better than French. Pavarotti, who famously refused to make his debut at La Scala as Arnold because "the role would have ruined my voice", is in his full, effortless maturity here – there is simply no greater performance from him on disc. Mirella Freni is similarly beyond criticism, Sherrill Milnes is thrillingly heroic as Tell, and the remaining cast are all superb – especially John Tomlinson as the relatively minor Melchtal. The chorus and orchestra are excellent, driven along by a conductor who clearly loves the opera. This is a marvellously clear pre-digital recording, capturing the grandeur of the huge ensembles without sacrificing detail.

GAETANO DONIZETTI

b. BERGAMO, ITALY, NOVEMBER 29, 1797; d. BERGAMO, APRIL 8, 1848.

"Music for the Italians", noted Berlioz, "is a sensual pleasure and nothing more. For this noble expression of the mind they have hardly more respect than for the art of cooking. They want a score that, like a plate of macaroni, can be assimilated immediately without having to think about it." If any one composer could be said to live up to this prej-

MARY EVANS

Gaetano Donizetti, creator of seventy three operas

udice, it is Gaetano Donizetti, the master of opera as vocal exhibitionism. Donizetti's note-spinning melodramas fell from favour very soon after his death, as the qualities that had ensured their enormous success during his lifetime – their easy tunefulness, undemanding plot lines and simple characterization – came to be perceived as faults. Along with Rossini and Bellini, Donizetti recovered some of his respectability during the bel canto revival of the 1950s, yet his stock remains unfairly low compared to the other members of the bel canto trinity. Surface might prevail over substance in the operas of Donizetti, but there are few more gorgeous operatic surfaces than the one he created in works such as *L'elisir d'amore* and *Lucia di Lammermoor*.

His family were poor and the young Donizetti was fortunate to find a teacher in Simon Mayr, who taught him for ten years without once accepting payment. As a destitute student in Bergamo, he was forced to undertake every commission that came his way, no matter the fee or the theatre, and not until Mayr pushed some Venetian commissions his way did he begin to establish some provincial celebrity. A batch of comic operas written for Naples brought him to the attention of La Scala, who in 1830 commissioned Donizetti to write *Anna Bolena* – his first international success. In 1832 he composed his great comedy *L'elisir d'amore*, following it with three dramatic masterworks: *Lucrezia Borgia*, *Maria Stuarda* and, most famously, *Lucia di Lammermoor*. By the decade's end he was Italy's pre-eminent composer.

However, in 1838 his patience with life in Italy began to wear thin, chiefly on account of the interference from the censors. After *Poliuto* was banned during rehearsals for its premiere, Donizetti began to consider moving to France, a leap he made later the same year, when Mercadente beat him to the directorship of the Naples conservatory. Acceptance in Paris wasn't easy, but 1840 was a breakthrough year, for it saw the premiere of his hugely popular comedy *La fille du Régiment* and of *La favorite*, his first successful Grand Opéra.

In 1842 he was appointed *Hofkapellmeister* to the Habsburg court in Vienna and for a while, despite his worsening syphilis, he was able to divide his time between France and Austria. He composed his comic masterpiece, *Don Pasquale*, in 1843, but in the following year his health finally began to collapse and he was confined to an asylum, where he was visited by Heinrich Heine: "While his magical tunes bring joy to the world, he sits a terrible picture of insanity in a lunatic asylum near Paris. Until some time ago, he had kept a childish consciousness of clothes: he had to be attired carefully every day in full dress, his tail coat decorated with all his orders." His condition worsened until, physically and mentally paralyzed, he was moved back to Bergamo, where he died five months after his fifty-first birthday.

When told that Rossini had composed the *Barber of Seville* in two weeks, Donizetti replied, "That does not surprise me, he has always been lazy." Donizetti produced seventy-three operas, and they constitute only a fraction of his output. He wrote too quickly, and chose some terrible libretti, but he was astute enough to recognize that for many people the opera house was a place to hear the world's greatest singers, rather than the world's greatest composers. Though never an innovator, he did much to relax the divisions between aria and recitative, he increased the role and widened the expressive range of the chorus, and he helped establish the cavatina (a languid, melancholic song) and the cabaletta (a quick, rhythmically urgent showpiece) as features of Romantic opera. He was under no illusions as to his place in the great scheme: "My heyday is over", he wrote in 1844, "and another must take my place. . . . I am more than happy to give mine to people of talent like Verdi."

L'elisir d'amore

The Elixir of Love

Composed 1832.
First performed May 12, 1832.
Libretto by Felice Romani, after Scribe and Malaperta.

Synopsis

Act I

Nemorino, who is in love with Adina, entertains himself and his farm workers by telling them the tale of Tristan and Isolde and the love potion. Sergeant Belcore gives flowers to Adina, who then upsets the sensitive Nemorino, firstly by showing Belcore too much affection and then by revealing that she could never love him. Nemorino, remembering Isolde's story, buys a potion from the quack Doctor Dulcamara, who claims it will work within only 24 hours. Buoyed by the wine (for that is the potion's prime ingredient), Nemorino grows in confidence, but this is shattered when he hears Adina agree to marry Belcore.

Act II

The wedding is postponed when Nemorino fails to attend. Penniless but desperate to buy more elixir, Nemorino enlists in Belcore's regiment. After taking more of the potion he is mobbed by the local village girls, who have heard of his inheritance, and so he assumes that the potion is working. Adina is shocked at his evident attractions but, after being told about the potion by Dulcamara, she claims that her own charms are more than a match for his trickery. Soon, however, Adina realizes that she loved Nemorino all along and, after buying back his commission, she confesses her feelings. The village celebrates as Dulcamara leaves, convinced that his potion works.

L'elisir d'amore has fared better than most of Donizetti's operas – it was the most frequently performed during his lifetime, and then, after fifty years of neglect, was revived by Enrico Caruso and kept alive by numerous other star tenors, famously Gigli, Tagliavini and Pavarotti. Written to a libretto that was adapted by Bellini's poet Felice Romani from a text by Scribe, its mixture of sharp comedy and heartfelt pathos make it one of the most beguiling confections of the nineteenth century.

The tunes almost tumble over one another, and, unlike Rossini's operas, which tend to begin much better than they end, *L'elisir* gets steadily more remarkable. The hard-hearted Adina (soprano), the spineless Nemorino (tenor) and the loquacious Dulcamara (baritone) are each ascribed melodies that pinpoint, more precisely than Romani's libretto, the changes taking place within them. Thus Nemorino's languid concluding romance, "Una furtiva lagrima" (the primary reason for Caruso's interest in the opera) starts with a gentle, hesitant phrase which is then developed into a broad, declamatory release of emotion, illustrating Nemorino's sudden growth in confidence more accurately than any number of words. The same applies to all the other big numbers – notably Adina's "Quanto Amore" (championing her charms above those of any potion) and Dulcamara's "patter" song – and if the comic interaction lacks the spark of Rossini's *Barber* or Mozart's *Figaro*, Donizetti nonetheless creates a work that has considerably greater vitality than the outline of its plot might suggest.

RECORDINGS OVERVIEW

There are a dozen studio recordings of *L'elisir d'amore*, but only one of them generates anything like the sort of atmosphere you might get in the theatre, while the small batch of live recordings are unevenly cast. Although Carlo Bergonzi, the greatest Nemorino of all, was taped on stage on a couple of occasions, no complete recording of a Bergonzi *L'elisir* is available on CD; however, you can sample his portrayal on two concert excerpts on the Memories label.

Sutherland, Pavarotti, Cossa, Malas; Ambrosian Opera Chorus; English Chamber Orchestra; Bonynge.
(Decca 414 461-2DH2; 2 CDs).

Recorded in 1969, when Pavarotti was at the height of his abilities, this is a dream performance: his sweet, effortless, and characterful voice makes for intoxicating listening. As always, his partnership with Sutherland is engagingly spontaneous and even if she is a little solemn, her technical brilliance – best heard in the thrilling aria "Nel dolce incanto" (which Donizetti added later for Maria Malibran; see p.162) – sets the music alight. Dominic Cossa is a swaggering, full-throated Belcore, Spiro Malas is an amiable Dulcamara, and Bonynge conducts with equal measures of verve and sentimentality. The recording is fresh and well balanced.

Lucrezia Borgia

Composed 1833.
First performed December 26, 1833.
Libretto by Felice Romani, after Victor Hugo.

Synopsis

Prologue

Gennaro leaves his friends and falls asleep on a terrace. He is discovered by Lucrezia Borgia, who is masked. He wakes and, charmed by her concern, tells her of his life and how he was raised by a lowly fisherman. He is horrified, however, when his friends tear off her mask and reveal that she is the infamous Lucrezia Borgia.

Act I

Lucrezia's fourth husband Alfonso suspects her of infidelity but she is only seeing Gennaro – who is in fact her son by a previous marriage. Gennaro is ignorant of his mother's identity and, keen to show his hatred of Lucrezia's crimes, he cuts off the first letter of her name from the palace gates, leaving only "orgia" (orgy). Enraged by this insult, Lucrezia demands revenge. Alfonso brings in Gennaro and forces him to take poison but, realizing the identity of the culprit, Lucrezia administers an antidote and begs him to leave the city.

Act II

At a banquet in Ferrara, Gennaro and his friends mock Lucrezia. She appears and informs them that they have all drunk poisoned wine, but when she sees her son she clears the hall and offers him an antidote. Revolted by her actions and shattered by her claim that she is his mother, he refuses the potion and dies. Crushed by his rejection, she drains the poisoned cup.

Victor Hugo's highly fictionalized account of the life of the much-traduced Lucrezia Borgia presented Donizetti with an irresistibly melodramatic character. The score is dominated by Lucrezia, a fearsome presence who is brought to the opera house only when a firebrand soprano wishes to parade her bag of tricks. Originally, Lucrezia dominated the opera even more than she does now, as Méric-Lalande, the first Lucrezia, insisted on ending her character's life with an aria-finale. The composer attempted to persuade her that it was idiotic to have Lucrezia singing a cabaletta while standing over the corpse of her murdered son, but she was adamant that the audiences were looking to her for their entertainment rather than to the composer, and so the indomitable diva had her way. However, taken by the beauty of Giovanni Mario's high tenor, Donizetti later replaced Méric-Lalande's finale with an emotional arioso for Gennaro – "Madre, se ognor lontano" – thereby giving the tenor his solitary opportunity to express his character's tragic predicament. For the rest of the opera Gennaro joins the rest of the cast in the wake of Lucrezia, as she charts her crazy path from the prologue's deeply affectionate "Com' è bello! quale incanto" to her anguished, hysterical final scene.

Caballé, Verrett, Kraus, Flagello; RCA Italiana Chorus and Orchestra; Perlea (RCA GD86642; 2 CDs).

Taped in 1965, this was the first studio recording of *Lucrezia* and it remains preferable to the solitary alternative, recorded by Sutherland for Decca twelve years later. Caballé's performance was taped shortly after her revival of the opera, in concert at Carnegie Hall, a performance from which her international stardom can be dated. The concert sometimes turns up on bootleg CDs, and if you find it you should get it – Caballé gives an accurate, sweet-sounding portrayal in the studio, but the live performance is an emotional typhoon. As for the rest of the RCA cast, Shirley Verrett's mezzo Orsini is outstanding, and the bass Ezio Flagello is a solid Alfonso, but the real star is the tenor Alfredo Kraus, whose delicious turns of phrase and mournful tone make you wonder why he never achieved the megabuck status of Pavarotti, Carreras and Domingo.

Maria Stuarda

Mary Stuart

Composed 1834.
First performed October 18, 1834.
Libretto by Giuseppe Badari, after Schiller.

Synopsis

Act I

In Westminster Palace, the arrival of Queen Elizabeth is eagerly anticipated. It is rumoured that she intends to unite England and France through marriage. Elizabeth doubts the constancy of Leicester, her favourite, and is upset when he asks her to grant an audience to her cousin, Mary Queen of Scots, a prisoner at Fotheringay.

Act II

Leicester rides to Fotheringay, where he helps prepare Mary for her meeting with the Queen. Elizabeth makes no secret of her hatred for her cousin, who in turn spits abuse at the Queen. Mary is duly condemned to death.

Act III

The Queen debates the wisdom of signing the death warrant but is encouraged to do so by Cecil. Leicester arrives only to be told that he is to witness Mary's execution. Mary receives her warrant without emotion, but turns to Talbot and confesses her sins. She begs her friends to pray for those who have done her wrong and, with Leicester looking on, she is taken to her death.

In 1834 Donizetti signed a contract with Naples in which he agreed to provide one opera seria every year for the Teatro San Carlo. By September he had finished the first one: a two-and-a-half-hour setting of Schiller's treatment of the life and death of Mary Queen of Scots. However, the Bourbon censors objected to an opera that ended with the execution of a monarch, and so Donizetti set the same score to an entirely new libretto, calling the opera *Buondelmonte*. The first performance was ruined by two sparring sopranos, who literally came to blows on stage. *Maria Stuarda* was eventually performed, thanks to the interest of the soprano Maria Malibran, at La Scala on December 30, 1835.

This too was a disaster and the work – now known as "the opera that not even Malibran could save" – remained unperformed for some 120 years. Not until 1971, when Montserrat Caballé sang the role in Milan, London and New York, did *Maria Stuarda* finally enter the repertoire alongside *Lucia* and *Lucrezia*.

Like *Lucrezia Borgia*, *Maria Stuarda* is dominated by the title soprano but essentially it's famous for a single, intensely powerful scene: the meeting of the two queens at Fotheringay (a confrontation that owes nothing to historical fact). The violence of this exchange, heightened by the delicacy of Mary's preceding aria, is without precedent in Italian opera, with Mary's frenzied stream of invective including such unmonarchial abuse as "bastarda". The other great scene occupies an entirely different emotional ground and comes at the conclusion, beginning with Mary's touching prayer "Deh! tu di un umile preghiera"; terrified by the second of the three cannon shots (anticipating her execution), Mary makes a final, desperate plea of her innocence ("Ah, se in

THE RISE OF THE TENOR – A CAUTIONARY TALE

It was not until the start of the nineteenth century that the tenor voice attained pivotal importance in opera, but the first bel canto tenors – Rubini, García, David and their ilk – were not exponents of modern-style tenor heroics. Rather, they were masters of line and the beautiful turn of phrase, and produced a small, flute-like sound. By the time Donizetti wrote *Lucia di Lammermoor*, however, audiences and composers were looking for a heavier and more dramatic voice, capable of filling the new large-scale theatres (such as the San Carlo in Naples, which Barbaia rebuilt along much grander lines after it was burnt down in 1816; see p.154) and of competing with the ever-larger orchestras.

Whereas Rubini and the rest had used a falsetto voice for everything above the stave, singers like **Domenico Donzelli** (1790–1873) produced a bigger sound by singing from the chest – as is common today. But this placed great strain on the throat, the lungs and the cardiovascular system, with calamitous results for singers lacking the technique and training of Donzelli. In 1831, while giving a performance of a Pacini opera in Rome, one Americo Sbigoli came to a phrase that Donzelli had famously articulated in full-throated glory. Sbigoli stepped manfully towards the footlights and, with all the force he could muster, declaimed his piece. However, he was unable to sustain the punishment of the music: as he reached the peak of tension a blood vessel burst in his neck and, before the startled audience, he fell down dead – a martyr to tenor machismo.

However, the most famous casualty of the fashion for dramatic tenors was Donzelli's great French contemporary **Adolphe Nourrit** (1802–39). Nourrit was an outstanding artist, a fine actor as well as a superlative singer. But in 1837, while at the height of his powers, his reign as the leading Parisian tenor was brought to an end when **Gilbert Duprez** (1806–96) was engaged at the Opéra in one of Nourrit's most famous roles – Arnold in *Guillaume Tell*. The fateful moment was described by Berlioz: "A number comes during which the daring artist, accenting each syllable, gives out some high chest notes with a resonance, an expression of heart-rending grief, and a beauty of tone that so far no one had been led to expect." During "Asile héréditaire", Duprez sang the first ever high C from the chest, the sort of sound produced today by Pavarotti, Alagna and Lopardo – a full and powerful high C, not the floated wisp generated by the early bel canto singers. In the audience were Rossini (who thought it an awful noise, referring to it as the "squawk of a capon whose throat is being cut"), Donizetti and, tragically, Nourrit, who came to the swift conclusion that his career was over. He resigned from the Opéra and moved to Italy, where the sound of Duprez's voice haunted him. Less than two years after that epoch-making night, unable to bear the pain of his inability to match that famous sound, he threw himself to his death from the third floor of his apartment in Naples.

The tenor had become a stunt man, whose performances had audiences on the edge of their seat because of the unconscious fear that they might crack under the pressure. And even today, the high C remains a test for every aspiring tenor and the ultimate thrill for fans of the male voice.

giorno da queste ritorte"), but with the final shot she stands tall and walks calmly to her death. *Maria Stuarda* may be an opera of isolated highlights, but they are concentrated and memorable highlights.

Sutherland, Tourangeau, Pavarotti, Soyer; Bologna Teatro Comunale Chorus and Orchestra; Bonynge.
(Decca 425 410-2DM2; 2 CDs).

Each of the four studio recordings of this opera features a strong leading lady (the other three are Sills, Gruberova and Janet Baker) but none reaches the heights touched in Joan Sutherland's 1974 account. In blistering form, she does some mind-boggling acrobatics (many of them improvised) while remaining sensitive to her character – her growling "vil bastarda" is especially memorable. The appeal of her delicate voice is heightened when heard against the rich and chesty soprano of Huguette Tourangeau, whose use of the language is inspired – in particular, her pronouncement of death is chilling. Pavarotti as Leicester is once again in startling form, setting standards that no later tenor in the bel canto field has matched.

Lucia di Lammermoor

Lucy of Lammermuir

Composed 1835.
First performed September 26, 1835.
Libretto by Salvatore Cammarano, after Scott.

Synopsis

Act I

Scotland, late sixteenth century. Lord Henry (Enrico) Ashton is determined that his sister, Lucy (Lucia), should marry Arthur (Arturo) Bucklaw, as their alliance would strengthen his political situation. But she loves Sir Edgar (Edgardo) Ravenswood – the family's greatest enemy. Edgardo wants to ask for her hand in marriage but Lucia is frightened of her brother's temper. Edgardo further complicates matters by telling Lucia that he has to travel to France on political business. They exchange rings.

Act II

Enrico forges a letter from Edgardo in order to prove his infidelity, and begs Lucia to agree to marry Arturo (his political difficulties having worsened). Devastated by the letter's contents and weakened by her responsibilities to her family, Lucia agrees. As the ceremony is about to begin Edgardo returns to claim Lucia – but she has signed the wedding contract.

Act III

Enrico challenges Edgardo to a duel. The wedding celebrations are shattered by news that Lucia has murdered Arturo. Deranged, Lucia appears carrying a blood-spattered knife and, hallucinating that she is about to marry Edgardo, she falls down dead. Edgardo awaits Enrico, but when he hears of Lucia's death he stabs himself.

Lucia di Lammermoor was a hit with the critics and the public as long as Donizetti was alive, but it wasn't long before it was relegated to the status of a mere showcase for coloratura display. Early in the twentieth century, however, *Lucia* was resurrected, as much for its leading tenor role as for the soprano part, and it has now been staged and recorded more than all his other operas combined.

Though it does suffer from floridness, *Lucia* is one of the most exhilarating Italian operas of the nineteenth century. The structure is fluid, the orchestration – with its bittersweet amplification of the brass – is as ripe as anything before Verdi's *Don Carlo*, and Donizetti's melodies are expressive as well as attractive. As in none of his other operas, Donizetti here applied harmony as a means of psychological representation, and the tonality of each act brings real gravity to the characterization. The opera's violent contrasts, both musical and theatrical, are thrillingly immediate – this was the opera from which Verdi learned and borrowed most.

Lucia's soprano and Edgardo's tenor dominate the opera, of which the best-known highlights are Lucia's astonishing mad scene and Edgardo's mournful concluding recitative and aria. But every scene has at least one instantly memorable idea, and several episodes are masterpieces of musical theatre, notably the "Wolf's Crag" duet between Enrico and Edgardo in Act III and the Act II sextet, which sent the audiences into a frenzy when Caruso sang it at the Met. One critic wrote, "Rarely have I witnessed such excitement. . . . A policeman in the lobby, thinking a riot of some sort had broken loose in the auditorium, grabbed his night stick and pushed through the swinging doors – only to find an audience vociferously demanding an encore." *Lucia* is opera at its most emotive, with passions painted in primary colours and characters who behave with determined irrationality. If badly performed – and, considering the difficulties of the soprano and tenor roles, this is not unlikely – it can seem little more than tuneful histrionics; but performed well, *Lucia* becomes the greatest of Italian Romantic operas.

RECORDINGS OVERVIEW

Though *Lucia* was one of the first operas to receive a complete recording, thanks to Mercédès Caspir's attempt in 1929, it didn't come alive on record until 1953, when Maria Callas transformed the title role. After Callas came a string of fine Lucias, including Roberta Peters (RCA), Renata Scotto (EMI), Anna Moffo (RCA), Joan Sutherland (Decca), Beverly Sills (EMI) and Montserrat Caballé (Philips), but there have been no really satisfactory recordings since the advent of digital sound. Great claims were made for the 1992 Domingo and Studer vehicle, but neither star is at all comfortable in this music.

Callas, di Stefano, Panerai, Zaccaria; La Scala Chorus; Berlin RIAS Orchestra; Karajan.
(EMI CMS7 63631-2; 2CDs).

Callas officially recorded *Lucia* three times. Twice in the studio (1953 and 1959, both with Serafin and both on EMI) and once in a live performance, conducted by Herbert von Karajan at the Berlin State Opera on September 29, 1955. All three have remarkable qualities, but the Karajan account just has the edge: Callas brings a passion and immediacy to the role that no other soprano this century has equalled. Her recreation of Lucia's emotional and mental collapse is of such intensity that, to paraphrase one critic, you are really not aware that she's singing. Callas is well partnered by Giuseppe di Stefano, whose tenor is ringing and full-bodied. Karajan creates ideal support for Callas's blinding performance. The mono sound quality is poor, but that's easily forgotten.

Caballé, Carreras, Sardinero, Ramey; Ambrosian Opera Chorus; New Philharmonia; López-Cobos.
(Philips 446 551-2PM2; 2 CDs).

This 1976 production was the "authentic" version of Lucia, in that it restored the bits traditionally edited out, but it was far from authentic in its rejection of ornamentation and cadenzas. However, Caballé is in gorgeous voice and makes much of her beautifully dark and expressive tone. Her voice sits perfectly next to the ardent young Carreras, whose powerfully heroic and secure singing gives Edgardo a rare strength. López-Cobez is an uneven conductor, enjoying the dramatic outbursts but seeming to lose patience during quieter passages, but he has a symphonic conception of *Lucia*, and New Philharmonia contribute much to the sense of gravitas. A bargain.

Moffo, Bergonzi, Sereni, Flagello; RCA Italiana Opera Chorus and Orchestra; Prêtre.
(RCA GD86504; 2 CDs).

Where Callas throws convention to the wind, sacrificing beauty to drama, Anna Moffo considers beauty a prerequisite. Moffo is a very pretty soprano, skipping her way through even the dizziest phrases, but by the time she reaches the mad scene you might find yourself thinking that a lovely voice is not quite enough. This recording's primary strength is Carlo Bergonzi's Edgardo, arguably his best studio portrayal. Powerful but flexible, he produces some of the most seductive singing of any tenor this century, but never loses his awareness of the character. His diction and sense of line are unsurpassed, and in ensemble he is stupendous – the Wolf's Crag scene, with the resounding Mario Sereni, has irresistible energy. Never famous for melodrama, Prêtre here breaks his own mould and delivers inventive, dynamic support.

Sutherland, Pavarotti, Milnes, Ghiaurov; Royal Opera House Chorus and Orchestra; Bonynge.
(Decca 410 193-2DH3; 2 CDs).

This 1971 recording, Sutherland's second Lucia, is one of her lasting achievements. Textual meaning is glossed over more than should have been allowed, but the voice is magnificent, more vibrant and varied than in 1961, and richer in character. Pavarotti is in young, resonant voice, while Sherrill Milnes and Nicolai Ghiaurov are in roaring good form as Enrico and Raimondo. Bonynge's conducting is more exhilarating than was Pritchard on Sutherland's first attempt, if less vital than Prêtre for RCA.

Poliuto

Composed 1838; revised 1840.
First performed November 30, 1848.
Libretto by Salvatore Cammarano, after Corneille.

Synopsis

Act I

Poliuto, a Roman, has decided to accept baptism from Nearco. The service is witnessed by Paolina, Poliuto's wife and the daughter of the Roman governor of Armenia, Felix. Severo, the Roman proconsul and an ex-fiancé of Paolina, is soon to arrive in Armenia. Though she wishes otherwise, she still loves him.

Act II

Severo is angry that Paolina has married but she remains loyal to her husband. They are overheard by Poliuto but before he can interrupt he is told of Nearco's capture, and rushes to the temple of Jupiter, where Nearco is being tried. In order to help his friend, Poliuto overturns the altar and confesses his Christian conversion.

Act III

Poliuto is visited in prison by Paolina who is so moved by her husband's dignity that she agrees to adopt the new religion. Together they enter the arena where, as Christians, they are martyred.

Poliuto was composed in 1838 as part of the contract with Naples, specifically for the "electrifying" talents of the tenor Adolphe Nourrit, but the censor refused to allow the presentation of Christian martyrdom on stage and banned the show in mid-rehearsal. After his move to Paris Donizetti took up a new libretto by Eugène Scribe, made various cuts, added an overture and various high-tension choruses and presented the revamped work in Paris as the *Les martyrs* – this time featuring the "dazzling" French tenor Gilbert Duprez. The French were nonetheless not hugely impressed and *Les martyrs* disappeared soon after the 1840 premiere. *Poliuto* was eventually premiered, at San Carlo, six months after Donizetti's death.

Though it's encumbered by loads of oom-pah-pah accompaniments and lumpy choruses (one of which, the Priest's Chorus in Act II, Verdi plundered for his triumphal chorus in *Aida*), *Poliuto* does contain some exciting music. The Act II finale is a corker and the Act III love music is amazingly potent, but most of the high-quality stuff is allocated to the famously difficult title role, which necessitates a range from a low F to a high C sharp. Poliuto's cabalettas are especially fine, as are his duets with Paolina, notably "Il suon' dell'arpe angeliche", in Act I.

RECORDINGS OVERVIEW

The best *Poliuto* is currently unavailable. Featuring the rare partnership of Maria Callas and Franco Corelli, it was recorded at La Scala on December 7, 1960, one of the most famous nights in the house's history (the theatre was decorated by Balmain with 16,000 carnations and seats were going for £150 each). This recording is bound to find its way onto CD again, and when it does it will be a clear first choice, for it's one of the most exciting displays of dramatic Italian singing on record.

Carreras, Ricciarelli, Pons, Polgár; Vienna Singakademie Chorus; Vienna Symphony Orchestra; Caetani.
(Sony M2K 44821; 2 CDs).

This live Viennese concert performance is a recommendation by default, for Carreras's voice is not a patch on what it was when he recorded *Lucia* (see p.176). With raw tone, widening vibrato, ugly phrasing and tight high notes, his performance makes difficult listening. His Paolina, Katia Ricciarelli, is in much better form, and Juan Pons is impressive as the proconsul Severo. On balance, though, wait for the Callas/Corelli set unless you're dying to get to know *Poliuto*.

La fille du régiment

The Daughter of the Regiment

Composed 1839.
First performed February 11, 1840.
Libretto by J.F.A. Bayard and J.H. Vernoy de Saint Georges.

Synopsis

Act I

Marie has been raised in a regiment by the amiable Sergeant Sulpice. Her eye has been caught by the young captain Tonio, who once saved her life, but little does she know that her affection is reciprocated. Tonio has been following her regiment, but even though they love each other they can never marry, because her husband has to be a member of the regiment. Tonio duly enlists but their love is again threatened when the Marquise de Birkenfeld, believing soldiers to be unsuitable companions for a young woman, orders Marie's removal from the regiment.

Act II

At the Marquise's château, Marie is growing tired of dancing and etiquette lessons. Her only pleasure is the presence of the recuperating Sulpice. Harassed by the Marquise's insistence that she embrace "respectability" and marry a foppish duke, Marie is overjoyed when her regiment visits the château. Tonio, who has been promoted for acts of valour, confronts the Marquise, demanding that he be allowed to marry Marie, but the Marquise is adamant. However, at dinner she shocks everyone by revealing that she is Marie's mother and consenting to her marriage. The opera ends with a hymn of praise to France.

Of the five operas Donizetti wrote to French texts, easily the most enjoyable is *La fille du régiment*, which was so well received in Paris that the first production ran for nearly fifty performances and the concluding "Salut, à la France" was raised to the status of unofficial national anthem. Today, it has regained its place in the affections of audiences across the world, and is staged whenever a satisfactory cast can be assembled. *La fille du régiment* is the best French opera not written by a Frenchman.

Marie and Tonio are gloriously simple comic characters, and Donizetti gave them music of joyful beauty. Of the countless good tunes, Marie's regimental song, "Chacun le sait", and her farewell to Tonio, "Il faut partir" (one of the opera's few plaintive episodes), are particularly fine, but it is Tonio's Act I "Pour mon âme ... ah mes amis" that is the great *tour de force*. One night at Covent Garden in 1966 Pavarotti made himself a superstar with his rendition of the ten-minute burst of riotous fun, in which the tenor is required to execute almost every barnstorming trick in the book – including a finale with nine consecutive high Cs.

The overall tone of the orchestral music is militaristic, as you might expect, but in contrast to the straight-faced martial setting of *Poliuto*, this is sardonic stuff, with Donizetti using the marching-band stereotype as a foil to the pretensions of the Marquise's polite society. But as with all of Donizetti's operas, the singing is the thing, and once you've heard the tumbling run of hit songs you might know what Mendelssohn meant when he controversially remarked that he wished he had composed *La fille du régiment*.

Sutherland, Pavarotti, Malas, Sinclair; Royal Opera House Chorus and Orchestra; Bonynge.
(Decca 414 520-2DH2; 2 CDs).

When the young Sutherland and Pavarotti made this recording in 1967 they were the perfect combination: not only did they possess the technique for the horrifically demanding main roles, they had a subtle comic interaction that was perfectly suited to the schooldays freshness of the young lovers. Pavarotti strolls through the opera with a unique combination of charm, wit and skill: his breathtaking "Ah mes amis" is perhaps his greatest moment on disc, while his ensembles with Joan Sutherland are the last word in élan. Of Sutherland's performance it's sufficient to say that she tackles the obstacle course of Marie's music with equal fluency. In short, everyone sounds as if they are having a whale of a time, and the recording itself is fresh and immediate.

Don Pasquale

Composed 1842.
First performed January 3, 1843.
Libretto by Giovanni Ruffini and the composer, after Anelli.

Synopsis

Act I

Don Pasquale, a wealthy old bachelor, is determined to disinherit his rebellious nephew Ernesto, who has fallen in love with the widow Norina. He asks Dr Malatesta to help him find a wife so that he can leave his fortune to his own children. Malatesta, a friend to both nephew and uncle, agrees to help Pasquale marry "Sofronia", supposedly Malatesta's sister, but in fact Norina in disguise.

Act II

Sofronia is presented to Pasquale; he is smitten by the veiled lady, whose only hobby is sewing. A wedding contract is drawn up in which the Don leaves half his worldly goods to his bride. As the ink is drying on the page, Sofronia reveals her true nature and begins to make her husband's life a misery, demanding every extravagance his money can buy.

Act III

Their relationship continues to disintegrate. Don Pasquale discovers that his wife has an assignation with a stranger, and prepares to catch the adulterers red-handed. Sofronia and Ernesto are surprised by the Don and Malatesta: although Pasquale is angry at having been made to look a fool, he is so delighted to be free of Sofronia that he readily agrees to bless his nephew's marriage.

Continuing the tradition of *Il matrimonio segreto* (see p.84) and *La serva padrona* (see p.42), *Don Pasquale* is the latest opera buffa to remain in repertoire. Its light orchestration and delicate vocal writing, harking back (with a hint of autumnal melancholy) to the comic operas of Mozart, suggest a radical re-evaluation after a lifetime's devotion to hearty extroversion.

It's a quick-witted opera, in which episodes of buffa humour are swiftly tempered by pathos, and vice versa. The third act provides a good example, when Norina, having slapped Don Pasquale during their quarrel over her intended visit to the theatre, expresses her remorse ("Via, caro sposino") at having driven the old fool to such despair; the sudden explosion of energy that follows, brought about by the exasperated Don's discovery that his wife is to meet another man, is typical of the composer's habit of quickly changing the emotional temperature.

The swiftness of pace is enhanced by the use of string-accompanied recitative, but Donizetti still takes time to indulge his passion for bel canto, and the melody grows progressively richer until, in the opera's solo highlight, Ernesto sings his idyllic "Com' è gentil". Tradition has it that this exquisite tenor cantilena was a last-minute addition: Donizetti allegedly took it from a box of miscellaneous music and sent it to Giovanni Mario, the tenor in the first performance, advising him to use it for his serenade to Norina. It was an immediate sensation, as was the opera as a whole, partly because the first-night cast featured not just the great Mario but also three of the so-called "Puritani Quartet" – his lover Grisi, plus Tamburini and Lablache.

RECORDINGS OVERVIEW

There have been fifteen recordings of *Don Pasquale*: many are extremely good, and two of those currently on CD are outstanding. Of those that might resurface, look out for the following: Cetra's 1949 set, with a beautiful Ernesto from Cesare Valletti and an affable title role from the character-bass Sesto Bruscantini; EMI's deliciously sung 1978 production with Sills and Kraus as the lovers (a bargain at mid-price); and Nuova Era's excellent live 1988 performance with Alessandro Corbelli as an outstanding Don Pasquale. The big-name productions with Muti (1982) and Gabriele Ferro (1988) are solid and reliable, but neither is a match for the following pair.

Corena, Sciutti, Oncina, Krause; Vienna State Opera Chorus and Orchestra; Kertész.
(Decca 433 036-2DM2; 2 CDs).

The Piccola Scala staged a famous production of *Don Pasquale* in 1959, building it round the talents of Graziella Sciutti, who was by then the world's most famous soubrette. Decca recorded her in the role of Norina not long after, and her performance set the mark against which all others have been measured – her voice is light, brilliantly flexible and shimmering with personality. Similarly convincing are Fernando Corena and Tom Krause as Pasquale and Malatesta. István Kertész, in one of his few operatic recordings, strongly suggests he should have made more. Good stereo and well priced.

Badini, Saraceni, Schipa, Poli; La Scala Chorus and Orchestra; Sabajano.
(Music Memoria MM30231; 2 CDs).

Taped in 1932, this was the first of the fifteen or so recordings of *Don Pasquale* and it remains a must. The primary charm is Tito Schipa's Ernesto, the only complete role he recorded: he is in glorious, smooth and aristocratic voice, and to this day he remains the finest exponent of the role on disc. There are other attractions to the set: Afro Poli's Malatesta is warm and purposeful, Adelaide Saraceni is young and flirty as Norina – and even the rusty La Scala Orchestra sounds beguiling on this old recording.

VINCENZO BELLINI

b. CATANIA, SICILY, NOVEMBER 3, 1801; d. PARIS, SEPTEMBER 23, 1835.

Bellini was born into an age when a composer was expected to complete an opera within a matter of weeks and not, as was the case half a century later, within a matter of years. When he died at the age of 34 he had completed ten operas – an impressive number, but at the same age Rossini had written thirty-nine, while Donizetti created thirty-five. The statistics are significant. Whereas Rossini and many of his bel canto successors could dash off an opera in days by falling back on habitual routines and not worrying too much about the correlation between text and music, Bellini tried to give more time and effort to his work. His Italian contemporaries generally saw themselves above all as creators of seductive melodies, and were content for the libretto and orchestra to effectively operate independently of each other. Bellini, however, strove to create well-

LEBRECHT COLLECTION

Vincenzo Bellini – "a sigh in pumps and silk stockings"

proportioned and poised dramas that appealed to the emotions rather than simply to the ear. Modern audiences sometimes have a problem with his abundance of oom-pah-pah orchestral passages, bombastic choruses and outbreaks of solo histrionics, but it's worth persevering, for he was, as Wagner wrote after Bellini's death, "all heart".

After studying with his father, Bellini moved in 1819 to Naples, where three years later he began lessons with Nicola Zingarelli, director of the Conservatorio di San Sebastiano and a noted composer of opera seria. Zingarelli introduced Bellini to the instrumental works of Mozart and Haydn and to the operas of Vivaldi and Scarlatti, and instructed the boy in counterpoint, harmony and melody. His concentration on the construction and use of song was fundamental to Bellini's development. Ironically for a composer famous for producing operas at incredible speed, Zingarelli shielded his pupil from Rossini's mellifluous note-spinning, and Bellini did not actually see one of the great man's operas until 1824, when, having already formed the foundations of his style, he attended a production of *Semiramide*. This imposed isolation was Zingarelli's single greatest gift to his student.

Bellini's graduation opera, *Adelson e Salvini*, performed at the Conservatorio in 1825, led to a commission from the Teatro San Carlo, where his *Bianca e Fernando* was produced the following year. This in turn led to an invitation from La Scala and an introduction to Felice Romani, Italy's most respected theatrical poet. It was the start of one of opera's most productive collaborations, from which emerged seven of Bellini's eight mature operas. Their first venture, *Il pirata*, marked the final, most glorious age of bel canto and secured Bellini's reputation overnight. Before long he had consolidated his fame with three masterpieces – *I Capuleti e i Montecchi*, *La Sonnambula* and *Norma* – but early in 1833 Bellini and Romani fell out over another of their collaborations, *Beatrice di Tenda*, a failure which appeared in print prefaced by Romani's apology for the poor standard of his work.

As his relationship with Romani collapsed so too did his private life: his protracted affair with the married Giuditta Turina ended when her husband discovered their relationship and all but forced the composer to leave the country. Bellini fled to London, where he assisted in the production of three of his operas. Loath to return either to Romani or Turina, Bellini remained in northern Europe, making his first visit to Paris in 1834. His stay brought him peace of mind and a commission for a grand opera seria from the Théâtre-Italien. Bellini's creative struggles with the composition of *I Puritani* – due in large part to the libretto by the dauntingly talentless Count Carlo Pepoli – were greatly relieved by his friendship with Rossini, who, though retired, continued to dominate the Parisian operatic world. Rossini convinced Bellini to persevere with his opera despite the weaknesses of the text, and the work was staged in January 1835 – eight months before Bellini's death from acute gastroenteritis.

His passing was mourned as a national tragedy. Within just eighteen months of arriving in the capital, Bellini had achieved a place in French musical life that was, according to one of his own letters, "second only to Rossini". Yet by the 1860s, with Wagner becoming Europe's most popular living composer, audiences had tired of Bellini's ingenuous emotionalism, although Wagner himself thought highly of Bellini's dramatic gifts – "he is one of my predilections because his music is strongly felt and intimately bound up with the words", he once wrote. Bellini did not return to the repertoire until the "bel canto revival" of the 1950s, when the likes of Callas and Caballé built their international reputations on his music, and the music of his more florid contemporaries. He has remained popular since then, but on record rather than on stage, chiefly because it's increasingly difficult to find singers who have the equipment for bel canto – lyric tenors, in particular, seem to be nearing extinction.

By the time Bellini hit his stride the demand for opera across Europe had become enormous and, as Meyerbeer and Rossini had proved, fortunes were there for the making. Like those two, Bellini submitted to the deadlines imposed by the impresarios who had become the masters of patronage, but he never lost the image of himself as a creative artist. Indeed for many he was the hypersensitive embodiment of the Romantic aesthetic – "a sigh in pumps and silk stockings" is how Heine acidly described him. His letters reveal that he saw himself in much the same way as Beethoven had, as the instrument of some divine force, a creator of life-changing art – and, again like Beethoven, he ensured that his genius was well paid. The most scrupulous of the bel canto composers, he used solid classical principles as the basis of a headily emotional style that exalts melody as an expression of character. In short, Bellini's work is the apotheosis of singer's opera, and whereas but a fraction of Donizetti's more flamboyant output is performed today, few of Bellini's operas have fallen out of circulation.

I Capuleti e i Montecchi

The Capulets and the Montagues

Composed 1830.
First performed March 11, 1830.
Libretto by Felice Romani, after Matteo Bandello and Luigi Sceola.

Synopsis

Act I

Capello, the chief of the Capuleti, refuses to agree to a pact through which his daughter Giulietta would marry Romeo of the Montecchi clan, and orders that her marriage to Tebaldo should go ahead immediately. Romeo fails to persuade Giulietta to elope, and so he and his supporter enter the city and disrupt the marriage celebrations.

Act II

Giulietta is informed by Lorenzo, the family doctor, that the only way to secure her freedom from Tebaldo is to take a sleeping draught that will give the impression that she is dead. She will be revived in the family vault, where he and Romeo will be waiting. The plan backfires when Lorenzo is arrested. Romeo believes Giulietta to be dead and takes poison but as he lies dying Giulietta wakes up. Hoping to avert the tragedy Lorenzo rushes in but he is too late: Romeo and Giulietta are lying dead in each other's arms.

Of the first Florentine production of *I Capuleti e i Montecchi* Hector Berlioz wrote in his memoirs: "Everyone was saying how good the music was; but the libretto too was well spoken of. This surprised me somewhat; the Italians as a rule pay little attention to the words of an opera. Perhaps I was about to hear a real Romeo at last, after all the lamentable attempts that had been made, a Romeo worthy of Shakespeare's genius. . . . In due course the principals appeared. Of these, all sang out of tune with the exception of two women, one of whom, tall and substantial, played Juliet. The other, short and thin, played Romeo." The dramatically absurd fashion for transvestite Romeos had long passed, but Bellini's tutor Zingarelli had written a part for a cross-dressed Romeo back in 1796, and his pupil inherited his belief that female voices in partnership are better suited to the expression of romantic love than the more naturalistic male/female coupling. It has since become common practice to substitute the mezzo-soprano Romeo with a tenor, but aside from the fact that this is not what Bellini intended, the tenor transposition is so arduous that only a specialist lyric voice, in the bloom of youth, can ever get away with it.

The assignment of the male lead to a female voice was not the only weatherbeaten feature of *I Capuleti e i Montecchi*. The libretto was reworked by Romani from a text he had written for Vaccai in 1825, and was set in a hurry by Bellini when the management of La Fenice asked him to write a piece for the carnival season, after Vaccai failed to deliver. It's hardly surprising, in view of the rush, that the final product fell some way short of the best of Bellini, but it has some moments of startling beauty.

The vocal writing has a lot of Rossinian vigour, with episodes that anticipate the warmth and spaciousness of Bellini's mature style – Juliet's soulful Act I romanza, "O quante volte", is a fine example. Other highlights include the characterful instrumental preludes, Tebaldo's opening romanza and the finale of Act I, in which the lovers sing a poignant cantabile melody in unison. It's true that Bellini here relies too much on conventional shifts into minor keys for moments of high drama, and that the music mirrors little beneath the characters' surface. Within just twelve months, however, his technique had become markedly more sophisticated.

Gruberova, Baltsa, Raffanti, Howell, Tomlinson; Royal Opera House Chorus and Orchestra; Muti.
(EMI CMS7 64846-2; 2 CDs).

This 1984 recording, taped live at Covent Garden, follows the original casting of both lovers as women, with a big mezzo Romeo and a light soprano Giulietta. Agnes Baltsa and Edita Gruberova are both exellent, with the former producing some spine-tingling tone, but their performances are dominated pretty much throughout by Riccardo Muti, whose discipline allows for little spontaneity. Dano Raffanti, a genuine lyric tenor, makes Tebaldo's Act I aria one of the recording's highlights, while John Tomlinson, in the small role of Lorenzo, shows off the diversity of his bass. This well-executed if not especially dramatic account makes the best introduction to Bellini's Shakespearean venture.

Scotto, Aragall, Pavarotti, Ferrin; La Scala Chorus and Orchestra; Abbado.
(Butterfly Music BMCDO12; 2 CDs).

If it were not for its poor sound quality and problematic availability, this remarkable recording would be a clear first choice, for it captures a trio of superb performers in their prime, in music that ideally suited their talents. Scotto's Giulietta is rich, impassioned and youthful, Aragall's Romeo is lucid, ringing and fluid right through his range, and Luciano Pavarotti, here singing Tebaldo, is simply magnificent. Add Abbado's loving attention to orchestral legato and the excellent La Scala Chorus, and you have a rare example of first-class modern-day bel canto.

La Sonnambula

The Sleepwalker

Composed 1831.
First performed March 6, 1831.
Libretto by Felice Romani, after Scribe.

Synopsis

Act I

The inhabitants of a small Swiss village are celebrating the forthcoming marriage of the orphan Amina and the wealthy farmer Elvino. The feudal lord Rodolfo, who is returning home after the death of his father, arrives to stay at the inn, where he flirts with Lisa, the hostess. Suddenly a window opens, through which enters Amina. Lisa, jealous of Amina and her engagement to Elvino, hurries off to tell him of his fiancée's seeming assignation with Rodolfo. Rodolfo realizes that Amina is sleepwalking and, moved by her somnambulistic declaration of love, he leaves her on his couch. Lisa and Elvino arrive to denounce Amina as an adulteress. Elvino calls off the wedding.

Act II

The village rallies round the distraught Amina and marches towards the castle to beg Rodolfo for verification of Amina's innocence. Amina is met on the way by Elvino, who rejects her and takes back his ring; he has decided to marry Lisa, who publicly rejoices in her good fortune. Rodolfo attempts to explain the truth but Elvino is unconvinced by the tale of his fiancée's somnambulism. The crowd is then distracted by the sight of Amina walking across the roof of the mill; when she reaches the ground she is heard praying for the return of Elvino's love. Moved by her devotion, Elvino replaces the ring on her finger. She wakes to find Elvino kneeling at her feet, and the crowd rejoices as the lovers head towards the church and their wedding.

Bellini's operas were written with particular singers in mind, and it was through his music that these artists established their reputations. The five or six singers for whom he wrote his finest music have gone down in history as some of the most gifted operatic performers there have ever been, and perhaps the greatest of all was Giuditta Pasta, for whom the roles of Amina and Norma (see p.184) were created. A lyric-dramatic soprano, Pasta's voice "electrified the soul", according to Stendhal, while Bellini praised her "encyclopaedic artistry". Certainly the disparity between *I Capuleti e i Montecchi* and *La Sonnambula* suggests that Pasta presented the composer with hitherto unattainable opportunities: the scale, colour and difficulty of the music were of a new order, and early performances of *La Sonnambula* were, as Glinka remarked, enough to drive "audiences to tears of emotion and ecstasy".

Amina is simply one of the most perfect soprano roles in Italian opera, possessing a strength of character that transcends the implausibilities of the plot. She is called upon to detonate a warehouse of coloratura fireworks, but her music has a variety and a pensive quality that anticipate the intricacy of many of Verdi's heroines. Her cavatina in Act I, for example, takes her through ecstasy, introversion and anxiety before arriving at an archetypal glittering bel canto display. Elvino is a lighter creature but his music is notable for its unusually lengthy melodies, a feature soon to become characteristic of Bellini's work, and he does have one effortlessly beautiful and outrageously sentimental aria, "Prendi, l'anel ti dono", also in Act I. Composed for the tenor Giovanni Rubini, Elvino is scored for an exceptionally high voice and nowadays his arias and ensembles are transposed down – even the megastars can't manage the part as written.

Sutherland, Pavarotti, Ghiaurov, Buchanan; London Opera Chorus; National Philharmonic Orchestra; Bonynge.
(Decca 417 424-2DH2; 2 CDs).

The second of Sutherland's two recordings of *Sonnambula* was recorded in 1980, eighteen years after her first. You might assume that, in her fifty-fourth year, the delicate requirements of Amina would be beyond her, but she floats above the stave with amazing sweetness and catches the high E flats with a grace and elegance most singers half her age could not manage. Her Elvino, Luciano Pavarotti, was past his best when he made this recording, but he is a true stylist, sweetening most shifts with sensual portamento, and giving Arturo a real grace and innocence. Bonynge makes all the right choices of tempo and balance, and the recording has good digital sound.

Callas, Monti, Zaccaria, Ratti; la Scala Chorus; La Scala Orchestra; Votto.
(EMI CDS7 47378-8; 2 CDs).

This 1957 recording is all about Callas, who is so forceful a presence that she tends to unbalance the opera. True to the composer's style, she produces some flowing, beautifully expressive lines, and though Votto's slow tempi allow for some questionable indulgences, she spurs the pace when pyrotechnics are needed. Unfortunately, the rest of the cast can't live with her, not even Nicola Monti, whose light and agile voice was well suited to this music, as he proved when recording the role again with Sutherland in 1960.

Pagliughi, Tagliavini, Siepi; Italian Radio Chorus and Orchestra; Capuana.
(Fonit Cetra CDO 16; 2 CDs).

There is only one reason for buying this recording, but it is a very good reason. Feruccio Tagliavini, who died in 1995, was a great lyric tenor who, like so many other post-war lyric tenors, ruined his voice through singing unsuitable but more exciting repertoire. His most successful performance on disc is his Elvino on this 1953 set, perhaps the finest recorded example of modern bel canto tenor. Although the music is transposed down, Tagliavini's singing is of a purity and effortlessness that comes as close to capturing the style of Bellini's time as anything you'll hear.

Norma

Composed 1831.
First performed December 26, 1831.
Libretto by Felice Romani, after Soumet and Chateaubriand.

Synopsis

Act I

Gaul during the Roman occupation. Pollione, the Roman consul, has abandoned Norma, the Druid high priestess (by whom he has two sons) in favour of Adalgisa, an acolyte. Norma is unaware of Pollione's infidelity. Despite ominous dreams, Pollione decides to take Adalgisa back to Rome and marry her. Norma is shattered to discover that Adalgisa's lover is none other than Pollione, while Adalgisa is horrified to learn that Pollione is intending to abandon Norma.

Act II

Norma wrestles with her conscience as she contemplates the murder of her children. She manages to restrain herself and decides to entrust them to Adalgisa's care. Adalgisa renounces Pollione to Norma and, swearing never to love him again, promises to persuade him to return to the mother of his children. When Norma learns of Adalgisa's failure to achieve this goal, she incites the Gauls to war against the Romans: all that is needed is a sacrifice. Pollione is captured breaking into the virgin's temple and is sentenced to death, but he still refuses to disown Adalgisa. Norma, driven to despair, orders the funeral pyre to be lit – she will take Pollione's place as the sacrifice. Her selflessness forces Pollione to reconsider and he realizes that he does in fact love Norma after all. But it is too late: after consigning her children to her father's care, she mounts the pyre, where she is joined in death by Pollione.

Bellini craved a good libretto so that he could "portray the passions in the liveliest manner", and for *Norma* he did receive an outstanding text, perhaps the finest he ever worked with. His obsession with the integration of words and music (an obsession for which he was dubbed "filosofica" by admiring contemporaries) led him to demand numerous revisions from Romani, so that he could produce an opera in which the verbal and musical accents coincide throughout, without diluting the lyrical quality of the work as a whole. *Norma* marks the zenith of dramatic bel canto, and for many it's the finest singers' opera ever written.

Norma achieves its power through uncomplicated means. Bellini was unmoved by the self-consciously expert technique of Rossini and was bored by much of Donizetti's loquacious melodrama. And whereas his German contemporaries Spohr and Weber experimented with ever more complex chordal and harmonic patterns, Bellini supported *Norma*'s finest vocal writing with no more than three or four chords. The vocal writing is very exposed, with extremely long, carefully unfolded melodies emerging organically from the recitative – the scene that opens the second act is a perfect example, with its heart-gripping build-up of tension through recitative into song. Similarly, Bellini sustains a remarkable continuity between outbursts of emotion and frequently melancholic introversion: in Act I, for example, a seamless half-hour span encompasses the tenor Pollione's self-assured showpiece, "Mecco all'altar di Venere", Norma's languid and exquisitely poignant prayer for peace, "Casta Diva", and her ecstatic resolution to elope with the proconsul, "Va, crudele".

The title role served as the model for many of Verdi's tragic heroines, and when he came to write *Tristan und Isolde*, Wagner expressed his wish that Isolde would become his Norma, acknowledging the power of Bellini's creation. And like *Tristan*, *Norma* is an opera of extremes, demanding absolute surrender from an audience – it cannot be appreciated, as can Mozart's operas, by a detached observer. If you listen to this piece sung by a top-quality cast, the last twenty minutes, with their tragic duets for Norma and Pollione, are likely to move you to tears.

RECORDINGS OVERVIEW

The title role of *Norma* is horribly arduous, but the reason so many recordings of the opera have failed has more to do with the demands of the role of Pollione: Sutherland, Caballé and Sills were all let down by their male leads, while Mario del Monaco's assault on the part, recorded for Decca in 1967, produced some of the ugliest and loudest singing ever committed to disc. Maria Callas, by contrast, had the good fortune to be well-matched on both her thrilling forays into *Norma*.

Callas, Stignani, Filippeschi, Rossi-Lemeni; La Scala Chorus and Orchestra; Serafin.
(EMI CDS7 47304-8; 3 CDs).

Callas's 1954 recording of *Norma* was one of the highlights of her career, and it's a performance in which her remarkable contribution is part of an even more remarkable whole. Her Norma is a powerful, frequently astonishing display of theatrical singing, with the blood-curdling outbursts balanced by moments of tender introspection. Mario Filippeschi was underrated and under-recorded, but his open-throated tenor is ideally placed for Pollione and there is something hypnotic in his old-fashioned, melancholic sound. Ebe Stignani's soprano was too light for the role of Adalgisa, but she is conscientiously dramatic and presents a defined and consistent character. Serafin is in marvellous form, inciting a searing account from the forces of La Scala.

Callas, Ludwig, Corelli, Zaccaria; La Scala Chorus and Orchestra; Serafin.
(EMI CMS7 63000-2; 3 CDs).

The reason for this remake, only six years later, was the emergence of the tenor Franco Corelli, whose Pollione is one of the most moving examples of heroic tenor singing on record. If you think Pavarotti is exciting, listen to this – Callas rarely came so close to being outshone by her leading man. Christa Ludwig is also outstanding: rich and creamy in the low register, and truly dramatic above the stave, she is unrivalled in the role of Adalgisa. Callas's voice is not what it was, with some shrill high notes and plentiful outbreaks of the notorious late-Callas vibrato, but as a singer-actress she has no equal, and there are some wonderful episodes – not least the final duets with Corelli. Serafin is again conscious of the need for theatrical support but he is more subtle and less inclined to rush than in the '54 version. Excellent stereo.

I Puritani

The Puritans

Composed 1834–35.
First performed January 25, 1835.
Libretto by Carlo Pepoli, after Walter Scott.

Synopsis

Part I

Plymouth, England, during the Civil War. Charles I's widow, Queen Henrietta (Enrichetta), is being held captive in a fortress governed by the Puritan Lord Walton. His daughter Elvira loves Lord Arthur (Arturo) Talbot, a Cavalier. Although they are given permission to marry, Elvira is secretly loved by the Puritan enemy of Arthur, Sir Richard (Riccardo) Forth. Arthur helps the widowed Queen to escape by dressing her in Elvira's bridal veil. Elvira, believing she has been betrayed, loses all reason.

Part II

Lord Walton's brother George (Giorgio) enters with news of Elvira's ravings. He is followed by Richard, who announces that Arthur has been sentenced to death by Parliament. The mad Elvira arrives, singing of her lost love. George urges Richard to save Arthur's life, for if he and Elvira are not soon reunited, she will surely die. Richard reluctantly agrees, but swears that, should Arthur join the Royalist ranks in battle the following day, he will exact revenge for the pain Arthur has caused Elvira.

Part III

Arthur, though aware of the danger, returns to Elvira. They embrace but Elvira, terrified that he will again disappear, cries out. Her screams bring Richard and a group of Puritan soldiers to the scene. Richard pronounces Arthur's death sentence but this brings Elvira back to her senses and the two are united for what seems the final time. At the last minute, soldiers announce the Stuarts' defeat and the end of the war. A universal pardon is issued, leaving Arthur and Elvira free to marry.

"Carve in your head in letters of adamant: the music-drama must draw tears, inspire terror, make people die." So the exasperated Bellini wrote to Count Carlo Pepoli, his ill-chosen librettist for *I Puritani*. Bellini first met Pepoli at the Paris salon of an Italian princess, but their collaboration was brought about by Rossini, who had used some of Pepoli's poetry for songs of his own. Bellini should have known better, given that Rossini's attitude towards the relationship between language and music was rather more devil-may-care than his own, and he certainly regretted his decision. Even after the opera had been lauded as a masterpiece, Bellini continued to lament Pepoli's "repetitive, commonplace and sometimes stupid turns of phrase".

Whatever the failings of the Count's literary efforts, the premiere was a sensation, due in large part to the fact that it was performed by four of the finest singers of any era, the so-called "Puritani" quartet of Grisi (soprano), Rubini (tenor), Tamburini (baritone) and Lablache (bass). Almost every number was encored, forcing Bellini to cut the opera so that the audience's demands might be accommodated, and it's in this truncated form that the work is heard today.

I Puritani is something of a bel canto manifesto, with a spectrum of expression that goes a long way towards compensating for Pepoli's shortcomings. From languid cantabile such as Arturo's haunting "A te o cara" to sparkling coloratura such as Elvira's lustrous "Son vergin vezzosa", this opera flaunts an array of set-pieces that's without equal in the bel canto repertoire, and the only reason *I Puritani* doesn't come around very often is that there are very, very few singers able to sing the lead roles. "A te o cara", with which Arturo makes his first entrance, calls for a high C sharp; his exuberant duet with Elvira, "Vieni, fra questa braccia", has two high Ds; and, as if that weren't enough, the final, tear-jerking duet with Elvira, "Credeasi, misera", calls for (but rarely receives) a high F – a fifth above the top note of "Nessun Dorma". ("Credeasi, misera" was sung at the composer's funeral, when Rossini and Cherubini were among the pallbearers.) To stabilize the vocal coruscations, Bellini provided an unusually sophisticated orchestral accompaniment, with expressive changes in key and metre, and harmonies that are much more adventurous than in his previous works. *I Puritani* may lack the dramatic cohesion of *Norma*, being marred by some offputting changes in pace, but judged as an assemblage of vocal highlights, this is one of the most enjoyable operas of its period.

RECORDINGS OVERVIEW

More than *Norma* or *Sonnambula*, Bellini's last opera is a work of ensemble, featuring prominent roles for tenor, baritone and bass as well as the soprano heroine. It's the uneasiness of her colleagues that makes Callas's 1953 EMI recording less than ideal, though Callas fans won't want to be without it. Bellini completists might want to check out the 1986 Fonit Cetra set, which recreates Bellini's revision of the score for Maria Malibran; the composer and Malibran both died before the performance could take place, and the score lay unperformed until these discs were made.

Sutherland, Pavarotti, Cappuccilli, Ghiaurov; Chorus of the Royal Opera House; Orchestra of the Royal Opera House; Bonynge.
(Decca 417 588-2DH3; 3 CDs).

Sutherland's habit of recording everything twice didn't often produce improvements, but her second reading of Elvira, taped in 1974, is greatly superior to the first, made eleven years earlier. The first attempt is certainly an exciting display of bravura technique, but second time round she gets behind the role, with a bite to her diction and a darker sonority that brings a lot to Elvira's character. Moreover, she sings with an ensemble that has never been bettered. Pavarotti is in sumptuous voice, distributing the high notes with bewildering panache – the impact is stunning when, after a gathering of high Cs and a clutch of Ds he launches himself into the high F in "Vienni fra questa braccia". Cappuccilli and Ghiaurov are similarly well placed for the roles of Riccardo and Giorgio, while Bonynge ensures that momentum is maintained.

Caballé, Kraus, Manuguerra, Hamari; Ambrosian Opera Chorus; Philharmonia Chorus; Muti
(EMI 769663-2; 3 CDs).

Excellent though the cast may be, the crux of this recording is Riccardo Muti's extremely detailed and thoughtful reading of the score. The stars are kept in their place, which makes a pleasant change in this sort of music. Caballé is in superb voice, and thanks to Muti she only rarely resorts to the creamy, expressionless tone which blights a number of bel canto recordings. Alfredo Kraus's tenor, on the other hand, could do with more bite – his dreamy voice produces passages of intoxicating but almost meaningless vocalism.

MICHAEL BALFE

b. DUBLIN, IRELAND, MAY 15, 1808; d. ROWNEY ABBEY, OCTOBER 20, 1870.

With few exceptions, the history of British opera is the history of foreign imports – perhaps because the British tend to agree with Dr Johnson's definition of the genre as an "exotic and irrational entertainment". During the nineteenth century, the roll-call of opera composers from the British Isles comprised only writers of light opera, and of these just two, Michael Balfe and Arthur Sullivan, achieved any lasting popularity.

Balfe received his early training in Wexford (where his works are often performed at the annual opera festival) and in London, but he learned most from his years in Italy and France where, as a baritone as well as a composer, he received encouragement from Rossini and Cherubini. In 1835, in London, he staged his first English opera, *The Siege of Rochelle*, which was almost immediately eclipsed when he wrote *The Maid of Artois* and produced it at Covent Garden, with the great soprano Maria Malibran (see p.162) in the title role. On the basis of these two hits, Balfe rashly announced a season of English opera at the Lyceum theatre; weeks later it closed. He moved to Paris in 1841 but two years later Drury Lane became the English Opera House, for which Balfe composed the best of his 29 operas, *The Bohemian Girl*.

By the end of the year his name was known throughout Europe and he began to divide his time between Paris and London, composing music for both cities. In 1864, after successful productions in Berlin, Vienna and St Petersburg, and far less successful involvement with the Pyne-Harrison Project for the "foundation and promotion of an English Opera", Balfe retired from music, turning his attentions towards farming on his vast estate in Hertfordshire.

Balfe was the only nineteenth-century English-speaking composer to thrive overseas, but despite the claims made by zealots of the British musical tradition, his work palls in comparison to that of Donizetti, Rossini and Verdi, the composers to whom he was most indebted. The appeal of his operas lies wholly in their ballads, melodic and generally sweetly melancholic creations, which are perhaps best regarded as high-class drawing-room or music-hall songs, rather than as full-blown operatic arias.

The Bohemian Girl

Composed 1843.
First performed November 27, 1843.
Libretto by Alfred Bunn.

Synopsis

Act I

In Pressburg, a grand festival is organized in honour of the Austrian Emperor but all turns sour when Count Arnheim's six-year-old daughter, Arline, is abducted by gypsies.

Act II

Twelve years later Arline is living in a gypsy camp. She is in love with Thaddeus, a Polish aristocratic officer who is taking shelter in her camp; but the Gypsy Queen is violently opposed to their union because she too loves Thaddeus. She plots against Arline but at her trial Arline is recognized by the judge, who, fortunately for her, is her father.

Act III

The Gypsy Queen decides to murder Thaddeus but is killed in the attempt. The Count agrees to his daughter's marriage, and the opera ends amid much rejoicing.

Alfred Bunn was a leading impresario of his day, and was proudly responsible for promoting the London debuts of Wilhelmine Schröder-Devrient (one of Wagner's favourites) and Maria Malibran (whom he paid the mad sum of £3,375 – more than £100,000 in today's currency – for nineteen performances in 1833). He was also a frightful librettist, and it's a testament to Balfe's abilities that he was able to make something, if not much, out of Bunn's anti-theatrical waffle and cardboard characters (very loosely based upon a short novel by Cervantes). The music is typically frothy with a disproportionate number of ballads, but some of the songs for Arline and Thaddeus have a glutinous sentimental charm, and two of them, "I dreamt that I dwelt in marble halls" and "When other lips and other hearts", have remained justifiably famous.

Thomas, Power, Cullen, Summers, German; RTE Philharmonic Chorus; Ireland National Symphony Orchestra; Bonynge.
(Argo 433 324-2ZH2; 2 CDs).

Taped in Ireland in 1991, this recording has much to recommend it, not least Bonynge's spirited, good-natured conducting. The cast revel in Bunn's daft libretto, and stroll sure-footedly through Balfe's undemanding music. The orchestra plays with gusto and brilliance, the chorus is bright and nicely balanced and the recorded sound is exceptional. The composer could have hoped for nothing better.

5

VERDI, WAGNER AND THEIR CONTEMPORARIES

VERDI, WAGNER AND THEIR CONTEMPORARIES

In the first half of the nineteenth century, Italian opera was sustained by a trio of top-rank composers: Rossini, Bellini and Donizetti. In the second half, one man dominated the scene: **Giuseppe Verdi**. The creator of a succession of vehement and tunefully melodramatic operas that have never lost their ability to pull in the crowds, Verdi was more than a musician – deeply involved in the political struggle to unify the Italian nation, he became a totemic figure for his audiences, who heard in his operas "the voice of the Italian soul", in the words of one of his collaborators. Through such works as *Rigoletto*, *Il Trovatore*, *La Traviata*, *Aida*, *Falstaff* and *Otello*, he dominated Italian opera from 1845 until his death in 1901, by which time Italy had been liberated and united, and Verdi's work was being enjoyed more for its dramatic potency than for its political undertones. Few other Italian composers were able to attract much limelight away from a man whose music was spread into every corner of the country on thousands of hurdy-gurdies and barrel-organs and became a staple of every European and American opera house during his lifetime. Of those who did, the best known are **Arrigo Boito** and **Amilcare Ponchielli**. Though most widely celebrated as the best of Verdi's librettists, Boito was a composer of considerable ability and his setting of Goethe's *Faust* has managed to find a place in the international repertoire. Ponchielli's solitary triumph, *La gioconda*, has been a perennial vehicle for dramatic singers ever since its premiere in 1876.

5

In Germany at this time the roost was ruled, absolutely, by **Richard Wagner**, one of the most influential musicians in history. Wagner revolutionized opera, blending music, poetry and stagecraft in enormous music-dramas that derived their subject matter from myths and ancient epics. In their ambition, atmosphere and construction, works such as *Tristan und Isolde* and the gargantuan *Ring* cycle have next to nothing in common with Verdi's thrilling romances, but for all their complexity (and, some would add, portentousness), Wagner's creations contain some of the most emotive and theatrical music ever written. Like Verdi, Wagner was a stifling presence, and only three of his German-speaking contemporaries wrote operas that have survived to the present day. Two of these, Friedrich von Flotow (see p.151) and the short-lived Otto Nicolai (see p.149), had hit their peak many years before Wagner's heyday. The third, **Johann Strauss the Younger**, could not have been more unlike Wagner. Known primarily for waltzes such as *The Blue Danube*, he made his major contribution to the genre of opera with *Die Fledermaus* and *Der Zigeunerbaron*, two frothy concoctions that are the epitome of decadent Viennese *joie de vivre*.

While Strauss spiced up his operettas with passing allusions to the folk music of eastern Europe, in the Czech lands a more serious approach to indigenous culture was manifested in the work of **Bedřich Smetana**, who gave his country an operatic language quite distinct from that of the dominant Austro-German influences. The same process was under way in Russia as well, a development heralded by **Mikhail Glinka**, the first to forge a Russian voice that was not a mimicry of European models. Glinka's operas, with their speech-based vocal melodies, innovative instrumentation and epic scenarios, were a source of inspiration for Russian musicians. *Ruslan and Lyudmila* and *A Life for the Tsar* were played throughout Europe, and within seven years of the composer's death the reforming Tsar Alexander II had established the St Petersburg and Moscow conservatories, institutions that played a crucial role in fostering the intensely patriotic group of musicians known as "The Five" or "The Mighty Handful": Mily Balakirev, Cesare Cui, **Alexander Borodin**, **Modest Mussorgsky** and **Nicolai Rimsky-Korsakov**. In musical terms, Borodin's *Prince Igor* is the least Russian of the operas produced by this group, though its subject matter is rooted in his homeland. In Rimsky-Korsakov's fairy-tale operas, however, you encounter a panoply of Russian effects, principally non-western harmony and orchestration and a lavish use of pictorial imagery. At the opposite extreme to the sprightliness of Rimsky-Korsakov stands Mussorgsky, whose single completed opera, the louring *Boris Godunov*, is considered by many to be the greatest of all Russian operas. Its rivals to this title are *Eugene Onegin* and *The Queen of Spades*, the masterworks of **Pyotr Tchaikovsky**. The most famous of all Russian composers was also the most complex. Antipathetic to the sometimes strident nationalism of "The Mighty Handful", Tchaikovsky fused the very best of both worlds, refining his talents through the study of such diverse composers as Mozart, Meyerbeer and Bizet, while drawing his material from Russian sources ranging from folk tales to Pushkin.

In France, meanwhile, the excesses of Grand Opéra were giving way to dramas that were more modest in scale while lacking nothing in emotional impact. **Charles Gounod**, the master melodist of French Romantic opera, created the single most popular French opera of the nineteenth century with *Faust*. **Ambroise Thomas** similarly had a skill for emotive and languid melodies, but the real innovator in France at this time was **Georges Bizet**, who struggled hard and long for success in the opera house, and died without knowing that he had achieved it with *Carmen*, a work that has remained in the repertoire of every opera company in the world. Packed with tunes and sounds that evoke the Mediterranean with unprecedented vivacity, this hard-hitting tale of lust and murder was to prove hugely influential – the shockers written by Puccini and his *verismo* compatriots are all the offspring of *Carmen*.

Though no other French composer of the period wrote anything that packed the same sort of punch as *Carmen*, the scene in France was more diverse than it was in Italy and Germany, as there was no single composer who exerted a degree of influence comparable to that of Verdi and Wagner. **Camille Saint-Saëns** produced one opera that has lasted, *Samson et Dalila*, while **Leo Delibes**, famed chiefly as a ballet composer, created *Lakmé*, an exotic tale that is home to one of the best-known tunes in all opera and that exemplifies the French predilection for delicate tissues of sound. **Edouard Lalo**, **Emmanuel Chabrier** and **Ernest Chausson** all produced operas that to some extent married the scale and weight of Wagner's work to the lyricism of Gounod, Delibes and Bizet – though Chabrier is now remembered mainly for a very un-Wagnerian comedy, *Le roi malgré lui*. Paris's undisputed king of comedy was **Jacques Offenbach**, scourge of Second Empire pretensions and the father of French operetta. Though his one serious opera – *Les contes d'Hoffmann* – has maintained its place into the CD era, his reputation rests on *Orphée aux enfers* and his other coruscating parodies of Napoleon III's self-indulgent and self-mythologizing regime.

Offenbach's engaging mixture of frivolity and satire bears more than a passing resemblance to the operettas of **Arthur Sullivan**, who with librettist William Gilbert embarked on a stupendously successful career just as Offenbach was nearing the end of his. Gilbert and Sullivan's so-called Savoy operas – named after the theatre in which they were first performed – might not feature on the period's roster of great works of art, but they provide a pleasurable diversion from *Tristan*, *Rigoletto* and the other giants of the second half of the nineteenth century.

GIUSEPPE VERDI

b. BUSSETO, ITALY, OCTOBER 9, 1813; d. MILAN, JANUARY 27, 1901.

The story of Italian opera from 1850 to 1900 is the story of Giuseppe Verdi. Born into one of the most exciting periods in Italian musical history, he reached maturity in the 1840s, when things had begun to look decidedly bleak: Rossini was in retirement, Bellini was dead and Donizetti was dying. Over the next fifty years, through the composition of nearly thirty operas, Verdi revitalized Italian music, giving it an identity as strong as that created for German music by Wagner. More than that, he was a figurehead for those endeavouring to constitute a nation from a country that had been divided up by the European superpowers in the aftermath of the Napoleonic wars. When, during the 1850s, audiences chanted "Viva Verdi", they were celebrating him, his music, and the idea of unified Italy, for Verdi was also the acronym of "Vittorio Emmanuele, Rè d'Italia" – Victor Emanuel, King of Italy. "What is too dangerous to say in words can be sung in music", wrote Beaumarchais with reference to the censorship of his own work, and Verdi made the most of this licence by employing a musical language that spoke with an unrivalled immediacy and conviction to the majority. Verdi's extra-musical status was eloquently confirmed at his funeral, when the crowd of thousands struck up the "Chorus of the Hebrew Slaves" from *Nabucco*.

Verdi's parents owned a tavern in the village of Le Roncole, close to Busseto in the Parma region of northern Italy. Just months after he was born, Russian troops rooting out pro-French factions smashed their way into the local church of San Michele and butchered a dozen women and children. Verdi's mother hid with Giuseppe in the belltower and escaped unharmed; the incident had an obvious formative effect. Though the Verdi family was poor, the boy's musical talent quickly flourished: by the time he was twelve he had been appointed organist at San Michele and was soon dividing his time between Le Roncole and Busseto, where he undertook formal musical studies.

In June 1832, under the patronage of the trader and music-lover Antonio Barezzi (who commissioned pieces from the young Verdi, for his Busseto Philharmonic Society), he travelled to Milan to sit the entrance exam for the conservatory. To everyone's astonishment, above all his own, he failed. He nonetheless remained in Milan and began private lessons, staying with friends of Barezzi, who found him a boorish lodger. He managed to find work conducting (at what is now the Piccola Scala) and began to make some sort of reputation, as a conductor and musical jack-of-all-trades, then in 1835 came back to Busseto to apply for the job of director of the Philharmonic Society. He was successful, receiving his official appointment in February 1836, just three months before he married Barezzi's daughter Margherita. Life pro-

Giuseppe Verdi – the figurehead of Italian opera in the second half of the nineteenth century

gressed uneventfully, and he spent most of his time hankering after the big stage in Milan. In 1839 his ambition got the better of him and he resigned from his post in Busseto and moved back north, where he submitted his first extant opera, *Oberto*, to the La Scala management.

For someone with no track record as a composer it was a remarkably confident gesture, typical of a man increasingly known for his taciturn single-mindedness and self-belief. Thanks largely to the intervention of the young soprano Giuseppina Strepponi, La Scala accepted the unsolicited offering, and though the staff of the opera house were to be sorely tried by Verdi's determination to prove he owed nothing to anybody (having lived for so long off Barezzi) and was better than any scholarship winner, *Oberto*'s success made up for any personal differences. Indeed, such was its success that La Scala offered Verdi a contract for a further three operas.

However, the deaths of his son, daughter and wife in 1840 sent him into a spiralling depression. He tried and failed to extract himself from the La Scala contract, and his unhappiness was compounded by the disastrous failure of his comic opera *Un giorno di regno* later the same year. Yet this flop provided confirmation that his talents lay with high-minded seriousness rather than with comedy. In 1842 he produced *Nabucco*, a biblical tale with a political message that the long-suffering Italian people easily identified; it secured Verdi's fame throughout Italy. There followed a string of commissions from Milan, Rome, Naples and Venice, and during the next eight years he composed thirteen operas, most of them tragic and nearly all rooted in historical fact. This use of history as a commentary on the current struggle of the occupied Italian nation struck a resounding chord with audiences, and through such works as *I Lombardi alla prima crociata*, *Ernani*, *I due Foscari*, *Attila*, *Macbeth*, *Luisa Miller* and *Stiffelio* Verdi cemented his reputation as his country's pre-eminent composer of opera.

By the time Verdi completed *Stiffelio* in 1850 he and Strepponi were three years into a relationship that would last for half a century (they married in 1859). A woman of great generosity and patience, she was witty and tactful where Verdi was blunt and rather humourless, and she had a profound influence on his personality and his work. She translated and edited source material for him and gave him the courage to set texts that might aggravate the authorities – one such, Victor Hugo's *Le roi s'amuse*, became *Rigoletto* (1851), the first of a series of operas that made him an international name.

After the big trio of *Rigoletto*, *Il Trovatore* and *La Traviata*, Verdi followed through with *Simon Boccanegra*, *Un ballo in maschera*, *La forza del destino*, *Don Carlos* and *Aida* – the most consistently popular body of operas produced in the period between Mozart and Puccini. After *Aida* was completed in 1871 he wrote no new opera for fifteen years, but these years were far from fallow. He was elected to Italian senate in 1874 (he served for five years) and he devoted a lot of energy to the revision of many of his earlier operas – including *Macbeth*, *La forza del destino*, *Simon Boccanegra* and *Don Carlos* – as well as creating his one great non-operatic work, the *Requiem* (1874), described by the German conductor Hans von Bulow as "the best opera Verdi never wrote".

The revision of *Boccanegra* in 1880 benefited from the involvement of the poet and composer Arrigo Boito, and it was to the team of Boito and Shakespeare that Verdi turned for the two operas that stand as the apotheosis of his life's work: a tragedy, *Otello* (1887); and a comedy, *Falstaff* (1893). After writing a series of sacred works, including the *Quattro Pezzi Sacri* (Four Sacred Pieces), he devoted his last two years to the establishment of the Casa di Riposa, a retirement home for musicians in Milan, funded by his enormous royalties. In 1901, aged eighty-eight, Verdi died of a stroke. The world's most famous and wealthy composer had modestly prescribed for his funeral "One priest, one candle, one cross", but it was turned into an occasion for national mourning. A huge orchestra, conducted by Arturo Toscanini, played at his burial in the grounds of the Casa di Riposa; a quarter of a million people attended the cortège.

In terms of sustained popularity, Verdi belongs in the highly select company of Mozart, Wagner and Puccini, with at least a dozen of his works in constant circulation. The reasons for this can be summarized in just three words: drama and melody. Verdi's operas deal with basic human emotions – love, envy, jealousy, loyalty and hatred – in a manner that is immediately empathetic, no matter how unusual (or in some instances unlikely) the circumstances in which the protagonists find themselves. Verdi's earlier operas were admittedly crude in their conception of drama: *Macbeth* is typical in its reliance on crashing music, violent contrasts and lavish spectacle, a style that was indebted to the melodramas of the likes of Meyerbeer and Donizetti. With *Rigoletto*, however, Verdi's musical language changed. Whereas the early works were characterized by repetitive rhythms, percussive orchestration, vast choruses and sudden contrasts between lyrical and declamatory passages, the later operas are marked by a far more sophisticated and fluent style. This fluency is quite different from the river-like structure of Wagner's great operas: in Verdi's work there are distinct arias, as in any traditional Italian opera, but the structure is as tight as a well-made play: whereas a Donizetti set-piece often seems to be begging for applause, a Verdi aria adds substance to the drama and impels the action onward.

And just as Verdi's manipulation of structure became far more adroit, so did his exploration of the expressive and illustrative character of melody – it's a long way from the barking, square manner of *Nabucco* to the lucid, unbroken, almost conversational lines of *Otello*. From *Rigoletto* onwards, Verdi showed an unerring ability to devise melodies that were both apposite and dazzling, expressing the profoundest of emotions without ever sacrificing the tunefulness that was the hallmark of nineteenth-century Italian opera. Isaiah Berlin summarized the appeal of Verdi when he wrote: "Noble, simple, with a degree of unbroken vitality and vast natural power of creation and organization, Verdi is the voice of a world that is no more. His enormous popularity among the sophisticated as well as the most ordinary listeners today is due to the fact that he expressed permanent states of consciousness in the most direct terms, as Homer, Shakespeare, Ibsen and Tolstoy have done."

Nabucco

Nebuchadnezzar

Composed 1841; revised 1842.
First performed March 9, 1842.
Libretto by Temistocle Solera.

Synopsis

Part I

King Nabucco's invading army has forced the Jews to hide inside Solomon's Temple. The high priest Zaccaria has kidnapped Nabucco's daughter Fenena, who is entrusted to the care of Ismaele (Ishmael). Unknown to Zaccaria, Ismaele and Fenena are lovers, having met when Ismaele was sent to Babylon as an emissary. Another of Nabucco's daughters, the warrior Abigaille (who is also in love with Ismaele), smashes her way into the temple and offers him a chance to save his people: if he will leave with her, the Jews will be spared. Nabucco then rides into the temple, at which point Zaccaria threatens to kill Fenena. Ismaele manages to save her and, as she runs to Nabucco, he and Abigaille call for the destruction of the Jews and their city. The Jews condemn Ismaele.

Part II

The Jews have been taken captive to Babylon. In the city palace, which is being governed by Fenena, it emerges that Abigaille was born to slaves, not royalty, and that she has stolen the solitary document of proof. She is supported by the High Priest of Baal, who begins a rumour that Nabucco has been killed and calls for Abigaille's coronation. In another room of the palace Zaccaria prays for wisdom and reveals that Fenena has become a Jew. Nabucco arrives and proclaims himself a god, but is struck by a thunderbolt and turned mad – whereupon Abigaille snatches the crown.

Part III

As Babylon salutes Abigaille, the High Priest demands the execution of all Jews – beginning with Fenena. Nabucco, still mad, tries to reclaim the crown but is dismissed by Abigaille, who then manages to trick him into signing Fenena's death warrant. When he realizes what he has done, Nabucco is horrified – doubly so when he sees Abigaille destroy the proof of her lowly birth. On the banks of the Euphrates, the Jews sing of their homeland. Zaccaria prophesies the fall of Babylon.

Part IV

Nabucco emerges from madness to realize that Jehovah is the one true God and, after kneeling in prayer, he calls for his warriors. Fenena and the Jews also kneel in prayer and when, after Nabucco's arrival, the statue of Baal crumbles to dust, everyone praises Jehovah. Meanwhile, Abigaille has taken poison and, after begging her sister's forgiveness, she dies in terror of God's judgement.

Having failed with *Un giorno di regno*, Verdi was seriously considering giving up his ambition to be a composer when, in January 1841, the manager of La Scala, Bartolomeo Merelli, presented him with Solera's text of *Nabucco*. Just three months later he had completed the opera that really marked the beginning of his career. One of the Milanese papers hailed it as a "clamorous and total success", and by the end of the year it had clocked up 65 performances in the city. The theme of freedom born of oppression made the opera popular in occupied Italy, where the Chorus of the Hebrew Slaves – "Va Pensiero" – was swiftly adopted as a surrogate national anthem.

However, "Va Pensiero" is something of an isolated musical highlight in a work that is somewhat under-endowed with the sort of thrills you might expect of nineteenth-century Italian opera. Nabucco's Act I denunciation of the Jews, "Tremin gl'insani", might be one of Verdi's finest baritone showpieces, but Ismaele is a scrawny tenor role, and essentially the show depends on the chorus and the staging. A direct ancestor is Rossini's Grand Opéra *Mosè*, which tells a similar story with similar casting, and there are no fewer than four scenes for on-stage band, a regular feature of Grand Opéra. But there's also something oratorio-like about *Nabucco*, with its heavy orchestration and brass-accompanied recitatives, a style befitting both the biblical subject and its sombre political subtext. Verdi's priorities are clear in his treatment of the love interest – where Solera had written a pivotal duet for Ismaele and Fenena, Verdi insisted on inserting instead a prophecy from Zaccaria, and he locked his librettist in a room until he got what he wanted. Verdi would soon abandon the ceremonial stasis of *Nabucco* for a more supple style, but for all its stiffness *Nabucco* marked an important step forward for the composer, not simply because of its success, but because it confirmed that tragedy and high drama were his métier. Not until the end of his life, some fifty years later, would he break his own mould.

RECORDINGS OVERVIEW

There have been just four professional recordings of *Nabucco*, of which two are available. The first was not taped until 1951, when Previtali conducted a broadcast performance for Cetra as part of the celebrations attached to the fiftieth anniversary of the composer's death. There followed a marvellous performance from Decca in 1965 and, twelve years later, a superbly conducted (but currently unavailable) reading from Riccardo Muti on EMI – by far the best in terms of atmosphere yet made. The most recent set, and the only one in digital sound, was released by Deutsche Grammophon in 1982, but Sinopoli's conducting is a huge turn-off, in spite of fine performances from Dimitrova and Cappuccilli.

Gobbi, Suliotis, Carral, Prevedi, Cava; Vienna State Opera Chorus; Vienna Philharmonic Orchestra; Gardelli. (Decca 417 407-2DH2; 2 CDs).

This lavish production is by far the best available, spiritedly conducted by Lamberto Gardelli and outstandingly played and sung by the Viennese forces. Despite some strained high notes, Tito Gobbi is a theatrical and uniquely complex Nabucco, while Elena Suliotis is a caution-to-the-wind Abigaille, throwing herself into the role with tremendous intensity. Bruno Prevedi does what he can to the one-dimensional Ismaele.

Attila

Composed 1845–46.
First performed March 17, 1846.
Libretto by Temistocle Solera and Francesco Maria Piave, after Werner.

Synopsis

Prologue

Atilla and his hordes are destroying the Italian city of Aquileia. Odabella, leader of the enemy women, impresses the Hun with her courage and he accepts her into his entourage. Ezio, emissary of the Roman Emperor, proposes to Attila that the Huns be ceded all the world except Italy, which Ezio would retain for himself; Attila rejects him, and Ezio declares the defiance of Rome. In the meantime, Foresto, Odabella's lover, arrives in Rio-Alto and urges his fellow refugees from Aquileia to stand their ground and build a new city.

Act I

Odabella and Foresto meet, and he accuses her of betraying their people. She claims she is awaiting her moment to kill Attila. Attila has a dream in which an old man warns him not to continue towards Rome; on waking, he is confronted by a procession headed by an old man (Pope Leo in disguise) who repeats the words he had heard in his dream.

Act II

Foresto and Ezio plot to overthrow the Huns. At a banquet, to which Ezio has been invited, Odabella saves Attila from death by poison. For this, he declares that she will be his bride.

Act III

Attila and Odabella are about to be married but during the ceremony the Romans surround the Huns' camp; as they attack, Odabella buries a knife in Attila's chest.

In March 1845 Verdi and Piave met in Venice (the city that grew from Rio-Alto) to work on a production of *I due Foscari*, and soon decided that Zacharias Werner's *Attila* would make an ideal subject for their next opera for La Fenice. Freely rewriting history (the real Attila was not murdered), it carried an obvious nationalist message in its tale of the survival of the Italian capital in the face of barbarians from the north, and came oven-ready with crowd scenes and a head-on contest between good and evil. However, Verdi made the mistake of engaging Solera rather than Piave to write the libretto; Solera abandoned the project before completing the third act, obliging the exasperated composer to ask Piave to finish the text. Verdi came through a bout of gastric fever to complete the music "virtually on my deathbed", and the first performance went ahead on schedule. Within twelve months it was his most popular opera, its blatant *Risorgimentale* message gaining a boost with the election of Pope Pius IX, a liberal pontiff whom audiences readily conflated with the Hun-repelling Pope Leo of Verdi's opera.

Attila is a tub-thumping opera that is direct to the point of artlessness. Yet it marks something of a step forward – for one thing, despite having plenty of excuses for such a stunt, Verdi rejected the "provincial nonsense" of the on-stage band, refusing to provide the cod-military marches that had wowed the audiences for *Nabucco*. More importantly, the melodies, though never exactly beautiful, are much more expressive and considerably better constructed than anything Verdi had previously written – this is the first appearance of the arch-like cantilenas for which middle-period Verdi became famous. Attila himself is a powerhouse bass role, demanding a singer who can manage both bravura and the ocassional foray into pathos. And for all the orchestral pile-ups, thunderous accompaniments and *Risorgimentale* choruses, there is a fair amount of memorable solo writing here – Odabella's defiant "Allor che i forti corrono", Foresto's kaleidoscopic "Ella in poter del barbaro!" and their reunion duet "Si, quell'io son, ravvisami!" are sweepingly emphatic creations. The musical scene-painting that would contribute so much to *Rigoletto*'s success is also strongly in evidence, notably during the prologue's evocative storm and Odabella's Act I moonlit "Oh! nel fuggente nuvolo". For all that, *Attila*'s charms are rarely so subtle, and the pleasures of this opera lie in its youthful vitality and almost camp theatrics.

VERDI IN REHEARSAL

For much of the nineteenth century, Italian opera houses had something of a reputation for shoddy production values, a situation due in large part to the fact that their main concern was to keep their public fed with a constant flow of new work in a familiar style. Turnover was so rapid that there wasn't time for proper rehearsal – and anyway, as most of the operas followed well-established formulas, they didn't require all that much preparation. Premieres were staged using the sets and the costumes of an entirely unrelated work that might be set in a different century and on another continent. Full orchestral rehearsals were something of a wearisome ancillary to the public event, and singers were often obliged to learn their parts just days before the opening night. In some instances this was too tough a task, and soloists either made up the words to fit the music, or relied on a prompter to call out the words before every line. (The latter habit persisted well into the twentieth century, as numerous live recordings attest.)

Verdi set out to change all this. Like Wagner, he wanted his singers to interpret rather than parrot their words, and so demanded that each creator of a new role study the entire score, so as to get a grasp of the meaning of the whole work. Verdi made no attempt to hide his generally low opinion of performers, and was particularly unimpressed by most of the conductors he encountered – "no one has ever, ever been able, or known how, to draw out all the effects conceived by me", he wrote. Thus wherever possible he took control himself, and his dictatorial manner came as something of a shock for those used to a fair amount of creative licence. He would scream and shout his way through even the least significant scene and singers were expected to tolerate his outbursts for the "good of the art". Eugenio Checchi remembered the preparations for the premiere of *Macbeth*: "the implacable Verdi spared no thought for his artists: he tired and tormented them with the same number for hours on end, and he never moved to a different scene until they had managed to perform the piece in a manner which fell least short of his ideal. He was not much loved by the multitude, for no word of encouragement, no 'bravo' ever passed his lips, not even when the orchestral players and members of the chorus believed they had done everything possible to content him."

Twenty years later, Jules Claretie watched Verdi supervising rehearsals for a performance of *Don Carlos*. "His sense of hearing is doubly, triply acute. He questions everything. In this thundering harmony he can hear the faintest of notes. He can hear everything at the same time: the chorus, the brass, the aria and all that happens on and off the stage. He gets up, beats time, snaps thumb against middle finger, and this strident, bright, terse note, this noise like the sound of castanets is heard above the orchestra and the chorus, goads them on, drives them forward like lashes from a whip."

It was a regular complaint from Verdi's conductors that their copy of the score would end up blotched by the sweat that dripped from the composer in rehearsal, and Verdi kept up his relentless pace right up to the end of his life. Sir John Barbirolli's father and his grandfather both played violin in the first performance of *Otello*, the rehearsals for which were punctuated by Verdi's furious outbursts and "that tremendously loud clicking of his thumb and second finger" whenever the performances failed to meet his expectations. The despotic style and quick-thinking mind made an indelible impression on a young cellist in that orchestra, a man who was to become the twentieth-century's incarnation of Verdi's ideal "man of the theatre" – Arturo Toscanini.

Ramey, Studer, Zancanaro, Shicoff; La Scala Chorus and Orchestra; Muti.
(EMI CDS7 49952-2; 2 CDs).

This is one of the best-cast Verdi recordings of recent years. The ex-policeman Giorgio Zancanaro (Ezio) has a bass-baritone that could shatter steel, while Sam Ramey swaggers his way through Attila in a performance that gets more contrast into his character than most basses could create. Studer is a little uncertain as Odabella and Shicoff is no more than efficient as Foresto, but Muti has an iron grip on the score – indeed, his driven conception of the work gives it greater weight than it perhaps deserves.

Raimondi, Deutekom, Milnes, Bergonzi; Ambrosian Singers; Royal Philharmonic Orchestra; Gardelli.
(Philips 426 115-2PM2; 2 CDs).

The main appeal of this 1972 recording (the only alternative to Muti's) is Ruggiero Raimondi's Attila – a role he has made his own on stage. He dominates the recording, as should be the case, and produces some genuinely terrifying sounds. This is also one of the last worthy performances recorded by the tenor Carlo Bergonzi, that paragon of Verdian style. Although his is a relatively minor role, he delivers Forresto's music with effortless beauty and control. Cristina Deutekom (Odabella) and Sherrill Milnes (Ezio) lend able support, but the performance is let down by Gardelli's pedestrian conducting and an overmiked recording.

Macbeth

Composed 1846–47; revised 1864–65.
First performed March 14, 1847; April 21, 1865.
Libretto by Francesco Maria Piave, after Shakespeare.

Synopsis

Act I

Macbeth and Banquo (Banco) come across three witches who predict Macbeth's ascension to the Scottish throne but address Banquo as "the father of kings". At Dunsinane, Lady Macbeth reads a letter relating the witches' prophecy but questions her husband's ambition. When Macbeth and King Duncan arrive she persuades her husband that Duncan must be killed; spurred on by a vision of a bloody dagger, he carries out the deed. Macduff and Banquo discover the murder.

Act II

Macbeth is crowned king and, remembering the witches' prophecy, he orders the murder of Banquo and his son Fleance (Fleanzio). Banquo is killed, but Fleance escapes. During a banquet, Macbeth is haunted by a vision of Banquo. Macduff leaves to join the Scottish exiles.

Act III

Macbeth returns to the witches and demands to know his future. They warn him against Macduff but reassure him that not until Birnam Wood comes to Dunsinane need he fear for his life, and that he will be invulnerable to any man "born of woman".

Act IV

Macduff is horrified to hear of the murder of his family, and swears revenge. In the castle, Lady Macbeth sleepwalks, remembering the murders she and her husband have committed. News of her death is brought to Macbeth who, lost in guilt, is unmoved. The exiles advance on the castle, camouflaged by branches from Birnam Wood, and Macduff tells Macbeth that he was "from his mother's womb untimely ripp'd"; the tyrant, realizing all is lost, falls to Macduff's sword.

Having suffered a life-threatening illness while writing *Attila*, Verdi was ordered to rest for at least six months. During this enforced withdrawal he began to contemplate producing a music-drama in which stagecraft was as important as the words and the music. His choice of subject when he came to apply this notion was Shakespeare's *Macbeth* ("one of mankind's greatest creations", he thought), and he demanded from his librettist a text that would have "extravagance, originality . . . brevity and sublimity". Having secured the services of the celebrated actor-baritone Felice Varesi, Verdi personally rehearsed the cast with maniacal diligence. The first Lady Macbeth, Marianna Barbieri-Nini, later remembered she had "for three months, morning and evening" to attempt to impersonate "someone who speaks in her sleep, who (as the maestro put it) utters words . . . almost without moving her lips, the rest of the face motionless." No-one had ever paid such attention to the acting of opera – and Verdi even cast Duncan and Fleance as non-singing roles.

As Verdi had confidently predicted, *Macbeth* was a triumph. Audiences and critics alike were amazed by the despair and ferocity of the work – indeed in Italy *Macbeth* became known as "l'opera senza amore" (the loveless opera). Right from the outset, Macbeth is characterized by chilling atmospherics. The F minor overture (no previous Italian opera had contained so many minor tonalities) is a masterpice of scene-setting, leading into the storm and a bizarre flurry of sniping woodwind and cackling witches. Most terrifying of all is the sleepwalking scene, in which Lady Macbeth's drained and icy vocal line, broken by interjections of hatred and remorse, is accompanied by a heaving, sighing orchestra.

The version that's performed today is a revision that Verdi prepared in 1864–65 for a production at Théâtre-Lyrique in Paris. Upon returning to the score, Verdi undertook a substantial re-write, re-arranging the orchestration (notably for the apparitions) and introducing a number of vocal changes and additions – most successfully Lady Macbeth's chilling "La luce langue" at the end of the first scene of Act II, when she and her husband resolve to kill Banquo. To comply with French tastes Verdi also added the customary ballet scene, but the first performance fell flat. "I thought I had done something passable, but evidently I was mistaken," commented the composer; time has proved him right, and the revised *Macbeth* remains among his most frequently staged operas.

RECORDINGS OVERVIEW

There are eight complete recordings of *Macbeth* in the catalogue at the moment, and several of them are excellent. Unfortunately, none of them features arguably the finest Lady Macbeth of the twentieth century, Inge Borkh. However, her extremely rare live performances do periodically appear on CD; if you've become a Verdi fan and you come across a Borkh disc, be sure to give it a listen.

Cappuccilli, Verrett, Ghiaurov, Domingo; La Scala Chorus and Orchestra; Abbado.
(Deutsche Grammophon 449 732-2GOR2; 2 CDs).

Abbado's is a thoughtful, unshowy reading of *Macbeth*: his tempi are cautious and he treats Verdi's markings with religious devotion. The result of this is that he emphasizes the approaches to the climaxes more than the climaxes themselves, creating a more cogent reading than conductors who go for an earth-moving approach. His cast is excellent, with Cappuccilli and Verrett hamming it up marvellously as husband and wife. Domingo is in generous voice as Macduff, while Ghiaurov's bass is ideal as Banguo – even if Ghiaurov's acting talents are not. The score is uncut, the sound is excellent and La Scala provides responsive support.

Warren, Rysanek, Hines, Bergonzi; New York Metropolitan Chorus and Orchestra; Leinsdorf.
(RCA GD 845 16; 2 CDs).

Unlike Abbado, Leinsdorf thunders his way through the score, applying speed as a substitute for drama. The beauty of this recording is its singing. Based on the 1958 Met production – which made a series of unnecessary but traditional cuts – it has a cast that was well used to each other and the music by the time they entered the studio. Bergonzi is in swooningly beautiful voice as Macduff, Warren delivers some beguiling sounds, presenting a carefully thought-out interpretation of the title role, and Rysanek is a hair-raising Lady Macbeth, prone to a shrill tone but very expressive. The stereo is primitive and, at times, boomy, but there is no mistaking the qualities of this "golden age" cast.

Mascherini, Callas, Tajo, Penno; La Scala Chorus and Orchestra; de Sabata.
(EMI CMS7 64944-2; 2 CDs).

This live recording has become something of a legend, uniting two of the greatest operatic talents of the century, Callas and de Sabata (who can be heard to comparable effect in *Tosca*). Together they bring almost supernatural tension to Lady Macbeth's disintegration. Enzo Mascherini is a guttural, jittery Macbeth, and Italo Tajo makes an enduring impression as Banguo, but the opera is dominated by the soprano and conductor. Despite the poor recorded sound, this comes close to dramatic perfection.

Rigoletto

Composed 1850–51.
First performed March 11, 1851.
Libretto by Francesco Maria Piave, after Hugo.

Synopsis

Act I

Rigoletto, the hunchbacked court jester, mocks Count Ceprano, whose wife is being seduced by the lecherous Duke of Mantua. Some courtiers suggest to Ceprano that he could gain revenge by abducting the jester's own mistress – but they don't realize that this woman is not Rigoletto's lover, but his daughter Gilda. Count Monterone attacks the Duke for seducing his daughter and is duly arrested; he curses the jester for laughing at him. Rigoletto's journey home is interrupted by the assassin Sparafucile, who offers his help, should he ever need it. Gilda greets her father, who, concerned for her safety, urges her never to leave the house on her own. She says nothing of her clandestine meetings with a local student who, unknown to her, is the Duke in disguise. The courtiers then congregate outside Rigoletto's house; having been tricked into allowing himself to be blindfolded, he unwittingly helps abduct his own daughter.

Act II

The Duke is overjoyed to hear of Gilda's abduction and leaves to comfort her. It dawns upon the jester that the members of the Duke's court might be responsible for his daughter's kidnapping and he marches to the ducal palace, where he condemns the courtiers for their actions. Rigoletto's worst fears are confirmed when, ashamed and tearful, Gilda rushes into his arms. Everyone, including the courtiers, is horrified to learn the identity of the jester's "mistress", and the act ends with Rigoletto swearing vengeance.

Act III

Rigoletto and Gilda visit Sparafucile's inn on the outskirts of town. Rigoletto has contracted the Duke's murder; unaware of this, Gilda maintains that she still loves the Duke, even though he deceived her. Rigoletto asks her how she would feel if he revealed to her the Duke's true nature; he then takes her to a tavern where the Duke is seen flirting with Sparafucile's sister, Maddalena. Maddalena has fallen in love with the Duke and manages to persuade her brother not to kill him. Instead, he agrees to murder the first stranger to come into the inn.

Sparafucile hands Rigoletto a sack containing the body of his victim, but just before he throws it into the river the jester hears the Duke's voice in the distance. Realizing he has been betrayed, he tears open the sack to find his daughter on the point of death. She begs his forgiveness and dies in his arms. Monterone's curse has been fulfilled.

"*Le Roi s'amuse* is the best plot and perhaps the best play of modern times ... it cannot fail ... make sure the censors accept this story." Verdi's letter to Piave, written on May 8, 1850, led to a formal decree from Venice's Department of Public Order: "His excellency the Military Governor Gorzkowski deplores the fact that the poet Piave and the great maestro Verdi have not been able to find any scope for their talents other than the disgusting immorality and obscene triviality of the plot titled *La Maledizione* [*Rigoletto*'s working title]. . . . His Excellency has decided to refuse absolutely the request for its performance." Not until January 26 the following year did the censors finally agree to the production of *Rigoletto*, and only then after many of the more "repellent" details had been diluted. The Austrian censor's fury at the proposed use of Hugo's play (which had been removed from the Paris stage after its first performance in 1832) was due principally to its depiction of royalty, an objection that Verdi and Piave removed by transplanting the action from the court of François I to the court of an anonymous Duke of Mantua. Once this change had been effected, the authorities seemed able to tolerate the lechery and violence of the opera, though some producers were more squeamish. At least one theatre had Gilda emerging from her sack fit as a fiddle, an emendation that forced the opera some way off its axis.

Yet *Rigoletto* was a huge success, receiving nearly three hundred performances during its first ten years. It remains the earliest of Verdi's operas to have never left the repertoire because the libertine anti-hero, the guileless heroine, the evil assassin and the tragic jester are among the most vivid creations in all opera, thanks largely to Verdi's unflaggingly brilliant music. The Duke's "La donna e mobile" might be the best-known moment, but the whole of *Rigoletto* is a parade of highlights, reaching a peak with the Act III quartet "Bella figlia dell'amore", in which all three protagonists plus Maddalena express their contrary emotions through a song of exquisite tenderness.

Rigoletto overturns many of the formulas of Italian opera: it has a brief prelude rather than a full-blown overture, the chorus is all male, and there are no entrance arias, ensemble finales or conventional recitatives. Characters are not delineated in a single self-proclaiming aria (as the character of Banguo is in *Macbeth*, for example), but are unfolded and explored over the course of the entire opera. And the entire opera is bound together by the figure of Rigoletto himself, described by Verdi as "grossly deformed and absurd but inwardly passionate and full of love". Mocked for his deformity, but revelling in the humiliation of others, he is a man of corrupted nobility, a being whose paradoxes are illuminated in a series of impassioned songs and intense encounters. This opera's musical sophistication – its complex harmony, for instance, and its sinister orchestration (notably the storm of Act III) – always serves the portrayal of character, and in Rigoletto Verdi created a heartbreakingly tormented central figure.

RECORDINGS OVERVIEW

With nearly thirty commercial recordings (four of them produced before 1920) and a fistful of pirates on CD, *Rigoletto* is among the most recorded operas of all time. Many of these sets have great highlights – notably Jussi Björling's Duke for RCA in 1956, Renato Capecchi's Rigoletto for Philips in 1959, Giulini's conducting for Deutsche Grammophon in 1979 and, most impressively, Giorgio Zancanaro's Rigoletto for EMI in 1988. Yet too many of them are ultimately unsatisfying as a whole, due to the record companies' tendency to concentrate on assembling a few star names rather than on getting the balance of the ensemble right. However, the exceptions reviewed below are stupendous.

Gobbi, Callas, di Stefano, Zaccaria; La Scala Chorus and Orchestra; Serafin.
(EMI CDS7 47469-8; 2 CDs).

Bergonzi, del Monaco and di Stefano, the three star Italian tenors of the 1950s, all recorded the Duke, but only the last achieved the right mix of licentiousness, cruelty and charm. Giuseppe di Stefano is in beautiful voice, elegant in "Bella figlia dell'amore", swaggering in "La donna e mobile" and thrilling in "Ella mi fu rapita". The other lead roles are similarly superb: Callas is by far the most convincing Gilda on disc (the death scene is sickeningly real), and Gobbi is the most subtle Rigoletto – tormented and vengeful, but tender and loving. Serafin gives smooth and attentive support. Dated mono sound, but so what?

Milnes, Sutherland, Pavarotti, Talvela; Ambrosian Opera Chorus; London Symphony Orchestra; Bonynge.
(Decca 414 269-2DH2; 2 CDs).

This 1971 recording was Pavarotti's first go at the Duke, and it's infinitely better than his 1989 re-make. His firmness of tone, confident extension (listen to the unending high C in "La donna") and beautiful portamento make this Duke a dangerously beguiling villain. Sherrill Milnes is outstanding too – a wounded, roaring, spitting Rigoletto – and Sutherland produces some lovely floated head notes, giving a gorgeously light reading of "Caro nome", even if her characterization of Gilda is paper thin. The conductor allows Verdi's music all the freedom it needs to let the magic do its work, and the production values are faultless.

Paskalis, Scotto, Pavarotti, Washington; Rome Opera Chorus and Orchestra; Giulini.
(Butterfly Music BMCD001; 2 CDs).

This live recording suffers from poor sound quality but it is notable for the amazingly sensual singing of a young Pavarotti as the Duke and an even younger Renato Scotto as Gilda. She is in wonderfully supple form, with none of the shuddering vibrato that was to affect her later work – in particular, her performance of "Caro nome" is one to die for. Together, she and Pavarotti make a remarkable partnership and their wonderfully sweet performance of "Bella figlia" is without equal. Giulini is a powerful presence, allowing liberties that less persuasive artists would not have warranted. A set to indulge in once you've got to know the opera well.

Il Trovatore

The Troubadour

Composed 1851–53.
First performed January 19, 1853.
Libretto by Salvatore Cammarano and Leone Emanuele Bardare, after Gutiérrez.

Synopsis

Act I

Spain, the fifteenth century. Ferrando, the Count di Luna's captain of the guard, recounts how di Luna's infant son fell ill after a gypsy woman was found peering into his cradle. The gypsy was condemned to death, for which her daughter Azucena abducted di Luca's younger child in revenge. The charred remains of a child were found at the site of the gypsy's execution, but the boy's father refused to accept that his baby was dead and ordered a search "without end". This was maintained after his death by his son, the present Count di Luna.

The Duchess Leonora, a lady-in-waiting to the Princess of Aragon, and the warrior troubadour Manrico are deeply in love. When the Count attempts to seduce her, Manrico rushes to her rescue and challenges the Count to a duel, which he wins – although a voice "as if from heaven" urges him to spare his life, for little do they know they are brothers.

Act II

The gypsy camp. Azucena tells Manrico of her mother's death and of her own son's accidental death by fire. Manrico is horrified, having always thought Azucena to be his mother; but she manages to convince him that he is in fact her son. A messenger arrives and informs Manrico that, believing him to be dead, Leonora is to enter a convent.

The Count and his followers sneak into the convent to abduct Leonora. At the last minute Manrico makes a heroic entrance, snatching her from di Luna's evil clutches.

Act III

Looking for Manrico, di Luna's guards arrest Azucena on charges of spying. The Count rejoices when it is revealed that she is Manrico's mother and orders her to be tortured and burned before the walls of Manrico's fortress. News of his mother's arrest and threatened execution interrupt Manrico's marriage to Leonora; he rushes to Azucena's rescue.

Act IV

Manrico is defeated and arrested. Leonora offers herself to di Luna if he will release him and – unaware that she will kill herself rather than be unfaithful to Manrico – he agrees. Manrico is overjoyed to see Leonora but suspects her of treachery when she tells him that he is to go free; when she falls into his arms, having taken poison, he realizes the sacrifice she has made and breaks down with remorse. The Count enters, finds Leonora dead and orders Manrico's immediate execution. Looking on from her prison cell, Azucena informs di Luna that he has just killed his own brother.

Verdi had originally intended to follow *Rigoletto* with a setting of Shakespeare's *King Lear*, but although Verdi and his librettist Cammarano both prepared extensive notes for the project, it never got further than that. Verdi then suggested Cammarano might take a look at *El trovador* by the Spanish playwright Garcia Gutiérrez – a work described by the composer as "very beautiful, imaginative and full of strong situations". The composer bullied the writer into adapting the play into something that would give him the maximum of creative leeway: "the more he provides me with originality and freedom of form the better I shall be able to do." The end product, even after the attentions of the young poet Leone Emanuele Bardare, was famously littered with inconsistencies and unlikely coincidences, but in the end it made no difference – *Il Trovatore* was for years Verdi's most popular opera. Essentially an out-and-out Romantic drama in the manner of Meyerbeer and Donizetti, it's packed with crowd-pleasing solo turns, big choruses, thrilling climaxes and complex ensemble finales – and, unlike *Rigoletto*, it requires next to no acting ability. Crucially, however, as Caruso remarked, it does demand "the four greatest singers in the world".

Il Trovatore is a roller-coaster of frenetic passions, in which the lyrical episodes are there to provide a bridge between histrionics and more histrionics. Manrico is a textbook heroic tenor, whose character is distilled in the Act III cabaletta, "Di quella pira", an act-ending show-stopper that concludes with an amazing high C. Verdi did not actually write this note into the aria, but the tenor Enrico Tamberlik, with Verdi's permission, stuck it onto the end, and it has now become a challenge that no tenor would dare shirk. The opera's other main focus is Azucena – perhaps the greatest mezzo-soprano role in Italian opera. From the demonic "Su l'orlo dei tetti", which ends the first scene of Act I, through the Act II cabaletta "Perigliarti ancor" to the chilling "Deh, rallentate, o barbari", when she is condemned to death, this role provides career-making opportunities.

Wonderfully tuneful music occurs throughout the opera – perhaps the most famous episode is sung by the chorus of gypsies who, in Act II, get to pound their anvils in time with the music. But the most moving passages are created through dialogue, notably the Act IV "Miserere" duet between Manrico and Leonora, in which she sings to the imprisoned troubadour above a chorus of praying monks, and the final exchanges between the lovers, beginning with the tenor's fearsome outburst "Parlar non vuoi". It is moments such as these that raise *Il Trovatore* way above the level of period-costume melodrama.

RECORDINGS OVERVIEW

The dates of *Trovatore* recordings are a reflection of the current "tenor crisis". From 1951 to 1983 there was a new set every three or four years; but since 1983 there have been just two – star vehicles for Domingo (his third go) and Pavarotti (his second), neither of them wonderful. The sets reviewed below are wonderful, however, and a couple of others are very interesting: the 1952 New York/RCA production with Milanov and Björling, which is notable for the Swedish tenor's beautiful account of Manrico; and Karajan's first reading of the opera for EMI, with Callas a charismatic Leonora. You might also come across a sensational bootleg of Corelli and Price making their Met debuts. Deutsche Grammophon's 1983 recording with Carlo Maria Giulini is worth hearing for the conductor's curiously slow tempi (based, he claims, upon a study of the composer's manuscript), but it is neither exciting nor exceptionally well sung.

Bonisolli, Price, Cappuccilli, Obraztsova; Berlin Chorus; Berlin Philharmonic Orchestra; Karajan.
(EMI CMS7 69311-2; 2 CDs).

As with many of his opera recordings, Karajan's second version of *Il Trovatore* was taped after a Salzburg produc-

tion – this one in 1977. As with his *Don Carlo*, the passions are unrelievedly intense and the violence of the orchestral playing is electrifying – all hell is let out for the day during the final act. Such a background places enormous strain on the soloists, but Leontyne Price as Leonora is more than up to the challenge and gives a glowing performance, while Obraztsova is a forthright Azucena, rich in voice and vital in character. Bonisolli is no Corelli and his tenor is too thick to give the music its natural ring, but he manages the notes and copes well with Karajan's tense direction. Cappuccilli is a disappointingly flaccid di Luna, but that's the single flaw in this thrillingly recorded, uncut production.

Corelli, Tucci, Merrill, Simionato; Rome Opera Chorus and Orchestra; Schippers.
(EMI CMS7 63640-2; 2 CDs).

The Karajan *Trovatore* is a legendary interpretation; this 1964 recording captures a legend in full cry. Franco Corelli was the most famous Manrico of his day, and rightly so – the thrill and zing of his voice is not easily forgotten and he makes a sultry, erotic and blisteringly powerful hero. Gabriella Tucci sings well but is too light for Leonora, and she's lost next to Corelli; Simionato, a throaty Azucena, tries too hard; but Robert Merrill is grand and nasty as di Luna. There are some strange cuts, and the conducting is solid rather than inspired, but Corelli's performance would make up for greater weaknesses than these.

Bergonzi, Stella, Cossotto, Bastianini; La Scala Chorus; La Scala Orchestra; Serafin.
(Deutsche Grammophon 445 451-2GX2; 2 CDs).

A budget-price recording with full-price singing, albeit in a production that uses a savagely cut score. Taped in 1962, it features Carlo Bergonzi as Manrico, which is recommendation enough, plus Fiorenza Cossotto as Azucena – one of the best interpretations of the role on disc. Antonietta Stella is a blandly beautiful Leonora, while Bastianini shouts his way through – and over – Verdi's music, but he does so with tremendous character. Serafin is, as ever, a master of subtle discipline and he conducts with natural inflection.

Domingo, Price, Milnes, Cossotto; Ambrosian Opera Chorus; New Philharmonia; Mehta.
(RCA RD86194; 2 CDs).

Placido Domingo's first Manrico, taped for RCA in 1969, was his first complete recording of an opera, and it captured his dark lyric tenor in full bloom. If you want to know why the cognoscenti regard the Three Tenors circus as a travesty of the man's art, this is a must. He is well matched by Leontyne Price as Leonora and Fiorenza Cossotto as an intimidatingly forceful, almost armour-clad Azucena. Sherrill Milnes is in typically smooth form as di Luna, and Mehta conducts a characterful account of the uncut score, though the engineering makes the voices too close.

Corelli, Price, Bastianini, Simionato; Vienna Philharmonic Orchestra; Vienna State Opera Chorus; Karajan.
(Deutsche Grammophon 447 659-2GX2; 2 CDs).

This recording, made at the 1962 Salzburg Festival, captured one of those rare occasions on which everything worked. Karajan was in enthralling form, propelling the Viennese forces to a frenzy of excitement. Corelli was at his magnificent best, and he just about takes off during "Di quella pira". Price, also in her prime, gives an extraordinary performance. Both Bastianini and Simionato impress as di Luna and Azucena. If the sound isn't perfect, then the performance is.

La Traviata

The Fallen Woman

Composed 1853; revised 1854.
First performed March 6, 1853; May 6, 1854.
Libretto by Francesco Maria Piave, after Dumas.

Synopsis

Act I

Paris, 1850. A party in the house of the courtesan Violetta. The hostess, who is visibly suffering from tuberculosis, is introduced to an admirer, Alfredo; after the guests leave he urges her to abandon her profligate way of life and offers his love, but she is unwilling to entertain a serious relationship and dismisses him. Left to herself, however, she begins to think that Alfredo might, in fact, be her redeemer.

Act II

Alfredo and Violetta have been living together, unmarried, for three months. While Alfredo is away from their apartment his father, Germont, arrives and begs Violetta to leave his son: the scandal of their relationship is threatening the success of his daughter's wedding. She loves Alfredo but agrees, leaving a note of farewell. Alfredo is distraught but tracks down Violetta at a party, where she is partnered by her former protector Baron Douphol. Alfredo confronts Violetta but she begs him to leave, fearful that the Baron will challenge him to a duel. Alfredo hurls a fistful of money at her; Germont arrives and berates Alfredo for his behaviour.

Act III

Some weeks later, Violetta has only hours to live. She receives a letter from Germont in which he confesses to having told his son of her sacrifice. Alfredo duly bursts in and begs for her forgiveness. They talk of her recovery and their future happiness, but she is clearly beyond. She rises briefly to her feet, then falls dead.

Verdi spent much of his time between 1847 and 1852 in Paris, where he may well have seen the first run of Alexandre Dumas' *La dame aux camélias*. With *La Traviata*, the opera that came out of Dumas' play, Verdi moved from *Trovatore*'s world of hot-blooded historical drama to something approximating to contemporary social realism, albeit glamorous upper-crust realism. Composed to a commission from La Fenice, this tale of familial strife and disease-blighted love inevitably ran into trouble with the conservative censors, but, partly owing to the leading Venetian theatre's excellent contacts, the only substantial revision demanded by the authorities was that the action be transplanted from the present day to 1700.

The first run was one of the composer's rare failures. The audience is said to have found the corpulent Fanny Salvini-Donatelli an unlikely consumptive (see p.207), but the overall lack of enthusiasm had more to do with the blunderbuss performance of Felice Varesi, the man who had first sung Verdi's Macbeth and Rigoletto and was now creating the role of Germont. Stung by the attitude of the critics, he felt forced to pen a letter of self-defence to *L'Italia Musicale* – Verdi was the "real reason for the opera's failure", he insisted, as he had not provided him with a part as interesting as Rigoletto. He concluded: "For a composer who used to declare that the thermometer of success was the box office takings at the sixth performance, this (the third) was a poor omen. Clearly *La Traviata* has not taken off." Verdi's characteristic reply was: "My fault, or that of the artists? Time will tell."

Indeed it has: nowadays *La Traviata* is the most frequently performed and most extensively recorded of Verdi's operas. Part of its appeal, as with all Verdi's mature works, is the sheer quality of its big tunes: Violetta's soprano, Alfredo's tenor and Germont's baritone are perfect celebrity vehicles, and the history of *Traviata* is studded with great three-part partnerships, notably that of Callas, di Stefano and Gobbi. Equally important, though, is the concentration of the drama, for although *Traviata* has its share of choruses and set-pieces it is, in essence, a chamber opera. There are only three important characters – one of whom, Germont, does not appear until nearly an hour into the work – and each role is constructed to play off the others, raising the tension to the tragic pitch of the final scene. The economy of Verdi's writing is evident from the start: in contrast to, say, *Rigoletto* or *Trovatore*, very little actually happens during the first act and yet it encompasses an amazing range of emotions and moods. The ethereal prelude (material from which is repeated at the opening of Act III) presents a portrait of the heroine as a compound of delicacy and decadence; her exchanges with Alfredo emphasize their disparate characters (Alfredo languid and civilized, Violetta effervescent and fickle) until they are joined in a duet which, on and off, lasts for the remainder of the act; and her final coloratura show-piece "Sempre libera degg'io" (ending with a startling E flat), in which she surrenders herself to a life of capriciousness, is a psychological portrait of great vividness, heightened by Alfredo's impassioned, off-stage reminders of his love.

Constructed to maximize emotional impact without resorting to raucousness, *La Traviata* is the Verdi opera that is likeliest to make converts of the uninitiated. That is what Verdi meant when, asked some years later which of his operas he liked best, he replied, "Speaking as a professional, *Rigoletto*; as an amateur, *La Traviata*."

RECORDINGS OVERVIEW

Although there have been more than two dozen recordings of *La Traviata*, there are rather too many that amount to star recitals rather than fully developed dramatic readings. That said, in addition to the sets we've recommended, there are others that feature star performances so fine as to justify the investment for the Verdi fan. Victoria de los Angeles's 1959 reading for EMI, with Serafin conducting, is one such recording; Carlo Bergonzi's second recording, made just five years after the one reviewed below, is similarly beautiful. There's even a recording worth hearing in spite of the singing – the one conducted by Carlos Kleiber for Deutsche Grammophon. His typically eccentric and perfectionist reading inspires exquisite sounds from his orchestra, but the Violetta of Ileana Cotrubas is not exactly seductive, and Domingo is no Alfredo.

Callas, di Stefano, Bastianini; La Scala Chorus and Orchestra; Giulini.
(EMI CMS7 63628-2; 2 CDs).

Callas recorded the role of Violetta several times, but this live recording of the famous 1955 Visconti production stands out for its completeness and intimacy – indeed, many would rank this as her greatest Verdi performance. At once naive and worldly, she creates an image as varied and contradictory as Verdi intended, and her voice contains a rainbow of tones, with none of the steel to which it was later prone. For all the forcing and curious diction, di Stefano is a worthy lover, and Bastianini's Germont is a powerful reading. Giulini shapes and phrases with intelligence, and the entire production hums with energy.

Sutherland, Bergonzi, Merrill; MMF Chorus and Orchestra; Pritchard.
(Decca 411 877-2DM2; 2 CDs).

This 1962 recording was the first uncut *Traviata* and it remains one of the most enjoyable. Sutherland is especially fine, with a glorious coloratura and some delicious phrasing, although she is never exactly subtle. Bergonzi is an ideally warm and ardent Alfredo, while Robert Merrill, making his second appearance on record as Germont, fleshes out all the contradictions of the old man's character and is in consistently attractive voice. Pritchard captains a tight ship, as alert to the tragedy as to the passion, and the recorded sound is near ideal.

Gheorghiu, Lopardo, Nucci; Covent Garden Chorus and Orchestra; Solti.
(Decca 448 119-2; 2 CDs).

Violetta was the role that established the international reputation of Angela Gheorghiu, and this 1992 recording shows what the fuss is all about – she has a gorgeous voice, but like Callas she does much more with that voice than merely convey the notes. She acts with every inflection. Her Alfredo is the fledgling superstar Frank Lopardo, whose youthful and warm voice is one of the few great hopes for modern Italian tenor singing. Leo Nucci is a bland Germont, but the octogenarian Georg Solti gives a splendidly vital and well-paced account of the score. Marvellously recorded.

Albanese, Peerce, Merrill, Stellman; NBC Symphony Orchestra and Chorus; Toscanini.
(RCA GD60303; 2 CDs).

A collector's item, perhaps, but this is a world-famous recording. The great conductor's personality shines through every bar (his voice comes through occasionally too), even if his furious energy at times seem unwarranted. The cast is perfectly in tune with him, Licia Albanese in particular – she uses the language with Callas-like intelligence, but produces a less mannered tone. Jan Peerce is a muscular Alfredo, with an ardent tone that's well suited to the excitable mood of the performance as a whole, and Robert Merrill is in wonderful form as Germont. It is a great shame that NBC's engineers were unable to capture this legendary event (recorded from two broadcasts in 1946) in better sound.

Simon Boccanegra

Composed 1856–57; revised 1880–81.
First performed March 12, 1857; March 24, 1881.
Libretto by Francesco Maria Piave, after Gutiérrez; revised by Boito.

Synopsis

Prologue

Genoa, the fourteenth century. The new Doge is about to be elected. The goldsmith Paolo urges Pietro, leader of the plebeian party, to vote for the common-born Simon Boccanegra. Boccanegra hopes that his election will enable him to marry the noble-born Maria Fiesco (daughter of Doge Jacopo Fiesco), with whom he has already had a child. The child, also named Maria, is missing. News arrives of the mother's death and Simon discovers her corpse just as the crowd proclaim him Doge.

Act I

Twenty-five years later. Simon's daughter has been brought up as Amelia Grimaldi by his political enemies. Father and daughter meet and Simon soon dis-

IT'S NOT OVER TILL THE FAT LADY SINGS

One of opera's most enduring stereotypes is the fat soprano, and though there are plenty of slimline sopranos on the circuit nowadays, it's an image that's been well earned. The history of opera is littered with examples of sopranos whose physical form didn't tally with the character being portrayed, and in this roll-call of humiliations the premiere of *La Traviata* looms large.

Verdi's concerns over his "considerable" leading soprano, **Fanny Salvini-Donatelli** (1815–91), were such that he had a clause in his contract with La Fenice that allowed him to replace her with a singer of his choosing, as long as he informed the management before the middle of January. As the conductor failed to reveal the extent of the problems created in rehearsal by Salvini-Donatelli's prosperous frame, the composer missed his deadline, and so was forced to suffer the spherical Salvini-Donatelli as his ailing Violetta. The first night was an ordeal for Verdi, but it was much worse for poor Salvini-Donatelli. She sang well during the first act, and it seemed her pretty voice might win round the sceptical audience. During Act II, however, the performance began to come apart at the seams as Varesi (the baritone) and Graziani (the tenor) did their best to bring the curtain down, the former yelling his head off, the latter going hoarse. But the audience reserved its hostility for the final act, when Salvini-Donatelli struggled to portray a frail young woman expiring from the ravages of tuberculosis – while weighing "precisely 130 kilograms". Her lumbering gait and palatial girth provoked laughter at every reference to her illness, and when it was announced that Violetta had just hours to live, a heckler took issue with the doctor's diagnosis – "I see no consumption, only dropsy!".

Salvini-Donatelli's most famous successor as Violetta was the equally rotund **Luisa Tetrazzini** (1871–1940), a singer described in E.M. Forster's *Where Angels Fear to Tread* as "stout", which was putting it kindly. A great friend of Caruso's, she shared his love of food, and her eating habits became the stuff of legend. She would breakfast on a whole chicken, plus porridge, kippers and oysters, and it was common for her to eat "for two" after each show. It was also normal for her to load up before the show. On one occasion, shortly before having to sing Violetta at the Met, she met Caruso for an Italian meal so huge that she was forced to remove her corset, so that when her Alfredo, John McCormack, encountered her on stage, he was met by the awesome sight of Tetrazzini "unrestrained". Required to lift her from her bed during the last act, McCormack felt "as though my arms were fondling a pair of Michelin tyres". Tetrazzini cared nothing for dieting ("If I diet, my face sags", she claimed), a fact which a Philadelphia newspaper, covering her farewell tour, publicized with the sensitive headline: "SURE TETRAZZINI IS FAT, DOESN'T CARE WHO KNOWS IT!'.

But in the twentieth century sopranos came under great pressure to conform to more conventional body images, a process most famously reflected in the changing form of **Maria Callas**. In 1953, when she appeared on stage as a "robust and healthy-looking" Violetta, she weighed over 200 pounds. Not exactly obese, but the Metropolitan Opera tactfully suggested she lose some weight, whereupon Callas shed an astonishing 100 pounds in the course of just one summer, thanks partly to giving up her favourite treat of fried eggs, potatoes and cheese. Many thought it was the biggest mistake of her life, attributing her vocal decline to the strain of fanatical dieting. Certainly, her voice after this drastic weight loss was noticeably different, but if slimming removed something from the quality of her tone, it enabled her extraordinary acting ability to blossom.

However, there's no direct link between girth and vocal technique – contrary to what many might think, huge circumference does not necessarily mean huge lung power. That said, while the number of overweight sopranos seems steadily to be diminishing, the number of great sopranos seems to be diminishing as well.

covers that Amelia is his long-lost Maria. Paolo, one of Simon's courtiers, is in love with Amelia, who detests him; when the Doge tells him to abandon all hope of a relationship, Paolo plans to abduct the girl. Gabriele Adorno, who is also in love with Amelia, murders the man who carried out the abduction. This starts a riot, which interrupts a meeting of the Doge's council. Gabriele denounces Simon, claiming that whoever the abductor was, he must have been working on the Doge's behalf. With Amelia's intervention to prevent

Gabriele murdering the Doge, the scene becomes even more chaotic, but Simon manages to restore order. He then commands Paolo to find the traitor.

Act II

Paolo blackmails Gabriele into helping him kill the Doge and secures his loyalty by telling him that Amelia and the Doge are lovers. While Gabriele looks on, Amelia and her father meet. She begs him to forgive Gabriele, and when Gabriele steps out to kill Simon once again she saves her father's life. Discovering that Amelia is Simon's daughter, Gabriele begs forgiveness. The Doge pardons him and blesses his marriage to Amelia.

Act III

Paolo has joined a rebel army, and when they are defeated by the plebeians he is led to his execution. He confesses to having abducted Amelia and attempted to kill Simon. Amelia is reunited with her grandfather Jacopo Fiesco, who embraces Simon as he begins to die from a slow poison Paolo has administered. Falling to the ground, he names Gabriele as his successor.

Verdi began *Simon Boccanegra* desperate for "another *Trovatore*", and he had high hopes that Garciá Gutiérrez's factually based drama would secure him such success. But so complicated was the libretto and so gloomy the music that it did not go down at all well, even though one critic considered it superior to anything by Wagner (who by then had already finished *Tannhäuser* and *Lohengrin*). Even Verdi came to accept that it was "too sad, too desolate", but twenty-three years later, after renewing his friendship with Arrigo Boito, he decided to rewrite the work for La Scala.

Verdi approached Boito about a revision of the libretto at the end of 1880, when Boito had already begun work on Verdi's late masterpiece, *Otello*. Minor changes were made throughout the opera, plus one vast addition – the interruption of the Doge's council, which came to occupy almost half of Act I. Boito himself was satisfied with his contribution, but no more than that, and he refused to allow his name to be attached to the new edition of "poor Piave's" work. Certainly the rewrite didn't completely dispel the rather depressing and dry atmosphere of the piece as a whole, but the revamped first act was very well received, creating what turned out to be well-justified anticipation of future Verdi–Boito collaborations.

As with many of Verdi's operas, *Simon Boccanegra* focuses on a father-and-daughter relationship, and it's conventional enough in its sub-plot of the rivalry between two suitors. However, *Simon Boccanegra* is unusual in that the tenor role, Gabriele Adorno, is the weakest of the male leads, for all the thrills of his Act II aria "O inferno!...Sento avvampar nell'anima". The thoroughly nasty Paolo, a baritone part, is considerably more gripping, especially during the extraordinary conclusion to Act I, in which Simon forces him to curse the kidnapper – ie, himself. The heart of the opera, of course, is the title character, one of the most testing baritone roles in all opera, and one of its noblest figures. Simon's address to the people at the end of the first act, "Plebe! Patrizi! Popolo!", is a unique phenomenon in opera – a rousing display of political rhetoric, equivalent to Mark Anthony's "Friends, Romans and countrymen" speech. Simon is a plum role for an operatic actor rather than a pure singer, for it's dominated by great tracts of declamation and dialogue and syllabic text settings that demand more of the artist's enunciation than of his technique. Of Simon's final duet with Fiesco, his only floridly Italianate music, one commentator wrote, "At last, real passion and not just a dull combination of notes!", but it's this overriding restraint – in line with the qualities of an elder statesman – that makes the title character of *Simon Boccanegra* such a weighty creation.

RECORDINGS OVERVIEW

Of the six studio versions of *Boccanegra*, the Abbado set is the first and last choice. However, two superb live recordings also periodically emerge on small labels. The more recent was made during the 1960s with Carlo Bergonzi as a white-hot Gabriele – no other tenor made so much out of the part. The other, the better all-round performance, is the 1939 Met recording with Elisabeth Rethberg as Amelia, Lawrence Tibbett as Simon, Ezio Pinza as Fiesco, Leonard Warren as Paolo and Giovanni Martinelli as Gabriele. No greater cast has ever been assembled, and it is a must for anyone interested in Verdi.

Cappuccilli, Freni, Carerras, Ghiaurov, van Dam; La Scala Chorus and Orchestra; Abbado.
(Deutsche Grammophon DG415 692-2GH2; 2 CDs).

Taped in 1977 in the wake of Giorgio Stehler's La Scala production, this account of *Boccanegra* boasts a perfectly integrated cast, each one of whom turns in a superlative performance, from Mirella Freni's technically perfect and emotionally rounded Amelia to Ghiaurov's towering Fiesco. If one contribution demands special mention, it is Cappuccilli's Simon, the recorded performance of his career. Abbado has done nothing better and his wonderfully fluent direction gives shape and life to this troublesome opera.

Un ballo in maschera

A Masked Ball

Composed 1857–58.
First performed February 17, 1859.
Libretto by Antonio Somma, after Scribe.

Synopsis

Act I

Riccardo (Richard), the governor of Boston, is planning the guest list for a forthcoming ball. The list includes the name of his beloved Amelia, the wife of his best friend Renato, who suddenly interrupts him with news of a plot against Riccardo's life. A judge then brings a petition for the exile of the fortune-teller Ulrica; but Oscar, a page, urges the governor to show clemency. Against Renato's better judgement, Riccardo proposes a visit to the woman, disguised, before passing sentence. He asks her about the plot and demands to know who will be his assassin, to which she answers, "Whoever shall first shake your hand." Laughing at her prediction, Riccardo is joined by Renato – who shakes him by the hand.

Act II

Standing beside the gallows at midnight, Amelia is torn between her love for Riccardo and her responsibility to Renato. When Riccardo arrives she resists for a while, but then they fall into each other's arms. Renato appears, to warn Riccardo that the plotters are lying in wait for him nearby. Amelia covers her face, fearful that her husband will realize that she is Riccardo's lover. Renato offers to take the mysterious woman home; on the journey they are duly waylaid by the conspirators who, during the ensuing scuffle, reveal Amelia's identity. Renato is furious and sides with the conspirators.

Act III

Renato and the conspirators draw lots to see who will kill the governor at the masked ball: Renato forces Amelia to draw for him and she pulls his name from the hat. At the ball, Riccardo tells Amelia of his plans to send her and Renato to England as envoys. As he bids farewell to Amelia, Renato approaches and bids his own farewell, shooting Riccardo in the back. Dying, Riccardo proclaims Amelia's innocence and begs that his death go unavenged.

Of all Verdi's operas to have suffered censorship, *Un ballo in maschera* suffered the most. He composed it for the San Carlo Theatre in Naples, where it was to have been staged during the 1858 carnival season. Based upon a Scribe libretto that Auber had used for his opera *Gustave III, ou le Bal Masqué*, Verdi's opera told the true story of the liberal King Gustavus III, who was shot on March 16, 1792, at a masked ball in Stockholm. On January 14, 1858, Felice Orsini made an attempt on the life of Napoleon III, and so the authorities in Bourbon-ruled Naples refused to sanction any opera dealing with regicide. Verdi refused to compromise, and *Un ballo* was withdrawn from the theatre's schedule, which sent thousands onto the streets crying "Viva Verdi!" The censor suggested the composer change his title and relocate the action to (in the words of the preface to the first English translation of the libretto) "the distant and, to the author, little-known city of Boston".

This historical solecism evidently satisfied the Bourbons, but the opera failed to establish a place next to the big three of Verdi's middle years. Perhaps *Traviata* had led audiences to expect greater subtlety. *Un ballo in maschera* marked a move sideways for Verdi, for although it superficially resembles *Traviata*, in that it's a tale of love and death in a high-society milieu, its superheated drama is closer to that of *Trovatore*. The passions are exaggerated to the point of caricature and the characters are strangely depthless: Amelia, Riccardo and Renato create a somewhat diagrammatic entanglement, and at the end of it all you have little sense of who they are. Gabriele d'Annunzio pithily summarized the strengths and weaknesses of this flawed masterpiece when he described *Un ballo* as "the most operatic of operas".

This is a fair assessment of a work that hinges on a magnificent, tightly strung ten-minute duet in Act II, in which Riccardo manages to convince Amelia that their love is more important than her good name. Switching between heaving passion and elegant lyricism, this strikingly beautiful episode is typical of Verdi's predilection for manic fluctuations and surprises – just as it seems the lovers are sated, the duet once more picks up speed before galloping towards the obligatory high C. Renato's great monologue "Eri tu", at the beginning of Act III, is another example of this opera's sudden extremes: having confronted Amelia, he is left alone to ponder how and why his friend could have betrayed him, and the music bursts from him in savage key shifts that vividly convey his torment and uncertain allegiances. It is Riccardo who spans the widest range of feeling. His Act I romance

"La rivedrà nell'estasi" is a jolly, clockwork-like invention; his Act III aria "Forse la soglia", in which he realizes that he must leave Amelia to Renato, is dark and gloomy; while his ensuing outburst "Si rividerti Amelia" borders on the hysterical.

There's an element of humour to offset the swooning and wailing, mainly through the wispish Oscar and the pantomime witch Ulrica (whose scene in Act I opens with three sinister hammer-blow chords) – even Riccardo has a laughing aria, "È scherzo od è follia", in which the song's rhythm imitates laughter as Riccardo mocks Ulrica's prophesies. In the final analysis, however, *Un ballo* is all about steamy passion, hence its nickname, "Verdi's *Tristan*".

RECORDINGS OVERVIEW

For an experience that does justice both to Verdi's orchestral writing and to the heroic vocals, pick one of the three sets reviewed below. Of those recordings currently in the catalogue but not reviewed here, three warrant a special mention: Toscanini's astonishingly conducted 1954 reading for RCA; Karajan's mid-price set for Deutsche Grammophon (1989), with Placido Domingo in fine form; and the Votto/EMI set from 1956, where Callas puts in a startling performance as Amelia. You should also keep an eye out for a couple of recordings that have dropped out of the catalogue for the time being. The first is Serafin's 1943 reading for EMI, which is magnificently sung by Maria Caniglia, Beniamino Gigli, Fedora Barbieri and Gino Bechi. The other is Decca's 1961 account, in which Georg Solti galvanizes an extraordinarily multinational cast of celebrities; the great Wagnerian soprano Birgit Nilsson was an unlikely choice for Amelia but she has no equal on disc, and she is more than matched by Carlo Bergonzi, who turns in perhaps his greatest recorded performance of a Verdi role.

Arroyo, Domingo, Cappuccilli, Grist; Royal Opera House Chorus; New Philharmonia; Muti.
(EMI CMS7 69576-2; 2 CDs).

This mid-70s effort benefits from determined, characterful direction, with Riccardo Muti generating animation through an almost pedantic attention to detail and structure. Crescendi, ritenuti and rubati are perfectly handled, and the pauses for air are splendidly paced – in short, every moment has its thoughtfully considered place within the overall drama. Muti's cast is dominated by Domingo in a role that suited his youthful, technically secure voice, and the love duet is loaded with languorous eroticism. Arroyo is a fine Amelia, with an ideal balance of declamation and sweetness; Fiorenza Cossotto is a powerful, ominous Ulrica; and Piero Cappuccilli is a conscientious Renato.

Price, Bergonzi, Merrill, Grist, Verrett; RCA Italiana Opera Orchestra and Chorus; Leinsdorf.
(RCA GD86645; 2 CDs).

Bergonzi's earlier Decca recording of *Un ballo* is not currently available, but his 1966 remake is a satisfactory alternative. Apart from Bergonzi's gorgeous tenor voice, the charms of this set are Leontyne Price's husky Amelia, Robert Merrill's thrilling Renato and Shirley Verrett's over-ripe Ulrica. Some may balk at Leinsdorf's conducting, which seems in a perpetual state of nervous agitation – especially during the final act, where he pushes Riccardo's "Si rividerti Amelia" into the realms of hysteria. It is an undeniably exciting ride, however, and is captured with bright if close sound.

Tebaldi, Pavarotti, Milnes, Donath, Resnik; Santa Cecilia Academy Orchestra and Chorus; Bartoletti.
(Decca 440 042-2DM02; 2 CDs).

This 1970 recording is notable for capturing the very end of one great career and the very beginning of another. Renata Tebaldi – whose prime occurred some twenty years earlier – made few recordings after this, and it doesn't do her glorious voice full justice; but for most of the second act and all of the third she produces a warmth of tone that is hard to resist. The young Pavarotti is in sensational form, giving Riccardo an ideal balance of naïveté and courage, and the voice itself is one to die for. Sherrill Milnes, mid-career, relishes the role of Renato and he sings with outstanding security and power. Bruno Bartoletti is no Toscanini and there are passages – especially during the love duet – where the tension flags, but he provides expressive accompaniment and the sound is both fresh and realistically spaced.

La forza del destino

The Force of Destiny

Composed 1861.
First performed November 22, 1862.
Libretto by Francesco Maria Piave, after de Saavedra and Schiller.

Act I

The Marquis of Calatrava stumbles upon his daughter, Leonora, eloping with her lover Don Alvaro. Surrendering, Don Alvaro throws his pistol to the ground; it goes off, killing the Marquis. With his last words, Calatrava curses his daughter.

Act II

The lovers are separated in their escape. Disguised as a man, Leonora begins her search for Alvaro at an inn where she sees her brother Don Carlo, disguised as a student. He tells Leonora that he is looking for Alvaro, whom he intends to kill in revenge for the death of his father. Leonora becomes convinced that Alvaro has deserted her and leaves for the monastery of Madonna degli Angeli. The monks allow her to live in a nearby cave where they will bring her food daily. In case of danger, there is a bell for her to ring.

Act III

Believing Leonora dead, Alvaro has joined the Spanish army under an assumed name. He hears a call for help and, running to the rescue, he finds Don Carlo, who has been attacked by a gang. Neither knowing who the other really is, they swear eternal comradeship. In the ensuing battle Alvaro is badly wounded and Carlo helps him to safety, where Alvaro hands him some papers that must be destroyed should he die. Carlo becomes suspicious of Alvaro's identity and, after finding a portrait of his sister in his pocket, he challenges Alvaro to a duel. Alvaro reminds him of their oath, but Carlo is implacable. A passing patrol manages to separate them: Carlo is dragged away and Alvaro enters a monastery – the Madonna degli Angeli.

Act IV

Five years on, Alvaro, now known as Father Raphael, lives a life of fasting and self-denial. Carlo enters the monastery and provokes a fight with Alvaro, during which Carlo is mortally wounded. Alvaro rushes to the local hermit for absolution, at which point he and Leonora recognize each other. When he tells her of her wounded brother she rushes to Carlo's side, but as she leans over to attend to his wounds, Carlo stabs her and dies. Alvaro curses heaven for having brought such pain to their lives. Believing that she and Alvaro will one day be reunited in heaven, Leonora dies – thus fulfilling the curse with which the opera began.

𝄞 By 1860 Verdi was extremely wealthy, extremely well known, and was considering retirement. Then he received a letter from the Italian tenor Enrico Tamberlik, asking him to provide an opera to coincide with the singer's forthcoming engagement at the Imperial Theatre in St Petersburg: "I have heard . . . that it might not be impossible to induce you to add another gem to the splendid crown of your operas, the series of which you are threatening to close." Tamberlik was one of the century's most popular singers and it is a measure of his influence that Verdi was spurred into action by his request.

After some prevarication, Verdi settled on a "huge and singular drama" by Angel de Saavedra, called *Alvaro, o La fuerza del sino*. Piave quickly constructed a libretto from the synopsis that Verdi had prepared, and on November 27, 1861, Verdi and his wife were on their way to Russia. However, on arrival they found the singers' voices unsuitable (Tamberlik had clearly found the Russian winter less than conducive); the staging was cancelled, but in September the following year the Verdis returned to Russia where *La forza del destino* was given its premiere, with Tamberlik creating Alvaro. The Russian audiences seemed to have found it excessively brutal, while the critics were disinclined to praise the work of a foreigner at a time when a distinctly Russian style was being forged. In 1869 Verdi replaced the prelude with an overture, re-ordered Act III and revised the ending, which had caused as much outrage in Italy as it had in Russia, but these changes had little effect. *La forza del destino* remains the black sheep of Verdi's maturity.

Convinced that the "opera of cavatinas, duets etc" was defunct and that the "opera of the future" was "the opera of ideas", Verdi produced in *La forza* a work that has no parallel in the rest of his output. The abstract title is a clue to its nature: *La forza* is populated by people whose actions seem to be governed by something other than the imperatives of character. In a work which might more justly be titled *The Force of Coincidence*, each of the three leading characters occupies an isolated place in the drama's universe, and tragedy ensues whenever their paths cross. So loose is the structure that Leonora does not even appear during Act III and she only returns to the opera for the final scene – just in time for her death. What cohesion the opera possesses comes from the use of leitmotif, such as the "Fate theme" – first heard as a pugilistic brass call at the beginning of the overture – and the haunting allusions to Leonora's Act II prayer. Otherwise, the opera rambles from highlight to highlight.

Reflecting Tamberlik's celebrated strength and technique, Alvaro is a horrifyingly arduous tenor role. Verdi provides him with a leviathan recitative and aria ("O tu che in seno agl'angeli") at the beginning of Act III, and his subsequent duet with the baritone Don Carlo, "Solenne in quest'ora" (a piece famously recorded by Caruso and Scotti) is equally gripping, albeit darker. Don Carlo's role in general is less taxing, while Leonora is an extravagantly tragic figure, a characteristic accentuated through the doom-laden minor-key properties of much of the music that surrounds her. When tranquility seems about to dawn, at the close of the second act, the forbidding music that follows her ensemble "La Vergine degli Angeli" hints that her rest is only temporary. In Act IV, her reverential prayer "Pace, pace, mio dio", with its sweeping phrases set above an undulating accompaniment (much like Alvaro's big aria), glows with a radiance that gives her an almost angelic demeanour. For a moment it appears as if her prayers have been answered – but, once again, fate catches up. As shouting is heard off-stage, it becomes immediately clear that not even a hermit can escape the path of destiny.

RECORDINGS OVERVIEW

La forza del destino has been recorded only six times since the coming of stereo, the reason being the extreme demands of the three leads – notably Alvaro, a swine of a part. Perhaps the finest Alvaro of the century, Placido Domingo, has recorded the role twice. Few other big names feature on the roll-call of first-rate recordings of this opera: Pavarotti has steered clear of it, Bergonzi recorded it several years past his prime, and Franco Corelli – an ideal protagonist – was ignored in favour of Richard Tucker by EMI in 1954. There are, however, one or two bootlegs of Corelli in live performances, and they more than justify the search.

Price, Domingo, Milnes, Giaiotti; John Alldis Chorus; London Symphony Orchestra; Levine.
(RCA RD8 1864; 3 CDs).

This 1976 production (of an uncut score) is justifiably among the most famous of all Verdi recordings. Levine shows a secure grasp of structure, giving the work's disparate elements a cumulative cohesion that no other conductor has managed. Domingo is the finest postwar exponent of Don Alvaro – his vocal weight and grand phrasing are nowhere better heard than in the big aria, which he pulls off with unflustered virtuosity. Leontyne Price sounds magnificent, singing Leonora with great intelligence and feeling, while Milnes gets the measure of Carlo's twisted, hateful personality. All in all there is no finer Verdi on disc.

Callas, Tucker, Tagliabue, Rossi-Lemeni; La Scala Chorus and Orchestra; Serafin.
(EMI CDS7 47581-8; 3 CDs).

Leonora is another of those roles that Callas was born to play: her kaleidoscopic range of inflection brings real tragedy to this portrayal, and her development of the character from lover to hermit is beyond comparison. Richard Tucker is by no means perfect as Alvaro but he is vigorous and smooth throughout and makes a good stab at the vicious "O tu che in seno agl'angeli". Tagliabue and Rossi-Lemeni are more than acceptable, although the latter was already past his best when this recording was made in 1954. Serafin's direction is well balanced and quite energetic.

Tebaldi, del Monaco, Bastianini, Siepi; Chorus and Orchestra of Academy St Cecilia, Rome; Molinari-Pradelli.
(Decca 421 598-2DM3; 3 CDs).

This solid recording captured one of opera's greatest partnerships – del Monaco and Tebaldi – in its prime, although the performance as a whole is inferior to both of those recommended above, because the conductor simply meanders through the score. Anyway, the singing is out of this world. Mario del Monaco attacks his role with all the delicacy of a panel-beater, but for testosterone there's no-one to beat him. Similarly, Tebaldi might have given more thought to what she was singing, but she is gloriously womanly. An unapologetic self-indulgence.

Don Carlos

Composed 1866–67; revised 1882–83.
First performed March 11, 1867; January 10, 1884.
Libretto by Joseph Méry and Camille du Locle, after Schiller and Cormon.

Synopsis

Act I
Madrid, 1558. Spain and France have been at war, but peace is at hand – so long as Don Carlos, the heir to the Spanish throne (occupied by his father Philip II), marries Elisabeth de Valois, the daughter of the King of France. Elisabeth and Don Carlos (who has travelled to France to catch a glimpse of his betrothed) meet during a hunt in Fontainebleau forest. He introduces himself as a member of the Spanish envoy's staff, and she questions him over the character of the man she will have to marry. When he shows her a portrait of the Prince, she realizes that this is the person she is talking to, and they rapturously declare their love for one another. But their ecstasy is short-lived for the Spanish envoy arrives with a formal request, on behalf of the King of Spain, for Elisabeth's hand in marriage. Urged by her courtiers to bring an end to the war, she agrees to marry Philip instead.

Act II
In the monastery of San Yuste, Spain, a friar kneels in prayer before the tomb of Charles V, Carlos's grandfather. Carlos proclaims his love for Elisabeth (who

has since married Philip) to his friend Rodrigo, Marquess of Posa. Rodrigo advises him to forget her and apply himself to defending the people of Flanders, who are being brutally persecuted by Philip. By the gates of the monastery, Tebaldo and Princess Eboli (Elisabeth's lady-in-waiting), together with the ladies of the court, shelter from the sun. They are joined by the Queen, and then Rodrigo, who gives her a note from Carlos in which he requests an audience. She dismisses her entourage (including Eboli, who secretly loves Carlos) and greets the Prince, who proclaims his enduring love for her. She offers to ask Philip to send him to Flanders, but will not allow him to embrace her. As Carlos leaves, Philip arrives; in the course of a long exchange Rodrigo tells him his suspicions about Carlos and Elisabeth. Philip orders him to keep an eye on them.

Act III

Carlos receives an anonymous note requesting a meeting. He assumes it is from Elisabeth, and is shocked when he finds that its sender is Princess Eboli. She realizes that he loves Elisabeth and threatens to inform Philip; Rodrigo now enters and attempts to persuade her that Carlos is unwell. Unconvinced, Princess Eboli leaves, swearing revenge. Rodrigo forces Carlos to hand over any incriminating documents. At a public burning of heretics, a Flemish deputation – headed by Carlos – arrives to beg for an end to Philip's persecutions, but they too are arrested. When Philip refuses to give him control of Flanders, Carlos draws his sword. Rodrigo springs to Philip's defence and Carlos is arrested.

Act IV

Prompted by the Grand Inquisitor, the King determines to put his son to death and agrees that Rodrigo should be handed over to the Inquisition. After the Inquisitor leaves, Elisabeth rushes in looking for a lost jewel case. Philip produces the box and opens it – revealing a miniature portrait of Carlos. He accuses her of adultery; when she faints, he summons Princess Eboli and Rodrigo. When the Queen and Eboli are left alone, the Princess confesses to having stolen the case. She also claims to have been the King's mistress. Elisabeth is appalled and demands that she enter a convent.

Rodrigo visits Carlos in his cell and reveals that he has implicated himself as the leader of the Flemish rebels, hoping that this sacrifice will gain Carlos his freedom. Two of the King's men enter the cell and shoot Rodrigo. Before dying, he manages to tell Carlos that Elisabeth will be waiting for him at the monastery of San Yuste.

Act V

At San Yuste, the following day, Carlos and Elisabeth meet. He promises to devote himself to the Flemish. As they make their farewells, Philip and the Grand Inquisitor emerge from the shadows. The King orders their arrest, but as Carlos draws his sword and begins to retreat towards the tomb of Charles V, the friar who appeared at the beginning of Act II leads Carlos to safety. The King, the Inquisitor and the guards exclaim that the friar must be the ghost of Charles V.

Having overseen the French premiere of his revised *Macbeth* on June 7, 1865, Verdi returned to Italy, where the theatre in Busseto, begun six years earlier, was nearing completion. Verdi was of course pleased that it was to be christened the Teatro Giuseppe Verdi, but was decidedly irked to discover that he was expected to give the management handsome donations for its upkeep. As Verdi's wife put it: "To the minor and modest composer Coppola the citizens of Catania are coining a gold medal worth 1227 francs as a token of their joy at his return after fifteen years' absence. Giuseppe Verdi, who has filled the world with the glory of his music, the citizens of Busseto have rewarded by poisoning his life with every sort of vileness." This was perhaps overstating the case, but the wrangling over funds for the theatre certainly brought about the end of Verdi's close friendship with his benefactor Giovanni Barezzi, and Verdi never set foot inside the theatre to which he eventually contributed 10,000 lire as a sort of severance payment.

So, when the Paris Opéra commissioned a new opera from him, Verdi leapt at the opportunity to get away from his native town and spend time in the French capital, where he signed a contract in November. Work did not begin until the following year, when he threw himself into Schiller's drama, determined to remain as true to the spirit of the play as he had been to the spirit of Shakespeare's. However, he no more followed the letter of the play than Schiller had followed the letter of history. Schiller took a proto-Hollywood attitude towards the facts when dramatizing the life of Don Carlos, who in reality was an epileptic psychopath, quite rightly feared and loathed by all around him. Verdi followed Schiller in painting Carlos as a man of honour, torn between his responsibility to the downtrodden and his love for an ideal woman, and added lashings of extra material – notably from Eugène Cormon's play *Philippe II, Roi d'Espagne*, the basis of Act I.

The score that was finally delivered to the Opéra was by far Verdi's longest, and although it was pruned during rehearsals, *Don Carlos* tried the patience of the Paris audiences – as Bizet wrote, "Verdi is no longer Italian, he is following Wagner." It limped on for about eight months, then disappeared from the repertoire for fifteen years, until Verdi produced an Italian version – dropping the "s" from the title, translating the libretto into Italian and scything much of the music, including the entire first act. It was reborn as a masterpiece, and ever since then *Don Carlo* has been the preferred edition, although recent productions and recordings have favoured an Italian-language version of the five-act form, originally published in 1886.

The Grand Opéra qualities of *Don Carlos* are misleading – yes, it's a very long opera, complete with dance music and big choruses, but more significant is the intimacy of its finest music and the scale of its central drama, aspects in which it most closely resembles *Otello*. The intertwined relationships between the Queen, Don Carlos and Philip II are expressed through music of remarkable delicacy, in which gentle phrasing and close intervals carry a sincerity and inwardness that is every bit as powerful as the thrashing and crashing of the choruses and ensembles. As is generally the case in Verdi, characterization is direct and uncomplicated. Philip is a one of the most grotesque of Verdi's creations: a tenebrous bass role, his shadow falls across the opera just as Iago's stains *Otello*. The two dominant female roles – Eboli's mezzo and Elisabeth's soprano – are well opposed, one dark and volatile, the other naive and idealistic; while Carlos himself is an unusually sensitive tenor, so that when he does lose his cool – as when he draws his sword on his father – the impact of the moment is overwhelming.

Tension is the crucial characteristic of *Don Carlos*, an opera in which the unveiling of lyrical ideas is often cut short by unexpected outbursts. One of the most shocking instances of this comes during the confrontation between Philip and Rodrigo that ends the second act: the King and Rodrigo's exchange about Philip's self-styled "peaceful" treatment of Flanders is ripped apart by Rodrigo's cry of "A horrible, dreadful peace", the words being roared above low brass and thunderous chords. This scene is a highlight of the opera, a masterpiece of characterization in which Philip raises himself to his full and horrible height, and the passage in which he warns Rodrigo to beware the Inquisitor is spine-chilling – as is his calm disgust at the behaviour of his son in the following act. *Don Carlos* might be a tad too long, and some people find the ending frustratingly inconclusive, but the dynamism of its relationships and its wealth of expressive melodies make it an absorbing experience for those with the requisite stamina.

RECORDINGS OVERVIEW

The bigger they are the more they cost, so it is a testament to the quality of *Don Carlo/Don Carlos* that it has received a dozen recordings – but only two in the original French. However, not until 1965, when Solti conducted one of his international spectaculars for Decca, did the opera receive a fair trial. All but two of the succeeding productions (EMI and Sony, both 1992) were very good, and three were outstanding. Claudio Abbado's account of the French-language version of the opera, for years the only one in the catalogue, now takes second place to EMI's 1996 set.

Carreras, Freni, Baltsa, Cappuccilli, Ghiaurov, Raimondi, van Dam, Gruberova; Berlin Opera Chorus; Berlin Philharmonic Orchestra; Karajan.
(EMI CMS7 69304-2; 3 CDs).

Karajan's 1978 recording of the four-act version of *Don Carlo* is arguably the most aggressive classical recording ever made. This might not sound like the start of a recommendation, but the intensity of Karajan's passion makes this an unbelievably intense experience. He gets the huge Berlin forces to produce waves of rich, bass-heavy sound, providing an amazing backdrop for his almost perfect cast. The young Carreras is in magnificent voice, easily the most impressive Don Carlo on record, while soprano Freni and mezzo Baltsa spark off each other as Elisabeth and Eboli. Ghiaurov, Raimondi and van Dam are equally impressive and reach almost hysterical levels of dramatic tension (one passage has Cappuccilli actually screaming his lines). The sound quality is a model for recording engineers.

Bergonzi, Tebaldi, Bumbry, Fischer-Dieskau, Ghiaurov, Talvela; Royal Opera House Chorus and Orchestra; Solti.
(Decca 421 114-2DH3: 3 CDs).

Despite the over-pushy direction of Georg Solti, this is the best of the various five-act versions of *Don Carlo*. Carlo Bergonzi is an excellent Carlo – powerful enough to bestride the opera as Verdi intended, but sensitive enough to justify Elisabeth's love. Not everyone will warm to Fischer-Dieskau's Rodrigo, but he brings an intelligence to the role that's lacking in the performances of many Italian baritones. Tebaldi and Bumbry generate a lot of excitement, though they pale in comparison with Freni and Baltsa, and the rest of the cast likewise cannot match the Karajan team.

Alagna, van Dam, Hampson, Mattila, Meier; Orchestre de Paris; Pappano
(EMI 5 56152 2; 3 CDs).

Claudio Abbado's French *Don Carlos* was a difficult act to match, boasting as it did a cast that included Domingo, Ghiaurov and Ricciarelli, but Antonio Pappano's recording – made during a superb production at Paris's Chatelet theatre – does manage to trump it. Pappano's conducting has the edge on Abbado's, while Roberto Alagna at the very least deserves to be ranked alongside Domingo. José van Dam is a fine Philip as well, but the outstanding performance is the gorgeous and very moving Elisabeth of Karita Mattila. The orchestral sound isn't top-class, but really that's the only problem with an interpretation that looks set to stand as the first-choice *Don Carlos* for many years.

gives himself up as a traitor – a tactic that allows Aida and her father to escape.

Act IV

Amneris visits Radamès in his cell and promises him his freedom if he denounces Aida. Unrepentant, he is sentenced to be buried alive; and as the stone is rolled above his head he declares his misery at never seeing Aida again. But she has hidden herself in the tomb so that they might die together; as Amneris is heard praying for Radamès, the lovers die in each other's arms.

Aida

Composed 1870–71.
First performed December 24, 1871.
Libretto by Antonio Ghislanzoni, after du Locle.

Act I

The Ethiopian people have begun to fight back against the occupying Egyptians, and their King Amonasro has crossed the border into Egypt at the head of his army. A messenger arrives in Memphis with news that the sacred city of Thebes is threatened by the Ethiopians. The priests ask the god Isis to whom they should entrust their armies; Radamès, an Egyptian commander, hopes he will be chosen. He is also hopeful that he might one day marry his beloved Aida, an Ethiopian slave girl assigned to Amneris, the daughter of the Pharaoh. But there are complications, for Amneris also loves Radamès. At a temple ceremony, the commander has his armour blessed by the High Priest Ramfis.

Act II

Amneris suspects Aida's love for Radamès and tricks her into a confession. Amneris swears that Aida and Radamès will never be together and taunts her by forcing her to watch Radamès ride into the city with the routed Ethiopian army in chains. The city stops to greet the Egyptian hero and when he is offered any reward, he asks that the Ethiopian slaves be released. All except Amonasro, who has confessed to being Aida's father (but not to being the King of Ethiopia), are set free. As further reward, Radamès is offered Amneris's hand in marriage.

Act III

Aida comes down the Nile to meet Radamès. Amonasro persuades his daughter to obtain from Radamès details of the Egyptian army's plans, as he intends to lead the Ethiopians against Egypt. When Radamès arrives, Aida begs him to elope; before they can flee, Amneris and Ramfis intervene, and Radamès

In November 1869 Khedive Ismail, the ruler of Egypt (who three years later would contribute handsomely to the fund for Wagner's theatre in Bayreuth). announced plans to open a new opera house in Cairo as part of the celebrations surrounding the opening of the Suez Canal. He asked Verdi to compose an "inaugural hymn" for its opening night, which was planned for November 1870; Verdi wasn't keen on this idea, but in April 1870 he responded enthusiastically to Ismail's alternative suggestion that he compose an opera on an ancient Egyptian subject. Verdi set to work, but that summer war broke out between Prussia and France, and the props and scenery for *Aida*, which were being made in the French capital, could not be taken out of the city – an incidental inconvenience, it turned out, as Verdi couldn't finish the music on time. The Cairo opera house opened instead with a performance of *Rigoletto*, and Verdi eventually finished work in December 1871, just weeks before the premiere in Egypt.

Verdi had taken extraordinary care over the preparation of Ghislanzoni's libretto, providing specific metrical requirements, and he was equally fanatical over the orchestration and stagecraft, in order to produce an opera "in a strictly Egyptian style". He studied Egyptian history, geography and religion, and went so far as to commission the construction of "Egyptian" flutes and trumpets for the ritual scenes. But for all his efforts, critics were dismissive of what they saw as another regression to the conventions of Grand Opéra. In some respects they had a point: *Aida* wallows in its exoticism and its continued popularity rests largely on the pomp and circumstance epitomized by the famous triumphal march, "Gloria all'Egito", which opens the second scene of Act II. This opera's scope for de-Mille like extravagance has made it a perennial fixture of the Verona opera festival, staged in the city's vast ancient Roman arena.

Yet *Aida* is a psychological drama rather than a cast-of-thousands show, and its tone is considerably more intimate than its best-known moment suggests. The opera opens discreetly, with a prelude of softly spun strings, with which Verdi brilliantly evokes both the Egyptian scene and the tormented psyches of the protagonists. And although the opera's first aria, the tenor Radamès' punishingly difficult "Celeste Aida", is introduced by a blaring trumpet fanfare, this Grand Opéra flourish is, typically for this opera, a setting against which the hero's melancholy song appears yet more intensely personal.

Radamès could not be numbered among Verdi's most complex creations, but there are degrees of intricacy in the other principal roles. Amonasro, for example, is pretty ruthless in the pursuit of his cause, and yet is capable of bursts of tearful compassion. Similarly, the spiteful Amneris undergoes a few U-turns: upon finding Radamès with Aida and Amonasro it is she who condemns him as a traitor, but in the following scene (the first of Act IV) she begs him to allow her to save his life. After he rejects her, she turns on him once again, threatening revenge in a powerful solo, "Chi ti salva, sciagurato"; but as he is led away, Amneris slumps in despair, blaming herself for his downfall, and when Radamès refuses to answer his accusers in court, she prays for his deliverance.

For all Amneris's roller-coastering, *Aida* is dominated by its title role, another empathetic personification of Verdi's preoccupation with the parent-child relationship. Riven between her love for Radamès and her responsibility to her father, she commands the spotlight with two great arias in Act I ("Ritorna vincitor!") and Act III ("O patria mia") and a series of powerful duets, culminating with the heart-breaking entombment scene. The final moments of Aida and Radamès are amazingly calm, with each secure in the knowledge that, through death, they will be united forever. There is, of course, an obvious similarity to the ending of *Tristan und Isolde*, but the mood could not be more different. Whereas Wagner ended his lovers' lives in voluptuous ecstacy, Verdi repeats the same, even-metred phrase some twelve times, closing the drama with music of gentle resignation. It is an unforgettably magical conclusion.

RECORDINGS OVERVIEW

The best recordings of *Aida* come from the period between 1949 (the year of the RCA/Toscanini set) and 1970 (RCA/Leinsdorf). Performances by Tebaldi (Decca, 1952 and 1959), Milanov (RCA, 1955), Price (Decca, 1961) and Nilsson (EMI, 1967) set the benchmarks for the interpretation of the title role, just as del Monaco (Decca, 1952), Björling (RCA, 1955), Bergonzi (Decca, 1959) and Corelli (EMI, 1967) set the highest standards in the role of Radamès. The two accounts below are comprehensively fine introductions to the opera, but if Zubin Mehta's performance for EMI, with Nilsson and Corelli, comes back into the catalogue it will become an equal first choice.

Tebaldi, Bergonzi, Simionato, MacNeil; Vienna Singverein; Vienna Philharmonic Orchestra; Karajan.
(Decca 414 087-2DM3; 3 CDs).

Karajan's first attempt at *Aida*, recorded in 1959, was also the first in stereo, and it has never been surpassed. Tempi are swift, but not unduly so, and Karajan ekes some gorgeous sounds from the VPO. Renata Tebaldi and Carlo Bergonzi, a well-matched pairing, produce consistently beautiful tone. Tebaldi's voice may lack the clarity and security of Callas and Milanov, and Bergonzi doesn't have Björling's rush or Corelli's bite, but they both give unerringly stylish and intelligent readings. MacNeil's Amonasro is suitably forthright and Simionato is a fantastically exciting Amneris. The sound is lush but it does not favour the voices, leading to a tendency for the orchestra to stampede some of the finer vocal detail. Nonetheless, at mid-price, this is a dream-ticket.

Milanov, Björling, Barbieri, Warren; Rome Opera Chorus and Orchestra; Perlea.
(RCA GD86652; 3 CDs).

This 1955 set unites five of the greatest singers of the century, a vocal cornucopia that more than compensates for the anonymous conductor and his scrappy orchestra. The dramatic soprano Zinka Milanov is in soaring form, paying careful attention to Verdi's scrupulously prepared dynamic markings. The same could be said of Jussi Björling, whose open-throated, ardent tone makes his Radamès a display of lyrical-heroic tenor singing at its very best. Leonard Warren and Fedora Barbieri are excellent as Amneris and Amonasro, while the roaring Boris Christoff makes much of Ramfis's extended lines. The mono sound is fine, as is the price.

Otello

Othello

Composed 1884–86.
First performed February 5, 1887.
Libretto by Arrigo Boito, after Shakespeare.

Synopsis

Act I

Othello, Venetian governor of Cyprus, is expected back on the island after defeating the Turks. His ship fights its way through a storm and the people celebrate when he steps ashore. He is greeted by Iago, his ensign, who wants to destroy the Moor for having promoted Cassio to lieutenant. Wine is brought out and Iago encourages Cassio to drink. He has also primed Roderigo, a Venetian gentleman, to mock Cassio – this leads him to pick a fight with Othello's predecessor, Montano, who is merely trying to keep the peace. Montano is wounded in the fracas, which wakes Desdemona, Othello's wife. Furious, Othello dismisses Cassio and appoints Iago in his place.

Act II

Iago tricks Othello into believing that Cassio is having an affair with Desdemona, then urges her to persuade her husband to release Cassio from prison, which serves to increase his suspicion. Iago steals Desdemona's handkerchief (given her by Othello) and tells Othello he has seen it in Cassio's hands. This drives Othello into a frenzy, and the act ends with Othello and Iago pledging to prove Desdemona's guilt.

Act III

Othello confronts his wife over the handkerchief (which she cannot find) and dismisses her repeated requests that Cassio be released. With Othello hiding, Iago enters with Cassio and the two men talk of Cassio's lover Bianca; but Othello cannot hear the woman's name and assumes that the woman referred to is his wife. After Cassio leaves, Othello and Iago vow to kill the unfaithful pair that very night. They are interrupted by the arrival of ambassadors, who announce that Othello is to be recalled to Venice, leaving Cassio in charge. At this, he strikes his wife and orders everyone from the room except the triumphant Iago.

Act IV

Alone in her room, Desdemona sings her "Willow Song", recalling the story of another woman who was similarly rejected. Othello appears and, ignoring her pleas of innocence, chokes her to death. Emilia

Jon Vickers as Otello – perhaps the greatest interpreter of the role since the war

(Desdemona's maidservant and Iago's wife) bangs on the door and cries out that Cassio has killed Roderigo, who was in love with Desdemona. The truth slowly dawns on Othello. As everyone gathers in Desdemona's chamber, Othello draws his sword. Realizing he is beaten, he admits his crime, removes a dagger from his belt and stabs himself. After one final kiss of his wife's lips, he dies by her side.

During the spring of 1879 – some eight years after the first performance of his previous opera – Verdi was invited to dinner by the publisher Giulio Ricordi and the conductor/composer Franco Faccio. As Ricordi later recalled: "Quite by chance I steered the conversation on to Shakespeare and Boito. At the mention of *Othello* I saw Verdi look at me with suspicion – and interest." The publisher arranged a meeting between Verdi and Boito, during which they discussed the possibility of working together on a setting of *Othello*. Although the two men had met during Boito's student years in Paris, they had later fallen out and Verdi was wary of committing himself to a collaboration with him, having not been overly impressed by Boito's *Mefistofele* (see p.225). All that came out of the session was Verdi's suggestion that Boito go ahead and start a libretto anyway, as it would "always do for me, or for you or for someone else".

Not unsurprisingly, nothing came of it, and nearly two years passed before Verdi, urged by Ricordi, asked Boito if he would help him in revising *Simon Boccanegra*. The 1881 revision was a big hit, and Verdi was highly impressed by Boito's alterations to the libretto. Talk again returned to *Othello*, but another three years were to pass before Verdi finally made his mind up. *Otello* was begun in March 1884 and Boito, in cutting the 3500 lines of Shakespeare's play down to 800, gave Verdi a drama perfectly suited to a man with a taste for absolutes. The composer responded in kind, creating what many believe to be his greatest score.

The La Scala premiere, conducted by Faccio, was one of the most reported events in Italian musical history, attended by critics from every European nation – it was, after all, Verdi's first new work for some fifteen years. The build-up was not without its stresses. The great Francesco Tamagno, in the title role (he later recorded extensive excerpts), provoked Verdi into writing to Faccio expressing the hope that he might persuade the tenor to sing "something approximating to what I have written". Romilda Pantaleone was not everyone's first choice as Desdemona (but Faccio had a non-musical interest in her), and the French baritone Victor Maurel, for whom the part of Iago was specifically written, kept announcing that he was "senza voce" (voiceless), though Verdi took solace from his acting ability – "So long as Maurel can speak I would rather he did Iago than anyone else." In the event it all came right – the critic Ugo Capetti wrote of the premiere, "Musical Italy is not yet lost!".

In *Otello* Verdi used an orchestra of Grand Opéra dimensions, but marshalled it with a rare fastidiousness. Fusing Italianate melody with the through-composed techniques that were typical of Germanic opera, he created a musical fabric in which divisions between numbers barely existed, manipulating leitmotifs and key association to underline points of detail – such as the exquisite "kiss" motif first heard during the love duet, and later used to tragic effect during Otello's death scene. Verdi's attention to word-setting was scrupulous too: for example, when Iago first mentions the word "jealousy", Verdi accompanies it with a chilling succession of parallel chords to mark the turning point. Stravinsky once quipped that it would be a good idea to throw all Verdi's best arias into a single, two-hour show, but with *Otello* every line plays a part in the development of the drama.

The depiction of Otello's decline epitomizes the sophistication of Verdi's art: whereas Verdi might previously have charted Otello's demise through a series of set numbers, each one detailing a distinct step in his downfall, here the emotional complexion changes within each episode. During his harrowing Act III monologue "Dio mi potevi scagliar", for example, Otello moves from half-sobbing despair via nervous regret to a bestial eruption of rage. Similarly, his final monologue, "Niun mi tema", is full of rapid mood shifts, ending with one of the most poignant deaths in all opera. Iago is a protean monster, courteous as the occasion demands, but emerging into blazing villainy with his "Credo", a thrillingly malevolent rant, while Desdemona, whom Verdi considered a "type of goodness, of resignation, of self-sacrifice", is assigned music of old-fashioned lyricism – her Act IV "Willow Song" stands out for its childlike simplicity. Ultimately, however, it is the name role – the most taxing tenor role in Italian opera – that dominates, from his opening vainglorious cry of "Esultate!" to his final achievement of self-knowledge.

SHORTENING OTELLO

The great Austrian tenor Leo Slezak was a famous source of operatic anecdotes. His best-known escapade occurred during a performance of *Lohengrin* in which, at the end of the final act, the swan swept up to the tenor and promptly departed way ahead of schedule; Slezak calmly inquired of his audience, "What time is the next swan?". However, his favourite tale concerned a performance at Houston opera house, where he was due to sing Otello, a role for which he was celebrated. Slezak knew that American opera houses had pioneered the exploitation of sponsorship and advertising, but he was nonetheless unprepared for the lengths to which the Houston had gone on behalf of Crisco, manufacturers of a brand of shortening (baking fat). The house programme looked like this:

OTHELLO

Opera in Four Acts, by Giuseppe Verdi

Act I.

The people of Cypria on their knees are praying for the safety of Othello, whose ship is fighting the elements. The danger passes. Othello arrives and greets the people with the words:

USE CRISCO, THE BEST SHORTENING

"Rejoice! The Turk is vanquished and drowned in the sea." The people hail Othello:

CRISCO IS UNSURPASSED

Iago, jealous of Cassio, who enjoys Othello's confidence, tries to render Cassio drunk. A drinking song:

CRISCO HAS NO RIVAL

is heard and Cassio, by now quite drunk, attacks Montano. Othello rushes in and calls out:

CRISCO IS ECONOMICAL

"Down with your swords!" Cassio is being demoted. Desdemona, Othello's bride, appears in the doorway to the castle. Othello takes her hand and they sing a lovely duet:

CRISCO USERS ARE SATISFIED

which belongs to the best Verdi wrote, and is considered one of the pearls of operatic music.

And so it continued, right through to the finale:

After Othello has strangled Desdemona, he plunges his dagger into his breast and, dying, sings the touching phrase:

ASK ONLY FOR CRISCO, THE FAMOUS SHORTENING

"Kiss me, kiss me again!" He dies. End of the opera.

RECORDINGS OVERVIEW

There have been a number of outstanding exponents of the role of Otello in the era of recording, including its creator, Francesco Tamagno, who recorded a series of excerpts during the first decade of the century (Opal CD9846). His immediate successors in the role were Giovanni Zenatello (who can be heard on a whole series of Pearl CDs), Renato Zanelli (whose thundering tenor can be heard on Nimbus NI7856) and, most famously, Giovanni Martinelli – whom you can hear in a complete Met broadcast made in 1938 (Music and Arts MACD-645). Martinelli was followed by arguably the greatest of them all, Ramón Vinay (of whom more below) and the man who was without question the loudest of them all – Mario del Monaco, whose two performances for Decca are unflinchingly full-blast. Thereafter the roost was ruled by McCracken, Vickers and Domingo. Pavarotti gave concert performances of the opera in 1991 in Chicago; Decca recorded them – Pavarotti it may well be, but Otello it isn't.

Domingo, Studer, Leiferkus, Vargas; Paris Opéra-Bastille Chorus and Orchestra; Chung.
(Deutsche Grammophon 439 805-2GH2; 2 CDs).

Myung-Whun Chung's reading of *Otello* upset a lot of reviewers when it was released in 1993, primarily because he took what was deemed to be an unduly creative approach to Verdi's markings. And it's true that his tempi and phrasing are, to say the least, unconventional. However, his choices usually sound like right choices, and he drives the drama to an unprecedented frenzy, with a vast dynamic and expressive range. The balance of soloists and orchestra is expertly maintained too. The title role is taken by Placido Domingo, who has effectively established a monopoly of the part since the 1970s. This is his third recording of it, and after a hurried "Esultate" – Otello's opening cry of triumph – he settles into what turns out to be one of the greatest performances of his career, even if his vocal resources are not what they used to be. Studer makes a light, somewhat brittle Desdemona, but she gives a touchingly vulnerable reading of the "Willow Song". The obviously Russian Leiferkus is a vulpine Iago, and easily the most interesting Iago to feature on a Domingo recording.

Vickers, Rysanek, Gobbi, Andreolli; Rome Opera Chorus; Rome Opera Orchestra; Serafin.
(RCA GD8 1969; 2 CDs).

For some reason, few of the top postwar Otellos have been Italian. Vinay was Chilean, McCracken was American, Domingo is Spanish and arguably the best of the lot was a Canadian – Jon Vickers. This recording was made in 1960, before he had performed the role on stage, but there is not even a hint of insecurity here. Although he possessed one of the most powerful tenor voices of his day, Vickers is a vulnerable rather than an heroic Otello: the love duet is achingly moving, and his death scene has a haunting dignity. Leonie Rysanek is too grand for Desdemona, but Gobbi – using his open-throated voice to great effect – is a thrilling, pungent Iago, especially during the "Credo". Serafin's approach is a little too spacious, but he coaxes some fine playing from the Roman forces.

Vinay, Nelli, Valdengo, Assandri; NBC Chorus and Orchestra; Toscanini.
(RCA GD60302; 2 CDs).

Toscanini played cello in the very first performance of *Otello*, so there can be no denying the historical importance of this recording, made in 1947. It also boasts the dark and noble presence of Ramón Vinay, without question the greatest Otello of the century. Originally a baritone (to which voice he would later revert), he brings unsurpassed gravity and vocal weight to the part, and has an ability to turn a phrase in a way that loads even the slightest gesture with significance. The remainder of Toscanini's casting was highly suspect, but the clarity and urgency of his authentically Verdian approach, and the glorious voice of Vinay, make this a trifling consideration.

Vinay, Martinis, Schöffler, Dermota; Vienna Philharmonic Choir and Orchestra; Furtwängler.
(EMI CHS 565751-2; 2 CDs).

With Vinay as Otello and Furtwängler at the helm, this was bound to be something magical. Vinay is in towering form, a veritable beast of a man, and he makes the final scene unutterably painful. Dragica Martinis, Paul Schöffler and the Vienna choir and orchestra provide excellent support, but of course the other star of this session is the conductor. Furtwängler's perception of the work's architecture has a magisterial finality to it, making this performance a unique fusion of passion and intellect. Good sound for a 1951 Salzburg Festival broadcast.

Falstaff

Composed 1889–90; revised 1893 and 1894.
First performed February 9, 1893.
Libretto by Arrigo Boito, after Shakespeare.

Synopsis

Act I

At the Garter Inn, Dr Caius accuses Sir John Falstaff of brutalizing his servants and complains that Falstaff's retainers Bardolph (Bardolfo) and Pistol (Pistola) have robbed him. Falstaff laughs it off and announces to his men that he intends to seduce the wives of Ford and Page. He commands Bardolph and Pistol to carry letters to the women but they refuse, claiming the action is dishonourable. Passing the notes to a page, Falstaff lectures them on the subject of honour.

In Ford's garden, with Nannetta (Ford's daughter) and Mistress Quickly listening on, Alice Ford and Meg Page read identical letters from Falstaff, and determine to teach him a lesson.

Act II

Back at the Garter, Mistress Quickly arrives with an answer to Falstaff's letters. He has won both women's hearts, but only Alice can see him – between two and three any afternoon, when her husband is away. Meanwhile, Ford (disguised as "Fontana") introduces himself as a wealthy man who has fallen in love with Ford's wife. He has tried to seduce her, but to no avail, and offers Falstaff gold if he will help his cause. As Sir John is to meet her that very day he willingly agrees. While Falstaff leaves to dress for the assignation Ford fumes with jealousy. In Ford's house, Falstaff arrives and begins wooing Alice; when Ford storms in looking for the intruder, Falstaff hides in a laundry basket, while Nannetta and Fenton hide, in each other's arms, behind a screen. While Ford searches the house, Falstaff – in his laundry basket – is dragged to the window and dumped in the river.

Act III

Outside the Garter, Falstaff is licking his wounds when Mistress Quickly arrives with news of another assignation with Alice, this time in Windsor Forest at midnight. However, this time he must go disguised as the "Black Huntsman". Their conversation is overheard by the other wives, Ford, Caius and Fenton – who plan the evening's fun. Later that night, with Sir John standing by Herne's Oak, Nannetta invokes the forest spirits (the local children) to prick and pinch Sir John as they stage the masque of the Fairy Queen, in the course of which Nannetta and Fenton are married. Ford is philosophical when he realizes his daughter has thwarted his wishes through trickery, and Sir John leads the company in a chorus – "Jesting is man's vocation. Wise is he who is jolly."

In 1879 the sculptor Giovanni Dupré published his memoirs, excerpts of which were printed in the Ricordi house magazine. There Verdi read Dupré's quotation of Rossini's comment that "Verdi was incapable of writing a comic opera". In response Verdi wrote to his publisher with news of a comedy that had come to his attention, but made it clear that, if he set it, the rights would go to another publisher. Ricordi apologized for the slight, but in truth Verdi had shown almost no flair for comedy, and Verdi probably knew it – that's the likeliest explanation for the fact that, when he finally decided to set *The Merry Wives of Windsor* at the age of seventy-five, he kept the project a secret between himself and Boito. For four years they worked, on and off, on the project, doing their best (but ultimately failing) to keep it from the outside world. When news did leak out, Verdi insisted he was setting the play to amuse himself and had no real wish to see it performed. In the event, he threw himself into preparations for the La Scala premiere, and he conducted the first night, where the opera was greeted as a masterpiece – although he later made extensive revisions in March 1893 and January 1894.

In most respects, *Falstaff* is the perfect antidote to *Otello*'s ferocious intensity. Where *Otello* relied extensively on solos (*Otello* is no less a singer's opera than *Rigoletto*), Falstaff is essentially a work of ensemble – when it does put the spotlight on one figure, as in Ford's monologue, it does so in a parodic manner. Melodies are handed about like batons, with duets, quartets and – most remarkably – fugues contributing as much to the opera's comic fizz as do the situations themselves. The whole cast is the star in *Falstaff*.

Just as the libretto squeezed "all the juice from that Shakespearean orange without letting any of the useless pips fall into the glass" (Boito), so Verdi crammed a life's experience into his final work. And he did not leave without paying his respects to some of his major colleagues and predecessors: homage is paid to everyone from Mozart (the concluding fugue) and Weber (the fairy music of Act III), to Delibes (in the gentle bustle of Act II), Bizet (Fenton's elegant "sonetto") and even Wagner – whose *Meistersinger* is honoured in the closing scenes of Act I.

Each scene contains some gem of comic writing: famously Falstaff's colourful self-portrait in Act I and his recollection of the ducking, which is accompanied by an extraordinary orchestral trill to remind him of the water's nip. But Verdi was careful to play the humour against a slight strain of melancholy, coming closer to the autumnal temper of Shakespeare's plays than any other musical treatment. Enjoyable as a display of orchestral virtuosity or simply as a riotously paced comedy, *Falstaff* is a perfect fusion of humanist realism and light-hearted fantasy – and the perfect testament to the multifaceted genius of Giuseppe Verdi.

RECORDINGS OVERVIEW

Toscanini's legendary 1950 NBC radio broadcast of *Falstaff* set a standard that only Karajan's recording for EMI has surpassed. Yet there are several other accounts that have very strong qualities, notably Solti's 1963 effort, which is memorable for Geraint Evans' characterful performance of the title role; and Leonard Bernstein's 1966 recording for CBS numbers one of his greatest achievements as a conductor, even if Fischer-Dieskau's Falstaff is vocally under-nourished and theatrically over-cooked. Of later attempts, you might want to check out the one conducted by Carlo Maria Giulini in LA in 1982. Marking Giulini's return to live opera after a fourteen-year hiatus, the performance is based on Verdi's own instructions on performing style – the result is intriguing, but to modern ears rather lethargic.

Gobbi, Panerai, Schwarzkopf, Moffo, Alva; Philharmonia Chorus and Orchestra; Karajan.
(EMI CDS7 49668-2; 2 CDs).

There is still no finer set than Karajan's first account, made in 1956 with a superlative cast. Technically Tito Gobbi is less well equipped for the title role than many, but the verve and sensitivity of his portrayal lift him clear of his rivals. Panerai's Ford (a role she recorded four times) is brilliantly sung and extremely funny, while Moffo is a light and youthful Nannetta, Luigi Alva is charming as Fenton, and Schwarzkopf shines as Alice. Karajan is remarkably attentive to the balance and application of instrumentation, and the ensembles are perfectly paced – especially the finale.

Valdengo, Guarrera, Nelli, Stich-Randall, Madasi; Robert Shaw Chorale; NBC Symphony Orchestra; Toscanini.
(RCA GD60251; 2 CDs).

For many, this is Toscanini's finest achievement on disc. Recorded in 1950, it has served as a point of reference for every succeeding conductor of the opera: the subtlety of expression, the timing and sense of architecture, and the delicacy of colouring are out of this world. The casting is weak, but this is a performance that thrives regardless. A legendary document but, more importantly, a legendary performance.

AMILCARE PONCHIELLI

b. PADERNO, ITALY, AUGUST 31, 1834; d. MILAN, JANUARY 17, 1886.

So comprehensive was Verdi's domination of Italian music during the middle-to-late years of the nineteenth century that all but a handful of his contemporaries have fallen into obscurity. Along with Boito and Catalani, Ponchielli is one of that handful, and his survival into the twentieth century is due solely to the merits of a single work, *La gioconda*, a typically Italianate display of passionate emotionalism.

A gifted child, he was enrolled at the Milan Conservatory shortly before his tenth birthday. After graduating in 1854 he returned to his birthplace near Cremona, where, two years later, he completed his first opera, *I promessi sposi*. Despite its provincial success, the work attracted no outside interest. Neither did his next two operas and not until the first performance of his revision of *I promessi* in 1872 did he achieve any widespread fame. The production led directly to a commission from La Scala for a ballet which, in turn, led to a publishing contract with Ricordi. In 1876 Ponchielli completed *La gioconda* for La Scala; he went on to compose two further operas but neither was especially popular, and he devoted the remaining years of his life to teaching at the Milan Conservatory, where his pupils included Puccini and Mascagni.

Ponchielli developed an operatic style that owed some debt to French Grand Opéra, but inevitably his chief reference point was his great contemporary and compatriot, Giuseppe Verdi. In his music you can hear something of the melodic voice of middle-period Verdi, and in his conception of modern opera as a form in which aria and chorus were less important than the dramatic whole he was moving along the same lines as Verdi – indeed, had he lived to see it performed, *Otello* would almost certainly have struck him as the realization of his ideal.

La gioconda

The Joyful Girl

Composed 1874–75; revised 1876, 1877, 1880.
First performed April 8, 1876.
Libretto by Arrigo Boito, after Hugo.

Synopsis

Act I

Venice, seventeenth century. Barnaba propositions the street-singer La Gioconda, but she rejects him. Furious, Barnaba turns the crowd against her blind mother, La Cieca, by telling them that she is a witch. She is saved by Enzo, an exiled Genoese noble disguised as a fisherman, and the Venetian Inquisitor Alvise disperses the crowd – in gratitude for which La Cieca gives Alvise's wife Laura a rosary. Enzo suddenly recognizes Laura as a past love, just as Gioconda begins to fall in love with the mysterious fisherman. Realizing who the fisherman really is, Barnaba offers to help Enzo and Laura revive their affair. At the same time, he writes to the Council of Ten informing them that an exiled nobleman is in town.

Act II

On board his boat, Enzo greets Laura and there follows a passionate duet. When he leaves to arrange for their departure, Gioconda emerges and confronts her rival. But Laura is more worried by the approach of her husband's ship, and she prays for help – removing La Cieca's rosary. Recognizing the necklace, Gioconda realizes that Laura is the wife of her mother's saviour and she alerts Enzo to the danger. After setting fire to his ship, he and Gioconda escape.

Act III

Alvise, bent on revenge against his unfaithful wife, forces her to take poison – but Gioconda has replaced the potion with a sleeping draught. Believing his wife dead, Alvise holds a banquet at his mansion where guests are entertained by the "Dance of the Hours". Disgusted by his cruelty, Enzo attacks Alvise but he is overpowered and arrested. Gioconda agrees to yield to Barnaba if he will save Enzo from death.

Act IV

When he is released Enzo forgets Gioconda's altruism and flees with Laura. Desolate, Gioconda prepares to submit to Barnaba but as he embraces her, she stabs herself. Thwarted, the evil Barnaba reveals to the dying woman that he has killed Gioconda's mother.

The playwright Albert Innaurato wrote of *La gioconda* that it was an opera in which "the expressive potential of music is used rather coarsely, and not harnessed to insights of an intellectual sort. But I think there is something fundamental about its dramaturgy that may make it a litmus test to differentiate those who like opera from those who adore it." Plenty of people have adored it – indeed Toscanini thought so highly of it that he chose the Prologue for his solitary postwar concert appearance at La Scala in 1948. However, the qualities that once endeared it to so many – its pungent orchestration, extended tunes, fizzing climaxes and superheated emotions – are no longer irresistible, and today it's rarely staged.

This is a pity, for the title role has featured on the curriculum vitae of many of the great dramatic sopranos since Maddalena Mariani-Massi created the role in Milan, and the quality of the vocal writing extends down to the secondary roles, especially the lustful baritone Barnaba, the calculating mezzo Laura and the doomed contralto La Cieca. The score of *La gioconda* is best known for its ballet divertimento "The Dance of the Hours" (taken from Alvise's banquet) and Enzo's big Act II romanza "Cielo e mar" – one of the most impassioned tenor songs in the romantic Italian canon. But there are a number of fine episodes, the most successful of them being the wild and stirring duet between Enzo and Laura that follows "Cielo e mar" (a confrontation as emotionally loaded as anything by Puccini), and the final, sickening sequence between the gloating Barnaba and the suicidal Gioconda, in which she ends her life to music of gut-wrenching despair.

RECORDINGS OVERVIEW

Of the sopranos to pick up the gauntlet of La Gioconda, the most successful were Maria Callas, Anita Cerquetti and Renata Tebaldi. They were also the best partnered, best recorded and best conducted, and for all the big names to grace the catalogue (eg Milanov/di Stefano, Caballé/Pavarotti), this trio's recordings stand clear of the crowd. Maria Callas recorded the role twice, once for Cetra in 1952 and again for EMI seven years later. The former is a barnstorming portrayal, but is only sporadically available as an import; the later effort has a more piercing tone that some might find taxing, but it is powerful stuff and readily available.

Callas, Ferraro, Cappuccilli, Companeez, Cossotto; La Scala Chorus and Orchestra; Votto.
(EMI CDS7 49518-2; 3 CDs).

Callas's 1959 Gioconda is marred by some booming chest notes, scrawny head tones and unpleasantly wide vibrato, yet the performance is awe-inspiring. No other soprano has managed to project such intensity in the studio – her singing of "Suicidio!" and the monologue that follows it are without rival. Piero Cappuccilli's Barnaba is beautiful if a little benevolent; but Pier Ferraro's woolly tenor is an unconvincing Enzo, particularly when heard next to Fiorenza Cossotto's forceful Laura. Cossotto's real-life husband Ivo Vinco is in good form as her stage husband Alvise, and Antonino Votto – who conducted Callas for Cetra – is again a steady presence, relishing the superior La Scala forces.

Cerquetti, del Monaco, Bastianini, Simionato; MMF Chorus and Orchestra; Gavazzeni.
(Decca 433 770-2DMO2; 2 CDs).

Recorded in 1957, this was Mario del Monaco's greatest moment in the studio, for here he found himself surrounded by sympathetic musicians in music that brought out the best from his steam-hammer tenor. Remarkably, he shades his tone in places, introducing some genuinely sensual phrasing, and he even produces one or two moments of quiet singing, but he is generally at full stretch throughout and, but for a questionably tuned "Cielo e mar", he is magnificently exciting. Anita Cerquetti, in the only complete role she recorded in the studio, is a vibrant Gioconda – hers is a tightly controlled and brilliantly phrased performance, at once tender, rich and theatrical. Simionato is a dream, and in her duets with del Monaco the sparks fly as if the performance were live. Gavazzeni, an unsung conductor, binds the whole with panache, fathoming the opera's construction as completely as the detail. The score is cut but the stereo is excellent.

Tebaldi, Bergonzi, Merrill, Horne; Santa Cecilia Academy Chorus and Orchestra; Gardelli.
(Decca 430 042-2DM3; 3 CDs).

Ten years after the del Monaco and Cerquetti *La gioconda*, Decca produced another recording, as a showcase for the talents of Renata Tebaldi and the tenor Carlo Bergonzi. Where the earlier set had highlighted the opera's melodrama, this recording brought out the lyrical qualities. Tebaldi's voice is creamy and indulgent, while Bergonzi's articulate, effortless tenor is delicious, even if his voice is too light for some of the second act's more furious exchanges. Marilyn Horne, singing one of her few late Romantic roles, is effulgent as Laura and Robert Merrill is rich if incongruously sweet as Barnaba. Lamberto Gardelli conducts this first uncut recording with a refined awareness of texture, though he lacks Gavazzeni's passion.

ARRIGO BOITO

b. PADUA, ITALY, FEBRUARY 24, 1842; d. MILAN, JUNE 10, 1918.

Novelist, poet, critic, conductor and composer, Arrigo Boito was one of the cultural luminaries of late nineteenth-century Italy. Initially an ardent Wagnerian, he was converted to the music of Verdi, for whom he wrote two libretti, the basis of his reputation today. On the whole his music is less accomplished than these libretti, but there is one great exception – *Mefistofele*, arguably the most ambitious setting of Goethe's *Faust*.

He studied at the Milan Conservatory where he won a scholarship to Paris, as did his lifelong friend Franco Faccio. There he met Verdi and provided him with the text for a cantata, but after returning to Milan he concentrated mainly on his own music, in particular his setting of Goethe. In 1863 Faccio commissioned Boito to write the libretto for his opera *I profughi fiamminghi*, a work that prompted Boito to declare that Faccio would "cleanse the altar of Italian opera now stained like the walls of a brothel" – a hot-headed remark that Verdi took personally, causing a rift that endured for years. In 1866, shortly after Austria had ceded Venice to the embryonic Kingdom of Italy, Boito and Faccio joined Garibaldi for the final push to achieve complete Italian unification. After three months of posturing, Boito left for Poland, where he completed *Mefistofele* in 1867.

The premiere at La Scala, conducted by the twenty-six-year-old composer, was a catastrophe. It was badly sung and shambolically conducted, and when the show dragged on past midnight, critics and audience conceded defeat. By the time the curtain came down at 1.30am the theatre was half empty. The Scala management divided the opera into two parts ("just like the poem", they pleaded) and spread the second performance over two nights; this did little to help and Boito withdrew the score from production before the third performance. During the ensuing period of disillusionment he devoted himself to writing libretti for other composers, including Catalani and Ponchielli, and to translating existing works, including *Tristan* and *Ruslan and Lyudmila*. But in 1875, seven years after its first performance, a revised and greatly abbreviated *Mefistofele* was received in Bologna as enthusiastically as the original had been condemned.

In 1879 Verdi and Boito were reconciled and began one of the greatest writer-composer relationships in operatic history, producing the triumphs of Verdi's *Otello* and *Falstaff*. Though Verdi urged Boito to renew his musical career, Boito failed to finish *Nerone*, an opera he had first begun in 1862. Toscanini saw to its completion and conducted the first performance in 1924, two years before conducting the first performance of Puccini's last, incomplete opera, *Turandot*.

Mefistofele

Mephistopheles

Composed 1860–67; revised 1875 and 1881.
First performed March 5, 1868.
Libretto by the composer, after Goethe.

Synopsis

Act I

After a prologue in which the Devil wagers God that he can win Faust's soul, the elderly philosopher is followed by a friar who reveals himself to be the Devil. He restores Faust's youth and urges him to sign a contract selling his soul in return for a single moment of divine happiness.

Act II

Mephistopheles (Mefistofele) flirts with Marta while Faust, introducing himself as Enrico, courts her friend Margherita. She agrees to meet him later, and Faust gives her a draught to keep her mother asleep so that they will not be disturbed. Mephistopheles takes Faust to witness the Witches' Sabbath (Walpurgis Night), during which he sees a vision of Margherita in chains.

Act III

Margherita, who is deranged, has been imprisoned for poisoning her mother (with Faust's draught) and for drowning her son by Faust. He visits Margherita in her cell and offers to free her, but she rejects his help and, after renouncing the Devil (who makes a late appearance beside Faust), she dies resolute in her Christian faith.

Act IV

Mephistopheles transports Faust to ancient Greece where he meets Helen of Troy (Elena). Faust offers his love, and they leave together, disappearing from sight.

Epilogue

Disillusioned and longing for death, Faust repents. He is pitied by God who, regardless of Mephistopheles' demands for his soul, welcomes him into heaven.

Based on both parts of Goethe's *Faust*, Boito's *Mefistofele* was an attempt to tackle the philosophical issues that Gounod and Berlioz chose to jettison when setting the poem – perhaps an unrealizable goal. The original 1867 version was a sorry example of ambition outstripping ability, and even after his major revision of 1875 – for which he changed Faust from a baritone to a tenor, cut much of the philosophical rambling, re-wrote the final scene and added two powerful arias – *Mefistofele* remained an episodic piece, and some producers try to tighten things up by axing the final act, linking Act III directly to the Epilogue. On the other hand, Boito's overhaul was successful in that he retained all of the finest music and further concentrated attention on the title role.

In naming his setting of Goethe's poem after the Devil rather than after its human protagonist, Boito was signalling that his primary concern was the metaphysics of the "bargain between God and the Devil" – a somewhat more lofty conception than Gounod's populist setting. The extraordinary half-hour Prologue confirms that Boito was aiming very high. Constructed of four separate movements, it begins with angelic voices and a noble (much repeated) theme of Wagnerian intensity, then continues with a roguish "pizzicato" scherzo (accompanying the Devil's arrival before God), a chorus of cherubs (sung by twenty-four trebles) and a psalmody of spirits scored for a huge orchestra and chorus – and all this before the opera has even begun.

The problem is that Boito lacked the technique, discipline and imagination to sustain his opera at this pitch, with the consequence that ideas lie dotted about the score like half-eaten carcasses. Sometimes it's hard to resist the suspicion that Boito was making it up as he went along. Ironically, much of the more successful music is small-scale, as if Boito was at his best when not worrying about making an impression. The first scene of the second act, for example, when Margherita asks Faust if he believes "in religion", is notable for the effortless beauty of their exchanges. The other strength of the opera is of course Boito's Devil, a marvellously menacing creation, nowhere more so than during his chilling proclamation in Act I, "Sono lo spirito che nega sempre tutto" (I am the spirit that denieth) and the remarkable "Ecco il mondo", at the close of the Witches' Sabbath. Mefistofele dominates the proceedings, even though Faust and Margherita are both given some lovely music – notably, in addition to the opening of the second act, Faust's pious "Dai Campi, dai prati" (Act I), his "Colma il tuo cor d'un palpito" (Act II), and the prison scene, in which he and Margherita sing the duet "Lontano, sui flutti d'un ampio oceano". Neither of the opera's premieres benefited from star singers, but the scale and personality of Boito's devil soon came to attract just about every bass with the technique to sing it. It's chiefly thanks to the likes of Fyodor Chaliapin, Nazzareno de Angelis (who sang the title role 987 times), Ezio Pinza, Boris Christoff and, most recently, Sam Ramey, that the opera has survived.

RECORDINGS OVERVIEW

Of the nine complete recordings, the first choice – Julius Rudel's 1973 performance for EMI with Norman Triegle and Placido Domingo in the male leads – is at present unavailable, but the runner-up is excellent (see below). There are also some curiosities well worth investigating. Boris Christoff's only studio performance of the title role, taped in 1955 by EMI, with Vittorio Gui conducting, is miraculous – but the text is heavily cut. Produced three years later, Decca's first recording of *Mefistofele* provides a remarkable shouting match between Cesare Siepi's Devil and Mario del Monaco's Faust, a contest given a degree of balance by the superb Margherita of Renata Tebaldi. The 1996 recording from RCA, with Muti conducting a patchwork of performances at La Scala is good fun, and Sam Ramey is the most devilish Devil to sing the role since Christoff, but the supporting cast veers between the weak and the ugly.

Ghiaurov, Pavarotti, Freni, Caballé; Trinity Boys' Chorus; National Philharmonic Orchestra; de Fabritiis. (Decca 410 175-2DH3P; 3 CDs).

Oliviero de Fabritiis is in full command of this mighty score: although his tempi are broad, he shapes the music well and provides sensitive support to his outstanding cast. Pavarotti is in blithely magnificent form as Faust, capturing the philosopher's pain, passion and hope with unequalled radiance. Caballé's Helen is also wonderfully sung, and she spins an irresistible magic during her grand duet with Faust. Freni catches the full scope of Margherita's character, fervent in her love music and genuinely terrified by the appearance of Mephistopheles in prison. Nicolai Ghiaurov lacks the brutal wit demanded by "Ecco il mondo", and "Son lo spirito che nega sempre tutto" is much more frightening in Christoff's hands, but he is beautiful sounding throughout. The full price is a shame, but the documentation is good and the recording excellent.

RICHARD WAGNER

b. LEIPZIG, MAY 22, 1813; d. VENICE, FEBRUARY 13, 1883.

Richard Wagner was a one-man artistic movement, a figure so massive that his influence was felt by all his contemporaries and nearly all his major successors. Some imitated him, some rejected him, and some were almost paralyzed by the immensity of what he had done. The composer Hugo Wolf wrote in 1883, "What remains for me to do? He has left me no room, like a mighty tree that chokes with its shade the sprouting young growths under its widely spreading branches." No other composer provoked such extreme antipathy nor such adulation. Ernest Newman, author of a four-volume biography of the composer, was not alone in his opinion when he wrote that Wagner's work was the creation of "the simultaneous functioning . . . of a composer's imagination, a dramatist's, a conductor's, a scenic designer's, a singer's, a mime's. Such a combination had never existed in a single individual before; it has never happened since, and in all probability it will never happen again."

When Wagner was born Beethoven had yet to make his definitive revision of *Fidelio* and Weber would not compose *Der Freischütz* for another eight years. At his death, opera had been reinvented as music-drama, a form of musical theatre in which arias and ensembles had been supplanted by huge, slowly unfolding strcutures that continued without interruption. In the works upon which Wagner's reputation rests, each constituent part of the musical fabric, whether harmonic or melodic, carries meaning, and the interaction of the principal themes – the leitmotifs ("leading ideas") – constitutes an ever-evolving drama in itself. So complex is the resultant texture that the destruction of Valhalla at the end of *Götterdämmerung*, for example, takes place against a sort of symphonic recapitulation into which some ninety leitmotifs are blended. Wagner's operas are dramas of epic grandeur, suffused with an extraordinary energy – the "Ride of the Valkyries" is too much of a set-piece to be typical of Wagner's work as a whole, but it's a perfect gauge of his virtuoso control of the orchestra's resources.

Then again, while his mastery of the orchestra is the key aspect of Wagner's achievement, it is but one component of what he described as his *Gesamtkunstwerk* ("total work of art"), a project in which music, poetry, drama and the visual arts were synthesized, an art form in which every detail from the instrumentation to the colours of the set served a dramatic purpose. Wagner is often travestied as a bombastic bore (Oscar Wilde: "I like Wagner's music. It is so loud that one can talk the whole time without other people hearing what one says."), but this is way off target – his work is characterized by a maniacal attention to detail, a precision that's as much in evidence in his scenes of idyllic calm as in the better-known scenes of torrid passion or bellicose mayhem. Wagner's stagecraft transformed the production of opera, just as his music took the vocabulary of Romanticism to the very brink of dissolution, heralding the revolution headed by Schoenberg.

By most accounts, the man who did all this was a monster. Analyzing Wagner from a safe distance in 1872, Theodor Puschmann, a Munich psychiatrist, concluded that the composer suffered from "chronic megalomania, paranoia . . . and moral derangement". He was a vicious racist and an infamous womanizer, fathering countless illegitimate children. He tyrannized his first wife then stole another man's wife, finding in her an echo of his limitless self-adoration (he habitually referred to himself in the third person). He was an animal-loving vegetarian (like Hitler), but behaved abominably to anyone who treated him with less than unquestioning devotion, and he seemed oblivious to the welfare of his family, cultivating an obsession for silks and other luxuries that kept them in perpetual debt. As far as Wagner was concerned, his genius excused everything, and remarkably, many people did excuse him. According to his lifelong enemy Eduard Hanslick, he "exercised an incomprehensible magic in order to make friends, and to retain them; friends who sacrificed themselves for him, and three times offended, came three times back to him".

Wagner's parentage has never been conclusively established, but his father was either his mother's husband, Carl Friedrich Wagner, or her lover, the actor and painter Ludwig Geyer, whom Wagner's mother, Johanna Rosine, married soon after Carl Friedrich died in 1814. (Problematic parentage was to be a recurrent theme in Wagner's operas.) Not altogether surprisingly, Wagner was initially interested in the theatre and he wrote a blood-and-guts drama, *Leubald*, in 1828; but after seeing Wilhelmine Schröder-Devrient's performance as Leonore in Beethoven's *Fidelio*, he decided to take music lessons. Having gained some command over the piano and learned the rudiments of theory, at the age of nineteen he wrote the text and began the music for his first opera, *Die Hochzeit* (The Wedding). Only fragments survive, but it is clear from these that Wagner developed swiftly in the couple of years separating *Die Hochzeit* from *Die Feen* (The Fairies), which he wrote while working as a chorus master in Würzburg. Very much in the mould of Weber and Marschner, it was an unremarkable work, and only Wagner was surprised when the Leipzig opera house rejected it.

LEBRECHT COLLECTION

Richard Wagner in Napoleonic mode

He began to study music by his non-German contemporaries, including Meyerbeer, Auber, Cherubini, Spontini and Bellini, as it became clear that, for all the impact that Weber's *Der Freischütz* had made, there was still no such entity as a current school of German opera. This study of Italian music was reflected in the bel canto melodies and general lightness of touch of his next opera, *Das Liebesverbot* (The Ban on Love), a work that flopped at its first performance in Magdeburg. Soon after, in 1836, he married the actress Minna Planer, travelling with her to Riga, where he began *Rienzi*, and later to Königsberg. Heavy debts forced him to keep on the move, and in 1839 he headed for London, where he managed to complete *Rienzi*; the next year he and Minna took their battle against poverty to France.

Rienzi was finally staged in 1842 in Dresden, where it was enormously popular. But before then Wagner had decided that he had reached a creative impasse and that a radical break with tradition was needed. As Nietzsche later put it, Wagner lacked schooling but "possessed courage: he made a principle of what he lacked – he invented a style of music for himself". Within a year of completing *Rienzi* Wagner had remade himself and German opera through *Der fliegende Holländer* (The Flying Dutchman), a work that inaugurated a succession of music-dramas that were to change the course of western music. In 1843 he was appointed conductor of the Dresden Opera, where he produced *Holländer*, and during the next five years he composed *Tannhäuser* and *Lohengrin*, prepared a draft of the text for *Die Meistersinger von Nürnburg* (The Mastersingers of Nuremberg), began the poetry for what would become the *Ring* cycle and read Wolfram von Eschenbach's poem *Parzival*. And so, with the exception of *Tristan und Isolde*, his entire life's work had now begun to take shape in his mind.

Meanwhile he had begun to involve himself in left-wing politics, though the mainstay of his incoherent, quasi-anarchistic philosophy seemed to be that a revolution by and for "the common man" was necessary to create a state in which his operas could be fully understood. He was implicated in the fighting that broke out after the Dresden rebellion of May 1849, and a warrant was issued for his arrest. Aided by Franz Liszt, a steady ally and inspiration, Wagner escaped to Zurich, where he wrote "The Work of Art of the Future" and "Opera and Drama", essay-manifestos presenting in great detail his theories on the relationship between words, music and the stage.

In 1850 Liszt conducted the first performance of *Lohengrin* in Munich, and two years later Wagner completed the poetry for the four mighty episodes of the *Ring*: *Das Rheingold* (The Rhinegold), *Die Walküre* (The Valkyrie), *Siegfried* and *Götterdämmerung* (Twilight of the Gods). He began the music in 1853, commencing a task that would take him a quarter of a century, but he was soon distracted by Mathilde, wife of Otto Wesendonck, a wealthy Swiss businessman and patron of the arts. There followed a passionate affair, out of which grew the typically self-mythologizing opera *Tristan und Isolde*, a work for which he suspended his labours on the *Ring* cycle in the hope that it would finance the construction of the unique theatre he now realized would be necessary for the staging of the *Ring*.

All the while, the hapless Minna, though suffering from a heart condition, did her best to tolerate his relationships with Mathilde and countless other women, and she spent much of the 1850s either seeking cures or following Wagner around his various lodgings, trying to win him back. The marriage finally collapsed in the early 1860s when Wagner fell in love with Liszt's daughter Cosima, who happened to be the wife of the conductor Hans von Bülow, one of Wagner's closest friends and his most tenacious champion. The conductor was distraught but sacrificed himself to Wagner's career, allowing Wagner to pursue Cosima while von Bülow continued to champion his "master's" music.

But not even von Bülow could staunch Wagner's profligacy, and by 1864 the composer's finances were in disarray. Salvation came in the shape of the benignly deranged King Ludwig II of Bavaria, whose enthusiasm for Wagner's operas was such that he created shrines to the composer in his castles in the Bavarian Alps, and discussed plans through which he might use the country's money to further the cause of "this god among men". Wagner encouraged Ludwig's infatuation and in return Ludwig threw ever larger sums of money at the composer – "He feels a king's power ought to suffice to protect me from all that is base, to leave me wholly free for my Muse," wrote Wagner to a friend, "and to provide me with all the resources I need to perform my works, when and as I wish." At the king's insistence *Tristan* was given its premiere at the Munich Court Opera in 1865, but when Ludwig discovered that Wagner and Cosima von Bülow had become lovers (the composer is said to have confronted the conductor with the words "I want you in my pit, and your wife in my bed") he was outraged, and there was a temporary falling out. Von Bülow continued to tolerate his humiliation, conducting the first production of *Die Meistersinger* in 1868, and the following year his marriage to Cosima was annulled. In 1870 Wagner and Cosima finally married, having already produced three children, and with the affair legalized the composer and the monarch were reconciled. Indeed, such was Ludwig's passion that he insisted that the first two parts of the *Ring* be produced in Munich in 1868 and 1870, even though Wagner wanted to wait until the cycle was ready for performance in its entirety. With *Die Walküre* premiered, Wagner renewed his attempt to convince Ludwig to fund the construction of a theatre devoted solely to his music at Bayreuth, near Nuremberg. Ludwig was unable to find the money to cover the whole costs, but made a handsome donation to get the ball rolling.

In 1871 the Bayreuth authorities gave Wagner a plot of land above the town and in May 1872, thanks once again to the last-minute support of Ludwig, the foundation stone was laid. Though his expenditure was carefully supervised by his government, Ludwig did manage to pay for a residence to be built in the centre of town. Wagner named it "Wahnfried", meaning "Peace From Illusion", and moved in with his family in 1873, prior to a serious falling-out with his patron, who was both appalled by Wagner's ruthless egoism and dejected by the realization that the composer was never going to reciprocate his sexual passion. With Ludwig refusing all communication, all seemed lost, but on January 25, 1874, the king had a change of heart, and the Bayreuth theatre was finally completed in time for the first performance of the complete *Ring* in 1876.

After that the theatre lay unused for six years, but in 1877 Wagner began work on the music for *Parsifal*, concurrently attempting – in vain – to establish a music school for the instruction of singers, instrumentalists and conductors "in the correct manner of performing music-dramatic works in the true German style" (his own music, in other words). The rest of his life was devoted to *Parsifal*, the premiere of which was given at Bayreuth six months before his death in Venice.

Wagner's body, and the chair upon which he died, were returned to Bayreuth, where he was buried in the grounds of Wahnfried. Cosima took over the running of the theatre, to be succeeded by her son Siegfried and his English-born wife Winifred. Under Winifred's control, Bayreuth became one of the holy places of the Third Reich: her friend Adolf Hitler and his cronies made pilgrimages to Wagner's theatre to applaud music which they took to be the embodiment of the true Teutonic spirit. Even the most right-thinking Wagnerite could not deny that there is much in the man's music (and even more in his writings) that prefigures the monstrous triumphalism of the Third Reich. Similarly, only the most blinkered anti-Wagnerite could maintain that his operas can be dismissed as nationalist and racist propaganda. But the legacy of the Nazi era continues to haunt Wagner's work, despite the corrective process that began right after the war, when Winifred's son Wieland banned his own mother from the theatre and set about purging all Bayreuth productions of the horned-helmet-and-breastplate clichés. There can be no end to this process of rehabilitation, because there is so much in Wagner's art that resists rehabilitation. It was only in 1993 that Wagner's music was first heard in Israel, and the event provoked massive controversy. At the same time, there can be no end to the exploration of Wagner's music-dramas: each generation discovers its own version of Wagner.

Der fliegende Holländer

The Flying Dutchman

Composed 1840–41; revised 1842, 1846, 1852, 1860.
First performed January 2, 1843.
Libretto by the composer.

Act I

The Norwegian coast, the eighteenth century. Daland's ship is forced by bad weather to take shelter in a cove seven miles from home. He curses the storm for keeping him from his daughter Senta. Through the storm appears the blood-red sail of the Flying Dutchman's ship. The Dutchman has been condemned to travel the seas until the Day of Judgement, unless he can achieve salvation through the love of a woman – he is allowed onto land once every seven years to seek such a woman. The Dutchman offers Daland enormous wealth in return for shelter and the chance to woo Senta. Daland agrees.

Act II

In Daland's house, surrounded by the village women at their spinning wheels, Senta sings the ballad of the Flying Dutchman, in which she considers herself as the source of his salvation. The hunter Erik announces Daland's return and begs Senta to persuade her father that he is a worthy suitor. He tells her of his dream in which, confronted by two men – one Daland, the other a dark and mysterious stranger – Senta throws herself towards the latter. The door opens and in walk Daland and the stranger of Erik's dream. The Dutchman and Senta are immediately smitten, and although he warns her of the sacrifices she will have to make if she takes him as her husband, she is adamant that she is the right woman.

Act III

Daland's ship is anchored alongside the Dutchman's, from which there is no response until a storm flares up around it, whereupon the Dutchman's crew sing of their fate – Satan has cursed them to sail the seas for eternity. Daland's crew flee in horror. Erik, appalled to hear of Senta's decision to marry the Dutchman, confronts her, reminding her of their embraces. The Dutchman overhears and assumes that she has been unfaithful. She fails to convince him otherwise and, as he leaves, he reveals his true identity. Desolate, Senta hurls herself into the sea. The doomed sailor is redeemed by her sacrifice, and the opera ends with the Dutchman and Senta heaven-bound.

Der fliegende Holländer was Wagner's first step towards creative autonomy, beginning the transformation of the formulas of opera into the Wagnerian universe of music-drama. In place of conventional divisions between arias, ensembles, accompaniment and so forth, each component – whether a vocal line or an instrumental part – was now subsumed into what Wagner called "a musical and poetic unit, entirely homogeneous". And for the first time, everything that happened on the stage and in the pit, from the instrumentation and harmony to the stage movement and lighting, was to serve a dramatic purpose. Wagner marked almost every bar of the score with some instruction – nothing was to be left to chance.

With Meyerbeer's help the first performance was to have taken place at the Court Opera in Berlin, but management wrangles and other difficulties forced Wagner to remove it. It was eventually given just four performances in Dresden (conducted by the composer), all of which were coolly received. Despite praise from Louis Spohr (see p.136) – "This work is full of imagination, of noble invention, well written for the voice, very difficult, and too much loaded with instrumentation, but overflowing with new effects" – *Holländer* was only a moderate success. It was briefly revived later the same year in Riga and Kassel, and then was produced in Berlin before falling from the repertoire for several years. Wagner revised the orchestrations in 1846 for a performance that never happened, and it remained on the publisher's shelf until April 1852, when Wagner again revised it for his own production in Zurich. A final revision in 1860 changed little beyond the ending, to which he added a motif signifying redemption, in the style of *Tristan*. To further complicate things, Wagner originally intended the opera to be played in a single unbroken span (itself a revolutionary idea), but for the premiere and later performances he subdivided it into three acts, which involved writing end-cadences for each act. Nowadays most opera houses opt for a version without a break – in other words, a form of *Der fliegende Holländer* that Wagner never saw.

Even when not performed in a single uninterrupted span, the *Dutchman* can still be overpowering for audiences who have come to opera via Mozart or Rossini. The whole score has a sort of monolithic fluidity, creating the impression of an organic whole in which everything is subservient to the interests of the drama. This is primarily created thanks to the atmospheric orchestration which, carrying the bulk of the thematic material, frequently relegates the voices – even the Dutchman's tormented baritone – to an almost supplementary role, reversing the traditional polarity in which the orchestra accompanies the voice. There's a supernatural hue to parts of this work, a feature that relates back to the work of Marschner, Weber and their kin; but nature, in particular the sea, is the all-pervasive influence – Franz Lachner once complained of "the wind that blows at you whenever you open the score". The overture (in which the pivotal struggle between damnation and redemption is first portrayed), the storm music, the Steersman's tenor song and the Sailor's Chorus all evoke the implacability of the elements, which in turn mirror the passions of the characters. Like so much else in Wagner's operas, Man and Nature are indivisible in *Der fliegende Holländer*.

In this opera many of Wagner's key ideas are developed extensively for the first time. Wagner was greatly taken by the notion of a man's redemption through the love and devotion of an "ideal woman" (his words), and he fused this idea with the idea of Christ's sacrifice to come up with the typically extreme Wagnerian concept of the *Liebestod*, the love-death in which the surrender of life itself was the consummating act of love. The ending of the *Dutchman* is Wagner's draft of what was to be a pivotal concept in the *Ring* cycle, and the very *raison d'être* of *Tristan und Isolde*. The strong-willed Senta is a sister to Isolde and Brünnhilde, Wagner's embodiments of his "ideal woman", while the Dutchman himself is conceived as a blood-brother to the Wandering Jew, whose burden it is to carry the guilt for the murder of Christ – a stereotype that would surface again forty years later in *Parsifal*, in the female guise of Kundry. Finally, of course, the Dutchman is also the Artist: with *Der fliegende Holländer* the twenty-nine-year-old composer erected the first great monument to the cult of himself.

RECORDINGS OVERVIEW

There are no bad recordings of *Der fliegende Holländer*, and the best are all readily available, a unique situation when it comes to Wagner. In addition to those recommended below (all of which use a three-act text), there are two studio sets that warrant a special mention: Klemperer's 1968 EMI recording, with the remarkable coupling of Anja Silja and Theo Adam, is notable for its intense orchestral playing and for Silja's fearsomely exciting Senta; while Solti's Decca production, recorded eight years later, boasts some marvellous conducting, though the leads are comparatively weak.

Estes, Balslev, Salminen, Schunk, Clark; Bayreuth Festival Chorus and Orchestra; Nelsson.
(Philips 434 599-2PH2; 2 CDs).

This 1985 recording brilliantly captures the cohesion and fluency of *Der fliegende Holländer*. Made at the end of Harry Kupfer's long-running Bayreuth production, with Woldemar Nelsson conducting pretty much the same cast he had been directing since 1981, the performance has a conspicuous unity of vision. Simon Estes' full-voiced, bass-baritone Dutchman, closely supported by the Bayreuth Orchestra, has an anguish and desperation rarely matched on record. Lisbeth Balslev may lack Anja Silja's primitive emotion, but her cultured approach sits well opposite Estes' luxurious voice. Most of the remaining cast sing superbly, especially Matti Salminen's resonant Daland. Obtrusive stage noises might prove irritating but there is no more exciting performance on record.

Crass, Silja, Greindl, Uhl, Paskuda; Bayreuth Festival Chorus and Orchestra; Sawallisch.
(Philips 442 103-2PM2; 2 CDs).

Sawallisch's 1961 Bayreuth recording features leads in roles for which they are famous. Anja Silja is electrifying as Senta, and her ringing tone and hammer-like high notes would have eclipsed a lesser talent than Franz Crass – conveying all the exhaustion that immortality has brought the Dutchman, Crass produces the most ominous and moving interpretation on disc. The Bayreuth Chorus again proves itself to be the greatest on earth, and the orchestra responds to Sawallisch with exceptional dramatic attention. The German tenors Georg Paskuda and Fritz Uhl are superb in the minor roles of the Steersman and Erik.

Muff, Haubold, Knodt, Seiffert; Austrian Radio Symphony Orchestra and Chorus; Steinberg.
(Naxos 8660025-6; 2 CDs).

This offering from Naxos is a powerful, beautifully recorded performance, with Pinchas Steinberg getting an ardently animated performance from his orchestra. Alfred Muff is a resonant, large-sounding Dutchman, and the little-known Ingrid Haubold is more than a match for him, although there are moments where she forces the tone. The big name here is Peter Seiffert, who sings Erik, a role that is usually given to too light a voice, but there are no real weaknesses in casting. At budget price, this is remarkably good value, even if it lacks the stature of the other recordings listed here.

Hotter, Ursuleac, Hann, Ostertag, Klarwein; Bavarian State Opera Chorus and Orchestra; Krauss.
(Preiser 90250; 2 CDs).

This classic mono recording was taped in the studio in 1944. Krauss's reading is all about the horror and brutality of the tale, and while there is much else to be found in the score, his approach is unequivocally effective. Hans Hotter, only thirty-five at the time, is strikingly secure as the Dutchman, delivering a horribly chilling performance. Krauss's wife, the soprano Viorica Ursuleac, is an uneasy Senta, but Karl Ostertag is an impressively committed Erik. Poor sound, but a thrilling interpretation.

Tannhäuser

Composed 1843–45; revised 1859–61.
First performed October 19, 1845; March 13, 1861.
Libretto by the composer.

Synopsis

Act I

Thuringia, the early thirteenth century. Inside the Venusberg (Venus's mountain), sirens, naïads, nymphs and bacchantes dance themselves into a frenzy. Tannhäuser sings of his malaise – he has enjoyed Venusberg's delights, but longs to return to the real world – and when he utters the name of the Virgin Mary he is transported to the valley of the Wartburg. A group of knights, accompanied by Landgrave Hermann and Tannhäuser's friend Wolfram, are astonished to encounter Tannhäuser, who disappeared twelve months earlier, and they invite him to rejoin them. Hearing of the unhappiness his disappearance caused Elizabeth, the Landgrave's niece, he agrees to accompany them back to the Wartburg castle.

Act II

Elizabeth is overjoyed when she and Tannhäuser are finally reunited, but Wolfram is fearful that he will now lose Elizabeth, with whom he is in love. She is concerned when Tannhäuser refuses to tell where he has been for the past year, but she is comforted by her uncle, who announces a song contest in which each of the contestants (including Tannhäuser) is challenged to capture love in a single song. Tannhäuser's song extols the joys of the flesh, rather than the spirit, which provokes a violent outcry. For his crime he is exiled to Rome, where he must seek the Pope's forgiveness. Hearing the voices of pilgrims in the distance, he kisses Elizabeth's hem and rushes to join them.

Act III

Back in the Wartburg valley, several months later. Elizabeth waits for Tannhäuser and beseeches the Virgin Mary to release her from her suffering. As she prepares for death, Wolfram prays for her soul, imploring the evening star to welcome Elizabeth as she enters heaven. As night falls, Tannhäuser returns. He tells Wolfram of the Pope's condemnation ("just as this staff can never blossom, so you can never be redeemed") and, convinced of his damnation, he decides to return to Venusberg. But when Wolfram calls out Elizabeth's name, he reminds Tannhäuser of her love. Tolling bells are heard and a funeral procession comes down the mountain. Redeemed through Elizabeth's death, Tannhäuser dies in Wolfram's arms. [Revised ending: Tannhäuser announces his decision to return to Venusberg and the goddess herself appears, urging his return. But when Wolfram proclaims Elizabeth's name, and Elizabeth's funeral procession passes by, Venus disappears and Tannhäuser, redeemed, falls dead onto Elizabeth's body. The Pope's staff is carried in by pilgrims and, as it sprouts leaves, the sun rises to bathe everyone in a new morning's light.]

During the last months of Wagner's stay in Paris, when he was completing *Der fliegende Holländer*, the homesick composer began to immerse himself in German history, hoping that a fitting subject for a new opera would emerge from his reading. A friend suggested the tale of Tannhäuser, as told by the poet Ludwig Tieck. Wagner was at first repelled by the story (the notion of "the pure individual" was becoming something of a fixation with him), but after his return to Dresden he picked up Tieck's poem, along with Heine's *Tannhäuser* and writings by E.T.A. Hoffmann and the thirteenth-century poet Wolfram von Eschenbach, then took to the mountains of Bohemia. There, enthused by his surroundings and by a chance encounter with a group of pilgrim monks, he underwent a change of heart and began to map out a plot. Back in Dresden he devoted himself to the libretto and then the music – in his memoirs he was to write that he had "no recollections of any importance" from this period, so intense was his immersion in the subject. He completed the music for his "Grand romantic opera" in October 1845; later that month, he conducted the first performance at the Royal Saxon Court Theatre in Dresden.

Wilhelmine Schröder-Devrient, singing Venus, was baffled by the opera ("You are a man of genius, but you write such eccentric stuff that it is impossible to sing"), and Joseph Tichatschek, who created the title role, was barely able to comprehend what the composer wanted, far less satisfy him. The audience was equally perplexed (half the scenery had failed to arrive, which didn't help) and the reception was no more than polite. Wagner immediately began extensive revisions, but despite the arrival of the sets and a hasty abbreviation of the title role, the second performance on October 27 was given to a half-empty theatre.

In 1859 Wagner offered the work to the Paris Opéra, for whom he began revising the score, but two years were to pass – by which time he was living in Paris with Minna – before he managed to persuade the management to mount a production. Wagner had to accede to the house's written rule that any opera played on its stage had to be in French, and he was advised to accede to its unwritten rule – enforced by the yobbish Jockey Club – that the second act must contain at least one ballet sequence, so the club members could enjoy the sight of the dancers' legs while eating their mid-opera meal. But Wagner's dance sequence (which he lengthened) arrived early in Act I and, as far as he was concerned, it was going to stay there. During each of the 163 rehearsals the management implored him to acknowledge the power of the Jockey Club claque; Wagner remained steadfast. Consequently, the Jockey members disrupted the performance at every possible turn, despite the presence of the Emperor and Empress. It was a disaster (although Gounod wrote at the time "God, give me a failure like that") and *Tannhäuser* disappeared from the French stage for thirty-four years; but a couple of years after the debacle, while starting work on *Die Meistersinger*, Wagner revised the Paris version of *Tannhäuser*, translating the libretto back into German. The end result of all these alterations was an opera that was not as well-knit as it had been, but had a sound-world that was far more sophisticated – and easier on the ear – than the first draft.

With *Tannhäuser*, Wagner took another major step forward. Though the solos for Tannhäuser (his tribute to Venus), Wolfram (the "Prayer to the Evening Star") and Elizabeth (her haunting "Dich, teure Halle") are unforgettable set-pieces, this opera marks a further erosion of the aria/ensemble divisions that continued to provide the backbone for the work of his contemporaries. Crucial to the elimination of these divisions was Wagner's development of the technique of leitmotif and his paring-down of the orchestra. Although the overture and the bacchanal might not have been out of place in a Grand Opéra production, Wagner approached the opera's instrumentation with a new-found subtlety, notably toning down the noisier sections of the orchestra (obviously the brass) to allow the voices greater room for clarity. Equally important was Wagner's determination to make the meaning of his text take precedence over melody. As he wrote in his memoirs, the decision to set the Song Contest as a competition in dramatic poetry (rather than a concert of arias) was conditioned by his intention "to force the listener, for the first time in the history of opera, to take an interest in a poetic idea" and to prevent the distraction of "unnecessary changes in modulation and rhythm". Much of the vocal writing in *Tannhäuser* is notated in *Sprechgesang* ("speech-voice"), a term coined by Wagner to describe the opera's semi-declamatory vocal line; newcomers to Wagner can find this a bit wearying, and some critics at the time had problems with it. In typical style Wagner blamed the inability of the singers to adapt to his radicalism – "In order to ensure my success in the future, I now had to confront the exceptional difficulty of making opera singers understand how to interpret their parts precisely in the way I desired."

Writing about *Tannhäuser*, Wagner presented himself as a man repelled by the pleasures of "the material present" and "yearning for appeasement in a higher, nobler element, an element which . . . could but appear to me in the guise of a pure, chaste, virginal love". The opera itself tells a somewhat different story. Chaste spirituality is embodied by Elizabeth, whose music – with the exception of her greeting of the Wartburg Hall, "Dich, teure halle" – isn't material that's likely to win any audience to her cause. By contrast, the hedonistic delights of Venusberg and the goddess herself are represented by sounds that glow with feeling – a contrast that's especially notable during the final great scene of Act III, when the apparition of Venusberg is accompanied by music that warms up the stark narrative of Tannhäuser's journey to Rome. Though the lengthy overture sets out the opposition of the spiritual and physical as a fairly even contest, it's difficult to respond to Tannhäuser's salvation as strongly as to his misdemeanours.

RECORDINGS OVERVIEW

Though it's the least recorded of Wagner's mature works, *Tannhäuser* has fared well on record. Many of the most successful performances are live, and it was a live Bayreuth *Tannhäuser* that set the benchmark in 1960, when Sawallisch conducted Wieland Wagner's production for Philips (see below). Sawallisch's standard was met by Solti's 1970 recording, which remains its chief rival, though the catalogue has a trio of sets that you might want to sample: Giuseppe Sinopoli's reading for Deutsche Grammophon, on which Placido Domingo's Tannhäuser offers a performance that some enthuse over (while others grind their teeth); Konwitschny's mid-price EMI recording, which is well conducted and features the young Fritz Wunderlich; and Teldec's set, conducted by Janowski, featuring a lovely Elizabeth from Kiri Te Kanawa. In addition, if you're lucky you might find a copy of the 1954 Bayreuth performance, conducted by Keilberth, with a revelatory cast headed by the Chilean bari-tenor Ramón Vinay. The mono sound is ropy, but the interpretation is unsurpassed.

Windgassen, Silja, Waechter, Bumbry, Greindl, Stolze; Bayreuth Festival Chorus and Orchestra; Sawallisch.
(Philips 434 599-2PH2; 3 CDs).

For his two productions of *Tannhäuser* in 1954 and 1961 – the latter recorded here by Sawallisch – Wieland Wagner experimented with his own mixture of the Dresden and Paris editions. Smoothing out the stylistic inconsistencies was not an entirely successful process, but Sawallisch imposes a secure direction and extracts some subtle singing from his patchy cast. Wolfgang Windgassen is a tired and emotional Tannhäuser, pinched and breathy, but Grace Bumbry is a compelling Venus and Eberhard Waechter as Wolfram is rivalled only by Fischer-Dieskau. The star of the show, however, is Anja Silja's Elizabeth, a touching portrayal of innocence and conviction. If Tannhäuser himself has been better served, then the opera as a whole is given a reading of consistent care, and it's well recorded, in rich stereo.

Kollo, Dernesch, Braun, Ludwig, Sotin; Vienna State Opera Chorus and Orchestra; Solti.
(Decca 414 581-2DH3; 3 CDs).

This account of the Paris text is the best studio recording of *Tannhäuser*. In the title role, René Kollo gives the performance of his life, floating the languid line with ease and security and portraying love, anger and despair with equal sensitivity. Helga Dernesch is too grand as Elizabeth, but Christa Ludwig is a glorious Venus, with all the mustard and none of the ham. Solti gives another one of those manic performances for which his work is generally celebrated, and often this is just what is required (especially during orchestral solos), but he tends to rush his singers, especially when accompanying Elizabeth. Generally, however, this is the most exciting performance beside the elusive Keilberth set.

Lohengrin

Composed 1846–48.
First performed August 28, 1850.
Libretto by the composer.

Synopsis

Act I

Early tenth century. King Heinrich der Vogler (Henry the Fowler) arrives in Brabant looking for men to defend Saxony against the Hungarians. Brabant is in chaos because Count Friedrich von Telramund, guardian of the dead Duke of Brabant's children, Elsa and Gottfried, is claiming that Elsa has murdered Gottfried. Accordingly, she has no right to the crown, which he duly claims. The king ordains trial by combat between Telramund and whoever may appear to champion Elsa. Elsa has a vision of her rescue by a heaven-sent knight, and no sooner has the herald called for a champion to step forward than a swan-drawn boat comes into view. In the boat is Lohengrin. Elsa throws herself at his feet and, after she accepts his conditions (she must never ask his name, or whence he came), he defeats Telramund.

Act II

Telramund and his wife Ortrud are banished. They determine to make Elsa doubt Lohengrin; tricking her way into Elsa's chambers, Ortrud offers her friendship. As dawn breaks, the crowds begin to gather for Lohengrin's marriage to Elsa. On the minster's steps, Ortrud and Telramund claim Lohengrin used evil magic to win the duel. Elsa reassures Lohengrin of her faith in his purity, although she has begun to doubt him.

Act III

Elsa, unable to stand the tension any longer, demands to know Lohengrin's name and origin. At this, four nobles, led by Telramund, burst in and attack Lohengrin. Telramund is killed, and Lohengrin announces that he will reveal everything. Before Heinrich and his court on the banks of the Scheldt, Lohengrin announces that he is one of the Knights of the Holy Grail. His father was Parsifal. He tells Elsa that, had he been able to spend just twelve months by her side, the Grail's power would have returned Gottfried to her. He leaves a sword, a ring and a horn to Elsa, to be handed to her brother should he one day return. Ortrud then boasts that it was she who abducted Gottfried and turned him into a swan. Lohengrin walks towards the water's edge where his boat is seen arriving. The dove of the Grail descends over the swan, which is transformed into Gottfried. Ortrud sinks to the ground, while Lohengrin steps into his boat which, drawn by the dove, disappears into the distance. Elsa falls lifeless into her brother's arms as her soul rises to heaven.

Having completed the first version of *Tannhäuser*, Wagner announced that he would be taking a recuperative sabbatical from his duties as *Kappellmeister* in Dresden. In 1845 he journeyed to the spa of Marienbad in western Bohemia, taking with him a small library consisting mainly of texts on the myth of the Holy Grail. The decision to write an opera about Lohengrin came to him while sitting in his bath: leaping from the water, he ran to his rooms where, in one of his typical marathons of creativity, he wrote the prose sketch (which ran to thirty pages when printed in a Bayreuth programme), mapped out the score and drafted the overall staging.

After the distraction of the ill-starred premiere of *Tannhäuser*, he threw his energies into *Lohengrin*, but it was another three years before the score was completed. Plans for the Dresden premiere were abandoned after Wagner involved himself in the revolt against the king of Saxony: troops came looking for him, and so he fled to Weimar and Franz Liszt, later crossing the border into Switzerland. As *Kappellmeister* in Weimar, Liszt gave the first performance of *Lohengrin*, the music of which was well received by the public but savaged by the critics, one of whom wrote, "Wagner reveals himself in this work to be completely unmusical. He has given us, not music, but noise." The French poet Gérard de Nerval, however, was more astute. "The music of this opera is very remarkable," he wrote. "It is a bold and original talent that has revealed itself to Germany, and which has as yet said only its first words. . . . He has been reproached for having given too much importance to the instruments, and having, as Grétry said, put the pedestal on the stage and the statue in the pit; but he has undoubtedly kept to the character of the poem . . . with the form of a lyric drama, rather than an opera."

In some respects *Lohengrin* is possibly the most accessible of all Wagner's operas. Avoiding the gloomy enigmas of the *Dutchman* and the ripe fantasy of *Tannhäuser*, *Lohengrin* tells a simple tale in which good and evil battle it out against a background of royal pageantry and intrigue. To this relatively straightforward yarn Wagner applied music that has the tone of an even-tempered narrative all the way through from the haunting orchestral Prelude. The unity of mood is maintained through a highly developed system of leitmotif: whereas in previous operas a musical idea or fragment had been called upon to remind the audience of a character or episode, Wagner was now using musical signatures to illustrate abstract ideas. For example, when Lohengrin first orders Elsa never to enquire of his name or origin you hear the theme of "the forbidden question", an eight-bar passage that recurs, complete or in part, throughout the opera – even during ensemble passages, such as the duet in Act III – until she finally defies Lohengrin's wishes and asks his name. The motifs have yet to reach the sophistication of the *Ring*, in which an interval or harmonic progression might carry dramatic significance, but they nonetheless provide a solid foundation for the narrative.

There are some outstanding moments – notably the rumbustious Prelude to Act III, the beautiful Bridal Chorus (which quickly found its way, to Wagner's amusement, into churches across the world), and Ortrud's magnificent call for vengeance in Act II, "Entweihte Götter!" – but it's only fair to say that *Lohengrin* lacks the emotional punch and eventfulness that make *Tristan* and the *Ring* so remarkable. On the other hand, Wagner intended this opera to be more like a religious ceremony than a theatrical event, and his deployment of the orchestra sustains a suitably devotional atmosphere, albeit with the vivacity of Wagner's instrumentation often compensating for the demure pace (groups of violins are set against each other, while the woodwind is treated as a group of individual voices). In its tone, pace and subject, *Lohengrin* foreshadows *Parsifal*, albeit in cruder form, and there are many Wagner fans who prefer the intimacy and reserve of *Lohengrin* to the fireworks of the *Ring*.

RECORDINGS OVERVIEW

Aside from the three recommended below, there are two currently unavailable sets that warrant a mention. Philips' live recording from Bayreuth in 1962 has Astrid Varnay as Ortrud, a fresh-voiced Anna Silja as Elsa, another excellent Lohengrin from Jess Thomas and a chillingly intense Telramund from Ramon Vinay – a first choice if it returns to the catalogue. The other, conducted by Rafael Kubelik for Deutsche Grammophon in 1971, is notable for James King's powerful title role and Kubelik's energetic conducting, though Gundula Janowitz's wishy-washy Elsa and Gwyneth Jones's ear-splitting Ortrud are not relishable. The Deutsche Grammophon recording conducted by Claudio Abbado is worth investigating for an excellent Lohengrin from Siegfried Jerusalem, a singer often touted as the "the last of the *Heldentenors*".

Thomas, Grümmer, Ludwig, Fischer-Dieskau, Frick; Vienna State Opera Chorus; Vienna Philharmonic Orchestra; Kempe.
(EMI CDS7 49017-8; 3 CDs).

This *Lohengrin*, produced in Vienna in 1962, is a triumph on every count, capturing as it does five of the finest Wagner singers at their peak. Jess Thomas is a formidably secure Lohengrin, powerful, confident and yet able to communicate the suggestion of human frailty and the inner quiet of the role. Elizabeth Grümmer was some years past her prime when she recorded Elsa but she is a passionate force, while Christa Ludwig is as vicious as Ortrud can get, and Fischer-Dieskau has done nothing better than this Telramund, presenting an almost charming face to the madman. The Viennese forces are as earthy as the characterizations, and they work superbly for the ever inventive Kempe. There is one, traditional cut, after Lohengrin's narration in Act II; combined with Kempe's swift tempi, this means the opera fits onto three CDs – so at mid-price, this is a bargain *Lohengrin*.

Windgassen, Steber, Uhde, Varnay, Greindl; Bayreuth Festival Chorus and Orchestra; Keilberth.
(Teldec 4509-93674-2; 4 CDs).

Joseph Keilberth's 1953 recording stars Wolfgang Windgassen, who takes great liberties with line, metre and dynamics, but is in marvellous and intimate voice. The American Eleanor Steber is a fragile Elsa, winsome and virginal: the floated high A during her pledge to Lohengrin in Act I is breathtaking, and she proves herself an unusually subtle Wagnerian throughout. Similarly convincing is Astrid Varnay's Ortrud: her meaty tone, sharpened by a steely top, bring real vitriol to her portrayal. Hermann Uhde and Josef Greindl are comparably theatrical as Telramund and Heinrich, and both benefit from Keilberth's attentive direction. The mono sound is erratic.

Domingo, Norman, Randová, Nimsgern, Sotin; Vienna State Opera Chorus; Vienna Philharmonic Orchestra; Solti.
(Decca 421 053-2DH4; 4 CDs).

This jet-setting studio production is a very sound performance – some even rate it as the best. Solti is comparatively restrained, directing a beautifully paced Act I Prelude, but he can't help himself during the third act, when the line is lost amid unwarranted surges and outbursts. Jessye Norman is too knowing, and her voice too luxurious, for Elsa, while Placido Domingo's warmth makes him too much the Latin lover, but the beautiful tone that flows out of this pairing is hard to resist. Add the gushing Viennese forces to the equation and you have one of the most beautiful-sounding performances of *Lohengrin* on disc.

Der Ring des Nibelungen

The Ring of the Nibelung

Das Rheingold

The Rhinegold

Composed 1851–54.
First performed December 26, 1862.
Libretto by the composer.

Synopsis

Scene I

Deep beneath the Rhine, the Nibelung dwarf Alberich lusts after the Rhinemaidens, the three guardians of the Rhinegold – to which Alberich's eye is drawn. Whoever fashions the gold into a ring will become master of the world, but to do so he must first renounce love. After the maidens mock his deformity, Alberich forswears love and steals the gold.

Scene II

Wotan, chief of the gods, has had Valhalla built by the giants Fafner and Fasolt, but is unable to pay them for their work. Consequently, he has promised to give them Freia, the goddess of youth, but Loge, the cunning god of fire, tells Wotan about Alberich and the stolen gold; Loge suggests they sieze the ring and give the giants the treasure that the ring's possession will have brought Alberich. The promise of such riches satisfies Fafner, who agrees to the terms but takes Freia as hostage. The gods, whose youth is preserved through the agency of Freia, begin to age.

Scene III

In a cavern, Alberich torments his brother Mime as he watches him forge the Tarnhelm – a helmet that will give its wearer the power to change shape. Wotan and Loge, who have been looking on, applaud Alberich as he changes himself into a dragon, but Loge challenges him to take the shape of a smaller creature; when he changes into a toad Wotan and Loge capture him.

Scene IV

Alberich, forced to give up the ring, the Tarnhelm and his treasure, curses everyone who wears the ring. Wotan dismisses the dwarf and his curse and offers the treasure (measured to Freia's height) to the giants; seeing a gap in the stack of treasure, they demand the ring be added. Wotan's wife, Fricka, urges him to comply, but only after the intervention of the earth goddess

TELDEC

Siegfried and Brünnhilde in the opening moments of Götterdämmerung – the Ring moves towards its climax

THE BUILDING OF BAYREUTH

The **Bayreuth Festpielhaus** looks remarkably unprepossessing – Stravinsky called it a "crematorium, and a very old-fashioned one at that", and the locals dismissively refer to it as a "factory". But functional plainness is exactly what Wagner wanted for the theatre he long dreamed of building for the production of his own music. A couple of decades before he finally came to lay the foundation stone in 1872 he had become convinced that his music-dramas could be properly served only in a purpose-built structure that disavowed the traditional luxury of European theatres. When his vision became a reality, he was adamant that the theatre be as simple as possible: just thirty rows of spartan seating with no carpets or ornaments, no columns to obscure the sight-lines, and a cowl over the orchestra pit to direct the sound outwards while hiding the musicians from the audience. Such was Wagner's absolutism that he originally intended the building to stand only for the first performance of the *Ring* cycle in 1876, after which, its sacred purpose fulfilled, it would be destroyed. In the event, Bayreuth remained intact beyond the first *Gotterdämmerung*, and in 1882 it saw the premiere of Wagner's final opera, *Parsifal*. After that, under the supervision of Wagner's family, summers at Bayreuth were often devoted to programmes of his music, and since World War II the Bayreuth Festival has been the most prestigious annual event in Germany's opera calendar.

Wagner would never have raised his theatre without the largesse of the eccentric **King Ludwig II** of Bavaria (1845–86). Their relationship was a strange inversion of the customary power relationship between patron and artist, but they made a perfect couple, both sitting precariously on the fence separating madness from sanity, and each dependent upon the other, although the nature of their needs was very different. Wagner wanted Ludwig's money and Ludwig wanted Wagner, whom he worshipped in as many ways as he could devise. Ludwig constructed huge Wagner-grottoes in his castles, painted the walls of his bedroom with images from Wagner's operas, and did all he could to devote his life – and the state's coffers – to the furtherance of the Wagner legend. Wagner was careful not to discourage the hapless king's sexual desires, although it is remarkable that Ludwig persisted with his fantasies in spite of the composer's well-publicized heterosexual prowess.

Wagner was perenially desperate for money, and he was thus delighted when, in 1864, Ludwig not only offered to help him out of his immediate crises, but agreed to help build the theatre that Wagner had hinted at in the foreword to the published text of the *Ring*. Determined to get every last drop from this "unbelievable miracle", Wagner moved to Munich, where Gottfried Semper, the preeminent German architect of the day, was initially engaged to design the "shrine" for a site in the city.

Before long Wagner had decided that Munich was too grand a setting for his theatre – he wanted to raise it in a town where his theatre would dominate the landscape, and Bayreuth proved perfect, because there was "no other reason for anyone wanting to visit the place". After the town council gave Wagner an area known as the Green Hill to build on, new architects – Wilhelm Neumann, and later Otto Brückwald – were given the responsibility of bringing Wagner's ideas to fruition, while Ludwig donated enough money to get the ball rolling and to build Wagner's private residence alongside the theatre. But Ludwig's advisors wouldn't allow him to bankroll the whole thing, so Wagner was soon producing "patrons' certificates", which, for an enormous sum, would ensure a seat for the debut of the *Ring*. When these proved unable to cover the steadily mounting costs, desperate appeals were made to the public for money to support this "great artistic act of German genius", to quote Nietzsche's appeal to the German people. In the end, Ludwig came to the rescue once more, writing to the composer, "No, no and again no, it should not end thus! Help must be given! Our plan dare not fail. Parcival [sic] knows his mission and will offer whatever lies in his powers." These powers stretched to 100,000 taler, and the *Ring* went ahead. Inevitably the opening production failed to meet the composer's standards, but his unflinching patron was ecstatic. After the final night of the first *Ring*, Ludwig wrote to Wagner: "You are a god-man, the true artist by God's grace who has brought the sacred fire from heaven to earth to cleanse, sanctify and redeem it!"

Erda does he relent. Freia is released and the gods are once more immortal; but the curse of Alberich takes effect as Fafner kills Fasolt in an argument over the ring. The gods cross a rainbow bridge to their castle and, to the lamenting voices of the Rhinemaidens, Loge predicts the downfall of Valhalla and its occupants.

Die Walküre

The Valkyrie

Composed 1851–56.
First performed December 26, 1862.
Libretto by the composer.

Synopsis

To ensure the protection of Valhalla, Wotan has fathered nine warrior daughters – Valkyries – by Erda. These women also bear the bodies of fallen warriors to Valhalla where they, in turn, are used to defend the castle. Descending to earth, Wotan fathers Sieglinde and Siegmund in the hope that the latter might one day kill Fafner and return the ring to the Rhinemaidens. Brother and sister are separated – Sieglinde is married to Hunding and Siegmund follows the life of a nomad.

Act I

Hunding's forest hut, in the middle of which grows a mighty ash tree. Sieglinde is disturbed by the arrival of a dishevelled stranger, but soon they are mysteriously drawn to each other. Hunding returns and, recognizing the stranger as the murderer of his kinsmen, he challenges him to a fight, which is postponed until the following morning. Sieglinde drugs her husband and takes Siegmund over to the ash tree, in which the sword Notung has been embedded by Wotan. Siegmund extracts the sword and flees with Sieglinde.

Act II

Wotan is aware that his children are running from Hunding, whom he knows will catch them. He sends his best-loved Valkyrie, Brünnhilde, to protect them and orders her to ensure that Siegmund is victorious in battle. Fricka, as the goddess of marriage, insists on Hunding's right to vengeance and berates the incestuous union of Wotan's children. Wotan is talked into allowing Hunding to prevail, but Brünnhilde upsets the plan by protecting Siegmund. Wotan is astonished and causes Notung to shatter, leaving Siegmund defenceless. Wotan, sickened by Siegmund's death, strikes Hunding down. After picking up the fragments of Notung, Brünnhilde rides off with Sieglinde – hotly pursued by Wotan.

Act III

The Valkyries gather on a mountain top. They are surprised when Brünnhilde arrives carrying a woman, but refuse to offer their protection; Brünnhilde sends Sieglinde away to a forest, where she will give birth to the noblest of heroes – the son fathered by Siegmund. Wotan arrives and confronts his errant daughter. Brünnhilde defends her actions, claiming that she knew how much he loved his son. Moved by her compassion, he spares her life, but consigns her to a magic fire through which only the most noble and innocent of heroes might pass.

Siegfried

Composed 1851–71.
First performed August 16, 1876.
Libretto by the composer.

Synopsis

Sieglinde dies giving birth to the hero Siegfried – who is found by Mime, Alberich's long-suffering brother. Mime and Siegfried live in a cave near Fafner who, having changed his shape into a dragon, guards the Ring and the Rhinegold.

Act I

A forest cave. Mime is unable to bind the fragments of Notung – the only weapon strong enough for Siegfried to kill Fafner. Siegfried mocks Mime, who is patently not his father, and demands to know his true identity. He is thrilled by Mime's story, and after urging the dwarf to mend the sword he rushes into the forest. The Wanderer (Wotan) appears and, through a series of riddles, tells Mime that only one "who has never felt fear" can mend Notung. Siegfried returns and begins forging the sword, but as he works, Mime prepares a poison – to be used on Siegfried after he has killed Fafner. Upon completing the blade, Siegfried slices the anvil in two.

Act II

Waiting outside Fafner's cave, Alberich is met by the Wanderer, who taunts his old adversary. Siegfried approaches the cave with Mime, and with one thrust of Notung he kills Fafner, who dies warning the naive warrior of Mime's treachery. Some of the dragon's blood spills onto Siegfried's finger and gives him the ability to understand bird song. A Woodbird tells him to search for the hoard and the ring, and when he emerges from the cave, Mime is waiting with a goblet. Sensing his guardian's intentions he strikes him dead with a single blow of Notung. Alberich's laughter is heard in the distance. The Woodbird tells Siegfried of Brünnhilde and her imprisonment, and agrees to lead him to her rock.

Act III

The Wanderer wakes the earth godess Erda from a deep sleep and asks her how to slow down the god's decline. Her head is cloudy "with the deeds of men" and so the Wanderer leaves to greet his grandchild. Their meeting is good-natured until the Wanderer begins to mock Siegfried for failing to know who created Notung; he leaves when Siegfried slices his spear in two. With a mighty blow on his horn, Siegfried marches into the flames around Brünnhilde, to find what he thinks at first is a male warrior. Kissed by Siegfried, Brünnhilde wakes to bless the earth and the sun. In a radiant duet they sing of their mutual love, and of the gods' imminent demise.

Götterdämmerung

Twilight of the Gods

Composed 1865–74.
First performed August 17, 1876.
Libretto by the composer.

Synopsis

Prologue

Three Norns, daughters of Erda, spin the golden rope of world knowledge, once tied to the World Ash Tree, which was desecrated by Wotan when he used it to make his spear, thereby establishing his rule over the universe. The rope snaps – breaking the connection between past and future – and the downfall of the gods is predicted. Siegfried and Brünnhilde, leading her horse Grane, emerge from a cave. Siegfried departs to pursue his heroic destiny, after putting the Ring of the Nibelung on her finger.

Act I

The hall of the castle which Alberich's bastard son Hagen occupies with his half-brother Gunther, the Lord of the Gibichungs, and his half-sister Gutrune. Hagen devises a scheme to kill Siegfried and bring down the gods. He will administer a potion to the hero, making him forget his past – including Brünnhilde – and then send him to bring back Brünnhilde as Gunther's wife. In turn, he will have the ring for himself and Siegfried will marry Gutrune – with whom he will (under the potion) fall passionately in love. Wholly duped, Siegfried leaves to find Brünnhilde. Meanwhile, the Valkyrie sits before her cave, awed by the wonder of the ring. She is approached by her sister Waltraute who tells her of Wotan's resignation to the downfall of Valhalla, but Brünnhilde will not return the ring to the Rhinemaidens, as it symbolizes her eternal love for Siegfried. She hears the hero's horn but is terrified when a man in the form of Gunther appears through the flames, tears the ring from her finger.

Act II

Gunther drags Brünnhilde into Gibichung Hall. Hagen calls for a double wedding; when Brünnhilde sees the ring on Siegfried's finger she accuses him of passing himself off as Gunther, but Siegfried is adamant that he has never seen Brünnhilde before. As proof, he swears on Hagen's spear that he is not who she claims. Hagen is triumphant and, accepting Brünnhilde's support, plans Siegfried's death.

Act III

Siegfried is drawn to the riverbank where the Rhinemaidens warn him that he will die that day if he does not remove the ring. He scorns their advice and delights to see Hagen. Hagen restores Siegfried's memory with a potion and then asks him to talk of his adventures. As Siegfried remembers his love for Brünnhilde, Hagen thrusts a spear into his back. Siegfried dies, and his body is carried to the Gibichung Hall. Gutrune is horrified to find her betrothed dead, and Hagen kills Gunther when they argue over the ring. Brünnhilde arrives and orders the construction of a pyre. She takes the ring from Siegfried, placing it on her own hand, and rides into the flames, bringing the hall crashing down around her. The Rhine overflows and, trying to snatch the ring from Brünnhilde, Hagen is dragged beneath the waves by the Rhinemaidens. As Valhalla burns, the kingdom of the gods is destroyed.

Wagner intended the *Ring* to "involve all life", and his fifteen-hour epic does indeed encompass a spectrum wider than any other opera, from superhuman rage and self-annihilating heroism to the meanest of base emotions. No other opera gives such sustenance for exegesis: Bayreuth productions have presented it as a timeless exploration of the eternal verities of love and death, and as a parable of the collapse of high capitalism (this was the central intrepretive notion of the centenary *Ring*). For the Nazis the *Ring* was a celebration of the indomitable Teutonic spirit, though it's hard to see how a tale in which the gods are brought crashing down by their own stupidity could ever have been seen as suitable to the glorification of the Aryan race. In an ironic twist, the last wartime concert given by the Berlin Philharmonic on April 12, 1945, before an audience that included Speer, Dönitz and Goebbels, ended with the finale from *Götterdämmerung*. It was also the last concert Goebbels ever heard.

Wagner's first documented reference to the *Ring* dates back to April 1, 1848. Inspired by the Europe-wide revolutions that had begun earlier that year, Wagner looked for a subject that would provide a suitably large-scale vehicle for his vision of contemporary society and German destiny. He found what he was looking for in the Norse-Germanic legend of Siegfried, through whom a corrupt world is destroyed and replaced by one founded on love and hope. Wagner quickly sketched the plot of *Siegfried's Tod* (Siegfried's Death), but soon recognized the need to elaborate upon the events leading to the hero's demise. Accordingly he wrote the text of *Der junge Siegfried* (The Young Siegfried), which became *Siegfried*, then expanded the tale with a prelude to Siegfried's life, *Die Walküre*, and a prelude to the entire three-opera sequence, *Das Rheingold*. Having completed the poems in reverse order, he composed the music in sequence, beginning in 1853.

In 1857 he broke off work on the cycle to write *Tristan* and *Die Meistersinger* but finally returned to *Siegfried's Tod*, renamed *Götterdämmerung*, in 1865, around the time of *Tristan*'s premiere in Munich's Hofoper. No traditional theatre was adequate for the presentation of Wagner's music-dramas – their stages were cramped and their flamboyance distracted attention from the stage, as did the visibility of the musicians crammed into the orchestral pit. By the time he came to write *Götterdämmerung*, Wagner had resolved that a special theatre would need to be built if the cycle were to be performed in line with his wishes, a resolution that was strengthened when he was obliged by Ludwig to arrange the performance of the first two parts of the *Ring* in the Hofoper in 1869 and 1870. He was adamant that the same fate would not befall the second two, and his theatre was duly standing by the beginning of 1876. The first *Ring* went ahead in August.

The premiere of the completed work, conducted by Hans Richter, was attended by phalanxes of the great, the good and the creative. Bruckner, Liszt, Saint-Saëns, Nietzsche and Tchaikovsky all attended, as did several monarchs, including Kaiser Wilhelm I, Ludwig II and Pedro II of Brazil – who noted his occupation on the hotel register as "Emperor". When it was over, most thought the staging was over-ambitious (could Wagner seriously have expected Fricka to arrive on stage in a chariot drawn by rams?), and that the work was too long – upon leaving the theatre for the last time Tchaikovsky wrote "it was like being released from prison". Some hated it: "It is not a theatrical work; it is literally a complete hallucination, the dream of a lunatic, who thinks to impose upon the world a most frightful sort of art, " wrote *Le Figaro*. Others, more open-minded, were amazed. The critic Wilhelm Mohr. who had dismissed Bayreuth as "cloud-cuckoo land", left comparing Wagner to the "two masters of all masters, Shakespeare and Beethoven".

Reduced to its barest elements, the *Ring* is a mock-folkloric epic about the beginning and end of the world, and a parable of the consequences of greed. Certain themes recur throughout the tetralogy – the abuse of power, the immutability of fate, the need for atonement and redemption, the status of love as the "final true and knowing redeemer". But a work of this scale, composed over so great a period of time, resists the imposition of any definitive – indeed any completely self-consistent – interpretation. You have only to look at the figure of Wotan to realize that Wagner's world view had undergone major changes in the course of writing the *Ring* – the deceitful, anti-heroic Wotan of *Das Rheingold* is not the creation of the same mind as the one who created the suffering, penitent Wanderer of *Siegfried*, a tragic figure eager to sacrifice himself and his kingdom for the good of the many. Such is the complexity of the *Ring* that directors have plausibly presented it both as a Jungian psychodrama and as a critique of high capitalism. Wagner might have seen his Nibelungs as the embodiment of the world's "slave races" and Siegmund, Brünnhilde and Siegfried as the "master race", but his multi-faceted creation can be read as a refutation of his odious racial theories, and it takes no great ingenuity to portray Alberich and his relatives as the political underclass, just as the denizens of Valhalla can be seen as ruthless politicians chasing their own selfish interests to the detriment of the many.

As a musical construct the *Ring* is an awesome accomplishment, but one that is commonly misunderstood by those who have never heard it, or heard only "highlights" such as the "Ride of the Valkyries". The Ring is not all big women, loud men and blaring trumpets – although all three elements do feature. Rather it is a work of huge variety and expressivity, in which there is as much introspection as there is bombast and in which every major episode has ramifications throughout the entire cycle. Indeed, the integration of the *Ring* is a staggering feat. Some two hundred harmonic and melodic themes, most of them derived from the

STAGING THE RING

For many people the name of Wagner brings to mind the image of a vast soprano in horned helmet, plaited blond wig and gleaming armour, and yet it is now about half a century since anyone attempted to play the *Ring* as Wagner envisioned it – with gods walking across rainbows, heroes slaying scaly dragons, and Valkyries flying across the stage in medieval garb. On the other hand, Wagner's legacy of detailed instructions left little room for revisionist manoeuvre, and at his theatre in Bayreuth obedience to the master's wishes was the paramount concern right up to World War II. Wagner went so far as to commission a disciple to sit in on the 1876 rehearsals and "note down everything I say, even the smallest details, about the interpretation and performance of our work, so that tradition goes down in writing", and his wife Cosima refused to countenance any deviation from this scripture while she was in charge of the theatre.

Cosima eventually handed over control to her son Siegfried, upon whose death in 1930 the reins were handed over to his English wife Winifred. Her directorship heralded the darkest period in the history of Bayreuth as she all but turned the theatre over to the Nazi Party, who used it to propagate the mirage of German cultural and racial supremacy. It was a case of "One Reich, one People, one staging style". The 1933 *Meistersinger* looked more like a Nuremberg rally than an opera production, while the 1936 *Lohengrin* was a grotesquely triumphalist show, with a chorus of three hundred, a lead character presented as the Messiah of Teutonic culture, and lots of flag-waving.

Until 1945 , when the theatre was closed, Wagner's Bayreuth was Hitler's Bayreuth, but in 1951 a new era dawned when Wieland Wagner – Cosima's grandson – reopened the Bayreuth Festival with a minimalist production of *Parsifal* from which almost every piece of scenery and every prop was removed, turning the opera into what *Die Welt* described as "nothing more than oratorio and optic-melodrama". The conductor Hans Knappertsbusch was asked by one incensed old-guard Wagnerite how he could have given his support to such an aberration. He replied that he had directed the rehearsals thinking the sets had yet to arrive.

Wieland gave the *Ring* a similarly stripped-down production, purging the stage of any literalist trappings and consigning to history the Aryan junk that had tainted Bayreuth during the Nazi period. The action took place on a central circle that could be raised or lowered, as a whole or in segments, by hydraulic pumps. Through the use of ingenious lighting effects (another Wieland Wagner trademark), these segments were transformed into a different abstract environment for each

simple wave-pattern that opens *Das Rheingold*, unite and direct every event, character and emotion, mutating through contact with each other so that the forms are constantly re-invented. A particularly audible and significant leitmotif is the "Nature Motif" – the melodic idea first heard as the depiction of the waters of the Rhine. Much of the thematic material of the subsequent fourteen hours is evolved from this simple two-bar notion, with especially notable derivatives being Erda's motif (a minor key variation), from which Wagner forges the motif of Wotan's wandering, which in turn eventually mutates – through inversion – into the theme of the gods' destruction.

The use of thematic linking in *Rheingold* is relatively primitive (sometimes the motifs amount to little more than calling cards), but by the time Wagner came to compose *Götterdämmerung*, his technique had reached an extraordinary complexity, so that each key, modulation and harmony was designed to play a dramatic role, responding to and pointing towards some action or emotional state or idea. After hearing *Götterdämmerung* for the first time, Mahler is said to have remarked, "It is the devil's own work. No mortal could have created such a thing." But Wagner is not making inhuman demands of his audience: he did not intend every listener to recognize all these motifs, and he had no wish for the fabric of the score to advertise its own ingenuities. The majority of the thematic pointers and signatures provide a subliminal backdrop, subtly scene, with the singers performing in a frame of darkness that placed the action in an otherworldly setting.

But by the time of Wieland's death in 1965, his productions had lost their iconoclastic edge. Having gone to great lengths to depoliticize the *Ring*, producers now began to restore the sense of historical location that had caused such problems during the 1930s. In the 1970s, however, the revolution arrived not in Bayreuth (where Wolfgang imitated his brother), but in Kassel and Leipzig. In Kassel Siegfried was a hippy, Wotan was a Texan oil millionaire (surrounded by decrepit gods in wheelchairs), the Nibelungs lived in a concrete bunker and the Gibichungs were decked out as Nazis. The Norns' broken rope at the beginning of *Götterdämmerung* was a crashed computer. The anti-capitalist line was furthered in Leipzig: Wotan was now a mad industrialist, the gods lived in a decaying Grecian temple, Fafner and Fasolt got a crowd of oppressed factory workers to build Valhalla, and the wedding in *Götterdämmerung* took place on a turbine-factory floor, surrounded by yet more Nazi thugs. In similar vein, the most famous modern *Ring* of all was that produced by Patrice Chéreau for the centenary Bayreuth Festival of 1976. A no-expense-spared production, it had the Rhinemaidens cavorting in front of a hydro-electric dam, Alberich presiding over an underground factory full of slaves, Mime's forge as a massive steam-press and Fafner as a tank. (You can get this *Ring* on video.)

Whereas there was something of a consensus to the major *Ring* productions of the 1970s, there's been a greater variety of approach since then. In the mid-1980s the Bayreuth management invited Peter Hall and his British team to stage a new *Ring* – and what they got was a doggedly literalist production that started with the Rhinemaidens splashing around in a vast swimming pool. The tree in Hunding's hut looked like it would test the muscles of a team of lumberjacks, but interpretively this *Ring* offered very little substance. The same could not be said of the next Bayreuth *Ring*, directed in 1988 by Harry Kupfer, who employed a battery of lasers to project a fatalistic and violent world view. This highly praised production looked stunning (it's on video from Teldec), was well thought through, and was brilliantly conducted too – as you can hear for yourself on Daniel Barenboim's *Ring* recordings. No *Ring* of the 1990s has had quite the same impact as Kupfer's, and the economics of present-day opera makes it unlikely that any opera house except Bayreuth will come up with anything to challenge it. That said, Richard Jones's 1995 Covent Garden staging – with its company of steroidal Rhinemaidens, roadsign-wielding gods and drug-addicted Gibichungs – did cause something of a flurry. The decades may pass, but some people will always want Viking costumes and scaly dragons.

imposing a unity that transcends the serpentine complications of the text. When Siegfried, on the brink of death, recalls his life with Brünnhilde, you don't need to have perfect recall of the events and words he is remembering, for the music insinuates the complex tone of his memories. There is not a single bar of "accompaniment" in the *Ring* – indeed, often there is more going on in the pit than on the stage, as, for example, at the start of *Götterdämmerung*, where the Norns' potentially wearying narrative is enlivened by the orchestra's recapitulation of the action to which the singers are referring.

The orchestra is the major actor in the *Ring*, but this is not to say that the singers are in any way superfluous – the *Ring* is an organic creation in which everything means something, and the vocal score is one of the richest ever created. According to Wagner the "words float like a ship on the sea of orchestral harmony", for only rarely do the singers sing the leitmotifs that are the basis of the orchestral score. Instead the vocal writing is an infinitely flexible line that mirrors and amplifies the inflections of the German language – the musical phrases are short and declamatory, or rhapsodically extended, or whatever the situation demands. Suppleness is the key: Wagner wanted lyrical singers who knew how to punctuate, not shouters. Fluidity is a key element to the entire project, as you might expect from a work that begins and ends with the image of the Rhine. The momentum of the

Ring is like the course of a river, and there is nothing in all opera to beat the sensation of completion that comes with the final bars of *Götterdämmerung*, in which the waters of the Rhine engulf everything.

For all this talk of high artistic purpose and achievement, it can't be too strongly stressed that the Ring is superlative entertainment, to use a word Wagner detested. The cycle is a thrilling ride through a self-contained universe. The ominous undulating music of the Rhine; the clangorous anvil-music of Nibelheim; the gods' march towards Valhalla; the charged love-duet between Siegmund and Sieglinde; the "Magic Fire" music; Siegfried and Brünnhilde's fervent duet; the tragic-triumphant music of Siegfried's death and funeral march; Brünnhilde's immolation – these are just glimpses of the *Ring*'s treasure. And virtually every member of the immense cast is a vividly etched creation: the bilious Alberich, the doomed god Wotan, his embittered wife Fricka, the warring giants Fasolt and Fafner, the ingenuous Siegmund and Sieglinde, the tragicomic Mime and Gunther, the snarling Hagen and, most important of all, the lovers Siegfried and Brünnhilde – they are all solid characters, providing singer-actors with inexhaustible challenges.

Charles Baudelaire, one of Wagner's most ardent disciples, provided perhaps the best encapsulation of what the *Ring* has to offer: "His is the art of translating, by subtle gradations, all that is excessive," he wrote. "On listening to this ardent and despotic music one feels at times as though one discovered again, painted in the depths of a gathering darkness torn asunder by dreams, the dizzy imaginations induced by opium."

RECORDINGS OVERVIEW

Until the invention of the LP, the recording of the *Ring* was impossible – on 78s it would have required some 240 sides. The first cycle was to have been conducted by Wilhelm Furtwängler for EMI but he died after recording just one part, *Die Walküre*. Decca then planned their own cycle, with Clemens Krauss, but then he died and it became clear that younger blood was needed if a set was to be completed with a single name at the helm. Decca therefore turned to the young Hungarian Georg Solti, who began the stereo cycle in 1958 and completed this milestone in the history of recording seven years later. There are now a dozen complete sets in the catalogue, and another in progress from Decca, with Christoph von Dohnányi conducting the Cleveland Orchestra and a prominently American cast.

The first three of our recommended *Ring* recordings are available in two forms: as one big box, generally priced at the top end of the mid-price bracket; and as individual operas, all at full price. In other words, buying a complete *Ring* will cost about the same as buying *Die Walküre* and *Siegfried* separately, so our advice would be to be bold and plunge in at the deep end.

In addition to these complete cycles, there are a good number of outstanding isolated recordings. A famous *Die Walküre*, recorded in 1961 with Vickers, Brouwenstijn, Nilsson and London and conducted by Leinsdorf, is available at mid-price from Decca, and it makes a good alternative to top-of-the-list recordings by Böhm and Solti. Fritz Reiner's remarkable 1935 Viennese recording of the first act of *Die Walküre* with Melchior and Lehmann offers a thrilling experience – it's available from EMI. Music and Arts have released Arthur Bodansky's breathtaking 1937 Met broadcast of *Siegfried* with Melchior and Flagstad, a performance that has never been equalled. Finally, EMI's four-CD set called *Les Introuvables du Ring* contains live and studio excerpts of some of the greatest Wagner singers of the century; and as a curiosity you might want to sample the few recordings made by Lilli Lehmann (1848–1929), who created the roles of Woglinde and the Woodbird in 1876 – they are available from Pearl and Nimbus, although the latter's transfers are preferable.

⊙ Various Artists; Bayreuth Festival Chorus and Orchestra; Böhm. (Philips 446 057-2PB14; 14 CDs).

Karl Böhm's *Ring*, recorded live at Bayreuth between 1966 and 1967, is the most viscerally exciting ever made. The casting is outstanding, the sound is vital, and Böhm's identity is stamped on every page. You might not like this identity – some find it too calculating – but few other performances of the complete work carry such a weight of personality, and an overriding personality is essential to a convincing *Ring* cycle. The casting overlaps with the Solti set (both have James King as Siegmund, Nilsson as Brünnhilde, and Windgassen as Siegfried, for example) but the live set captures these remarkable voices in richer, more theatrical form. The whole is considerably less beautiful than Solti's set and the brass is too closely miked, but the feeling of narrative cohesion is unsurpassed. The voices of Windgassen, Nilsson and Adam ring with especially startling intensity in the last two operas, but it would be hard to fault the general vocal fabric – right down to the secondary casting (the Rhinemaidens and the Valkyries, for example), this is an admirably sung *Ring*. To celebrate the centenary of the conductor's birth, this set was released as a bargain-price box, albeit without libretto. The odds are that it will revert to mid-price once stocks are exhausted, but it will still be a bargain.

Various Artists; Vienna State Opera Chorus; Vienna Philharmonic Orchestra; Solti.
(Decca 414 100-2DM15; 15 CDs).

The first *Ring* is for many the finest: the sumptuous orchestral presence, the superb singing, the sound quality and the special effects (eighteen real anvils for *Rheingold*) have never been bettered. As an overall conception, however, it falls slightly short of the Böhm *Ring*, for incident rather than structure seems to have been the preoccupation of conductor and producer. With Wagner regulars Nilsson, King and Windgassen in outstanding form, there is no more impressive-sounding *Ring*, but Solti's aggressive tempi, excessive punctuation and fractured line tend to have a dislocating effect. You just have to accept the rough with the smooth, and considering the superb quality of the smooth, this is not terribly difficult. The first two operas are given better readings – in fact a mixture of Solti's and Böhm's performances would constitute an ideal, if expensive *Ring*.

Various Artists; Bayreuth Festival Chorus and Orchestra; Barenboim.
(Teldec 0630-10010-2; 14 CDs).

Recorded live in 1993 at Bayreuth, where Daniel Barenboim has been a regular since making his debut in 1982, this *Ring* is the most rewarding since Böhm's. The carefully prepared voices, sublime orchestral sonorities and clear, naturally balanced sound would satisfy the most pedantic score-follower, but the spirit of Wagner's gothic imagination is also present throughout, with some remarkably percipient and imaginative conducting. The jewel in the crown is the *Götterdämmerung*, perhaps the finest yet recorded, thanks to a superb Siegfried from Jerusalem, a magnificently horrible Hagen from Paul Kang, and one of the greatest displays of Wagner conducting recorded since the war.

Various Artists; La Scala Chorus and Orchestra; Furtwängler.
(Music and Arts CD914; 12 CDs).

Furtwängler's legendary La Scala performance (not to be confused with the Rome broadcast recordings released by EMI) is a grim and fatalistic vision of the *Ring*, deliberately paced, dark-hued, saturated with a sense of tragic inevitability. Concentrating on the orchestra, Furtwängler allows his singers unusual freedom, an approach that leads to some inspired performances – not least from the mighty Kirsten Flagstad, whose exultantly regal Brünnhilde is the vocal highlight. Her colleagues rise to the challenge, flinging themselves with amazing energy into the music. There's a lot of ambiguous intonation and ragged ensemble work here, the mono sound is hazy and the Italian orchestra is woefully inferior to any Bayreuth band, but Furtwängler has everyone performing out of their skins in what remains a uniquely vital interpretation. In addition to the Music and Arts set (which was beautifully remastered in 1995), this *Ring* is usually available as a lower-quality small-label release, sometimes at an amazingly low price – a couple of years back you could pick up the Virtuoso box for the cost of just two full-price CDs.

Various Artists; Bayreuth Festival Chorus and Orchestra; Krauss.
(Gala/BMG GL999791; 15 CDs).

Clemens Krauss died before he could conduct any of the projected Decca *Ring*, but he did leave behind this magnificent live production of the cycle, recorded at Bayreuth in 1953, the year before his death. Krauss is the very antithesis of Furtwängler: the tempi are quick (his *Siegfried* is probably the quickest ever) and the articulation makes everything flow with an almost Italianate grace. In comparison to doom-laden Furtwängler, Krauss can seem superficial, but this is an exhilarating ride, lifted into a very special class by the quality of the singing. On balance, this is the most impressively cast *Ring* you can get. Outstanding contributions include a young, remarkably weighty Siegfried from Windgassen, a threatening Wotan from Hans Hotter, an explosive Siegmund from Ramón Vinay (surely the mightiest German tenor voice of the century) and a heart-stopping Brünnhilde from Astrid Varnay, one of the greatest Wagner sopranos. The mono sound is excellent for the time.

WARNER

Daniel Barenboim – the new master of Bayreuth

Tristan und Isolde

Tristan and Isolde

Composed 1856–59.
First performed June 10, 1865.
Libretto by the composer.

Synopsis

Act I

The Irish Princess, Isolde, is on her way to marry King Marke of Cornwall, escorted by Tristan. Isolde tells Brangäne how she nursed Tristan after he was wounded in a struggle with her betrothed, Morald, who was killed in the fight. When Isolde realized who it was she was aiding, she raised a sword to kill the wounded Tristan, but looking into his eyes she found herself unable to strike. Seeing death as the only escape from the dishonour into which she has already nearly fallen, Isolde orders Brangäne to prepare a poison; but Brangäne substitutes a love potion, and when Isolde and Tristan drink from the goblet their true feelings for each other emerge.

Act II

Outside King Marke's castle, Isolde meets Tristan while her husband and his courtier Melot are out hunting. Brangäne advises them to be careful, suspicious that Melot (supposedly Tristan's best friend) has set a trap, but they are oblivious and fall into each other's arms. Their ecstasy is interrupted by the sudden arrival of Kurwenal, who warns the lovers of King Marke's approach. Marke is horrified to find himself deceived, but he is too distressed to act. Isolde and Tristan assure each other of their eternal love and Melot, drawing his sword, attacks Tristan.

Act III

Tristan's castle in Brittany. A shepherd plays a melancholy tune while the wounded Tristan mourns Isolde's absence. Kurwenal tries to console his master but Tristan can think only of Isolde. The mournful pipe continues until a joyful tune announces the arrival of Isolde's ship. Tristan leaps to his feet and tears off his bandages, to fall dead into Isolde's arms. Melot and Marke arrive to pardon Tristan but Kurwenal attacks Melot, killing him and receiving a mortal wound in the process. Isolde proclaims her eternal love for Tristan, and falls dead into Brangäne's arms.

Wagner wrote to Liszt in 1854: "Since I have never enjoyed the real happiness of love in my life, I want to erect another monument to this most beautiful of dreams in which love will be properly sated from beginning to end." *Tristan und Isolde* was the fulfilment of that ambition. Shocked by its eroticism, men at the first performance removed their women from the Munich theatre, and a priest was seen to cross himself before fleeing in horror. Wagner himself was terrified by his own opera, writing to Mathilde Wesendonck, "This Tristan is turning into something fearful! That last act!!! . . . I'm afraid the opera will be forbidden . . . only mediocre performances can save me. Completely good ones are bound to drive people mad." George Ander, who was to have sung Tristan, did indeed go mad studying the role, but at least he survived – Ludwig Schnorr von Carolsfeld, who sang the first Tristan, died a few weeks after the premiere, and Felix Mottl and Joseph Keilberth, two of the twentieth century's finest conductors, died conducting the second act. *Tristan und Isolde* is the most extreme opera ever written.

Tristan und Isolde came about through the confluence of three elements in Wagner's life. In the autumn of 1854 he read Arthur Schopenhauer's masterwork *The World as Will and Representation*, and its quasi-Buddhistic notion that renunciation of the world offered the only salvation from suffering had a profound effect on the composer – he later wrote, "For years Schopenhauer's book was never completely out of my mind." The vehicle for this philosophy – Gottfried von Strassburg's medieval poem *Tristan* – was suggested by his friend Karl Ritter, but the emotional impetus came from his illicit infatuation with Mathilde Wesendonck (the wife of one of his patrons), with whom Wagner became infatuated during the summer of 1854. Inspired by her beauty and – crucially – her enthusiasm for him and his music, he dropped work on the *Ring* at the end of the second act of *Siegfried*, and in 1857 embarked on two uninterrupted years of obsessive work. The new project was rooted in Schopenhauerian notions of self-abnegation and suppression of the will, but turned it into what is essentially a four-hour love song, in which death is transformed into an experience of orgasmic transcendence.

In 1859 he moved to Paris (where he was joined by the ailing Minna), where he attempted in vain to get *Tristan* staged. But Dresden Opera agreed to mount it the following year. After seventy-seven rehearsals the production was abandoned, with the tenor on the brink of mental collapse. The opera remained unperformed until the Munich Royal Court Theatre and King Ludwig II came to the rescue in 1865 and helped stage the premiere. Hans von Bülow conducted, the leads were taken by the husband-and-wife team of Ludwig and Malvina Schnorr con Carolsfeld, and Wagner supervised the staging – removing the first row of the stalls to accommodate the enormous orchestra.

The orchestral score of *Tristan* is full of unimaginably complex chromatic harmonies, thick with dissonances and unresolved suspensions. When you listen to a Mozart overture the harmonic structure tells you that a resolution is not far away, but with the prelude to *Tristan* you have no sense of when the experience is going to end. Dragging tonality to the most extreme limits, Wagner creates a musical narrative in which conventional notions of time and space are jettisoned. Less a tale than a psychodrama, *Tristan* is an unprecedentedly symphonic opera, a huge triple-movement construction within which each pause and silence serves a dramatic function, intensifying the claustrophobically erotic atmosphere. Dozens of motifs (between forty and sixty, depending on how you analyze them) bind the protagonists and project the flux of their emotions: every chord of *Tristan* draws the audience into the lovers' all-annihilating passion.

Despite its exorbitant length, *Tristan* is the most streamlined of operas: the cast is small, comprising just two characters plus a few ancilliaries, and the music describes a single arc through three monolithic acts in which very little external action occurs. Beginning with an unresolved chordal progression that remains unresolved until the very end, the opera moves with a sense of tragic inevitability towards Isolde's final "Transfiguration" – commonly known as the "Liebestod" or love-death. What makes *Tristan* such a breathtaking score is the tightness of its construction – the way in which the elements of harmony, melody and instrumentation are deployed in unison as registers of the central relationship. Thus, for example, when Isolde sings her final monologue, her music is dominated by the motif that, during the prelude to the second act, was used to symbolize her joy at the prospect of reunion with Tristan. Now, greatly extended, it symbolizes a more exalted cosmic union with Tristan, with whom she is to be united through death. The opera ends with the entire orchestra playing the motif of longing, with the voices of an oboe and a coranglais emerging from the swell of sound – the motif, and the instruments, with which the opera began.

Tristan is a relentlessly intense opera, in which Wagner's "endless melodies" (his words), sweeping orchestrations, surging rhythms and opulent harmonies create the sense of a self-contained universe. Its eroticism reaches its desperate pitch in the amazing second-act love duet, for many people the greatest single episode in all of Wagner. This nocturnal coupling lasts nearly three-quarters of an hour and culminates in the most blatant coitus interruptus in all music, as the disruptive force of their passion crashes against the forces of reason and order, represented by Marke's monologue (a clash anticipated at the end of the first act when the chromatic music of the love potion is challenged by the triadic fanfares that announce Marke's arrival).

There was simply no precedent for *Tristan*, an opera so revolutionary that Schoenberg credited it with "the emancipation of the dissonance". It is a measure of Wagner's genius that he anticipated the radicalism of Schoenberg and his cohorts way back in 1856 – less than thirty years after the death of Beethoven.

RECORDINGS OVERVIEW

Tristan und Isolde is the most difficult of Wagner's operas to successfully cast because it is made up of almost nothing but exposed episodes, most of them for the leading tenor and soprano, both of whom need extreme power, uncommon range and preternatural stamina. Of those equipped with these abilities, many – such as Max Lorenz, Franz Völker, Ramón Vinay, Helen Traubel, Astrid Varnay and Inge Borkh – never recorded *Tristan* in the studio, though there are rare live recordings of each of these artists (a blistering 1960 performance with Vinay and Nilsson, conducted by Böhm, has been seen on CD).

However, the catalogue currently boasts some very fine recordings. In addition to those recommended below, you might want to check out Carlos Kleiber's brilliantly conducted and gorgeously played Deutsche Grammophon recording – the Tristan of René Kollo is what keeps it off our listings. Bootleg live performances conducted by Karl Elmendorff (the first ever, 1928), Erich Kleiber, Carlos Kleiber, Hans Knappertsbusch, Fritz Reiner and Karl Böhm are all worth owning, as are any excerpts conducted by Victor de Sabata and Albert Coates – two of the greatest but least-recorded Wagner conductors. EMI also issue a fascinating composite of a 1937 Beecham performance and a 1936 performance conducted by Fritz Reiner. Act II and the opening of Act III are conducted by Beecham, the rest by Reiner, but the split presents few problems, for the conductors are united in their obvious fondness for their lead singers – Lauritz Melchior (regularly voted the greatest of all *Heldentenors*) and the regal Kirsten Flagstad. The only turkey, to be avoided even if it is the last recording in the shop, is Leonard Bernstein's self-indulgent account – the tempi are agonizingly slow, the detail is over-stressed, the dynamics are underlined in blood, and the leads sound nasal and pressured.

Windgassen, Nilsson, Ludwig, Talvela, Waechter; Bayreuth Festival Chorus and Orchestra; Böhm.
(Philips 434 425-2PH3; 3 CDs).

Karl Böhm was capable of boring the pants off an audience, especially as he got older, but this live 1966 Bayreuth production captured him in fearsome form: such is the pace he takes it at that he manages to fit each of the three acts onto a single CD, where everyone else needs four. The barnstorming performance (also available as a more expensive Deutsche Grammophon set) comes from the mighty Birgit Nilsson, whose steam-whistle soprano rips through the score. Wolfgang Windgassen's tenor was beginning to thin out by 1966 but he is a superb stylist, and he keeps going strongly – which, considering Böhm's relentless direction, is a miracle. Christa Ludwig's vibrant Brangäne is exquisite while Eberhard Waechter and Martti Talvela round off a vocally sumptuous, theatrically intense, perfectly recorded performance.

Suthaus, Flagstad, Thebom, Greindl, Fischer-Dieskau; Royal Opera House Chorus; Philharmonia; Furtwängler.
(EMI CDS7 47322-8; 4 CDs).

This *Tristan*, Furtwängler's only complete performance of the work, is a classic – some may carp about the details, but everyone agrees that it's great. The slow tempi and dark orchestral atmospherics create an extraordinary vision of souls in torment, and Furtwängler's flexibility and sense of line give the long-postponed climaxes the sort of impact that no amount of thundering can ever replace. The casting has always been a matter of debate, however. The Isolde is Kirsten Flagstad, past her prime in 1952 (Elizabeth Schwarzkopf sang the high Bs and Cs) but bringing a profoundly moving seriousness to her interpretation. Ludwig Suthaus's Tristan lacks the warmth of a man possessed by love, but his voice is ideal for the sufferings of the third act. There can be no quibbling, however, about the grandeur of Furtwängler's conception of this opera, which the mono sound captures in all its intimacy and passion.

Vickers, Dernesch, Ludwig, Ridderbusch, Berry; Berlin Deutsche Opera Chorus; Berlin Philharmonic Orchestra; Karajan.
(EMI CMS7 69319-2; 3 CDs).

Like many of Karajan's EMI opera recordings, this 1972 *Tristan* is an essay in violence, highlighting the pagan, ritualistic quality of the lovers' communion. Many may wince at the insistent aggression and exploding climaxes – many of which simply do not exist on the page – but this is the most orchestral *Tristan* of them all, dominated by a Berlin Philharmonic that reveals every detail bared to the world. Incomparably weighty and muscular, Karajan's reading sacrifices architecture to sonic impact, exerting an almost repulsive seductiveness. His cast produce suitably tenebrous performances, sealing an experience that is available nowhere else.

Jerusalem, Meier, Lipovsek, Salminen, Struckmann; Berlin Staatsoper Chorus; Berlin Philharmonic Orchestra; Barenboim.
(Teldec 4509-94568-2; 4 CDs).

This 1995 studio recording has much to commend it, primarily the singing of Siegfried Jerusalem and Waltraud Meier. Neither of them forces their tone – thanks to some sympathetic conducting from Daniel Barenboim – and both make much of the composer's conscientious expressive markings. Jerusalem's slightly husky tenor is especially successful during Act III, and he copes well with the demands of Act II. On the other hand, there is little of the spontaneity that the same cast generated on the Bayreuth stage later the same year, and Barenboim is a surprisingly diffident presence, which obviously is not ideal with so symphonic an opera. That said, the fine singing, the playing of the Berlin forces and the superb digital stereo make this a notable addition to the catalogue.

Melchior, Flagstad, Thorborg, Kipnis, Huehn; New York Metropolitan Opera Chorus and Orchestra; Leinsdorf.
(Music and Arts MACD-647; 3 CDs).

Flagstad and Melchior sang *Tristan* together on dozens of occasions. One of the most celebrated was during the Met production in 1941, when they were joined by the great Alexander Kipnis as Marke and Toscanini's ex-assistant Erich Leinsdorf as conductor. Leinsdorf's lunging gestures and extreme speeds reveal little of the subtleties of the score, but this is a passionate reading, and the love duet ignites as on no other recording. Not one for first-timers, but essential once you've caught the bug.

Die Meistersinger von Nürnberg

The Mastersingers of Nuremberg

Composed 1861–67.
First performed June 21, 1868.
Libretto by the composer.

Act I

Nuremberg, middle of the sixteenth century. Midsummer's Eve. The Franconian knight Walther von Stolzing is in love with Eva, the daughter of the blacksmith Pogner. Magdalene tells Walther that Eva's father has promised her hand to whoever wins the song contest to be held by the Guild of the Mastersingers the following morning. Walther decides to join the Guild. He has the rules explained to him by David and although Pogner is flattered that a nobleman wishes to join them, the Guild members – Hans Sachs among them – are sceptical when Walther tells them that his singing teacher was an ancient book. It is agreed that the initiate should be allowed a formal trial, adjudicated by Beckmesser the town clerk (who is also in love with Eva). Walther fails, but Sachs is impressed nonetheless.

Act II

Eva has heard the news of Walther's failure and when he arrives they decide to flee together. Their path is blocked by Sachs and Beckmesser, who wants to sing his prize song to Eva; she manages to switch places with Magdalene (David's betrothed). During the performance Sachs hammers his anvil every time Beckmesser makes a mistake so that he is forced to sing ever louder. This wakes up David, who sees Beckmesser serenading his beloved. A riot ensues, during which Walther and Eva try once again to escape. Sachs stops them and, forcing Eva upon her father, takes Walther into his own home.

Act III

David visits Sachs in his workshop and apologizes for the previous night. Walther enters and sings a tune that came to him in a dream, for which Sachs writes the first two stanzas. Sachs is excited by this new-sounding song and is convinced that it will be the prizewinner. Eva's arrival inspires Walther to write a third verse but when Beckmesser arrives he finds the manuscript and thinks it is Sachs's prize song. He allows Beckmesser to take the sheet – omitting the name of its real author. Everyone congregates in the festal meadow. Beckmesser steps forward and sings the song – very badly – but when Walther sings it he wins both the prize and Eva's hand in marriage. Sachs tells Walther of the Mastersingers' purpose in keeping the tradition of German song alive, and with this Walther is inducted into the Guild.

With the exhausting *Tristan* finished, Wagner decided to write a comedy. For his libretto he returned to a scenario he had prepared in 1845 as a successor to *Tannhäuser* – like *Tannhäuser* the action focused on a song contest, but this time the adjudicants were the Mastersingers, societies that thrived in Germany between the fourteenth and sixteenth centuries and believed themselves to be the guardians of the integrity of the German song tradition (the Mastersingers enumerated some thirty-two different failings to be avoided in their competitions). Hans Sachs (1494–1576), the hero of *Die Meistersinger*, was a Nuremberg cobbler who became famous for writing some six thousand poems and four thousand songs, pieces that have intermittently been exalted in some quarters as the very distillation of the German soul. His writings were a major source for the opera, but Wagner also drew from E.T.A. Hoffmann's story *Master Martin the Cooper and his Apprentices*, Johann Deinhardstein's play *Hans Sachs* and, most importantly, Goethe's poem "An Account of the Old Woodcut Showing Hans Sachs's Poetic Calling", a work which brought about a renewal of interest in Sachs across Germany. Wagner dovetailed all this material, but added love interest in the form of Eva, plus two emblematic characters in Walther von Stolzing – the embodiment of innovation – and Beckmesser – the embodiment of stale conservatism. The latter was initially named Hans Lick in the libretto, after the critic Eduard Hanslick, a man who missed no opportunity to praise Brahms and denigrate Wagner; when Hanslick walked out of a read-through to which he had been invited, Wagner changed the character's name. As for Stolzing, nobody could be under any misapprehension as to whom Wagner had in mind as a model.

Wagner wrote the libretto in 1861–62 and composed most of the score over the succeeding three years, but preparations for the premiere of *Tristan* put the new work on hold until 1866, when he brought it to completion. (Thus *Die Meistersinger* interrupted Wagner's work on *Siegfried* and prefaced his composition of the music for *Götterdämmerung*.) The Munich premiere was enthusiastically received by the hand-picked audience and Wagner, who was sitting beside King Ludwig, was called after each scene to acknowledge the applause. But criticism was, as ever, mixed, and the old attacks against Wagner's poetic aspirations caused him continued grief – one critic wrote: "Yes, Richard Wagner is superior to Beethoven in so far as he is a poet; and yes he is superior to Schiller, in so far as he is a musician."

The music of *Die Meistersinger* is as bright as *Tristan* is dark, but its overt celebration of the German *Volk* and its climactic warning against the taint of foreign influence made it a Nazi favourite, an association it has never quite lived down. (At Bayreuth in 1938 Sachs's Act III hymn to "holy German art" brought the audience to its feet, right arms extended.) And you could argue that Wagner labours the point in places, and that an hour could be lost from the running time without too much damage to the integrity of the drama. Yet *Meistersinger* is the least intimidating of all Wagner's operas, for it has closer affinities with the listener-friendly conventions of pre-Wagnerian opera than any Wagner opera after *Der fliegende Holländer*.

Whereas the orchestra hogs the limelight for much of the *Ring* and *Tristan*, the voices win the day here. Walther's four tenor arias (the most beautiful of these, known as the "Prize Song", wins him the competition), Beckmesser's baritone serenade, Pogner's bass "Address", David's tenor song and Sachs's two bass monologues serve as focal points, and many of them are announced during the course of the rip-roaring overture. This overture is the opera's most popular episode, but was famously denounced by Hanslick as "an invention in which the leitmotifs of the opera are dumped consecutively into a chromatic flood and finally tossed about in a kind of tonal typhoon. . . . The only thing which prevents one from declaring it to be the world's most unpleasant overture is the even more horrible prelude to *Tristan und Isolde*."

The chorus work is remarkably clear and imaginative – especially those sung by the apprentices – and the engaging use of Lutheran Chorales, fugues and Bach-like counterpoint generate a comfortably enveloping old-world atmosphere. That said, there are some sizable exceptions to the antiquarian rule, notably the prelude to Act III – a ghostly, serious-minded symphonic portrait of Sachs, anticipating his abdication to the new generation personified by Walther.

Die Meistersinger is Wagner's most nationalistic opera, and the xenophobic banner-waving makes it unpalatable for many people. Its enormous length can be another deterrent – the third act lasts as long as *Das Rheingold*. But the wealth of melody, the delightful scenarios (*Die Meistersinger* can actually raise laughs), the vivid characterization (Hans Sachs is Wagner's most rounded and human character) and the sheer sweep of the music usually win over anyone who gives it a chance.

RECORDINGS OVERVIEW

Despite being the most accessible of Wagner's late works, *Die Meistersinger* has only been recorded on ten occasions in the studio – four times by EMI, the most recent of which was released, with Sawallisch conducting, in 1995. Prior to this it had not been commercially recorded for nearly two decades. The earliest sessions were conducted by Furtwängler in 1943, with an almost perfect Walther from Max Lorenz, but the CD transfers are difficult to find (Lys and the less expensive Grammofon 2000 both produce versions). An even finer historic live recording is the one conducted by Hermann Abendroth, which in its concision and energy is rivalled only by the first of the studio recordings, conducted by Knappertsbusch. Kempe's second production has probably the finest cast of any recording, and just pushes Karajan's second EMI recording off the top of the stereo-era rankings. Performances by Keilberth, Varviso, Jochum and Solti also have much to recommend them, but none is superior to those listed below.

Schöffler, Treptow, Gueden, Edelmann, Dönch, Dermota; Vienna State Opera Chorus; Vienna Philharmonic Orchestra; Knappertsbusch.
(Decca 440 057-2DM04; 4 CDs).

This 1951 studio recording captured the uniquely creative but comparatively rare coupling of Hans Knappertsbusch and the Vienna Philharmonic Orchestra, and together they produce a light, swiftly

moving platform for the cast. Paul Schöffler's Sachs is less beautiful than on the set reviewed below, the tone having begun to narrow, but the intelligence and sensitivity are unmistakable. Hilde Gueden is a sweet, dramatically potent Eva and Anton Dermota makes a superb David, riding the high tessitura with ease and charm. Karl Dönch is a cartoon-character Beckmesser and Günther Treptow is a resonant Walther, although like most tenors he finds the high writing uncharitable. The mono sound should not put you off, for this is a memorable recording.

Schöffler, Suthaus, Scheppan, Dalberg, Kunz, Witte; Bayreuth Festival Chorus and Orchestra; Abendroth.
(Preiser 90174; 4 CDs).

Hermann Abendroth's collaboration with the Nazis put paid to his reputation, but his recordings testify to an eccentrically inventive talent. His one extant opera recording, taped at "Hitler's Bayreuth" in 1943, has a momentum that no other conductor managed to generate. The subtle turns of phrase, graphic punctuation and disciplined control create a striking sense of freshness. This immediacy is compounded by a superb cast headed by Paul Schöffler, for many the finest Sachs of all. Dalberg and Kunz are excellent as Pogner and Beckmesser – Kunz making great mileage from the arch comedy – and Scheppan sings with loving, lyrical tenderness as Eva. Ludwig Suthaus is a rich, luxurious Walther and the mono engineering brings the voices, as well as the heavy contrapuntal texture, bursting to life. The full price tag is the only thing wrong.

Frantz, Neidlinger, Grümmer, Höffgen, Schock; Chorus of the Berlin Municipal Opera and Deutsche Opera; Berlin Philharmonic Orchestra; Kempe.
(EMI CMS7 64154-2; 4 CDs).

Recorded in 1956, in mono, this is overall a superbly cast performance, from the principal roles right down to the minor part of the Nightwatchman, sung here with great beauty by a very young Hermann Prey. Elizabeth Grümmer (Eva) and Marga Höffgen (Magdalene) are an exquisite, rich-sounding coupling, and Rudolph Schock is probably the finest studio Walther there has ever been. The only weakness – and, unfortunately, a prominent one – is Ferdinand Frantz's Hans Sachs. The dignity and humanity are there, but the voice is not. There are notable contributions from Gottlob Frick as Pogner and Gustav Neidlinger as Beckmesser, and Kempe draws some glorious tone from the Berlin Philharmonic.

Adam, Evans, Kollo, Donath, Hesse; Dresden State Opera Chorus and Orchestra; Karajan.
(EMI CDS7 49683-2; 4 CDs).

Karajan's 1970 *Meistersinger* features a much less starry company than his 1951 version, but the atmosphere is noticeably more theatrical. Theo Adam (a celebrated Wotan) brings his usual weight and intensity to his performance as Sachs, while Karl Ridderbusch glows as Pogner, giving one of the performances of his life. Geraint Evans sings beautifully as Beckmesser, but doesn't give much punch to the characterization, while René Kollo is in tinny form as Walther. The women are uniformly superb, however, with Helen Donath swooningly lovely as Eva and Ruth Hesse delightful as Magdalene. The stereo is excellent, the price shocking.

Parsifal

Composed 1865–82.
First performed July 26, 1882.
Libretto by the composer.

Synopsis

Act I

A forest close to Monsalvat, the Grail castle. Gurnemanz tells a group of young knights about Amfortas, the keeper of the Grail, and his vision in which "a pure fool made wise through pity" will one day become King of the Grail. Kundry, a woman condemned to perpetual penance after mocking Christ, brings balsam for Amfortas's never-healing wound – sustained after she seduced him and led him to the garden of the wizard Klingsor, who struck Amfortas with the spear that had pierced Christ's side. As they look on, Amfortas is taken by stretcher to the lakeside to bathe his wound, which only the sacred spear can cure. The young knights bring in a boy who has just killed a swan. Gurnemanz suspects he is the "pure fool" and takes him to the castle to see the ceremony in which, instructed by his father Titurel, Amfortas unveils the Grail. The young man is moved but uncomprehending, and Gurnemanz sends him away.

Act II

Klingsor's magic castle. The magician orders Kundry, who is under his spell, to ensnare the boy, who is transfixed when Kundry calls him by the name given him by his mother – Parsifal. Kundry kisses him, whereupon he understands the consequences of lust, and now pities Amfortas, having understood his weakness. Rejected, Kundry calls on Klingsor, who hurls the sacred spear at Parsifal. It stops in mid-air; Parsifal seizes it and makes the sign of the cross, bringing Klingsor's castle to the ground.

Act III

Good Friday, many years later. Amfortas is refusing to unveil the Grail, and the knights are ailing in consequence. Kundry, near death, goes to fetch water for

Amfortas. She sees a knight dressed in black armour and carrying a spear: it is Parsifal. Kundry bathes Parsifal's feet and Gurnemanz anoints him King of the Grail. Parsifal then baptizes Kundry and all three leave for the castle, where Parsifal touches Amfortas's wound with the spear. As he raises the Grail a white dove hovers above his head, and Kundry falls lifeless to the ground. The knights end the opera with the words "Redemption to the Redeemer".

In the years following the successful premiere of *Die Meistersinger* in 1868 many of Wagner's dreams began to come true: he finally married Liszt's daughter Cosima in 1870, he completed the music of his mighty *Ring* cycle in 1874, and even managed to build his theatre at Bayreuth for the premiere of the *Ring*. He talked about composing a series of single-movement symphonies (which came to nothing), and considered writing an opera about Christ or Buddha or Moses; but he was haunted by Wolfram von Eschenbach's *Parzival*, which he had first read while writing *Lohengrin* more than thirty years earlier.

Of course, Wagner saw that there was much room for improvement in von Eschenbach's 24,000-line poem about the knight who became Lord of the Grail; a letter from 1859 complained: "All that matters is senselessly passed over by our poet, who merely took his subject from the sorry French chivalric romances of his age, and chattered gaily after them like starlings. . . . I shall have to invent absolutely everything." In the event he didn't so much invent the scenario as supplement von Eschenbach with material from other sources, including the poem *Percival le Galois* by Chrétien de Troyes and the collection of medieval Celtic tales known as the *Mabinogion*. He wrote a prose scenario in 1865, but – distracted by such matters as *Tristan*, and *Die Meistersinger*, and the *Ring* – didn't get round to completing the poem until twelve years later. The score also took much longer than anticipated: he began it in 1877, but it was not finished until early in 1882. However, he was quick to organize the premiere and *Parsifal*, subtitled "Ein Bühnenweihfestpiel" (A Stage Dedication Festival), was performed, under Wagner's direction, just thirteen months before his death.

Hermann Levi conducted (Wagner insisted the Jewish conductor accept Christian baptism before touching the score; Levi refused) – and he selected his singers from theatres across Germany. Convinced that no single cast could effectively bring the work to life for "a month at a stretch", he chose two basses for Gurnemanz, three tenors for Parsifal, two basses for Klingsor and three sopranos for Kundry. Regarding the work as a quasi-religious ritual of absolution, and his theatre as a temple of virtue, Wagner asked the audiences not to applaud the performers (most of whom refused payment, considering their selection honour enough) and stipulated that, as the subject was too serious for production in any ordinary theatre, it was never to be performed anywhere but Bayreuth. Wagner's overweaning demands were first flaunted in 1903 by the Met, after which nearly every opera house capable of staging it defied the composer's wishes.

In *Parsifal* the legend of the Holy Grail, a subject always close to Wagner's heart, is reappraised in the light of Schopenhauerian ideas on suffering, the denial of the Self and redemption, which here comes about not through love-death, but through the compassion of a Holy Fool. There is a grotesque subtext to all this. In conjunction with the opera, Wagner published a polemical essay entitled "Heroism and Christianity", a demented work in which he argued that the Aryans, the "German leaders of mankind", evolved from the gods, whilst everyone else – "the lesser races" – descended from the apes. The notion of a religion based upon the worship of a Jew repelled him, and thus, in *Parsifal*, he sought to re-invent the Christ figure in his own Aryan image, while representing the ungodly Jewish world as Klingsor's Garden. Even if the anti-Semitism were not there, there is still something distinctly unpalatable about the liturgical services that punctuate the drama and in the character of Kundry, a Mary Magdalene figure with an extra misogynistic spin, who presents a foil and motivation for the monastic company of the knights. And there's a lot of bad faith in an opera that celebrates asceticism through music of extraordinarily voluptuous beauty – pain has never seemed so delicious, and neither has hatred been so beguilingly packaged. Nietzsche, hardly a friend of Christianity and a longstanding admirer of the composer, was appalled by *Parsifal*, damning it as "Christianity arranged for Wagnerians . . . a work of malice, of vindictiveness . . . an outrage on morality".

What makes *Parsifal* the most problematic of Wagner's creations is that you can be repelled by its decadent religiosity while being simultaneously seduced by what you are hearing, for *Parsifal*, more than any other of Wagner's operas, brought words, music and drama into perfect communion. With its intimate play between leitmotif and language, its austerely choreographed stage action, and its slow-moving, contemplative music, *Parsifal* is an opera in which absolutely nothing is superfluous. The prevailing hushed atmosphere is established at the outset, through a sixteen-minute prelude in which the opera's three most resonant motifs are first heard – the climactic theme being the "Dresden Amen", a stirring cadence that dates back to the sixteenth century. Although it resembles *Tristan* in that the lengthy prelude establishes tensions that are released only at the opera's conclusion, *Parsifal* has nothing of *Tristan*'s impetuosity – indeed, its progress is so stately that it tends towards a condition of stasis. The use of chant-like themes for the chorus creates an air of monastic tranquility, and even the carnality of Klingsor's Flower Maidens is of a passive, almost solipsistic kind. At times the action comes to a dead halt, with the epic narrations of Gurnemanz, who is required to spell out what has happened prior to the point at which we join the story.

Where *Tristan*, the *Ring* and *Meistersinger* show Wagner's imagination at its most complex, with many lines of musical thought running concurrently, *Parsifal* returns to the mysterious uncertainties of *Lohengrin*, but with a far greater sense of gravity and inwardness. What sets the mood-painting of *Parsifal* apart from anything Wagner wrote before is the economy of its means and the use of silence as a positive element in the score. Parsifal is an exercise in suspension, relying more upon the accumulation of suggestion than the thrill of effect, and so anticipates the shifting, twilit world of Debussy's *Pelléas et Mélisande*. There is no getting round the fact that some people find *Parsifal* a long haul – Mark Twain once remarked: "The first of the three acts occupied two hours, and I enjoyed that in spite of the singing." But if you can suspend judgement on the repugnant philosophy, you'll find this opera contains some of the most subtle and ethereal music Wagner ever composed.

RECORDINGS OVERVIEW

There's only a handful of successful recordings of *Parsifal*, two of which are conducted by the same man, Hans Knappertsbusch. The strongest modern *Parsifal* is conducted by Armin Jordan, though Daniel Barenboim's lush, warm-sounding performance has great strengths as well – the scene transformations and the Good Friday Music are superbly played, the ambience is extremely atmospheric, and Siegfried Jerusalem projects a real authority in the lead role. On balance, however, it doesn't quite have the sense of purpose that makes Barenboim's *Ring* so distinctive, and neither does the cast have such quality in depth. As for the other contenders, Pierre Boulez's Deutsche Grammophon recording is notable for a commanding Parsifal from James King and some incisive ideas from Boulez, while Karajan's movingly conducted account for the same label is let down by weak casting; the reverse is the problem with Solti's 1972 recording for Decca.

Hans Knappertsbusch

As a footnote, recordings were made by three members of the 1882 cast of *Parsifal*: Marianne Brandt (Kundry); Luise Belce (one of the solo Flowermaidens); and, most importantly, Hermann Winckelmann, the first Parsifal. Primitive technology and advancing years make the first pair's sessions of historical value only, but Winckelmann's excerpts from *Meistersinger*, *Lohengrin* and *Tannhäuser* give a reasonably good idea of what the tenor Wagner chose to create Parsifal sounded like. At the moment, none of these sessions has been transferred onto CD.

Thomas, London, Hotter, Dalis, Neidlinger, Talvela; Bayreuth Festival Chorus and Orchestra; Knappertsbusch.
(Philips 416 390-2PH4; 4 CDs).

This 1962 Bayreuth recording, one of the best-selling Wagner records, is a triumph of vision and execution. Not only are the performances faultless, but the early stereo is extraordinarily beautiful, capturing the Bayreuth sound to perfection. This is a quicker, more cultured and slightly lighter reading than Knappertsbusch's 1951 account (see below). It's also better sung, with a genuine *Heldentenor* Parsifal from Jess Thomas and a remarkably moving Amfortas from George London. Hans Hotter's Klingsor and Martti Talvela's Gurnemanz are classic performances, while Irene Dalis's Kundry, hurling caution to the wind, is the most compellingly dislocated interpretation on disc. The remaining cast are all superb – any account that could afford to cast such fine tenors as Gerhard Stolze and Georg Paskuda in minor roles (two Squires) was always likely to secure legendary status.

Windgassen, London, Weber, Mödl, Uhde, van Mill; Bayreuth Festival Chorus and Orchestra; Knappertsbusch.
(Teldec 9031-76047-2; 4 CDs).

There are six known recordings of *Parsifal* conducted by Hans Knappertsbusch, all of which are live. This is the first, recorded at Bayreuth in 1951 – the year of his Festival debut – when he was already sixty-three years old. It's the slowest ever recorded – taking well over four hours – but it is never dull or flabby, for Knappertsbusch understood the opera's intricate web of motifs and character relationships as well as anyone, and uses them to keep the opera animated no matter how slow the basic pulse or speed. George London is a perfect Amfortas, Martha Mödl a dark Kundry, and the only questionable presence is Windgassen's lightweight Parsifal. The orchestral and choral support have never been bettered, and the mono sound is a model for its time.

Goldberg, Lloyd, Schöne, Minton; Prague Philharmonic Chorus; Monte Carlo Philharmonic Orchestra; Jordan.
(Erato 2292-45662-2; 4 CDs).

This is the most convincing stereo recording of *Parsifal*. Jordan adopts quicker tempi than Knappertsbusch and voices the inner parts with great delicacy and detail – in short, where Knappertsbusch looks to the shadows, Jordan looks to the light. Yvonne Minton is breathtaking as Kundry, while Robert Lloyd comes across as the most commanding Gurnemanz since Hans Hotter. Reiner Goldberg is no *Heldentenor*, but he tries hard and there are isolated episodes in which he manages both gravity and sweetness. The supporting cast (especially the Flowermaidens) are magnificent – as is the recorded sound.

JOHANN STRAUSS THE YOUNGER

b. VIENNA, OCTOBER 25, 1825; d. VIENNA, JUNE 3, 1899.

Just as Offenbach's operettas embodied the spirit of the French Second Empire in its terminal phase, so Johann Strauss the Younger's dance music epitomized the riotous twilight of the Austro-Hungarian Empire. Strauss's father Johann was himself one of Europe's most famous musicians, having been the first to raise the waltz to the level of art music, but was not keen for his son to follow him into so precarious a profession. But after Johann senior left the family home in 1842, Johann junior's talents were cultivated by his mother, and he learned quickly: before his twenty-fifth birthday he was conducting his own orchestra. He composed almost nothing but dances before the mid-1860s. Then Offenbach's operettas arrived in Vienna and their enormous popularity persuaded Strauss to contemplate writing for the opera house.

His first effort never made it into production, but his second, *Indigo und die vierzig Räuber*, first performed in 1871, was a great success, receiving performances throughout Germany. Remarkably, the critics nonetheless thought he should stick to dance music and, even more remarkably, neither these critics nor the Viennese public were especially moved by the first performance, in 1874, of *Die Fledermaus*. Within six years, however, it had been mounted in 180 German theatres, a level of popularity he came close to matching only

GUS ONG

once more: with *Der Zigeunerbaron*, composed in 1885. His remaining theatre music, while initially popular, has not lasted the distance, with the exception of the sporadically revived *Wiener Blut*, a shapeless patchwork of waltz tunes, famously denounced by Julius Korngold as a "slab of bleeding chunks".

Strauss modelled his stage works on Offenbach's operettas (indeed Offenbach's librettists provided the source for *Die Fledermaus*), but founded a distinctively Viennese tradition, characterized by musical fluidity and sentimental charm rather than by satirical bite. Admired by the likes of Wagner, Liszt, Brahms (who regretted that he hadn't written the *Blue Danube* himself) and Richard Strauss (no relation), Strauss was the consummate master of light music. There are no hidden depths to *Die Fledermaus* and *Der Zigeunerbaron*, but on the strength of their musical panache and comic verve they continue to hold their place in the opera houses of the world alongside the heavyweight work of Mozart and Wagner.

Die Fledermaus

The Bat

Composed 1873–74.
First performed April 5, 1874.
Libretto by Carl Haffner and Richard Genée, after Meilhac and Halévy.

Synopsis

Act I

A spa near Vienna. Eisenstein is to go to prison for offending the tax collector. His wife Rosalinde is being wooed by a former lover, the opera singer Alfred. Eisenstein is furious with his lawyer but his friend Dr Falke – who is supposed to escort Eisenstein to prison – cheers him up by reminding him of the time Eisenstein left him to walk home after a party, in broad daylight, dressed as a bat. Falke suggests that they now go to Prince Orlovsky's party, just as long as Eisenstein makes it to the prison before six o'clock the following morning. Adele, Rosalinde's maid, asks her mistress if she can have the evening off to visit her sick aunt (in reality to attend Orlovsky's party) but she refuses. Eisenstein tells Rosalinde that he is about to begin his sentence and they bid each other an insincere farewell – she is looking forward to Alfred's return. Rosalinde and her lover are disturbed at dinner by Frank, the prison governor, who, assuming that Alfred is Eisenstein, drags the protesting singer off to jail. Conscious of the potential scandal, Rosalinde plays along with the misunderstanding.

Act II

At the party Dr Falke tells the Prince of the "Bat's revenge", his plan to get his own back on Eisenstein for the humiliation he caused him. The victim, Eisenstein, is announced as Marquis Renard. Eisenstein recognizes one of the guests as Adele, but she denies she is who he thinks she is. Renard is introduced to Chevalier Chagrin (Frank) and then to a Hungarian countess (Rosalinde), with whom he flirts. He then begins to boast of his now famous practical joke. After much good-natured celebration, the clock strikes six and Eisenstein and Falke leave for prison.

Act III

In jail Alfred is annoying the jailer Frosch with his singing. Frank, drunk, falls asleep at his desk. Adele has followed the "Chevalier" as she believes he will help her acting career. Eisenstein and Falke arrive to hear that the prisoner has already begun his sentence. Furious at the thought of an impostor, Eisenstein disguises himself as Alfred's lawyer and questions Alfred and Rosalinde. Ever more furious, he reveals his identity but before he can become too self-righteous, his wife engages her

Hungarian accent and produces a watch she took from him at the party. The remaining guests arrive and Falke admits the entire scenario as his "Bat's revenge". The opera ends in praise of champagne, on which the previous evening's numerous indiscretions are blamed.

The decadence of the capital of the Austro-Hungarian Empire is perfectly mirrored in *Die Fledermaus*, an opera in which luscious music disguises a mordant critique of the audience at which it's aimed. The management of the Theater an der Wien found it too close to the knuckle (they insisted that a prostitute be written out of the script, for one thing), and even after editing it caused something of a scandal, while those with more robust constitutions had problems with the unintelligible plot. Within two years, however, it was being performed throughout Europe and America, and in 1890 the Vienna Opera took the extraordinary step of adding this operetta to its repertoire.

Gingered up with bits of quasi-Hungarian local colour, the score has all the sparkle you'd expect from the creator of the *Blue Danube*, and Strauss demonstrates a brilliant handling of structure and pacing, as well as a flair for character-drawing: each of the cast has reason for behaving as he or she does, which is not the case with most operettas. Whereas Offenbach's caricatures were often targeted at real-life individuals, Strauss's satire is more generic, which is not to say that it's less acute: Orlovsky is an unforgettable image of aristocratic degeneracy, adroitly cast by Strauss as a mezzo in drag, a device that gives the character an overtone of slippery sexuality. Moreover, Strauss couches his satire in a more "cultured" musical language than that employed by his French colleague. Indeed, *Die Fledermaus* is the most operatic of operettas. The orchestra here plays a far more prominent role than in most operettas, presenting principal themes and defining character rather than merely serving as accompaniment. Similarly, the vocal score is decidedly grown-up: only the comic role of Frosch can be played by an untrained voice, and only the very greatest singers can hope to tackle Adele or Rosalinde, whose Hungarian-style aria in Act II is an absolute blinder.

Strauss's analysis of his society is cynical, but the way he presents it is full of generosity and vivaciousness. No matter what deception or dishonesty is occurring, the music is all about fun and escapism, as exemplied by such highlights as Adele's laughing aria "Mein Herr Marquis", Orlovsky's toast to champagne, "Im Feuerstrom der Reben", and Falke's hymn to love, "Brüderlein und Schwesterlein". Constructed with a classical precision of which Mozart might have approved, *Die Fledermaus* is, in short, something of a Trojan Horse.

RECORDINGS OVERVIEW

Nearly twenty recordings of *Die Fledermaus* have been made, but only half that number are currently available on CD. Of the unavailable ones, the most desirable is Decca's 1950 mono set – the first since the premiere recording of 1907. Conducted by Clemens Krauss, the performance has a spontaneity unrivalled on disc: the Vienna Philharmonic are superb, the cast is top-drawer (Gueden, Lipp, Dermota and Patzak), and the sound is clear. Others to keep any eye out for are the RCA set from 1963, with probably the best cast of the stereo era (Leigh, Rothenberger, Stevens, Waechter, London and Kónya), and the Eurodisc *Fledermaus* of 1964, with Robert Stolz conducting the Vienna Symphony Orchestra and another classic cast (Lipp, Steiner, Berry and Schock).

Gueden, Köth, Kmentt, Zampieri, Berry, Resnik, Waechter; Vienna State Opera Chorus and Orchestra; Karajan.
(Decca 421 046-2DH2; 2 CDs).

This was a very heavily promoted recording when it was produced in 1960, and it is easy to hear why. Karajan gives an un-self-conscious and beautifully integrated reading, the Vienna Philharmonic are on lush form, and the world-class cast are consistently true to the opera's character and style. There's a huge bonus in the star-studded gala recital inserted at the interval. Björling, del Monaco, Corena, Sutherland, Berganza, Leontyne Price and Ljuba Welitsch all produce typical fare; but Birgit Nilsson sings "I could have danced all night", Tebaldi has a go at "Vilja's Song" and, most eccentrically, Simionato and Bastianini, two of the greatest Italian bel canto singers of all time, sing "Anything you can do, I can do better". Surreal.

Varady, Popp, Prey, Kollo, Weikl, Rebroff; Bavarian State Opera Chorus and Orchestra; Kleiber.
(Deutsche Grammophon DG 415 646-2; 2 CDs).

Carlos Kleiber reinvents almost every score he turns his mind to, and this is no exception. It is also one of his best-sung recordings, with a glorious Rosalinde from Julia Varady and an exacting Adele from Lucia Popp. René Kollo is thin and nasal as Alfred, and Hermann Prey is too smooth to be true, but the characterizations are nicely pointed and Prey's big duet with Bernd Weikl's Falke is excellent fun. The one gaffe is the casting of coloratura bass Ivan Rebroff as a falsetto Orlovsky. The excellent sound and the inclusion of the ballet "Donner und Blitz" make this a fascinating experience.

Der Zigeunerbaron

The Gypsy Baron

Composed 1885.
First performed October 24, 1885.
Libretto by Ignaz Schnitzer, after Jókai.

Synopsis

Act I

The exiled Sandor Barinkay returns to Hungary to claim his lands. His palm is read by an old gypsy who says that he will find both money and a wife. Zsupán, a wealthy illiterate, thinks Sandor an ideal husband for his daughter, Arsena, but she loves Ottokar, the son of her governess Mirabella. Arsena rebuffs Sandor but says that she would change her mind if he were a baron – but even when it transpires that Sandor is, in fact, a gypsy baron, Arsena still turns him down. Sandor turns to the old gypsy and asks to marry her daughter Sáffi instead.

Act II

Sandor and Sáffi are in love. Her mother Czipra helps them locate a casket of buried treasure. When Arsena, Ottokar and Zsupán are told that Sandor and Sáffi are married they denounce the marriage as illegal – sentiments intensified when the lovers claim they were married by the birds of the forest. However, all this is forgotten when provincial governor Count Homonay arrives on a recruiting drive for soldiers to fight against Spain. Zsupán and Ottokar take the draft, and when Czipra reveals that Sáffi is in fact descended from the last Pasha of Hungary, Sandor realizes that he is beneath her as well, and so he too joins the army.

Act III

With war at an end, Vienna heralds the victorious soldiers – among them the less than gallant Zsupán (who picked the pockets of the dead) and Sandor, whom Homonay creates a real baron. Returning to Sáffi, he then blesses the marriage between Arsena and Ottokar.

The idea for an "ethnic" Hungarian operetta began to take shape at a party in Budapest in November 1882, at which Strauss entertained everyone with a selection of Hungarian pieces at the piano. By February he had received the encouragement of Franz Liszt and been introduced to the author Maurus Jókai, who suggested his story *Saffi* as the basis for a stage work. Within a matter of weeks a libretto had been commissioned from Ignatz Schnitzer, but Strauss's prior commitments delayed completion of the project until October 1885, shortly before he conducted the first performance. The response was remarkable: it remained on the stage for 87 consecutive nights, and was staged by no fewer than 140 theatres during Strauss's lifetime.

The celebrated anti-Wagnerite Eduoard Hanslick wrote of the new work that the "music has retained the unaffected naturalness and healthy naiveté that strikes us as the principal characteristic and cardinal virtue of Strauss's music". He was not wrong, but there's more to *Der Zigeunerbaron* than simple charm, for in this work more than any other Strauss breaks down the traditional barriers between serious opera and operetta by applying a serious composer's resources to the genre. For example, he wanted at least eighty soldiers on foot and horseback for his chorus, and provided them with music of grand opulence – along the lines established by *Die Fledermaus*, but with none of that work's self-conscious sophistication. Indeed, he saw his opera as an earthy celebration of the cultural unification of Austria and Hungary, fusing the high artistic values of Vienna with the ethnic vivacity of Hungarian folk song. In a series of irresistible marches, polkas, mazurkas and czardas, Strauss mixes royalty and gypsies in a delightful conflation of rural and cosmopolitan life.

Lippert, Coburn, Schasching, Holzmair; Schoenberg Choir; Vienna Symphony Orchestra; Harnoncourt. (Teldec 4509-94555-2; 2 CDs).

Harnoncourt is best known for his work on heavyweights from Bach to Schubert, but here he shows himself just as adept in operetta. His gift for flexible beat and elastic phrasing imparts a sense of spontaneity, and his cast relish the opportunity to let their hair down. Wolfgang Holzmair is outstanding as Homonay, while Herbert Lippert (Barinkay) and Pamela Coburn (Sáffi) are disarmingly charming. The bright-sounding VSO augment the warmth of the set. The alternative choice is EMI's mid-price recording with Prey and Gedda.

JOHANN STRAUSS
DER
ZIGEUNER
BARON
THE GYPSY BARON
LE BARON TZIGANE
WIENER SYMPHONIKER
NIKOLAUS
HARNONCOURT

AMBROISE THOMAS

b. METZ, FRANCE, AUGUST 5, 1811; d. PARIS, FEBRUARY 12, 1896.

Ambroise Thomas was the embodiment of the Second Empire musical establishment, writing operas that were calculated to appeal to the middle-class taste for dramatically naive, melodically sweet operas. With two operas – *Mignon* and *Hamlet* – he hit the jackpot, but nowadays they are very much an acquired taste, requiring the services of a star coloratura soprano to make them palatable.

Thomas was taught at the Paris Conservatoire by Jean-François Le Sueur, the fiercely conservative tutor of Berlioz, and between 1837 and 1843 he composed nine works for the stage, mainly comic operas in imitation of Auber and Boïeldieu. Denounced by the composer-musicologist François Fétis as "whipped cream for breakfast, lunch and tea", they were lavishly tuneful and little else. Only *Le songe d'une nuit d'eté* (which featured parts for Shakespeare, Falstaff and Elizabeth I) anticipated the deft elegance of *Mignon* and *Hamlet*, which he produced in 1866 and 1868.

These were to be his only lasting successes, and he devoted the remaining years of his life to the Paris Conservatoire where, as director from 1871, he became his country's most influential teacher. Though his values were attacked by many for their extreme conservatism, this did little to affect the enthusiasm of audiences, who continued to flock to *Mignon* and *Hamlet* until well into the 1930s. No French or Italian soprano's recording catalogue was complete without at least one 78 of "Connais-tu le pays", and until the 1950s it was common for a budding coloratura soprano to launch her career as Mignon.

Thomas was a composer for whom critical prestige mattered considerably less than commercial prosperity. His weakness for melodies that were either languorous and sugary or brilliant and sparkling (but nothing in between) brought him into conflict with the supporters of Verdi and Wagner, and later into disrepute when Debussy's star began to rise. For all that, Thomas was a high-class craftsman with an expert understanding of the human voice, as *Mignon* and *Hamlet* demonstrate at length.

Mignon

Composed 1866.
First performed November 17, 1866.
Libretto by Michel Carré and Jules Barbier, after Goethe.

Act I

Wilhelm, a student, and Lothario, a man driven half-mad by the search for his long-lost daughter, save a young girl named Mignon from a gang of gypsies. Looking on are two musicians, Laërte and Philine. The latter begins to fall in love with Wilhelm as Mignon starts singing of her childhood. This makes Mignon jealous; Wilhelm nonetheless engages her as his maid.

Act II

Philine and Laërte are engaged to perform in the theatre at Rosenberg castle. Frédérick, the nephew of the castle's owner, who is in love with Philine, quarrels with Wilhelm. After the play, Mignon sees Wilhelm with Philine, which pitches her into a jealous gloom, but then the theatre is set on fire and, rushing into the flames, Wilhelm again saves Mignon from death.

Act III

Mignon is recovering from the ordeal in an Italian country palace. Lothario prays for her recovery while Wilhelm listens to a servant recount the family history of the castle's owner, Marquis Cypriani. Believing his daughter drowned, he left Italy after his wife died. The name Cypriani stirs dim memories in Lothario, just as Mignon begins to wake from her fever. She speaks of the palace as if she had lived there many years before, and when Wilhelm and Mignon confess their love for each other they are interrupted by Lothario, who has changed into noble finery: he is Marquis Cypriani and Mignon is his long-lost daughter Sperata. The opera ends in great rejoicing.

In its own terms, *Mignon* succeeded perfectly: the opera was performed one hundred times in its first year alone, and it remained a solid part of the repertoire in Paris until World War II, by which time it had clocked up 1600 performances at the Opéra-Comique alone. But not everyone was impressed – Chabrier was far from alone when he pronounced that there were three types of music, "good, bad, and Ambroise Thomas". The fact is that *Mignon* was out of date at the time of its premiere: the absurd plot, unlikely characters and self-consciously difficult vocal score harked back to a time when opera was regarded above all as a nicely staged singing show. Largely bereft of motive and personality, *Mignon* is basically a string of sugar-coated arias, and it is no surprise that Mignon's Act I number, "Connais-tu le pays", was one of the most recorded items in the era of early 78s.

Thomas tempers the bel canto fireworks with a distinctly French kind of lyricism – whereas his Italian precursors would always have entrusted the lead role to a coloratura soprano, Thomas goes for a mezzo, carefully exploiting the darker tone of that lower vocal range. Nowhere is this more impressive than during the second scene of Act II when, rejected, despondent and about to kill herself, Mignon sings the powerful aria "Elle est là, près lui". Philine sits at the other end of the soprano scale, all jollity and brilliance; somewhere between the two comes gallant, lightweight Wilhelm, a role loved by many a great lyric tenor, thanks to the opportunities it offers for unbridled gushing, as in his "Adieu, Mignon".

For its London premiere in 1870 Thomas reduced the conclusion, replaced the spoken dialogue with recitative and added some new music. Whenever *Mignon* is revived, it is this version that is performed.

RECORDINGS OVERVIEW

Irritatingly, neither of the two complete recordings of *Mignon* is currently available. The first set, taped in 1953 by Decca, has more than a modicum of Gallic charm, but Geneviève Moizan's title performance is laboured and Georges Sebastian's conducting is uninspired. Much better is the 1977 CBS recording, well conducted by Antonio de Almeida, with the unlikely casting of Marilyn Horne in the title role. In spite of her advanced years, she is in glorious voice, and the remaining cast, particularly Alain Vanzo as Wilhelm, are excellent.

Hamlet

Composed 1867–68.
First performed March 9, 1868.
Libretto by Michel Carré and Jules Barbier, after Shakespeare.

Act I

Elsinore, Denmark. Prince Hamlet is disgusted by the hasty marriage of his mother Gertrude to his uncle Claudius, so soon after the death of his father, the king. Laertes (Laërte) entrusts his sister Ophelia (Ophélie) to Hamlet's care, as he has to leave Denmark. Hamlet is told that his father's ghost has been seen. On the castle battlements, the king appears and tells his son how he was murdered by Claudius. Hamlet swears to avenge his death.

Act II

Hamlet has begun to act strangely and this alarms Ophelia, who turns to the queen for comfort. At Hamlet's invitation, a troupe of actors perform a play in which a king is murdered; during the show, the guilt-stricken Claudius rises to leave. Hamlet snatches his crown.

Act III

In the castle chapel, Hamlet overhears the king's confession of guilt. Gertrude urges her son to marry Ophelia but he refuses, provoking Ophelia to return their engagement ring. Forcing his mother to look at portraits of his father and Claudius, Hamlet reveals that he knows the truth. His father's ghost appears and demands vengeance against Claudius, but implores Hamlet to spare Gertrude.

Act IV

Ophelia hears peasants dancing by a lake; having lost all reason, she walks into the water and drowns.

Act V

At the cemetery Hamlet considers Ophelia's madness – though both he and the gravediggers are unaware of her death. Laertes returns and challenges Hamlet to a duel, but as they draw their swords, a procession, headed by the king and queen, passes with Ophelia's bier. The ghost appears for the last time and demands Claudius's death. Hamlet kills his uncle and is pronounced king.

Michel Carré and Jules Barbier provided libretti for most of the popular composers working in Paris during the middle years of the nineteenth century, including Bizet, Gounod, Meyerbeer and Offenbach. They were particularly fond of Shakespeare (in translations by the elder Dumas), preparing *Roméo et Juliette* for Gounod and providing Thomas with a pruned and sweetened version of *Hamlet*. The end product is of zero interest as a re-appraisal of Shakespeare's problematic tragedy, but it again hit the button with the Paris public, providing Thomas with his only success at the Opéra and remaining in its repertoire for seventy years. The resurgence of light-lyric sopranos during the 1960s brought it back off the shelf, and both of the twentieth century's most celebrated Ophelias, Joan Sutherland and June Anderson, have recorded it.

Writing for the more exalted Opéra, Thomas attempted to create something with greater weight than *Mignon*, but what he came up with was not so much a consistent drama as a sequence of highly melodic outbursts of action. But if narrative and characterization were never Thomas's strong points, he knew how to write a good tune, and his *Hamlet* is littered with sprightly dances, hearty choruses and moments of deeper significance – the Act I love music is really beautiful, and the great soliloquy "Ètre ou ne pas être" carries unexpected force. Thomas scored the title role for a baritone, hoping to give the prince a seriousness that might have eluded a tenor voice, but the show belongs to the coloratura Ophelia, whose mad-song is a shameless pitch for the services of a show-off diva.

Hampson, Anderson, Kunde, Graves, Ramey; Ambrosian Opera Chorus; London Philharmonic Orchestra; de Almeida.
(EMI CDS7 54820-2; 3 CDs).

Recorded in 1993, this is the most recent recording of *Hamlet*. Its only rival, also on CD, has Milnes and Sutherland in the main roles, and while the former clearly enjoys hamming it up, the latter is past her best. June Anderson is not only closer in age to the character she is playing, but she sounds it. Using imperious soprano with laudable restraint, she sings beautifully, especially in duet with Thomas Hampson, who is ideal in the title role. Orchestra and supporting cast are excellent, and the recorded sound is faultless. However, three full-price discs make this an expensive luxury for all but the most ardent fans of French lyric opera.

CHARLES GOUNOD

b. PARIS, JUNE 18, 1818; d. SAINT-CLOUD, OCTOBER 18, 1893.

During the first half of the nineteenth century, Paris was Europe's chief musical centre, but this situation arose more from the city's ability to attract foreign talent such as Chopin, Liszt and Meyerbeer than from any fostering of native talent – as Berlioz never ceased to complain. Charles-François Gounod was the first home-grown composer to achieve the same success as the illustrious immigrants: chiefly responsible for leading French opera away from the elephantine spectaculars of Meyerbeer, he became the most popular operatic composer in the country's history.

As a young man Gounod had determined to take holy orders, but he was encouraged to pursue his musical talents by the soprano Pauline Viardot. His first attempts for the stage were weak pastiches of Gluck, and not until 1859 did he hit upon a subject that really stimulated him – Goethe's *Faust*. It was hugely popular, and so sustained was the clamour for tickets at the Théâtre-Lyrique that the Opéra offered to stage it in 1869 – but only after he had re-scored the spoken dialogue as recitative and added ballet interludes.

Keen to build upon *Faust*'s success, Gounod produced *Philémon et Baucis*, *La colombe* and the five-act *La Reine de Saba*; but the last of these attracted accusations of "Wagnerism", a cardinal offence in Paris. The opera was an overnight failure, and its successor, *Mireille*, was similarly rejected after its first performance in 1864. It began to look as if Gounod would never repeat the glory of *Faust*, but in 1867 his reputation was saved by Shakespeare – *Roméo et Juliette* was vigorously promoted by the Théatre-Lyrique, who were desperately in need of critical prestige, and both theatre and composer got the hit they needed.

In 1870, fleeing the Franco-Prussian war and the scandal generated by his adultery, Gounod made an extended visit to England, together with his long-suffering wife and children. He was warmly received as "the composer of *Faust*", notably at Buckingham Palace, as Queen Victoria was an admirer of his music. She became an admirer of the man, until in February 1871 the composer's eye lit upon the amateur singer and society hostess Georgina Weldon. Before the end of May, Anna Gounod had admitted defeat and taken her children back to Paris. Gounod remained, growing in popularity thanks to his stream of

ANDRÉ LECOZ/LEBRECHT COLLECTION

Gounod's Faust – it's not hard to see why it still packs them in

archetypally Victorian pious slush, much of which he wrote for his mistress's questionable talents. However, their relationship began to suffer when the composer embroiled himself in Weldon's schemes to establish a music school in Bloomsbury, and the scales were finally tipped in November 1873 when, increasingly desperate for money, Weldon was said to have attempted to blackmail the Queen of England.

Gounod left both Weldon and England six months later. Upon his return to Paris he wrote three new operas, but his sentimental style was by now sounding dated. Grudgingly, he retired from opera composition, returning to liturgical music. He continued, nonetheless, to be fêted as one of the few to maintain a distinctively French style, and in this respect he was to be seen as an exemplary figure to many later French composers, such as Massenet and Ravel.

Faust

Composed 1856–59.
First performed March 19, 1859.
Libretto by Jules Barbier and Michel Carré, after Goethe.

Synopsis

Act I

Lonely and despairing, Faust summons Méphistophélès. In return for his soul, the Devil agrees to satisfy Faust's sensual desires. Faust hesitates until the Devil conjures a vision of Marguérite sitting at her spinning wheel. Transformed into a young and handsome nobleman, Faust sings of his future and the joys that await him.

Act II

In the town square Valentin entrusts his sister, Marguérite, to the care of his friends while he is away with his regiment. Méphistophélès appears and ridicules Marguérite, provoking Valentin into attacking the Devil, who makes his sword break in mid-air. Valentin and the villagers flee, making the sign of the cross. Méphistophélès is joined by Faust, who offers Marguérite his arm – which she modestly rejects.

Act III

Faust pays homage to Marguérite's lodgings and the sheltering care of nature. Méphistophélés leaves a jewel box in her room, and when she tries on the jewels she is overcome with joy. The Devil and Faust enter her rooms. Goaded by Méphistophélès (who has caught the eye of Marguérite's guardian Marthe), Faust seduces Marguérite.

Act IV

Nine months later, Marguerite has given birth to Faust's child and been ostracized by all but her closest friends. Valentin returns from the war and fights a duel with Faust. As Valentin lies dying he damns his sister for eternity. She hurries to a church where she attempts to pray, but the Devil – and his demons – continually interrupt her, causing her to faint at the altar.

Act V

In the Harz mountains, on Walpurgis Night. Faust is affected by visions. Eventually he sees Marguérite's image and determines to find her; she is in prison for having murdered her baby. She rejects Faust's suggestion that they leave together; and after appealing to God for forgiveness, she dies. As Marguérite's soul rises to heaven Faust is dragged to hell by a triumphant Méphistophélès.

Performed in more than fifty countries and translated into twenty-five languages, *Faust* has been a hit since the day of its premiere. Indeed, it was so popular that an English critic complained in 1863 – "Faust, Faust, Faust, nothing but Faust. Faust on Saturday, Wednesday and Thursday; to be repeated tonight, and on every night until further notice." The craze for *Faust* drove publishers into overtime: aside from printing constantly re-packaged editions of the opera in short and full score, dozens of piano reductions, song arrangements, instrumental fantasies and ballad compilations were produced to satisfy French, German and English enthusiasts. The work's popularity long outlasted its composer. It received its 2000th Parisian performance in 1934, and it remains among the three or four most popular French operas ever written.

Based chiefly on Michel Carré's play *Faust et Marguérite*, a distant relative of Goethe's poem, *Faust* is a prime example of the opéra lyrique, a derivation of Grand Opéra in which the five-act form, the ballets and the choruses were retained, but the spectacle was played down to create a more song-based work of musical theatre, with greater emphasis on character motivation. The libretto was originally offered to Meyerbeer – the composer whose reign over French musical life *Faust* did much to end – but even he balked at the "molestation of Germany's greatest poem". Gounod had no such qualms, and set about writing music to a text that reduced Goethe's metaphysical epic to a tussle between the libido and righteousness.

As ever, the Devil has the best tunes, or at least most powerful ones. Where Faust is all lyric sweetness (a quality typified by his "Salut, demeure et chaste et pure") and romantic gushing (notably during his duets with Marguérite), Méphistophélès is a roaring, jubilantly sensual creation, and by far the most human character in the opera, with a rather appealing cynicism that's encapsulated in the alarmingly jaunty "Golden Calf" aria of Act III. The disparity between the lovers and their matchmaker is clear from their opening words: Faust's first utterance is "Nothing", Marguérite's is "No", but Méphistophélès enters with a splendidly assertive "Here I am". Marguérite, the weakest of the central trio, is an implausible lust object, embodying a sickly Christianity that is all about incense and bells, but Gounod observes the protocol by apportioning her some coloratura showpieces (famously the "Jewel Song"), and he makes the most of the voice in a series of exhilaratingly over-the-top ensembles.

Like many of his contemporaries, Gounod found it difficult to resist an opportunity for rampant sentimentality – Marguérite's final-act cry for divine protection, "Anges purs! anges radieux", is particularly difficult to take. But generally the high-quality melodies keep coming at such a rate that these lapses are soon forgotten. Whether through solos, ensembles, ballets or choruses (you will probably recognize the thumping "Soldiers Chorus"), Gounod gives every scene a tune that is at least enjoyable while it lasts and at best highly memorable. For many of the more ardent passages make use of the trick of gradually raising the melody in pitch and intensity until a high note can be milked for all its worth – the final love music, "Qui, c'est toi je t'aime", is a conspicuous example. But in its marriage of the calculated and the emotive, this set-piece defines the quality that continues to make *Faust* such a popular opera. Gounod was a sentimentalist who knew exactly what he was doing.

RECORDINGS OVERVIEW

Unsurprisingly, *Faust* has been well served by the record companies, with some sixteen complete studio recordings floating in and out of the catalogue – and a seventeenth, with Roberto Alagna and Angela Gheorghiu, on the way. In matters of style, EMI's 1930 Parisian production, conducted by Henri Büsser, is one of the truest guides to the approach that the composer would have recognized (it's available on Pearl). There followed an intriguing Marguérite from Géori Boué (for Beecham) in 1948 and a magnificent Méphistophélès from Cesare Siepi (for Cleva) in 1951, but sadly neither is currently on CD. In 1953 and 1958 EMI made two recordings with the same cast (see below), and in 1966 Bonynge directed a wilfully unauthentic but gloriously sung production for Decca. Thereafter, the standard has dropped, with generally weak Fausts and sloppy conducting – though the Marguérites have been preferable, with Caballé and Freni in beautiful form for Erato and EMI respectively. The best all-round productions are discussed below.

Gedda, de los Angeles, Christoff, Blanc; Paris Opera Chorus and Orchestra; Cluytens.
(EMI CMS7 69983-2; 3 CDs).

In 1953 EMI taped a mono studio recording of *Faust* with the same orchestra, chorus, conductor and leads as those on this set. Five years later, thanks to the advent of stereo, they had another go. Generally speaking, the latter is the better performance, with brighter, more incisive conducting and a more theatrical atmosphere. Gedda's Faust is beautifully stylish and Gallic, with a range of expression available on no other recording. De los Angeles's Marguérite projects a purity fully in keeping with the character, while the demonic Boris Christoff gives the over-the-top performance of his life, roaring and bawling his way through the score. The French forces play with great enthusiasm.

Corelli, Sutherland, Ghiaurov, Massard; Ambrosian Opera Chorus; London Symphony Orchestra; Bonynge.
(Decca 421 240-2DM3; 3 CDs).

Bonynge was able to command the cream of European vocal talent when he made this recording in 1966, and he directs a thrilling ride through the score. Franco Corelli's French is appalling and his swooping and sobbing are an affront to Gallic style, but he stirs the heart as the composer must surely have intended. Joan Sutherland is also free with Gounod's notation and her French is no model of accuracy, but the wealth of expression and sweetness of tone are more than compensation. The Bulgarian bass Ghiaurov is a top-rank Méphistophélès, bringing equal measures of wit and menace to the role.

Roméo et Juliette

Composed 1865–67.
First performed April 27, 1867.
Libretto by Jules Barbier and Michel Carré, after Shakespeare.

Synopsis

Act I

At a Capulet masked ball, Juliette is admired by the guests, among whom are Roméo and his Montague friends. Juliette talks of how she has no interest in marriage, but when she and Roméo meet, she realizes that their destinies are linked.

Act II

Roméo steals into Juliette's garden and eulogizes Juliette. He announces himself and, after expressing their love for each other, they decide to marry.

Act III

Frère Laurent marries the young lovers. The page Stéphano incites tension between the two families and during the ensuing fight, Roméo fatally wounds Tybalt. For the Capulet's death, the Duke of Verona banishes Roméo.

Act IV

Roméo and Juliette have spent the night together. Roméo is woken by the song of a lark and, after he has left, Juliette is informed by her father that she is to marry Paris. She turns to Frère Laurent, who suggests how she and Roméo might escape: first Juliette must take a sleeping potion that will give the impression that she has died. She drinks from the bottle and while walking up the aisle with Paris, she collapses.

Act V

Roméo has not received news of Laurent's ruse and, believing his wife to be dead, he takes poison. As he lies dying Juliette awakes and, finding Roméo close to death, she stabs herself.

Having gone to Germany's national poet for *Faust*, Gounod and his librettists turned to England's finest for *Roméo et Juliette*, and again axed a large amount of their source to concentrate on the love-story element. To increase the theatrical impact, they also made a number of alterations, notably waking Juliette in time for the lovers to bid farewell to each other, and a few additions – such as an entirely new character called Stéphano (Roméo's page) and the wedding scene (which most producers now cut). Many critics didn't react well to this tampering, and there's no question that the original play is considerably more varied than Gounod's version, but it's hard to understand the widely held opinion that *Roméo et Juliette* was tuneless. Nothing could be further from the truth: *Roméo* is just as melodic and memorable as *Faust*, and it is both less sentimental and dramatically tighter.

In Acts I and II the lovers are given sumptuous arias and duets (famously Roméo's cavatina to Juliette's balcony "Ah, lève-toi, soleil"), and the duet that ends Act II carries some of the most sensual music in all French opera. The opera's highlight is the lover's final duet, which occupies the whole of Act V. Nearly twenty minutes long, it demands outstanding singers and a conductor able to balance the pacing towards Roméo's final, heartbreaking soliloquy, "Console-toi, pauvre âme". The passions far exceed the lovers' state of health – the near-dead Roméo would have been neither willing nor able to bash out a high C – but the music comes closer to the pathos of Shakespeare than any other operatic adaptations of his plays outside the work of Verdi. Indeed, when Verdi came to write the Act I love duet of *Otello*, he must have been conscious of the opening of *Roméo*'s Act IV, in which a strikingly moving passage for divided cellos characterizes the lover's lingering nocturnal embrace. This delicate, effortlessly lyrical scene is typical of Gounod, a man who might have been writing about himself when he wrote: "France is essentially the country of precision, neatness and taste, that is to say the opposite of excess, pretentiousness, disproportion, longwindedness."

RECORDINGS OVERVIEW

The two most recent of the five studio recordings of *Roméo et Juliette* – EMI's 1983 set with Malfitano and Kraus, and RCA's 1996 account with Domingo and Svensen – are the only ones that can't be recommended. Of the various live recordings that have been transferred onto CD, the most famous and the best sung was taped in 1947 at the Met, with Emil Cooper conducting an all-star cast, headed by the most famous Roméo since the war, Jussi Björling. It is a devil to find, but well worth the effort.

Corelli, Freni, Depraz, Gui; Paris Opera Chorus and Orchestra; Lombard.
(EMI CMS5 65290-2; 2 CDs).

This jet-setting production, taped in 1968, captured the most famous stage Roméo and Juliette of recent years, Franco Corelli and Mirella Freni, in an opera they did much to popularize in the US during the 1960s. Neither was comfortable with the French (Corelli really messes the vowels around to suit his voice), but both singers give incredibly passionate readings. The incidental cast are not in the same league (though they are French), and Lombard doesn't so much conduct as defer to his stars, but the excellent sound adds to the emotional immediacy.

Jobin, Micheau, Ricquier, Rehfuss; Paris Opera Chorus and Orchestra; Erede.
(Decca 443 539-2LF2; 2 CDs).

This stylish 1953 set is an outstanding recording, among the very best from Decca's years as the dominant producer of recorded opera. Heading the Francophone cast, forceful Raoul Jobin (who was christened Roméo) is a rich and sultry tenor, with easy top notes and an effortless line; Janine Micheau does not have the technique for some of the higher, lighter writing and her tone lacks variety, but she perks up when singing next to Jobin. Although he sings his benediction beautifully, Heinz Rehfuss is a little flat as Laurént, but conductor Alberto Erede is in good form, allowing his singers just enough room to enable a genuine sense of French style.

JACQUES OFFENBACH

b. COLOGNE, JUNE 20, 1819; d. PARIS, OCTOBER 5, 1880.

Jacques Offenbach made operetta an international art form, paving the way for Lehár, Sullivan and the musicals of the twentieth century. Fusing dialogue and highly theatrical set-pieces in productions of great verve and satirical bite, he deflated the morals and manners of Second Empire – and became, in the process, a symbol of the very civilization he was attacking.

Born the seventh of ten children of a synagogue cantor in Cologne (he later signed himself "O. de Cologne"), Offenbach was sent in 1833 to Paris, where, his father believed, Jews were better treated than in Germany. Jacob changed his name almost immediately and, as Jacques, he was enrolled – with Cherubini's blessing – at the Conservatoire. Joining the orchestra of the Théâtre Ambigu Comique and, later, the Opéra-Comique, Offenbach published waltzes and concert pieces for his own instrument, the cello, but not one of his stage works was performed. As his reputation as a salon musician improved, so Offenbach's humour worsened. He even considered emigrating to America but in 1850 his luck changed when he was appointed conductor of the Théatre Français. *Oyayaie, ou La reine des îles* was successfully staged later that year but his reign as the preferred entertainer of "Le tout Paris" did not begin until 1855 when, on the back of the Paris International Exhibition, he hired a tiny theatre on the Champs-Elysées and promoted his own three-character, one-act musical comedies alongside operas by Adam and Delibes.

Offenbach's creations were funnier than anything being offered by the Opéra-Comique, and he was soon France's most popular composer. His company made an acclaimed visit to London in 1857, prompting a number of imitations (not least from Arthur Sullivan), but Offenbach lived beyond his means, and debt forced him to leave Paris for a few months. Upon his return he completed his first full-length operetta, *Orphée aux enfers*, the reception of which persuaded Offenbach to commit his energies entirely to composition. All but one of his greatest works date from the 1860s, but in 1871, after the horrors of the Franco-Prussian war and the suppression of the Paris Commune, the national mood changed and Offenbach found himself out of favour, branded "the great corrupter". Unperturbed, the irrepressible Offenbach invested his considerable fortune in the Théatre de la Gaîté. The gamble didn't work: in 1875 he closed just short of bankruptcy and made his long-threatened move to the promised land of the United States. He soon tired of America and returned in 1878 to Paris, where he died leaving his only serious opera, *Les contes d'Hoffmann*, unfinished. It became the most frequently performed of Offenbach's 106 works.

GUUS ONG

Though Offenbach brought the cancan into the world, his music was the product of a sophisticated mind. His work was often self-referential, scattered with references to his earlier creations – and it says a lot about his popularity that audiences were able to appreciate these frequently subtle allusions. Moreover, he took great pleasure in parodying the most popular current music through association: Orpheus's poor musicianship, for example, is illustrated by his playing an excerpt from Strauss's *Skater Waltz*. And beneath all the merriment and face-pulling, Offenbach displays a cynicism that makes him more modern than many of his contemporaries.

Orphée aux enfers

Orpheus in the Underworld

Composed 1858.
First performed October 21, 1858; revised 1874.
Libretto by Hector Cremiuex and Ludovic Halévy.

Synopsis (revised version)

Act I

Orpheus is a deluded composer whose music and violin playing incite intense hatred in his wife Eurydice. She, in turn, is a slut who is having an affair with Areistaeus, a strapping shepherd (in fact Pluto in disguise). Desperate to get rid of his wife, Orpheus – unbeknown to Eurydice – has struck a deal with Pluto, who arranges for her to die by a snakebite. Triumphant, Pluto takes her down to Hades. Orpheus is overjoyed, but Public Opinion insists that he visit Olympus, home of the gods, and beg for her return. Reluctantly, he agrees.

Act II

On Mount Olympus the gods are bored with their lives and, in particular, the diet of Nectar and Ambrosia. The gods mutiny against Jupiter, who is the only one who ever has any fun. When Orpheus arrives and makes his petition, Jupiter decides that they should all have a look at Hades, and transports his entire family there to see what all the fuss is about.

Act III

Eurydice is tired of Pluto's company and has decided she would rather be back on earth. Disguised as a fly, Jupiter falls in love with Eurydice and they decide to elope.

Act IV

At the farewell party for the gods, who have to return to Olympus, Jupiter agrees that the reluctant Orpheus may now rescue his wife, provided he does not turn to look at her on the way out. However, on the journey back Jupiter lets loose a lightning bolt, causing Orpheus to turn and look at Eurydice. Everyone, with the exception of Public Opinion, is delighted as Eurydice is returned to hell as a Bacchante.

Until 1858 Offenbach's theatrical licence, provided by Napoleon III's government, limited him to staging one-act operas with no more than four characters, but in that year, after months of negotiations, he obtained a new licence that allowed for several characters as well as a chorus. He decided to celebrate with an attack on the Second Empire's predilection for neoclassical pomposity (a trait that would reach its peak in 1861 with Garnier's colossal Opéra building) and the vogue for Gluck's operas, which were presented at the Comédie-Française as paragons of classical virtue. While young Napoleon, inspired by the memory of his uncle's First Empire, was busy rebuilding Paris, expressions of discontent with his extravagance, his increasingly heavy taxation and his dangerous foreign policy (which would lead to the disastrous Franco-Prussian war and his own downfall) met with a harsh response from a repressive police force. The time was ripe for the satire of *Orpheus in the Underworld*.

As his partner in this parodic offensive Offenbach recruited Ludovic Halévy, the composer's son – though because the twenty five-year-old Halévy was politically ambitious (he had just been appointed secretary-general to the ministry of Algeria), he begged Offenbach to omit his name from the credits. Their work was topical and hard-hitting: it criticized social repression by pitting Public Opinion against the gods; it mocked the government through figures like John Styx, a send-up of a notoriously dim minister of justice; and it blatantly caricatured Napoleon, deriding him for his ugly appearance, his selfish use of public funds, his obsession with expensive ceremony and his infamously roving eye. If nothing else, the Emperor had a sense of humour, for not only did he refuse to censor the work (the fame of which inspired a fashion for *Orphée* fancy-dress parties), but within eighteen months of the premiere he requested a command performance, after which he personally congratulated the composer. Rather less pleased were the conservative critics who objected to Offenbach's treatment of venerated composers – there was a highly public battle between Offenbach and a certain Jules Janin, who attacked Offenbach's mocking of Gluck's "Che faro senza Euridice" as a "desecration".

Orphée is Offenbach's most accessible, witty and tuneful opera, boasting some of the funniest dialogue and daftest situations in French opera. A number of these, such as Jupiter's transformation into a fly, are difficult to translate onto the stage, but Offenbach's score is so rich in pictorial effects that the music overrides the technical problems – Jupiter's metamorphosis, for example, is accompanied by the buzzing "Fly duet". There are dozens of memorable scenes for the fourteen central players, with each of the principal gods, as well as John Styx and Public Opinion, assigned songs in parodic styles that cover the field from Mozart to Wagner. Preferential treatment is given to Eurydice's soprano, who carries many of the best tunes, such as her gushing "Ah, when a woman's heart is yearning" and her "Hymn to Bacchus". The best-known episode is of course the final act's riotous *galop infernal*, or "infernal cancan" – "At last, something you can dance to," sing the party-goers. But this accounts for just a couple of minutes of an opera that lasts a hundred, and the entire work has just as much élan as this famous highlight. In fact, there is no more enjoyable example of light opera.

Orphée aux enfers was written twice, first in 1858 for the Bouffes-Parisiens and again in 1874, when Offenbach divided the two acts into four, expanded the text and added considerably to the orchestration for its premiere at the Théâtre de la Gaîté. The two-act version originally prevailed, but since the 1970s – when the four-act version came into vogue – productions have favoured a hybrid score.

Sénéchal, Mesplé, Burles, Trempont; Toulouse Capitole Chorus and Orchestra; Plasson.
(EMI CDS7 49647-2; 2 CDs).

This excellent 1978 recording, the only one available in French, perfectly captures the wild decadence of Offenbach's operetta. Using the expanded 1874 text, Plasson conjures a bubbling, stylishly played performance that benefits from some wonderfully arch singing from Mady Mesplé as Eurydice, Michel Sénéchal as Orpheus and Charles Burles as Pluto. A fruity wind band and booming percussion add to the fun – especially during the cancan – and the engineers have captured the whole in generous sound.

Fieldsend, Patterson, Suart, Hegarty; D'Oyly Carte Opera Chorus and Orchestra; Edwards.
(Sony SM2K 66616; 2 CDs).

This 1994 production of Jeremy Sams's hilarious translation of the 1858 edition was the first non-Gilbert & Sullivan work ever recorded by the D'Oyly Carte Company. Barry Patterson is completely over the top as Pluto and he curls his Scottish brogue around the ridiculous verse with tremendous wit; David Fieldsend is a lovably smug Orpheus; and Mary Hegarty (whose brilliantly flexible soprano is the recording's highlight) tramps her way through Eurydice. The words are clearly enunciated and Jonathan Edwards conducts a brisk, perfectly overstated performance that's sure to leave you smiling.

La belle Hélène

Beautiful Helen

Composed 1864.
First performed December 17, 1864.
Libretto by Henri Meilhac and Ludovic Halévy.

Synopsis

Act I

Sparta, before the Trojan War. The marriage of Helen (Hélène) to King Menelaus (Ménélaus) is floundering, for which Helen blames the Fates. Venus has announced that Paris, disguised as a shepherd, will win the hand of the most beautiful woman on earth. Calchas, the High Priest of Jupiter, reveals to Helen that he has heard rumours of a beauty competition. The kings of Greece enter and there follows a game of charades, the winner of which will receive his prize from Helen. When Paris is triumphant Helen invites him to dinner. Calchas tricks Menelaus into leaving the couple alone.

Act II

Helen initially resists Paris, but when he returns to her bedchamber at night, she thinks she is dreaming and the two begin to kiss. They are interrupted by Menelaus, who banishes Paris.

Act III

The kings have all left for their holidays in Nauplia, where they argue over what to do about Helen and Paris. Venus is furious that Paris has left and everyone blames Menelaus. However, Menelaus announces that he has invited the High Priest of Venus from Cythera to make amends on their behalf. The priest arrives and announces that only if Helen goes with him to Cythera will Venus forgive them. As they sail away, the priest reveals himself to be none other than Paris, thus setting off the Trojan War.

La belle Hélène, written six years after *Orphée*, again in collaboration with Ludovic Halévy, was just as sharp in its satire of Napoleon and French high society. The absurd game of charades won by Paris in Act I was a swipe at the Emperor and Empress, whose taste for party games was notorious; the royal excursion to the beach lampooned the Emperor's predilection for vacations, which were thought insensitive in view of the increasing tensions between France and Prussia; and the opera's last act, in which the king relies on the intervention of a third party to clear up the mess created by his own stupidity, was considered particularly critical of the Emperor, an expert at passing the buck for failed policies.

Chromatic harmonies, fizzing instrumental counterpoint and intriguingly developed melodies mark a departure from the simple verse structures of *Orphée*, and *La belle Hélène* also differs from its predecessor in its concentration on ensemble numbers rather than solos. Though there are some lovely solo numbers – not least Paris's delightful tenor cantilena "Au mont Ida" and Helen's lushly melancholic "Amours divins" – *Hélène* is, first and last, an operatic farce, driven by the usual apparatus of mistaken identities, manic exchanges and screaming caricatures. And as with *Orphée*, Offenbach's illustrious musical forebears and contemporaries are included in the roster of targets. To accompany the parade of the monarchs in Act I he ridicules the tournament music from Wagner's *Tannhäuser* (which Menelaus passes off as "German music I commissioned for the ceremony"); and when, during the final act, Agamemnon and Calchas attempt to convince Menelaus that he must give up Helen, Offenbach sets their trio to music that satirizes the chest-beating patriotism of Rossini's *William Tell* and Auber's *La Muette de Portici*. *Tell* suffers yet further humiliation when Paris, arriving disguised as a priest, breaks into Tyrolean yodelling. It is all completely daft, but it is also, as Bernard Shaw wrote, "wicked . . . abandoned stuff; every accent is a snap of the fingers in the face of moral responsibility".

Norman, Aler, Burles, Bacquier; Toulouse Capitole Chorus and Orchestra; Plasson.
(EMI CDS7 49647-2; 2 CDs).

Michel Plasson made this outstanding recording of *La belle Hélène* in 1984 as part of a series of Offenbach recordings. Jessye Norman is a little po-faced and grand as Helen, but there's never been a more beautiful-sounding interpretation of the part. John Aler is another whose voice might seem unsuited to Offenbach's flummery, but he uses his tenor to hilarious affect as Paris – yodelling and all. The sound is well balanced, and the orchestra play with zip and fizz.

La Périchole

Perichole

Composed 1868.
First performed October 6, 1868.
Libretto by Henri Meilhac and Ludovic Halévy, after Mérimée.

Act I

Peru, mid-eighteenth century. Don Andres (Andrès), the viceroy, is celebrating his birthday. Outside the Three Cousins Inn, Don Andres (in disguise) watches two gypsy singers, La Périchole and Piquillo. Unable to resist her beauty, the viceroy asks Périchole to be his Lady-in-Waiting. She agrees and pens a letter of farewell to Piquillo. However, form demands that she has to be married if she is to take the post, and so Don Andres arranges for a husband – he selects Piquillo, who is thus rescued from the brink of suicide.

Act II

Périchole is now Countess of Tabago, Lady-in-Waiting. Formality demands that she be presented to the viceroy by her husband; but Piquillo, not realizing that the Countess is Périchole, is less than keen to marry a complete stranger. However, when he realizes that Périchole is the Countess, and that she would have married anyone selected for her by the viceroy, he furiously denounces her for her treachery – and with such force that the viceroy sends him to prison where, to his horror, he meets a number of other recalcitrant husbands.

Act III

Locked in his cell, Piquillo wonders whether or not his wife will help. She duly arrives and melts his heart, and together they plan to bribe the jailer. Unfortunately, the jailer turns out to be the viceroy in yet another of his disguises and, in revenge, he chains Périchole to the wall opposite her husband. With the help of another prisoner, they abduct Don Andres and escape. Eventually, they give themselves up; Périchole appeals to the viceroy's good nature, and all three are granted their freedom.

Liberally adapted from a play by Prosper Mérimée, *La Périchole* is one of the most cutting of Offenbach's farces, and Napoleon III is once again at the centre of Offenbach's satirical universe, being ridiculed in the form of the self-important Don Andres. The opera was first performed in two acts (the third was added for the revival in 1874) at the Théâtre Variétés, where, thanks partly to the performance of Hortense Schneider as the soubrette Périchole, it triumphed. It was, nonetheless, to be the composer's last big success. By July 1870 France was at war with the expansionist Prussia; the following year the French were defeated, Napoleon was out, and the Second Empire came to an end. Offenbach spent the war in Spain, England and Austria, and when he returned he found the war-scarred French public was rapidly losing its taste for this kind of music.

La Périchole is the definitive French light opera, fusing a witty text to music that skips along with great flair. Incidents like the finale of Act I, in which Périchole gets herself drunk ("Ah, quel diner"), or the wonderfully absurd end of Act II, in which Offenbach creates an idiotic waltz from the individual syllables of the word "recalcitrant", are typical of his frivolous brilliance. But, anticipating the sobriety of *Les contes d'Hoffmann*, this work also has a serious tone that surprised critics and audiences who had come to expect Offenbach to serve up lashings of tuneful irreverence. *La Périchole* marked something of a departure in its realistic characterization of the volatile young lovers, who are given some of Offenbach's finest music to sing: Périchole's appeal to the viceroy's better nature ("La Clémence d'Auguste") is a ballad of perfect lyrical sweetness, while her farewell to the absent Piquillo, "O mon cher amant", is genuinely mournful, just as Piquillo's subsequent expression of despair avoids any hint of the broad irony which was an Offenbach trademark. Moreover, in his creation of Spanish colour through a series of boleros, seguidillas and fandangos, Offenbach strongly influenced Bizet when he came to write *Carmen* – another opera with a libretto derived by Meilhac and Halévy from a Mérimée play.

Crespin, Vanzo, Bastin, Friedmann; Rhine Opera Chorus; Strasbourg Philharmonic Orchestra; Lombard
(Erato 2292 45686-2; 2 CDs).

The first and, in most respects, the best recording of *La Périchole* was taped in 1976. The cast is French and Alain Lombard oversees a lively if somewhat detached performance, throughout which the delightful voices of Régine Crespin and Alain Vanzo shine – the latter is a warm and characterful Piquillo, while the former captures just the right amount of exaggeration as the sly, headstrong heroine. Jules Bastin is a fruity Don Andres, rich and nicely overdone, and the remaining cast all rise to the high standards. The sound is excellent, although the spoken dialogue has been omitted.

Le contes d'Hoffmann

The Tales of Hoffmann

Composed 1877–80, completed by Guiraud 1881.
First performed February 10, 1881.
Libretto by Barbier and Carré, after Hoffmann.

Synopsis

Prologue

Luther's Nuremberg wine cellar. Andrès, the servant of the prima donna Stella, and Lindorf, a Councillor of Nuremberg, enter the tavern. The latter discovers that the poet Hoffmann has arranged to meet with the singer after that night's show. The tavern is flooded with students during the interval of *Don Giovanni*, who plead with Hoffmann to sing them a story. He begins the tale of the hunchback, knock-kneed Kleinzach, but keeps breaking into a romance about Stella. He gestures towards Lindorf, informing the crowd that the Councillor has always tried to frustrate his love affairs and, drinking from the bowl of punch, he agrees to tell the story of his three great loves.

Act I

The first was called Olympia. The curtain rises on the room of the inventor Spalanzani. He has created a life-like mechanical doll that he hopes will make his fortune, but fears that his rival Coppélius, is planning to steal her. Hoffmann arrives and is intrigued by Olympia, whom he mistakes for the inventor's daughter. First Hoffmann's friend Niklausse arrives, and then Coppélius, who sells Hoffmann a pair of spectacles that make him fall in love with the doll, and then forces Spalanzani to recognize his share in the doll's success: he supplied the eyes. At dinner, Olympia begins to sing but her mechanism keeps winding down, obliging Spalanzani to keep turning the key in her back. Hoffmann is puzzled by her behaviour, but remains devoted nonetheless. Coppélius marches in, convinced that Spalanzani has tried to cheat him; after Hoffmann and Olympia dance a wild waltz, Coppélius destroys the doll. Hoffmann is saved.

Act II

Munich. The singer Antonia, a consumptive, has been hidden away by her father Crespel to escape Hoffmann, whose love has only made the girl's condition worse. Her father has ordered her not to sing, as this will endanger her life, but when Hoffmann arrives with Nicklausse it's not long before Hoffmann and Antonia are singing a passionate duet. The evil Dr Miracle arrives to examine Antonia. Crespel despises him as he thinks he killed his wife, and fears that he will do the same to his daughter. Hoffmann, now aware that singing is dangerous for Antonia, urges her not to sing, but the doctor tricks her into one last song; as he plays the violin her voice rises higher and higher until her strength gives way and she falls dead.

Act III

Venice. Hoffmann has renounced women – he would rather drink and listen to Giulietta sing. Even so, Nicklausse warns him that at the first sign of his falling in love he will drag him away. The mysterious Dappertutto enters, bearing a huge diamond which immediately transfixes Giulietta. He offers it to her in return for Hoffmann's soul (just as she helped steal Schlemil's), which she can gain only by making him look into Dappertutto's magic mirror. She easily seduces Hoffmann and gets him to look in the mirror. After fighting a duel with Schlemil for Giulietta's hand, Hoffmann finds that she has abandoned him in favour of the deformed Pittichinaccio.

Epilogue

Luther's tavern. Nicklausse suggests that the three women were all really Stella in disguise but he is too drunk to care and when she arrives he does not even recognize her. Lindorf rises to leave, and Stella joins him. The Muse of Poetry appears by Hoffmann's side and claims him for herself.

Le contes d'Hoffmann, Offenbach's first and last true opera (it's the only work he wrote to be sung throughout), was started in 1877 as a piece for the Thêatre de la Gaîté, but the vast project lasted longer than his theatre, which folded in 1878. Offenbach continued working on his opera and in May the following year he arranged for a private performance of some of its songs – in the presence of Léon Carvahlo, impresario of the Opéra-Comique. Carvahlo agreed to stage the premiere, but only if Offenbach replaced the sung recitative with spoken dialogue and only if the roles were rewritten for the company singers. Offenbach had originally written the title role for the baritone Jacques Bouhy (the first Escamillo), but he was now forced to rewrite it for the tenor Jean-Alexandre Talazac. He also rescored the three female leads – which were originally to be taken by the one singer – for coloratura, lyric and dramatic sopranos, making it necessary to cast each of them separately.

Offenbach's death in October the following year left much incomplete, including most of the orchestration. Ernest Guiraud was brought in to fill in the gaps from the composer's sketches, and it was ready for production by the end of January 1881, albeit in a mutilated form. It was a triumph, so much so that by the end of the year they were celebrating the one hundredth performance; but not until 1907 was it revised, again by Guiraud, in line with the composer's intentions – restoring the Venetian act and replacing the dialogue with recitative.

Having spent much of his life composing operettas, Offenbach was more or less obliged to tackle the more arduous genre of through-composed opera, now that the audience for his satires of Second Empire life had gone the way of Napoleon III (to say nothing of his desertion by Meilhac and Halévy). And to a great extent he succeeded, creating through Hoffmann's tales a much darker – even sinister – work of music-theatre, in which humour plays a relieving rather than a defining role. Hoffmann's failure to find love is the unifying motif of this proto-surrealist drama, for which Offenbach adapted his fizzing style to create longer, more complicated numbers that move in sympathy with the changing moods and situations of the text.

Inevitably, Offenbach did occasionally give in to the temptation to indulge in a comic turn, as in Olympia's coloratura "mechanical" aria "Les oiseaux dans la charmille", in which her voice drops in a huge glissando from high above the stave every time her mechanism runs low, and the aria given to the minor character Frantz in Act IV, in which he fails to make the high notes at the end of his scales. But this opera's finest moments are those in which the composer catches the dreamy melancholia of Hoffmann's tales. Antonia's touching "Elle a fui, la touterelle" is one such moment, but the two best-known examples are Hoffmann's opening aria ("The Legend of Kleinzach"), in which his jubilant tale is interrupted by his elegiac recollection of the face of his beloved, and the atmospheric intermezzo (better known as the Barcarole), which returns Hoffmann to the tavern and his despair in Act IV.

Offenbach knew he was dying when he wrote *The Tales of Hoffmann*. He had spent his life compromised: a master craftsman playing the music-hall, a German playing the Frenchman, a Jew pretending to be a Christian. His opera was a last-ditch attempt to undo some of these self-confessed "aberrations" and to gain critical respect. At the last, he did indeed prove himself to be an opera composer of the first rank.

RECORDINGS OVERVIEW

Of the ten complete recordings of *Les contes d'Hoffmann*, the very first remains a clear first choice, regardless of the mono sound; its chief rival is the first all-round stereo success, recorded by Decca in 1971 with the young Domingo as Hoffmann and the not-so-young Sutherland tackling all three soprano leads. In addition to these, performances conducted by Beecham (in English) and Monteux (live from the Met) have much to recommend them, as do EMI's 1965 studio recording (despite Schwarzkopf's awful Giulietta), and Kent Nagano's 1996 recording with Roberto Alagna and Sumi Jo. Jeffrey Tate's version for Philips (1991), on which the recitative is replaced with spoken dialogue, is an interesting approximation to the score played at the first production.

Jobin, Doria, Bovy, Musy; Paris Opéra-Comique Chorus and Orchestra; Cluytens.
(EMI CMS5 65260-2; 2 CDs).

More than any other, this 1948 recording captures the opera's native style: nothing is exaggerated and no-one tries to outdo anyone else (which is what happens on many later sets). The production has a tightness that is largely due to André Cluytens, whose direction is quick and spontaneous, urging some remarkably fruity playing from the Paris orchestra. Conductor and players create an ideal atmosphere for the perfect cast: Raoul Jobin is in splendid form; Renée Doria's Olympia is superbly sung and witty as well; and Vina Bovy's Giulietta is memorably lively. The remaining cast are excellent, and the mono sound is bright and well focused.

Domingo, Tourangeau, Sutherland, Bacquier; Suisse Romande Radio Chorus; Suisse Romande Orchestra; Bonynge.
(Decca 417 363-2DH2; 2 CDs).

This was one of Placido Domingo's first complete studio recordings and this set is above all a monument to the twenty-nine-year-old tenor. Joan Sutherland takes on the difficult task of singing all three heroines, as well as Stella in the Epilogue: she is triumphant as the coloratura Olympia, but gives somewhat flat performances as Giulietta and Antonia. That said, the voice is enjoyable whatever its limitations when it comes to characterization. Gabriel Bacquier is outstanding as all four villains, straining only when playing the bass Lindorf, and Bonynge gives a sprightly account of the score, though he replaces the recitative with spoken dialogue.

EDOUARD LALO

b. LILLE, FRANCE, JANUARY, 27 1823; d. PARIS, APRIL 22, 1892.

Edouard Lalo completed only two operas, but he always believed himself to be born to the theatre and, for all his fame as a composer of orchestral and chamber music, it was the first production of his opera *Le Roi d'Ys* in 1888 that brought him the greatest fulfilment of his career.

A gifted violinist, Lalo studied the instrument in Paris, having fled home to escape his dictatorial father, and soon took up composition lessons. Though he played for local orchestras and worked with Berlioz, his own compositions were almost exclusively in the genres of chamber music, and so it remained until 1866, when the announcement of an opera competition spurred him to return to writing music after a protracted period of depression. His entry, *Fiesque*, failed to win first prize and was never staged. Refusing to accept defeat, Lalo paid for the vocal score to be published and, continuing to prize the work above all his others, he made frustrated references to it in later compositions, notably his G minor symphony. In the 1870s his fame spread, mostly through the popularity of his *Symphonie espagnole*, but, for all his success in the concert hall, he was determined to write for the stage.

In 1875 he began to set *Le Roi d'Ys*, a libretto by Edouard Blau, and six years later he gave concert performances of excerpts from the opera. Yet no theatre showed any interest in staging it until 1888, when the Opéra-Comique agreed to put it on. Its huge popularity in France has survived into this century, and in Lalo's homeland it is for *Le Roi d'Ys* rather than the *Symphonie espagnole* that he is remembered. In 1891 he began a third opera, *La Jacquerie*, but he died having finished only the first act. Even though the material was almost entirely drawn from the previously rejected *Fiesque*, the bosses of the Monte Carlo opera house were suitably impressed to commission its completion, and in 1895 they mounted the first production.

Le Roi d'Ys

The King of Ys

Composed 1875; revised 1886.
First performed May 7, 1888.
Libretto by Edouard Blau, after the Breton legend of Ys.

Synopsis

Act I

Outside the palace of Ys, the people are celebrating the end of war – a peace brought about by the engagement of the king's daughter Margared to their enemy's leader Karnac. Margared is confronted by her sister Rozenn who is concerned that she appears so unhappy on the day that her wedding is announced. Margared admits that she is in love with a soldier who sailed with the hero Mylio on a ship of which no-one has heard anything since the cessation of hostilities. She then confesses her hatred for Karnac. Rozenn advises her to free herself before the contract is signed and then, left on her own, she sings of her love for Mylio – who suddenly appears by her side. At the wedding Rozenn tells Margared of Mylio's return. Assuming that her lover must also be with him, Margared denounces Karnac and refuses his hand in marriage. At this, Karnac swears revenge but then Mylio steps forward and vows to defend the city. To Margared's astonishment, she recognizes Mylio as the man with whom she fell in love.

Act II

Both sisters love the same man, but Rozenn has been given permission to marry Mylio if he is victorious. The jealous Margared plans with Karnac to destroy Ys by opening the floodgates protecting the city from the sea.

Act III

Rozenn and Mylio are married, and Margared and Karnac plot Ys's destruction; but when Margared hears her father and sister praying for her return, she is struck by remorse. Karnac has opened the gates, for which she kills him, and she then warns her family of their impending fate. The crowd pray for deliverance as half the city is washed away. Margared realizes that the waters need a sacrifice and hurls herself into the sea; the waters recede.

Lalo was primarily a master of small forms, specializing in chamber music and songs, many of which were inspired by and composed for his wife, Julie de Maligny. But it was difficult to make it as a composer in Paris without writing for the stage, and Lalo looked upon *Le Roi d'Ys* as something of a make-or-break. In the event the gamble paid off, even if some critics did carp about Lalo's "Wagnerism". The critics did have a point when they traced this opera's through-composed structure and outbreaks of surging orchestration to the influence of Wagner, and of course the plot has decidedly Wagnerian undertones. Furthermore, Lalo was to make his affiliations plain by consorting with the cabal known as *Le petit Bayreuth*. Nonetheless, *Le Roi d'Ys* is not a mere homage to Wagner, for in its melodies and sensuous harmonies it typifies the delicacy and musical epicurianism that is characteristic of much French music.

At times Lalo's lightness of touch is at odds with the gravity of the drama, notably during the sisters' confrontation and during the scene in which Margared and Karnac plot to destroy the city. However, Lalo's predilection for sweet sounds is often to the opera's advantage: Mylio's tenor aubade "Vainement, ma bien-aimée" is a delight, and the choruses heard during the wedding scene are among the most beautiful in all French opera. And occasionally Lalo toughens up his act, as when Margared begins to lose her grip on reality – her confession of guilt shortly before throwing herself into the raging orchestral waters is suitably harrowing.

Le Roi d'Ys is a schizophrenic opera: there's a bit of Wagner in the mix, while the melodies look back to Gounod and the scented harmonies look forward towards Debussy. It's not one of the seminal works of the nineteenth century, but it's an entertaining piece, best approached once you've got to know *Pelléas et Mélisande* (See p.361).

Hendricks, Ziegler, Villa, Courtis; French Radio Chorus and Philharmonic Orchestra; Jordan.
(Erato 2292 45015-2; 2 CDs).

Le Roi d'Ys is a comparatively little known opera outside France, but this luxuriant recording might bring about a change in its fortunes. The orchestra revels in the opulence of Lalo's score, but Armin Jordan keeps a firm control over the performance. The voices of Dolores Ziegler (Margared) and Barbara Hendricks (Rozenn) are ideally placed against one another, the former dark and theatrical, the latter light and graceful. Eduardo Villa brings a suitably heroic, if small-scale tenor to the fiendishly high-lying role of Mylio, and the lower voices, especially the evil Karnac (sung by Marcel Vanaud) are engagingly melodramatic.

CAMILLE SAINT-SAËNS

b. PARIS, OCTOBER 9, 1835; d. ALGIERS, DECEMBER 16, 1921.

By any standards Camille Saint-Saëns was a freakishly gifted child. As a two-year-old he could read and write and was picking out melodies on the piano. Shortly after his third birthday he began composing, and by the age of five he had given his first piano recital. At seven he was reading Latin, studying botany and developing what was to become an eighty-year interest in lepidoptery. As an encore after his formal debut as a concert pianist, the ten-year-old Camille offered to play any of Beethoven's thirty-two sonatas from memory. In short, his childhood suggested Mozartian potential, and yet it was a potential that was never fully realized. He once remarked that composing was as natural as "an apple tree producing apples". And there lay the problem. Like Mendelssohn, the technique came so easily to him that it virtually extinguished all inspiration.

That said, for many years he dominated French musical life and was widely considered to be France's greatest musical revolutionary, a reputation that grew more from his outspoken support of other composers' music – especially Wagner's – than from any work of his own. He is commonly remembered for his concert music, particularly the third symphony, but he composed for almost every conceivable instrument and situation, including the opera house. However, only one of his thirteen operas, *Samson et Dalila*, achieved any lasting success – a failure acutely regretted by Saint-Saëns, who believed his operatic music to be among his very best.

The heart of the problem with Saint-Saëns' operas is the absence of theatrical flair, even in a work tackling the lurid tale of Samson and Delilah. Haunted by the ghost of Mozart, he rejected the Wagnerian aesthetic of through-composition in favour of old-fashioned melody and closed-form arias and ensembles. His operas embody many of the traditional qualities of French music – neatness, clarity and elegance – but the concentration is on form at the expense of characterization and dramatic impact. Saint-Saëns wrote of himself that he "ran after the chimera of purity of style and perfection of form", echoing Berlioz's assessment that "he knows everything but experience".

Samson et Dalila

Samson and Delilah

Composed 1866–77.
First performed December 2, 1877.
Libretto by Ferdinand Lemaire.

Synopsis

Act I

The Jews lament their persecution by the Philistines. Samson calls upon his people and strengthens their weakening resolve. Their defiance provokes Abimélech, the satrap of Gaza, who scorns the Israelite God. Infuriated, Samson kills the satrap. The temple gates open and the High Priest of Dagon enters, surrounded by guards. A group of Philistine maidens, headed by Dalila, approach Samson, ostensibly to celebrate his valour; oblivious to warnings from the elders, Samson finds himself drawn to her.

Act II

Dalila is pursuaded by the High Priest to find the secret of Samson's strength. Samson arrives; though reluctant to reveal his secret, he is mesmerized by Dalila and betrays himself. Her cries of triumph summon the Philistines and, deprived of his hair, Samson is overpowered.

Act III

In a Gaza prison, Samson has been blinded. He is tormented by the voices of the Hebrews who sing of his apparent betrayal of them. Led by a child, the once mighty Samson is paraded into the temple before the mocking Philistines. He asks to be led to the temple's two central columns and, praying to God for the return of his strength, he brings the temple crashing down, burying himself and his people's oppressors.

𝄞 Deeply impressed by the English oratorio tradition, and in particular by Mendelssohn's *Elijah*, Saint-Saëns originally intended to use the Samson myth as the subject for an oratorio. However, the poet and dramatist Ferdinand Lemaire saw theatrical potential in the story and convinced Saint-Saëns to turn it into an opera. In 1870 Liszt agreed to produce the work in Weimar if Saint-Saëns ever completed it and, amazingly, he kept his word nearly eight years later. The French premiere didn't come until 1890, for despite Saint-Saëns' reputation, the Paris Opéra refused to stage a work based upon material from the Bible.

Although *Samson et Dalila* has the trappings of Grand Opéra – ballets, big choruses, lengthy ensembles and a fair amount of spectacle – it is otherwise typical of the composer's cerebral approach to opera. At times the piece seems more suited to a church than an opera house, and Saint-Saëns' taste for allusions to other composers (Bach for the Hebrews, Handel for the Philistines, a passing reference to Gounod as the satrap is killed) often suggest a man less interested in drama than in proving his cleverness. That said, much of Act III is sensationally dramatic, opening with Samson's melancholic treadmill aria "Vois ma misère, hélas" before plunging into the barnstorming barbarism of the bacchanal – Saint-Saëns' most impressive orchestral showpiece.

Some French critics attacked what they perceived as the tunelessness of *Samson*, a complaint that can most charitably be described as perverse. Samson's ardent tenor and Dalila's rich mezzo-soprano carry some of the most beautiful vocal music in French opera – music that was later to become central to the repertoire of Parisian organ grinders. Dalila's great Act II seduction aria, "Mon cœur s'ouvre á toi" (which becomes a duet with Samson), is rightly the best-known music, but her "Printemps qui commence" (at the end of Act I) and her vibrant, sensual call to love, "Amour! Viens aider ma faiblesse" (at the beginning of Act II), are no less fine. For moments such as these it is easy to forgive Saint-Saëns his somewhat calculated manner.

RECORDINGS OVERVIEW

There has not been a single professional recording of *Samson et Dalila* with a French tenor playing the hero, and there has only been one recording with a French heroine – the very first. Fortunately that performance is available on CD, as is the clear first-choice recording, conducted by Georges Prêtre. Of later efforts, Domingo's early version is preferable to his 1991 one, while Colin Davis's 1989 recording for Philips boasts Agnes Baltsa's outstanding Dalila but suffers from a strained, agonizing Samson from José Carerras.

Vickers, Gorr, Blanc, Diakov; René Duclos Chorus; Paris Opéra Orchestra; Prêtre.
(EMI CDS7 47895-8; 2 CDs).

Jon Vickers, one of the very genuine *Heldentenors* of his generation, made regrettably few complete opera recordings, but those he did make are all absolutely invaluable. This 1962 recording of a role with which he was synonymous is startling for the power and commitment of his singing, and he brings tragic grandeur to his death scene (as he did with Verdi's *Otello*). Rita Gorr is up against a formidable partner, but she wisely chooses not to go over the top – it is her dignity as much as her sexuality that conquers the hero. Ernest Blanc as the High Priest and Anton Diakov as both Abimélech and the Old Hebrew (a minor part) are more than satisfactory. Prêtre gives an unusually passionate reading, hurling caution to the winds during the second act, but this show is ruled from start to finish by the Canadian tenor. There are few more epic performances of French opera on CD.

Luccioni, Bouvier, Cabanel, Cambon; Paris Opéra Chorus and Orchestra; Fourestier.
(EMI CMS5 65263-2; 2 CDs).

Though Samson is sung by an Italian tenor, José Luccioni, this 1946 set is the closest any recording has come to capturing the French style and spirit of Saint-Saëns' opera. Fourestier phrases the music beautifully and the Opéra orchestra produces a warm and sensual Gallic sheen that's entirely distinctive. Hélène Bouvier's Dalila is unsentimental, her variations in tone giving her a dignity missing on later "evil harlot" interpretations. Luccioni made few recordings (competition was stiff in the '40s), but he was a dynamic, silky and beguiling tenor, even if he does sometimes overdo the heroics. The supporting cast and chorus are excellent and the transfers are outstanding.

Domingo, Obraztsova, Bruson, Thau; Paris Chorus and Orchestra; Barenboim.
(Deutsche Grammophon DG 413 297-2GX2; 2 CDs).

One of Barenboim's earliest recordings as an opera conductor, this 1978 *Samson et Dalila* has a Spanish Samson, a Russian Dalila, an Italian High Priest and a British Assur – the one concession to the opera's country of origin is Pierre Thau's Abimélech. Thanks to the fact that it was produced soon after a stage production in Orange, the performance has a cohesion that compensates for the dire pronunciation and lack of French style, and Barenboim's roller-coaster conducting certainly makes the bacchanal very exciting, even if his way with the text is a bit over-imaginative. Obraztsova is prone to wobble, but she's the most powerful Dalila on disc, while Domingo is in outstandingly energetic form.

LEO DELIBES

b. SAINT-GERMAIN-DU-VAL, FRANCE, FEBRUARY 21, 1836; d. PARIS, JANUARY 16, 1891.

Friedrich Nietzsche said he liked Leo Delibes because he had "no pretensions to depth", and Tchaikovsky preferred his music to that of Brahms and Wagner. Like his teacher Adolph Adam, who wrote "my only ambition is to compose music that is transparent, easy to understand and amusing to the public", Delibes was a committed populist, and his music is full of personality – albeit the personality of Meyerbeer, Gounod, Lalo, Bizet, Bellini and countless others, rather than his own. He may have possessed no strong musical identity, but Delibes achieved considerable fame during his lifetime and is the founder of modern symphonic ballet music. As a composer of opera he has just one enduring claim to fame, *Lakmé*.

After having worked as a chorister (singing in the first performance of Meyerbeer's *Le Prophète*) and later as a chorus master (assisting Gounod, Bizet and Berlioz), Delibes composed a string of enormously successful comic operas and operettas, mostly in the style of Offenbach. In 1870 he completed the ballet *Coppélia*, a work that displays his musical gifts at their most engaging, but although he now gave most of his time to dance music, Delibes did not entirely neglect the opera. Beginning in 1873, he wrote a trio of works for the Opéra-Comique, culminating in 1883 with the hugely successful *Lakmé*, a delightful orientalist confection.

Lakmé

Composed 1883.
First performed April 14, 1883.
Libretto by Edmond Gondinet and Philippe Gille, after Loti.

Synopsis

Act I

India, mid-nineteenth century. Two English army officers, Gérald and Frédéric, are in a sacred Brahmin grove, where Gérald becomes captivated by Lakmé, a Brahmin priestess. Her father, Nilakantha, spies the trespassers and swears revenge on Gérald for violating the holy ground.

Act II

Gérald and Frédéric are wandering through a local bazaar. Nilakantha forces his daughter to sing a Brahmin song to draw Gérald into the open. Lakmé warns Gérald of her father's plans, but later, during a procession, Nilakantha stabs Gérald.

Act III

Lakmé tends Gérald in a forest hut. She passes him a cup filled with a "magic" water that will ensure their eternal love; but Gérald is torn between his desire for Lakmé and his duty to his regiment. Frédéric stresses this responsibility to the army and when Lakmé realizes that Gérald is going to leave, she takes poison and dies.

Lakmé was first performed the year after the premiere of Wagner's *Parsifal*, but it comes from an entirely different world. It is a thoroughly conservative opera, constructed from separate numbers (including ballets) that are supported by an orchestra that rarely strays from the role of accompanist. Its survival owes everything to the melodic richness of the conventional soprano/tenor relationship between Lakmé and Gérald, and to Act I's sweetly expansive "Flower Duet" (used by *British Airways* and countless other advertisers), a set-piece that sounds like the work of an opium-smoking Bellini – indeed, *Lakmé* resembles an Italian bel canto opera as closely as it resembles any French opera. Gérald's "Fantasie aux divins mensonges" is one of the great French lyric tenor showpieces, and Lakmé's sparkling "Bell Song" (sung at the bazaar) not only reveals the composer's flair for Italianate melody and coloratura effect, but also his sensitive ear for orchestration. *Lakmé*'s delicate, very French and rather camp sound-world is all pastel shades, at its most alluring when providing a flutteringly orientalist accompaniment to the dialogue. However, the seductive lyricism of the vocal music is the key to *Lakmé*, the title role of which has long been a vehicle for celebrity sopranos – since the 1880s every lyric soprano, including Patti, Tetrazzini and Sutherland, has had a go.

Sutherland, Vanzo, Bacquier, Berbié: Monte Carlo Opera Chorus and Orchestra; Bonynge.
(Decca 425 485-2DM2; 2 CDs).

This 1967 recording was mounted as a showcase for the astonishing voice of Joan Sutherland, and "La Stupenda" is at her stupendous best here. She might just as well be singing the weather forecast for all the sense she makes of the text, but her larynx is so startling an instrument that it's futile to carp about niceties of characterization. There is much else to enjoy here, too. Alain Vanzo's slight but easy tenor navigates Gérald's high writing with grace and character, and Jane Berbié's mezzo Mallika provides some much-needed French style – where Sutherland shapes the sound, Berbié shapes the words. Bonynge keeps the ship moving steadily forward, holding the sentimentality in check.

GEORGES BIZET

b. PARIS, OCTOBER 25, 1838; d. BOUGIVAL, JUNE 3, 1875.

Like many other nineteenth-century opera composers, Georges Bizet attained immortality through the success of a single work. But whereas most of the others lived to enjoy their good fortune, and in some cases thrived off it for the rest of their lives, Bizet's triumph was posthumous. *Carmen* was given its first, calamitous performance in March 1875, and although it received many more performances during its first run than any of his previous works, the composer was badly affected by the adverse criticism *Carmen* had received. Plagued by illness and obsessed by what he took to be his failure, he died in June; it wasn't long before *Carmen* began its unstoppable rise to international popularity. At his death Bizet was acclaimed as a composer of concert music who had regrettably dabbled with the theatre. However, he had devoted the greater part of his short life to opera, and it was for the stage that he wrote his greatest music.

Bizet was frighteningly precocious, reading music by the age of four and playing the piano to "a high standard" by the time he was six. Three years later he was playing Mozart sonatas from memory, and before his tenth birthday he was admitted to the Paris Conservatoire, where he was to study with Jacques-François Halévy (whose daughter he later married). He learned most through his private lessons with Charles Gounod during the 1850s, and by the time he was sixteen there was little basic theory that Gounod could teach him. Instead he gave him other composers' music to arrange, including his own, and assisted in the gestation of Bizet's first major work, the *Symphony in C*, which was composed in 1855. Bizet's first operas date from around this time, but they were Italianate creations which Bizet later disowned, along with almost everything from this period.

By the 1860s the influence of Gounod, Meyerbeer and Halévy was beginning to take the place of Donizetti and Rossini, as was clear from his first important opera, *Les Pêcheurs de Perles* (The Pearlfishers), in which a distinctive lyrical voice emerged from amid the Grand Opéra clutter. His next work for the theatre, *La Jolie Fille de Perth* (completed in 1866 and first performed the following year), compounded the success of *Les Pêcheurs de Perles* and it seemed as if Bizet was getting into his stride. However, not one of his next five projects got any further than sketches, and only after finishing Halévy's *Noé* in 1869 did he complete his next opera, the one-act *Djamileh*. First performed at the Opéra-Comique in 1872, it so impressed the theatre's director, Camille du Locle, that Bizet was invited to collaborate on a full-length work with the librettists Henri Meilhac and Ludovic Halévy

(Offenbach's former sidekicks). Bizet suggested they adapt Prosper Mérimée's novella *Carmen*, and by the summer of 1874 the orchestration was complete. He had no doubts as to his opera's quality: "They make out that I am obscure, complicated, tedious, more fettered by technical skill than lit by inspiration. Well this time I have written a work that is all clarity and vivacity, full of colour and melody."

Unfortunately, the Parisian critics – fired by du Locle's embittered co-director De Leuven, who had resigned over the obscenity of showing the murder of a woman on "his" stage – did not share his opinion. Headed by Léon Esçudier, who wrote "the composer has made up his mind to show us how learned he is, with the result that he is often dull and obscure", they littered their attacks with words such as "vulgar", "undramatic", "unoriginal", "suffocating" and "contemptible". A small band of devotees hailed *Carmen* as a masterpiece, but Bizet was shattered. Three months and two heart attacks later, he died, aged thirty-six.

In an age dominated by Verdi and Wagner, Bizet was one of the very few opera composers to create a genuinely individual style. His music might have evolved from the *opéra lyriques* of Gounod and Delibes, but with *Carmen* he took French opera into a new dimension. In his homeland it was Massenet who most strongly continued where Bizet had left off, and in Russia his legacy is clear in the operas of Tchaikovsky, but it was in Italy that Bizet had the biggest impact, for *Carmen* can truly be called the very first verismo opera, even though it precedes the verismo era by two decades.

Les Pêcheurs de Perles

The Pearlfishers

Composed 1863.
First performed September 30, 1863.
Libretto by Eugène Cormon and Michael Carré.

Synopsis

Act I

A group of pearlfishers have gathered on the Ceylonese coast in preparation for an expedition. They choose Zurga as their chief and swear absolute obedience to him. Zurga's friend, the hunter Nadir, then enters and the two remember their last meeting, when they both fell in love with a beautiful priestess (Leïla), whom they agreed never to pursue, thus ensuring the security of their friendship. A canoe arrives, from out of which steps a veiled priestess, who has been sent to bless the fishermen and their new season. It is Leïla, and within minutes she and Nadir have fallen in love.

Act II

The high priest Nourabad warns Leïla that she risks death if she breaks any of her vows (primarily virginity); she defends her good name, but is soon singing a passionate love duet with Nadir. They are discovered by Nourabad, who curses them both. Zurga upholds his right to be their judge; when he lifts Leïla's veil and sees who she is, he is inflamed by rage and condemns them to death.

Act III

Left to himself, Zurga regrets his decision. Leïla begs him to save Nadir, but this only intensifies his jealousy. However, he has noticed the necklace she is wearing: it is the one he gave years ago to the girl who hid him from his enemies. Nourabad leads Leïla to the funeral pyre, but Zurga has set fire to the fishermen's camp; as the fishermen flee, Zurga releases the prisoners and reveals that he was the fugitive whose life she had saved. He helps the lovers onto a boat and pushes them to safety, remaining to die in the flames.

Les Pêcheurs de Perles, Bizet's second opera to reach the stage, lasted just eighteen performances, for few critics shared Berlioz's opinion that it contained a "considerable number of beautiful, expressive pieces filled with fire and rich colouring". *Le Figaro* wrote that "there were no fishermen in the text and no pearls in the music", and the first part of the complaint is fairly close to the target – upon hearing the music, Bizet's librettists expressed embarrassment at having palmed him off with such a feeble text, though to be fair to them they had been saddled with a composer who kept prevaricating about exactly what is was he wanted. Bizet's own judgement of *Les Pêcheurs* as "an honourable, brilliant failure" is a fair summary of an opera whose appeal depends to a large extent on the audience's ability to ignore what the singers are singing about.

The opening prelude and choruses are cast in the Grand Opéra mould, and the Grand Opéra tradition is a strong presence throughout *Les Pêcheurs*, with its plethora of lusty choruses, "scenic" introductions (which establish the context while leading into a dramaturgically pointless solo or ensemble) and big-scale orchestrations. But Bizet transcends these clichés, using spicy harmonies and uneven rhythms to conjure a plausibly exotic setting, and by spicing the score with some of the sweetest songs in all French opera – like his teacher Gounod, to whom the vocal score of *Les Pêcheurs* is much indebted, Bizet was primarily a melodist. Nadir's lyrical Act I aria "Je crois entendre encore", famous for its hypnotic momentum and beautifully placed high As, is perhaps the finest moment, although the most famous is the duet, also in Act I, between Nadir and Zurga, "Au fond du temple saint" (the refrain of which is used as a "friendship" motto throughout the score). Also striking is Bizet's recitative, in which the tension of the sentiment rises in parallel with the pitch of the line – as during Nadir's "A cette voix", in which he laments what appears to be his and his lover's imminent execution.

For all the beauty of their music, however, neither Zurga nor the unfortunately christened Nadir is much developed, and it is difficult to feel much sympathy for them or their dilemma. Indeed, Bizet himself sometimes seems to have taken his eye off the action: Zurga's sacrifice, the opera's emotional climax, is preceded by an unsuitably jubilant trio, and the repetition of the "friendship" motif (by Nadir and Leïla) as Zurga goes up in smoke is frankly absurd. Unlikely characters in impossible situations are part of the fun of Grand Opéra, but the best parts of *Les Pêcheurs* hint that Bizet was capable of something vastly superior – and with *Carmen* he was to prove it.

RECORDINGS OVERVIEW

There's half a dozen versions of *Pearlfishers* on CD, of which the two listed below give the best all-round account of the opera. Should you fail to track down either of them, or find the idea of mono recordings intolerable, good alternatives are EMI's budget-price 1977 recording, with Cotrubas and Vanzo swooningly impressive as the lovers, or EMI's mid-price 1961 set with Micheau and Gedda.

Alarie, Simoneau, Bianco, Depraz; Brasseur Chorus; Lamoureux Concert Orchestra; Fournet.
(Philips 434 782-2PM2; 2 CDs).

This is one of the most sublime examples of lyric tenor singing on record. Leopold Simoneau's performance as Nadir is effortlessly beautiful, and he takes his time over even the most exacting phrases, with not even a suggestion of a break between the vocal registers. Pierrette Alarie is a likable, sweet-toned Leïla and René Bianco makes a solid if unremarkable Zurga. Fournet's conducting of the stylish Lamoureux Orchestra downplays the bluster, and the 1953 mono sound is more than acceptable.

Angelici, Legay, Dens, Noguera; Opéra-Comique Chorus and Orchestra; Cluytens.
(EMI CMS5 65266-2; 2 CDs).

Taped two years later than the Philips set, this account is especially notable for Cluytens' conducting – his feel for shape, colour and detail is without equal, while the luscious tone of the Opéra-Comique Orchestra, with their reedy wind section and soupy strings, is an irresistible sound. The cast is a classic ensemble gathering of the 1950s. Martha Angelici's light and fluttery Leïla and Henry Legay's almost femininely smooth Nadir are enjoyable, but the real gem is baritone Michael Dens's Zurga, a classic portrayal for which he was famous long before making this recording. You'll soon forget the limitations of the mono sound.

Carmen

Composed 1873–75.
First performed March 3, 1875.
Libretto by Henri Meilhac and Ludovic Halévy, after Mérimée.

Synopsis

Act I

In Seville's town square Micaëla is trying to find Don José, a corporal in the army. He arrives just as the girls leave the cigarette factory for their break. One of them, Carmen, sings of her fickle attitude towards love and throws a flower to Don José before returning to work. Micaëla brings Don José a letter in which his ailing mother urges him to take Micaëla for his wife. José is about to throw the flower away when Carmen comes running out of the factory, having cut a girl's face in a fight. After refusing to answer Captain Zuniga's questions, she is arrested. Don José is chosen to guard her cell; unable to resist her charms, he allows her to escape and is himself arrested.

Act II

Carmen is dancing in Lillas Pastia's inn. Zuniga tells her that Don José is about to be released after a month in prison, then in bursts Escamillo, the champion bullfighter. He and Carmen are immediately drawn to one another but Carmen chooses to remain faithful to Don José, although she tells Escamillo not to lose hope. After the bar empties, the smugglers Le Remendado and Le Dancaïre arrive and inform

Carmen of their plans for the evening. To their amazement, she refuses to accompany them, claiming to be in love. Carmen is reunited with Don José, but her joy turns to fury when he tells her that he is expected back at his barracks. Zuniga arrives, hoping to find Carmen alone. Don José attacks him, but the arrival of two other soldiers prevents the violence from ending in murder. Having threatened a senior officer, Don José is now a wanted man, and so he agrees to run away with Carmen.

Act III

In the mountains, Carmen has begun to tire of Don José. They are constantly arguing and he begins to regret having broken his promise to his mother that he would marry Micaëla. Escamillo and Don José fight over Carmen and the toreador's life is only just saved by Carmen. Micaëla visits Don José and tells him that his mother is dying. They leave together.

Act IV

The day of Escamillo's bullfight in Seville. Carmen has been warned that Don José is in the crowd, desperate for revenge. They meet behind the ring. Don José begs her to join him, but she is scornful and throws his ring to the floor. He stabs her to death as the crowd salutes the victorious Escamillo.

𝄞 Bizet once wrote in a letter – "I tell you that if you were to suppress adultery, fanaticism, crime, evil and the supernatural, there would no longer be the means for writing one note." This credo was given substance with *Carmen*, an opera that came as a shock to the first-night audience at the Opéra-Comique, a theatre in which the traditional diet was somewhat lighter than this tale of erotic obsession and murder. *Carmen* is the great forerunner of verismo opera, the hot-blooded genre typified by *Cavalleria rusticana* and *I Pagliacci*, but there's far more to *Carmen* than the venting of extreme passions – its earthy vitality is the product of a hugely sophisticated musician.

"If you want to learn how to orchestrate, don't study Wagner's scores, study the score of Carmen.... Every note and every rest is in its proper place". So wrote Richard Strauss, and indeed Bizet's orchestration is outstandingly inventive. Whereas wind instruments had conventionally just provided a bit of colour, here they are used to state leading themes, as in the "Seguidilla" and the "Flower Song", while violins are used to imitate guitars and mimic a sliding vocal manner. Instruments are also used to emphasize character (Carmen is symbolized by the flute), and the complicated use of motif – such as the augmented second associated with inexorable fate – help tie the score together. Local colour is achieved with spicy dissonances, sliding harmonies, and some of the liveliest rhythms to be heard in all opera. The dances and gypsy songs create a thrilling synthesis of Spanish culture, but most of the "authentic" tunes are the composer's own invention.

Carmen herself is frequently rated as the most successful mezzo role in all opera, and her manipulative and magnetic personality is articulated through music of graphic sensuality – her opening habañera and seguidilla are especially sexy. Her hyperbolic sensuality emphasizes the plodding egotism of the muscle-bound baritone Escamillo, whose music is typified by the swaggering "Toreador" song. Similarly, the simplicity of the conceited bullfighter highlights the complexities of the impulsive tenor Don José, the emotional axis of the drama. Don José's disintegration – revealed through music that moves from the tender Act I duet with Micaëla, "Parle-moi de ma mère", via the impassioned plea to Carmen, "La fleur que tu m'avais jetée" (the "Flower Song"), to the ravings of his final confrontation with his "demon" – is a masterpiece of progressive characterization. The tempestuous relationship between Don José and Carmen culminates in one of opera's most gripping finales. Resisting the temptation to end his work with an unbroken song (which is what Gounod, Delibes and Saint-Saëns habitually did), Bizet constructs a duet of short and powerful exchanges, a fitful dialogue that conveys the fracturing of José's mind as powerfully as it does the shallowness of Carmen's affections. The culmination, in which he howls one final wounded cry of devotion to the corpse at his feet, is amazingly intense.

By 1905 *Carmen* had received over a thousand performances at the Opéra-Comique alone, and nowadays it is securely placed as one of the dozen most frequently played operas in the world. It's a drama that has something for just about everybody, charting extremes of emotions with which everyone can sympathize through a series of irresistible tunes. As Nietzsche enthused: "Bizet's music seems to me perfect. It comes forward lightly, gracefully, stylishly.... This music is wicked, refined, fatalistic."

RECORDINGS OVERVIEW

Put on disc twice in 1928, *Carmen* was one of the first operas to be recorded complete, and new versions have emerged at least every five years since the 1950s. Famous Carmens include Risë Stevens, Victoria

CARMEN THE BODICE-RIPPER

The American soprano **Minnie Hauk** (1851–1929) was a very successful singing-actress – so successful that she could afford to buy Wagner's villa at Triebschen for her retirement. She was widely celebrated for her performances as Carmen, but it is unlikely that she would have wanted to be remembered for this one, given in 1880 and recorded in the memoirs of the impresario James Henry Mapleson.

"It was in the middle of the third act, when Don José, the tenor Ravelli, was about to introduce an effective high note which generally brought down the house. Carmen rushed forward and embraced him – why, I could never understand. Being interrupted at the moment of his effect, he was greatly enraged, and by his movements showed that he had resolved to throw Madame Hauk into the orchestra. But she held firmly onto his red waistcoat, he shouting all the time "Laissez-moi, laissez-moi!", until all the buttons flew off. . . . Ravelli rushed forward and exclaimed "Regardez, elle a déchiré mon gilet!" [Look, she's ripped my jacket!] and with such rage that he brought down thunders of applause, the people believing this genuine expression of anger to be part of the play."

Ravelli remained in a fury about his ruined high note and outfit, and the newspapers reported that the show featured a tenor who "was always threatening to murder the primadonna". The primadonna's husband duly felt obliged, as Mapleson records, to "take up a position at one of the wings bearing a revolver with which he proposed to shoot the tenor the moment he showed the slightest intention of approaching the personage for whom he is supposed to entertain an ungovernable passion." Mapleson's account of this bizarre *Carmen* concludes: "it was an understood thing between the singers impersonating these two characters that they were to keep a respectful distance from one another. Ravelli was afraid of Minnie Hauk's throttling him while engaged in the emission of a high B flat; and Minnie Hauk, on her side, dreaded the murder with which Ravelli again and again had threatened her. Love-making looks, under such conditions, a little unreal."

de los Angeles, Grace Bumbry and, of course, Maria Callas. Some might find it a little odd that we haven't recommended Callas's 1964 reading, but with such competition her undeniably exciting performance (one she never gave on stage) is not enough to justify putting up with Nicolai Gedda's Don José and Robert Massard's Escamillo. Masochists might want to sample Decca's 1963 *Carmen* with Regina Resnik and Mario del Monaco. Resnik's Carmen is angry and little else, del Monaco's tenor would have brought Jericho to its knees, the "Flower Song" contains three accurately pitched notes and the final duet is little more than a shouting match. A candidate for the title of Worst Opera Recording Ever.

Price, Corelli, Freni, Merrill; Vienna State Opera Choir; Vienna Philharmonic Orchestra; Karajan.
(RCA GD86 199; 3 CDs).

Very few of the twenty-odd records of *Carmen* have featured French principals, but this set might seem to be taking things too far: it has an American Carmen and Escamillo, an Italian Don José and Micaëla and an Austrian conductor directing an Austrian orchestra and chorus. However, with Karajan in thrilling form, Leontyne Price a glowing Carmen, Franco Corelli a testosterone-driven Don José – interpolated high notes and all – and Mirella Freni a fragile but yearning Micaëla, the chemistry of this set is uniquely explosive. Some find Karajan's tempi slow, and everyone agrees that whatever Corelli is singing it isn't French, but for vocal splendour, unity of conception and high production values, this *Carmen* tops the bill.

Berganza, Domingo, Cotrubas, Milnes; Ambrosian Singers; London Symphony Orchestra; Abbado.
(Deutsche Grammophon DG 419 636-2GH3; 3 CDs).

This is a superbly professional *Carmen*, featuring some of the best singers the world had to offer in 1977. Domingo is a smooth but powerful Don José, Teresa Berganza is a very sexy Carmen, vocally magnificent and suggesting a youthful capriciousness so often missing from modern interpretations. Sherrill Milnes struts through the role of Escamillo and delivers his "Toreador Song" with splendid oomph, while Ilena Cotrubas is a vibrant, if unusually weighty Micaëla. The London forces provide precise support, and if the momentum sometimes flags slightly (the sessions were rather protracted), it doesn't detract too much from what is the most Spanish *Carmen* on record.

Michel, Jobin, Angelici, Dens; Paris Opéra-Comique Chorus and Orchestra; Cluytens.
(EMI CMS5 65318-2; 2 CDs).

This 1950 *Carmen* is the only French performance currently available, and it amply proves how much is to be gained from the French style of phrasing, pronunciation and pacing. The sweetness of the voices and the smoothness of the momentum are marvellous and there is a unique character to the French orchestra, with its biting wind section and sliding strings. Solange Michel is a light-voiced Carmen but she possesses an agile, flirtatious voice and is engagingly temperamental. Raoul Jobin is the most Gallic Don José on record, virile and dangerous but with an elegance of line that gives his "Flower Song" rare tenderness. André Cluytens was a stalwart of the Opéra-Comique and he gives a brisk reading of an edited score.

EMI
CLASSICS
Bizet
Carmen
Solange Michel
Raoul Jobin
Martha Angelici
Michel Dens
André Cluytens
l'Opéra-Comique

EMMANUEL CHABRIER

b. AMBERT, FRANCE, JANUARY 18, 1841; d. PARIS, SEPTEMBER 13, 1894.

Owing partly to the anti-German feeling engendered by the hostilities that came to a head with the Franco-Prussian war, French composers were resistant to Wagner until the early 1880s, by which time he was dead. Things then changed rapidly. As Romain Rolland wrote in *Musicians of Today*: "From 1885, Wagner's work acted directly or indirectly on the whole of artistic thought, even on religious and intellectual thought of the most distinguished people of Paris. . . . Writers not only discussed musical subjects, but judged painting, literature, and philosophy, from a Wagnerian point of view." The greatest of Wagner's French disciples was Emmanuel Chabrier, and yet as a composer of opera he is remembered nowadays chiefly for *Le roi malgré lui*, a work that owes nothing to Wagner.

Chabrier's parents, like Berlioz's, thought music an unsuitable career for their son, and they forced him into studying law. Nonetheless he persisted with private musical studies, and even after taking a position in the Parisian civil service he spent all his free time with artistic luminaries: among his friends were the poets Paul Verlaine and Catulle Mendès (both of whom would later provide him with libretti), Manet and various other painters, and a number of France's most celebrated composers, including Fauré, Chausson, Duparc and D'Indy – the circle that would later form "Le Petit Bayreuth", the core of the French Wagnerian movement.

In 1880, a year after seeing a performance of *Tristan und Isolde* in Munich, Chabrier resigned his government post to concentrate on composition. Financial necessity at first compelled him to write operettas – a genre in which he had already enjoyed success with *L'étoile* (1877) – but in 1883, after working on some of Wagner's music as a chorus director in Paris, Chabrier began his first obviously Wagnerian opera: *Gwendoline*. It was first performed in 1886 but failed to bring him the acclaim he had hoped for – partly because a sizable portion of the Parisian public was still not keen on anything that smacked of Germanic music. Meanwhile, Chabrier commenced an opéra comique, *Le roi malgré lui*, the premiere of which, in 1887, succeeded where *Gwendoline* had failed, broadcasting his name overseas. Both the opera and the composer were championed by the star tenor Ernest van Dyck and the conductor Felix Mottl, and in 1889, thanks to the enthusiasms of the latter, *Gwendoline* was played throughout Germany – notably in Munich and Leipzig. At his death Chabrier was working on a Wagnerian lyric drama named *Briséïs*.

The operas produced by "Le Petit Bayreuth" have not survived in good shape – within ten years of Chabrier's death Debussy was to show the way out of the dead-end of French Wagnerism by creating an opera that was innovative and unequivocally French. Chabrier has maintained a place in the opera house on the strength of one major excursion from the Wagnerian path.

Le roi malgré lui

King, Despite Himself

Composed 1886.
First performed May 17, 1887.
Libretto by Emile de Najac, Paul Burani and the composer, after Ancelot.

Synopsis

Act I

Poland, 1574. Henry of Valois is about to be crowned king of Poland when he hears of a plot to abduct and expel him from the country. Although he would rather be in France, duty compels him to remain; disguised as his friend Nangis (whom he has arrested to get him out of the way), he attends a local ball.

Act II

There he meets Count Laski, the Archduke of Austria's aide, who has been promoting his master's cause as rival for the crown. Thanks to the unwitting help of Alexina, the Duchess of Fritelli, Henry worms his way into Laski's conspiratorial ring and is forced to take part in a lottery to see which of the conspirators is to kill the king. Henry draws the short straw and is given the honour of assassinating himself. Nangis is helped to freedom by the Polish slave Minka, who believes him to be the king.

Act III

The Archduke flees when his scheme is discovered. At an inn Henry (still disguised as Nangis) hides as Minka bursts in, desperate to find the king, and when she is told that he is dead she prepares to stab herself. At the last minute, the real Nangis enters and Henry, though determined to return to France, is persuaded to accept the Polish crown.

The plot of *Le roi malgré lui* is so complicated that you have to keep the libretto close at hand if you want to make sense of what's happening. But the grace, gaiety and lyricism of Chabrier's last completed opera make it his masterpiece, as critics of the time proclaimed – indeed Maurice Ravel went so far as to proclaim that he "would rather have written *Le roi malgré lui* than the *Ring of the Nibelung*".

Chabrier's score is packed with playful rhythms and sprightly melodies (the Act II dance music, *Fête Polonaise*, is great fun) and decorated with splashes of Polish and Hungarian local colour, a memorable episode being the spicy mazurka of Act III. The pace is frequently frenetic, especially as the acts draw to a close: Act I ends in a flurry of exclamations that bring Offenbach to mind, and the crazy contrapuntal bustle of Act II's finale might have come from the out-takes from Berlioz's *Béatrice et Bénédict*. Showing a very un-Wagnerian sense of humour, Chabrier assigns to Laskia a parodically doleful mazurka in the first act ("Le Polonais est triste et grave"), puts sarcastic references to Berlioz's *Marche Hongroise* in Alexina's absurd outbursts during Act III, and even takes a swipe at the composer of *Tristan* by aping that opera's portentous opening.

In amongst the knockabout stuff there's some rather touching music, the best of it being for women's voices. The Act II interlude, with its small female chorus and a stirring solo from Minka, is particularly lovely, and the duet between the sopranos Minka and Alexina in Act III is simply exquisite. A darker mood appears in Laski's bass romance "L'amour, ce divin maître", but the opera is otherwise distinguished by its sweetness and good nature – qualities not normally associated with one of the pillars of the French Wagnerian movement.

Hendricks, Garcisanz, Quilico, Jeffes; French Radio Chorus and New Philharmonic Orchestra; Dutoit.
(Erato 2292-45792-2; 2 CDs).

It is a shame that Dutoit conducts the first and only recording of *Le roi malgré lui* with a heavily cut score and all the linking recitative omitted. Nonetheless, this attentive performance should help spread the word about this opera beyond France. As ever, Barbara Hendricks is an irresistible presence and her sparkling performance as Minka sits comfortably next to the flowing tenor of Peter Jeffes (Nangis). Gino Quilico's Henry and Isabel Garcisanz's Alexina are no less captivating (the latter's Act III duet with Hendricks is a gem), and all four leads revel in the fluent melodies. The recorded sound is clear and well-spaced.

ERNEST CHAUSSON

b. PARIS, JANUARY 20, 1855; d. LIMAY, JUNE 10, 1899.

Ernest Chausson completed only one opera, *Le roi Arthus*, but it is arguably the most successful of all the French homages to Wagner. It wasn't hugely popular in Chausson's homeland (the French public never fell for Wagner as did some French composers), and nobody would argue that it is a masterpiece, but it does constitute a fascinating document – the last flaring of Wagner's influence in France before the arrival of the deeply un-Wagnerian talent of Debussy.

Born into a wealthy family, Chausson was a talented child and throughout his teenage years displayed a gift not just for music but for painting and poetry as well. Yet his father, like the progenitors of so many composers, did not think music a suitable career for his son and forced him into studying law. In 1877 Chausson duly qualified as a barrister but, having fulfilled his family's wishes, he refused to go into legal practice. Reluctantly, his father now agreed to support him in his desire to pursue a life in music and in 1879 Chausson began his studies, first with Massenet and later with César Franck. In the same year he travelled to Munich, where he witnessed a production of the *Ring* cycle; the influence of Wagner was strengthened in 1880, when Chausson saw *Tristan und Isolde*, and in 1882, when he managed to get a ticket for the first performance of *Parsifal*.

He and his wife, Jeanne Escudier (dedicatee of his tone-poem *Viviane*, subtitled "On a Legend of the Round Table"), spent their honeymoon at Bayreuth, then settled into a quiet and easy existence, in which *Le roi Arthus* occupied him on and off for nine years from 1886. Although Chausson never played anything more than a peripheral role in French musical life, his soirées, which brought together the likes of Mallarmé, Debussy and Albéniz, were famous. He died, aged only forty-four, in a fall from his bicycle, a bathetic end for one of the last great French Romantics.

Le roi Arthus

King Arthur

Composed 1886–95.
First performed November 30, 1903.
Libretto by the composer.

Synopsis

Act I

Arthur (Arthus) celebrates victory over the Saxons and embraces his first knight Lancelot, little realizing that Lancelot is having an affair with his wife Guenevere (Gueniѐvre). Mordred discovers the lovers together; in the ensuing fight Mordred is wounded by Lancelot but manages to escape. Arthur is horrified by the news of his wife's adultery and sends for Lancelot, who ignores the King's summons and elopes with Guenevere.

Act II

Arthur visits his wizard Merlin, who confirms his wife's love for Lancelot and then tells him his kingdom is doomed to fall. Arthur swears revenge and, taking up Excalibur, he leaves Camelot. When the two men confront each other Lancelot refuses to fight and flees. Guenevere is horrified at his refusal to champion her and strangles herself with her own hair.

Act III

Arthur has lost his throne to Mordred and he and Lancelot have one final battle in which Lancelot is mortally wounded. Arthur forgives the dying knight and steps onto a skiff that will bear him to Avalon.

At various stages in his life Chausson contemplated at least ten different operatic projects, including pieces based on writings of Shakespeare, Cervantes and Schiller, but it is no great surprise that the one completed opera by this dedicated Wagner fan should have been based upon the legend of Arthur and Guenevere. The score builds to C-major choral apotheosis, like *Parsifal*, but the clearest debt is to *Tristan*, with its series of opulent love duets for tenor and soprano (the first, in Act I, directly quotes the prelude of *Tristan*), and its focus on three love-torn characters, mirroring the *ménage à trois* of Tristan, Isolde and Marke. But the atmosphere of *Le roi Arthus* is quite unlike the morbid air of *Tristan*, for Chausson takes the Arthurian narrative straight, rather than as an opportunity for deep pyschosexual exploration.

Chausson's treatment of Lancelot and Guenevere highlights how unlike his hero he was. In Wagner's masterpiece the eroticism of the relationship between Tristan and Isolde saturates almost every bar of the score and governs the structure of the entire piece, delaying its climactic moment to the very end of the drama. Here the soprano and tenor voices reach their highest pitch in Act I, and though there are more duets to come Lancelot and Guenevere don't form the axis of the work in the same way as Wagner's lovers do – indeed, Guenevere doesn't even survive into the final act. Moreover, the music they sing is ardently lyrical, anticipating Massenet rather than echoing Wagner, just as the orchestral music is immediately recognizable as the product of a French composer. True, Chausson's technique has Wagnerian features: he uses leitmotifs to tie things together; he steadily charges the atmosphere by piling layers of rising chromatic melody on top of one another; and his orchestrations are remarkably heavy by French standards, using the contrapuntal drama of the orchestra to illuminate the feelings of his protagonists. For all that, Chausson's writing has a frankness that's far removed from the sometimes neurotic fervour of Wagner, a guileless quality that's typified by Arthur's profoundly moving forgiveness of Lancelot, and the following sequence, which leads to his stepping aboard the Avalon-bound ship – an unforgettable passage, awash with delicate string textures.

Quilico, Zylis-Gara, Winbergh, Massis; French Radio Chorus; New Philharmonic Orchestra; Jordan.
(Erato 2292 45407; 3 CDs).

This 1986 recording (the only version of *Arthus* in the catalogue) has a somewhat washy sound that perfectly suits Chausson's music. Armin Jordan is an enthusiastic protagonist and he phrases the large orchestral lines with a fine ear for colour – especially during the finale, where he creates a wonderfully mystical atmosphere. Gino Quilico is a warm-sounding King, underplaying the madness that grips him when he discovers his wife's adultery; Gösta Winbergh, regardless of the light, Mozartian character of his tenor, injects heroic stature into Lancelot's music. Teresa Zylis-Gara was twenty years past her best when she recorded Guenevere and her soprano is not seductive enough, but she can turn up the tension when required.

ARTHUR SULLIVAN

b. LONDON, MAY 13, 1842; d. LONDON, NOVEMBER 22, 1900.

Arthur Sullivan, the composing half of Gilbert and Sullivan, was England's most significant native composer since the death of Purcell, a century and a half before Sullivan's birth. While he failed to revitalize England's musical reputation abroad (Bernard Shaw's obituary stated, "they trained him to make Europe yawn"), Sullivan's witty burlesques were as typically English as Offenbach's were French and Strauss's were Austrian. Learning from Balfe's mistakes, Sullivan reached the conclusion that English composers were wasting their time by trying to match the Italians or the Germans at their own game, and turned back to the example set by John Gay and his *Beggar's Opera* to provide his English audiences with works that appealed to the national predilection for satire and parody. He was tempted just once to establish a serious English opera, launching the Royal English Opera House in 1891 with his *Ivanhoe*;

but the venture failed. Another fifty years would pass before English opera discovered a new voice.

The son of an Irish bandmaster, Sullivan studied at the Royal College of Music and at the Leipzig Conservatory. Most of his early work was steeped in the German tradition, then in 1871 he met the playwright William Gilbert, with whom he collaborated on the "Operatic extravaganza" *Thespis, or The Gods Grown Old*. When this failed they parted company, going their separate ways until 1875 when the impresario Richard D'Oyly Carte engineered another meeting between composer and playwright, and commissioned a one-act operetta to precede a staging of Offenbach's *La Périchole*. The result, *Trial by Jury*, was a triumph, and the pair embarked on the most long-lasting partnership in English music. D'Oyly Carte's Savoy Theatre – established purely as a showcase for Gilbert and Sullivan – became the venue for a string of hugely popular social comedies, such as *H.M.S. Pinafore*, *The Pirates of Penzance* and *The Mikado*.

Sullivan placed much store by his serious music – especially *Ivanhoe* – but his talents were better represented by the Savoy operas, in which his subversive pastiches were perfectly matched by Gilbert's satirical and whimsical word-play. Though both men were subject to typically Victorian lapses into sentimentality, more often than not their mawkishness was of an engagingly self-conscious variety, and, as with the operettas of Offenbach, their best work has episodes of sincere heart-on-sleeve emotion.

H.M.S. Pinafore

Composed 1878.
First performed May 25, 1878.
Libretto by W.S. Gilbert.

Synopsis

Act I

Aboard *H.M.S. Pinafore*, Ralph, a humble sailor, reveals his love for Captain Corcoran's daughter Josephine – but she is to marry the First Lord of the Admiralty, Sir Joseph Porter. Upon his arrival, Porter sings of his life and how he managed to rise to his current eminence. Meanwhile Ralph has threatened suicide if Josephine does not admit her feelings for him. She duly confesses her love. With the exception of Dick Deadeye, Ralph's crewmates agree to help the lovers.

Act II

Thinking he is promoting his own cause, Sir Joseph explains to Josephine that Love is the ultimate leveller. She attaches this theory to her feelings for the lowly Ralph and determines to be his wife. Deadeye has tipped off Corcoran, who catches the lovers as they are about to elope. Ralph pleads his case but is thrown into the hold. Mrs Cripps announces that, years before, she was nurse to both Ralph and Corcoran, and that she mixed the infants up. The group are now paired off: Cripps with Corcoran, Ralph with Josephine and Porter with his cousin Hebe.

Having had a hit with a parody of the British legal system (*Trial by Jury*), Gilbert suggested to Sullivan that they train their sights on another British institution – the navy – for their next operetta. Gilbert's father had been a naval surgeon and liked to claim descent from the Elizabethan navigator Sir Humphrey Gilbert, but as far as Gilbert himself was concerned, the navy was the very epitome of the English class system and its attendant snobbery. Sir Joseph Porter serves as the work's fulcrum, being the embodiment of upper-class ineptitude ("Stick close to your desks and never go to sea, And you all may be Rulers of the Queen's Naveee!") and little-England pomposity ("I am an Englishman", begins his finest set-piece). The victim of his purblind theories on class and society, Dick Deadeye, is virtually forced into the role of villain simply because, as he sings: "From such a face and form as mine the noblest sentiments sound like the black utterances of a depraved imagination." Gilbert had seen a production of *The Merchant of Venice* shortly before writing *Pinafore*, and he must surely have been influenced by the character of Shylock, whose line "Is not my love as good as another's?" is more than once paraphrased by Dick.

Aside from Porter and Dick, this work's charm is, uniquely among G & S's popular operettas, predominantly musical. Nicely spiced with hornpipes and plausible nautical airs, the score draws on the Italian bel canto for its lyrical moments, notably during Ralph's tenor romances. Sullivan's line in musical satire – affectionate for Handel, cruel for Thomas Arne, composer of "Rule Britannia" – provides further compensation for Sullivan's lazy preference for "rum-ti-tum" accompaniments.

RECORDINGS OVERVIEW

There are no fewer than six available recordings of *Pinafore*. The clear first choice is listed below, but all the rest have their qualities, with Malcolm Sargent's 1930 recording (which omits the dialogue) being notable for a famous performance by Sir Henry Lytton as Sir Joseph Porter. Sargent's later recording of the work for EMI, from Glyndebourne, is better recorded but it lacks the authentic feel of the earlier performance. Sir Charles Mackerras's recent version with the forces of Welsh National Opera is great fun, and very well sung, but as it omits the dialogue it cannot be considered in favour of Isidore Godfrey's classic 1960 recording.

Reed, Skitch, Round, Hindmarsh, Adams; D'Oyly Carte Opera Chorus; New Symphony Orchestra; Godfrey.
(Decca 414 283-2LM2; 2 CDs).

Godfrey's reading of *Pinafore* is a delight from start to finish – the vigour of his conducting is remarkable, and not even Mackerras has such a way with the ensembles. John Reed is a suitably aristocratic Porter and Jeffrey Skitch is a likable Corcoran, just as Thomas Round convinces as Ralph. Donald Adams is a villainous Deadeye and Jean Hindmarsh is a uniquely charming Josephine. Chorus and orchestra capture the spirit down to the last detail, and the recording quality has more than stood the test of time.

The Pirates of Penzance

Composed 1879.
First performed December 31, 1879.
Libretto by W.S. Gilbert.

Synopsis

Act I

Frederic has completed his apprenticeship and is now a member of the pirate band. However, he decides to jump ship and join the Pirate King's enemies. His nursemaid Ruth wishes to marry him – and has high hopes of success, as he has never seen another woman. Unfortunately, he wanders across a group of young, attractive ladies – the daughters of the Major-General – and one of them, Mabel, very decently agrees to be his wife. The pirates are about to abduct the women when the Major-General arrives; he persuades them to leave his children alone by telling them he is an orphan and couldn't bear to see his children orphaned in turn.

Act II

Feeling guilty about his lie, the Major-General cannot sleep. Meanwhile Frederic is about to lead a police raid against the pirates. He is confronted by the Pirate King and Ruth, who explain that as he was born on February 29th, a leap year, his apprenticeship – which is to run until his 21st birthday – will therefore not elapse for decades. Frederic agrees to return to the pirates and bids farewell to Mabel. Having been informed of the Major-General's deception the pirates now want revenge, but after defeating the police they yield "in Queen Victoria's name". It is then revealed that the pirates are not, in fact, pirates but noblemen who have gone wrong. They are forgiven ("peers will be peers") and Frederic and Mabel prepare to marry.

The inspiration for *The Pirates of Penzance* came first from the popularity of Stevenson's *Treasure Island*; second from the occasion in Gilbert's childhood when he was kidnapped by Neapolitan bandits; and third from the playwright's less-than-respectful feelings for the army, the police and the House of Lords. Building on the English tradition of turning the highwayman into a lovable, misguided rogue (see Gay's *Beggar's Opera*, p.64), Gilbert put his pirates at the opera's moral centre, where they display a courage and a dignity notably lacking in the authorities. The Pirate King is the very model of decency, with a nice line in vicious social commentary: "I don't think much of our profession, but, contrasted with respectability, it is comparatively honest." His attitude is justified when it turns out that the pirates are really misdirected noblemen – the fawning Major-General then announces to the now respectable band of thieves: "Resume your ranks and legislative duties, And take my daughters, all of whom are beauties."

The characterization of *Pirates* is both more varied and better developed than in *Pinafore*. The Pirate King, one of the few wholly likable Gilbert creations, presents an entirely credible mixture of frankness and cynicism. Opposite stands the Major-General, who is a pantomime oaf – albeit an oaf with more than one side, as revealed by his famous virtuoso patter aria "I am the very model of a modern Major-General", which shows that he is versed in almost every field except the one to which he has been appointed.

Sullivan again plagiarizes effectively, using Italian sources for romances such as Frederic's bel canto tenor lament "Oh is there not one maiden here", and employing Victorian oratorio pastiche for the first act's lovably pompous

"Hail, Poetry!". The array of marches and dance tunes (famously Mabel's coloratura waltz "Poor Wandering One") adds much to the work's appeal, and the rich orchestral support is both more expressive and more pictorial than in anything Sullivan had written before, revealing – as one critic commented at the time – a "power of making his instruments almost laugh with his text".

RECORDINGS OVERVIEW

Pirates too is well served on record, with seven performances on CD, and once again Godfrey takes the top slot. Sargent's 1929 recording provides classic entertainment, but as with all but one of the recordings, he omits the dialogue. His later recording of the work is splendidly sung, as is Sir Charles Mackerras's Telarc recording, which boasts such luminaries as John Mark Ainsley as Frederic and Richard van Allen as the Police Sergeant. Were it not for the omitted dialogue, the Mackerras would be first choice – but for first-time listeners the dialogue is essential.

Reed, Adams, Masterson, Brannigan; D'Oyly Carte Opera Chorus; Royal Philharmonic Orchestra; Godfrey.
(London 425 196-2LM2; 2 CDs).

Godfrey achieves a wonderful sense of theatre, and were the singing and orchestral playing not so perfect, and the sound so clear, you might think it was a live set. Donald Adams is magnificent as the Pirate King and – like his colleagues – he is as convincing with his spoken dialogue as he is with the sung parts. Owen Brannigan is gloriously over the top as the Police Sergeant and John Reed is secure as the Major-General, but the vocal highlight is Valerie Masterson's Mabel – a wonderfully affectionate, even seductive portrayal. Production standards are very high, and Godfrey draws some elegant playing from the RPO.

The Mikado

Composed 1884–85.
First performed March 14, 1885.
Libretto by W.S. Gilbert.

Synopsis

Act I

The troubadour Nanki-Poo arrives in Titipu to learn that his intended, Yum-Yum, has become engaged to her guardian Ko-Ko – the Lord High Executioner. Yum-Yum and her friends Pitti-Sing and Peep-Bo taunt the mighty Pooh-Bah ("Lord High Everything Else"). Nanki-Poo tells Yum-Yum that his father is the Mikado (the king) and that he is fleeing from the attentions of the ageing Katisha. As Ko-Ko prepares to order the day's decapitations, Nanki-Poo considers suicide, but the two make an arrangement : Nanki-Poo can marry Yum-Yum if he agrees to lose his head to Ko-Ko in one month's time. Not even the arrival of Katisha can dampen Nanki-Poo's good spirits.

Act II

While preparing for her wedding, Yum-Yum sings of her happiness, but this is soon dampened when Ko-Ko announces that he has discovered a law stating that when a man is executed his wife must be buried alive. When the Mikado arrives Ko-Ko tells him of a recent execution – the victim of which the Mikado believes to have been his son. The punishment for murdering the heir is "something lingering, with boiling oil in it". Nanki-Poo will not come back to life (his father thinks he is dead) unless Ko-Ko agrees to marry Katisha, but this distresses the Executioner almost as much as the prospect of a painful death. Reluctantly, Ko-Ko persuades Katisha to accept him as her husband, at which point Nanki-Poo and Yum-Yum appear as husband and wife. Even the Mikado is happy.

After the failure of *Princess Ida* in October 1884 Sullivan wrote to D'Oyly Carte announcing that he would compose no more operas for the Savoy Theatre. "My tunes are in danger of becoming mere repetitions of my former pieces, my concerted movements are getting to possess a strong family likeness", he wrote. But just a few weeks later he was toying with the idea of writing an operetta that would appeal to the vogue for "something Japanese". Both Gilbert and Sullivan had attended a Japanese exhibition in London, which had led to friendships with a number of Japanese expatriates, whose reports of life back home helped G & S in their creation of Titipu, setting of *The Mikado*. But Titipu was essentially England in oriental clothing, and most of its absurdities were parodies of English custom and pretension – just as the musical fabric, for all its oriental overtones, owes most to English music (especially madrigals). Pooh-Bah, in particular, is an uproarious embodiment of corruption and the evils of privilege, revelling in his ability to trace his "ancestry back to a protoplasmal primordial atomic globule".

Gilbert's text was well judged to serve his partner, providing templates for a huge variety of musical forms and numbers, including some inspired jokes – such as Katisha's "Oh faithless one, this insult you shall rue", in which she attempts to reveal Nanki-Poo's identity only to be drowned out at every turn by the chorus. Gilbert created lines that invited Sullivan to indulge his love of musical parody, notably of Bach, Handel and Beethoven, though there are allusions to at least half a dozen of his more serious contemporaries. Victorian ballads are nicely set against more acerbic pastiches, and the essential cruelty of much of Gilbert's text is perfectly balanced by the overall sunniness of Sullivan's sparkling music. Many of the work's best numbers have lodged in the English collective unconscious: Ko-Ko's "Tit-willow" refrain, for example, will be recognized by many who think they don't know any Gilbert and Sullivan. The statistics bear out the quality of *The Mikado*: surviving for 627 consecutive performances at the Savoy, it was the longest running of Gilbert and Sullivan's collaborations, and over a century later, it remains the most frequently translated opera by an English composer.

RECORDINGS OVERVIEW

Irritatingly, not a single recording of *The Mikado* on CD has included the dialogue – not even Isidore Godfrey's recording for Decca. This opens the field up, and in spite of the charm of Godfrey's conducting, Mackerras's cast has the upper hand.

Adams, Rolfe Johnson, Suart, van Allen, McLaughlin; Welsh National Opera Orchestra and Chorus; Mackerras. (Telarc CD80284; 1 CD).

This is the finest of Mackerras's G & S recording for Telarc, and is certainly the best-sung *Mikado* on disc, with a world-class operatic cast letting their hair down without resorting to cringe-inducing opera-luvvy vocalizing. However, not only is the dialogue omitted, but the overture is cut as well, and though there's an economic benefit to editing the score to fit onto a single CD, you are left with a savagely trimmed object. That said, Mackerras is in sparkling form, and the performances are universally marvellous – Richard Van Allen's Pooh-Bah and Anthony Rolfe Johnson's Nanki-Poo are especially lovable. Marie McLaughlin is at ease as Yum-Yum and Felicity Palmer has a whale of a time as Katisha.

BEDŘICH SMETANA

b. LITOMYŠL, BOHEMIA, MARCH 2, 1824; d. PRAGUE, MAY 12, 1884.

Although Prague was one of the great musical centres of the eighteenth century (it saw the premieres of Mozart's *Die Zauberflöte* and *Don Giovanni*, for example), the Czech lands didn't have a native operatic tradition until the middle of the nineteenth century, when Bedrich Smetana came along. Smetana's style owed much to Italian opera and to Wagner, but his absorption of his country's folksongs, chiefly through the use of their characteristic rhythms, marks him as the first Czech to bring his nation's musical culture to Europe-wide attention.

Born the son of a brewer, Smetana showed exceptional ability as a child: he was playing in a string quartet from the age of five and three years later he produced his first symphony. He was educated at the Proksch Institute in Prague, where he wrote some Liszt-like tone-poems that received little recognition. Obliged to teach in order to make ends meet, he was almost penniless when Liszt prompted him to try his fortune in Sweden, away from the oppressive atmosphere of Austrian-ruled Prague. From 1856 to 1861 he lived in Gothenburg and it was there that he composed his first successful tone-poem, *Richard III*, a heavily Germanic work. In 1861, with the easing of the Austrian regime, Smetana returned home. His financial instability forced him to tour as a pianist, but in January 1862 the opening of the Provincial Theatre, the first theatre specifically set aside for the production of Czech opera, prompted

Smetana to begin his first opera, *The Brandenburgers in Bohemia*. Premiered in January 1866, it was notable for a vocal style that mirrored the cadences of the spoken language, and was immediately successful.

Encouraged by Smetana's popularity, the Provincial Theatre appointed him director and chief conductor, a post he was to hold for eight years, in the face of interference from a conservative management who disapproved of his supposed Wagnerism. Smetana strove to improve every aspect of the house's working practices, from orchestral standards to stagecraft, and to build up a core Czech repertoire. He made a major contribution to this dream later in 1866, when his *The Bartered Bride* was premiered at the Provincial Theatre. In its original two-act version, with spoken dialogue, it fared only moderately, but in 1870 a three-act revision was unveiled, cementing Smetana's position as his country's foremost composer. In the interim he had produced a third stirring opera, *Dalibor*, and begun work on yet another patriotic flag-waver, *Libuše*.

He continued to run the Provincial Theatre until 1874, when an almost complete loss of hearing, brought on by syphilis, forced him to resign. Astonishingly, the traumatic period after his resignation was highly creative, producing the majority of Smetana's greatest music, including the *String Quartet No. 1* and the tone-poem *Ma Vlast*. He also completed a further three operas (*The Kiss*, *The Secret* and *The Devil's Wall*) but early in 1884 he was committed to Prague's lunatic asylum where, on May 12, he died. Like Weber in Germany and Glinka in Russia, Smetana had pioneered a national style of opera; he was, as Liszt wrote to a colleague, "a composer with a genuine Czech heart."

The Bartered Bride

Composed 1863–66; revised 1869–70.
First performed May 30, 1866; September 25, 1870.
Libretto by Karel Sabina.

Synopsis (revised version)

Act I

A Bohemian village, nineteenth century. Mařenka and Jeník are in love but Mařenka's father, Krusina, has demanded she marry Vašek, son of Tobias Micha, the town's wealthiest citizen. Krusina and his wife Ludmila are hounded by the marriage broker Kečal, who tells them that Tobias had another son, by an earlier marriage, but that he has long since disappeared and is now thought dead. He stresses that modesty has prevented the future husband from coming to meet them (in reality he is a simpleton); Ludmila would rather her daughter chose a husband for herself. When Mařenka arrives, she surprises her parents and alarms Kečal when she confesses to having become engaged to Jeník. Kečal determines to find this "obstacle".

Act II

Vašek enters the local inn, nervous and stammering. His mother Hata has threatened him with humiliation if he should fail to marry Mařenka. Mařenka arrives and soon realizes that Vašek is her intended, but she does not let on her identity. Rather, she expresses her amazement that such a handsome lad would marry such a pain as Mařenka, who will make his life a misery once they are wed. Vašek is frightened of what his mother will say and do, but Mařenka points him towards another, much prettier girl, whom he tries to embrace. She avoids him and he leaves the inn in her wake. Meanwhile, Kečal is attempting to bribe Jeník into rejecting Mařenka. They agree on a price of 300 gulden, but Jeník only consents on the condition that the money is paid to the long-lost elder son of Tobias Micha. The victorious Kečal leaves, unaware that this son is none other than Jeník; he returns with Krusina, who is to witness their agreement. When the town hears that he has given up his beloved for money there is a storm of protest. Even Krusina is shocked.

Act III

Vašek falls in love with a visiting circus dancer, Esmeralda, who persuades him to dress as an "American Bear" for that night's show. When Mařenka hears about Jeník's bargain with Kečal, she decides to marry Vašek, who is delighted. When Jeník arrives she denounces him for his behaviour and even Kečal is alarmed at his callousness; but he agrees to pay up the 300 gulden the moment Mařenka has signed the marriage contract with Vašek. Furious, she signs and the money is paid. But when Hata and Tobias recognize Jeník as their missing son, everyone is delighted by the trick and Kečal storms off in a fury. Jeník has the money and his wife, but the celebrations are cut short by news of an escaped bear. Everyone begins to panic, but Vašek soon calms the situation by removing his circus costume.

Smetana had already been working on the score of *The Bartered Bride* for some three years when *The Brandenburgers in Bohemia* was first performed on January 5, 1866, and he had reason to believe that the warm reception given to his first opera would be repeated at the premiere of *The Bartered Bride* in May. He was to be disappointed, but he correctly surmised that the problem lay not with his music but with the sheer length of the two acts, and his use of spoken dialogue. Accordingly he recast it as a three-acter with recitative, a form in which it instantly achieved classic status. By 1927 it had been performed over a thousand times in Prague alone.

As with most of Smetana's music, *The Bartered Bride* is built from simple basic material, which is then often developed in a sophisticated manner. A fine example of this is the Act I love duet between Mařenka and Jeník: it is made up of ideas taken from Czech folksong (like all this opera's vocal melodies), but Smetana enhances the intensity of the moment through the use of a flowing orchestral undercurrent and rich harmonic patterns, turning the duet's central theme into a "love" motif that runs through the whole opera. Smetana's technical expertise is never obtrusive or complicated – not a single line of the opera is beyond the efforts of a good amateur singer, which is how it had to be, given the resources of the young Provincial Theatre. And though there are elements of Italian fluency and German declamation in Smetana's style, the metre and the pulse of the vocal parts are dictated by the unique character of the Czech language. The stuttering, lovelorn Vašek, the bossy mother, the earnest but canny lovers and the cheerfully scheming Kečal are empathetic characters with authentic-sounding voices, and it is this sense of authenticity – along with the opera's bold contrasts of mood and atmosphere (thought by Smetana to be a "Czech quality") – that propelled *The Bartered Bride* to international popularity.

RECORDINGS OVERVIEW

Of the eleven complete recordings of *The Bartered Bride*, only five are in Czech. Another five are in German – the language in which it is most frequently performed outside the Czech Republic – and one in Russian, which comes closer than German to the metre, but only just. Not surprisingly, the Czech label Supraphon has led the way in matters of recording, with three complete sets, produced in 1952, 1961 and 1981. Without much hesitation, the clear choice is the most recent.

Beňačková, Dvorský, Kopp, Novák; Czech Philharmonic Chorus and Orchestra; Košler.
(Supraphon 103511-2; 3 CDs).

Recorded between 1980 and 1981, this outstanding performance of *The Bartered Bride* was made to accompany a film of the opera, which can now be found on video. Zdeněk Košler is an eager, imaginative conductor and he generates some exquisite playing from the Czech Philharmonic. The casting is dominated by the sweet tenor voices of Peter Dvorský (better known for his singing of Italian bel canto) and Miroslav Kopp as Jeník and Vašek – neither shows the slightest strain. Gabriela Beňačková is similarly refined as Mařenka but Richard Novak, as the doddery Kečal, is outrageously over the top. Superb digital sound completes the attractions of one of the brightest jewels of the Supraphon catalogue – although fifteen years after it was made, the full price tag is a little unreasonable.

Dalibor

Composed 1865–67.
First performed May 16, 1868.
Libretto by Josef Wenzig and Erwin Spindler.

Synopsis

Act I

Prague, fifteenth century. Dalibor, a Czech knight, is on trial before the king for having murdered the Burgrave of Ploskovice in revenge for the execution of his friend Zdeněk. At the trial, the king calls upon the Burgrave's sister, Milada, who demands his execution. As Dalibor is brought in, the crowd rises in support of him. When Dalibor tells of his friend's capture and murder the court reduces his sentence from death to lifetime imprisonment. Milada painfully realizes that she is falling in love with Dalibor and, in collusion with Jitka (an orphan befriended by the knight), she resolves to set him free.

Act II

Milada enters the prison disguised as a boy and finds employment with Dalibor's jailer, Beneš. She charms Beneš into allowing her into the dungeon where Dalibor is being held. The knight greets her with jubilation and, in a passionate duet, they sing of their love for each other.

Act III

They plot to bribe Beneš, but the jailer informs the king of their attempted escape. Taking the advice of his council, the king orders Dalibor's death. Milada, waiting outside the prison, hears the tolling of the bell that signals Dalibor's execution. Accompanied by her followers, she storms the castle, where, after rescuing Dalibor, she is wounded and dies in his arms. Dalibor stabs himself and is united in death with his beloved. (An alternative ending has Dalibor executed before Milada can rescue him.)

Whereas *The Bartered Bride* makes constant allusions to Czech folk music, *Dalibor* is much more closely tied to German high culture. The text bears an obvious similarity to Beethoven's *Fidelio*, even though Smetana's opera ends tragically. Just as striking is a musical fluency and opulence that can be traced to Wagner, with Smetana's manipulation of the opera's dominant theme bringing the composer of *Lohengrin* to mind with particular force. When the theme is first heard, soon after the opening fanfare, it represents Dalibor's destiny; it is later modified (and modulated) to depict his valour, and from this idea grows the theme of Zdeněk, his murdered friend; yet another derivation reveals the motif of deliverance.

In its martial tone and its subject matter, however, this opera is profoundly Czech. Based on a semi-legendary figure who has the same sort of resonance for the Czech people as Joan of Arc has for the French, *Dalibor* provided a number of anthems for the Czech liberation movement of the late nineteenth century. In particular, the principal melody of Milada's rousingly heroic aria in the Act II dungeon scene was adopted as a call to freedom by a people consigned to the prison of Austro-Hungarian domination.

Přibyl, Jindrák, Kniplová, Švorc; Prague National Theatre Chorus and Orchestra; Krombholc.
(Supraphon 112185-2; 2 CDs).

Many of Supraphon's complete opera recordings were produced in conjunction with the Prague National Theatre, whose ensemble casting usually brings with it a laudable commitment and enthusiasm. This 1967 recording of *Dalibor* is a decent example of their approach. Vilém Přibyl's ardent tenor is the star turn, and the rest of the cast contribute to the charged atmosphere – though Nadezda Kniplová is a nasal and pinched Milada. The Prague Orchestra is scrappy and noisy, but Jaroslav Krombholc does his best to remain on top of the work. Unremarkable stereo and a full price tag detract from the recording's appeal.

Libuše

Composed 1869–72.
First performed June 11, 1881.
Libretto by Josef Wenzig and Erwin Spindler.

Synopsis

Act I

Radmilla introduces a case over which Libuše, as Queen of Bohemia, must arbitrate: it concerns Radmilla's brothers, Chrudoš and Šť'áhlav, who are fighting over their dead father's estate. When Libuše finds for Šť'áhlav, Chrudoš refuses to obey the judgement of a woman. Libuše is upset by his reaction and vows to take a husband to whom she can entrust her country's rule.

Act II

Krasava loves Chrudoš, but she has treated him poorly. She confesses this to her father Lutobor, who agrees to forgive her if she can reconcile her differences with Chrudoš and persuade him to bow before Libuše. Šť'áhlav, who overhears Krasava's confession, is in turn reconciled with his brother. Deep in the countryside, Premsyl – a peasant farmer – is told that he has been chosen as Libuše's husband. He willingly agrees to the honour.

Act III

While waiting for her husband-to-be, Libuše blesses the reconciliation between Št'áhlav and Chrudoš. Premsyl promises the people he will do his best to lead them and, in his first act as ruler, he demands that Chrudoš apologize to Libuše. As he bends low Premsyl embraces him as a man of honour. Libuše falls into a trance and receives a vision of the Czech future in which kings and heroes are paraded before the audience. The opera ends with the promise of a golden future.

Though asserting that *Libuše* was "not an opera of the old type but a festive tableaux", Smetana was equally adamant that it was a successful piece of musical theatre – "I regard this as my most perfect work in the field of higher drama and, I can say, as a completely original work." Even in his homeland, however, there were to be few who shared his estimation of this musical apotheosis of Czech nationhood.

He originally composed *Dalibor* to be played in honour of the coronation of Franz Josef as king of Bohemia, but it was decided that the opera should be held back for the opening of the Czech National Theatre, the foundation stone of which was laid, before a crowd numbering tens of thousands, in 1868. When it was eventually completed in 1881, the building duly opened with the premiere of *Libuše*; the theatre burned to the ground just a few months later, and *Libuše*'s future wasn't exactly illustrious. Though well received, it was too stately a piece to lodge itself in the opera repertoire, and was too staunchly Czech to have much international appeal. Nowadays it gets dusted down for official ceremonial occasions, but is otherwise rarely aired.

A sense of ritual pervades the entire score, in which the prevalent tone is more like that of an oratorio than an opera. Characterization takes second place in Smetana's mission to proclaim the Czech love of justice, reason, the motherland and Nature (typified by the idyllic pastoral scene of Act II). Only at the opera's close, when Libuše sings her profoundly moving, physically exhausting prophesy, does Smetana strike the rich melodic seam for which the earlier works are so remarkable. *Libuše* remains something of a curiosity, worth sampling for an understanding of the culture that produced it, but unlikely to gain converts to its creator's cause.

Beňačková, Zitek, Švorc, Vodička; Prague National Theatre Chorus and Orchestra; Košler.
(Supraphon 11276-2; 2 CDs).

Supraphon's second recording of *Libuše* was taped live on the opening night of the reopened National Theatre on November 17, 1983 – 102 years after the first National Theatre opened with a performance of the same piece. The performance is atmospheric and the casting suitably world-class, with Gabriela Beňačková in powerful (if wobbly) form as Libuše. The bass Antonin Švorc and the tenor Leo Vodička are passionately Slavic as Chrudoš and Št'áhlav, and the orchestra and chorus of the Prague Theatre play with spirit and a fair measure of precision. The live sound is fresh and generally free of intrusive stage noises.

ANTONIN DVOŘÁK

b. NELAHOZEVES, BOHEMIA, SEPTEMBER 8, 1841; d. PRAGUE, MAY 1, 1904.

As a composer of opera, Dvořák is wholly overshadowed by his compatriots Smetana and Janáček, but he did write at least one fine opera – *Rusalka*, a work loved by Czech adults and children in much the same way as *Hänsel und Gretel* is loved in Germany.

Dvořák's first intense experience of opera came in 1862, when he became a violist in the orchestra of the newly opened Provincial Theatre, where Smetana was chief conductor from 1866. In 1863 he played in a concert of Wagner's music directed by the composer, and in 1870 – the year before he left the orchestra to devote himself to composition – Dvořák completed his first opera. He went on to compose a further nine but he seems to have always been aware that his talents lay elsewhere. During his three-year stay in the United States (1899–1903) he wrote to a friend that he regretted having wasted so much of his time writing for the stage.

In essence, the problem with Dvořák's operas is twofold: he was stronger on the musical depiction of atmosphere than on character, and he wore his influences on his sleeve. Chief among these was the Wagner of *Tannhäuser* and *Lohengrin*, works which lie behind Dvořák's early operas and the late *Armida*, which was composed when the model had been out of date for some twenty years. Some of the later work is also clearly indebted to Meyerbeer and to the German operettas of Nicolai and Lortzing, and only *Rusalka* has anything like the personality that comes through so strongly in his concert music. Seven of his ten operas have been recorded, but six of these are no more than a curiosity for those with a passionate interest in this otherwise outstanding composer.

Rusalka

Composed 1900.
First performed March 31, 1901.
Libretto by Jaroslav Kvapil, after Fouqué.

Synopsis

Act I

Rusalka, a water-nymph, wants to become human so that she can earn the love of the Prince. She invokes the help of the witch Jezibaba. who agrees to help her on two conditions: first, Rusalka must remain silent, never uttering a word to the Prince; and second, he must always remain true. If either of these promises is broken they will both be damned. The Water Goblin warns her against the pact, but Rusalka is determined, and when she and the Prince see each other, they fall instantly in love.

Act II

At the Prince's court, the mute Rusalka is plotted against by the evil Foreign Princess, who convinces the Prince to reject her.

Act III

Rusalka is a wreck, broken by the Prince's rejection and damned by the witch's curse. The repentant Prince returns to Rusalka. She explains her silence and tells him she can be released by a single embrace, but that it would cost him his life. He urges her to free them both and they kiss; the Prince dies and Rusalka returns to the water.

In 1899, shortly after completing his comedy *Kate and the Devil*, Dvořák announced that he was looking for another libretto. Jaroslav Kvapil provided him with a text inspired by Fouqué's libretto for Hoffmann's *Undine* (see p.135), by the medieval French legend *Melusine*, and, more obviously, by Hans Christian Andersen's *Little Mermaid*. Dvořák set Kvapil's fairy tale without making a single alteration, and it gave him his one and only international operatic triumph.

Dvořák's conception of the spirit world and the material world is not exactly original: the former is glittering and ethereal, the latter is passionate, direct and emphatically symphonic. But it's a beautifully cultivated cliché, and Dvořák comes up with some wonderful sounds as Rusalka is gradually drawn into the arms of a mortal and the two worlds begin to blend – especially during the second act, when the pounding dances are interrupted by the melancholy song of the Spirit of the Lake. It is only right that the opera is celebrated above all for Rusalka's elegiac Act I "Hymn to the Moon" – with its haunting glissando string motif, it has become a regular on anthologies. But there is a wealth of fine music elsewhere in the score, notably the Nymphs scene of Act III, in which the first Nymph sings the delightful folk-ballad "Golden Is My Hair", a wonderful example of the lyrical skills that make this one of the most poignant fairy tales in all opera.

Beňačková, Novak, Soukupovă, Ochman; Prague Philharmonic Choir; Czech Philharmonic Orchestra; Neumann. (Supraphon 10 3641-2; 3 CDs).

This set – the only complete version widely available – is uniformly successful, with some beautiful, gently placed singing from Gabriela Beňačková in the title role. Vera Soukupová is a pantomime witch, revelling in the low-written, chesty register, while Wieslaw Ochman is a suitably heroic Prince. The Czech Philharmonic and Prague Philharmonic Choir are superb, and the recorded sound is fresh and realistically balanced.

MIKHAIL GLINKA

b. NOVOSPASSKOYE (NOW GLINKA), JUNE 1, 1804; d. BERLIN, FEBRUARY 15, 1857.

Glinka was the father of Russian musical nationalism, the founder of the Russian operatic tradition and the first Russian composer to gain widespread acclaim in the rest of Europe.

Born to minor aristocracy, he studied casually in St Petersburg, then in 1824 abandoned music in favour of a post at the Ministry of Communication. However, he continued to compose and give recitals as an amateur singer, and in 1830 he moved to Italy, where he immersed himself in that country's music. Determined to write an opera rooted in the culture of his homeland, Glinka left for home in 1833, travelling via Vienna and Berlin, where he studied for five months. The following year he began work on *A Life for the Tsar*, the first serious attempt at genuinely Russian opera. The work's successful production in 1836 proved that Glinka had struck a chord, and his subsequent appointment as Imperial *Kapellmeister* cemented his position as Russia's most important composer.

For the text of his next opera Glinka turned to *Ruslan and Lyudmila*, a poem by his friend Pushkin, but in January 1837, before a proper collaboration could begin, Pushkin was fatally wounded in a duel. The libretto passed through various hands before reaching what Glinka called its "wretched completion" and, more than anyone, Glinka was surprised by the interest of composer/conductors such as Liszt and Berlioz, both of whom conducted performances of the work. Dejected by the failure of *Ruslan* to gain a wider audience, in June 1844 Glinka left Russia for France, where the richness of Parisian musical life – and in particular, the support of Berlioz – helped to lift his spirits. A year later he was on his way to Spain, where he remained for two years before embarking on a grand tour of Europe that lasted, on and off, until May 1852, when he finally settled in St Petersburg.

Three years later he began a third opera, *Dvumuzhnitsa* (The Bigamist), but he was sidetracked by his interest in liturgical music and in 1856 he set out once more for Berlin, where he made a study of music by Lassus and Palestrina. On January 21, 1857, he heard Meyerbeer conduct the Trio from *A Life for the Tsar* and he died just three weeks later, from influenza.

Glinka once remarked, "when I settle into work, I involuntarily hear the music of others, and this distracts me". Most of his early compositions were plainly modelled on operas by Rossini and Bellini, but, as he wrote in his memoirs, "a longing for my own country led me gradually to the idea of writing in a Russian manner". When Glinka did finally resolve to do this, he had to contend with a situation in which European culture was so powerful an influence that even Russian folksongs were beginning to suffer contamination from the music of Mozart and Bellini. Delving back into a period before such infiltration had occurred, he produced a distinctly Russian sound-world in *Ruslan and Lyudmila*, a sound dominated by pungent harmonies, an oriental richness of orchestration (in which brass and wind instruments were given prominence) and a fluent vocal line that close-

GUUS ONG

ly mirrored the inflections and rhythms of Russian speech. Glinka was the first composer to recognize that the future of Russian opera depended on its truth to what Dostoyevsky called "the spirit of the people", and as a declaration of independence, *Ruslan and Lyudmila* has a claim to be the most important opera in Russian musical history.

A Life for the Tsar

Composed 1834–36.
First performed December 9, 1836.
Libretto by Georgy Rosen.

Synopsis

Act I

Russia and Poland, winter 1612. The peasants celebrate as news arrives that a Tsar has been elected, but Antonida is dejected as she sits waiting for her betrothed, Bogdan Sobinin, to return from the army. Her father, Ivan Susanin, arrives with news of a Polish uprising against Moscow and tells his daughter that there can be no wedding until the Poles are defeated, but when Sobinin finally enters he announces that the Poles have been defeated. Susanin still refuses to agree to a wedding until the coronation of the Tsar has taken place, but when Sobinin announces that Mikhail Romanov, their landlord, is the man to be crowned in Moscow, Susanin relents.

Act II

At a ball in a Polish commander's residence, a messenger bursts in with news of their defeat and the election of Romanov. The majority stay to dance, but a group of Polish soldiers determine to kidnap Romanov from the monastery in which he is living.

Act III

During preparations for Antonida's wedding Polish soldiers break in and demand that Susanin lead them to the Romanov's monastery. Susanin sends his son ahead to warn Romanov and then, pretending to agree to the Pole's demands, he leaves with them for the forest. Antonida is distraught to see her father leave with his enemies, but he tells her to stay and enjoy her wedding in his absence. Sobinin gathers some friends and together they leave to rescue Susanin.

Act IV

Susanin tricks the Poles by leading them into the heart of the Enchanted Forest. When he confesses his deception, he is killed.

Epilogue

In Kremlin Square the new Tsar praises the bravery of his supporters, and after mourning the death of Susanin, all rejoice in their victory over the Poles.

𝄞 The story of the peasant who saved the life of the first Romanov Tsar was suggested to Glinka during a visit to Moscow in 1834. As he later wrote, "many themes and even details of their workings flashed into my head at once"; indeed so excited was he by the idea that he frequently overtook his librettist, forcing the unfortunate Rosen to fit his words to Glinka's music. They worked together on the opera for two years, then in 1836 they rehearsed it in the presence of the Tsar himself, who was so taken by its fervent patriotism that he proposed the alteration of its name from *Ivan Susanin* to *A Life for the Tsar*. Its success was immediate and it remained the most performed opera in Russia until the 1917 revolution, when it was heavily revised and given its original title again.

A Life for the Tsar is Russian in its subject matter, but it is basically a western European opera. The large-scale scenes owe a clear debt to the Grand Opéra of Meyerbeer and his contemporaries, the harmony is Germanic and the vocal writing is, for the most part, Italianate, although one critic "tried to recall from which Russian song this or that motif was taken, and could not discover the original" – probably because Glinka borrowed only two traditional melodies, both of which were heavily diluted. In its recitative, *A Life for the Tsar* was more innovative, for all previous Russian opera had used spoken dialogue, whereas Glinka devised a style of recitative that reflected the colour and character of his native language. The resulting fluency was further enhanced by Glinka's use of variation and repetition to accompany references to particular characters and incidents: Susanin's Act IV farewell, for example, contains eight thematic allusions to music associated with his family, while the final scene carries some twenty quotations from earlier in the score. The music of *A Life for the Tsar* is varied and energetic, and the battling nations are differentiated through unambiguous musical characterization: the Poles are portrayed by "shallow" national dances, while the Russians are portrayed, for the most part, by slow and elegiac arias and ensembles. If Glinka rarely achieved the sense of momentousness that the story deserved, his first opera nonetheless was a crucial stepping-stone – indeed, the choral theme of the Epilogue became something of a Russian anthem.

Martinovich, Pendachanska, Merritt, Toczyska; Sofia National Opera Chorus; Sofia Festival Orchestra; Tchakarov.
(Sony S3K 46487; 3 CDs).

EMI's classic *A Life for the Tsar*, with Boris Christoff as Ivan and Nicolai Gedda as Sobinin, is currently unavailable; but Emil Tchakarov's Bulgarian production, using a post-Revolution edition of the text, is a worthy stopgap. The performance has a lively attention to rhythm and shape, and a real feeling of ensemble. Chris Merritt's tenor is on the light side for Sobinin and Boris Martinovich has a monochromatic and uncertainly pitched bass, but the female singers are much better – especially Alexandrina Pendachanska, whose soprano packs considerable punch.

Ruslan and Lyudmila

Composed 1837–42.
First performed December 9, 1842.
Libretto by Konstantin Bakhturin, Valerian Shirkov and various others, after Pushkin.

Synopsis

Act I

Lyudmila, daughter of the Prince of Kiev, is to marry one of three suitors – the knight Ruslan, the poet Ratmir or the cowardly warrior Farlaf. She chooses Ruslan, but at a banquet to honour their engagement, Lyudmila vanishes. The Prince offers his daughter's hand and half his kingdom to whoever can bring her back.

Act II

The magician Finn tells Ruslan that Lyudmila has been abducted by the dwarf Chernomor and advises him to beware the evil enchantress Naina. After defeating a giant head (who turns out to be Chernomor's brother and one of the dwarf's victims), Ruslan is bequeathed a magic sword which the head tells him is the only weapon that will defeat the evil dwarf.

Act III

In Naina's palace Ruslan is tricked into love by her sirens, but the spell is broken by Finn.

Act IV

Ruslan and Chernomor fight – offstage. The good knight defeats the dwarf by cutting off his beard – the source of all his power – but his triumph is shortlived, for Chernomor has placed Lyudmila in a trance. He nonetheless takes her back to her father.

Act V

Farlaf steals Lyudmila from Ruslan and returns her as his prize, but he fails to wake her. With a magic ring given to him by Finn, Ruslan successfully brings her around. He takes Lyudmila as his bride, and half the Prince's kingdom as his dowry.

While in Berlin, Glinka came into contact with Weber's work, and *Der Freischütz* in particular made a deep impression on him, giving him a taste for the operatic fusion of the fantastic and the naturalistic. His contribution to this sub-genre was *Ruslan and Lyudmila*.

Very freely adapted from the poem by Pushkin, Bakhturin's outline for a rescue-drama (devised "in a quarter of an hour while drunk") delighted Glinka, but as Bakhturin was neither available nor suitable to such a protracted project, it was handed over to the young officer and poet Valerian Shirkov. Shirkov failed to stay the distance and in stepped a succession of three amateur writers, whose collective procrastination dragged the process out over five years. To make matters worse, Glinka's personal life during the opera's gestation was pretty miserable, owing to the infidelities of his wife, who separated from him at the end of 1839, bigamously remarried in March 1841, then dragged him through the divorce court. All things considered, it's surprising that *Ruslan* isn't more of a mess.

As with *A Life for the Tsar*, Glinka completed substantial sections of the opera before receiving the words to fit the music. Setting scenes piecemeal rather than consecutively, Glinka found himself writing something that was not so much an integrated opera as a series of related tableaux. But whatever *Ruslan* lacks in cohesion it makes up for in vivacity. Glinka's incorporation of genuine and synthetic folksong gives this work a much more "ethnic" flavour than *A Life for the Tsar*. Drawing upon various elements of Russia's complex cultural heritage, Glinka uses arabesques and Persian melodies to conjure the fantastic settings, and he heightens the magical atmosphere by the use of pungently dissonant harmony, explosive rhythms and some of the oddest instrumentation to be found in any opera of its period. Indeed, *Ruslan*'s defining quality is its kaleidoscopic orchestral score, which is typified by the riotously energetic and enduringly popular overture. Perhaps the greatest innovation is Glinka's self-styled "shifting background", in which a fixed tune is repeated against an ever-changing orchestral setting – this device was to prove central to the evolution of Russian music, and as such, it would be impossible to imagine a work as progressive as the *Rite of Spring* without *Ruslan and Lyudmila*.

Ognovienko, Netrebko, Diadkova, Bezzubenkov, Gorchakova; Kirov Opera; Gergiev
(Philips 446 746-2; 2 CDs).

This 1996 release, the latest in Philips' series with Valery Gergiev and the Kirov, is the only recording of *Ruslan* in the catalogue, and it's so good that it's unlikely anyone will try to challenge it. The intensity of the orchestral playing is everything you'd expect of this team, and all the soloists are outstanding. Sound quality isn't perfect – there's a fair amount of audience noise – but that's a minor quibble in the context of a performance of such all-round quality.

ALEXANDER BORODIN

b. ST PETERSBURG, RUSSIA, NOVEMBER 12, 1833; d. ST PETERSBURG, FEBRUARY 27, 1887.

The history of Russian nationalism begins with Glinka and continues with the work of five composers known as "The Five" or "the mighty handful": Balakirev, Cui, Mussorgsky, Rimsky-Korsakov and Borodin. All were amateurs. Borodin studied music as a child but pursued a career in chemistry and went on to become a professor at the Academy of Medico-Surgery in St Petersburg. As a student he maintained his musical education with guidance from Mussorgsky, but not until 1862, when he met Mily Balakirev, the chief idealogue of Russian music, did he begin to exercise his musical talents. Rimsky-Korsakov remembered how Borodin juggled his two lives: "as soon as he was free he would take me into his living rooms and there we occupied ourselves with music and conversation, in the midst of which Borodin would rush off to the laboratory to make sure nothing was burning or boiling over, making the corridor ring as he went with some extraordinary passage of ninths or seconds. Then back for more music and talk." Yet Borodin was adamant that music should not interfere with what he saw as his chief vocation, and the result was a rate of composition that often slowed to almost stationary.

He completed just one opera – *The Bogatyrs*, which was little more than a series of excerpts from operas by Rossini, Verdi and Meyerbeer – and took eighteen years not to finish *Prince Igor*, a mighty work to which he devoted almost all his spare time. When he died, aged only 53, the overture was unfinished, many of the vocal numbers were incomplete, very little had been orchestrated and the third act was missing both text and music. Despite the frequently inspired efforts of Rimsky-Korsakov and Glazunov (who scored the overture from his memory of Borodin's extemporizations), *Igor* remains a sequence of tableaux rather than a coherent piece of music-theatre. However, as a work of music it is among the very greatest by a Russian composer, filled to bursting with exciting orchestral and choral show-pieces – notably the celebrated choral "Polovtsian Dances" that bring Act II to its sensational end.

Prince Igor

Composed 1869–87.
First performed November 4, 1890.
Libretto by the composer, after Stassov.

Synopsis

Prologue

Poutivl town square, 1185. In spite of the ominous eclipse of the sun and regardless of the pleas of his wife Yaroslavna, Igor, accompanied by his son Vladimir, leaves with his army to pursue the Polovtsi, a Tartar tribe who were originally hunted by Igor's father, Prince Sviatoslav of Kiev.

Act I

Inside the house of Yaroslavna's brother, Prince Galitsky. The Prince boasts of his profligate life, for which he is popular with the people of Poutivl, whose governor he has been appointed. Two drunken deserters from Igor's army, Skula and Eroshka, try to stir up trouble in Igor's absence, demanding to know why Galitsky should not be their ruler. Yaroslavna sings of her dreams and fears for the future of herself, her husband and their country. Boyars enter her house and announce that Igor has been defeated and taken prisoner. Polovtsi then begin attacking the town.

Act II

The Polovtsian leader Khan Konchak treats his captives with kindness and respect. Vladimir falls in love with Khan's daughter, Konchakovna, but Igor yearns for Yaroslavna. Konchak orders his slaves to entertain the captive prince with dancing and singing (Polovtsian Dances).

Act III

Poutivl is ransacked and when news of his town's destruction reaches Igor, his thoughts turn to escape. The Khan offers to let him go if he promises not to wage war against the Polovtsi again. Igor refuses but manages to escape, earning the Khan's admiration. Reluctant to leave Konchakovna, Vladimir remains in the Polovtsian camp and is welcomed by Khan as his son-in-law.

Act IV

Yaroslavna bemoans her husband's absence and the destruction of Poutivl. However, she then sees two horsemen riding towards the town, and recognizes one of them as her husband. They embrace and the opera ends in celebration.

Borodin once wrote that in opera "bold outlines only are necessary; all should be clear and straightforward". *Prince Igor* is indeed a work in which bold outlines dominate, and its grand gestures and melodramatic passions give it the same place in Russian culture as Verdi's *Don Carlos* has in Italian. However, *Igor* is a curious mixture of influences whose Russianness is of a less pronounced kind than that of *Boris Godunov*. Borodin was, at heart, a lyrical composer, unmoved by the "mystical ramblings" of Mussorgsky's folk-based dramas, and although Stassov's plot carried a powerful nationalist message (as did the majority of operas produced by "The Five"), Borodin was more interested in drama for its own sake than in proselytizing. As Rimsky-Korsakov later remarked, Borodin was, at best, a "reluctant patriot".

Viewed as a spectacle, *Igor* is clearly a descendant of Grand Opéra. It comes complete with love interest, rival armies, extravagant crowd scenes, dances and a celebratory denouement – all standard fare at the Paris Opéra. As for the music, Borodin's love for Italian opera is manifest throughout the essentially up-beat score – for example in the smooth bel canto lines of Vladimir and Konchakovna's love music, or in the comic passages involving Skula and Eroshka (of which the composer was extremely proud), which smack of Italian opera buffa. The barnstorming Polovtsian Dances are rather more Russian with their slightly piquant harmonies, brittle rhythms and smattering of un-western intervals, but there's nothing in this opera to compare to the "authenticity" for which Mussorgsky strove.

Igor's weakness is not its music, which tears along with great melodic vigour, but its construction, which was undoubtedly marred by the opera's eighteen-year gestation period, during which Borodin patched together his libretto while repeatedly reworking the music. Each act breaks down into a series of closed units which, while impressive in themselves, fail to cohere as a work of narrative theatre. This sense of dislocation is exacerbated by Borodin's inconsistent handling of characters: for what purpose, you might ask, did the composer create Prince Galitsky if he had no intention of taking him any further than the first act? For all its lumpiness, however, *Prince Igor* is an epic work, and much easier to digest than many epics, thanks to a verve and warmth that's rare in Russian opera of this period.

Kit, Gorchakova, Grigorian, Ognovenko, Minjelkiev; Kirov Theatre Chorus and Orchestra; Gergiev.
(Philips 442 537-2PH3; 3 CDs).

Recorded in conjunction with the Kirov's 1993 production in St Petersburg, this was the first recording of *Igor* in which all the constituent parts, from the engineering to the casting and the conducting, are as they should be. Gergiev gives a dynamic, sometimes ferocious reading of the score, animating even the weakest scenes. Mikhail Kit's ringing bass lacks definition, but he is a formidable presence as Igor. Galina Gorchakova's dramatic soprano has a glorious bloom and she brings sweetness and dignity to Yaroslavna. Gegam Grigorian sometimes tries too hard as Vladimir, but Olga Borodina is a likable and sensitive Konchakovna. The high production standards, with outstanding orchestral and choral performances from the Kirov, complete one of the great opera recordings of the 1990s.

MODEST MUSSORGSKY

b. KAREVO, RUSSIA, MARCH 21, 1839; d. ST PETERSBURG, MARCH 28, 1881.

Although they were almost exact contemporaries, Borodin and Mussorgsky embodied precisely opposite principles, the former advocating beautiful sound above all else, the latter promoting the cause of absolute drama and theatrical veracity. As Mussorgsky wrote to a colleague: "Music is a means of communication between men, and not an end in itself – the pursuit of beauty alone, in the literal acceptance of the word, is a childish stupidity, a rudimentary form of art." Mussorgsky saw it as his mission to illuminate the lives and history of his people, and he is to Russian music what Verdi is to Italian and Wagner to German. Unlike either of those contemporaries, however, Mussorgsky wrote little, and what he did write was either sloppily put together (he had almost no training) or left unfinished. All of it was misunderstood. While recognizing that Mussorgsky was "talented, original, full of so much that was new and vital", Rimsky-Korsakov could not come to terms with the "absurd, ugly part-writing, sometimes strikingly illogical modulation (and) unsuccessful orchestration". When, after Mussorgsky's death, Rimsky-Korsakov was invited to prepare the unfinished scores for performance and publication he set out to level the eccentricities, sanding down the very qualities that were at the heart of Mussorgsky's unique musical personality.

ROYAL COLLEGE OF MUSIC

Modest Mussorgsky – permanently worse for drink

He was born into a wealthy landowning family and led an early life that can best be described as dilettantish. In 1855 he joined the Cadet School of the Guards in St Petersburg, where his life-long and highly destructive love of vodka was born, and he met Mily Balakirev, the founder of the group of Russian nationalist musicians known as "The Five". Balakirev encouraged him to pursue music, giving him the only formal lessons of his life, and within a matter of months Mussorgsky felt confident enough to leave the army. For five years he devoted himself to song-writing, producing pieces that demonstrated a genuine empathy with the lowest of Russia's social strata, and forging a style based upon the colour and rhythms of Russian speech. His operatic music owes everything to these experiments with song – indeed, he and Richard Strauss remain the only great song composers to have achieved comparable success in the opera house.

Mussorgsky enjoyed life out of the army and made good headway in his private studies, but in 1861, after Nicholas I's emancipation of the serfs bit heavily into his private income, he was forced to take a job in the civil service. As with so many Russian composers of the time, composition was now a part-time activity for Mussorgsky, but during the 1860s he nonetheless began to concentrate increasingly on operatic projects. His first attempts included a treatment of the Oedipus myth, a setting of Flaubert's historical novel *Salammbô* and, most importantly, a word-for-word setting of Gogol's play *The Marriage*. None of these was completed, but *The Marriage* was nonetheless a profoundly important work. Completed in 1868 and subtitled "an experiment in dramatic music in prose", it was conceived as a continuous drama dominated by recitative-like speech-melody, encapsulating Mussorgsky's growing antipathy to the insipid "musical mathematics" of western classical music.

In the same year a colleague suggested Pushkin's poem *Boris Godunov* as a suitable basis for a libretto, and Mussorgsky seized upon it as the ideal vehicle for an intrinsically Russian opera. He completed it in 1869, revised it in 1871–72 and helped supervise the first performance the following year, when, despite a warm reception from the audience, *Boris Godunov*'s irregular and unmelodious music was savaged by the critics. Dejected by this dismissal and bored witless by the prospect of a life within the civil service, Mussorgsky lapsed into depression and suicidal bouts of drinking. (Tolstoy once refused even to talk about him, claiming "I like neither talented drunks nor drunken talents.") He died leaving two operatic projects incomplete, *Khovanshchina* and *Sorochintsy Fair*.

Boris Godunov

Composed 1868–69; revised 1871–72;
revised 1896 by Rimsky-Korsakov.
First performed February 8, 1874.
Libretto by the composer, after Pushkin.

Synopsis

Prologue

Russia and Poland, 1598. In 1591 Dimitri, heir to the Russian throne, was murdered by the boyar Boris Godunov. The weak Fyodor was made Tsar and Boris his regent, but when Fyodor dies the people visit Boris at his monastery retreat and implore him to take the crown. Despite his guilt, Boris relents and is crowned Tsar.

Act I

Six years later, the monk Pimen is completing a history of Russia. He tells the novice Grigori of Dimitri's murder; Grigori, who realizes that had he lived he and Dimitri would have been the same age, is so moved by the story that he resolves to exact revenge against Boris. He leaves for Poland, where he begins to raise an army. At an inn on the Lithuanian border Grigori, now claiming to be Dimitri, meets two monks – one of whom, Varlaam, tells the story of Ivan the Terrible's victory at Kazan. Police arrive with a warrant for Grigori's arrest, but he escapes.

Act II

Boris's rooms in the Kremlin. He sings of his love for his children but memories of his crime rise to the surface. Prince Shuisky, a counsellor, brings news of a "resurrected" Dimitri. He gives a detailed account of the boy's features, causing Boris to collapse into a grief-stricken, hallucinatory frenzy.

Act III

A Polish castle. Princess Marina has fallen in love with Dimitri. Her Jesuit priest urges her to marry him and ensure Russia's conversion to Catholicism. In an extended duet they sing of their love for one another. [Rest of this act dropped in 1871/2 revision.] Outside St Basil's Cathedral in Moscow, the people are gathering to beg the Tsar for bread; a simpleton accuses the Tsar of murder.

Act IV

The deranged Boris interrupts an emergency state meeting in the Kremlin. News arrives of a miracle performed at the tomb of Dimitri and, once again, Boris collapses. He comes to, but is unable to rise. After making his peace with God, he dies. In a forest near Kromy the people taunt a half-dead boyar but they are distracted by the arrival of Dimitri. He leads them to Moscow and, left to himself, the simpleton sings of his country's bleak future.

The evolution of *Boris Godunov* was tortuous. The first version, composed in 1869, had just seven scenes, no leading female role and a small cast that was utterly dominated by the title bass. Two years later, having failed to secure a performance, Mussorgsky began rewriting: he widened the character base to include Dimitri and Marina, excised the St Basil scene, and inserted the Kromy Forest episode. Then, after Mussorgsky's death, Rimsky-Korsakov tried to get the opera back into the Russian repertoire by making it a little less indigestible: he not only re-orchestrated the entire score but "improved" the rhythm, metre and harmony, and even tried to westernize the vocal writing – the very essence of the opera. The composer's own revised version has now been returned to the repertoire and every recording since 1976 has been of Mussorgsky's 1872 edition.

Rimsky-Korsakov acted out of the best of intentions, for Mussorgsky's *Boris* was never likely to make its author a household name. It's an austere, often bleak creation, in which the tortured characters are starkly delineated in tableaux-like scenes – albeit tableaux that are carefully linked through the use of recurrent motifs. Above all else, the vocal style is staunchly uningratiating. Basing his melodies on the metre of spoken Russian, Mussorgsky attached highly detailed markings to the score, to ensure that the singers adhered to the style he termed *glukho* – something like singing-speech, requiring the singer to blur the written line by exaggerating certain syllables to emphasise the meaning of the text. It occurs at its most extreme during Boris's sinister hallucination, but the style colours most of the opera's solo music – even the quasi-folksong that

MUSSORGSKY HITS THE BOTTLE

Even in a culture where a capacity for vodka was taken as an index of virility, Mussorgsky's intake of liquor was a cause for comment. The famous painting of him by Repin shows, with alarming detail, just how drunk Mussorgsky looked when sober – it's the picture on p.300. His alcoholism might have contributed to the extraordinarily original character of his music, but it left many works incomplete, and in the end it killed him: his death occurred as a consequence of a severe epileptic fit that came in the wake of a particularly arduous drinking spell.

Yet Mussorgsky drunk was capable of things that few people are capable of in any condition. His physician, Vasily Bertensson, left an account of the time he hired the tenor Ravelli to give a concert of Italian arias, with Mussorgsky as accompanist. "On the day before the concert Ravelli told me that he wished to meet his piano accompanist and asked me to bring him around next day for an early rehearsal. Having obtained Mussorgsky's consent the day before, happily finding him in a lucid period, I went to him once more to carry out Ravelli's commission. But to my horror I found Mussorgsky drunker than wine. No persuasions or pleas of mine had any effect, and with the stubbornness of the drunken he went on saying 'No sir, no; at the moment it is not possible. This evening I shall be alright.' At that time Mussorgsky lived in a small, slovenly room. On the dirty table stood some vodka and some scraps of miserable food. In saying goodbye to me he got up with difficulty, but saw me to the door and bowed me out in a manner which, though not quite worthy of Louis XIV, was quite amazing for someone so completely tight. . . . Sure enough, Modest showed up promptly at 7 at Kononov's hall where the concert was to take place.

Unfortunately, he remained long enough in the green-room to sample all the drinks on the table there, growing drunker and drunker. Suddenly my Italian tenor . . . decided that his voice was a little strained and would therefore be compelled to sing his entire programme a half or even a whole tone lower than usual. This was all we needed.

I rushed to Mussorgsky to ask him whether he could do this for Ravelli. Rising from his chair with a certain gallantry, Mussorgsky calmed me with the words 'Why not?' To prove his assuring words he suggested that the tenor at once run through his whole programme mezza-voce. Mussorgsky, who was probably hearing all Ravelli's Italian stuff for the first time, so charmed the Italian with his refined performance and his ability to transpose to any key that the tenor embraced him, saying repeatedly 'What an artist!'."

emerges during the coronation scene. Even today the effect can be harrowing, and it is hard to imagine what contemporary audiences must have made of it.

These vocal lines are supported by a comparably primitivistic harmonic palette, and as there is little instrumental counterpoint the musical landscape is often spartan. Although the coronation scene is potently scenic, with a famous passage for real and imitated bells, this opera is a world away from Borodin's *Igor*, with its seductive colouristic effects. Mood and atmosphere are communicated in this opera by the voices – indeed they predominate to such an extent that when the singer's line is interrupted, the orchestra often stops with it. As with the use of *glukho*, the place of silence within *Boris* strongly anticipates the work of later composers, notably Debussy.

The presence of Boris saturates the opera, even though Mussorgsky ended up giving him just two major scenes. A towering representation of demonic madness, this role is the summit of the dramatic bass repertoire. The remaining characters are more than mere foils. The heroic tenor Dimitri and the dramatic soprano Marina generate some of the opera's most upbeat passion, with the former's aggressive ambition and the latter's youthful stubborness forcefully depicted, and Mussorgsky invested the same degree of care in his representation of even the least significant personality. For example, the chorus in Act I is depicted as a collective of individuals rather than a mere mob, and the boyar Tchelkalov – who sings no more than thirty bars of music – emerges a fully rounded creation, whose thoughts and actions serve a pivotal dramatic purpose.

Boris Godunov is a morbidly gloomy creation, but from the opening bars it draws you into a fully defined and convincing world. Its finale is one of the most powerful in all opera: alone on a darkened stage, the simpleton laments his country's fate: "Weep, ye people; soon the foe shall come, soon the gloom shall fall, woe to our land; weep, Russian folk, weep, hungry folk!"

RECORDINGS OVERVIEW

There have been nearly twenty recordings of *Boris Godunov*, an astonishing number in view of the fearsome demands of the title role. The catalogue contains magnificent interpretations of Boris from Ivan Petrov (for Melodiya), Nicolai Ghiaurov (Decca) and Martti Talvela (EMI) – all well worth hearing, after the sets reviewed below.

Raimondi, Polozov, Vishnevskaya, Plishka; Washington Choral Arts Society; Washington National Symphony Orchestra; Rostropovich.
(Erato 2292-45418-2; 3 CDs).

This 1987 performance remains the most authentic yet produced, thanks primarily to Rostropovich's fanatical attention to detail, shape and expression. Ruggiero Raimondi's baritonal Boris lacks physical weight and he is prone to uncalled-for lyricism, but the intensity with which he portrays Boris's vertiginous fall is unforgettably haunting. Vyacheslav Polozov hurls himself into the tenor role of Dimitri and the conductor's wife Galina Vishnevskaya sings her second Marina (the first being for Karajan) with often brutal passion. The remaining cast, which includes Nicolai Gedda as the Simpleton and Kenneth Riegel as Shuisky, are outstanding, and the recorded sound is beyond fault.

Kotscherga, Larin, Lipovšek, Ramey, Nikolsky, Langridge; Slovak Philharmonic Choir; Berlin Philharmonic Orchestra; Abbado.
(Sony S3K58977; 3 CDs).

It is a testament to Abbado's affinity for Mussorgsky's music as well as his firm sense of style that he managed to fuse what was little more than "celebrity casting" into something so brilliantly theatrical. Anatoly Kotscherga – star of the same conductor's recording of *Khovanshchina* – is a formidable Boris, although he sometimes delivers the words with excessive force. Marjana Lipovšek is a little mature as Marina and Sam Ramey struggles with the language as Pimen, but both give lyrical performances that contrast with Kotscherga's declamatory approach. The rest of the cast are splendid (Sergei Leiferkus is notable in the small role of Rangoni), but the show really belongs to Abbado and his sonorous BPO. It is the richest sounding of all the orchestras to have recorded *Boris* and in such a potentially spartan work this is a huge advantage. Ideal sound.

Christoff, Gedda, Zareska, Bielecki; Paris Russian Chorus; French National Radio Orchestra; Dobroven.
(EMI CHS5 65192-2; 3 CDs).

If you want to own a version of Rimsky-Korsakov's less arduous and more colourful edition, this is the one to choose. The first and best of Boris Christoff's interpretations of Godunov is a rightly celebrated recording. His enormous, colourful bass (quite the opposite of Raimondi) has the sort of grandeur that Fyodor Chaliapin gave to the title role, and although the tone can widen to something close to a bawl, the rawness is magnificent. (Christoff also takes the minor roles of Varlaam and Pimen – but no matter his attempts at disguising the fact, both sound like Boris.) Eugenia Zareska also doubles up, singing both

Marina and Feodor, but she is more successful in differentiating between her roles. Gedda's Dimitri is virile and exciting and the sound is more than acceptable for a 1952 mono recording.

Khovanshchina

The Khovansky Affair

Composed 1872–80.
First performed February 21, 1886.
Libretto by the composer.

Synopsis

Act I

The boyar Shaklovity dictates a letter warning Tsar Peter that the reactionary Prince Ivan Khovansky and his son Andrei, aided by their troops (the Streltsy), are plotting a rebellion. When Khovansky arrives at the head of the Streltsy (many of whom are Old Believers) he falsely announces his intention to crush all enemies of the Tsar. Meanwhile, Andrei begins chasing Emma, a young German girl, but his fun is interrupted by Marfa (an Old Believer and one of Andrei's former lovers), who dismisses his childish behaviour. Andrei argues with his father for showing an interest in Emma, but the monk Dosifei (the leader of the Old Believers) restores order and Marfa takes Emma into her care, as Dosifei and the Old Believers fall to their knees in prayer.

Act II

Prince Golitsyn reads a love letter from his ex-lover, the Regent Sophia (Peter's half-sister), but he suspects that this might be some sort of ploy. He has invited Marfa to his house so that she might tell his future; when she predicts scandal and disaster for him, Golitsyn throws her out and then orders her death. In marches Khovansky, angry that Golitsyn has been interfering with his duties as advisor to Sophia. The two men argue until Dosifei calms them by urging a return to the ways enshrined in the ancient books. They are interrupted by Marfa, who bursts in desperate for sanctuary from Golitsyn's servant, who has tried to drown her: she tells them how she was saved by Tsar Peter's bodyguard, whose presence in Moscow alarms Golitsyn. Shaklovity then enters and announces that the Khovanskys have been denounced to the Tsar as traitors.

Act III

Marfa remembers her love for Andrei, for which Susanna criticizes her as a sinner. Dosifei offers comfort, but his calming words are shattered by the arrival of the drunken Streltsy guards. They are told that foreign mercenaries have been seen attacking women and children on the outskirts of the Streltsy camp. The soldiers raise Khovansky and ask him to lead them against the mercenaries, but he urges them to disperse for it is now obvious that Tsar Peter has taken absolute control of the country.

Act IV

Dancing Persian slaves are entertaining Khovansky when Shaklovity arrives demanding that he attend a council of state; as Khovansky prepares himself for the journey, Shaklovity stabs him to death. Golitsyn is exiled from Moscow, as Andrei and Marfa argue over Emma. Marfa dares him to summon the Streltsy – which he does – but they arrive carrying the blocks for their own executions. Andrei is spirited away by Marfa, as a herald announces that the Streltsy have been pardoned.

Act V

A pine wood in Moscow. With Khovansky dead, the Old Believers' cause is lost, but they will die rather than yield to the Tsar. Entering a chapel in the forest clearing – where they are joined by Dosifei, Andrei and Marfa – the Old Believers immolate themselves just as the Tsar's soldiers arrive.

Before writing a note of *Khovanshchina* Mussorgsky devoted a lot of time to the study of Russia during the reign of Peter the Great, intending to compact a number of real events in the hope of constructing a drama that would be a microcosm of seventeenth-century Russia – and an allegory of contemporary Russia, where the reforms of Tsar Alexander II (notably the abolition of serfdom) were widely resented by reactionary nobles. But concision was never really on the cards for the vodka-riddled Mussorgsky, who ended up rambling all over the place, revising completed episodes before he'd finished the first draft of others. When he died the ends of Acts II and V were left incomplete and little beyond two short scenes in Acts III and IV were orchestrated. Once again, in stepped Rimsky-Korsakov, who completed the score for the 1886 premiere, but also axed large amount of music and re-composed much that seemed to him ugly. These cuts were later restored by Shostakovich, who in 1958 made a revision that took its cue from the composer's vocal score; it is this edition that you're most likely to hear performed today. (An intriguing footnote to the story is that Diaghilev brought Stravinsky and Ravel together to collaborate on a revision for the Paris premiere in 1913; tragically, their efforts have been lost, with the single exception of Stravinsky's subdued setting of the final chorus.)

Whereas Verdi might have made such a subject into a chest-beating thriller, Mussorgsky is all high seriousness, and this opera is predominantly dark and slow moving – right from the prelude, a tranquil and beautiful evocation of the windswept dawn landscape around Moscow. Mussorgsky's flair for atmospheric description provides compensation for the lack of pace (notably during the second scene of Act IV, when a melancholy pattern grows from the double-basses to signify Golitsyn's long march into exile), and there are a few episodes to raise the temperature: for example, the stirring "Dance of the Persian Slaves", the murder of Khovansky and the final immolation. His creation of distinct musical characteristics for each of the conflicting parties (Golitsyn; Khovansky and the Streltsy; Dosifei and the Old Believers) is another attraction, and for all the gloom, Mussorgsky's writing for Dosifei's bass, Golitsyn's tenor, Khovansky's bass and Marfa's mezzo-soprano is rather more ingratiating than the speech-like line he deployed in *Boris*. *Khovanshchina* lacks the grandeur of the earlier work, but is definitely more accessible.

RECORDINGS OVERVIEW

Remarkably, for a work that is so rarely staged, *Khovanshchina* has been recorded four times. The two most recent, both using the Shostakovich revision, are the best; the other account available on CD is an old Bolshoi set, released by Chant du Monde, which uses Rimsky-Korsakov's edition.

Haugland, Atlantov, Popov, Lipovšek; Vienna State Opera Chorus and Orchestra; Abbado.
(Deutsche Grammophon DG 429 758-2GH3; 3 CDs).

Abbado is regarded by many as the world's finest conductor of Mussorgsky's music, and this live recording comes closer to the heart of *Khovanshchina* than any other. The atmosphere, orchestral tone and fluid conducting help you forget how fragmented the opera really is, and the cast is uniformly superb. Vladimir Atlantov is thunderous as Golitsyn and Marjana Lipovšek radiant as Marfa. In the title role, Aage Haugland's bass is suitably powerful, and while it lacks Russian bite, his reading of the character is gripping throughout. For the final scene, Abbado uses Stravinsky's revision in place of that by Shostakovich.

Minjelkiev, Galusin, Steblianko, Okhotnikov; Kirov Chorus and Orchestra; Gergiev.
(Philips 432 147-2PH3; 3 CDs).

Whereas Claudio Abbado draws fluency and beauty from Mussorgsky's gloomy score, Valery Gergiev – using the Shostakovich edition – goes at it like a man possessed, opting for animal passion rather than sophistication. As is the case with all the Gergiev/Kirov/Philips recordings, the cast are all in excellent form, providing a solid ensemble base, and the orchestra and chorus are stunning throughout. The Gergiev approach might give some people a bit if a headache, but it's a fine representative of the traditional Russian way of tackling Mussorgsky.

PYOTR IL'YICH TCHAIKOVSKY

b. VOTKINSK, RUSSIA, MAY 7, 1840; d. ST PETERSBURG, NOVEMBER 6, 1893.

If any composer can be said to have embodied the essence of Russianness it is Pyotr Il'yich Tchaikovsky, and yet he was the one major nineteenth-century Russian composer who cannot be bracketed with the nationalist school. Though initially associated with "The Five" (or "The Mighty Handful") – led by his friend Mily Balakirev – he soon followed an independent path, and he paid dearly for his determination. Few major artists have ever suffered the sort of critical savaging meted out on a regular basis to Tchaikovsky. It is now hard to understand why his music aroused such antipathy, for he is one of the most powerful and direct of composers, whose music is characterized above all by its tunefulness and grand passion. He was prone to bombast and sentimentality, but these weaknesses are the obverse of his chief strength, which is his sincerity. Today he is chiefly remembered for his ballets, symphonies and concertos, but the turbulence of his extraordinary life is vividly mirrored in his operas, to which he gave more of his time than he gave to any other genre.

He was born some six hundred miles east of Moscow in the provincial town of Votkinsk, where his father was a mining engineer. His tuition began at home, where his parents played him pieces by Mozart, Bellini and Rossini, and his passion for the theatre was first excited when, at the age of ten, he was taken by his mother to a performance of *Don Giovanni*. The family moved the same year to St Petersburg, where in 1854 his mother died; Tchaikovsky sought refuge from his grief in opera, but none of his early opera sketches (including a setting of a scene from Pushkin's *Boris Godunov*) was enough to convince him or his tutors that he should concentrate on music. In 1859, after extensive law studies, he left school to work as a clerk at the Ministry of Justice, and it was during his time there that he came to regard music as his vocation. After three years at the ministry he enrolled at the Conservatoire, where he was taken under the wing of the composer/pianist Anton Rubinstein. So rapid was his development that, within just four years, he was recommended to Anton's brother Nicolai at the Moscow Conservatoire, where Tchaikovsky was appointed professor of harmony.

In Moscow he came into contact with Balakirev, Rimsky-Korsakov and their cabal of young nationalists. For a while he shared their devotion to Russia's folk heritage, composing a nationalist opera called *The Voyevoda* in 1867 and titling his second symphony "The Little Russian" in 1872. But even before "The Little Russian" his cosmopolitan instincts were begining to prevail, and in 1869 and 1870 he wrote two western-influenced operas, *Undina* (based on the fairy tale previously set by Hoffmann and Lortzing) and *Oprichnik*. By the end of 1875, with another opera (*Vakula the Smith*) and his first piano concerto finished, his style had begun to settle.

But personal crises were coming to the boil. Homosexual acts were punishable by death in Russia, and Tchaikovsky was not always careful where and with whom he conducted his affairs. In 1877 he took the reluctant step of marrying one of his pupils, Antonina Milyukova, a young woman with her own share of psychological problems. It was a disaster and they separated within just nine weeks, leaving Milyukova bitter and Tchaikovsky suicidal. He resigned his post in Moscow and devoted himself entirely to composing, a move made possible by Nadezhda von Meck, a wealthy widow and patron of the arts (and later a friend of Debussy), who had begun to support him the previous year. Throughout the fourteen years of their relationship she never once met the composer, but she commissioned numerous pieces from him and provided him with an annuity. Thanks to her support, Tchaikovsky had been able to see the first *Ring* cycle in Bayreuth in 1876 and to attend a performance of Bizet's recently premiered *Carmen* in Paris. Deeply impressed by the epic scale and cohesion of the *Ring* and by *Carmen*'s fiery naturalism, Tchaikovsky applied himself to opera, beginning his fifth, the great *Eugene Onegin*, in 1877, and his sixth, *The Maid of Orleans*, the following year.

By 1880 his work was popular throughout Europe and America. By his own standards he was happy, and by anyone's standards he was wealthy, but his next two operas – *Mazeppa* (1881–83) and *The Sorceress* (1885–87) – were uneven efforts, set to poor libretti. In 1885 he bought himself a country estate at Klin, where he remained in isolation until an invitation to make his debut as a conductor drew him back to Moscow in 1887. In this capacity he toured Europe during 1889, and the following year he stopped in Florence, where he composed what many regard as his finest opera, *The Queen of Spades*. The first performance was one of the composer's triumphs, and though his relationship with von Meck foundered at this time, his career continued its upward trajectory: an exceptionally successful visit to the United States followed in 1891, when he conducted the inaugural concert of what was to become Carnegie Hall. Somewhat bewildered, he wrote to his brother: "I am a much more important person here than in Russia."

Tchaikovsky in 1877 – the year he began Eugene Onegin

In 1892 he completed *Yolanta*, an unsuccessful opera and his last. The following year, soon after completing his tragic sixth symphony, Tchaikovsky died, in circumstances that remain controversial to this day. The official version was that he had died from cholera after drinking unboiled water. Many people surmised that he had hoped this reckless act would bring about his death, but then in the 1970s a Russian scholar produced a new account of the composer's death which, he claimed, established that it was suicide. Shortly before his death, the story went, Tchaikovsky had been caught *en flagrante* with a nephew of a high-ranking official. Tchaikovsky's law-school colleagues, determined to avert a scandal that would reflect badly on them, summoned the composer to a "court of honour" on October 31 and ordered him to kill himself. Two days later, he took arsenic.

Tchaikovsky's operas are the distillation of what he termed his "lyrical idea", the notion that everything can be characterized or made real through melody. His technique was always at the service of melody and his music was first and foremost conceived for the voice – whether or not it was actually written for the voice, his music can always be sung. Tchaikovsky was not, however, an effortless tunesmith, and he worked hard at honing his skills, making an intensive, life-long study of his European precursors. He was also unusually practical and unpretentious in his approach, writing in 1874 that in order to "hold the attention of the theatregoer" the composer must employ a style that is "simple, clear and colourful". The infuence of Italian bel canto and of Mozart is plain in each of his operas, and in his two most successful works, *Eugene Onegin* and *The Queen of Spades*, you can detect the presence of his "god" Bizet, whose *Carmen* served not only as an inspiration for the composer, but as a confirmation of life's tragedy.

Eugene Onegin

Composed 1877–78.
First performed March 29, 1879.
Libretto by the composer, after Pushkin.

Synopsis

Act I

At the Larins' country estate, Olga expresses concern over the health of her sister, Tatyana. Suddenly, their neighbour Lensky arrives, accompanied by his friend Onegin. Tatyana, who has been reading a romantic novel, immediately recognizes Onegin as the man that Fate has chosen for her, while Lensky sings of his love for Olga. During the night, Tatyana writes a gushing letter to Onegin; but the following morning Onegin reproaches her for her impudence and proposes they see no more of each other, leaving Tatyana humiliated.

Act II

Lensky and Onegin have been invited to Tatyana's birthday party. Onegin does not want to be there and is angered when a group of elderly women begin to gossip about him and Tatyana. To annoy his friend – whom he blames for dragging him to the party – he dances with Olga. To Lensky's horror, she encourages the flirtation and when Lensky reprimands her she petulantly takes another dance with Onegin. Lensky challenges his friend to a duel and is killed.

Act III

After six years of self-imposed exile, Onegin returns to St Petersburg. Tatyana has married Prince Gremin. At one of the Prince's balls, Onegin reflects on his past and he recognizes Princess Gremina as Tatyana. He realizes that he does, after all, love her and begs a meeting. She agrees to see him and although she cannot deny her love, she rejects his suggestion that they elope. After one final embrace, she demands he leave. Despairingly, he accedes.

In May 1877 Tchaikovsky received a love letter from the besotted young Antonina Milyukova. Later that month, a friend suggested to Tchaikovsky that he write an opera of Pushkin's great verse-novel *Eugene Onegin*. He was initially unconvinced of the poem's suitability as a libretto, but then he came to the passage in which Tatyana, the heroine of the story, writes a letter to Onegin, declaring her love for him. Tchaikovsky began to set the scene to music, and by July, when he married Antonina, he had already completed two-thirds of the opera. However, the rapid deterioration of his marriage delayed completion of the opera until the end of 1879, some time after he and Antonina had parted.

Tchaikovsky referred to his *Eugene Onegin* as "lyrical scenes in three acts and seven tableaux", making it clear from the outset that he was concerned much more with emotional timbre than with a narrative of events. Whereas Pushkin precisely delineated the discrepant social environments of Tatyana, the country girl, and of the suavely aristocratic Onegin, Tchaikovsky kept the spotlight on the chief protagonists, simplifying the material to portray the transformation of Tatyana from a "fragile creature" into a woman, and of Onegin from "gentleman" into a man. Tchaikovsky wrote to his brother that "clarity [and] definition of character" were paramount, and subtlety of characterization was what he wanted his performers to concentrate on – which is why he chose students to give the premiere rather than seasoned opera singers, fearing the latter would think their job well done if they just made a beautiful sound.

Initially, the serious-minded but ingenuous Tatyana is defined by music of rustic charm and simplicity, open-hearted, rhythmically upbeat and generally major key. Onegin is the very opposite – as is clear when they first set eyes on each another, Tatyana looks upon Onegin as the man chosen for her by Fate (for which Tchaikovsky created a descending leitmotif, an idea borrowed from *Carmen*), and her music reflects her naive infatuation; his patronizing response is accompanied by stark, minor-key phrases, underlining an incompatibility that is again reinforced by the great "Letter Scene" and its aftermath. As Tatyana writes her innocent declaration of love, she sings a song that is positively Italianate in its warmth and fluency; Onegin's denunciation of her "childish ways" is dressed appropriately in sounds of pompous formality. By Act III, however, the situation has changed drastically, as is evident when the married Tatyana enters to an *écossaise*, a cosmopolitan dance that would never have been heard in the Larins' country house. When she comes face to face with Onegin, she is now the dominant figure, and Onegin, now a "boy in spellbound passion", unburdens himself to Tatyana in a manner that bears little relation to the reined-in style of Act I, just as Tatyana's music conveys a bitterness foreign to the susceptible young girl with whom the opera opened.

Lensky too is nicely transformed. Initially no more than a foil to Onegin, he is sketched by writing that is light and good natured, but when he realizes that he is to face Onegin in a duel he sings the darkly mournful "Faint echo of my heart", one of Tchaikovsky's most pain-filled songs. It's an outburst that's typical of Lensky's frankness but unrepresentative of a work in which, until the histrionic finale, the action is swathed in a palpable atmosphere of self-repression.

RECORDINGS OVERVIEW

Onegin has had a long and impressive history on record, with ten complete studio recordings and at least as many live versions having been produced since the first sessions in 1936. There is one outright first choice and two very fine contenders, and one other set – currently out of the catalogue – that has much to recommend it: Mstislav Rostropovich's 1970 recording. Made in Paris while on tour with the Bolshoi company, it is notable above all for a big-sounding Lensky from the young Vladimir Atlantov and some intense direction from the conductor. Its drawback is Vishnevskaya's tired performance of Tatyana – to hear her at her best in the role for which she is probably most famous, buy the set listed below.

Vishnevskaya, Avdeyeva, Lemeshev, Belov, Petrov; Bolshoi Theatre Chorus and Orchestra; Khaikin.
(Melodiya 74321 17090-2; 2 CDs).

This is one of the greatest recordings of Tchaikovsky's music ever made. Little-known Boris Khaikin has so remarkable a feel for the score's nuances of mood and texture that his conducting alone would make this a fabulous set, even if the singing were not as wonderful as it is. Vishnevskaya is in stunning form: sensual and perceptive, she presents a graphic transformation from girlish coyness to womanly confidence. Yevgeny Belov is a masculine, committed Onegin and Sergei Lemeshev, though long past his prime, is a suitably heroic Lensky. The Bolshoi orchestra play with equal measures of passion and sweetness, and the sound, though mono, is excellent for 1955.

Hvorostovsky, Focile, Shicoff, Borodina; St Petersburg Chamber Chorus; Paris Orchestra; Bychkov.
(Philips 438 235-2PH2; 2 CDs).

This 1990 set offers the rare coupling of intelligent conducting and intelligent, beautiful singing. Though it is partly intended as a showcase for the prize-winning talents of bass-baritone Dimitri Hvorostovsky, the casting is well assimilated, with no-one trying to steal the limelight. Hvorostovsky's voice is a glorious thing and he knows it, but he shapes the character of Onegin well, charting the transformation from prig to love-struck desperado with admirable imagination. Nuccia Focile is an impressively Italianate Tatyana, phrasing Tchaikovsky's lines with persuasive gentility; and Neil Shicoff – in his second recording as Lensky – shows himself to be one of the most unfairly neglected talents of the Pavarotti generation. Excellent sound quality.

Allen, Freni, Shicoff, von Otter; Leipzig Radio Chorus; Staatskapelle Dresden; Levine.
(Deutsche Grammophon DG 423 959-2GH2; 2 CDs).

This is completely unlike Bychkov's reading. Levine conducts the work very much from the heart, and for all the eccentricities and overstatements (the "Fate" motif is blazed in neon lights), it all adds up to a marvellously exciting performance. This is due, in no small measure, to Thomas Allen and Mirella Freni who, while clearly not Russian, bring vivid personality to the music: Allen's Onegin is a genuinely nasty piece of work and Freni's Tatyana conveys both the character's youth and tragedy. Neil Shicoff's Lensky is a dream as well, accentuating the insecurities of his character in keeping with the overall tone of this fraught interpretation.

The Queen of Spades / Pique Dame

Composed 1890.
First performed December 19, 1890.
Libretto by Modest Tchaikovsky and the composer, after Pushkin.

Synopsis

Act I

St Petersburg, late eighteenth century. Herman, an officer, is in love with Lisa, the granddaughter of the Countess – a famous gambler once celebrated as "The Queen of Spades". However, Lisa is engaged to marry Eletsky, another officer. Tomsky, a friend of Herman's, reveals that the Countess was once given the secret of three cards that would guarantee uninterrupted success at gambling. Little suspecting that Lisa secretly loves him, Herman swears that Eletsky will never have Lisa. As she sings of her "secret passion" Herman walks into her room; after the Countess nearly catches them together, they finally embrace.

Act II

Desperate to learn the Countess's secret, Herman breaks into the Countess's bedroom at night and demands the answer. Drawing a pistol, he threatens the old woman, frightening her to death. Lisa is distraught, believing that Herman has been wooing her to get close to her grandmother and the secret of the three cards. Desperate, she orders him to leave.

Act III

The ghost of the Countess appears and gives him her secret: "Three... seven... ace". Herman, though terrified, is delighted. Lisa still loves Herman and she begs him to meet her later that night. Herman, however, is obsessed with putting his secret to the test and doesn't turn up. Heartbroken, she drowns herself. Meanwhile, Herman has staked everything on three, and wins. He then gambles all his winnings on the seven, and wins again; but when he places everything he has on the ace, his card turns out to be the Queen of Spades. As the Countess's ghost makes another appearance, Herman loses his reason and stabs himself. The chorus pray for the forgiveness of his soul.

In 1888 Tchaikovsky's brother Modest wrote to him about an idea for a libretto based on Pushkin's short novel *The Queen of Spades*. Having triumphed with Pushkin's *Onegin* it was reasonable for Modest to assume that this might rouse some interest, but Tchaikovsky was unmoved by the subject and replied that he was more concerned with his new symphony. No further mention was made of the project until the end of 1889 when Tchaikovsky, in St Petersburg for rehearsals of *The Sleeping Beauty*, met the Director of the Imperial Theatres, who prompted him to reconsider his brother's unfinished libretto, thinking it might make a vehicle for the talents of his star singers, the tenor Nikolay Figner and his soprano wife, Medea. An agreement was soon reached and in January 1890 he settled in Florence, where he completed the score in June. The first performance was a huge success, but because of Medea Figner's pregnancy it was dropped from the Mariinsky Theatre just two months after the premiere.

Tchaikovsky had only agreed to turn Pushkin's story into an opera on the condition that a number of changes were made, notably to its conclusion. Pushkin's tale ended with Lisa surviving the tragedy to marry the son of her grandmother's steward, and Herman going mad and being consigned to an asylum, where he endlessly repeats the words "three ... seven ... ace; three ... seven ... queen". Such a conclusion was too open-ended for Tchaikovsky, who elected to kill them both, then add insult to injury by forgiving Herman after his suicide. His treatment of *Eugene Onegin* had attracted criticism from guardians of Pushkin's sacred flame, and his drastic rewriting of *The Queen of Spades* (also known by the French title *Pique Dame*) provoked outrage. Tchaikovsky was convinced of the validity of his reinvention of Pushkin. "Unless I'm terribly mistaken, the opera is a masterpiece", he wrote to his brother, and the wider public shared his opinion – it was soon Tchaikovsky's most performed opera.

The Queen of Spades is in many respects a more sophisticated work than *Eugene Onegin*. It is a propulsive drama rather than a series of lyrical scenes, with Tchaikovsky keeping his characters just short of boiling point as the hand of Fate guides them towards their doom – somewhat as Bizet had done in *Carmen*. Yet the music of *The Queen of Spades* bears no resemblance at all to the steamy setting of Bizet's melodrama, for this opera constantly evokes the world of Mozart and the Rococo style of Catherine the Great's St Petersburg, through music that is permeated by a generalized longing for the past. The juxtaposition of intense emotion and delicate, archaic music is the dramatic principle of *The Queen of Spades*. For example, the death of the Countess, the most disturbing scene in all Tchaikovsky's operas, is preceded by a gentle passage in which she sings an eighteenth-century air by Grétry, just as the Act II masked ball provides a sophisticated backdrop against which Herman's passions appear ever more extreme, or, in the first scene of the final act, the pious song of a church choir forms the setting for Herman's fevered recollection of the Countess's corpse winking at him.

Instrumental to the momentum of this opera is Tchaikovsky's perfectly harmonized system of themes, which at crucial points reinforce the notion that the action is heading inexorably towards tragedy. Again, a "Fate" motif figures prominently, but it is Herman's hypnotically intense leitmotif (set to the words "Three cards, three cards, three cards", first heard in Act I) that is most significant. Seeming to drive Herman towards psychosis and death, it appears modified more than thirty times throughout the opera before reaching its resolution in the heartbreaking finale.

A sort of half-brother to Bizet's Don José, Herman inspired Tchaikovsky to write his most forceful and dramatic operatic music. Initially a dignified, if rather excitable, member of the officer class, Herman begins the opera singing the sort of sweet, sophisticated music you'd expect of a romantic tenor lead, but by the time he comes to play his final hand, he is a psychotic paranoiac, and his music has become shockingly high and declamatory, full of wild intervals that are both grotesque and thrilling. Lisa is a more tepid creation. Her love music is pretty enough and her discovery of Herman in her grandmother's room is gut-wrenching stuff, but she is not exactly Tchaikovsky's most impressive heroine and she loses presence as the opera progresses – indeed the music that Tchaikovsky gives to her suicide suggests that he too was not profoundly engaged by her. The dominant female is the Countess, whose dark, low-written mezzo is one of the most theatrical characters in Russian opera. She is typical of a work which, as the Tchaikovsky scholar David Brown has noted, provides evidence of "the composer's increasing occupation with emotions bordering on hysteria".

RECORDINGS OVERVIEW

There have been nine complete recordings of *The Queen of Spades*, all but three of them produced in Russia. Of those that are currently unavailable, keep an eye out for the re-emergence of Deutsche Grammophon's stormy account and highly engaging recording, conducted by Mstislav Rostropovich; Galina Vishnevskaya is some years past her best as Lisa, but Resnik's fearsome Countess is unchallenged on record. Incidentally, Nikolay and Medea Figner both lived long enough to make records – their early 78s have been issued on CD by Pearl, a fascinating document of the original Herman and Lisa.

Atlantov, Freni, Forrester, Leiferkus, Hvorostovsky; Tanglewood Festival Chorus; Boston Symphony Orchestra; Ozawa.
(RCA 09026 60992; 3 CDs).

This 1992 set is one of the finest of all Tchaikovsky records. Maureen Forrester's Countess is less mysterious than Resnik's, but she is considerably nastier and she sounds the right sort of age (she was sixty when this record was made). Mirella Freni was way too old to be playing Lisa, but she sings beautifully throughout, rising magnificently to the challenge in her love duets with Atlantov. Leiferkus and Hvorostovsky are outstanding as Tomsky and Yeletsky, but the show is stolen by the astonishing tenor of Vladimir Atlantov: having already proved himself as Herman in 1974 (for Philips), he presents here a much darker, more troubled account of the role. Ozawa keeps the action fluid and the contrasts pointed, and the Boston orchestra, while over-polished, are clear and well balanced. The recorded sound is rich, but annoyingly close.

Grigorian, Gulegina, Arkhipova, Putlin; Kirov Theatre Chorus and Orchestra; Gergiev.
(Philips 438 141-2PH3; 3 CDs).

Recorded a year after the Ozawa version, this was another triumph in the run of marvellous Kirov/Gergiev/Philips opera productions. Taking the lead throughout, Gergiev drives the opera with tremendous force, encouraging his singers to give tremendously physical performances. Gegam Grigorian's tenor is a little reedy here, but his Hermann is a nicely judged portrayal, making much of the tragic ending. Maria Gulegina's lyrical, youthful soprano is ideally suited to the role of Lisa and the remaining cast are all solid. The production standards are faultless.

NIKOLAI RIMSKY-KORSAKOV

b. TIKHVIN, RUSSIA, MARCH 18, 1844; d. LYUBENSK, JUNE 21, 1908.

If Mussorgsky represents the fatalistic side of the Russian soul, Rimsky-Korsakov epitomizes the fantastic. Regarding opera as "essentially the most enchanting and intoxicating of lies", he drew on his country's rich folk heritage to create a fairy-tale world in which the fanciful and commonplace were fused through extravagant orchestral virtuosity and fervently Romantic vocal writing.

Born into an aristocratic family, he received a standard musical education, but his first ambition was to join the navy. In 1856 he did so, and was stationed in St Petersburg, where he was deeply affected by the music of Glinka and was encouraged by Balakirev to begin a symphony, despite Rimsky-Korsakov's tenuous grasp of basic theory. In 1865, after two and a half years at sea, he began to apply himself to the study of harmony, counterpoint and orchestration, and resumed work on his symphony. Four years later he completed Dargomyzhsky's opera *The Stone Guest*, the first of many such completions of other composers' works, and in 1871 he was appointed professor of composition and orchestration at the St Petersburg Conservatory. Still ignorant of the finer details of the subject he was now teaching, he worked in private to obtain a better knowledge and not until the mid-1870s, when he began editing a collection of Russian folksongs, did he perfect his technique.

He composed his first opera two years after joining the Conservatory, but *The Maid of Pskov* was a realistic costume drama that swiftly became a cause for regret. With his next opera, *May Night*, first performed in 1880, he established the model to which most of his succeeding operas would conform, mixing supernatural elements into a folk setting. He attempted much the same fusion with *The Snow Maiden* in 1882, then, after the failure of his village comedy *Christmas Eve* (a tale previously set by Tchaikovsky as *Vakula the Smith*), produced the spectacular and exotic *Sadko*. Strangely he followed the quintessentially Russian extravaganza with a neoclassical drama, *Mozart and Salieri* (1889), a piece based on the Pushkin play that perpetrated the myth that Salieri killed the irritatingly perfect Mozart. But Rimsky-Korsakov was uncomfortable with pastiche, and in 1899 he returned to costume drama with *The Tsar's Bride*. There followed three further fantasies, the last of them, *The Golden Cockerel*, being finished just weeks before his death.

Even if he had written no operas of his own, Rimsky-Korsakov's place in the history of the genre would be assured, for it was through his services that some of Russia's most important works reached a performable form. In 1876 he assisted Balakirev with the preparation of Glinka's operas for publication. Six years later he began revising Mussorgsky's music, including the mighty *Boris Godunov*, and after Borodin's death in 1887 he helped Glazunov complete *Prince Igor*. His revisions might not have been always faithful to the creator, but he was the only one of "The Five" to immerse himself in the practicalities of composition and the only one really to master the orchestra: indeed he contributed as much to the craft of orchestration in Russia as Berlioz did in France and Wagner in Germany.

Sadko

Composed 1894–96.
First performed January 7, 1898.
Libretto by the composer and Vladimir Ivanovich Bel'sky.

Synopsis

Tableau I

The merchants of Novgorod are holding a banquet to celebrate their prosperity. Sadko, a troubadour, sings of his love for Novgorod but reminds them that there are many lands beyond their port worth exploring. They dismiss him and return to their feast.

Tableau II
On the shores of Lake Ilmen, Sadko sings of his disillusionment, but he is distracted by the approach of swans who begin to transform into women. Among their number is Volkhova, the Sea Princess (daughter of the King and Queen of the Ocean), who predicts his future, telling him that he will retrieve three golden fish from the lake. She promises to wait for him while he is away.

Tableau III
Sadko's wife, Lubava, is overjoyed to see him return but she is broken-hearted when he announces that he must leave almost immediately.

Tableau IV
On Novgorod's busy quayside, Sadko tells the mocking crowd of the three golden fish and bets his head against their collected wealth that he will be able to bring them up from the deep. As predicted, his nets produce three golden fish and when he returns to port he invites all those brave enough to join him on a journey. Sadko then asks three traders – a Viking, a Venetian and an Indian – to sing of their lands so that he may decide which to visit. He eventually settles on Venice and commends Lubava to the care of the Novgorod people.

Tableau V
Twelve years later, laden with treasure, Sadko's ships begin their return to Novgorod, but midway home they are becalmed. Sadko steps onto a floating log. As he does so the winds pick up and he is left stranded. A mist rises.

Tableau VI
When the mist clears, Sadko finds himself at the bottom of the sea as the guest of the King and Queen of the Ocean. Sadko is to marry Volkhova, and their wedding is attended by every creature of the deep. Sadko sings, and a tumultuous dance follows that creates such a storm that one of Sadko's ships is sunk. He and Volkhova leave.

Tableau VII
On the shores of Lake Ilmen, Volkhova sings a lullaby to the sleeping Sadko. She bids farewell to her sleeping lover and turns herself into the mighty river Volkhova. He is woken by Lubava, who has been waiting patiently ever since he left. For a moment he thinks that everything has been a dream but when he sees his fleet moving up the river he realizes that he is the richest man in Novgorod. The city welcomes him with triumphant celebrations.

In 1867 Mussorgsky suggested to Rimsky-Korsakov that the eleventh-century epic the *Novgorod Cycle* might make a good subject for a tone-poem. Rimsky-Korsakov agreed, but chose to concentrate on painting a "musical portrait" of the poem's seafaring hero rather than on the drama as a whole. After revising this tone-poem in 1892 he decided to turn the tale of Sadko into a series of epic musical tableaux. *Sadko* is a pageant, a celebration of national identity, somewhat like Smetana's *Libuše*, but unlike *Libuše* it is a strikingly theatrical creation.

Rimsky-Korsakov handles the interplay between fantasy and reality with dazzling skill, illustrating the hearty camaraderie of Novgorod and the shimmering magic of the lake through music that displays an amazing ear for harmony and orchestral timbre. The use of chromaticism for the fantastic elements and diatonicism for the earthly world clearly delineates the two domains (they remain distinguishable even when mashed together in the sixth tableau), and the personalities of the principal roles are vividly etched by repeated themes. This manipulation of motifs might be pretty basic in comparison with the protean motifs used by Wagner, but Rimsky-Korsakov takes second place to nobody in the brilliance of his orchestration. *Sadko* is above all else a virtuoso display of picture-painting in music, and Rimsky-Korsakov is just as adept at evoking the sombre beauty of the moonlit shores of Lake Ilmen (in the second tableau) as he is at capturing an undersea party and a riot of storms and hurricanes (in the sixth). Similarly the songs of the Viking, the Indian and the Venetian present seductive images of worlds that existed chiefly in the imagination of Rimsky-Korsakov, augmenting the escapist fun of the proceedings. *Sadko* is, in other words, the polar opposite of Mussorgsky's granite-hewn *Boris Godunov* – an operatic fairy tale in which, for once, the music is convincingly fantastic. Painfully self-critical though he was, Rimsky-Korsakov considered it among his best works, later writing, "all my operas after *Sadko* have, I think, only temporary interest".

Galusin, Tarassova, Alexashkin, Tsidipova; Kirov Chorus and Orchestra; Gergiev.
(Philips 442 138-2; 3 CDs).

This live recording is one of the highlights of the Philips/Kirov series. The performance is remarkable for its closely knit ensemble singing, yet Vladimir Galusin, one of the world's highest-rated tenors, shines as Sadko, giving a muscular reading of the title role. Valentina Tsidipova's Princess and Sergei Alexashkin's Sea King play their supernatural characters with athlet-

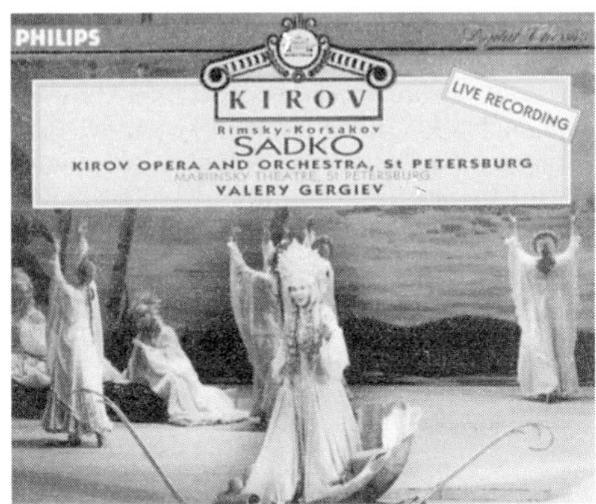

ic flair – doing much to make Tableau VI seem like the best thing the composer ever wrote – and the rest of the cast, down to the Jesters, Soothsayers and Gold-Finned Fishes, are no less excellent. Valery Gergiev gives a splendidly colourful reading of the score, and the Kirov forces are outstanding. The whole is captured with fresh and vibrant sound.

The Golden Cockerel

Composed 1906–07.
First performed October 7, 1909.
Libretto by Vladimir Ivanovich Bel'sky, after Pushkin.

Synopsis

Act I

After a Prologue in which The Astrologer warns the audience that there is a moral to his tale, he reveals the palace of the Tsar Dodon. The Tsar asks his two sons, Guidon and Afron, what he should do about a threatened attack and when both fail to suggest anything of any use, they begin to argue whether or not an augury should be consulted. At this, the Astrologer re-appears and presents the Tsar with a cockerel. It will crow if there is to be peace but if danger threatens it will point its head in the direction of its approach. For this, the Tsar offers the Astrologer anything his heart desires. During the night the bird raises the alarm twice and on the second occasion the Tsar assembles his army and rides out to battle.

Act II

The Tsar is defeated and both his sons lie dead. No-one knows the identity of the victorious foe, but as the sun rises they see a mighty tent and, assuming that it belongs to the enemy general, they bombard it. Their weapons prove useless. A maiden emerges and sings in praise of the sun. She turns out to be the Queen of Shemakha and, besotted by her beauty, Dodon offers her his hand in marriage.

Act III

To general rejoicing, the Tsar and his Queen process back into the city, but the festivities are cut short by the Astrologer, who demands the Queen as his heart's desire. Dodon refuses and strikes him with his sceptre, killing him. When he tries to embrace the Queen, she laughs and pushes him away. Thunder and lightning portend doom and, sure enough, the Tsar is killed – by the cockerel, who lands on his head and pecks him to death. When the storm passes, the Queen and her Cockerel have vanished. In the Epilogue the Astrologer returns to explain that he and the Queen were the only real people and that all the others were nothing more than "a pale illusion, emptiness".

The Golden Cockerel, based on Pushkin's 1834 poem, was Rimsky-Korsakov's last opera. It was also his most provocative. In 1904 the Japanese government, despairing of ever being able to persuade the Russians to give them back Manchuria, launched a naval attack on Port Arthur. The Russian defences were disorganized and lost not only the opening battle, but the majority of the ensuing conflicts, with the army and navy humiliated by a country thought incapable of organizing any serious military threat. Shortly after the Japanese victory in 1906, Rimsky-Korsakov began *The Golden Cockerel*, using a libretto that turned Pushkin's original tale into a satire of military incompetence, aristocratic stupidity and political corruption. When he completed the score in September of the following year he was forced to submit it to the censor; the result was that it was barred from production, and Rimsky-Korsakov died without ever having heard the opera performed. When it finally reached the Moscow stage in 1909, it was with substantial changes imposed by the censor.

A tightly drawn and corrosive satire, *The Golden Cockerel* is the most succinct of Rimsky-Korsakov's operas. His predilection for exotic and sensual sound-worlds is still in evidence (spitting brass, reedy wind and brittle percussion contribute towards a sinister, otherworldly atmosphere), but the orchestration is noticeably more reserved than in *Sadko*, with a less indulgent harmonic palette. The melodies are more stringent, and much of the text setting has a sharpness of inflection that anticipates the work of his illustrious pupil, Igor Stravinsky.

In contrast to the delights of *Sadko*, this opera's dominant tone is rather ominous, a quality that particularly informs the character of the Astrologer, whose menacing and flamboyant Prologue and Epilogue frame the action. His music – characterized by a motif of arpeggiated, staccato glockenspiel chords – is scored very high in the tenor range, creating an effect which, like Schoenberg's Aaron, often sounds instrumental rather than vocal. Similarly, the Queen of Shemakha is identified with a slippery, descending chromatic pattern, a motif highly in keeping with her cruel personality (it plays a prominent role in her seduction of Dodon), and the edginess of the opera is increased by the role of the Golden Cockerel (played by a soprano), a part associated with a trumpet theme of jumpy, nervous tension. Though Dodon's bass and the Queen's radiant coloratura are memorable for their folk-based arias (the Queen's "Hymn to the Sun" is the most celebrated), this is an unconventionally acerbic and disturbing work.

RECORDINGS OVERVIEW

There have been two recordings of *The Golden Cockerel*, although the preferable reading – produced in 1962 by Melodiya with a mixed-bag cast conducted by Aleksei Kovalev – has yet to make its way onto CD. The later recording, taped live at the Bolshoi in 1988 and released on CD by MCA, is a mess, despite some quick-witted conducting from Yevgeny Svetlanov. Wait for the Kovalev set.

6

OPERA IN TRANSITION

THE GENERATION OF PUCCINI, MASSENET AND DEBUSSY

OPERA IN TRANSITION

THE GENERATION OF PUCCINI, MASSENET AND DEBUSSY

Several major composers reached their peak in the years between the heyday of Verdi and Wagner and the mould-breaking works of Strauss, Schoenberg, Berg and their contemporaries. Some of their operas might be described as belonging to a deliquescent phase of Romanticism, others can be seen as harbingers of modernism, and a few of the best known belong to a genre that was born and died in the decades preceding and following 1900 – verismo.

Verismo was born in Rome, which in 1870 became capital of the newly created Kingdom of Italy. At that date Rome was but a pale shadow of its former greatness, with a population of less than 200,000, around half that of Naples. In keeping with its restored status, Rome needed a new opera house, and in 1888 the Teatro Costanzi appointed its first manager, the publisher Edoardo Sonzogno, who promptly stole a march on the more successful firm of Ricordi by announcing a competition for one-act operas to be staged at his theatre. Remarkably, there were no fewer than 73 entrants, but the jury was quick to decide upon three winners, one of which, **Pietro Mascagni**'s *Cavalleria rusticana*, inaugurated the brief era of verismo ("realistic") opera.

Mascagni's work was based upon a story by Giovanni Verga, whose tales of low-life debauchery and violence – in many respects resembling the work of Emile Zola and Dumas – were to become something of a quarry for verismo composers. Verismo was all about shock, presenting grittily realistic characters in situations of extreme stress, and telling its tale through brief, illustrative bursts of music. In its purest form, verismo dealt with the lives of the underclass – characters far removed from the knavish or saintly rustic caricatures who had figured so frequently in bel canto. *Cavalleria rusticana*, an opera of rough-hewn peasants, adulterous passion and murder, prompted a flood of imitations, most of them conforming to the one-act, quick-punch model.

From this deluge of new work emerged **Ruggero Leoncavallo**'s *I Pagliacci*, a work that not only matched the worldwide box-office takings of *Cavalleria rusticana* but became shackled to it in the most successful double-bill in opera history. However, just as verismo didn't require its audiences to concentrate for long stretches of time, so it was too extreme and restricted a form to engage the attentions of its creators for long. Mascagni quickly moved on to lyrical comedy with *L'amico Fritz*; **Umberto Giordano**, having achieved notoriety with his "outrageous work of blasphemy", *Mala Vita* (Wicked Life), produced *Andrea Chénier*, an opera that might be described as a verismo romance, then lapsed entirely from real-life drama with the soppy but hugely lucrative *Fedora*; and **Francesco Cilea**, another Sonzogno discovery, abandoned the blood-and-guts routine for the lyrical elegance of *Adriana Lecouvreur*.

As was the case with Giordano, Leoncavallo and the more serene **Alfredo Catalani** (composer of the song-filled *La Wally*), Cilea's career featured just the one big triumph. By contrast, **Giacomo Puccini** hit the top early on, and stayed there. In 1889, when Puccini had produced just two operas, Cilea wrote bitterly to a friend, "I know that Puccini has to be 'the successor of Verdi' ", and indeed Puccini achieved a position in Italian musical life as dominant as Verdi's had been, writing music that married the virtues of Italian lyrical opera to the thrilling theatricality of verismo. Puccini's name was made with the premiere of *Manon Lescaut* in 1893, the first in a series of massively tuneful and often sensationalist operas that have remained central to the repertoire of every opera house on the planet and that included *La Bohème*, *Tosca* and *Madama Butterfly*. Richard Strauss became just as rich, but Puccini was the last opera composer to be as highly regarded by the person in the street as by the cognoscenti.

In France, the thoroughly different figure of **Jules Massenet** reigned supreme. Following in the footsteps of Gounod and Thomas, Massenet composed somewhat maudlin dramas that have survived chiefly on account of the sincerity and attractiveness of their vocal melodies, rather than on their qualities as music-drama, though the vitality and colour of his style shows an awareness of the work of more aggressively theatrical composers. While Massenet represented the final stand of the old guard, and **Gustave Charpentier** scored his main success with a lyrical French version of verismo opera, **Claude Debussy** cut a path out of the thickets of fin de siècle excess. Disgusted by the "saccharine abandon" of Gounod, Thomas and Massenet, and fascinated by the "serenity and resignation" of Wagner's *Parsifal*, Debussy turned the notion of melody-driven, character-led, plot-bound opera on its head with his setting of Maeterlinck's *Pelléas et Mélisande*. If one opera can be said to mark the cusp between late Romanticism and modernism, this is it.

In Germany, in the years separating *Parsifal* from Strauss's *Salome*, only one new composer managed to excite the German opera-going public. **Engelbert Humperdinck** was a lifelong devotee of Wagner, yet his finest hours were inspired not by Norse myth or Christian allegory, but by fairy tales. His gloriously melodic setting of *Hänsel und Gretel* brought him international celebrity, and he more than equalled its musical qualities (if not its income) with the tear-jerking *Königskinder*. Meanwhile **Frederick Delius**, a rootless Englishman, was writing his best-known opera – *A Village Romeo and Juliet* – in a distinctly German style and then overseeing its production in Germany. By the time both *Königskinder* and *A Village Romeo and Juliet* reached the stage, however, the German scene had been shaken by the arrival of Richard Strauss. But his story belongs to the twentieth century.

ALFREDO CATALANI

b. LUCCA, JUNE 19, 1854; d. MILAN, AUGUST 7, 1893.

Whereas a number of French composers tried to assimilate Wagner's music into their own work, nearly all Italian composers were resistant to the German's influence. The best known of those who weren't was Alfredo Catalani.

His earliest studies were with Puccini's uncle Fortunato Magi, after which he moved to Paris, where he undertook private studies with the ultra-conservative François Bazin. Returning to Italy, he settled in Milan, where he completed his studies at the Conservatory and then, in 1875, wrote a one-act opera to a libretto by Arrigo Boito. Like Boito, Catalani became involved with Scapigliatura, a gathering of progressive artists whose members included the music publisher Giovannina Lucca. Lucca began to support the composer, commissioning *Elda* in 1880, *Dejanice* in 1882 and *Edmea* in 1886, but when her company was absorbed by Ricordi, Lucca found herself forced to promote the works of Puccini – and Catalani was abandoned.

He achieved some success with the lush *Edmea*, as did its neophyte conductor, Arturo Toscanini, but the revision of *Elda* as *Loreley* (a legend previously set by Mendelssohn and Bruch) in 1890 was ignored by Ricordi, who didn't care for its indebtedness to Wagner. Frustrated by the popularity of verismo and Puccini's inexorable rise, Catalani took the extraordinary step of using his own money to pay for a libretto (it was normal for a text to come via a publisher or from the librettist) and he spent a year working on the score of *La Wally*. In 1892 he secured its first production at La Scala, where it established his reputation overnight. But it was to be a short-lived reputation: a year and a half later, two months after his thirty-ninth birthday, he was dead.

Catalani wrote modest, aristocratic and lyrical music, but ultimately Verdi and Wagner presented him with too many attractive influences for a strongly personal style to evolve. Unable to match the emotional intensity of his verismo colleagues and Puccini, and possessing little flair for theatre, he was destined to remain a slight figure to all but a few, and nowadays he's entrenched as one of the nineteenth century's lesser one-hit wonders.

La Wally

Composed 1890–91.
First performed January 20, 1892.
Libretto by Luigi Illica, after Wilhelmine von Hillern.

Synopsis

Act I
The Tyrol, 1800. At his seventieth birthday party Stromminger insults Hagenbach of Sölden, who strikes the old man to the ground. Wally rushes to her father's side and recognizes Hagenbach as the man she has secretly loved from afar. Her suitor Gellner warns Stromminger that his daughter is in love with his enemy and so Stromminger orders her to marry Gellner within the month. When she rejects Gellner she is expelled from the house.

Act II
Many years later at the Eagle tavern in Sölden. Stromminger has long since died, Wally has inherited his fortune and the landlady Afra is engaged to marry Hagenbach – whom Wally still loves. At a dance she confesses her feelings to Hagenbach, who then proceeds to mock her. Wally, enraged, seeks out Gellner and asks him if he still wants her. He does, but in return for her love Wally demands that he kill Hagenbach.

Act III
Both Wally and Hagenbach regret their actions, but Gellner carries out Wally's wishes, throwing Hagenbach down a ravine. Wally is horrified by the news and rushes to the edge of the ravine, where she helps bring the unconscious Hagenbach to safety. She turns to Afra and wishes them happiness together.

Act IV

Wally, wandering high in the Alps, prepares to end her life when she hears Hagenbach's voice in the distance. He has recovered from his injuries and is on his way to declare his love. She tells him of her part in his assault, but he doesn't care and they embrace. As they prepare to head back down the mountain, a storm blows up, setting off an avalanche in which both are killed.

The plot of *La Wally* is one of the daftest ever created, and stylistically the opera is something of a mongrel. In keeping with the Alpine setting, Catalani made use of Swiss folksongs – notably the sickly *Edelweiss* (as in *The Sound of Music*) – and gave the village dances a rustic feel that sits awkwardly with the sophisticated harmonic twists to which the composer was prone. This harmony is frequently Wagnerian in its thick, contrapuntal chromaticism, and the prevalent use of motifs is reminiscent of Wagner, but *La Wally's* type of through-composition owes more to Verdi's *Otello* than to Wagner's *Tristan*; and the tunes bear the unmistakable fingerprints of Verdi.

The most impassioned and most celebrated of these tunes is Wally's ethereal Act I aria "Ebben? Ne andro lontan", and throughout the opera the title role has the finest music in a score whose earthy power commanded the affection of no less a judge than Toscanini – indeed, he was so moved by Catalani's heroine that he lumbered the second of his two daughters with her name. The soprano Renata Tebaldi regarded Wally as the finest role in her repertoire, but Catalani gave little time to the heroine's colleagues: Hagenbach's tenor is a lacklustre creation, with no great tunes, and Gellner is a wimpish also-ran. This opera's success in performance depends almost entirely on the quality of its lead soprano.

Tebaldi, del Monaco, Cappuccilli, Diaz; Turin Lyric Chorus; Monte Carlo National Opera Orchestra; Cleva.
(Decca 425 417-2DM2; 2 CDs).

During the 1950s and 1960s, Renata Tebaldi demonstrated a unmatched ability to transform this far-fetched yarn into something truly moving, and her performance here captures the gravity of her voice in its full maturity. The lush and evocative timbre are utterly distinctive, and the joy with which she tackles the intensifying drama of "Ebben? Ne andro lontan" is priceless. Mario del Monaco barks and roars his way through Hagenbach; this is the sort of tenor that provokes extreme reactions, but either way you have to admire Tebaldi's courage – he cannot have been easy to sing next to. Cappuccilli does his best as Gellner but it is clear that neither he nor conductor Fausta Cleva felt able to do much with the role. Cleva's tempi are generally swift throughout but it is nice to hear him slam on the brakes whenever Tebaldi decides to enjoy herself. Wonderful, over-miked 1960s Decca sound, and excellent value.

PIETRO MASCAGNI

b. LIVORNO, ITALY, DECEMBER 7, 1863; d. ROME, AUGUST 2, 1945.

Of the various elements that fed the intense, brief-burning flame of verismo opera, one of the most significant was the literary realism of writers such as Dumas, Zola and the Sicilian author Giovanni Verga. Italian composers were particularly taken by Verga's violent novellas, and in 1889 his *Cavalleria rusticana* grabbed the attention of the young Pietro Mascagni, who translated the sensationalism of the story into a punchy operatic style that gave Italian opera a new direction.

Uninterested in working in his family's baking business, Mascagni at the age of nineteen entered the Milan Conservatory, where he briefly studied with Ponchielli and became friends with Puccini. Expelled in his second year, he travelled around Italy with a touring opera company, then supported himself by playing the double-bass at a theatre in Milan. In 1885 he conducted an operetta season in Parma, later moving to Cerignola as a piano teacher, but in 1889 he was attracted by an advertisement for a one-act opera competition promoted by the publisher Sonzogno. He immediately turned to Verga's story of rustic love and death, and completed the music of his seventy-minute masterpiece within a matter of weeks. Seized with doubts as to the opera's quality, he prepared to send in the fourth act of a full-length opera he'd written called *Guglielmo Ratcliff*; but without his knowledge his wife submitted the score of *Cavalleria* instead. As one of three winners, it received its first performance in front of a half-empty but wildly enthusiastic house. Within months it was one of the world's most frequently performed contemporary operas.

Mascagni was soon championed as the leader of the *veristi*, but for his next opera he abandoned the primary colours of his one-act shocker

LEBRECHT COLLECTION

Pietro Mascagni (third from the left) with the first-night cast of Cavalleria rusticana

PIETRO MASCAGNI

for the light and delicate pastoral comedy of *L'amico Fritz*. It was successful but not on the scale of *Cavalleria*, and for all his efforts Mascagni failed to recapture his youthful dazzle, even though a few of the later works contain some fine music. As he later remarked: "It was a pity I wrote *Cavelleria* first. I was crowned before I was king." Mascagni did not lapse into obscurity, however. An adroit opportunist, in 1929 he succeeded Toscanini as music director of La Scala, where he cheerfully launched each performance with the fascist hymn – indeed he was swiftly adopted by Mussolini's government as their official composer. Though this move earned him the obloquy of the victorious allies, by the 1950s *Cavalleria* had made a solid return to the stage. The colossal success of this one opera had made much of Mascagni's life an ordeal. On one occasion his aggravation reached such a pitch that he refused to conduct a selection of highlights from *Cavalleria* at a high-society function in London; in the end he relented, but no sooner had he regained his composure than he was introduced to Queen Victoria, whose opening gambit was "Signor Mascagni, I hope you will soon write another *Cavalleria*." It was a sentiment that dogged him for half a century, but as he once conceded, it was "better to have conquered once, than never to have conquered at all".

Cavalleria rusticana

Rustic Chivalry

Composed 1889.
First performed May 17, 1890.
Libretto by Giovanni Targioni-Tozzetti and Guido Menasci, after Verga.

Synopsis

Easter morning in a Sicilian village. Turiddù has been away with the army. Before leaving he had an affair with Lola, who has now married Alfio. Turiddù is upset by this, but has found consolation through a brief affair with Santuzza, whom he has made pregnant. For this, she has been excommunicated. As the curtain rises Turiddù sings of Lola. Alfio meets Turiddù's mother Lucia and asks her where her son is. She replies that he has gone to fetch wine for the family inn; but when Alfio tells her that he has seen him near his house, Santuzza quickly tells Lucia to say nothing of Turiddù's interest in Lola. After the villagers enter the church for the Easter service Santuzza tells Lucia how her son made her pregnant and then abandoned her. Lucia enters the church, leaving Santuzza to face Turiddù. They meet, and she begs him to honour his obligation, but he is distracted by Lola's arrival. When Lola enters the church, Santuzza implores Turiddù to return her love; he throws her to the ground and follows Lola into the church, leaving Santuzza to thoughts of revenge. She tells Alfio that Turiddù has been unfaithful with Lola, driving Alfio into a rage. After the service Turiddù encourages the villagers to drink his mother's wine. He offers a glass to Alfio – who refuses to drink – and when it becomes clear that a fight is imminent the women leave. Alfio challenges Turiddù to a duel. Turiddù goes to his mother, whom he asks to look after Santuzza should he die. He leaves to face Alfio; they fight offstage, then a female voice is heard screaming that Turiddù has been killed.

The pairing of *Cavalleria rusticana* and Mascagni's *Pagliacci* – the double bill known in the trade as "Cav and Pag" – was initiated in New York in 1903, and the two operas have been inseparable ever since. There are obvious similarities between them (the duration, the themes of adultery and revenge) but Mascagni's is the more realistic story, and although his score lacks the carnal immediacy of *Pagliacci*, *Cavalleria rusticana* is the more ingratiating piece of music. Even when the heat is turned right up, Mascagni's melodies never crack under the pressure.

For example, Turiddù's opening number, the offstage "O Lola", is intended to convey his lustful obsession with Alfio's wife – yet Mascagni's music is pleasant and lilting (compare this to the nervy opening of *Pagliacci*). Similarly Turiddù's ingenuous tribute to the joys of wine, "Viva il vino spumeggiante", comes as a respite from the sense of impending mayhem, and his duet with Santuzza – one of the most exciting in Italian opera – is as lyrical an episode as you could wish for. Although the opera moves at a swift pace, it does so on its own terms, never rushing through ideas that warrant a little musical indulgence.

The final scene is Mascagni's most remarkable achievement: while the villagers are in the church, the famous orchestral intermezzo – used in a dozen advertising campaigns – lulls the audience into a false sense of security, before Mascagni cranks the opera up a gear, propelling it towards the fatal duel. Breaking point is reached with Turiddù's farewell to his mother,

"Mama, quel vino e generoso" – a haunting lament which marks one of the pinnacles of verismo tenor writing. It's typical of Mascagni that his final scene should leave the audience breathless while providing a mattress of beautiful sound to fall back on.

RECORDINGS OVERVIEW

Cavalleria rusticana is a conductor's opera, in that it can survive weak singing but not bad conducting. Many of the thirty or so complete recordings of *Cavalleria rusticana* suffer from self-indulgent conducting, some of it perpetrated by maestros who elsewhere have proved themselves brilliantly capable. The composer himself gave a low-key reading when he recorded it in 1940 with Gigli as Turridù (a set now available on Nimbus), while at the other end of the scale the 1966 Decca recording, with Elena Souliotis and the indestructible Mario del Monaco, was a performance of supernatural loudness and vulgarity. Some of the most promising combinations – Milanov/Björling/Cellini (RCA), Simionato/del Monaco/Serafin (Decca) and de los Angeles/Corelli/Santini (EMI) – turned out to be the most disappointing, and today's superstars have rarely fared well. That said, Domingo's 1978 recording of the work for RCA under James Levine (the first of Domingo's three) would be a fourth choice after the sets reviewed below.

Evstatieva, Aragall, Tumagian, di Maurao; Slovak Philharmonic Choir; Bratislava Radio Symphony Orchestra; Rahbari.
(Naxos 866002; 1 CD).

This 1992 budget-price recording is as good as any in the catalogue. The mercurial Alexander Rahbari gives the performance of his career, with quick, finely calculated tempi that avoid the customary bombast without placing undue strain on the singers. In terms of technique and beauty of tone, Giacomo Aragall cannot compete with the likes of Corelli, Domingo or Pavarotti, but he responds well to Rahbari's direction and clearly enjoys working alongside Evstatieva, who gives a penetrating account of Santuzza. Similarly the Czech forces are not a patch on Karajan's La Scala (see below), but Rahbari understands this music perfectly, and for dramatic integrity this interpretation cannot be beaten.

Cossotto, Bergonzi, Guelfi, Martino; La Scala Chorus and Orchestra; Karajan.
(Deutsche Grammophon 419 257-2GH3; 3 CDs – with *I Pagliacci* and various opera intermezzi).

Karajan's *Cavalleria rusticana* is exquisitely, almost suffocatingly beautiful, with its slow tempi and oversized orchestra. Bergonzi is in big, confident voice and his final scene is thrillingly performed (sobs and all), while Fiorenza Cossotto's chesty soprano brings a dark and brooding quality to the wretched Santuzza. The lush orchestral wash is accentuated by a rich, glowing sound quality that makes every moment a sumptuous experience. The Karajan sound isn't without its critics, but this set is an easily acquired taste. However, at full price and on three CDs, it is an expensive set.

Callas, di Stefano, Panerai, Canali; La Scala Chorus and Orchestra; Serafin.
(EMI CDS7 47981-8; 3 CDs – with *I Pagliacci*).

Serafin was better known for his work with bel canto opera than with verismo, but this mono *Cavalleria* is an exciting and committed account, notable for the enthusiastic and detailed playing from La Scala's orchestra and the scorching Santuzza of Maria Callas – these 1953 sessions captured her soprano in secure form, with a tight vibrato and few brittle high notes. Rolando Panerai is an impassioned Alfio and di Stefano, though ill-suited to the role of Turiddù, makes the best of it, shining in his final scene. The sound was boxy on LP and EMI's transfer has made little difference, but the determined conducting and thrilling singing make this a tempting proposition. The accompanying *Pagliacci* doesn't have the same flair, but at mid-price this set is still good value.

L'amico Fritz

Friend Fritz

Composed 1890–91.
First performed October 31, 1891.
Libretto by Nicola Diaspuro, after Erckmann and Chatrian.

Synopsis

Act I

Fritz complains to David that, once again, he has been asked to provide the dowry for two neighbours who wish to marry. He cannot understand romantic love or why anyone would want to enter wedlock. Suzel, the daughter of one of Fritz's tenants, arrives with flowers and they sit together, listening to a gypsy play the violin. David wagers Fritz that the latter will soon be married.

Act II

In a cherry orchard Suzel throws cherries down to Fritz, who praises her singing. He is captivated by her, and they sing the so-called "Cherry duet". David arrives and, in Fritz's absence, he discovers that Suzel would happily marry Fritz. When he tells Fritz that he has found Suzel a husband, Fritz – not knowing that he is the man in question – is horrified but realizes there is nothing he can do.

Act III

David asks for Fritz's consent to Suzel's marriage. He refuses it. Suzel arrives and Fritz asks her if it is true that she is going to marry. She says she is unhappy at the prospect of an arranged marriage and this encourages Fritz to confess his love. David has won his bet and the chorus congratulate the couple on their engagement.

With *Cavalleria* breaking box offices across the world, Mascagni's admirers anticipated that its follow-up would be the same species of opera. However, conscious of the limitations of the slam-bang format of verismo, and resentful of suggestions that *Cavalleria* owed its success to the quality of its libretto, Mascagni determined to compose an opera in which the music rather than the drama was dominant. As he wrote to Sonzogno, he wanted "a simple libretto, with almost a flimsy plot, so the opera could be judged on the music alone", and he was duly provided with a text that Verdi described as "the worst libretto I have ever seen". For Mascagni, it was ideal.

L'amico Fritz could hardly be less like *Cavalleria*: it is a benign comedy, the characters are agreeable, and the vocal writing is in the bel canto mode, complete with arias and ensembles and deliciously sweet melodies. Fritz himself is unrealistically wholesome but his high-lying tenor is a gem of a part – and he has the distinction of being one of the few middle-aged tenor heroes, presenting rare opportunities for characterization. From the "Cherry duet" onwards, his music has a magical and refined beauty, reaching its peak with the expansive Act III aria "O amore, o bella luce del core", a touching creation that ends with a wallowing climax for orchestra and soloist. Suzel's music is generally less memorable than Fritz's, but her part in the "Cherry duet" and her principal Act III aria "Non mi resta che il pianto" are gorgeously tuneful.

Tagliavini, Tassinari, Pini, Meletti; EIAR Chorus and Symphony Orchestra; Mascagni.
(Fonit Cetra; CDO 18; 2 CDs).

Mascagni's 1942 recording of this undervalued opera is a delightful performance – perfectly phrased and beautifully sung, with subtle instrumental shading, intuitive rubato, and fizzing climaxes. Most seductive of all is the young tenor voice of Ferruccio Tagliavini, whose elegantly varied but slightly husky tone is used with admirable tastefulness; from the amorous declamation of the "Cherry duet" to the incremental passions of "O amore, o bella luce del core" he is in magnificent voice. Saturno Meletti is a vital David, Amalia Pini a delightful Beppe, and Pia Tassinari a shy but yearning Suzel. The superb singers are ably supported throughout by the composer, who evidently enjoyed his cast almost as much as his opera.

Pavarotti, Freni, Gambaradella, Sardinero; Royal Opera House Chorus and Orchestra; Gavazzeni.
(EMI CDS 7 47905-8; 2 CDs).

Recorded in 1968, Gavazzeni's aristocratic reading lacks the warmth and good humour that characterizes Mascagni's set, but Pavarotti – making his first studio recording – glides irresistibly through this music, and his phrasing is a model of sweetness, breathing and declamation. Mirella Freni – also a studio debutante – is a little detached for Suzel, and the remaining cast do no more than satisfy the basic requirements, but the London forces are a big improvement on the EIAR orchestra and chorus, just as EMI's stereo marks a huge advance on Cetra's mono.

RUGGERO LEONCAVALLO

b. NAPLES, MARCH 8, 1857; d. MONTECATINI, AUGUST 9, 1919.

Verismo was initiated by Mascagni's *Cavalleria rusticana* in 1889 and perfected by Leoncavallo's *I Pagliacci* two years later. The epitome of every hot-blooded Italian operatic cliché, *Pagliacci* is one of the most elementally exciting operas ever written and its international popularity has never waned from the day of its premiere.

Leoncavallo began his musical life as a devotee of Wagner, though it was not so much the music as the literary and dramatic substance that he admired. At the age of thirty he began writing *Crepusculum*, a Renaissance trilogy "à la Nibelungen", but he was sidetracked by *Chatterton*, an opera about the suicidal young English poet that had occupied him since his student days. When the promoter of the premiere disappeared with the composer's money shortly before the first night (causing the production to be abandoned), Leoncavallo approached the publisher Ricordi with a view to getting the score printed. Ricordi, however, thought Leoncavallo a better librettist than composer and commissioned him to write the text for Puccini's *Manon Lescaut*; Puccini, unimpressed by Leoncavallo's progress, had him removed from the project.

In 1891, after two years of further dissatisfaction, Leoncavallo found his inspiration in the limelight of Mascagni's recently premiered *Cavalleria rusticana*, a work he greatly admired. Taking as his raw material a murder case his magistrate father had once judged (as he revealed after Catulle Mendès sued the composer for alleged plagiarism of his play *La Femme de Tabarin*), Leoncavallo worked flat out on his new creation: "I shut myself in my house . . . and in five months I wrote the poem and music of *Pagliacci*." Toscanini gave the first performance, and Leoncavallo's fame and fortune were made overnight. On the back of this success he took the peculiar and ill-advised step of arranging the premiere of *I Medici*, the first part of his *Crepusculum*, but, despite the blaze of pre-publicity, the venture was savaged by the press and ridiculed by the public.

His reputation was in tatters and from then on Leoncavallo was embroiled in a losing battle with Puccini for the affections of the Italian people. Leoncavallo's interpretation of *La Bohème*, staged almost a year after Puccini's, met with some initial success, but inevitably faded from the scene as Puccini triumphed. He was one of the first composers to take a serious interest in the gramophone, and he composed the song "Mattinata" expressly for the G&T company, recording it with Caruso in April 1904.

Leoncavallo spent the rest of his life attempting to recreate *Pagliacci*'s burst of glory, or to live it down. He grew so weary of his hit that he once accompanied a performance of *Pagliacci* at Forlì opera house with a running commentary on its failings, assuring his neighbour that it was "great rubbish and unoriginal", that "this particular aria was stolen from Bizet, that another motive was from Wagner, and that such-and-such a bit was taken from Verdi" . The following day the local paper reported his analysis under the headline "Leoncavallo on his own opera *Pagliacci*". After that he made sure never again to disparage his own work in public, but Leoncavallo's life went steadily downhill after *Pagliacci*. The man who had once proposed writing a music-drama to rival Wagner's *Ring* spent his dying months composing an operetta entitled *A chi la giarettiera?* or "Whose garter is this?".

I Pagliacci

The Clowns

Composed 1891–92.
First performed May 21, 1892.
Libretto by the composer.

Synopsis

Act I

After a prologue in which Tonio informs the audience that what they are about to witness is a true story, the

ARTURO TOSCANINI

The premieres of *I Pagliacci*, *La Bohème*, *Turandot* and dozens of other operas were conducted by **Arturo Toscanini** (1867–1957), a musician whose reputation retains such an aura that in the early 1990s RCA released an 82-CD set of Toscanini-led recordings. He shot to fame aged just nineteen, when, on tour in Brazil with an Italian orchestra, he was promoted from cellist to conductor to lead a performance of *Aida* at very short notice. On this as on almost every subsequent engagement, Toscanini did his job without the aid of a score, for having read through a score he could recall every note with such precision that decades later he could correct wind or string parts that players had failed to read correctly from the pages in front of them. But memory alone doesn't make a great conductor. It was his charisma, his energy and his fiercely disciplined attitude towards performance and the composer's intentions ("com'è scritto!" – "as it's written!" – he used to scream) that made him such a force and influence. It's an indication of how quickly Toscanini achieved mastery of his art that in 1892 Giuseppe Verdi, never the most generous of critics, approached the twenty-five-year-old after he'd conducted *Falstaff* and simply enthused – "Grazie! Grazie! Grazie!"

Taking Verdi as his model, Toscanini made himself into the ultimate tyrant of the podium. To get what he wanted he would rant, stamp his feet, tear his scores to shreds, snap his baton, sulk and even assault his musicians – he once grabbed hold of a soprano's breasts and shrieked, "if only these were brains!". Regarding musicians as the servants of the composer, he hated the star system and frequently got into confrontations with his celebrity singers – most famously when, during a performance of *Un ballo in maschera* at La Scala in 1903, he denied the tenor Giovanni Zenatello the opportunity to encore "È' scherzo od è follia". The audience booed and Toscanini stormed out of the pit, leaving the performance incomplete and refusing to return to La Scala for three years.

He had been conducting at La Scala since 1896, and in 1898 he had been made the theatre's principal conductor. In spite of his difficulties with the management, the singers and the public – he would yell at anyone who dared talk during the performance or, worse still, arrived late – he stuck it out until 1908, when "the world's most thrilling conductor" was appointed artistic director of New York's Metropolitan Opera, where he made his debut conducting *Aida*. His stay at the Met was no less stormy than his stint at La Scala (thanks partly to a passionate affair with the soprano Geraldine Farrar and his constant rows with Caruso and his fellow stars), but he brought about a remarkable rise in standards and refreshed the repertoire – not least the world premiere of *La Fanciulla del West* with Caruso and Destinn in the leading roles. But in 1915 he resigned, embarking upon life as an itinerant conductor-for-hire, all the while enhancing the myth of "maestro" Toscanini, the man who could play every instrument in the orchestra and whose ear was infallible.

The modern cult of the conductor was born with Toscanini, and his prestige sometimes irri-

Calabrian villagers assemble to greet the strolling players. The players are directed by Canio, who invites the crowd to attend their performance. Canio's wife Nedda is wooed by the deformed Tonio, one of the players, but she cruelly rejects his advances. Her lover, Silvio, arrives and they arrange to meet later. Their exchanges are overheard by Tonio, who alerts Canio to the assignation. He is furious and demands to know her lover's identity but she denies she is having an affair; as Canio prepares for that evening's performance, he unburdens himself of his grief.

Act II

The protagonists enact a drama that mirrors their own situation. Canio does his best to maintain his composure but when Colombine (Nedda) refuses to reveal her lover's identity, he can no longer contain himself. Nedda mocks him and, insane with jealousy, he stabs her to death. When Silvio comes to her aid, Canio kills him as well. Turning to the audience he announces "La commedia è finita!" – the comedy is over.

The first performance of *I Pagliacci* must have been momentous. The soprano Adelina Stehle (Verdi's Nannetta) sang Nedda, the tenor Ludovico Giraud (Debussy's Italian Pelléas) sang Canio, the baritone Victor Maurel (Verdi's Iago and Falstaff) sang Tonio, and the young Toscanini conducted. As "a tated those who had a more valid claim to be true creators. For example, when it was rumoured that Toscanini was to conduct Puccini's works in London in the 1919 season, the composer wrote to his friend Sybil Seligman: "I don't want that pig of a Toscanini. . . . I won't have this God. He's no use to me."

Not until 1920, when La Scala tempted Toscanini back to Milan, did he take up another permanent appointment. But fascism was on the rise, and disputes with Mussolini soon developed. Il Duce complained that the conductor's well-publicized arguments with his players reflected badly on the leading opera house of the "New Italy", and tension came to a head with Toscanini's refusal to conduct the fascist anthem, the "Giovinezza", although Mussolini had made it law that it must always be played after the national anthem. Toscanini again left his homeland for the United States in 1929, when he was appointed joint head of the New York Philharmonic. The following year he became the first non-German to conduct at Bayreuth, but just three years later his anti-fascist principles forced him to break off relations with the Wagner family. His loathing of anti-Semitism was underlined when he conducted the inaugural concert of the Palestine Symphony Orchestra (later the Israel Philharmonic) in Tel Aviv in 1936.

Although he never gave up his Italian citizenship, he finally settled in the USA in the following year, and embarked on the final phase of his career as a figurehead of American high culture, exploiting the ever-expanding broadcast media so adroitly that his fame was soon as great as the president's. The first conductor to make the covers of *Life* and *Time* magazines, he was also the first to devote as much time to the recording studio as to the concert platform, and millions tuned to hear his radio broadcasts for NBC – the network which, in 1937, formed an orchestra especially for his exclusive use. From 1948 to 1952, despite his great age, NBC broadcast twice-yearly live TV concerts of Toscanini and his NBC Orchestra, raising his exposure to a level that was unprecedented and remains unmatched. It's been estimated that one in three of New York's TV sets was tuned in to each show, and that the concerts reached an aggregate audience of 80 million. In 1954 his final concert was broadcast as if it were some sort of state occasion, and millions saw the maestro falter under the emotion of it all, dropping his baton and – horror of horrors – losing his place in the score. By that stage RCA had sold an incredible twenty million Toscanini records. Four years later, following his death, RCA joined forces with the Book of the Month Club to launch the RCA Victor Record Club on the back of the Toscanini back-catalogue; subscribers were enticed with a bargain-priced set of the Beethoven symphonies conducted by Toscanini – and within the first three months some 340,000 customers signed up. But perhaps the most significant indicator of Toscanini's impact on the American scene is the fact that in 1953 – the year before his retirement – the National Music Club registered 30 million paid admissions for classical concerts, drawing receipts of $45 million. The same year, major league baseball welcomed 15 million through the turnstiles, banking $5 million less.

bleeding slice of life", to quote Tonio's prologue, the opera required an unbroken dramatic flow, but the premiere was repeatedly halted by the applause of the audience. Nowadays the punters tend to stay in their seats for the full hour of *Pagliacci*'s emotional turmoil, but it has not lost its capacity to thrill. Musically it may lack the finesse of *Cavalleria rusticana*, but *Pagliacci* is the apogee of verismo: rarely has such intensity of feeling been condensed into so brief a passage of time.

The aggrieved husband, the faithless wife, the treacherous colleague and the spurned lover may not be the most complex operatic creations but Leoncavallo gives them an almost unbearable immediacy. The clown Canio is one of the most exhilarating Italian tenor roles, requiring a singer with equal measures of stamina, dexterity and power: he and the opera in general are celebrated for the brief lament "Vesti la giubba . . . ridi Pagliaccio", an outburst of shivering self-pity, but his opening "Un tal gioco" and concluding, feverishly passionate "Non, Pagliaccio, non son!" have even greater dramatic impact. The rest of the cast – the spitting, hissing, seductive Nedda, the creepy Tonio, the deeply unlovely Silvio – make sure that the action stays way over the top. There is no subtlety in the text or music of *Pagliacci*; for a short, sharp operatic shock there is nothing to beat it.

RECORDINGS OVERVIEW

Pagliacci has been recorded dozens of times, but few of these recordings do the piece justice. The catalogue contains a number of casts that, on paper, seem to guarantee success, and yet, despite some marvellous highlights, the "benchmark" recordings with Pacetti/Gigli, de los Angeles/Björling, di Stefano/Callas, Caballé/Domingo, Freni/Pavarotti and Scotto/Carreras don't quite burn with the intensity of the performances listed below. There is one superb but currently unavailable set: Erede's 1952 Decca recording, with the young del Monaco thunderously exciting as Canio, plus Clara Petrella's savage Nedda and Afro Poli's earthy Tonio. Del Monaco's ear-splittingly loud 1959 repeat is available, but to be avoided.

Corelli, Amara, Gobbi, Zanasi; La Scala Chorus and Orchestra; Matacic. (EMI CMS7 63967-2; 2 CDs, with *Cavalleria rusticana*).

Recorded in 1960, this set captures two of the century's most exciting singers – Franco Corelli and Tito Gobbi – in their prime. Corelli's electrifyingly powerful tenor shines throughout, ringing like a struck bell and hitting the high notes as if they were a third lower than they are. Purists may object to the Gigli-esque sobbing and heaving, but these tricks of the tenor's trade are perfect for a melodrama like this. Gobbi has a great time as Tonio, and although his tone is forced he delivers a stupendous A flat at "Al pari di voi" during the Prologue. Matacic's tempi are fast but nicely judged, and the orchestral playing and recorded sound are ideal. There are not many opera recordings in which everything works, but this is one of them. The accompanying *Cavalleria rusticana*, however, is slack and inconsistent, with Corelli in unacceptably brash form.

Bergonzi, Carlyle, Taddei, Panerai; La Scala Chorus and Orchestra; Karajan. (Deutsche Grammophon 449 727-2GOR; 1 CD).

As with the first-choice performance of *Cavalleria rusticana* with which it's coupled, Karajan's 1965 recording of *Pagliacci* is fabulously lush, a fine testament to his transformation of the Scala forces from a second-rate band into the most expressive opera orchestra ever to record the work. Carlo Bergonzi's voice might have lacked some steel, but this is a menacing portrayal of Canio, and the weight and fluency of his phrasing are intoxicating. Joan Carlyle's light soprano is vital and beautifully produced, and Giuseppe Taddei is a feverish Tonio, but the overwhelming influence is Karajan's. In addition to this mid-price re-issue, this great recording is also available as part of a full-price three-CD box with a superb *Cavalleria rusticana* and a miscellany of Italian operatic overtures and intermezzi.

GIACOMO PUCCINI

b. LUCCA, ITALY, DECEMBER 22, 1858; d. BRUSSELS, NOVEMBER 11, 1924.

It has been said that Wagner's music is better than it sounds. Conversely, Puccini's often sounds better than it is. Possessing a taste for high drama, a highly developed sense of theatre, an uncanny facility for memorable melodies and a genius for emotional manipulation, Puccini soon settled upon the most effective means to achieve his ends, and stuck to them so firmly that from his third opera, *Manon Lescaut*, to his twelfth and last, *Turandot*, his style evolved very little. He was often accused of decadence and shallow showmanship, as he still is, but judged by box-office receipts he is the most successful composer to have written opera in the twentieth century.

Puccini was born into a long line of musicians and benefited greatly from early encouragement. His initial studies were with his father (himself a pupil of Donizetti) and then his uncle, but upon entering the Milan Conservatory in 1880 he began tuition with Ponchielli, who steered him away from the family tradition of church music and towards the stage. With Ponchielli's encouragement Puccini

Torre del Lago Puccini - Villa Puccini - Il Maestro al pianoforte

Puccini relaxes at home in Torre del Lago

entered Sonzogno's competition for a one-act opera (as did Mascagni and Giordano), and though *Le Villi* failed to receive even an honourable mention, it did secure a commission for another, full-length opera from the publisher. Six years later, *Edgar* was given its first performance, conducted by Franco Faccio, an important figure in the careers of Ponchielli and Verdi. Yet this too was a failure and it was another four years before Puccini produced his first successful opera, *Manon Lescaut*.

The fusion of high passion and sweet melodies led Bernard Shaw to proclaim Puccini the rightful heir to Verdi, and by the time his next work, *La Bohème*, was given its premiere in 1896, he was Italy's most talked-about musician. His reputation was further enhanced by his next opera, *Tosca*, first performed in 1900, and though his rise was briefly interrupted by the disastrous first performance of *Madama Butterfly* in 1904, that too was acclaimed a masterpiece after Puccini's revision. By now, he was wealthy enough to indulge his tastes for sports cars and expensive property and to devote as much time to shooting and fishing as he wanted, frequently to the detriment of prearranged work schedules. But he was in an unhappy marriage and he was forever drifting in and out of affairs; in a notorious case, one of his servants was driven to suicide by Elvira Puccini's accusations that the girl was sleeping with the composer. An autopsy revealed that, for once, Puccini had not had his way, but his reaction – he dismissed her death as the actions of a "silly girl" – was indicative of a streak of cruelty that dismayed even those who loved him. But while his attitude to other people frequently suggested a character akin to a steamroller, Puccini was prone to fits of self-doubt and would sometimes go through dozens of different ideas before reaching what was invariably an uncertain conclusion.

This trait was never more obvious than when it came to writing a follow-up to *Butterfly*, and several months passed before he eventually settled on *The Girl of the Golden West*, a play by David Belasco, author of the text from which *Butterfly* had been derived. After the New York premiere of *La Fanciulla del West* in 1910 the composer once again dithered over his latest project, before receiving from Vienna's Carl Theater a commission for an operetta; though no admirer of the operetta tradition, he was encouraged by the offer of vast sums of money to write a comic opera "like *Rosenkavalier*, but more amusing and more organic". But *La Rondine* turned out to be no *Rosenkavalier*, and its early success has not endured. For his following work he revived an earlier project for a triptych of one-act operas, and produced a verismo thriller, *Il Tabarro*, a sentimental religious drama, *Suor Angelica*, and a comic farce, *Gianni Schicchi*. All three (performed together) were big hits, but only *Gianni Schicchi* has secured a place in the repertoire. Puccini died from throat cancer before completing his last opera, *Turandot*, and so Toscanini engaged Franco Alfano to complete the final duet. It was first performed in front of an ecstatic Milanese audience on April 25, 1926, almost two years after the composer's death.

Puccini's immediately recognizable and accessible style grew out of the music of Verdi and of verismo, a genre he transmuted by moving away from its shock tactics to create something that was in effect a reinvention of the bel canto tradition. Puccini is the confluence of bel canto fluency and verismo realism, but where the proponents of verismo were concerned above all to be "true to life", Puccini regarded beauty as the ultimate criterion of value. It can't be denied that Puccini has his weaknesses: he often lapses into glutinous sentimentality; there's more than a hint of misogyny in his preference for helpless heroines dominated by despotic men; and his plots are sometimes feeble or trivial. But for most audiences these weaknesses are beside the point, for his operas contain some of the most enjoyable music ever written, carrying into the twentieth century the legacy of Bellini, Donizetti and Verdi.

Manon Lescaut

Composed 1889–1892; revised 1893 and 1922.
First performed February 1, 1893.
Libretto by Leoncavallo, Praga, Oliva, Illica and Giacosa, after Abbé Prévost.

Synopsis

Act I

Des Grieux, a young Chevalier, sits with friends in an inn. He mocks the vagaries of love and celebrates his life of selfish pleasure; but when Manon Lescaut arrives (on her way to a convent, accompanied by her brother) he falls immediately in love with her. One of Manon's travelling companions, Géronte, tells Lescaut of his interest in his sister, and Lescaut blesses his plan to take her as his wife to Paris. Both are fooled when des Grieux manages to convince Manon to elope with him. They steal Géronte's carriage.

Act II

Manon has left des Grieux for Géronte, tempted by his wealth. Des Grieux finds Géronte's house, where he and Manon rekindle their love, but they are discovered by Géronte, who is sent packing by Manon. As des Grieux and Manon prepare to leave, her brother arrives and warns them that Géronte has summoned the police; Manon tries to take Géronte's jewels with her, but the police burst in and arrest her for stealing.

Act III

Manon is to be deported from Le Havre. Des Grieux and Lescaut are waiting for sunrise, at which point they will rescue her. When their plan fails, des Grieux hurls himself at the feet of the captain and begs to be allowed to accompany her. As the order for departure is given, he steps on board.

Act IV

Manon and des Grieux are again on the run, this time in Louisiana. Manon is dying from exhaustion and des Grieux leaves to find water. He returns, alone and empty-handed, to find Manon at death's door. She swears her love to the end, and dies in his arms.

𝄞 In 1890, with the failure of *Edgar* weighing heavily upon him and with a wife and two children to support, Puccini considered leaving Italy for Argentina, where his brother was living. Unable to afford the passage, he resumed the struggle with his debtors and his work, briefly considering a Shakespeare adaptation (Verdi had recently triumphed with *Otello*) before alighting on Prévost's *Manon Lescaut*. He wrote to Ricordi: "Manon is a heroine I believe in; she cannot fail to appeal to the hearts of the public." Leoncavallo began sketching a text, but Puccini had him dumped from the project, initiating a reciprocal, life-long and public hatred. There followed a stream of librettists, none of whom satisfied Puccini's increasingly difficult demands (he wanted a text with minimum similarities to Massenet's popular treatment of the same story), but eventually, Luigi Illica and Giuseppe Giacosa completed a draft, and within twelve months of its first performance, in Turin, *Manon Lescaut* was premiered in England and America.

Puccini's final act is a confusing mess, and the music suggests that he thought so as well, but the strengths of the first three acts are more than ample compensation. *Manon*'s primary quality is its precipitous onward movement –

an intermezzo at the beginning of the third act just about gives the audience time for a breather before the nervous tension of the scene at Le Havre. Rarely pausing for a traditional number (des Grieux's ardent Act I ballad "Donna non vidi mai" is an exception), *Manon* is a rush of mood-swings and theatrical coups: Manon's Act I duet with des Grieux is brutally cut short by Lescaut's outburst; their eighteen-minute love duet in Act II is shattered by Géronte's arrival; and their mournful exchanges in Act III are ended by a rifle shot and Lescaut's despairing news that his escape plans have failed. Compared to *La Bohème* and *Tosca*, *Manon Lescaut* might be a somewhat gauche creation, but its naive passion makes it a considerably more exciting treatment of Prévost's text than Massenet's more faithful adaptation.

RECORDINGS OVERVIEW

The very first recording of *Manon Lescaut*, conducted by Lorenzo Morajoli and taped in 1931 by EMI, offers an exciting example of how *Manon* was perceived shortly after the composer's death and, should it be released, it would be a valid first choice. Decca's 1954 account (see opposite) marked something an interpretative shift, reducing the orchestral presence in favour of the singers, as nearly all modern recordings tend to do. It is pipped to the post by RCA's outstanding account, produced the same year, with Björling and Albanese. Callas's brilliantly temperamental account, dating from 1957, received fine support from di Stefano and Serafin, but her tone is likely to deter the non-partisan. Placido Domingo, a blistering des Grieux in the right circumstances, has three versions of the role in the catalogue: a rather earthbound one with Caballé; a better-conducted interpretation for Deutsche Grammophon under Giuseppe Sinopoli; and the comprehensively superior live performance listed opposite. One other recording must be mentioned. Featuring Carlo Bergonzi and Dorothy Kirsten as the lovers, Fausta Cleva's 1960 New York Met performance is the most electrifying version on record; it has been available on Golden Age of Opera, and might reappear at some date – if it does, get it.

Björling, Albanese, Merrill, Calabrese; Rome Opera Chorus and Orchestra; Perlea.
(RCA GD 60573; 2 CDs).

This is just about the greatest recording Licia Albanese ever made. Some find her technique mannered, but she is a remarkably intelligent singer and she reveals the different stages in Manon's decline with sometimes alarming naturalism. Jussi Björling is in splendid, velvety form, and – unusually – he conveys more than just the beauty of his voice, giving the character room to develop. Robert Merrill is a little blunt as Lescaut, but the voice is hard not to enjoy; and the chorus and orchestra are excellent – in no small part thanks to Jonel Perlea's tightly drawn direction. Unforgettable.

Tebaldi, del Monaco, Boriello, Corena; Santa Cecilia Academy Chorus and Orchestra; Molinari-Pradelli.
(Decca 430 253-2DM2; 2 CDs).

Like a schoolmaster new to his class, Molinari-Pradelli seems intimidated by his singers, and he is a detached presence throughout this highly strung performance. Renata Tebaldi is in typically glowing form as Manon, and she makes her music flow like no other singer. She strives with touching delicacy to phrase her line throughout the love-duet, but she's up against the des Grieux of the turbocharged Mario del Monaco, so the result sounds less like a lovers' exchange than an argument. But while del Monaco suggests little of his character's confusion or fear, there is no denying the thrill of hearing him smash his way through music as emotive as this. Mario Boriello also lacks charm as Lescaut, but he suggests considerably more of his character's complex, unlovable personality.

Olivero, Domingo, Fioravanti, Mariotti; Verona Arena Chorus and Orchestra; Santi.
(Foyer 2-CF2033; 2 CDs).

This set was recorded live in Verona in 1970, when Placido Domingo was still barely known, and it captures him in fantastically exciting form – if you want proof that he's one of the century's greatest voices, just listen to this. He's placed alongside one of the finest sopranos, Magda Olivero, and the sparks really fly. Nello Santi, never a first-rank conductor, was inspired by his singers on the night: the pacing and inflection are much less pretty than in Cleva's Met production, but this is an exhilarating show. Good sound, wild audience.

La Bohème

The Bohemians

Composed 1893–95; revised 1896.
First performed February 1, 1896.
Libretto by Giuseppe Giacosa and Luigi Illica, after Murger.

Synopsis

Act I

Paris, the Latin Quarter, Christmas Eve, c. 1830. Marcello, an artist, and Rodolfo, a poet, are joined in their garret by the philosopher Colline and the musician Schaunard, who bring food and drink. Rodolfo burns some of his manuscripts to keep them warm. The landlord Benoit arrives, demanding rent, but they ply him with wine and trick him into believing that they are, in fact, well-off. He leaves empty-handed. All leave for a café, except Rodolfo, who promises to join them when he has finished a piece he is writing. Left to himself he is interrupted by a knock on the door. It is Mimi, a consumptive seamstress, in need of a light for her candle. Within minutes, they have fallen in love.

Act II

At the Café Momus Rodolfo introduces Mimi to his friends, including Musetta, who is attended by an elderly admirer, Alcindoro. When she notices Marcello, an ex-lover of hers, Musetta creates a scene to get rid of Alcindoro. When the bill arrives, no one can pay it. As a military band passes, they escape into the crowd. Alcindoro returns to find nothing but the Bohemians' huge bill.

Act III

A few weeks later, Mimi comes to the inn looking for Rodolfo, but finds Marcello instead. She tells him of Rodolfo's terrible jealousy, but when Rodolfo arrives she retreats to hear him give Marcello his version of their problem: he at first calls her a "heartless creature", but then reveals his inability to endure life with a woman who is incurably ill. When her coughing alerts Rodolfo to her presence, they agree – albeit regretfully – to part company. Simultaneously, Marcello and Musetta begin squabbling over the latter's infidelity, and they too decide to split up.

Act IV

In their garret Rodolfo and Marcello unhappily remember the women they have abandoned. The atmosphere warms when Colline and Schaunard arrive, but their good humour is shattered by news that Mimi is alone and near death. She has asked to spend her last hours with Rodolfo. When she is brought in, Marcello leaves to sell Musetta's earrings for medicine, and Colline decides to sell his coat. Mimi dies as Rodolfo is looking out of the window. Thinking she is asleep, Rodolfo attends to her comfort until he realizes that Mimi is dead. Sobbing, he throws himself on top of her body.

Puccini originally intended to follow *Manon Lescaut* with a setting of *La Lupa* (The She-Wolf), a novel by Giovanni Verga, whose *Cavelleria rusticana* had already furnished Mascagni with spectacularly successful material. He sketched out a few ideas and visited the author in Sicily (where he was arrested as a spy after taking pictures of the naval fortifications), but even before leaving the island he began to feel his inspiration ebbing away. On the ferry home he met Countess Beaudine Gravina – Cosima Wagner's daughter by her first marriage – and her distaste for Verga's "drama of sensuality and crime" seems to have tilted the balance. Puccini had no problems with sex and violence, but the countess's reaction to the blasphemous element of Verga's tale was probably crucial for a composer to whom the contentment of the Italian public was an overriding concern. He promptly abandoned Verga in favour of Henry Murger and his novel *La vie de Bohème*, a decision that accelerated the disintegration of Puccini's relationship with Leoncavallo, who had shown Puccini a libretto based on Murger's book long before Puccini's trip to Sicily. The rival composers battled in public over the rights to the novel, and Puccini, fired up by the confrontation, was first to the finishing line, completing his score in 1895. Toscanini – who had been dragged into the battle by both composers – conducted the first performance of Puccini's work in Turin, three years to the day after the premiere of *Manon Lescaut*. The maudlin hand-wringing, the comic touches and the relatively steady pace surprised those expecting a repeat of *Manon*'s fire, but within six months it was the composer's most popular work, a position from which it has never faltered.

From the opening ensemble the opera is dominated by an astonishing melodic richness, with the big-hitting arias emerging fluidly and with great dramatic impact from the fast-moving "conversational" dialogue. From the bustling camaraderie of the bohemians in Act I rise two of the most popular operatic songs ever written: Rodolfo's "Che gelida manina" (aka "Your tiny hand is frozen" – during which Caruso once forced a hot sausage into the hand of his Mimi, Nellie Melba), and Mimi's rejoinder "Mi, chiamano Mimi". These two arias, recalled through the repetition of motifs or more subtle echoes, dominate the entire opera, tying it together in a way that distinguishes the structure from the rough-and-ready assembly techniques of verismo. The free-flowing dialogue and strictly organized four-act construction further mark out *Bohème* from the concentrated hysteria of contemporary fashion, but the most conspicuous difference lies in the quality of the vocal lines. For example, when the coquettish Musetta is introduced during the opening of Act II, she announces herself through an erotic cantilena, "Quando me'n vo", that could almost be a song by Bellini, although it's framed by a frantic ensemble that could only be Puccini's.

The long-suffering Marcello, the vampish Musetta, the capricious Rodolfo and the fragile, guileless Mimi have more substance than the customary verismo crew, and even the blustering Benoit and the philosophical Colline (who sings a famous song to his coat in the final act) are well-defined musical personalities. The audience's engagement with Puccini's protagonists gives the final tragedy a poignancy unmatched by any other Italian opera of the period. The sense of loss and of the belated onset of responsibility is heightened by music in which the material first heard in Act I returns as a reminiscence of earlier happiness. Only the hardest of hearts could remain untouched.

RECORDINGS OVERVIEW

Unsurprisingly, *La Bohème* was one of the earliest operas to receive a complete recording – care of EMI in 1917 – and it has since been recorded nearly thirty times. Of these, some have earned classic status, and we've listed them below, along with the pick of the newer recordings (the 1996 Bohème with Roberto Alagna is more remarkable for its conducting than its singing). Maria Callas's Mimi of course has her fans, but she is not the most convincing consumptive, and she's paired with Giuseppe di Stefano's strained Rodolfo. Domingo/Caballé/Solti (RCA) and Scotto/Krauss/Levine (EMI) produce some beautiful singing but both suffer from manic conducting, while José Carreras's first Rodolfo, well conducted by Colin Davis (Philips), is weakened by Carreras's fellow lead soloist. To be avoided are Deutsche Grammophon's two accounts, conducted by Votto and Bernstein, and Carreras's embarrassing second set, recorded in 1987 by Erato.

Tebaldi, Bergonzi, d'Angelo, Bastianini; Santa Cecilia Academy Chorus and Orchestra; Serafin.
(Decca 448 725-2DF2; 2 CDs).

Taped in 1958, this was the first stereo *Bohème*. Conducted with lyrical vigour by Puccini's friend and champion Tullio Serafin, the performance has an exuberance rarely captured on record. Carlo Bergonzi, recently converted from singing baritone, is here singing one of his first complete roles as a tenor. With his youthful, firm tone and old-fashioned technique, he has the perfect balance of grace and weight for Rodolfo. An inimitable stylist, he gives an interpretation that is graced with entirely appropriate inflections: the horribly difficult *subito piano* (sudden drop in dynamic on a fixed note) near the beginning of "Che gelida manina", for example, is remarkable. Renata Tebaldi is a resonant Mimi, a little doughty perhaps for a dying consumptive, but vocally compelling. Bastianini is a virile Marcello and the feisty Gianna d'Angelo is a flagrantly flirtatious Musetta. The sound is warm and exciting but the orchestra is over-miked, leaving the singers distant – and no libretto.

de los Angeles, Björling, Amara, Merrill; RCA Victor Chorus and Symphony Orchestra; Beecham.
(EMI CDS7 47235-8; 2 CDs).

This 1952 recording is the most celebrated *Bohème* on record, thanks to its two stars. Jussi Björling makes a glorious Rodolfo, stirring a rush of emotion with each succeeding phrase, and there is an innocent abandon to his performance that reinforces the legend that he neither knew nor cared what he was singing about. Victoria de los Angeles is similarly effusive as Mimi, revelling in her voice rather more than in the character of Puccini's heroine. Lucine Amara is a light but spicy Musetta and Robert Merrill is a charming, good natured Marcello. Beecham's direction is too reserved – you can't help wondering what would have happened had a less laconic conductor been teamed with the passionate Björling and de los Angeles – but the RCA orchestra provides sensitive support, and the mono sound is bright and well balanced.

Te Kanawa, Leech, Titus; London Symphony Chorus and Orchestra; Nagano.
(Erato 0630-10699-2; 2 CDs).

The casting of Erato's 1995 recording seemed inauspicious (a mature soprano, novice tenor and a conductor with no track record in this sort of music), but this is the most successful *Bohème* for many years. American tenor Richard Leech has a powerful and honeyed Italianate style that recalls the young Carreras, and he makes an outstanding Rodolfo (especially during the final act), injecting just the right measure of emotion into his voice without distorting the line. Kiri Te Kanawa sounds half her age and she makes a divine Mimi, kaleidoscopic in colour and expressive in shape. Alan Titus is a senior Marcello, but he too has manufactured a beguiling Italian sweetness. Rounding off a fine achievement, Kent Nagano's conducting has a strong drive and yet is delicately phrased.

Albanese, Peerce, Valentino, McKnight; NBC Symphony Orchestra and Chorus; Toscanini.
(RCA GD 60288; 2 CDs).

This classic recording of *Bohème* was taken from two live broadcasts made by Toscanini in 1946 exactly fifty years after he conducted the first performance, and it's a life-affirming reading of a score about which he knew more than anyone else. Jan Peerce is a masculine Rodolfo, his earthy tenor well suited to the conductor's no-nonsense approach. Licia Albenese is a lovable Mimi – indeed the final scene is achingly moving, despite the hurry that Toscanini imparts to the proceedings. The sound is rough and boxy, but for anyone with a deep interest in the opera it is as essential as if the composer himself were conducting.

Freni, Pavarotti, Harwood, Panerai; Berlin Deutsche Oper Chorus; Berlin Philharmonic Orchestra; Karajan.
(Decca 443 204-2DH11-2; 2 CDs).

This recording has won extravagant plaudits ever since its release in 1972. The voices are indeed ideal, with Freni and Pavarotti singing beautifully as Mimi and Rodolfo; furthermore, the sound is rich and instrumental detail is amazingly clear. But Herbert von Karajan's tempi are the most sluggish and self-indulgent on record, and his pacing disrupts the structure while placing considerable strain on his singers – God knows where Pavarotti found the air to complete the penultimate phrase of "Che gelida manina". As with too many of Karajan's recordings, beauty is everything, and there are some exquisite episodes, but despite the voluptuous voices of Freni and Pavarotti this is not a first-choice *Bohème*.

Tosca

Composed 1896–99.
First performed January 14, 1900.
Libretto by Giuseppe Giacosa and Luigi Illica, after Sardou.

Synopsis

Act I

Rome, June 1800. Angelotti, an escaped political prisoner, has taken refuge in the church of Sant'Andrea della Valle. He approaches his old friend and sympathizer Mario Cavaradossi, a painter, who is at work on a picture of Mary Magdelene. Cavaradossi agrees to help, but they are disturbed by the arrival of Tosca, a celebrated singer and Cavaradossi's lover. Cavaradossi hurries Angelotti into a nearby chapel. Tosca is jealous when she sees that Mario's model for the portrait is the Marchesa Attavanti. He manages to assure her of his love and, after a lengthy duet, she finally leaves. A cannon signals the discovery of Angelotti's escape and so Cavaradossi agrees to take him into hiding at his villa. Meanwhile, the choristers celebrate the news that they are to be paid extra for that evening's Te Deum, but their good spirits are quashed when the police chief Scarpia bursts in and orders a search of the chapel. When Tosca returns, Scarpia is waiting. He tells her that Cavaradossi has run away with the Marchesa, provoking the furious Tosca to leave for his villa – followed by one of Scarpia's men. Left alone, Scarpia gloats over his plans to destroy Cavaradossi and seduce Tosca.

Act II

Cavaradossi is imprisoned in Scarpia's castle. The police chief summons Tosca to join them. As Cavaradossi is tortured, Scarpia questions Tosca. Unable to bear her lover's cries of pain, she reveals Angelotti's hiding place; as Scarpia triumphantly summons Cavaradossi, it is announced that Napoleon has been defeated at Marengo. Cavaradossi delights at the news, then is removed to prison. Scarpia and Tosca are again left alone. She agrees to give herself to him if he will let her and Cavaradossi go free. Scarpia tells her that, to save face, the painter must undergo a mock-execution, and he signs their safe-conduct pass; but before the ink is dry she stabs him with his table knife, taunting him as he dies.

Act III

Shortly before dawn, Cavaradossi is awaiting his execution. Tosca assures him that the soldiers will be using blank cartridges, and she produces Scarpia's safe-conduct pass. The executioners fire, and Cavaradossi falls dead – Scarpia has tricked them even in death. The soldiers have now discovered Scarpia's body and they chase Tosca towards the ramparts. Defiant to the end, she hurls herself from the castle walls.

Puccini first considered setting Sardou's play *La Tosca* way back in 1889, two years after the play had been given its first performance with Sarah Bernhardt in the title role. Ricordi dissuaded Puccini from pursuing the idea, forcing him to concentrate on *Manon Lescaut*, but when, in 1895, Puccini heard that Alberto Franchetti had been asked – by Ricordi – to set a libretto based on *La Tosca*, he demanded he be given the project. By devious means, Puccini and Ricordi convinced Franchetti that the story was unsuited to the operatic stage; the day after Franchetti relinquished his rights to the play, they were placed in Puccini's name.

Both librettists found collaboration with Puccini something of a strain, owing to his habit of going fishing and shooting while they slaved over revisions, but by 1899 the score was complete. The premiere in Rome was a success with most of the audience – "E lucevan le stelle" was encored and Puccini was required to make six entrances onto the stage – but the press were scandalized by this "shabby little shocker". However, thanks mainly to Toscanini's performances in Milan later that same year, *Tosca* was soon a staple of the Italian opera scene.

Crucial to *Tosca*'s notoriety is the monstrous figure of Scarpia, whose motif is announced in the work's forbidding opening chords and whose desperate passion for Tosca, for whom he would give up his "place in heaven", is the mainspring of the opera. Incapable of finding pleasure except in conquest, Scarpia is a depraved sadist who delights in proclaiming his own depravity – his twisted "Credo" at the close of Act I thunderously states his case as he broods on his lust for Tosca and fantasizes about Cavaradossi's bloody execution. The tension is heightened by the accompaniment of a Te Deum, to which he eventually joins his voice before a tumultuous orchestral explosion brings the act to an end. With the "Credo" finished he has no further arias, but rather a string of thickly accompanied arioso passages in which the instrumentation and harmony conjure a sense of evil comparable to the characterization of Hagen in Wagner's *Götterdämmerung*.

The relationship between Scarpia and Tosca is the axis upon which the drama spins, and yet their exchanges are almost entirely confined to the second act. With the exception of

TOSCA TAKES A TUMBLE

No opera has generated as many anecdotes as *Tosca*, the most passionate and most accident-prone of operas. Sometimes the sheer verve of the performance has ensured a place in operatic folklore. Reporting on a 1920s' production at the Met, Ernest Newman wrote: "It was the roughest Tosca within my experience. Never have I seen two characters mix it like this. Other Scarpias allow themselves to be counted out after the first jab from the table knife. Mr Scotti rose at the count of eight and the uppercut with which he was at last put to sleep was a beauty. The winner left the ring without a mark. The weights were not given in the programme, but Madame Jeritza has the advantage in reach." It is said that Franco Corelli's imitation of a man killed by a firing squad was so convincing that on one occasion one of the executing officers dropped his musket and ran across the stage to see if he was all right. Conversely, an absence of verve has sometimes provoked comment. During a Covent Garden performance, the larger-than-life tenor Pavarotti was awaiting execution. The house was gripped as the muskets fired; but Pavarotti was slow in falling. Indeed, his knees were giving him problems at the time and, as if settling into his favourite chair, he hesitantly crouched, shuffled and, finally, sat on the floor before rolling onto his side. The audience was audibly unconvinced.

A couple of *Tosca* stories have acquired the status of urban myths. The first of these – and the one likeliest to be based on fact – is said to have occurred in Buenos Aires during a performance conducted by Erich Kleiber. The first two acts had gone very well, but during the brief intermission the stage director discovered, to his horror, he had no guards to chase Tosca to the battlements. In a panic, he rushed out to a café around the corner where he asked for five volunteers; five lads stepped forward and the director rushed them to the dressing rooms, where they were rapidly prepared. By the time they were ready, the final act was almost over and they gathered in the wings just as Tosca discovered her lover Mario lying dead at her feet. With no time to spare he pointed to the sobbing heroine and issued the command "Follow that woman!". As they rushed out to chase her, Tosca threw herself off the battlements – promptly followed, lemming-like, by the five volunteers.

The most famous *Tosca* disaster has as its protagonist a soprano who had been a pain in the neck throughout the production – the name of the prima donna varies from teller to teller. The story goes that she whinged endlessly about the inadequacy of the padding used to cushion her fall from the battlements. The long suffering stage hands finally snapped and replaced the padding with a trampoline. The unsuspecting audience were gripped as Tosca sang her final words "O Scarpia, avanti a Dio!", leapt off the castle wall – and then bounced back into full view, several times.

Cavaradossi's "Vittoria!", a heart-stopping denunciation of Scarpia, and Tosca's sole aria, the brief but harrowing "Visi d'arte", this act is given over to the morbid, quasi-ritualistic duel between heroine and anti-hero, in which Puccini sustains a tension between Scarpia's long, minatory phrases and Tosca's rapid, apprehensive interjections. The outer acts conform more closely to the traditional "numbers" structure, rather like *La Bohème*. In particular, the first act is notable for Cavaradossi's aria "Recondita armonia" and the grand love duet between Cavaradossi and Tosca. Cavaradossi might be no more than a cipher, an inspiration to Tosca and a pawn for Scarpia, but he is one of Puccini's most beautiful tenor roles. The third act contains the tenor's heartbreaking "E lucevan le stella" and another touching duet, "O dolci mani", but it is little wonder that Ricordi thought the final act a disappointment, for while the music is undeniably attractive, the drama is effectively dead the moment Scarpia dies.

Benjamin Britten once spoke of being "sickened by the cheapness and emptiness" of *Tosca*, and many others have found it a disgusting tale. But there is a sincerity to Puccini's shallowness that redeems even the cheapest theatrical trick – and music this tuneful is difficult to reject.

RECORDINGS OVERVIEW

Tosca is the most recorded of Puccini's operas, with no fewer than eleven mono recordings made before Leinsdorf conducted the first stereo effort in 1957. Of these, two are superlative: de Fabritiis's 1938 EMI recording with Gigli's incomparable Cavaradossi and Maria Caniglia's blazing Tosca; and Maria Callas's first recording, conducted by Victor de Sabata in 1953. Only the latter is currently available. Of the later productions, several are notable for individual performances – notably Björling's Cavaradossi for Leinsdorf (RCA; 1957), Taddei's Scarpia for Serafin (Philips; 1957), Bergonzi's Cavaradossi for Prêtre (EMI; 1965) and Zancanaro's Scarpia for Muti (Philips; 1992). But with de Sabata's performance casting a long shadow, good modern *Toscas* have been thin on the ground.

Callas, di Stefano, Gobbi, Calabrese; La Scala Chorus and Orchestra; de Sabata.
(EMI CDS7 47 175-8; 2 CDs).

There is no argument about this 1953 set: it is and will almost certainly remain the finest *Tosca* on record. It was de Sabata's first and last studio recording of an opera, and it reveals exactly why his name inspires such reverence among the cognoscenti: the feeling for structure and momentum is uncanny, while his awareness of detail gives every motif and phrase its proper emphasis. Callas produces what is quite simply the most moving portrayal of Tosca ever recorded – volatile but dignified, as inclined to love as to hate – and her singing is staggeringly forceful. Gobbi defined Scarpia for every subsequent interpreter of the role: though vocally raw and prone to opening the throat beyond its natural limits, Gobbi is nonetheless the nastiest Scarpia there has ever been, and his presence is mesmerizing. The only real weakness, and then a slight one, is di Stefano's Cavaradossi, who strains his delicate tenor to compete with the high-octane singing from Callas and Gobbi. Regardless of this quibble, and the mono sound, this is an essential Puccini recording.

Nilsson, Corelli, Fischer-Dieskau, Maionica; Santa Cecilia Academy Chorus and Orchestra; Maazel.
(Decca 440 051-2DM02; 2 CDs).

Maazel's 1966 account is an example of celebrity head-hunting at its very best – Decca teamed two of the greatest operatic voices of the century with a young and headstrong conductor and hoped for the best. It was worth the gamble, for this is the most impressively sung *Tosca* of them all, if not the best characterized. Nilsson is clearly not Italian, but her fearsome power, range and colour are such that you can overlook the lack of perception. Corelli's smooth extension (applied to some dizzy heights, especially during the "Vittoria!"), hammer-blow declamation, lyrical fluency and hammy masculinity put his Cavaradossi right at the top of the league. Supported by Maazel's urgent, temperamental conducting, Corelli and Nilsson (who were more than good friends at the time) set the performance alight. The mistaken casting of Fischer-Dieskau as Scarpia is the one limitation of an immensely entertaining performance.

Caballé, Carreras, Wixell, Ramey; Royal Opera House Chorus and Orchestra; Davis.
(Philips 438 359-2PM2; 2 CDs).

This is probably the most satisfying recent *Tosca*. With Davis playing a cool hand for much of the time, the principal attraction is the young José Carreras tearing his way through Cavaradossi. Carreras was at his very best in 1976, and his ringing, gushing Latin voice makes the ideal love-interest. Ingvar Wixell is a fascinatingly different Scarpia from Gobbi's maniacal creation: this is an intelligent, self-knowing man, and his beautiful voice is a joy. Caballé is too lyrical to communicate the angst of Tosca, and she tends to enjoy herself at the expense of dramatic intent, but Davis sometimes impels her into a greater commitment. All in all, nothing to rival de Sabata, but a worthy alternative to Maazel.

Madama Butterfly

Composed 1901–03; revised 1904.
First performed February 17, 1904; May 28, 1904.
Libretto by Giuseppe Giacosa and Luigi Illica, after Belasco.

Synopsis (revised version)

Act I

Nagasaki, c. 1904. Pinkerton, an American naval officer, has taken out a 999-year lease on a little house, in which he intends to live with his Japanese wife, the fifteen-year-old Butterfly. The wedding ceremony is disrupted by members of her angry family, but when it is over the two sing a passionate love duet and prepare for their first night alone.

Act II

Part I

Several years later. Shortly after their wedding Pinkerton abandoned Butterfly and returned to America. Butterfly confidently awaits his return, having since borne him a son. Sharpless, the American consul, has received a letter from his friend informing him that he has married an American woman called Kate, with whom he is returning to Nagasaki. Sharpless doesn't have the heart to tell Butterfly, who remains convinced of her husband's fidelity. A cannon is fired, announcing the arrival of Pinkerton's ship; Butterfly prepares to receive him.

Part II

When Pinkerton arrives – accompanied by Kate – Butterfly is asleep; Pinkerton leaves, unable to face the woman he deserted. When Butterfly wakes she finds Kate, together with Suzuki, her handmaid, and Sharpless. They break the news to her that Kate is married to Pinkerton and that he will never remain in Japan. Butterfly agrees to give up her son if Pinkerton will collect him. She then asks to be left alone, and stabs herself as Pinkerton bursts into the room calling her name.

Puccini had good reason to expect the premiere of *Madama Butterfly* to be a success. *Tosca* was well established in the repertoire, and the personnel engaged for the new work could hardly have been bettered. The cast was headed by the ideal trio of Storchio as Butterfly, Zenatello as Pinkerton and de Luca as Sharpless; the conductor was the much-respected Campanini; the producer was Ricordi's son, Tito; and Lucien Jusseaume, one of France's finest designers, had prepared the sets. However, Puccini's enemies – including the embittered Franchetti – had packed the La Scala audience with hecklers, who proceeded to disrupt the show at every opportunity. The wondrous Act I love duet was greeted with catcalls, hissing and booing, and when Butterfly's kimono billowed before her, one member of the audience yelled "Butterfly is pregnant". Come the twittering birdsong that concludes Butterfly's "vigil", the house virtually collapsed with laughter and the performance was almost abandoned.

In truth, the opera would probably have encountered problems with any Italian audience. The original version was too long, it contained no tenor aria (an inexplicable omission considering Zenatello's abilities), and orientalism, so popular in France, was not an Italian taste. Furthermore, the tale of a fifteen-year-old Japanese girl giving birth to an American's baby (a true-life event, dramatized by David Belasco) was an invitation to outrage, and the score's through-composed structure – divided into only two acts – was

LEBRECHT COLLECTION

Rosina Storchio – the first Butterfly

likely to tire an audience used to the bite-sized chunks of verismo. Puccini withdrew the opera, returned his fee to the astonished La Scala, and set about revising his score, adding a tenor aria and cutting Act II into two smaller units (the latter is sometimes labelled Act III). Three months after the fiasco of La Scala, Puccini oversaw the second premiere in Brescia, with only one cast change. The new *Madama Butterfly* triumphed: Puccini was again Italian opera's top dog.

The character of Butterfly gives plenty of ammunition to Puccini's detractors: this is the "weaker" sex at its weakest, with none of Tosca's strength or Manon's resilience, and she embodies some thoroughly distasteful racial attitudes. For a lyrico-dramatic soprano, however, she presents one of the most demanding roles in the Italian repertoire, requiring a transition from ingenuous youth to melancholy maturity within the space of just two hours. Along the way lies some intensely poignant music – notably the famous "Un bel dì", her "Flower Duet" with Suzuki, and her painful monologue on the brink of death – but the highlight of the whole opera is Butterfly's moment of bliss, her Act I duet with Pinkerton. Lasting nearly a quarter of an hour, it begins with delicate exchanges and builds towards tremendous unison phrases that culminate in a shared high C of rapturous devotion. Nothing else in the opera compares with this remarkable passage, although the final trio is beautifully written – with one extraordinary phrase in which a floated B flat from Pinkerton rises through the voices of Sharpless and Butterfly.

Pinkerton himself is at first all bluster and bonhomie, traits signalled by lusty quotations from the "The Star Spangled Banner" (just as Butterfly and her family are tagged with music that uses the oriental-sounding pentatonic scale). It doesn't take long, however, for him to emerge in his true colours as a self-righteous racist, whose primary interest in Butterfly is utterly basic – as he gloats to Sharpless, the marriage agreement is not even binding. Callously detached from the suffering he causes, Pinkerton is assigned music that resembles that of the standard Italian romantic tenor lead, an approprate incongruity that intensifies his cruelty. (Unlike the traditional tenor lead, however, he gets only a set-piece aria, "Addio fiorito asil", which comes shortly before the end.)

Puccini couches Pinkerton's cruelty and Butterfly's suffering in music that's entirely in character with Puccini. Some might regret that he didn't make an effort to dramatize Butterfly through music that was more in character with a young woman pushed to suicide by a cold-hearted seducer, but Puccini was always better at empathizing with oppressors and avengers than with life's victims. Above all he had a genius for well-turned tunes, and *Madama Butterfly* has lashings of them.

RECORDINGS OVERVIEW

Surprisingly, the first recorded *Butterfly* was made in English, by EMI in 1924, with Eugene Goosens conducting; but the first great *Butterfly* was recorded (again by EMI) in 1939 – with the incomparable coupling of Toti dal Monte and Beniamino Gigli, conducted by a young Oliviero de Fabritiis. Not until 1954 was a worthy rival produced, once more by EMI, with the youthful de los Angeles and di Stefano conducted by Gavazzeni. None of these recordings is currently available. The earliest good recording to find its way onto CD is Callas's 1955 account, but although she produces some extraordinary singing, she is poorly supported by Herbert von Karajan and ineffectually partnered by her Pinkerton, Nicolai Gedda. There followed the two classic recordings recommended below, and Bergonzi's second account of Pinkerton, conducted by Barbirolli – a fine performance, but Bergonzi is less firm and passionate than in his earlier version, and Renata Scotto's tone can't be compared to Tebaldi's. Thereafter, Pavarotti, Domingo and Carreras have all had a go at Pinkerton, and Caballé, Freni and Scotto have all recorded Butterfly (the latter two twice), but none of these couplings can rival the performances recommended below.

Tebaldi, Bergonzi, Sordello, Cossotto; Santa Cecilia Academy Chorus and Orchestra; Serafin.
(Decca 425 531-2DM2; 2 CDs).

The first stereo *Butterfly* is a wondrous thing, starring the two leads who had already made the definitive *La Bohème* for the same label. Conducted by Serafin in a sweeping symphonic manner that's perfectly in keeping with the composer's instructions, this performance uniquely encompasses the opera's tenderness as well as its cruelty. The sound favours the orchestra above the soloists and so there is some loss of clarity, but Tebaldi is in sumptuously expressive form, without a sign of strain until strain is called for, whereupon the emotional floodgates are opened. Bergonzi is an aristocratic Pinkerton and his vibrant, warm tenor sails through the role. The love duet is perhaps too slow – as are many of Serafin's tempi – but it is the most beautifully sung version on disc. With the bonus of a pleasing Sharpless from Sordello, this is an indispensable *Butterfly*.

Price, Tucker, Maero, Elias; RCA Italiana Opera Chorus and Orchestra; Leinsdorf.
(RCA RD86 160; 2 CDs).

Recorded in 1962, this is the most energetically conducted *Butterfly*. Leinsdorf concentrates less on line than on pulse, colour and gesture, drawing a remarkably pungent performance from his singers and his orchestra. Price, a vocally luscious Butterfly, revels in Leinsdorf's obsession for detail – the way she lightens then swells the tone during "Un bel dì", all in one breath, is amazing. Her Pinkerton, Richard Tucker, is a powerful, virile tenor – less seductive than Bergonzi but, driven by Leinsdorf, more exciting. Their love duet trumps all others, not in elegance or sweetness, but in theatricality: it's a feverish outburst of passion, leaving you wondering who is seducing whom.

La Fanciulla del West

The Girl of the West

Composed 1908–1910.
First performed December 10, 1910.
Libretto by Guelfo Civinini and Carlo Zangarini, after Belasco.

Synopsis

Act I

California, 1850. At the Polka Saloon, a group of gold miners are playing cards. It is revealed that the bandit Ramerrez is on the loose and that a $5000 reward is on offer for his capture. The local sheriff, Jack Rance, makes advances to the bar's owner, Minnie, but she rejects him, explaining she will settle only for true love. At this point a stranger, Dick Johnson, arrives. Minnie remembers that they met long ago, and she falls in love with him – not realizing that he is the bandit Ramerrez. Although it was his plan to raid the miner's gold, his feelings for Minnie (who guards the gold) hold him back.

Act II

Johnson and Minnie get together in Minnie's rooms, but Rance then arrives and produces a photo of Johnson, warning her that he is none other than the bandit Ramerrez. When Rance leaves, Johnson tries to explain how he came to be a bandit, but his tale cuts no ice with Minnie, who demands that he leave. Shortly after, gunfire is heard: Ramerrez has been shot. Minnie drags him to safety in her loft, but Rance forces him to descend, whereupon Johnson collapses. Desperate, Minnie turns to Rance and suggests a game of cards to decide the bandit's fate – the stake, Johnson's life. Minnie cheats and wins, forcing Rance to abandon his prey.

Act III

In a nearby forest, Rance and his men are told that Ramerrez has been captured. The miners drag in Johnson and prepare to hang him; in a moving speech, he asks them to tell Minnie that he escaped to freedom. However, Minnie arrives just in time and, holding the miners back with a pistol, she begs her friends to spare his life. Their love for Minnie compels them to free the bandit, and Ramerrez and Minnie ride off to start a new life together.

Having been put out by the Milanese reaction to *Madama Butterfly*, it was with some hesitation that Puccini approached his next opera. For a while he considered Hugo's *Hunchback of Notre Dame*, then was sidetracked by the notion of writing a triptych of operas based on the writings of Gorky, for the Russian bass Chaliapin. When Ricordi dismissed that idea Puccini turned to *Marie Antoinette*, a project that had intermittently engaged him for years, but this also came to nothing. He considered setting a sado-masochistic novel called *The Woman and the Puppet*, but the recent scandal surrounding Strauss's *Salome* (see p.378) persuaded Puccini – fearful of censorship and restricted income – to abandon this as well. Numerous other ideas came and went until 1907, when he visited New York to see the Met's US premiere of *Butterfly*, his first encounter with the tenor Enrico Caruso. During his stay he also saw a performance of Belasco's play *The Girl of the Golden West*, which he read in translation on his way back through London. By the time he was back in Italy he and the playwright had agreed terms.

Progress was badly hindered by serious marital difficulties and the scandal surrounding the suicide of Puccini's serving girl, and he failed to complete the score until 1910 – almost seven years after *Butterfly*. Rehearsals were problematic, provoking Puccini to write of Caruso, "he won't learn anything, he's lazy and he's too pleased with himself – all the same his voice is magnificent". But the first performance – the Met's first world premiere – was a sensation, and *La Fanciulla* secured Puccini fame and wealth that put him in a two-man stratosphere with Richard Strauss.

Yet *Fanciulla* has long been seen as something of a weak link in Puccini's career: in Europe it never generated the sort of enthusiasm it initially produced in America, where it soon lapsed from the core repertoire. You can understand why it hasn't matched the success of *Bohème* or *Tosca*: the Italianized Wild West setting ("Whisky per tutti!" etc) can be tiresome, and the relationship between Johnson and Minnie has none of the fire of Tosca and Scarpia, or the delicious romance of Mimi and Rodolfo. Furthermore, although *Fanciulla* has some disarmingly beautiful episodes – Minnie's first entrance, Rance's bitter "L'amore è un altra cosa", Minnie's poignant "Io non son che una poverta fanciulla", her rich duet with Johnson and, most of all, Johnson's impassioned plea that Minnie never be told of his death ("Ch'ella mi creda") – only the last of these could be described as a showstopper. Yet therein lies a clue to the strengths of this opera: the melody is thoroughly integrated into an orchestral and thematic framework, so that the songs grow from the orchestra and the orchestral passages from the songs. As never before in Puccini's work the edges are blurred, so that it's almost impossible to carve highlights from the whole. In short, *Fanciulla* is not the place to start if you're new to Puccini, but once you've got to know his work well, you might well end up preferring *Fanciulla* to any other of his operas.

RECORDINGS OVERVIEW

Record companies have tended to shy away from *La Fanciulla del West*. The first recording – which set a precedent for making cuts in the first act – was not made until 1950, when Cetra made a pig's ear of the score with an absurdly unsuitable cast. Eight years later EMI took the inspired step of engaging Birgit Nilsson to play Minnie, and despite the failings of her co-lead this remains one of the two strongest contenders, just behind Decca's inevitable del Monaco/Tebaldi recording of the same year. This remained the last studio version for nearly twenty years, until Deutsche Grammophon recorded Domingo in his first reading of the work – notable for its completeness and some fine conducting from Zubin Mehta but little else. Two 1992 recordings from RCA and Sony did little to challenge the earlier performances.

Tebaldi, del Monaco, MacNeil, Tozzi; Santa Cecilia Academy Chorus and Orchestra; Capuana.
(Decca 421 595-2; 2 CDs).

This is the most exciting and well-rounded *Fanciulla* on disc. Mario del Monaco is in excellent form, and though he thunders his way through the love duet he does generally observe markings such as "piano" and "crescendo" and successfully conveys the softer edges that make Johnson such a lovable bandit. Tebaldi is the perfect singer for the maternal Minnie, and is equally convincing as the gun-toting saviour of Act III. Cornell MacNeil's enormous baritone matches the volume produced by Tebaldi and del Monaco: menacing but noble, he remains the definitive sheriff. Franco Capuana and the Decca engineers lose much of the orchestral sonority to the thunderous singing, but the pace never slackens.

Nilsson, Gibin, Mongelli, Zaccaria; La Scala Chorus and Orchestra; Matacic.
(EMI CMS7 63970-2; 2 CDs).

Considering who was available at the time, it's a pity that EMI selected João Gibin to sing Johnson opposite Birgit Nilsson's Minnie, the very personification of the tough bar owner that Puccini envisaged. She mollifies her tone throughout, generating some exquisitely gentle phrasing, but when she opens her throat the rush of sound engulfs him, and on occasion everybody else. Gibin's voice is pleasant enough, for all its lack of metal, and Andrea Mongelli is a masculine Rance, but the performance is dominated by the soprano, whose presence would seem to have intimidated the conductor into allowing her all the rhythmic freedom she wanted.

Il Trittico

The Triptych

Il Tabarro

The Cloak

Composed 1915–16.
First performed December 14, 1918.
Libretto by Giuseppe Adami, after Gold.

Synopsis

On a barge moored beside the Seine, Michele sits and watches the stevedores finish work for the day, while his wife Giorgetta does her chores. As the stevedores walk past the barge on their way home, Giorgetta steals a few moments with one of them, Luigi, who is her lover. Michele looks on suspiciously, but does nothing, enabling the lovers to arrange a meeting later that night. Once Giorgetta is back on board, Michele tries to embrace her, but she pushes him away and goes inside the barge. He is convinced of her infidelity and as he sits alone on deck he lights his pipe – the flare from which is mistaken by Luigi for Giorgetta's signal. He climbs on board only to encounter Michele, who forces the stevedore to confess the affair. He then strangles him to death and hides his body beneath his overcoat. When Giorgetta appears on deck and walks towards her husband, he slowly opens his coat to reveal her lover's corpse.

Suor Angelica

Sister Angelica

Composed 1917.
First performed December 14, 1918.
Libretto by Giovacchino Forzano.

Synopsis

A convent, late seventeenth-century Italy. The curtain rises on a group of nuns busy with their chores. Everyone is cheerful – except Angelica, who has been seven years in the convent and has heard nothing from her family in all that time. Suddenly, however, the Abbess informs her that her aunt, a princess, has come to see her. Angelica rushes to greet her, but is coldly received by the princess. It emerges that Angelica was sent to the convent by her family as punishment for having an illegitimate child; the princess has come not to forgive, but to inform her that her child has died. The princess leaves, and as Angelica sings of her longing to join her child in Heaven, her sister nuns raise their voices in praise of the Virgin Mary. Left alone, Angelica drinks poison, but then it dawns on her that her suicide will result in damnation – and thus separation from the child she never knew. She prays despairingly to the Madonna, and this time her voice is joined by those of angels. As the song rises to a height of ecstasy, the Madonna herself appears – with Angelica's child – to lead her into Heaven.

Gianni Schicchi

Composed 1917–18.
First performed December 14, 1918.
Libretto by Giovacchino Forzano, after Dante.

Synopsis

Florence, late thirteenth century. The scene is the bedroom of the recently deceased Buoso Donati, a rich old gentleman with a large and greedy family. This family is gathered about his bed, pretending to mourn his passing, until it is suggested by one of their number that he has left the entire fortune to the local monastery. They rush about the house in search of the will. Rinuccio finds it, but will not reveal its contents until they agree to his marrying Gianni Schicchi's daughter, Lauretta. They agree but are appalled when the will confirms their fears: it is all to go to the church. Rinuccio then suggests turning the problem over to his future father-in-law, who is famed for his cunning. Despite mocking his lowly birth, the family agrees; at first, Schicchi refuses to help but when Lauretta intercedes he agrees to sort out the problem as long as everyone plays along with his plan. He will pretend to be Buoso and rewrite his will – but they must never reveal the deception, as the punishment under Florentine law is severe. When the notary arrives, Schicchi awards the money and the estate to his "devoted friend" Gianni Schicchi. The horrified relatives are helpless, and once the notary has left Schicchi drives the family from his newly acquired home. Rinuccio and Lauretta remain, singing of their love; looking on, Schicchi ends the opera delighting at the way in which Buoso's money has been used.

In Paris in 1912 Puccini saw a one-act play by Didier Gold called *La Houppelande* (The Cloak) and immediately decided to set the hard-hitting drama to music. By 1913 he'd reached an agreement with Gold (whose work was eventually turned into a libretto by Giuseppe Adami), but he felt this "red stain" of a text needed to be flanked by pieces that would "contrast with it". The solution came from the 29-year-old playwright Giovacchino Forzano, who proposed that he complete the triptych by writing a sentimental tragedy and a buffa comedy. Puccini was delighted with Forzano's idea and commissioned him to write the libretti for *Suor Angelica* (a tale of Forzano's devising) and *Gianni Schicchi* (derived from the thirtieth canto of Dante's *Inferno*). After many delays the composer finally set to work on *Il Tabarro* in 1915 and completed the final pages of *Gianni Schicchi* shortly before the triptych's premiere, at the Met, in 1918.

Il Trittico is a testament to Puccini's versatility and his talent for concision – played in sequence, the three contrasting mini-operas last as long as Beethoven's *Fidelio*, and each one constructs an entirely plausible world. At 55 minutes, *Il Tabarro* is a full-throttle verismo opera of jealousy and revenge, in which Puccini creates a set of believable and sharply defined characters, bringing even minor figures – such as the stevedore Il Tinca – into sharp focus. Using realistic touches such as a motor horn, the call of a music-seller, the moan of a foghorn and the whirrings of an organ grinder, Puccini economically conjures a menacing atmosphere. There are few real numbers, but the love music is graphically passionate, and Michele's brooding aria "Nulla! Silenzio!" captures, with horrible intensity, his descent through seething jealousy into suicidal despair.

Suor Angelica is completely different, not merely because the cast is entirely female. For all the crude ecclesiastical trappings, this work is nothing like as atmospheric as *Il Tabarro*, and neither is there the same concentration of theatrical incident. The dramatic crux is the conflict between Angelica and her aunt, an episode of great menace and foreboding, the intensity of which is heightened by the sickly-sweet piety of the preceding scene. The spiteful princess is brilliantly captured, and the clash of her stark and declamatory contralto and Angelica's warm and ingenuous soprano beautifully creates a tense prelude to the opera's one true aria – Angelica's profoundly moving and dignified "Senza Mamma". *Suor Angelica* is the weakest wing of the triptych, but its dollops of saccharine are much more palatable if consumed between *Il Tabarro* and the riotous *Gianni Schicchi*.

The final part of the triptych opens superbly: Puccini has both the cast and orchestra sighing and sobbing for the dead Buoso, only for the atmosphere to change in an instant the moment mention is made of the will's possible contents. It is typical of an opera constructed as a series of quickfire scenes, in which situation rather than character is the mainspring of the action. There is only one real character, Gianni Schicchi, whose comic patter and monologues are the finest examples of the buffa tradition since Donizetti's *Don Pasquale* – the scene in which he dictates the spurious will of Buoso Donati is hilarious. However, his contribution is primarily theatrical, and the musical highlights come from Rinuccio, whose announcement of Schicchi's arrival harks back to the jollity of *La Bohème*, and from Lauretta, whose winsome plea to her father for his compliance, "O! mio babbino caro", is one of the best-known tunes ever written. The denouement is perhaps the finest ensemble finale in Italian opera after Verdi's *Falstaff* – and it suggests that Puccini made a mistake in never considering a full-length comic opera.

RECORDINGS OVERVIEW

There's a wide array of recordings of the separate operas from *Il Trittico*, but it is best to experience the work complete and in the hands of a single conductor – which rules out EMI's set, which is handsomely cast but has three different conductors, locations and dates. Bruno Bartoletti's set for Decca, though well conducted, is poorly cast, with stars who are either too old (Mirella Freni) or not old enough (Roberto Alagna) in the central roles.

Wixell, Scotto, Domingo, Sénéchal/Scotto, Horne, Payne, Cotrubas/Gobbi, Cotrubas, Domingo, di Stasio; New Philharmonia/London Symphony Orchestra; Maazel.
(Sony M3K 79312; 3 CDs).

Recorded between 1976 and 1977, this set shows both Lorin Maazel's legendary attention to detail and his grasp of the bigger picture. *Il Tabarro* is slow but highly charged, and in particular the love duet between Domingo and Scotto is blisteringly intense. Maazel encourages Scotto and Horne to milk the sentiment of *Suor Angelica*, but not to the detriment of the overall structure as do some readings. He and his cast are equally at home with the buffa jolliness of *Gianni Schicchi* and while Tito Gobbi was well past his prime in 1977, he was still a great vocal actor and he plays the title role with perfect timing and inflection. The sound is excellent.

Merrill, Tebaldi, del Monaco/Tebaldi, Simionato, Pace/Corena, Tebaldi, Lazzari; MMF Chorus and Orchestra; Gardelli.
(Decca 411 665-2DM3; 3 CDs).

This excellent set, produced in 1961 as a vehicle for Decca's leading soprano Renata Tebaldi, has much to recommend it throughout the three operas – most of all Tebaldi's glowing voice, which is nicely moulded to play three disparate leading characters. She is well served by her colleagues, with the stentorian Mario del Monaco as Luigi, Giulietta Simoniato as the princess and Fernando Corena as Gianni Schicchi. Gardelli's conducting is a sometimes semi-detached, but the standard of singing is remarkable. The sound quality is dated, but this is a superb, good-value set.

Turandot

Composed 1920–24; completed by Franco Alfano 1925–26.
First performed April 25, 1926.
Libretto by Giuseppe Adami and Renato Simoni, after Gozzi.

Synopsis

Act I

The evil Princess Turandot has announced that she will marry whoever can answer her three riddles.

Failure will be punished by death. In a Peking square the crowd is awaiting the execution of yet another suitor. Among them is Timur, the deposed King of Tartary, who sees his long-lost son Calaf in the crowd. Timur's servant girl Liù loves Calaf but he has fallen for Turandot. Despite the protestations of his father and Liù, Calaf resolves to solve the riddles.

Act II

The Emperor Altoum also tries to convince Calaf of the folly of his quest, but Calaf is adamant. Turandot is similarly sure that no one will ever succeed, but when Calaf answers her riddles correctly she begs Altoum to release her from her oath. Calaf turns the table on Turandot by agreeing to go to his execution if she can guess his name before sunrise the following day.

Act III

Turandot has threatened to put the people of the city to death if they do not reveal the stranger's name. The crowd then turn on Calaf and his father. Turandot arrives to question Timur but Liù comes forward, confessing that she alone knows his name. Fortified by her love for Calaf she refuses to betray him and, before she can be executed, she takes her own life, telling Turandot that through her death Turnadot will learn the nature of love. The sun has still not risen but Calaf confronts Turandot and passionately kisses her. She begs him to leave, but he refuses and, as the trumpets announce the coming of dawn, Calaf reveals his name. His life is in her hands and, overwhelmed by his sincerity, Turandot tells her father that the stranger's name is Love.

𝄞 As with *La Fanciulla*, Puccini arrived at *Turandot* by a circuitous route. In 1911 he saw a Max Reinhardt production of Gozzi's play *Turandot* while staying in Berlin, and decided that "the passion of Turandot, who for so long has been suffocated beneath the ashes of her immense pride", was ideal operatic material. But he wasn't to act on this flash of inspiration for several years, having in the interim contemplated setting Shakespeare's *Taming of the Shrew*, Belasco's *The Son-Daughter* and Dickens's *Oliver Twist*. In 1920, three years after Busoni had made an opera out of the same play, Puccini introduced his librettist Giuseppe Adami to Renato Simoni, a Gozzi scholar and playwright, and asked them to prepare a text. The process was protracted by Puccini's cancer, his severe demands on his librettists (at one point he wanted a complete rewrite) and by his regular losses of confidence: "My life is a torture because I fail to see in this opera all the throbbing life and power which are necessary in a work for the theatre if it is to endure and hold," he wrote in one typical outbreak of despair. According to the composer's biographer, Puccini remarked at one point – "My opera will be staged incomplete, and then someone will come onto the stage and say to the public: 'At this point the composer died'".

Turandot – an irresistible temptation for any producer with money to burn

In the event, that is exactly what happened. A throat tumour necessitated a gruesome operation under local anaesthetic, and he died less than a week later, with the final duet of *Turandot* still incomplete. Puccini asked his family to invite Zandonai to finish the work from his sketches, but Puccini's son didn't like the idea of a famous composer completing his father's opera and insisted that the minor talent of Franco Alfano be employed instead. It took him six months and the final result was rather good, but Toscanini was unhappy with his work and at the first performance he ended the performance at the point where Alfano's work began. Only on the second night was the completion played.

With *Turandot* Puccini's mastery of orchestral sound reaches its pinnacle: this is a ripe, opulent, *fin de siècle* score, in which deep washes of colour are applied to a profusion of melodic ideas. Dramatically, *Turandot* marks a return to the more conventional structures of *Tosca* and *Butterfly*: the arias tumble over each other as if Puccini knew he was about to die and was desperate to unburden himself of the tunes he had stored up. His central characters, Calaf and Turandot, are as intensely delineated as Tosca and Scarpia, and it is their relationship that monopolizes the opera. Ever since the 1990 World Cup half the planet has known Calaf's "Nessun Dorma", a tune first heard when Calaf asks his question of Turandot. It's far from being an isolated highlight: Calaf's "Non pangiere Liu" and his answers to the three riddles are hair-raising numbers, but the most scintillating episode of the whole work is his final duet with the Princess, beginning "Principessa di morte", a stentorian pronouncement that leads into a series of high-octane exchanges between the lovers (Alfano's completion).

Turandot is similarly given a succession of memorable melodies, not least her icy "In questa regia", a *tour de force* that begins as a monologue and ends with Calaf joining his voice to Turandot's in an ever-rising duet that finishes with two of the most thrilling high Cs in all Italian opera. As with Scarpia, you can't help feeling that Puccini revelled in the creation of this deeply repellent character, and *Turandot* is unquestionably a nasty drama – the composer's treatment of the hapless Liù is prima facie evidence of extreme misogyny. But the decadent luxuriousness of Puccini's orchestral music and the visceral charge of his vocal writing prevail over the doubts of most audiences, and *Turandot* is a thoroughly appropriate full stop to Puccini's long and astonishingly successful career.

RECORDINGS OVERVIEW

Turandot has been very successful on record – indeed, of the many versions currently in the catalogue, only the Roberto Abbado set, recorded for RCA, is beyond the pale. The first sessions were taped by Cetra just eleven years after the world premiere, with Gina Cigna and Francesco Merli as Turandot and Calaf, and it remains one of the best. Decca's 1955 stereo recording with Borkh and del Monaco set a very high standard of singing. It was followed two years later by Callas's account, which has its fans, but preferable are Birgit Nilsson's two studio performances: the first was released in 1959 by RCA, then six years later she tackled it again with Franco Corelli, in what remains the greatest studio performance. A live recording of the same pair conducted by Leopold Stokowski, made from a 1961 broadcast from the Met, is the finest performance ever recorded – it is very hard to track down, but is worth every effort and any price. In 1972 Pavarotti and Sutherland broke away from their customary bel canto repertoires to make a fine recording for Decca with Zubin Mehta; later big-name efforts never really took off.

Nilsson, Corelli, Scotto, Mazzini; Rome Opera Chorus and Orchestra; Molinari-Pradelli.
(EMI CMS7 69327-2; 2 CDs).

This recording was made four years after Corelli and Nilsson headed the Met's first revival of *Turandot* for thirty years, and their performances were responsible for bringing the opera wider popularity in the US. Franco Corelli's stupendous, wildly emotional Calaf is the finest ever recorded, and the combination of him and the equally powerful Nilsson produces a performance that beggars description. Molinari-Pradelli might have kept a tighter grip on the reins, but he gets some lovely phrasing and colouring from the orchestra. If you buy just one Puccini opera set, make it this one.

Borkh, del Monaco, Tebaldi, Corena; Santa Cecilia Academy Chorus and Orchestra; Erede.
(Decca 433 761-2DMO2; 2 CDs).

Both Mario del Monaco and Inge Borkh had the equipment to do this music justice. Borkh boasted one of the most exciting dramatic sopranos of the 1950s and '60s, and if del Monaco was rarely capable of dropping his tone below a yell, this is what much of *Turandot* demands. Unfortunately, both these fine singers are let down by some sloppy conducting from Alberto Erede: a firmer hand is required if the flesh is to stay on the bone. Nonetheless, this is magical singing and a fine mid-price alternative to the benchmark performance from Corelli and Nilsson.

Pavarotti, Sutherland, Caballé, Ghiaurov; John Alldis Choir; London Philharmonic Orchestra; Mehta.
(Decca 414 274-2; 2 CDs).

This all-star recording, made in London in 1972, was one of Pavarotti's earliest ventures into the heavy repertoire with which he is today associated, and it remains one of the most successful. His pure, easily produced tenor lacks weight but he uses it with great musicianship and the high notes are uniquely spine-tingling. Sutherland never sang Turandot on stage and, like Pavarotti, her voice is best in lighter music, but here she manages superbly, producing some meatily theatrical tone. Caballé's Liù – a logical piece of casting – suffers from some lazy pronunciation, but she gives a distinctive, potent reading. The supporting cast – including none other than the aristocratic Sir Peter Pears as the Emperor Altoum – are all fine, and Zubin Mehta conducts with tremendous flair, encouraging some exquisite playing from the LPO.

UMBERTO GIORDANO

b. FOGGIA, ITALY, AUGUST 28, 1867; d. MILAN, NOVEMBER 12, 1948.

Umberto Giordano's *Andrea Chénier* is not a typical verismo opera: for one thing, it's a period-costume drama, and for another it lasts considerably longer than *Cavalleria rusticana* or *I Pagliacci*. But the historical setting amounts to little more than fancy dress for a volatile love story, and this opera is not so much a lengthy structure as a string of short ones. With its straightforward and sympathetic characters and its unrelenting succession of melodramatic outbursts, *Andrea Chénier* can truly be said to represent the fulfilment of everything Mascagni had in mind when composing *Cavalleria rusticana*.

Typically for a nineteenth-century Italian composer, Giordano was immediately attracted to the stage. By the time he graduated from Naples Conservatory in 1890 he had already completed his first opera, *Marina*, which he entered for the Sonzogno competition that Mascagni won. While it fared no better than sixth place out of seventy-three submissions, *Marina* impressed the jury ("when a boy has begun like this he should go far"), one of whom secured him a commission for a full-length drama from Sonzogno. The resulting work, *Mala vita*, was sensationalist even by the standards of verismo, telling the story of a labourer who vows to reform a prostitute if the Virgin Mary will rid him of his tuberculosis. It was violent, crude and, for a short time, enormously popular – considerably more so than his next work, *Regina Diaz*, which was abandoned after only two performances.

Sonzogno dropped his protégé and Giordano found himself looking for work, initially as a bandmaster and then as a fencing instructor. But in 1894 Sonzogno had a change of heart and invited Giordano to set Luigi Illica's *Andrea Chénier* for a performance in Milan. Premiered just two months after the first production of Puccini's *La Bohème* (also in Milan and also to an Illica libretto), *Chénier* inevitably came off second best, but it nonetheless brought Giordano wide-reaching acclaim. His next work, *Fedora*, was almost as popular, giving rise to the witticism "Fedora fè d'oro" (Fedora made money), but the opera was a prime example of a whole amounting to considerably less than its parts. Of his subsequent operas, only *Madame Sans-Gêne* achieved any success, and that was thanks to the combined presence of the tenor Martinelli and the conductor Toscanini. In 1930 he composed his last opera, *Il re*, and his remaining nineteen years were devoted to teaching and the composition of songs and salon pieces (including a fanfare for Italian radio news). At his death he was remembered as the composer of *Andrea Chénier*, an opera he had completed more than half a century earlier.

Andrea Chénier

Composed 1894–96.
First performed March 28, 1896.
Libretto by Luigi Illica.

Synopsis

Act I

At the Contessa de Coigny's fête, her daughter Maddalena is struck by the sincerity and passion of the poet Andrea Chénier who, in an improvised verse, denounces the selfishness and greed of the ruling classes. He is interrupted by a group of rebellious peasants, led by one of the Contessa's servants, Gérard, who tears off his livery. They leave, and calm returns, the party resuming as if nothing had happened.

Act II

Five years have passed and Chénier is distraught at the violence of the revolutionaries. One of his friends, Roucher, has secured him a passport and begs Chénier to leave while he can; but the poet reveals that a woman has sent him a note, requesting a meeting that evening. It is from Maddalena. When they meet, Maddalena confesses her love for Chénier – which he reciprocates – but they are spied upon by Gérard (now working for Robespierre), who tries to abduct Maddalena. In the ensuing fight, Gérard is wounded by Chénier; but when Gérard is asked to name his attacker, he pretends not to know.

Act III

Chénier has been arrested. In an impassioned monologue, Gérard sings of his disillusionment, of his corrupted patriotism and his desire for Maddalena. Driven by this desire, he signs Chénier's indictment. Maddalena begs Gérard to let Chénier go, even offering herself to him in return, but at the trial neither Chénier's assured self-defence nor Gérard's publicly stated change of heart can save him from the guillotine.

Act IV

In his prison cell, Chénier writes his final poem. Before he is called to his death, Maddalena convinces Gérard to allow her to take the place of another female prisoner so that she and Chénier may meet their deaths together.

𝄞 Giordano died a wealthy man, but during the two years it took him to write *Andrea Chénier* he lived the life of a pauper. Having moved to Milan to be near Illica (who in turn was living in Milan to be near Puccini), he could only afford a single room with a solitary window and an upright piano – in, of all places, a funeral parlour. Surrounded by corpses, headstones and wreaths, he started creating the elegant, decadent household of the Contessa de Coigny, a project he completed in Switzerland. He wrote to Illica: "I assure you that it is beautiful stuff, because I've written it with enthusiasm. . . . I'm very much in love with Act Two. . . . Ah, if *Chénier* goes well!", but for a while, it seemed as if *Chénier* would not go at all. Sonzogno, uneasy about certain aspects of the score and the political radicalism celebrated by the opera, at first rejected the work, until Mascagni demanded that the publisher honour his obligation to the young composer. The first-night reception was ecstatic: Chénier's Act I aria "Un di all'azzuro spazio" had to repeated and the audience interrupted the flow at every pause. After the American premiere later that year, Sonzogno telegrammed the composer: "CHENIER TRIUMPHANT. LAST ACT AROUSED FANATICAL ENTHUSIASM. BOOM. BOOM. BOOM."

The bravura of *Andre Chénier* has much in common with Puccini's work, though Giordano didn't possess Puccini's talents as a dramatist. Puccini would never have come up with anything like the prison finale, in which the lovers sing in gushing unison while being transported in a tumbrel to their deaths, or the court scenes, in which Chénier conducts himself in a manner that suggests a failure to grasp the gravity of the situation. But such is the splendour of Giordano's music that you're unlikely to trouble yourself over such technicalities as plausibility. Chénier's terrifyingly difficult tenor role, a cornucopia of heart-tugging melodies and show-stopping climaxes, dominates the work from "Un di all'azzuro spazio", through a succession of magnificent arias, duets and monologues, to the concluding dam-buster of a duet with Maddalena ("Vicino a te"). The role was first sung by Borgatti, a tenor whose mighty voice was later devoted to singing Wagner, and hugely influenced the style of verismo singing. The earnest role of Maddalena is crowned by her moving "La mamma morta" (used to great effect in the film *Philadelphia*), while Gérard's baritone reaches its zenith in the defiant hymn "Nemico della patria", an outrageously overstated piece of operatic rhetoric. In all, *Andrea Chénier* contains more than a dozen memorable arias and duets, and the opera's absence from the stage has more to do with a dearth of genuine heroic tenors than with any intrinsic musical weakness.

RECORDINGS OVERVIEW

Most of the top tenors of the last fifty years have had a go at Chénier, but the golden age for this opera was the 1950s and 1960s. Of the recent big names, neither Pavarotti nor Carreras – both of whom recorded the role late in their careers – possessed the gravity for the central role, though Domingo has turned in a creditable performance. If you're lucky, you might come across the obscure Verona label's recording of Mario del Monaco and Maria Callas singing *Chénier* on January 8, 1955 at La Scala. The sound is atrocious but this performance will leave an indelible impression. Del Monaco is in awesome form, producing an unimaginably massive sound: his rendition of "Un di . . ." is so thrilling that before the final notes have been sung the audience erupts into a frenzy that lasts almost as long as the aria. The performance comes to a halt and Callas is shouted down so that del Monaco can march to the footlights and receive further adoration. This is opera as a spectator sport.

Corelli, Stella, Sereni, De Palma; Rome Opera Chorus and Orchestra; Santini.
(EMI CMS5 65287-2; 2 CDs).

This 1963 recording would have been enough on its own to ensure Franco Corelli's immortality. Andrea Chénier is the part he was born to play, and here he plays it at the peak of his form. Full and baritonal, his voice is nonetheless capable of glass-breaking heights, smacked out with a verve that shakes your teeth in their sockets. "Un di . . ." is sung with all the self-indulgent mannerisms for which his performances were so memorable, while the "Credo" and the final "Vicino a te" are uniquely moving, even if Antonietta Stella is so outweighed that the final duet is more like a tenor solo with soprano accompaniment. Mario Sereni is the finest Gérard on disc: rasping and indignant, he delivers "Nemico della patria" with unstoppable bravura. In short, this is one of the greatest Italian opera recordings ever made.

Domingo, Scotto, Milnes, Sénéchal; John Alldis Chorus; National Philharmonic Orchestra; Levine.
(RCA GD82046; 2 CDs).

This is the best post-Corelli recording, thanks largely to the intelligent conducting of Levine. The driving tempi, quick phrase-turning and subtle instrumental pointing reveal Giordano's talent for orchestration in all its sumptuous glory. Domingo is a rather phlegmatic Chénier, but powerful nonetheless, while Scotto, though past her best, still revels in Maddalena's passions. Sherrill Milnes makes an aggressive Gérard and copes well with Levine's velocity. The London pick-up band plays superbly.

FRANCESCO CILEA

b. PALMI, ITALY, JULY 23, 1866; d. VARAZZE, NOVEMBER 20, 1950.

Few verismo operas lasted much more than an hour. The glory of verismo composers did not last much longer. Mascagni, Leoncavallo and Giordano achieved early celebrity with one particular opera and spent the remainder of their lives striving to repeat the act, and the verismo constellation was illuminated by even more evanescent luminaries, such as Tasca, Sebastiani and Spinelli. One of the better known one-opera wonders of the era was Francesco Cilea, a composer of considerable talents, today remembered solely for *Adriana Lecouvreur*.

Before leaving the Naples Conservatory in 1889, Cilea produced his first opera, *Cigna*, achieving enough local success to secure a publishing contract from Sonzogno. Both publisher and composer were captivated by verismo, but the first performance of *La Tilda*, in 1892 (the year of *Pagliacci*), was a painful failure, and Cilea abandoned opera for the next five years. In 1897 he composed *L'Arlesiana* (after a play by Daudet for which Bizet had composed incidental music in 1872), and this time he had a hit, due in part to Caruso's impassioned contribution. But the success was shortlived and, despite various revisions, the work soon fell from the repertoire. Another five years passed before the first performance of *Adriana Lecouvreur*, a work which at last brought Cilea the fame and recognition for which he had long been labouring, and made a star of Caruso. After *Gloria* closed in 1907 after only two nights – despite Toscanini's conducting – Cilea made one last attempt at opera, *Il matrimonio selvaggio*, but it was never performed. For the remaining forty-three years of his life he earned his living as a teacher, and though he revised his operas his only new works were for the church and the concert hall. Indeed, he was one of the first Italian composers of the period to seriously occupy himself with non-operatic music.

Adriana Lecouvreur

Composed 1901–02.
First performed November 6, 1902.
Libretto by Arturo Colautti, after Scribe and Legouve.

Synopsis

Act I

Backstage at the Comédie theatre. The actress Adriana Lecouvreur tells stage manager Michonnet that she loves Maurizio (Comte de Saxe) – who, unknown to her, is a pretender to the Polish throne. They meet just before she goes onstage, when she gives him a bouquet of violets. Later on, a note to Maurizio, requesting a meeting, is intercepted by the Prince de Bouillon, who assumes that it is from Maurizio's mistress, the actress Duclos, while it is in fact from the Princess de Bouillon.

Act II

The Princess de Bouillon awaits the arrival of Maurizio. When he arrives she demands to know if he is seeing another woman. He says not, and calms her down by giving her the violets given to him by Adriana. As the guests arrive for a party thrown by the Princess's husband, she hides in an adjoining room until she is helped to escape by Maurizio and, unwittingly, Adriana. While neither says anything, both women suspect the other of being their rival.

Act III

At the Princess's party, Adriana's voice is recognized by the Princess as that of the woman who, with Maurizio, helped her to freedom. Vengefully, she shows Adriana the now fading bouquet of violets and, in return, Adriana quotes a verse from Racine, hinting at the Princess's immorality. For this, the Princess swears revenge.

Act IV

At the Comédie, the company are celebrating Adriana's birthday. One of her gifts is an anonymous delivery of violets. She assumes that they are from Maurizio and breathes deeply from their scent. However, they are from the Princess, who has soaked them in poison. Maurizio arrives to find her dying.

Nobody would claim that *Adriana Lecouvreur* is a first-rank example of music-theatre. Its libretto – distantly based on real-life events in eighteenth-century Paris – began life as one of the most confused ever written, and was made even worse at rehearsals when Cilea cut some sections that he thought confusing. The merit of this romantic fantasy lies entirely with Cilea's music, in which the fervour of verismo is tempered by a delicate, eighteenth-century quality, a contrast first employed by Giordano in *Andrea Chénier* (see p.348). Cilea's sparkling orchestration, rich with small-scale detail, has an intimacy that strikingly offsets the heaving and wailing of the opera's verismo stereotypes, a crew possessing few psychological subtleties. Adriana herself is an impressive, low-lying soprano role, however. Her contribution, which reaches its climax during the death scene with Maurizio, is the crux of this opera's appeal, and perhaps more than any other verismo opera, *Adriana Lecouvreur* succeeds or fails through the abilities of its soprano. As Magda Olivero proved – unfortunately never in the studio – the title role has enough weight to justify the opera's place beside the works of Mascagni, Leoncavallo and Giordano.

RECORDINGS OVERVIEW

Of the five complete recordings made of *Adriana* only one, Levine's 1977 account, can be said to have succeeded completely, though the earlier Tebaldi/del Monaco vehicle has its plus points. One to avoid, despite the praises from some sectors of the music press, is the 1990 Decca set, produced by the team of Joan Sutherland, Carlo Bergonzi and Richard Bonynge. All three have made many superb recordings, but this drag of a show is emphatically not one of them.

Scotto, Domingo, Milnes, Obraztsova; Ambrosian Opera Chorus; Philharmonia; Levine.
(CBS CD79310; 2 CDs).

Levine's animated and imaginative conducting makes Cilea's music sound really fresh, enhancing the flaming passions and the period elegance alike. Domingo is a reverberant, heady Maurizio, and Scotto similarly gets under her character's skin, although her timbre is weaker than Tebaldi's. Milnes is a muscular Michonnet and yet he produces some delicate nuances, while Obraztsova's big mezzo is excellent for the Princess – Levine makes her hold back the tidal wave of sound that might have swamped everybody around her. An exciting and touching performance, and the strongest possible argument for the return of this opera to the repertoire.

Tebaldi, del Monaco, Fioravanti, Simionato; Santa Cecilia Academy Chorus and Orchestra; Capuana.
(Decca 430 256-2DM2; 2 CDs).

Franco Capuana is rarely able to control his forces in the way Levine does, but Tebaldi's Adriana is unrivalled for beauty, colour and expression. Mario del Monaco, on the other hand, is like a pilotless plane spiralling out of control, and his refusal to adjust the volume of his voice to anything below fortissimo is exhausting – even if there are some thrilling episodes. Simionato and Fioravanti are less impressive than Milnes and Obraztsova, and Capuana only just manages to keep things moving. But at mid-price, it's worth the investment for Tebaldi's unique Adriana.

JULES MASSENET

b. MONTAUD, FRANCE, MAY 12, 1842; d. PARIS, AUGUST 13, 1912.

While the likes of Chabrier and Chausson tried to convert French music to the way of Wagnerian righteousness, Jules Massenet remained true to the lineage of French lyric opera. Building on the work of Charles Gounod and Ambroise Thomas, Massenet tightened their suavely elegant vocal style in music that represents one of the last great flowerings of operatic Romanticism.

After studies with Ambroise Thomas, Massenet won the Prix de Rome in 1863. He spent three years in Italy, where he came to know Liszt, and on his return he was engaged as timpanist in the orchestra at the Paris Opéra. As he later wrote in his memoirs, this spell taught him much about the mechanics of orchestration and within two years he was equipped to write his first opera, *La grand'-tante*. His first notable successes, however, were the oratorios *Marie-Magdelaine* and *Eve*, creations characterized by what Vincent d'Indy termed a "pseudo-religious eroticism". This quality was to colour much of Massenet's later operatic work, but his next stage work marked a return to earlier conventions. Written in 1876–77 for the extravagant new Paris Opéra, *Le roi de Lahore* was an exotic Grand Opéra, and its success made Massenet's name in France.

His reputation was further enhanced by the first production in 1881 of *Hérodiade*, a version of the Salome legend in which Massenet's semi-declamatory melodies to some extent anticipated Debussy's *Pelléas et Mélisande*. *Hérodiade* was followed three years later by his most lasting success, *Manon*, which was in turn followed by the grandiose *Le Cid* and two of his most lasting failures, *Esclarmonde* and *Le mage*. In 1892 he produced his masterpiece, *Werther*, the first of a string of verismo-influenced dramas, including the sensationalist *La navarraise*, in which the heroine murders the hero, then goes mad. *Sapho*, premiered in 1897, marked his return to the fluid lyricism for which he was most widely celebrated, and was his last commercial success, though he experienced an Indian summer in 1909, when he composed *Don Quichotte*, a meditative, valedictory work that was not his last opera (he composed four more), but which might well have been.

LEBRECHT COLLECTION

Jules Massenet

Massenet's operas mirror many of the various tendencies of the preceding half-century, but he was in essence a conservative, remaining true to the tuneful vocabulary of the lyric tradition, even when he veered off into the terrain of verismo or Grand Opéra. His melodies are sweet, sometimes cloyingly so, but their sincerity is undeniable and their tender, sensuous melancholy has continued to attract the greatest singers. Massenet's world is defined by song, even when nobody is singing, for all his major operas have lengthy passages in which the orchestra sings as fluently as the singers. His somewhat saccharine style fell from popularity within months of his death, and he continues to suffer from the condescension of the high-minded. Nonetheless, Massenet's best music has now regained something of its former standing, and his luscious, emotional operas are the mainstays of his reputation.

Hérodiade

Herodias

Composed 1878–81.
First performed December 19, 1881.
Libretto by Paul Milliet, Georges Hartmann and Angelo Zanardini, after Flaubert.

Synopsis

Act I

Salome, stepdaughter of Herod (Hérode), confesses to the astrologer Phanuel that she has fallen in love with John the Baptist (Jean), who has been travelling the land predicting the arrival of the Messiah. He has also been denouncing Herod's marriage to Herodias (Hérodiade), Herod's brother's wife, for which Herodias has come to despise the preacher.

Act II

Herod becomes ever more obsessed with Salome's beauty, and Herodias grows ever more jealous. Unbeknown to her, Salome is in fact her long-lost daughter.

Act III

Herod attempts to seduce Salome. She resists, and in his fury he orders her to be beheaded alongside John the Baptist, whose death has been demanded by Herodias.

Act IV

As they await their deaths, Salome and John hope that their love will thrive in heaven. Salome sings of her hatred for Herodias, who is responsible for John's imminent execution. When it is revealed that Herodias is her mother, Salome kills herself.

Massenet's *Hérodiade*, the first major operatic setting of the Salome story, is quite different from Strauss's better-known treatment, thanks primarily to Milliet's loony innovation of having the Baptist and Salome fall in love. The director of the Paris Opéra, presented with the score by Massenet's publisher, considered the work indecent and refused to have anything to do with this heady cocktail of sex and religion, just as he had rejected Saint-Saens's "amoral" treatment of the Samson story. It proved to be an expensive rejection, for when it was staged at the Théâtre de la Monnaie in Brussels it was an instant hit, remaining one of the composer's most popular works long after the colossal successes of *Manon* and *Werther*.

Critics praised the way in which Massenet's music set the evil of Herod and Herodias against the noble goodness of John and Salome (though the dichotomy is the musical equivalent of "white hat/ black hat" Westerns), and the love music in the dungeon scene was considered by one commentator to be "the finest in the lyric tradition since *Roméo et Juliette*". Massenet created the Baptist and Salome as a typical romantic tenor and soprano duo, but in their long and boldly shaped phrases there is a strong sense of Massenet pulling away from the inflexible "numbers" formula beloved of Gounod – indeed, there is a conversational tone to the lovers' music that anticipates the delicate sensuality of *Manon*. Similarly, the ensemble passages unfold much more fluently within the narrative framework (which is bound together by some neon-lit leitmotifs), even if the choruses and ballets (of which there are far too many) have an old-fashioned feel that sometimes harks back to Meyerbeer. The title role is the mainspring of the action, but Herodias's music isn't what you take away from this opera. That said, she's given some powerful declamatory singing in the low-lying regions of the mezzo range, and by Massenet's standards she's a fruity and red-blooded creation.

Domingo, Fleming, Zajik, Pons; San Francisco Opera Chorus and Orchestra; Gergiev.
(Sony S2K 66847; 2 CDs).

This live recording was one of the first to be made by San Francisco Opera after Domingo's appointment as

its director, and it has all the energy one would expect from an opera company with him at its helm. He finds some of Jean's music rather taxing, but his is still an extraordinarily beautiful tenor voice, and the love music is ravishingly sung. Renée Fleming is a passionate, full-voiced Salome (suggesting little of the character's youth) and Juan Pons and Dolora Zajik make a colourful pair as Herod and Herodias. Russian specialist Valery Gergiev shows a surprising affinity with Massenet's sound-world, and if he is prone to force the volume the choruses benefit from his theatrical flair.

Manon

Composed 1882–83.
First performed January 19, 1884.
Libretto by Henri Meilhac and Philippe Gille, after the Abbé Prévost.

Synopsis

Act I

France, second half of the eighteenth century. At an inn in Amiens Lescaut greets his cousin Manon, who is on her way to join a convent. Manon is wooed by the old lecher Guillot while her cousin fetches her luggage, but when Lescaut returns he sees Guillot off and warns Manon to beware "unwelcome strangers". Manon is captivated by her busy, cosmopolitan surroundings, and her attention is then caught by the entrance of the young and handsome Chevalier des Grieux. He introduces himself and they fall instantly in love. Stealing Guillot's coach, they elope together.

Act II

In the apartment he shares with Manon, des Grieux writes to his father telling him of his future wife. Suddenly, Lescaut storms in, accompanied by his nobleman friend de Brétigny. Des Grieux assures him that he intends to marry his cousin, and produces the letter he has just written as proof; but while they argue, de Brétigny begins to lure Manon away from her humble life with des Grieux, with tales of pleasure and riches. She cannot resist. Lescaut and de Brétigny leave, followed shortly after by des Grieux who is off to post his letter. While he is away Manon bids farewell to her life with des Grieux; when he returns he tells her of his daydream in which all was paradise – except that Manon was not there. He is interrupted by a knock at the door and when des Grieux answers he is abducted by Lescaut and de Brétigny. Though grief-stricken, Manon does nothing to stop them.

Act III

Lescaut, Manon and de Brétigny are enjoying the good life. Des Grieux's father, the Count, tells de Brétigny of his son's conversion, and of his intention to take holy orders. He is to preach that evening at St-Sulpice. In St-Sulpice, the Count congratulates his son on his excellent sermon; but after he leaves, des Grieux soliloquizes that his religious faith is still tested by visions of Manon. He goes into the church and returns to find Manon. They fall instantly into each other's arms and, once again, escape together.

Act IV

Lescaut and his friends are taken aback when Manon and des Grieux enter the room in which they are gambling. They urge des Grieux to join the game, and with the encouragement of Manon (who is again bewitched by affluence) he takes a seat. When Guillot loses to des Grieux he storms off and summons the Count and the police: des Grieux and Manon are arrested for cheating.

Act V

Des Grieux has been released, but Manon is to be deported as a "woman of easy virtue". Lescaut's plan to free her fails; he then bribes the guards to allow Manon time alone with des Grieux. She is too weak to escape, and dies in des Grieux's arms.

Abbé Prévost's *L'histoire du Chevalier des Grieux et de Manon Lescaut* provided the source for Puccini's third opera, as well as an inspiration to Auber and, less obviously, Hans Werner Henze (see p.514). But of all operatic treatments of Manon's decline from child-like innocence to complete degradation, Massenet's is the most penetrating. Such was his affection for the soldiering and novel-writing Abbé that he composed part of the score in the house where the writer lived while staying in the Hague, and the sentimental affinity inspired what many believe to be Massenet's greatest work. Massenet once remarked, "we must always agree with the public". The comment may not have been entirely sincere, but he knew what the public wanted and in the luscious emotionalism of *Manon* he gave them more of it than in any other of his operas. Even though the initial run was cut short by the death of the soprano Marie Heilbronn, *Manon* received its thousandth performance only seven years after the composer's death in 1912.

As with Strauss, the majority of Massenet's finest music was written for the female voice, and the role of Manon is perhaps the fullest illustration of Massenet's facility for developing character: just compare her fragile first aria, "Voyons, Manon, plus de chimères", an ingenuous passage revealing Manon's innocent enthusiasm for a life of which she knows nothing, with her Act III seduction aria "N'est-ce plus ma main que cette main presse", an urgent episode underlit with a sensuality that's light years from the child-like creature of Act I.

Manon's fall from grace is set against a generally light orchestral backdrop by which Massenet – skilfully employing Baroque forms such as minuets and gavottes – conjures atmospheres as different as the devotion of St-Sulpice and the sleaze of the gaming rooms. For all the colour of its scene-painting, however, it is its emotional directness that makes *Manon* such a captivating opera. When it is successfully performed, you can almost understand why Thomas Beecham once pronounced that he would "happily give up all the *Brandenburg Concertos* for *Manon*".

RECORDINGS OVERVIEW

The first of the six complete recordings of *Manon*, taped by Pathé at the Opéra-Comique in 1923, is the most authentic: many of the orchestra would have played for Massenet himself and at least three of the singers were personally known to him. Five years later EMI made the first of their four complete recordings, the best of which was made in 1955, with Victoria de los Angeles and Henri Legay conducted by Pierre Monteux. At the moment this is not on CD, and neither is EMI's fine 1970 performance with Beverly Sills and Nicolai Gedda. A notable curiosity is a single CD from Myto that contains bleeding chunks recorded in the 1940s, with Giuseppe di Stefano as a strikingly beautiful des Grieux.

Cotrubas, Kraus, Quilico, van Dam; Chorus and Orchestra of the Capitole de Toulouse; Plasson.
(EMI CDS7 49610-2; 3 CDs).

Michel Plasson's longstanding partnership with the Capitole players produces a real sense of cohesion and unity of purpose in this 1982 set. Ileana Cotrubas is a lyrical, beautifully paced but nicely theatrical Manon, even if she lacks the darker qualities needed for the last two acts. Ever-stylish Alfredo Kraus is the stereo era's closest approximation to Georges Thill, and Gino Quilico is a huge success as Lescaut, making much of Massenet's rather one-dimensional material. The supporting cast are all excellent and the recorded sound is fresh and flexible.

Freni, Pavarotti, Ganzarolli, Zerbini; La Scala Chorus and Orchestra; Maag.
(Butterfly BMCD004; 2 CDs).

This outstanding live recording of a heavily cut score, taped in 1969, is about as French as Inspector Clouseau, but it is nonetheless the most beautifully sung *Manon* after Monteux's 1955 recording. Mirella Freni has an open-throated warmth that many French singers would envy, and the sweet, Italianate phrasing and brittle declamation have an irresistible charm. Pavarotti is similarly inclined to Italianate gestures, such as the interpolated sob, aspirate and jumped cadence, but he sings des Grieux's great aria, "Ah, dispar vision", with an ecstasy and vocal splendour unrivalled on disc. The conductor maintains an urgent pace, even if the La Scala forces don't quite pass muster.

Le Cid

Composed 1884–85.
First performed November 30, 1885.
Libretto by Adolphe d'Ennery, Louis Gallet and Edouard Blau, after Corneille.

Synopsis

Act I

Spain, eleventh century. Rodrigue, soon to be knighted by the king, is to marry the Comte de Gormas's daughter Chimène. At the wedding in Burgos cathedral, a fight breaks out between the Comte and Rodrigue's father, Don Diègue, over the latter's appointment as the Infanta's tutor.

Act II

Rodrigue champions his father and kills Gormas, provoking Chimène to demand revenge from the king; but when war breaks out with the Moors, the king sends Rodrigue to head his armies.

Act III

Despite her vengeful feelings, Chimène cannot prevent herself from falling into Rodrigue's arms. He is visited by a vision of St James of Compostela, in which he is promised victory, and the Moors are duly defeated.

Act IV

Rodrigue is rumoured to be dead, but then returns as The Cid ("The Conqueror"). Chimène forgives him and abandons her right to justice. Rodrigue is racked with guilt and attempts suicide, but he is saved by Chimène, who again proclaims her love for him.

Le Cid is Massenet's grandest opera, a spectacular attempt at rejuvenating the middle-century style of Meyerbeer and Halévy. The formulas are frequently over-familiar, but the substance is fresh, exotic and colourful, with a Spanish hue which – as with *Carmen* – owes as much to the composer's invention as to the indigenous music of Spain, although Massenet made a trip to that country before beginning *Le Cid*. Extravagant fanfares and marches pepper the action, but the opera's primary attraction is, once again, its vocal writing. The scene at the end of Act I between Rodrigue and Don Diègue is a thrillingly impassioned exchange, bolstered by some sensational, percussive orchestration; Chimène's aria at the beginning of Act III and the ensuing duet with Rodrigue are equally gripping; and the highlight of the entire opera is Rodrigue's astonishing Act II tenor aria, "O souverain, ô juge, ô père". Famously recorded by Caruso in 1916, this graceful showpiece is typical of Massenet's smooth, even-tempered style of tenor writing in his pre-*Werther* period. In Gormas Massenet created one of the greatest and certainly the most flamboyant of all his bass roles (the antithesis, in many respects, of the gentle Don Quixote), and it calls for a mighty *profondo* voice. It was created by Pol Plançon, whose amazing voice can be heard on CD, albeit not singing *Le Cid*.

Bumbry, Domingo, Plishka, Voketaitis; Byrne Camp Chorale; New York Opera Orchestra; Queler.
(CBS CD79300; 2 CDs).

This is a big-name, big-sounding *Le Cid*. Grace Bumbry is a loud, uncompromising Chimène and Paul Plishka roars his way through Gormas, but the star of the show is Placido Domingo's Cid, a gripping presence. His pronunciation is crisp and his phrasing disciplined, and "O souverain, ô juge, ô père" is attacked with a rare candour. The sound is boxy and the balance is frequently artificial, but the general enthusiasm and Domingo's resonant performance make this is a valuable set. It has literally no competition.

Werther

Composed 1885–87.
First performed February 16, 1892.
Libretto by Edouard Blau, Paul Milliet and Georges Hartmann, after Goethe.

Synopsis

Act I

Frankfurt, around 1780. July. An unnamed Magistrate is rehearsing his children in a Christmas carol. As his wife has died, he is cared for by the eldest of his daughters, twenty-year-old Charlotte. Two of his friends arrive and inform him that the poet Werther is about to leave to take up an ambassadorial position and that Charlotte's fiancé Albert has arrived back in town. Werther arrives and watches Charlotte as she tends to her siblings. The Magistrate introduces him to his family, after which they all leave for a Christmas ball. While they are away, Albert finally arrives. Werther and Charlotte return arm in arm, the former obviously now deeply in love. His advances are interrupted by her father's voice, informing her that Albert has arrived, at which she tells Werther that, having made the promise to her dying mother, she has to marry Albert. Werther is distraught.

Act II

September. Albert and Charlotte are contentedly married. Werther returns to the village and sees them walking together into church. He curses Albert's good fortune, and bemoans his own unhappiness. When Albert comes out of the church, he meets Werther and suggests Charlotte's sister, Sophie, as a possible bride. Charlotte tells Werther to go, a rebuff that makes him consider suicide. Before he leaves he tells Sophie that he will not be returning; she relays this news to Charlotte, whose reaction convinces Albert that Werther's passion for Charlotte is reciprocated.

Act III

Christmas Eve. As she rereads Werther's letters to her, Charlotte realizes that she is in love with Werther. Sophie attempts to console her, and as Charlotte prays to God for help, Werther appears. They fall into each other's arms but Charlotte is stricken by guilt and rushes from the room. Werther also leaves, but not before sending a request to Albert for his pistols, which he will need on his journeys overseas. Realizing what is happening, Charlotte rushes after Werther.

Act IV

Christmas night. In his study, Werther lies mortally wounded, a pistol by his side. Charlotte revives him and, after confessing that she does love him, they kiss for the first and only time. As he dies, he mistakes the sound of singing children for angels.

The protagonist of Goethe's *Sorrows of Young Werther* is the archetypal Romantic hero, eternally searching for truth and beauty; the protagonist of the opera Massenet made from the novel is simply a victim of frustrated love. Yet if the more complex *Manon* is Massenet's greatest work of opera, *Werther* is his greatest work of music.

He completed the score in 1887 but its production was delayed, first by the Opéra-Comique's management, who thought the work too depressing, and then by a gas-lamp which burnt down the theatre. It was eventually given its premiere in Vienna, where it was very well received. "Goethe said that 'where words leave off, music begins'. In the score of *Werther*, words and music are so closely allied as to seem born of one and the same inspiration", wrote one critic. The title role was created by the Belgian tenor Ernest van Dyck, a spherical man who was blessed with a magnificent voice (his recordings are available on CD) and an impossible vanity – despite his great popularity, Mahler later dismissed him from the Vienna Staatsoper. Van Dyck's lyric tenor was ideally suited to the role's wide intervals and declamatory phrasing: with the principal exception of the ecstatic aria "Pourquoi me réveiller?" (at the end of Act III), Werther is characterized through urgent, unstable and sometimes hysterical writing.

By contrast, Charlotte's struggle to resolve the claims of love and loyalty is bathed in music of great sweetness, although Massenet successfully conveys something of her inhibition, presenting her as Werther's opposite until she finally confesses her love for Werther – a moment that breaks with Goethe's novel but which comes as a great relief musically as well as dramatically. Werther's orchestrations are richer and weightier than in *Manon*, but they are never overbearing: rather the instrumental writing carries the vocal line with perfect fluency, creating a cohesiveness that is further underlined by Massenet's inventive use of motif. All loose threads are audibly resolved during the final scenes in which, to music of throat-catching pathos, Werther is raised to heaven.

RECORDINGS OVERVIEW

Reflecting *Werther*'s postwar return to popularity, all but one of the complete sets was made after 1950. However, it is the first recording – made in 1931 – that continues to dominate the opera's history on record. Later Werthers – including Gedda, Kraus and Domingo – can't really be bracketed with Georges Thill, although Victoria de los Angeles, partnering Gedda on the 1969 EMI set, is a delightful Charlotte. There are some outstanding live Italian performances to be found with Bergonzi and Corelli singing the title role – but they are hard to track down and, naturally, both sing in Italian.

Thill, Vallin, Roque, Féraldy; Opéra-Comique Orchestra; Cohen.
(EMI CHS 7 63195-2; 2 CDs).

This is one of the greatest of all French operatic recordings, notable for its old-fashioned style and glorious singing. Georges Thill maintains a powerful sense of line and heroic timbre whilst remaining alive to the sensuality of the language – a master singer, he is perfect in every respect. Ninon Vallin's soprano has an urgency that perfectly compliments Thill's regal sophistication. The support is excellent and Elie Cohen encourages the Opéra-Comique orchestra to revel in the singing tone and vibrant textures of the old-fashioned instruments (wooden flutes, French bassoons, gut strings etc). The sound is fine for the year, but the full price is an imposition nearly seventy years after it was first released.

Kraus, Troyanos, Manuguerra, Barbaux; London Philharmonic Orchestra; Plasson.
(EMI CMS7 69573-2; 2 CDs).

Although working with a London band, Plasson does his best to get them to adopt French tone and phrasing, allowing the heavy orchestrations their due without letting them overwhelm things. His stylistic inclinations are well served by the mellifluous Alfredo Kraus (although the Spanish tenor's pronunciation is frequently very wide of the mark), and he and Tatiana Troyanos make a perfect couple, with the latter's naturally rapid vibrato and dark tone nicely placed against Kraus's lighter voice. Manuguerra does well to hold back his formidable baritone as Albert, and he conveys just the right level of arrogance and cruelty. The sound is excellent and the price fair.

Carreras, von Stade, Allen, Buchanan; Royal Opera House Chorus and Orchestra; Davis
(Philips 416 654-2PH2; 2 CDs).

This 1980 recording, made after a Covent Garden production, is belligerent reading, with four-square phrasing and overcooked singing from Carreras, who hurls himself into the character with overdone bravura. The elegantly placed soprano of Frederica von Stade is the primary source of pleasure, and her singing of the final act is a performance to die for. Thomas Allen's beguiling baritone well serves Albert's role as suitor. All in all a decent set, but the headstrong Carreras demotes it to third place.

Don Quichotte

Don Quixote

Composed 1908–09.
First performed February 19, 1910.
Libretto by Henri Cain, after Cervantes.

Synopsis

Act I

The townspeople are enjoying a fiesta. Dulcinée is serenaded by four suitors – one of whom, Juan, mocks Don Quixote when he and his servant Sancho Panza arrive. Juan challenges the knight to a duel but Dulcinée intervenes and sends Juan on his way. However, she then begins to taunt the Don, demanding that he prove his love for her by retrieving a necklace that she lost to bandits. He accepts the challenge and leaves with Sancho Panza.

Act II

Out looking for the bandits, Sancho Panza sings a polemic against women, but the Don is preoccupied by what he takes to be a group of giants but is in fact a bank of windmills. To Sancho's dismay, his master charges off to attack the enemy and is caught up on one of the sails.

Act III

Having proceeded with their search, Don Quixote and Sancho Panza fall asleep. When they are woken by the noise of the bandits, Sancho runs away, but the Don stands his ground. He is overpowered and the bandits prepare to kill him, but they are moved by his noble prayer to God. When he tells him that he is a knight errant on a quest for a beautiful lady, they return the necklace. Don Quixote gives them his blessing.

Act IV

Dulcinée entertains the crowd. Don Quixote promises Sancho Panza an island in return for having accompanied him on his adventures. He returns Dulcinée's necklace (to everyone's amazement) and asks her to marry him. When the crowd laughs at this, she sends them away but, nonetheless, turns down his offer: she is a free spirit and does not want to be tied down. The Don is grateful for her gentleness and honesty but he cannot disguise his disappointment. When the crowd returns and mocks the knight, Sancho berates them for their cruelty and leads his master to safety.

Act V

The Don is beaten, his heart is broken and he prepares to die. He apologizes to Sancho that the only island he can give him now is the one in his dreams and, lying in Sancho's arms, he sees a vision of Dulcinée. Deaf to his servant's tearful demands that he remain, Don Quixote dies.

Massenet's adaptation of Cervantes' immense picaresque novel was primarily inspired not by the text itself but by images derived from the book, notably the engravings of Gustave Doré, who created a memorably simplistic, sometimes maudlin portrait of the hero and his servant. Convinced he was dying, and racked with rheumatic pain, Massenet threw himself into the creation of a work whose protagonist, he wrote, had entered his life "like gentle balm". Undoubtedly he saw himself in the character of the Don, who clung to the chivalric code as

Massenet clung onto tonality in the face of adventurous works such as Debussy's *Pelléas* and Strauss's *Elektra*.

Massenet conceived the title role for the Russian bass Fyodor Chaliapin, an extraordinarily charismatic actor-singer, who twenty-three years later was to revive the role for Georg Pabst's 1933 film of the opera. Massenet's Don is an upright character, spared the more extreme humiliations that Cervantes meted out to his hero, and his scenes with Sancho Panza are exquisitely poignant – indeed it would be hard to find a more loving partnership in all opera. The lyrical score, which is notable for its plausibly Iberian instrumentation, is dominated by their bass/baritone combination, and the final act, which lasts no more than twenty minutes, is perhaps Massenet's finest moment. Avoiding the emotional blackmail of earlier works, the death of Don Quixote is a dignified and subdued scene, in which the music is permeated by a profound melancholy and tenderness. With Don's Quixote's death, Massenet also took his final bow, crowning his life's work with music of genuine pathos.

RECORDINGS OVERVIEW

The most precious recordings of music from *Don Quichotte* are those made by Chaliapin (see p.592), who created the title role and later recorded the final scene. Christoff and Ghiaurov are superlative singers, but neither of the two recordings listed below quite attains the nobility of Chaliapin's 78s.

Ghiaurov, Bacquier, Crespin; Suisse Romande Radio Chorus and Orchestra; Kord.
(Decca 430 636-2DM2; 2 CDs).

Decca's *Don Quichotte* is an enchanting account of Massenet's swan song. Nicolai Ghiaurov's forthright, sanguine Don wrings every last drop of feeling from his character without ever stooping to cheap tricks. Gabriel Bacquier's vibrant, fruity baritone beautifully complements Ghiaurov's lavish bass, while Régine Crespin flirts and chides effectively. The final scenes are handsomely done, thanks partly to Kord, whose grip is always steady. This touching, excellently recorded account is an obvious first choice.

Christoff, Badoli, Berganza; RAI Chorus and Symphony Orchestra; Simonetto.
(Fonit Cetra CDAR 2025; 2 CDs).

This live 1957 Italian broadcast of a primarily Italian cast singing *Don Quichotte* in Italian is of interest for the Don of Boris Christoff, Chaliapin's true heir and the most celebrated Quixote of the postwar years. Deploying his enormous bass with remarkable imagination and wit, he presents a superb reading, and his death scene is even sadder than Ghiaurov makes it. Good orchestral support and a fine Dulcinée from the youthful Teresa Berganza complete a treasurable recording.

GUSTAVE CHARPENTIER

b. MEURTHE, FRANCE, JUNE 25, 1860; d. PARIS, FEBRUARY 18, 1956.

Despite the precedent of Bizet's *Carmen* and the unflinchingly clear-eyed novels of such writers as Flaubert and Zola, most French composers were inclined to leave operatic realism to the Italians. There are a few exceptions: Massenet made a rare departure from the exotic with *La navarraise*, while his pupil Charpentier explored the Bohemian demimonde of Montmartre in *Louise*, the only work for which he is known but one that has managed to retain its popularity – at least in France – since its premiere in 1900.

While studying at the Paris Conservatoire with Massenet he unexpectedly won the coveted scholarship, the Prix de Rome, which allowed him to study in Italy, and it was while there, from 1887 to 1890, that he sketched much of his subsequent music, including the first act of *Louise*. It took Charpentier ten years to complete it, and it was finally accepted by the Opéra-Comique, where it was produced by Albert Carré with designs by Lucien Jusseaume and conducted by Andre Méssager – the same team that was to produce *Pelléas et Mélisande* two years later. The opera was a huge success. Mary Garden, who was to be Debussy's first Mélisande, took over the title role after eight performances, and both she and Charpentier were launched to international celebrity.

Though Charpentier produced a sequel, *Julien*, in 1912, *Louise* was to remain his only real success, so much so that by the mid-1930s it had been performed over a thousand times in Paris alone. In 1935 Charpentier reduced the score for recording purposes, then three years later he returned to it once again, this time to supervise the music for a film version directed by Abel Gance, starring Georges Thill and Grace Moore. Charpentier was a lifelong socialist of a particularly idealistic type (he loved music hall songs and refused to write chamber music because he thought it was elitist), and much of his energy was devoted to the Oeuvre Mimi Pinson, an organization that provided working women with tickets to the opera. After 1902 it became the Conservatoire Populaire Mimi Pinson, a school providing free tuition in both music and dance.

Louise

Composed 1889–96.
First performed February 2, 1900.
Libretto by the composer and Saint-Paul-Roux.

Synopsis

Act I

Louise, a dressmaker, is in love with the poet Julien, who tries to persuade her to elope with him. Louise's parents think he is a layabout and will not consent to their marriage.

Act II

The new day begins with the cries of street vendors. The Noctambulist tells of the desire of the poor to improve their lot. Julien traces Louise to her place of work, where he tries to persuade her to abandon her family. Eventually she agrees to go with him.

Act III

Louise has settled into Bohemian life and in a mock coronation is crowned Queen of Bohemia and the Muse of Montmartre. The celebrations are interrupted by the arrival of Louise's mother, who demands she return home as her father is terribly ill.

Act IV

Her father recovers and when Louise prepares to return to Montmartre her parents do all they can to persuade her to remain. Her father eventually loses all patience and tries to bar her way. Louise manages to escape while her parents curse Paris for having taken their daughter away.

Louise has obvious similarities to *La Bohème*, which was written at the same time, but unlike Puccini's opera it has a contemporary setting and presents a more wide-ranging picture of life on the margins. At its premiere some critics hailed it for its radical and honest look at working-class life, and indeed Charpentier knew the reality of Montmartre well, having lived there since his student days in fairly abject poverty. The strange figure of the Noctambulist – the personification of "the pleasure of Paris" – looms over the action, whose protagonists were obviously modelled on real people (most of Charpentier's characters sing in a Parisian dialect). Not everyone was convinced: Debussy for one remarked that Louise was "a thousand times more conventional than *Les Huguenots*. . . . And they call this life. Good God! I'd sooner die."

Richard Strauss, Janáček, Mahler and Massenet, on the other hand, all thought that *Louise* was a work of great merit, but Debussy was right to point out that *Louise* is not as musically daring as some made out. On the whole the story is told through gentle, illustrative music which doesn't touch the intense heights of true verismo, and most of the melodies are typical of opéra-comique, with a sweep and charm that you might expect from a pupil of Massenet. Fluid and highly characterful, *Louise* boasts two delightful roles in the title soprano and Julien's high tenor, but the detailed period atmosphere plays an equally important role in making this one of the most beguiling French operas of the last hundred years.

RECORDINGS OVERVIEW

There have been only five recordings of Charpentier's "Parisian Novel". The earliest, made in 1935, has near-perfect casting, with Georges Thill and Ninon Vallin outstanding as the lovers, but the score was heavily cut by the composer especially for record. Philips's 1956 Opéra-Comique recording sounds authentically French but is let down by unnecessary cuts and a weak title performance from Berthe Monmart. Twenty years later Prêtre conducted a performance for CBS, with the heavy-duty voices of Domingo and Cotrubas making heavy weather of the lyrical music. The following year EMI recorded what is still the most secure performance of the complete opera, with Sills and Gedda in excellent form. Erato recorded a live and extremely noisy performance in 1983 with Felicity Lott and Jerome Pruett as the lovers, but it presents little competition to the earlier sets – despite the digital stereo.

Gedda, Sills, van Dam, Dunn; Paris Opéra Chorus and Orchestra; Rudel.
(EMI CMS5 65299-2; 3 CDs).

Nicolai Gedda throws himself into Julien's opening phrases with great passion, and goes on to give one of his finest portrayals on record, perhaps inspired by the sweet coloratura of Beverly Sills. They make a remarkably convincing pair of lovers. Mignon Dunn's Mother and José van Dam's Father are both excellent, conveying both the fear of loss and the pain of regret, and the Parisian atmosphere is recreated with real imagination by Rudel. A superb recording.

Thill, Vallin, Pernet, Lecouvreur; Les Choeurs Raugel and Orchestra; Bigot.
(Nimbus NI 7829; 1 CD).

Nimbus have made a marvellous transfer of the 1935 recording, which though heavily cut still functions as rather more than a highlights disc. Thill and Vallin were the outstanding French singers of the time – Charpentier thought her the best-ever Louise – and they are both in exquisite form. Thill's fervent tenor is perfectly matched by her more demure and pure-toned soprano, and André Pernet makes a convincingly gruff but sympathetic Father.

CLAUDE DEBUSSY

b. ST GERMAIN-EN-LAYE, FRANCE, AUGUST 22, 1862; d. PARIS, MARCH 25, 1918.

As the nineteenth century came to its close, French music writers were in the habit of bewailing the fact that their nation's music was mortgaged to foreigners, notably Wagner. But in 1902, twenty years after the first performance of *Parsifal* and two years before Strauss's *Salome*, Debussy's *Pelléas et Mélisande* was given its first performance – an occasion, according to Romain Rolland, that was "one of the three or four red-letter days in the history of our lyric stage". Offering the first viable alternative to the thundering passions of late-century opera, *Pelléas et Mélisande* is at once the distillation of Romantic yearning and a forebear of musical modernism.

Pelléas was Debussy's only completed full-length opera but he was preoccupied with the stage, in one form or another, for most of his working life. Like Puccini he found it difficult to find a subject capable of stimulating him throughout months of composition, and he wrote sketches for settings of the Tristan story and Shakespeare's *As You Like It* as well as toying with more than twenty other schemes in the course of his life. Having almost completed the Wagner-influenced *Rodrigue et Chimène* and visited the Wagner festival in Bayreuth, Debussy began in 1889 to map out his ideal opera. As he wrote to a former teacher: "The ideal would be two associated dreams. No place. No time. No big scene. No compulsion on the musician who must give body to the work of the poet. Music in opera is far too predominant. Too much singing and the settings are too cumbersome. The blossoming of the voice into true singing should occur only when required. My idea is of a short libretto with mobile scenes. No discussion or arguments between the characters, whom I see at the mercy of life or destiny."

Three years later he began setting Maeterlinck's play *Pelléas et Mélisande*, a piece set in a twilit world of half-expressed emotion and elusive symbols, the obverse of the forthright mythologies of Wagnerian theatre. It took several years for Debussy to get his opera staged. It was originally accepted by the Opéra-Comique in 1898, but they then delayed the premiere, announcing it in 1901. During this hiatus the composer made a number of alterations to his score, not least the addition of interludes to accompany the frequent scene changes. These additions irritated Maeterlinck, who went ballistic when Debussy announced that he'd contracted the Scottish soprano Mary Garden for the premiere – Maeterlinck had promised the role to his mistress, Georgette Leblanc. The playwright wrote to *Le Figaro*, expressing the hope that the opera would flop, and printed a satirical synopsis of Debussy's "arrangement" of his text (though Debussy had changed barely a word), handing it out at the first public dress rehearsal. And this wasn't the end of the controversy. During one rehearsal a Conservatoire professor berated the "filthy score" for its "errors of harmony" (a Conservatoire pupil was later expelled for having been found in possession of *Pelléas*), while admirers of the composer brawled with detractors in the cafés and restaurants (a punch-up obliged one place to close early the night before the premiere). Meanwhile some sections of the press pilloried the Debussy acolytes known as the Pelléastres: "Beautiful young men with long hair carefully brushed over their foreheads, with dull, smug faces and deep set eyes. They wear velvet collars and puffed sleeves . . . precious rings of Egypt or Byzantium on their little fingers (for they all have pretty hands). . . . Beneath the spell, they whisper in each other's ears, and their whispers descend deep into the soul." Yet the first performance went off without too much trouble, and many of the critics hailed it a masterpiece, albeit a perplexing one. Typical was the reaction of one Gustave Bret: "This music overwhelms you, drives deep into your heart with a power of inspiration that I admire but cannot fully understand."

Having thus found his feet, Debussy was expected to follow *Pelléas* with another drama in the same vein. Like so many of his French contemporaries, he had great affection for the tales of Edgar Allen Poe, whose morbid imagination found its echo in Debussy's own writings – "The colour of my soul is iron-grey," he once wrote to Chausson, "and sad bats wheel about the steeple of my dreams." For the rest of his life he intermittently considered and worked on two Poe stories which he thought suitable for translation into one-act operas – *The Devil in the Belfry* and *The Fall of the House of Usher* – but they came to nothing as Debussy chose to concentrate on instrumental works and, in particular, a formidable body of piano music. Debussy, like Beethoven, was to remain the creator of a single, overwhelmingly important opera.

Pelléas et Mélisande

Composed 1893–95.
First performed April 30, 1902.
Libretto by Maurice Maeterlinck.

Synopsis

Act I

Golaud, one of King Arkel's grandsons, is walking through a forest when he comes across a mysterious young girl. She is lost and is weeping over the loss of her crown, which she will not let him retrieve from the pool into which it has fallen. After much persuasion, she reveals her name, Mélisande, and agrees to return with him to his castle. Six months pass, during which time the widower Golaud, who already has a son by a previous marriage, marries Mélisande. Golaud writes to his half-brother Pelléas about his new wife, and invites him to visit. His mother Geneviève reads Golaud's letter to Arkel, who tells Pelléas to accept.

Act II

Pelléas and Mélisande are sitting by a fountain. She lowers her long braids into the water and plays with the ring given to her by Golaud. As a distant clock strikes noon, she drops the ring into the water. At exactly the same time as the ring hit the water, Golaud falls from his horse. While tending to her husband's wounds, Mélisande complains of being miserable in the castle; initially concerned for his wife's happiness, Golaud is enraged when he sees her ring is missing. He demands she find it, and insists she take Pelléas as an escort. While searching at the well they are frightened by three blind and starving beggars asleep on the ground.

Act III

Mélisande is combing her hair at her window; Pelléas persuades her to let it fall into his arms so that he can caress it. Golaud chastises their "childishness" and, taking Pelléas into the castle vault, warns him to stay clear of his wife – who is now pregnant. Later, he uses his son Yniold to spy on Mélisande; Yniold reports that

ZOË DOMINIC

The big hair scene in Act III of Pelléas

she and Pelléas are merely sitting in silence, but Golaud is nonetheless inflamed by jealousy.

Act IV

Pelléas has decided to leave, and arranges to meet Mélisande for one final time. Finding them together, Golaud drags his wife away by her hair; Pelléas and Mélisande manage to meet once more and, this time, they confess their love for each other. Listening in the dark is Golaud, who rushes out and kills his half-brother.

Act V

Arkel, Golaud and the Doctor wait beside Mélisande's bed where, having given birth to a daughter, she lies dying. Golaud is abject with remorse for the murder of Pelléas but he cannot rid himself of his jealousy; in spite of his wife's condition, he questions her about the nature of her love for Pelléas. She answers that she did nothing wrong, but Golaud does not believe her and he repeats the question. This time, however, she fails to respond; Mélisande is dead.

When Debussy began setting Maeterlinck's poetry – starting with the final scene of the fourth act – he found it difficult to exorcise the influence of Wagner: "the ghost of old Klingsor keeps peeping out". The influence of *Parsifal* was to remain clear in Debussy's harmony and, most obviously, his use of leitmotifs to signal changes in mood, but he radically revised his approach to text-setting, reaching conclusions of extraordinary radicalism. As he wrote to Chausson: "I have satisfied myself with a technique which seems to me quite extraordinary, that is to say, Silence (don't laugh!) as a means of expression, perhaps the only way to give the emotion of a phrase its full power!"

Discretion, understatement and subtlety, what Rolland referred to as "Debussy's genius for good taste", are the key to an opera that has only four fortissimos in its entire three and a quarter hours, and has little by way of traditional melody. In an article published in *Le Figaro* two weeks after the premiere, Debussy explained his thinking thus – "Melody, if I dare say so, is anti-lyrical. It cannot express the varying states of the soul, and of life. Essentially it is suited only to the song that expresses a simple feeling." Over a shifting tonal palette, marked by complex, centreless harmonies, Debussy's vocal lines carry the text in long, soft declamation that sets one syllable to one note. Completely rejecting the conventional lyricism of Italian, French and German opera, Debussy gives absolutely no opportunities for vocal display: the vocal writing in *Pelléas*, like the light but intricate orchestration, is a means of creating mood and atmosphere, rather than a way of expressing character or furthering the action.

In fact "action" is not the appropriate word: hardly anything happens in *Pelléas*, except in the sense that memories happen. "I shall always prefer a subject where, somehow, action is sacrificed to feeling," Debussy once wrote. For some people, however, the lack of incident and tight structure makes *Pelléas* an unreal experience – some, indeed, find it catatonically boring, as did the *New York Post* writer who ironically praised Debussy for his "simple yet original process of abolishing rhythm, melody and tonality from music and thus leaving nothing but atmosphere". On the other hand, Stravinsky was drawn to the aristocratic sensuality of Debussy's score, and the fearsomely progressive Pierre Boulez has long championed the modernity of its destabilized sound-world. To begin to appreciate it, you need to jettison as many preconceptions as possible, for immediacy of experience is everything here. In the composer's own words: "When we really listen to music, we hear immediately what we need to hear. . . . We must agree that the beauty of a work of art will always remain a mystery. . . . We must at all costs preserve this magic, which is peculiar to music and to which, by its nature, music is of all the arts the most receptive."

RECORDINGS OVERVIEW

Debussy's opera has received almost as many recordings as Beethoven's *Fidelio*, and most of them have been very good – the least satisfactory is Charles Dutoit's stainless steel account for Decca. Aside from those recommended below, recordings worth a mention include the first, conducted by Roger Désormière in 1941 for EMI, and Armin Jordan's account for Erato in 1979; Claudio Abbado's 1992 Deutsche Grammophon recording is marred by Maria Ewing's singing, but is otherwise of high quality.

Jansen, de los Angeles, Souzay, Froumenty, Collard; Raymond St Paul Chorus; French Radio National Orchestra; Cluytens.
(Testament SBT3051; 3 CDs).

Recorded by EMI in 1956, this spacious, languid and luxuriant *Pelléas* boasts some of the sweetest casting on record: the cool-voiced de los Angeles as Mélisande; the throaty mezzo Jeannine Collard as Geneviève; the smoothly gallic Jacques Jansen as Pelléas; and Gerard Souzay as Golaud, his only recorded operatic role. Famed as a Lieder singer, Souzay might be a touch too precise and civilized for some tastes, but the solemnity of his approach sits nicely in the overall texture. The mono sound is nicely balanced, and the engineer's experimentation with mike placing gives the singers a beguiling sense of movement.

Grancher, Michel, Jansen, Roux; Lyric Chorale; RTF National Orchestra; Inghelbrecht.
(Disques Montaigne TCE8710; 3 CDs).

Désiré Inghelbrecht was a good friend of Debussy, and if any recording of Péllèas can be said to be authentic, it is this 1962 production, which was taped at the end of a long series of concert performances of the opera. The conductor draws out the music smoothly while maintaining tempi that are brisker than most, and his casting is unbeatable. Micheline Grancher is a light, classically Gallic Mélisande, and Jacques Jansen's evenly produced Pelléas is perfectly set against Michael Roux's rougher-sounding Golaud. The sound is less than perfect, but this is a beautifully shaped, elegantly sung performance.

Mollet, Danco, Rehfuss, Vessières, Bouvier; Suisse Romande Orchestra; Ansermet.
(Decca 425 965-2DM2; 2 CDs).

Although some prefer Ansermet's 1964 recording (also for Decca) thanks primarily to the stereo, his first production, taped twelve years earlier, is better sung and better played. Ernest Ansermet was nineteen when *Pelléas* was first performed and his close association with the opera was famed long before he made his name as one of Stravinsky's champions. His is a swift, crisp and deliberate reading, which imparts a degree of urgency without losing the mystery of Debussy's score. Danco's naturalistic diction brings real gravity to Mélisande, a character whose gauzy quality is often seen as the opera's weakness. Pierre Mollet is a straightforward Pelléas, and Heinz Rehfuss does his best as Golaud, but the role's suppressed violence is beyond him.

Shirley, Söderström, McIntyre, Ward, Minton; Royal Opera House Chorus and Orchestra; Boulez.
(Sony SM3K47265; 3 CDs).

Of modern recordings, this is the most convincing, best recorded and most compellingly sung. The clarity, depth and resonance of the Royal Opera House Orchestra is a revelation, and Boulez's concern for detail tears open Debussy's score, highlighting much that earlier performances failed to grasp. Elizabeth Söderström wallows as Mélisande, and George Shirley thrives as a baritonal tenor Pelléas, rich in low voice but sweet and even above the stave. Yvonne Minton gives a vocally rich but emotionally lightweight performance as Geneviève, and the remaining cast are satisfactory. Not a first-choice performance, then, but one to make you rethink the opera.

ENGELBERT HUMPERDINCK

b. SIEBURG, GERMANY, SEPTEMBER 1, 1854; d. NEUSTRELITZ, SEPTEMBER 27, 1921.

With the death of Wagner, some composers endeavoured to maintain the good name of German opera through flagrant imitation, a process typified by August Bungert's demented six-opera cycle *Homerische Welt* (Homeric World). Soon, however, two other schools emerged: "Volksoper" (popular opera) and "Märchenoper" (fairy-tale opera). The latter marked a return to the early Romantic style of Weber and Marschner, and produced some fine music, the foremost example being Engelbert Humperdinck's *Hänsel und Gretel*.

LEBRECHT COLLECTION

Engelbert Humperdinck – the original

Humperdinck was a highly gifted child and began composing operas before formal studies at Cologne University, where he won dozens of prizes. His first published music was written for the concert hall and not until 1880, when he met Wagner in Naples, did he renew his interest in opera. Wagner invited Humperdinck to Bayreuth to work as an assistant, and in 1881–82 he helped prepare *Parsifal*, composing music for a scene change at the first performance.

After leaving Bayreuth he journeyed to Barcelona, returned to Cologne, worked for the music publishers Schott, then tried his hand at teaching and music criticism. In 1890 he returned to composition and three years later Humperdinck's friend and champion Richard Strauss – then the enfant terrible of German music – conducted the first performance of *Hänsel und Gretel* in Weimar. The opera's popularity was enormous, and it made the composer a household name in Germany almost overnight. (The reception abroad was initially less rapturous; the English impresario Augustus Harris hardly helped when he introduced the opera to an American audience as "the wonderful work of this great composer Pumpernickel".) The royalties from *Hänsel und Gretel* allowed Humperdinck to devote the remaining years of his life to composition, his major later achievement being *Königskinder*. At his death he was acknowledged as one of the last great Romantic composers, through whom the line of Beethoven could be traced through Wagner and on to Richard Strauss.

Hänsel und Gretel

Hansel and Gretel

Composed 1890–93.
First performed December 23, 1893.
Libretto by Adelheid Wette, after the Brothers Grimm.

Synopsis

Act I

Hänsel and Gretel have been given chores by their mother Gertrud, who is furious upon her return to find the tasks incomplete. She sends them out to pick strawberries in the wood, but when their father Peter comes home drunk and hears that his children are in the forest he tells Gertrud of a child-eating witch. They leave together to search for them.

Act II

Hänsel and Gretel have eaten all the strawberries. They begin to grow fearful and from out of the mist emerges the Sandman, who throws sand in their eyes. They kneel to say their prayers, then fall asleep. They are watched over during the night by fourteen angels.

Act III

In the morning, having been woken by the Dew Fairy, they find themselves near a house made of gingerbread and sweets. Unable to resist the temptation, they eat little pieces from the house. The Witch who lives there captures the children; she puts Gretel to work in the kitchen and begins to fatten Hänsel for eating. Gretel tricks the Witch and pushes her head-first into her own oven, causing it to explode. Around the house, gingerbread men turn into children and all the children whom the Witch has baked in the oven rise from the earth. The witch is pulled from the ruined oven, having been baked into a gigantic honey cake; the opera ends with a hymn of thanksgiving.

Humperdinck's first and most successful opera began life as a commission from his sister Adelheid Wette, who asked him to write music for a children's play she had adapted from the Brothers Grimm tale *Hänsel und Gretel*. He initially provided his sister with just four songs but was soon convinced of the fable's operatic potential, and three years later came up with a work that Strauss described as "a masterpiece of the highest quality . . . all of it original, new and so authentically German". Strauss was not alone in seeing *Hänsel und Gretel* as the salvation of German opera, bringing relief from the murky Wagnerian depths of Teutonic myth and initiating a return to the shimmering world of the fairytale. It has remained one of Germany's most popular operas, and in 1923 it became the first complete opera to be broadcast on radio from Covent Garden; eight years later it became the first to be broadcast from the New York Met.

Humperdinck's opera is steeped in the guileless world of folksong: the children's songs and dances, the idyllic forest scenes, the comically supernatural material and the central thematic "chorale" are all rooted in German traditional music. Just a couple of things detract from the effortless charm of the score: the dense Wagnerian orchestration, which is often overcomplicated for such subject matter, and the tendency to thematic repetition. The main theme of the overture is particularly insistent, cropping up a dozen times later on, famously in the siblings' duet. That said, the three orchestral interludes – in particular, the breathtaking Witch's Ride (Act I) and the haunting Dream Pantomime (Act II) – are exceptional displays of imagination and technique.

This opera is above all a showcase for the female voice, as the Father is the only male part, although the mezzo-soprano Witch is sometimes taken by a character tenor. The siblings themselves are captivatingly sugary soprano roles, to whom the majority of the opera's pivotal music is assigned. The Witch is great fun, and her low-lying music gives a suitably theatrical singer every opportunity to hurl out her words in a semi-sung style.

RECORDINGS OVERVIEW

Hänsel und Gretel has been recorded thirteen times since the first foray in 1943, and while only eight of those are currently available, the prevailing standard is extremely high. Karajan (see overleaf) and Solti (Decca, 1978) are the only superstar conductors to have tackled the piece, leaving the field for some of Germany's unsung *Kappelmeisters* to show that a provincial conductor can often bring a greater intimacy – and rehearsal time – to the score than the jet-setters can manage. Most recently, the underrated Scottish conductor Donald Runnicles has given a fascinating, symphonic reading for Teldec – but he is poorly served by his cast. The two performances recommended overleaf are the best of a very good bunch.

Moffo, Donath, Fischer-Dieskau, Augér, Ludwig; Tolz Boys Choir; Munich Radio Orchestra; Eichhorn.
(RCA 74321 25281-2; 2 CDs).

The casting of the radiant Helen Donath as Gretel, the ham-theatrical Christa Ludwig as the Witch and the noble but lovable Dietrich Fischer-Dieskau as the Father would have been sufficient to secure this recording's fame, but to cast Lucia Popp as the Dew Fairy and Arleen Augér as the Sandman, both tiny roles, was a master stroke. With such an array of vocal riches, Kurt Eichhorn might have simply let them get on with it, but instead he produces a reading that accentuates the detail and colour of the score more than any other, drawing out the richness of the instrumental part-writing with astonishing success. The one failing is the frequently shrill Hänsel of Anna Moffo, who was one of RCA's flagship sopranos during the 1960s and 1970s, and consequently required to sing an unfeasibly wide range of roles. Nonetheless, this is an almost faultless recording.

Grümmer, Schwarzkopf, Metternich, Schürhoff; Bancroft's School Choir; Philharmonia; Karajan.
(EMI CMS7 69293-2; 2 CDs).

It would be perverse not to recommend Karajan's 1953 *Hänsel und Gretel*, a performance famed for the conductor's insight into the symphonic texture of the orchestral score. If his achievements in this respect have been subsequently matched, the same cannot be said of Elizabeth Grümmer's Hänsel, for this remains one of the most beautiful vocal performances ever recorded. Her sumptuous, perfectly placed soprano, rich with old-fashioned portamento, is intoxicating, and rather overshadows the wispily self-conscious Gretel of Elizabeth Schwarzkopf. With the exception of Else Schürhoff's exhausted-sounding Witch, the remaining cast are reliable.

Königskinder

Royal Children

Composed 1908–10.
First performed December 28, 1910.
Libretto by Elsa Bernstein-Porges.

Synopsis

Act I

The Goose-Girl is imprisoned and spellbound in a forest by a Witch who, wishing to teach her the black arts, forces her to bake a deadly magic loaf. The Prince comes to rescue her and he gives her a crown as a token of his love, but when it becomes clear that the spell prevents her from leaving the forest he abandons her. The townsfolk send the Broom-Maker and the Wood-Cutter to the Witch's hut to ask how they might find a king. She tells them that their king will be the first person to walk through the town gates on the stroke of twelve. Meanwhile, the Fiddler has spied the Goose-Girl and, together, they break the Witch's spell and leave to seek out the Prince.

Act II

At noon the Goose-Girl enters the town, wearing the crown the Prince had left her. The townspeople brand her an imposter and when the Prince comes to her defence, they are both driven out of the town.

Act III

It is winter and the Fiddler has moved into the Witch's abandoned hut. The Broom-Maker and the Wood-Cutter beg him to return to the town, where the children are rebelling against the adults. Cold and starving, the Prince and Goose-Girl come to the hut where they find the Wood-Cutter. They barter the now broken crown for shelter and food – the Witch's loaf. When the Fiddler returns, they are lying dead in each other's arms.

Königskinder was first performed at New York's Metropolitan Opera, with Geraldine Farrar (Puccini's Angelica) as the Goose-Girl and Hermann Jadlowker (Strauss's Bacchus) as the Prince. It was, by all accounts, one of the greatest nights in the house's history, and the quality of the performance must have contributed considerably towards the opera's warm reception, which started with a fifteen-minute ovation at the final curtain. Disappointingly for Humperdinck, this reception was not repeated in Germany, where most compared it unfavourably to *Hänsel und Gretel*.

Like *Hänsel und Gretel*, *Königskinder* began life as something other than an opera. In 1897 Humperdinck turned the fairytale into a melodrama with music that was midway between speech and song, so that it could be performed as successfully by an actor as by a singer: "The notes for the spoken word generally indicate the relative, not the absolute pitch," he wrote. But when he came to turn the melodrama into an opera, Humperdinck reverted to a more conventional style, prompting one contemporary to describe the work as "a warm bath of song", although the Wagnerian melody is so extended that "song" might give the wrong impression – the melodic ideas, all linked to the prevalent leitmotif, are rather like the workings of a boa constrictor.

Königskinder and *Hänsel und Gretel* emerge from the same folkloric world, but the two are quite different. The later work is moody, sinister and restless, its textures thicker, its musical lines longer and more demanding, and there is no hint of archness in its simplicity. Received opinion tends to prefer the earlier work, but *Königskinder* is a more inventive and expressive opera: in particular, the final act, culminating in the Fiddler's intense baritone monologue, constitutes one of the most moving musical episodes in post-Wagnerian German opera.

Dallapozza, Donath, Prey, Ridderbusch; Bavarian Radio Chorus and Orchestra; Wallberg.
(EMI CMS7 69936-2; 3 CDs).

Throughout this famous (and solitary) recording of *Königskinder* the voice of Hermann Prey dominates as the Fiddler, one of the most formidable baritone roles in the German repertoire. Reaching its apex with the Act III monologue and the final heartbreaking song, this is one of Prey's career highlights on record. As the Prince, Adolf Dallapozza is secure if somewhat dry, but Karl Ridderbusch is superb as the Woodcutter and Helen Donath is in sublime form as the Goose-Girl. Wallberg provides fresh and urgent direction. Good sound and an inviting price make this a desirable set.

FREDERICK DELIUS

b. BRADFORD, ENGLAND, JANUARY 29, 1862; d. GREZ-SUR-LOING, FRANCE, JUNE 10, 1934.

Born in England to a German father, Frederick Delius turned to composing while in Florida, but spent most of his working life in rural France. His music is similarly cosmopolitan and difficult to classify, but it was largely inspired by a mystical response to nature, whose beauty and impermanence Delius evoked in rich, diaphanous orchestral textures, full of shifting chromatic harmonies. The richly atmospheric nature of his harmonic language has led to his being labelled an "Impressionist", but his chromaticism owes much more to Wagner than it does to Debussy, the composer such a tag usually suggests.

Delius was brought up in Bradford, the son of a prosperous wool-merchant who insisted that the boy join the family business, even though it had no appeal for him. He left England in 1884 for Florida in order to run an orange plantation, and it was the workers' songs which he heard wafting across the St John River that made him determined to become a composer – and were later to inspire his third opera, *Koanga*. He took some lessons with a local organist named Thomas Ward, and spent eighteen months at the Leipzig Conservatory between 1886 and 1888. He always claimed that Leipzig taught him little, but it did bring him the friendship and support of Edvard Grieg, who managed to persuade Delius's father that his son's future was as a composer. Delius came to regard Norway as his spiritual home, and his bohemian years in Paris in the early 1890s were largely spent in the company of Scandinavian artists, including the painter Edvard Munch and the playwright August Strindberg.

It was in Paris that he met Jelka Rosen, a Prussian artist whom he later married. In 1897 the couple moved to the village of Grez-sur-Loing, near the forest of Fontainebleau. In contrast to his dissolute years in Paris, Delius's life at Grez was reclusive, an environment which allowed him to develop his own individual style. His music gained initial success in Germany, but its biggest following was in England (a country he claimed to despise), principally through the advocacy of his greatest interpreter, Thomas Beecham, who organized major Delius festivals in 1929 and 1946 and conducted the English premieres of *A Village Romeo and Juliet*, *Koanga*, and – belatedly – his first opera, *Irmelin*. The latter stages of Delius's life, however, were marked by increasing ill-health, which eventually left him blind and paralyzed, the result of syphilis contracted in his youth.

Of his six completed operas, only three – *Koanga*, *A Village Romeo and Juliet*, and *Fennimore and Gerda* – were performed in his lifetime, and all three were premiered in Germany and in German versions. *Koanga* (1898), set on a sugar plantation in Louisiana, contains a wealth of sumptuous music with especially lyrical writing for the title role. It suffers, however, from a clumsy libretto, as does Delius's final opera *Fennimore and Gerda*, which even Beecham felt was too awkward to perform. *A Village Romeo and Juliet* is generally regarded as Delius's finest opera: it was the only one to be performed in England during his lifetime, and it is the only one regularly performed anywhere nowadays.

A Village Romeo and Juliet

Composed 1899–1901.
First performed February 21, 1907.
Libretto by the composer, after Gottfried Keller.

Synopsis

Scene I

Marti and Manz are farmers whose land is separated by an overgrown tract. The tract is up for sale because the owner, the Dark Fiddler, has no legal right to it, owing to his illegitimacy. The farmers' children – the boy Sali and girl Vreli – play together in the woods. The Dark Fiddler tells them to beware of anyone who ploughs up the land separating their fathers' plots. Marti and Manz begin to argue and warn their children to avoid the Fiddler.

Scene II

Six years later, the children are grown up and, despite the hatred between their fathers and the poverty that has befallen them, they decide to resume their friendship.

Scene III

The Dark Fiddler invites Sali and Vreli to follow the life of a wanderer like him. When Vreli's father arrives and begins to drag her away, Sali attacks him and knocks him to the ground.

Scene IV

Sali's blow has caused Marti to lose his mind and he is confined to an asylum. The two children fall asleep in each other's arms and dream of marriage. When they wake they visit the fair in Berghald.

Scene V

Their happiness at the fair is disturbed by the staring crowds, and they head for the Paradise Garden, where they can be alone.

Scene VI

At an inn in the Paradise Garden, Sali and Vreli are joined by the Fiddler, who implores them to share his life, mocking their respectability. They leave the Fiddler and take a barge, deciding to "drift away forever". Sali pulls the plug from the bottom of the boat and, lying clasped in each other's arms, they sink to their deaths.

In 1894, five years before he began composing the score to *A Village Romeo and Juliet*, Delius wrote to a friend, "I want to tread in Wagner's footsteps. . . . For me dramatic art is almost taking the place of religion." *A Village Romeo and Juliet* was his monument to this belief, revelling as it does in a Wagnerian sound-world and putting a rural (almost suburban) slant on Wagner's tale of obsessive love, *Tristan und Isolde*. Unlike *Tristan*, however, the passions of Delius's opera are subdued and spiritual, with both the orchestral and the vocal music casting an autumnal shadow over the work's sensuousness. Basing his piece on a story by the Swiss writer Gottfried Keller, Delius wrote his own libretto (having rejected attempts by two other writers), changing Keller's emphasis on moral responsibility into something much more dreamy and fatalistic.

For its 1907 premiere, at the Komische Oper in Berlin, the opera was performed as *Romeo und Julia auf dem Dorfe* in a German translation made by Delius's wife Jelka. (Except in English-speaking countries, this is the version most widely used.) Though the Berlin audience was better used to the more strident music of Strauss, Mahler and Schoenberg, it was well received, even if Delius's dense orchestration was obviously not the work of a natural theatre composer – the voices are prone to disappear in performance. The various orchestral sections – of which "The Walk to the Paradise Garden" is the most famous – create the strongest impression and contain some magical sounds: their glowing, hypnotic textures really establish the mood of the work. Characterization was not as important to Delius as atmosphere, and neither of the lovers is particularly sympathetic –

although their final love-duet, "See, the moon-beams", is thrilling. The baritone role of the ominous Fiddler, the character most closely identified with the energy of Nature, provides Delius with a good excuse for less restrained vocal writing, and as a result is far more compelling.

When *A Village Romeo and Juliet* received its English premiere in 1910 several critics were less than overwhelmed. Thomas Beecham's defence elegantly summarizes the opera's charm: "It is an idyll with something of the other-world or dream quality of a pastoral or fairy play. The characters are types rather than personages and express themselves with a brevity and a reticence that is almost epigrammatic. . . . The music, as befits the subject, is lyrical and consistently poetical, with a recurring strain of tenderness."

Mora, Dean, Linay, Davies, Hampson; Schoenberg Choir; Austrian Radio Symphony Orchestra; Mackerras.
(Argo 430 275-2ZH2; 2 CDs).

Apart from his Janáček recordings, this English-language version of *A Village Romeo and Juliet* is Charles Mackerras's finest operatic work on disc. His shaping of Delius's orchestral phrasing is superb and his attention to colour, line and contrast could not be bettered. He perhaps lacks Beecham's idiomatic grace but this is a small objection considering the fluency and beautiful singing of his lovers, Arthur Davies and Helen Field – the former is in particularly brilliant form. Thomas Hampson's sumptuous voice perhaps lacks the requisite moral ambiguity as the Fiddler. Typically for Argo recordings, the sound is kaleidoscopic and well spaced, capturing just enough instrumental detail without seeming over-miked.

Dowling, Sharp, Soames, Dyer, Clinton; Chorus; Royal Philharmonic Orchestra; Beecham.
(EMI CMS7 64386-2; 2 CDs).

Beecham's 1948 complete recording of his favourite composer's most favoured opera (in German) is a treat. He produces an extraordinarily vocal tone from the RPO, making them sing through even the most densely scored passages. His cast also float through their parts – René Soames (Sali) and Lorely Dyer (Vreli) are outstanding – and the overall performance has a warmth from which not even the poor mono sound can detract.

7

THE ERA OF MODERNISM

THE ERA OF MODERNISM

As the new century began, the figure of Richard Wagner still cast a long shadow over opera. Thus when **Richard Strauss** burst onto the operatic scene in Germany, he was pushing Wagnerism to extremes with the loud and lurid *Salome* (1905), a work he followed up with the even more shocking *Elektra* (1908). At that point he pulled back from the brink, becoming the most successful opera composer of his day by writing operas that harked back, with a mixture of irony and nostalgia, to the world as it was before Wagner's music-dramas changed the landscape. In their very reversal of the principles of Wagner's legacy, works such as *Der Rosenkavalier* were as potent a testimony to his influence as the most densely orchestrated, leitmotif-laden homage.

Of those who saw themselves as disciples of the Bayreuth master, none was more devoted than **Hans Pfitzner**, whose masterpiece, *Palestrina* (for which he also wrote the libretto, as Wagner would have done), presents a picture of the artist as a divinely inspired upholder of tradition. Hailed by some as the authentic voice of German art, Pfitzner soon degenerated into racist and reactionary polemic, much of it directed against the rigorously modernist **Arnold Schoenberg**, a composer who followed to its logical conclusion the process begun by Wagner's abandonment of clearly defined tonal centres. Believing that the whole diatonic basis of western music was exhausted and that a completely new musical language had to be found to replace it, Schoenberg looked for it first of all in atonality – that is music that is no longer based on the system of major and minor scales. In the theatre Schoenberg used atonalism to express heightened psychological and emotional states, most effectively in his Expressionist monodrama *Ewartung*, a work of such extremity that, though written in 1909, it was not performed until 1924. Schoenberg soon realized that the complete expressive freedom of atonalism was in itself an aesthetic cul de sac, and began to compose music using the self-imposed discipline known as serialism, a method that underpinned his incomplete full-length opera, *Moses und Aron* (1945). Schoenberg's pupil **Alban Berg** produced one of the century's most overwhelming musical statements in his opera *Wozzeck* (1922), a richly textured score which combines extreme dissonance with rhapsodic lyricism. This combination of qualities is also present in Berg's other opera, *Lulu* (1935), which like *Moses und Aron* was governed by the principles of serialism and was left unfinished at its creator's death.

The desire to break away from Austro-German musical dominance led many composers from central Europe to explore their indigenous musical heritage in a rather less superficial manner than their immediate forebears had done. In Hungary, after a relatively conventional conservatory training, **Béla Bartók** set out, with his friend and colleague **Zoltán Kodály**, to make a systematic record of the folk music of central and eastern Europe. This ethnomusicological research fed directly into both men's compositions, not simply by moulding melody and rhythm (as had largely been the case with the likes of Brahms and Dvořák) but also by helping to forge a harmonic language based on an older modal system of scales. (Their compatriot, **Franz Lehár**, made a fortune writing music that made lighter use of his country's folk heritage, revitalizing the world of Viennese operetta with works such as *Die lustige Witwe*.) In England a similar programme of folk music research and composition was being pursued by **Ralph Vaughan Williams**, but whereas none of Vaughan Williams's six operas has made it into the international repertoire, and Kodály's *Háry János* remains something of a Hungarian speciality piece, Bartók's *Bluebeard's Castle* (1911) is now regularly performed around the world. Yet *Bluebeard's Castle* was a one-off in Bartók's career; by contrast, opera was central to the output of the great Czech composer **Leoš Janáček**, who also drew on indigenous music (in his case Moravian song) as he evolved a highly original vocal style based on a careful study of speech rhythms and patterns. Janáček's work ranges widely in subject and tone, from the bloody melodrama of *Jenůfa* (1903) to the cartoon-inspired high spirits of *The Cunning Little Vixen* (1923), and is also notable for the preponderance of powerful and strong-minded heroines. Even more prolific than Janáček was the idiosyncratic **Bohuslav Martinů**, whose operas don't often show him at his best, though *Julietta* (1938) is a fine work and the postwar *Ariadne* and *The Greek Passion* also have lasted well.

A different strand of modernist opera is represented by **Igor Stravinsky**, whose route away from the emotional and orchestral excesses of late Romanticism and Expressionism led him to a leaner and more "objective" music based on eighteenth-century models – unlike Strauss, not for reasons of nostalgia, but in order to rediscover the clarity and precision imposed by the old "closed" forms. Neoclassicism was the name given to this return to the formal precedents and lighter textures of the eighteenth century, but Neoclassicism encompasses as great a diversity of work as any other label. In Stravinsky's case the term can be applied to his two finest stage works: *Oedipus Rex* (1927), in which he employed a spare and angular style to give a ritualistic quality to the ancient tragedy; and *The Rake's Progress* (1951), a caustic social comedy written in collaboration with W. H. Auden. The principal operas by the major German Neoclassicist, **Paul Hindemith**, are both concerned with the social role and the psychology of the artist. The earlier work, *Cardillac* (1926), uses a pastiche polyphonic style as a commentary on a mystery story set in the seventeenth century; *Mathis der Maler* (1935), on the other hand, is a sombre, often austere meditation on the subject, which is marked by the atmosphere of political crisis in which Hindemith was working. Similar concerns lie at the heart of *Doktor Faust* (1924), the unfinished masterpiece of **Ferruccio Busoni**, self-proclaimed standard-bearer of "Young Classicism", who was born in Italy but enjoyed most of his success as an opera composer in Germany.

Other German composers in the 1920s turned to popular music as a means of replenishing opera. *Jonny spielt auf* (1926) by **Ernst Krenek** combined jazz-inspired music with more conventional styles to produce a fine example of what the Germans termed *Zeitoper* – opera set in the present, addressing topical issues in an accessible manner. *Jonny* was one of the most successful operas of the century, but its fame was short-lived; a more durable example of the *Zeitoper* genre was *Die Dreigroschenoper* (1928), the most celebrated of **Kurt Weill**'s collaborations with Berthold Brecht. Weill was to end up working in the USA, driven out of his native land by the Nazis, who long before they came to power began targeting musical events of which they disapproved, shouting down works by Jewish composers such as **Franz Schreker**. Now best known for his early operas *Die ferne Klang* and *Die Gezeichneten*, Schreker was broken by Nazi persecution; even more brutal was the treatment of **Victor Ullmann** and **Ervín Schulhoff**, both of whom died in Nazi camps. Spain's greatest opera composer, **Manuel de Falla**, fled Franco's fascist Spain and died in exile in Argentina.

In the Soviet Union a not dissimilar process of repression was underway: avant-garde artists who had put their work at the service of the Revolution found themselves, after the ascendancy of Stalin, forced to conform to the guidelines laid down by the cultural commissars of the Communist Party. The potentially brilliant operatic career of **Dmitri Shostakovich** was cut short when Stalin attended a performance of his opera *Lady Macbeth of Mtsensk* (1932), a raw and powerful depiction of oppression and frustrated sexuality which was denounced as a decadent "noise" in the pages of *Pravda*. **Sergei Prokofiev**, having left his homeland, eventually returned, only to have his career as an opera composer similarly stunted by Stalinist dogma.

The exodus of composers and musicians from Europe did much to enrich the cultural life of the countries to which they fled – notably Britain and the United States – but the lack of opportunities for contemporary opera in those countries was largely unchanged by the influx of new talent. Despite the fact that California could boast the presence of Krenek, Schoenberg and Stravinsky, none of the state's opera houses saw fit to commission new works from them. When it came to music-theatre, the most successful emigré, Kurt Weill, looked to America's indigenous music-theatre for direction. Inspired by the example of **George Gershwin**, whose masterpiece *Porgy and Bess* (1935) he knew well, Weill wrote mainly for the commercial theatre and in several works – most notably *Street Scene* (1947) – managed to combine the immediacy of the Broadway musical with the depth and symphonic sweep of opera. The only other contemporaneous American composer to have created something that still lives on the opera circuit is **Virgil Thomson**, creator of the whimsical and enigmatic *Four Saints in Three Acts*.

Completing the roll-call of this chapter are four composers whose operas remain less well known than their concert-hall music: **Maurice Ravel** and **Paul Dukas**, the creators of the best French operas of the period; **Karol Szymanowski**, the most prominent Polish composer of the twentieth century; and **Sergei Rachmaninov**, whose operas belong chronologically to the twentieth century but aesthetically to the nineteenth.

RICHARD STRAUSS

b. MUNICH, JUNE 11, 1864; d. GARMISCH, SEPTEMBER 8, 1949.

Richard Strauss was the last great German Romantic, but the trajectory of his career was more convoluted than such a definition suggests. Having burst onto the scene as the composer of feverishly ardent orchestral pieces, he went on to produce operas as progressive and discomforting as any of their time, before switching to a decorous, slightly decadent and often ironic conservatism. However, through each phase of Strauss's long life – from the electrifying brilliance of the early tone poem *Don Juan* to the delicate eighteenth-century charm of the late opera *Capriccio* – there runs a fundamentally consistent harmonic and melodic style, marked above all by a Mozartian tunefulness. Like Mozart, Strauss possessed an amazing technical facility, and if his abilities did sometimes lead to passages of superficial note-spinning, he was incapable of writing anything slipshod. Often depicted as the traditionalist opponent of modernism, even the epitome of bourgeois complacency (few composers ever enjoyed Strauss's financial success), he has now come to seem like a prophet of the postmodern age, in which irony and pastiche are seen as radical procedures. His work is dismissed as shallow kitsch in some quarters, but such critical disapproval has not affected his standing as one of the most popular – and frequently performed – of all twentieth-century opera composers.

Strauss was the only son of Franz Strauss, the brilliant principal horn player in the Bavarian Court Opera. Strauss senior was an arch-conservative who hated the music of Wagner (even though Wagner loved his horn playing) and brought up his son with a profound reverence for Bach, Mozart and Beethoven and a healthy respect for Mendelssohn, Schumann and Brahms. Strauss junior took piano lessons from the age of four, began composing two years later and – requiring no formal musical training – received a traditional, rounded education at the Ludwigsgymnasium in Munich. After the composition of his Brahmsian *Symphony No. 1* in 1880, he scored a sufficient success with his *Serenade* for wind instruments for the great conductor Hans von Bülow to commission a suite from him in 1882. By this stage, Strauss had succumbed to Wagner fervour (von Bülow called him "Wagner's revenge") and, after a few months as von Bülow's assistant, he succeeded him as principal conductor at Meiningen in 1885, a post he left the following year to journey to Italy, where he composed his first symphonic poem, *Aus Italien*. Upon his return he was appointed conductor at the Munich Opera and later that year shot to celebrity as the composer of *Don Juan*. His rise seemed unstoppable and it was only a matter of time before he turned his attention towards the theatre.

In 1894 Strauss's first opera, the Wagnerian *Guntram*, was conducted by the composer at Munich, with his pupil and future wife, Pauline de Ahna, taking the principal soprano role. Despite a third act full of good tunes, the opera was a failure, due in part to an inadequate tenor and an uncooperative orchestra. It was Strauss's first critical upset and he vowed to avenge himself on what he perceived to be the philistinism of Munich. His next opera, *Feuersnot* (Fire Famine), written seven years later, was set in twelfth-century Munich and concerned a young sorcerer who, humiliated by the woman he loves, extinguishes all the town's fires until she acknowledges him. Though still showing an obvious debt to Wagner, *Feuersnot* was more lightly and inventively scored than *Guntram* and revealed a more individual voice. Its premiere in Dresden was relatively successful, but nothing like the *succès de scandale* generated by his third opera, *Salome*. Strauss had seen a German version of Oscar Wilde's play – itself inspired by Gustave Moreau's bejewelled and exotic paintings of the subject – and he responded to its claustrophobic decadence with an astonishingly rich and chromatic score. It was premiered in 1905, again in Dresden, and its combination of biblical setting with perverse eroticism upset the church and irritated the Kaiser, but it made Strauss's name and brought him sufficient money to build a villa in the mountain resort of Garmisch.

Strauss was now the most talked about composer since Wagner – although the Wagnerites had denounced him in favour of Pfitzner (see p.391) – and he needed a suitable subject with which to capitalize on the success of *Salome*. In 1905 he attended a performance of Hugo von Hofmannsthal's powerful adaptation of Sophocles' *Elektra*, a play he thought ideal for operatic treatment. The two men had met earlier, when the writer had proposed working on a ballet together, but it was the performance of *Elektra* that opened Strauss's eyes to the young playwright's potential as a librettist. The following year he wrote to him: "I would ask you urgently to give me first refusal with anything composable that you write. Your manner has so much in common with mine; we were born for one another and are certain to do fine things together if you remain faithful to me." Strauss's judgement was correct: though Hofmannsthal's sensibility was more complex and intellectual than his, it was complemented by Strauss's rather more practical sense of theatre, and the two men collaborated on six of Strauss's fourteen operas, beginning with *Elektra* in 1909 and ending with *Arabella* in 1933. In *Elektra* Strauss took what seemed to be another daring step towards the abandonment of tonality, but Hofmannsthal's literary gifts were to steer him away from the avant-garde towards a more urbane and sophisticated art, typified by *Der Rosenkavalier*.

Strauss's operas with librettists other than von Hofmannsthal are generally less interesting, although most contain some superb music. *Intermezzo* (1924), for which he wrote his own words, is closely based on his turbulent relationship with his domineering wife and is notable for its contemporary subject matter, though the music is rather less colourful. *Die Schweigsame Frau* (The Silent Woman, 1935) was his first opera after Hofmannsthal's death and, despite a fine libretto from Stefan Zweig, is largely uninspired. *Friedenstag* (Peace Day, 1938) is his weakest opera, a tawdry, half-hearted denunciation of war, but *Daphne* (1938) is the most animated of his later works, and is notable for two of the most exciting tenor roles in German opera. *Die Liebe der Danae* (The Love of Danae, 1940) failed to capitalize on the popularity and musical ingenuity of *Daphne*, and not until 1942 did he rekindle the old magic with the gentle *Capriccio*.

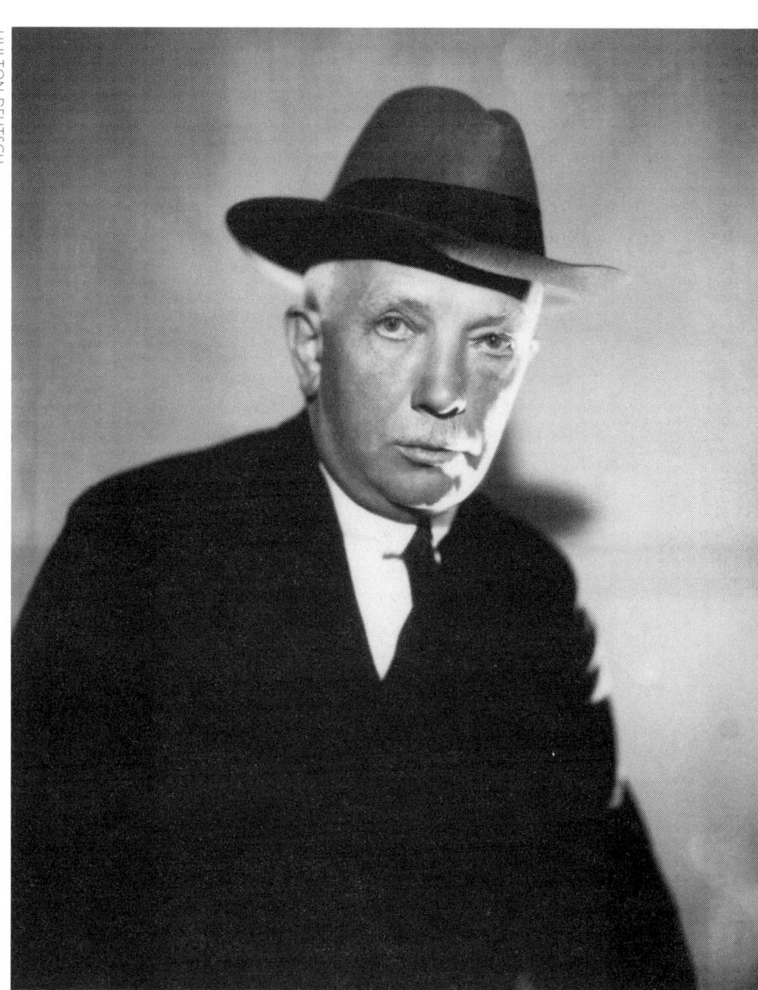

HULTON DEUTSCH

Richard Strauss – believe it or not, once the wild man of German music

Since his death, Strauss's reputation has had to contend with the inevitable reaction against the grand gestures of late Romantic music and, more seriously, his refusal to leave Germany following the rise of the Nazis. An arrogant and often insensitive man, Strauss felt himself to be above politics and he chose to remain in Germany, believing that he could serve German music without serving the Reich itself. But in 1933, without consulting him, the Nazis appointed Strauss President of the Reichsmusikammer – making him, in effect, the official representative of German music. In the same year he stepped in to conduct the Berlin Philharmonic when the Jewish Bruno Walter was forbidden to, and similarly replaced the anti-fascist conductor Toscanini for the fiftieth anniversary performance of *Parsifal* at Bayreuth. In both instances Strauss argued that he was acting out of loyalty – not to the Reich but to the orchestras and singers involved. Perhaps his willingness to kowtow to the party was also motivated by fear for his Jewish daughter-in-law and his beloved grandchildren. He clearly believed that his eminence would allow him a certain degree of artistic freedom and respect, but when two years later he refused to give up his Jewish librettist Stefan Zweig, and continued to correspond with him when the latter was in exile, the Nazis forced him to resign from the Reichsmusikammer. Though now merely tolerated by the regime, he continued to live in Garmisch until the war's end, when he was investigated as a Nazi collaborator and acquitted. After a few years' exile in Switzerland, Strauss and his wife returned to their villa in Garmisch, where he died shortly after his eighty-fifth birthday.

Like Puccini, Strauss composed music intended, first and foremost, to tug the heartstrings, but his style was incomparably more varied, and his inspiration more eclectic. On the one hand he worshipped Mozart above all others, and on the other he wrote some of the most hedonistic and unbridled music of the century. Even Romain Rolland – one of Strauss's most prominent supporters – called him "a Shakespearean barbarian: his art is torrential, producing at one and the same time, gold, sand, stone, and rubbish: he has almost no taste at all, but a violence that borders on madness." To his supporters it is precisely this shameless enjoyment of the physicality of music that makes him the most pleasurable of all twentieth-century opera composers.

Salome

Composed 1904–05.
First performed December 9, 1905.
Libretto by the composer, after Lachmann's translation of Oscar Wilde.

Synopsis

King Herod's Palace in Jerusalem. The guard Narraboth lusts after the King's stepdaughter Salome. From the cistern where he is imprisoned comes the voice of Jokanaan (John the Baptist) denouncing the marriage of Herod and Herodias and prophesying the coming of the Messiah. Salome, who is thrilled by the sound of his voice, persuades Narraboth to release him. To the prophet's disgust she sings of her physical longing for him. Narraboth kills himself and Jokanaan urges Salome to repent and seek salvation. He returns to his cell as Herod and his party arrive. Herod, who also desires Salome, asks her to dance for him; when she refuses he offers her anything she wants. After her Dance of the Seven Veils she asks Herod for the head of Jokanaan. He begs her to change her mind but she is adamant. Jokanaan is executed and his head is brought up from the dungeon on a shield. Grabbing it in both hands, Salome sings a long and delirious song – finally kissing the head's bloody lips. Herod is disgusted and orders his soldiers to kill her. They rush forward and crush her with their shields.

𝄞 Strauss first saw Max Reinhardt's production of Wilde's *Salome* (in German translation) in 1902, by which stage he had already started sketching ideas for an operatic setting, having earlier been sent a copy of the play by the Austrian poet Anton Lindner. Wilde's highly stylized, exotic and erotic text appealed to Strauss, who determined to match its violence and grotesquerie with a musical language of primitive feeling. To that end he assigned the dominant role to the 105-strong orchestra – indeed both *Salome* and *Elektra* are often referred to as "stage tone-poems". Every scene from the opening clarinet arpeggio (there is no prelude) through to Salome's deranged final monologue maintains a constant tension, thanks chiefly to Strauss's manner of setting lyrical vocal melodies over an outlandishly chromatic and contrapuntal foundation. The resultant charge between the strident sound-base and the melodious vocal line is typified by the mounting frenzy of

THE BIRTH OF SALOME

Not since the premiere of Wagner's *Tristan und Isolde* had an opera aroused so much anger and consternation as Strauss's *Salome* did. When, long before the first rehearsals, word got out that Strauss was setting Oscar Wilde's play, it was thought that the composer of the old-fashioned *Guntram* would be bringing similarly familiar techniques to bear on his text. The new work turned out to be perhaps the most controversial opera of the century.

It was controversial even before the first night. The cast were terrified by the music's demands, and Maria Wittich, who sang the title role, considered the whole thing "disgusting". She agreed to sing the work, but she barely acted a single scene and refused to do The Dance of the Seven Veils or kiss the severed head: "I'll do no such thing! I'm a decent woman," she insisted.

Opinions of the show ranged widely. Cosima Wagner thought it "madness", Felix Weingartner considered it "indescribably beautiful", and newspaper cartoonists had a field day. One cartoon featured Salome saying to John, "Wait and see, John, they're going to cut your head off," with John replying, "That's not as bad as being made into an opera by Strauss." The Catholic Church condemned *Salome*, and Kaiser Wilhelm refused to allow the work to be performed in Berlin unless the Star of Bethlehem was seen to appear at the end to herald the birth of Christ – which was a curious innovation, since the adult Christ had earlier been baptized by John. The Kaiser later remarked of Strauss: "I like him otherwise, but with this he will do himself a great deal of harm." The harm, Strauss noted, allowed him to build a lavish villa in Garmisch, and he received the enormous fee of 60,000 marks from his publishers for the opera's rights.

In London the question of whether or not the work should be performed was brought before Parliament, and Strauss's most prominent British champion, Thomas Beecham, was granted an audience with Prime Minister Asquith, whom he attempted to convince that there was nothing wrong in staging *Salome* to a few thousand enthusiasts. However, when the press revealed that permission to stage *Salome* was being considered by the Lord Chamberlain, thousands of letters of complaint were received, mostly protesting at the very idea of presenting a biblical character on the operatic stage. When Beecham pointed out to the Lord Chamberlain that both Samson and Delilah had long been favourites of the opera-going public, he was told: "There is a difference. In one case, it is the Old Testament and in the other, the New."

Some four years after the Dresden premiere, Beecham eventually received permission to edit the work for a Covent Garden production, and the first of his alterations was to change the name of John to "The Prophet", an alteration that seemed sufficiently non-specific to appease some of the objectors. The issue of The Prophet's head was rather more problematic, as Beecham later remembered. "Some substitute had to be found for the offending member. . . . It was settled that Salome be given a blood-stained sword. But this time it was the prima donna who put her foot down, objecting that the gruesome weapon would ruin her beautiful gown and flatly refused to handle it at all. . . . The best and final concession we could obtain was that Salome should have a large platter completely covered with a cloth." At least this was a braver attempt than the pitiful spectacle with which the audience at a later regional production was presented: when the lid of the platter was lifted, it was to reveal not a bloodied head but a freshly steamed pudding.

"Salome's Dance", a wild orchestral showpiece, in which the music imitates Herod's ever quickening heartbeat. The ratchet is tightened even further as Herod's delight turns to horror upon realizing that Salome will take nothing but John's head as her reward. With each succeeding offer, his tenor rises higher and higher, and the music becomes ever more fraught until, exhausted, he concedes despairingly to his stepdaughter's gruesome demand.

Strauss wanted Salome to be sung by "a sixteen-year-old Isolde", and it is certainly one of the most extraordinary and taxing of all roles, demanding an equal measure of delicacy and power. Salome's vocalizing oscillates between bestial ferocity and child-like compassion and culminates in a glowing stream of sound – the chilling declaration of love that precedes her death. Saint-Saëns, himself the composer of a controversial biblical opera (see p.274), summarized this opera when he wrote: "From time to time, the cruellest discords are succeeded by exquisite suavities that caress the ear with delight. While listening to it I thought of those lovely princesses in Sacher Masoch who lavished upon young men the most voluptuous kisses while drawing red-hot irons across their ribs."

RECORDINGS OVERVIEW

As one of the most demanding of all soprano roles, Salome has received only a handful of successful performances on record. The most famous Salome of the century was Ljuba Welitsch, who recorded excerpts for EMI in the 1930s as well as a complete, live performance at the Met in 1949, conducted by Fritz Reiner. The latter is probably the finest portrayal on record, with a strong supporting cast which includes Elizabeth Höngen as Herodias, Set Svanholm as Herod and Hans Hotter as Jokanaan. It is not currently available, but would be a first choice if released on CD. A live recording of Inge Borkh, conducted by Joseph Keilberth in 1951, is available on Orfeo and makes fascinating listening. Also worth hearing is a live concert performance of Birgit Nilsson performing the final scene, currently available on a budget-price Deutsche Grammophon sampler of the singer – she's possibly the least plausible sixteen-year-old on record, but as a display of stunt-singing it will set every hair of your body on end. The sets you're likeliest to find in the shops are the recent ones from Decca and Philips, conducted by Christoph von Dohnányi and Seiji Ozawa respectively; Dohnányi's conducting is impressive, but Catherine Malfitano's vibrato will put many people off, while Ozawa's version is a showcase for Jessye Norman's Salome, an overpowering performance that's too statuesque for the role.

Behrens, van Dam, Böhme, Baltsa, Ochman; Vienna Philharmonic Orchestra; Karajan.
(EMI CDS7 49358-2; 2 CDs).

Though Behrens was nearer the beginning than the end of her career in 1977 when she made this impressive recording, she has the capacity to sound almost naive at the most worrying moments, such as after Narraboth's suicide. van Dam is a little sweet as John, lacking the bite of Waechter's performance for Solti, but he is utterly convincing in his denunciations of the royal couple. Baltsa and Ochman are excellent as Herodias and Narraboth, the latter chillingly desperate, and Karl-Walter Böhme brings an uncommon sense of fear to his portrayal of the King. Karajan is the only conductor apart from Böhm and Reiner to have captured the score's instrumental intricacies as powerfully as the huge symphonic sweep, and despite a muddy recording, he brings warmth and clarity to Strauss's fearsome score.

Nilsson, Waechter, Stolze, Hoffman, Kmentt; Vienna Philharmonic Orchestra; Solti.
(Decca 414 414-2DH2; 2 CDs).

This is one of Solti's most famous recordings and, thanks to Decca producer John Culshaw, it is sonically outstanding. Solti launches himself at the score with characteristic zeal, thrashing his way through it as if he were conducting with a scythe. Much of the instrumental voicing is lost and the clarity of the string writing is submerged beneath the vast Viennese forces, who sound as if a second orchestra has been brought in to provide extra muscle. Nilsson sounds like a Valkyrie masquerading as Salome and the enormous power of her voice, while undeniably impressive, is just too big to sound like anything other than Birgit Nilsson. Stolze is the most gripping Herod on disc, angrily barking the death sentence to his soldiers, while Eberhard Waechter makes an incandescent John, sounding genuinely prophetic. This may not be a recording that is faithful to the music, but it is undeniably sensational.

Elektra

Composed 1906–08.
First performed January 25, 1909.
Libretto by Hugo von Hofmannsthal, after Sophocles.

Synopsis

Outside the walls of the Royal Palace at Mycenae, Elektra mourns for her father, Agamemnon, who has been murdered by her mother Clytemnestra (Klytemnästra). As Elektra calls on her father's spirit for help, she is interrupted by her sister Chrysothemis, who warns her that her mother and her new husband Aegisthus (Aegisth) plan to imprison her. Clytemnestra arrives and asks Elektra what sacrifice she must make to get rid of her nightmares. Elektra tells her that her brother Orestes (Orest) will kill her and Aegisthus with the sacrificial axe. Horrified at first, Clytemnestra begins to laugh hysterically when news is brought of Orestes' death. Elektra is dismayed and exhorts her sister to join her in killing their mother but she runs away. A stranger arrives with news of Orestes' death: it is Orestes himself, and brother and sister embrace before Orestes heads for the palace and murders Clytemnestra. Aegisthus arrives and

Elektra lights his way towards the palace, where he too is murdered. With Orestes acclaimed king Elektra dances for joy; she is urged by her sister to come inside the palace, but Elektra is lost in delirious triumph and falls dead as Chrysothemis calls her brother's name.

In 1903 Max Reinhardt followed his long-running production of Wilde's *Salome* with a version of Sophocles' *Elektra* by Hugo von Hofmannsthal. Strauss saw the production two years later and was struck by the musical potentialities of the play, which in true *fin de siècle* style pushed the ancient tragedy to dysfunctional extremes. However, he was worried by the obvious similarities between Hofmannsthal's reworking of Sophocles and his own recent setting of biblical myth. Hofmannsthal reassured him: "The blend of colour in the two subjects strikes me as quite different in all essentials; in *Salome* much is, so to speak, purple and violet, and the atmosphere is torrid. In *Elektra*, on the other hand, it is a mixture of might and light, or black and bright."

LEBRECHT COLLECTION

Lucille Marcel in the title role of the 1909 Vienna production of Elektra

Clytemnestra, for whom Strauss composed his only atonal music, must rank as the most revolting creation in his entire output. In the immediacy of Elektra's hatred for her mother, her love for Orestes and her disgust with her sister Chrysothemis, the composer was inspired to levels of inventiveness that he was never to equal – if Salome needs a sixteen-year-old Isolde, then Elektra needs a twenty-year-old Brünnhilde. Orestes is a less substantial creation, but he is the only source of light or hope in the work, and the Recognition Scene between brother and sister – the one unequivocally major-key episode – is the poignant climax of the opera, the point at which the drama finally turns to Elektra's advantage.

The first performance brought the Dresden Opera House to its feet, but audiences elsewhere were baffled by the immense, dissonant score, failing to detect the lyricism beneath, or above, what one critic referred to as the "horrible din". The score of *Elektra* is indeed noisy, exceptionally complicated and demands an immense concentration from performers and audience alike, but it is arguably the best and most tightly constructed of all Strauss's operas. It begins with a central, binding theme from the orchestra (suggesting a cry of "Agamemnon!") and develops as one huge crescendo. Elektra's opening monologue, which takes her from despair through defiance to love and ecstasy, states all the opera's various leitmotifs, which are gradually intensified until the glorious duet with Chrysothemis, in which the opera's main ideas are finally resolved as Elektra loses herself to the music in her head, dancing what is surely the most demonic waltz ever written.

RECORDINGS OVERVIEW

Unlike *Salome*, there are several versions of *Elektra* on record but only five of them were studio produced. Of live recordings, the earliest, with Rosa Pauly as Elektra, is the best, even though it is heavily abridged. The passion and stamina are impressive, while the expressive range defies belief, and conductor Artur Rodzinsky is alone in capturing the unrestrained joy of the concluding waltz; available on the Eklipse label, this is a valuable record of a performance that was greatly admired by Strauss himself. Astrid Varnay's 1952 account with Fritz Reiner conducting at the Met is another thrillingly sung, tightly conducted performance, but Inge Borkh outshone even Varnay when she sang it for Mitropoulos in Vienna five years later, when her Chrysothemis was another great Strauss interpreter, Lisa della Casa. The former is available on the Myto label, the latter on Memories. Also worth checking out is Teldec's 1995 recording, not so much for the singing as for Daniel Barenboim's exciting direction.

Borkh, Madeira, Schech, Uhl, Fischer-Dieskau; Dresden Staatskapelle Opera Chorus and Orchestra; Böhm.
(Deutsche Grammophon 445 329-2GX2; 2 CDs).

One of the century's greatest recordings, this 1960 Deutsche Grammophon production captured Inge Borkh in her prime. Her soprano is not especially big, certainly not compared to Nilsson's, but it is more dramatically projected and the variety of tone enables the character to develop as the events overtake her – the woman who sings the opening monologue is not the same as the woman singing herself to death in the final scene. Clytemnestra is sung by Jean Madeira, and no singer has ever conveyed so convincing an impression of disintegrating sanity, and all with the most amazing technical assurance. In support, Fischer-Dieskau makes a powerful and emotional Orestes and Marianne Schech is an intense Chrysothemis. Controlling all this talent is Karl Böhm, whose feel for the internal pulse of Strauss's score brings the opera throbbingly to life.

Nilsson, Resnik, Collier, Stolze, Krause; Vienna State Opera Chorus; Vienna Philharmonic Orchestra; Solti.
(Decca 417 345-2DH2; 2 CDs).

Nilsson's Elektra is the most vocally impressive interpretation of them all. However, it is precisely because the voice is so remarkable that her portrayal remains problematic: the voice is sometimes too healthy to convey Elektra's fractured mental state. Unlike Böhm, whose performance is taut and percussive, Solti goes for orchestral beauty, an approach that tends to undercut the anguish, but this is irresistible music-making, with the Vienna Philharmonic in glowing form. The casting is generally outstanding, and the recording quality unrivalled. The score is performed without cuts.

Der Rosenkavalier

The Knight of the Rose

Composed 1909–10.
First performed January 26, 1911.
Libretto by Hugo von Hofmannsthal.

Synopsis

Act I

In Vienna, during the reign of the Empress Maria Theresa (known as the Marschallin), the wife of the Field Marshal Werdenberg has spent the night with her seventeen-year-old lover Count Octavian. Voices alert the young man, who disguises himself as "Mariandel", a maid, just as Werdenberg's cousin, Baron Ochs, arrives. He boorishly asks the Marschallin to choose a Knight of the Rose to present the silver rose to his fiancée, Sophie von Faninal. Octavian decides it is time to leave but he catches the eye of the lascivious Ochs, who decides that "Mariandel" is prettier than Sophie. Back in his own clothes, Octavian is worried by the Marschallin's conviction that, at 32, she is growing too old and that their relationship will never last. After a formal parting, she sends the rose after him.

Act II

In the von Faninal family home, Sophie and her duenna Marianne await the presentation of the silver rose. But the moment Sophie and Octavian lay eyes on each other, they fall in love. Ochs barges in, outraging Octavian with his rudeness; the younger man demands satisfaction for the insult. During their duel, Ochs is slightly wounded, and in the ensuing commotion Sophie's father threatens to make her enter a convent if she does not marry Ochs. Octavian is desperate to win her for himself and tricks Ochs into a rendezvous with "Mariandel".

Act III

"Mariandel" and Ochs meet at an inn, where Octavian has prepared all sorts of traps to scare Ochs. He even arranges for the arrival of a mystery woman who claims to be his wife and the mother of the children she has with her. Ochs calls the police and general tumult ensues as the law, servants, the Faninal family and the Marschallin all arrive. The Marschallin clears the inn and, bringing Octavian and Sophie together, she leaves them to their love.

Der Rosenkavalier was conceived by Hoffmannsthal as an eighteenth-century comedy of manners, in the style of Molière and the Mozart/da Ponte operas – above all the *Marriage of Figaro*. Baron Ochs is an aristocratic lecher in the vein of Count Almaviva (a "rural Don Giovanni" in Strauss's words), Octavian (sung by a soprano) is close to Cherubino, while the Marschallin is a more *simpatico* and less passive version of the Countess. But the vision of this opera is nostalgic and essentially romantic, celebrating the *ancien régime* rather than criticizing it. On receiving the first act, Strauss pronounced Hoffmansthal's libretto as a masterpiece, and he set it to music that was "like oil and melted butter". Although Strauss thought sections "too delicate for the mob", both composer and librettist thought the opera's charm and light humour were destined for success. For the premiere the brilliant designer Alfred Roller was employed, and, after problems with the original producer, Max Reinhardt was brought in to oversee the show. Even so, no-one could have predicted quite how successful the opera was to be. Indeed, with special "Rosenkavalier" trains being run to Dresden from all across Germany, it soon made Strauss a very rich man. Once again he was the toast of German audiences – if not of German critics, who generally agreed that the composer had capitulated to the lure of the box office.

Urged by Hofmannsthal to create a "Viennese comedy, not a Berlin farce", Strauss devised a delicious concoction laced with some of his most moving and passionate vocal writing, most of it conceived in a surprisingly conversational manner. This relaxed, almost ingenuous quality disguises the opera's remarkable complexity – there are more subtly interconnected leitmotifs in *Der Rosenkavalier* than in any other of his operas – but for most people the structural ingenuity takes a distant second place to the simple beauty of the vocal score. With the uproarious prelude over, *Der Rosenkavalier* is dominated by its melodies, most of which are written for the nigh-perfect soprano roles of Octavian, Sophie and the Marschallin.

On one level the work is a celebration of the soprano voice, and sopranos have queued up to display their mettle in such glorious episodes as the final scene of Act I, the Act II "Presentation of the Rose" and the famous final trio of Act III, in which Strauss entwines all three soprano leads in a seven-minute scene of intoxicating beauty. Of the male voices, Ochs is a Falstaffian buffo caricature of aristocratic pomposity, and his music is suitably gruff and outsized, but Strauss's lyrical proclivities are given vent in such interludes as the Italian Tenor's aria (a Mozart pastiche sung by a nameless walk-on). For all the succulence of the voices, *Der Rosenkavalier* is also a celebration of the waltz, a form with which the opera anachronistically abounds. Derived from the music of Schubert, Lanner and Johann Strauss the Younger, the opera's dance music is so refined and plausible that you might be tricked into thinking that they must have been a feature of eighteenth-century musical life. *Der Rosenkavalier* may not be Strauss's greatest opera, but it is surely his most captivating, deserving more than any other Debussy's approbation: "There is sunshine in the music of Strauss . . . it is not possible to withstand his irresistible domination."

RECORDINGS OVERVIEW

Der Rosenkavalier is harder to cast successfully than either of the preceding operas, not just because three leading sopranos are required but because even the most incidental roles demand world-class character singers. It is surprising, therefore, to find that so many fine versions have been recorded. EMI's abridged 1933 recording with Lotte Lehmann as the Marschallin, Elizabeth Schumann as Sophie, Maria Olszewska as Octavian and Richard Mayr as Ochs (a role he created in 1911) is a fascinating and characterful document. In more recent times, Solti's 1969 account with Crespin, Donath and Minton in the female leads is a sumptuous if over-inflated interpretation while Haitink's 1990 recording for EMI, with Te Kanawa, Hendricks and von Otter, is among the most vocally beautiful and best recorded, though the conducting is a little detached. Both of these are well worth considering, but the following three recordings are unsurpassed.

Ludwig, Troyanos, Mathis, Adam; Vienna State Opera Chorus; Vienna Philharmonic Orchestra; Böhm.
(Deutsche Grammophon 445 338-2GX3; 3 CDs).

Karl Böhm recorded *Rosenkavalier* in the studio in 1958, but that set pales beside this 1969 live recording from the Vienna Staatsoper. The beauty and warmth of Christa Ludwig's Marschallin, the urgency of Tatiana Troyanos's Octavian and the fragile innocence of Edith Mathis's Sophie have never been bettered. Theo Adam's Ochs is a complicated, intelligent creation, affluent and likable throughout, and Böhm's favourite tenor, Anton de Ridder, delivers the goods as the Italian singer – although the conductor's dilatory tempo suggests that he hated the character. Böhm's feel for the opera's overall shape, orchestral texture and phrasing is unequalled. From start to finish, this is the most consistently beautiful performance on record.

Schwarzkopf, Ludwig, Stich-Randall, Edelmann; Philharmonia Chorus and Orchestra; Karajan.
(EMI CDS7 49354-2; 3 CDs).

This is a famous recording, and rightly so, but it is not without its faults. Unlike Böhm, who is alert throughout to the sudden changes in mood, Karajan sails through the score seemingly oblivious to the opera's finer colouring. But the performance's real qualities are to be found in the casting. The Marschallin was one of Elizabeth Schwarzkopf's finest roles, and her performance here provided the benchmark against which all others have been measured. Occasionally she sounds mannered, with a tendency to over-articulate her words, but even so this is still one of the finest performances of her career. Christa Ludwig and Teresa Stich-Randall shine as the lovers and Otto Edelmann makes a blustering Ochs. The early stereo is slightly misty but this almost adds to the other-worldly quality of this memorable production. EMI also release this *Rosenkavalier* as a full-price mono recording (two sets of masters were made), a process that brings the voices to the fore in a manner that newcomers to the opera might find a bit too obtrusive.

Reining, Jurinac, Gueden, Weber; Vienna State Opera Chorus; Vienna Philharmonic Orchestra; Kleiber.
(Decca 425 950-2 DM3; 3 CDs).

Erich Kleiber's 1954 studio recording is justly considered a classic. The three sopranos are all outstanding, combining beautiful tone with a direct and largely unsentimental approach to the music. Jurinac and Gueden are beautifully matched as the young lovers, and if Maria Reining's outrageously old-fashioned-sounding Marschallin will not be to everyone's liking, the warmth and sincerity of the interpretation are irresistible. The same could be said of Weber's Ochs, vocally too old for the role but brilliantly characterized all the same. Best of all is Kleiber's conducting, his effortlessly natural sense of phrasing allowing the story to unfold as if for the first time. The sound is rather monochromatic but not worryingly so.

Ariadne auf Naxos

Ariadne on Naxos

Composed 1911–12; revised 1916.
First performed October 25, 1912.
Libretto by Hugo von Hofmannsthal.

Synopsis

Prologue

At the house of Vienna's richest man, two opposing theatre companies are gathered for a banquet. The Music Master is furious that his pupil's opera seria, *Ariadne auf Naxos*, is to be followed by a burlesque. However, not all is going well for the Composer: the violins and soprano are missing and the tenor does not like his wig. Zerbinetta, the leader of the commedia dell'arte group, arrives; despite her dismissal of the absurd traditions of opera seria, she captures the Composer's heart. But there is further uproar when the Major-domo announces that the two works, opera and burlesque, will have to be performed simultaneously in time for the fireworks at nine o'clock. The Dancing Master suggests a compromise: the two works are to be combined – although the Composer regrets his decision the moment he sees the comedians skipping about the stage.

The Opera

On the island of Naxos, Ariadne – abandoned by Theseus – is sleeping, watched over by three nymphs. She wakes and cries for death but Zerbinetta, finding the whole thing ridiculous, tries to cheer her up, singing of the love of life. Ariadne is inconsolable and so Zerbinetta clears the stage and sings a long showpiece through which she tries to illustrate that there are other fish in the sea. After a brief show from the comedians, the Nymphs announce the sudden arrival of Bacchus. Ariadne emerges from her cave and the two stalk each other, neither sure who the other is. Before long they are infatuated and the opera ends with Zerbinetta confirming that the new is always better than the old.

By 1911 Strauss seems to have been happy to leave it to Hofmannsthal to come up with ideas for operas, although their correspondence reveals that the more enthusiastic the composer's response to his librettist's suggestions, the more doubtful Hofmannsthal became – as if approval from the ultimate bourgeois was the last thing he wanted. *Ariadne auf Naxos* was their most problem-filled collabo-

ration, and ultimately one of their greatest achievements.

It was begun with Max Reinhardt's theatre company in mind, since both Strauss and Hofmannsthal wished to express their gratitude for the uncredited work that Reinhardt had put into the premiere of *Rosenkavalier*. Hofmannsthal had seen Molière's *Le bourgeois gentilhomme* in Paris and thought he would write an operatic divertissement to be inserted at the end of the play, linked to it by a short prose scene. The work's gestation generated much acrimonous debate between the two collaborators before the premiere of the first version in Stuttgart in 1912. Reinhardt's company performed Hofmannsthal's version of the Molière play, with incidental music from Strauss, then came the opera. The evening lasted over six hours and was not deemed a success: those coming to hear the play were irritated by the opera, while those coming to hear Strauss's music were bored by Molière. One critic, Richard Specht, suggested that the play be turned into a prologue with music – and, four years later, that is exactly what happened.

Shifted from the seventeenth to the nineteenth century, *Ariadne* became a gently satirical artistic debate, contrasting the artificial conventions of opera seria with the direct, knockabout humour of the commedia dell'arte. For Hofmannsthal, however, the opera was essentially about Ariadne's heroism in remaining faithful to a lost ideal, as opposed to the rather more human and earthbound Zerbinetta's determination to get on with life – a view of the piece that reflects his and Strauss's respective characters. Thus, whereas Strauss was worried by the intellectual baggage with which he felt his librettist weighed down the characters, Hofmannsthal had his doubts about Strauss's perceived frivolities, such as making the role of the Composer a soprano part. In fact, far from belittling the character as Hofmannsthal thought it would, Strauss's writing invests him with an ingénue charm – in the manner of Octavian – that is hard to imagine being conveyed by the tenor that Hofmannsthal wanted.

As always with Strauss, the most memorable parts are sung by women. Ariadne herself is an engaging portrait of Romantic excess, and her long, arching lines of song demand a voice of power and sensitivity in equal measure, notably for one exquisite octave leap to a pianissimo high C. Appearing in the Prologue as the Prima Donna (just as Bacchus appears as the Tenor), Ariadne dominates the work, but Zerbinetta – a point of light and humanity amidst the seria earnestness – is a coloratura soprano of exquisite personality and spirit, being provided with some of Strauss's most impressive melodies. Her long solo "Grossmächtige Prinzessin" is the most difficult coloratura aria ever written and provides the musical, if not the emotional, climax of the whole work.

Ariadne is a chamber opera, with a small cast and an orchestra of just thirty-six, playing music which sparkles through every imaginable instrumental combination before letting rip with full-bloodied Wagnerian passion in the closing duet. Much of this colouristic variety can be lost if the opera is performed – as it often is – in a large-opera house, but produced on the right scale *Ariadne* can seem the most brilliant of all Strauss's operas.

RECORDINGS OVERVIEW

Of the nine complete recordings of *Ariadne auf Naxos*, only two are completely unsatisfactory: Solti's Decca recording of 1977 and Levine's for Deutsche Grammophon in 1988. The remaining seven sets all have their strengths. Böhm's first recording of 1944 boasts the extraordinary combination of Maria Reining, Alda Noni, Irmgard Seefried and Max Lorenz, while Karajan's 1954 EMI recording is notable for Seefried's remarkable Composer and an outstanding Bacchus from Rudolph Schock. In 1988, Philips recorded the wonderful Jessye Norman as Ariadne with Julia Varady equally impressive as the Composer. Directed by Kurt Masur, this is arguably the best-conducted version, but the supporting cast let the production down. In terms of all-round success the following two sets emerge as the leaders.

Janowitz, Zylis-Gara, Geszty, King; Dresden Staatskapelle, Kempe.
(EMI CMS7 64 159-2; 2 CDs).

Recorded in 1968, this is one of Rudolph Kempe's great successes as an opera conductor, not least because of his cast. Ariadne is a role in which beauty of tone is of greater importance than interpretive complexity, and beautiful tone is what Gundula Janowitz has in abundance, with a creamy voice that cascades over Strauss's melodies. Sylvia Geszty's Zerbinetta is technically awe-inspiring, but witty as well as acrobatic. James King, in the short but extremely difficult role of Bacchus, may lack Schock's style and sensitivity, but he possesses a matchless incision and ardour. Kempe's handling of the Dresden forces is a model of balance, attention to detail and imagination, and while he emphasizes the work's textural lucidity it is never at the expense of momentum. This recording demonstrates true ensemble opera at its most successful.

della Casa, Seefried, Gueden, Schock; Vienna Philharmonic Orchestra; Böhm.
(Deutsche Grammophon 445 332-2GX2; 2 CDs).

This recording comes second on the list simply because, as a live recording made in 1954, the sound is not ideal. Böhm had an instinctive sense of theatre, and this, plus his timing, his feeling for texture and his sensitivity to his singers, made him the perfect interpreter of Strauss. He generates an unfailingly congenial atmosphere, with della Casa an elegant but highly sensual Ariadne. She alone, on record, tackles the awkward octave leap perfectly, landing on the most delicate and accurately pitched pianissimo C imaginable – a highly graceful moment that is typical of her performance as a whole. Seefried is a characterful Composer, the young Hilde Gueden fizzes as Zerbinetta and Rudolph Schock purrs as Bacchus. The Vienna forces play with great gusto but also respond with wit and imagination to the flexibility of Böhm's conducting.

Die Frau ohne Schatten

The Woman Without a Shadow

Composed 1914–17.
First performed October 10, 1919.
Libretto by Hugo von Hofmannsthal.

Synopsis

Act I

The Emperor of the Eastern Islands once nearly killed the daughter of Keikobad, lord of the spirits, while out hunting. He married her but, neither human nor spirit, she has borne her husband no children. The Nurse looks upon the Emperor and his wife before they are awoken by news that Keikobad will turn the Emperor to stone and take back his daughter if she does not "cast a shadow" within the next three days. Knowing that a shadow can be obtained only from a human woman, the Nurse takes the Empress to see the Dyer, Barak, a poor man with three deformed brothers. The Dyer's Wife is unhappy, having been unable to provide her husband with children. This the Nurse turns to her advantage, offering the woman a life of luxury in return for her shadow. First, however, she must resist Barak for three days, during which the Nurse and the Empress will act as her servants. Barak returns from the market to find a single bed.

Act II

The Nurse conjures the young man of the wife's dreams. When Barak returns she refuses the food that he brings. Meanwhile, awaiting his wife, the Emperor sees her in the world of the humans and decides to kill her, but he cannot bring himself to fire the arrow. Barak too is driven to thoughts of murder when his wife tells him of her pact with the Nurse, but as he raises the sword above his head, he and his wife are swallowed up by the earth.

Act III

Separately imprisoned, Barak and his wife are released by the spirits in order to find each other. Since being alone, they have come to realize that they love one another. The Empress, realizing that the Nurse is using deception and trickery to win her a shadow, rejects her help and, in defiance of the Nurse's advice, she enters Keikobad's temple, where she can hear the voices of Barak and his wife as they search for each other. The Nurse is banished and The Keeper of the Threshold offers the Empress a drink, after which she will have the Dyer's Wife's shadow. But the Empress refuses to steal the shadow, even after she is shown an image of the Emperor turned to stone. At this point the stage goes dark and when the light returns the Empress casts a shadow as she has learned the importance of compassion. All are forgiven, Barak and his wife are reunited and the opera ends with singing from the voices of unborn children.

In the four years that separated the two versions of *Ariadne*, Strauss and Hofmannsthal made extensive headway on their fourth opera. *Die Frau ohne Schatten* is thought by some to be Strauss's greatest opera – it is certainly his most convoluted. Having relaxed with two comedies, Hofmannsthal was keen to return to the psychological nether world of *Elektra* and, having already suggested fairy tales to Strauss as possible sources, he was hopeful that the composer would respond to his densely allegorical quest-drama. Strauss was initially reluctant: "Characters like the Emperor and Empress and also the Nurse can't be filled with red corpuscles in the same way as the Marschallin or Ochs. My heart's only half in it". Hofmannsthal dismissed the composer's concerns and urged him to get to work, suggesting that the drama should be seen "in general terms, to *Zauberflöte* as *Rosenkavalier* is to *Figaro*". Strauss finally began sketching the music in July 1914 but did not complete the full score until 1917, when the war was at its height.

Hofmannsthal's reputation as a librettist was based on his skill in transforming already existing texts – such as *Elektra*, *Oedipus* and *Le bourgeois gentilhomme* – into parables of contemporary relevance, and *Die Frau ohne Schatten*, as he acknowledged, owes a clear debt to *Die Zauberflöte*. Like Mozart and Schikaneder's masterpiece, it tells of the spiritual journey of two contrasted couples, and in the figure of Kaikobad it contains a semi-divinity similar to Sarastro. But unlike the couples in *Die Zauberflöte*, the relationships of the two couples are established at the outset, and both are profoundly damaged, ostensibly because of the absence of children. But if fulfilment through childbirth seems to be the opera's main message, it is the psychological dynamics of the relationships that really concerned Hofmannsthal, and these dynamics reveal a lot about the sexual politics of the time, just as the emphasis on repopulation bears witness to the ravages of World War I. Barak's wife was largely based on Strauss's strong-willed wife Pauline, and was meant to be, in Hofmannsthal's own words: "a bizarre woman with a very beautiful soul. . . strange, moody, domineering and yet at the same time likable". On one level this exposes Hofmannsthal's feelings for Pauline Strauss, but *Die Frau* also represents the uncertainty of male attitudes towards women, who were now beginning to take control over their lives and bodies – a development that receives quite different treatment in Apollinaire's exactly contemporary *Les mamelles de Tirésias* (see p.498). The complexity and confusion of the text stems, in part, from Hofmannsthal's inability to make up his mind as to whether or not independent womanhood was a good or a bad thing.

Strauss's response to his librettist's confusion was typically independent, and regardless of his inability to fathom what Hofmannsthal was getting at, he produced a blockbuster of a score, over three and a half hours long, boasting a huge orchestra and the most inventive musical characterization in all Strauss's operas. In places the music seems to mark a return to *Elektra*, though here the rootless harmony is largely used to enhance the mystery of the Emperor's spirit world, in contrast to the warm conventionalities of Barak's earthly existence. As with *Elektra* it is the orchestra that dominates – indeed you could argue that *Die Frau* is less an opera than a huge Romantic tone-poem with obbligato voices. Of these voices, the Emperor's tenor and the Empress's soprano stand out as two of Strauss's most perfect roles, the former carrying the opera's haunting "Falcon" theme – an arresting, omnipresent leitmotif, typical of this opera's penchant for musical symbols and labels.

Without doubt *Die Frau* contains moments of profound obscurity teetering on pretentiousness. But it is a work that rewards perseverance, for its pages of painful dialogue are punctuated regularly by tumults of ravishing song. As Newman wrote of Strauss: "He was the most consistently inconsistent composer of the century."

RECORDINGS OVERVIEW

All five recordings of *Die Frau ohne Schatten* are worth having, although each is distinguished in different ways. The first was produced with Karl Böhm conducting the Vienna Philharmonic and a starry cast that included Rysanek, Hopf and Schoeffler. It remains for many the best of them all, but Decca's primitive stereo and the opaque atmosphere make Böhm's later live recording for Deutsche Grammophon marginally preferable. Joseph Keilberth's 1963 recording, also for Deutsche Grammophon, has the merit of Inge Borkh's Dyer's Wife, Martha Mödl's Nurse and Jess Thomas's incomparable Emperor, but it is currently unavailable. In 1987 Sawallisch produced one of his best opera recordings but was let down by a weak cast, in particular René Kollo's nasal Emperor.

Varady, Domingo, Behrens, Van Dam, Jo; Vienna State Opera Chorus; Vienna Philharmonic Orchestra; Solti.
(Decca 436 243-2DH3; 4 CDs).

One of the great recordings of the 1990s, this set took two years to produce, due to the organizational problems of assembling its magnificent cast. It epitomizes jet-set opera production (none of the players had worked on the opera in the theatre) but the quality of the leading performers is such that the final product sounds like the product of two years' preparation rather than two years' production. Domingo is radiant as the Emperor, while Varady's dark and low-lying voice is perfect for the Empress. Behrens makes an outstanding Dyer's Wife, Reinhild Runkel brings real power to the role of the Nurse, and José Van Dam is a gentle Barak. The Vienna forces are captured in perfect sound, and Solti's attention to colour, if not to shape, is laudable.

Rysanek, King, Nilsson, Berry, Vienna State Opera Chorus; Vienna Philharmonic Orchestra; Böhm.
(Deutsche Grammophon 445 325 2GX3; 3 CDs).

Of all Strauss's operas, *Die Frau ohne Schatten* is the one that suffers most from cutting, but Böhm wilfully slices his way through the second and third acts. And yet he is an unquestionable master of what's left, and this 1977 set should be approached as a document of a great performance, rather than a true picture of the

opera. Leonie Rysanek's Empress and Birgit Nilsson's Dyer's Wife give carefully detailed and tonally sumptuous readings, and Walter Berry's Barak is palpably human in his suffering. Ruth Hesse comes close to suggesting the Nurse's true instincts without letting on too soon, and James King is the only tenor apart from Thomas to really sing the Emperor. Böhm shapes the huge score well and the Vienna Philharmonic play with beauty and sensitivity.

Arabella

Composed 1930–32.
First performed July 1, 1933.
Libretto by Hugo von Hofmannsthal.

Synopsis

Act I

During the Carnival of 1860, in a hotel in Vienna, the impoverished Count Waldner and his wife discuss their future prospects. Their one hope is to find a rich husband for their daughter Arabella (their other daughter, Zdenka, has been brought up as a boy, Zdenko). A young officer, Matteo, is in love with Arabella, little realizing that the letters he has been receiving from her are, in fact, from Zdenka/Zdenko. Waldner has sent a portrait of his daughter to a rich former army colleague, Count Mandryka. When Mandryka arrives, he turns out to be the old man's dashing nephew, who has inherited the title.

Act II

At the Cabbies' Ball, Mandryka and Arabella are introduced and fall instantly in love. Matteo is assured of Arabella's affections by Zdenka, who hands him an envelope with Arabella's bedroom door key inside. Mandryka overhears and is astonished when Arabella excuses herself for the evening. Mandryka gets drunk and insults the Waldners before going home with them.

Act III

Matteo is seen emerging from Zdenka's room. He is under the impression that he has spent the night with Arabella and is amazed to see her walking up the stairs. He approaches her, hinting at their recent intimacy, but Arabella is confused. When Mandryka arrives he sees Arabella and Matteo together and orders his bags to be packed. Zdenka runs down the stairs in her nightdress and bids farewell to her family, intending to jump into the river. The truth of her relationship with Matteo emerges, then Mandryka apologizes, urging the Waldners to accept Matteo as their son-in-law. Arabella and Mandryka are left together and the opera ends with their embrace.

"I am completely cleaned out! So please, write some poetry. It may even be a 'second *Rosenkavalier*' if you can't think of anything better. If the worst comes to the worst, a little stop-gap job. . . to keep my hand in." So Strauss wrote to Hofmannsthal in September 1927, one week before completing the score of *Die Ägyptische Helena*. Hofmannsthal responded by preparing a synopsis of "a three-act comic opera, indeed almost an operetta . . . which in gaiety does not fall short of *Fledermaus*, and without any self-repetition is related to *Rosenkavalier*". The opera was provisionally entitled *Arabella, or the Cabbies' Ball*, and it was to be the final collaboration between the two men. After completing the final draft of Act I, nearly two years later, Hofmannsthal suffered a fatal stroke while dressing to attend the funeral of his son Franz, who had committed suicide. Strauss decided to continue with the opera, partly as a tribute to their long collaboration, though he dedicated the opera not to Hofmannsthal but to the theatre director Alfred Reucker and the conductor Fritz Busch, who were to be responsible for the first production in Dresden. However, with Hitler coming to power in January 1933, the Jewish Reucker and the anti-Nazi Busch were dismissed; Strauss tried to withdraw the work, but Dresden's management forced him to honour his contract.

With its Viennese setting, aristocratic milieu and abundance of waltzes, *Arabella* was dismissed by most critics as a mere imitation of *Rosenkavalier*. And yet it's far more tightly structured than the earlier work, and Hofmannsthal never created a more human set of characters nor Strauss a more delightful score. The flowing melodies, achingly beautiful soprano lines and soft orchestral fabric are among the most emotionally direct in all Strauss's operas. Only the most hardened classicist could resist such an episode as Arabella's gushing Act I solo "Aber der Richtige" (an aria based on a Croatian folk song), which develops into a soprano duet that's as luscious as the "Presentation of the Rose" in *Der Rosenkavalier*. This romantic excess is all very calculated – the first Arabella, Viorica Ursuleac, said that Strauss was somewhat embarrassed at having written something so self-consciously sentimental – but it sets the dreamy, lyrical tone of much to follow, not least the tender expressions of love between Arabella and the baritone Mandryka "Un du wirst mein Gebieter sein" (early in Act II) and the touching final scene in which they are reunited. Arabella and her suitor dominate the show, but there is fine music for the high soprano of Zdenka and the equally high tenor of Matteo, who has one scene of enormous bravura during Act III.

Lisa della Casa

In fact, the voice plays a more prominent part in *Arabella* than in any other Strauss opera, for the orchestra is generally so subdued that it provides an accompaniment to the voices rather than constituting a voice in itself. There are some weak moments – primarily at the end of Act II – but the comic situations and regular bursts of unforgettable melody make this the most simply pleasurable of all the Strauss–Hofmannsthal works.

della Casa, Rothenberger, Fischer-Dieskau, Paskuda; Bavarian State Opera Chorus and Orchestra; Keilberth.
(Deutsche Grammophon 437 700-2GX3; 3 CDs).

Lisa della Casa recorded Arabella – her most celebrated role – twice: in the studio with a rather perfunctory Solti in 1957 and live with Keilberth in 1963. The latter is miraculous. Della Casa is in ravishing form, producing impeccably seamless yet varied tone in a performance that is choked with emotion – her duet with Fischer-Dieskau's tender Mandryka is one of the most heartfelt declarations of love you're ever likely to hear on disc. Much of the glory belongs to Keilberth, who is a model of sensitivity, encouraging all the singers to revel in the music. His tempi veer from rapid to snail's pace but they always seem appropriate to the flow of the music. Anneliese Rothenberger is a pure and lyrical Zdenka and Georg Paskuda is a powerful, urgent Matteo. The recorded sound is ideal.

Capriccio

Composed 1940–41.
First performed October 28, 1942.
Libretto by Clemens Krauss and the composer.

Synopsis

At an eighteenth-century Paris salon, the widowed Countess Madeleine listens to a sextet, composed for her birthday by the composer Flamand. The poet

Olivier has written a play, which La Roche is to direct. A debate arises as to which is more important – words or music – and both composer and poet look to the Countess to decide the issue. Both secretly declare their love to the Countess. She agrees to meet Flamand at eleven the following morning, in the library. La Roche brings on a ballerina and then two Italian singers, whose love duet is praised for its music, but the words of which are derided as meaningless. The arguments continue until it is decided that composer and poet should collaborate on an opera. Various subjects (including Ariadne) are proposed before the Countess suggests a contemporary drama – about themselves. This is agreed and the theatre companies leave for Paris. The Countess is eventually left alone. She receives a message from Olivier, who wants to know how the opera will end, and will meet her in the library at eleven the following morning. The Countess ponders the respective qualities of words and music, wondering whom she loves more – Flamand or Olivier. She cannot decide and leaves for supper, humming.

The relationship between words and music preoccupied Strauss throughout his life, but the idea of making this the subject of an opera came from Stefan Zweig who, in 1935, had come across Abbate Casti's 1786 libretto *Prima la musica, poi le parole* (First the music and then the words) while researching in the British Museum. Strauss asked Zweig's friend Joseph Gregor for help in reworking Casti's text but eventually decided that Gregor was not up to the task and turned, instead, to his friend the conductor Clemens Krauss, who conducted the premiere at the Bavarian State Opera in October 1942, at the height of the Allied bombing of Munich.

Strauss was seventy-six years old when he composed *Capriccio*, and was seen by many – not least the government – as a relic of the nineteenth century, to be wheeled out whenever German culture was a point of debate. In fact he was entering one of the most creative periods of his life, a period that produced not just *Capriccio* but also the second horn concerto, the wind sonatinas, the *Oboe Concerto* and the haunting *Metamorphosen*. *Capriccio* was his operatic swan song: it nostalgically celebrates a life in theatre but in a way that is tinged with melancholy. It ends with a question mark, undecided as to which element of opera is the more important, but as the Countess leaves the stage humming, Strauss was surely pointing his audience towards his own preference.

This is Strauss's most delicate and touching work, even though he had originally thought of it as a self-indulgent academic exercise, of little interest to the audience of whom he was usually so conscious. He described it as a "theatrical fugue", and, indeed, it is a virtuosic display of technique in emulation of the eighteenth century, with several octets, parodies, complex ensembles, fugues etc. Yet *Capriccio* is a delightful and affecting chamber opera, from the opening string sextet to the aching melancholy of the Countess's final scene. A model of economy and balance, it is the very antithesis of the work with which he announced his arrival upon the operatic scene nearly forty years earlier. He announced after the first dress rehearsal, "I can do nothing better than this", and when Clemens Krauss tried to tempt him into continuing with a series of small-scale music-dramas Strauss made it clear that *Capriccio* was the end of his life as a composer of opera – "Isn't this D flat major the best winding-up of my theatrical life-work? One can only leave one testament behind."

RECORDINGS OVERVIEW

Capriccio has been recorded only three times complete – most recently with Kiri Te Kanawa in the title role, on Decca, in a less than ideal production. Sawallisch's 1957 version, which is just pipped to the post by Böhm's stereo production, has a heavyweight cast that includes Schwarzkopf as the Countess, together with Ludwig, Gedda, Fischer-Dieskau, Wächter and Hotter as Olivier – a role he created at the premiere. You can hear excerpts from the original 1942 production on a Myto CD – Krauss's conducting is superb, as is the singing of his wife, Viorica Ursuleac, as the Countess.

Janowitz, Fischer-Dieskau, Schreier, Prey; Bavarian Radio Symphony Orchestra; Böhm.
(Deutsche Grammophon 445 347-2GX2; 2 CDs).

Recorded in 1971, this is an outstanding account. Janowitz might be imprecise with her diction, but the ripeness of her tone makes her an irresistible Countess. Schreier and Prey are a delightfully impulsive pair as Flamand and Olivier, and the Italian Singers – Anton de Ridder and Arleen Augér – ham up the Metastasian duet with great gusto. Böhm accentuates the autumnal warmth of the work and, in the slightly dewy-eyed finale, comes closer than anyone else to capturing the feeling of regret with which Strauss ended his life as an opera composer.

HANS PFITZNER

b. MOSCOW, MAY 5, 1869; d. SALZBURG, MAY 22, 1949.

Though Jewish luminaries like the conductor Bruno Walter spoke up in his defence, Hans Pfitzner's reputation was largely destroyed by his involvement with the Third Reich. Preoccupied with the idea of producing a purely Germanic music, he explored the nature of Germanness in works such as his cantata *Von deutscher Seele* (Of the German Soul) and expended a lot of energy on anti-modernist polemics and clashes with progressives such as Busoni and Schoenberg. As the author of an essay entitled "The New Aesthetic of Musical Impotence", which equated modern music with Bolshevism and concluded that German culture was threatened by international Jewry, it's hardly surprising that Pfitzner was adopted as a figurehead by Nazi "intellectuals", who upheld his music as the epitome of the best in the German tradition and used it as a stick with which to beat the "degenerate" Richard Strauss when the latter fell from favour. Pfitzner, a difficult and acutely jealous man, was happy to work for anyone who promoted his music above that of his rival, for until the premiere of Strauss's *Salome* in 1905, Pfitzner had been considered Germany's leading opera composer, along with Humperdinck. Pfitzner's music has failed to overcome its negative political associations, but his eclectic style – combining the fulsomeness of late Romanticism with an elevated awareness of classical structure – at least deserves to be sampled, and his opera *Palestrina* is the place to sample it.

It's ironic that such a proudly German composer was born in Moscow, where his father was working as a violinist. Moving to Frankfurt as a child, he studied at the conservatory until 1890, then took up a succession of teaching posts, including a spell at the Stern Conservatory in Berlin, where he taught composition and conducting. His first two operas, *Der arme Heinrich* (Poor Heinrich, 1891–93) and *Die Rose vom Liebesgarten* (The Rose from the Garden of Love, 1897–1900), were Wagnerian exercises in Germanic-Christian medievalism and were both widely admired – indeed Mahler conducted the first Viennese performance of *Die Rose*. In 1907 Pfitzner moved to Strasbourg to become director of the conservatory, and three years later he was also made director of Strasbourg Opera, where he employed as his assistant – and then fell out with – Otto Klemperer.

In 1917 he triumphed with *Palestrina*, and in 1921 he struck gold with his mighty *Von deutscher Seele*, going on to further endear himself to the Nazis in 1929 when he composed another jingoistic choral piece, *Das dunkle Reich* (The Dark Realm). Until the end of the war – when his house in Munich was bombed flat – he remained a darling of the Reich, and though the Vienna Philharmonic arranged for him to move from his pensioners' home into a private house, there were few to praise him once the war was over.

Palestrina

Composed 1912–15.
First performed June 12, 1917.
Libretto by the composer.

Synopsis

Act I

Rome, 1563. Palestrina's pupil Silla plays his latest composition, written in the new Florentine style. Palestrina's son, Ighino, expresses concern about his father since the death of his wife Lucrezia. Palestrina enters with Cardinal Borromeo, who expresses horror at Silla's music and asks Palestrina's opinion. When the composer replies that it is "the music of the future", Borromeo tells him that the Council of Trent is almost certain to ban polyphonic music from the church and he asks him to write a Mass that will prove to the Pope that polyphony is still able to express sober religious devotion. Palestrina refuses and Borromeo storms from the room.

While sleeping, Palestrina is visited by the greatest of his musical forebears, who tell him that his ultimate duty is yet to be fulfilled. As the composers depart their place is taken by angels, who dictate the music of his Mass – and as he reaches the height of inspiration, a vision of his wife appears before him, bearing a message of peace. As dawn breaks Palestrina collapses, exhausted, before the manuscript of his *Missa Papae Marcelli*. Ighino and Silla arrive and are delighted to see that the master has been at work and are astonished when they realize an entire Mass has been written.

Act II

The Council of Trent is about to recommence. Borromeo has had Palestrina thrown into jail for refusing his request. Some time into the talks, the subject of sacred music is raised and Borromeo announces that Palestrina has been commissioned to write a Mass. Provoked by the Spanish envoy, the conference soon collapses into nationalist squabbling and is adjourned; but the Spanish servants, believing their master insulted, start a fight. Papal soldiers begin killing all involved while survivors are dragged to the torture chambers.

Act III

A fortnight later Palestrina is told that his Mass is being performed before the Pope at St Peter's. Having heard the music, the Pope and Borromeo ask Palestrina to devote the remainder of his life to their service. The Pope blesses Palestrina, then Borromeo and the composer embrace. Palestrina is told that Silla has left for Florence (in other words, gone over to the modernists); as the crowd calls his name offstage, Palestrina walks first to a portrait of his wife and then to his organ, where he plays softly until the curtain falls.

Although it was written before Pfitzner engaged in his fractious polemics against modernism, *Palestrina* is effectively his artistic credo, expressing an unwavering belief in the traditional artistic values represented by Palestrina himself, as opposed to the experimentation represented by his pupil Silla. (Ironically, the "modernists" to whom Silla is drawn were the very people who "invented" opera.) In the published score Pfitzner inserted an epilogue from the philosopher Schopenhauer that asserts the intellectual's position outside of society: "alongside world history there goes, guiltless and unstained by blood, the history of philosophy, science, and the arts". *Palestrina* is thus a role-of-the-artist opera like Hindemith's *Mathis der Maler* (see p.413) but occupying a different ideological position: where Mathis's artistic ideas are directly challenged by the political events that surround him, Palestrina clings to cultural tradition as a source of continuity and stability in a changing world. Indeed when this tradition is renewed – in the composition of the *Missa Papae Marcelli* – it occurs as something God-given, with Palestrina simply serving as the privileged channel of a chorus of angels.

When *Palestrina* was first performed in 1917 it was singled out by Thomas Mann as exemplifying the idealism of German culture, and its first conductor Bruno Walter described it as "the mightiest musical-dramatic work of our time". If experienced away from the theatre, however, Pfitzner's profoundly serious work can be heavy going. The roles of Ighino and Silla are assigned to female voices, but otherwise the world of Palestrina is a male one, and only the factional squabbling at the Council of Trent hints at any humour. The musical and spiritual language is very much rooted in the world of *Parsifal*, with the addition of angular counterpoint to suggest the music of the seventeenth century (though Pfitzner has no qualms about supplying anachronistic harps for the angelic rendition of Palestrina's Mass). At moments, for instance the prelude to Act II, the dark melodies are completely persuasive, but dramatic pacing isn't Pfitzner's strong point: the opera's climax occurs during Act I's "composition" scene, nearly two hours before the opera's conclusion, and nothing following this remarkable passage can compare with it. The immediacy of the central characterizations, particularly the tenor of Palestrina and the baritone of Borromeo, is sometimes smothered by the mass of extras commanded to march on and off the stage – as well as the substantial chorus, there are sixteen named and five unnamed singing characters, more than a dozen silent actors, and thirteen singing apparitions. In short, *Palestrina* is without doubt Pfitzner's finest achievement, but for every listener who finds its lyricism and sincerity involving, there will be half a dozen for whom the overelaborate polyphony and high moral seriousness make for a ponderous and undramatic experience.

Gedda, Ridderbusch, Fischer-Dieskau, Fassbaender; Bavarian Radio Chorus and Symphony Orchestra; Kubelik.
(Deutsche Grammophon 427 417-2GC3; 3 CDs).

This outstanding recording, made in 1972, brought its composer out of the cultural wilderness for the first time since the war. It is no longer alone in the catalogue (Berlin Classics released a recording in 1993) but it remains superior in every respect. Featuring three of the finest male voices of recent years, the casting is near perfect, with Nicolai Gedda and Dietrich Fischer-Dieskau superbly matched as Palestrina and Borromeo. Karl Ridderbusch as the Pope and Brigitte Fassbaender as Silla are no less impressive, while Kubelik succeeds in generating a high degree of tension, shaping the expansive orchestral music with Wagnerian patience and detail.

ALEXANDER ZEMLINSKY

b. VIENNA, OCTOBER 14, 1871; d. LARCHMONT, USA, MARCH 15, 1942.

Zemlinsky has suffered the misfortune of being pushed to the margins of musical history, both during his lifetime and since his death, despite the advocacy of his pupil Arnold Schoenberg. "I have always believed he was a great composer," Schoenberg wrote in 1949, but maybe he wasn't the most useful champion. Basically Zemlinsky's music fell between two stools, being too advanced for his conservative contemporaries, but not interesting enough for the radicals. However, after a long period of neglect, the last fifteen years have seen a reassessment of Zemlinsky's lushly *fin de siècle* music and particularly his operatic output – the double bill of his two one-act operas has proved particularly successful. But with stage productions a rarity the only practical way of discovering this music is on disc.

Zemlinsky was a typical product of Viennese multiculturalism: his father was Slovakian, his mother from a Sarajevo Bosnian-Jewish family. After training at the Vienna Conservatory, Zemlinsky became one of the circle of musicians around Gustav Mahler, the reforming force in the city's musical life. Opera dominated Zemlinsky's career both as composer and conductor. *Sarema*, the first of his eight operas, was performed in Munich in 1897, and his second, *Es war einmal* (Once Upon a Time), was premiered by Mahler at the Court Opera in Vienna in 1900. Zemlinsky became conductor at the Carltheater in 1899, then moved on to the Volksoper, where he gave the Viennese premieres of *Salome* and *Tosca*. His star seemed to be rising under the patronage of Mahler, who appointed him as director of music at the Court Opera and planned the premiere of his next opera, *Der Traumgörge* (Görge the Dreamer). However, after numerous disagreements with the management, Mahler resigned in 1907, prompting Zemlinsky to walk out in protest. *Der Traumgörge* wasn't performed until 1980.

UNIVERSAL

Alexander Zemlinsky – the forgotten man of Viennese modernism

After another spell at the Volksoper, where his comic opera *Kleider machen Leute* (Clothes Make the Man) was performed, in 1911 Zemlinsky went to work at the Neues Deutches Theater in Prague, where he was to remain for sixteen years. Under his direction it became one of the most important opera houses in Europe – Stravinsky, usually highly restrained in his praise, described hearing Zemlinsky conduct Mozart as one of the most satisfying experiences of his life. This was the most successful period of Zemlinsky's life as a composer as well. It was in Prague that he wrote his best operas, *Ein florentinische Tragödie* and *Der Zwerg* (revised as *Der Geburtstag der Infantin*), as well as the *Lyric Symphony*, his most famous work. In 1927 he went to work with Otto Klemperer at the Kroll Opera in Berlin, where his last completed opera, *Der Kreidekreis* (The Chalk Circle), was performed in 1934, before being suppressed by the Nazis. Zemlinsky went first to Vienna, where he virtually completed *Der König Kandaules* (King Candaules), and then fled to America, where he died a forgotten man.

Es war einmal

Once Upon a Time

Composed 1897–99.
First performed January 22, 1900.
Libretto by Maximilian Singer, after Holger Drachmann and Hans Christian Andersen.

Synopsis

A Prince comes with his companion Kaspar as the latest in a long line of suitors for the hand of a Princess. Bored with the usual gushing praise, she rejects him. He decides to subdue her pride and win her over by disguising himself as a poor Gypsy and tricking her into loving him with the help of a magic kettle. When she finally realizes she loves the Gypsy, he reappears as the Prince and claims her as his bride. She refuses his riches, claiming she has found true love. Finally she discovers that he is her Gypsy lover after all, and they can become Prince and Princess as husband and wife.

Zemlinsky, along with many other opera composers of the period, had a predilection for fairy tales, with *Es war einmal*, *Der Traumgörge* and *Der Kreiderkreis* being the most obvious examples in his output. In *fin de siècle* Vienna these tales often came with subtexts – this was the city of Freud, after all – but in his early operas Zemlinsky's approach seems to be remarkably childlike and innocent. *Es war einmal* (based on Andersen's "The Swineheard") is presented as pure escapism, but the craft of the piece is remarkable and it contains some of Zemlinsky's most beautiful music. The orchestral writing is glitteringly transparent, with a prelude that transports the listener to a distant, fairy-tale land, while the vocal lines are lyrical and emotionally charged at the key moments. To avoid the danger of sickliness, Zemlinsky pokes fun from time to time, bringing out the boredom of the Princess and her father at the endless succession of suitors and creating a pantomime-like episode when the Prince and his companion disguise themselves as a Gypsy and his mother. The delightful music for the Princess and her companions in the palace gardens anticipates the music for the Infantin in Zemlinsky's more focused masterpiece, *Der Zwerg*.

While he was working on *Es war einmal*, Zemlinsky showed the score to Mahler, who was to conduct the premiere at the Vienna State Opera. Mahler suggested various alterations and reworked the finale of Act I himself. The closing bars are thus a rare example of surviving music composed for the stage by Mahler.

Johansson, Westi; Danish National Symphony Orchestra and Chorus; Graf.
(Capriccio 60 019-2; 2 CDs).

For the foreseeable future this is probably the only way to discover a score that deserves to be staged but never is. The Danish tenor and soprano Kurt Westi and Eva Johansson are excellent as the Prince and Princess, although his voice seems exaggerated and overstretched at moments. The supporting roles are good and the orchestral playing and balance make this a very fine recording.

Ein florentinische Tragödie

A Florentine Tragedy

Composed 1916.
First performed January 30, 1917.
Libretto by Max Meyerfeld, after Oscar Wilde.

Synopsis

Simone, a Florentine merchant, comes home to find his wife Bianca entertaining Guido Bardi, her lover. Simone feigns ignorance of the situation and uses the opportunity to sell Bardi some of his robes and fabrics. Guido and Bianca maintain a pretence of propriety until Simone leaves the room, whereupon the lovers embrace and Bianca urges him to kill her husband. As Guido takes his leave Simone hands him his sword and a duel begins. Simone kills Guido and, in a surprising twist, Bianca finds her love for Simone rekindled by his exploits.

The idea of emotional turmoil beneath a respectable exterior had a particular fascination for Viennese composers of this period: *A Florentine Tragedy* is one such psychological study, and Schreker's *Die Gezeichneten* is another (see p.403). For Zemlinsky there was also a highly personal dimension to the choice of plot, which has affinities with the relationship between Mathilde Schoenberg (Zemlinsky's sister) and the painter Richard Gerstl, who committed suicide in 1908 after Mathilde returned to her husband.

Like the opening of Strauss's *Der Rosenkavalier*, the opera begins with an extended orchestral prelude depicting the two lovers. Structurally, the opera somewhat resembles a Strauss tone-poem, as Zemlinsky ties the music together through a number of recurrent ideas linked to the themes of love and death, motifs that develop as the music moves through different moods. It turns darker from the moment Guido offers to buy Bianca, becomes more dramatic as Bianca urges Guido to kill Simone, and then flowers into glorious love music charged with shimmering violins. The duel at the end is like a rousing symphonic finale, and then Zemlinsky concludes his most concise and integrated operatic score by assigning Bianca and Simone the same music for the first time, a device that makes Bianca's volte-face believable rather than merely opportunistic. Gone is the ingenuous fairy-tale world of the composer's earlier operas. This is Zemlinsky packing a punch (or a sabre), and it leaves a powerful impression of dark, invidious and passionate forces.

Soffel, Riegel, Sarabia; Berlin Radio Symphony Orchestra; Albrecht.
(Koch Schwann CD 11625; 1 CD).

The conductor Gerd Albrecht has been one of the prime movers in the revival of Zemlinsky's operas and this is one of the finest introductions to his music. Appropriately enough, it's the bass, Guillermo Sarabia (Simone), who comes over most strongly here, revealing that ultimately he is master of the situation. Doris Soffel and Kenneth Riegel are well matched as the lovers, although Riegel's slightly eccentric voice is better suited to the dwarf (in *Der Geburtstag*) than Guido.

Der Zwerg / Der Geburtstag der Infantin

The Dwarf / The Infanta's Birthday

Composed 1921.
First performed May 28, 1922.
Libretto by Georg Klaren and Adolf Dresen, after Oscar Wilde.

Synopsis

It is the birthday of the Infanta of Spain and amongst her presents is a hideous dwarf. The dwarf, who has no idea how ugly he really is, is entranced by the Infanta's beauty. She plays him along and he attempts to kiss her. Ghita, her favourite maid, warns her not to be cruel. The Infanta dances with the dwarf and then leaves him alone. When he catches sight of himself in a mirror he realizes how hideous he is and dies of a broken heart. The Infanta says that next time she wants a toy without a heart and returns to the dance.

The power of this piece may derive from Zemlinsky's personal identification with its central character. An unprepossessing man, he fell in love with Alma Mahler, who uncharitably described him as a "horrid little dwarf – chinless, toothless and stinking of the coffee-houses". Wishing to write a piece about the "tragedy of the ugly man", he commissioned a libretto from Franz Schreker, who had composed a dance-pantomime based on the Wilde story in 1908; the resulting libretto became Schreker's own *Die Gezeichneten*, while Zemlinsky set a text that departs significantly from Wilde's story. Zemlinsky's Infanta is deliberately cruel, and the figure of the dwarf is a far more civilized being than Wilde's forest creature.

The music is permeated, as Berg said, by a "wonderful flow of glorious melody", and it was the composer's most successful opera in its day, with performances in Berlin, Prague and Vienna quickly following the Cologne premiere. Its weak point, though, was perceived to be Georg Klaren's flowery libretto, which was full of inconsequential details. So for the 1981 Hamburg revival a new libretto by Adolf Dresen was prepared, sticking much closer to Wilde's source story, *The Birthday of the Infanta*: although pretty much identical to *Der Zwerg* in musical terms, this version was renamed *Der Geburtstag der Infantin*.

The Infanta and her girlfriends at the court are characterized by an unemotional, neoclassical style of writing, very pretty, but brittle and diatonic, like a musical box. Ghita, the Infanta's maid, is given more lyrical and expressive music, but inevitably the emotional heart of the piece is in Zemlinsky's music for the dwarf. This is sublimely beautiful, with the searing melody and chromatic harmony of a cor anglais reflecting the dwarf's "natural" character.

"I know of no other composer since Wagner", wrote Schoenberg after Zemlinsky's death, "who was more competent at giving noble shape and substance to what the theatre needs. His ideas, his forms, sonorities and every turn of phrase are directly inspired by the dramatic action and the voice of the singer concerned, and have a clarity and precision of the very highest order." High praise indeed, and *The Birthday of the Infanta* earns it.

Nielsen, Riegel; Berlin Radio-Symphony Orchestra; Albrecht.
(Koch Schwann CD 11626; 1 CD).

As with all Zemlinsky's operas there is no alternative recording, but in this case no alternative is called for. Kenneth Riegel makes the role of the dwarf his own, Inga Nielsen is excellent as the Infanta, and the other roles are well cast (Cheryl Studer pops up as one of the Infanta's maids). Gerd Albrecht is very much at home in this quintessentially central European repertoire, and this piece offers a challenging series of atmospheric scenes which he brings off with great poetry and dramatic pacing.

Der Kreiderkreis

The Chalk Circle

Composed 1931–32.
First performed October 14, 1933.
Libretto by Zemlinsky after Klabund.

Synopsis

Act I

Haitang is sold by her widowed mother to work as a prostitute in a tea-house. There she is seen by Prince Pao, who falls in love with her, and Ma the wicked mandarin, who forced her father into suicide. Ma outbids Pao and takes her away.

Act II

Ma has become a better man through his love for Haitang and she has given him a son. Ma has turned away from his first wife Yu-Pei and she has grown to hate Haitang. When Yu-Pei discovers Ma is planning to alter his will in favour of Haitang, she poisons Ma and throws the suspicion on Haitang, who is arrested.

Act III

Yu-Pei bribes the judge, claims that the child is her own and that Haitang poisoned her husband. Haitang is condemned to die, but a messenger comes from Peking with news of the emperor's death. The new emperor, Pao, has suspended all death sentences and demands to hold the trial himself. He draws a chalk circle on the floor, places the child in the centre and instructs each wife to take one of the child's arms. The true mother will be the one who pulls the child out of the circle. Haitang lets go so as not to hurt the baby and shows herself to be the true mother. What's more, Emperor Pao confesses to Haitang that on the night she was sold to Ma he crept into the mandarin's house and made love to Haitang while she slept. She had thought it was only a dream, but in fact the child is the son of Haitang and the emperor; she is elevated to empress.

Klabund's play *Der Kreiderkreis* was a huge success in Berlin from 1925, thanks to a production by Max Reinhardt, and it became one of the most performed of German plays – to become even more famous in Brecht's version, *The Caucasian Chalk Circle*. Zemlinsky, with his predilection for fairy tales and dichotomies of good and evil, turned it into an opera that was scheduled to be premiered simultaneously in the opera houses of Berlin, Frankfurt and Cologne in the spring of 1933. It should have been the culmination of Zemlinsky's career, but it fell victim to the new Nazi cultural policies. In April 1933 the bosses at the opera houses in Berlin, Cologne, Dresden, Frankfurt, Hamburg, Leipzig and several other cities were sacked and several preformances cancelled, including *Der Kreiderkreis*. The premiere finally took place in Zürich in October 1933, although there was a production the following year at the Staatsoper in Berlin, where for a while the repertoire was less regimented than in other German opera houses.

Musically, the score is a radical departure from Zemlinsky's lush, lyrical style – here the musical language is sparer and winds predominate over the strings. The opening, set in the brothel-cum-tea-house, is quite remarkable: featuring tenor sax, clarinet, brushed cymbal and kettledrums, it is China evoked through the distorting mirror of cabaret Berlin.

Haitang has the lion's share of the expressive melodic lines (Pao gets some as well), but spoken or recitative-like parts predominate in the rest of the cast, which makes this opera rather uningratiating – indeed, the most compelling music comes in the orchestral preludes to the various scenes. Concluding with the message "Justice shall be your highest aim, that is the lesson of the Chalk Circle", this is a very serious-minded work, even if it lacks the passion of *Ein florentinische Tragödie* and *Der Geburtstag der Infantin*. You might well come away from it regretting that Zemlinsky didn't find a way of combining the brittleness of *Der Kreiderkreis* with the concision of his one-act operas, but many of Zemlinsky's latter-day advocates rate it very highly, and to get the measure of this intriguing composer you should at least give *Der Kreiderkreis* a listen.

Behle, Goldberg, Hermann, Ottenthal; Berlin Radio Symphony Orchestra; Soltesz.
(Capriccio 60 016-2; 2 CDs).

This is the only recording available of this opera, and Renate Behle in the central role of Haitang holds it together well. Stefan Soltesz makes the most of the drama and lyrical moments, and clearly enjoys the chinoiserie. The weak point is the exaggerated and flowery voice of Reiner Goldberg as Pao.

ARNOLD SCHOENBERG

b. VIENNA, SEPTEMBER 13, 1874; d. LOS ANGELES, JULY 13, 1951.

In 1909 Arnold Schoenberg wrote his *Three Pieces* for piano, Op. 11, the first wholly atonal music and arguably the most significant composition of the twentieth century. In these three epigramatic works, Schoenberg abandoned the traditional methods of musical expression – tonal centres, key signatures and the traditional application of harmony – in favour of one in which all the notes of the chromatic scale were assigned equal importance. It was the most radical departure from tradition in the history of western music, and even today there are many people who find his subsequent work violent and incomprehensible. His music demands a concentrated response, but perhaps the easiest route into Schoenberg's world is via his two main operas, *Ewartung* (Expectation) and *Moses und Aron*, which are creations of enormous immediacy and power.

Born in Vienna to Jewish parents, Schoenberg first learned the violin and cello and taught himself theory until 1894 when Alexander Zemlinsky – whose sister he later married – began instructing him in counterpoint. By the time he was twenty-five, Schoenberg had seen each of Wagner's operas more than twenty times and although his earliest music reflects an admiration for Brahms' classical discipline, Wagner's influence soon became all-consuming, as was clear from the opulent string sextet *Verklärte Nacht* and the grandiose choral work *Gurrelieder*. With the first part of the latter project under his arm he applied for a teaching post in Berlin. On Richard Strauss's recommendation he was accepted at the Stern Conservatory, where he stayed for three years, a period during which he composed his Straussian tone-poem *Pelléas und Mélisande*.

But whereas Strauss and Pfitzner seemed content to live off the harmonic legacy of Wagner, to Schoenberg it seemed evident that Wagnerian chromaticism had exhausted the conventional vocabularies without offering any way forward. Between 1900 and 1910 Schoenberg set off in a new direction: developing a style from which he gradually moved towards a more economical and increasingly personal musical language. With the *String Quartet No. 2*, written in 1907, he came to the brink of composing music that was in no identifiable key, and with the *Three Pieces* of 1909 he finally made the complete break with tonality, following it up, in the same year, with the bleak, atonal opera *Ewartung*.

LEBRECHT COLLECTION

Arnold Schoenberg

By the following year, Schoenberg and Strauss (by now estranged) were the *enfants terribles* of European music, but whereas Strauss was hugely successful, Schoenberg was the subject of venomous derision – though he had two devoted supporters in his pupils Anton Webern and Alban Berg (see p.405), the other members of what came to be known as the Second Viennese School. The Viennese premiere of *Pierrot Lunaire* in 1912 produced outright hostility, in marked contrast to the premiere of *Gurrelieder* later the same year, which was an unqualified success. Schoenberg served in the ranks during World War I and immediately after the war he returned to Vienna where, together with Berg and Webern, he organized and played in concerts of new music, events from which the critics of the Viennese press were barred. He composed little until 1924 when he announced his "re-emergence" with the creation of twelve-tone serialism, the method by which he brought order to the potential chaos of atonality. Whereas pure atonalism gave the composer the freedom to select notes at will from the entire chromatic scale, the twelve-tone technique arranged the twelve notes in a specific sequence (or tone-row) for each piece. The tone-row could be played note by note, simultaneously, even upside down, but no note could be repeated until the whole series had been played. By giving all twelve notes of the chromatic scale equal value, the conventional sense of movement to and from the tonic was eliminated, as it had been with atonalism, but this new method gave modern music a sense of focus that had been lacking in atonal compositions.

In 1925 Schoenberg moved to Berlin, where he taught composition at the Academy of Arts, but with the advent of Nazism he was dismissed from his post. He left Germany in 1933 and eventually emigrated to the United States, where he settled in Los Angeles and taught at the University of California. In the remaining years of his life he produced a large body of music in a range of styles. In 1944 he applied for a Guggenheim grant to allow him to complete *Moses und Aron*, which he had begun in 1930; his application was rejected, and he died leaving the third act incomplete.

Erwartung

Expectation

Composed 1909.
First performed June 6, 1924.
Libretto by Marie Pappenheim.

Synopsis

Scene I

In the moonlight, a woman approaches a forest looking for her lover. She enters the forest despite her feelings of fearful expectation.

Scene II

In the darkness, she feels something moving and hears weeping. Alarmed by a bird, she runs and trips over what she thinks is a body. Turning to look she sees that the body is just a tree trunk.

Scene III

The woman enters a clearing and is terrified by her own shadow. She calls for help but there is no response.

Scene IV

At the forest's edge, exhausted and tattered, the woman finds blood on herself. She stumbles across the body of her lover, and tries to awaken him. Imagining it is day and that the moonlight is sunlight, she lies down beside the man and kisses him. Veering from grief to anger she accuses him of infidelity and wonders what she is to do with her life. Eventually, she leaves.

Marie Pappenheim, the librettist of *Ewartung*, was a medical student as well as a poet, and her dramatized monologue has many of the qualities of a Freudian case history – without the analysis. The language is a terse and elusive stream of consciousness, and the listener has no way of measuring the veracity of what is being said since there is no-one with whom the woman interacts. The story, if it can be called that, emerges through fragments of information. The only thing that is clear is the sense of the woman's psychological dislocation and instability caused by the loss (real or imaginary) of the object of her love. Pappenheim's libretto was partly influenced by a terrible emotional crisis in the Schoenberg household. The year before *Ewartung* was begun, the painter Richard Gerstl – who taught both Schoenberg and his wife Mathilde – committed suicide after Mathilde had terminated her affair with him and returned to her husband.

Schoenberg worked on the opera at white-heat intensity, completing the draft score in just fifteen days, but so disturbed were producers and conductors by its music and psychological rawness that he had to wait until 1924 for the first performance, conducted by Zemlinsky in Prague. He matched the text perfectly with the most improvisatory and expressionistic music he ever wrote, and he set the text to an extreme form of *Sprechgesang* ("speech-song"), a style of expressive vocal declamation midway between speech and singing, in which the voice briefly touches the indicated pitch without sustaining it. The rapidity of the mood swings – moments of lucidity next to near-incoherence – are brilliantly communicated by the music's extraordinary rhythmic freedom, while the absence of a clear pulse, like the absence of tonality, contributes to a sensation of rootlessness and timelessness, as if the whole opera were taking place within the woman's head. The orchestra is large but the instruments are used in richly varied chamber-like combinations, rather than en masse, creating an atmospheric commentary on what is happening. Vocally, *Erwartung* is a *tour de force*, demanding a soprano with a capacity for tenderness and hysteria and the lung capacity to keep going for more than half an hour with scarcely a break.

Norman; New York Metropolitan Opera Orchestra; Levine.
(Philips 426 261-5PH; 1 CD).

The size of Jessye Norman's voice might have been thought too immense for the solo role of *Erwartung*, but this 1993 recording is a great achievement, beautiful and nightmarish at the same time. Levine succeeds not only in producing a luscious wash of sound from the Met Orchestra but also in highlighting the internal mechanics and overall structure of the score. This is harrowing music, but sung and played as dramatically as it is here, it makes an ideal introduction to the composer's more difficult work. It's accompanied by remarkably witty performances of Schoenberg's *Cabaret Songs*.

Moses und Aron

Composed 1930–32.
First performed March 12, 1954 (concert); June 6, 1957 (staged).
Libretto by the composer, after the Old Testament.

Synopsis

Act I

Moses is instructed by God, through the burning bush, to lead the Israelites from slavery in Egypt to the Promised Land. Moses fears his inadequacy but God tells him that his brother Aaron will be his mouthpiece. Moses and Aaron meet in the Wasteland and discuss their task; they are confronted by the increasingly doubtful Israelite priests who do not believe that Moses and his God will deliver them from Pharaoh. Moses begins to believe that he has failed in his task but Aaron takes his brother's staff and, in God's name, performs miracles. The Israelites are united but concerned that they will starve in the wilderness. Moses tells them that they will live off "pure contemplation", but Aaron promises that God will "turn the sand into fruit" – thus betraying Moses's ideals, but convincing the Israelites to follow Moses into the Wasteland.

Act II

At the foot of the Mountain of Revelation. The Israelites have grown uneasy in Moses' absence and despite Aaron's attempts at reassurance they threaten to kill the priests if Aaron does not help give their gods definable form. They dance before the Golden Calf which Aaron has created for them and embark on an orgy that leads to suicide, rape and murder. Moses comes down the mountain carrying the tablets of God's law and destroys the golden image. Terrified, the people flee, leaving Moses and Aaron alone. Aaron defends his actions by claiming that he was doing no more than was asked of him: interpreting Moses's word in terms they can understand. Infuriated, Moses sees the tablets as just another image and smashes one onto the rocks. As a pillar of fire leads the people onwards through the desert, Moses despairs.

Act III

Moses and Aaron are together, the latter in chains. Before the elders, Moses repeats his belief in the ideal nature of the Godhead and condemns Aaron's misrepresentation of that ideal. Eventually, Aaron is freed but as his chains drop to the floor, he dies.

An unresolved need for communication with God was central to Schoenberg's personality, and for most of his life he was racked by the problems of self-knowledge and religious belief. His regular conversions to and abandonment of Judaism were indicative of the anguish he suffered, and in *Moses und Aron* he wrestled with the issue of humanity's inability to deal with absolute truth – as given to Moses by God. The work was left incomplete at his death, not because of shortage of time, but because Schoenberg found it impossible to create music for the final act, in which Moses berates Aaron for his devotion to the Image rather than to the Idea. Schoenberg wrote in 1950 that he "agreed the third act may simply be spoken, in case I cannot complete the composition", but the first staged performance – supervised by the composer's widow and conducted by Hans Rosbaud – omitted the act completely, a solution that is perfectly convincing and is now standard practice.

Even incomplete, this is still Schoenberg's largest staged work and the most complete dramatic expression of his serialist techniques. The twelve-tone system, even when used with the flexibility that Schoenberg gives to it, brings with it a number of problems – primarily in the delineation of character, because the tone-row makes it difficult to construct distinct soundprints for each protagonist. But Schoenberg generates a dramatic charge by writing the baritone role of Moses in *Sprechgesang* while creating Aaron's part as a fully scored role for a very high tenor, as far from the style of Moses as could be imagined. As a result an almost delirious intensity is generated in the clashes between Moses, the believer in God as "pure thought", and Aaron, who doubts that anyone loves what "they dare not imagine". But although the drama hinges on their exchanges, and it is their relationship that drives the narrative, the musical interest is dominated by the huge chorus, part of which is used (in the form of six voices) to represent the voice of God. Indeed, there are few operas more dependent upon the skill of its chorus. Only in the Stravinskian "Dance around the Golden Calf" – where Schoenberg relieves the tension of the tone-row with music of sumptuous colour – does the orchestra dominate the proceedings. Otherwise, as with *Erwartung*, Schoenberg uses his orchestral forces with great economy, brilliantly controlling the contrasts of scale between the symphonic and the chamber-like. However, the music is so complex that Schoenberg doubted whether the opera would ever be performed, and it does need to be heard a number of times before even the most basic structural threads begin to reveal themselves. Yet for all the difficulty of the music, the emotional power of *Moses und Aron* is as direct as anything by any of Schoenberg's more traditional contemporaries.

RECORDINGS OVERVIEW

There are currently just three recordings of *Moses und Aron*, all of them on CD. The first was recorded in 1974, with Pierre Boulez conducting a vigorous cast headed by Richard Cassilly and Günter Reich; the second, and still the finest, was made just two years later; and the most recent was taped in 1984, conducted by the over-aggressive Georg Solti with a pressured cast. Pierre Boulez has re-recorded the opera for Deutsche Grammophon, and this set promises to be something special – especially for Chris Merritt's Aaron, for it's rarely the case that the role is assigned to a tenor with the necessary range, which Merritt certainly has.

Haseleu, Goldberg, Mróz, Krahmer; Leipzig Radio Chorus and Symphony Orchestra; Kegel.
(Berlin Classics 001162BC; 2 CDs).

Made in East Germany in 1976, this recording has only become more widely available relatively recently. It is a truly sensational performance, boasting two outstanding protagonists in Reiner Goldberg's powerful Aaron and Werner Haseleu's bleak and unsettling Moses. The frustration and anger of Moses as he returns from the mountain is one of the highlights, matched in intensity only by the exuberance of the "Dance around the Golden Calf". Kegel is attuned to the intricacies of the work but he manages to generate real dramatic momentum as well – never does the tension slack.

FRANZ SCHREKER

b. MONACO, MARCH 23, 1878; d. BERLIN, MARCH 21, 1934.

In the 1910s Franz Schreker was regarded as the third member of German music's avant-garde triumvirate, alongside Richard Strauss and Arnold Schoenberg. Nowadays he has become little more than a footnote to the history of modern music, even though his operas – especially *Der ferne Klang* (The Distant Sound) – are among the most intriguing works of the early twentieth century. At times reminiscent of both Richard Strauss and Debussy, Schreker creates an impressionistic sound-world of ever-changing moods and colours, a style perfectly suited to the post-Freudian psychology of his subjects. But if his music deserves to regain its former reputation, his lurid and overwrought libretti – which he wrote himself – have always had their critics.

Born in Monaco to Austrian parents, Schreker lived most of his life in Vienna where, in 1892, he was enrolled at the conservatory. He studied with Peter Fuchs, a friend of Brahms and the teacher of, among others, Sibelius, Mahler and Zemlinsky. As the founder-director of the Vienna Philharmonic Choir he received considerable attention as a musician, but his first success as a composer came in 1908 with *Der Geburtstag der Infantin* (The Birthday of the Infanta), a ballet based on a story by Oscar Wilde. Four years later the premiere of the first of his major operas, *Der ferne Klang*, established him as a leading modernist. Both Schoenberg and Berg expressed great admiration for the score, with the latter making a piano reduction of it. For a short time Schreker's influence on the development of new music was crucial. He conducted the premiere of Schoenberg's *Gurrelieder* in 1913, and in 1920 was appointed to the prestigious position of director of the Hochschule für Musik in Berlin, where he presided over an impressive teaching staff that included Hindemith.

Two more operas, both written during World War I, consolidated his reputation: *Die Gezeichneten* (The Branded Ones) and *Der*

Franz Schreker

Schatzgräber (The Treasure Seeker) were two of the most frequently performed operas of the immediate postwar period, but by the mid-1920s Schrecker's opulent style was rapidly going out of fashion as the more acerbic manner of composers like Weill and Hindemith began to find favour. He produced four more operas but his later works were not well received despite being championed by conductors of the calibre of Otto Klemperer and Erich Kleiber. The first performance of *Christophorus* in 1931 was cancelled as a result of Nazi pressure, but the premiere of *Der Schmied von Gent* (The Blacksmith of Ghent) the following year was allowed to continue – only to be shouted down by an anti-Semitic mob.

In 1932 the composer Max von Schillings became the new President of the Prussian Academy of Arts, accepting the task of purging the Academy of all "racially undesirable" members. Schreker was duly dismissed from his teaching post and he found himself at the mercy of some of modernism's most virulent opponents. Quite apart from any musical criticism, he was attacked for "sexual deviancy", with disastrous consequences. Condemned for his religion, his homosexuality and his music, Schreker suffered a fatal heart attack, dying just two days short of his fifty-sixth birthday. Only in very recent years has there been any serious attempt to reassess his achievements as an opera composer.

Der ferne Klang

The Distant Sound

Composed 1901–10.
First performed August 18, 1912.
Libretto by the composer.

Synopsis

Act I

Fritz, a musician, will not marry his beloved, Grete, until he has discovered the source of the "distant sound" that plagues his imagination. Grete's father, a drunkard with considerable debts, "loses" his daughter in a card game. Rather than marry the innkeeper who claims her, Grete runs away to the forest and contemplates suicide before a mysterious old woman appears, promising her wealth and happiness.

Act II

Ten years later, Grete has become a high-class prostitute, working in an elegant Venetian bordello. She continues to think lovingly of Fritz but nonetheless offers to marry whichever of her eager suitors sings the most affecting song. Fritz arrives and is astonished to find Grete there, but the moment he understands her profession, he abandons her once again.

Act III

Five years later at a cafe, the distant sounds of Fritz's new opera can be heard coming from the theatre across the street. Grete – now a street-walker – is helped from the theatre where she has been deeply moved by the music. As the audience emerges they complain of the opera's weak ending. Grete falls into a faint but when she hears of Fritz's illness she begs to see him. Fritz believes he has ruined Grete's life as well as his own but he is desperate to see her. When they finally meet, they fall into each other's arms and Fritz understands that the "distant sound" – the natural world, the power of love, Grete – was within his grasp all the time. He decides to rewrite the finale of his opera but dies in Grete's arms.

The incredible critical success of *Der ferne Klang* following its first performance in Frankfurt established Schreker as one of Germany's leading modernist composers. Retrospectively, however, it is possible to see why his prestige was short-lived, for this opera presents the acceptable face of modernism. The saturated texture and sometimes fussy internal decoration suggest an affection for Schoenberg's experiments, but *Der ferne Klang* is emphatically tonal: for all the daring of its subject matter and Schreker's advanced harmonic language, this is essentially a Romantic work, characterized by muscular instrumentation and almost boastful orchestration (sometimes a little overwhelming for Schreker's arioso vocal style) and extremely atmospheric sonorities that augment the moods and emotions of the protagonists. In terms of dissonance it is not as extreme as Strauss's *Elektra*. which was composed around the same time, and it was the opera's luxuriant and diaphanous textures that so appealed to contemporary audiences. One critic, William Ritter, described the music as "like the murmuring that can be heard in the inner recesses of sea shells . . . sounds of harps, sounds of spun glass, sounds of water-filled wine glasses stroked by a moistened finger".

But at the very heart of *Der ferne Klang* lies an ambivalence about such hyper-refinement: Fritz the composer seeks his inspiration in some exotic "distant sound", and his escape from the real world results in an opera that is rejected by its audience and in the rejection of the woman he loves. Obliged to face the harsh realities of life and try to make her own destiny, Grete is a much more modern character than the decadent Fritz, and it is in her story, rather than in the heady opulence of its music, that *Der ferne Klang* looks forward to one of the great monuments of modernism in opera – Berg's *Lulu*.

Schnaut, Moser, Nimsgern, Helm; Berlin Radio Chorus and Symphony Orchestra; Albrecht.
(Capriccio 60 024-2; 2 CDs).

There are two recordings of *Der ferne Klang* but Gerd Albrecht's is preferable in most respects, with a rich, indulgent sound and a fine orchestra, to whom the music is clearly second nature. Gabriele Schnaut is a powerful, chesty mezzo and she copes well with Grete's difficult music. Thomas Moser is reliable in the baritone role of Fritz but no more, and the remaining cast all give solid – if not top-flight – performances, clearly relishing the rich ensemble writing. Albrecht's affinity for this music is always apparent and his conducting is the recording's main appeal.

Die Gezeichneten

The Branded Ones

Composed 1913–18.
First performed April 25, 1918.
Libretto by the composer.

Synopsis

Act I

The hunchbacked nobleman, Alviano Salvago, is obsessed with his own ugliness. He has created an island pleasure garden, "Elysium", which he plans to donate to the people of Genoa. In an underground grotto on the island, young noblemen, among them Vitelozzo Tamare, hold orgies with women abducted from the city. Tamare is in love with Carlotta, the consumptive daughter of the mayor, who is more fascinated by Alviano and wishes to paint his portrait.

Act II

Tamare is determined to seduce Carlotta and decides to take her by force if necessary. While painting Alviano, Carlotta confesses her love for him. Alviano is overwhelmed but restrains himself and in that one moment of ecstacy she finishes the portrait.

Act III

The people of Genoa visit the island of Elysium. Alviano is now their hero but Carlotta is no longer interested in him. Carlotta is seduced by Tamare and taken to the grotto. The police arrive and denounce Alviano, who leads them to the grotto, where he discovers the lovers. Alviano kills Tamare but is then rejected by the weakened Carlotta, who dies calling for Tamare. Alviano goes mad.

The idea for *Die Gezeichneten* was not Schreker's own: in 1911 Alexander Zemlinsky (see p.395) had asked him for a text about "the tragedy of the ugly man" along the lines of Oscar Wilde's story *The Birthday of the Infanta*, which Schreker had set as a ballet in 1909. Having complied, Schreker decided to set the text himself, and worked on it throughout World War I. Before starting work on *Die Gezeichneten* Schreker conducted careful research into Renaissance Genoa, where the opera is set, but the period setting never really tallies with Schreker's main concerns, which are pathological sexuality and the spiritual isolation of physical disfigurement. The extraordinary reaction to *Die Gezeichneten* – there were more than twenty productions throughout Germany and Austria before the opera was banned in 1933 – suggests that its emotive depiction of moral stagnation through music of almost mystical euphoria struck a profound chord in war-ravaged Germany. One critic called it a "grand mental and moral house-cleaning in Germany".

The mood of *Die Gezeichneten* is immediately established by the opera's remarkable prelude, which alone deserves to guarantee its composer's reputation. It opens with a mysteriously shimmering chord before stating the main leitmotifs of the opera, motifs that evoke as much by dazzling orchestral colour as by melody. The orchestra remains the main musical protagonist, with the solo voices mostly adopting a free-flowing parlando style which is wrapped around by delicate and evocative instrumental detailing. This reaches a thrilling climax in Act I, with Carlotta telling Alviano of her desire to paint his picture in ever more fervent and soaring tones. Thinking that he is at last loved, Alviano is overwhelmed, but Carlotta's feelings arise from a mixture of her own suppressed desires and an idealization of Alviano's plight. As in *Der ferne Klang*, throughout this opera there is an implicit critique of art – and indeed the pursuit of pleasure – as some kind of escape from reality, and as such *Die Gezeichneten* makes an interesting parallel with the contemporary *Doktor Faust* of Busoni (see p.429), although that opera ends with at least some kind of hope for the future.

As with Faust, the narrative construction of *Die Gezeichneten* is at times haphazard, and the last act, set on the pleasure island, is especially fractured and kaleidoscopic (or demented), as the line between fantasy and reality becomes ever more blurred: nobles leap out of bushes disguised as fauns, the good burghers of Genoa call enthusiastically for Alviano, who ignores them as he desperately searches for Carlotta. In the opera house it would be a producer's nightmare, and it's a measure of Schreker's brilliance that his music makes the whole absurd situation so compelling.

Kruse, Connell, Pederson, Muff; Berlin Radio Chorus; Berlin Symphony Orchestra; Zagrosek.
(Decca 444 442-2; 2 CDs).

This is one of the highlights of Decca's "Entartate Musik" (Degenerate Music) series, even if Zagrosek tends to wallow in the instrumental textures to the detriment of the opera's shape – the overture, for example, is never allowed to take off in the way it should. However, the conductor's ear for sonorities is magnificent, and he provides excellent support for his cast. Heinz Kruse is a Wagner tenor in the making and he throws himself into the role of Alviano, tackling the high tessitura with ease and confidence, while Monte Pederson clearly enjoys the Tamare's devil-may-care recklessness. The highlight of the set, however, is Elizabeth Connell's glorious portrayal of Carlotta, which captures her rise to and fall from emotional freedom with exquisite tenderness and strength.

ALBAN BERG

b. VIENNA, FEBRUARY 9, 1885; d. VIENNA, DECEMBER 24, 1935.

In the midst of the experimentations of the modernist era, Alban Berg was one of the few to cultivate a musical language that was both highly original and immediately communicative. Berg's music is usually grouped with that of Schoenberg and Webern under the heading of the Second Viennese School, but he was never as doctrinaire as his colleagues and many of his compositions – notably his two operas, *Wozzeck* and *Lulu* – reveal a strong affinity with the more refulgent sound-worlds of Richard Strauss and Gustav Mahler.

Berg was born into a wealthy and highly cultured Viennese family. Despite the absence of any formal musical education, he began to compose songs when he was fifteen and in 1904, on the strength of his intellect rather than his musical talent, he was accepted as a student by Schoenberg. As a composer Schoenberg was a radical innovator, but as a teacher he believed in a traditionally thorough grounding in harmony and counterpoint. Even so both Berg and Anton Webern – a student at the same period – came to share Schoenberg's enthusiasm for the expressive possibilities inherent in atonality. With the *String Quartet* of 1910, the last score to be written under Schoenberg's guidance, Berg reached maturity as a composer, bringing an immediately identifiable approach to this new musical language. Even though a performance of two of his *Altenberg Lieder* in 1913 was brought to a close by the audience's rioting, Berg's flexible, expansive and above all lyrical version of atonality was soon attracting critical praise.

LEBRECHT COLLECTION

Berg at work

In May 1914 Berg saw a performance of George Büchner's *Woyzeck*, a fragmentary, proto-Expressionist drama that was in turn based on a true story. Berg was so impressed that he instantly determined to make the play the subject of his first opera. His efforts were interrupted by military service but in 1921 he finally completed *Wozzeck*, a piece that's generally regarded as his greatest score. Extracts were performed in Frankfurt in 1924 but the first staging – with an unprecedented amount of artistic control in the hands of the composer – took place a year later at the Berlin Staatsoper, conducted by Erich Kleiber. The *succès de scandale* of *Wozzeck* brought Berg international recognition, and he settled into a period of intense creativity.

In searching for a suitable text for his next opera he first considered Gerhart Hauptmann's play *Und Pippa tanzt* (which Schoenberg had once thought of setting) before finally settling on the sexually daring "Lulu" plays of Frank Wedekind – *Der Erdgeist* (Earthspirit) and *Die Busche der Pandora* (Pandora's Box). By 1934 the short score of *Lulu* was finished, but before completing the orchestration he was moved to write his *Concerto for Violin* to commemorate the death of Manon Gropius, the eighteen-year-old daughter of his close friend Alma Mahler. The effort severely weakened him, and just four months later he died – through blood poisoning from an insect bite. On hearing the news, Schoenberg wrote to Webern that the greatest of their number had died and that they were "now alone".

For all his modernity, Berg was also a traditionalist: his music preserves the foundations of diatonic melody, often includes quotations from the work of others – including Bach and Wagner – and relies heavily upon classical notions of structure. His genius was perhaps best summarized by Stravinsky when he wrote: "the essence of his work is thematic structure, and the thematic structure is responsible for the immediacy of the form. . . however 'mathematical' these forms are, they are always born of pure feeling and expression."

Wozzeck

Composed 1914–21.
First performed December 14, 1925.
Libretto by the composer, after Büchner.

Synopsis

Act I

Wozzeck, a soldier, is shaving the Captain, who despises him. Wozzeck is resigned to his superior's lecturing, only responding when the Captain questions his morality. Quoting the Bible, Wozzeck defends himself as one of the "poor folk". In a field outside the town Wozzeck and his friend Andres chop sticks. Wozzeck is alarmed by odd sounds and half-visions. Wozzeck's mistress Marie flirts with a passing Drum-Major; her neighbour Margret comments on Marie's interest in the Drum-Major. A doctor is experimenting on Wozzeck, who tells him of his visions; the Doctor is so pleased that he gives Wozzeck a raise. Meanwhile at home, Marie invites the Drum-Major into the house.

Act II

In her room, Marie admires the earrings given to her by the Drum-Major. Wozzeck enters and wonders where she got them. He hands over his pay and leaves Marie. In a side street the Captain meets the Doctor; as Wozzeck passes, they hint at Marie's infidelity. Wozzeck goes to her house and confronts her, but she denies the allegation. Watched by Wozzeck, Marie dances with the Drum-Major in a tavern garden. An idiot reads the future and smells blood on Wozzeck. In his bed at the barracks, Wozzeck is plagued by visions of a flashing blade and the sound of voices. The Drum-Major enters, boasting of his "conquest" of Marie. Attacking the Drum-Major, Wozzeck is knocked to the floor and beaten.

Act III

In her room, Marie reads to her child from the Bible. Later Wozzeck and Marie are out walking. Wozzeck stabs Marie in the throat. At an inn, Wozzeck is trying to drown his sorrows, but Margret draws people's attention to the blood on his hand. He runs to a pond, into which he throws the murder weapon. However, frightened by the blood-red moon, he goes to fetch the weapon in order to throw it deeper into the pond and drowns. Passing by, the Captain and Doctor are disturbed by the sound of the drowning man and move on. Outside Marie's door, her child is playing with his hobby-horse; the other children begin to taunt him with news of his mother's death.

Georg Büchner's play – which was more than seventy years old when Berg first saw it – is a powerful indictment of military brutality and a painful unravelling of the social pressures that might lead an ordinary man to murder. Berg used it more or less word for word as his libretto, telescoping the action into fifteen fast-moving cinematic scenes, with often just seconds of music joining them. Each of the characters is sharply drawn, and each adult is to some extent implicated in Wozzeck's tragedy. Only the child is innocent, but with his mother dead, the other children predict that he too is doomed to a life of pain and submission. It was this fatalistic conclusion, as much as the abrasively modern music, that angered the Nazis, who banned the opera in 1933.

Wozzeck is Berg's most Expressionistic work, with a largely dissonant score that creates an atmosphere of mounting paranoia and oppressiveness. But the music is more varied than such a summary suggests, for there are outbreaks of a more reassuring and lyrical style – in Marie's lullaby, for instance – as well as a Mahlerian tendency to parody simple musical styles for ironic effect, above all in the nightmarish tavern scene. Throughout the work Berg makes brilliantly subtle use of *Sprechgesang*, a type of speech-song in which the rhythm and pitch of every note is carefully prescribed. Unlike Schoenberg's harsh use of the technique in *Pierrot Lunaire*, however, Berg's approach favours a more fluid vocal manner which leaves the choice of tonal colour up to the performer.

The three acts (lasting one and a half hours) are performed without intervals, with terse orchestral interludes played during scene changes. Berg makes use of certain musical forms, such as a sonata or a fugue, to unify each component of the individual scenes, and employs leitmotifs to tie the whole work together. The most prominent motif is the one associated with Wozzeck's predicament as a poor man who cannot afford morality – a motif that acquires new potency in the final interlude, a luscious post-Romantic summation of the entire tragedy. To respond to *Wozzeck*, however, it's not necessary to be able to detect this painstaking structural cohesion. In fact, the composer insisted that "No matter how thorough one's knowledge of the musical forms which are to be found within the opera. . . from the moment when the curtain rises until it falls for the last time, nobody in the audience ought to notice anything of these forms – everyone should be filled only by the idea of the opera, an idea which far transcends the individual fate of Wozzeck."

RECORDINGS OVERVIEW

Eric Kleiber recorded only extracts from the score he premiered, and the first complete recording of *Wozzeck* was made live in New York in 1951, with Mitropolous conducting an error-strewn performance, but one in which the atmosphere (and tangible audience hostility) is remarkable. The first studio recording was made in 1965 by one of the composer's greatest champions, Karl Böhm, and this was followed by Pierre Boulez's 1966 CBS set, notable for the Wozzeck of Walter Berry. Abbado's 1979 recording for Deutsche Grammophon is overcalculated, and with Boulez's recording currently unavailable, the choice rests between Böhm and Dohnányi – though that may change with the release of Daniel Barenboim's eagerly awaited account on Teldec.

Waechter, Silja, Winkler, Laubenthal, Zednik; Vienna State Opera Chorus; Vienna Philharmonic; Dohnányi.
(Decca 417 348-2DH2; 2 CDs).

Eberhard Waechter's portrayal of Wozzeck is an apocalyptic vision of fear and desperation. His attention to pitch is extremely conscientious and through varying the quality of his voice he gives a chilling impression of Wozzeck's instability without falling to the sort of barking and wailing found on some other recordings. Anja Silja's Marie, a powerfully lyrical portrayal, is perfectly suited to Dohnányi's viscerally exciting view of the score. The excellent engineering brings orchestra and voices into ideal focus.

Fischer-Dieskau, Lear, Melchert, Wunderlich, Stolze; Berlin Deutsche Opera Chorus and Orchestra; Böhm.
(Deutsche Grammophon 435 705-2GX3; 3 CDs; includes *Lulu*).

Brilliant, glowing textures abound in this benchmark Berlin production. Böhm's tempi may be slow – and there is clearly some tension between stage and pit – but from start to finish the performance is marked by his conviction that the pain and suffering of Wozzeck are revealed as clearly through the orchestral score as through the solo writing. The casting is almost ideal – with lyric tenor Fritz Wunderlich in the role of Andres – and the only slight failing comes with Fischer-Dieskau's baritone, which is simply too healthy and suave for the role of Wozzeck. The accompanying performance of Berg's incomplete draft of *Lulu* makes this a very valuable set.

Lulu

Composed 1928–35.
First performed June 2, 1937 (incomplete); February 24, 1979 (completed by Friedrich Cerha).
Libretto by the composer, after Wedekind.

Synopsis

The Prologue

The Animal Trainer presents the animals in his menagerie. The snake, represented by Lulu, appears last.

Act I

Lulu is having her portrait painted, watched by Dr Schön. Left alone, the Painter attempts to seduce Lulu; as he drags her to the floor her elderly husband, Dr Goll, beats down the door. Finding them together, he has a stroke and dies. The Painter takes advantage of Lulu's shock.

The Painter, now wealthy, has married Lulu. The front doorbell rings, announcing the arrival of Schigolch, a decrepit old tramp who may be Lulu's father. Schön arrives, wishing to break off the affair that he has been having with Lulu. He confesses as much to the Painter, who then kills himself. As Schön calls the police, Lulu insists that he marry her.

At the theatre where she performs, Lulu tells Schön that she is planning to marry a Prince; when he hears the news Schön breaks off his own engagement and agrees to marry Lulu.

Act II

At the home of Schön and Lulu, the lesbian Countess Geschwitz arrives to invite Lulu to a ball but is told to leave by Schön. While Schön is out, several of Lulu's admirers arrive, including Schigolch, Schön's son Alwa, the Countess and a schoolboy. Alwa confesses his love for Lulu. Schön returns, brandishing a pistol. He takes Alwa outside and returns, handing Lulu the pistol and telling her to kill herself. Schön discovers the Countess and locks her in a room; when he returns to demand Lulu commit suicide, she kills him.

Interlude: A silent film shows Lulu's arrest, trial, conviction, imprisonment and escape, disguised as the Countess. Lulu deliberately contracts cholera but eventually she and Alwa declare their love.

Act III

In a Parisian casino, Lulu is threatened by a Marquis with life as a prostitute, but she escapes with Alwa to London where, nonetheless, she lives as a prostitute. Alwa and Schigolch await her return with a client, the Professor; while he and Lulu are together, they go through his pockets. After the Professor leaves, the Countess enters with the portrait of Lulu painted in the first scene. Lulu returns, with another client, who kills Alwa over a disagreement about money. The Countess leaves, then returns threatening suicide. Lulu enters with a third client, Jack the Ripper, who murders Lulu and then the Countess.

While Strauss's *Salome* epitomizes the fantasy of the destructive allure of female sexuality, Berg's *Lulu* is a rather more complex and less paranoiac representation of that *fin de siècle* archetype, the *femme fatale*. Frank Wedekind's plays were regarded as so shocking that they were banned in Germany between 1905 and 1918. Berg first saw them in a private performance in 1905, and immediately recognized a world-view that was congruent with his own, and which he later sketched in a letter to his fiancée Helene Nahowski: "sensuality is not a weakness, does not mean a surrender to one's own will. Rather it is an immense strength – the pivot of all our being and thinking." If the world is a menagerie, as the opening of *Lulu* suggests, then sexuality is the wheel that turns it. But the character of Lulu, unlike Don Giovanni, is an amoral representation of the pleasure principle – she is the embodiment of pure desire rather than of immoral transgression. Moreover Lulu, though in many ways inscrutable in her motives, is a self-determining woman, and it is her very independence, her refusal to abide by the rules of men, that leads to her death. Karl Kraus, who produced the first staging of the opera, was adamant that Lulu was the real victim of a text he described as "the tragedy of the hounded and eternally misunderstood grace of woman, permitted by a benighted world only to climb into the Procrustean bed of its own moral concepts".

Berg decided to stick closely to Wedekind's text, a decision that almost overloads the opera with a host of demi-monde archetypes: bloated plutocrat, aspiring artist, down-and-out, etc. As in *Wozzeck*, Berg imparts cohesion to this melée through a wealth of structural devices – sonata form, rondo, variations – that make connections which operate principally on a subliminal level. Only the most skilled can consciously detect all these constructions underneath the welter of sound, but the opera's cohesion depends to a great extent upon them, and upon the less covert operation of the various leitmotifs that guide the audience through the maze of counterpoint and tone-rows. If you study the score of Lulu it appears as something of a masterclass in compositional technique; heard in the theatre or on record, its impact derives from its almost overwhelming sonic richness, as it ranges from Straussian full-orchestra density to pared-down cabaret-style instrumentation – indeed Stravinsky once identified "... the saxophone's juvenile-delinquent personality" as the key component of "the vast decadence of *Lulu*".

When Berg died with only four-fifths of the orchestration for *Lulu* complete, his widow asked Schoenberg and then Webern to complete the work, but neither was prepared to accept the responsibility. After their refusal, she became emphatically opposed to the completion of the opera, and at the Zurich premiere only fragments of the last act were performed, to which the singers mimed. This proved a disappointment, for the last act was crucial to Berg's original plan – Lulu was to form a musical and dramatic arch, with characters and music from the earlier parts of the opera returning at the close, where Lulu's three customers were to be played by the same singers as her earlier lovers. Only after Hélène Berg's death in 1976 was the opera completed by Friedrich Cerha; the first full performance was given at the Paris Opéra by Pierre Boulez in 1979.

RECORDINGS OVERVIEW

Though the Boulez version of *Lulu* is the clear first choice, the other performances in the catalogue are also worth investigating. Karl Böhm's live recording is of the incomplete text and has some irritating extraneous noises, but it's a sensitive and superbly sung performance, and comes coupled with his superb *Wozzeck* (see p.407). Christoph von Dohnányi's 1976 production for Decca (currently out of the catalogue, but you might find copies lying around) is notable for Anja Silja's title performance and the virtuosity of the Vienna Philharmonic, while EMI's 1991 set, recorded live with Jeffrey Tate conducting, is an intense reading which would head the field if it weren't for Boulez.

Stratas, Mazura, Riegel, Minton, Tear; Paris Opera Orchestra; Boulez.
(Deutsche Grammophon 415 489-2GH3; 3 CDs).

Pierre Boulez's studio recording of *Lulu*, made in the wake of his stupendous premiere of the completed opera in Paris, is one of the highlights of his conducting career – there is a freedom and spontaneity to the performance, an ease and inevitability to the changes of pacing and the subtleties of rubato that is simply breathtaking. Teresa Stratas was famous for playing neurotic heroines and, like Anja Silja, she has long been associated with Lulu. Her interpretation is exceptional, and the supporting cast more than rise to the challenge, especially Gerd Nienstedt, whose performance as the Animal Trainer is successfully disgusting. Thrillingly played, richly recorded, this ranks as one of the classic recordings of twentieth-century music.

PAUL HINDEMITH

b. HANAU, GERMANY, NOVEMBER 16, 1895; d. FRANKFURT, DECEMBER 28, 1963.

Paul Hindemith was one of the twentieth century's greatest musical polymaths, equally adept as string player, conductor, theorist and composer. His style was similarly varied, ranging from the dense Expressionism of his early one-act operas to the sinewy contrapuntalism of his neo-Baroque maturity. Like several of his fellow composers during the inter-war period, Hindemith saw himself as an opponent of bourgeois culture, with a political commitment to the idea of making music that was direct and accessible ("for people with ears my stuff is really easy to grasp"), and throughout his life he wrote regularly and extensively for amateurs. His standing as one of the seminal figures of modern music was partly undermined by his extraordinary facility (it took him less than six hours to write *Trauermusik* to commemorate George V's death) and by his stylistic diversity, but if his reputation sharply declined at his death, it has undergone a steady reappraisal since the late 1980s, with *Mathis der Maler* once more appearing on opera-house stages and recording schedules.

Hindemith came from a poor, working-class background but his father, recognizing his children's talent, had them coached in music: Paul and his sister Toni learnt the violin and their younger brother Rudolph learnt the cello. Between 1909 and 1914 Paul studied at the Hoch Conservatory in Frankfurt and then, at the start of the war, got a job in the Frankfurt Opera orchestra and the position of second violinist in the string quartet of his teacher, Adolf Rebner. It was while at the Frankfurt Opera that Hindemith came to the attention of the conductor Fritz Busch, who was looking for new operas by up-and-coming composers. Busch gave the premieres of Hindemith's first two operas, *Mörder, Hoffnung der Frauen* (Murder, Hope of Women) and *Das Nusch-Nuschi* at Stuttgart in 1921. Both were extreme works, the first a setting of a violent play by the Expressionist painter Oscar Kokoscha, the second containing a castration scene. Busch drew the line at conducting Hindemith's third one-act opera, *Sancta Susanna*, which centred on the sexual fantasies of a young nun.

Such shock tactics made Hindemith's name but in the 1920s he began to review his musical language, gradually developing a more disciplined style based on Baroque composers like J.S. Bach, which first appeared in *Kammermusik No. 1* of 1921 and can be heard in his fourth opera *Cardillac*. His ability to startle, however, had not deserted him: *Neues vom Tage* (News of the Day, 1929) was, like the near-contemporary *Intermezzo* of Strauss and *Von Heute auf Morgen* of Schoenberg, an opera about the disintegrating relationship of a married couple. Unlike the other two, it had a scene featuring the wife in her bath (which upset Hitler) as well as a fashionable jazz element to the score. Hindemith then undertook another change of direction, writing a series of staged cantatas (including *Lehrstück*, with a text by Brecht) in which thinly disguised political messages were set to archly neo-Baroque music. None of this endeared him to the Nazis when they came to power in 1933 and they began what was at first a sporadic campaign of denigration. This was the climate in which his opera *Mathis der Maler* was written.

Like *Cardillac*, *Mathis der Maler* addressed the subject of the artist's relationship to his own work and to society, but it was also a highly emotional reaction by Hindemith to the violence and oppression that surrounded him. The possibility of its being staged in Germany was always remote, and Hindemith's standing became even more precarious when in November 1934 the conductor Furtwängler published a vigorous defence of him, ending his article by questioning the Nazis' right to censure artistic activity. The successful premiere of the symphony that Hindemith wrote for Furtwängler, using material from the opera, further irked Hitler and his followers.

In 1937, following a complete ban on his music, Hindemith left Germany for Switzerland, where *Mathis der Maler* was premiered in 1938. Two years later he moved to the USA, becoming a professor at Yale (where he organized a performance of Monteverdi's *Orfeo*) and taking American citizenship in 1946. He composed two further operas: *Die Harmonie der Welt* (The Harmony of the World, 1957), about the life of the Renaissance astronomer Johannes Kepler, and *The Long Christmas Dinner* (1961), to an English libretto by Thornton Wilder. Neither has succeeded in entering the repertoire.

LEBRECHT COLLECTION

Paul Hindemith photographed at Yale in 1942

THE KROLLOPER

The hugely influential **Berlin Krolloper** was built in 1844 by the entrepreneur Josef Kroll, who intended it to be used for nothing more than puppet shows and popular plays. But the fine acoustics and large stage made it ideal for opera, and during the 1850s it became a venue for the work of composers like Lortzing (who gave famous performances of *Zar und Zimmerman* and *Undine* here) and performances by touring stars like Adelina Patti. In 1927, however, the Krolloper changed direction when the far-sighted Prussian Ministry of Culture decided to fund a showcase for new music and production techniques, and awarded the contract to the Krolloper, under the artistic directorship of the conductor **Otto Klemperer**. The conductor's contract stated that he was to "establish the Kroll with its own ensemble on as independent a basis as possible", but no-one could have predicted the lengths to which Klemperer would go in his quest for artistic autonomy.

Having tuned down the directorship of the Berlin Staatsoper in 1921 because of his refusal to accept artistic interference, he determined to make the Kroll his own, and one of his first moves was to engage Alexander Zemlinsky and Fritz Zweig as assistant conductors and the radical artist Ewald Dülberg as his designer. He then set about "diverting a river through the filth of the repertoire system", concentrating on establishing a solid company with whom he could produce both new and old works with ample rehearsal time. Determined to bring an end to the naturalistic production style inherited from the nineteenth century, Klemperer allowed Dülberg a free hand in designing the staging of his first show, Beethoven's *Fidelio*.

The rehearsals lasted three months, and by the time the first night came around, the cast and orchestra were, as one critic noted, "wonderfully drilled". But the severity of the sets was not to everyone's liking, and neither was Klemperer's emphasis on the liberation of the masses rather than on the individual victory of Leonore. When one writer suggested that Klemperer simply didn't understand Beethoven's masterpiece, the conductor replied that his modern-dress production of Beethoven was nothing compared to what he had in store. First off he mounted a daring production of a Stravinsky triple-bill, consisting of *Marva*, *Oedipus Rex* and *Petrushka*. This he followed up with productions of Hindemith's *Cardillac* and *Neues vom Tage*, Schoenberg's *Erwartung* and *Die glückliche Hand*, Janáček's *From the House of the Dead* and Weill's *Der Jasager* and *Royal Palace*.

All this modern stuff was startling enough, but it was the Krolloper's radical 1929 production of Wagner's *Der fliegende Holländer* that left the deepest mark on German operatic life. Departing completely from Wagner's explicit staging instructions, Klemperer provoked so furious a reaction from the self-appointed guardians of the German tradition that two hundred police officers were sent to the theatre on January 15, the night of the premiere, to prevent Nazi thugs from smashing the place to pieces. The *Allgemeine Musikzeitung* led the critical onslaught: the Dutchman looked like "a Bolshevist agitator", Senta was "a fanatical Communist harridan", Erik "a pimp" and Daland's crew resembled "port vagabonds". It was, in short, "a total destruction of Wagner's work". In fact, it was a triumph of experimental theatre, and its impact was such that it is now considered the forerunner of Wieland Wagner's amazing postwar Bayreuth productions.

Klemperer and his theatre continued to promote contemporary music and avant-garde theatre for as long as their subsidy remained, but it was inevitable that the constant press criticism, the Machiavellian antics of the reactionary rival opera-house boss Heinz Tietjen ("that terrible, terrible man" as Klemperer called him) and the growing pressure from the Right would eventually take their toll. Just four years after taking over, Klemperer was moved sideways to the Staatsoper and the Kroll was closed. In April 1933, as the Nazis began hounding Jews and radicals, Klemperer emigrated. Many years later, he was asked if he thought he had succeeded as director of the Kroll: "No. It was only a beginning . . . you can't build a palace in four years," he commented. Even so, it was one of the greatest and most adventurous centres of activity in the history of opera, and it set an example to which most modern managers and producers can only aspire.

Cardillac

Composed 1926; revised 1952.
First performed November 9, 1926.
Libretto by Ferdinand Lion after E.T.A. Hoffmann.

Synopsis

Act I

Paris, late seventeenth century. The goldsmith Cardillac is so mesmerized by his own work that he cannot bear to part with it. Whenever customers persuade him to sell a piece, he kills them in order to retrieve it. The crimes have created turmoil in the city and people have begun to suspect the jeweller. A Lady offers her favours to a Cavalier in exchange for a piece of Cardillac's jewellery. When the Cavalier brings a golden belt to her rooms, a stranger bursts through the window, kills him and steals the belt.

Act II

Cardillac receives a visit from a gold merchant who suspects the jeweller might be the murderer. Cardillac's daughter intends to elope with an Officer. The King and his entourage visit the shop but are rudely treated by Cardillac. Cardillac consents to his daughter's marriage and the Officer insists on buying a gold chain from him but is then followed out of the shop.

Act III

The Officer is attacked and wounded but he recognizes his assailant as his future father-in-law. The Officer refuses to denounce Cardillac and tries to blame the attack on the gold merchant. When Cardillac eventually confesses, he is killed by the crowd.

Cardillac was Hindemith's first full-length opera, and in the spirit of the anti-Romantic aesthetic of the German avant-garde he composed it as an old-fashioned "numbers" opera in three acts, scored for a large chamber-orchestra rather than for a Wagnerian assembly. The music is spartan, with a neo-Baroque delicacy that generates its moments of drama almost exclusively through sudden and unlikely contrasts (particularly between strings and wind) but spreads a palpable air of tension and unease over the whole work, right from the opening prelude prior to the arrival of the crowd. The *Grand Guignol*, melodramatic story – derived from a tale by the arch-Romantic E.T.A. Hoffmann (see p.135) – would have lent itself well to Hindemith's earlier Expressionist style, but by opting for a more austere and antiquated manner Hindemith achieved a distance from his material that's akin to Brecht's "alienation effect", a quality that is at its most calculated in the Act I "pantomime", where an extended flute duet takes the place of the expected love duet between the Cavalier and the Lady.

Cardillac's psychopathology makes an intriguing comparison with the more human and rational hero of Hindemith's next opera, *Mathis der Maler* – the one is an almost solipsistic obsessive, while the other acknowledges his connection to a world outside of himself. In both characters there is a mixture of the flawed and the heroic, but it is significant that in his post-war revision of *Cardillac*, Hindemith attempted to make his protagonist less of a type and more of a person. However, the earlier version of the opera is dramatically stronger (for one thing, Hindemith lumbered the revision with an unnecessary arrangement of music by Lully), and it's not as frigid and cerebral as some critics maintain. Indeed the opera culminates in an exceptionally beautiful and moving passacaglia: Cardillac's daughter and the Officer have broken through the mob to find the jeweller on the edge of death; as they raise him up a shudder of life passes through the jeweller's broken body and, raising his head, he moves to kiss, not his daughter, but his chain. The passacaglia ends with a lush lament for his death, in marked contrast to the stringent polyphony that characterizes the rest of the work.

Fischer-Dieskau, Kirchstein, Grobe, Kohn; Cologne Radio Chorus and Symphony Orchestra; Keilberth.
(Deutsche Grammophon 431 741-2GC2; 2 CDs).

This recording of the original version of *Cardillac* was taken from a 1960s radio broadcast and it captures a sparkling and vital performance from Joseph Keilberth and his Cologne orchestra. Favouring steady tempi that accentuate the emphatically Baroque style, Keilberth nonetheless injects a nerviness into the scenes between Cardillac, his daughter and the Officer. As the jeweller, Fischer-Dieskau is outstanding, presenting an exceptionally emotional characterization that arouses unexpected compassion. As his daughter, Leonore Kirchstein is no less credible and the Officer is wonderfully sung by the tenor Donald Grobe. The sound is fresh and lively, if a little noisy, and the accompanying highlights from *Mathis der Maler*, with Fischer-Dieskau and Pilar Lorengar, are an excellent bonus.

Mathis der Maler

Mathis the Painter

Composed 1934–35.
First performed May 28, 1938.
Libretto by the composer.

Synopsis

Scene I

During the Peasants' Revolt of 1524 the painter Mathis is working at St Anthony's monastery in Mainz. The rebel leader Hans Schwalb and his daughter Regina arrive there. Schwalb challenges Mathis's commitment to art in such troubled times. To help them escape the pursuing Catholic troops, Mathis gives them his horse. When the troops arrive, Mathis admits to an officer, Sylvester von Schaumberg, that he has helped the rebels.

Scene II

In the palace of the Cardinal-Archbishop of Mainz, the Cardinal and his advisors discuss the riots in the city. Mathis is in love with Ursula, the daughter of the Lutheran Riedinger. Riedinger asks the cardinal for an end to the book-burning. Mathis – accused by Sylvester of colluding with the rebels – pleads the rebels' cause. Telling the Cardinal that he can no longer paint, he resigns his service.

Scene III

Amid preparations for a burning of Lutheran books, Mathis and Ursula pledge their love. Her father wishes her to marry the Cardinal as a means of reconciling Lutherans and Catholics.

Scene IV

Mathis witnesses the rebels sacking a village, and denounces their brutality. The rebel army is massacred by Catholic troops and Schwalb is killed. Mathis and Regina survive.

Scene V

Ursula offers herself to the Cardinal as his wife. Initially appalled, he is won over by her integrity and faith, and decrees that Lutherans can now openly practise their religion.

Scene VI

Mathis and Regina are in hiding in a forest. While she sleeps, Mathis experiences a series of visions in which he is tempted (in the manner of St Anthony) by figures from his past; the figure of the Cardinal (as St Paul) exhorts him to return to painting.

Scene VII

In Mathis's workshop Regina is dying, tended by Ursula. Mathis and the Cardinal meet for the last time, after which the painter puts away his tools, in preparation for his own death.

𝄞 Matthias Grünewald (1460–1528) was a German painter whose work – most famously the Isenheim Altarpiece – is characterized by intensely heightened colour and graphic depictions of physical suffering. In the early years of the twentieth century there was a revival of interest in his work, and for Expressionist painters he became an almost talismanic figure. The idea of writing an opera about him was suggested to Hindemith by his publisher, but he was initially reluctant and only began working on it in 1933 – the year the Nazis came to power.

The composer wrote his own libretto after reading more than a hundred books on the bitter struggles between Catholics and Lutherans in sixteenth-century Germany. Hindemith intended his audience to draw parallels with their own times, describing Mathis as a man "blessed with the highest mastery and understanding of his art, yet at the same time plagued by the devilish torments of a doubting, seeking soul, who experiences . . . the breakdown of a new era with its inevitable destruction of existing traditions." A projection of all Hindemith's own doubts and struggles, Mathis seeks to discover what the artist must do in a brutal and unstable political climate. Returning to his work and attempting to express the reality that surrounds him, he makes a choice not to look the other way – like Hindemith, who remained true to his talent but not at the expense of wider truth.

Drawing on Gregorian chant and old German folk sources (most clearly heard in the Prelude, "The Concert of Angels" as it's known), Hindemith produced a score that is cast in a series of unbroken set-pieces, in a style that is consistently contrapuntal but far less terse than in *Cardillac*, reaffirming Hindemith's faith in sung melody. The seven scenes are based on the chromatic rise from the key of C sharp to E major and back again, rigorously mirroring the shifts in Mathis's mental state with an unremitting intensity. This registration of mental states is sometimes achieved at the expense of narrative momentum, and in the theatre the three and a quarter hours can seem considerably longer. But *Mathis der Maler* is full of glorious moments – notably Mathis's opening baritone monologue and the two haunting scenes with which the opera ends – and is undoubtedly Hindemith's operatic masterpiece.

Hermann, Protschka, von Halem, Winkler; Cologne Radio Choir and Symphony Orchestra; Albrecht.
(Wergo WER6255-2; 3 CDs).

This set has an immediacy and atmosphere that comes as close to the live element as could be wished from studio conditions. Gerd Albrecht spurs his orchestra to play with an intensity that never obscures the detail of the score. His cast is less starry than on the alternative, but Roland Hermann is much more emotional in the title role – and in *Mathis*, a committed lead tenor is a fundamental requirement. Joseph Protschka is no James King, but he is expressive enough, and the sense of ensemble unity cannot be faulted.

Fischer-Dieskau, King, Feldhoff, Schmidt; Bavarian Radio Chorus; Bavarian Radio Symphony Orchestra; Kubelik.
(EMI CDS5 55237-2; 3 CDs).

This recording looks good on paper but in reality is slightly disappointing and not a patch on the extracts conducted by Leopold Ludwig on the *Cardillac* disc. The problem is partly Kubelik's over-respectful conducting, which can make the rather knotty counterpoint sound more academic than it actually is, and partly Fischer-Dieskau's voice, which is not at its best. However, this is an intelligent performance and a decent alternative to the pricier Wergo set.

KURT WEILL

b. DESSAU, GERMANY, MARCH 2, 1900; d. NEW YORK, APRIL 3, 1950.

Just as Roman audiences in 1890 had been astonished by the first performance of Mascagni's lurid *Cavalleria rusticana*, so Berlin audiences were scandalized four decades later by the premiere of Kurt Weill's *Die Dreigroschenoper* (The Threepenny Opera), which thronged the stage with prostitutes, pimps and thieves who rejoiced in the thrills of the low life. This modern reworking of *The Beggar's Opera* (see p.64), the first in a series of satirical works written to texts by Berthold Brecht, brought Weill international celebrity almost overnight, and so popular was it that by 1933, only five years after the premiere, it had been performed 10,000 times.

Weill's father was Dessau's chief cantor, himself a composer, and young Weill was tutored in music by – among others – Humperdinck and Busoni. As a student he flirted with the atonalism of Schoenberg, but Weill was by nature drawn to less esoteric principles. Despite the commercial success of his operas *Der Protagonist* and *Der Zar lässt sich photographieren* (The Tsar Has His photograph Taken), Weill felt restricted by the conventions of the opera house and began, as he put it, "to dream of a special brand of musical theatre which would completely integrate drama and music, spoken word, song and movement".

Weill first began working with Brecht in 1927, giving the playwright his first taste of success when they produced the *Mahagonny Songspiel* (a song-setting of a group of Brecht poems) in Baden-Baden. *Die Dreigroschenoper*, *Happy End* (1929), *Aufstieg und Fall der Stadt Mahagonny* (1930) and *Der Jasager* (1930) followed, but the hugely productive relationship then began to deteriorate, first because it became clear that Weill was the dominant force in the partnership, and second because Weill was not prepared to "set the Communist manifesto to music", as the composer's wife Lotte Lenya later remembered. (It should be added that the literary contribution made by Brecht's various female admirers, most notably Elisabeth Hauptmann, was of a somewhat greater order than Brecht gave them credit for.) Weill then turned to the

ENTARTETE MUSIK

The prominence and influence of avant-garde Jewish composers such as Schoenberg and Weill were a source of great embarrassment to the ideologues of Nazism, whose loathing bore poisonous fruit in 1937 with the compilation of a list of music by composers it considered unacceptable – a list that included nearly every published Jewish composer. In May 1938 the Nazis decided to make their point even more emphatically through an exhibition in Düsseldorf, in which photographs and portraits of offending contemporary composers would be displayed next to appraisals of their weaknesses and failings. Directed by Heinz Ziegler, one of Goebbels' stooges, the exhibition was called **Entartete Musik** (Degenerate Music), taking its name from the Entartete Kunst (Degenerate Art) exhibition that had been opened by Hitler in Munich the previous year, in which progressive art had been shown alongside the daubings of the insane, prior to its destruction by the Nazi arbiters of German culture.

Ziegler defined his exhibition as "a veritable witches' sabbath portraying the most frivolous intellectual and artistic aspects of Cultural Bolshevism . . . and the triumph of arrogant Jewish impudence". Calling the German people to arms, he paraphrased *Mein Kampf*: "The human being who recognizes a given danger, who sees with his own eyes the possibility of remedy, has the duty and obligation not to work on the quiet, but openly to meet and overcome the sickness." In this moral crusade the enemies of the healthy Reich were Jews such as Schoenberg (whose *Erwartung* was highlighted as an especially perfidious creation) and Schreker, and non-Jewish "Bolsheviks" like Stravinsky and Hindemith. Even the popular operetta composers Oscar Strauss and Leo Fall were included in the roll-call of the condemned.

As evidence of the insidious influence of the Jewish/Bolshevik axis, the exhibition displayed writings by Adorno and other proponents of atonalism and serialism, lists of the composers and musicians represented by the Jewish agent Wolff, copies of various composers' theoretical works (notably Schoenberg's *Harmonielehre*, which would have made little sense to anyone not fully trained in music), and a large number of scores annotated to draw attention to those episodes considered typically corrupt. Among these were every one of Hindemith's completed operas, Weill's *Der Dreigroschenoper* and *Mahagonny*, both Berg's operas, Schreker's *Die Gezeichneten* and Krenek's *Jonny spielt auf*.

In the centre of the main hall stood a huge pillar on which were printed bilious attacks on jazz music, with distorted photographs of black American performers (including Louis Armstrong) alongside those European composers whom Ziegler and the Ministry of Culture considered responsible for importing this "corrupting" influence – chiefly Weill and Korngold. One panel suggested that jazz had been created as a Jewish disease to infect German music, while a caption to a portrait of Stravinsky implied that the jazz-tainted Russian composer might in fact be Jewish as well. Among the offensive illustrations in the pamphlet accompanying the exhibition was one of a grotesquely caricatured black American, with a star of David on his shirt, playing a saxophone. Should anyone remain unconvinced by this drivel, patrons were invited to retire to one of six booths in which they could hear the awful degeneracy of music by Hindemith, Weill, Krenek and others.

Some of those singled out for abuse had already left Germany. Others were soon to leave. Some stayed, and lost their careers in music. Others lost far more than that – see p.423.

Expressionist playwright Georg Kaiser, with whom he had worked in his pre-Brecht days, for the libretto of *Der Silbersee* (1933), which was premiered simultaneously in three different cities. But this tremendous fame was not to last. Early performances of *Silbersee* were disrupted by Nazi thugs, and within weeks of the Reichstag fire Weill and Lenya fled to Paris.

In Paris, he met up again with Brecht, with whom he wrote the song cycle *Die sieben Todsünden* (The Seven Deadly Sins), but just eighteen months after arriving in France he left for America, where he remained for the rest of his life, composing a large variety of music for Broadway and, less memorably, Hollywood. Weill warmed instantly to a country he thought would offer a way out of what he saw as the dead end of the European avant-garde, stating in an interview in 1943: "I never felt the oneness with my native country that I do with the United States; the moment I landed here I felt as though I'd come home."

However, Weill's experience was to fall short of his expectations, for the American theatre system placed commercial concerns above all else, and American audiences weren't as keen on his style of social and political critique as they had been back in Germany. Frequently, the quality of the work – which brilliantly assimilated American folk, jazz and dance music into well-integrated orchestral scores – brought critical success but box office failure. Works such as *Love Life* (1948) – an analysis of marriage in the context of industrialized society – and *Lost in the Stars* (1949) – which was based on the anti-apartheid classic *Cry, the Beloved Country* – were not the sort of thing to get investors rushing, however sophisticated the product. That said, his best stage works hit all corners of the market, and with *Street Scene* (1946) he created his American masterpiece, a work he described as "a real blending of drama and music, in which the singing continues naturally where the speaking stops, and the spoken word as well as the dramatic action are embedded in overall musical structure".

As he confessed shortly before his death in 1950, Weill had never really found the new public which he was so desperately seeking. In Germany he had known incredible success before the Nazis decided that he was a danger to the Reich. So fearful were they of his music that not only were performances banned in Germany, but diplomatic channels were used in an attempt to destroy all scores and recordings. In America he was attacked for his scandalous and satirical treatments of contemporary society, while many of his former admirers believed he had sold out to the commerical temptations. However, for Weill there was no discontinuity in his life, for he had always seen himself as a composer with a social mission. As he told an interviewer in 1940 – "Schoenberg has said that he is writing for a time fifty years after his death. . . . For myself, I write for today. I don't give a damn about writing for posterity."

Die Dreigroschenoper

The Threepenny Opera

Composed 1928.
First performed August 31, 1928.
Libretto by Berthold Brecht and Elisabeth Hauptmann.

Synopsis

Act I

London, Soho. In the Prologue, the Streetsinger respectfully recalls Macheath's crimes in the "Ballad of Mack the Knife". The opera begins with Mr and Mrs Peachum standing before their mob of thieves and evil-doers. They are alarmed to notice that their daughter, Polly, is missing, and horrified to be told she has eloped with Macheath (Mack), whom they regard as an unsuitable son-in-law. Mack and Polly celebrate their wedding in a stable. Among the guests is Mack's old schoolfriend, the police chief Tiger Brown, who, after reminiscing about their days in the army together, wishes him well. Polly returns to her parents and attempts to explain away the ring on her finger, but they are not going to accept Mack as a son-in-law and determine to persuade Brown to arrest the miscreant.

Act II

Back at the stable Mack and Polly say goodbye: Mack has business to attend to. Meanwhile, Mrs Peachum bribes the prostitute Jenny to betray Mack to the police. Mack is duly arrested and sent to the Old Bailey; after singing "The Ballad of the Good Life", he is helped to escape by Brown's daughter Lucy.

Act III

Peachum threatens Brown that, if Mack remains at large, his band of criminals will disrupt the imminent coronation. Brown has his old friend rearrested and returned to the Old Bailey. Polly fails to provide the necessary bribe to have her husband released, and so Mack is executed. However, Peachum has thought of a different conclusion to the story: in honour of her coronation, the Queen has decided to grant Mack absolution, a peerage, a castle and a pension. The chorus ends the opera with the refrain "Don't prosecute crime: it will die out of its own accord."

The Beggar's Opera, written by Gay and Pepusch in 1728, played the realities of London's seedier side against the pompous conventions of opera seria. When Brecht and Elisabeth Hauptmann transported the work two hundred years down the line into the Germany of brownshirts and political hooliganism, the *modus operandi* remained the same: *Die Dreigroschenoper* paints a picture of German life that deflates the Aryan fantasies espoused by the National Socialists. As Hauptmann and Brecht set out to undermine the self-deluding niceties of Germany's bourgeoisie, so Weill's music aimed at "the complete destruction of the concept of music-drama", being cast in verse-song with pauses for spoken dialogue and any necessary action. In essence, the style was like a high art version of the hugely popular Berlin cabaret genre, yet both the authors and most of the cast suspected that it would flop – especially as the composer continued to make changes even while the premiere was in progress. But even though the first night failed to make a full house, the word spread through Germany like wildfire, and *Die Dreigroschenoper* remained on the stage pretty much without interruption until the Nazis banned it and its composer in 1933.

What makes *Die Dreigroschenoper* so effective is the way in which Weill wraps the mockery of the text in the sweetest and most insinuating music, so that the words have a sort of delayed action effect. A fine example is the libidinous "Ballad of Sexual Dependency", which so shocked the first Mrs Peachum that she refused to sing it, but best of all is the sexily murderous "Mack the Knife", a slinky number made famous through performances by Louis Armstrong and Frank Sinatra. The caustic ironies of *Die Dreigroschenoper* are a world away from the contrapuntal extravagances of Wagner, Strauss and Schreker, and all those composers for whom Evil was a diminished seventh and Good a rising fourth.

RECORDINGS OVERVIEW

It is a measure of *The Threepenny Opera*'s appeal that it has been recorded on no fewer than ten occasions, the first in 1954. The most powerful of these is Brückner-Rüggeberg's 1958 set, made for CBS under the supervision of the composer's widow Lotte Lenya, and with herself cast as Jenny. It has been on CD, but is currently out of the catalogue; in the meantime, for a taste of what the composer really heard, there is a Teldec CD of a set of highlights recorded in 1930, with Lenya and various other members of the original 1928 cast – all led by the original conductor Theo Mackeben.

Kollo, Lemper, Milva, Adorf, Dernesch; Berlin RIAS Chamber Choir and Orchestra; Mauceri.
(Decca 430 075-2DH).

This is not the complete opera (the spoken dialogue has been heavily cut) and there has been some liberal tampering with the score to accommodate the cabaret voices of Ute Lemper as Polly and Milva as Jenny, the latter of whom sings some of her numbers an octave down. However, both are consummate professionals, and if their tone sometimes sets your teeth on edge, bear in mind that this is how the composer wrote the music. As such both René Kollo and Helge Dernesch are fish out of water, and neither sounds right in the roles of Mack and Mrs Peachum. Mauceri is the work's main success, and he directs a sprightly account of the score which will more than suffice until CBS's first recording is re-released.

Aufstieg und Fall der Stadt Mahagonny

Rise and Fall of the City of Mahagonny

Composed 1927–29.
First performed March 9, 1930.
Libretto by Berthold Brecht.

Synopsis

Act I

An American desert. A beaten-up old truck drives onto the stage and breaks down. Inside are Fatty, Begbick and Trinity Moses – white slave traders on the run from the law. Standing above a dried-up riverbed, Begbick states that it is easier to steal money than grow it, and so they decide to build themselves "a city of nets" – Mahagonny. Jenny and her friends are the first to arrive, having smelled the money that everyone thinks will soon flood in. Four lumberjacks from Alaska enter – Jimmy Mahoney, Jake, Bill and Joe – and are immediately offered their choice of girls. Jimmy buys Jenny for thirty dollars. All goes smoothly until the city begins to enter a recession, and Jimmy laments that everything has gone too quiet; but an approaching typhoon soon threatens to liven things up. As they wait for it to hit the city, Jimmy presents his idea of a perfect city – a city where total permissiveness reigns, a city where every man looks after himself.

Act II

Mahagonny is spared destruction by the typhoon, and so the city decides to follow Jimmy's ideal: Jakes eats himself to death (Gluttony), Begbick takes over a brothel (Lechery), Jimmy loses all his money backing Joe in the boxing ring, in which he is killed by Trinity Moses (Sloth and Aggression), and Jimmy buys drinks for which he is unable to pay. When Begbick demands the money be paid, Jimmy turns to Jenny for a loan – which she refuses, quoting his motto "every man for himself". He is thrown into prison.

Act III

In court, Toby Higgins is released from his charges of murder, after buying off the court. Jimmy asks Bill for the money to do the same, but Bill says that friendship is one thing and money is another. Jimmy is accused of many crimes – the worst of which is the inability to pay – and is sentenced to death. On the way to his execution, Jimmy exhorts the people of Mahagonny to continue living life to the full. He has no regrets. He is strapped to the electric chair. After he has died, the people begin to complain of the cost of living, and the city is set on fire. As the flames rise, Jimmy's possessions are paraded as relics.

Unlike *The Threepenny Opera*, which was classed by its creators as a "play with music", *Mahagonny* is a true opera and was written for operatic voices – the first performance was to have been given at the progressive Kroll Opera House, with Otto Klemperer conducting. However, the theatre was unable to raise the composer's fee and, more importantly, Klemperer considered the work immoral. Coming from a man whose own lack of sexual inhibition was the stuff of legend by 1930 this seems odd, but he was not alone in finding *Mahagonny* disturbing – the Act II scene in which a group of men queue up outside a brothel was removed when Gustav Brecher conducted the premiere in Leipzig.

In an attempt to justify his opera to Klemperer, Weill wrote to the conductor on August 6, 1929: "After [Stravinsky's] *Oedipus* . . . *Mahagonny* is the most decisive expression of a new musical theatre. . . . Naturally it contains much that is critical of the status quo." Indeed it does, for Brecht and Weill went out of their way to make sure their second collaboration with Weill sounded the funeral knell of "culinary opera", as Brecht contemptuously labelled the standard opera-house fare of the post-Wagner era. *Mahagonny* is a classic *Zeitoper*, blending ragtime, operetta and swing in a score that supports a hard-hitting depiction of current corruption. Whereas *The Threepenny Opera* was redolent of cabaret sophistication, *Mahagonny* came on like a militant music-hall burlesque, its attitude exemplified by the famous pidgin-English "Alabama Song". As far as Brecht was concerned, the message should have taken precedence over the medium, but *Mahagonny* is a considerably more complex – and absorbing – piece of music than any of Weill's previous works, and the issue of precedence was to be the source of much friction between the two men. Catchy tunes still prevail here, but they are now set within an intricately structured framework and against a complicated harmonic canvas that makes *Mahagonny* much less of a song-cycle than the *Threepenny Opera* had been.

Lenya, Sauerbaum, Günter, Litz; NW German Radio Chorus and Orchestra; Brückner-Rüggeberg.
(CBS CD77341; 2 CDs).

This 1956 recording has much to recommend it, although some might have problems with the idiosyncratic voice of Lotte Lenya, who was no opera singer. When she played Jenny in the 1931 Berlin production, she sang it in the soprano register, whereas here she employs her bizarre tenor-like register and, on occasion, even drops her part an octave. It's a provocative and intelligent reading, but sounds rather incongruous alongside colleagues whose voices are more conventionally beautiful. Gisela Litz is a delightful Begbick and Heinz Bauerman is haunting as Jimmy Mahoney. Brückner-Rüggeberg's conducting is professional and energetic, but the sound is poor, and the set may well soon drop from the catalogue.

Street Scene

Composed 1946.
First performed January 9, 1946.
Libretto by Elmer Rice and Langston Hughes.

Synopsis

Act I

A tenement block in New York City. The inhabitants, who together complain about the heat, are introduced: the gossip Mrs Jones, the milk deliverer Mr Sankey, the bookish Sam Kaplan, who is in love with Rose Maurrant, daughter of the adulterous Anna (one of whose lovers is Mr Sankey); Sam's father Abraham and his sister, the teacher Shirley; Mr Buchanan, whose wife is about to give birth; and, finally, Frank Maurrant, an inarticulate, reactionary theatre electrician and husband of Anna. Mr Fiorentino, the ice cream salesman, arrives, comparing one of his cones to the Statue of Liberty's torch – the first thing that all immigrants see when they enter New York

Harbor; he is followed by Jennie Hildebrand, who is returning from her graduation ceremony. Everyone rejoices in her success, although the entire block knows that she and her family are to be evicted for non-payment of rent. Mr Maurrant leaves for a night's drinking as his daughter arrives with Harry Easter, a man from her office who intends to make Rose his mistress. His offers are not accepted, however. When her father returns, she takes leave of Harry. Mr Buchanan's wife begins labour, Anna Maurrant rushes to help and Rose and Sam sing a duet in which they look to a better life.

Act II

Early the following morning, Buchanan thanks Anna for helping while Rose implores her father to be nicer to her mother. Rose then tells Sam about Harry Easter's advances, at which they consider eloping together. Easter then arrives to accompany Rose to the funeral of an office colleague. As Anna invites Mr Sankey up to her apartment, city marshals begin throwing the Hildebrands' possessions onto the street. Suddenly, the suspicious Frank returns from work to find Anna with Mr Sankey. Shots are heard and Maurrant is seen fleeing. Rose arrives to see her dying mother being carried from the building. Mr Sankey has also been killed. Two hours later, two uptown nursemaids are seen with their charges. They express amazement at the double murder. Frank Maurrant is caught and as he is dragged away he confesses to Rose that he killed them out of jealousy. Rose is left alone with Sam. She prepares to start a new life – without Sam, for she cannot, after such tragedy, make any commitments. She leaves, and two prospective tenants for the Hildebrand apartment arrive. The opera ends with the neighbours complaining about the heat.

Soon after Weill arrived in America, he was introduced to the playwright Elmer Rice, whose 1929 play about life in a tenement block he had seen while still in Germany. Rice, who was famously reluctant to let composers near his work, took a liking to Weill and gave him the rights to *Street Scene* in 1945. Rising to the "great challenge" of creating music to match "the stark realism of the play", Weill commissioned the poet Langston Hughes to write song lyrics (which are excellent) and convert the play into viable operatic dialogue (of which there is perhaps too much). Hughes in turn took Weill on a research trip around Harlem, but their collaboration was frequently quite rocky, and the first performance in Philadelphia was nearly delayed by their inability to see eye to eye. The first run was received so coldly that it almost didn't make it to New York, but once it was mounted at the Adelphi Theatre, with a cast of opera singers, its future seemed secure, and it ran for 148 consecutive nights.

It's easy to understand why the Philadelphian audience were taken aback by *Street Scene*, for it is a unflinching story of apathy, intolerance, poverty and alienation. Beginning and ending with the line "Don't know what I'm gonna do", it is populated by people for whom drugs, sex and alcohol are means of escape from a life in which disaster seems always imminent. It is a testament to Weill's remarkable skills that he was able to bring such expression to such a wide variety of suffering people, in a song-filled score that achieves a perfect balance between gritty reality (for example, minor key laments such as "Pain, nothing but pain") and spirited humour (Jennie's joyful "Wrapped in a ribbon"). Indignant at the huge social divide that exists within just a single block, Weill never patronizes his characters, whose beleaguered dignity survives even the unhappiest of endings, where a quiet victory is implied by the return to the old lament "Ain't it awful, the heat". As an operatic study of working-class life *Street Scene* remains unparalleled – Charpentier's *Louise* looks stagey by comparison.

Ciesinksi, Kelly, Bullock, Bottone, van Allan; English National Opera Chorus and Orchestra; Davis.
(That's Entertainment TER 21185; 2 CDs).

This recording was made on the back of an ENO production at the Coliseum, although Carl Davis did not conduct it in the theatre. The production values and casting are less high than on the rival Decca set (conducted by Mauceri, with Barstow, Ramey and Hadley), but the atmosphere and cohesion are far greater, for the entire cast is obviously used to the work and each other. Christine Ciesinksi as Anna and Richard van Allan as her husband are splendid, moulding their voices well to the musical-operatic character of Weill's songs; Janis Kelly and Bonaventura Bottone are also excellent as the doomed lovers. The chorus is a little ropey, but the orchestra plays marvellously.

ERNST KRENEK

b. VIENNA, AUGUST 23, 1900; d. PALM SPRINGS, CALIFORNIA, DECEMBER 23, 1991.

The term *Zeitoper* arose from the German avant-garde of the 1920s to describe an opera in which the spirit of the time was reflected in both the choice of subject matter and in the musical style, in an attempt to replace the subjectivity of Expressionism with something more "objective" and popular. The works of Kurt Weill are the best-known examples of the genre, but for a brief period between 1927 and 1930, Ernst Krenek's *Jonny spielt auf* – the only one of his twenty operas to remain in circulation – was the musical phenomenon of its day. In Germany it was performed in more than thirty different theatres during its first season alone and within two years of its premiere it was staged in more than twenty different countries. Although Krenek was later to dismiss it as a "reactionary mistake", none of his later works brought him anything like the same success.

Born in Vienna, Krenek studied with Franz Schreker (see p.401), following him to Berlin when Schreker moved to the Hochschule in 1920. From the beginning his dramatic works displayed their composer's concern with, in his own words, "the idea of social freedom from oppression and personal freedom from inhibitions". His scenic cantata *Die Zwingburg* (1922) was an Expressionist critique of tyranny whose dissonant style led to a break with Schreker. It was followed the next year by *Der Sprung über den Schatten* (The Leap over the Shadow), a comedy in which Krenek parodied both Expressionism and psychoanalysis and attempted to incorporate jazz elements (although in Weimar Germany the term "jazz" usually meant whatever American popular music a composer was familiar with). His third opera, *Orpheus und Eurydike* (to a libretto by the painter and writer Oskar Kokoschka), was a return to Expressionism, but a visit to Paris and contact with the more carefree and ironic musical environment of Milhaud and Poulenc helped to loosen his style. He also benefited enormously from his work as assistant to Paul Bekker (a leading champion of new music) at the Kassel opera house. Krenek was involved in every aspect of production and it was at Kassel that *Jonny spielt auf* was written.

Jonny was followed by three short *Zeitopern*, all premiered at Wiesbaden, but in 1929 Krenek changed direction once again, this time adopting a neo-Romantic style with *Leben des Orest*. Between 1931 and 1933 an even more spectacular transformation occurred when he received a commission from the Vienna State Opera. The result was *Karl V*, an historical work about the Holy Roman Emperor Charles V, which offered a specifically Catholic challenge to the encroaching barbarism of Nazism. Its most radical aspect, however, was the fact that it was the first opera to employ the serial techniques of Schoenberg, even though Krenek had been initially dismissive of them. However, its antinationalist sentiments led to its being banned even before its first performance, and Krenek was forced into exile in 1934. Four years later he moved to the United States, where found great success as a teacher, writing chamber operas for his students and keeping abreast of practically every contemporary trend – including electronic music. With his American operas attracting little real interest, from the 1960s he was, in his own words, "tragically forgotten".

The remarkable emotional, intellectual and stylistic range of Krenek's operas is without equal in twentieth-century German music, but it's arguable that this very diversity precludes an overriding sense of an autonomous artistic personality. Employing every conceivable means of contemporary expression, from the stark serialism of *Karl V* to the more populist manner of *Jonny spielt auf*, Krenek has becomes stranded in something of a musical no-man's-land, as the very qualities that make him so fascinating have contributed most to his present isolation.

Jonny spielt auf

Jonny Strikes Up

Composed 1925–26.
First performed February 10, 1927.
Libretto by the composer.

Synopsis

Part I

The young and rather serious composer Max meets the opera singer Anita on top of a mountain. They begin a passionate affair which leads to the creation of his new opera, which Anita will perform in Paris. At a hotel in Paris Jonny, a black jazz musician, has his eye on the violin of the virtuoso and notorious philanderer Daniello. Anita is seduced by Daniello, Jonny steals his violin but the chambermaid, Yvonne, gets the blame and is sacked. Anita takes her back to Germany as her maid. Having stowed the violin in Anita's banjo case, Jonny follows them.

Part II

Max is distraught to hear of Anita's affair and returns to the glacier where they met. Jonny retrieves the violin. A radio broadcast of Anita singing his music stops Max from taking his life, and just as he decides upon a reconciliation, Jonny's jazz band comes on the air. Daniello, who is also listening to the broadcast, recognizes his violin. Jonny hides the violin in the luggage of Max and Anita, who are leaving for America, and Max is arrested. Daniello arrives and will not allow Yvonne to clear Max's name. Daniello falls under a train, Max escapes with Anita to America and Jonny strikes up a tune while standing on the station clock, which has turned into a globe.

Like Weill, Hindemith (for a time), and other left-wing composers of the time, Krenek sought to redefine opera by bridging the divide between art music and popular music. *Jonny spielt auf* is a typical *Zeitoper* brew, mixing references to Strauss and Schoenberg with jazz stylings, for which Krenek had developed a taste after hearing Duke Ellington's music for the revue "Chocolate Kiddies" in Frankfurt. It seemed radical stuff back then, but Krenek's assimilation of black American music was extremely superficial, amounting to little more than the deployment of repeated rhythms and syncopation, plus a dash of jazzy instrumentation.

The opera is scored for a large orchestra and on-stage jazz band, and the music fizzes with metamorphic energy, changing its colour, tone and character with remarkable ease and inventiveness, culminating in a kind of ragtime chorale for the finale. But Krenek's eclecticism is used primarily for symbolic and parodic purposes: Jonny the jazz man represents the vital energy and the lack of inhibition of the New World; Max is like a caricature of Krenek's teacher Schreker, with Anita getting some suitably lyrical and overblown moments written for her; while the violinist Daniello is surely a shot at the cult of the virtuoso, with music that is both insinuating and meretricious. The problem with *Jonny spielt auf* is that, aside from the novelty of the orchestration, much of the music is rather dull and you soon begin to yearn for some of the satirical bite and anger of the Brecht/Weill collaborations. *Jonny* is mild when compared to *The Threepenny Opera* or *Mahagonny*, and any pertinent points about the role of the modern artist are obscured by now-stale topical jokes (like the craze for Alpine scenery) and ham-fisted Americanisms (Krenek had yet to visit the country).

The incredible success of *Jonny* can be put down to a number of causes. Most obviously it enlivened the traditional operatic repertoire, not just musically but by a daring use of stagecraft – the last scene, for example, presented a railway station (plus trains) on stage. The fact that it made a black man the hero of the opera (albeit a blacked-up white singer for nearly all the early productions) made it a cause célèbre for radicals and a bugbear to the cultural right – indeed the Nazis adapted the poster of Jonny playing the saxophone as the symbol of their notion of "Degenerate Music" (see p.415). Krenek disliked the sobriquet "jazz opera", preferring to think of the work as an exercise in musical regeneration but, seventy years on, it seems now little more than a historical curiosity.

Kruse, Marc, St Hill, Kraus; Leipzig Opera Chorus and Orchestra; Zagrosek.
(Decca 436 631-2; 2 CDs).

Produced after a live 1990 production in Leipzig, this recording of *Jonny* is the only one since the first LPs were released in the 1960s, with Lucia Popp and Heinrich Hollreiser. Sadly, however, the performance is unremarkable, repeatedly failing to capture the spark that is the score's main attraction. The jazzy bits are sluggish and the big orchestra glides where it should skip, wallows where it should gloat. This is almost entirely the fault of the conductor, Lothar Zagrosek, since the Leipzig orchestra and the singers are generally excellent, with Alessandra Marc's powerful Anita and Krister St Hill's engaging Jonny providing especially committed performances.

VIKTOR ULLMANN

b. TESCHEN, SILESIA, JANUARY 1, 1898; d. AUSCHWITZ, PROBABLY OCTOBER 17, 1944.

The name of Viktor Ullmann is inextricably linked with the concentration camp of Terezín (Teresienstadt), from where – along with the rest of the camp's extraordinarily large number of highly talented musicians and composers – he was transported to Auschwitz. His reputation still rests mainly on the twenty or so compositions he wrote in Terezín, including his opera, *Der Kaiser von Atlantis* . The opera stands as a testament to a composer whose reputation has been marginalized by the brutality of twentieth-century history, and to his extraordinary creativity in appalling circumstances. "Our desire to create", wrote Ullmann, "matched our will to live."

Ullmann was born into a German-speaking family in Teschen (now Těšín) on the Moravian-Polish border, but received his musical education in Vienna, where he joined Schoenberg's composition class in 1918. He was well connected in Viennese musical life, and Alexander Zemlinsky, Alban Berg and Arnold Schoenberg were strong musical influences as well as personal friends. Ullmann's music is very Viennese in style – it is often highly chromatic, but resists the atonality and serialism of Schoenberg.

From 1920 to 1927 Ullmann worked as assistant to Zemlinsky at the Neues Deutsches Theater (now the Smetana Theatre) in Prague, before taking posts in Aussig (Ústí nad Labem) and Zurich. He became passionately interested in Rudolf Steiner's anthroposophical theories of self-knowledge and for a while gave up his musical career to run the Anthroposophic Society's bookshop in Stuttgart. Hitler's rise to power forced him back to Prague in 1933, and in the ensuing years he started composing more seriously. He won a prize for his first published composition, the *Schoenberg Variations*, and another for his 1936 opera *Der Sturz des Antichrist* (The Fall of the Antichrist), which remained unperformed because the central character could have been interpreted as a reference to Hitler – an idea Ullmann was to develop in *Der Kaiser von Atlantis*. (It was finally performed and recorded in the mid-1990s by the CPO label – not an essential disc, but one to turn to after the one recommended on p.424.) Other important works, dating from the years just before the Nazis invaded, and therefore unperformed in Ullmann's lifetime, are the delightful *Piano Concerto* and the one-act comic opera *Der zerbrochene Krug* (The Broken Jug), based on a play by Heinrich von Kleist and premiered in Dresden in 1996.

In September 1942 Ullmann was transported to Terezín, where his official duties were to organize concerts and work as a music critic. This concentration of musical activity made his years in Terezín the most productive of his life as a composer: he wrote three piano sonatas, several song-cycles, a string quartet, an orchestral piece and the astonishing allegorical opera *Der Kaiser von Atlantis*. This was rehearsed but not performed, as the SS realized it was a savage parody of Hitler and an allegory of his downfall – this was one of the few cases of censorship in a town that masqueraded as a "Paradise ghetto" to fool the outside world about the fate of the Jews. On October 16, once it was deemed they had served their useful purpose, most of the musicians and composers of Terezín were transported to Auschwitz. Ullmann was one of those sent immediately to the gas chambers.

Der Kaiser von Atlantis

The Emperor of Atlantis

Composed 1943.
First performed December 16, 1975.
Libretto by Peter Kien.

Synopsis

Life and Death have lost their meaning as the power-crazed Emperor Overall tries to overrun the world.

TEREZÍN

Terezín, about 60km northwest of Prague, was built by the Habsburg Emperor Josef II in the 1780s and named in honour of his mother, Maria Theresa. From November 1941 until the liberation in May 1945, it was used by the Nazis as a concentration camp for the Jews of central Europe. Conditions at **Theresienstadt** (its German name) were appalling and transports left regularly for Auschwitz, but the town was administered by the Jews themselves, who created an incredible cultural life within the ghetto, organizing lectures, cabaret, theatre, music and opera performances in cellars, attics, and wherever else there was space. The inmates were more or less left to get on with their performances unhindered, and by 1944 the artistic life of the ghetto was being officially encouraged by the Nazis, who saw it as a propaganda tool for fooling the visiting Red Cross delegations. A film was even made that included footage of the world première of the *Study for Strings* by **Pavel Haas** and a scene from the children's opera *Brundibár* by **Hans Krása**, the most popular piece performed in the ghetto.

There were four composers of significance imprisoned in Terezín: Haas, Krása, **Viktor Ullmann**, and the young **Gideon Klein**. Ullmann was the most established of the four and was the most prolific in Terezín, but each of the others produced some wonderful compositions in the ghetto. These are works that are interesting not only because of the circumstances in which they were written, but as pieces of high quality in their own right.

Pavel Haas (1899–1944) was from the Moravian city of Brno, where he was a pupil of Janáček. The influence of his mentor can be heard in the string quartets, the wind quintet and the opera *Sarlatán* (The Charlatan), which he wrote before the war. In Terezín he composed *Four Songs to Chinese Poetry* for voice and piano, which evoke the isolation and homesickness felt there, and the *Study for Strings*, which was conducted there by Karel Ančerl, who survived Auschwitz and went on to direct the Czech Philharmonic after the war.

Hans Krása (1899–1944) was perhaps the most interesting and idiosyncratic of these composers. Before the war, his *Symphony* was performed in Paris and by the Boston Symphony Orchestra. He also wrote an opera, *Verlobung in Traum* (Betrothal in a Dream), which won a Czechoslovak State Prize in 1933 and has been recently revived in Prague. His children's opera, *Brundibár*, was written in 1938 and performed in secret in a Jewish orphanage in Prague. In Terezín it was rescored and played a remarkable 55 times. In the ghetto he wrote the wild and rhythmic *Tanz* for string trio and an accompanying *Fantasy and Fugue*, plus *Three Songs* for baritone, clarinet, viola and cello, and an overture for small orchestra.

The pianist and composer Gideon Klein (1919–45) was only 22 when he arrived in Terezín and until recently it was thought that he had written nothing very much before his arrival in the ghetto. In 1990, however, a locked suitcase was discovered in Prague containing quite a number of manuscripts of astonishing craftsmanship and maturity: songs, an octet and pieces for string duos and quartet. His masterpiece from Terezín, a string trio, was completed just a few days before he was transported to Auschwitz.

The majority of the musicians and composers in Terezín were transported to the gas chambers of Auschwitz on October 17, 1944. Their music is now finding its place on concert programmes and on disc – Koch International have embarked on a series of nine CDs documenting all the surviving music written in Terezín.

His agent, a Drummer-girl, conveys his orders, but Death, tired of this mechanized killing, decides to go on strike. The ill or mortally wounded are unable to die. A soldier and a girl from the opposing camp meet each other on the battlefield and, unable to kill each other, fall in love. The Emperor, unnerved by events, pleads with Death to return to work. There is one condition – the Emperor must be his first victim.

Written to an incisive libretto by Ullmann's fellow inmate Peter Kien, *Der Kaiser von Atlantis* is scored for a chamber orchestra of thirteen players (including banjo, saxophone and harpsichord and harmonium), as dictated by the resources available in Terezín. The music is an eclectic mixture of Weill-style cabaret, operetta, sumptuous late-Romanticism and direct pastiche of various sources. There is a daring send-up of the German national anthem *Deutchland über alles*, barely disguised in a minor key as the Drummer-girl declaims the Emperor's endless conquests. Other significant quotations include the opening trumpet motif (a unifying theme throughout the opera) and a version of the death motif from Josef Suk's *Asrael Symphony*, which would have been familiar to a large part of the audience. And the opera ends with a moving hymn based on the Lutheran chorale *Ein feste Burg*, re-set to the words "Komm Tod, du unser werter Gast" – Come Death, our welcome guest. It has the effect of an apotheosis, just like the chorale theme at the end of the *Violin Concerto* by Ullmann's friend Alban Berg, a composer he particularly admired.

Some of the most striking music is reserved for Death. He is not a fearsome character, but an honourable soldier – "an old-fashioned craftsman of dying" – a faithful friend, merciful and welcoming. The music of his second aria is ecstatically beautiful, dripping with suspensions and sumptuous harmonies. In stark contrast is the angular and rather over-academic writing of the Emperor's farewell, which precedes the closing chorale. This aria exists in two versions: a bleaker, more universal message written by Peter Kien, in which war is temporarily stopped, but is certain to return; and an alternative text written by Ullmann himself, which is more enigmatic but more of a release. Ullmann's ultimate message is one of hope mingled with resignation as Death is held up as a relief from life's torment: "It's not the other side we need fear, but rather this world that is veiled in darkest shadow."

Ullmann left the score of *Der Kaiser* with his friend H. G. Adler, who survived and moved to London after the war. After lying neglected for years it was taken up by the conductor Kerry Woodward, who prepared a performing version for the world premiere in 1975. It has since been performed quite widely in revised versions closer to the original score.

Kraus, Berry, Vermillion, Lippert; Leipzig Gewandhausorchester; Zagrosek.
(Decca 440 854-2; 1 CD).

This is the premiere recording of *Der Kaiser* and for that reason is very welcome indeed. It is not ideal, though. The serious moments are very well done, but the lighter ones lack the sense of dangerous fun that this score really needs. Unfortunately Walter Berry as Death is too old and crusty and doesn't bring over the lyrical seductiveness of his music. That said, the other voices are well suited, and Michael Kraus is deeply powerful in the Emperor's farewell aria, which is very difficult to bring off (both versions are included). The closing chorale is unutterably moving. Included as a fill-up are Ullmann's three *Hölderlin-Lieder*, also composed in Terezín, well performed by Iris Vermillion, the Drummer-girl in *Der Kaiser*.

ERVÍN SCHULHOFF

b. PRAGUE, JUNE 8, 1894; d. WÜLZBURG, GERMANY, AUGUST 18, 1942.

In the years between the wars, Schulhoff was a well-known name in contemporary music circles, ranked alongside his near-contemporaries Hindemith and Bartók. His orchestral scores were played by illustrious conductors such as Erich Kleiber, George Szell, Ernest Ansermet and Václav Talich. But having the misfortune to be both a communist and a Jew when the Nazis invaded Czechoslovakia, he was despatched to an internment camp in Bavaria, where he died of tuberculosis. His work suffered an eclipse for half a century, and it is only in the last few years that interest has reawakened in his extensive output.

Schulhoff was born into a prosperous German-Jewish family in Prague and showed an early talent for music, impressing Dvořák and entering the Prague Conservatory aged ten. His musical career was interrupted by World War I, when he was called up to serve in the Austrian army. The experience of war affected him profoundly: he became a pacifist and politically moved sharply to the left. In his diary of 1916 he wrote: "I can only place the years 1914, 1915, 1916 on humanity's lowest rank."

After the war he joined artists Otto Dix and Georg Grosz in their Dadaist attacks on bourgeois society. He heard jazz for the first time (allegedly in the apartment of Grosz, who had a large collection of American 78s) and rapidly absorbed it into his music, along with charlestons, foxtrots and shimmys. "I am boundlessly fond of night-club dancing," he wrote in 1921, "so much so that I have periods during which I spend whole nights dancing with one hostess or another." The 1920s and early 1930s marked the peak of his career. He wrote six symphonies, a great deal of piano and chamber music (including the *Hot Sonata* for saxophone and piano), a *Double Concerto for Flute, Piano and Orchestra*, a *Concerto for String Quartet and Wind Orchestra*, two adventurous dance pieces, a jazz oratorio and his only opera, *Flammen*.

In the early 1930s he joined the Communist Party and endorsed the socialist-realist ideal of appealing to a broad working-class audience. He simplified his style and wrote one of his most notorious works, the *Manifesto Cantata*, to texts by Marx and Engels. Schulhoff lost his job as a radio pianist in 1939, when the Nazis invaded Czechoslovakia. Two years later he took Soviet citizenship, but he never got out. He was placed under house arrest in June 1941, transported to the Wülzburg camp at the end of the year, and died eight months later.

Flammen

Flames

Composed 1927–29.
First performed January 27, 1932.
Libretto by Karel Beneš and Max Brod.

Synopsis

Act I

A series of scenes in which Don Juan encounters and lusts after women, pursued by a chorus of shadows and Death (La Morte) in the form of a woman.

Act II

At a nighttime carnival Don Juan dances a foxtrot with Donna Anna which turns nightmarish as he stabs to death her husband (not father, as in the Mozart), the Commendatore. Donna Anna commits suicide. Don Juan pursues a group of shadowy women in flames until La Morte appears. Don Juan is in love with her and she is in love with him, but says he is more tangible for her alive. "I love you too much to be able to destroy you." The Commendatore condemns him to eternal life. Don Juan shoots himself and instead of dying turns into a young man. The scene returns to the opening: La Morte, in love with Don Juan, pursues him eternally.

This reworking of the inexhaustible story of Don Juan started when Schulhoff went to visit the writer Max Brod (who was a great friend of Janáček and German translator of his operas) and happened to mention he was interested in the theme. By a strange coincidence Brod happened to have on his desk a play on the subject of Don Juan by Karel Beneš. The composer and writer met and Beneš reworked the play into a libretto, which Brod then translated into German. The result – a nightmare fantasy on erotic love, death, sin and punishment – sounds surprisingly like a 1920s version of Schnittke, mixing jazz bands, tangos and sumptuous late-Romantic sounds with ghostly echoes of Mozart. Lust without end is here presented not in the form of drama, but as a series of imaginatively scored surreal scenes and dances, replete with gongs, vibraphone and other percussion. Some of the music is beautifully transparent, delicately scored and chamber-like, but Schulhoff lets rip at times: there are some extraordinary transitions, as when La Morte plays a solemn Gloria on the organ which somehow transforms itself into a delirious jazz combo with muted trumpets and rattling xylophone. The vocal writing is far less rewarding than the orchestral parts, but the music for La Morte and the Chorus of Shadows gives the score a remarkable spectral ingredient. It would be great to see it staged.

Westi, Eaglen, Vermillion; Deutsches Symphonie-Orchester Berlin; Mauceri. (Decca 444 630-2; 2 CDs).

Attentively conducted by the versatile John Mauceri, this is another highly recommendable release in Decca's "Entartete Musik" series. The performances are first-rate, with Kurt Westi masterfully navigating Don Juan's angular vocal line. Jane Eaglen is fine as Donna Anna (and various other women he seduces) and Iris Vermillion is very striking as the eerie apparition of La Morte. All in all, a fascinating exploration for anyone interested in the further reaches of twentieth-century opera.

FERRUCCIO BUSONI

b. EMPOLI, ITALY, APRIL 1, 1866; d. BERLIN, JULY 27, 1924.

Ferruccio Busoni is one of the forgotten men of twentieth-century music, a situation largely due to the diversity of his talents and his resistance to easy classification. The child of professional musicians, Busoni was born in Tuscany but spent most of his professional life in Germany where, although he always regarded himself as primarily a composer, his early fame was achieved as one of the greatest pianists of his generation. Like Schoenberg – with whom he enjoyed a mutually respectful relationship – he was a formidable theoretician, and his *Outline of a New Aesthetic of Music* (1907) established him as one of the leading figures of the avant-garde and the first modern musician to espouse microtonality (music with 36 notes to an octave) and electronic music. His theories on new music made him the target of musical conservatives, most notably Hans Pfitzner, who attacked him for his "sterile intellectualism". Yet Busoni was never able to escape the pull of tradition and his more daring notions were never incorporated into his own compositions. Instead he preferred to write music that looked back to the eighteenth century for inspiration, an approach he termed "Young Classicism" and defined as "the mastering, sifting and exploitation of all the achievements of preceding experiments".

Busoni made several false starts in the field of opera and did not complete his first, *Sigune*, until 1892 and then never orchestrated it. The 1890s were mainly dedicated to playing the piano, but in 1893 the first performance of Verdi's *Falstaff* revitalized his faith in Italian music. Around this time he first thought of an opera on the Faust myth, an idea that was to preoccupy him for twenty-three years but which he only began making a reality in 1916. By then he had completed three operas: *Die Brautwahl* is a confused setting of a Hoffmann novella, but

HULTON DEUTSCH

Ferruccio Busoni (seated) with admirers – including, on the far left, Paul Hindemith

Arlecchino and *Turandot*, both written under the influence of "Young Classicism", are brilliant examples of Busoni's eclectic but highly individual style. He died leaving his masterpiece, *Doktor Faust*, incomplete – it was finished by Philipp Jarnach, one of his pupils, and given its first performance just ten months after the composer's death. In recent years a revised edition of the score, by Anthony Beaumont, has revealed *Doktor Faust* as one of the most powerful and mysterious of all modern operas.

Arlecchino

Composed 1914–16.
First performed May 11, 1917.
Libretto by the composer.

Synopsis

Scene 1 (Harlequin the rogue)
Arlecchino (Harlequin) flirts with the beautiful Annunziata while her old husband, Ser Matteo, is reading Dante. Arlecchino tells the old man that the town is under attack and locks him in the house. When Cospicuo the Abbot and the Doctor walk past the house, they are alarmed at the old man's news and decide to tell the mayor; in the end they finish up in the local tavern.

Scene 2 (Harlequin the warrior)
Arlecchino tells Ser Matteo that he has been called up for the army and grants him permission to take his copy of Dante with him.

Scene 3 (Harlequin the husband)
Arlecchino is about to enter Matteo's house when his wife, Colombina, begins berating him for his infidelity. After he makes his getaway, a wandering minstrel, Leandro, appears and begins serenading Colombina. Arlecchino overhears and challenges him to a duel.

Scene 4 (Harlequin the victor)
Cospicuo and the Doctor return from the tavern and fall over Leandro's body, which they haul into a donkey cart. With everybody gone Arlecchino returns in order to elope with Annunziata. Ser Matteo comes home and waits patiently for his wife.

Since *Die Brautwahl* Busoni had become increasingly interested in anti-naturalistic forms of theatre, in particular the commedia dell'arte and the marionette theatre. The hour-long *Arlecchino* was originally conceived by him as a comic intermezzo that would form part of

Doktor Faust, but it gradually came to take on a life of its own. The libretto, Busoni's own, was written in 1913 and was partly inspired by a visit to Bergamo – the traditional home of Harlequin and the opera's setting – as well as by a performance of Schoenberg's *Pierrot Lunaire*. As in *Pierrot*, Busoni employs a type of speech-song for Harlequin that is strictly notated as regards rhythm but not as regards pitch. It establishes the eponymous anti-hero as someone who operates by a different set of rules to everybody else, a character who prevails out by cunning and guile.

The score is full of references to various musical genres, encompassing styles as diverse as Gluck and ragtime, and on one level it functions as a kind of anti-opera – above all in Leandro's music, which mimics the kind of expressive bombast that Busoni found so objectionable in verismo opera. However, this element of parody has begun to evaporate by the fourth scene, at the end of which triumphant Harlequin declares, "Now shines my star. The world stands open! The earth is young! Love is free!". According to Busoni, some people found this conclusion "scornful and inhuman", and certainly *Arlecchino* is not a warm opera. But for all the Neoclassical acerbity it is an engrossing work, upholding the composer's declaration that "Just as melody is supreme among all the composer's resources, the human voice remains the most important and expressive of sound media."

Richter, Mentzer, Mohr, Holzmair, Dahlberg; Lyon Opera Chorus and Orchestra; Nagano.
(Virgin VCD7 5913-2; 2 CDs; with *Turandot*).

Since recording this set for Virgin in 1992, Kent Nagano has gone on to greater things, but this relatively early product is still remarkably impressive. It's tightly drawn and features some splendidly idiomatic playing from the Lyon orchestra, and if Ernst Richter and Susanne Mentzer over-play their hands as Arlecchino and Columbina, the baritone Wolfgang Holzmair, as Cospicuo, suggests something of the tremendous talent that has since thrust him into the international limelight. The sound is superb and the accompanying *Turandot* is more than satisfying (see p.429).

Gester, Malbin, Wallace, Evans, Dickie; Glyndebourne Festival Orchestra; Pritchard.
(EMI CMS5 65284-2; 2 CDs; with *Barber of Baghdad*).

This 1954 recording of *Arlecchino* has been re-released at mid-price, accompanied by Leinsdorf's 1956 recording of extracts for Carl Cornelius's *Barber of Baghdad* (1858). While Pritchard lacks Nagano's feel for Busoni's orchestral palette, he does have the stronger cast, and there is something to be said for his gentler approach. Kurt Gester is beautifully understated in the title role, and Cospicuo and Leandro are unforgettably captured by Geraint Evans and Murray Dickie. The sound is OK for the time.

Turandot

Composed 1917.
First performed May 11, 1917.
Libretto by the composer, after Gozzi.

Synopsis

Act I

Having been separated from his servant Barak following his father's defeat in battle, Prince Kalaf is reunited with him in Peking. Barak tells Kalaf of the Princess Turandot, who poses three riddles to her suitors and executes them if they cannot answer. When Kalaf sees her portrait he rushes to the palace, where the Emperor Altoum fails to dissuade the prince from his pursuit of Turandot. Kalaf answers the final riddle and when Turandot refuses to marry him, he counters with his own riddle: What is his name?

Act II

Adelma, who still loves Kalaf from afar, betrays his name to Turandot in the hope that she might win him for herself. When Turandot appears she announces his name and Kalaf realizes he is doomed. But Turandot, though dressed in mourning, has realized that she loves him after all and, to the crowd's astonishment, she welcomes Kalaf as her husband. The opera ends in praise of Buddha and the virtues of love.

Like Puccini's far better known opera of the same title, Busoni's *Turandot* is a version of a piece by the eighteenth-century playwright Carlo Gozzi, who employed the stock characters of commedia dell'arte in a rather more fantastical manner than his contemporary Goldoni. Busoni composed incidental music for the play in 1905, and its success in Max Reinhardt's celebrated Berlin production six years later prompted Busoni to set the tale as an opera, intending it to form a double-bill with *Arlecchino* under the heading *La nuova commedia dell'arte*.

Busoni remained much truer to Gozzi's original than did Puccini, and the spirit of his opera is that of a comedic fantasy with a moralizing and affirmative ending. The Princess is less an ice-maiden than an intelligent woman trying to control her own destiny – albeit by cruel means. When composing *Turandot* Busoni drew heavily from a book containing examples of musical styles from Arabia, India and China, and the oriental colour is not only more pronounced but more realistic than in Puccini's opera. But it is also much less melodic and more brittle and febrile – so much so that many will find this opera rather heavy going.

Gessendorf, Dahlberg, Selig, Sima; Lyon Opera Chorus; Lyone Opera Orchestra; Nagano.
(Virgin VCD7 593 13-2; 2 CDs; with *Arlecchino*).

Aside from his recording of Prokofiev's *Love for Three Oranges*, this 1991 set is Kent Nagano's finest moment on record as an opera conductor. His sense of timbre and nuance is shown to great effect, bringing real verve to Busoni's curious orchestrations. His cast generate a fair measure of spontaneity: Stefan Dahlberg's Kalaf and Mechtild Gessendorf's Turandot are exceptional, both vocally and theatrically, and the remaining singers clearly relish the opportunity to impress.

Doktor Faust

Composed 1916–24; completed by Philipp Jarnach 1925.
First performed May 21, 1925.
Libretto by the composer.

Synopsis

Prelude I

At Wittenberg the scholar Faust is working in his study when Wagner, his servant, announces three students from Krakow, who present him with a magic book.

Prelude II

Using the book, Faust summons the demon Mephistopheles, with whom he strikes a pact: in exchange for almost limitless powers, Faust will ultimately surrender his freedom to Mephistopheles.

Scenic Intermezzo

In a chapel the body of Gretchen, a suicide whom Faust seduced, is watched over by her brother, who swears revenge. Mephistopheles arranges the brother's murder.

Scene 1

The Duke of Parma is celebrating his wedding. Faust is presented as a world-famous magician. He creates three magic tableaux: Samson and Delilah, Solomon and the Queen of Sheba, and Salome and John the Baptist. The Duchess becomes mesmerized by Faust and leaves with him.

Scene 2

In Wittenberg, Faust presides over a dispute between Catholic and Protestant students but only causes further conflict. Mephistopheles enters carrying the body of the child the Duchess has borne Faust, which he sets on fire producing from the flames a vision of Helen of Troy. Faust is excited by her beauty but cannot grasp her. The students return to inform him that he will die at midnight.

Scene 3

The nightwatchman (Mephistopheles) calls the hour and the students celebrate Wagner's appointment as Faust's successor as rector of the university. Faust, wishing to perform a good deed, gives money to a beggar-woman who turns out to be the Duchess. She urges him to complete his work, and he transfers his soul into the body of the dead child. Faust falls dead as the clock sounds midnight; the child rises and strides away into the night – Mephistopheles has been conquered.

Like Strauss's *Die Frau ohne Schatten*, Busoni's *Faust* is an extremely complex opera that defies brief explication. Unlike the better-known setting by Gounod, Busoni's interpretation is rooted not in Goethe – although his debt to the richness of Goethe's language and style are unmistakable – but rather in the sixteenth-century puppet plays through which Faust first became known to the German public. He also acknowledged a debt to the 1592 play by Christopher Marlowe in constructing a version of the Faust myth that could serve as a platform for his own ideas and beliefs. Busoni's Faust is the archetypal restless scholar, but he is also a representation of the misdirected Romantic artist, isolated from the world by his overweaning arrogance, convinced of his superiority to conventional morality. For all the supernatural elements of the story, Mephistopheles is an expression of Faust's own desires, and Faust's escape from the clutches of Mephistopheles is achieved not through religion but through a more secular decision to transfer the better part of himself into his child, the symbol of the future. This opera is the summation of Busoni's career, and he devoted the last eight years of his life to its completion; even so, at his death two major scenes – the vision of Helen of Troy and the final scene – were still incomplete.

Like Berg's *Wozzeck*, which was premiered only four months after *Faust*, each section of this opera is governed by a traditional musical form, such as a fugue, scherzo or chorale. (Busoni plundered much from his earlier formula-bound works – thus the study scene is an adaptation of the *Sonatina Seconda* for piano, while parts of his *Toccata* occur with the first appearance of the Duchess.) To these conventional forms Busoni applied a no less conventional predilection for operatic "numbers", but these arias and duets are set against some of the most complex polyphonic counterpoint in all opera, generating a Straussian conflation of simplicity and complexity that gives the opera its curiously discomfiting quality. At its most expansive, *Faust* is one of the masterpieces of late Romantic opera. Although Edward Dent's opinion that "*Doktor Faust* moves on a plane of spiritual experience far beyond that of even the greatest of musical works for the stage" is difficult to support, *Faust* is an exquisitely rich work and a profoundly disquieting one.

Fischer-Dieskau, Cochran, de Ridder, Hillebrecht; Bavarian Radio Chorus; Berlin Radio Symphony Orchestra; Leitner. (Deutsche Grammophon 427 413-2GC3; 3 CDs).

This 1969 recording – the only version of Busoni's *Faust* in the catalogue – boasts a sensational Duke of Parma from the under-rated tenor Anton de Ridder, but the show is stolen by Dietrich Fischer-Dieskau's Faust, a role for which he was long celebrated. He gives a penetrating impression of the character's changing personality, and, for once, he is as secure vocally as he is dramatically, spinning a seductive, wonderfully expressive line. Hildegard Hillebrecht and William Cochran are striking as the Duchess and Mephistopheles – although neither makes exactly pleasant listening – while Ferdinand Leitner and the Bavarian forces provide consistent and intense support. Excellent value, but a new recording incorporating Beaumont's more satisfactory completion is now long overdue.

LEOŠ JANÁČEK

b. HUKVALDY, MORAVIA, JULY 3, 1854; d. OSTRAVA, CZECHOSLOVAKIA, AUGUST 12, 1928.

Janáček's operas are amongst the most powerful, accessible and distinctive ever written: once he had found his voice in *Jenůfa*, his personal style – terse, lyrical, pungently characterized, full of colourful orchestration and rhythmic bite – was recognizable in every bar he wrote. Though Janáček was born the year after Verdi completed *La Traviata*, his best music belongs decisively to the twentieth century: the last four operas and several other masterpieces were composed in an astonishing burst of creativity in the last decade of his life.

Janáček was the ninth of thirteen children born into a poor teacher's family in northern Moravia. He was educated in Brno, the Moravian capital, and spent most of his life there, after unsuccessful studies at the conservatories of Leipzig and Vienna. He worked as a teacher in Brno, where the National Theatre premiered all his operas except *The Adventures of Mr Brouček*, while the Czechs in Prague preserved a cool indifference, viewing him as a provincial eccentric who was not to be placed alongside their beloved Smetana and Dvořák. This attitude stills persists today.

As with so many central European composers, folk music was the liberating ingredient in his career. In 1888 he set off on a tour of northern Moravia with the ethnographer František Batoš, and this intense encounter with indigenous culture led to a decisive change in his compositional style. Certain folk tunes found

LEBRECHT COLLECTION

Leoš Janáček – his best years came late

their way into his orchestral and choral compositions, but more profoundly the short, irregular melodic phrases of Moravian music became integral to Janáček's musical language, and echoes of folk ensembles influenced his orchestral sound. A scrupulous observer of people, Janáček also noted down people's speech in musical notation, and these naturalistic "speech melodies" honed his dramatic vocal writing so that it approached the ideal that he had defined: "to compose a melodic curve which will, as if by magic, reveal immediately a human being in one definite phase of his existence". The outcome of all these observations wasn't just a musical liberation, but a national one as well, as folk culture gave him a symbolic means of casting off the German domination of his country. He was an ardent patriot, and the foundation of the Czechoslovak Republic in 1918 was a factor behind the amazing fecundity of his last years.

The other dominating feature of Janáček's later music is its erotic charge. His marriage, to a pupil ten years his junior, was never very successful – they were formally separated in 1917, when Janáček had an affair with Gabriela Horvátová, singer in the Prague production of *Jenůfa*. Soon afterwards he began the crucial relationship of his last decade, when he met Kamila Stösslová, a married woman half his age. Janáček developed an all-consuming but unreciprocated passion for Kamila, to whom he wrote over 700 letters, the most passionate ones being written at an almost daily rate in the last sixteen months of his life. (They have been published in English, edited and translated by John Tyrrell). Janáček's song-cycle, the *Diary of One Who*

Disappeared, was the first work to be inspired by Kamila, who was then transformed into the heroines of three of his finest operas, *Kát'a Kabanová, The Cunning Little Vixen* and *The Makropolus Case*. He died in 1928 from pneumonia while putting the finishing touches to the scoring of his last and most original opera, *From the House of the Dead.*

Janáček's success came late in life. *Jenůfa* was premiered in 1904, when he was fifty years old, and twelve more years were to pass before he finally succeeded in getting the piece staged in Prague. The Prague production launched the composer's international career: performances in Vienna, Berlin and New York soon followed, and by the year of his death *Jenůfa* had been seen in sixty theatres outside Czechoslovakia. Yet, despite these successes, it is only in the last couple of decades that Janáček's operas have firmly established themselves in the international repertoire. This is due in no small measure to the work of the conductor-scholar Sir Charles Mackerras, who prepared editions of the composer's original scores, several of which had been "tidied up" to make them less abrasive. Truly ahead of his time, Janáček has now found his rightful place as one of the true originals of twentieth-century music.

Jenůfa

Její pastorkyňa (Her Foster-Daughter)
Composed 1894–1903.
First performed January 21, 1904.
Libretto by the composer, after Gabriela Preissová.

Synopsis

Act I

The Buryjovka family mill. Autumn. Jenůfa is pregnant by her unreliable cousin Števa, who may be conscripted, leaving the child illegitimate. In the event he is not taken into the army, but the celebrations are interrupted by Jenůfa's stepmother, the Kostelnička (sacristan), who says the couple must wait a year before they marry, to test Števa's sobriety. Laca, who has long been in love with Jenůfa, is jealous and warns Jenůfa off his rival. She rejects him and he slashes her cheek with a knife.

Act II

The Kostelnička's cottage five months later. Winter. Discovering that Jenůfa is pregnant, the Kostelnička has hidden her away to have the baby. Števa is not interested now that Jenůfa's face is scarred, and the Kostelnička tells Jenůfa the child would be better dead. Laca still wishes to marry Jenůfa but doesn't know about the child. The Kostelnička drowns the baby in the river and tells Jenůfa it died soon after the birth.

Act III

The Kostelnička's cottage. Spring. The wedding of Jenůfa and Laca is about to take place. Števa and his new fiancée arrive. The party is disturbed by shouts from the river where a baby's body has been found under the ice in the mill stream. The Kostelnička confesses and explains that she was acting out of concern for Jenůfa's future. Jenůfa says Laca would be better off without her, but he prevails and they agree to face everything together.

Gabriela Preissová, an important figure in the history of Czech theatre, lived in the Moravian-Slovakian border region from 1880 and used her experience of village life in her unromanticized, slice-of-life dramas. Her two early plays, *The Farm Manager's Woman* and *Her Foster-Daughter*, both caused a stir and were transformed into successful operas – the first into Josef Foerster's *Eva* and the second into *Jenůfa*. Janáček's work was the first Czech opera to set prose rather than verse, and it has a prose-like consistency, rejecting individual operatic numbers in favour of a continuous form.

In its dramatic power and hard-hitting subject matter, *Jenůfa* has affinities with the work of Puccini, whose operas were regularly performed in central Europe at that time – indeed the premiere of *Jenůfa* in Brno was followed the next night by a performance of *Tosca*. However, the musical styles of Puccini and Janáček are sharply contrasted, partly for linguistic reasons: Italian is full of long vowels which in music get translated into sustained melodic lines, while Czech is heavy with consonants and percussive rhythms which suggest short but powerful musical phrases. The musical representation of natural speech is a crucial aspect of this opera. "At the time *Jenůfa* was being composed," Janáček wrote, "I drank in the melodies of the spoken word. Furtively, I listened to the speech of passers-by, reading the expression of their faces, following with my eyes every raised voice, noticing the speakers' environment, their company, the time of day, whether it was light or dark, cold or warm. I also rejoiced quietly at the beauty of these speech melodies, at their aptness and the ampleness of their expression. I could see far deeper into the soul of a man to whose speech I listened through its speech melody." Thus Janáček's vocal lines are declamatory rather than conventionally melodic, laid over strong orchestral blocks that add greatly to the emotional impact.

When Janáček had completed *Jenůfa* he submitted it to Karel Kovařovic at the National Theatre in Prague, who turned it down, possibly remembering a savage review Janáček had written of an opera of his some years earlier. It was successfully staged in Brno, where Kovařovic eventually came to see it on the ninth invitation, but still refused to take it up. Only in 1915, after a lot of pressure from Janáček's friends and admirers, did he agree, on condition that he be allowed to make some cuts and revise the orchestration. Janáček agreed and his rough-hewn score was duly given an elegant late-Romantic gloss, a revision that seems to have helped the opera's rapid acceptance abroad. It was only with the reconstructive work of Charles Mackerras in the 1970s that the original Janáček version became the preferred score.

Söderström, Randová, Dvorsky, Ochman; Vienna Philharmonic Orchestra; Mackerras.
(Decca 414 483-2; 2 CDs).

As will become apparent from these listings, Charles Mackerras's recordings of Janáček's principal operas are unsurpassed. In this 1982 recording of *Jenůfa* he brings the necessary emotional drive and rhythmic bite to the proceedings. Elisabeth Söderström and Eva Randová are splendid foils as Jenůfa and the Kostelnička; likewise Petr Dvorský and Wieslav Ochman as the two men. The great moments, such as Jenůfa's lament for her dead child, the dramatic ending to Act II and Jenůfa's final address, are all exceptional, and the Kovařovic version of the final scene is included by way of comparison. Also included is an aria in which the Kostelnička outlines her difficult marriage – Janáček cut it, as it holds up the action, but it adds a nuance to our understanding of the character.

Beňačková, Kniplová, Krejčík, Přibyl; Brno Janáček Opera Orchestra; Jílek.
(Supraphon 10 2751-2; 2 CDs).

This is a very acceptable 1978 recording of the Kovařovic version. Textual considerations aside, Mackerras has the edge in drive and recording clarity, but Gabriela Beňačková is a wonderfully clear-voiced Jenůfa. Vilém Přibyl as Laca sounds a bit of a drip, but that could be considered in character.

Fate

Osud

Composed 1903–05.
First performed September 1, 1934.
Libretto by the composer and Fedora Bartošová.

Synopsis

Act I

A busy summer's day in the spa town of Luhačovice. At the centre of attention is the beautiful Míla, who meets the composer Živný, her former lover and father of her child. She explains that her mother forced her away from him in favour of a richer suitor. The couple are obviously still in love.

Act II

Four years later Míla and Živný are living together with their four-year-old son, Doubek. Živný is still wrestling with his opera in which Míla is jealously portrayed as unfaithful. Míla's insane mother is living with them and in a mad struggle falls down the stairs to her death, dragging Míla with her.

Act III

Eleven years later at the conservatoire where Živný teaches. Students are preparing to perform his unfinished opera. He talks at length about his love for Míla and his music. A storm breaks out and as lightening strikes the room Živný collapses and dies, saying the last act of the opera is in the hands of God.

If the plot of *Osud* seems strange, the story of its conception is equally bizarre. Janáček began it in 1903 after the death of his only surviving child, Olga, had effectively severed the remaining bond between the composer and his wife. He took a holiday in the fashionable Moravian spa town of Luhačovice – where we was to become a regular visitor and eventually meet his great inspiration, Kamila Stösslová. On this occasion he fell for a young woman called Kamila Urválková, whose voice "was like that of a viola d'amore". She told Janáček how Ludvík Čelanský had unfairly portrayed her as a superficial flirt in his opera *Kamila*, and asked him if he'd write her into a more sympathetic scenario. Astonishingly, Janáček agreed. His liaison with Kamila was broken off while he was working on the opera – and so her operatic counterpart, Míla, gradually disappears from *Osud* and dies suddenly at the end of Act II. The glow of lost love remains, though, and it ends as a vehicle for Janáček's preoccupations about love and music.

Not surprisingly the opera has had a difficult history. It was accepted by a theatre in Prague where, ironically enough, Ludvík Čelanský was music director, but the production never took place. Janáček eventually lost interest, moved on to other things, and never saw *Osud* staged. But despite the strange plot (which is a lot more fragmentary and confused than a brief synopsis can suggest), the opera contains some glorious music, as is often the case when Janáček was writing from a powerful personal drive. In the third act, for instance, you get a fascinating insight into Janáček's preccupations as Živný explains the creation of his opera: "All her beauty melted into the dream of that music! And when beautiful truth ended, he used fantasy to find the rhythm of his hungry senses. The libretto came to life again, rousing him and rousing joy, laughter and sorrow."

Far removed from the Moravian peasant world of *Jenůfa*, the scenario of *Osud* could be described as cinematic, with short scenes and much of the action relayed through short encounters and snippets of conversation. The opening scenes are an extraordinary construction of inconsequential and occasionally consequential exchanges, underlined by waltz music that evokes the highly charged social atmosphere of the spa that Janáček so enjoyed. Although the language and imagery are often obscure, *Osud* is an important experiment in Janáček's concept of fast-moving, non-linear drama created by juxtaposition and collage. It is the first step towards the idiosyncratic dramaturgy he was to develop in *The Cunning Little Vixen* and *From the House of the Dead*, although it was not a path he followed consistently – his experimental scores alternate with more conventional dramas like *Kát'a Kabanová* and *The Makropulos Case*. *Osud* and his next opera, *Brouček*, are significant in showing how innovative Janáček could be, for they both predate Berg's *Wozzeck*, the work which is often credited with introducing cinematic and expressionist techniques into opera. What's more, they are very enjoyable in their own right.

 **Straka, Ághová; Czech Philharmonic; Albrecht**
(Orfeo C 384 951 A; 1 CD).

This 1995 recording, from a live concert performance in Prague, is the best way to discover this fascinating score. Both Peter Straka and Lívia Ághová are more relaxed and lyrical than Vilém Přibyl and Jarmila Palivcová in the alternative Supraphon version. The only weakness is Marta Beňačková (not to be confused with Gabriela Beňačková) as the mad mother, who is disturbingly flat for her big moment. The orchestral playing is terrific.

The Adventures of Mr Brouček

Composed 1908–17.
First performed April 23, 1920.
Libretto by V. Dyk and F. S. Procházka, after Svatopluk Čech.

Synopsis

Act I

Mr Brouček staggers out of the Vikárka Inn below Prague castle and attempts to find his way home. He gets caught up in a tiff between the two lovers Málinka and Mazal. Once they are reconciled everyone waves Mr Brouček off for the night and he goes home to sleep. In fact he gets transported to the moon and finds it colonized by pretentious artists and aesthetes who eat flowers – all strangely reminiscent of his friends in the pub. He shocks them all by eating sausages and leaves the artists singing hymns in the Temple of the Arts. Back at the inn day is breaking: the customers are leaving and hear that Mr Brouček had to be carried home. Málinka and Mazal embrace, having spent the night together.

Act II

Once again Mr Brouček is leaving the inn, but after a conversation about fifteenth-century Prague he finds himself lost in one of the city's medieval tunnels. The author Svatopluk Čech appears and laments the declining heroism of the Czech nation. Brouček finds himself in fifteenth-century Prague amidst the holy wars between Jan Hus and the Holy Roman Empire and displays exceptional cowardice for which he is sentenced to death. His plea that he is a child of the future and not yet born carries no weight and he is put into a barrel to be burnt. Back in the pub, the landlord hears groaning from the cellar and finds Brouček drunk in a barrel. He tells the landlord how he helped liberate Prague, but begs him not to tell anyone.

𝄞 *The Adventures of Mr Brouček*, another oddity in Janáček's output, underwent substantial changes in its nine-year process of composition. Its source lies in Svatopluk Čech's satirical tales about Mr Brouček, which had been popular in the 1880s. Janáček decided to set *The Excursion of Mr Brouček to the Moon* in 1908, soon after the poet's death, finding something highly conducive in Čech's treatment of the "moon creatures", his parodic doubles of the pretentious artistic and literary types of Prague. Janáček devised a scenario in which the babbling moon characters had their counterparts in the Vikárka Inn that Brouček frequented (and is still to be found in Prague), but the composer went through several librettists without getting a text he felt was satisfactory, and lost interest in the project in 1914.

Janáček's confidence revived when *Jenůfa* was finally performed in Prague to great success in 1916, and he resumed work on *Brouček*, adding a second part to the opera, the *Excursion to the Fifteenth Century*, as a patriotic statement at a time of Czech aspirations for a national state. Here, though, the subject of the satire was different. In the first part the joke was at the expense of rarified artists, but in the second it is directed at the weak-willed Brouček (which means "beetle"), the representative of those who vacillated at a time of national crisis. The opera was dedicated to Masaryk, the first president of the new Czech Republic.

Like *Osud*, *The Adventures of Mr Brouček* is a flawed work, but it deserves to be seen more often than it is, for its contrasted halves contain some very good music. The love music of Málinka and Mazal anticipates the mood of *Kát'a Kabanová*, the orchestral depiction of Brouček's return from the moon is a glorious episode and the second part contains superb choral writing. Although the piece lacks the concision and drive of Janáček's subsequent operas, it is once again radical in its cross-cutting construction. Though there are similarities with developments in avant-garde theatre, Janáček's approach seems to have been instinctive rather than theoretical and probably grew out of a musical style which was becoming increasingly molecular. By this stage his scores were built up of musical cells and motivic patterns which are repeated, varied, juxtaposed and superimposed. It doesn't all hang together in *Brouček*, but it's always a lot of fun.

Přibyl, Novakák, Švejda, Jonášová, Krejčík; Czech Philharmonic Chorus and Orchestra; Jílek.
(Supraphon 11 2153-2 612; 2 CDs).

This is a very good recording indeed and can be firmly recommended to anyone wanting to explore beyond Janáček's established operas. Apart from Vilém Přibyl as Brouček, all the other roles are small but well characterized, with lots of doubling up. František Jílek captures not only the satire, but the lyricism and heroism as well. The choral singing, which carries so much of the patriotic fervour of part two, is spectacular. The alternative recording (on Orfeo), recorded at the first German performance in Munich in 1959, is little more than a curiosity, despite the presence of the great Fritz Wunderlich as Mazal.

Kát'a Kabanová

Composed 1919–21.
First performed November 23, 1921.
Libretto by the composer, after Ostrovsky.

Synopsis

Act I

The Kabanov household is dominated by the quarrelsome old woman Kabanicha, whose weak-willed son, Tichon, is married to Kát'a. Another man, Boris, has his eyes on Kát'a. Varvara, an orphan adopted into the household, sees Kát'a's unhappiness and urges her to follow her impulses. Tichon goes away to market.

Act II

The women are left in the house and Kabanicha starts her habitual complaining. Varvara organizes a tryst in the garden for Kát'a and Boris, as well as for herself and her lover Kudrjáš. When Kát'a meets Boris she is afraid at first, but finally lets herself go. The two couples are in love.

Act III

It is two weeks later and there is a fearful storm. Tichon has returned and Kát'a is overwhelmed by guilt; despite the attempts of Varvara and Kudrjáš to stop her, she confesses she has spent every night with Boris. She rushes out into the storm. Varvara and Kudrjáš decide to elope, while Kát'a wants to see Boris once more. They find each other and embrace. He has to go to a trading post in Siberia and they say farewell. Kát'a throws herself into the Volga. The family arrive and Tichon, for the first time, gets angry with Kabanicha and blames her for destroying Kát'a. Kabanicha is unmoved.

After the eccentric subjects of his previous two operas, Janáček returned in *Kát'a Kabanová* to a conventionally constructed play and a more traditional menu of operatic ingredients. It is a logical development from

Jenůfa, although Janáček's writing is now more economical and works through a much tighter juxtaposition of lyrical and dramatic moments. Its literary source was *The Storm*, a play by Alexander Ostrovsky, the leading Russian dramatist of the mid-nineteenth century and, like Janáček, an artist interested in rural dialects and singing traditions. It is easy to see why Janáček was attracted to the play, but the composer's principal inspiration was more personal.

In 1917 Janáček, aged 63, had met the 25-year-old Kamila Stösslová in Luhačovice and had fallen in love with her. In his letters to Kamila he frequently referred to his identification of her with his operatic heroines, and in *Kát'a Kabanová*, the first of his operas to be inspired by her, the element of wish fulfilment is clear – the central character is a married woman who has an affair while her husband is away. The other characters are relatively two-dimensional, whereas Kát'a is a far more rounded and dominating character than in the Ostrovsky play, and she has the opera's most radiant music. The Kamila connection is underlined by the inclusion of a part for viola d'amore, an instrument with blatant romantic associations – though in performance the part is usually taken by a conventional viola, as it's impossible to make the instrument heard. Just in case anyone missed the point, Janáček dedicated the opera to Kamila Stösslová.

The opening sets the mood with a brooding orchestral prelude in which the melodic line keeps turning in on itself before reaching the glorious melody that is associated with Kát'a throughout the opera. The timpani then burst in ominously with a motif that returns at decisive moments throughout the score, particularly in the storm music. As you'd expect from the plot, there is plenty of passionate music here – most of it in the orchestral accompaniment around the vocal lines. Janáček's terse cellular style and lyrical intensity are perfectly balanced in this score, which glows with a dark and dreamlike quality.

Söderström, Dvorský, Kniplová; Vienna Philharmonic Orchestra; Mackerras.
(Decca 421 852-2; 2 CDs).

Made in 1976, this was the first of Mackerras's Janáček opera recordings, and he returns to Janáček's original score – even, with the help of the Decca engineers, including the viola d'amore. This performance perfectly conveys the pent-up passion of this piece: the orchestral writing is controlled with great sensitivity and the singing is faultless, with Elizabeth Söderström outstanding in the complex title role. The opera comes with the eccentric *Capriccio* and *Concertino* for piano and orchestra as valuable fill-ups.

The Cunning Little Vixen

Composed 1921–23.
First performed November 6, 1924.
Libretto by the composer, after Rudolf Tešnohlídek.

Synopsis

Act I

Animals and insects are playing in the forest. The Gamekeeper enters and lies down to sleep. A young vixen chases a frog, which lands on the Gamekeeper's nose and wakes him up. He takes the vixen home for his children. At the Gamekeeper's house the vixen talks to the dog and hens who enjoy the domesticated life there. The vixen kills a cock and escapes from the Gamekeeper back into the forest.

Act II

The vixen evicts a badger from his sett and makes it her home. She watches the activities of the Gamekeeper and his friends; the Gamekeeper shoots at the vixen. She meets a fox, they fall in love and marry.

Act III

The Gamekeeper sets a trap, but the vixen and her new family make fun of it. They eat the chickens of a poultry dealer and the vixen is shot dead. The Gamekeeper and friends complain about the passing of time. In a return to the opening scene, the Gamekeeper lies down to sleep on his way home and dreams of a young vixen. He tries to catch her, but succeeds only in grasping a frog. The frog says it was his grandfather last time round and he'd told him about the Gamekeeper.

After the angst-ridden *Kát'a Kabanová* came *The Cunning Little Vixen*, Janáček's most sunny and tuneful opera. Kamila was again an important factor in its creation (she's transmogrified into the resourceful vulpine wife and mother), but the opera's immediate origins lie in the *Bystrouška* (Sharp-ears) stories, a popular cartoon strip in Brno's liberal daily paper *Lidové noviny*. Focusing on the vixen and the Gamekeeper, these stories – unlike many anthropomorphic tales – were not satirical in intent, but simply an evocation of country life in Moravian dialect, which obviously appealed to the composer, who in 1921 had bought a house in his native village of Hukvaldy, where walks in the surrounding countryside provided relaxation and inspiration. Once his attention had been drawn to the strip, Janáček arranged to meet the writer, Rudolf Tešnohlídek, and started a special study of animals, noting down, no doubt, their "speech melodies". Janáček fashioned his own libretto, a practice to which he was now accustomed, and achieved a melding of the human and animal worlds that enabled them to interact without coyness or pomposity. But he made a significant departure from Tešnohlídek's collection of stories, which ends with the vixen's courtship and wedding: Janáček kills the vixen in Act III and thereby expands his subject into the cycle of birth, death and rebirth.

In keeping with its rural theme, *The Cunning Little Vixen* relies much more on folk-like melodies than its predecessor, but it is also one of the more experimental of Janáček's scores. The piece moves between opera, ballet, mime and substantial orchestral interludes, with a number of recurring melodic patterns and motifs unifying the whole work. The predominant sound is of the luscious strings that evoke the forest, while specific creatures are characterized by idiosyncratic figures in the woodwind and solo violin. The whole effect is novel, fresh and life affirming – the seventy-year-old Janáček speaks through the Gamekeeper, who observes as he falls asleep that "men and women will walk with heads bowed, and realize that a more-than-earthly joy has passed that way." The composer requested that the final scene be played at his funeral, as indeed it was.

Popp, Randová, Jedlička; Vienna Philharmonic Orchestra; Mackerras. (Decca 417 129-2; 2 CDs).

This 1981 recording is demonstration-quality Janáček, as Mackerras peels away some Talich re-orchestrations to give us the original score. Lucia Popp, as the vixen, is very youthful and mercurial; Eva Randová is restrained and respectful as the fox and Dalibor Jedlička as the Gamekeeper is refreshingly down-to earth. Particular highlights include Popp's rapture as the vixen becomes aware of and revels in her beauty; the joyful wedding, complete with the wordless, singing forest; and Jedlička's matter-of-fact final remarks. Luxuriant and permeated with a glowing warmth, this recording is probably the place for newcomers to Janáček to start.

The Makropulos Case

Composed 1923–25.
First performed December 18, 1926.
Libretto by the composer, after Karel Čapek.

Synopsis

Act I

The offices of the lawyer Dr Kolenatý. The outcome of the century-old inheritance case of Gregor vs Prus is expected today. Kolenatý outlines the case at length to the famous opera singer Emilia Marty, who reveals an uncanny knowledge of past events concerning Elian MacGregor, the mistress of "Pepi" Prus, and directs them to an unknown will. Emilia Marty wants a document in Greek from Albert Gregor, who is attracted by her.

Act II

Backstage at the opera house. After a triumphant performance Emilia Marty holds court for her admirers. Prus and Gregor intrigue over various documents that will affect the case. Both men are now fascinated by Marty. Prus agrees to bring her the Greek document she wants if she will meet him that night.

Act III

Emilia Marty's hotel room. Baron Prus has spent the night with Marty, but claims she is cold and unfeeling. She asks for the document. Various people arrive with questions as her past catches up with her. Emilia Marty tells her story: She was born Elina Makropulos in 1585 to the alchemist at the court of Rudolf II. Her father invented a potion to prolong life and tested it on her. She has lived for over three hundred years and changed her name several times, keeping the initials E.M. She needs to take the formula again to stay alive. But, she says, infinite life has no meaning: it only has a value when it is finite. The formula is burnt and Emilia Marty dies.

Karel Čapek was sceptical when Janáček approached him for the rights to *The Makropulos Case*: the legalistic paraphernalia at the centre of his play did not seem to lend itself to operatic treatment, and the modern-day setting of offices, theatres and hotel rooms seemed especially unconducive to a composer of Janáček's folkloric proclivities. "That old crank," he joked, "soon he'll be setting the local column in the newspaper." (Janáček had already done just that, of course, with *The Cunning Little Vixen*.) But when the playwright saw the premiere in Brno he was obliged to admit – "He did it a hundred times better than I could ever have imagined." In complete contrast with the sprightliness and optimism of *The Cunning Little Vixen*, this opera is a poignant evocation of world-weariness.

The opera opens with a wonderful prelude full of sweeping strings, brass and timpani, with offstage fanfares and drums harking back to the distant world of Rudolf's court. Having deployed his full resources in this effusive, lyrical outburst, Janáček holds it all back, keeping the music dry and rather spare until the conclusion – there are no duets or ensembles, and there's a high level of dissonance, making this one of the composer's more arduous scores at first hearing. Janáček saves the most heartfelt music for the end, with Emilia's overwhelming confession and renunciation of her immortality. The brass and drums of the opening return with an incredible feeling of inevitability, and Janáček brings it all out of reserve as warm and cathartic string phrases surge beneath Emilia's cool resignation, making her seem for the first time human and vulnerable. Janáček is determined to warm up a heroine he described as "the icy one" – clearly reflecting the composer's ambivalent feelings about Kamila Stösslová, whom he had come to realize would never reciprocate his affection.

Söderström, Dvorský, Zítek; Vienna Philharmonic Orchestra; Mackerras. (Decca 430 372-2; 2 CDs).

Emilia Marty should dominate the proceedings throughout, and that is exactly what Elisabeth Söderström does in this classic 1978 recording. But the supporting male roles of lawyers, clerks and claimants are well sung by artists who are regulars on these Mackerras recordings: Petr Dvorsky, Vladimir Krejčik, Václav Zítek and Dalibor Jedlička. Beno Blachut is excellent in the one comic role, Emilia's former lover Hauk-Šendorf. As usual Mackerras is assured in the dramatic pacing, so important in this piece. Like all in this Decca series, the set has very full essays by John Tyrrell, the leading expert on Janáček; the early *Lachian Dances* are included as a fill-up.

From the House of the Dead

Composed 1927–28.
First performed April 12, 1930.
Libretto by the composer, after Dostoyevsky.

Synopsis

Act I

A Siberian prison camp in winter. Prisoners emerge from the barracks to wash and eat. An argument breaks out. Petrovich, a new prisoner, arrives. He is interrogated by the Commandant, who orders him to be flogged. The prisoners tease an eagle with a broken wing, but admire its defiance in captivity. Some prisoners go to work, others recount their stories. Petrovich is brought back after his flogging.

Act II

By the banks of a river, the following summer. Petrovich strikes up a friendship with Alyeya, a Tartar boy. It is a feast day and a priest comes to give a blessing. The prisoners perform two plays on an improvised stage. Another fight breaks out and Alyeya is injured.

Act III

The prison hospital. Alyeya is sick. Various prisoners tell their stories. The Commandant informs Petrovich he is to be released. The prisoners release the eagle and celebrate its freedom as it flies away before they are ordered back to work.

Janáček's last opera is his most extraordinary. Unlike all his others there is no central character and it is written for a cast of male voices, except for the young boy Alyeya and the brief appearance of a prostitute. The subject matter itself – life in a Siberian prison camp – is hardly standard operatic material, but Janáček makes from it a richly coloured collage of characters and images. Preparing the Czech libretto directly from Dostoevsky's Russian text as he went along, Janáček worked frenetically at what he knew would be his final work. "So I am finishing one work after another," he wrote, "as if I had to settle my accounts with life. With my new opera I hurry like a baker throwing loaves into the oven." By his 74th birthday, in July 1928, the work was pretty well complete, apart from some scoring revisions to the third act, which he was still working on at his death a month later.

A performing version was prepared by Janáček's pupils Břetislav Bakala and Osvald Chlubna. Looking over the chamber-like score, with its eccentric orchestration (the staves simply disappeared whenever instruments fell silent), they came to the conclusion that the work was substantially unfinished. Acting with the best of intentions, Chlubna thickened out the orchestration with lush woodwind and harp, and gave the opera a more optimistic tone by finishing with a reprise of the "freedom" chorus instead of with Janáček's brusque call to work. This is how the work was premiered in 1930 and continued to be played until Rafael Kubelík and then Charles Mackerras did the necessary work to get back to the original version.

It's not surprising that Bakala and Chlubna were misled. The work is indeed much more spare and harsh than Janáček's previous operas. There is less blending of instrumental textures, and the work is built up from small-scale motifs dynamically intercut with great severity, as in the late chamber pieces, taking to its conclusion the process begun in *Osud*. Strange combinations of instruments and of sounds at opposite ends of the register had always been a characteristic of Janáček's orchestral style, but they are much more extreme in this piece (high piccolos and low trombones), and the music also features some distinctive percussion instruments – a rattle, an anvil and, most notably, prisoners' chains. It makes it a brittle and spiky score, but absolutely appropriate in the context.

In his operatic writing Janáček had been relying increasingly on monologues and here he takes the technique to its conclusion, writing a sequence of monologues for the prisoners' stories, juxtaposed with choral passages that underline the collective nature of the piece. Despite the seemingly gloomy subject, Janáček gets great contrasts of mood into the opera: there are sudden moments of lyricism, and the second act, set outside the prison camp, brings relief with its festive atmosphere and lightheartedly tuneful music for the prisoners' plays. And every page of the score is imbued with Janáček's all-embracing humanism, a philosophy encapsulated in an article found after Janáček's death. In it he wrote: "Why do I go into the dark, frozen cells of criminals with the author of *Crime and Punishment*? Into the minds of criminals and there I find a spark of God. You will not wipe away the crimes from their brow, but equally you will not extinguish the spark of God. Into what depths it leads – how much truth there is in their work!"

Jedlička, Žídek, Blachut; Vienna Philharmonic Orchestra; Mackerras. (Decca 430 375-2; 2 CDs).

This recording from 1980, the last in Mackerras's series of Janáček recordings, is as exemplary as the others. In what is essentially a company piece with no leading roles, it makes no sense to single anyone out – suffice it to say that the characterization and choral work is first-rate throughout. The recording is very clearly focused, which is important for the detailed textures and timbres in this piece. As a valuable contrast, two of Janáček's most joyous works from his old age – *Mládí* and *Říkadla* – are included.

BOHUSLAV MARTINŮ

b. POLIČKA, BOHEMIA, DECEMBER 8, 1890; d. LIESTAL, SWITZERLAND, AUGUST 28, 1959.

After Janáček, Martinů was the leading Czech composer of the twentieth century and he was immensely prolific, with fifteen or so operas amongst his four hundred compositions. Although Martinů's operas were not always successful, they do reveal a composer trying something fresh and they open the door to his more idiosyncratic music. They have rarely been seen on stage but several have been recorded, and *Julietta*, *Ariane* and *The Greek Passion*, in particular, deserve to be more widely heard.

Martinů was born in the little town of Polička in the Bohemian-Moravian highlands, an area of remarkable musical riches (Smetana and Mahler were born nearby). He came from a humble family, but thanks to local donations was able to attend the Prague Conservatory, where he was not a very successful student. In 1923 he took advantage of a small grant from the Czech Ministry of Education and went to Paris, where he stayed for over seventeen years, absorbing elements of the music hall, jazz and the musical avant garde. The most inspired of his early operas, *Les Trois Souhaits* (1929), takes place in a film studio during the shooting of a silent movie, and calls for a jazzy band of flutes, saxophones, banjo, piano and accordion – clearly showing the influence of Krenek's *Jonny spielt auf* (see p.420).

After a few years in Paris, Martinů also started to draw on the folk traditions of his native Czechoslovakia, and his third completed opera, *Hry o Marii* (The Miracles of Mary) was a follow-up to his very successful Czech fairytale ballet, *Špalíček*. After that he produced a couple of operas for the new medium of radio, most notably *Veselohra na mostě* (Comedy on the Bridge), a typically Czech absurdist morality tale. Two years later, in 1937, came Martinů's best opera, *Julietta*. It was one of Martinů's favourite scores: he carried it with him his whole life, quoted its main motif in his *Symphony No. 6*, and was working on a French version immediately before his death in 1959.

In 1940, soon after the premiere of his magnificent *Double Concerto* (his finest work), Martinů was blacklisted by the Nazis and his music was banned in occupied Czechoslovakia. Martinů and his wife fled Paris with no more than a suitcase and the score of *Julietta*, and went to America. After the war ill-health prevented Martinů from returning to Czechoslovakia, and with the arrival of the Communist regime in 1948 he reluctantly decided to stay in the US. Having composed two new television operas, he returned to Europe in 1953 and settled in France. He wrote an Italian-style comic opera, *Mirandolina*, after Goldoni, but the major operatic scores of his last years were *Ariane* and *The Greek Passion*. Martinů died in a Swiss hospital before either of these two pieces had been performed. His body was transferred to the family grave in his beloved Polička in 1979.

Julietta

Composed 1936–37.
First performed March 16, 1938.
Libretto by the composer, after Georges Neveux.

Synopsis

This opera is in effect a sequence of unconnected episodes with a huge range of surreal characters, but a rough outline might run as follows:

Act I

Michel returns to a small seaside town in search of Julietta, a young girl whose voice he heard at an open window on a previous visit and has obsessed him ever since. Everyone in this strange world has lost their memory and when Michel tells them about a toy duck he had as a child he is declared mayor of the town – a fact immediately forgotten by everyone. He finally finds Julietta and they arrange to meet in the forest.

Act II

Several men are looking for Julietta in the forest. A fortune-teller reveals the past, not the future; a travelling merchant offers memories for sale. Julietta and Michel meet and declare their love, but never manage to understand each other. She tries to leave and Michel shoots at her as she goes. Michel is uncertain whether the shooting was a dream or not. Sailors who go in search of Julietta only find her scarf. Michel goes to her house, but no one knows of her there. Michel leaves on a ship and hears Julietta's voice again from her window.

Act III

Michel is at the Office of Dreams. Various characters come in pursuit of their dreams and in all of them a Julietta appears. Michel wants to stay in the Office of Dreams, but the clerk says he must leave and shows him the grey, faceless creatures that are trapped there with their dreams. Michel hears Julietta calling from behind a door. The night-watchman locking up shows Michel there is nobody behind the door and he is about to leave when he hears the voice again. Michel is determined to go back and the opera returns to the beginning as he re-enters his dream.

Julietta is Martinů's operatic masterpiece and it was a work to which he was deeply attached – the subjects of longing and wandering had an obvious resonance for a composer who was an exile for so much of his life. Compounding the personal significances, the figure of Julietta was associated not only with his wife Charlotte but also with his student Vítězslava Kaprálová, with whom he may have been romantically involved. When she died in 1940, aged only 25, her last words were "Julietta, Julietta".

Neveux had granted the rights for an operatic version of his story to Kurt Weill, but he received an invitation from Martinů to come and hear the first act of *Julietta* at his home. Before the play-through he didn't have the courage to tell Martinů that the rights had already been taken, but by the end Neveux was overwhelmed: "For the first time in my life I had really entered the world of *Julietta,*" he wrote. "Martinů had made such a masterpiece of it that I was dazzled. The next day I wrote to Weill's American agent that there had been a misunderstanding and my play was not free." Martinů's score enhances the atmosphere of nostalgia and longing with yearning string passages and poignant snatches of half-forgotten melodies on the accordion. However, this is no easy-listening mood music. Apart from a few recurring motifs or chord progressions, the score is built up from short sections and the often unrelated statements of dozens of different characters – even the two central fiigures, Julietta and Michel, have very little in the way of extended solos or arias. This fragmentary quality makes *Julietta* quite hard work for a new listener, making his more conventional *Greek Passion* a better introduction to Martinů's operatic world.

Tauberová, Žídek; Prague National Theatre Chorus and Orchestra; Krombholc.
(Supraphon 10 8176-2; 3 CDs).

This classic account dates from the opera's revival at the Prague National Theatre in 1965. The conductor Jaroslav Krombholc was a close collaborator with Václav Talich, who conducted the premiere performances, and succeeded him as chief conductor at the National Theatre. There are no weak links in the substantial cast, which is led by Maria Tauberová as the intangible Julietta and Ivo Žídek as the troubled dreamer Michel.

Ariane

Ariadne

Composed 1958.
First performed March 2, 1961.
Libretto by the composer, after Georges Neveux.

Synopsis

Tableau I

Athenian youths arrive at Knossos to kill the Minotaur. Amongst them is Theseus, who meets Ariadne (Ariane). He turns out to be the unknown lover she is waiting for.

Tableau II

Burun, one of Theseus's companions, ridicules him for being vanquished by a woman when they have come to fight the Minotaur. Burun is slain by the Minotaur and Theseus avenges his death. The Minotaur takes the form of Theseus himself and the hero has to kill his alter-ego, the Theseus who fell in love and married Ariadne.

Tableau III
Theseus leaves with his companions. Ariadne sings her farewell.

Amazingly, *Ariane* was composed within just one month, as a sort of diversion from *The Greek Passion*. It was specifically intended for Maria Callas and so, unlike *Julietta*, Martinů's other Neveux opera, it is packed with gloriously lyrical coloratura vocal lines. Martinů's wife Charlotte remembered: "One evening I was listening to the radio and suddenly I heard a marvellous voice. It was Maria Callas, who was giving a recital at the Paris Opera. Bohuš was reading in the next room, but when he heard her voice, he came in and listened, thoroughly impressed." In the event, however, Callas never sang the role of Ariadne.

Martinů constructed his own libretto (in French) from Neveux's play *Le voyage de Thésée*, and the charm of the piece lies in its simplicity and the ambiguity of a scenario in which Theseus and the Minotaur might be one and the same creature. It's a disquieting take on a story that has been set in different versions by a great many composers, including Monteverdi (the score is lost except for the lament), Handel and, of course, Richard Strauss. Martinů, in one of his most attractive Neoclassical scores, refers back to Monteverdi (in the lament) and to the Baroque world of Martinů's compatriot Jiří Benda, who wrote a melodrama called *Ariadne* in 1775. The opera is constructed on a formal scheme with a sinfonia introducing each of the three tableaux, the first two of which basically consist of extended duets for Theseus and Ariadne, while the last is largely devoted to Ariadne's final aria. Restrained rather than dramatic, but lyrical and transparent throughout, the music features some very imaginative instrumental scoring – the third tableau, from the extraordinary sinfonia beginning (with harp and high woodwind) to the concluding aria, contains some of Martinů's most beautiful music.

Lindsley, Phillips; Czech Philharmonic Orchestra; Neumann.
(Supraphon 10 4395-2; 1 CD).

The American singer Celina Lindsley is no Maria Callas, but she brings off Ariadne's demanding role splendidly, likewise the baritone Norman Phillips as Theseus. Some of the other roles are less assured, but this is an enjoyable recording of a very appealing score.

The Greek Passion

Composed 1956–59.
First performed June 9, 1961.
Libretto by the composer, after Nikos Kazantzakis.

Synopsis

Act I
In the Greek village of Lycovrissi the priest, Grigoris, announces the cast of villagers for next year's Passion play. They include Manolios as Christ, the widow Katerina as Mary Magdalene, Yannakos as Peter and Panait as Judas. As they think about preparing for their roles, a group of refugees arrives in the village. They are repulsed by the priest, but helped by Manolios, Katerina and others.

Act II
Yannakos is pursuaded by the miser Ladas to buy valuables from the refugees at a knock-down price. Manolios is approached at the well by Katerina. She confesses her love, but Manolios rejects her. Yannakos goes to the refugees to get their gold, but seeing their situation just gives them his money.

Act III
Manolios is tormented by dreams about being worthy to portray Christ. When he wakes his fiancée Lenio comes to him, but he rejects her. She goes off with a shepherd boy. Manolios goes to Katerina, who thinks he's come to love her. He says he can't and she decides to follow him spiritually. Manolios preaches to the village to help the refugees, while Grigoris and Panait plot against him.

Act IV
Lenio and the shepherd Nikolios get married. At the height of the festivities Grigoris excommunicates Manolios, who passionately speaks up for the refugees. Led on by the priest, the villagers close in and Panait kills Manolios. Katerina leads the refugees in a call for mercy and they move on again.

Written in the very last years of Martinů's life, *The Greek Passion* looks back to his early opera *The Miracles of Mary* in making use of a mystery play and a folk-influenced musical language. But whereas that was an essentially static and ritualistic work, this one is about a real community tearing itself apart. It's based on the novel *Christ Recrucified* by Nikos Kazantzakis; Martinů had originally wanted to set his *Zorba the Greek*, but took the author's advice that *Christ Recrucified* would make a better libretto.

Martinů makes some attempt to evoke the Greek setting – there's a plangent reedy melody at the beginning of Act III, the sounds of a folk band at the wedding, and the use of Orthodox choral music (the composer visited Greek churches and noted down the chants in his sketch books). But the overall sound – reflecting Martinů's desperate homesickness for Czechoslovakia and his native village of Polička – is a distinctively Czech infusion of folk-based melody and lyricism, a sound which characterizes much of his late work and is most evident in the four folk cantatas written at the same time.

Martinů underplayed the specific politics of a story set in Turkish-occupied Greece, wanting to write a piece which universalized the problems of refugees. Expressing his deep sadness at his twenty-year exile, Martinů laboured at this opera over an uncharacteristically extended period, producing a piece that has a religious quality rare in his work and is equalled only in the *Field Mass*, written when Czechoslovakia was overwhelmed by the Nazis in 1939. In *The Greek Passion* Martinů gives unprecedented weight to the choral writing in his powerful depiction of a community in conflict, and the interaction of its cast makes it Martinů's most dramatic and realistic opera, in a nineteenth-century sense.

Mitchinson, Field, Davies, Tomlinson; Brno State Philharmonic Orchestra; Mackerras.
(Supraphon 10 3611-2; 2 CDs).

This recording derives from the Welsh National Opera production of *The Greek Passion* in 1981 and uses Martinů's English libretto, intended for the abortive Covent Garden premiere. The soloists, excellently led by John Mitchinson, Helen Field and John Tomlinson, are predominantly British and they work very well, apart from some unnervingly strong Welsh accents. Sir Charles Mackerras is the perfect conductor in this repertoire. For your first exploration of Martinů's operas, this is the place to start.

ERICH KORNGOLD

b. BRNO, MORAVIA (NOW CZECH REPUBLIC), MAY 29, 1897; d. HOLLYWOOD, NOVEMBER 29, 1957.

Erich Wolfgang Korngold, the son of the leading Viennese music critic, Julius Korngold, was one of the most astonishing musical prodigies of the century. At the age of nine he wrote a cantata, *Gold*, which so impressed Gustav Mahler that he proclaimed the boy a genius and arranged for him to study with Zemlinsky. His ballet-pantomime *Der Schneemann*, written in his thirteenth year, was premiered under Zemlinsky's baton and subsequently performed all over Austria and Germany. Both Puccini and Strauss – the dominant influences on his style – were admirers, the latter remarking that "this firmness of style, this sovereignty of form, this individual expression, this harmonic structure – one shudders with awe to realize these compositions were written by a boy."

Korngold's first two operas, *Der Ring des Polykrates* and *Violanta*, were produced in 1916 as a double bill at the Munich Staatsoper, conducted by Bruno Walter. Both were emotionally charged works employing a rich post-Wagnerian chromaticism that became even more intense for his next opera, *Die tote Stadt* (The Dead City), which is generally considered his masterpiece in the genre. *Die tote Stadt* was staged simultaneously at Cologne and at Hamburg (where Korngold was musical director) to huge acclaim.

Throughout the 1920s Korngold was involved with the renowned producer Max Reinhardt, making new arrangements for him of operettas by Johann Strauss the Younger and Offenbach. He also wrote another opera, *Das Wunder der Heliane* (1924–26), which he considered his finest work but which was overshadowed by the extraordinary success of Krenek's *Jonny spielt auf* (see p.421). Even so, in 1928 the *Neue Wiener Tagblatt* conducted a poll which named Korngold and Schoenberg as the two greatest living composers. But his success in Germany was not to last. By the early 1930s the growing intensity of anti-Semitism in Germany led his publishers, Schott, to warn him that future performances of his music would be extremely difficult. In 1934 Max Reinhardt invited him to accompany him to Hollywood to work on a film version of *A Midsummer Night's Dream* for which Korngold re-scored Mendelssohn's incidental music. He returned briefly to Vienna to work on his final opera, *Die Kathrin,* before returning to Hollywood, where over the next twelve years he was to write eighteen outstanding film scores, mainly for Warner Brothers, two of which – *Robin Hood* and *Anthony Adverse* – were to win him Oscars.

Yet the American years ruined his career. Leaving Hollywood for Vienna in 1949, he was now disparaged as much for having worked in the cinema as for the old-fashioned style of his music. After the critics panned the belated Viennese performance of *Die Kathrin* (the Nazis had cancelled the 1937 production), he gave up the idea of a sixth opera and he devoted the remaining years of his life to orchestral music, including a violin concerto which was performed and recorded by Jascha Heifetz. Many of these later works employed material previously used in his film scores.

Korngold is one of several candidates for the title of "last of the great Romantics", for as a boy he brilliantly assimilated a late Romantic style from which he never later deviated. His work is full of warm and expansive melodies and the lushest of harmonies ("more corn than gold" was how one critic snidely described his violin concerto), while lacking the contrapuntal adventurousness of Strauss or Pfitzner. But in the last twenty years there has been a major revival of interest in his work: *Die tote Stadt* was staged at the Met in 1975 and several young virtuosi have added the violin concerto to their repertoire. The hothouse emotionalism of his operas will not appeal to everyone, but those unafraid to wallow will not be disappointed.

Die tote Stadt

The Dead City

Composed 1917–19.
First performed December 4, 1920.
Libretto by Erich and Julius Korngold, after Rodenbuch.

Synopsis

Act I

Paul is in mourning for his dead wife, Marie. He rarely leaves their house and preserves her room as if she were still alive. A close friend, Frank, persuades him to leave the house for a few hours and, while out walking, he meets Marietta. He is struck by her resemblance to Marie and invites her back to his home. Paul and Marietta dance and he places Marie's shawl across her shoulders and begins to believe that his wife has returned. Marietta sees Marie's portrait and realizes what is happening. She mocks the increasingly desperate Paul, who is torn by his feelings for her. In a vision Marie implores him to "see and understand".

Act II

The entire act, which is dominated by Marietta, unfolds in Paul's imagination. He sees her being seduced by Frank, rising from the dead and exorcizing the ghost of her rival, Marie.

Act III

The nightmare continues into the final act in which Marietta desecrates Marie's possessions, driving Paul to strangle her with a length of his wife's hair. When he awakes, the plait is in his hands, but Marietta is nowhere to be seen. He understands Marie's riddle and, changing out of his black suit, he leaves the city.

Puccini declared *Die tote Stadt* "among the most beautiful and the strongest hope of new German music", but Korngold's masterpiece has inexplicably failed to achieve the worldwide popularity of the majority of Strauss's operas, even though the line dividing it from, say, *Die Frau ohne Schatten* is almost invisibly thin. The libretto of *Die tote Stadt*, based on George Rodenbuch's symbolist novel *Bruges-la-Morte*, was credited to Paul Schott, a mysterious individual who in fact turned out to be Julius and Erich Korngold. Their adaptation retains the dreamy atmosphere of the original but relegates the deathly and brooding presence of the city to the background, making the psychological vulnerablity and anguish of the protagonist its main concern. The trauma of World War I lies just under the surface.

The score veers between a quasi-religious profundity and a honeyed sweetness which to many ears comes dangerously close to kitsch, but Korngold marshals his huge orchestral forces with great precision, and the opera also contains some powerful melodic writing – as in the Act I aria "Gluck, das mir verblieb", sung first by Marie and then by Paul. This inspired episode, made famous by Lotte Lehmann and Richard Tauber, illuminates Paul's despair with wonderful clarity and is the opera's finest vocal moment. The range and requisite stamina of the vocal writing, especially Paul's tenor, may represent one of the main reasons for the opera's undue neglect – this work's unabashed lyricism and brilliant orchestral colour warrant more regular attention from the world's leading opera companies.

Kollo, Neblett, Luxon, Wageman, Prey; Bavarian Radio Chorus; Munich Radio Orchestra; Leinsdorf.
(RCA GD87767; 2 CDs).

This fine recording has never left the catalogue and, for many, it is the finest achievement of both René Kollo and Erich Leinsdorf. The tenor's voice is unstrained here and is both smoother and darker than on almost everything else he has recorded. Carole Neblett is in similarly glowing form, tapping the sentimentality with shameless abandon, and Benjamin Luxon makes a wonderfully tender, meditative Frank. Leinsdorf is clearly in love with Korngold's sweet orchestrations – holding suspensions beyond their natural length – and he revels in the chromatic wash. The 1975 recording might have brought more clarity to the lower frequencies but this is a slight quibble considering the magnificence of the performance as a whole.

Das Wunder der Heliane

The Miracle of Heliane

Composed 1924–26.
First performed October 10, 1927.
Libretto by Hans Müller, after Kaltneker.

Synopsis

Act I

In the kingdom of a harsh and despotic Ruler, a Stranger has been imprisoned for bringing joy and hope to the people. The Ruler visits him in his cell to tell him that the next day he will be executed. Later the Stranger is visited by the Ruler's pure and beautiful wife, Heliane, who wishes to comfort him. The Stranger falls in love with her and begs her to give herself to him. Heliane refuses but reveals her naked body before going to the chapel to pray. The Ruler returns and offers the Stranger his freedom if he can make his wife love him. The naked Heliane returns and the Ruler accuses her of adultery and orders the Stranger's death.

Act II

The Ruler's former mistress (the Messenger) incites him to have Heliane tried. Six judges appear, led by the blind Chief Justice. The Ruler gives Heliane his knife and tries to persuade her to kill herself. The Stranger refuses to testify at the trial but asks to be alone with Heliane. As he kisses her, he plunges the dagger into his own heart. Unable to discover the truth, the Ruler proposes a trial by God: if Heliane can bring the Stranger back to life it will prove her innocence. She agrees.

Act III

A crowd has gathered. Heliane is about to attempt the Stranger's resurrection when she breaks down and confesses that she loved him. She is condemned but the Ruler offers her freedom if she will only love him. She refuses, but while being led away the corpse of the Stranger rises up and Heliane runs to him. The enraged Ruler stabs her. The Stranger drives out the Ruler and blesses the people. Heliane and the Stranger enter heaven, united in their love.

Even judged by the standards of grand opera, *Das Wunder der Heliane* has a particularly ludicrous and symbolically overloaded plot. It was also written at a time when operatic taste was changing in favour of more modern subjects, like Krenek's *Jonny spielt auf* – a work that Julius Korngold went out of his way to denigrate in order to elevate his son's work. A cigarette manufacturer joined the fray by producing two new brands – the cheap and cheerful "Jonny" and the expensive and elegant "Heliane". In the event, neither product lasted long.

Erich Korngold's source was an unpublished play, *Die Heilige* (The Saint), by the Romanian author Hans Kaltneker, which had been written with operatic adaptation in mind. Kaltneker's work shows a very obvious debt to the mysticism of Richard Wagner, and the libretto strikes an uneasy balance between the symbolic and the literal. The stranger is a Christ-like figure who also represents the life force itself, while Heliane is both a Madonna and a sexual magnet who repels the advances of her husband because he represents darkness and death. The love of the stranger and Heliane is blessed by God (in the form of a decidely Hollywoodish angelic chorus) and is thus a kind of transcendental adultery à la *Tristan und Isolde*, having the power to overcome evil and heal and restore the nation. A particularly risible moment of the stranger's attempted seduction of Heliane has him gasping: "O give me your tiny white feet, so that I may kiss them until they come for me!"

All this is wrapped up in Korngold's most opulent and ambitious score, demanding immense orchestral forces and the very best singers. The thick chromaticism is harmonically daring by Korngold's standards: "By no means do I isolate myself against the harmonic enrichments which we owe to say, Schoenberg. But I will not give up claim to eminent possibilities offered by 'old music,'" he wrote. In fact it's the "old music" that makes the strongest impression, particularly the influence of Wagner, which is evident in the music's unstable tonal centres and generally rhapsodic tone. With each of the three acts lasting close to an hour, the dense orchestral writing can tire, and with the exception of Heliane's big Act II aria "Ich ging zu ihm" (made famous by Lotte Lehmann), few of the melodies have the memorability or simple beauty of "Gluck, das mir verblieb" from *Die tote Stadt*. But the tone is generally more dramatic and the music more intense than in any of the earlier works, and much of *Das Wunder der Heliane* offers the sonic equivalent of a warm bath.

Tomowa-Sintow, De Haan, Runkel, Welker; Berlin Radio Chorus and Orchestra; Mauceri.
(Decca 436 636-2; 3 CDs).

Alongside Schreker's *Die Gezeichneten*, this is one of the high points of Decca's "Entartete Musik" series. Mauceri gives a beautifully shaped and subtle reading of the elaborate score, drawing some ravishing sounds from the Berlin Radio Orchestra. The cast is outstanding, with Tomowa-Sintow radiant in the title role and the tenor John David de Haan showing great promise as the Stranger. Reinhild Runkel is impressive as the Ruler and Nicolai Gedda makes an engaging cameo as the Blind Judge. The sound is, if anything, too clean, and a little more space might have been introduced, but the recording is otherwise very good.

FRANZ LEHÁR

b. KOMÁRON, HUNGARY, APRIL 30, 1870; d. BAD ISCHL, AUSTRIA, OCTOBER 24, 1948.

Franz Lehár was the Andrew Lloyd Webber of his day, writing popular music-theatre for a very wide audience and making a great deal of money into the bargain. He revitalized the world of Viennese operetta and made himself a dollar millionaire with *Die lustige Witwe* (The Merry Widow) in 1905 and followed it up with several scores which, if not repeating that astonishing success, were hugely popular all round the world. Shows like *Der Graf von Luxemburg* (The Count of Luxembourg) and *Das Land des Lächelns* (The Land of Smiles) still keep a place in the repertoire, particularly in central Europe – as well they might, for they are wonderful examples of Lehár's gift for intoxicating melodies and his rich orchestral palette, which exploited the innovations of Debussy, Puccini and Richard Strauss.

The son of a military bandmaster, Lehár was a true product of the Austro-Hungarian empire. He spent his childhood stationed with his father's regiment in various towns across central Europe, and entered the Prague conservatory aged twelve to study the violin. Dvořák, no less, is reputed to have advised him: "Hang up your fiddle and start composing." When called up for military service he followed in his father's footsteps and served as a regimental bandmaster, then in 1902 settled in Vienna and started conducting at the Theater an der Wien, one of the city's two principal operetta houses (the Carltheater was the other). Lehár had composed four operettas for these theatres by the time he was given the libretto of *Die lustige Witwe* by Oscar Léon and Leo Stein, the authors of Strauss's hugely popular *Wiener Blut*. In fact Lehár was the second choice as composer: he got the job after being sent the lyrics for a song which he composed in a single day and played down the telephone to Léon.

After a slow start, *Die lustige Witwe* became a Viennese sensation and was rapidly produced across Germany and then in London and New York. The score inaugurated what has become known as the Silver Age of Viennese operetta, which was epitomized by Lehár and fellow Hungarian Emmerich Kálmán.

After a couple of flops Lehár scored another success with *Der Graf von Luxemburg* (1909) and then *Zigeunerliebe* (Gipsy Love) in 1910, both of which had international acclaim. But World War I put a brake on the worldwide success of Viennese music for a few years and Lehár seemed to lose his winning streak in subsequent works. The downturn in his career was overcome by his association with the tenor Richard Tauber, who became the most celebrated performer of Lehár's music and gave his name to the *Tauberlied*, hugely popular songs that have become more famous than the operettas that spawned them. The most famous of these, 'Dein ist mein ganzes Herz' (You are my heart's delight), comes from Lehár's last international triumph, *Das Land des Lächelns*, premiered in Berlin in 1929.

At Christmas 1930 some two hundred productions of *Das Land des Lächelns* were on in Europe, and in total five hundred different Lehár shows were being staged. As a crowning accolade his last major work, *Giuditta*, was premiered at the Vienna State Opera, the only operetta to have been given that honour in a city which is surprisingly snobbish towards the form. The show was relayed internationally, but the piece hasn't achieved a lasting success.

Many musicians who had Jewish blood were forced to emigrate when Hitler came to power, and many took their talents to enrich the development of American musical theatre. Lehár, although his wife was Jewish, stayed in Vienna: he was one of the favourite composers of the Führer, who as a young man went regularly to the Theater an der Wien to see *Die lustige Witwe*. After the *Anchluss* Lehár composed a new overture to the work, which he dedicated to Hitler to protect himself and his wife. This didn't help Lehár's Jewish colleagues, however, and Fritz Löhner-Beda, one of the librettists of *Das Land des Lächelns* and *Giuditta*, was murdered in a concentration camp while his work was playing in Vienna. After moving to Switzerland for a few years Lehár returned to his villa in Bad Ischl, where he died in 1948.

Operetta is looked down on by many opera fans, but often because they are unfamiliar with the music. It's true that Lehár's work lacks the dramatic power of contemporary through-composed operas (*Salome* had its premiere three weeks before *Die lustige Witwe*), but the genre can be fairly compared to the *Singspiel* speech-and-aria style of an earlier period. However, although the plots are no more ludicrous than in many operas and the music speaks to a much wider audience, the top directors and singers are rarely engaged for stage productions, which means the works are often best explored on disc.

In addition to the sets listed below, Lehár fans should check out EMI's *Composers in Person* disc (CDC 7 54838 2), a superlative selection conducted by Lehár himself. It starts with the 1940 overture to *Die lustige Witwe* and includes fine performances by Esther Réthy from *Zigeunerliebe* and *Paganini*, plus original-cast recordings of *Das Land des Lächelns* with Tauber and Vera Schwarz and *Giuditta* with Tauber and Jarmila Novotná in 1934. Some of these performances, particularly Tauber's, can seem overblown to modern ears, but these recordings give a wonderful sense of eavesdropping on a vanished age.

Die lustige Witwe

The Merry Widow

Composed 1905.
First performed December 30, 1905.
Libretto by Victor Léon and Leo Stein, after Henri Meilhac.

Synopsis

Act I

The Paris embassy of the Balkan kingdom of Pontevedro. Baron Mirko Zeta, the Pontevedrin envoy, is concerned that the fortune of Hanna Glawari, a young Pontevedrin widow, is going to be lost to the nation by her remarriage. He hatches a plot to marry her off to a young and eligible Pontevedrin bachelor, Count Danilo. It turns out that the two are former lovers, but Danilo is not interested, because a declaration of love would just put him alongside all the

Frenchmen who are after her money. In the ballroom Hanna has to choose a dancing partner, and selects the one man who appears to be ignoring her, Danilo. As a subplot we discover the love of Camille, a French aristocrat, for Baron Zeta's wife, Valencienne.

Act II

The following day Hanna hosts a party which begins with Pontevedrin dances and songs. Hanna sings the famous "Vilja Lied", about an alluring forest sprite. After various complications Hanna announces her engagement to Camille, a French aristocrat. Danilo, unable to disguise his grief, storms off to Maxim's, his favourite cabaret. Hanna realizes he loves her.

Act III

Hanna's house is decked out as Maxim's. Danilo asks Hanna not to marry Camille in order to save the Pontevedrin economy. Danilo and Hanna confess their love for each other.

Die lustige Witwe virtually defines the prerequisites for Silver Age operettas: a plot charged with tingling emotional encounters, plenty of misunderstandings, and preferably an exotic setting of some kind – in this case Parisian cabaret and the mythical Pontevedro. Yet this work didn't begin auspiciously, as the influential Wilhelm Karczag, director of the Theater an der Wien, was horrified by the sensuality of the score and offered Lehár five thousand crowns to withdraw it. Convinced that the piece would be a failure, the theatre management gave it the cheapest possible production, with old sets and tatty costumes. The premiere went well enough, but business was slow and free tickets were handed out to fill the house. Eventually, though, word got around and *Die lustige Witwe* began to break records. It was the first show to go in for "merchandising", and, particularly in the States, Merry Widow hats, corsets, cigarettes and cocktails were an industry in themselves. The show is still a regular fixture at the Theater an der Wien and along with *Die Fledermaus* it's the operetta most performed in opera houses.

The innovation of *Die lustige Witwe* lies in the size of the orchestra, which is a long way from the standard operetta pit band. Lehár was unusual among operetta composers in fully orchestrating his works, and this score calls for harp, glockenspiel and tambourine in the pit, plus guitar, tambourine and strings on stage, in addition to the sumptuous orchestra of quadruple woodwind and strings. The operetta is a study in flirtation and Lehár doesn't hold back on the shimmering strings. When Hanna and Danilo finally get together in Act III the solo violin and cello symbolically intertwine while the music slips into a seductive waltz that underpins their relationship throughout the piece. As in all his scores, Lehár shows himself a master of local colour: the Pontevedrin characters are allied to east-European style mazurkas, polonaises and kolos (including the "Dummer, dummer Reitersmann" duet in Act II, which was the number played down the phone to Oscar Léon); Paris is evoked through the gallop and cancan; while Viennese marches and waltzes occupy the middle ground.

Studer, Skovhus, Bonney, Trost, Terfel; Vienna Philharmonic; Gardiner. **(Deutsche Grammophon 439 911-2; 1 CD).**

John Eliot Gardiner makes the Vienna Philharmonic sound as if they have this music in their blood, but amazingly they hadn't touched it for forty years prior to this vivid and tinglingly seductive set. All the singers bring a quality of unforced clarity and ease to the vocal lines and show the wisdom of bringing opera singers into this repertoire – only Boje Skovhus (Danilo) has been a regular performer of operetta. The other great pluses of this recording are that it is contained on one CD, includes all the music and cuts the spoken dialogue down to a minimum. It's not surprising Gardiner was invited back to conduct the Vienna Philharmonic Ball after this.

Schwarzkopf, Waechter, Steffek, Gedda, Knapp; Philharmonia; Matacic. **(EMI CDS 7 47178 8; 2 CDs).**

This recording, dating from 1963, has long been the classic version of *The Merry Widow* and has only just been superseded by the Gardiner version above. From the very first notes of the introduction it sweeps you into the fantasy world of the score. Elisabeth Schwarzkopf is exemplary at conjuring the alluring mystery of Hanna, while Eberhard Waechter and Nikolai Gedda are suitable foils. This is the version for completists who want all the spoken dialogue.

Zigeunerliebe

Gypsy Love

Composed 1909.
First performed January 8, 1910.
Libretto by A. M. Willner and Robert Bodanzky.

Synopsis

Act I

A party is being held to celebrate the engagement of Zorika to Jonel, an eligible young man. But she feels restricted by this conventional match and is carried away by the tales and music of Jozsi, the gyspy fiddler. Whilst he is playing she remembers the superstition that a girl who drinks from the river on the night of her betrothal will have her future revealed. Her head full of romantic thoughts, she falls asleep and dreams.

Act II

In her dream Zorika has eloped with Jozsi and things are moving towards a gyspy wedding. But the situation is complicated by various jealousies, and Zorika is disowned by her father, who disapproves of the marriage.

Act III

The party of Act II continues. Jozsi declares that he will always be a roving gypsy, and Zorika is delighted to be reunited with her faithful Jonel.

Of Lehár's lesser-known operettas, *Zigeunerliebe* is the most deserving of a wider public. It has all the highly charged emotional power of *Die lustige Witwe*, and Lehár rises to the Transylvanian setting with luxuriant gypsy-style numbers: the composer was a mean violinist himself and shows it to good effect in numbers like "Ich bin ein Zigeunerkind" and "Hör' ich Cymbalklänge". The mood is distinctly Hungarian, imbued with the rhythm of the csardas and the dotted, dactylic rhythms that predominate in the language and music. In fact the piece was adapted by Lehár as a fiercely patriotic opera for the Budapest State Opera in 1943 to celebrate the brief wartime re-annexation of Transylvania to Hungary.

In the lush orchestral sound and emotionally charged vocal lines this score has much in common with the music of his Italian contemporary Puccini – particularly a sentimental piece like *Manon Lescaut*. (The same is true of Lehár's later scores like *Das Land des Länchelns* and *Giuditta*.) The composers were great admirers of each other's music – in *La Rondine*, Puccini sought to write a Lehár-style Viennese operetta, and when Puccini died in 1924, Lehár was suggested as a candidate for completing *Turandot*.

In *Ziegeunerliebe*, Zorika is torn between two men – the conventional noblemen to whom she is betrothed and the fiery gypsy fiddler who seems so much more romantic and alluring. Joszi, the gypsy, symbolizes the power of music, but is also an emblem of the unorthodox and risky. In the end she takes the safe option and marries her fiancé. Those who know Lloyd Webber's *Phantom of the Opera* will recognize the parallels in the plot and the enduring power of the dilemma.

Schramm, Schock; Berlin Symphony Orchestra; Stolz.
(Eurodisc 258 360; 1 CD).

With any operetta, highlights discs are generally better than complete recordings – the dialogue between numbers is no great loss. The Eurodisc Lehár series, conducted by Robert Stolz, is of a very high standard – he was, after all, the original conductor of *Die lustige Witwe* and the supreme champion on Viennese operetta all his life. Margit Schramm is a passionate Zorika and the two men are both sung by Rudolf Schock (suggesting an interesting psychological subtext), but what really sets it off are the highly charged strings, the solo fiddle playing (by Hans-Georg Arlt), the rippling clarinet and the cimbalom effects.

Das Land des Lächelns

The Land of Smiles

Composed 1929.
First performed October 10, 1929.
Libretto by Ludwig Herzer and Fritz Löhner-Beda.

Synopsis

Act I

Lisa, the daughter of Count Lichtenfels, is sick of the empty flirting at aristocratic balls. Ignoring the attentions of Lieutenant Gustl, she is struck by the Chinese prince Sou-Chong. He is suddenly summoned back to China to become Prime Minister, by which time he and Lisa have fallen in love.

Act II

Lisa has gone to China with Sou-Chong. Despite their love, the cultural differences begin to have their effect and Lisa feels constrained. Sou-Chong is reminded that by custom he must take four wives, despite his protestation that his whole heart belongs to Lisa. Gustl, who has come from Vienna in pursuit of Lisa, pursuades her to leave, but Sou-Chong forbids it and becomes her captor.

Act III

An escape plan is devised, but Lisa and Gustl run into Sou-Chong. Lisa pleads with him and finally he sadly agrees to let them depart.

Apart from *Die lustige Witwe*, this is the only Lehár operetta staged with any regularity outside central Europe, and it is the most successful of his later works for Richard Tauber. A reworking of *Die gelbe Jacke* (The Yellow

Jacket), which was a flop in 1923, *Das Land des Lächelns* was an international triumph and has a rarity value as a major operetta with an unhappy ending. The operetta counterpart of Puccini's *Madama Butterfly*, it is clearly the work of a more mature and serious man than the composer of *Die lustige Witwe* – this is a tougher piece than its glutinous hit song, "Dein ist mein ganzes Herz", would suggest.

At this time Lehár was writing his scores for Berlin, where the audience was much more demanding and less sentimental than in Vienna. It shows in the music, which begins with a Viennese style waltz that could have come from *Die lustige Witwe*, but by the second act the sound has become distinctly orientalist, with flute, tam tam and pentatonic melodies creating overtones of Puccini's *Turandot*. The end of Act II is grimly dramatic as Lisa sees that the cross-cultural marriage is impossible and finds herself under house-arrest. But, as ever, it is the romantic moments that linger – in this case Sou Chong's aria "Von Apfelblüten einen Kranz" and the magical duet "Wer hat die Liebe uns ins Herz gesenkt?", both of which return with a wistful irony at the end before Lisa and Sou Chong finally separate.

Schramm, Schock; Berlin Symphony Orchestra; Stolz.
(Eurodisc 258 373; 1 CD).

This highlights disc under the baton of Robert Stolz omits nothing essential, and the pairing of Margit Schramm and Rudolf Schock is, once again, excellent. Schock's mannerisms in "Dein ist mein ganzes Herz" may be a bit overblown for modern tastes, but they are nothing compared to Tauber. This is a score well worth getting to know.

BÉLA BARTÓK

b. SINNICOLAU MARE, HUNGARY, MARCH 25, 1881; d. NEW YORK, SEPTEMBER 26, 1945.

Bartók wrote just one opera, *Bluebeard's Castle*, but it occupies a similar standing to Debussy's *Pelléas et Mélisande* as one of the twentieth century's most powerful works of music-theatre. It is a short and intensely concentrated work which, with Kodály's *Háry János* and Ligeti's *Le grand macabre*, is one of very few Hungarian operas to have achieved international fame. Although a Hungarian national opera had been established by Ferenc Erkel in the middle of the nineteenth century, Bartók was not encouraged to study Hungarian music while studying at the Budapest Academy, but was instead steered firmly towards the German classics. As a young man he was a fervent admirer of Brahms and Wagner and almost all his early works reflect the central European tradition, with the influence of Richard Strauss especially prominent in his compositions prior to *Bluebeard*. Then in 1905 Bartók began his systematic exploration of Hungarian folk music, and his detailed field research inspired him to cultivate a musical style in which Magyar song was treated not as an atmospheric device but as raw material. This idea was central to all his subsequent work but the first, and for many the most impressive, example of his conception of Hungarian musical nationalism was *Bluebeard's Castle*.

Bartók entered *Bluebeard's Castle* for a competition shortly after its completion but it was rejected as unperformable. Even with revisions it had to wait until 1918 for its first performance – in a double bill with his ballet *The Wooden Prince*, written the previous year. The opera received no further Hungarian performances for nearly twenty years because the writings of Bartók's librettist, Béla Balázs, were prohibited by the reactionary Horthy regime and Bartók would not agree to performances if Balázs was denied credit for his libretto. Not surprisingly his enthusiasm for opera was rather dampened by these experiences, and he wrote just one more theatre piece, the ballet *The Miraculous Mandarin* (1918–19). Béla Balázs tried, at various times, to interest him in other operatic projects but Bartók henceforth concentrated almost exclusively on orchestral and instrumental music, and indeed vocal writing constitutes a very small fraction of his output.

Bluebeard's Castle

Composed 1911.
First performed May 24, 1918.
Libretto by Béla Balázs, after Perrault.

Synopsis

A short spoken prologue invites the audience to enter the realm of myth. The curtain rises on the hall of Duke Bluebeard's castle. Bluebeard enters with his new wife Judith. Curious about seven mysterious doors, she requests the keys for them and her husband reluctantly agrees. Unlocking the first, she finds Bluebeard's torture chamber. Claiming to be unafraid, she then opens four more doors in succession, discovering Bluebeard's armoury, his treasury, his garden and his kingdom. Bluebeard warns her not to open the sixth door but Judith cannot resist and finds a lake of tears. He begs her not to open the final door but when she asks him if he has ever loved other women before her, he refuses to answer. Finally he gives her the seventh key and on opening the door three women appear. Judith is astonished by their beauty; Bluebeard tells her that they are the brides of his morning, noon and evening. As they return to their room, Bluebeard crowns Judith as the bride of his night and she goes to join them. The door closes, leaving Bluebeard alone in the darkness of his castle.

Béla Balázs was a member of a group of Hungarian intellectuals called the Sunday Circle, who were aware of the latest developments of the European avant-garde but were also fascinated by their own, rapidly vanishing, folk culture – preoccupations that mirrored those of Bartók and his colleague Kodály, who were on the fringe of the group. Balázs's chief sources for his Bluebeard were Perrault's fairy tale and Maeterlinck's 1901 play *Ariane et Barbe-bleue* – set as an opera by Dukas in 1907 (see p.480). But he also looked at Transylvanian ballads, specifically *Anna Molnár*, and the language of his libretto has a regular folk-like metre which

Heart of darkness – an early production of Bluebeard's Castle

is sometimes emphasized by Bartók and at other times disguised.

Bartók, whose introversion bordered on the pathological, evidently empathized with the text he was given. He dedicated *Bluebeard's Castle* to his new bride Márta, a rather ominous dedication in view of the work's affirmation that loneliness is the essential quality of the human condition. The immensely rich and detailed score emphasizes the gulf between Judith and Bluebeard chiefly through the way they sing: dramatic grandeur for her, stark repression for him. Unity is achieved through the statement and repetition of pivotal motifs: for example the theme associated with blood, the interval of a minor second, is employed as the opera's central motif and it accompanies the revealing of every room. For the opening of the various doors Bartók composed highly expressive, miniature tone-poems which encapsulate the contents of each room. The opening of the fifth door is the work's highlight. To convey the white light bursting from Bluebeard's kingdom, there is a simple but staggeringly loud C major chord for orchestra and organ. It is a spine-tingling moment and, although it leads to Bluebeard's most fervent and lyrical music, from this episode it is evident that Judith's fate is sealed.

Bluebeard's Castle is at once static and extremely dramatic: its single setting provides a claustrophobic intensity while the gradual unlocking of the doors creates an almost unbearable suspense. Bluebeard and Judith are both seeking a new beginning to their lives, but from the start there is a sense that each of them is on the edge of the void, surrounded by a literal and a metaphorical darkness. It's a mood of anxiety and impending horror similar to that of Schoenberg's contemporary *Erwartung* (see p.399), a work quite often staged as a double bill with *Bluebeard*.

RECORDINGS OVERVIEW

Bartók's *Bluebeard* has fared well on record, a situation that has much to do with its relative cheapness as an opera project – it has a cast of just two and can be fitted onto a single CD. There have been twelve complete versions made since the first, in 1955, when Walter Susskind conducted a recording engineered and released by the composer's son Peter. But while many of these are competently conducted, few have suitable soloists, and there can be no denying the advantages of stereo in this work – preferably digital.

Ramey, Marton; Hungarian State Orchestra; Fischer.
(CBS CD44523; 1 CD).

This 1987 digital recording of *Bluebeard* is not just sonically spectacular but contains the finest Duke and Judith since the war. Eva Marton's soprano is at its best when the throttle is pushed to the floor, but she is able to touch upon lighter textures and darker moods without sounding strained or out of character. Ramey's voice is as large and powerful as Marton's but he too handles the lighter music with care – the fifth door is especially lyrical. Fischer's accompanies his singers well, with tempi less driven than on the Kertész set, and the effect is generally brighter and more romantic – not least because of the glowing recorded sound. Above all this recording leaves one with an overriding sensation of partnership between the performers.

Berry, Ludwig; London Symphony Orchestra; Kertész.
(Decca 443 571-2DCS; 1 CD).

Kertész's vision of *Bluebeard* is entirely different from Fischer's: here all is febrile, restless and edgy. His conducting pays a great deal of attention to detail which, combined with his manic and fluctuating tempi, makes the score sound less flowing than it really is – but it is an approach that works well. The husband and wife team of Walter Berry and Christa Ludwig sing with their usual strength and commitment, though the former's tone is sometimes almost too smooth and generous. Nonetheless, this is a fine stereo alternative to the Fischer recording and extremely good value at mid-price.

Tomlinson, von Otter, Elès; Berlin Philharmonic Orchestra; Haitink.
(EMI 5561622-2 CDC; 1 CD).

This outstanding live recording, made in Berlin in 1996, has a dream-like quality that's established at the outset by Sandor Elès's intonation of the sepulchral (and rarely recorded) spoken prologue. Haitink's sudden gear-changes and strange instrumental highlighting can sound a little contrived at times, but there is an unpredictability to this reading that vividly embodies the nightmare of Bluebeard's shadowy domain. Anne Sofie von Otter is a light-voiced Judith and John Tomlinson does not really have the range to tackle the higher writing, but both singers bring superlative tone and expression to the roles.

ZOLTÁN KODÁLY

b. KECSKEMÉT, HUNGARY, DECEMBER 16, 1882; d. BUDAPEST, MARCH 6, 1967.

Like Bartók, Kodály composed just one opera, and like *Bluebeard's Castle*, Kodály's *Háry János* reflects its composer's immersion in his homeland's indigenous culture. In fact, more a Hungarian *Singspiel* than an opera, *Háry János* is one of the most profoundly Hungarian pieces of twentieth-century music. Kodály was fundamentally self-taught, learning the basics of music theory before moving to Budapest and the Liszt Academy. While in Budapest he met and became friends with Béla Bartók, whose interest in Hungarian and Magyar songs coincided with his own studies. As Kodály later remembered: "This vision of an educated Hungary, reborn from the people, rose before us. We decided to devote our lives to its realization." Together they collected, catalogued, analyzed and, eventually, published thousands of these songs, and Kodály later used this research as the basis for his Method, a theory of music teaching that continues to serve the modern Hungarian curriculum.

With Bartók, he formed a society for the promotion and performance of contemporary music, a scheme that met with official hostility and public indifference, and their attempts to promote folksong were no more successful. In 1923, however, Kodály's fortunes changed with the widespread success of his cantata *Psalmas Hungaricus*, written to celebrate the fiftieth anniversary of the unification of Buda and Pest. In 1925, having signed with the publishers Universal Edition, he set to work on his opera *Háry János*.

Kodály remained in Hungary during World War II, and after Bartók's death in 1945 he was hailed as Hungary's greatest living composer, being inundated with invitations to head colleges and universities and to conduct his and Bartók's music around the world. In spite of the more radical musical fashions of the 1950s and 1960s, Kodály's popularity remained undimmed and in 1961 Ferenc Fricsay, one of the composer's more public champions, gave a speech in which he said of Kodály: "His life has been devoted to the task of giving this nation a cultural identity through music."

Kodály's style was founded on nineteenth-century ideas of scale and expressivity, and he was devoted to melody and to the singing voice. His work is distinctive thanks largely to the rich mix that went into it – in addition to folksong, he was fascinated with Debussy, Bach and Palestrina, and nearly everything he wrote has an accessibility that makes his music more immediately rewarding than Bartók's. In 1921 Bartók himself paid tribute to his colleague: "Kodály's compositions are characterized in the main by rich melodic invention, a perfect sense of form, a certain predilection for melancholy and uncertainty . . . everything in it is based on the principle of tonal balance."

Háry János

Composed 1925–26; revised 1927.
First performed October 16, 1926.
Libretto by Béla Paulini and Zsolt Harsányi, after Garay.

Synopsis

Háry sits at a bar in his village, Nagyabony, and talks of his fantastic adventures. The first involves him moving a border guardhouse across the Russian-Hungarian frontier, enabling him to free the Austrian Emperor's imprisoned daughter Marie-Louise – who is none other than Napoleon's wife. In gratitude, she invites Háry and his girlfriend Ilka to stay at the Imperial Palace. Upon arriving he successfully tames a wild horse and then proceeds to cure Marie-Louise's father, the Emperor, with a magic balm carried from Nagyabony. Háry is enlisted and almost immediately promoted to the rank of colonel. He leads the Emperor's army against Napoleon and, during the Battle of Milan, he defeats the French army single-handedly, taking Napoleon captive. At this, Marie-

Louise offers to leave her defeated husband if Háry will have her – and she throws in a dowry of half her kingdom. But Háry loves Ilka and decides to return to Nagyabony.

Just as Faust, Don Giovanni and Till Eulenspiegel are all said to have actually lived, so János Háry (Hungarians put the surname first) is believed to have fought during the Napoleonic wars, after which he is supposed to have related his adventures to the poet János Garay – on whose narrative poem "The Veteran" Paulini and Harsányi based their libretto. Kodály was immediately drawn to the folk hero and his Munchhausen-like escapades, seeing his tales less as the fantasies of a congenital liar than as a reflection of his country's deep-rooted oral tradition. "Háry is the personification of the Hungarian story-telling imagination," he wrote. "He does not tell lies; he imagines stories, he is a poet. What he tells us may never have happened, but he has experienced it in spirit, so it is more real than reality."

Like Kodály's two semi-staged narrative dramas, *The Transylvanian Spinning-Room* and *Czinka Panna*, *Háry János* (or *János Háry's Adventures from Nagyabony to the Vienna Burg*, to give it its full English title) is a *Singspiel*-narration, with an episodic score made up from numbers separated by spoken dialogue. Kodály had not set out to write an opera in the western tradition, but instead sought to create a place for unadulterated Hungarian folksong in the theatre. The story is told and enacted by a narrator whose words are illuminated and characterized by songs and orchestral interludes (the latter being later combined to form the famous concert suite), and are prefaced by an orchestral "sneeze", designed to warn the listener that what they are about to hear is not entirely true.

Kodály's consistently witty and good-natured score incorporates a variety of song forms (including gypsy tunes and Hussar melodies) and shows a virtuosic control of the orchestral palette. A kaleidoscope of instrumental colour is brilliantly used to distinguish between the simple but wholesome Hungarians and the sophisticated but benevolent Austrians, and a whole host of sound effects, including charging horses and mighty crowd scenes, are conjured to give depth and character to a work that is, after all, dramaturgically one-dimensional.

Ustinov, Melis, Szönyi, László; Edinburgh Festival Chorus; London Symphony Orchestra; Kertész.
(Decca 443 488-2DF2; 2 CDs; *includes Variations on a Hungarian Folk Song* and *Psalmus Hungaricus*).

This CD transfer of Kertész's 1968 recording of *Háry János* is the only official version in the catalogue (there is also a marvellous performance conducted by Ferenc Fricsay in Rome in 1955 floating about on CD). Kertész's reading is great fun, with Peter Ustinov hamming it up in English and an excellent Hungarian cast revelling in the earthy spirit of Kodály's folksong melodies. Kertész himself is in bombastic form, and the LSO are well caught by Decca's engineers. The accompanying performance of *Psalmas Hungaricus* is a classic – but note that there are neither texts nor translations.

KAROL SZYMANOWSKI

b. TYMOSZÓWKA, UKRAINE, OCTOBER 6, 1882; d. LAUSANNE, SWITZERLAND, MARCH 29, 1937.

Karol Szymanowski, the most prominent Polish composer of the twentieth century, is comparable to Bartók in the way he forged a distinctive style out of the folk music of his native land. And like Bartók he wrote just one opera, although Szymanowski's *Król Roger* (King Roger) is a world away from *Bluebeard's Castle*: Bartók's works are highly structured and rigorously crafted, but Szymanowski's tend to be rhapsodic and visionary creations – in fact, if any music could be said to be heavily perfumed it is Szymanowski's.

He was born into a Polish family in territory annexed to the Russian Empire and was always a Polish patriot. His childhood on the Tymaszówka estate seems to have been a continuous round of dances, plays and music. The poet Jarosław Iwaszkiewicz, with whom Szymanowski later worked on *King Roger* and the ballet *Harnasie*, left accounts of the elaborate fancy-dress balls for which Karol and his elder brother Felix composed the music. Of the five children in the family, three went on to become professional musicians – his sister Stasia became an opera singer and starred as Roxana in the first performance of *King Roger*.

In his early years Szymanowski found little to inspire him in Poland, a country then partitioned between Germany, Russia and the Habsburg Empire. His musical interests lay with foreign composers such as Wagner, Richard Strauss, Debussy, Scriabin and Stravinsky, and he felt a deep affinity with Italy and North Africa, regions he explored in 1911 and 1914 with Stefan Spiess. The cultures of ancient Greece, Norman Sicily and the Arab world had a huge influence on his music.

World War I and the Russian Revolution overturned Szymanowski's world: the house at Tymaszówka was destroyed by the Bolsheviks in 1917. Unable to compose during the turmoil of the war, Szymanowski worked on a novel (now lost) that appears to have been an exploration of religious faith and homosexual love, themes which – like its Sicilian location – link it to *King Roger*.

LEBRECHT COLLECTION

Karol Szymanowski

The independent Poland that emerged out of the chaos of World War I coincided with Szymanowski's artistic maturity. He gained an international reputation with the *Symphony No. 3*, the *Violin Concerto No. 1* and *King Roger*, all of which are exotic and hedonistic in style. Then, under the influence of Stravinsky, his music became more self-consciously nationalistic. During the 1920s he spent more and more time in the Polish mountain resort of Zakopane, where he absorbed the distinctive sounds of *gorale* (highland) music – the ballet *Harnasie* was the main work to grow out of his folk-music research, but the masterpiece of this period (indeed of his entire career) was the austerely beautiful *Stabat Mater* (1926). His last years were a story of failing health, financial hardship and neglect in Poland, but at least he had growing success abroad – *King Roger* was triumphantly received in Prague, and *Harnasie* likewise in Paris. Szymanowski died in a sanatorium in Lausanne and received a huge state funeral in Kraków.

Król Roger

King Roger

Composed 1924.
First performed June 19, 1926.
Libretto by Jarosław Iwaszkiewicz.

Synopsis

Act I

King Roger II with his wife Roxana and advisor Edrisi attend High Mass in the cathedral of Palermo. The archbishop warns against a heretic – a handsome young shepherd who is trying to topple the authority of the church. The Shepherd is led in and given the chance to explain himself. "My God is as young and beautiful as I am," he exclaims. The archbishop demands death for this blasphemy, but Roger, Roxana and Edrisi are impressed and invite the Shepherd to the palace, where he will be judged by the King.

Act II

Roxana is increasingly attracted by the Shepherd and asks Roger to be indulgent with him. When the Shepherd is led in he entrances the whole court and leads them in an abandoned dance, despite Roger's attempts to have him bound. All except Roger and Edrisi follow him, but the King is under his spell too, and decides to follow him as a pilgrim, not a king.

Act III

Roger and Edrisi arrive in the ruins of the ancient amphitheatre of Syracuse. The King calls Roxana, who tells him that only the teachings of the Shepherd can free Roger from his troubles. They light a sacrificial fire and the Shepherd now appears as Dionysus. Roxana and the crowd worship him ecstatically. They exit as dawn breaks and Roger is left singing a hymn of praise to Apollo and the rising sun.

The extraordinary opening scene of *King Roger* was described by the composer in the following words: "The last rays of the setting sun and the light of many candles dimly illuminate the church. In the diffuse light, the gold of the mosaics and the sumptuous vestments of the priests shimmer now and again." Dark resonant chords and powerful choral singing richly evoke the incense-laden glow of the ritualized Byzantine church, and it's the conflict between this church and the Shepherd's liberating paganism that powers this opera, in which each act features a confrontation between Roger and the Shepherd. It's true that Szymanowski's best music is contemplative rather than dramatic (this is probably the reason *King Roger* is a rarity in the opera house), but the philosophical antagonism of Roger and the Shepherd (who can, of course, be seen as two facets of the same character) is beautifully conveyed in the music. The first appearance of the Shepherd really sets up the opposition of moods, with a transparent C major harmony following the heavy ecclesiastical sounds. The Shepherd introduces himself and describes his faith with a simple, lyrical phrase – and the solo violin imitating it goes soaring into the stratosphere. Throughout the opera the Shepherd is evoked with sultry violin writing and the sort of highly charged, exotic flavouring found in Szymanowski's first violin concerto.

Szymanowski had recently become familiar with Ravel's *Daphnis et Chloe*, and there are clear affinities between that luminous score and *King Roger*'s evocation of an idealized classical world – though Szymanowski's luxuriant melody and orchestral colour often create a quite different, quasi-orientalist atmosphere. What anchors the score is Roger's more earthbound music and the opera's oratorio-like structure as a series of set pieces: the opening choral section and the Shepherd's song in Act I; Roxana's aria (which has a separate existence as a concert aria and in an arrangement for violin solo) and the wild dance of the Shepherd and his followers in Act II; and climactic scenes of Roxana and the Shepherd, and Roger's hymn to Apollo and the sun. Whereas Iwaszkiewicz's libretto had Roger being won over by the Shepherd, the composer changed it so that Roger remains aloof, keeping Dionysus and Apollo in balance – an alteration that says a lot about Szymanowski's personal preoccupations.

RECORDINGS OVERVIEW

Despite its rarity on stage, *King Roger* is represented by three versions in the current catalogue. Two of these are very good, but neither of them contains a libretto. If you need to follow this opera word by word, get hold of the recording issued by Koch Schwann (314014; 2 CDs), but bear in mind that this is the least idiomatic recording, despite Barbara Zagórzanka's fine performance as Roxana.

Hiolski, Ochman, Zagórzanka; Polish State Philharmonic; Stryja.
(Marco Polo 8.223339-40; 2 CDs).

The newest *King Roger*, made in 1990 under Karol Stryja, is the finest: the score really benefits from a digital recording and the glittering sonorities come across well in a clear acoustic. The three principal voices are well characterized: Andrzej Hiolski as Roger has an authoritative presence, Wieslaw Ochman as the Shepherd is a good foil, and Barbara Zagórzanka just melts into her seductive aria. Despite what it says on the box, there is no libretto, only a synopsis. Incidental music to Tadeusz Micinski's play *Prince Potemkin*, written immediately after *King Roger*, is included as a fill-up.

Hiolski, Pustelak, Rumowska; Choir and Orchestra of the National Opera House; Mierzejewski.
(Olympia OCD 303; 2 CDs).

This was for a long time the best recording of *King Roger* and in the ritual splendour of its opening scene it still beats the others. Andrzej Hiolski is Roger as in the version above; Kazimierz Pustelak is a glorious Shepherd, but Hanna Rumowska's Roxana is slightly shrill. On the plus side are the price and the substantial fill-up of the highland ballet *Harnasie*.

SERGEI RACHMANINOV

b. SEMYONOVO, RUSSIA, APRIL 1, 1874; d. BEVERLY HILLS, MARCH 28, 1942.

Sergei Rachmaninov was a displaced person in more than one sense – a Russian who spent much of his life outside his native country, and a Romantic who embodied a brooding stereotype that belonged to a previous era. Though a piano virtuoso of Liszt-like abilities, he spent much of the first half of his life writing for and working in the opera house, striving to uphold the nineteenth-century traditions embodied by Tchaikovsky, his idol and Russia's most successful composer of opera. His three one-act operas are conservative, expressive and melodic pieces, but they are dogged by weak libretti, and are now generally considered as curiosities of operatic history. The finest of the three, and the only one to have been staged in recent years, is *Francesca da Rimini*.

He was born into wealth, but his father was profligate, so by the time Rachmaninov was nine the family was left with nothing. In 1885 he moved to Moscow where he began piano lessons, which in turn led to his first attempts at composing. In 1889 he began sketching his first opera, *Esmeralda*, a setting of Victor Hugo's *Hunchback of Notre Dame*, but this, and many other operatic projects, remained incomplete. Similarly, when he joined the Moscow Conservatory he continued to begin and leave unfinished a number of operatic works, and not until 1893, when he presented *Aleko* to the examining board at the conservatory, did he complete his first work for the stage. Praised by Tchaikovsky, *Aleko* was relatively successful, and it won the composer the Great Gold Medal of the Moscow Conservatory. This highlight was overshadowed by the grim failure of his first symphony, but his success as a pianist kept his spirits aloft, and from 1897 he threw his energies into a conducting position with the Moscow Private Russian Opera Company. It was in this capacity that he made his first professional trip abroad, when he journeyed to London in 1899.

In 1903 he began another opera, a setting of Pushkin's *The Miserly Knight*, as a vehicle for his friend, the bass Fyodor Chaliapin. Halfway through writing the music (after he was appointed conductor at the Bolshoi) he resumed another opera, *Francesca da Rimini*, to a libretto by Tchaikovsky's brother Modest. He completed both works around the same time and they were performed at the Bolshoi, with the composer conducting, as a double-bill.

In 1906 he considered turning Flaubert's *Salammbô* into an opera, and he later completed the first act of a setting of Maeterlinck's *Monna Vanna*. This turned out to be his last operatic venture. Commitments as a pianist and a composer of concert music drew him away from the theatre, and after he settled in America in 1917 he became so famous as a virtuoso that he could hardly find the time to visit an opera house, far less write for one.

Francesca da Rimini

Composed 1900–05.
First performed January 24, 1906.
Libretto by Modest Tchaikovsky, after Dante.

Synopsis

Prologue

The ghost of Virgil comforts the fearful Dante as he descends towards the Abyss. They are met en route by the ghosts of Paolo and Francesca who, entwined in each other's arms, promise to tell their story.

Tableau I

The Malatesta Palace in Rimini. Lanciotto Malatesta, a warrior in the service of the Pope, is preparing for battle, but he is terrified of leaving his wife Francesca alone in the palace. Old and unpopular, he tricked her into marrying him by having his younger brother Paolo woo her on his behalf. Aware that she still loves his brother, he decides to leave her to Paolo's care and wait to see what happens.

Tableau II

Paolo and Francesca are alone together. He reads to her the story of Lancelot's love for Guinevere, and becomes so moved that he falls sobbing at her feet. They embrace, then Malatesta rushes in with his dagger drawn. Both are killed.

Epilogue

The lovers' spirits are swept away by the winds of Hell. Dante, overcome with grief, faints to the ground.

It was in 1898 that Rachmaninov first thought of making an opera from the fifth canto of Dante's *Inferno*, a tale that Tchaikovsky had earlier turned into a "symphonic fantasy". Two years later Tchaikovsky's brother provided him with a libretto, but the huge and rambling drama was sent back with requests for something more concise. When Rachmaninov received the revised libretto he complained that it was now too short, and although a compromise was finally reached between composer and writer, the final text was too disjointed to work effectively (the Prologue, for instance, is much longer than either Tableau).

If *Francesca* is weak dramatically, then it is musically the strongest thing the composer ever wrote for the stage. The evocation of Hell, with its voiceless choir and ominous harmonies, is particularly impressive, and the depiction of the Infernal Winds (high-written strings entwined with moaning, sometimes screaming voices) is genuinely unsettling. Malatesta and the lovers, on the other hand, sing music of an intensity that perfectly offsets the rootlessness of Hell. Keen to make the most of Chaliapin's lyrical qualities, Rachmaninov turns the first tableau over to the warrior's monologue, in which he unburdens himself of love for Francesca, only to turn around at the very end and reveal his murderous intention. The second tableau is dominated by the lovers' duet – an Italianate, tremendously exciting ten-minute outburst of passion that more than makes up for the tedium of the preceding "reading scene". If only for this duet and the soundscape of Hell, *Francesca* deserves a hearing.

Rechetniak, Vassiliev, Matorin, Lapina, Tarastchenko; unnamed orchestra; Chistiakov.
(Le Chant du Monde LDC 288 081; 3 CDs; with *Aleko* and *The Miserly Knight*).

This 1992 recording of Rachmaninov's *Francesca* is far from ideal – the singing is provincial, and the orchestra produces some painfully thin string tone. But the fervour with which the singers, orchestra and conductor throw themselves into the music is hard to resist. In particular, the love duet really takes off, with the tenor Vitaly Tarastchenko and the soprano Marina Lapina generating the requisite unbridled emotion. The rest of the singing is solid enough, with Nikolaï Vassiliev splendid as Dante. The set comes with recordings of both of the other operas, which are no less enthusiastically brought to life.

IGOR STRAVINSKY

b. LOMONOSOV, RUSSIA, JUNE 17, 1882; d. NEW YORK, APRIL 6, 1971.

More than any other composer, Igor Stravinsky exemplifies the stylistic plurality of twentieth-century classical music. His first great score, the ballet *The Firebird* (1910), was written in an exotically opulent, late-Romantic style that owed much to his teacher Rimsky-Korsakov. Three years later another ballet, *The Rite of Spring*, shocked audiences unprepared for its primitive sound and daringly irregular rhythms. A colossal orchestral work, *The Rite* was closely followed by pieces such as *The Soldier's Tale* and the *Octet for Wind Instruments*, which used small, unconventional combinations of instruments in a cool and sardonic manner that enabled audiences to perceive the autonomy of each element of the music. This economy of means dominated Stravinsky's output for the next thirty years, a period commonly referred to as his Neoclassical period, since it marked a rejection of the pictorialism and subjectivity of Romanticism in favour of the uncluttered musical language of the eighteenth century, and which culminated in the opera *The Rake's Progress* of 1951. The stylistic volte-face that then occurred was perhaps the most remarkable of all: introduced to the key serial works of the Second Viennese School, Stravinsky was particularly impressed by the crystalline scores of Anton Webern and began employing the twelve-tone method with characteristic inventiveness and vigour, typified by the creation of the ballet *Agon* (1957).

Of the twenty or so works that Stravinsky wrote for the stage, only three – *Le Rossignol* (The Nightingale), *Mavra* and *The Rake's Progress* – are unequivocally operas, the rest being either ballets or hybrid combinations of dance and singing, often involving a speaking role. Yet Stravinsky was almost ideally qualified to be an opera composer: his father Feodor was the leading bass of the celebrated Mariinsky Theatre in St Petersburg, and the young Igor was familiar with much of the mainstream repertoire from a very early age. On his father's death in 1902 Stravinsky was all but adopted by Rimsky-Korsakov, who was then Russia's leading opera composer. But

LEBRECHT COLLECTION

Stravinsky in 1914 – the year he finished Le Rossignol

OPERA AS A VISUAL ART

During the nineteenth century many opera houses hardly bothered with set design at all, while those that did tended to use the same scenery and costumes for any number of different works. The bigger the star, the less important the scenery or stagecraft (there are accounts of star soloists hauling props to the front of the stage to use as seating for their more arduous solos), and not until the second half of the century did the balance of priorities change. Even though Wagner's approach to staging sent a shockwave through the world's opera houses, a theatre as important as Covent Garden was still producing Wagner in the 1920s with almost no stage direction, a single spotlight and very basic backdrops.

However, things were different in France during the first quarter of the twentieth century, when Serge Diaghilev and Igor Stravinsky brought about a new rapprochement between opera and the visual arts. When Stravinsky began working with Diaghilev in 1910, on *The Firebird* ballet, the impresario brought into the team the designer and artist Leon Bakst, who had already produced exotic costumes and sets for performances by Diaghilev's Ballet Russes. However, the first performance of *Le Rossignol* in May 1914, in a production conducted by Pierre Monteux and designed by Alexandre Benois, took the partnership between music and visual arts a step further. Benois later remembered the Chinese March in Act II: "As the procession appeared from the wings, each link made two rounds of the stage and sank down on the floor within the space lit up by lanterns, thus forming a gorgeous and motley carpet of living flowers who emphasized by their movements the principal points of the action. In the light of the huge blue lanterns the fantastic costumes stood out vividly against the background of white and blue china columns, and when the Emperor, sparkling with gold and jewels, stepped forward from under his gigantic umbrella and the crowd fell down to worship him, the effect was so great that for the first time in my life I felt genuinely moved by my own creation."

Such was the popularity of Benois's work that Diaghilev approached Henri Matisse – against Stravinsky's wishes – to design a production of *Chant du Rossignol*, a staged piece edited down from *Le Rossignol*. Stravinsky later complained that, although he liked the painter, "the production, and especially Matisse's part in it, were failures. Diaghilev hoped Matisse would do something very Chinese and charming. All he did do, however, was to copy the China of the shops in the rue de la Boëtie . . . Our Matisse collaboration made Picasso very angry: 'Matisse!

Rimsky-Korsakov discouraged his pupil's enthusiasm for opera, until 1908, when Stravinsky began work on a short fairy-tale opera, *Le Rossignol*. The first act was finished in 1909, but Stravinsky then abandoned the project to work on *The Firebird* for Diaghilev's Ballet Russes, and only completed *Le Rossignol* in 1914 – by which time his style had changed somewhat.

For the next eight years Stravinsky experimented with conventional theatrical practice in ways that often suggested an ironic distancing from his material: *The Soldier's Tale*, for instance, was written for actors, narrator and chamber orchestra, and was designed to be toured on the back of a lorry. *Les Noces* (The Wedding) was a ritualized ballet depicting a typical Russian wedding with songs and choruses that suggest overheard scraps of conversation. *Renard* (1915) was a fifteen-minute "burlesque for singing and acting" set in a farmyard, in which the action was created by dancers, with vocal parts sung from the orchestra pit. The first performance in 1922 was on a bill which included *Mavra*, his first real opera since *Le Rossignol*. Created as a reaction to the "inflated arrogance" of Wagner, and dedicated to Tchaikovsky, Glinka and Pushkin, this work paid homage to "the vocal style and conventions of the old Russo-Italian opera". Neither *Renard* nor *Mavra* was deemed a success, however, and both are very rarely performed today.

Stravinsky's desire to produce a more large-scale and serious dramatic work came to

What is a Matisse? A balcony with a big red flower-pot falling all over it.'"

After Diaghilev quarrelled with Bakst over money, responsibility for the design and setting of *Mavra* was handed to the unknown painter Survage, but after this act of faith backfired, Diaghilev never again approached any but the best known and most controversial painters. With Cocteau's help Picasso was engaged to design Stravinsky's ballet *Pulcinella* in 1920 and, in 1924, for a production of Darius Milhaud's *Le Train bleu*, Diaghilev combined the talents of Pablo Picasso, Jean Cocteau, Coco Chanel, Henri Laurens and Bronislava Nijinska.

Diaghilev continued to promote the Paris Opera House as a home for the best in contemporary art, engaging André Derain to design works by Satie and Milhaud, and Marc Chagall to create a now legendary production of *The Firebird*. After Diaghilev's pioneering efforts, opera producers routinely turned to the big names of the art world to give added lustre to their shows. In 1933 Giorgio de Chirico was invited to design *I Puritani*, the inaugural production of Florence's Maggio Musicale festival; Oskar Kokoschka was brought to the Kroll by Klemperer and by Furtwängler to Salzburg; Menotti invited Henry Moore to his Spoleto Festival, to design a *Don Giovanni*; and John Piper, Maurice Sendak and David Hockney all created celebrated productions for Glyndebourne – the last of the three was particularly successful, designing an unforgettable *Rake's Progress* in 1975. Chagall continued to work in the opera house well into his eighties (he painted the ceiling of the Paris Opéra in 1965), and John Piper designed most of the sets and costumes for Benjamin Britten's stage premieres, doing notably fine work for *A Midsummer Night's Dream* in 1960.

The results of such high-profile collaborations have not always been successful (hence the move to full-time in-house designers) but most have been memorable. Salvador Dalì's 1950 *Salome* for Covent Garden created one of the greatest uproars in British theatre history, for although Dali was kept on a fairly tight lead, he nonetheless had the characters marching about in surreal costumes, and he decked out the stage with pomegranates and peacock-feathers. This was as nothing, however, compared to his 1963 production, for La Fenice, of an obscure work by Alessandro Scarlatti, in which one character had to sit on stage watching television, while the air filled with perfumed soap bubbles and the artist splashed himself with paint – all in front of a backdrop dominated by a huge weeping eye and elephants with legs a hundred feet long.

fruition in 1925 when Stravinsky asked Jean Cocteau to rework Sophocles' *Oedipus*. The text was then translated into Latin, for Stravinsky wanted a language "not dead but turned to stone", in the belief that it would thereby "contain an incantatory element that could be exploited in music". The use of masks and a speaking narrator lent this opera-oratorio (as Stravinsky termed it) an hieratic formality that did not appeal to its early audiences, but *Oedipus Rex* is one of Stravinsky's most powerful and dramatically effective works.

The Rake's Progress, Stravinsky's most celebrated opera and his only full-length one, marked the climax of Stravinsky's operatic career and the end of his exploration of classical forms. Of the theatre works produced in his late serial style, only the ballet *Agon* can really be deemed a success. His final work, *The Flood* (1961–62), was a one-scene musical play commissioned for television: unfortunately Stravinsky's tendency to compression in his late style produced a score that was densely worked but undramatic to the point of tedium. Other opera projects were considered, including a proposed collaboration with Dylan Thomas on the rebirth of the world after a nuclear Holocaust, but nothing came to fruition. Stravinsky died in New York but was buried in Venice near the grave of Diaghilev, the man who – more than anybody else – had enabled him to become one of the century's greatest composers for the theatre.

Le Rossignol

The Nightingale

Composed 1908–14.
First performed May 26, 1914.
Libretto by the composer and Stepan Mitusov, after Hans Christian Andersen.

Synopsis

Act I

In a forest by the sea, a Fisherman listens to the beautiful song of a Nightingale, unaware of the presence of the Emperor's chamberlain, who has been sent to fetch the bird. The Nightingale points out that his voice sounds sweetest in the forest, but agrees to the Emperor's request.

Act II

At the palace the Nightingale sings to the Emperor, delighting all those present, but when Japanese ambassadors arrive with a mechanical nightingale, the real bird flies away. Angered, the Emperor banishes the bird and appoints the Japanese imitation "First Singer of the Bedside Table on the Left". The Fisherman's voice is heard again.

Act III

On his deathbed the Emperor is visited by the ghosts of past deeds. Death arrives, wearing the Emperor's crown, and prepares to take his life just as the Nightingale returns. So entranced is Death by the song of the Nightingale that the Emperor is allowed to live if the song continues. At dawn, Death leaves and the Emperor reinstates the Nightingale, who agrees to sing for the Emperor but only at night. The Fisherman is heard for the final time, proclaiming the song of the Nightingale as the voice of Heaven.

Stravinsky was first introduced to Stepan Mitusov, the librettist of *Le Rossignol*, at Rimsky-Korsakov's house in 1904, and it was Mitusov who in turn introduced Stravinsky to the circle of intellectuals and connoisseurs associated with *The World of Art* – a journal published by Diaghilev. This eclectic artistic milieu espoused a particularly Russian form of Symbolism, which looked to both the naive and the exotic aspects of folk art for inspiration, and it is therefore unsurprising that Mitusov and Stravinsky's operatic collaboration should be a picturesquely simple tale of magic and morality. But the project was abandoned in 1909, when Diaghilev asked Stravinsky to write *The Firebird*, and it was not taken up again until 1913 when the recently established Free Theatre of Moscow commissioned him to compose a three-act opera. Stravinsky was reluctant to return to a work he had begun under Rimsky-Korsakov's tuition, but the offer of an enormous fee of 10,000 roubles was "unrefusable", and after revising the first act by thinning the harmony and the orchestration, he composed the other two acts by March 1914. Meanwhile the Free Theatre had closed and so Stravinsky took the opera to Diaghilev, who arranged the first performance in Paris, with particularly sumptuous designs by Alexandre Benois.

Although the composer's style had evolved rapidly over the intervening five years, the stylistic division between the first act and the rest of the work is never a problem: indeed it turns the lyrical first act into something of a prologue to the rest. Stravinsky's changing attitudes can be heard through the tightening of the vocal line, the increasing asceticism of the Nightingale's coloratura song and the gradual simplification of the harmony, but the changes are nowhere near as striking as they would have been if he had returned to the opera two years later. Though the pageantry of the chinoiserie (recalling Rimsky-Korsakov) and the opulent Forest Music of Act I provide moments of late-Romantic richness, *Le Rossignol* is a delicately scored piece, with a remarkably imaginative use of unlikely instrumental colourings, notably the combination of mandolin and guitar for the dialogue between Death and the Nightingale – the most exquisite moment in the entire opera.

Bryn-Julson, Caley, Palmer, Tomlinson; BBC Singers and Symphony Orchestra; Boulez.
(Erato 2292-45627-2; 1 CD).

Boulez's light tempi and gentle phrasing emphasize the composer's fastidious part-writing without making the music sound calculating, and the BBC orchestra finds a perfect balance between the warmth of the first act and the encroaching tartness of the conclusion. Phyllis Bryn-Julson and John Tomlinson stand out as the Nightingale and the Chamberlain, and Felicity Palmer makes a youthful impression as the Cook. The sound is natural and well balanced.

Oedipus Rex

Composed 1926–27; revised 1948.
First performed May 30, 1927 (concert); February 23, 1928 (staged).
Libretto by Jean Cocteau (French) and Jean Daniélou (Latin), after Sophocles.

Synopsis

Act I

The Narrator introduces the tragedy of Oedipus: "At the moment of his birth a snare was laid for him – and you will see the snare closing." The men of Thebes bemoan the plague that is killing their town, and ask their king, Oedipus, to free them from it. His brother-in-law Creon returns from Delphi, where he consulted the oracle who revealed to him that King Laius's murderer is still at large and living in the city. Oedipus accuses the seer Tiresias of the murder, suggesting that he and Creon are in league, but Tiresias knows the truth and retorts that it was another king who killed Laius. The arrival of Jocasta, Oedipus's wife, is announced.

Act II

Jocasta demands the brothers stop quarrelling and accuses the oracle of lying. It is known that Laius was killed at the crossroads between Daulis and Delphi by robbers. The word crossroads fills Oedipus with foreboding and he confesses to Jocasta that he killed an old man at that very point; although he is not Laius's son, he is appalled at his crime. A messenger announces the death of King Polybus: he reveals that Oedipus was not the son of Polybus, as he has always thought, but that he was found abandoned as a baby and brought up by a shepherd. Jocasta tries to leave but Oedipus accuses her of shame at the news that he is of lowly birth. Painfully it is spelled out to Oedipus that he is the son of Laius and Jocasta and has therefore been guilty of both parricide and incest. The narrator announces that Jocasta has hanged herself and that Oedipus has put his eyes out with his wife/mother's brooch. The Thebans banish Oedipus from their city.

Composed in secret as a gift to celebrate Diaghilev's twenty years as an impresario, *Oedipus Rex* was first performed in a concert performance flanked by two fully staged ballets – inappropriate programming that did not endear it to the audience. Diaghilev seems to have been mystified, cryptically pronouncing it "un cadeau très macabre", and it is certainly one of Stravinsky's most paradoxical works. Developing his idea of theatre as ritual, Stravinsky built into his "opera-oratorio" a number of highly formal devices that were designed to distance the spectator from the action: the inhabitants of the drama sing in Latin, wear masks and are statically grouped in a shallow tableaux, while the narrator wears contemporary evening dress and recites, in French, what is about to unfold on stage.

Such a rigid-sounding scenario might suggest cool and calculated music, but although the score is largely in Stravinsky's Neoclassical manner, and although Stravinsky treats the words phonetically (often breaking them up in a way that disguises their meaning), the music of *Oedipus Rex* is surprisingly varied, with extreme fluctuations of mood to accompany the opera's revelations. Deploying a somewhat Italianate manner for the soloists and a declamatory style for the chorus (which dominates the proceedings, even though each of the six soloists is accorded an aria), Stravinsky re-creates the impact of cumulative disaster as the music evolves into ever-larger, more complex forms, and the narration, which begins the opera separate and detached, becomes integrated into the monumental musical fabric. *Oedipus* is a relentless work and it has always divided critics – Schoenberg disliked it intensely – but it can be highly effective, especially in a small theatre, a fact established by the brilliant 1928 staging at the Krolloper in Berlin conducted by Otto Klemperer, a production which did much to make its reputation.

Cole, von Otter, Estes, Sotin, Gedda; Swedish Radio Chorus and Symphony Orchestra; Salonen.
(Sony SK48057; 1 CD).

The main strength of Essa-Pekka Salonen's 1991 recording of *Oedipus Rex* is its cast. Had Stravinsky had access to such talent, his own recordings of the work would have more than just historical interest. Vinson Cole is in excellent, effortless form, as is Anne Sofie von Otter, whose mezzo is the most fluent and expressive on the recording. The conductor's clear-eyed approach to the score is exemplified by the remarkable precision and concentration of the chorus, which in turn gives the soloists' words and music an even greater impact. Superbly recorded.

The Rake's Progress

Composed 1947–51.
First performed September 11, 1951.
Libretto by W. H. Auden and Chester Kallman.

Synopsis

Act I

Eighteenth-century England. In the garden of Trulove, his daughter Anne and her betrothed Tom Rakewell sing of their love while Trulove looks on. He hopes that his misgivings about Tom are unfounded and implores him to find work. Tom sings of his need for money, whereupon a stranger, Nick Shadow, appears with news that Tom has inherited a fortune. Nick asks to be taken as Tom's servant and, after agreeing to be paid one year and a day after his engagement, they leave for London.

In Mother Goose's brothel Nick and Mother Goose begin to instruct Tom in the ways of vice, but he falters at the mention of love. Mother Goose then takes him to her bed and Tom quickly forgets Anne. However, Anne cannot forget Tom and determines to rescue him from his life of sin.

Act II

At his house in London, Tom bemoans the tedium of his life of fashion and high society. Nick suggests that if he marry the famous bearded lady Baba the Turk, he will be free from "those twin tyrants of appetite and conscience". Tom is convinced and agrees to marry Baba. Anne arrives at Tom's house but cannot enter. When Tom arrives in a sedan chair she is horrified to see that he has married. Tom begs her to leave him to his fate, while Baba entertains the crowd with a sight of her beard. In their rooms, Tom and Baba are left alone; when she fails to appeal to his "finer feelings" she begins to smash their china. Tom silences her with his wig and falls asleep, during which time Nick presents a "bread-making machine" to the audience. Tom awakes, having dreamed of just such an invention, which he believes will bring an end to all misery.

Act III

Tom's house is now a mess of filth and cobwebs. His possessions are up for sale and the auctioneer, Sellem, announces the lots, among which is Baba. Anne is looking for Tom, and Baba advises her to go to him. In a churchyard Tom and Nick meet for the final time. It is a year and a day since Tom employed Nick, who now wants Tom's soul as his wages. He tells Tom that he must kill himself on the stroke of midnight, but with three seconds to go Nick relents and suggests they play a game of cards to decide Tom's fate. He listens to the voice of love (Anne offstage) and wins, but Nick takes his revenge by condemning Tom to madness.

An inmate of Bedlam, Tom imagines himself to be Adonis awaiting Venus. Anne arrives and sings him to sleep after which she leaves with her father. When Tom wakes, he finds himself alone – "Venus" having left him – and he dies from grief. The curtain falls and the principals appear and sing the work's moral: "For idle hands, and hearts and minds, The Devil finds a work to do."

𝄞 Inspired by Hogarth's eight satirical paintings entitled *The Rake's Progress*, which he saw in Chicago in 1947, Stravinsky asked W. H. Auden – like him, a resident of the US – to write a libretto based on the pictures. Auden and his collaborator came up with a text that mixed in references to other Hogarth images (such as the *Idle and Industrious Apprentices* and *Marriage à la Mode*) and beefed up the scope of their morality tale with allusions to *Don Giovanni*, Faust, and Venus and Adonis, while paying tribute to writers such as Congreve and Gay in the clarity of its verse.

Stravinsky worked on the score, to the exclusion of all else, for three years, and his creative relationship with Auden – a fellow Christian – was extremely successful. Upon hearing the first performance in Venice, Dylan Thomas was moved to remark, "Auden is the most skilful of us all", and the libretto of *The Rake's Progress* did indeed give Stravinsky the perfect vehicle for a savagely ironic piece, in which the music of the eighteenth century is placed in inverted commas, as it were. Constructed from solo and ensemble numbers which are accompanied by a small, beautifully scored chamber orchestra and strung together by recitatives accompanied by harpsichord, this opera constantly invokes Mozart and *The Beggar's Opera*. However, there are references to the bel canto style in some of the arias, and the action commences with a fanfare that invokes the opening of Monteverdi's *Orfeo*, while there's a distinctively modern and Stravinskian feel to the often odd metrical emphasis and the spare and angular harmony. With its subtle anachronisms the music mirrors a world in which the natural order – epitomized by marriage, the family and country life – is subverted by Tom's feckless career, and in its extremely knowing (some might say cold-hearted) exploitation of opera's heritage, *The Rake's Progress* marks the culminating point of Stravinsky's Neoclassical style.

RECORDINGS OVERVIEW

Of the four recordings currently available, only one is conducted by the composer, even though he recorded it three times in all. The first, no longer available, was taped live at the premiere in 1951 with Stravinsky conducting badly and Schwarzkopf singing beautifully. His two later recordings were both made in the studio, one in 1953 and one in 1964. Both are interesting, but the latter is better conducted, even if Judith Raskin is no replacement for the 1953 Anne, Hilde Gueden. Riccardo Chailly's 1983 Decca recording boasts Samuel Ramey's magnificent Nick, while Robert Craft's effort is brilliantly conducted, but neither can match the newest *Rake*, released in 1996 by Erato.

Hadley, Upshaw, Ramey, Bumbry; Chorus and Orchestra of Lyon Opera; Nagano.
(Erato 0630-12715-2; 2 CDs).

Kent Nagano has made *The Rake's Progress* something of a speciality, and his studio recording pretty much redefines the standard, presenting an ideally cast and exactingly prepared performance that gets as close to the opera's mercurial character as anything yet recorded. Jerry Hadley is an ardent Tom Rakewell and Dawn Upshaw is the most ravishing Anne since Schwarzkopf. Samuel Ramey has made a career out of playing devils, and his Nick Shadow is exceptional, carrying just the right amount of menace; and while Grace Bumbry is some years past her best (which occurred somewhere around the mid-1960s), she has the measure of Baba. The playing of the Lyon Orchestra is first class, and the sound is expertly balanced and refreshingly clear.

Young, Raskin, Reardon, Sarfaty; Sadler's Wells Opera Chorus; Royal Philharmonic Orchestra; Stravinsky.
(Sony SM2K 46299; 2 CDs).

Stravinsky was not a great conductor and many of his recordings are disappointing. This 1964 *Rake* is an exception. Most of the cast had recently performed the opera and so were familiar with the music's intricacies, which are well served by a clear, well-produced recording. The mild disappointments are Judith Raskin, who is a rather stodgy Anne, and John Reardon, whose lack of edge makes Nick Shadow almost likable.

SERGEI PROKOFIEV

b. SONTSOVKA, UKRAINE, APRIL 23, 1891; d. MOSCOW, MARCH 5, 1953.

Though he was regarded as impossibly avant-garde in his youth, Sergei Prokofiev belongs to the same great tradition of Russian music as Tchaikovsky and Mussorgsky, a tradition resonant with a sense of their country's history. In general, he clung to the classical forms of the symphony, concerto and sonata, just as his great contemporary Stravinsky was so pointedly rejecting them, and he wrote in an immediately recognizable style which reconciled progressive technique with melodic traditionalism. His music is among the most accessible and popular of the twentieth century, an achievement all the more remarkable in view of the fact that much of it was achieved in the face of the dogmatic repression of Stalinism and in the midst of Russia's terrible suffering in World War II. As an opera composer he was dogged by disappointment and failure, but he left behind at least three operas that deserve to be heard: *Love for Three Oranges*, *The Fiery Angel* and *War and Peace*.

Born in the Ukraine, Prokofiev soon displayed prodigious talent as a composer and as a pianist, as well as a somewhat overdeveloped sense of his own importance. He was encouraged by the composer Glière, under whose guidance he completed two childhood operas, composing a third before his sixteenth birthday. At the St Petersburg Academy, where he studied with Rimsky-Korsakov, he proved rebellious, disruptive and totally unsuited to the discipline of academic study, earning the hostility of, among others, Glazunov. In 1911 he composed his first mature opera, *Maddalena*; but in 1914, stifled by the cultural conservatism of Russia, he packed his bags and left for a spell in London, where he met Diaghilev and Stravinsky. The latter's music had a deep and lasting impact on him, although the two men's relationship was always mutually suspicious and competitive. From Diaghilev he received a commission for three ballets and was encouraged by the impresario to stay away from Russia. He also began an opera after Dostoyevsky's *The Gambler*, which was completed in 1917, just in time for a promised performance at the Mariinsky Theatre in St Petersburg. But the political turmoil and Prokofiev's anti-lyrical score – which fused conversational melodies to stark instrumental textures – led to postponement for several years. Prokofiev decided to tour America as a pianist and in 1919, after a sensational recital in Chicago, he was invited by the opera house to write an opera after Gozzi's play *The Love for Three Oranges*.

When performances of his Chicago opera were delayed, Prokofiev turned his attentions to a new opera, *The Fiery Angel*, which was to occupy him, on and off, for the next thirty years. He moved to Paris in 1920, where the performance of his ballet *Chout* was a notable success, before returning to America the following year for the premiere of *The Love for Three Oranges* and a series of concert tours that left the composer "with a thousand dollars in my pocket and an aching head". His resolve not to return to his homeland held out until 1926 when, homesick and curious as to how his homeland had evolved during his long absence, he agreed to an extensive tour of western Russia. To his surprise, Prokofiev was greeted as a celebrity and a hero of Russian music, and a permanent return must have seemed increasingly attractive. In the event it was another seven years before he bowed to the inevitable: in 1933 Prokofiev and his family left Paris and returned to Russia forever. It was almost certainly the worst decision of his life.

Prokofiev could have stayed in the west – as had Stravinsky and Rachmaninov – but he saw himself as an apolitical artist and disregarded the political implications of his return, believing that the Soviet authorities would grant him immunity as an internationally famous composer. He genuinely felt that the pressures being brought to bear on other composers would not apply to him. His timing could not have been worse: by 1936 the musical establishment was being run by politicians and when he arrived in Moscow, Prokofiev was at the mercy of a system that now expected composers – without exception – to write music for "the people", extolling the brave new world of Soviet socialism. The ensuing years were extremely hard and his relationship with the authorities rapidly disintegrated. Like Shostakovich, he suffered frequent humiliation, often having to thank the authorities for belittling him and his music in the press. When war broke out, ill-health and deep-seated resentment towards his country prevented him from taking any involvement and in 1941, his relationship with a 25-year-old student, Mira Mendelson, ended his marriage.

Opera continued to occupy him during the years of repression, but even the positive and accessible *War and Peace*, considered by the composer to be among his greatest achievements, fell foul of the authorities, being attacked at the 1948 Moscow Congress of Composers for "formalism" – a catch-all term applied to any music that had no immediately utilitarian function. Prokofiev, and other "errant" composers such as Shostakovich, were charged with "anti-democratic tendencies that are alien to the Soviet people and its artistic tastes". Unequivocal apologies were wrung from each of the accused, and Prokofiev's final operatic project, *The Story of a Real Man* (1948), was a crudely patriotic work aimed at pacifying his superiors. Listened to by Soviet cultural officials behind closed doors, even this was dismissed as "anti-melodic" and refused performance. Prokofiev was utterly crushed and, for all the support he received from friends such as Mstislav Rostropovich, David Oistrakh and Sviatoslav Richter, his last three years were miserable ones. He died just a few hours before Stalin, an irony that might, perhaps, have appealed to him.

The Love for Three Oranges

Composed 1919.
First performed December 30, 1921.
Libretto by the composer, after Gozzi.

Synopsis

Prologue

Advocates of different theatrical genres (Tragedy, Comedy, etc) demand to be entertained by their particular favourite. A chorus of The Ridiculous People chase them off and the opera begins.

Act I

The King's son and heir is suffering from terminal melancholy and while the King will do anything to cure him, the Prince's enemies – including his niece Princess Clarice and Prime Minister Leandro, who are secretly engaged to marry – are equally committed to his destruction. The King and his son are protected by Tchelio, Clarice and Leandro by Fata Morgana. The King's doctors advise him that laughter is the only medicine able to cure the Prince and so he orders huge and lavish entertainments. Leandro feeds the Prince a diet of Tragic Verses but Clarice is impatient, especially as the clown Truffaldino looks as if he might succeed in bringing a smile to the Prince's lips. Fata Morgana announces that she will attend the festivities.

Act II

The Prince refuses to laugh at Truffaldino and vomits up the Tragic Verses. He refuses to attend the entertainments, but the clown pushes him out the door. At first, he is unmoved by the jollity and his face remains a picture of misery. However, when Fata Morgana crosses the room, slips on the shiny floor and falls sprawling, the Prince bursts into laughter. Everyone laughs – except Leandro, Clarice and Morgana, who casts a spell on the Prince: he will fall in love with three oranges and spend the rest of his life looking for them. The Prince leaves immediately, followed by Truffaldino.

Act III

Tchelio discovers that the Prince is heading for Creonte's castle, where the oranges are kept. Tchelio is unable to break Morgana's spell but he advises the Prince not to open the fruit unless he is near water, and gives him a magic ribbon. The Prince and Truffaldino use the ribbon to distract Creonte's giant cook and they steal the three oranges and make their escape. However, the further they move away from the castle, the larger the fruits become, and the Prince and his clown become exhausted. Forgetting the warning, Truffaldino cuts open the first orange – to reveal a princess who begs him for a drink – and then another – which reveals the same. The clown runs away screaming, leaving the princesses to die. When the Prince wakes, he realizes his hopes are with the last orange; he cuts it open and a third princess – Ninetta – steps out. The Ridiculous People arrive with a bucket of water and save Ninetta from her thirst. Back at the palace, Fata Morgana's servant Smeraldina turns the princess into a rat and takes her place. When the court arrive they agree that she is the one the Prince should marry.

Act IV

The Ridiculous People lock Fata Morgana into a prison so that Tchelio can return to the palace. When the court enter for the Prince's wedding they are met by the sight of a giant rat sitting on the King's throne. The soldiers begin to fire at it but Tchelio realizes who it is and turns the animal back into Ninetta. The King now realizes that Smeraldina, Leandro and Clarice are traitors and orders them to be executed. They manage to escape with Fata Morgana and the opera ends with The Ridiculous People drinking a toast to the Prince and Ninetta.

Having failed to get *The Gambler* onto the stage, Prokofiev's need for operatic success became a major preoccupation during his concert tour of America. When a commission materialized it was from Cleonfonte Campanini, the director of the Chicago Opera, with whom Prokofiev signed an agreement in January 1919 for a production of *The Love for Three Oranges* later that year. But the work was postponed when Campanini resigned his directorship, and it remained unperformed until the soprano Mary Garden was appointed director for the 1921–22 season. Although Garden was a champion of contemporary music (she had been in the premiere of *Pelléas et Mélisande*), she was taken aback by the harshness of much of Prokofiev's score. Nevertheless, the production went ahead, conducted by the composer, and was deemed a great success in Chicago – although a single performance in New York received a critical mauling.

In choosing to set Carlo Gozzi's *Fiaba dell'amore delle tre melarancie* Prokofiev was following in the wake of Busoni and Puccini, who had already turned to the eighteenth-century dramatist for the tale of *Turandot*. The engagingly lunatic libretto was written by the composer from a translation into French by the Russian director Meyerhold, whose theories on "the diminution of the role of the actor" and the need to "challenge conventional audience relationships" had an influence on this anti-naturalistic and self-consciously avant-garde opera. Musically, however, *The Love for Three Oranges* is something of an amalgam of the rhythmically driven world of Prokofiev's *Scythian Suite* and the more refined and elegant language of his *Classical Symphony*. These two very different aspects of the composer are, on the whole, successfully synthesized, and the music – while never easy – perfectly captures the frenzy and unreality of the drama. Each of its unlikely characters is characterized through broad orchestral strokes: diatonic and well-ordered music for the forces of good (Prokofiev the classicist), chromatic and unstable for evil

(Prokofiev the modernist). The vocal writing is subjugated to the French text in a manner that makes the tunes fragmented and brittle – short, acerbic phrases predominate to such an extent that this opera favours the casting of singing actors, rather than of singers who are able to act.

Amidst the riot of activity, which continues almost without interruption, Prokofiev provides a light and simple orchestral background – the famous March and Scherzo in Act II (frequently played in concert) are decidedly atypical in their bravura. For all the witty ensembles, especially the high-speed finale, *The Love for Three Oranges*, like Busoni's *Turandot*, is a strangely detached piece, presenting many intriguing faces but never for long enough for a lasting image to develop.

Bacquier, Viala, Perraguin, Le Texier, Gautier; Lyon Opera Chorus and Orchestra; Nagano.
(Virgin VCD7 59566-2; 2 CDs).

This award-winning performance has remained in the catalogue since it was first released in 1989 and is one of the most notable opera recordings of the past decade. Played and sung by a French company who have learnt the work in repertoire, it has a palpable unity of intent from the outset and Nagano perfectly judges the character of the farce, never overplaying it but nonetheless allowing his cast to enjoy themselves. His direction is precise and ideally paced, and although on occasions there is a tendency to exaggerate the more aggressive episodes, he is remarkably successful in smoothing the stylistic jumps. His singers are outstanding and the recording is a model of clarity and balance.

The Fiery Angel

Composed 1919–23; revised 1926–27.
First performed November 25, 1954.
Libretto by the composer.

Synopsis

Act I

Renata believes that she has a protecting angel called Madiel. She has been living with Prince Heinrich – whom she believed to be Madiel – but he has left her and now she spends her time looking for him. She explains her situation to Ruprecht, who is in love with her and agrees to help her.

Act II

Renata and Ruprecht consult books of black magic in their quest for the Prince. In the process they conjure evil spirits. A leading sorcerer, Agrippa, refuses to help them.

Act III

Renata catches up with Heinrich but he rejects her for a second time. Incensed, she urges Ruprecht to defend her honour and he challenges the Prince to a duel. However, Renata sees the Prince bathed in a flood of light and again thinks that he must be Madiel. Concerned, she urges Ruprecht not to hurt him. As a consequence he is himself badly wounded. Struck by remorse she promises to love him and nurse him back to health.

Act IV

Ruprecht recovers and Renata leaves him, telling him that she intends to enter a convent, where she thinks she can find salvation. Ruprecht is met by Faust and Mephistopheles, and the latter offers to protect him.

Act V

Renata is still obsessed with Madiel and she has brought her visions with her to the convent. She has also brought demons and spirits, who terrorize the nuns. She is sent before the Inquisition who fail to exorcise her evil spirits. In the presence of Ruprecht and Mephistopheles, Renata is sentenced to death as a witch.

Having moved from the bitter realism of Dostoyevsky's *The Gambler* to the comic fantasy of Gozzi's *The Love for Three Oranges*, Prokofiev turned for his next opera to the novel *The Fiery Angel* by the Russian Symbolist Valery Bryussov. Prokofiev began the work in the belief that Mary Garden would mount it in Chicago, but even after her departure he continued to work on the score, convinced that this extravagant spectacle would provide him with the operatic success that had so far eluded him. In 1926 Bruno Walter, as conductor at the Berlin Städtische Oper, offered to mount the premiere but failed to honour his agreement. In the end the first staged production did not occur until 1955, two years after Prokofiev's death, at La Fenice in Venice.

Tales of obsession fascinated Prokofiev for most of life and many of his operas present some new slant on obsessional behaviour, but *The Fiery Angel* is unique in Prokofiev's output, not merely in its affinities with the work of his progressive contemporaries (notably Berg's *Wozzeck*), nor simply for its brutality. Rather it is the intensity of emotion that gives it its special appeal, and of all Prokofiev's operas it's the one that comes closest to revealing the man within. There is something profoundly moving in the concentration with which he tells Renata's tale, doubtless inspired by his own feelings for Lina Llubera, whom he had recently married. Renata's internal conflict between the spiritual (Madiel) and the physical (Heinrich) animated Prokofiev "as nothing before", but like most great works of Expressionist musical theatre, the questions that stand at the work's heart (does Renata really see Madiel, or is she hallucinating?) are left unanswered.

The five-act form is divided into tableaux and the entire score is based upon a series of linking chromatic motifs. Two of these, heard in Act I and associated with Renata, pervade the entire score and provide an anchor amidst the contrapuntal complexity. Indeed, the music for *The Fiery Angel* is startlingly busy and richly voiced, most dramatically in the finale, where the confusion of the nuns' voices is set against the chant of the Inquisitor. Amid these shifting and coagulating textures, in which divided strings play a remarkably effective part (notably during the chilling conjuring of the spirits), float some of Prokofiev's most lyrically intense vocal writing. Unconventional in their great length and simplicity, the extended lines (such as the radiant theme that accompanies Renata's declaration of love for Madiel) are made all the more arresting by the turmoil of the accompanying instrumental counterpoint, and it is this fusion of lucidity and opulence that makes *The Fiery Angel* such a gripping opera.

Leiferkus, Gorchakova; Kirov Chorus and Orchestra; Gergiev.
(Philips 446078-2; 2 CDs).

You will love or hate this no-holds-barred recording. Gergiev lets loose the dogs of war from his orchestra, and an atmosphere of violence and menace pervades the entire proceedings. Renata's neuroses are brought to life with thundering intensity – Gorchakova is stunningly impressive in the role, not least because she has one of the most beautiful voices of her generation. Sergei Leiferkus is equally splendid as Ruprecht, and the remainder of the well-integrated cast more than rise to the occasion. Fearsomely powerful stuff.

Secunde, Lorenz, Zednik, Salomaa, Moll, Terfel; Gothenburg Pro Musica Chorus; Gothenburg Symphony Orchestra; Järvi.
(Deutsche Grammophon 431 669-2GH2; 2 CDs).

This, the only other recording of *The Fiery Angel* currently available, might appeal if you find Gergiev's approach too manic. However, it has its problems. Järvi has a fine sense of shape, and there are some extraordinarily impressive interludes, but he is prone to let the work sink into balmy lushness. That said, Nadine Secunde achieves wonders in the extremely demanding role of Renata, while Siegfried Lorenz as Ruprecht and Kurt Moll as the Inquisitor deliver nicely pointed vocal portrayals. The sound is impressive but, in the vital question of balance, completely artificial.

War and Peace

Composed 1941–43; revised 1946–52.
First performed October 16, 1944.
Libretto by the composer and Mira Mendelson, after Tolstoy.

Synopsis

Part I: Peace

1810. The recently widowed Prince Andrei Bolkonsky is cheered when he hears Natasha Rostova singing of the coming spring. At the New Year's Eve ball, they fall in love – although the scheming Prince Anatol has plans of his own.

Two years later the lovers are engaged, but the Prince's father, Nicolai, refuses to accept her. Andrei has to go away for a year – leaving Natasha to the married Anatol, who soon succeeds in convincing her to forget Andrei. Ignoring his friend Dolokhov's advice, Anatol and Natasha attempt to elope, but their attempt is foiled and Anatol only just escapes. Natasha is told by an old family friend, Count Pierre, that Anatol is already married, and she is further shocked when Pierre, who is also married, confesses that he too is in love with her. Later that night Pierre demands that Anatol give up Natasha and leave Moscow. News arrives of Napoleon's march into Russia.

Part II: War

August 25, 1812. While the Russian volunteer army assembles, Andrei considers his future. Convinced that he must forget Natasha, he enlists, rejecting the offer of a desk job. Later the same day, Napoleon expresses astonishment at the fervour and organization of the Russian resistance and begins to suspect that fate is turning against him. Field-Marshal Kutuzov decides to relinquish Moscow to the French, so as to give themselves time to regroup.

In French-occupied Moscow the streets are empty. Pierre learns that Natasha and her family have also fled – taking with them a small group of wounded Russian soldiers, including (although she does not know it) Andrei. Natasha eventually discovers that Andrei is among them and although she begs his forgiveness and promises faithfulness in the future, it is too late and he dies.

November 1812: the French are in retreat, taking their prisoners back with them; those who cannot keep up are shot. A party of Russian soldiers attacks the French column, freeing the prisoners – among them Pierre. He discovers that Natasha is unwell, but hopes that, once she is better, she will return his love. Kutuzov is cheered by the people, whom he congratulates for defeating the French.

As far as Prokofiev could see, the best way he could fufill the morale-boosting role he was expected to play in wartime Russia was to promote Russian culture and history through his music, and in resolving to turn Tolstoy's epic novel *War and Peace* into an opera, he believed he was doing more than merely toe the line. As always, however, the line was hard to define and, in May 1942, after submitting eleven of the thirteen scenes of *War and Peace* to the much feared cultural censor Andrei Zhdanov, he was subjected to ruthless criticism. *War and Peace* was one of the pillars of Russian literature and was held up as a model for socialist realist artists, but Prokofiev's score was a long way from fulfilling the quota of heroics expected of an operatic translation. On top of this, Prokofiev failed to modify his musical vocabulary to the satisfaction of the Soviet officials and, as well as being told to beef up the drama, he was requested to add more tunes. Secretly, Prokofiev had initially intended the opera to be small in scale, concentrating on Pierre and Natasha to the exclusion of Kutuzov and the Russian people, but it was soon made clear that in order to set Peace, he had first to set War. He did so, presenting Napoleon as a caricature of Hitler and Kutuzov as Stalin. The first performance, at the Bolshoi in Moscow, was planned for 1943 but this failed to materialize and not until June 1946 was any of the opera (an augmented Part I) staged. Thereafter, the political climate precluded any further performances and, thanks to the tyrannical Zhdanov, Prokofiev died before he could hear the work performed complete.

In setting *War and Peace*, Prokofiev resurrected the tableaux format of *The Fiery Angel* but, in compliance with the demands of his "superiors", he introduced conventional "numbers" and set-pieces. Part I recalls the Tchaikovsky of *Eugene Onegin*, with its languid melodies and dance music, while Part II is indebted to the Mussorgsky of *Boris Godunov*, with large ensemble scenes and a solemn bass role (Kutuzov) dominating the proceedings. The style throughout is heavily melodic (Napoleon's inarticulate quasi-*Sprechstimme* is one obvious exception), and avoids the complexities of earlier works. The result is less concentrated (there are, after all, nearly seventy named characters), but it is considerably more accessible, with a typically Russian predilection for meaty, militaristic choruses and grand dances (there are strong echoes of Glinka's *A Life for the Tsar*). Working with the film director Eisenstein on *Alexander Nevsky* and *Ivan the Terrible* evidently honed Prokofiev's skill at creating big, emotive scenes – as is evident from the battle episodes and the scene in which Anatol hears the sound of blood rushing in his ears as he lies dying.

The vocal writing is consistently persuasive and prevents the four-hour length from seeming like it. Each of the four primary voices (Andrei, Natasha, Pierre and Kutuzov) is beautifully characterized, with the General especially grand and Natasha and Andrei suitably passionate. The opera is most notable, perhaps, for its remarkable fusion of the private and the public, its touches of pathos within the sweep of a narrative in which the interests of the common citizen are thrust into conflict with the interest of the state. It was a struggle that Prokofiev well understood.

RECORDINGS OVERVIEW

Remarkably, the longest Russian opera ever written has been recorded six times – although only the two most recent (discussed overleaf) are complete.

Of the first four, the outstanding one is Melodiya's first set, recorded on the back of the Bolshoi's premiere production in 1959. Featuring a superlative Natasha from Galina Vishnevskaya, it's superior to her later recording under the baton of her husband, Mstislav Rostropovich, but is not on CD at the moment.

Gergalov, Prokina, Kannunikova, Gregoriam, Marusin, Okhotnikov; Kirov Theatre Chorus and Orchestra; Gergiev.
(Philips 434 097-2PH3; 3 CDs).

In 1992 Gergiev and the Kirov produced this extraordinary recording on the back of a series of magnificent live performances (one of which has been released on video). Gergiev pushes where Rostropovich savours, and the younger conductor manages to generate an irresistible sense of theatre, applying rapid, fluently maintained tempi throughout (he gets the whole thing onto three discs). The battle scenes are astonishingly vivid and the chorus work is among the finest ever captured on a recording of a Russian opera. The repertoire casting is faultless, but it is the feeling of immediacy, the live element, that makes this such a gripping recording.

Vishnevskaya, Miller, Ciesinski, Ochman, Gedda, Ghiuselev Ghiavrov; French Radio Chorus; French National Orchestra; Rostropovich.
(Erato 2292-45331-2; 4 CDs).

Rostropovich was asked by the composer on his deathbed to bring *War and Peace* to life for the world, and some thirty years later he was able to keep his word, conducting the first ever complete recording of the opera. Sadly, however, Rostropovich's performance is fragmented and uneven, and is blighted by passages of crass sentimentality. The saving grace is the casting: Vishnevskaya's Natasha, for all the strain in the voice, is a genuinely moving reading; Nicolai Gedda is similarly up against the ravages of time, but he brilliantly acts his way through Anatol's oiliness; and Wieslaw Ochman's sweet-toned tenor is ideal for the naive and selfless Pierre. Nicolai Ghiaurov in the idealistic role of Kutuzov does well to underline the General's indulgent melancholia. In short, a well-recorded, well-sung but inconsistent effort.

DMITRI SHOSTAKOVICH

b. ST PETERSBURG, SEPTEMBER 25, 1906; d. MOSCOW, AUGUST 9, 1975.

Unlike Prokofiev, who grew up and was educated in tsarist Russia, Shostakovich spent almost his entire life as a citizen of the Soviet Union. The Soviet system nurtured him as a composer but it also regularly humiliated him whenever his music was deemed to have failed to fulfill the banal criteria of the Soviet cultural commissars. Shostakovich's first opera, *The Nose*, was completed in 1928, and was typical of the creative freedom that existed during the early years of the Soviet regime, but by the time *Lady Macbeth of Mtsensk* was staged, the political climate had long since changed. In January 1936, two years after its first performance, *Lady Macbeth* was condemned in a *Pravda* editorial as "A Muddle instead of Music". The attack continued: "If by chance the composer lapses into simple, comprehensible melody, he is scared at such a misfortune and quickly plunges into confusion again. . . . All this is coarse, primitive and vulgar." This criticism, a direct expression of Stalin's opinion, almost broke Shostakovich, whose career as an opera composer then almost ground to a halt.

Shostakovich's musical life began in earnest when he enrolled, at the age of thirteen, at the Petrograd (St Petersburg) Conservatory, where he studied piano under Nikolayev and composition under Steinberg and Glazunov. The artistic atmosphere was essentially conservative but the more adventurous students, including Shostakovich, had access to scores by Bartók, Schoenberg and Stravinsky. In 1926, Shostakovich's diploma work – the *Symphony No. 1* – established his reputation after performances in Moscow and Leningrad (the renamed Petrograd), and it was taken up abroad by such conductors as Toscanini and Bruno Walter. Despite the emergence of Stalin, the mid-1920s was still a time of extraordinary experimentation, as the new forms of the avant-garde were felt by many to be the most appropriate artistic language for the post-Revolutionary era. The young Shostakovich was closely involved with some of the most radical artistic figures in Russia. In 1927 he met the brilliant theatre director Vsevolod Meyerhold, and the following year he became the musical director of Meyerhold's theatre in Moscow. It was around this time that he wrote *The Nose*, a setting of Gogol's satirical short story presented as a series of very brief scenes linked by orchestral interludes, in a manner similar to Berg's *Wozzeck*.

Reactions to *The Nose* were mixed, and anti-modernist groups like the Russian Association of Proletarian Musicians were becoming increasingly influential. Though Shostakovich still believed that complex, even difficult, music was reconcilable with Communist ideals, *Lady Macbeth* marked a tempering of his style in the way it mixed the abrasive language of *The Nose* with moments of lyricism. But the compromise was to no avail. Shostakovich's response to the savaging he received from *Pravda* was to write the accessible *Symphony No. 5*, subtitled "a Soviet artist's creative reply to just criticism", and from now on his principal means of expression – still subject to political scrutiny – were the symphony and the string quartet. His mediation between political expediency and aesthetic integrity during the Stalin years is one of the most admirable feats of twentieth-century music.

During World War II, Shostakovich wrote two other operas, *The Silly Little Mouse* (1939) and *The Tale of a Priest and his Servant Balda* (1941). Both were turned into animated films but unfortunately their scores have been lost. In 1940 he abandoned plans for an opera based on Tolstoy's *Resurrection* and two years later he left his setting of Gogol's *The Gamblers* incomplete because, according to his memoirs, he found the subject "morally unacceptable" in wartime Russia. In 1958 he wrote a lightweight operetta called *Cheryomushki*, then in 1962 – in the middle of the Khrushchev thaw – his almost complete rehabilitation was marked by the production of *Lady Macbeth* in a revised and toned-down version entitled *Katerina Ismailova*.

Lady Macbeth of Mtsensk

Composed 1930–32; revised 1958.
First performed January 22, 1934.
Libretto by the composer and Alexander Preys, after Leskov.

Synopsis

Act I

Katerina is the bored and unfulfilled wife of the merchant Zinovy. Boris, her father-in-law, keeps an eye on her and continually pesters her about providing an heir. While her husband is away a new labourer, Sergei, is employed. Sergei instigates an assault on the cook, and when Katerina intervenes he wrestles her to the ground. That night when Katerina is in bed, Sergei knocks on the door and asks to borrow a book. They start to make love.

Act II

Boris, lurking around Katerina's window, catches Sergei as he leaves the house. In a rage, he beats Sergei and then demands food from Katerina. He eats mushrooms which Katerina has laced with rat poison, dying horribly some moments later, but not before he has revealed the crime to a priest. When Zinovy returns and tries to beat his wife, Sergei and Katerina murder him and hide the body in the cellar.

Act III

Katerina and Sergei are to be married. A peasant, desperate for alcohol, finds the body of Zinovy and tells the police, who are resentful at not being invited to Katerina's wedding. The police descend on the wedding feast and arrest the newlyweds.

Act IV

Katerina and Sergei are prisoners, marching on the road to Siberia. Sergei rejects Katerina, blaming her for their predicament. Sergei now has a new woman, Sonyetka, who demands Katerina's stockings. When Sonyetka and the other women convicts taunt Katerina she pushes Sonyetka into the river and then jumps in herself. The convicts continue along the road.

Lady Macbeth of Mtsensk was first produced in two separate productions in January 1934: one at the Maly Theatre in Leningrad and the other at the theatre of Nemirovich-Danchenko in Moscow (under the title *Katerina Ismailova*). Despite the dissonant modernity of the music, both productions were very successful and were rapidly followed by others throughout the world, including at the Met in New York. In 1935 and the early 1960s the composer revised the score. The latter revision was the more complete, involving the excision of episodes that the over-sensitive Russian authorities still considered unacceptable (such as Katerina's lovemaking with Sergei in Act I), the thinning out of the orchestrations and the rescoring of numerous melodies, making them generally easier on the voice as well as the ear. But the original version of *Lady Macbeth* is Shostakovich's operatic masterpiece, for only in his first draft does the music match its subject.

Originally conceived by Shostakovich as the first of three works portraying the hardships and triumphs of Russian women (the plan never came to fruition), the opera was intended to "preserve the strength of Leskov's novel, and yet, approaching it critically, to interpret its events from our modern point of view". What this meant was that whereas Leskov's Katerina is a cruel, selfish and guiltless character, Shostakovich presents her as a victim of circumstances, oppressed by the squalor and brutality of those who surround her, and pulled down to their level largely out of sexual frustration. The sexual content of the opera was always going to be controversial, and there's still something startling about Shostakovich's musically graphic sex scene in Act I which culminates in post-coital glissandi on the trombones. Over and again the music is brilliantly employed to illustrate the specific weaknesses of the various characters, like the crude waltz that signals the desire of Boris for his daughter-in-law, or the passionless and insipid music that characterizes Zinovy.

Much of the strength of *Lady Macbeth* comes from its extraordinary orchestral score, a brilliantly garish fusion of primary colours, cruelly driving rhythms and wild dissonances that culminates in the splendidly grim passacaglia (one of six orchestral interludes) in Act II, which quotes from the opera's opening and communicates a strong sense of events starting to run out of control. But there are also moments of real comedy, including the utterly convincing drunken peasant, the priest's song over the dying Boris and, best of all, the chorus of policemen – compared by one New York critic to the Keystone Kops. Stravinsky thought *Lady Macbeth* "lamentably provincial. . . in a very embarrassing realistic style", and it is a crude work, in the sense that it is raw and sometimes brash, but it is also profoundly moving, with a final scene that encapsulates centuries of Russian suffering and deprivation. It also contains one of the greatest soprano roles of modern opera, a role which pushes the expressive range of the voice to extremes in order to convey, in the words of Galina Vishnevskaya, "the recklessness and elemental power of a passion that make us identify with that strong young woman and forget all her evil deeds".

Vishnevskaya, Gedda, Petkov, Krenn; Ambrosian Opera Chorus; London Philharmonic Orchestra; Rostropovich. (EMI CDS7 49955-2; 2 CDs).

This is one of Rostropovich's most successful recordings as a conductor: his sensitivity to the vivid orchestral colours and his vigorous tempi perfectly serve the opera's sudden contrasts and black humour. Vishnevskaya sings with a thrilling, elemental power and although Gedda was past his prime in 1978 he works wonders with the text, being precise where another tenor might have resorted to shouting. The rest of the large cast is fine and the electric atmosphere is perfectly captured by EMI's engineers.

CARL NIELSEN

b. SORTELUNG, DENMARK, JUNE 9, 1865; d. COPENHAGEN, OCTOBER 3, 1931.

Opera in Denmark got off to a bad start: in 1689 a fire swept through the Amalienborg Theatre in Copenhagen during a performance of *Der vereinighte Götterstreit*, killing 180 people. Povl Schindler's *Der vereinighte Götterstreit* was the first full-length opera by a Danish composer to be performed in Denmark, but it was written in German and Germany continued to be the dominant musical influence on its northern neighbour for many decades. Carl Nielsen was the first Danish opera composer to establish a pan-European reputation, but even he is better known for his cycle of six symphonies than for his two fine operas, *Saul og David* and *Maskarade*, neither of which is often performed outside Denmark. Both were written relatively early in Nielsen's career. Although he continued to compose many delightful songs in Danish as well as incidental music for the theatre, the last twenty-five years of his life were largely taken up by orchestral writing. His involvement in opera continued, however, as principal conductor of the Royal Theatre in Copenhagen from 1908 to 1914.

Like Richard Strauss, Nielsen's operatic models were Mozart and – initially at least – Richard Wagner. In 1890, having already found work as a second violinist at the Royal Theatre, he won a scholarship that enabled him to travel to Dresden and Berlin, where performances of Wagner's *Ring* and *Die Meistersinger* greatly impressed him, though he was later to reject Wagner's use of leitmotifs, dismissing it as "spoonfeeding". Brahms, whom he met in 1894, was another influence, particularly on his early symphonies, and guidance also came from the Norwegian composer Johan Svendsen (his predecessor as conductor of the Royal Theatre), but arguably the most important sources for Nielsen's combination of the lyrical and the dynamic were the songs his mother used to sing to him as a child, and his father's village dance band, in which the young Carl played violin. Nielsen always recalled his childhood among the peasants of eastern Denmark with great affection, and both his operas are marked by their down-to-earth humanity. Much of their dramatic effectiveness derives from the directness and clarity of their story-telling, an operatic priority that first struck Nielsen in 1894: "The plot must be the pole that goes through a dramatic work; the plot is the trunk, words and sentences are fruit and leaves, but if the trunk is not strong and healthy, it is no use that the fruits look beautiful."

Saul og David

Saul and David

Composed 1898–1901.
First performed November 28, 1902.
Libretto by Einar Christiansen, after the Book of Samuel.

Synopsis

Act I

King Saul carries out a sacrifice which only the prophet Samuel should perform. The prophet enters and foretells the end of Saul's reign over Israel. Saul's son Jonathan asks the shepherd David to sing to the king. David tells Saul's daughter Mikal that he loves her.

Act II

David is singing to Saul when news arrives that the defeated Philistine army has regrouped and is being led by the giant Goliath. The Philistines are defeated when David kills Goliath; the people praise David, provoking the king's jealousy. David is banished.

Act III

David is pursued by Saul. At night in Saul's camp, David enters the king's chamber as he sleeps, but spares his life in order to prove his loyalty. Samuel anoints David as the chosen King of Israel and then dies.

Act IV

Saul visits the Witch of Endor and asks her to summon Samuel's spirit. It is prophesied that Saul and Jonathan will die at the hands of the Philistines. In fulfilment of the prophecy Jonathan is killed, but rather than die at the hand of another, Saul takes his own life. David is acknowledged by the Israelites as their king.

The devoutly religious Nielsen first considered the tale of Saul and David as a subject for an opera in 1896 but only approached his librettist, the playwright Einar Christiansen, two years later. From then on the work became an obsession for him and he worked on little else during its composition: ". . . it stirred and haunted me, so that for long periods I could not free myself from it, no matter where I was – even when I was sitting in the orchestra with my second violin, busy with ballets and vaudeville." Above all, it was the relationship of the two main characters that fascinated him, although it turned out that the tragic figure of Saul (bass-baritone) monopolized much of the action and got most of the best music. Saul represents a defiant and erratic individualism while David's conformism stands for tradition – and it is always clear that Nielsen's sympathy is with the former, whose final desperate stand leads to a death scene of great darkness and poignancy. David is rather less appealing: written for a high tenor and providing a lyrical contrast to the brooding Saul, he often seems an insipid and unheroic hero.

Nielsen's breathtakingly rich and percussive orchestral score reaches a peak of excitement during the battle scenes – the writing for David's defeat of Goliath is particularly powerful. There are numerous other intensely theatrical scenes, notably the opening scene of Act I. A fiery military prelude introduces the king and his son impatiently awaiting the arrival of Samuel. Saul can wait no longer and, in Samuel's absence, he prepares to make a sacrifice to God. The solo voices, heightened by fear, are joined by a sober background of sacred choral music, and as the mass of voices reach a crescendo of passion, they are cut short by the arrival of Samuel, who pronounces Saul an outcast. It is a superbly powerful construction, and if the work as a whole has little of the melodic appeal for which Nielsen's early symphonies are famous, then the brutal directness of the drama has a compelling intensity.

Haugland, Lindroos, Kiberg, Westi; Danish National Radio Chorus and Symphony Orchestra; Järvi.
(Chandos CHAN8911-2; 2 CDs).

Chandos made this excellent recording in 1990 with Danish musicians and an all-Danish cast. Aage Haugland's Saul steals the show – as should be the case – although Peter Lindroos brings to the role of David almost more than it deserves. The remaining cast are all solid (Anne Gjevang is a pantomime-lurid Witch of Endor), and Järvi conducts brightly and efficiently.

Maskarade

Masquerade

Composed 1904–06.
First performed November 11, 1906.
Libretto by Vilhelm Andersen, after Ludvig Holberg.

Synopsis

Act I

Copenhagen, 1723, at the house of Jeronimus. A marriage has been arranged between Leander, Jeronimus's son, and Leonora, the daughter of Leonard, a family friend. Unfortunately both Leander, who is present, and Leonora, who is not, resist the match, having fallen in love with other suitors at the previous evening's masquerade. Jeronimus confines his family to the house.

Act II

Leander and his servant Henrik manage to escape from the house by outwitting Jeronimus's idiotic servant Arv. Leander and Leonora meet in the street on the way to another masquerade. Unaware of each other's identity, they fall in love with each other, while their two servants – Henrik and Pernille – flirt.

Act III

At the masquerade Jeronimus's wife, Magdelone, flirts with Leonard, Leander and Leonora continue their declarations of love, while a drunken Jeronimus attempts to seduce a ballerina. When the masks are removed at midnight all is resolved to everyone's satisfaction.

Nielsen's second opera makes a complete contrast to the psychological intensity of *Saul og David*. Its source was a play by Ludvig Holberg, an eighteenth-century Danish playwright whose knockabout farces are similar in tone to the plays of his Venetian contemporary Goldoni. Holberg was a cultural icon to be approached with caution, and so Nielsen chose as his librettist the Holberg scholar Vilhelm Andersen, whose adaptation of *Maskarade* makes such extensive use of rhyme and punning that the text resembles the work of a Scandinavian W. S. Gilbert. The opera is also frequently described as Mozartian, but in fact it is much closer in feel to early intermezzi like Pergolesi's *La serva padrona* (see p.42), with its simple plot and two-dimensional representations of the various social classes. The character that functions best is the wily man-servant Henrik, whom Nielsen described as "... quite modern in his feelings, after all, he even says socialistic things". In the end true love wins out, but not before the elderly and the respectable have been exposed as hypocrites and shown to be just as susceptible to foolishness and passion as those younger and socially inferior to themselves.

The opera's sound-world evokes the eighteenth century by being bright, direct and uncluttered, but there is rarely any sense of pastiche. There are no arias or big set-pieces, but Nielsen's vocal style has a highly communicative simplicity and a naturalness, and is enlivened by some vivid instrumental characterization: Jeronimus as stern paterfamilias in Act I gets to sing a chorale-like denunciation of the masquerade, but as would-be seducer in Act III gets to loosen up considerably. The lyric tenor of Leander has the opera's most passionate moments: his two duets with Leonora – the first rhapsodic, the second more subdued – have a lyricism that Richard Strauss might have been proud of. *Maskarade* is a major achievement, and as a twentieth-century reworking of an eighteenth-century model is scarcely inferior to *Der Rosenkavalier*.

Hansen, Landy, Johansen, Plesner, Bastian, Brodersen; Danish National Radio Chorus; Danish Radio Symphony Orchestra and Chorus; Frandsen.
(Unicorn DKPCD 9073/4; 2 CDs).

Though made in the 1970s, this recording is beginning to sound rather long in the tooth – not least in the rather broad handling of the comic scenes. Conductor Frandsen is adequate but does not really possess the requisite lightness of touch nor does he keep all his singers under control. However, Gert Bastian and Edith Brodersen (as Leander and Leonora) have a real sweetness of tone and theirs are the best moments – particularly the rapturous duet in the second act.

RALPH VAUGHAN WILLIAMS

b. DOWN AMPNEY, ENGLAND, OCTOBER 12, 1872; d. LONDON, AUGUST 26, 1958.

With his friend and colleague Gustav Holst, Vaughan Williams spent many years researching and cataloguing English traditional songs that had never previously been written down, thereby spurring a resurgence in English music comparable to the folk-inspired movements within eastern and central Europe. Both men were also keen to find success as English opera composers, but in the early years of the twentieth century this was still a near-impossible task, as Vaughan Williams acknowledged when writing to a friend in 1910: "I see hardly any chance of an opera by an Englishman being produced, at all events in our lifetime." This was slightly too gloomy, for in that very year Thomas Beecham's first opera season at Covent Garden included two works by English composers, *The Wreckers* by Ethel Smyth and *A Village Romeo and Juliet* by Delius. However, the opera that Vaughan Williams began writing in 1910, *Hugh the Drover*, didn't reach the stage until fourteen years later. Beecham once remarked that the English are not, by nature, an operatic race, and it is a testament to

Vaughan Williams's tenacity that he persisted in the face of received opinion, creating at least a couple of operas that warrant investigation.

As a composer Vaughan Williams was something of a late starter. In 1897, having graduated from the Royal College of Music, he travelled to Germany to study with Max Bruch, and as late as 1908 he was in France for much-needed lessons in orchestration from Ravel. But by 1914 he had produced a considerable body of music, including *Hugh the Drover* and two symphonies, and was beginning to find an audience. After World War I – during which he served in the military corps and the artillery – he threw himself into music, not just composing but also conducting the Bach Choir and Handel Society, and teaching at the Royal College, where nearly all his operas were give their first performances. Much of Vaughan Williams's immediate postwar music has an intensely rhapsodic and spiritual quality, exemplified by *The Shepherds of the Delectable Mountain* (1921–22), a short but fervent setting of a passage from Bunyan's *The Pilgrim's Progress* – a text that preoccupied him, on and off, for more than half his life.

ROYAL COLLEGE OF MUSIC

Ralph Vaughan Williams and friend

The 1920s was the period of his most intense operatic activity, with three operas being written at the same time: *Sir John in Love*, begun in 1924, was based on Shakespeare's Falstaff; the grimly realist *Riders to the Sea* was a setting of the play by J. M. Synge; while *The Poisoned Kiss* was a comic romance, close in style to an operetta. Since none of these works was commissioned, Vaughan Williams had difficulties in getting them professionally performed: the only Vaughan Williams opera to get a performance at Covent Garden during his lifetime was *The Pilgrim's Progress*, which was finally staged as part of the Festival of Britain in 1951. The production was execrable and the work's formal pageant-like quality was criticized for unshapeliness and lack of dramatic drive, a judgement from which it has never really recovered. Its failure was a grave disappointment to Vaughan Williams but it did not prevent him from starting work on a new opera, *Thomas the Rhymer*, which was incomplete at his death.

Hugh the Drover

Composed 1910–14; revised 1924, 1933, 1955.
First performed July 4, 1924.
Libretto by Harold Child.

Synopsis

Act I

At a small market town in the Cotswolds during the Napoleonic Wars, a fair is taking place. Mary is heard singing mournfully of her coming marriage to John the Butcher. He is the strongest and richest man in town but she does not love him. When Hugh the Drover arrives it is love at first sight and when he asks his "Sweet little Linnet" to join him on his travels, Mary agrees without hesitation. When John finds out he challenges Hugh to a fight.

John loses and retaliates by denouncing Hugh as a French spy. Mary is scornful of such silliness, but the patriotic crowd is not so sure and Hugh is dragged to the stocks by Mary's father, the Constable.

Act II.
Early the following morning, Mary steals the keys for the stocks and frees Hugh. John has brought flowers for Mary and when he discovers she is not at home he walks to the stocks where, to his amazement, Mary has locked herself in next to Hugh. Soldiers arrive and John urges them to try Hugh for treason, but the sergeant recognizes Hugh as an old comrade and press-gangs John, promising to make a soldier of him. The townspeople beg Hugh's forgiveness and ask him to stay, but he does not like town life, preferring the "windy wolds of life where man has to do or die"; Hugh and Mary depart.

The primary appeal of *Hugh the Drover* is its evocation of a rural way of life that was being eroded by the ever-encroaching towns and cities during the early years of this century. Vaughan Williams was deeply attuned to the rhythms and the pace of English country life, but unfortunately his librettist, Harold Child, took a rather more stereotypic view of things rustic and peopled the opera with patronizing characterizations straight out of a *Punch* cartoon. The composer struggled to amend the text but was never entirely happy with it (the character of John is particularly underdeveloped), and the opera's return to favour in the 1990s is entirely due to Vaughan Williams's wonderfully adroit assimilation of folk melodies into an operatic framework. *Hugh the Drover* abounds with simple, singable tunes, albeit wrapped in rich and full-bodied orchestration. It also reveals Vaughan Williams's admiration for Puccini: there is an Italianate lyricism to much of the music, and the slightly embarrassed eroticism of Hugh and Mary's love duet is unique in English opera. England's nearest equivalent to Smetana's *Bartered Bride*, this piece is a delightful exercise in nostalgia, with a freshness and spontaneity that make it difficult to resist.

Bottone, Evans, van Allan, Opie, Walker; New London Children's Chorus; Corydon Singers and Orchestra; Best.
(Hyperion CDA 66901-2; 2 CDs).

Hyperion have made an excellent job of Vaughan Williams's jolly tale. Matthew Best conducts a highly spirited account, encouraging excellent performances from the tenor Buonaventure Bottone as Hugh and the bass-baritone Richard van Allan as the Constable. Alan Opie is outstanding as John the Butcher, while Sarah Walker revels in her cameo as Aunt Jane, but the highlight of the casting is the Mary of Rebecca Evans. It was an inspired idea to engage an operetta voice for the role, and she works wonders in her love music with Bottone.

Riders to the Sea

Composed 1925–32.
First performed December 1, 1937.
Libretto by John Millington Synge.

Synopsis

On the Isle of Aran, Nora asks her sister Cathleen to help her identify some clothes taken from the body of a man found down by the sea. Having lost their father and four brothers, they are terrified that they belong to another brother, Michael. They decide to hide the clothes from their mother, Maurya, who is sleeping next door. However, Maurya is awake worrying because her son, Bartley, intends to take horses across the sea to Galway Fair. When Bartley leaves, his sisters are angry with their mother for not giving him her blessing and they send her after him. In her absence they fetch down the bundle of clothes and discover that they are indeed Michael's. They compose themselves for their mother's return and once again hide the bundle. Maurya tells them that she saw Michael riding behind Bartley and when they tell her of Michael's death, she realizes that her vision was an omen. Sure enough Bartley's body is carried in; despite her loss, Maurya expresses relief that the sea can cause her no more pain.

The musical style of *Riders to the Sea* owes little to Vaughan Williams's earlier operas, for there is only the vaguest suggestion of folk melody here – instead the composer allows himself to be guided by the language of Synge's one-act play of the same name, which he sets almost word-for-word. The symphonic score evokes a consistently bleak picture of the life of the Aran islanders, and the haunting character of Maurya, who dominates the opera, is memorably portrayed through music of almost liturgical simplicity. Her concluding dirge, "No man at all can be living", is placed against the wailing of the women's voices as Bartley's body is carried into the house, a moving episode that is sometimes compared to the great lament from Purcell's *Dido and Aeneas*. The melancholic treatment of all four female voices – Bartley's baritone is the only male – creates a poignancy that's absent from the earlier work, but it is the general evocation of ghostly atmosphere and of nature, with the wind and the sea a permanent presence, that makes *Riders* so compelling. Musically this is the composer's most effective opera, but its awkward length (forty minutes) makes it a troublesome work to stage.

Burrowes, Price, Watts, Luxon; Ambrosian Singers; London Orchestra Nova; Davies.
(EMI CDM7 64730-2; 1 CD).

Made in 1970, this EMI recording captures five of Britain's finest postwar singers at their very best. Norma Burrowes and Margaret Price are in ringing form as Nora and Cathleen, while Benjamin Luxon throbs manfully as Bartley. Best of all is Helen Watts's Maurya, an incredibly intense reading, with her lament providing a chilling climax. The one weakness is the conducting of Meredith Davies, who fails to capitalize on the score's elemental drama – the sense of the sea's unremitting energy never really materializes. Ultimately this recording is entirely carried by its brilliant singing, but a more comprehensively powerful performance would be a welcome addition to the catalogue.

PAUL DUKAS

b. PARIS, OCTOBER 1, 1865; d. PARIS, MAY 17, 1935.

Although now known chiefly for his orchestral fantasy *L'apprenti sorcier* (The Sorcerer's Apprentice), thanks to its use in Disney's *Fantasia*, Paul Dukas was a highly respected contemporary of Debussy and Ravel, albeit a conservative one who never achieved the same degree of success or notoriety. Like Ravel, he came to regret having devoted so much time to refining works that had been perfect in the first place, and like Debussy his sole significant opera was an adaptation of a Symbolist play by Maurice Maeterlinck.

He was born to an exceptionally musical mother and showed acute musical sensibilities at an early age – he later claimed to have breast-fed "in 9/8 time". He began composing at the age of sixteen, an overture based on *King Lear* being his first major piece; the following year he was befriended by Debussy and became attached to the French Wagnerian movement. After studying at the Paris Conservatoire, where he came within a single point of winning the 1888 Prix de Rome, he scored his first real success with a decidedly Wagnerian orchestral setting of Corneille's *Polyeuchte*. By the time he began his first opera, *Horn et Rimenhild*, he was, by his own admission, utterly in thrall to "visions of Bayreuth".

However, *Horn et Rimenhild*, for which he had written his own libretto, got no further than the first act, and not until 1899 did he turn again to opera, with *L'arbre de science*, a tale based on Hindu legend. This too was left incomplete when, to Dukas' surprise, Maeterlinck gave him permission to set *Ariane et Barbe-bleue*. The first performance was given in 1907, at the Opéra-Comique. Thereafter, he composed comparatively little and devoted most of his time to teaching, notably at the Conservatoire, where he taught composition between 1910 and 1913, and from 1928 until his death – Albéniz and Messiaen were among his pupils.

Ariane et Barbe-bleue

Ariadne and Bluebeard

Composed 1899–1906.
First performed May 10, 1907.
Libretto by Maurice Maeterlinck.

Synopsis

Act I

Ariadne (Ariane), the new wife of Bluebeard (Barbe-bleue) arrives at the castle accompanied by her nurse. She is alarmed by the local peasants, who rail against her husband. She enters the castle carrying seven keys, but she discards the first six (which are picked up by the nurse), holding onto the seventh, the one key she has been told not to use under any circumstance. The Nurse, however, opens each of the first six doors, revealing piles of precious stones. Ariadne eventually opens the final door, from which emerges the wailing song of Bluebeard's first five wives. At this, Bluebeard enters, and begs her not to pass through the seventh doorway. Suddenly, the crowd bursts through the castle gates and rushes into the hallway; Ariadne swears that Bluebeard has not harmed her.

Act II

Ariadne cannot suppress her curiosity and descends the steps leading from the seventh door. At the bottom, she finds her predecessors. They are reluctant to defy Bluebeard, but Ariadne reassures them and leads them up the stairs and into the light.

Act III

The wives are dressing themselves in fine clothes and jewellery when Bluebeard returns to the castle. Offstage, he is attacked by the peasants, who bring him in bound with ropes. Thinking that his wives will see to his execution, they leave; but the women start tending to his injuries and begin to flirt. Ariadne releases Bluebeard and, after inviting each of the women to join her, she leaves alone with the Nurse.

When Maeterlinck wrote his libretto for *Ariane et Barbe-bleue* he hoped it would end up being set by Edvard Grieg. That Dukas became the lucky recipient was perhaps not unrelated to the composer's willingness to allow Georgette Leblanc to create the role of Ariane, for Leblanc was none other than Maeterlinck's wife – whom Debussy had rejected in favour of Mary Garden as creator of the title soprano for *Pelléas et Mélisande*. As with Debussy's setting of *Pelléas*, Maeterlinck's text remained virtually unaltered, but unlike *Pelléas*, *Ariane* presents a busy, action-led narrative in which the description of off-stage events and the chorus-like interruptions of the townspeople provide a sharp counterpoint to the misty uncertainties of Bluebeard's castle. In short, Dukas' version of the Bluebeard myth is a more conventionally dramatic creation than Debussy's masterpiece and Bartók's psychodramatic setting of the same tale.

Furthermore, although Dukas' music makes allusions to Debussy's opera and to *La Mer* (the setting of moody whole-tone scales against bright pentatonics is particularly Debussy-like), the world of *Ariane* is quite unlike the half-lit vagueness of *Pelléas*, a score Dukas knew well from his friend's private piano-led performances of the score. With its heady chromaticism, the underlying tone is Wagnerian, but the score is unsettlingly disparate – there are numerous quotations from French folksong in the mix (famously "Claire de Lune") as well as a strong Russian flavour to the orchestrations, reminiscent of Rimsky-Korsakov. However, for all the orchestral references and quotations, *Ariane*'s vocal score is more personal, suggesting something of a cross between the ardent fluency of Grand Opéra and the intimate inflection of French song. Though Bluebeard gets first billing, female voices predominate: Ariadne is on stage for almost the entire two-hour duration, and even the Nurse and the four singing wives (the fifth is silent) all play a greater role than Bluebeard.

Ciesinksi, Bacquier, Panouva, Blanzat; French Radio Chorus and Orchestra; Jordan.
(Erato 2292 45663-2; 2 CDs).

On this 1991 production Katherine Ciesinksi and Gabriel Bacquier are suitably powerful in the title roles, although both are able to tone down their voices as required. Mariana Panouva is a little wobbly as the Nurse, but the chorus is excellent, and the close-miked recording brings tremendous definition to the multicoloured orchestrations. Armin Jordan provides spirited and sensitive direction.

MAURICE RAVEL

b. CIBOURE, FRANCE, MARCH 7, 1875; d. PARIS, DECEMBER 28, 1937.

Everything that Ravel wrote is still in the concert-hall and opera-house repertoire, but in a career spanning some four decades he wrote just a few hours' worth of music. He frequently devoted absurd amounts of energy to the refinement of compositions that were already finished, and he relied excessively on spontaneous inspiration, a precarious thing at the best of times, made more so by his extreme self-criticism. As he admitted: "I can be occupied for several years without writing a single note. . . one must spend time in eliminating all that could be regarded as superfluous in order to realize as completely as possible the definitive clarity so much desired." Later in his life he bitterly regretted having composed so little and, in particular, wished that he had spent more time writing for the stage. He completed just two operas, but both are superb examples of the distinctive style of a fastidious composer who combined the classical with the contemporary, expressing enthusiasms that ranged from Rameau to gypsy music, jazz and Spanish culture.

Ravel spent his childhood in Paris and enrolled at the Conservatoire in 1889. In the course of the next six years he studied with Fauré, among others, and developed a personal style that was characterized above all by unconventional harmonies. His progressiveness offended his conservative elders, and his four attempts to win

HULTON DEUTSCH

Maurice Ravel entertains – that's George Gershwin on the far right

the Prix de Rome all ended in failure. This setback did not inhibit Ravel's creativity, and the next ten years saw the composition of many of his best works, including the *Rhapsodie espagnole* for orchestra, his piano masterpiece *Gaspard de la nuit*, his opera *L'heure espagnole* and the ballet *Daphnis et Chloé*. With the outbreak of World War I Ravel became an ambulance driver – the army and air force having turned him down – but was discharged in 1916 after suffering a complete physical collapse. The death of his mother the following year seemed to push him into a slow, inexorable decline and despite being fêted as France's greatest living composer (Debussy died in 1918), his creativity was drying up. His last two decades were largely spent tampering with earlier compositions, but in 1920 he wrote the wonderful *La Valse* for orchestra and reluctantly agreed to collaborate with the novelist Colette in writing a second opera, *L'enfant et les sortilèges*; it took five years to complete, but the result was the most vivid and enchanting of all his works. In 1933 Ravel began to suffer from the effects of a degenerative brain disease and after four years of increasing agony he agreed to surgery, from which he never regained consciousness.

L'heure espagnole

Spanish Time

Composed 1907–09.
First performed May 19, 1911.
Libretto by Franc-Nohain (Maurice-Etienne Legrand).

Synopsis

Act I

The watchmaker Torquemada has to leave his wife, Concepción, alone with the mule driver Ramiro while he regulates the town clocks. Concepción is worried because she is expecting her lover, the poet Gonzalve. She manages to clear Ramiro out, telling him to take a clock to her bedroom just as Gonzalve arrives. When Ramiro comes back down, she tells him that she wants the clock back downstairs. She hides Gonzalve in another clock which she then commands Ramiro to carry upstairs. Don Inigo, a banker, arrives to court Concepción but decides to hide in the first clock. Concepción returns and demands the removal of the second clock, and during his absence Don Inigo attempts to seduce her. Oblivious, Ramiro again carries the first clock back upstairs. Gonzalve emerges from his clock but returns when he hears Ramiro approaching. Concepción once again demands the removal of the first clock and in Ramiro's absence she bemoans the lunacy of the situation. Ramiro returns with the first clock – in which Don Inigo finds himself stuck – and Concepción suggests that she and Ramiro go upstairs together. When Torquemada arrives home he finds two men locked in his clocks. They explain that they are interested in his work and, after reluctantly agreeing to purchase the timepieces, they are freed by Ramiro.

Ravel's warm but waspish personality found its ideal vehicle with Franc-Nohain's comedy, a piece described by one critic as a "mildly pornographic vaudeville". The central idea of the play (which Ravel set almost in its entirety) is that sexual appetite is comparable to the workings of a clock, and throughout Ravel's opera the incessant tickings and whirring of clocks and automata act as a counterpart to the to-ings and fro-ings of Concepción and her lovers. Ravel's great skill as a musical farceur is to draw attention to the machine-like nature of the characters while, at the same time, making their predicament seem genuinely human. As in so much of his work, he looked to the eighteenth century for precedent: "I've tried to . . . breathe new life into the Italian *opera buffa*, " he wrote. "I wanted to express irony through the music above all, through harmony, rhythm and orchestration."

Ravel's Spanish-tanged orchestration is brilliantly inventive throughout, with a marvellously eccentric percussion section that includes three metronomes, castanets, a whip and a mechanical cuckoo. He also employs some unusual instruments like the double bassoon and the Sarrusophone – a cross between a bassoon and a saxophone – for moments which require a rich and gravelly tone colour. Much of the humour is achieved by the music conveying a sense of things being slightly out of kilter: clocks tick at different speeds; harmonies and instrumental colour are unpredictable; Gonzalve and Concepción's longed-for embrace is forestalled by the repetition required by his *da capo* aria. But for Concepción's lament "Ah, la pitoyable aventure" and some of Gonzalve's affectedly lyrical musings, there are no traditional "numbers", with the singers declaiming rather than singing, in the "quasi-parlando of Italian buffo recitative". The wit of Franc-Rohain's double-entendres and Ravel's music are beautifully complemented by the delicate Spanish flavour, and all three qualities reach their sublime climax in the grand but mocking "Scene and Habañera" quintet finale that spells out the moral – "in the pursuit of love, eventually the muleteer will get his turn".

Danco, Derenne, Hamel, Rehfuss; Suisse Romand Orchestra; Ansermet.
(Decca 433 400-2DM 2; 2 CDs; with *L'enfant et les sortilèges*).

Ansermet was more commonly associated with the music of Stravinsky and Debussy, but he did much to popularize Ravel's operas. His was the first of two recordings of this opera made in 1953 (the other, conducted by Cluytens, has been withdrawn by EMI), and nearly half a century later it remains the most engaging. The imaginative Ansermet – who knew the composer – has a sure grasp of the score and he builds steadily towards the opera's climax, which zips along with amazing zest. The cast are not only the most authentic sounding, but they are the most emotionally convincing. Suzanne Danco's mezzo is ideal for Concepción, and André Vessières's Don Inigo is delightfully over the top.

Berbié, Sénéchal, Giraudeau, Bacquier; French Radio Chorus and Orchestra; Maazel.
(Deutsche Grammophon 423 718-2GH; 2 CDs; with *L'enfant et les sortilèges*).

Maazel's rival pairing of Ravel's operas is also excellent, but whereas Ansermet's set is marginally stronger in the earlier work, with Maazel it's the other way round. The primary asset of his 1965 *L'heure espagnole* is Jane Berbié's Concepción, one of the most enchanting examples of stylized French character singing on record. Michel Sénéchal is excellent as Gonzalve, and the ever resourceful Gabriel Bacquier is a riot as Ramiro. Maazel is as attentive to the work's colour as to the general sweep, and this remains one of the conductor's most enduring operatic achievements.

L'enfant et les sortilèges

The Bewitched Child

Composed 1920–25.
First performed March 21, 1925.
Libretto by Colette.

Synopsis

A bored little boy defies his mother's request to do his homework. After scolding him for his rudeness, his mother leaves him and he flies into a tantrum, attacking everything in the room including the walls, the fireplace, the furniture, his books and the family cat. To his astonishment, the victims of his temper – including the shepherds from the wallpaper – come to life and agree that they will put up with him no more. As he tries to sit down, the chairs recoil and begin to dance with one another, the fairy from his book of tales flies up at him and the cat begins to sing a duet with his mate. The scene moves from the house to the moonlit garden: the trees moan from the wounds the boy's pocket knife has inflicted on their bark and the dragonfly bemoans the fate of his mate, pinned to a board. The squirrel criticizes him for his cruelty to all the animals, and an animal ballet takes over the garden. Frightened and ashamed, the child calls for his mother but some of the unforgiving creatures begin to bear down on him. In the mêlée that ensues, a squirrel with a bleeding paw approaches the boy, who bandages the injury with a ribbon. Responding to this display of kindness the garden forgives the boy his wicked past and, together, they help call for his mother. A light goes on in the house and as his mother opens the door the boy calls to her affectionately.

Ravel's second opera is a brilliant evocation of childhood and one of the most enchanting operas ever written. Colette's libretto began life in 1917 as a scenario for a ballet to be written by Ravel, but by 1920 the ballet had become an opera. Typically for Ravel, work was slow but in November 1924 he completed the orchestration and sent the score to the conductor Victor de Sabata, who conducted the first performance at Monte Carlo. Considering the bizarre demands of the staging – singing crockery, funiture and animals, and a six-year-old boy sung by a mezzo-soprano – it was perhaps a miracle that Ravel's "lyric fantasy" was performed at all. As Dallapiccola suggested in an essay to coincide with the opera's Italian premiere in 1939, "the ideal medium would. . . be a great Walt Disney colour cartoon. Only in this form could *L'enfant et les sortilèges* find its definitive expression – free from compromise, open and clear."

Ravel stated that "The emphasis is on melody, allied to a subject which I chose to treat in the spirit of American musical comedy. . . The vocal line is the important thing." Indeed, *L'enfant* is overflowing with melody: each of the animated inanimate objects is provided with delicately scored vocal numbers, and the musical characterization is a virtuosic demonstration of technical mastery. For example, the dance of the two armchairs is a sprightly minuet, the duet between the teapot and the china cup (denoted in the score as "Wedgwood noir") is a charming foxtrot, the fire's aria is a "rondò a capriccio", and the scene where the mathematician leaps from the boy's schoolbook is a classical ostinato. In particular, the scene between the pot and the cup is one of the composer's wittiest achievements: a flood of high-pitched parallel intervals in the Chinese pentatonic scale accompanies the cup's pronunciation of random oriental phrases – *Mah-jong*, *Kong-kong*, *harakiri* etc. But perhaps the opera's most magical moments are the scenes in the garden in which, through highly original instrumental colour, Ravel creates an utterly convincing world that is both seductive and sinister.

Ogéas, Collard, Berbié, Gilma; French Radio Chorus and Orchestra; Maazel.
(Deutsche Grammophon 423 718-2GH; 2 CDs; with *L'heure espagnole*).

Maazel's *L'heure espagnole* is very good, but his *L'enfant et les sortilèges*, recorded in 1960, is even better – he moulds a performance that's both animated and ravishingly beautiful, displaying an amazing attention to detail without sounding affected. Jane Berbié is, once again, in excellent form, with the treble Françoise Ogéas excelling as the child. The sound quality is light and well focused and adds to the overall sense of innocence lost and found.

Wend, de Montmollin, Touraine, Danco; Geneva Motet Chorus; Suisse Romande Orchestra; Ansermet.
(Decca 433 400-2DM 2; 2 CDs; with *L'heure espagnole*).

This 1954 recording of *L'enfant* is a delight. Ansermet takes his time more than Maazel, refusing to rush through the myriad orchestral effects, toning down the wind and brass to keep the textures light and the balance clear. His cast are uniformly faultless, although Susanne Danco stands out as the mother. The sound is dated, but the performance is as fresh as when it was first released.

MANUEL DE FALLA

b. CADIZ, NOVEMBER 23, 1876; d. ALTA GRACIA DE CÓRDOBA, ARGENTINA, NOVEMBER 14, 1946.

Until the twentieth century the history of Spanish music-theatre is largely the history of *zarzuela*, a form of light opera with spoken dialogue. While some Spanish composers did adopt French and Italian operatic models – notably Martin y Soler in the eighteenth century – their successes were achieved for the most part away from their native land. The first real attempt to promote a national operatic style – as distinct from *zarzuela* – came in the late nineteenth century with Felipe Pedrell, who wrote operas in Spanish and exhorted his contemporaries to follow his example in replenishing their musical heritage. Pedrell's most famous pupil was Manuel de Falla, who had already written six *zarzuelas* when in 1904 he won a competition for a one-act opera with the exuberant *La vida breve* (Life Is Brief). Significantly the organizers of the competition, the Royal Academy of San Fernando in Madrid, reneged on their agreement to stage the work, which had to wait until 1913 for its premiere in Nice – sung in French.

Born in Cadiz into a prosperous family, Falla was encouraged to immerse himself in music from an early age, receiving piano lessons first from his mother and then from an array of eminent teachers. He was about seventeen when he decided to become a composer, around the time that he first heard the music of Grieg. Impressed by Grieg's efforts towards the establishment of a national musical identity, Falla conceived "an intense desire to create one day something similar with Spanish music". After a brief spell as a student at the Madrid Conservatory, Falla began to take lessons with Pedrell, who encouraged him to develop a style based on folk music, and showed him how to achieve this within a wider European framework.

In 1907 he bought a one-week return train ticket to Paris but ended up staying for seven years. He immersed himself in the city's musical life, forming friendships with Debussy, Ravel and Dukas (from whom he received informal tuition) and re-evaluating his style in the context of Impressionism. The first fruit of this process was *Noche sen los jardines de Espana* (Nights in the Gardens of Spain, 1911–15), a lush and atmospheric composition for piano and orchestra. At the outbreak of World War I Falla returned to Spain, where he wrote two hugely successful ballet scores, *El amor brujo* (Love the Magician) and *El sombrero de tres picos* (The Three-Cornered Hat), both of which derive their character from the *cante jondo*, the highly evocative song style of Andalusia. In 1919, on the death of his parents, he moved to Granada, where he gathered around him a circle of intellectuals, the most notable of whom was the writer and poet Lorca. Inspired by the Neoclassicism of his friend Stravinsky, he refined his style to a lapidary perfection which culminated in the small-scale theatre piece *El retablo de Maese Pedro* (Master Peter's Puppet Show, 1919–22). Never one to repeat himself, Falla then embarked on *Atlántida*, a huge patriotic and religious oratorio for soloists, chorus and orchestra. This was the most ambitious work he had ever undertaken and he was to devote the rest of his life to it, but it remained unfinished and was not performed until 1962, in a version completed by his pupil Ernesto Halffter. Falla's last years were lived out in self-imposed exile in Argentina, where the composer had moved to escape the fascist regime of General Franco.

La vida breve

Life Is Brief

Composed 1904.
First performed April 1, 1913.
Libretto by Carlos Fernández Shaw.

Synopsis

Act I

In the gypsy quarter of Granada, Salud, who lives with her grandmother, is waiting for Paco, a local playboy who has promised to marry her. Salud's grandmother tries to comfort her, assuring her that Paco will turn up, but Salud is despondent and sings a mournful folk song. Paco arrives and the lovers sing a duet, but Salvador, Salud's uncle, tells the grandmother that Paco is to marry another girl in the morning.

Act II

Singing and dancing take place in celebration of Paco's marriage to Carmela. Salud arrives to find Paco in the arms of Carmela. She is overcome and prays for death but her uncle tries to comfort her, cursing Paco and everyone around him. Salud insists that she must speak to Paco and after an interlude the scene moves to the courtyard of the house where Paco and Carmela are awaiting the family speeches. Paco is nervous, having heard Salud's voice. Salud enters the courtyard with Salvador and after denouncing Paco's treachery, she falls dead at his feet.

Written at great speed, to a text by one of the leading writers of *zarzuela* librettos, *La vida breve* is a Spanish verismo opera, originally in one act but later divided into two, in the same way that *I Pagliacci* is an unbroken work in two acts. With its sprinklings of "real life" effects – like the cries of street vendors at the beginning of Act I – it shows Falla's familiarity with Charpentier's *Louise* (see p.359), and in its intensity and directness it owes clear debts to Bizet's *Carmen* and the Italian verismo works then sweeping through Spanish theatres. Unlike his Italian contemporaries, however, de Falla turned to his ancestors' music for inspiration, and there is a powerful seam of folk song running throughout the opera, with many of the more potent melodies (such as the forge-men's song and Salud's mournful "The man that's born of a woman, is born on an evil day") paraphrasing Andalusian folk tunes. Similarly, there is a rustic immediacy to the linking music, such as the sinewy dance (known in transcription as "Spanish Dance No. 1") which takes place during the wedding celebrations, and the brief intermezzo/interludes in Act II.

Like *Cavalleria rusticana*, to which *La vida breve* is often compared, the velocity of the action and the simplicity of the characterization make for gripping music-theatre – nowhere more so than in the scenes that connect the wedding scene with Salud's discovery of Paco with Carmela. The hurtling transition from jollity through horror-struck disillusionment to unassuagable grief is absolutely riveting.

Berganza, Iñigo, Nafé, Carreras, Pons; Ambrosian Opera Chorus; London Symphony Orchestra; Navarro.
(Deutsche Grammophon 435 851-2GH; 1 CD).

All three recordings of *La vida breve* are now available on CD, but the most successful was recorded in 1978 by Deutsche Grammophon with a starry cast that includes Teresa Berganza as Salud, José Carreras as Paco and Juan

Pons as Uncle Salvador. All three are in youthful voice – Carreras's ardent tenor is especially appealing – and while Berganza lacks the crystalline delicacy of de los Angeles she presents a more earthy account of the heroine. Garcia Navarro propels the story along and supports the voices well, and the sound is rich and well spaced.

El retablo de Maese Pedro

Master Peter's Puppet Show

Composed 1919–22.
First performed March 23, 1923.
Libretto by the composer, after Cervantes.

Synopsis

In the stable of an inn, the puppeteer Master Peter invites the guests (among whom are Don Quixote and Sancho Panza) to join him for a production of the story of "Melisendra's Deliverance". Each of the six episodes is narrated by Master Peter's boy.

Scene 1
At the court of the Emperor Charlemagne, Gayferos is seen playing chess with Roland. Charlemagne rebukes him for neglecting the plight of his wife, Melisendra (Charlemagne's daughter), who is held captive by the Moors at Saragossa. Gayferos calls for his armour.

Scene 2
Melisendra scans the horizon from the tower where she is held. She is approached by a Moor, who kisses her. Marsilius, the Moorish King, orders her assailant to be punished.

Scene 3
The man is beaten 200 times, and when the boy informs the audience that he was tried without legal representation Don Quixote interrupts, telling him to get on with the story.

Scene 4
Gayferos crosses the Pyrenees on horseback, blowing on his hunting horn.

Scene 5
Melisendra, who does not at first recognize her husband, leaps from the tower into his arms.

Scene 6
The Moors chase the husband and wife; when the boy wishes them every happiness, he is rebuked by Master Peter for deviating from the text. When he then suggests that bells rang to sound the alarm Don Quixote complains that "among Moors is no ringing of bells, but beating of drums and squealing hautboys". Master Peter claims artistic licence but when the boy describes how the Moors are about to overtake the heroes, Don Quixote can stand no more and, mounting the stage, he cuts the puppet Moors into pieces, destroying both the set and Master Peter's livelihood.

El retablo de Maese Pedro was commissioned by the society hostess and patron of the arts Princess Edmond de Polignac as a chamber opera to be performed privately at her house. When living in Granada Falla had arranged some music for puppet shows devised by his friend Lorca, and he now suggested a puppet opera to the Princess, proposing as its subject a chapter from Cervantes' *Don Quixote*. The half-hour work was written to be performed by two sets of puppets: large ones for the puppeteers and their audience, small ones for the puppets themselves. The first "staged" performance took place in the drawing room of the Princess's Paris home with the tenor Thomas Salignac singing the title role and Wanda Landowska at the harpsichord.

At this stage of his career, Falla had pared down his style considerably, and *El retablo* has the same kind of economy and directness as Stravinsky's contemporary *The Soldier's Tale* – a work which he knew well. The music also reflects careful study of the medieval and Renaissance music of Spain, particularly in the vocalizing of Master Peter's boy, which Falla wanted to be "nasal and rather forced – the voice of a boy shouting in the street", and which he derived by combining Andalusian street cries with plainsong. Falla's fastidious orchestral technique is used to brilliant effect – each scene has an orchestral character of its own, despite the relatively spartan tonal palette. While *El retablo* might be somewhat disconcerting after the lushness of *La vida breve*, there are few more enchanting works of small-scale music-theatre.

Smith, Oliver, Knapp; London Sinfonietta; Rattle.
(Decca 433 908-2DM2; 2 CDs).

There are several successful recordings of *Master Peter's Puppet Show*, but this one is the most appealing, thanks partly to the accompanying works – all by Falla, including the ballet *El Amor Brujo*, excerpts from *La vida breve* and the *Harpsichord Concerto*, all conducted by different people. Under Simon Rattle's control Falla's puppet-opera trips along with infectious grace and wit, and it would be difficult to find a more natural performance of this jumpy work. All three singers give excellent, idiomatic performances and the sound is fresh and sensitively balanced.

VIRGIL THOMSON

b. KANSAS CITY, NOVEMBER 25, 1896; d. NEW YORK, SEPTEMBER 30, 1989.

Virgil Thomson is a dominant but paradoxical figure in twentieth-century American music. In *Four Saints in Three Acts* (1933) he produced what is arguably the first really significant American opera, but it's a work that eschews conventional narrative and is very rarely staged. As a young man in Paris he aligned himself with the artistic avant-garde but, under the influence of Erik Satie, pared down his musical language into something simple and direct that drew heavily on the popular and religious music of Protestant America.

He came from a Southern Baptist background, and his childhood was rich with music: while still a boy he gave concerts, played the organ in the Episcopalian and Baptist churches of his home town, and provided the accompaniment to silent movies. After narrowly missing action in World War I, Thomson entered Harvard to study music and, against the grain, became a committed Francophile, immersing himself in a study of modern French music. As a member of the Harvard Glee Club he travelled to France and decided to settle in Paris, where he became the first of Nadia Boulanger's American students (Philip Glass was a rather late one) and met Cocteau, Les Six and his hero Satie. He returned to America and graduated in 1923, but France tempted him back in 1925 and he was to remain there, on and off, until 1940.

In 1926 Thomson met the experimental writer Gertrude Stein, whose *Tender Buttons* he had read while at Harvard. They became instant friends ("Gertrude and I got on like a couple of Harvard boys") and Thomson suggested that they collaborate on an opera. After rejecting Stein's suggestion of George Washington as a subject the pair settled upon the vague idea of a group of Spanish saints in a Spanish rural setting. Stein completed her libretto in June 1927 and Thomson completed the short score just a year later – although he did not get round to orchestrating it until 1933. The first performance, presented by the Friends and Enemies of Modern Music, took place at the Wadsworth Athenaeum in Hartford (concurrently with the first Picasso retrospective in America) with an all-black cast that Thomson had auditioned in Harlem. It was produced by John Houseman and choreographed by Frederick Ashton, and the designer Florence Stettheimer daringly employed the new industrial material of cellophane for the sets. With such impeccable avant-gardiste credentials the show became a hot ticket and transferred to Broadway, where it ran for sixty performances and made Thomson and Stein highly fashionable – albeit briefly.

Returning once more to Paris, Thomson spent the next seven years perfecting the craft of composition and briefly turning his back on the folksy elements that had been such a major part of his music-making hitherto. These were soon to re-surface in a series of scores which included the music for the documentary film *The Plow that Broke the Plains* (1936) and for the ballet *Filling Station* (1937). When World War II broke out Thomson returned to America and in October 1940 he was appointed music critic of the *New York Herald Tribune*. Thomson's literary style mirrored his musical one, with consistently sharp appraisals expressed in down-to-earth and unpretentious prose.

He continued to compose and in 1946, just months before her death, Stein completed another libretto for Thomson, this time with a marginally clearer "plot". *The Mother of Us All* was loosely based on events in the life of the pioneering American feminist Susan B. Anthony; like *Four Saints*, the score was a compendium of musical Americana, but for many critics it was a more dramatically effective – if less radical – marriage of music to words. Thomson's final opera, *Lord Byron*, was commissioned in 1960 by the Koussevitzky Foundation. With his librettist Jack Larson, Thomson worked on it for seven years but the intended production at the Metropolitan Opera never materialized and the work only received its premiere at the New York Lincoln Center in 1972. It is by far the most conventional of

Thomson's three operas, much less detached from its material and with a surprisingly overt emotionalism.

In all three operas Thomson's language is tonal and melodic. Though he regarded himself as a modernist he readily acknowledged the traditional basis of his work: "there is no law against the common chord. It usually creates a scandal when music is supposed to be bumpy. The press is beginning to discover that I am a conservative composer because my music is quite often grammatical." The simplicity of his musical idiom has divided critics – for some it constitutes a refreshingly American alternative to the grandiosity of the operatic tradition, while others have found it irritatingly faux-naif. It is true that he lacks the quirky originality of his major inspiration Satie, but in *Four Saints* his plundering of the American vernacular and his brilliant musical accommodation of Stein's incantatory prose style creates a refreshingly exuberant and unusually theatrical experience. To hear *Four Saints* is to realize just how much a debt future American opera composers – especially so-called minimalists like Adams and Glass – owe to its un-self-conscious eclecticism and its hypnotic use of rhythmic repetition.

Four Saints in Three Acts

Composed 1927–28.
First performed May 20, 1933.
Libretto by Gertrude Stein.

Synopsis

Prologue

Chorus and saints announce "A narrative of prepare for saints". Two independent commentators – the compère and the commère – discourse inconsequentially on saints and numbers.

Act I

The act – set in Avila – is made up of seven tableaux. Saint Teresa II paints eggs "half in and half out of doors". She is photographed by St Settlement. Both Terasas ask "can women have wishes?". St Ignatius presents flowers to Teresa II. Ignatius and Teresa admire a model of a heavenly mansion. Teresa II is revealed in ecstasy. Teresa II holds an imaginary baby.

Act II

The countryside near Barcelona. The compère and commère observe the action from a distance. They are joined by Teresa and Ignatius. There follows A Dance of Angels and a party game, after which everyone – except the compére and commére – leaves. They enact a love scene – watched with pleasure by the two Teresas. A telescope is brought on through which the two Teresas see a vision of a heavenly mansion.

Act III

A monastery garden on the sea coast. The male saints are fixing a fishing net. Saint Ignatius, the two Teresas and Saint Settlement begin discussing the monastic life. Ignatius describes a vision of Holy Ghost ("Pigeons on the grass alas"). A heavenly chorus is followed by the voice of Saint Chavez lecturing the men. There follows a Spanish dance and a prediction of the Last Judgement by Saint Ignatius. In a prologue to act four the compère and commère discuss whether there should be another act.

Act IV

The curtain rises on the saints assembled in Heaven. The commère asks "Who makes who makes it do?", and the chorus reply "St Teresa and St Teresa too". The compère proclaims "Last Act", and the entire cast answers "Which is a fact".

The appeal of Stein's writing for Thomson is not hard to understand: her work was linguistically clear but semantically elusive and shared with the music of Satie a matter-of-factness and lack of rhetoric that, occasionally, teeters on the banal. The freedom of thought that her language suggests has been compared to the automatic writing of the Surrealists, but its fragmentary and elliptical vision ("to tell what could be told if one did not tell anything") more closely resembles the work of the Cubist painters – which Stein collected. It is also intensely musical in the way words are often chosen to emphasize sound more than sense, and in the way repetition and the slight varying of phrases are used to create complex aural patterns.

Three years after the opera was staged, Stein explained her choice of subject matter: "A saint a real saint never does anything, a martyr does something but a really good saint does nothing, and so I wanted to have four saints who did nothing and I wrote *Four Saints in Three Acts* and they did nothing and that was everything." The text that she sent Thomson was so amorphous that he asked his friend Maurice Grosser to impose some kind of structured scenario around it. Even so it would be wrong, as Grosser pointed out, to suggest that Stein's words mean nothing at all. On one level her text functions as a meditation on being as opposed to doing (since a saint "does nothing"). Stein's saints populate the landscape of the opera as if in a joyous state of grace, unconcerned as to the unfolding of time: it is only the compère and commère (Thomson's suggested additions) who – in their oblique commentary and questioning – emanate any sense of unrest. Though she was not religious, it is very clear that Stein is mirroring the repetitive and insistent chanting found in both ritual and private prayer to create a similar sense of reassurance and common purpose.

Thomson cut about a third of Stein's text but, even so, rarely can a librettist have found so enthusiastic and empathetic a setter of their words. His compositional method was designed to capture the spirit of immediacy in which the libretto had been conceived, and he would place the text on the piano and improvise over and over until, repeating himself, he knew he had the kernel of the work under his belt. It was Thomson's own idea to divide the role of Saint Teresa between two sopranos in order that she could sing duets with herself. He also felt that "with meanings already abstracted, or absent, or so multiplied that choice among them was impossible, there was no temptation towards tonal illustration". Instead he provided an extraordinarily eclectic but consistently lively score, in which parlando rhythms and the earnest harmony of Anglican chant are placed next to the oom-pah-pah of a brass band.

In the sheer immediacy and accessibility of its musical language, *Four Saints* often seems far closer to a musical than to an opera, and, indeed, many of the Act I choruses would not have sounded out of place on Broadway. But the musical content – for all its borrowings – is not pastiche and the matching of music to words is often inspired. The phrase "He asked for a distant magpie" sung to a simple hymn tune is moving partly because of its incongruity but also precisely because it is so mysterious and inexplicable. Certainly there are moments when the opera flags, when the circularity of the proceedings seems merely nonsensical, and many have found its whimsicality infuriating, but when taken on its own terms it can be an uplifting experience which, in the words of John Cage, can take us into "the world in which the matter-of-fact and the irrational are one, where mirth and metaphysics marry to beget comedy".

Allen, Matthews, Thompson, Dale, Quivar; Chorus and Orchestra of Our Time; Thome.
(Nonesuch 79035-2; 2 CDs).

This recording was made in 1983 in the US and is currently only available there. The all-American cast are more than adequate if not outstanding, and there are times when one feels that the singers might have responded more feelingly to the nuances of the words and their associative power. But there is no doubting the enthusiasm for the project, and conductor Joel Thome maintains the fresh-faced vigour of the work throughout.

GEORGE GERSHWIN

b. NEW YORK, SEPTEMBER 26, 1898; d. HOLLYWOOD, JULY 11, 1937.

Like many other songwriters who held sway over American popular music in the 1920s and 1930s, George Gershwin was a New Yorker of European-Jewish extraction. During his boyhood his family was constantly on the move from one Manhattan tenement to another, and his parents were too busy trying to support their children to have much time for cultural pursuits. The young George, however, had a homegrown artistic partner in the shape of his older brother Ira, who in later years was to write the lyrics to most of his classic songs. The purchase of a piano by the Gershwins in 1910 was to change George's life: originally intended for Ira, it was soon taken over by George, and by the age of sixteen he had dropped out of business school and was working on Tin Pan Alley as a plugger of other people's songs. In 1919 he had his first hit with *Swanee*, taken from his comedy *La La Lucille*. It was the start of a long roll-call of popular music highpoints, including *Fascinatin' Rhythm*, *Someone to watch over Me*, and *Lady Be Good*.

But despite his growing success as a popular composer, Gershwin was not satisfied. Fascinated since childhood by classical music, he started to entertain the idea of writing extended instrumental works that would use American musical forms – like ragtime, blues and jazz – to depict the vibrant everyday life of America. The catalyst for this new departure was provided by the band leader Paul Whiteman, who commissioned Gershwin to write a piece for a concert advertised as "An Experiment in Modern Music". In under a month Gershwin wrote his *Rhapsody in Blue*, performing the piano part himself at the premiere in 1924. Attended by the likes of Toscanini, Stravinsky and Rachmaninov, the concert was a sensation and it made Gershwin famous overnight.

Gershwin's first venture into opera occurred quite early in his career when he wrote a twenty-minute jazz opera called *Blue Monday*, for the revue *George White's Scandals* in 1922. The first-night audience disliked the tragic ending and it was dropped for the remainder of the run, but Gershwin's triumphant series of musicals continued throughout the 1920s. Largely self-taught as a composer, Gershwin undertook a sustained period of study with Joseph Schillinger from 1932 to 1936, and the techniques he acquired – notably how to develop thematic material – bore fruit in what has proved his most durable stage work, the opera *Porgy and Bess*. Gershwin had first read DuBose Heyward's novel *Porgy* in 1926 and was keen to set the story to music but had to wait seven years before he and Heyward reached a "mutually beneficial" agreement. Both men were emphatic that the story be treated operatically, and Gershwin relied heavily on his studies with Schillinger to give the drama a far greater weightiness than his Broadway work. *Porgy and Bess* opened at New York's Alvin Theater in October 1935 with the classically trained Todd Duncan and Anne Brown in the title roles. It ran for 124 performances – an amazingly long run for an opera – but the critical reaction was lukewarm and, at best, condescending. Today *Porgy* is regarded as the greatest of all American operas and Gershwin's premature death from a brain tumour two years after its completion remains one of the great tragedies of modern music. Among those who felt the loss most keenly was Arnold Schoenberg, who said of Gershwin: "Music was what made him feel, and music was the feeling he expressed. Directness of this kind is given only to great men, and there is no doubt that he was a great composer."

Porgy and Bess

Composed 1934–35.
First performed October 10, 1935.
Libretto by DuBose Heyward, with additional lyrics by Ira Gershwin.

Synopsis

Act I

The action is set in Catfish Row, a poverty-stricken black tenement in Charleston, South Carolina. His

Saturday night and a card game is in progress. Jake, a fisherman, sings to his wife Clara and their baby. The residents welcome the crippled Porgy, just as the brutish stevedore Crown arrives with his woman Bess. Crown joins in the game of cards but an argument breaks out and Crown kills one of the players, then flees. Porgy takes Bess in. The residents console the dead man's widow.

Act II

Weeks later, Jake leads the fishermen in a song as they work on their nets. Meanwhile Porgy muses on how Bess has changed his life. Sportin' Life, a smooth-talking drug-dealer, tries to peddle his "happy dust" and fake lawyer Frazier offers to free Bess from Crown. Bess is invited to a picnic on an island but wants to stay with Porgy, who tells her to go and enjoy herself. Crown confronts Bess at the picnic and begs her to return to him: she finally gives way. Some time later Jake and the fishermen leave for a trip. Bess can be heard calling out – delirious since being found on the island. When she recovers, Bess tells Porgy that she wants to stay with him and he tells her that she has nothing to fear. A storm rises and many take refuge – including Crown – but when Jake's boat is found empty, Clara runs out to look for him. Crown follows her into the hurricane.

Act III

After the storm, Bess is about to be reclaimed by Crown when Porgy kills him. The police receive no assistance from the residents of Catfish Row but they take Porgy to identify the body. While he is away, Bess is tricked and then drugged by Sportin' Life into leaving with him for New York. When Porgy returns from jail he is told that Bess has left with Sportin' Life; he resolves to find her and, as the curtain falls, he prepares to make the journey north.

Gershwin's strong sense of identification with the poor and the oppressed – already evident in *Blue Monday*, which was set in Harlem – received its fullest expression in his collaboration with DuBose Heyward, a native of Charleston. Though a white man, Heyward had a close knowledge of the lives of the downtrodden black people of South Carolina, and his novel was widely praised for its sympathetic and realistic depiction of black life. Even so, Heyward had no hesitation in suggesting Al Jolson for the role of Porgy nor in considering handing over the music rights to Jerome Kern after promising them to Gershwin. Gershwin rejected the idea of Jolson – ". . . the sort of thing I had in mind for Porgy is a much more serious thing than Jolson could ever do" – and the threat of losing the project to Kern seems to have galvanized him into action. He wrote *Porgy and Bess* in eleven months, visiting Charleston in June 1934 to ensure the accuracy of a project that was a labour of love. He stipulated that his "American folk opera" should always be performed by a black cast, but his sincerity was not enough to deflect some black critics. No less a figure than Duke Ellington dismissed "Gershwin's lampblack Negroisms", commenting that "the music does not hitch with the mood and spirit of the story".

Gershwin conceived *Porgy and Bess* as a fusion of classical and popular musical traditions, a reconciliation of the structural demands of through-composed opera with the populist forms of the musical. But although his achievement of this goal is now acknowledged on both sides of the musical divide (due in part to landmark productions at the Met and Glyndebourne in the 1980s), *Porgy and Bess* didn't initially achieve the respect it's due. While jazz fans were dismissive of his use of African-American music, opera critics sniffily complained that Gershwin's "opera" was basically just a string of hit tunes. Gershwin responded to the latter charge by pointing out that "nearly all of Verdi's operas contain what are known as 'song hits'", and he might have gone on to point out that very few twentieth-century composers of any type have written songs as tuneful and powerful as "Summertime", "I Got Plenty o' Nuttin'", "Bess, You Is My Woman" and "It Ain't Necessarily So". He might have been pitching it a bit high when he said his masterwork would "resemble a combination of the drama and romance of *Carmen* and the beauty of *Meistersinger*", but *Porgy and Bess* is emphatically a true opera: its music is continuous, its score is rigorously structured and threaded with leitmotifs, and the highly developed melodies call for a classical singing technique – especially Porgy, whose role is frequently cut to lessen the strain. Achieving a feeling of authenticity not through cheap stunts but primarily through "blue note" harmony and syncopated rhythm (the only orchestral effects are a banjo and African drums), Gershwin created what remains opera's only successful treatment of African-American experience.

RECORDINGS OVERVIEW

The earliest recording of *Porgy and Bess* was made by CBS in 1951, but is currently out of the catalogue. It contained several of the original Broadway cast but replaced most of the principal roles; its main asset is the fine Porgy of Lawrence Winters. The original

Sportin' Life, John. W. Bubbles, appears on an RCA highlights disc from 1963, which also has Leontyne Price in fine voice as Bess. The two recordings below are the best of the complete sets, though the Lorin Maazel's lush interpretation for Decca features Barbara Hendricks as an outstanding Clara and Willard White as an extremely affecting Porgy.

White, Haymon, Blackwell, Clarey, Evans; Glyndebourne Festival Chorus; London Philharmonic Orchestra; Rattle.
(EMI CDS7 49568-2; 3 CDs).

This 1988 recording follows a much-praised production at Glyndebourne and boasts an exceptionally strong cast. Once again Willard White takes on the role of Porgy and if anything is even more authoritative than on the Decca recording. The Bess of Cynthia Haymon is sympathetic, if a little thin toned, but Harolyn Blackwell's Clara is wonderfully alluring. The hard-to-cast role of Sportin' Life gets an energetic performance from Damon Evans. The LPO play beautifully, although there are times when Rattle's tendency to overemphasize can be a little exhausting.

Albert, Dale, Lane, Shakesnider, Marshall; Houston Grand Opera Chorus and Orchestra; DeMain.
(RCA RD 82109; 3 CDs).

RCA's recording of Houston Grand Opera, like the EMI recording, has the advantage of being based on a successful stage production. This is not such a hard-driven performance, and its energy and sparkle make it sound rather closer to a Broadway musical. Its greatest asset is the wonderful sense of ensemble – Catfish Row has never more convincingly come across as a complex community. There are also some very good performances, particularly in the female roles, with an outstanding and deeply moving Bess from Clamma Dale and a fine Clara from Betty Lane. Conductor John DeMain holds it all together with an idiomatic flair, allowing his singers just the right amount of space in which to develop well-rounded characterizations.

8

OPERA SINCE WORLD WAR II

OPERA SINCE WORLD WAR II

After World War II a new generation of composers emerged whose experiences of the war would have a direct bearing on the kind of operas they would write. The nightmare of totalitarian oppression haunted many composers, and is perhaps most nakedly expressed in *Il prigioniero* by **Luigi Dallapiccola**, an Italian who combined the serialism of Schoenberg with his own lyrical intensity. At exactly the same time – in the immediate postwar years – the Austrian **Gottfried von Einem** was writing *Dantons Tod*, a more epic treatment of political tyranny in which the volatility of popular feeling is conveyed by brilliant writing for the chorus. Similarly dynamic choral writing is used in the contemporary *Peter Grimes* of **Benjamin Britten** to express the claustrophobia of group conformity, which in this case is pitted against a troubled and troubling outsider. One of the major figures of postwar opera, and the first British opera composer to establish an international reputation, Britten returned repeatedly to the themes of the abuse of power and the corruption of innocence in works such as *Billy Budd* and *The Turn of the Screw*, achieving a degree of success that was to act as a catalyst for several British composers. The most prominent of these British contemporaries is **Michael Tippett**, whose *The Midsummer Marriage* is almost unique among operas written in the aftermath of the war for the way it presents a life-affirming vision of rebirth and renewal. His next opera, however, was markedly less optimistic: *King Priam* (1961) is a powerful indictment of war, but one in which the contradictions of human behaviour are never simplified.

All of the above composers were born in the first two decades of the century and, though their styles are diverse, they are similar in that each of them pursued a largely undoctrinaire and individualistic approach to composition. The next generation to make a significant impact on opera were committed to a profoundly radical reappraisal of the whole genre – when they were interested in it at all. From the early 1950s the European avant-garde were primarily concerned with the structure and organization of pure sounds – a project antithetical to the traditionally expressive realm of opera. Pierre Boulez – the most rigorous and dogmatic of the postwar modernists – has never written an opera at all and once facetiously suggested that all opera houses should be blown up. The first truly experimental composer to tackle the theatre was **Luigi Nono**, whose *Intolleranza 1960* uses a whole range of sounds and devices, including taped electronic music, to tell the story of an immigrant worker and the hostility he faces. Although Nono does not completely reject narrative, much of his material is presented as a montage of fragmentary images and ideas, using a variety of different texts. This approach can also be found in *Die Soldaten* by **Bernd Alois Zimmermann**, an anti-military satire in which the music quotes from different historical styles while several layers of action occur simultaneously.

The music-theatre of **Luciano Berio** is less overtly political than that of Nono or Zimmermann and is, above all, preoccupied with the versatility of the human voice and with the symbiotic relationship between performer and audience – concerns encapsulated in his opera *Un re in ascolto* (A King Listens). The other seminal figure of the postwar avant-garde, **Karlheinz Stockhausen**, did not commit himself to theatre work until the late 1970s, when he embarked on *Licht* (Light), a projected series of seven operas designed to be performed on each evening of a week. Epic in scale, each episode is a mystical and didactic spectacular, with a strong ritual aspect replacing a clearly coherent narrative.

In Eastern Europe under communism, those composers who were not merely timeservers had few opportunities for writing opera. Since the early 1960s, however, the Polish **Krzysztof Penderecki** has forged an international career as an opera composer by combining an expressive and highly wrought musical language with dramatically extreme subject matter – as in his first opera, *Die Teufel von Loudon* (The Devils of Loudun). A more exploratory and inventive approach can be found in the work of the Hungarian **György Ligeti,** who emigrated to the west in 1956. His one opera, *Le grand macabre*, combines a helter-skelter of stylistic references within an anarchically satirical vision – as, indeed, does *Life with an Idiot*, a scabrous satire on the decline of the Soviet Union written in exile by Russia's major composer of the period, **Alfred Schnittke**.

Of all the composers of the Stockhausen/Boulez generation, **Hans Werner Henze** has maintained the greatest enthusiasm for opera, having written over fifteen of them. Musically he is receptive to a huge diversity of musical idioms, from jazz to Donizetti, but he has tended to assimilate these into his own style rather than present them as self-conscious quotation or pastiche in the way that Schnittke does. From the late 1960s Henze adopted a militantly leftist political stance, but all of his operas contain rich, sensuous music while sustaining an incisive theatricality. In Britain, a similarly eclectic approach has been evident in the work of **Peter Maxwell Davies**. Mixing a vocal style derived essentially from Schoenberg's with an array of aggressive parody, Davies fashioned a raw and confrontational music-theatre in which social and political evils are generally the focus of attention. His friend and contemporary **Harrison Birtwistle** developed a similar sound-world with his violent and strident *Punch and Judy*, before developing a more ritualistic, formal and richly orchestrated kind of theatre with rugged works like *The Mask of Orpheus* and *Gawain*.

In the USA, a lusher and traditional tonal approach has been the norm, due largely to the paucity of state subsidies and competition from the Broadway musical. The operas of **Gian Carlo Menotti**, **Samuel Barber**, **Leonard Bernstein** and **John Corigliano** have earned enthusiastic receptions on their home soil, but though Menotti's *Amahl and the Night Visitors* has become a Christmas favourite in many countries, their style hasn't really travelled well. This is far from the case with those American composers bracketed together as "Minimalists", whose music is accessibly tonal but has a driven and often hypnotic quality that allies it more with progressive popular music than with the classical tradition. The most successful of these, **Philip Glass**, made his theatre debut with *Einstein on the Beach*, a bizarre and patience-testing collaboration with Robert Wilson, a guru figure on the US progressive drama scene; later works have been less offbeat, and *Akhnaten* has established itself on the repertoire of more enterprising opera houses. Glass's compatriot **John Adams** has a more wide-ranging and "American" style (you can hear traces of Copland and Thompson in his work), and is virtually alone in turning to contemporary history for his subject matter, in operas such as *Nixon in China* and *The Death of Klinghoffer*.

In Britain, the time-suspending techniques of Minimalism have been put to quite different uses by **John Tavener**, whose *Mary of Egypt* is less a music-drama than a staged exercise in spiritual contemplation. In its uncompromising purity of expression and devout spirituality Tavener's work might be compared to **Olivier Messiaen**'s colossal opera on the life of Saint Francis of Assisi – apart from the works of **Francis Poulenc**, the only postwar French opera to have attained any sort of reputation outside France. The sheer diversity of modern opera is exemplified by the contrast between the work of **Judith Weir**, who studied with Tavener, and her contemporary **Mark-Anthony Turnage**. Whereas Weir has fashioned a sequence of witty and ironic parables such as *A Night at the Chinese Opera* and *Blond Eckbert*, Turnage's *Greek* – a transposition of the Oedipus story to London's East End – is as savage and visceral an opera as you're ever likely to hear. You might rather drift on Philip Glass's rafts of sound or wrestle with Stockhausen's complexities than submit yourself to a battering from Turnage, but whatever your preferences, there can be no doubting that the challenges of the postwar world have prompted some fascinating operatic work.

FRANCIS POULENC

b. PARIS, JANUARY 7, 1899; d. PARIS, JANUARY 30, 1963.

For years Francis Poulenc was pigeonholed as the playboy of French music, and superficially there is some justice to the charge. He was born into money and had a privileged social position. Through his piano teacher Ricardo Viñes he gained access to the fashionable Parisian artistic scene, and became a key member of a group of iconoclastic young composers called Les Six, who, spearheaded by the writer Jean Cocteau, rejected not only the inflated Romanticism of Wagner but also what they regarded as the imprecision of Debussy and Ravel. Of all the group, Poulenc seemed the most facile and clownish, the man with the permanent grin on his face. But he was also a serious craftsman, who had made a careful study of counterpoint and was the only member of Les Six to develop in new directions. By no stretch of the imagination could Poulenc be described as a modernist, yet he always had a keen interest in the international scene and in 1921 travelled to Vienna with Milhaud (another member of Les Six) in order to meet Schoenberg and his pupils.

Like many young French composers of the interwar years, Poulenc was immensely taken by the irony of Stravinsky's early Neoclassical works. His masterstroke was to take this irony and turn it into something beguilingly French. In this project, the influence of Cocteau was never far away, and the rather brittle, jewel-like works of these years showed Poulenc taking to heart Cocteau's principle that artists must aim for a coolly elegant modernity, braced with a classical sense of proportion. There was artifice aplenty in the *Aubade* for small orchestra and the ballet *Les Biches* (written for Diaghilev's Ballets Russes), but there was also much ingenuity in the way he achieved fresh sounds with conventional materials.

In the 1930s a series of disastrous love affairs (mostly with younger men) precipitated a return to the Catholic church, and a spate of powerful religious works followed, most notably the *Litanies à la vièrge noire* (1936). He also began his lifetime association with the baritone Pierre Bernac, who became the greatest interpreter of his songs and introduced him to the surrealist poet Paul Eluard, many of whose poems he later set. Eluard, whose surrealism was of a decidedly emotional and sensual strain, encouraged Poulenc to modify his rather detached Stravinskian style and embrace the spicier sound-world of Chabrier and Ravel.

Arguably Poulenc's greatest strength was as a lyrical melodist and a writer for the voice: few could match the exquisite delicacy of his word-setting, which displayed a feeling for every nuance of his native tongue. But, despite a childhood wish to be an opera singer, he turned to opera relatively late in his career. *Les mamelles de Tirésias*, composed during World War II, was a setting of Apollinaire's surrealist comedy and epitomized Poulenc at his most ebullient and lighthearted. It was followed, nine years later, by a work utterly different in tone and mood. *Les dialogues des Carmélites*, based on the true story of a group of nuns persecuted and executed during the French Revolution, confirmed Poulenc's transformation from young turk to arch conservative, but it was also one of the most direct and heartfelt of all his compositions. Whereas *Les dialogues des Carmélites* celebrates faith and the spiritual strength of a religious community, Poulenc's final opera, *La voix humaine*, chronicles the psychological disintegration of a desperate woman as she converses on the telephone with her apparently indifferent lover. It is Poulenc's rawest and most extreme work, and the one in which he reveals – with extraordinary honesty – the vulnerability and pain of his own emotional life.

Les mamelles de Tirésias

The Breasts of Tiresias

Composed 1944.
First performed June 3, 1947.
Libretto by the composer, after Apollinaire.

Synopsis

Act I

The Theatre Director appears before the curtain and announces the work's motto: "You must make babies now as you never have before". The curtain then rises on the main square of Zanzibar. Thérèse, who is fed up with being a woman, with her husband, and the fact that she can't be a soldier, decides to change sex. She opens her corset, releasing her breasts which she bursts as her face starts to sprout hair. Her husband assumes she has been murdered but his former wife explains that she is now Tirésias and they leave together with the husband dressed in her old clothes. After witnessing a shooting the Police Chief attempts to seduce the husband, who decides that if the women won't produce children, the men should.

Act II

The husband has produced 40,049 children in one day. A journalist wants to know how he does it and how he supports them. Another child is born who turns out to be a journalist. The Cartomancer (Tirésias in disguise) supplies them with ration cards. Arrested by the Police Chief, she strangles him, before revealing her identity to her husband. As the Police Chief recovers, the husband attempts to turn Tirésias back into Thérèse by supplying breasts in the form of balloons. She releases them into the sky and the opera ends with a repetition of the initial motto.

Apollinaire's absurd and witty play was written at the end of World War I, when the idea of repopulating the world and challenging the conventional roles of men and women was more than just a fanciful idea. His introduction to the play marks one of the first uses of the term "surrealism", and *Les mamelles* is a kind of operatic free association that combines the apposite with the bizarre, the serious with the ridiculous. Poulenc was attracted to it for precisely these reasons: ". . . if my music succeeds in producing laughter while still allowing some moments of tenderness and real lyricism, my aim will have been fully attained; thus I shall not have been false to Apollinaire's play in which the most violent buffoonery alternates with melancholy." Poulenc wrote it during World War II and at rehearsals for the first performance at the Opéra-Comique the work's message was reinforced when the first two sopranos entrusted with the leading role both had to withdraw because of pregnancy.

The score represents something of a tribute to Poulenc's forebears. It owes its immediate influence to Chabrier (see p.282), Poulenc's "true grandfather", who was one of the first to legitimize vulgarity in serious French music, but the fingerprints of numerous other composers are also strongly in evidence: Offenbach's operettas provide the basic formula, both Gounod and Bizet make guest melodic appearances, while the dominant harmonic presence is that of Stravinsky. This might make it sound like a derivative hodge-podge, but almost the opposite is true and Poulenc manages to knit the whole thing together by a lightness of touch and an unfailing feel for the truly comic. It's a work that succeeds best in the theatre but at just under an hour long it is difficult to programme, and performances outside of France are relatively rare.

Duval, Giraudeau, Rousseau; Paris Opéra-Comique Chorus and Orchestra; Cluytens.
(EMI CDS5 65565-2; 1 CD; with *Le bal masqué*).

Made in 1953, this recording is a unique document of the fresh and characterful voices of the Opéra-Comique in its heyday. As in all the following recommended recordings, this disc is dominated by the sparkling tone of Poulenc's favourite soprano, Denise Duval, who brings an effortless sense of style to the role of Thérèse. It's paired with *Le bal masqué*, a cantata for solo voice and chamber ensemble, written and premiered in 1932.

Les dialogues des Carmélites

Dialogues of the Carmelites

Composed 1953.
First performed January 26, 1957.
Libretto by the composer, after Bernanos.

Synopsis

Act I

At the height of the French Revolution, Blanche, a young and fearful aristocrat, announces to her family that she wishes to join the Carmelite convent at Compiègne. On arriving, she is cross-questioned by the Prioress before being accepted at the convent. Blanche is cleaning with Constance, a simple novice, who tells of her dream that she and Blanche will die together. The Prioress is slowly dying in great pain, attended by the devout and loyal Mother Marie, who is shocked by her blasphemy. Blanche witnesses the Prioress's death.

Act II

Blanche's nervousness is fuelled by the terrible events occurring outside. She is calmed by Mother Marie. Blanche's brother arrives and fails to persuade her to leave the convent. As Mother Marie warns the sisters against pride and the temptation of martyrdom, an angry mob arrives at the gates. Agitated by what is happening, Blanche drops a statue of Jesus.

Act III

The convent has been attacked and desecrated. Mother Marie proposes that the nuns secretly vote whether to take the vow of martyrdom or not. The sisters prepare for death. Blanche escapes disguised as a servant. When the nuns are publicly executed one by one, Blanche watches from the crowd before stepping up to the guillotine to join them.

The true story of the Carmelite order of Compiègne was first told by Mother Marie, the only one of their number to survive the Terror. The nuns were later canonized and in 1931 their story was turned into a novel. When, just after World War II, it was decided to film the book, the Catholic writer and polemicist George Bernanos was asked to write the screenplay, which he completed shortly before his death. It is this screenplay that forms the basis for Poulenc's opera, which was written at a time of great stress for the composer, whose lover was then dying.

Bernanos' text is the most simple and direct expression of his recurrent theme of the struggle against evil. The opera is dominated by female voices, which articulate a range of responses to the horror of the world and the imminence of death, from the serenity of Mother Marie to the terror of Blanche. For a non-Catholic audience, the celebration of self-sacrifice and the welcoming of death at the opera's conclusion can be hard to take, but there is never any doubt about the intensity and sincerity of the feelings expressed.

Poulenc's score once again reflects his eclecticism. The essential structure of the work, its balance between recitative and *arioso*, is Verdian, but the recitatives themselves owe much to Monteverdi in their sensitivity to the natural rhythms of speech. The vocal writing is highly lyrical, as ever, although some of the solo lines are cast in quasi-melodic declamation. Supporting these lines is a continuously changing but lucid orchestral palette that's often beautiful but generally very understated. The opera's most powerfully dramatic moment comes at the end, when the mob chorus is drowned out by the nun's voices. With the exception of this and the episode of the Prioress's death, the *Dialogues* is a tranquil opera, in which Poulenc dramatizes not the external incidents but rather the emotional and philosophical implications of those extreme situations. The opera stands as a testament to both his lyrical gifts and his solid religious faith.

Duval, Créspin, Berton, Scharley, Gorr; Paris Opéra Chorus and Orchestra; Dervaux.
(EMI CDS7 49331-2; 2 CDs).

This 1958 recording was made a year after the Paris premiere and features the original cast. There is much superb singing here, particularly the intense Blanche of Denise Duval, the sparky Constance of Liliane Berton and the wonderfully reassuring mezzo of Rita Gorr's Mother Marie. Dervaux's conducting brings out the richness of the score and stresses the work's contemplative aspects, without lapsing into dullness, but this set is valuable above all as one of the great recordings of postwar French singing.

Dubosc, Gorr, Fournier, Dupuy, Van Dam; Lyon Opéra Chorus and Orchestra; Nagano.
(Virgin VCD7 59227–2; 2 CDs).

Recorded in 1992, this is yet another splendid set from the Nagano/Lyon stable. Having learned the work for a staged production, everyone from the chorus to the orchestra brings a sense of unity of purpose to the proceedings. Nagano gets great colour and variety out of the potentially static score, shaping phrases and moulding tempi with real imagination. Catherine Dubosc is superb as Blanche, and Brigitte Fournier is uniquely likable as the flippant Constance. Veterans Rita Gorr (as the Prioress) and José Van Dam (as the Marquis) are in superb form, and everything – not least the swishing blade of the finale – has been captured in first-class sound.

La voix humaine

The Human Voice

Composed 1958.
First performed February 6, 1959.
Libretto by Jean Cocteau.

Synopsis

A woman (simply referred to as Elle) answers the phone and begins a conversation with her lover. During the conversation – which is interrupted by several crossed lines and wrong numbers – it becomes apparent that he no longer cares for her and her responses become increasingly desperate and self-pitying. Eventually she wraps the flex around her neck and goes to bed whispering words of love into the earpiece.

Cocteau's play, written in 1930 as a vehicle for the Comédie Française actress Berthe Bovy, is an extremely demanding monologue, requiring the performer to convey a great deal that is not actually stated in addition to what is, as she wheedles, cajoles and lies to her indifferent lover. Poulenc's operatic version of the play lasts just forty minutes but is no less gruelling. It was written specifically for the dramatic soprano Denise Duval, who for many years made the part almost exclusively her own. She described the role as "a killer because the phrasing – sometimes long, sometimes short, always in a low key, half singing, half parlando – is a *tour de force* of no small order. It lies better really for a darker voice . . . but that sort of instrument cannot quite produce the hysterical impression that is so essential." This wide range of expressive vocal styles and techniques is presented both unaccompanied and with a large orchestra, which Poulenc employs to bathe the vulnerable voice in a warm and sensual glow. In a great performance the work is almost unbearably painful and places the audience in the role of powerless voyeur – indeed Poulenc, who was separated from his lover at the time, called *La voix humaine* "a sort of musical confession".

Duval; Paris Opéra-Comique Orchestra; Prêtre.
(EMI CDM5 65156-2; 1 CD; with Cocteau's *Bel indifférent*).

This recording, by the role's creator, was made shortly after the first performance, and is the benchmark against which all subsequent recordings have to be measured (though rival recordings have been few and far between). Duval's light French voice articulates the words with such truthfulness it's as if she were making them up as she went along. The way she registers minute changes of feeling and mood creates an extraordinary intimacy. Prêtre supports her with subtlety and discretion. As a filler, EMI have included the 1953 recording of Jean Cocteau's monodrama *Bel indifférent*, with the ever-remarkable Edith Piaf in typically fervid form.

OLIVIER MESSIAEN

b. AVIGNON, FRANCE, DECEMBER 10, 1908; d. PARIS, APRIL 28, 1992.

The greatest twentieth-century French composer after Debussy, Messiaen was an intriguing mixture of the ascetic and hedonistic. He was a devout Roman Catholic who found inspiration in medieval chant and wrote a vast opera on the life of Saint Francis of Assisi, and yet his music is also an ecstatic celebration of earthly life, deriving much of its material from the natural world. When Messiaen went on a pilgrimage to the Holy Land in the last decade of his life, he spent the time between prayer transposing the songs of the local birds – "I doubt that one can find in any human music, however inspired, melodies and rhythms that have the sovereign freedom of bird song." The inventor of a thrillingly sensuous music which strives to create aural equivalents of glowing colour, Messiaen single-handedly forged a new musical vocabulary that was eagerly seized on by postwar composers such as his students Pierre Boulez and Karlheinz Stockhausen.

Born in Avignon, Messiaen was composing by the age of seven. He attended the Paris Conservatoire, where he studied the organ with Marcel Dupré and composition with Paul Dukas. His brilliant piano playing won all the available prizes there, while in private he began studying eastern musical scales and rhythms. His first major composition, *Preludes* (1929), owed much to Debussy but shimmered with the exotic sound of what he termed his "modes of limited transposition" – special scales which lent his music a strange harmonic richness. It was during this period that he was appointed organist at the church of La Trinité, where he was to play for more than five decades. As professor of music at the École Normale in Paris, he founded a group, La Jeune France, devoted to the propagation of a wholly French musical aesthetic.

During World War II he was interned by the Germans in a prisoner of war camp where he wrote an eight-part quartet, *Quator pour le fin du temps* (Quartet for the End of Time), which tried to "Bring the listener closer to eternity in space, to infinity." Throughout the 1950s he committed himself to notating the sounds of birds, roaming rural France with pen and paper in hand, transposing every song. The project bore fruit with the massive piano piece *Catalogue d'oiseaux* (1956–58), in which he utilized Greek and Indian rhythms to convey the calls of numerous different species.

Messiaen completed his one and only opera in 1983 when he was seventy-six years old and – as far as most commentators were aware – completely indifferent to the genre. *Saint François d'Assise* represented the culmination of Messiaen's life work and is entirely coloured by his deeply felt Catholic faith. There had always been a theatrical element to many of his works, in particular his vast symphonic narrative the *Turangalîla Symphony* (1948), but in the more simplified language of *Saint François* the emphasis is on a slow ritualistic unfolding of events through a series of tableaux, and there is considerably less dramatic drive to the opera than in, say, Bach's *St Matthew Passion*. The opera was commissioned by Rolf Lieberman, the Swiss Intendant of the Paris Opéra, and was given a lavishly staged premiere in 1975, conducted by Seiji Ozawa. Its length and the vast forces needed to perform it means that there have been no subsequent fully staged productions.

Saint François d'Assise

Saint Francis of Assisi

Composed 1975–83.
First performed November 28, 1983.
Libretto by the composer.

Synopsis

Act I

Francis and Brother Leo discuss the importance of suffering for their faith. Through prayer Francis confronts his revulsion to the ugliness in the world, in particular his fear of leprosy. He meets a leper and tries to teach him acceptance. An angel sings of God's love and Francis embraces the leper, who is cured.

Act II

The brothers are addressed by a visitor whom they treat dismissively until Brother Bernardo realizes that it is an angel come to visit Francis. When Francis meets the Angel he is overcome by celestial music and is found in a swoon by the brothers. Francis preaches to the birds on the hillside, commending their freedom and abandonment to the will of God.

Act III

Francis is nearing the end of his life and has taken to living in a cave devoid of all comforts. He prays for blessing and receives the stigmata. He bids farewell to the distraught brothers and dies. The stage is bathed in a blinding light.

The ritualistic and highly formal quality of *Saint François d'Assise* has led some critics to deny it operatic status and to describe it rather as a liturgical oratorio that would be better served by performance in a cathedral rather than an opera house. Certainly the work is not conventionally dramatic, although it does tell a story – the story of Saint Francis's journey of spiritual development through his attainment of grace to his final union with the divine. The work is made up of three acts divided into eight self-contained scenes, all of which strive for the simplicity and solemnity of an early Renaissance painting. Though the drama is essentially internal and meditative, the music is often highly active, full of shifting colours and often frenetic with birdsong. So dense is the scoring, that the character's thematic motifs – Francis has at least five – are often lost beneath Messiaen's incredibly intricate orchestral counterpoint, even though the entire orchestra (120 musicians) is only used on a few occasions. One such occasion is the opera's powerful ending, when Francis's death is followed by a celebratory chorale sung by the entire 150-strong chorus of monks.

Messiaen once declared that melody is the "point of departure" of his music, and melody dominates his depiction of the Saint's interior drama, albeit deployed in a way that's closely akin to plainchant. The most insinuating sounds come from the ethereal ondes martenot, the electronic instrument featured so prominently in the *Turangalîla Symphony*, here used to underline the wordless communications of the Angel (soprano). There are two exclusively orchestral interludes: the first a frenetic dance of triumph by the cured leper; the second a concert of the birds, made up of numerous instruments all playing different melodies, with the instrumentalists choosing their own tempi and creating a dense wavering mass of sound. If you surrender to its unruffled pace and grandeur, *Saint François d'Assise* can be an overwhelming experience; if not, its four-and-a-half-hour length – in particular its highly static second act – can seem an eternity.

van Dam, Eda-Pierre, Riegel, Philippe; Paris Opéra Chorus and Orchestra; Ozawa.
(Cybelia CY 833/6; 4 CDs).

This live recording was made by Radio France during the work's original run at the Paris Opéra. Ozawa, a Messiaen specialist, achieves miracles in bringing out the inner luminosity of the score but the recording's chief glory is José van Dam. In the enormous and vocally taxing role of Saint Francis he sustains an amazing sense of fervour and intensity, and makes the Saint's struggles seem real. There is a certain degree of stage noise, but it's largely tolerable. The set is currently available only in France.

LUIGI DALLAPICCOLA

b. PISINO, ISTRIA, FEBRUARY 3, 1904; d. FLORENCE, FEBRUARY 19, 1975.

Shortly after the first performance of his opera *Il prigioniero* (The Prisoner) in 1949, Luigi Dallapiccola was asked by the conductor Igor Markevitch why so many of his works were concerned with prisons and the suffering of prisoners. Only then did it occur to the composer that, for the ten years between 1938 and 1948, he had been "living spiritually among prisons and prisoners". His preoccupation with liberty and persecution, which is central to *Il prigioniero*, was engendered in 1917 when he and his family were arrested and interned at Graz by the occupying Austrian forces for "suspected nationalist sympathies". The family remained in Graz until after the war, when Istria was transferred back to Italy. This loss of liberty profoundly affected the boy and its consequences can be traced throughout Dallapiccola's work, especially in his operas *Il prigioniero*, *Job* (1950) and *Ulisse* (1968).

Dallapiccola's formative musical experiences were at the opera house in Graz, and in particular a performance of *Der fliegende Holländer* determined him to become a composer. After the war he began to pursue his musical studies with greater seriousness, making weekly visits to Trieste for lessons in piano and harmony. Around 1920 the music of Debussy made a deep impression on him and his enthusiasm for the French composer's *Pelléas et Mélisande* coincided with his exposure to early Italian music by Monteverdi and Gesualdo. In 1922 Dallapiccola moved to Florence and enrolled at the conservatory, where two years later another decisive event – a performance of Schoenberg's *Pierrot Lunaire* – led him to make a thoroughgoing analysis of Schoenberg's twelve-tone system. Dallapiccola's first opera, the one-act *Volo di notte* (Night Flight), written in the late 1930s, was based on Antoine de Saint-Exupéry's book about night-time aviators in Latin America. It is his only opera with a contemporary setting but it deals with his perennial theme of escape – although in this case the release is spiritual.

Promoted by the composer Casella, Dallapiccola's music began to reach a wider audience and his reputation spread throughout Italy, but the rise of Mussolini and the horrors of the Spanish Civil War obsessed the composer. As he wrote, "the world of . . . carefree serenity closed for me, and without the possibility of return . . . I had to find other timber in other woods". Fascist anti-Semitism, though not as extreme as in Germany, placed Dallapiccola's Jewish wife Laura in great danger. Dallapiccola responded with the defiant and highly political *Canti di prigionia* (Songs of Imprisonment), and managed to avoid persecution by keeping on the move, even giving concerts in neutral countries.

With the war over, Dallapiccola completed *Il prigioniero*; and his life began to return to its "carefree serenity". Another short opera, *Job*, followed in 1950. By now he had become a world figure, feted by many of the finest conductors and instrumentalists, and after being invited by Koussevitzky to give masterclasses at Tanglewood, he became a regular visitor to America, touring as a lecturer and teacher. In 1968 his last work, *Ulisse*, was given its first performance at the Berlin Deutsche Oper, conducted by Lorin Maazel. This is Dallapiccola's only full-length opera and it deals with Homer's hero not simply as the wandering hero but as a seeker after truth. The use of serialism (partly in homage to Schoenberg's *Moses und Aron*) is even more pronounced than in *Job* and the opera's predominantly bleak musical language may explain its subsequent lack of success, despite the fact that Dallapiccola regarded it as his greatest work. Thereafter he devoted himself to compiling his writings for publication, composing little but exercising an ever greater influence as the elder statesman of twentieth-century Italian music.

Il prigioniero

The Prisoner

Composed 1944–48.
First performed December 1, 1949.
Libretto by the composer, after Villiers de l'Isle-Adam.

Synopsis

In a prologue before the curtain, the Prisoner's Mother sings of her nightly dream in which Philip II is transformed into the figure of Death. The curtain rises on a prison cell in Saragossa. The Prisoner is telling his mother of the torture he has suffered and of how the Gaoler – who calls him "fratello" (brother) – has helped restore his faith in life. Alone again, the Prisoner is suddenly visited by the Gaoler, who tells him that Flanders is in revolt and that Philip's reign and the Inquisition are doomed. He then leaves, having deliberately failed to lock the door behind him. The Prisoner slowly makes his way out of the cell down a series of corridors, past two monks – one a torturer – who fail to notice him, until finally he reaches a nocturnal garden. Ecstatic, he runs towards a cedar tree and throws his arms around it. As he does so, arms shoot out from the tree and grab him with the chilling statement: "Fratello". It is the Grand Inquisitor who, having disguised himself as the Gaoler, has administered to the Prisoner the ultimate torture – hope. A fire begins to glow in the background, towards which the Inquisitor leads the Prisoner.

When Mussolini's government implemented anti-Jewish legislation in 1938, Dallapiccola noted in his diary: "I should have liked to protest, but I was not so ingenuous as to disregard the fact that, in a totalitarian regime, the individual is powerless. Only by means of music would I be able to express my indignation." His immediate response was to write the *Canti di prigionia* but the more enduring reaction came in 1944, when he began setting his own libretto of *Il prigioniero*, based on Villiers de L'Isle-Adam's story *La torture par l'esperance* (Torture by Hope). Dallapiccola completed the work in 1948 and Hermann Scherchen – one of the composer's most committed advocates – conducted the first concert performance, broadcast live by Italian radio. He also directed the first staged production in Florence the following year.

From the outset, the score is dark and unstable, opening with a garish Bartók-like fanfare to which each of the succeeding seven scenes makes reference. Fundamentally the opera is based on three twelve-tone rows, each of which is used symbolically: the first is connected to the Prisoner's prayer; the second with the Gaoler and his use of the word "brother"; and the third – the most conventionally tonal – is linked to the Gaoler's announcement of the Flemish revolt and, as a consequence, to the idea of freedom. As the Prisoner makes his journey down the corridor towards the light, all three rows are invoked in spare orchestration that creates a remarkable effect of tension, until the Prisoner bursts forth with the cry "Alleluia" – the prelude to the bitter finale. Though the soprano role of the Mother employs a mild sort of *Sprechgesang*, the part of the Prisoner is marked by an almost Straussian lyricism, and while the opera may be bleak, with a truly horrifying climax, the simplicity of the music and its directness make it one of the most concentrated and effective operas of the postwar period.

Hynninen, Haskin, Bryn-Julson; Swedish Radio Chorus and Symphony Orchestra; Salonen.
(Sony SK 68323).

This 1995 recording is the first since Antal Dorati's for Decca in 1974. Esa-Pekka Salonen's excellent performance is not only better cast but incomparably recorded by Sony's engineers. The imposing, thrillingly projected baritone of Jorma Hynninen is the dominant presence and – despite the difficult range of the role – he brilliantly communicates the pathos of the character, largely through subtle alterations of vocal colour. Phyllis Bryn-Julson makes a suitably distraught Mother, and Howard Haskin brings great intelligence to the dual roles of Gaoler and Inquisitor. The chorus are outstanding, producing an organ-like resonance, and the orchestra follow Salonen's shaping of the work with power and sensitivity. The remaining twenty minutes of the single CD are given over to the *Canti di prigionia*.

LUIGI NONO

b. VENICE, JANUARY 29, 1924; d. VENICE, MAY 8, 1990.

In the last years of World War II, Luigi Nono was a member of the Italian Resistance, fighting against the Nazis. After the war he joined the Italian Communist Party, and in 1975 he was elected to its Central Committee. If this direct political engagement leads you to expect Nono's music to adopt the tenets of postwar socialist realism, your expectations will be frustrated by what he actually wrote. For Nono was a member of that generation of composers, now often derided in the era of minimalist accessibility, who saw no contradiction between avant-garde modernism and revolutionary politics. His operas give direct expression to his beliefs, and their librettos (for want of a better word) make use of the writings not only of Brecht, Mayakovsky and Rimbaud, but also of Marx, Lenin, Castro, Che Guevara and Gramsci.

Nono was born into a cultured family, and studied law in Padua as well as taking composition lessons from Malipiero in Venice. Later teachers included Bruno Maderna and Hermann Scherchen, who introduced Nono's work to Darmstadt, the crucible of European postwar modernism. Nono adopted Schoenberg's serialism (and also married his daughter Nuria), but he regarded technique as the servant of political radicalism, to which end he also deployed chance methods, *musique concrète* and electronics. His rejection of aesthetic and political compromise won him enemies, and the premiere of *Intolleranza 1960* was disrupted by neo-Fascists who accused Nono of contaminating Italian music – and of having a name which was a double negative.

Wanting to create a theatre of ideas, Nono looked to Russian theatre of the revolutionary period for his models. Though only two of his operatic projects ever made it into the theatre, text was always vital to his music. A long collaboration with the philosopher Massimo Cacciari led to *Prometeo* (1981–85), originally conceived for the theatre but finally labelled a *tragedia dell'ascolto* – a tragedy for listening. Other works for voice included *La Victoire de Guernica* (1954) and *A Spectre Rises over Europe* (1971), using words from the Communist Manifesto. Apart from *Intolleranza 1960*, the only other "opera" Nono completed was *Al gran sole carico d'amore* (In the Great Sun, Heavy with Love), a piece conceived in collaboration with director Yuri Lyubimov, designer David Borovsky and conductor Claudio Abbado, and premiered in 1975. Celebrating the Paris Commune and the Russian Revolution (particularly the part played in them by women), *Al gran sole* was later described by its composer as an "elephant". It certainly proposed a model that few later composers have felt inclined to adopt.

Intolleranza 1960

Composed 1960–61; revised 1970.
First performed April 13, 1961.
Text by the composer, after Angelo Maria Ripellino, Brecht, Mayakovsky, Sartre and others.

Synopsis

Part I
An Emigrant worker longs to leave the mines and return home. His wife/lover begs him to stay, but he sets off on his journey. Caught up in a demonstration, he is arrested, tortured and sent to a concentration camp, from which he escapes with an Algerian.

Part II
The Emigrant meets a woman, with whom he confronts intolerance. Eventually they reach a mighty river beyond which the Emigrant sees his homeland. The river rises, bursts its banks and engulfs everything. A final chorus urges the audience to an act of remembrance.

In 1958 Nono went to Prague, where he met Alfred Radok, creator of the Magic Lantern Theatre. Shortly after he read about

Mayakovsky's ideas for a revolutionary theatre. The conjunction of these two discoveries led him to conceive of an opera in the form of an *azione scenica*, in which narrative would largely be supplanted by the juxtaposition of episodes and found materials. That opera became *Intolleranza 1960*, in which an emigrant's story provides a vehicle for the exploration of the themes of oppression and intolerance.

For a 1990s audience, it's a difficult work to assess, since it is rarely staged, and spectacle is central to its conception. Listened to on CD, *Intolleranza 1960* seems shrill, both musically and politically, yet there is no doubting the force of Nono's orchestral writing, which moves from the subtlest colourations to the most abrasive, high-volume wall of sound. At the moment the opera seems trapped in a moment in history, but time's dialectical motion might one day allow it to escape.

Rampy, Koszut, Harries; Stuttgart Opera Chorus; State Orchestra; Kontarsky.
(Teldec 4509 97304-2).

Alfred Andersch's German version of the opera was recorded in 1993 at live performances in Stuttgart. The recording's theatrical origins mean that balances are not always ideal, but David Rampy throws everything he has into the role of the Emigrant, and Kontarsky harnesses Nono's fearsome orchestral energies. For some reason, the spoken section that opens Part II is missing, although the CD booklet includes the original text, as well as the substitute text (by Heiner Müller) that this production used to convey "the absurdities of life".

LUCIANO BERIO

b. ONEGLIA, ITALY, OCTOBER 24, 1925.

Of all the leading figures of his generation, Luciano Berio is the most prodigal and encyclopaedic, drawing on a range of influences that reaches from the poetry of Dante to the politics of Martin Luther King and from the operas of Monteverdi to the riffs of modern jazz. His output includes beautiful settings of traditional folksongs, yet has also embraced all the major musical developments of its time, including electronic music, music-theatre, and works using quotation and collage. Above all his music possesses a dynamic lyricism which links him to the great Italian tradition of Verdi and Puccini.

After lessons from his singing-teacher father, in 1945 Berio entered the Milan conservatory where, for six years, he divided his time between study and work as an accompanist and conductor in provincial opera houses. Berio's formative years, the 1950s, were spent as much in the studio as in the concert hall, and in early works such as *Omaggio a Joyce* and *Visage* he produced some of the seminal electronic music of the period. Both these pieces incorporate the recorded voice of Berio's then wife, Cathy Berberian, a mezzo-soprano whose vocal gifts were matched by a vivid stage presence that was exploited to the full in other works Berio wrote for her – *Recital*, for instance, in which the performer is asked to enact the nervous breakdown of a concert singer. But Berio's vocal music is not just concerned with theatrical role-playing or with re-creating the beauties of Italian bel canto for the twentieth century. It's also interested in the very nature of language and speech, as in *Circles* (also written for Berberian), in which the singer's movement in a circle around the stage is mirrored by a musical circle in which three poems by e e cummings are progressively deconstructed into their constituent phonetic parts and then reconstructed. A similar idea underpins the beautiful *O King* (1967) for mezzo and five instruments, in which the words "O Martin Luther King" are gradually constructed out of their vowel sounds.

O King was later incorporated into *Sinfonia* (1969), one of three major vocal and orchestral works from the 1960s – with *Epiphanie* (1962) and *Laborintus II* (1965) – that perfectly demonstrate the omnivorousness of Berio's music. *Ephiphanie* sets words by Proust and Brecht (among others) in a variety of vocal styles ranging from the extravagantly ornamented to the monotonously spoken, interleaved with orchestral movements, while *Laborintus II* uses speaker, singers, orchestra and jazz musicians to explore a welter of texts organized around the poetry of Dante. Berio's appropriation of other people's words and music hasn't always aspired to the complexity found in *Sinfonia*, however: folk music was an important source of material in works such as *Voci* (1984), a haunting recomposition of Sicilian folk melodies for viola and orchestra, and, more elaborately, in *Ritorno degli snovidenia* (1977), for cello and orchestra.

Berio's taste for recomposition and collage runs throughout his work, as does his love of the theatrical. This theatrical element looms large in the *Sequenza* cycle, a series of solo pieces which launch an innovative and sometimes zany investigation into the virtuosic and dramatic possibilities of musical performance, ranging from the vocal extravaganzas of *Sequenza III* for voice to the instrumental buffoonery of *Sequenza V* for trombone. Later, some of these pieces were themselves recomposed in yet another cycle of works, called *Chemins*, in which new layers of musical "commentary" are added to the original *Sequenza*.

Such "commentary" techniques, both literary and musical, also appear in the first of Berio's three "operas", baldly entitled *Opera* (1970), which uses the techniques developed in *Epiphanie*, *Laborintus II* and *Sinfonia* to interweave three distinct narratives drawn from the sinking of the Titanic, Monteverdi's *Orfeo* and a contemporary American drama about the care of the dying. *Opera* suffers from a certain musical and dramatic incoherence, but in his two later operas, *La vera storia* (The True Story; 1981) and *Un re in ascolto* (A King Listens; 1984), Berio has achieved a remarkable synthesis of extended theatrical techniques and large-scale musical means, albeit one which owes little to traditional operatic models.

BETTY FREEMAN/LEBRECHT COLLECTION

Luciano Berio listens

At the moment, unfortunately, none of Berio's "operas" are available on CD, but *Un re in ascolto* has been performed in several opera houses, and of all Berio's large-scale works it's the one you're likeliest to encounter.

Un re in ascolto

A King Listens

Composed 1979–84.
First performed August 7, 1984.
Libretto by the composer, after Italo Calvino, W.H. Auden, Friedrich Gotter and Shakespeare.

Synopsis

Part I

In his theatre (his island), Prospero auditions three singers, hoping to find three female protagonists for his new production. He fears he will never find the "otherworldly" woman for whom he is searching. Things then go from bad to worse as the Producer hired to bring Prospero's work to life begins to turn it into an extravaganza completely at odds with Prospero's conception. Despairing, Prospero begins to tear down the Producer's scenery, but collapses.

Part II

Prospero is dying. Realizing this, his friends and colleagues go through the pretence of caring for him in his hour of need. Prospero is immersed in visions and dreams, and he looks upon his "kingdom" not as lights and scenery, but as a "sea of music". Strengthened by these visions, he resolves to find his ideal female protagonist. She enters his mind and presents an assessment of everything that has happened to him. He can never win her and he dies alone, having failed, on the island of his stage.

The idea for *Un re in ascolto* first came to the composer through discussions with Italo Calvino, with whom Berio had earlier collaborated on *La vera storia*. Calvino proposed the creation of a modern parable about a king who hears of his kingdom's collapse and his queen's infidelity through court gossip; Berio turned the king into a dying impresario named after the central figure in Shakespeare's *The Tempest* – "an inevitable shift of perspective", commented the composer, for whom this work was to become something of a retrospective manifesto.

Un re in ascolto is subtitled "a musical action in two parts" and it opens with Prospero's claim "I have dreamt a theatre", a line that encapsulates its creator's view of operatic convention. For Berio the opera of narrative, dialogue and explication is over, and *Un re in ascolto* is an attempt to create a new sort of theatre, a theatre of the mind. Like Strauss's *Capriccio*, *Un re in ascolto* is an operatic discussion of what opera is and what it should be, and the rift between Prospero and the Producer can be read as recapitulations of the struggle between Moses and Aron in Schoenberg's opera – the latter is a passionately articulate man who wants to see the stage erupt with life, thus satisfying the masses, while the former is withdrawn, thoughtful, and fearful of simplification.

Narratively very little happens in *Un re in ascolto*, and yet the stage is frantic with activity for much of the duration – there is a powerful sense of the action illuminating the music, a reversal of the traditional arrangement. Circus acts, a chorus of stiffly moving caricatures and a grotesque Caliban-like figure called Friday keep the stage teeming, but it is Berio's music that gives the work its focus. Both acts are shaped from classical formulas, such as arias, duets and ensembles, and the overall score owes an unmistakable debt to Monteverdi, with each scene expanding from a single dramatic or musical idea. The resemblance is scarcely audible, however, for Berio's germinal ideas are often just a single chord or a single word. As Nicholas Kenyon wrote after the premiere – "precisely imagined chords fall like white sheets, and on them Berio spatters vocal lines, splashes of instrumental colour with pitches that always relate and make sense". The almost romantic unfolding of the vocal lines, especially in Prospero's five monologues, are exquisitely beautiful and Berio's writing for the human voice brings pinpoint definition to Calvino's open-ended texts. There is a suspicion during the second act that he is rambling – the shapeless chord sequences and stuttering vocal lines seem to lead nowhere – but for Prospero's death scene Berio was invigorated to create one of the most touching, if disturbing, scenes in all twentieth-century opera. There is, unfortunately, no recording at the moment.

GOTTFRIED VON EINEM

b. BERNE, SWITZERLAND, JANUARY 24, 1918;
d. OBERNDURENBACH, AUSTRIA, JULY 12, 1996.

Of all German-speaking postwar composers, Gottfried von Einem had the greatest success in the opera house, even if the esteem in which his best works are held in Europe has not travelled much further afield. His first opera and his finest work, *Dantons Tod* (Danton's Death), re-opened the Salzburg Festival in 1947 and was immediately hailed as a major work: its theme of an individual and a society being destroyed by ideological extremity was especially pertinent, and it remains one of the most satisfying musical adaptations of a great play.

Einem was born in Berne, the son of the Austrian military attaché to Switzerland. In 1938, having attended music school in Holstein, he became a repetiteur at the Berlin Staatsoper and at Bayreuth. A year later he was arrested by the Gestapo for helping friends and colleagues escape from Germany but his influential contacts secured his release soon after. He remained in Germany during the war, studying with leading modernist composer Boris Blacher, who had swiftly recognized his pupil's "unique lyrical gift". In 1944 the success of Einem's ballet *Prinzessin Turandot* led to his appointment as resident composer and adviser to the Dresden Staatsoper. Three years later *Dantons Tod* led to Einem being championed in some quarters as the saviour of the German operatic tradition and Richard Strauss's successor. The critics were right to praise the opera in such terms but Einem never again tapped such a vein of inspiration.

His next opera, *Der Prozess* (The Trial), based on the Kafka novel, was produced at Salzburg in 1953 with Max Lorenz as Joseph K and Lisa della Casa singing all three female roles. It continued Einem's exploration of the plight of the individual oppressed by the state, but its stylistic pluralism didn't please everyone (critics identified too much Strauss, Orff and Stravinsky in the mix), and the grim monotony of the vocal style detracted somewhat from the sharply written orchestral backdrop.

The 1950s continued to be an extremely productive time for Einem but he composed no further operas until *Der Zerrissene* (1961), an untypically light work of comic fantasy. Another ten years passed before he returned to more familiar territory with *Der Besuch der alten Dame* (The Visit of the Old Lady), a satire on financial greed based on a play by Durenmatt (who also wrote the libretto). Commissioned by the Vienna Staatsoper, it was a notable success and was staged throughout Europe. *Kabale und Liebe* (1975), after Schiller, was rather less successful, while his final opera *Jesu Hochzeit* (1980) infuriated the Catholic church with its erotic representation of Jesus.

Einem's influence as a composer has waned since the 1950s, and he is now too often dismissed as a conservative throwback. It's certainly the case that his music represents the closing of an era, but if Einem lacks the modern edge of composers such as Henze, he nonetheless created in *Dantons Tod* an opera that repays repeated listening.

Dantons Tod

Danton's Death

Composed 1944–46.
First performed August 6, 1947.
Libretto by the composer and Boris Blacher, after Büchner.

Synopsis

Part I

1794, Paris. Danton is gambling with his friends. Desmoulins arrives and begins to denounce the reign of terror instigated by Robespierre. He asks Danton to attack Robespierre in the Convention. Outside, Simon rages over the luxury of the wealthy. The crowd abduct a young man and are about to hang him when he manages to save himself. Robespierre arrives and rouses the crowd with news of further executions. Danton, disgusted at Robespierre's methods, confronts him. After Danton's exit Robespierre, encouraged by Saint-Just, announces that both Danton and Desmoulins must die. In Desmoulins' house, Danton, Desmoulins and his wife Lucile discuss their social responsibilities. Danton is called away and returns with news that he is to be arrested; he decides not to flee – "I shall die courageously. It is easier than living."

Part II

Danton and Desmoulins are in prison. Outside their cell the crowd rages as Simon tells stories of Danton's wealth while praising Robespierre's virtue. At his hearing Danton reminds the court of his own revolutionary actions, and eventually turns the crowd against the regime and its dictator Robespierre. The hearing is postponed. In the square the mob sing and dance before the guillotine; having forgotten his words, they savour Danton's imminent death. A tumbril brings in Danton and Desmoulins; after a few words from each, they are beheaded. The crowd disperse and two executioners begin to clean up after the day's work. Lucile seems to have lost her mind and is arrested as she sings: "Es lebe der Konig" (Long Live the King).

Georg Büchner's proto-Expressionist plays had previously attracted some attention from opera composers, most notably Alban Berg, who turned *Woyzeck* (see p.406) into one of the masterpieces of modernism, but Einem was the first to tackle *Dantons Tod*. Working with Boris Blacher, he condensed the play's four acts into two parts, and its thirty-two "episodes" into six scenes, creating a libretto that is as much a commentary on the evils of dictatorship as on the specific dilemmas confronted by Danton and Desmoulins.

The score of *Dantons Tod* bears a close resemblance to the expressionism of Berg, but the shifting, metamorphic orchestrations are placed at the service of sensuous vocal writing that's dominated by arias and parlando-like dialogue. Danton, a Siegfried-like figure, possesses much of the opera's finest music: his monologue in the first part of the opera, which owes much to a similar scene in Strauss's *Die Frau ohne Schatten*, is one of the great moments in the baritone repertoire. Robespierre, on the other hand, is one of the nastier tenor roles and his music is genuinely disturbing – Einem's writing for his confrontation with Danton is particularly powerful. Central to the success of Einem's project is the prominence of the crowd, for which he provided brilliant choruses to place the actions of the central characters in context. The opera's musical climax occurs at Danton's trial, where the complicated choral writing brilliantly conveys the volatility of the crowd, culminating in the setting of the "Marseillaise" in counterpart with the "Carmagnole". Lucile is the more involved of the two female roles but Einem's writing for the female voice is generally less imaginative. Nonetheless, with its restless orchestration, vocal intensity, and the sense of individuals being swept away by events, *Dantons Tod* is deeply affecting, and it is astonishing that it has failed to secure a ready audience outside Germany.

Schöffler, Patzak, Klein, Witt; Vienna State Opera Chorus; Vienna Philharmonic Orchestra; Fricsay.
(Stradivarius STR 10067; 2 CDs).

This extraordinary recording of the first night of *Dantons Tod* is difficult to track down and the sound, taken from a broadcast, is not brilliant, but the performance is outstanding, with a perfect cast which includes Paul Schöffler, Julius Patzak, Ludwig Weber, Maria Cebotari and Rosette Anday. Schöffler stands out in the title role, but Patzak's Desmoulins and Cebotari's Lucile are no less remarkable. Fricsay gives vital, emotional direction and the Vienna forces are in top form. A wonderful opera given near-ideal treatment.

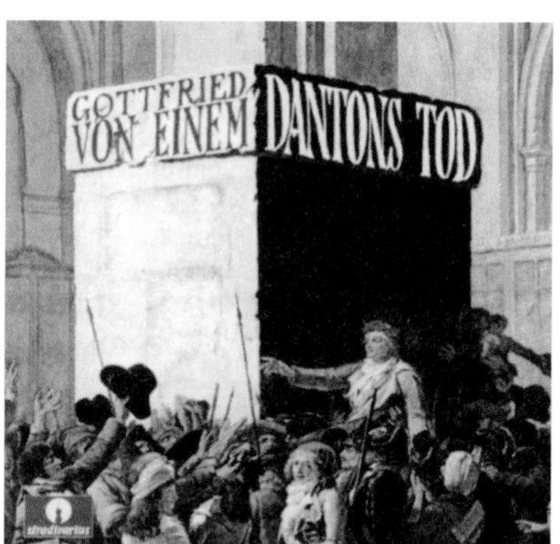

Adam, Hollweg, Gahmlich, Hiestermann, Laki; Austrian Radio Chorus and Symphony Orchestra; Zagrosek.
(Orfeo C102 842; 2 CDs).

Zagrosek's recording is also live from the Salzburg Festival, this time a concert performance held twenty-six years after the premiere. Although it lacks the electricity of the earlier account, it is extremely impressive and – of course – has considerably better sound. None of the soloists matches the dramatic intensity of their predecessors, but Werner Hollweg is a dignified and powerful Danton and Horst Hiestermann is suitably insinuating in the role of Robespierre. Zagrosek's conducting is dynamic enough but doesn't quite convey sufficient danger.

BERND ALOIS ZIMMERMANN

b. BLIESHEIM, GERMANY, MARCH 20, 1918; d. COLOGNE, AUGUST 10, 1970.

Zimmermann only wrote one opera, *Die Soldaten* (1964), but it is widely regarded as the most important German-language opera since Einem's *Dantons Tod* (1947), if not Berg's *Lulu* (1935). Zimmermann was an exact contemporary of Einem and like him was deeply involved with the notion of an Austro-German musical tradition, but – unlike Einem – his mature style was essentially atonal and embraced the technique of serialism as an organizational starting point. He also had close contact with the avant-garde of the 1950s and 1960s while maintaining a discrete distance from them – in short, he was an experimental composer but an independent one. *Die Soldaten* reflects this in the way it reworks a classic German text from a radical perspective, employing highly original stagecraft and substantial quotation from different musical sources.

Zimmermann's life was closely associated with the city of Cologne: he was born in nearby Bliesheim and it was while studying at the Cologne Music School that he was conscripted into the army and sent to fight in France. This was to be his one and only journey outside of Germany, and it was while there that he first encountered the contemporary scores of Stravinsky, Milhaud, Poulenc and Honegger. Their influence on his creative development was considerable and in 1942, on his return to Germany, he began composition lessons with Philip Jarnach – Busoni's former pupil. His music from this period is essentially Neoclassical but between 1948 and 1950 he attended courses given by Wolfgang Fortner and René Leibowitz at Darmstadt – the centre of the postwar German musical revival – and it was after this that he started to incorporate Schoenberg's twelve-tone techniques into his own work. His Darmstadt years encouraged him to concentrate more on composing, though his work teaching at Cologne University and then at the Cologne Music School often left him little time to write.

Perhaps the most distinctive aspect of Zimmermann's work throughout the 1950s was his increasingly bold use of musical quotation, a technique that can be compared to the collages of an artist like Kurt Schwitters, where the overlaying and juxtapositioning of disparate elements create richly powerful associations, as well as different levels of meaning. Sometimes quotations are so integrated into the fabric of the score as to be hardly perceptible, at other times their presence acts as a startling contrast or sets up a kind of dialogue within different sections of a piece. While composers like Boulez and Stockhausen were attempting a clean break with the music of the past (and dismissing opera as bourgeois), Zimmermann preferred to engage with it as a means of confronting and coming to terms with his country's history and identity. He was also very widely read in both literature and philosophy and this, no less than his wide-ranging musical knowledge, contributed to his pluralistic aesthetic.

Die Soldaten is the most ambitious and successful of Zimmermann's multilayered projects – if not the most extreme. In *Musique pour les soupers du roi Ubu* (1966) the entire work is made up of pre-existent music, while his last work, *Ich wandte mich und sah an alles Unrecht*, completed five days before he committed suicide, contains extensive quotation from the Bible, Dostoyevsky and Bach – specifically seven bars from the chorale *Es ist genug*, the same chorale used by Berg for his own last composition. At his death Zimmermann was working on an operatic setting of *Medea*.

Die Soldaten

The Soldiers

Composed 1958–60; revised 1963–64.
First performed February 15, 1965.
Libretto by the composer, after Lenz.

Synopsis

Act I

At Lille in the house of Wesener, a fancy goods merchant, his daughter Marie is writing to the mother of her fiancé Stolzius, a draper, in Armentières. Stolzius is seen being teased by his mother. Back at Lille a French officer, Desportes, is attempting to woo Marie but her father will not allow him to take her to the theatre. In Armentières, soldiers discuss what to do when off duty. Captain Haudy proposes the theatre in defiance of the chaplain Eisenhardt's criticisms. Back at Lille, Wesener is seen telling Marie not to discourage either of her suitors.

Act II

In an Armentières coffee house, Eisenhardt condemns Haudy's plan to seduce Marie away from Stolzius, who is then mocked by the soldiers who tell him that Desportes also has his eye on Marie. The second scene has three different, but simultaneous settings. In Lille Desportes seduces Marie, while (on another part of the stage) her grandmother sings of her ruin, and in Armentières Stolzius and his mother receive a letter from Marie – part written by Desportes.

Act III

Eisenhardt informs Captain Pirzel that Major Mary has arrived in Lille. Stolzius takes a job as Major Mary's servant. Mary then enters, with Stolzius, to take Marie for a drive. The Countess de la Roche then arrives in the knowledge that her son has also been involved with Marie; but she is interested only in helping the girl. In the final scene she enlists Marie as her companion.

Act IV

Marie has fled the Countess and returns to Desportes, who is in prison and wants to be rid of her. He sends her to his gamekeeper, who rapes her. At dinner, Mary and Desportes mock Marie. They are waited on by Stolzius, who has poisoned Desportes' food. As he lies dying, Stolzius kills himself with Mary's sword. By the river Lys Wesener is confronted by a beggar, whom he does not recognize as his own daughter. He gives her a coin, at which she falls to the ground.

Jakob Lenz's play of 1776, which forms the starting point of *Die Soldaten*, cast a critical eye on the morality of French soldiers in Strasbourg, and chronicled the downfall of the flighty Marie, who is treated as a plaything by several of them. (It was much admired by Georg Büchner, whose own *Woyzeck* owes much to its sentiments and construction.) Zimmermann widened Lenz's sights and directed his anxiety at soldiering and the military in general, implicitly asking the question "who protects against our protectors?" *Die Soldaten* was the summit of Zimmermann's pluralist aesthetic, blending past, present and future – sometimes simultaneously – in a grim parable of social disintegration. In an interview he gave in 1969 he defined the requirements of modern opera as "the concentration of all theatrical media for the purpose of communication in a place created specifically for the purpose . . . In my *Soldaten* I have attempted to take decisive steps in this direction." The opera was commissioned by Cologne in 1958, but on completion the work's complex requirements, which included twelve performance areas, were considered unperformable and it was only staged in 1965 after Zimmermann had simplified it.

The parallels between *Die Soldaten* and Berg's *Wozzeck* are many and obvious (not least in the association of each scene with a textbook form, such as the chaconne and toccata), but the basic character is quite different. For a start, Zimmermann's work is considerably busier, with much more to occupy the ear and the eye – the use of film and newsreel projected onto three large screens means that the audience is bombarded with a plethora of simultaneous images and ideas. This simultaneity and the sheer variety of quotation – which ranges from pop and jazz to Gregorian chant, Bach chorales and Mozart – makes it impossible to assimilate the information as in a traditional narrative, while many of the extra-musical sounds, which include screaming, shouted military commands, "hopeless moaning", whispering and "unrestrained weeping", make for difficult listening. Yet much of Zimmermann's score is economical, so the voices are rarely swamped by the orchestra, and in the hands of a forceful director *Die Soldaten* is an engrossing theatrical experience.

Vargas, Shade, Ebbecke, Cochran, Hoffmann; Stuttgart State Opera Chorus and Orchestra; Kontarsky. (Teldec 9031-727752; 2 CDs).

This 1991 recording of *Die Soldaten*, conducted by contemporary music specialist Bernhard Kontarsky, is a colossal achievement, capturing the scale and eclecticism of Zimmermann's enormous score with good singers and a near-perfect sound. The highlight comes from the veteran mezzo-soprano Grace Hoffmann, who gives a marvellous performance as Wesener's Mother, and is clearly an inspiration to her colleagues.

HANS WERNER HENZE

b. GÜTERSLOH, GERMANY, JULY 1, 1926.

Though his style has undergone many, frequently violent, changes, Hans Werner Henze has created some of the most approachable music written since 1945, and his operas occupy a prominent place in the modern repertory. As Andrew Porter wrote in 1962, he is an "inspiration, interpreter and prophet for those whose musical understanding was formed after the war. Then, Schoenberg and Stravinsky were the old gods, still speaking; but Henze speaks for, and with, us."

Henze's interest in the theatre was first engaged by a recording of the overture to Mozart's *Marriage of Figaro* but it was the friendship and tuition of Wolfgang Fortner that cultivated Henze's passion for opera. After military service – and a brief spell as a POW – Henze was encouraged by Fortner to acquire some practical theatrical experience. He was initially engaged as a staff member at the Deutsches Theater in Konstanz but within two years he was appointed music director and conductor of Wiesbaden ballet. He remained close to Fortner who, according to Henze, gave him a "thorough knowledge of early methods of composition, strict harmony, counterpoint and the art of the fugue . . . and a comprehensive introduction to the realm of modern music and its inherent problems." Always conscious of the need for a reconciliation between the traditional and the experimental, Henze has remained, in his own words, "a reluctant modernist".

His first opera, *Das Wundertheater* (1948), was a cabaret-style parody of the Nazi obsession with racial purity. In 1951 he composed *Boulevard Solitude*, his first full-length opera, a work of similar political commitment but displaying a bewildering stylistic prodigality. Two years later Henze moved to Italy, a country that has stimulated his work in many ways: through

NICK LUCKHURST/LEBRECHT COLLECTION

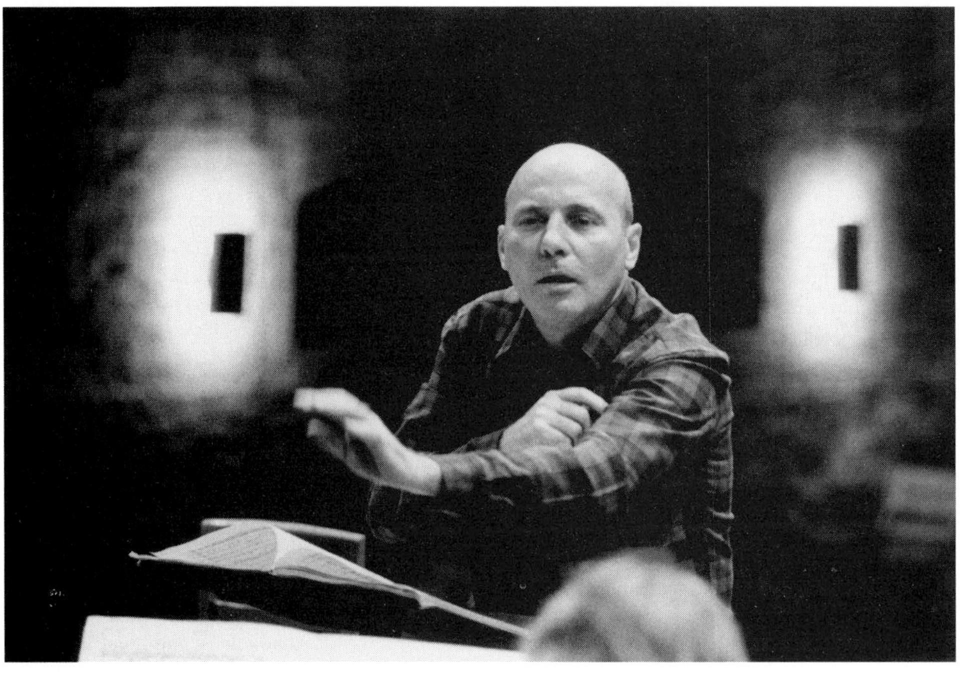

Hans Werner Henze conducting in 1982

its light and colour; through its freer attitude towards his homosexuality; and, perhaps above all, in its emphasis on community. The four-hour *König Hirsch*, based on a Gozzi fantasy, duly manifested the influence of Italian folk-song and the orchestrations of Puccini. It was followed by such works as *Der Prinz von Homburg*, in which Henze ridiculed Germanic militarism, *Elegy for Young Lovers*, a setting of a W.H. Auden and Chester Kallman libretto exploring the artist's relationship with society (an abiding Henze concern), *Der junge Lord*, a sort of tribute to opera buffa, and the sombre *The Bassarids*, another Auden/Kallman collaboration.

In the mid-1960s, however, Henze – in common with many of his contemporaries – underwent a radicalization of his politics. In works such as his oratorio *Das Floss der Medusa* (The Raft of the Medusa), with its invocations of Ho Chi Minh, Henze proclaimed his revolutionary socialism through music that rejected luxurious tonality and lyricism in favour of a stripped-back, hard-hitting, sometimes strident style. One of his best works from this period, *El Cimarrón*, was written during a sojourn in Cuba and took as its subject the autobiography of a runaway slave. As he stated in 1970: "My crisis was not so much about opera as about music, music making and people, and in this context I could see that I would contribute no more new operas . . . I feel opera is finished. Their decay, heralding the decay of present society, naturally also heralds the decay of its theatre."

Nonetheless, by the mid-1970s Henze was again writing for the conventional theatre: *We Come to the River* (1974) was followed by *Don Chisciotte della Mancia* (1976), *The English Cat* (1983) and *Das verraten Meer* (1990). *We Come to the River* was a huge project, with a named cast of over a hundred, and its extreme demands (three orchestras, three stages and a military band) have kept it out of production. The hard-edged political agenda of Henze and his librettist, Edward Bond, was also problematic in some quarters – the audience at the Covent Garden premiere certainly didn't take well to finding itself on the receiving end of a bluntly expressed anti-capitalist assault. The rather more successful *English Cat*, Henze's second operatic collaboration with Bond, is a modern ballad-opera along the lines of Stravinsky's *The Rake's Progress*. It is tremendous fun as a piece of theatre, with everyone dressed up as cats, rats and mice, but the heavily percussive score is still quite hard work. However, his next opera, *Venus and Adonis*, promises to mark a return to the sound-world of the early operas. Henze predicts "a very lush, almost tropical luxuriance. Everything will be extremely sensual, physical and atmospheric."

Boulevard Solitude

Composed 1950–51.
First performed February 17, 1952.
Libretto by Grete Weil, after Prévost.

Synopsis

Scene 1
Paris, the end of World War II. Armand des Grieux and Manon meet in a railway waiting room. He tells her of his miserable existence, and they leave together.

Scene 2
Armand and Manon sing of their happiness. Manon's brother, Lescaut, persuades Manon to take a rich lover, M. Lilaque, in order to fund his own extravagant lifestyle.

Scene 3
In Lilaque's mansion, Lescaut sees Manon's letters to Armand and fears his income may be in jeopardy. He robs the safe, but is caught and both he and Manon are thrown out.

Scene 4
Armand is obsessed with Manon, and disbelieves rumours about the robbery.

Scene 5
Armand takes drugs, supplied by Lescaut. Manon meets her new client, Lilaque's son.

Scene 6
Armand and Manon meet at the younger Lilaque's house. Lescaut steals a painting but Lilaque the elder discovers the theft and calls the police. Lescaut shoots him and forces the smoking gun onto Manon.

Scene 7
Armand sees Manon as she enters prison. The opera ends with a series of flashbacks to happier times.

𝄞 Although *Boulevard Solitude*, an instant success at its first performance in Hanover, is often held up as one of the most arresting examples of Henze's affinity with the Second Viennese School of Schoenberg and Berg, the opera's dominant influence is Stravinsky. Henze did not meet Stravinsky until two years after the first performance of *Boulevard Solitude*, but he had long been drawn to the elder composer's Neoclassicism. Inspired by the faultless craftsmanship and the "clarity, elegance and eloquence" of Stravinsky's "classical voice", Henze approached Prévost's eighteenth-century tragedy in a similar manner to the way Stravinsky was at the same time approaching the text of *The Rake's Progress*, setting the dramatic narrative within the classical formalities of arias and ensembles. However, anyone expecting something similar to Massenet's and Puccini's better-known treatments of the same story will be in for a surprise – even though Henze follows their precedents in scoring for a soprano Manon, a tenor Des Grieux and a baritone Lescaut.

Henze's Neoclassicism is aggressively parodic, and in splicing the formalities of classical structure to the heterogeneous music of big-band jazz, Parisian music-hall and the American-era Kurt Weill he created a vision of the eighteenth century in which his protagonists were "ravaged, violated and turned upside down". Henze uses harmony to differentiate between the drama's two planes of existence – the impoverished and painful world inhabited by the lovers is atonal, whereas the bourgeois, capitalist world that corrupts them is decadently tonal. His orchestrations are equally unambiguous, with instruments and groupings applied to different characters and settings. With its powerful neo-Bellini and neo-Schoenberg vocal writing, *Boulevard Solitude* is an extraordinary brew of various styles, typical of a composer for whom the reconciliation of the old and the new has always been a preoccupation.

Vassilieva, Pruett, Falkman, Salzman, Brewer; Rencontres Musicales Orchestra; Anghelow.
(Cascavelle VEL 1006; 2 CDs).

The versatility and variety of Henze's setting of *Manon Lescaut* is wonderfully caught by this unfortunately hard-to-obtain recording. None of the cast nor the orchestra or conductor are well known, but although the performance has a rather provincial feel to it, there is contagious enthusiasm here. Vassilieva and Pruett are a distinctive Manon and Des Grieux, and Falkman is a splendid Lescaut, but the star of the show is undoubtedly Anghelow, who manages to bring all the disparate voices, influences and colours together to form a convincing whole.

Der junge Lord

The Young Lord

Composed 1964.
First performed April 7, 1965.
Libretto by Ingeborg Bachmann, after Hauff.

Synopsis

Act I

Hülsdorf-Gotha, 1830. Sir Edgar (a silent role) arrives in town, shunning the people's reception and refusing to speak to the local dignitaries. The lovers, Wilhelm and Luise, begin a series of amorous duets. When a circus comes to town, Sir Edgar compounds his scornful attitude by addressing only the children and circus entertainers, whom he offers accommodation when their licence is revoked by the resentful councillors.

Act II

The Mayor investigates strange noises coming from Sir Edgar's house. Sir Edgar explains that it is his young nephew, Lord Barrat, who is learning German. At a party, the young Lord Barrat starts behaving oddly, and seduces Luise. They sing of their love, with Wilhelm looking disconsolately on. The rest of the party dances, but Lord Barrat soon dominates the floor, his movements growing more erratic until he wildly rips off his clothes, revealing that he is in fact an ape from the local circus. In the general confusion, Luise and Wilhelm rediscover their former love.

Der junge Lord was written in Italy, and can be seen as Henze's tribute to Italian opera – specifically, the bel canto style and the conventions of opera buffa. Henze takes a parable by the nineteenth-century German playwright Wilhelm Kauff and puts it into a traditional buffa framework, replete with memorable vocal music, in order to attack class hypocrisy. The revelation that the "real English Lord", over whom the petit-bourgeois townspeople have been fawning, is actually a circus monkey, is one of opera's great coups de théâtre. But it is the overall musical fabric, in which Mozartian elegance and opera-buffish clowning are modified by Henze's strikingly twentieth-century imagination, that makes *Der junge Lord* Henze's most popular opera.

It is no surprise that Henze attended a performance of Mozart's *Die Entführung aus dem Serail* the night before beginning work on *Der junge Lord* (there is even a burst of Turkish music played early during the first scene), but although Mozart's influence is clear in the economy and lightness of the orchestrations, Rossini's hectic brio is the more conspicuous element, notably during the ballroom party of Act II, when the guests start imitating the Young Lord's increasingly eccentric behaviour. Rossini's lyrical imprint is also unmistakable in the love duet between Wilhelm and Luise, which, for all the twentieth-century ironic twists, is one of the most ardent expressions of love in all opera.

Having only a single aria, *Der junge Lord* is an ensemble opera in which Henze deploys his cast with a skill and sense of timing of which Rossini would have been proud. The subversive undercurrent remains well disguised until the final scene, and the subversive sting in the tail is even more potent for the climate of decorum within which it occurs. *Der junge Lord* is a clever and extremely funny opera, but its sudden turn makes it also one of the most shocking operas written since the war.

Mathis, Driscoll, Grobe, Johnson; Berlin Deutsche Opera Chorus and Orchestra; Dohnányi.
(Deutsche Grammophon 449 875-2GC2; 2 CDs).

Dohnányi's performance of *Der junge Lord* numbers among his finest achievements on record. With an unerring sense of what is right for this music, he accentuates the lyrical qualities, drawing some glorious playing from the Berlin orchestra and some divinely fluid singing from Edith Mathis, Lisa Otto and Donald Grobe. The 1960s stereo is generous and nicely balanced.

The Bassarids

Composed 1965.
First performed August 6, 1966.
Libretto by W.H. Auden and Chester Kallman, after Euripides.

Synopsis

1st Movement

Pentheus, the new King of Thebes, hopes to convert the Bassarids (or Bacchae) from their irrational worship of Dionysus to monotheism. He bans the cult of Semele (the mother of Dionysus).

2nd Movement

Fearful of the cult, Pentheus arrests the Bassarids. He notices his mother, Agave, amongst the prisoners but cannot wake her from her ecstatic trance.

3rd Movement

The Bassarids escape when an earthquake hits Thebes. Under duress from Dionysus, Pentheus joins the group, disguised as a woman, but Dionysus then exposes him as a spy and he is torn to pieces. One of the murderers is Agave.

4th Movement

Leading the victory procession, Agave suddenly realizes what she has done, and bitterly chides the cult leaders. Dionysus and Semele prevail, and order the destruction of the Theban royal palace, regaining the absolute devotion of the Bassarids.

The Bassarids is a setting of Euripides's *The Bacchae*, a play that focuses on the conflict between the orderly world of King Pentheus of Thebes and the unrestrainable rule of the hedonistic god Dionysus. Auden and Kallman remained true to their source, but they placed greater emphasis on the solo cast (in Euripides the chorus is far more prominent) in order to underline the psychoanalytical components of the drama. In highlighting the mother–son conflict they also underpinned what Auden took to be the play's defining theme: "Our Pentheus's fall is occasioned not so much by his arrogant behaviour towards others as by his unawareness of his own nature, an ignorance which is the result of a philosophical error."

The Bassarids bears more than a passing resemblance to the sound-worlds of Schoenberg's *Erwartung* and *Moses und Aron*, but for all its angular atonality, it can also be read as something of a homage to the late nineteenth century. At the time, one critic referred to *The Bassarids* as "the opera Mahler never got round to writing" and there is a powerful contrapuntal density to Henze's score that's reminiscent of Mahler's late symphonies – indeed Henze explicitly asked Auden for an "opera in the mould of a four-movement symphony".

Played as a single uninterrupted act lasting two and half hours, *The Bassarids* begins with a movement in sonata form, presenting the two opposing elements of the drama: the hard, unsensual Pentheus and the heady, expressive Dionysus. A reliance on time-honoured formulas is maintained throughout the opera, with each successive "movement" adhering to an established musical structure, culminating in a grand passacaglia built upon a 43-note theme.

A complex system of quotations (notably from Berg and Mahler) and leitmotifs reinforces the span, but this is not a reductive exercise in technique. Praising the libretto he had been given, Henze wrote that Auden "understood the ability of music to forget itself . . . the crude shamelessness of musical expression", and *The Bassarids* abounds with shamelessly rich and expressive music. Agave's haunting description of her first exposure to the cult, the wild hunt of the Bassarids, and the appearance of Agave carrying her son's head are all extremely intense episodes, and throughout the opera the conflict between rationality and sensuality is mirrored in clashes between harmony and cacophony. The cumulative impact is extraordinary. The most original moment comes right at the end when, with disorder triumphant, Pentheus dead, Cadmus and his court banished, and Dionysus in total command, the music becomes subdued – a moment more dreadful in its calm acceptance of the new order than any Dionysian orgy.

Riegel, Schmidt, Burt, Tear; South German Radio Chorus; Berlin Radio Symphony Orchestra; Albrecht.
(Schwann SCHW 314006; 2 CDs).

Kurt Albrecht, one of the most prolific opera conductors on record, is a noted champion of Henze's music, and this 1986 performance of the German-language version of *The Bassarids* (Die Bassariden) is full of conviction and confidence. The casting is world-class, with the baritone Kenneth Riegel and Andreas Schmidt outstanding as Dionysus and Pentheus. The sound is full, capturing the sumptuous Berlin forces with clarity and warmth.

ARIBERT REIMANN

b. BERLIN, MARCH 4, 1936.

Reimann was three years old when war broke out and eight when Berlin was first blitzed; later he lost a brother in the Allied bombings and saw the family home reduced to rubble. His musical identity was formed amid the austerity and deprivation of postwar Germany, under the watchful eyes of his father, a noted organist and Bach scholar, and his mother, a concert singer and teacher. After studying at the Berlin School of Music, from 1958 Reimann began to establish himself as a composer and a pianist, and was soon in great demand from singers – most famously Dietrich Fischer-Dieskau – as an accompanist and coach, work that gave him a thorough knowledge of the human voice. The majority of his work is vocal, encompassing songs, choral works and opera.

His bleak childhood experiences strongly influenced his choice of material and each of his six operas is a tragedy. *Ein Traumspiel* (A Dream Play; 1965), which was based on a Strindberg play, was followed by *Melusine* (1971), the most lyrical but also the most vocally taxing of his operas. More famous, however, is *Lear* (1978), which grew from a suggestion by Fischer-Dieskau and made an enormous impact at its first performance in Munich, with Fischer-Dieskau in the title role. Since *Lear* Reimann has written three more operas: *Die Gespenstersonate* (The Ghost Sonata; 1983) is another Strindberg adaptation in which Reimann employs quarter-tone harmony to unnerving effect; *Troades* (The Trojan Women; 1985) is a tragedy derived from Euripides; while his last opera, *Das Schloss* (The Castle; 1991), is an adaptation of Kafka that experiments with a more acrobatic style of vocal writing. None of these works has had the same kind of impact as *Lear*.

Reimann is essentially an Expressionist composer: his music is dark, complex and brooding, with an emphatic use of brass, but it is also highly theatrical, with brilliant explosions of light amidst the gloom. Orchestral textures are inclined to be overwrought, his remarkable understanding of the singing voice

– which he frequently pushes to technical extremes – has given the vocal line a greater centrality than is found in much contemporary opera.

Lear

Composed 1976–78.
First performed July 9, 1978.
Libretto by Claus Henneberg, after Shakespeare.

Synopsis

Part I

King Lear abdicates and plans to divide the kingdom among his three daughters, Regan, Goneril and Cordelia – according to how much they love him. Cordelia refuses to praise her father beyond saying that she loves him as a daughter should. She is disinherited and banished but marries the King of France. Edgar, the son of the Duke of Gloucester, is accused of plotting against his father by his illegitimate half-brother Edmund. Goneril and Regan – the kingdom now theirs – attempt to keep their father under control. Humiliated, the old king departs with his Fool and the Duke of Kent. On a heath during a storm, the king raves against the elements. The king and his friends find Edgar, who pretends to be mad, hiding in a hovel. Gloucester saves the king and takes him to Dover to meet up with Cordelia.

Part II

Regan's husband, Cornwall, abducts Gloucester, blinds him and is himself killed by a servant. Goneril and Edmund plan to marry and to poison Regan. Edgar pretends to help Gloucester to kill himself but reveals himself as his son and saves him. Gloucester and Lear are reunited with Cordelia at Dover. Edmund captures father and daughter, and commands that Cordelia be strangled; Goneril poisons Regan and, after Edmund is killed by Edgar, she takes her own life. Carrying Cordelia's body in his arms, Lear dies from grief.

Shakespeare's *King Lear* was a major preoccupation of Berlioz, Verdi (who actually began work on a setting) and Debussy, and it has been turned into an opera by several composers, none particularly distinguished. According to David Littlejohn: "*Lear* is the most unconventional, the most nearly hysterical, the most outré and outrageous play Shakespeare ever wrote. It is so much a play dependent on medieval or Renaissance conventions, that Reimann's shrieking, snarling, crashing, no-holds-barred score probably suits its essence better than any more conventional musical idiom could do." Indeed, the unhinged sound-world of Reimann's *Lear*, with its huge percussion section, is the key to its effectiveness. But Reimann's scoring, reminiscent of Berg, is also remarkably accessible, being moulded around an intricately thought-out structure that allows for moments of lyrical tenderness – as in the terrible pathos of the final scenes. The wildly expressive title role was conceived for the talents of Dietrich Fischer-Dieskau – a baritone especially noted for the raw edge of his interpretations – and it demands enormous vocal stamina. All the other parts, with the exception of the Fool – a spoken role accompanied by string quartet – are equally vividly drawn. Of the three sisters, Regan is characterized by a highly elaborate vocal writing that suggests someone on the brink of hysteria, while Goneril's wide-intervalled outpourings are more sinisterly controlled. Cordelia's music, the most consistently lyrical role, is based on a twelve-tone row which, when reversed, provides much of the material for the equally sympathetic Edgar.

Lear is a deeply disturbing opera that fuses a hugely complicated orchestral score to some of the most extreme and violent vocal writing of the century. Many will find the brutality difficult to take, but its effectiveness in conveying – without rhetoric – the pain and despair at the heart of Shakespeare's play makes it one of the most powerful and moving of all postwar operas.

Lear was recorded by Deutsche Grammophon soon after its premiere and, for a contemporary opera, it sold remarkably well. Fischer-Dieskau delivered a high-voltage, fervently characterized reading of the title role, and the set as a whole generated a palpable air of excitement; inexplicably, however, it has not been transferred to CD and it is currently unavailable in any format.

KARLHEINZ STOCKHAUSEN

b. BURG MÖDRATH, GERMANY, AUGUST 22, 1928.

In today's global village of information superhighways and cultural cross-pollination, no composer occupies so pivotal a place as Karlheinz Stockhausen, the iconic figure of postwar modernity and the first electronic studio composer. Way back in the 1960s he was predicting "a music of the whole world" and in 1977 he announced that he was beginning a work that would fulfil that prediction: *Licht* (Light), a mammoth opera cycle of seven works, one for each day of the week, to be completed around the turn of the new millennium. *Licht*

HARALD FRONZECK FOTOGRAFIE

Karlheinz Stockhausen at work in the Stockhausen lab

marked Stockhausen's first venture into the genre. Though a number of his works from the 1950s and 1960s (notably *Gruppen* and *Momente*) had elements of theatricality about them, none of them could be described as dramas. But during the early 1970s, Stockhausen's experiences of Asian theatre strongly influenced his move towards a ceremonial music in which the musicians, performing on stage, became the embodiment of characters. Works such as *Trans* (1971), *Harlekin* (1975) and *Sirius* (1975–77) paved the way for something much more substantial.

Brought up in the environs of Cologne, Stockhausen spent his earliest years on the move, following the wanderings of his schoolteacher father, while absorbing music from his mother – who played piano and sang – and from the radio and gramophone. The war shattered his childhood: his mother, who had been recuperating in a mental home, fell victim to the Nazis' euthanasia programme; his father was reported missing and was never seen again. By the war's end, having witnessed terrible suffering as a stretcher-bearer, Stockhausen had become a devout Christian, and was playing jazz piano to American GIs to finance his courses at Cologne's music school and university.

Stockhausen made it his mission in life to break utterly with the past – both music and Germany had to start again. Already strongly influenced by Schoenberg and Webern, he began attending new music courses at Darmstadt, where he was entranced by the work of Messiaen, with whom he then studied in Paris and who proclaimed him a genius. In Paris also met Pierre Boulez and Pierre Schaeffer, both of whom were working on innovative forms of tape composition at the studio of ORTF Radio.

At the age of twenty-four Stockhausen was offered a job at the WDR radio station in Cologne to continue his search for a "pure electronic music". He experimented with electronics throughout the 1950s, gaining a reputation as the most advanced composer of his day with pieces such as the thirteen-minute *Gesang der Jünglige* (1956), a mix of electronic sound and boy-soprano voice that made the same sort of impact as Stravinsky's *Rite of Spring* had made back in 1913. In 1960 he began to apply his electronic studies in sound-colour and silence-duration to acoustic instruments, and he started to write for more traditional ensembles. Everything he saw, heard or in any way experienced – however trivial – was assimilated into a continuous production system in which events were meticulously annotated, logged and transcribed into music. In 1977, with the announcement of *Licht*, he began to channel every new creation, electronic and acoustic, into the enormous operatic project. Everything written since then has been incorporated into the cycle: when he was commissioned to write a work to celebrate the 800th anniversary of Saint Francis of Assisi's birth, for example, the new piece became the final scene of *Samstag*.

Licht

Light

Commenced in 1977, *Licht* will be completed by *Sonntag aus Licht*, which is planned for completion in 2002, by which time Stockhausen hopes to have built his own "Bayreuth" for the staging of the entire twenty-hour cycle. Comparisons between Stockhausen and Wagner are unavoidable. *Licht* is the grandest operatic project since the *Ring*, and like the *Ring* it is a huge metaphysical epic of which each component, though capable of standing as an independent work, will only reveal its full significance when experienced in the context of the other parts. All the cycle's seemingly disparate threads will be united in *Sonntag*, a *Götterdämmerung*-like apotheosis worthy of the new millennium.

Though the mythological and religious references of *Licht* are highly complicated, the underlying concern is simple: *Licht* is a parable of unification, of the struggles between the material and the spiritual. Central to the entire cycle are the Archangel Michael (humanity's protector), Eva (an Erda-like mother figure and the universal teacher) and Lucifer (humanity's challenger, a "brilliant, intuitive, extremely progressive" extremist of the intellect), each of whom is represented by a variety of characters, instruments and ensembles. Musically, *Licht* is phenomenally complex, but at the heart of all the parts is a series of three-note "formulas" somewhat like leitmotifs. Associated with characters and their defining instruments – Michael is linked to a trumpet, Lucifer to a trombone, Eva to a flute – these formulas constitute an armature around which Stockhausen accumulates a plethora of different instrumental textures. Sometimes the formulas emerge in stark, brief phrases, and on other occasions they generate entire sections of a score, as in "Lucifer's Dream" (*Samstag*), in which the harmonies of the formula are echoed and examined until an entirely new passage of music is created. *Licht* is nobody's idea of an easy ride: some of the operas are very long and slow-moving; the frequent recourse to onomatopoeic chanting can become trying; and you shouldn't expect the action to make immediate sense (the synopses make parts of *Licht* sound like retro-hippy rambling). But it's a unique adventure in sound, and the summation of the career of postwar Europe's riskiest musical intellect.

Discussed below are the days from *Licht* that are available on CD. In 1996 a fifth instalment, *Freitag aus Licht*, was premiered in Leipzig to generally unecstatic reviews; it has yet to be released on disc. All Stockhausen CDs – along with signed copies of books by and about Stockhausen, and posters from each of the premiere productions – are available from Stockhausen-Verlag, Kettenberg 15, 51515 Kürten, Germany. Very few record stores stock the recordings.

Montag aus Licht

Monday from Light

Composed 1984–88.
First performed May 7, 1988.
Libretto by the composer.

Synopsis

Act I

Monday is Woman's Day, a celebration of Birth. The opera opens with the "Nine Months of Pregnancy", which is followed by the birth of fourteen children, seven of whom are born with animal heads, and seven with grey hair. Three "Eva" sopranos give thanks in a birth aria. Lucifer is furious and condemns the children.

Act II

A second birth must take place, and Eva is fertilized by a piano piece played by a budgerigar-boy. When the new children are born, the women wash and dress them. One of them begins to teach the children to sing, leading them from single syllables to more complicated, extended patterns. Men arrive and attempt to contact the Lady of the Heart (a form of Eva), who is playing a basset horn. The women enter from all over the stage and tell the men that a stranger has arrived.

Act III

The women then flee to fetch the Children Catcher, who, like the Pied Piper, is a flautist. After a duet with the basset horn, he turns towards the children and bewitches them with his playing. The basset horn player withdraws into a figure of the Lady of the Heart, the men and women begin to leave and the Children Catcher flies off with the boys and girls, whose voices are transformed into birdsong.

According to the composer, *Montag* is Eva's day, which is why the piece "is characterized principally by female voices". Wanting to pay homage to "women as creators", Stockhausen presents an image of "Mother Earth surrounded by her flock" – an analogy that was reinforced at the premiere through the dominant use of green lighting, sets and costumes. *Montag* is one of the richest of the operas in terms of its range of expression: the libretto features a bizarre array of phonetics and verbal trickery, and the piece calls for a large chorus, more than twenty on-stage musicians, various choirs and smaller instrumental ensembles, and a huge panoply of electronic sounds. The music for *Montag* is among the most accessible so far written for *Licht*. It is at times as close to being traditionally harmonious as Stockhausen ever gets, and the sparkling use of instrumental textures to enhance the depiction of Nature marks a fascinating departure from his normal abstraction. At the end, for example, when the children's voices are transformed into birdsong, Stockhausen translates the mountains, shrubs, trees, flowers and streams into music of luminous beauty.

Meriweather, Isherwood, Clemens, Pike; Chorus of the Westdeutscher Rundfunk; Orchestra; Stockhausen.
(Stockhausen Verlag CD 36; 5 CDs).

Julian Pike and Helmut Clemens, accompanying Stockhausen regulars Annette Meriweather and Nicholas Isherwood, cope superbly with the taxing vocal parts and the electronics are truly magnificent. The final scene is definitely one for the repeat button. No recording can do justice to a work as visual as *Montag*, but the superb accompanying booklet comes complete with many stills from the production.

Dienstag aus Licht

Tuesday from Light

Composed 1977–91.
First performed May 10, 1992.
Libretto by the composer.

Synopsis

Act I

Dienstag is a spiritual battle between Michael and Lucifer, who is attempting to stop time. Eva can see the future and calls for peace, but Michael and Lucifer taunt each other, then agree to a more testing combat.

Act II

Two invasions by aircraft ensue, and three musical defences bring down the planes. Meanwhile, two instrumental armies chase each other about the stage and the auditorium. The Lucifer troupe cut into a huge wall and reveal a bank of glistening crystal. A piercing scream brings everything to a halt and a white flag appears from inside the crystal bank. It opens to reveal a nurse made of glass, accompanied by two other glass beings. Michael is killed but performs a haunting duet "Pietà" with Eva. A third invasion begins and Lucifer's army reaches the crystal bank, which gradually disintegrates as three explosions bring the crystal crashing down. The army disappears beneath the earth, the chorus return and the Synthi-Fou plays a comically virtuoso solo, which slowly winds down the opera.

Dienstag is one of the most exciting works of music-theatre written since the war. The Prologue begins, as one might expect of a passage entitled "Mars' Day", with a fanfare: played by nine tremolo trumpets above nine roaring, snarling trombones, it is almost as noisy as the war it is supposed to preface. There follows cacophony, then out of the crashing and thundering emerges the soprano voice of Eva, calling for calm and reason. The first act, titled "Jahreslauf" (The Course of the Years), was originally written for a Japanese royal wind and percussion ensemble in Tokyo, and Stockhausen's re-scoring of it for western instruments and electronics is remarkable, not least for the sense of humour that colours this weird war-game.

The real battle begins in Act II, subtitled "Invasion-Explosion with Farewell". Using multi-directional speakers placed around the hall (a Stockhausen invention he calls "Octophonie"), Stockhausen creates an extraordinary battle through music, imitating the sounds of planes swooping and diving about the hall. In performance Michael and Lucifer's respective armies of musicians invade the auditorium, firing off salvos of music at each other. The effect is at once thrilling and funny – especially the "zombie", a synthesizer toting maniac with speakers on his shoulders.

After all the lunacy, however, Stockhausen brings the audience back down to earth in the "Pietà", a funereal lament for braying flugelhorn and soprano which becomes more and more muted until the Synthi-Fou, sitting behind a huge bank of synthesizers, brings the opera to an end with a luscious, colouristic pastiche of virtuoso keyboard technique. A remarkable, kaleidoscopic work, and probably the finest of the *Licht* operas so far completed.

Meriweather, Pike, Isherwood; Leipzig Choral Ensemble; Orchestra; Stockhausen.
(Stockhausen Verlag CD 40; 2 CDs).

This recording goes as far as is humanly possible to capture the atmosphere of the performance. The Octophonic effects are inevitably muted on an ordinary two-speaker system (it works wonderfully in surround sound) but the battle sequences are tremendous and Annette Meriweather as Eva and Julius Pike and Nicholas Isherwood as the warring eternals are superb. Thrilling stuff.

Donnerstag aus Licht

Thursday from Light

Composed 1978–80.
First performed March 15, 1981.
Libretto by the composer.

Synopsis

Act I

Michael arrives on Earth and is taught by his parents the ways of mankind, in order to understand human suffering. He meets Mondeva, another astral visitor and, having passed a music exam, sets off on a voyage of musical discovery around the world.

Act II

The world appears as a huge globe on the stage. Michael emerges from different continents. In Africa he joins Mondeva, and the couple are reunited.

Act III

Michael and Eva meet when he returns to the stars. She showers him with gifts and they sing a hymn together, but are interrupted by the arrival of Lucifer, whom Michael is forced to conquer in a spectacular Dragon Fight. A vision, recapping the main events of the opera, is revealed to Michael.

𝄞 *Donnerstag* is the day in which kindness and charity, as the product of learning, experience and wisdom, are seen in the ascendant. The opera begins, in live performance at least, in the foyer of the theatre, where a hypnotic instrumental prelude is played as a "musical arch" through which the audience walk when entering the auditorium. Building on this material, the opera unfolds as a series of mini-scenes through which Michael is seen to learn, among other things, the mysteries of language, the pleasures of physical love, the deceptions of humanity, and the brevity of life. The relationship between the prepared tape and the fourteen live performers (three voices, eight instruments and three dancers) carries the listener through a uniquely mystical environment, immersed in a sound-world that has no precedent outside the work of Stockhausen. For example, the trumpet part for Michael requires the performer (originally the composer's son Markus) to apply a series of electronic filters and mutes to his instrument, creating an ever-changing spectrum of real and electronic sounds. Act II's "Terrestrial Pilgrimage" contains some intoxicating music – nearly an hour long, it accompanies Michael's journey with passages of music in keeping with the character of the regions from which he emerges. The ensuing love duet between Michael and Eva (this time playing a basset horn) is one of the most delightful and witty passages in all twentieth-century opera.

A masterly approach to what Stockhausen calls "composing the spaces" (ie writing music to be played in different parts of the auditorium) adds to the magnificence of the opera's scope. Nowhere more so than during the opera's coda, when trumpeters sitting near the roof of the theatre play out the Michael "formula" in all its unadorned glory.

Gambill, Angel, Sperry, Meriweather, Stockhausen; Rundfunkchor and Rundfunkorchester Hilversum; Ensemble InterContemporain; Eötvös, Stockhausen. (Stockhausen Verlag CD 30; 4 CDs).

Donnerstag is a dense, intricate score demanding, and here receiving, total commitment from its performers. Two of Stockhausen's children and the clarinettist Suzanne Stephens give astonishing performances of the composer's fiendish instrumental parts. The recording captures the live experience in perfect sound and the booklet, while unnecessarily complicated, should help explain much of the more obscure detail.

Samstag aus Licht

Saturday from Light

Composed 1981–84.
First performed May 25, 1984.
Libretto by the composer.

Synopsis

Scene I

Lucifer is asleep and dreams up a piece of music which tells of his desire to destroy time. But he finds it impossible not to let his performance be overcome by the beauty of Eva's theme of rebirth, and is so moved by it that he dies.

Scene II

He is mourned by Kathinka, a cat, who plays music for his spirit. Death does not last for long, however. Lucifer comes back to life exultantly, dancing around the on-stage band, which is tiered up on stage in the shape of a face.

Scene III

When Michael arrives, dressed for battle, Lucifer and Kathinka deride him and continue with their dance. Suddenly, the instrumental accompaniment begins to drop out: the musicians were only paid to play for a certain time and will not be persuaded to continue. Despite the rage of the conductor and a theatre official, order cannot be regained and chaos ends the scene.

Scene IV

The final scene is a setting of text by Saint Francis of Assisi, in which monks carry out the ritual acts of setting a bird free and breaking coconuts in front of the church.

𝄞 *Samstag* is the most personal of the days so far completed. Its main theme is death, fusing a close study of the Tibetan Book of the Dead with Stockhausen's own encounters with mortality as a child during the war. As you might expect from an opera that's so close to the bone, Stockhausen's musical language in *Samstag* is much less complicated than in the other operas, in that the ideas are not buried beneath waves of contrapuntal texture as they so often are elsewhere. However, while the musical ideas may be less difficult to absorb, they are jarringly unorthodox, incorporating microtonal inflections, yelping and screaming, as well as the real and imitated sounds of Nature – as occurs during the introduction, in which widely spaced brass choirs throw out an almost primeval fanfare. Against these pagan explosions are contrasted the most intimate piano solos and extended lines of instrumental music, and such oppositions are a feature of the whole piece. For example, in the second scene the solo flute of Kathinka the cat provides a mischievous counterpoint to the confrontational "Lucifer's Dance", a wild and thrilling passage for symphonic wind-band (which has been performed with great success in concert) lined up in ten groups of six on stage. "Lucifer's Dance" is the highlight of the entire *Licht* cycle to date, and the inclusion of an orchestral strike, with the players abandoning the show midway through, is one of the wittiest musical jokes since Haydn's *Surprise* symphony.

Hölle; University of Michigan Symphony Band; Stockhausen.
(Stockhausen Verlag 34; 4 CDs).

This is another extremely impressive recording of what is unquestionably very difficult music to perform. The baritone Mathias Hölle – the only vocal soloist – perfectly masters his exceptionally taxing role and the solo instrumental turns (especially Kathinka's flute solo) are magically brought off. The electronic music is ravishingly recorded, as is par for the course with Stockhausen's CDs.

GYÖRGY LIGETI

b. TIRNAVENI, ROMANIA, MAY 28, 1923.

Ligeti's life has been a series of exiles. He was born in Transylvania just as Hungary was about to lose that region to Romania, and left Hungary permanently in 1956 after the Soviet Union crushed the uprising there. Since then he has lived in Hamburg and Vienna, becoming an Austrian citizen in 1967. His work reflects this rootlessness – it is difficult to classify his music, as he's a composer who changes his style from piece to piece. His Hungarian years reveal the prevailing influence of Bartók and an almost complete ignorance of contemporary music outside of Eastern Europe. On arriving in Germany he submerged himself in the experiments of the avant-garde and for a time wrote electronic music at the WDR studios in Cologne. But despite this new experimental approach and his admiration of Stockhausen, he never conformed to any modernist dogmas and much of his music is informed by a neo-Dadaist sense of the ridiculous.

Ligeti's electronic work led him to conceive musical sound in a new way, a way that he continued in his non-electronic pieces. His is a highly abstract sound-world that simultaneously achieves a kind of monumental stasis and a sense of agitation by the use of great washes of contrasted sound made up of a dense web of swirling lines. This penchant for clashing clusters of instruments and the babble of opposed languages links both to the multiculturalism of his native land and to his wanderings. It can be heard most famously in *Lux Aeterna* (1965), a piece for unaccompanied voices which was used to great effect in Stanley Kubrick's film *2001: A Space Odyssey* – as was a superb Ligeti orchestral piece called *Atmospheres*. There is often a superficial resemblance between Ligeti and the music of the American Minimalists, but Ligeti's Central European background comes through in a variety of ways: a feeling of loss and nostalgia characterizes much of his output, often evoked by use of the strangely haunting five-

György Ligeti

note scale and half-tones of Transylvanian folk music. Equally important is Ligeti's absurdist humour, apparent in works such as his *Poème Symphonique* (1962), in which one hundred metronomes set at different speeds gradually wind down from their babble of tick-tocking to a single regular beat.

Ligeti's dark humour is the dominant element in his theatrical works, which consist of two short music-theatre pieces, *Aventures* and *Nouvelles aventures*, and an opera, *Le Grand Macabre*. *Aventures* and *Nouvelles aventures* were originally conceived as two independent concert works but were revised for staging in 1966. Littered with protracted silences during which both performers and audience are directed to remain absolutely still, both *Aventures* have "meaningless" texts made up of phonemes and fragments of words. The cast are instructed to sing down cardboard tubes while the percussion section have to burst paper bags, rub suitcases with sandpaper and scrape their feet against the floor. The result is both witty and sinister, seeming constantly to teeter on the brink of making sense. Ligeti's only opera began as a commission from Göran Gentele of the Stockholm Royal Opera in 1965. For several years he worked on a comic-strip version of *Oedipus* with Gentele as librettist, but abandoned it after Gentele's death. The replacement source-text, Michel de Ghelderode's play *La balade du grand macabre*, was suggested to Ligeti by the opera's eventual designer. The work's great success across Europe has not prompted the composer to attempt another opera, although there have been periodic rumours of proposed settings of Lewis Carroll's *Alice* books as well as of Shakespeare's *The Tempest*.

Le Grand Macabre

Composed 1974–77.
First performed April 12, 1978.
Libretto by Michael Meschke and the composer after Michel de Ghelderode.

Synopsis

Act I

In Breughelland, Piet the Pot sings in praise of his homeland. He is joined by Miranda and Amando, a couple in search of non-stop lovemaking. Nekrotzar the "Grand Macabre" announces his plan to destroy the world. He forces Piet to assist him. The astronomer Astradamors is making love to his wife Mescalina. While he gazes through his telescope, his wife implores Venus to send her a good lover. Nekrotzar appears and kills her with his violent love-making. Nekrotzar, Piet and Astradamors depart for the palace of Prince Go-Go.

Act II
At the palace of the young prince the politicians are arguing. The Chief of the Secret Police enters to warn of an impending catastrophe. Nekrotzar and his retinue arrive, causing panic. Piet and Astradamors embark on a drinking bout and try to get Nekrotzar drunk. Nekrotzar speaks the words which will end the world, then collapses. All the characters, alive, dead or merely very hung-over, slowly reappear. None knows quite whether the world has ended or not. Mescalina reappears and chases Nekrotzar. The two lovers from Act I also arrive, and their happiness becomes the prevailing mood of the assembled company – except for the deflated despot Nekrotzar, who melts away into nothingness.

Having abandoned *Oedipus*, Ligeti was still attracted to the idea of a comic-strip opera, one that was garish and direct with no aspirations to any psychological depth. The nightmare visions of painters such as Bosch and Pieter Breughel the Elder were an inspiration to Ligeti and so Ghelderode's play appealed to him both for its fantasy landscape and for having Death as the hero. Ligeti was less enthusiastic about its poetic language, however, and asked Michel Meschke (the opera's producer) to "Jarry-fy" it, that is to give it the absurdity and viciousness of the work of Alfred Jarry. The opera also functions as a kind of critique of 1960s hedonism, with its drug-named characters and the sexual preoccupation of its lovers (originally called Clitoria and Spermando) and Mescalina. Through the licentious world of Breughelland stalks the tyrannical but comical figure of Nekrotzar, "Le Grand Macabre" himself. The fact that Death doesn't triumph at the end cannot be taken to mean that Ligeti advocates the pursuit of pleasure as the overriding goal of life; indeed, he has written: "Life utterly devoid of fear, life devoted entirely to pleasure, is in fact profoundly sad." There is little reassurance in this opera's conclusion: "No-one knows when his hour will fall. And when it comes, then let it be . . . Farewell, till then, live merrily!"

Ligeti's score for *Le Grand Macabre* is suitably polymorphous. To emphasize the piece's irrationality, there is no consistent musical idiom, instead the music darts around all over the place, encompassing the shimmering orchestral textures which one associates with Ligeti's concert pieces, through moments of clamorous Expressionism, by way of parodies of and quotations from other works. Ligeti was trying to get away from the grandiloquent gestures of traditional opera: ". . . the dramatic action and the music should be riskily bizarre, totally exaggerated, totally crazy. The novelty of this form of musical theatre should be made manifest . . . in the inner quality of the music. The musical texture should not be symphonic. The musical and dramatic conception should be far removed from the territory of Wagner, Strauss and Berg." To establish a mock-heroic mood, the opera opens with a palindromic fanfare of car horns, before Piet the Pot enters singing the "Dies irae". The most lyrical passages in the opera are in the music given to the two lovers (both sung by sopranos), which resembles the most sensuous moments of Monteverdi's *Poppea* carried to absurd extremes of ecstatic ornamentation. Nekrotzar's entrance in Act II is accompanied by an orchestral interlude which is based on the finale of Beethoven's *Eroica Symphony*. Such use of allusion is incorporated into the fabric of the work in a way that Ligeti himself has compared to the use of "borrowed" material in Pop Art. Irony and knowingness are all, but *Le Grand Macabre* also possesses an exuberant energy and naiveté that ultimately makes it more enjoyable than comparable works like Zimmermann's *Die Soldaten* or Schnittke's *Life with an Idiot*.

Davies, Walmsley-Clarke, Fredricks, Smith; Austrian Radio Chorus and Symphony Orchestra; Howarth.
(Wergo WER 6170-2; 2 CDs).

Elgar Howarth, who conducted the first production, has made Ligeti's opera something of a personal crusade, having conducted most of its major European premieres since the first in 1978. With Eirian Davies dominating the cast in the dual roles of Chief of the Secret Police and Venus, the work's myriad colours and characters are brought to life with infectious enthusiasm. The Austrian forces are more than up to the extreme technical and expressive challenges, and they and the cast are captured in vital well-spaced sound.

KRZYSZTOF PENDERECKI

b. DEBICA, POLAND, NOVEMBER 23, 1933.

Penderecki first made his mark as a violinist, performing Vivaldi in public at the age of fourteen, and for a time he considered a career as a violin virtuoso. Having decided to devote his attention to composing while a student at Kraków Academy, in 1959 he won the first and the two second prizes in the composers' competition of the Polish Composers' Union, whose judges included Lutosławski. His early work was relatively avant-garde, but like his nearly exact contemporary Henryk Gorecki he soon tempered avant-gardism with elements of traditional styles, both archaic and romantic (albeit with different results). In much of his work since the 1970s, the romanticism has almost obliterated the innovation.

The voice has always been his first instrument, often at the service of his Christian beliefs, which have also been marked by political liberalism – his 1984 *Requiem* includes a movement written for the unveiling of a Solidarity monument. It was a piece of vocal music that marked Penderecki's arrival on the international scene – his *St Luke Passion* (1966), commissioned to celebrate the seven-hundredth anniversary of Munster Cathedral, received more than fifty performances within four years of its premiere. Since then he has written four operas: *Die Teufel von Loudun* (1969), *Paradise Lost* (1978), *Die Schwarze Maske* (The Black Mask; 1986), and *Ubu Rex* (1991). In their different ways, each of his stage works is a personal confrontation with tyranny, intolerance, fanaticism and death, and his expressive style makes formidable demands on his singers, who may be called on to spit and scream in addition to the more customary duties of the opera singer. Such vocal extremities, allied to the rubbing, tapping, squawking, and extensive use of glissandi and vibrato which he calls for from his instruments, contributes greatly to the power of his work, which has found comparatively large audiences around the world.

Die Teufel von Loudun

The Devils of Loudun

Composed 1968–69; revised 1972.
First performed June 20, 1969.
Libretto by Penderecki, based on Erich Fried's translation of John Whiting's dramatization of Aldous Huxley's book.

Synopsis

Act I

Jeanne, prioress of an Ursuline convent, is gripped by erotic obsession with Father Grandier, and has a vision of him in a heretic's shirt, his legs broken, a rope around his neck. She sings "The blood that will flow between us will make us one", but in a further vision sees Grandier in the arms of a young widow. Jeanne goes to Grandier's church, but when the priest enters, she screams and flees. Later she admits her obsession to Father Mignon. Meanwhile Adam and Mannoury plot to indict Grandier, and Jeanne's confession to Mignon becomes a useful weapon. Mignon sends for Barré, an exorcist. In the grip of the exorcism, Jeanne, in a man's voice, names the object of her obsession: "Grandier!"

Act II

The exorcism proceeds, culminating with an enema. The plot against Grandier gathers momentum, although the priest pleads that he has never seen Jeanne. Jeanne now alleges that Grandier forced her and her nuns to participate in a Black Mass, and the exorcism recommences, this time in public, in Grandier's church. Jeanne speaks in voices. Grandier enters, and is arrested by the king's special messenger.

Act III

Grandier is to be executed: he has been found guilty of being in league with the Devil, of debauchery and of blasphemy. He maintains his innocence. Jeanne plans suicide, but her nuns prevent her. Grandier is publicly tortured and his failure to confess taken as proof of a diabolical pact. As in Jeanne's initial vision, he is taken to the stake. While the flames engulf him, Jeanne is seen in silent prayer.

So great was the interest in Penderecki's new opera that it opened in two productions (Hamburg and Stuttgart) within the space of 48 hours, and an American production was mounted two months later. The combination of sexual and religious obsession is good box office, of course, but Penderecki's opera – which is based on the same source as Ken Russell's film *The Devils* – is no mere pot-boiler. The composer's libretto is meticulously constructed, breaking the action down to thirty short scenes which proceed from one to the next almost cinematically. Indeed, at the beginning of Act III there is a kind of split-screen effect, with action taking place simultaneously in three sections of the stage.

Penderecki has written much music for film and theatre, which no doubt taught him about shaping music to illustrate dramatic events, but there is nothing "incidental" about his music for *Die Teufel*, an opera which requires its protagonists to exert every vocal resource to match the emotional pitch of the orchestra. It is a huge orchestra, including four saxes, electric bass guitar, piano, organ, harmonium and tape, but for the most part Penderecki skilfully uses only small groups at any one time, generating a broad range of instrumental colour with no loss of power.

In fashioning his libretto, Penderecki stripped away much of the matter of John Whiting's play. If this leaves some of the political detail obscure, it clears a space for the ghastly trials visited on Jeanne and Grandier by their sexuality and by the doctrinal absolutism of their persecutors. This makes for a deeply pessimistic opera, one that would seem to compromise Penderecki's Christian faith. Perhaps he wrote the work precisely in order to test his belief; or perhaps he wrote it simply because he knew it would make a profound and serious opera.

Troyanos, Hiolsky, Ldaysz, Sotin; Hamburg State Opera Chorus and Orchestra; Janowski.
(Philips 446 328-2; 2 CDs).

Recorded shortly after the opera's Hamburg premiere, this presents virtually the same cast as those performances, but with Marek Janowski conducting, rather than Henryk Czyz. It is a powerful recording, made exceptional by the fine performance of Tatiana Troyanos as Jeanne. Troyanos is remembered mostly for her bel canto roles, but here she portrays sexual dementia with a ferocious intensity.

ALFRED SCHNITTKE

b. ENGELS, RUSSIA, NOVEMBER 24, 1934.

Schnittke's ethnic background set him apart from the start: his mother was a Volga-German, his father German-Jewish, and he spoke German as his first language. Until his emigration to Germany he remained something of an outsider in Russian society but became Russia's most celebrated contemporary composer, producing a vast number of diverse works that are characterized by irony and wild pastiche, with occasional excursions into the spiritual. His stance is typified by *Life with an Idiot*, an operatic requiem for the Soviet Union, and one of the most provocative, idiosyncratic and lewd scores of the last few years.

Schnittke's most distinctive works didn't appear until the 1970s, with the extraordinarily anarchic *Symphony No. 1* marking a turning point. Juxtaposing elements of Baroque, classical, Romantic, contemporary and popular music, it epitomizes Schnittke's "polystylistic" approach, in which snatches of Vivaldi might be followed by a dissonant tango or a popular song spiced with outbursts of atonal writing. For a composer whose work is often powerfully dramatic, it's odd that Schnittke came to opera so late in life: *Life with an Idiot*, his eagerly awaited first opera, was premiered in Amsterdam in 1992 and has been swiftly followed by *Gesualdo*, the Vienna State Opera's first new commission for over twenty years, and *Historia von D. Johann Fausten*, first performed at the Hamburg Opera in 1995.

Gesualdo is a spare and transparent piece, avoiding the large-scale gestures of many of Schnittke's scores, being introduced and concluded by five singers a cappella. Its seven scenes relate the betrothal and marriage of the Italian madrigalist to his beautiful cousin Donna Maria, her indifference to her husband's music, the seduction by her lover Don Fabricio and Gesualdo's murder of them after trapping them in flagrante delicto. In the final scene Gesualdo kills the child of his marriage, fearing it might not be his own. Schnittke's music is postmodern sixteenth-century pastiche, with organ, mandolin and theorbo giving a period flavour alongside the contemporary colouring of vibraphone and marimba. The vocal writing, though, is disappointingly monotonous, especially given the harmonic surprises and power of Gesualdo's own music – the score only takes off in the moments when Schnittke draws heavily on his subject's work.

Fifteen years in the writing, *Faust* bypasses Goethe and Marlowe, the preferred models for the other operatic settings, and goes back to the earliest version of the story published by Johann Spies in 1587, cataloguing Faust's sorcery and devilish transgressions. But despite this historical placing, Schnittke portrays Faust as a universal figure and throws quotes from Wagner and Shostakovich, plus some wild tango into his usual allusive mix. His vast orchestra includes saxophones, bass guitar and two synthesizers, plus marimba, vibes, krummhorn, lute and zither. Regrettably, however, the score is pretty leaden until it gets to Act III, which Schnittke composed back in 1983 – and which, as the *Faust Cantata*, has been recognized as one of his masterworks. Suddenly here is Schnittke at his blood-curdling, iconoclastic best, and the contrast with the rest of the opera reveals how far his powers have declined in the interim. The only things going for the 1996 recording of the complete opera (on BMG) is that the *Faust Cantata* is at last heard in its proper context, and that the performance of it is by far the best on disc, with its feverishly raunchy tango sung by a wild chorus of demons and the glorious Mephistophelia (a female Mephistopheles) of Hannah Schwartz. This episode, wrote the *New York Times* at the opera's premiere, "achieves a hurtling dramatic momentum that has not been seen in German opera since the death of Berg".

Life with an Idiot

Composed 1991–92.
First performed April 13, 1992.
Libretto by Victor Erofeyev.

Synopsis

Act I

There are three main characters: I, Wife and Vova. For some unspecified misdemeanour I has to take an Idiot into his apartment. He chooses Vova (a Lenin lookalike), who only utters the word "Ekh". The story of how I selected Vova is intercut with a premonition of what is to come. Vova cuts off the Wife's head with giant secateurs. "He was enchantingly bald" sing the chorus, "And the prominent forehead of the polemicist was lit up by a burning dream!"

Act II

Vova begins to wreck the lives of I and his Wife (who has survived her decapitation). He eats all the food, tears up books, shits on the floor, pisses in the fridge and rapes the Wife. Then the Wife falls in love with Vova and gets pregnant. She has an abortion, then Vova and I have a homosexual affair and beat up the Wife. Finally she demands Vova choose between her and I. Vova decapitates her with secateurs, puts her body down the rubbish chute and disappears.

𝄞 The librettist of this opera, Victor Erofeyev, lost his job at a literary institute and was expelled from the Writers' Union for his unofficial writings in 1979. It wasn't until Gorbachev's *glasnost* that Erofeyev was rehabilitated and his writings, including *Life with an Idiot*, were published in 1990. Schnittke heard the author read the story and conceived the idea of a satirical opera in the tradition of Shostakovich's *The Nose* (see p.471). Schnittke's friend and long-term champion, the cellist and conductor Mstislav Rostropovich, secured the commission for the Netherlands Opera and fired the composer into writing it. The whole team responsible for that premiere production had been persecuted by the Soviets: Erofeyev, Schnittke, the artist and designer Ilya Kabakov, director Boris Pokrovsky and Rostropovich. And thus it's hardly surprising that the overall impression created by this obscure allegory is of a group of former dissidents having a massive binge on all the taboos of Soviet life – sex, wife-beating, homosexuality and murder.

The above synopsis is misleadingly clear, for the fragmented narrative is told simultaneously from different perspectives and jumps around in time. The music is similarly difficult: its strengths lie in the choral writing (often allied to bells and brass, which gives it a real Russian feel) and in the parodic episodes, such as the splendid tango that emerges from the lurid premonition of the Wife's decapitation, or the appearance at the end of the Russian folksong "A Birch was Standing in a Field" (familiar from Tchaikovsky's *Fourth Symphony*), chanted as a ravaged echo of a lost world while Vova and the Wife grunt the monosyllable "Ekh!"

The writers see in the work more than a brutal and ribald comment on the collapse of an ideology in Russia. For Erofeyev, the idiot Vova is a permanent part of the human condition and Schnittke has always been interested in the juxtaposition of opposites and what he calls the profundity of the banal."*Life with an Idiot*", he says, "is about something which is totally absurd but at the same time totally serious and also naive. The simultaneous interaction of two entities – seriousness and frivolity – seems to me to be extremely important." The sense of desolation and futility at the end of the opera is powerful, but ultimately the work is a curiosity – like those Russian dolls depicting Soviet leaders nesting inside each other from Lenin to Yeltsin. It is a cartoon opera, and a fairly crude one at that, which can only be seen as a response to the collapse of communism. But all too often opera deals with mythical characters and remote events, and Schnittke and his collaborators should be congratulated on producing something that is an immediate and challenging response to a decisive moment in history.

Duesing, Ringholz; Rotterdam Philharmonic; Rostropovich.
(Sony S2K 52 495; 2 CDs).

This is a score better experienced on stage than on disc, but this recording is as good as they come. The soloists cope admirably with the demands of the music and Howard Haskin (Vova) gets all sorts of expressive variations into his one word, "Ekh!". Rostropovich has his moments to shine as soloist as well as conductor – on the piano in the Act I tango and the cello in the Act II intermezzo. There is a comprehensive libretto to help make sense of it all.

AULIS SALLINEN

b. SALMI, FINLAND, APRIL 9, 1935.

Opera is a relatively recent phenomenon in Finland. Sibelius, the country's greatest composer, wrote just one, short work, *The Maiden in the Tower* (1896), which he later withdrew, while the outstanding prewar Finnish opera, Merikanto's *Juha* (1922), was rejected by Helsinki Opera and not staged until 1958. In more recent years, however, there has been a huge upsurge of activity, and currently Finland has one of the most active and healthy operatic scenes in the world. Of all the present generation of opera composers, none has been more successful both at home and abroad than Aulis Sallinen. His style is markedly tonal and not especially original – the influence of Bartók, Britten and Shostakovich is discernible – but each of his five, very different, operas reveals real dramatic flair, and a brilliant capacity to create atmosphere through the accumulation of detail and clever orchestration.

Sallinen studied composition at the Sibelius Academy in Helsinki with Merikanto and Jonas Kokkonen. His early work, atonal and serialist, was superseded by an increasingly lyrical and descriptive musical language that owes much to Sibelius and to the equally pervasive influence of the bleak northern landscape. In the 1960s he worked for Finnish radio and between 1963 and 1976 taught at the Sibelius Academy. His first opera, *Ratsumies* (The Horseman; 1975), a commission from the prestigious Savonlinna Festival, is an epic exploration of national identity, with a husband and wife, Antti and Anna, symbolizing Finland's plight between the empire of Sweden and that of Russia. It's a dark work of rather overloaded symbolism but it was enormously successful and led the Finnish National Opera to commission another opera. Where *Ratsumies* is dreamlike and symbolist, *Punainen viiva* (The Red Line) is down-to-earth and realist, with a tighter dramatic structure and a correspondingly economic score. It is generally regarded as Sallinen's best opera to date, and following its premiere in 1978 Sallinen started to acquire a reputation abroad – to the extent that his next opera was a joint commission between the Savonlinna Festival, the Royal Opera House in London and the BBC. *Kuningas lahtee Ranskaan* (The King Goes Forth to France; 1984) is a continuation of Sallinen's rather jaundiced view of politics but this time in the form of a grim but comic fantasy. Set in a future ice age, the opera plots the deterioration of the King from idealist to megalomaniac and shows man's capacity for self-destruction through endless cycles of violence.

Asked to write an opera for the opening of a new opera house in Helsinki, Sallinen turned to Finland's great national epic, the *Kalevala*, specifically the episodes dealing with the tragic hero Kullervo who, Oedipus-like, brings death and destruction into his own family before killing himself in an attempt to expiate his guilt as his sister's seducer. In *Kullervo* (1988) Sallinen employs an even leaner and more precise musical language than before. The opera is comparable to Peter Maxwell Davies's near contemporary *Resurrection* in the way it blends violence and parody with a dash of sardonic humour (see p.560). As in *Resurrection* the monster that is spawned at the opera's end is clearly the product of the violence at the heart of society, although arguably Sallinen's vision is a more compassionate one than that of Maxwell Davies. Sallinen's latest opera, *The Palace*, was premiered at the Savonlinna Festival in 1995.

The Red Line

Composed 1977–78.
First performed November 30, 1978.
Libretto by the composer, after Ilmari Kianto.

Synopsis

Act I

In northern Finland a poor peasant family desperately struggle for survival. The crofter Topi, the head of the family, finds a sheep that has been killed by a bear, which he swears to kill. He dreams that he applies for poor relief to the local priest who instead offers a good deal on burying his three children. A pedlar from Russia tells of social unrest there, and Topi and his wife Riika attend a political meeting where a demagogue encourages the villagers to draw a red line on their voting slip in order for things to change.

Act II

Topi and his neighbours do not know how to register their vote. They hear the dogs barking – it is the bear awaking from its hibernation. When election day comes they all go off to vote, despite being told of the trouble it will cause. When Topi leaves to earn money logging, Riika waits for the promised changes to occur but instead sees her children die from malnutrition. Topi arrives home in time to bury them. News reaches the couple that the election has been won. Topi hears the sound of the dogs barking and the noise of his solitary cow – the bear has awoken and kills the cow. Topi goes out to fight with it, and later Riika finds her husband's body with a red line indicating his slit throat.

The Red Line is based on a classic Finnish novel by Ilmari Kianto, who specialized in highly critical and realistic depictions of rural poverty that explored the nature of the Finnish psyche. Published in 1909, it is set two years earlier, at the time of the first elections in which women were allowed to vote – this was in the wake of the Russo-Japanese war, when Russia's hold on Finland was severely weakened. The bare bones of the story suggest something unremittingly grim, but in fact neither opera nor novel is depressing – rather the peasant characters that inhabit them exhibit a dogged single-mindedness that borders on the heroic. The villains are those in authority: insensitive priests, and most damningly, an insinuating and complacent politician who effectively stirs up the people's feelings but is not around when the promised changes fail to materialize.

Sallinen's main achievement as a musical dramatist is in conveying, without a hint of condescension, the hardness of his characters' lives, their vulnerability and their hope for better times. Over and again there is an emphasis on just how debilitating poverty is, both to day-to-day life and to relationships – the inability to find food for their children leads to poignantly embittered exchanges between Topi and his wife Riika in the opera's early scenes. Topi is a rugged and inarticulate man who feels a sense of failure and angry frustration at being unable to support his family. His struggle with the marauding bear (on one level a symbol of the ever-present threat of Russia) represents the perennial problems that the rhetoric of politicians fails to address.

Both dramatically and musically, *The Red Line* is Sallinen's best work. Musically conservative he may be, but the way he finds just the right idiom or colouration to create character and to denote a change of mood is brilliantly theatrical and shows a composer in complete control of what he is doing. In one of the opera's most effective scenes, when the peasants assemble to hear what the political agitator has to say, Sallinen underlines both the man's attractiveness and his lack of substance by a clarinet tune that is oleaginous and oddly elusive. His oratory builds until it culminates in a crudely energetic but appealing revolutionary march, the emptiness of which is underlined by the searing intensity of the march in Act II, which accompanies the burial of Topi and Riika's children. Other telling touches include the off-stage chorus and brass used to denote the presence of the bear, the jaunty folk melody of the pedlar and the skewed chorale of the village priest. Above all it's the accumulation of such details and a sense of Sallinen's complete identification with his subject that makes *The Red Line* so compelling and convincing an opera.

Hynninen, Valjakka, Viitanen, Hietikko; Chorus and Orchestra of the Finnish National Opera; Kamu.
(Finlandia 1576-51102-2; 2 CDs).

Made in 1980 by Finland's major, state-subsidized, recording company, this performance makes an extremely strong case for this being one of the most powerfully written operas of the last twenty years. It is extremely fortunate to have Jorma Hynninen – arguably the greatest dramatic baritone singing today – in the role of Topi. There is a directness and a sincerity to Hynninen's voice that would enliven any score, but it is particularly appropriate for the gritty integrity of Topi. The rest of the cast are also very good: the soprano Taru Valjakka makes an intense and moving Riika, Usko Viitanen is a convincing rabble-rouser, while the sweet-toned Jaakko Hietikko brings great commitment to the relatively small role of the pedlar. In the pit Okko Kamu is responsible for much of the raw and passionate energy that comes across.

BENJAMIN BRITTEN

b. LOWESTOFT, ENGLAND, NOVEMBER 22, 1913; d. ALDEBURGH, DECEMBER 4, 1976.

Benjamin Britten was simply the most prolific and the most important British composer since Purcell, with almost one hundred major compositions to his credit, ranging from full-scale operas to accessible but unpatronizing music for children. His second opera, *Peter Grimes* (1945), is widely regarded as one of the masterpieces of postwar opera, and its premiere marked a turning point in the history of British opera. Prior to then, contemporary British composers had struggled to be taken seriously by opera-house managements, and the few opportunities they had were usually the result of personal initiative or the championship of the conductor and impresario Sir Thomas Beecham. The success of *Peter Grimes* changed all that: the proof that there was an audience for good contemporary work immediately galvanized composers such as Michael Tippett and William Walton, and encouraged institutions like Covent Garden to embrace new repertoire. *Peter Grimes* is also an encapsulation of many of the themes that were to preoccupy Britten in his dramatic works – the vulnerability of innocence, the abuse of power, and the susceptibility of the outsider to the pressures of society.

Britten was born on St Cecilia's day – appropriately, since she is the patron saint of music. His mother, a keen amateur musician and singer, was the formative influence in his early years, and by the age of five he was already composing. Britten went on to take lessons from the composer Frank Bridge, who introduced him to the music of progressive European composers such as Bartók, Berg and Schoenberg. After studying at the Royal College of Music, Britten worked for the Post Office film unit, producing the music for a number of innovative documentaries – most notably *Night Mail* – as well as writing the incidental music for several stage plays. The text for *Night Mail* was by the poet W.H. Auden, who was to be one of the most important influences in Britten's life, reinforcing his left-wing politics and his pacifism, and providing the text for his first important song cycle, *Our Hunting Fathers* (1936).

Discontented with life in England, Auden emigrated to America in 1939, followed a few months later by Britten and Peter Pears, the tenor who was to be Britten's partner for almost forty years – it's hard to find a relationship that so dominated the creative output of a composer as this one did. Britten and Pears spent nearly three years in America, where Britten wrote his first dramatic work, the operetta *Paul Bunyan* (1941), to a libretto by Auden. Despite Britten's brilliant assimilation of the vocabulary of popular American music-theatre, *Paul Bunyan* was not a success and it was set aside for more than thirty years. This period in the States was crucial in bringing out Britten's profound attachment to his English heritage, and his affection for his native East Anglia was heightened by reading an article by E.M. Forster on the eighteenth-century Suffolk poet George Crabbe.

Britten returned home in 1942 and had soon written some of his very best music – *A Ceremony of Carols* and a song cycle for Pears entitled *Serenade for Tenor, Horn and Strings*. But it was *Peter Grimes*, based on a poem by Crabbe, that put him firmly on the map, establishing him not just as a brilliant composer but also as an astute commentator on society – something that runs through most of his output. At the time of *Peter Grimes* there were only two established opera companies in Britain, so Britten turned to the medium of chamber opera, gathering around him a company of like-minded collaborators to perform them. Their first venture, *The Rape of Lucretia* (1946), staged in association with Glyndebourne, was written for a mere eight singers and twelve instrumentalists. It was followed by *Albert Herring* (1947), a brilliant bitter-sweet comedy using the same forces, and in the same year Britten founded the English Opera Group with the producer and librettist Eric Crozier and his regular designer John Piper. The annual Aldeburgh Festival (where many of his works were premiered) was established the following year in the Suffolk seaside town that he and Pears had made their home. Britten's next three operas were all outside commissions: *Billy Budd* was another full-scale work with a maritime setting, written for the 1951 Festival of Britain; *Gloriana* (1953), about Queen Elizabeth I, was written for the coronation of Elizabeth II (and was a critical disaster that has only recently started to recover); while *The Turn of the Screw*, from the ghost story by Henry James, was a commission from the 1954 Venice Biennale.

Britten also found the time to create two highly effective operas for children, *The Little Sweep* (1949) and *Noye's Fludde* (1957), both written for Aldeburgh – as was *A Midsummer Night's Dream* (1960), a magical adaptation of Shakespeare partly influenced in its orchestration by Britten's investigations into eastern music following a trip to Bali and Japan in 1956. The same trip also prompted a radical re-appraisal of his approach to drama after his experiences of Japanese Noh plays (slow-moving and highly stylized all-male plays), the effects of which were clear in the more ascetic style of his three Church "parables": *Curlew River* (1964), *The Burning Fiery Furnace* (1966) and *The Prodigal Son* (1968) were all conceived for performance in church and, in spirit, are really closer to ritual than to opera.

Like his friend Michael Tippett, Britten had been a conscientious objector during the war, and several of his works carry a pacifist message. His great *War Requiem* (1961) was one such, as was Britten's penultimate opera, *Owen*

Wingrave (1970), a work written for television. A few years later, the opening of the Snape Maltings just outside Aldeburgh allowed for larger-scale opera productions, and *Death in Venice*, a work based on the novella by Thomas Mann, was premiered there in 1973. The last of Britten's fifteen operas, it provided Pears – in the character of Aschenbach – with his most demanding stage role since Grimes.

Britten was an emphatically tonal composer and a committed melodist – although he was fearful of "sounding like Puccini", whose music he loathed. Despite the fact that he was only prevented from studying with Alban Berg by the Austrian composer's death, he was surprisingly impatient with atonality of any sort, infamously walking out of the first performance of Birtwistle's *Punch and Judy* at Aldeburgh. "It does not matter what style a composer chooses to write in," he once wrote, "as long as it has something definite to say, and says it clearly." His own style was unmistakably modern in its economy, clarity and energy; he was a brilliantly descriptive composer – the "Four Sea Interludes" from *Peter Grimes* are astonishingly evocative – but he rarely indulged in the uninhibited lushness of his contemporary Michael Tippett. In Britten's operas, in particular, there is a sense of austerity that seems to reflect an essentially pessimistic view of humanity, and his music is often powerfully elemental. As Yehudi Meuhin once memorably put it, "If wind and water could write music, it would sound like Ben's."

Peter Grimes

Composed 1944–45.
First performed June 7, 1945.
Libretto by Montagu Slater, after Crabbe.

Synopsis

Prologue

At the Moot Hall of the Borough an inquest is being held into the death of the apprentice of fisherman Peter Grimes. According to Grimes, they ran out of drinking water while at sea. The coroner finds him not

CATHERINE ASHMORE

Ben Heppner sings Peter Grimes at Covent Garden

guilty but advises him not to get another boy. Ellen Orford, the schoolmistress and a friend of Grimes, implores him to leave the Borough with her.

Act I

At the sea-shore, Grimes calls for help in dragging his boat ashore but only Balstrode, a retired sea captain, and Ned Keene, the apothecary, will help. Keene tells Grimes of a new apprentice he has found and Ellen leaves to fetch the boy. Balstrode advises Grimes to leave the Borough and join the merchant navy, but he is determined to stay and save enough money to settle down with Ellen. In the Boar Inn, each arrival tells of the damage being wreaked by the storm. Grimes bursts in soaked and dishevelled, and is attacked by the drunken Methodist fisherman Bob Boles. Keene intervenes and when Ellen arrives with the boy, John, Grimes takes him away to his hut on the cliffs.

Act II

In the High Street some weeks later, Ellen and John sit together watching the townsfolk attend church. She notices the boy's clothes have been ripped and that he has been injured. When Grimes arrives to take him out to sea, Ellen begs for the boy to have some rest. Grimes strikes her and runs after the boy – a scene witnessed by Keene and Boles. Ellen tries to defend him but is shouted down. The menfolk decide to visit Grimes. He is furious when he sees them coming towards his home, and when he opens the hut door the boy slips and falls down the cliff. The men arrive at the empty hut and are surprised to see everything in order.

Act III

Some days later, on a summer evening in the village street, Mrs Sedley tells Keene that she thinks the missing Grimes has murdered his apprentice. His boat has returned but there is no sign of either man or boy. Balstrode and Ellen (who has found the boy's jumper) determine to help Grimes but Mrs Sedley overhears their conversation and starts a manhunt. With the sound of foghorns and the searching crowd in the distance, Grimes enters – exhausted and demented. Balstrode tells him to take his boat out to sea and sink it. The following morning the coast guard reports a sunken vessel and life in the Borough returns to normal.

𝄞 Having been alerted to the poetry of George Crabbe by E.M. Forster's article in *The Listener*, Peter Pears managed to track down a copy of Crabbe's poem *The Borough* in San Diego. Britten immediately saw the theatrical possibilities of the sections involving the sadistic fisherman accused of murdering his apprentices, and was further encouraged by the offer of a commission of $1000 from the Koussevitzky Foundation. When Christopher Isherwood declined to write the libretto, Britten began working with Pears, "sketching out bits here and there". Britten and Pears identified with the outsider Grimes: "As conscientious objectors . . . we experienced tremendous tension. I think it was partly this feeling which led us to make Grimes a character of vision and conflict, the tortured idealist he is, rather than the villain he was in Crabbe". On arriving in Britain, Britten and Pears handed over their work to the playwright Montagu Slater, who took eighteen months to produce the libretto. Britten began the score at the beginning of 1944 and, some weeks before its completion nearly a year later, played excerpts of it to the soprano Joan Cross, who was then managing Sadler's Wells Opera. Cross was instantly gripped by the work and determined that it should re-open Sadler's Wells after the war. In the face of a generally sceptical company, Cross maintained her faith in the work and the opera opened just weeks after the war ended with Pears in the title role and Cross herself as Ellen Orford. Unexpectedly, the opera was immediately recognized as a major work and became the first by an English composer to enter and remain in the international repertory.

Peter Grimes continues to be Britten's most celebrated opera, but it is an extremely harsh and emotionally complicated work, which asks us to sympathize, if not identify with, a violent and irascible man simply because of the merciless way in which his community has judged and isolated him. While Grimes is the ostensible protagonist, it is the Borough itself – and the dynamics of that particular community – that exercises the most power, a largely negative power that even defeats Ellen Orford, whose love offers Grimes his one hope of redemption. Despite the conventional framework of orchestral interludes, a storm scene and a mad scene, *Peter Grimes* is a peculiarly twentieth-century opera in the way it depicts the central tragedy in terms of an intolerant society that victimizes non-conformity. Even so, Grimes is a morally disturbing character in a way that the central character of Berg's *Wozzeck* (a notable influence on Britten's opera) is not, and, although he's not the psychopath of Crabbe's poem, his precise involvement in the death of his first apprentice is left unclear. Certainly Britten gives him the finest music, with the enraptured vision of the soliloquy "Now the Great Bear and Pleiades" in Act I giving a crucial insight into his troubled psyche. But this poetic singularity is in stark contrast to the cruelty with which he treats his new apprentice in Act II, which in turn gives way to the poignant reverie "In dreams I've built myself some kindlier home".

Arguably it is precisely the ambivalence of *Peter Grimes* that gives it such an impact. Britten's extraordinary achievement as a composer was to create a completely convincing musical expression of the conflicting elements of the opera – Grimes' insularity, Ellen's tenderness, the bustling energy of the village. The characterization has a vitality and force that makes even the most absurd caricature (for instance the pompous Swallow) completely alive. Britten pulls the orchestral stops out in the six Interludes, used at the beginning and middle of each act, which are among the most brilliantly evocative music that Britten ever wrote and which help to establish the constant, overpowering presence of the sea as the opera's dominant force.

RECORDINGS OVERVIEW

The earliest recorded extracts of *Peter Grimes*, from the 1948 Covent Garden production, have been reissued by EMI. It's worth seeking out for Cross's authoritative Ellen Orford and the sweet tones of the young Peter Pears. Ten years later, when he made the Decca recording, Pears' voice had hardened slightly but his complete command of every nuance of the role makes this the yardstick recording. No new versions appeared until the Philips version twenty years on, with Jon Vickers bringing a startling brutality to the title role (a video of his Covent Garden performance is available). In the last couple of years there have been two fine recordings with two decidedly English tenors. For EMI Anthony Rolfe Johnson makes a beautiful sound but most of the work's ominousness and psychological tension is generated by Bernard Haitink's handling of the orchestra and the raw energy of the Royal Opera House Chorus. The Chandos recording, under Richard Hickox, cannot match the subtlety of the EMI version but it boasts a fine performance of startling intensity from Philip Langridge as Grimes (whose performance of the role at the English National Opera is available in a fine video).

Pears, Watson, Pease, Watson; Royal Opera House Chorus and Orchestra; Britten.
(Decca 414 577-2DH3; 2 CDs).

This is a marvellous recording. Symphonically rich and atmospherically evocative, Britten's reading creates a grandly powerful but deeply melancholy vision. Pears' voice is on the light side (originally Britten had planned it for a baritone), but he uses it with enormous intelligence, above all in conveying Grimes' complexity – the final scene has never been bettered in its poignant understatement of the tragedy. Claire Watson lacks the ardour and love-torn confusion demanded by Ellen's character (and supplied by Cross), but her voice is distinctive and touchingly lyrical. The remaining cast are all superb and the Covent Garden forces are in top form – especially the chorus, who provide an impressive impression of village solidarity.

Vickers, Harper, Bailey, Bainbridge; Royal Opera House Chorus and Orchestra; Davis.
(Philips 432 578-2PM2; 2 CDs).

Jon Vickers provides a complete contrast to Pears' approach, replacing the poetry and intelligence with greater brawn – both vocal and physical. Vickers' reading of the title role carries a mixture of violence, pain and fragility that at times has a Lear-like quality. The sweep of his voice and the power of his declamation is always thrilling and it is matched in urgency by Colin Davis's conducting, which constantly stresses the danger lurking beneath the surface – occasionally to excess. Heather Harper comes closer to the earthy quality found in Joan Cross's reading of Ellen, the supporting roles are all excellent and, once again, the Royal Opera House Chorus create a great sense of community.

The Rape of Lucretia

Composed 1945–46; revised 1947.
First performed July 12, 1946.
Libretto by Ronald Duncan, after Obey.

Synopsis

Act I

The Male and Female Choruses tell of Tarquinius Superbus's sacking of Rome and of how his warrior son, Sextus, has come to treat the city as his own. The curtain rises on an army camp where Collatinus, Junius and Tarquinius are arguing about a wager that took place the night before, which proved Lucretia – the wife of Collatinus – the only virtuous wife. Tarquinius determines to "prove Lucretia chaste" and he leaves for Rome. In her house Lucretia is seen sewing with her two servants Bianca and Lucia, when Tarquinius arrives and demands a room for the night.

Act II

Lucretia is asleep on her bed. Tarquinius approaches and kisses her. In her dreams she believes him to be her husband and draws him closer. When she wakes she tries to repel him but Tarquinius draws his sword and rapes her. (The choruses make reference to Christ's compassion.) In the morning Bianca and Lucia are arranging flowers. When Lucretia appears she gives Lucia an orchid to take to Collatinus "from a Roman harlot". As Lucia leaves Collatinus arrives and finds Lucretia in purple mourning. She tells Collatinus what has happened, but though he forgives her she stabs herself. The opera concludes with the moral that "Christ is all".

Reacting to changes in policy, in March 1946 Eric Crozier, Peter Pears and Joan Cross resigned from Sadler's Wells. Together with Britten they determined to set up their own company "dedicated to the creation of new works, performed with the least possible expense and capable . . . of being toured". Their first project, suggested by Crozier, was for an operatic version of André Obey's 1931 play *La viol de Lucrèce*, for which the American poet Ronald Duncan would supply the libretto. Glyndebourne staged the first performance with Kathleen Ferrier as Lucretia and, while the first run of thirteen performances was relatively successful, the provincial tour was a disaster. John Christie, the owner of Glyndebourne, bore the financial responsibility but he made it clear that, after honouring his agreement to stage *Albert Herring*, he had no wish to continue collaborations between his opera house and Britten.

Lucretia's status as a paragon of virtue in classical literature was taken up by Christian writers, who made her an almost Christ-like figure because of her self-sacrifice. Duncan and Britten make her an even more overloaded symbolic figure and as a result the opera is one of Britten's most problematic works. This is partly because of the way the choric commentary overwhelms the piece by drawing a specifically Christian moral from the story, but also because of Duncan's rather overpoetic text (like Tippett, Duncan was adversely influenced by the work of T.S. Eliot). Central to the opera's philosophical conundrum is the question first put by St Augustine: "If she is adulterous, why is she praised? If chaste, why was she put to death?" The opera offers no conclusive answer, simply the hope of Christian redemption. This religious aspect of the work irritated most critics. Ernest Newman thought it "rotten with insincerity and pretentiousness", while W.J. Turner thought "the pseudo-religious ending" was "appalling".

Paradoxically, despite a scenario with which it is difficult to feel involved, *The Rape of Lucretia* contains some of Britten's most lyrical vocal writing, notably the Female Chorus depicting Lucretia's sleep, Lucretia's plangent aria on the day after the rape, and the music as she approaches her husband – a glorious instrumental section on cor anglais and low strings. Above all, the opera's strength lies in the wonderful array of sonorities and colours that Britten gets out of his small orchestra of twelve instrumentalists. The piano dominates, but the harp has the most varied expression, ranging from the chirping crickets of the first scene to the domestic tranquillity of Lucretia working with her women.

RECORDINGS OVERVIEW

When *The Rape of Lucretia* was first performed it had two alternating casts, both of which were recorded. Extracts from these exist on CD and provide fascinating listening. For EMI – on the same set as the earliest *Grimes* recording – you can hear Nancy Evans as Lucretia under the scintillating direction of Reginald Goodall. Even better, and with substantially more music, is the recording licensed to the Music and Arts label. Made from a 1946 live performance conducted by Britten in Holland, the sound is not very good but the singing, above all from Kathleen Ferrier as Lucretia, is stunning, and for sheer inner dignity and warmth of sound Ferrier's performance has not been bettered. In 1970 Britten made a new recording for Decca with Janet Baker as Lucretia; as a complete version it remained unchallenged for twenty-three years until Chandos committed Jean Rigby's fine performance to disc. Rigby had played Lucretia in the English National Opera's revelatory staging in 1983, a production that is available on video.

Baker, Pears, Harper, Luxon; English Chamber Orchestra; Britten.
(London 425666/2LH2; 2 CDs).

As a singer Janet Baker was almost as favoured by Britten as her legendary predecessor Kathleen Ferrier, and their work together on this recording is a moving reminder of their affinity. Baker is a formidable presence, bringing tremendous weight to the role, and responding instinctively to Britten's animated direction. Peter Pears and Heather Harper are superb as the Male and Female Choruses and Benjamin Luxon makes a rounded, credible Tarquinius. The entire cast bring a splendid range of colour and expression to their contributions and the engineers capture them – and the responsive English Chamber Orchestra – in clear and vital sound.

Rigby, Robson, Pierard, Maxwell; City of London Sinfonia; Hickox.
(Chandos CHAN 9254/5; 2 CDs).

This recording of *Lucretia* was greeted with tremendous enthusiasm when it was first released in 1993, and rightly so. Jean Rigby is a superb, womanly Lucretia who, despite lacking Janet Baker's ripe tone, is a superb musician, shaping Britten's melodies with an impressive range of colour and expression. Nigel Robson is a vocally secure Male Chorus – more so than Pears for Decca – and Catherine Pierard's beautiful voice is perfectly suited to the Female Chorus. Donald Maxwell is in superb form as Tarquinius, revelling in the character's griminess. Though Richard Hickox is less animated than Britten, he gives a clear and nicely shaped account of the score, which is ideally presented by the Chandos engineers.

Albert Herring

Composed 1946–47.
First performed June 20, 1947.
Libretto by Eric Crozier, after de Maupassant.

Synopsis

Act I

Loxford, a small market town, during April and May 1900. At Lady Billows's house the Mayor, the Vicar, the Schoolmistress (Miss Wordsworth) and the Police Superintendent (Budd) are meeting to decide who should be the May Queen. Lady Billows announces a first prize of £25, but all candidates are vetoed as Florence Pike (the housekeeper) reveals some piece of scandalous information about them. Budd then suggests his mother's rather dim shop assistant Albert Herring and everyone agrees. At the Herring shop, Sid (the butcher's assistant) taunts Albert for being a mother's boy and tries to tempt him with the life of pleasure that awaits him when he breaks from her apron strings. Albert considers Sid's words but he is interrupted by the town committee who bring news of his election. Albert does not want to know, but Mrs Herring has heard about the £25.

Act II

Inside the festival marquee a large trestle table has been set for eleven. Sid has told his girlfriend Nancy that he intends to spike Albert's lemonade with rum. The town elders begin to arrive and the ceremonies begin. After singing and flower presentations, Albert calls for a toast in honour of Lady Billows, drains his glass and explodes with hiccups. Back at the shop, Albert remembers the food and drink he has just enjoyed. Hearing Sid walk past the shop, he listens to him tell Nancy that, once Albert has sown some oats, he'll be all right. Albert tosses a coin and then decides to leave.

Act III

The following afternoon everyone is looking for Albert at the shop. Sid and Nancy quarrel, and Lady Billows demands the intervention of Scotland Yard and Conan Doyle. They find Albert's crushed straw hat and everyone – assuming him to be dead – begins to intone a threnody ("In the midst of life"). As the music comes to an end, Albert enters, muddy and dishevelled. It transpires that he has spent £3 of his £25 on girls and drink. He has been ejected from one pub and started a fight in another. Albert scorns his repressive mother, as Billows predicts disaster. As the crowd disperse and Albert is left with Sid, Nancy and the village children, he throws his orange-blossom crown into the audience.

Britten began *Albert Herring* in 1946 as a companion piece to the much starker *Rape of Lucretia*, scoring both works for exactly the same chamber forces. But the work also reflects *Peter Grimes* – albeit from a comic perspective – in the way small-town Suffolk society deals with an oddball. Some were taken aback that the cosmopolitan musical-philosopher of the two earlier operas could turn his hand so abruptly to the trivialities of village life, but *Albert Herring* was immediately popular and it has remained one of the few enduring English comic operas outside the Gilbert and Sullivan oeuvre – to which it is more than a little indebted.

The opera's appeal is fairly straightforward. It is very funny, with a number of hilarious set-pieces and more than its share of visual wit. Eric Crozier was careful to provide the composer with plenty of opportunities for parody, and each of the characters is accompanied, at one point or another, by some type of musical quotation. The Vicar, for example, is set to music that fuses the Victorian hymn-tradition and "mummerset" folk song, while Miss Wordsworth is caricatured through the very worst of the ballad-tradition. Mrs Billows is, as her name suggests, outrageously pompous and her music veers from the grandiosity of Baroque opera to the banner-waving jingoism associated with Parry and Elgar. When Sid laces Albert's lemonade with rum, Britten quotes the love-potion theme from *Tristan und Isolde*.

The whole thing lasts over two and a quarter hours, and yet so swift is the pacing and so fluid the vocal writing that it seems to pass in less than half that time. For this reason, and reasons of scoring and character, *Albert Herring* has been compared to Strauss's *Ariadne auf Naxos*, and there is also something of Strauss's self-consciously flamboyant technique in Britten's use of complicated forms such as canon, fugue and passacaglia to accompany episodes of relative simplicity. But – unlike *Ariadne* – *Albert Herring* is touched by a melancholy that is rather like that of Mozart's *Così fan tutte*. This dark side is at its most poignant during the last act when, believing Albert to be dead, the opera's characters join voices in a threnody for nine voices that gives each individual the opportunity to be him or herself whilst remaining part of the group. It is a deeply moving episode, and English opera's closest thing to a lament for the passing of regional identity.

Pears, Fisher, Peters, Noble, Ward; English Chamber Orchestra; Britten. (Decca 421 849-2LH2; 2 CDs).

This is the only recording of *Albert Herring* (though a video of Peter Hall's 1985 production exists) and it is one of the composer's finest. Britten's conducting successfully handles the opera's awkward mood swings and, with his small chamber forces, achieves miracles of phrasing, texture and pacing. The cast is nearly ideal, with Pears in tremendous comic form as Albert (a role he was too old to play on stage by 1963) and Catherine Wilson and Joseph Ward both splendid as the free spirits Sid and Nancy. Sylvia Fisher, the only other survivor of the premiere on this recording, was also too old to play Billows but she gives a splendidly intimidating portrayal of the old dragon. The small group of ECO instrumentalists play with precision and character, and the sound is fresh and expressive.

Billy Budd

Composed 1950–51; revised 1960.
First performed December 1, 1951; November 13, 1960.
Libretto by E.M Forster and Eric Crozier, after Melville.

Synopsis

Prologue

Captain Vere, as an old man, looks back on his career and tries to recall the disturbing incident in "the summer of seventeen hundred and ninety seven".

Act I

The *H.M.S. Indomitable* receives newly press-ganged recruits taken from a merchant ship *The Rights o' Man*. One of them, the stammering Billy Budd, is sent to the crow's nest; Billy sings of his happiness, "Farewell, old Rights o' Man", which alarms the officers, who think he is referring to political rights. Claggart, the master-at-arms, instructs his corporal Squeak to make Billy's life difficult, and Billy is warned to stay out of Claggart's way. In Vere's cabin a week later, two officers tell him about Billy's song but he advises them not to worry. Below deck the men are singing when Billy leaves to fetch some tobacco from his kit bag. He finds Squeak going through his things; Squeak pulls a knife but Billy knocks him down. Claggart is forced to put his spy in chains. Left alone, Claggart sings of his hatred for Billy.

Act II

Claggart asks to register a complaint with the Captain – who is irritated by his sycophancy. They are interrupted by the call to engage. The French have been spotted but escape into the mist. Claggart returns to making his complaint and Vere agrees to talk to Billy. Back in Vere's cabin, Claggart formally accuses Billy of attempted mutiny. Billy is incensed and, unable to get any words out, strikes Claggart dead. Vere orders a court martial and Billy is thrown in irons. The following day, Dansker tells Billy that the ship is on the edge of mutiny, but Billy urges him to keep the peace – otherwise more will hang. Just before he is hanged Billy calls out his blessings on the captain ("Starry Vere, God bless you!").

Epilogue

Vere, now an old man, mourns his actions. He knows that he could have saved Billy, but takes some comfort from his final words.

Although *Billy Budd* was commissioned by the Arts Council for the 1951 Festival of Britain, Britten had already discussed turning Herman Melville's short story into an opera with E.M. Forster and Eric Crozier. Crozier was to research naval history and work on the dialogue, while Forster prepared "the big slabs of narrative" – he wrote it in prose, which, according to Britten, strongly influenced the opera's musical character. Once again Britten set a story that concerns a visionary individual, an "innocent" who is positioned both within and apart from a tightly-knit society. In this case conflict arises not between Billy and the crew (he is almost universally loved), but between him and another individual, Claggart. The drama is remarkably direct and the presentation of good and evil in the forms of Billy and Claggart is among the most intense in all opera, with Britten employing easily recognizable tonalities for each – B flat major for Billy and B minor for Claggart. A more complex duality informs Vere's musical representation, with his internal conflict mirrored throughout in music that is tonally unstable.

Much has been made of the homo-eroticism that runs through *Billy Budd* (the cast is exclusively male), and indeed the heaviness of Britten's orchestration does suggest a sense of sexual tension. But this is just one element among several that contribute to the claustrophobia of this opera. No less important are the rigid social hierarchy, the bitterness of Claggart as he is caught – Iago-like – between officers and men, the presence of death implicit in any warship, and the constant feeling of entrapment and potential mutiny. Into this pressure cooker comes Billy Budd, part child and part saint, whose beauty – both physical and spiritual – and intense joy in living both enriches and undermines the status quo.

In musical terms, *Billy Budd* is much more obviously symphonic than *Peter Grimes* and the richness of the harmony and weight of the counterpoint can make the opera feel rather clotted. But Britten clarifies the characterization and atmosphere through the repetition and development of relatively straightforward melodic themes, and through vivid use of instrumental and orchestral association. Using the largest orchestra he ever used for one of his operas (six percussionists are required), he applies massed wind to the sea-pictures, darker and more ominous textures (brass, low wind etc) for the evil Claggart, and a trilling trumpet and gulping wind section to announce the stammering Billy.

Glossop, Pears, Langdon, Shirley-Quirk; Ambrosian Opera Chorus; London Symphony Orchestra; Britten. (London 417 428-2LH3; 3 CDs).

Produced in 1967, this was another success for Britten's partnership with Decca, although the cast does suffers from two vital weaknesses: a rather gruff title performance by baritone Peter Glossop and a stiff and overvillainous reading of Claggart from Michael Langdon. Peter Pears makes a fine Captain Vere, perfectly balancing aristocratic sophistication with tortured conscience. The remainder of the cast is no less impressive and Britten brings extraordinary life to the kaleidoscopic score. Alternatively, you can track down the original 1951 cast recording on the American VAI label, or the video of the 1993 English National Opera production with Thomas Allen as Billy. Both are worth investigating but – given the wealth of fine Britten singers around today – a new recording is long overdue.

The Turn of the Screw

Composed 1954.
First performed September 14, 1954.
Libretto by Myfanwy Piper.

Synopsis

Prologue

A male Narrator introduces the opera, explaining how a woman became a governess to two orphaned children – on the condition she agreed never to contact their young guardian.

Act I

The Governess travels to the country house, Bly, where she is welcomed by the housekeeper Mrs Grose and the children Flora and Miles. News arrives that Miles has been expelled from school. Mrs Grose tells the Governess that the boy is naughty but never bad, and they agree not to tell the guardian. Strolling in the grounds of Bly, the Governess sees a man in the tower. Later, she sees him again outside the hall window. She describes him to Mrs Grose, who cries out "Quint! Peter Quint!" and proceeds to explain how the evil Quint – who is now dead – had been the guardian's valet, and how he had exploited his trust. At the lake, the Governess and Flora both see the ghost of Miss Jessel, the former governess. At night, Quint calls Miles from the tower and Jessel calls Flora from the lake. They are interrupted by the Governess and Mrs Grose.

Act II

Quint and Jessel bicker with each other and the Governess sings of her fears. Mrs Grose urges the Governess to contact the guardian, but she refuses. When Miles mentions "the others", the Governess decides that she must leave Bly. Entering the schoolroom, however, she finds the weeping ghost of Jessel and she decides to remain, writing to the guardian for help. In Miles' room the Governess begins to question him but is interrupted by Quint, who extinguishes the candle. Later, Quint gets Miles to steal the letter. Flora goes missing. The two women leave to find her by the lake – where Jessel appears once more. Mrs Grose decides to take Flora away from Bly. The Governess is left behind with Miles, who is listening for Quint. When she begins to ask him questions, Quint whispers to him not to betray their secrets but he becomes hysterical and confesses to having stolen the letter. The Governess insists that Miles tells her who it is he can see; he calls out "Peter Quint, you devil!", and dies in the Governess's arms.

Shortly after the grim reception accorded his coronation opera *Gloriana* in June 1953, Britten proposed a collaboration with Myfanwy

Piper, the wife of his regular designer John Piper. She suggested a setting of Henry James's *The Turn of the Screw*, a tale which, with its theme of the corruption of childhood innocence and its disturbing ambiguities, immediately struck a chord with Britten – he later described it as the "nearest to me of any I have chosen (although what that indicates of my own character I shouldn't like to say!)". The opera was commissioned by the 1954 Venice Biennale and Britten worked at a furious rate, writing with his left hand when an inflammation made his right hand unusable. The first performance was well received by the Italian audience and the first Sadler's Wells staging, shortly after, was no less successful.

Henry James's tale, published in 1898, has been a favourite with post-Freudian critics, who have found rich pickings in aspects of the story which James leaves tantalizingly unclear. Are the ghosts (which Mrs Grose never sees and Flora frequently denies seeing) real, or are they the products of the Governess's neurotic imagination? Is she, in fact, the source of the children's confused behaviour? This is a problem that anyone wishing to stage (or film) the story has to confront, and in the opera Quint and Miss Jessel not only speak but are visible to the audience. The other veiled, and more disturbing, aspect of the book is the question of what precisely went on between Quint, Miss Jessel and the children before the Governess arrived. Piper and Britten make the sexual implications of this much more explicit than James does – indeed, Mrs Grose tells the Governess "But I saw things elsewhere I did not like. When Quint was free with everyone, with little Master Miles! ... Hours they spent together . . . he made free with her too, with lovely Miss Jessel . . . He liked them pretty, I can tell you, Miss, and he had his will, morning and night." *The Turn of the Screw* is as much an opera about child abuse as it is about ghosts – a fact that few critics are prepared to confront. That a kind of abuse can be discerned in the supposedly nurturing but ultimately suffocating behaviour of the Governess (who finishes up alone with Miles and arguably causes his death) makes the opera doubly disturbing. On another level the opera continues the typically Britten themes – central to *Billy Budd* – of power and responsibility: Miles, like Billy, is destroyed by the evil and the weakness of those put in charge of him.

Musically, the opera is one of Britten's most complicated. It is founded upon a theme of twelve notes, built from rising fourths and falling minor thirds, but for all the surface similarity to Schoenberg's tone-row system, each of the theme's various occurrences is allied to a definite tonal centre. The two acts are sub-divided into seven and eight separate scenes, each one a variation of the theme of the first scene after the Prologue, and each one is given a sub-title, "The Journey", "The Welcome", "The Letter" etc. These variations are Britten's musical response to the title, for each consecutive variation signifies the gradual tightening of tension within Bly as the situation becomes more and more claustrophobic. As never before, Britten shows himself to be a master of manipulation and development, and the way in which he builds the opera from its simple twelve-note origins is a remarkable feat of technical skill. However, the greatness of this opera is not simply a matter of technique: the score's variety of expression is magnificent and Britten's writing for the chamber orchestra is incandescently beautiful – especially the use of low woodwind (in Miles's room), celesta (to announce Quint), bells and harp. Similarly, the use of children's nursery rhymes and the haunting writing for the ghosts – especially Quint's chilling bel canto – contribute to the opera's ethereal atmosphere. Ultimately, however, it is the central role of the Governess that makes *The Turn of the Screw* such a remarkable work. It is Britten's greatest female creation and her ardently lyrical letter scene, her invocation to the summer night as she strolls through the grounds of Bly, and her final Requiem for the dead Miles provide an unforgettable emotional and musical *tour de force*.

RECORDINGS OVERVIEW

A year after its premiere, *The Turn of the Screw* became the first complete Britten opera to be recorded. It was made by Decca, with whom Britten enjoyed a long working relationship, using the original cast and conducted by the composer. It's a masterly recording and remained unrivalled until 1981 when Colin Davis made a fine recording for Philips, with Robert Tear as Quint and Helen Donath as the Governess, which was used as the soundtrack for a gripping film version directed by Peter Weigl (available on video). But the main rival to the original recording comes from Britten's one-time assistant Steuart Bedford, who conducts an Aldeburgh-derived performance on the Collins label.

Pears, Vyvyan, Hemmings, Dyer; English Opera Group Orchestra; Britten.
(Decca 425 672-2LH2; 2 CDs).

The sense of tension in this recording is tangible throughout. Jennifer Vyvyan's performance as the Governess is exemplary, brilliantly conveying the character's disintegrating control over events. Peter Pears is splendidly creepy as Quint, especially in the insinuating melismas with which he ensnares Miles. David Hemmings (later to become a film star) gives a startlingly mature and considered reading of Miles's tortured personality. Britten provides subtle, seductive direction and his regular orchestra play with their distinctive clarity and virtuosity.

Langridge, Lott, Pay, Hulse; Aldeburgh Festival Ensemble; Bedford.
(Collins 7030-2; 2 CDs).

This 1994 recording is so wonderful it comes extremely close to superseding the above version. Felicity Lott is heroic and yet vulnerable as the Governess, and Philip Langridge is menacing and seductive as Quint – a role that perfectly suits his probing intelligence. As the two children, Sam Pay and Eileen Hulse are also extremely good. Much of the special atmosphere of this piece is created by the orchestral textures, which have never sounded so luminous as here.

A Midsummer Night's Dream

Composed 1959–60.
First performed June 11, 1960.
Libretto by the composer and Peter Pears, after Shakespeare.

Synopsis

Act I

The wood at twilight. Oberon, King of the Fairies, and his Queen Tytania have quarrelled over her attendant, the Indian boy. Oberon orders Puck to fetch him the juice of a herb which, when sprinkled on sleeping eyelids, will make the recipient love the first person that they see. Meanwhile, Hermia has been ordered by her father to marry Demetrius – even though she loves Lysander. In defiance of her father, she and Lysander escape Athens. As they leave, Demetrius and Helena enter. Demetrius tells Helena that he no longer loves her but instead loves Hermia. Puck returns with the herb and Oberon tells him his plan: he must anoint Demetrius's eyes and ensure that when he wakes he finds Helena. The rustics arrive to rehearse their play *Pyramus and Thisbe*. Lysander and Hermia get themselves lost and lie on the ground to sleep, then Puck enters and anoints Lysander's eyes. Helena enters and wakes Lysander, who falls in love with her and pursues her. Oberon finds Tytania asleep and sprinkles the juice on her eyes.

Act II

The wood. The rustics prepare for their performance. Bottom (who has been given the part of Pyramus) leaves the clearing, followed by Puck, who transforms his head into that of an ass. Tytania wakes and the first person she sees is Bottom. Hermia is pursued by Demetrius. Oberon enchants Demetrius with the juice and he awakes to find Helena – now both the young men are in love with her. Confusion reigns until Oberon orders Puck to restore order by sprinkling Lysander's eyes with the juice.

Act III

Next morning Oberon, having gained the Indian boy, frees Tytania – and Bottom – from their enchantment. The four lovers wake and find themselves reconciled: Lysander with Hermia and Demetrius with Helena. In Theseus's Palace, Theseus and Hippolyta are joined by the lovers. A triple wedding is planned at which the rustics present *Pyramus and Thisbe*.

Shakespeare has suffered some terrible operatic settings, and yet he has also inspired four or five of the greatest operas ever written. Arguably, one of these is Britten's adaptation of *A Midsummer Night's Dream*, a project that came into being in 1959, when it became obvious to Britten and Pears that there was no time to commission a new libretto for the planned opening of Aldeburgh's enlarged Jubilee Hall the following year. Necessity drew the two men to Shakespeare, and within just seven months the entire work was complete. Necessity also led them to cut the play by half, although the adding of new text and the redistribution of some lines (Puck's words often find themselves in the mouths of the fairies) met with some disapproval. Britten's response was typically confident: "The original Shakespeare will survive." Despite illness, the composer conducted the first night, having assembled many of his favourite singers – Jennifer Vyvyan as Tytania, Owen Brannigan as Bottom and, of course, Peter Pears, this time in the relatively minor role of Flute. Britten wrote the Oberon role for the great English counter-tenor Alfred Deller, and – in a brilliant touch – made the part of Puck a speaking one (it is often played by a dancer) accompanied by raps on a drum and trumpet cadenzas.

The atmosphere on the first night was, according to *The Times* critic Frank Howes, "that of being gripped by a spell, of being subjected to a dose of Oberon's own medicine". Continuing Britten's preoccupation with the disparate worlds of night and day, of waking and sleeping, of the natural and the supernatural, *A Midsummer*

Night's Dream is characterized by utterly distinctive and appropriate sound-worlds, as Britten uses his ever-developing gift for orchestration to achieve just the right effect for each group of characters. Harps, celesta, percussion and harpsichord are used to accompany the mysterious and sinister world of the fairies; strings and woodwind are associated with the lovers; bassoon and low brass define the bumbling rustics. The vocal score is one of Britten's richest, with the Fairies much spikier than might be expected, and Tytania's coloratura and Oberon's counter-tenor sounding suitably otherworldly. Oberon is especially remarkable in that there is a seam of decidedly human malevolence running beneath the surface, and his equivocal character – thought by David Drew to be "a more grimly effective horror than Quint" – allows the performer enormous scope in interpretation.

Of the various ensembles, the extraordinarily cocky Act I duet between Lysander and Hermia, "I swear to thee", which moves through twelve major triads before arriving at a gloriously rich C major, and the Act III quartet "And I have found Demetrius", are two of the opera's highpoints. But, as with *Peter Grimes*, you are left marvelling as much at the setting and the atmosphere of the work as at the characterization, and, in the end, it is the extraordinary evocation of the sighing, creaking, rustling forest that is the opera's most memorable feature.

Deller, Harwood, Pears, Veasey; London Symphony Orchestra; Britten.
(London 425 663-2LH2; 2 CDs).

This superb performance is celebrated for the composer's wonderfully youthful direction of the LSO, but the performances of Alfred Deller and Peter Pears (here singing Lysander) play as big a part in making this set so wonderful. The rustics are engagingly led by Owen Brannigan as an hilarious Bottom and the three female leads are ravishingly sung by Elizabeth Harwood, Josephine Veasey and Heather Harper. The sound is bright and the production standards are pretty well faultless.

Bowman, Watson, Graham-Hall, Herford; City of London Sinfonia; Hickox.
(Virgin VCD7 59306; 2 CDs).

This, the only other recording of the opera, has Richard Hickox conducting a carefully reduced chamber orchestra that allows for much greater intimacy between conductor, orchestra and soloists than on the composer's set. The casting is a delight, with Donald Maxwell a domineering Bottom, and Della Jones and Jill Gomez marvellous as Hermia and Helena. James Bowman, though less sweet in tone than Deller, is a more forceful presence as Oberon. There is a generally good-natured mood to the proceedings and the overall delicacy of presentation is a delight. The sound is superior to that on the Decca set.

Death in Venice

Composed 1971–73.
First performed June 16, 1973.
Libretto by Myfanwy Piper, after Thomas Mann.

Synopsis

Act I

Aschenbach, a widowed novelist, believes his life as a writer is over. He enters a Munich churchyard where he hears a Traveller sing of far-off lands and decides to take a holiday in the sun. Leaving on a boat for Venice he becomes aware of a group of youths leaning over the deck and shouting to the girls on shore. They are joined by a made-up old fop who encourages them in the popular song "Serenissima". Aschenbach is disgusted at the sight of him and goes inside. In Venice, while travelling by gondola, he passes a boatload of boys and girls also singing "Serenissima". At dinner in his hotel, he is captivated by the beauty of a young Polish boy called Tadzio; later, on the beach of the Lido, he watches Tadzio play. Back at the hotel, he decides to leave but is forced to stay when his luggage is sent to the wrong destination. The Manager has kept his room, and tells Aschenbach that the wind is now blowing some of the heat away. Aschenbach sees Tadzio on the beach once more; he cannot bring himself to approach him and winces when Tadzio walks past and smiles. Left alone, Aschenbach exclaims "I love you".

Act II

At the hotel barber's, Aschenbach is told of a disease passing through Venice. Again he stumbles across Tadzio with his family and follows them into St Mark's. Learning that the disease is cholera, he feels the need to warn Tadzio's mother but is unable to speak. While sleeping in his room, Aschenbach dreams of Apollo and Dionysus. He returns to the beach where Tadzio and his friends are playing. Later, Aschenbach visits the barber and gets him to dye his hair and paint his face. Feeling invigorated, he takes a gondola and follows Tadzio's family through the canal system. Losing them, he returns for the last time to the beach, where Tadzio loses a fight with one of his friends. Rising from his chair, Aschenbach cries out and Tadzio beckons, but Aschenbach falls back in his chair and dies.

Britten first considered turning Thomas Mann's novella *Death in Venice* into an opera some years before putting pen to paper, and it was not until November 1970 that he approached Myfanwy Piper for a libretto. He began the score in the spring of the following year, getting into his stride in October when he and Pears visited Venice with the Pipers. While working on the opera Britten's heart condition became extremely serious, and he knew this was likely to be his last major composition. Accordingly there is a strong autobiographical and valedictory feeling about the work. Five months after the opera's completion Britten suffered a stroke and woke to find his right hand partly paralyzed. He was unable to supervise rehearsals (conducted by Steuart Bedford) and missed the first performance at the Maltings, but was well enough to attend the first London performance at Covent Garden in October 1973. He was thus able to see Peter Pears in a role which he viewed as a public tribute to his life-long companion and greatest interpreter.

Once again, Britten approaches an operatic score primarily in terms of atmosphere and geographical setting, but though the creation of local colour is very effective, Britten and Piper tend to overemphasize the symbolic in their adaptation of the story: Aschenbach is led to his fate, for example, by a number of sinister characters representing Death, all played by one singer. It's also an opera in which the element of self-disclosure is at times too prominent: moments like "The Games of Apollo", in which Tadzio (who is played by a dancer) and his companions perform athletics while Apollo (a counter-tenor) sings of male beauty, are barely sublimated expressions of Britten's erotic impulses. But if the work is confessional about Britten's attraction to boys, it is also a statement about Britten's view of the predicament of the artist – the pursuer of truth and beauty, but also the observer from afar, the outsider unable to become involved.

Unfortunately, Aschenbach's extremely long and arduous music is a mixture of Baroque-recitative simplicity and shapeless *Sprechgesang* that can leave you cold. The most striking music in the opera is associated with Tadzio and his friends, who dance to seductive gamelan-like music played on timpani and tuned percussion, but even these sections can seem overlong, and the same is true of the opera as a whole. Despite the depth of the central role, in the final analysis, *Death in Venice* is the least engaging of Britten's major works because its vocal style owes little to the expressive, lyrical manner for which his music is celebrated.

Pears, Shirley-Quirk, Bowman, Bowen; English Opera Group Chorus, English Chamber Orchestra; Bedford.
(London 425 669-2LH2; 2 CDs)

This powerful reading by Peter Pears of his last operatic creation for Britten was made when the tenor was over sixty, and yet it is one of his finest recordings. He succeeds in creating a remarkably haunting impression of the character's inner life – a quality that is nicely set against the frequently extreme characterizations of John Shirley-Quirk, who plays various characters with whom Aschenbach comes into contact. Steuart Bedford provides solid, if somewhat reverential support, and the beautifully shaped orchestral playing is well served by Decca's engineers.

MICHAEL TIPPETT

b. LONDON, JANUARY 2, 1905.

Michael Tippett is one of the very few English composers to have established an international reputation as an opera composer. Inspired by the great success of his friend Benjamin Britten's *Peter Grimes* (1945), Tippett began his own opera *The Midsummer Marriage* in the following year. Although he had already written several short operas for children and amateurs, this was his first full-scale opera, and it aroused immediate controversy, largely because of Tippett's libretto, which most critics found perversely obscure and esoteric – a criticism that has been repeatedly levelled at his four subsequent operas. In fact *The Midsummer Marriage* is a continuation of many of the themes adumbrated in the composer's great oratorio *A Child of Our Time* (1941), most notably the idea of the reconciliation of opposites, which in *The Midsummer Marriage* take the form of the destructive and the creative impulses in human nature. Whereas Britten's operas tend to dwell on the power of evil and the loss of innocence, Tippett's operas – for all their dark moments – move towards a sense of healing and wholeness achieved through understanding, a philosophy partly derived from his fascination with Jungian psychology. All of Tippett's operas, with the exception of *King Priam*, deal with contemporary issues but from a perspective that brings out their mythic and archetypal aspects: it is this aspiration to universality, coupled with his tendency to embrace fashionable political issues in his later operas, that has led several critics to dismiss his work as pretentious and naive.

NIGEL LUCKHURST/LEBRECHT COLLECTION

Michael Tippett

Musically Tippett belongs to no category except his own. His style, which has undergone some radical changes of direction during his long life, is underpinned by a late-Romantic lyricism which is fused to a modern astringency, though only rarely has he embraced atonality or serialism. A late starter, he did not begin to study music seriously until he was eighteen, but then applied himself assiduously to the mechanics and fundamentals of composition, continuing his studies at the Royal College of Music. His first recognized score was not produced until he was thirty, and he attracted virtually no public recognition for another ten years. Much of his early musical career was spent as a teacher and a conductor, working largely with amateur groups like the London Labour Choral Union. He was also involved in left-wing politics, briefly working in a mining village in Yorkshire and, at one point, he planned to write an opera commemorating the Irish Uprising of 1916.

Tippett's most significant pedagogical work was as director of Morley College, London, where, as well as teaching, he programmed a series of concerts that became known for their great variety. During World War II he was a conscientious objector but was briefly imprisoned for failing to do stipulated war work. He retired from Morley College in 1951 in order to spend more time composing, in particular to complete *The Midsummer Marriage*, which he had already been working on for four years.

Tippett's second opera, *King Priam* (1962), marked an unexpected change of approach – its dissonant, aggressive language being the antithesis of the tonal patterns common to his earlier work. Four years after *King Priam*, Tippet began *The Knot Garden* (1969), a psychodrama that examined the inner workings of a loveless marriage and marked another phase in his development, with its absorption of popular music – an element crucial to much of his later work. His fourth opera, *The Ice Break*, was conceived after visiting the USA and it encapsulates many of the composer's most personal philosophies, fusing classical procedures to jazz, boogie-woogie and an idealistic libretto that asks "whether or not we can be reborn from the stereotypes we live in". Tippett thought of it as his last opera but in 1986 he began to contemplate a magnum opus which would contain his entire life's experiences. Initially conceived as a piece for the concert hall, the project crystallized as *New Year*, an astonishingly confused and confusing opera in which various modern musical idioms (including taped music and rap) are allied to a utopian fantasy that is occasionally touching but more often inane. Both *The Ice Break* and *New Year* are thick with embarrassingly dated colloquialisms and, for all their undoubted sincerity, they represent the composer at his most self-indulgent and unfocused.

The Midsummer Marriage

Composed 1946–52.
First performed January 27, 1955.
Libretto by the composer.

Synopsis

Act I

Morning on Midsummer's Day outside a woodland temple. Mark and Jenifer are to be married in the company of a chorus of their friends. They disperse on the arrival of dancers, led by Strephon, and the two Ancients. Mark asks for a new dance for his wedding but the He-Ancient orders a repeat of the old dance. Jenifer arrives and calls off the wedding – it is truth, not love, that she seeks. The couple argue and Jenifer climbs a nearby spiral staircase, claiming "the light" for herself, and Mark falls into a cave. Jenifer's father, King Fisher, arrives with his secretary Bella, looking for Jenifer. He asks Bella to get her boyfriend Jack to open the cave gates. His first attempt fails and when he raises his hammer for the second time a mysterious voice warns him not to interfere. The Ancients emerge and demand that Mark and Jenifer sing of their experiences. The two are still in disagreement but decide to share each other's experiences – Jenifer descends into the cave while Mark ascends the staircase.

Act II

Afternoon at the temple. Strephon listens to the voices of Bella and Jack. Since it is Midsummer's Day, Bella proposes to Jack and they sing of their future together. Three ritual dances take place: Bella is scared by their violence and cries out. Jack comforts her.

Act III

Evening and night. The chorus are celebrating Midsummer but King Fisher sends them to collect Sosostris his clairvoyant, whom he will pit against the Ancients and win back his daughter. The chorus return, not with Sosostris but with Jack in disguise. During the ensuing confusion the veiled figure of Sosostris emerges and tells of a vision in which Mark and Jenifer are making love. King Fisher is furious and commands Jack to unveil her, but he refuses. When King Fisher himself unveils her, he finds a lotus flower enclosing Mark and Jenifer in each other's arms. He aims a pistol at Mark but when the couple turn to look at him he falls dead. A fourth ritual dance of human sacrifice is performed in front of the transfigured couple. The lovers prepare to celebrate their wedding as the sun rises.

The Midsummer Marriage is a quest opera that makes obvious reference to two great fantasies: Mozart's *The Magic Flute*, in the way two contrasting sets of lovers undergo a trial – one spiritual, one psychological – before they can be united; and Shakespeare's *A Midsummer Night's Dream*, in the way that the world of the lovers overlaps with a supernatural world which may or may not be a dream. Tippett also pays tribute to his literary mentor, T.S. Eliot, by borrowing the Fisher King and the clairvoyant Sosostris from his poem *The Waste Land* – it was Eliot who encouraged Tippett to create his own texts, having declined to collaborate on *A Child of Our Time* on the grounds that a strong poetic presence might compete with the composer's work. Even more important is the debt to Carl Jung, whose concept of archetypes – those symbolic figures and signs that are recognized, according to Jung, by us all – dominates the opera's supernatural landscape.

The initial inspiration for the opera was a vision of Tippett's own: "I saw a stage picture . . . of a wooded hilltop with a temple, where a warm and soft young man was being rebuffed by a cold and hard young woman . . . to such a degree that the collective, magical archetypes take charge – Jung's *anima* and *animus* – the girl, inflated by the latter, rises through the stage-flies to heaven, and the man, overwhelmed by the former, descends through the stage floor to hell." In the opera Jenifer and Mark reach a spiritual maturity by recognizing those elements of each other that exist in themselves, and in this they are obliquely assisted by the He-Ancient and the She-Ancient – guardians of the temple in the woods – and opposed by Jenifer's father, the dark and materialistic King Fisher. Central to the work are the "Four Ritual Dances" that enact the constant seasonal cycle of death and rebirth, culminating in Strephon's death and Mark and Jenifer's spiritual union in the final dance, "Fire in Summer".

The premiere of *The Midsummer Marriage* took place at Covent Garden with a young Joan Sutherland as Jenifer and Richard Lewis (Walton's Troilus) as Mark. Undoubtedly much of the initial bafflement was due to the deliberate ambivalence and irrationality of the story, but it was compounded by Barbara Hepworth's over-reverent designs, which created far too abstract and rarefied a mood. What makes *The Midsummer Marriage* ultimately convincing and one of the masterpieces of postwar opera is the sheer vigour and richness of the music, which conveys – more clearly than the words – a sense of transcendence. At moments reaching extraordinary heights of ecstatic lyricism, on a purely musical level this work is hard to fault. Reflecting the beauty of English summertime, Tippett's score is determinedly tonal and lyrical, with its roots planted firmly in the English pastoral tradition – indeed the long, slow-moving peroration that Madame Sosostris sings in Act III sounds close to Elgar in the way its luscious harmonies maximize the spiritual intensity. It is true that, like a painter incapable of finishing a canvas, Tippett often adds more and more layers until the idea gets smothered, but ultimately this is one of the most joyous and affirmative of all postwar operas.

Carlyle, Harwood, Remedios, Burrows, Herincx; Royal Opera House Chorus and Orchestra; Davis.
(Lyrita SRCD2217; 2 CDs).

Recorded in 1971 by Philips, this fine performance has recently been re-issued on Lyrita and stands as one of Colin Davis's finest achievements. Resisting the temptation to wallow in the splendour of the writing, Davis's disciplined approach illuminates the often thickly Romantic orchestration. The Covent Garden orchestra's playing is shimmeringly beautiful and the cast is no less exceptional: Alberto Remedios brings a true sense of impetuous vitality to Mark, and is nicely matched by the delicate beauty of Joan Carlyle's Jenifer. Elizabeth Harwood's earthy portrayal of Bella is perfectly judged while Raimund Herincx is a commanding and arrogant King Fisher. It's a studio recording but the cast is the same as in the 1970 Covent Garden revival so there is a real sense of thought-out characterization here, and the Covent Garden chorus have rarely sounded better.

King Priam

Composed 1958-61.
First performed May 29, 1962.
Libretto by the composer.

Synopsis

Act I

In the royal palace at Troy, Queen Hecuba has given birth to a son, Paris. The Queen's bad dream is interpreted as a premonition that the child will cause his father's death. Hecuba wants the child killed but the boy's father, King Priam, is torn between his duties as a father and as a king. Paris is not killed but given to a shepherd. As a young boy he meets his father and brother Hector out hunting. Priam decides to accept him as his son. At Troy the two brothers are antagonistic and, after Hector's marriage to Andromache, Paris goes to Greece where he falls in love with Helen, the wife of Menelaus of Sparta. Paris must decide whether to abduct Helen and provoke a war. In a divine test, he has to choose which of three goddesses – Athene, Hera and Aphrodite – is the most beautiful. He chooses Aphrodite, the goddess of love, and the corollary of his choice is that he will elope with Helen.

Act II

In the war between the Greeks and the Trojans, the Greek warrior Achilles refuses to fight because of an argument with King Agamemnon. At Troy Hector taunts Paris for not fighting. Priam encourages both of his sons to fight the Greeks. Patroclus tells his friend Achilles that the situation is desperate. Achilles agrees to lend Patroclus his armour. Patroclus is killed by Hector and Achilles is finally roused to action.

Act III

Hecuba, Andromache and Helen are at odds with each other. Andromache anticipates the death of Hector who is, indeed, killed by Achilles. Paris brings the news to Priam, who in his torment remembers his decision (in the first scene) not to have Paris killed. Priam visits the Greek camp and begs Achilles to release the body of Hector. Achilles feels pity for the old man and does so. Priam withdraws into his own inner world and will talk only to Paris and Helen. Finally he is killed by Neoptolemus, Achilles' son.

𝄞 Tippett was in no way put off by the initially negative reaction to his first opera, but his second, *King Priam*, marked a quite radical shift from the lyrical and celebratory to the bitter and clamorous. It is a transformation that can be partly explained by the harsh and violent change of subject. On the advice of theatre director Peter Brook, Tippett turned to an ancient legend, that of the fall of Troy after ten years of war. It is a story and a landscape filled with the suffering and pain of seemingly arbitrary and pointless killing, but Tippett saw the tale in terms of the fundamental questions that he had begun to explore in his earlier work. Significantly, he presents the story from the perspective of the losers, concentrating on the way choices have profound and far-reaching effects beyond the individual who made them: Priam chooses to let Paris live even though he has been warned of the consequences, while Paris's decision to award the prize to Aphrodite and abduct Helen unleashes a cataclysmic war. Tippett does not really question the basic premise of Greek tragedy – that the destiny of the individual is inescapable. Instead he anatomizes the struggle that each individual decision presents, discussing its moral dimensions in Brechtian interludes that occur between each scene. There are no easy answers in *King Priam*, although the opera also highlights the fact that compassion and fellow-feeling are always present even in war. In the most powerful scene in the opera the warrior Achilles feels pity, if not remorse, when Priam supplicates him for the body of his son.

The most obvious musical difference between *The Midsummer Marriage* and *King Priam* is the way the lush and largely contrapuntal orchestral writing of the earlier work has been replaced by something leaner and more focused. But what hasn't changed is the way Tippett's abstract and poetical text is transformed, and at times overwhelmed, by music of searing power and intensity. The orchestra may have been divided into smaller units, rarely playing in its entirety, but the resulting clarity brilliantly spotlights the emotional character of each scene. The raucous fanfare of brass with which the opera opens sets the dark background mood for the whole piece, against which individual scenes are set in relief. In some instances Tippett allocates particular instrumental combinations for different characters, as in the sombre but sensual cello writing that he gives to Andromache, or the violin figure that is associated with Hecuba. But for characters of greater complexity – in particular Priam and Achilles – he employs a variety of musical signifiers. Achilles gets the most lyrical moment in the whole opera, the guitar-accompanied "O rich-soiled land", and also the most chilling, when – hearing of Patroclus's death – he puts on his armour and gives forth his terrible war cry. Priam, who is sung by a baritone, has a vocal style which is predominantly hard and declamatory but he also has moments of increasing serenity until, by the end of the opera, his music suggests a kind of inner peace.

King Priam was first performed at the Coventry Festival of 1962, which celebrated the building of a new cathedral from the ashes of the old one destroyed in World War II. The festival also saw the premiere of Britten's *War Requiem*. Both works are highly personal responses to the impact of war, but of the two it is *King Priam* that most fully confronts the contradictory and conflicting impulses that war generates.

Bailey, Harper, Allen, Palmer, Langridge, Minton, Tear; London Sinfonietta Chorus and London Sinfonietta; Atherton.
(Chandos CHAN 9406/7; 2 CDs).

This outstanding recording was originally issued on Argo in 1981, and it's hard to imagine it being bettered. It boasts a cast that represents the cream of English singing talent, with Norman Bailey bringing both authority and vulnerability to the role of Priam, and Robert Tear making a commanding Achilles. The extraordinary tension and violence of Tippett's score is brought out by conductor David Atherton with great energy and panache.

The Knot Garden

Composed 1966–69.
First performed December 2, 1970.
Libretto by the composer.

Synopsis

Thea and Faber are a thirty-something married couple, guardians of Flora, a problem adolescent. They invite the psychoanalyst Mangus to attend to Flora but he soon realizes that it is Thea and Faber's marriage that needs attention. Mangus prepares a "session" based on Shakespeare's *Tempest*: Faber plays Ferdinand and Flora Miranda, and two homosexual friends, Mel and Dov, take the roles of Ariel and Caliban. Mangus presides as Prospero but Thea is not included.

Act I

Each of the characters presents themselves: Mangus trying to summon a tempest, Thea and Faber arguing, Flora relieving herself of her various neuroses and Mel and Dov preparing for the imminent therapy session. The relative security of the process is shattered by the arrival of Denise, Thea's "freedom fighter" sister. Physically and emotionally mutilated by torture, she is disgusted by the "beautiful and damned" before her.

Act II

Each of the characters expresses their true feelings in a series of duets. The two most wounded by the process, Dov and Flora, remain alone and console each other.

Act III

Mangus prepares four charades and, with the exception of Dov and Mangus, who now sees the presumption of his behaviour, each of the characters comes to terms with themselves. Mangus stops the session and the cast moves to the foot of the stage where they sing of the human emotions and qualities that can bind them and the audience together.

With the myth and theatricality of *King Priam* behind him, Tippett's third opera marked a return to the obscure quasi-philosophical universe of *The Midsummer Marriage*. When the opera was first revived at Covent Garden in 1972, William Mann wrote: "One cannot call it realism. The charm and power of *The Knot Garden* is that it is a real play, not just a fake of real life behaviour." Inspired by the intricacies of Mozart's *Così fan tutte*, Tippett constructs a psychological maze for the opera's seven characters, and the interaction between the protagonists has a complexity that for most people will outweigh the weaknesses of Tippett's calculatedly "contemporary" exploration of such subjects as the family unit and political evil.

The score marks something of a reconciliation between the sweetness of his first opera and the harshness of the second. Fast-moving and free of narrative diversions, *The Knot Garden* is a traditionally constructed opera (arias and ensembles), and its brief duration (just over an hour) and use of popular music (including jazz and blues) give it an accessibility that's not too common in modern opera. Denise's harrowing entrance aria "O you may stare" is typical of the opera's more astringent music, but while such passages dominate, they are set against episodes of lyrical warmth – such as Dov's song to Flora at the end of Act II, and Flora's song to Dov, a magically orchestrated version of Schubert's "Die liebe Farbe". The resultant bittersweet tone pervades an opera that embodies Tippett's almost ingenuous openness to new ideas and sounds.

Gomez, Barstow, Minton, Tear, Herincx, Hemsley; Royal Opera Chorus and Orchestra; Davis.
(Philips 446 331-2PH2; 2 CDs).

This is a typically professional production from the company that created the opera in 1970. Although one might have asked for less self-conscious conducting from Colin Davis (who seems much less in his element than on his recording of *The Midsummer Marriage*), he generates marvellous energy, and both chorus and orchestra give magnificently committed performances. Robert Tear, Thomas Hemsley, Jill Gomez and Josephine Barstow are superb as the couples, and the many ensembles, notably the Act I septet and the concluding quintet, are brilliantly carried off.

WILLIAM WALTON

b. OLDHAM, ENGLAND, MARCH 29, 1902; d. ISCHIA, ITALY, MARCH 8, 1983.

Although he dabbled briefly with atonality in his early string quartet, William Walton was an unrepentant neo-Romantic for most of his life. By his late twenties he had settled on a style that reconciled the essentially lyrical Englishness of Elgar with the pungency of Prokofiev and Stravinsky, a style characterized by earthy rhythms, wide intervallic writing, colourful and unstable harmonies and a predilection for melancholy. Walton may not be the most challenging of modern composers, but his music is always extremely well crafted and two of his works – *Belshazzar's Feast* and the *Symphony No. 1* – have proved to be among the most durable of the twentieth century. The critical jury is still out on his two operas: *Troilus and Cressida* and *The Bear* both contain some marvellous music, but neither has succeeded in winning a permanent place in the modern repertoire, even in Britain.

The son of a choirmaster and singing teacher, Walton spent his formative years in Oxford, where he was a chorister at Christ Church Cathedral. It was there that he began to compose, and in 1918 he was taken up by the aristocratic and artistic Sitwell family, with whom he lived. Three years later he achieved notoriety with *Façade*, a superficially modernist "Entertainment" for instrumentalists and a speaker who recited the poems of Edith Sitwell through a megaphone. Walton's style reached its full maturity with *Belshazzar's Feast* (1931), a dramatic cantata which revealed both a powerful dramatic sense and an ability to write genuinely lyrical music. Although he had developed a passion for opera – particularly Italian opera – at an early age, Walton did not consider writing one himself until 1941, when the music historian Cecil Gray suggested collaborating on the life of the wife-murdering Renaissance composer Gesualdo. Although Gray completed the libretto, the project foundered after a few years. A rather more fruitful collaboration was with Laurence Olivier, for whom Walton wrote a number of brilliant film scores. Beginning in 1944 with *Henry V*, Walton's music for Olivier reveals his acute sensitivity to narrative pace and development, as well as a sure touch in creating exactly the right mood for a particular scene.

Walton's only full-length opera, *Troilus and Cressida*, was commissioned by the BBC in 1947 as an opera for broadcasting. The troubled relationship between Walton and his librettist delayed work and it was not until 1954, after Walton had married and moved to the Italian island of Ischia, that the score was finally completed. *Troilus* was premiered at Covent Garden in the same year, but the ungenerous reception was a terrible disappointment to Walton and put him off writing opera until 1965, when the Aldeburgh Festival commissioned him to write a one-act work. Where *Troilus* was an excercise in the grand style, *The Bear* was a witty caprice that went down very much better with reviewers than the earlier opera. Walton's librettist this time was the playwright Paul Dehn, whom he had met on Ischia and with whom he enjoyed a good working relationship. Unfortunately, Dehn's death soon after the premiere in 1967 put paid to any further collaborations, and a mooted companion piece for *The Bear* never materialized.

Troilus and Cressida

Composed 1947–54; revised 1955, 1963 and 1972–76.
First performed December 3, 1954.
Libretto by Christopher Hassall, after Chaucer.

Synopsis

Act I

Troy is under siege from the Greeks. Calkas, the High Priest, wants to surrender but Antenor decides to do battle. Troilus professes his love to Cressida, Calkas's daughter, and is offered help in wooing her by her uncle, Pandarus. Calkas deserts to the Greeks and Antenor is captured. Troilus goes to his rescue, taking a scarf as a love token from Cressida.

Act II

Pandarus schemes for Troilus and Cressida to meet whilst sheltering from a storm. When they do, they declare their love for each other. They are interrupted by a Greek prince, Diomede, who demands that Cressida return to Calkas in exchange for Antenor. Cressida and Troilus are forced to part and he returns the scarf to her.

Act III

Cressida has not heard from Troilus for weeks as, unbeknown to her, his letters have been intercepted by Calkas. Diomede finally succeeds in seducing Cressida and receives the scarf which she had previously given to Troilus. Pandarus and Troilus arrive to hear Diomede claim Cressida as his own. However she refuses to renounce Troilus and a fight ensues in which Troilus is fatally stabbed by Calkas. Both Calkas and Cressida are taken prisoner but, in order to cheat Diomede of his prize, Cressida kills herself with Troilus's sword.

Once Walton had decided on *Troilus and Cressida* as a subject, he became absolutely clear about the type of opera he wanted to produce: "If my aim . . . was a close union of poetic and music drama, it was also my concern to recreate the characters in my own idiom as an example of English bel canto, the parts carefully designed to bring out the potentialities of each voice according to its range – in the hope of adding another "singer's opera" to the repertory." The singer he had in mind for the role of Cressida was the soprano Elizabeth Schwarzkopf, but in the end she decided against performing the part, citing her poor English as her reason, though she was clearly unhappy with the opera as a whole. This inauspicious start to the opera's performing history was made worse when the conductor Malcolm Sargent – a leading exponent of Walton's work but an inexperienced opera conductor – failed to learn the music by the time rehearsals began. In the end the first Cressida was Magda Laszlo, a Hungarian singer whose English was so bad that she had to be coached by the composer's Argentinian wife. Walton remained bitter about the inadequacy of preparations for the premiere, which he felt contributed to the opera's lukewarm reception. Critics were polite but the consensus was that the work fell between stools – being old-fashioned but not sufficiently lyrical. Another problem was thought to be Hassall's libretto, which was rather self-consciously poetic and which Walton later had no qualms about altering.

In fact, apart from one or two rather gushing moments, which were cut when the opera was revised in 1976, Hassall's libretto has many fine episodes and inspired some of Walton's most heartfelt writing, notably in Cressida's two biggest arias ("Slowly it all comes back to me" and "At the haunted end of the day"). The bel canto inspiration is evident in the rather obvious echoes of Italian opera, which sound slightly rhetorical and hollow. Walton sweetened his customarily tart orchestration with some exceptionally rich scoring (two harps and a large percussion section), which he deployed with great subtlety. It is true that his high dramatic ambitions are not always attained: the material is unevenly developed, and at moments when some truly dramatic music is called for – the entrance of the Greeks in Act III, for instance – the response is often bathetic. Troilus is too ineffectual to be heroic, and Cressida's predicament demands a brilliant actress/singer to be at all moving. This was surely the reason that Walton rewrote the part for the mezzo Janet Baker when Covent Garden revived the opera in 1976, but though the part arguably gained a greater emotional depth with this alteration, it lost incisiveness and combined less well with the tenor of Troilus. For all its flaws and its inconsistency, *Troilus and Cressida* is an opera that contains some of Walton's most powerful music, and – despite his desire to create "a singer's opera" – its energy, for the most part, comes from the orchestral writing.

Howarth, Davies, Robson, Opie, Howard; Opera North Chorus; English Northern Philharmonic; Hickox.
(Chandos CHAN9370/1; 2 CDs).

This 1995 recording, made after a production by Opera North, keeps some of the composer's 1976 revisions but returns the role of Cressida to its original soprano – the more effective setting. Judith Howarth copes well with the broad range and wide intervals, giving a highly sensitive portrayal. Arthur Davies is a worthy heir to Richard Lewis (the first Troilus), producing a powerful, varied tone, and Nigel Robson is an intelligent Pandarus. Hickox conducts a brisk and fluent performance and the sound is tight and nicely focused. All in all, just about everything the opera deserves.

Baker, Cassilly, English, Luxon, Bainbridge; Chorus and Orchestra of the Royal Opera House; Foster.
(EMI CMS 565 550-2; 2 CDs).

Produced in 1976, this was the first complete recording of the opera. Using Walton's revised score, it features Janet Baker as Cressida, and though her voice is here past its prime, it is still a glorious performance, displaying all the warmth and strength of character for which she was famous. She is fairly well partnered by the American tenor Richard Cassilly, whose rich and high-lying voice is well suited to Walton's Italianate music but sounds rather strained in the lower register. The remaining cast are remarkably strong and conductor Lawrence Foster draws some lovely playing from the Royal Opera forces, even if he seems a little unsure of his direction at times.

The Bear

Composed 1965–66.
First performed June 3, 1967.
Libretto by Paul Dehn and William Walton, after Chekhov.

Synopsis

Widow Popova is in mourning for her husband and refuses to cheer up, despite her servant Luka's reminder that the deceased was unfaithful, unreliable and hardly deserving of her anguish. Smirnov, a debt collector, arrives and tries to force the widow to pay interest on her husband's debts. She is outraged by Smirnov's ruthlessness and eventually declares that the only solution is to fight for the money. They arrange a duel (after Smirnov has shown her how to hold and fire a pistol) but, at the crucial moment, neither can shoot. Smirnov admits that he is love with her, and she soon gives in to his advances.

The Bear was described by its creator as an "extravaganza" rather than an opera, and it marks something of a return to the wit and stylishness of his earlier *Façade*. Lasting a mere forty-five minutes, it is lightly scored for three singers (mezzo, baritone, bass) and a small orchestra augmented with a piano, a harp and percussion. The tenor Peter Pears suggested Chekhov's burlesque *The Bear*, for which Walton adopted a suitably light and parodic style, paying homage to Chekhov's satirical bite and sharply sketched characters by writing almost exclusively in rhythm-dominated quasi-recitative. Tunes are scarce but, as in *Troilus*, the orchestration is exceptionally clever and inventive. Walton also clearly enjoyed taking swipes at several composers (including ones he respected): from the mock-Debussian French of Smirnov's wheedling pleas, to hints of Tchaikovskian romanticism as the duellists eye each other over their loaded pistols, and even a small dig at Britten. Some have argued that almost all the jokes necessitate an existing knowledge of their musical targets, but this is to ignore Dehn's clear and caustic libretto, which provides Walton with some brilliant opportunities for sustained irony – as in Widow Popova's "I was a constant, faithful wife", in which the closing word of each verse is repeated with an almost obsessional bitterness.

Jones, Opie, Shirley-Quirk; Northern Sinfonia; Hickox.
(Chandos CHAN9245).

The performers on this recording would be almost impossible to better. Alan Opie, one of the best operatic baritones around, practically steals the show as Smirnov, hurling himself into the burlesque with great abandon, but Della Jones and John Shirley-Quirk are no less excellent as Popova and Luka. Hickox generates a lively pulse, coaxing an elegant, beautifully pointed performance from the Northern Sinfonia, and the sound is bright and full.

HARRISON BIRTWISTLE

b. ACCRINGTON, ENGLAND, JULY 15, 1934.

Despite acknowledged debts to Stravinsky and Varèse, Harrison Birtwistle's music sounds as if it has sprung into being from somewhere outside the mainstream of European music, evoking the ceremonies of Greek tragedy, the ritual violence of ancient myths, the bleak and depopulated landscapes of rural England. Many of Birtwistle's compositions have the massive, rough-hewn quality of a prehistoric monument, but he can also produce music of spare lyrical beauty and, on occasion, haunting delicacy.

During the 1950s, when Birtwistle began his musical studies, the English scene lay in the shadow of Vaughan Williams (see p.476) and other such pastoral composers, while recent events in European music were generally regarded with reactionary disdain. It was in this claustrophobic environment that the "Manchester School", consisting of composers Birtwistle, Alexander Goehr and Peter Maxwell Davies (see p.557), plus conductor Elgar Howarth and pianist John Ogdon, began their careers, looking to the latest developments on the continent for inspiration. Birtwistle bided his time, studying clarinet and keeping his ambitions as a composer to himself until 1957 when, with the wind quintet *Refrains and Choruses*, he launched himself as the most distinctive voice among his illustrious contemporaries. It was strikingly raw and hard-edged music, and it unfolded not by any conventional development but as a series of static blocks, evoking a kind of imaginary rite.

Birtwistle scored his first major critical success with the ensemble piece *Tragoedia* (1965) – the title, meaning "goat dance", is drawn from Greek drama, one of the principal influences on Birtwistle during this period. Birtwistle's works of the 1960s culminated in the notorious chamber opera *Punch and Judy*, which was premiered at the Aldeburgh Festival in 1968. Here the ritual violence of instrumental works such as *Tragoedia* was transferred to an explicitly theatrical context, depicting the career of a murderous and libidinous Punch. Typical of this and Birtwistle's subsequent works for the stage is the lack of progressive narrative: the story is not told in sequence from beginning to end, but re-enacted over and over again, each time from a slightly different angle (Punch commits no

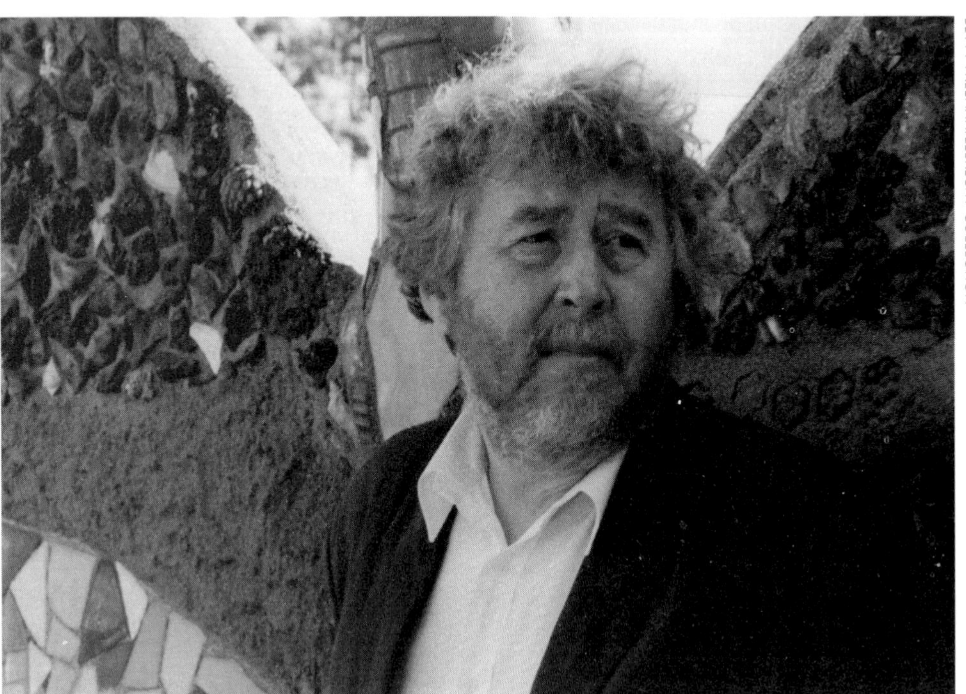

BETTY FREEMAN/LEBRECHT COLLECTION

Harrison Birtwistle

fewer than four murders), creating a tension between the heated, bloody subject matter and its cool, rather distanced presentation.

The work that really signalled the arrival of Birtwistle as one of the major composers of his generation was *The Triumph of Time* (1972), a monumental orchestral procession inspired by Brueghel's depiction of the remorseless progress of Time and Death. After this came a series of masterful works such as *Silbury Air*, *Secret Theatre*, *The Fields of Sorrow* and, in 1983, *The Mask of Orpheus*, a colossal opera which, with its masked and mythologized characters, represents the summation of Birtwistle's love of hieratic structures and repetitive narratives. Since the long-postponed premiere of *The Mask of Orpheus* in 1986, Birtwistle has increasingly turned his attention to opera. In 1988 came the "mechanical pastoral" *Yan tan tethera*, a supernatural tale of two shepherds, their sheep and the Devil, followed in 1991 by the monumental opera *Gawain*, in which he counterpoints the Arthurian hero's trials against the remorseless cycles of nature. His latest opera, *The Second Mrs Kong*, completed in 1994 and premiered at Glyndebourne, turned out to be a disappointment. Russell Hoban's libretto, with a cast list that included King Kong, a film mogul, a beauty queen, Vermeer, Orpheus and Euridice, is tortuous and pretentious (a charge that Birtwistle has always risked), and though the music is as approachable as anything by the composer – there is some dazzling, jazzy writing for piano accordion and saxophone – it doesn't project the strong sense of identity that *Gawain* does. It will be interesting to see how Birtwistle develops from what would seem to be a theatrical dead-end.

Punch and Judy

Composed 1966–67.
First performed June 8, 1968.
Libretto by Stephen Pruslin.

Synopsis

Punch is rocking the baby, then throws it into the fire. He stabs Judy to death when she finds the charred baby. Punch is now free to seek Pretty Polly, and he leaves on his horse. He finds her and offers her a flower, which she refuses, saying it was tarnished by his murder of the baby. The Doctor and Lawyer revile Punch, but they too are murdered and join Judy at the chorus gibbet. Punch again woos Pretty Polly, giving her a prism. Again she rejects him. Punch murders the Choregos, a narrator figure. This is a turning point in Punch's life. He is haunted by nightmarish images of his cruelty and a satanic wedding with Judy. Punch goes to the gallows for his crimes, but cheats the hangman. Pretty Polly reappears and the two sing a love duet around the gallows, now transformed into a maypole.

Birtwistle's first stage work was commissioned by and first performed during the 1968 Aldeburgh Festival, where it achieved instant notoriety by provoking the festival's guiding spirit, Benjamin Britten, to walk out in disgust. Many were appalled by all the wailing, clanging and violence, with one critic attacking *Punch and Judy* as "gratuitously offensive". For others, however, it constituted an uncompromisingly modern assault on the comfortable certainties of the English tradition – or rather, in its grotesque re-invention of end-of-the-pier children's entertainment, it revealed the barbarities lurking within certain aspects of traditional English culture.

Though the tale of *Punch and Judy* bears some resemblance to that of Monteverdi's *Coronation of Poppea* (a similarly disquieting opera in its day), and though its truncated toccatas, arias, recitatives, quartets and chorales apply the Baroque doctrine of "one mood per movement" to Punch's brutal progress, the sound-world of this *commedia dell'arte* horror-story is stridently new. The vocal writing requires the performers to sing way out of their natural ranges, and Birtwistle's characteristically aggressive score is especially notable for its percussive qualities, which can be thrilling in much the same way that a hailstorm can be. Providing some sort of anchor, various "musical signposts" punctuate the action: each murder is prefaced by the line "The sweetness of the moment is undeniably bitter"; the recurrent "Passion Chorales", in which Judy, the Doctor and Lawyer comment on what's just happened, are a distancing device that heightens the horror of Punch's rampage while invoking the precedent of ancient Greek drama; and duets, lullabies and dances act as lyrical counterpoints to the mayhem. *Punch and Judy* is modern opera's most frighteningly vivid portrayal of the Freudian id in all its cruelty and lustfulness.

Bryn-Julson, DeGaetani, Langridge, Roberts, Wilson-Johnson, Tomlinson; London Sinfonietta; Atherton.
(Etcetera KTC 2014; 2 CDs).

David Atherton, who conducted the first performance, gives a brisk and pungent account of this opera, with Stephen Roberts full-bloodedly horrible as Punch, and Jan DeGaetani a suitably tormented Judy. The recording quality is a bit flat, but that's the only reservation to be made about this intrepid venture.

The Mask of Orpheus

Composed 1971–84.
First performed May 21, 1986.
Libretto by Peter Zinovieff.

Synopsis

Act I

Euridice and Orpheus marry, but in running from the bee-keeper Aristaeus, who tries to rape her, Euridice is bitten by a snake and dies (two versions of this event are presented). After learning of her death, Orpheus visits the Oracle of the Dead in order to learn how he might be able to enter the Underworld.

Act II

This act is prefaced by another version of Euridice's death. Orpheus, the Man, dreams that Orpheus, the Hero, descends into the Underworld, passing through seventeen arches connecting life and death. He wakes up midway through "the dream", having failed to bring Euridice back, and hangs himself.

Act III

Nine versions of events in the myth are replayed, including the deaths of both lovers. Orpheus the Myth gradually overtakes Orpheus the Man and Hero. He is killed by Zeus for revealing divine secrets and is then sacrificially torn apart by the Maenads, followers of Dionysus, in the manner of Pentheus in the Bacchae myth. Eventually all that is left, his skull, becomes an oracle, but even this is silenced by Apollo.

The Mask of Orpheus is a remarkably complicated work, in which each of the principal characters appears in three guises: the mythical, the heroic and the human. Each is played by three performers: a singer (with a puppet double), a dancer and a mime. According to the composer, he wanted to examine "over and over the same event from different angles so that a multidimensional musical object is created, an object which contains a number of contradictions as well as a number of perspectives. I don't create linear music, I move in circles; more precisely, I move in concentric circles . . . to find a narrative to match this way of proceeding, I had to turn to myth, for only in myth do you find narratives that are not linear. Myths are multidimensional narratives containing contradictions and ambiguities. In telling a myth, you have to tell the whole myth, not just a part of it."

Act I is straightforward enough – largely expository, it presents the source material upon which Birtwistle elaborates in the next two acts. The rest of the opera, with its multiple time-shifts and character mutations, is considerably more demanding, as it elides, juxtaposes and reconstructs numerous readings of a myth that has been fertile ground for opera composers since the very beginnings of the genre. Each act is pivoted on a specific ritual (wedding, funeral and sacrifice), which serves as a point of fixity around which the opera revolves. The cyclical complexities of the text are reflected in the monumental score, in which "blocks of sound" are created by the fusion of live orchestral music with prepared tapes. Two years of intermittent labour at IRCAM in Paris went into the creation of the electronic score, which, in the words of David Atherton, "provides background auras (of summer, of winter, of bees etc)", as well as simulating the voice of Apollo, a great electronic belch that irrupts into the flow of the music.

Heard some seventy times during the opera's three and a half hours, Apollo's voice is an unforgettably impressive intervention. However, this is the only electronically produced vocal part. All the others are traditionally sung, with the range of colour and expression veering between song-like lyricism and urgent, grating *Sprechgesang*. Some of the more dream-like passages don't do much more than buoy up the words, which are frequently enigmatic to the point of incomprehensibility, but Birtwistle generally manages to maintain a sense of momentum as the opera returns again and again to the base material of the myth. Birtwistle's work is one of the most stimulating and ambitious of all operatic retellings of the tale of Orpheus – but unfortunately it's so ambitious that there's no recording of it, and no opera house has been brave enough to tackle it since its first run.

Gawain

Composed 1991.
First performed May 30, 1991.
Libretto by David Harsent, after *Sir Gawain and the Green Knight.*

Synopsis

Act I

A confrontation between Morgan le Fay, a sorceress, and Lady de Hautdesert is rapidly followed by scenes of King Arthur's court. Into the court comes a Green Knight, who challenges the court champion to decapitate him. Gawain does so, but the Knight picks up the head and rides off with it, having forced Gawain to promise to meet him next year so that he can return the blow. The seasons change and soon Gawain has to begin his journey to the distant Green Chapel.

Act II

Gawain is delayed on his journey to the Green Chapel when he stops at the castle of Bertilak. Here he is seduced by Lady de Hautdesert, and is attacked by the Green Knight. He survives the axe-wielding knight, only to realize that it is, in fact, Bertilak, who has succeeded in his aim to reveal Gawain to be no superhuman court champion, but an ordinary man with flaws, whose selfishness subverted the unity of Arthur's court.

Birtwistle's fascination with the changing seasons was first revealed in his dramatic pastoral *Down by the Greenwood Side*, which handled themes of death and rebirth with urgent, black humour. In *Gawain*, the passing year (represented explicitly in the Act I masque, "The Turning of the Seasons") takes on an added ritual significance as it marks out the year of waiting before Gawain can undertake his "rite of passage". With the slow revolution of the year and Gawain's arduous journey constituting the foundations of *Gawain*, Birtwistle's music has a greater sense of organic development than in his previous operas, and in its lush harmonies and complex, loud orchestration you might hear something of the sound-worlds of late Romanticism.

However, Birtwistle's counterpoint is so complex that there are, at times, a dozen separate strands at work simultaneously, and the end result is something like a sonic battering ram, as Birtwistle applies layer after layer of music in building one thunderous climax after another. There's the odd episode of tenderness, like the scene between Gawain and Lady de Hautdesert, but there is generally very little contrast throughout the opera's length – one critic characterized this as "music cast in chain mail". More than any other Birtwistle opera, *Gawain* has polarized opinion. At its premiere it became something of a battleground between proponents of the avant-garde and champions of a "back to melody" faction, who thought they were making a valuable contribution to British cultural life by heckling the performance. The hecklers, obsessed with what they took to be the cacophony of Birtwistle's score, overlooked what is a more serious problem with *Gawain*, which is that its modernity is only skin-deep. David Harsent's libretto is strewn with portentous mock-medievalisms – "This is the hour of vanity or choice / This is the hour of legacy or loss" is a typically oracular utterance – and Birtwistle's strenuous heroics similarly sound a little phony to some ears. It's difficult to resist the conclusion that underneath all the modernist trappings there lurks a nostalgia for a fabled time in which things were simpler than they are in the modern world – a nostalgia that links Birtwistle more closely with the Pre-Raphaelites than with the composers his sound-world often evokes.

Le Roux, Angel, Tomlinson, Walmsley-Clark; Chorus and Orchestra of the Royal Opera House; Howarth.
(Collins Classics 70412; 2 CDs).

This live recording was taken from a performance of the revised version at Covent Garden in 1994, in which the "Turning of the Seasons" was truncated. François Le Roux soars through the title role with noble ease; less secure is the soprano Marie Angel, who struggles with Le Fay's inconsiderately difficult writing. John Tomlinson does his usual scene-stealing act as the Green Knight and Elgar Howarth just about keeps on top of the enormous score.

PETER MAXWELL DAVIES

b. MANCHESTER, ENGLAND, SEPTEMBER 8, 1934.

Peter Maxwell Davies studied at Manchester's Royal Northern College of Music, where, with fellow students Harrison Birtwistle and Alexander Goehr, he formed a cell of composers seriously committed to the principles of the European avant-garde. At the same time Maxwell Davies was also exploring Indian ragas (the subject of his university thesis) and medieval music, developing a particular interest in the technique of basing the structure of a work on a pre-existent piece of plainsong. The lure of medievalism was not simply stylistic: much of Maxwell Davies's music confronts the notion of damnation, and his many theatre works frequently turn on the idea of an individual attempting to maintain authenticity in a morally confusing world.

After a spell as head of music at Cirencester Grammar School, and periods at Princeton and at Adelaide University, in 1968 Maxwell Davies founded, with Harrison Birtwistle, the Pierrot Players (later renamed the Fires of London). Before long he was writing most of his music for them, most controversially his *Eight Songs for a Mad King* (1969), a music-theatre spectacle which depicts the disintegrating inner world of King George III. In a work that is both harrowing and moving, Maxwell Davies transforms scraps of the King's words, tunes that he knew (and tried to teach his pet birds), and snatches from Handel's *Messiah* into an Expressionist collage of distorted foxtrots, bloodcurdling screams and demented instrumental chatterings. *Eight Songs* reveals Maxwell Davies's magpie-like plundering of different musical styles to create a disturbing picture of the world, and this talent for the using of parody to create several levels of meaning has remained a constant in his theatre music.

Maxwell Davies's long-standing fascination with the life and music of the sixteenth-century English composer John Taverner gave rise to two orchestral fantasias and *Taverner* (1962–70), an opera based on the historically dubious premise that, at the time of the English Reformation, Taverner abandoned composition in order to persecute Catholics. Davies uses much of Taverner's own music – in various transformations – as the thematic backbone of the opera, which has similarities with the violently parodic language of *Eight Songs for a Mad King*, though the orchestration has a richness and a complexity which suggests the influence of Mahler.

COLLINS CLASSICS/NICK WHITE

Peter Maxwell Davies

In 1971 Maxwell Davies moved to the solitary Orkney island of Hoy, where he has lived out the Romantic image of the reclusive composer while at the same time working hard to make his music of use to the local community. The sounds, landscapes, literature and history of the place have inspired many works, including his first and second symphonies (1976 and 1980), while his religious thought has taken on a more mystical hue, exemplified by his *Hymn to St Magnus* (1972), a work based on a twelfth-century psalm to the Orcadian saint. Crucial, too, has been the work of local writer George Mackay Brown, whose texts Maxwell Davies has frequently turned to, and whose novel *Magnus* formed the basis for the opera *The Martyrdom of Saint Magnus* (1973). Most of his stage works since his move have been shaped by the dramatic landscape and isolation of the island: *The Lighthouse* (1979) is his retelling of a true incident that occurred on the Flannan Islands at the turn of the century, while *Resurrection* (1986) shows the social and familial pressures placed on an individual to conform. More recently Maxwell Davies collaborated with producer/librettist David Pountney on *The Doctor of Myddfai* (1996), a commission from Welsh National Opera. Described by Maxwell Davies as his last full-scale theatre work, it encapsulates most of his life-long concerns, particularly in the way it uses an ancient story as a vehicle for truths about the corruption of modern politics and the stultifying power of officialdom.

The Martyrdom of Saint Magnus

Composed 1976.
First performed June 18, 1977.
Libretto by Peter Maxwell Davies, after George Mackay Brown.

Synopsis

Omens of war are muttered by Blind Mary, an oracle who represents the conscience of Orkney. During the Battle of the Menai Strait, Magnus refuses to fight but remains unharmed. Magnus is tempted five times but remains resolute. After years of civil unrest, Orkney is in a ruinous state. A meeting is arranged between the heads of the warring groups – Magnus and his cousin Hakon. Magnus foresees his own death followed by Hakon's treacherous plot to murder him and win control of Orkney. The time switches to the present day: reporters are jostling to relate the troubles of the island. The hanging of Magnus by Hakon and a henchman is represented as if in a concentration camp. The closing scene returns to the twelfth century and shows Blind Mary being healed by Magnus. But with her sight restored she sees only the audience's suffering and reminds us of Saint Magnus's sacrifice.

The Martyrdom of Saint Magnus was first performed at St Magnus's Cathedral in Orkney. Though the opera is similar to Britten's church parables in the way its ritualized solemnity creates a sense of detachment, it is far more political than the Britten works. Magnus, the son of the Viking ruler of Orkney, was a pacifist who himself eventually ruled Orkney with his cousin Hakon. In many ways *The Martyrdom of Saint Magnus* functions as an echo of the earlier *Taverner*, but whereas Taverner gives in to temptation and renounces his true nature to become an instrument of oppression, Magnus – like Taverner, sung by a tenor – resists temptation, renounces violence and becomes the victim of state oppression, a universal figure representing humanity in a brutal world. Depicting the hanging of Magnus in a contemporary context serves to reinforce – albeit clumsily – the work's political meaning, which is further rammed home by Blind Mary's confrontation of the audience in the final scene.

The opera is scored for five singers (who take several parts), supported by the forces of the Fires of London – flute, clarinet, viola, cello, percussion and keyboards – plus some stridently demonstrative brass. *The Martyrdom* is much less morally ambivalent than *Taverner*, and its music is also more economical and austere, with Gregorian chant recurring throughout as a kind of spiritual underpinning. Though there are moments of violence (largely reserved for the scenes set in the present day), the predominant mood is much calmer and more elegiac than in *Taverner*, and there are some finely detailed scene-setting instrumental interludes, of which the most adept is Magnus's stormy, premonition-laden crossing to Egilsay by boat. Magnus's lyrical declamation of his own impending death provides the most powerful moment in the whole opera, making Maxwell Davies's relapse into the Expressionistic agitprop of the final scenes all the harder to bear.

Dives, Gillett, Thomson, Morris; Scottish Chamber Opera Ensemble; Rafferty.
(Unicorn DKPCD 9100).

This recording was made on the back of a production by Music-Theatre Wales and each of the five soloists was involved in the stage performance. All the cast give well-characterized performances, although Christopher Gillett and Tasmin Dives are outstanding as the Prisoner and Blind Mary respectively. Michael Rafferty draws some imaginative colouring from the Scottish band and the engineered sound is open and unobtrusive.

The Lighthouse

Composed 1979.
First performed September 2, 1980.
Libretto by Peter Maxwell Davies.

Synopsis

In a brief prologue a court of inquiry investigates the mysterious disappearance of three lighthouse, keepers. The action then switches to the lighthouse where the three keepers, Arthur, Blazes and Sandy, quarrel over a game of cards then, in an attempt to lessen the tension, start singing. Their songs conjure up unwelcome aspects of their past. In the gathering mist of the sea the three are driven almost mad by their fantasies. Arthur starts the foghorn and mistakes the lights of a passing ship for the eyes of the Beast. Three officers from a passing supply boat arrive at the lighthouse and can find no trace of the keepers. The mystery remains unsolved.

Based on a real-life mystery, *The Lighthouse* is essentially a ghost story, albeit one – like *The Turn of the Screw* – in which the line between fantasy and reality is blurred, and seemingly straightforward protagonists gradually reveal a disturbed psychology. The moral ambivalence of the characters is emphasized by Maxwell Davies's casting, which requires each of the singers to take on the role of both lighthouse keeper and supply ship officer. An unnerving tension is maintained throughout, and the flashing of the automated lighthouse which ends the opera suggests that perhaps the supply ship officers are ghosts too, and that all the previous images have been hallucinations.

Theatrically *The Lighthouse* is Maxwell Davies's most effective work. It begins quite restrainedly, with the questions posed to the officers who discovered the abandoned lighthouse played by a solo horn placed in the audience. As the opera unfolds the music become more and more expressive, building to a climax in the psychological violence and claustrophobia of the card scene. The three men's songs bring to the surface the sense of trauma that has been lurking throughout: a music-hall ballad of increasing brutishness (accompanied by fiddle, banjo and bones) brings out the working-class violence that has tainted the childhood of Blazes; Sandy's maudlin love song is corrupted by the other two men; and Arthur's hymn – with Salvation Army-style acompaniment – reveals his religious guilt and violent impulses. As in Britten's *Peter Grimes*, the elemental power that surrounds the characters is depicted without sentimentality and *The Lighthouse* derives much of its tension from the implicit rhythms of the sea acting as a backdrop to the mounting hysteria of the keepers.

Mackie, Keyte, Comboy; BBC Philharmonic; Maxwell Davies.
(Collins Classics 14152).

Neil Mackie, Christopher Keyte and Ian Comboy produce performances which are almost as vivid on disc as they are on the stage. The explosive clashes between the sanctimonious Arthur and the aggressive Blazes are particularly well played, and emphasize the plaintive other-worldliness of Mackie's Sandy. The playing of the BBC Philharmonic is exemplary in all departments, fine-grained and richly variegated, so that even the densest textures have a focused luminosity. A splendid performance of a genuinely unnerving opera.

Resurrection

Composed early 1960s, completed 1986.
First performed September 8, 1994.
Libretto by the composer.

Synopsis

In a prologue the hero (a non-singing dummy with his back to the audience) is subjected to abusive advice from members of his family and various professionals. Representatives of moral authority – a vicar, a doctor and a headmaster – weigh in with their views but during a sanctimonious final chorale the hero's head explodes. The rest of the opera is an analysis of what went wrong: four surgeons begin a "moral dissection" of the hero, using capitalism, religion and socialism as cures for his lack of conformity. Just as the plot is dissolving into farce, an apocalyptic mood descends. The surgeons carry out more violent surgery, then sing a triumphant song celebrating their transformation of the hero. It is obvious, however, that what they have actually created is a gun-carrying Antichrist.

Whereas the musical parody of *The Lighthouse* is confined to three character-sketches towards the end of the opera, in *Resurrection* it intrudes into the musical texture to such an extent that it becomes the opera's defining feature. Violent swings in style replace cogent flow and development as the opera's guiding principle. The work was thirty-odd years in the making and there is something of the 1960s (in particular *A Clockwork Orange*) in its free-for-all critique of the nuclear family, authority figures and the crassness of consumer society. Revivalist marching hymns jostle with self-aggrandizing rock music, crackly Edwardian ballad with twee TV jingle, Mantovani strings and tinkling piano with shatteringly atonal nightmare music. Maxwell Davies is uncompromising and eclectic in his selection of material, and gloriously self-assured in his razor-sharp mockery. This is tempered by some beautiful, haunted lyricism that's reminiscent of Tippett (whose

Midsummer Marriage was an influence), and moments of intensely chilling and dark music. The major weakness of *Resurrection* is that its libretto cannot keep up with the tide of Maxwell Davies's musical imagination. Slogans about conformity and individuality seem merely clichéd in the context of such exuberantly anarchic music, while Maxwell Davies's identification of rock music with both the satanic and the banal seems worthy of the hero's reactionary oppressors. *Resurrection* was first performed at Darmstadt in a production thought to be so bad that it effectively killed off the opera's chances of success and it has never been staged since.

Jones, Robson, Hill, Jenkins, Herford, Finley, Best; BBC Philharmonic; Maxwell Davies.
(Collins Classics 70342).

Abandon all hope of following the plot, since the silence of the hero – around whom the opera revolves – makes the action seem even more convoluted on disc than it is on stage. Instead enjoy the dazzling partnership of Maxwell Davies and his orchestra and singers, who enter fully into the chameleon-like spirit of the work, traversing gospel music, jazz dances and jingles with breathtaking fluency. A sense of tension runs through the piece from beginning to end, conveying the real anger that feeds Maxwell Davies's satirical vision.

MICHAEL NYMAN

BORN LONDON, MARCH 23, 1944.

Michael Nyman's break as a composer came by way of Harrison Birtwistle, someone who might not seem too much in sympathy with Nyman's aggressive post-Minimalism. Nyman had already provided the libretto for Birtwistle's *Down by the Greenwood Side* (1968), when in 1977 Birtwistle, as musical director of London's National Theatre, asked Nyman to provide music for a production of Goldoni's play *Il Campiello*. At the time Nyman was known mostly as a critic (his superb *Experimental Music: Cage and Beyond* was published in 1974) and an editor of Purcell, and it was presumably his affinity with the Baroque that led to Birtwistle's request. Nyman put together the loudest band he could think of: banjo and soprano sax alongside rebecs, sackbuts, shawms and Nyman's own pumping piano. Nyman liked the sound so much that he kept the band together, first as the Campiello Band, then as the Michael Nyman Band. The outfit needed repertoire, Nyman had to provide it, and so began his full-time career as a composer.

At about this time he also wrote *1-100* for a film by Peter Greenaway, with whom he became a regular collaborator, providing music that the director would edit to suit his own cinematic priorities. So successfully did music and image marry that it now seems impossible to imagine films like *The Draughtsman's Contract* and *The Cook, The Thief, His Wife and Her Lover* without hearing Nyman's music (one H. Purcell is listed as "Music Consultant" for the former). In the end, the collaboration was terminated by mutual disagreement. Nyman has continued to write film scores, notably for Jane Campion's *The Piano* and for Volker Schlöndorff's *The Ogre*.

Success with film has not interrupted Nyman's other musical activities. He is a prolific composer, whether writing for his band, or for more conventional concert hall ensembles and soloists. His music is assertive, insistent, repetitive and tuneful, and work for the cinema has given him a sure grasp of timing and timbre. In addition to *The Man Who Mistook his Wife for a Hat*, he has written TV operas (*The Kiss*, 1985; *The Man Who Mistook his Wife for a Hat*, 1986; *Letters, Riddles and Writs*, 1991) and operas for the stage (*Orpheus's Daughter*, 1988; *Vital Statistics*, 1992) – though the latter pair remain in limbo, awaiting the composer's final thoughts – as well as *La*

Princesse de Milan (1991), a work occupying a middle-ground between opera and ballet. His most celebrated opera remains *The Man Who Mistook . . .* , but Expo 98 in Lisbon has commissioned an opera from him, and he has long nurtured a dream of turning Sterne's *Tristram Shandy* into an opera – so perhaps his major contribution to the genre lies ahead.

The Man Who Mistook his Wife for a Hat

Composed 1985–86.
First performed October 27, 1986.
Libretto by Christopher Rawlence, after Oliver Sacks.

Synopsis

In a spoken prologue, Dr S explains that he seeks a neurology that centralizes the patient's humanity rather than any perceived "deficit". Dr and Mrs P enter. Dr P is a professional singer who habitually makes silly visual gaffes. When, on leaving the surgery, Dr P grabs his wife's head instead of his hat, Dr S sees the problem.

Dr S visits Dr P at home. The two discover a mutual passion for Schumann. Although Dr P can no longer read music, his musical brain is intact; later he beats Dr S at chess. The neurologist notices that Dr P's paintings trace a path from naturalism to abstraction, a path that parallels the progress of his illness, but Mrs P views the change as artistic progress. She calls Dr S a philistine.

At the exclamation "Philistine!", Dr P, who has been humming to himself while eating, freezes into silence. Dr S sees in this a key to the illness, and suggests that Dr P continues to render his world coherent through music, making his own "internal soundtrack". In a spoken epilogue, Dr S tries to understand Dr P: "When the music stopped," he says, "so did he."

Few composers would see the raw material for an opera in Oliver Sacks' neurological case-study, but having grasped the potential, Nyman homes in on the heart of the matter, while his librettist Christopher Rawlence (who has also provided a libretto for Michael Torke's TV opera *King of Hearts*) makes dramatic what could easily be no more than diagnostic.

With three singers and an ensemble of seven players (strings, harp and Nyman's piano), the musical textures of *The Man* are thinner than usual with Nyman, but this gives the music a lightness and transparency not always present in his brasher scores. The vocal lines are not "expressive" in any conventional fashion, but they allow you to follow what is a moving and literate libretto. Nyman alludes frequently to Schumann in the score, and includes a complete performance of the song "Ich grolle nicht" (from *Dichterliebe*), but what emerges is distinctly Nymanesque: repetitive, even mechanistic, but carrying a real emotional weight.

Belcourt, Leonard, Westcott; ensemble; Nyman.
(CBS MK44669).

This was recorded shortly after the work's premiere at London's Institute of Contemporary Art. Mrs P was originally sung by Patricia Hooper; on this single disc (the opera lasts less than an hour) her part is taken by Sarah Leonard, who has been associated with Nyman's music for many years, and whose slightly antiseptic timbre suits the role perfectly.

JOHN TAVENER

b. LONDON, JANUARY 28, 1944.

In the early 1960s, John Tavener was regarded as something of a prodigy, taking the solo part in the premiere of his own *Piano Concerto* when only eighteen years old, and conducting the first performances of his opera *The Cappemakers* and his prizewinning cantata *Cain and Abel* at the ages of twenty and twenty-two, respectively. Then in 1968 a new contemporary music ensemble, the London Sinfonietta, played a work it had commissioned from Tavener for its inaugural concert. *The Whale*, a retelling of the Old Testament story of Jonah, was a highly theatrical piece, involving prerecorded tape, amplified metronomes and a narrator within an original, somewhat exotic instrumental line-up. Its success was immediate and, in new music terms, enormous – The Beatles came close to adopting Tavener as in-house composer for Apple Records, and issued a recording of *The Whale*.

With its flamboyance and wry humour, *The Whale* is far removed from the music that has made Tavener one of the most successful composers of the 1990s. Always religious, Tavener joined the Russian Orthodox Church in 1977, and ever since has seen his music as part of the tradition of Orthodox liturgy. For Tavener, innovation is a chimera, and almost the only twentieth-century composer he admits to admiring is Stravinsky. His iconic, static style is at its most concentrated in *The Protecting Veil* for cello and strings, the recording of which (by Steven Isserlis and the London Symphony Orchestra under Gennadi Rozhdestvensky) was an enormous hit in 1993.

A music which aspires to stasis is not innately theatrical, yet Tavener has written several stage-works, including the one-act opera *Thérèse*, premiered at Covent Garden in 1973, and described by the critic Stephen Walsh as "a kind of operatic *Dream of Gerontius* cum *Inferno* on the death agonies of St Thérèse de Lisieux". *A Gentle Spirit* (1977), based on a short story by Dostoevsky, was another stage-work with a libretto by Gerard McLarnon, himself a convert to the Orthodox faith.

In 1981 Tavener met Mother Thekla, Abbess of the Greek Orthodox Monastery of the Assumption in Buckinghamshire (she is now based in Yorkshire). Their meeting marked a turning point in the composer's life. Mother Thekla became his spiritual adviser, and although she professes herself unmusical, has provided the libretti for Tavener's two most recent stage-works, *Mary of Egypt* and *The Toll Houses* (still in progress). Since meeting her, Tavener has purified his music still further, to the point where some find it simply boring. Others, though, are immensely moved – and besides, critical denunciations of "Holy Minimalism" mean as little to Tavener as they do to the no less devout Arvo Pärt. Both composers continue along a way which may not be merry, but which is certainly functional and focused.

Mary of Egypt

Composed 1990–91.
First performed June 19, 1992.
Libretto by Mother Thekla.

Synopsis

Act I

Mary of Egypt is a prostitute in Alexandria; Zossima is a holy man in a monastery in Palestine. The two meet. Zossima poses the rhetorical question, "Am I not perfect in ascetic labour, in toilsome tasks outstripping my neighbour?" A chorus of Swine Women and Swine Men hymn the delights offered by Mary while ridiculing Zossima's self-righteousness. Mary joins a pilgrim band on its way to Jerusalem; a voice advises Zossima to find salvation in the desert.

Act II

Zossima joins a band of desert monks in their labours, while in Jerusalem Mary finds that entry to the church of the Holy Sepulchre is barred to her. She prays to the Mother of God, who replies that she must give up the pleasures of the flesh and go to the desert.

Act III

The Jordan desert, 47 years later. Mary and Zossima meet again. Zossima sees her "Perfection . . . the most gracious of your kind" and asks for her blessing. Mary replies that he must give the first blessing. They then sing an ecstatic duet. Mary tells Zossima to return in one year's time so that he can grant her wish for "the Blood and Body of our Christ".

Act IV

One year later. In mime, Zossima and Mary meet; Mary walks on water, and bids Zossima once again to return in one year's time.

Act V

One year later, Zossima returns, but can't find Mary. Suddenly he sees her dead body; beside it is written in the sand "Bury humble Mary". With the help of a chorus of "lion and animals" he does so. Mary has achieved her salvation; Zossima must continue to search for his.

Tavener describes *Mary of Egypt* as an "Ikon in Music and Dance", and we are invited to imagine the action in terms of a triptych, the panels of which open as the opera unfolds, and then close as it comes to an end. The lack of event such a description implies is certainly one of the opera's characteristics, but this ritualized parable is by no means untheatrical, and much of the music is highly appealing.

One of the opera's most striking features is the use of an overtone singer for the heavenly Voice which Mary and Zossima repeatedly hear, but the more conventional soprano part of Mary is also strikingly beautiful, as are the slow and sinuous lines within the orchestra. Raucous brass fanfares repeatedly break through the monochrome fabric, as if to wake anyone who might have drifted away into sleep. *Mary of Egypt* may not be opera as we know it, but it is one of Tavener's most typical works – seductive and frustrating, alluring and frozen.

Rozario, Varcoe, Goodchild; Ely Cathedral Choristers; Britten-Pears Chamber Choir; Aldeburgh Festival Ensemble; Friend.
(Collins Classics 7023-2; 2 CDs).

Recorded during the premiere performances at the 1992 Aldeburgh Festival, this set captures the heady incense of Tavener's strange creation. Patricia Rozario is one of the composer's favourite singers, and he has written several pieces for her, including the role of Mary. Her clear, bright voice dominates the performance, only upstaged when Chloe Goodchild's remarkable heavenly Voice blasts through the speakers. The CDs also include an interview with Tavener, who talks about the opera.

JUDITH WEIR

b. CAMBRIDGE, ENGLAND, MAY 11, 1954.

Judith Weir, one of Britain's most gifted opera composers, is on record as having declared: "I increasingly work with theatre and dance companies, who seem to have much more use for the living composer than opera houses do.". Yet she has written three full-length (but never long-winded) operas, as well as a dance/opera collaboration with choreographer Ian Spink (*HEAVEN ABLAZE in His Breast*; 1989); *The Black Spider*, an opera "suitable for performance by secondary school pupils" (1985); a "re-composition" of Mozart's *Il Sogno di Scipione* (Scipio's Dream; 1991); and *King Harald's Saga*, a "Grand Opera in Three Acts" lasting barely ten minutes. In addition, she has composed incidental music for Peter Shaffer's *The Gift of the Gorgon*, and for Caryl Churchill's *The Skriker*. Theatre in all its forms is what moves and excites her.

She studied at Cambridge with Robin Holloway, who has said that already there was nothing he could teach her. Earlier she had studied with John Tavener, and played the oboe in the National Youth Orchestra. "Any particular empathy I have with singers probably comes from those oboe-playing days I spent gulping in large lungfuls of air and (more urgently) trying to find opportunities to breathe it out again." The musical establishment has not been slow to make use of her talents. She has taught in Glasgow (1979–82), held a creative arts fellowship in Cambridge (1983–85), and been Composer in Residence at the Royal Scottish Academy of Music and Drama (1989–91). In 1995 she was appointed Composer in Association with the City of Birmingham Symphony Orchestra.

Her music shows a debt to Stravinsky and to Messiaen, but draws no less on folk traditions from her native Scotland, from elsewhere in Europe and from further afield. There is often an irony in her work, as if she were trying to undercut her deep Romantic affinities, which are most evident in her opera *The Vanishing Bridegroom* (1990); but her text-setting is always precise and imaginative, often being tailored to suit particular voices. She prefers to provide her own libretti: "I've never considered myself a poet, it's entirely a matter of expediency." In every other way she has proved to be a willing collaborator.

King Harald's Saga

Composed 1979.
First performed May 17, 1979.
Libretto by the composer, after the thirteenth-century Icelandic saga *Heimskringla*.

Synopsis

Act I

In 1066, King Harald recalls his military glories. Treacherous Tostig persuades Harald to invade England.

Act II

In a dream, Harald sees his dead brother, St Olaf, who counsels against invasion. Harald rejects the advice and sets sail, bidding his two wives farewell.

Act III

Harald lands with his army, fights the English and loses. His army is wiped out. Harald is among the dead.

Epilogue

A sage ponders Harald's death.

Less an opera than a virtuoso ballad, *King Harald's Saga* calls for the soprano soloist to take on eight solo roles, and impersonate an army, all in ten minutes. Weir skilfully finds ways of allowing a single voice to delineate different characters, provided the soloist has the resources. Many clearly do, for the piece has become a favourite showpiece in new-music circles, where such wit is a rare commodity. Weir asks her soloists to do a certain amount of parodying of new-music clichés, but there is also a gentle, rather wistful lyricism here – Weir's humour is rarely free of melancholy.

Manning.

(United 88040 CD; with *The Consolations of Scholarship* and *Missa del Cid*).

Weir wrote this piece especially for Jane Manning, a long-standing champion of new music, who here gives a definitive performance. The accompanying pieces are invaluable demonstrations of Weir's talent as a writer for the voice: *The Consolations of Scholarship* is a 25-minute song-cycle in which Weir, in her own words, "combined the dramatic elements of several Yuan dramas, and other Chinese sources, into a story-line which resembled a speeded-up opera with the singer taking all the roles and the narrative"; *Missa del Cid*, for ten unaccompanied singers, juxtaposes the Latin mass with a thirteenth-century account of the exploits of El Cid.

A Night at the Chinese Opera

Composed 1986–87.
First performed July 8, 1987.
Libretto by the composer, based on the thirteenth-century drama *The Chao Family Orphan* by Chi-Chou Hsiang.

Act I

Khublai Khan invades the city of Loyan. Chao Sun leaves, abandoning his wife and baby son, Chao Lin, who grows up to become a successful engineer. He is commissioned to build a canal through the region where his father is in exile. Chao Lin attends a performance of *The Chao Family Orphan*.

CATHERINE ASHMORE

A scene from Judith Weir's Chinese opera

Act II

The peformance of the play is interrupted when the Fireman and the Soldier burst in with news of an earthquake to the north. Chao Lin, deep in thought, has noticed striking resemblances between the play and his own life.

Act III

The morning after the play, Chao Lin sets off with a workers' convoy to build the canal. He tries to find his father, but is told that he died in exile. Chao Lin plots revenge against Khublai Khan's military governor, but is captured and sentenced to death. Now the actors gather again to rehearse the last part of their play, in which the Orphan of Chao is rewarded by the Emperor for thwarting a treasonous plot.

𝄞 Weir believes that, just as many of the West's scientific discoveries were prefigured in China, so what we look for in modern theatre "had been put down on the page by Chinese playwrights seven hundred years ago . . . with a dramatic cogency and a justification for the presence of music for which, on the whole, twentieth-century music is still looking". The result is not mere Chinoiserie. Although there are instances of what Weir calls "imaginative reconstructions of Chinese originals", she insists that "it was never my intention to attempt a reconstruction of . . . original performance styles". Though she provides directions on Yuan dramatic style for the play in Act II, and a note on role distribution in Chinese opera, what emerges is nonetheless distinctly a work by Weir.

The story-within-a-story is a Weir trademark, as are the brightly glittering surfaces of the opera's sound-world, where Western disciplines constantly collide with Eastern possibilities. Some have suggested that there is little substance beneath those surfaces, but this was the first full-length opera by a young composer, and its exuberance should not be mistaken for shallowness. Many composers might have made something ponderous from a story of a young man living through tyranny. Weir's way is wittier and wiser – but at the moment there is no recording to demonstrate the fact.

Blond Eckbert

Composed 1993–94.
First performed April 20, 1994.
Libretto by the composer, after Ludwig Tieck.

Synopsis

Act I

A bird tells a story to a dog. It is the story of Blond Eckbert and his wife Berthe, who are visited by Walther. Berthe tells Walther the story of her life: she ran away from cruel parents, and was taken in by an old woman whose only possessions were a dog, whose name Berthe no longer recalls, and a bird which lays jewels. Berthe, having tied up the dog, ran off with the bird, returned to her village, and met and married Eckbert. Berthe's story over, all three prepare for bed. Berthe and Eckbert are amazed to discover that Walther knows the name of the dog in the story. Eckbert fears that Walther intends to steal the bird's jewels.

Act II

In the prelude, we see Eckbert kill Walther. Berthe, disturbed by Walther's visit, is at death's door. Racked with guilt, Eckbert visits the nearby city, where he is befriended by Hugo. But Eckbert sees that Hugo resembles Walther, and rushes away in fear. He finds himself outside the house of the old woman from Berthe's story. The old woman reveals herself as both Walther and Hugo, and horrifies Eckbert with the news that Berthe was his long-lost sister. Eckbert goes mad and dies. The bird, having finished telling its story, flies away, chased by the dog.

𝄞 At one point in Act II, Eckbert sings of "The marvellous mingled with the commonplace", a precise description of Weir's imaginative world. She herself has called Tieck's story "a psychological thriller", "a Gothic mystery" and "a crime novel", and there are elements of all three in her typically epigrammatic telling of the tale. At times, perhaps, her music, particularly the vocal lines, seems to be treading water so as to allow the story to catch up, but there are moments of striking colour: the Act II prelude can't be said to be illustrative in any conventional sense, but it paints a bewitching picture nevertheless; while the opera's last scene, plainly labelled "At the End", has an intensity that is chilling. There remains the suspicion that Weir's music can't quite take Tieck's story seriously, but there is no doubt that the opera is the work of a gifted musical storyteller.

Jones, Owens, Ventris, Folwell; English National Opera Chorus and Orchestra; Edwards.
(Collins Classics 1461-2).

Inevitably this is a live recording, for in this day and age few record companies can afford the costs and risks of a studio recording for new operas. In any case, this single CD (the opera lasts 65 minutes) does full justice to Weir's score. Sian Edwards' conducting of the premiere was not well reviewed, but here, although the opera is deprived of Tim Hopkin's virtuoso production, the pacing and balance are fine, and the cast's commitment is exemplary.

MARK-ANTHONY TURNAGE

b. GRAYS, ENGLAND, JUNE 10, 1960.

For a time during the 1980s, Mark-Anthony Turnage enjoyed playing the role of Essex soul boy as a way of distancing himself from the new-music mainstream. It wasn't entirely a ruse, for Turnage has real affection for jazz-funk idioms – he grew up listening to it, and studied at Tanglewood with Gunther Schuller, who in the 1950s played with Miles Davis and coined the term "Third Stream" to describe his own and others' attempts to bring jazz and modern composition together. Schuller would seem to have had a profound influence on Turnage, whose admiration for Miles Davis verges on the idolatrous, and whose own music is imbued with the colouristic possibilities offered by jazz. In 1996 he went so far as to write a piece, *Blood on the Floor*, which placed improvising jazzmen within a straight-ahead chamber ensemble.

Greek, Turnage's first opera, was commissioned by Hans Werner Henze for the Munich Biennale, and took as its text Steven Berkoff's scabrous modern version of the Oedipus myth, published in 1980. Created with the help of Jonathan Moore, who directed the 1988 premiere, it was a brutal fable of Thatcher's Britain, and its foul language was a deliberate rejection of opera house decorum. From 1989 to 1993 Turnage was Composer in Association with the City of Birmingham Symphony Orchestra, where his music found a champion in Simon Rattle. The opportunity to work and experiment with the same group of musicians taught him much about how to write for the orchestra, and his music has grown in confidence since. In 1995 he was appointed Composer in Association to English National Opera, where he became closely involved with the company's Contemporary Opera Studio. If that seemed an odd position for someone with only one opera to his credit, Turnage quickly set about turning himself into a genuine opera composer: besides writing *The Country of the Blind* for the 1997 Aldeburgh Festival, he is at work on an operatic adaptation of Sean O'Casey's play *A Silver Tassie*, scheduled for performance by English National Opera in 1998.

Greek

Composed 1987–88.
First performed June 17, 1988.
Libretto by the composer and Jonathan Moore, after Steven Berkoff.

Synopsis

Act I

Eddy, an Oedipus for our times, wants to escape the mundane routines of his lumpen existence, and imagines himself in a more sophisticated milieu. Back in the real world, Dad tells his son about a gypsy prophecy that Eddy's father will die a violent death, and that – "something worse than death" – Eddy will have "a bunk-up with his Mum". Eddy, appalled at the idea, leaves home. He encounters police brutality, and seeks safety in a café. When service is slow, Eddy kicks the manager to death and falls in love with the dead man's wife. Wife tells her new man of her long lost infant son.

Act II

Ten years later, Eddy and Wife are now prosperous. Mum and Dad visit their café, reminding Eddy that a plague stalks the land. Outside the city, a Sphinx is killing all who cannot answer her riddle. Eddy sets off to tackle her, finds that there are two Sphinxes, answers their riddle, and beheads them. He is welcomed back as a hero, but to his horror learns that Mum and Dad are not his natural parents. Eddy realizes that Wife is his real mother, and that he is "the source of all the stink" that engulfs the city. In a Soliloquy of Regret he laments his situation and appears to blind himself. A funeral procession carries him away, but with a hearty "Bollocks to all that!" Eddy comes back to life and runs to rejoin his mother/Wife: "Exit from Paradise, Entrance to Heaven!" he exclaims.

Steven Berkoff has expressed dismay at the way Turnage and Jonathan Moore stripped his play of its mythic qualities, exaggerating its visceral invective for the sake of political immediacy. There's some justification for his dismay, for *Greek* the opera is very much a product of its time, a one-off that now looks rather dated in its rhetoric, whereas Berkoff strove to be, if not universal, then at least not parochial. Furthermore, impeccably trained opera singers have problems striving for the exaggerated vowels of "estuary English", and the best efforts of the cast are often undercut by Turnage's distancing irony. But what gives the opera its undoubted power is the orchestra, an ensemble of 21 players, most of them called on at one time or another to double on percussion. *Greek* is not the only opera where the real drama takes place in the orchestra, and here Turnage deploys every atom of his considerable skill to produce a score that is cinematic in its matching of colour to mood. The Prologue to Act II manages, in a brief two minutes, to encapsulate brooding anger, menacing tension and a certain emotional expansiveness, telling us things that the singers, their declamation vacillating between parlando and mob bellowing, can only hint at.

Hayes, Suart, Kimm, Charnock; Greek Ensemble; Bernas.
(Argo 440 368-2ZHO).

This must be one of the few opera recordings to be issued with a parental warning sticker. It's virtually an original cast recording, and benefits from the singers' familiarity with, and fierce commitment to, the piece. Still, it's the orchestra that impresses most: Richard Bernas conducts with an exact command of the nuances Turnage requires.

GIAN CARLO MENOTTI

b. CADEGLIANO, ITALY, JULY 7, 1911.

The career of Gian Carlo Menotti is one of twentieth-century opera's most spectacular cases of changing fashion. From 1945 through to the early 1960s his particular brand of tuneful verismo, with its dash of Hollywood style, made him the most successful opera composer in the USA. His short opera *The Medium* (1945) established his international reputation and was later made into a film under Menotti's direction. He consolidated his position with *The Consul* (1949) before achieving a kind of immortality with *Amahl and the Night Visitors* (1951), a charming if deeply sentimental tale, based on the story of the Three Kings. Though *Amahl* became a staple of Christmas TV schedules in the US, and remains a favourite of amateur opera groups far further afield, by the 1960s Menotti was regarded by many as hopelessly old-fashioned. He continued to write opera but productions of his work became increasingly sporadic and badly received. As a result, much of his energy went into his Festival of Two Worlds, an annual event at Spoleto in Umbria, which Menotti founded in 1958 to give young American and European musicians the chance to appear in world-class productions. It is still one of the world's great arts festivals.

Menotti was an exceptionally precocious child. He composed two operas before entering the Milan Conservatory at the age of thirteen, and in 1928, at the suggestion of Toscanini, moved to America and the Curtis Institute of Philadelphia. There he met and studied alongside Samuel Barber (see p.572), who became his companion and for whom he wrote libretti. After travels in Italy and Austria with Barber, Menotti began a one-act opera buffa, *Amelia Goes to the Ball* (1937), which was performed in Philadelphia and New York. Its popularity was such that the following year the Metropolitan Opera of New York staged it with Strauss's *Elektra* in a highly eccentric double bill. This led to a commission from NBC for a radio opera, *The Old Maid and the Thief* (1939), and a request from the Met for another opera, *The Island God* (1942), which made little impression. Menotti wrote no further operas until 1945, when he produced *The Medium* – a phenomenal success which was staged in London soon after its New York premiere and subsequently travelled the world. After *Amahl*, *The Medium* is Menotti's most frequently revived work.

One year later Menotti wrote a frothy comedy called *The Telephone* as a companion piece for *The Medium*, and followed it with *The Consul*, his first full-length opera. Its subject – state oppression – gave it a Cold War topicality, but unlike the contemporaneous *Il prigioniero* by Dallapiccola (see p.503) or Einem's *Dantons Tod*, the darkness of *The Consul* frequently seems melodramatic. Nevertheless, it ran for eight months in New York and won a Pulitzer Prize. The fine original cast recording, made in 1950, has long been unavailable, and reassessment of what some regard as Menotti's masterpiece is long overdue. *Amahl and the Night Visitors*, completed two years later, confirmed Menotti's box-office infallibility and, like Puccini forty years earlier, it seemed as if he could do no wrong.

The turning point in his fortunes came in 1956 when Joseph Kerman published his highly influential *Opera as Drama* and singled out Menotti's *The Saint of Bleeker Street* (1954) for particularly swingeing criticism: "Menotti is a sensationalist in the old style, and in fact a weak one, diluting the faults of Strauss and Puccini with none of their fugitive virtues." Menotti's reputation never really recovered, even though at its best the sheer theatrical know-how of his work and the passion of his music can be highly effective.

The Medium

Composed 1945.
First performed May 8, 1946.
Libretto by the composer.

Synopsis

Act I

In the parlour of Madame Flora – a medium known as Baba – her daughter Monica and Toby (a mute servant boy) are preparing for a seance. The clients for that evening are Mr and Mrs Gobineau (who are regulars) and Mrs Nolan, a widow who is attending for the first time. During the seance, Monica impersonates the spirit voices and Mrs Nolan thinks she recognizes her dead daughter's voice. Suddenly Baba becomes hysterical when a cold hand seems to touch her throat. Suspecting Toby (who operates the trick effects), she turns out her visitors and tries to interrogate him. Monica tries to soothe her by singing.

Act II

As Toby performs a puppet play for Monica, she realizes that he loves her. Baba enters drunk and resumes her accusations of Toby. The Gobineaus and Mrs Nolan arrive expecting a seance, and are disbelieving and horrified when Baba tells them that she is in fact a fraud. She turns them and Toby out of the house. Later Toby returns to see Monica and to collect his possessions. He makes a noise – which wakes Baba – and then hides in the puppet theatre. Baba grabs a pistol and, seeing the curtain of the theatre move, shoots at it. Toby falls dead to the floor as Baba cries: "I've killed the ghost!"

𝄞 Menotti can perhaps best be described as a Hollywood auteur who happens to be a musician. His most successful projects have been those over which he has exercised complete control, not just writing words and music but also directing and designing the show. And his operas have a pronounced Hollywood element to them in the way they combine realism with overcharged emotion, and in the way the music underlines the dramatic climaxes. By this analogy it is an operatic film noir, and in a good production it can pack almost as powerful a punch as Britten's *The Turn of the Screw*, even though the music is not as varied nor as imaginative. *The Medium* is also considerably shorter, and much of its impact is dependent on the speed with which the stability of Madame Flora's world begins to unravel.

The idea for the opera came to Menotti after attending a seance in 1936 and his intention was to create "a play of ideas . . . the tragedy of a woman caught between two worlds, a world of reality which she cannot wholly comprehend and a supernatural world in which she cannot believe". The house of Madame Flora is a world of illusion: she peddles hope to the bereaved, but has become estranged from her own charges, Monica and Toby, who themselves create a fantasy world in which to escape. The vocal writing is dominated by parlando-style recitatives, which are punctuated by occasional arias of a folk-like simplicity, like the song "Black Swan", which Monica sings in an attempt to calm her mother. But the overall musical impression is of a clever and eclectic composer rifling through the late-Romantic bag of tricks in order to give his dramatic scenario the maximum impact: such was his success in achieving this that *The Medium* (in harness with *The Telephone*) ran for an astonishing 211 performances on Broadway.

RECORDINGS OVERVIEW

Madame Flora provides a good dramatic mezzo with a great showcase, and the intensity of Marie Powers – who played Flora on Broadway – did much to contribute to the work's initial success. The CBS recording of the 1947 Broadway cast, with Evelyn Keller as Monica, was most recently re-issued (with *The Telephone*) in 1984 but has never appeared on CD. Marie Powers possessed a dramatic rather than a pleasing voice and a more satisfactory recording was made – again by CBS – in 1968 with the great American mezzo Regina Resnik as Madame Flora. Judith Blegen is a charming, fresh-faced Monica and both singers bring such a degree of interpretative subtlety to their roles as to completely hide the work's musical shortcomings. It has been issued on CD but is not currently available.

Amahl and the Night Visitors

Composed 1951.
First performed December 24, 1951.
Libretto by the composer.

Synopsis

Outside a hut, Amahl, a twelve-year-old with a crippled leg, is playing his pipe. The three Kings pass by and decide to stop at Amahl's house. When Amahl tells his mother, she rebukes him for lying. The Kings tell the woman that they are looking for a Child and describe their vision. In the morning Amahl's mother, seeing the Kings' wealth, tries to steal some gold but the Kings' page stops her. Woken by the noise, Amahl fights the page. Melchior – one of the Kings – restores order and tells Amahl's mother that she can keep the gold as the Child has no need of it. Moved by his description of the Child, the mother offers the gold back, saying that if she owned anything, she would give it. Amahl steps forward and offers his crutch. As he lifts it above his head everyone is astonished as he steps forward. Amahl dances about the room and each of the Kings asks to touch him. Amahl asks them if he can go with them to see the Child. They agree, as does his mother, and the opera ends with Amahl playing the pipe tune with which the opera began.

Menotti was initially unenthusiastic about the commission from NBC to write a television opera. But coming across Bosch's painting *The Adoration of the Magi* on a visit to the Metropolitan Museum of Art acted as a spur to action. Drawing also on aspects of his childhood in Italy, Menotti wrote the work quickly, and rehearsals began before it was complete. First relayed on Christmas Eve 1951, *Amahl* was instantly popular and has been broadcast annually ever since.

The music for each of the six named characters, especially the treble lead, is carefully written so as to put the opera within the reach of amateurs, but it is in no way simplistic or dull. Menotti writes naturally for the voice and *Amahl* is filled with good tunes, while the lightly balanced orchestral score is a delight. The "miracle" that forms the emotional climax of the opera is undoubtedly sentimental but there is also much humour – especially in the characterization of the Kings – which effectively personalizes the Christmas story in an extremely direct and effective way. This, and the work's tight theatrical construction, gives the opera a unique charm and, as a way of introducing children to the genre, there is almost nothing more certain to succeed.

Rainbird, Haywood, Dobson, Maxwell; Royal Opera House Chorus and Orchestra; Syrus.
(TER CDTER 1124).

This enjoyable performance was recorded after a production at Sadler's Wells by a team from Covent Garden. The largely excellent cast provide the sort of character and detail that is missing from both of the American recordings, and conductor David Syrus brings an appropriately light touch. Some of the singing is a little too operatic, in particular Lorna Haywood, whose wide vibrato sometimes leaves Menotti's vocal line choking for air. James Rainbird's treble is much more reliable and he uses his voice with amazing imagination and creativity. Best of all is the sympathetic Melchior of Donald Maxwell. The sound is fresh if a little close.

SAMUEL BARBER

b. WEST CHESTER, PENNSYLVANIA, MARCH 9, 1910; d. NEW YORK, JANUARY 23, 1981.

Back in the 1930s, while Samuel Barber was being lauded in some quarters as one of the most talented American composers of his generation, his music was being labelled as an anachronism by modernists. Totally unperturbed, Barber went on writing in his neo-Romantic vein, turning out essentially dramatic and lyrical works in a tonal language that was rooted in the late nineteenth century. As a young man, Barber possessed an excellent baritone voice, and when he undertook studies at the Curtis Institute his intention was to become a professional singer. It's thus hardly surprising that many of his compositions are for the voice, and that his operas display a great sensitivity to the potential of the voice, even if they are more notable for their unselfconscious effusiveness than for their qualities as music-drama.

After graduating from Curtis in 1932 Barber travelled to Vienna, where he studied singing, gave recitals, and recorded a number of his own songs, each of which displayed his gift for melody and text-setting. He was by now a confident composer with several highly accomplished works under his belt, including *Dover Beach* (a song singled out for praise by Vaughan Williams) and the *Serenade for String Quartet*. One of Barber's fellow students at Curtis was Gian Carlo Menotti (see p.569), who became Barber's companion for most of his life. But whereas Menotti turned readily to opera, Barber avoided the medium until 1953, when he composed the nine-minute miniature *A Hand of Bridge*, a witty caprice in which the private thoughts of two couples playing cards are expressed out loud. The libretto was by Menotti, who also collaborated with Barber on his first full-length opera, *Vanessa* (1957). Based on a short story by Isak Dinesen, *Vanessa* brought the composer wide-ranging American recognition as well as a Pulitzer Prize.

Almost ten years later, Barber was commissioned to compose a new opera for the re-opening of the New York Metropolitan Opera after its move to the Lincoln Center. In the event, *Antony and Cleopatra* was a calamity. Written to a libretto clumsily assembled from Shakespeare's play by Franco Zeffirelli, it was smothered by an excessively sumptuous and grandiose Zeffirelli production, and became the most expensive flop in the Metropolitan Opera's eighty-year history. Barber attempted no further operas or, in fact, much new work of any kind during the fourteen years that remained to him after the Met fiasco, though he constantly revised *Antony and Cleopatra* in the hope that it would finally be acclaimed as the masterpiece that, in his eyes, it had always been. Though Cleopatra's death scene is sometimes heard as a concert item, not even Menotti's sterling advocacy has been able to counter the critical obloquy that has accumulated around one of opera's most celebrated white elephants.

Vanessa

Composed 1956–57; revised 1964.
First performed January 15, 1958.
Libretto by Gian Carlo Menotti.

Synopsis

Act I

A country house in an unspecified northern country in the early years of the century. Vanessa and her mother, the Old Baroness, and the Baroness's niece, Erika, are awaiting the arrival of Vanessa's lover Anatol, who left twenty years earlier. A young man called Anatol arrives; he is an opportunist who turns out to be the original Anatol's son. He informs Vanessa that his father is dead.

Act II

Erika tells the Baroness that Anatol seduced her on the night of his arrival. Anatol and Vanessa are beginning to fall in love. Erika decides to reject Anatol.

Act III

At a ball Erika is dumbfounded by Anatol and Vanessa's public confession of their love.

Act IV

Erika discovers she is pregnant by Anatol and attempts suicide. Vanessa and Anatol marry and leave for Paris. Erika remains devoted to Anatol and settles down to wait for him, just as Vanessa had done for his father twenty years before.

Searching for a librettist for his first opera, Barber had already had discussions with various writers, including Dylan Thomas and Thornton Wilder, when his lover and fellow-composer Gian Carlo Menotti proposed himself as author. In many ways it was an ideal combination, given both men's predilection for lyrical and unstressful vocal music, and Menotti's libretto – loosely based on one of Isak Dinesen's *Seven Gothic Tales* – supplied Barber with words as direct and simple as he could have wished for. The scenario is a different matter, in that it aspires to a Chekhovian, *fin-de-siècle* wistfulness, but replaces the psychological astuteness of the Russian playwright with a rather crude emotionalism. In dramatic content and musical style *Vanessa* bears comparison to Korngold's *Die tote Stadt*: both operas possess a protagonist who is driven by a pathological obsession with a lost love whom they try to re-create in another person. In *Vanessa*, the tragedy lies in the way this cycle is continued – like an ancient curse – in the character of Erika. A common musical vocabulary links the two operas even more: both are characterized by long-phrased quasi-Straussian vocal writing and accompanying orchestral textures that are complex and thickly painted.

As the recording of the original cast well illustrates, Barber's opera provided ideal opportunities for suitably gifted singers and the first night was a triumph for Eleanor Steber in the title role. Though Barber had previously written the fine soprano-and-orchestra piece *Knoxville: Summer of 1915* for her, Steber was not the first choice for Vanessa: Callas had turned it down (allegedly on the grounds that she could not possibly be asked to fall in love with a man who had already slept with the mezzo-soprano), and Sena Jurinac abandoned the part six weeks before the first night. Steber filled the gap admirably, and she effortlessly sailed above Barber's often rather thick orchestration – most brilliantly in the coloratura skating aria in Act II. Perhaps the most representative moment in the opera is the powerful quintet with which it ends: Menotti's spare text ("To leave, to break, to find, to keep") is set by Barber as a complex canonical quintet, a climax which – though undoubtedly impressive – becomes less profound the more you hear it, something that is true of the opera as a whole.

Steber, Elias, Resnik, Gedda; New York Metropolitan Opera Chorus and Orchestra; Mitropoulos.
(RCA GD87899; 2 CDs).

This recording is a document of both historical and musical value. It was recorded in the studio shortly after the premiere and comes close to providing an ideal performance of *Vanessa*. Each of the leading performers were celebrated for their full-blooded performances of late-Romantic Italian opera, and the beguiling interplay between Eleanor Steber's dark soprano and Nicolai Gedda's smooth, charismatic tenor is irresistible. Regina Resnik's part as the Old Baroness is short but delivered with brilliant dramatic efficiency, while Rosalind Elias's sumptuous Erika heralded a stupendous talent that was never fully exploited. Mitropoulos and the New York forces indulge themselves to the full but with great attention to detail, which is well served by the early stereo.

LEONARD BERNSTEIN

b. LAWRENCE, MASSACHUSETTS, AUGUST 25, 1918; d. NEW YORK, OCTOBER 14, 1990.

A brilliantly dynamic conductor and a fine composer, Leonard Bernstein followed the lead of George Gershwin (see p.490) and Kurt Weill (see p.414) in trying to break down the division between the world of the American musical and the world of opera. If, in the end, he was less successful than either in creating a convincingly American operatic idiom, he did succeed in injecting into the musical a greater complexity and seriousness, above all in *West Side Story*. His conducting career was more controversial: for many, Bernstein got right to the heart of Beethoven, Mahler and Wagner, giving himself unreservedly to the music's emotional pulse; for others, the expansive personality of Bernstein always got in the way of the music.

Bernstein's big break is the stuff of legend: having studied conducting with Koussevitsky and Reiner, he substituted at short notice for a sick Bruno Walter at a New York Philharmonic concert in November 1943, and became famous overnight. By then his involvement in music-theatre had already begun – in 1939, while still at Harvard, he directed and performed in Marc Blitzstein's pro-union musical *The Cradle Will Rock*. Blitzstein's radical form of music-theatre was an important influence on Bernstein, and the older composer assumed the role of mentor and advisor for much of his life. Bernstein's own first success as a composer came – soon after his conducting break – with the ballet *Fancy Free*, about three sailors on shore leave. At the suggestion of choreographer Jerome Robbins, the storyline was adapted for a full-length musical, *On the Town* (1945) – a breezy show which contained substantial self-contained dance sequences and included the hit tune "New York, New York". Bernstein next turned his attention to opera, producing the one-act *Trouble in Tahiti* (1952), which was staged at Brandeis University in a double-bill with Blitzstein's translation of Weill's *Threepenny Opera*. At the time, comparisons between the two works did Bernstein's piece few favours, but in fact *Trouble in Tahiti* is a remarkably effective short opera which successfully marries popular styles (it opens with a radio trio crooning about the joys of suburbia) with more obviously operatic vocal techniques. Its plot, in which a breakfast argument with her husband leads a woman to seek comfort first with her psychiatrist and then at the movies, has been ridiculed as an example of Bernstein chic, but for all the seriousness of its subject the opera is never pompous, and the culminating movie sequence contains a wonderfully witty parody of *South Pacific* that gives the work its name.

After returning briefly to the musical with *Wonderful Town* (1953), Bernstein composed his comic-operetta *Candide*, which failed to take off on its initial Broadway run in 1956. Many years were spent by the composer (and a total of seven different writers) in trying to knock the work into definitive shape, and in its final transformation it is one of Bernstein's finest achievements. In 1957 Bernstein responded to an idea from his regular collaborator Jerome Robbins for an updated musical version of *Romeo and Juliet*. The result, *West Side Story*, was ground-breaking in the way the disparate elements of plot, singing and dancing were integrated, and it went on to become Bernstein's most successful stage-work, with a string of songs ("Maria", "America", "Tonight") that have deservedly achieved classic status.

Bernstein composed no more pieces for the theatre until 1976, when he produced his first complete failure, *1600 Pennsylvania Avenue*, a two-act musical about the White House domestic staff of successive presidents. His final stage work, *A Quiet Place* (1980–83), was a full-length opera conceived as a sequel to *Trouble in Tahiti*. Although it incorporates the earlier work within it (as well as deriving much of its musical material from it), the overall character of *A Quiet Place* is very different. Where *Trouble in Tahiti* turned a caustic gaze on the shortcomings of the American Dream, *A Quiet Place* tackles its theme of familial alienation and reconciliation with all the ponderous earnestness of a soap opera. Unfortunately, the fine CBS recording of *Trouble in Tahiti* is not currently available, so to listen to the work at all means extracting it from the 1986 Deutsche Grammophon recording of *A Quiet Place*.

Candide

Composed 1954–56; revised 1973, 1988–89.
First performed December 1, 1956.
Libretto by Lillian Hellman, after Voltaire; rewritten (1973) by Hugh Wheeler; lyrics by Richard Wilbur.

Synopsis

Candide, an unworldly youth from Westphalia, sets out on his travels round the world (Lisbon, Paris, Buenos Aires, Venice) firmly believing what his tutor, Pangloss, has taught him: that all is for the best in the best of all possible worlds. Disillusionment follows as the woman he loves (Cunegonde) is apparently killed and Pangloss is hanged by the Inquisition. His travels continue to the New World, accompanied by an Old Lady and the miraculously rescued Cunegonde. After visiting Eldorado and surviving a shipwreck, he returns to Westphalia where he abandons the teachings of Pangloss and decides to lead an honest life with Cunegonde.

Voltaire's *Candide*, first published in 1759, is a riposte to Leibniz's optimistic philosophy "that all is for the best in the best of all possible worlds". It was Lillian Hellman's idea to turn it into a work of music-theatre – she regarded it as "the greatest satire ever written, hitting out in all directions, enclosing all human nonsense", undoubtedly thinking of her own experiences at the hands of the virulent Congressional Committee headed by Senator McCarthy. Bernstein largely shared her left-of-centre liberal humanism, and on one level *Candide* functions as a critique of 1950s America, though a scene ridiculing McCarthy was removed and its ultimately positive ending differs from Voltaire's consistently sceptical vision.

Fans of the musical might, with some justification, rate the dramatic qualities of *West Side Story* above those of *Candide*, but the latter is the superior work in many respects, and it is a shame that its stylistic diversity has prevented it from taking root in the international repertory. Its failure on Broadway, despite several rave reviews, prompted Bernstein into revising and re-revising the score. The 1973 revision, masterminded by producer Harold Prince, trivialized the piece but was successful enough on Broadway for it to remain the standard performing version. Bernstein himself, however, regarded John Mauceri's 1988 version for Scottish Opera as the last word on the subject.

Candide is Bernstein's hectic homage to the richness of the European and American musical traditions. From the glittering overture (much performed as an independent piece), through solemn chorales to pastiche Offenbach and love songs that are off-cuts from *West Side Story*, *Candide* is a glorious rag-bag. Occasionally you begin to feel that the cake has been overegged, but on the whole the mixture of popular and classical is deftly balanced (tangos and waltzes sit prettily next to jazz riffs), and the orchestration is near-perfect – thrillingly so in the overture, a touch over-ripely in the schmaltzy finale. Vocal highlights include the coloratura aria "Glitter and Be Gay", a parody of the "Jewel Song" from Gounod's *Faust* with an irresistible charm all of its own. Some have found Bernstein's affection for parody a bit wearying, feeling that it comes across as musical bravado for its own sake, but there is so much beauty and sheer fun in *Candide* that you'd have to be a mean-spirited specimen to resist it completely.

Hadley, Anderson, Ludwig, Gedda, Green; London Symphony Chorus and Orchestra; Bernstein.
(Deutsche Grammophon 429 734-2GH2; 2 CDs).

John Mauceri produced an "opera house" version of *Candide* in 1982 (and recorded it for New World Records), but his final revision – carried out in conjunction with the composer – is the most successful, and here it receives a fine recording under the direction of Bernstein himself. Tenor Jerry Hadley in the title role and soprano June Anderson as Cunegonde both revel in the work's high spirits and sentimentality. Christa Ludwig is superb as the Old Lady (clicking her own castanets), and the rest of the cast – in multiple roles – are no less impressive, with the exception of Adolph Green, who sounds both too old and too arch as Pangloss and Martin. Bernstein's conducting is as florid as always, and the LSO indulge him to the full. It is a shame that John Wells' hilarious narration (which is on the video) has been omitted, but this is nonetheless great fun from beginning to end.

CARLISLE FLOYD

b. LATTA, SOUTH CAROLINA, JUNE 11, 1926.

Carlisle Floyd's third opera, *Susannah*, was a US-wide hit after its first New York production in 1956 and it became one of the very few home-produced operas to secure a place in the US standard repertoire. Although both *Susannah* and its composer suffered a lapse in popularity in the 1970s, a resurgence of interest in his work during the 1990s has resulted in a mini-wave of recordings and productions.

While studying at Syracuse University, Floyd composed and produced his first opera, *Slow Dusk*, which achieved considerable local popularity; but his second, *The Fugitives*, which he wrote and produced in Florida (where he was teaching), was taken off after a single performance. In 1953 a friend suggested making an opera from the apocryphal *Book of Susanna* (a text that was turned into an oratorio by Handel), and Floyd quickly set to writing his own libretto, even though, as he later confessed, he did not read the full text of the *Book of Susanna* until some time after the opera had been completed. It took him less than seven months to produce the fully orchestrated score, and just eighteen months after its first performance at Florida State University it was taken up by New York City Opera. Critics fell over themselves to praise it, with Winthrop Sargeant describing *Susannah* as "probably the most moving and impressive opera to have been written in America – or anywhere else as far as I am concerned – since Gershwin's *Porgy and Bess*".

After *Susannah*, Floyd was commissioned by Sante Fe Opera to translate Emily Brontë's *Wuthering Heights* to the stage. Initial reactions were unfavourable, but after major revisions it too became a success, touring widely across America. Later works failed to generate much enthusiasm, although Floyd's setting of John Steinbeck's *Of Mice and Men* has been regularly produced since its premiere in 1970.

Susannah

Composed 1953–54.
First performed February 24, 1955.
Libretto by the composer.

Synopsis

Act I

New Hope, in the Tennessee mountains. A dance is in progress outside New Hope church, during which the locals gossip about the young and beautiful Susannah Polk. Malicious Mrs McLean predicts a bad end for her and her brother Sam. A travelling preacher, Olin Blitch, arrives and shows an interest in Susannah. After promising to pray for her, he joins the dance. Susannah is accompanied home by Little Bat McLean, who loves Susannah even though her family disapproves. Susannah sings of her dreams of seeing the world, but these are forgotten when Sam arrives and they dance the night away. The following morning the town Elders stumble across Susannah bathing in a secluded pond. They return to the town where they denounce her "wickedness". By evening the gossip has escalated, turning her into a harlot, and everyone agrees that she has either to confess her sins or be expelled from the church. She arrives at the local picnic and is upset when she is made to feel unwelcome. Little Bat then tells her that he has been coerced into claiming that she seduced him.

Act II

Blitch invites Susannah to the church and Sam urges her to go, if for no other reason than to show that she is not intimidated. When Blitch welcomes all sinners to come forward and be saved, Susannah begins to walk in a trance towards the preacher, but when she realizes what she is doing she runs screaming from the church. Blitch follows her and puts his arm around her, leading her into her house, where he seduces her. To his horror, he discovers that she was a virgin. He summons the Elders and attempts to convince them of her innocence, without implicating himself. Left alone with Susannah,

Blitch begs forgiveness. She laughs and leaves him on the ground sobbing. Later that night, she tells Sam of her seduction by the preacher. Appalled, Sam grabs his gun and leaves for the pool where Blitch is baptizing converts. Sam kills Blitch and the townspeople march to Susannah's house and hurl abuse at her. She confronts them with her own gun, and laughs at them. Little Bat approaches, and is slapped by the semi-deranged Susannah.

Floyd saw in the tale of Susannah a reflection of American life in the 1950s, when anti-Communist paranoia was turning decent people into informers and malicious gossips. The analogy between Susanna and the Elders seemed too good to be true. McCarthyism, Floyd later recalled, "permeated everything at that time . . . accusation was all that was needed as proof of guilt. It terrified and enraged me." By changing the ending of the source, in which Daniel proves Susannah's innocence, Floyd paid homage to those who refused to roll over.

Like Aaron Copland, Carlisle Floyd turned to US folksong as a grounding for his music, and the modal simplicity of Quaker hymns permeates every page of *Susannah*, combining with the colloquial text and parlando melodies to create a convincing reflection of Midwestern life during the 1950s. In addition to Quaker melodies, there are plentiful square dances, gospel anthems and Appalachian ballads in the folky mix, and it is a testament to Floyd's skills as a dramatist that he was able to set so many four-square melodies into such a driving narrative – this opera rarely pauses for set-pieces. For all the reliance on folk melody, the musical language of *Susannah* belongs to the twentieth century: the overall fabric is very dense, setting the melodies within rich and contrapuntal textures which, during the climaxes, reach thrilling heights of late-Romantic passion.

Studer, Hadley, Ramey, Chester; Chorus and Orchestra of Lyon Opéra; Nagano.
(Virgin 7243 54503924; 2 CDs).

Produced under the supervision of the composer, this was the first professional recording of Floyd's finest opera. Uniting a high-profile American cast, Nagano has done both the composer and his work proud. Nagano clearly loves the opera, and every scene glows with feeling, especially in those passages dominated by the tragic heroine, sung here by Cheryl Studer. As her brother Sam, Jerry Hadley is in superb voice (although, like most of the cast, he fails to get the words across clearly), and Sam Ramey is a gloriously ringing, self-righteous Blitch.

PHILIP GLASS

b. BALTIMORE, MARYLAND, JANUARY 31, 1937.

The goal of Philip Glass is to escape the dead-end obscurities of the contemporary avant-garde and bring "serious" music back into the wider public domain. This he has achieved more successfully than any other composer of the contemporary era, even though many listeners are hostile to the radical simplicity of his "Minimalist" style, which is characterized above all by the repetition of small, cell-like phrases over long periods of time, imbuing his music with a powerful sense of suspended time. His works – especially his operas – unfold slowly, as patterns gradually grow and contract in restless development. Though often open to the accusation of being shallow and uneventful, Glass's music is unmistakably his, and at its best it's insidiously effective.

Glass grew up in Baltimore and acquired a taste for commercial music while selling Elvis Presley records in his father's music store. He was an accomplished flautist and violinist by the age of fifteen, when he attended Chicago University to study maths and philosophy. By the late 1950s he was at the Juilliard School in New York, from where he went on to study with Darius Milhaud and Nadia Boulanger. He seemed to be on his way to a conventional composerly career, but then in the mid-1960s he met sitarist Ravi Shankar, who introduced him to the additive structures of Indian music. Glass set off across India, the Himalayas and North Africa on a new musical quest.

Returning to New York in 1967, he threw himself into the art scene of Lower Manhattan, giving loft concerts with Terry Riley and Steve Reich, and forming the Philip Glass Ensemble. From this period came *Music In Similar Motion* (1969) and *Music In Changing Parts* (1970), both written for organs, flute, trumpet and saxes, and combining rock-type grooves with perpetual drones, all played at high volume. The breakthrough came when he met theatre conceptualist Robert Wilson, with whom he produced the hallucinogenic four-hour opera *Einstein on the Beach* (1976) – a sell-out at the Met, it pushed Minimalism into the mainstream.

Assisted by engineer Kurt Munkacsi, Glass built up a reputation for technical brilliance in the studio, and his first digital album, *Glassworks* (1982), was a smash right across the musical spectrum, from heavy metal fans to Dean Martin lovers. On a larger scale, the operas *Satyagraha* (1980) and *Akhnaten* (1984), drawing on the lives of Gandhi, Tolstoy, Martin Luther King and a sun-worshipping Egyptian pharaoh, completed the trilogy of "portrait" operas begun with *Einstein*, and thrillingly combined his trademark repetitions and overlappings with ceremonially grandiose staging.

Glass maintains a formidable rate of output – he was the first composer to develop a production-line system, using sampling techniques so that every musical sketch could be speedily turned into finished product. Following the trilogy, Glass has worked on many music-theatre and opera projects, including two "operas" based on films by Jean Cocteau, and *The Voyage* (1992), a discursive exploration of the idea of discovery, written for the 500th anniversary of Columbus's "discovery" of America.

Einstein on the Beach

Composed 1975.
First performed July 25, 1976.
Libretto by the composer, with Christopher Knowles, Lucinda Childs and Samuel M. Johnson.

Synopsis

Act I

A small boy tosses paper planes onto the stage. A dancer, dressed as Einstein, moves across the stage; on one side of the stage another Einstein chalks equations onto an invisible blackboard. A steam train inches across the stage as dancers begin to emerge from the shadows. In the second scene a young woman –

the Defendant – recites from a book, accompanied by Einstein on his violin. The trial follows no discernible process, though it skirts the subject of relativity.

Act II
A spaceship hovers in the distance. As the chorus chants abstract syllables, elegant Victorian couples mime love duets on stage. The couples board the steam train, which moves off into the distance.

Act III
Another trial, set in a prison. The Defendant lies on a bed, seeming to suffer a nightmare. She later re-emerges as a Patty Hearst figure, wielding a gun which she points at the audience. The spaceship begins to drift across the stage.

Act IV
The train changes into a building and Einstein is seen frantically scribbling in a notepad. The spaceship lights up and humanoids are seen inside. Orchestra members climb into the spaceship; the opera ends with the representation of an atomic explosion – as the curtain falls, it reveals the formula $E=MC^2$.

The initial inspiration for *Einstein on the Beach* was the dramaturge/performance artist Robert Wilson. In 1973, having seen Wilson's twelve-hour show *The Life and Times of Josef Stalin*, Glass felt an instant rapport with his work: "I understood then, as I feel I have ever since, his sense of theatrical time, space and movement." They decided to collaborate soon after, taking off from Wilson's fascination with figures of power and influence. Wilson suggested Charlie Chaplin as a possible subject; Glass countered with Gandhi, Wilson proposed Adolf Hitler, and finally they decided to embark on a trilogy of operas on major historical figures, starting with Einstein and the attendant issues of "science, technology and ecology".

The music for *Einstein* grew not from a libretto but from Wilson's sketches for the envisaged production. The finished piece of "Music-Theatre" has no dialogue and no narrative, but rather revolves around three central musical-visual themes: the first, a train, links Einstein's childhood toys with a common analogy used to explain his theory of relativity; the second, a trial, puts Einstein's discoveries in the dock; and the third, a spaceship, reflects on the positive potential of his life's work. It's played by an ensemble of two electronic organs and three wind players (doubling on saxophone, flute and bass clarinet), plus a solo soprano voice, with most of the vocal music sung by a choir of sixteen mixed voices. All of the performers are dressed as Einstein, but Einstein himself is played by a violinist who does not sing, though his three violin solos are central to the opera.

The texts were written by an autistic boy called Christopher Knowles, and these are played backwards and forwards, frequently dragging single syllables out over extended periods of the score. The score is absolutely tonal and its basic material is frequently beautiful, reaching a pitch of excitement in those passages in which the chord progressions gather pace. However, while *Einstein*'s reliance on "addictive repetition" makes it a *locus classicus* of Minimalism, the lack of incident is ultimately exhausting. It works best on CD, where you can pick and choose – indeed, Glass himself admits "I have never seen the entire work straight through without interruption".

Riesman; Philip Glass Ensemble; Glass, Gibson, Childs.
(CBS M4K 38875; 4 CDs).

This recording of the original 160-minute *Einstein* is a definitive account, but it may not be in the catalogue much longer. The newer version on Elektra (Glass's current label) is half an hour longer, and is technically a better recording, but the ensemble outbursts don't have the same thrill as on the spiky CBS set.

Satyagraha

Composed 1978–80.
First performed September 5, 1980.
Libretto by Philip Glass and Constance DeJong, after the Bhagavad-Gita.

Synopsis

Act I
Tolstoy. A battle from the Bhagavad-Gita is re-enacted, as a prelude to an outline of the philosophical basis of Satyagraha, seen in operation at Gandhi's ashram, Tolstoy Farm. The Satyagrahi resist British rule, and gain strength as a political and religious movement.

Act II
Tagore. Gandhi walks through an angry crowd, and is protected only by the wife of the police chief. The printing and distribution of *Indian Opinion*, the Satyagrahi newspaper, helps the collective resistance of the group, culminating in the burning of registration cards in defiance of the government.

Act III

King. Gandhi urges miners to strike as part of the protest against the government. Their agreement reflects the growing power of Satyagraha. The presence of American police dressed in the uniforms of Martin Luther King's time links the drama to the ongoing struggle for racial and political liberation, a keynote of the opera.

"Well, Philip, that was very interesting. Now, how would you like to write a real opera?" – thus Glass recalled the invitation extended him by Hans de Roo, director of Netherlands Opera, after *Einstein* was performed in Amsterdam. What de Roo wanted was a work that could be performed by an "orchestra, chorus and soloists, people trained and practised in the singing of traditional opera". Returning to one of their earlier ideas, Glass and Wilson based their new collaboration upon Gandhi's early years in South Africa, exploring "politics: violence and non-violence" through Gandhi's philosophy of Satyagraha or passive resistance. The Bhagavad-Gita, upon which the libretto is loosely based, is the Sanskrit religious text that Gandhi used as his "dictionary of daily reference".

Taking on board de Roo's requests, Glass and Wilson conceived the work along much more conventional lines than *Einstein on the Beach*. This time, the central figure, though not brought to life through anything so direct as a linear narrative, is the hub of a sequence of clearly defined tableaux. The drama of each act clusters around a figure who sits apart from the action. The figures come from Gandhi's past (Tolstoy, to whom Gandhi wrote as a young man), his present (the writer Rabindranath Tagore) and his future (Martin Luther King). Their purpose is to open out the ideological framework of the opera, for *Satyagraha* is a work about ideas rather than action, and Glass's music, with its hypnotically repetitive chord progressions, creates the atmosphere of an extended philosophical meditation on a core idea. *Satyagraha*, Glass's first major work to use a traditional orchestral line-up and a cast of solo vocalists, is the most beautiful Minimalist opera ever written, and the simplicity of the writing, especially for the soloists, perfectly encapsulates the simplicity and purity of Gandhi's teaching.

Perry, Cummings, Liss, McFarland, Reeve, Woods; New York City Opera Orchestra and Chorus; Keene.
(CBS M3K 39672; 3 CDs).

This is another excellent recording, with singers and instrumentalists all perfectly attuned to the unsentimental Glass style. Rhonda Liss brings a welcome warmth of tone to the role of Gandhi's wife, and Douglas Perry is a languid, vibrato-less Gandhi with a voice of evocative, mystical eeriness, which combines very beautifully with the lower strings.

Akhnaten

Composed 1983.
First performed March 24, 1984.
Libretto by Philip Glass with Shalom Goldman, Robert Israel and Richard Riddell.

Synopsis

Act I

The funeral of Amenhotep III is followed by the coronation of his son Akhnaten, in the presence of his wife, Nefertiti. The new pharaoh, strongly influenced by his mother, Tye, proves to be radical in his ideas: he denounces traditional gods, and draws mystic symbols in praise of the sun. His entourage dance in the old temple, to the horror of the priests.

Act II

Akhnaten destroys the ancient temples of Amon, and learns new creeds from Tye. He plans and builds a magnificent city, Akhetaten. Akhnaten and his followers celebrate the new city and worship the sun god. Akhnaten tries to touch the sun.

Act III

Scenes of happy family life are destroyed when Akhnaten begins to lose control of Egypt and his city is attacked by priests of the old regime. His family deserts him and, in the ruins of Akhetaten, he disappears. Moving to the present, tourists pick over the ruins of Akhnaten's city, but as they leave, it becomes evident that the doomed pharaoh's spirit still lingers.

The final part of Glass's historical triptych, a study of "religion, orthodoxy and reaction", was inspired by his reading of two books: Sigmund Freud's *Moses and Monotheism* and Immanuel Velikovsky's *Oedipus and Akhnaten*. The latter was particularly important in determining the approach of the opera, for in it Velikovsky attempted to trace the Oedipus myth and the "mother complex" back to the life of Akhnaten. Furthermore, though

Akhnaten's revolutionary monotheism was replaced by the old theology as soon as he was dead, Velikovsky argued that the Judeo-Christian belief system could ultimately be traced back to the pharaoh's doomed enterprise. Akhnaten thus became a figure whose life altered the world as radically as had the physics of Einstein and the politico-philosophical beliefs of Gandhi.

Like *Satyagraha*, *Akhnaten* makes use of obscure languages, in this instance Egyptian, Akkadian and Hebrew, although this time a narrator is employed to translate the words as they are delivered. Even more than *Satyagraha*, it explores the more lyrical side of the composer's Minimalism, particularly in the writing for Akhnaten (a counter-tenor), whose Act II duet with Nefertiti is an unprecedentedly ardent song. Glass also shows himself to be an adroit orchestral colourist, notably in the atmospheric evocation of the court and its rituals. Leitmotif-like themes herald the main characters and events, and the principal characters have distinctly delineated roles within a straightforward linear narrative – just compare the role of Akhnaten with the way the eponymous hero of *Einstein on the Beach* was treated. This is, in short, a more mainstream opera than anything previously attempted by Glass, so if you're approaching him with prejudices formed by classical music rather than by popular music, this is the place to start.

Esswood, Vargas, Liebermann, Hannula; Stuttgart Opera Chorus and Orchestra; Davies.
(CBS CD42457; 2 CDs).

Russell Davies here conducts many of the original cast from the Stuttgart premiere of *Akhnaten*. Paul Esswood is ideal as the pharaoh, and the remaining players are all well cast, giving characterful portrayals. However, *Akhnaten* is an opera in which the orchestra is the leading voice, and the Stuttgart players rise to the occasion. Well recorded and handsomely packaged.

JOHN CORIGLIANO

b. NEW YORK, FEBRUARY 16, 1938.

John Corigliano's writing for film, TV and radio and his works for the concert and operatic stage have established him as one of the most accessible composers of the postwar generation. Though his music is rarely original, its lyricism, vivid orchestration and witty pastiche have made him popular both with the major orchestras who have commissioned works and with the concert-going public. His opera *The Ghosts of Versailles* (1991) was the first premiere to be staged at the Metropolitan Opera since Samuel Barber's *Antony and Cleopatra* in 1966 (see p.572), and its comic inventiveness, starry cast and spectacular staging made it a huge success, though it has yet to be staged in Europe.

Corigliano comes from a musical background, and received his first musical tuition from his father, who led the New York Philharmonic for many years. His formal training as a composer began at Columbia University. For much of the 1960s he worked for radio and television both as a producer and as a composer, as well as teaching composition at two schools in New York. A series of witty and entertaining concertos brought him wider attention: his piano concerto was championed by Daniel Barenboim, who also premiered his first symphony – dedicated to AIDS victims – with the Chicago Symphony Orchestra. His multimedia rock opera called *Naked Carmen* (1970) was conceived as a record album and has never been performed on stage. Corigliano has also written incidental music, most vividly for Ken Russell's *Altered States* (1980) – a modern variant on the *Dr Jeckyll and Mr Hyde* story – for which Corigliano received an Oscar nomination.

Commissioned by the Metropolitan Opera to celebrate its centenary, *The Ghosts of Versailles* is typical of a composer who has long been preoccupied with the influence of art on history and, in particular, with the importance of music as social document. It requires a knowing audience for its parody and irony to work completely, but even for the uninitiated *The Ghosts of Versailles* makes an enthralling entertainment.

The Ghosts of Versailles

Composed 1980–91.
First performed December 19, 1991.
Libretto by William M. Hoffman, after Beaumarchais.

Synopsis

Act I

Beaumarchais announces a performance of his new opera as part of his courtship of Marie-Antoinette. This opera-within-an-opera begins with Figaro retelling his life story. The Queen's jewels are borrowed for the show, but both Beaumarchais and Bégearss, a revolutionary, aim to steal them. Beaumarchais tries to seduce the Queen, but is attacked by her husband, Louis XVI. In a finale at the Turkish embassy, Figaro takes the jewels.

Act II

Beaumarchais assures Marie-Antoinette that art can change history, but history cannot be contained: the script breaks down as Figaro exclaims "down with the Queen!" Marie-Antoinette accuses Beaumarchais of treachery. She asks for a re-trial, at which Beaumarchais is chief accuser. When Figaro comes to her aid he is surrounded by Bégearss's angry revolutionaries, who arrest some of the aristocracy. All except Marie-Antoinette are later rescued by Figaro and Beaumarchais. The Queen has resigned herself to her fate, and finds ultimate rest in paradise with the playwright.

The Ghosts of Versailles is loosely based on Beaumarchais' *La mère coupable* (The Guilty Mother), the third – and least successful – of his Figaro trilogy (it was set by Milhaud in 1965). Its dramatic energy derives from a series of overlaps between two central groups of characters: the ghosts of Marie-Antoinette and her court, and the reincarnated characters of the opera-within-an-opera. As their creator, the ghost of Beaumarchais is forever prompting his characters, or exploiting scenes for his own ends, capitalizing, for instance, on a romantic duet between Rosina and Cherubino in his attempt to seduce the Queen. The audience of ghosts see their embodied selves in the opera-within-an-opera, rub shoulders with each other at a ball, and finally witness their own imprisonment and rescue. At the climax of the opera, Marie-Antoinette witnesses her own execution.

Corigliano's music reinforces both the autonomy of the two groups and their interactions. The fabric of the opera-within-an-opera is essentially that of the Mozart/da Ponte collaborations, with various Neoclassical twists that suggest Stravinsky. The music of the ghosts, on the other hand, is wispy and atonal, yet full of strange echoes from the past. As the two groups collide, their musics mingle, history overtakes the farcical plot, and an atmosphere of tragedy overtakes the buffa characters.

In a work whose central theme is the celebration of history, it is appropriate that Corigliano should incorporate so much musical reference. He borrows not only from the Mozart and Rossini operas from which the Beaumarchais characters are taken, but also from Verdi, Puccini and Richard Strauss. Wagner's music dramas (a soprano in full Wagnerian armour arrives at the end of Act I to question the mayhem of the finale) are a constant target of parody, but despite the weighty themes, Corigliano's tone is light and brilliantly witty – as one character observes, "it's only an opera!" Despite some critical disdain, *The Ghosts of Versailles* is a splendidly ingenious opera and it is regularly revived at the Met.

Stratas, Horne, Clark, Quilico, Hagegård; Metropolitan Opera Orchestra and Chorus; Levine (Deutsche Grammophon Video 072 430-3).

It is something of an understatement to say that the staging of *The Ghosts of Versailles* was lavish, given the enormous cast, the period costumes and the stunning set-pieces and special effects – including an exploding Pasha the size of a Greyhound bus (see the back cover of this book). There has been no CD release but this video succeeds admirably in reproducing the total-theatre experience. The vividly drawn roles are treated with relish by all the performers. Teresa Stratas, as Marie-Antoinette, creates a perfect balance between elegy, bitterness and romance, her wistful tone giving form to the shadowy spirit-world of her dead courtiers. Graham Clark gives an absorbingly evil portrayal of the worm-like Bégearss. Gino Quilico (tenor and occasionally soprano) is a delightful, tongue-in-cheek Figaro, and Hakan Hagegård is resolutely pompous as Beaumarchais. Unfussy but sensitive filming enhances the fantastic designs, and high-quality stereo does as much for James Levine and his orchestra as could be expected from video.

JOHN ADAMS

b. WORCESTER, MASSACHUSETTS, FEBRUARY 15, 1947.

In a world of endless narrative possibilities, contemporary opera has frequently not known what stories it wants to tell. For many composers, Greek myth remains as rich a source as it was for opera's founding fathers: Harrison Birtwistle, for example, with *The Mask of Orpheus* (1986; see p.555), or John Buller, whose *The Bacchae* (1992) has a libretto in ancient Greek. Others seek solace in Shakespeare (eg Stephen Oliver's *Timon of Athens*; 1991), or some other canonical giant. It remains surprising, even shocking, how few contemporary composers have opted to make opera from the recognizable modern world.

One who consistently has is John Adams, who has said "the myths of our time are not Cupid and Psyche but characters like Mao and Nixon". European audiences may not quite see these figures as mythic, but Adams' point is well-made, the more so since his first opera *Nixon in China* showed just how powerfully more or less contemporary events could be turned into opera. What is perhaps even more surprising than Adams' creation of an opera that reflects on modern history is that *Nixon* found a large and appreciative audience, something most opera composers of the last half-century have had to do without. It toured the United States and Europe in 1987 and 1988, thrilling audiences and dividing critics wherever it went. If Adams' debut opera now seems to be in limbo, that is probably less to do with its ephemerality than with unimaginative opera houses: *Nixon* remains unseen in London, for example, except on TV.

Adams' work belongs to the history of Minimalism, but he has always been more interested in overt emotional expression than most other Minimalists, including Steve Reich and Philip Glass. He is a natural eclectic, as liable to write a piece inspired by 1950s animated cartoons (*Chamber Symphony*; 1992) as to produce a concerto in the grand Romantic tradition (*Violin Concerto*; 1993). Adams' father played clarinet, both jazz and classical, and he grew up in a house where, he says, "Benny Goodman and Mozart sat side by side on the same shelf, and there was no opprobrium attached to one or special honour applied to the other". For Adams, that is the American experience, and his music strives to honour it.

The idea for *Nixon* came from director Peter Sellars, who went on to stage the work, and Adams' next two operas. Sellars and Adams met in 1983 when the former was directing a production of Haydn's *Armida* – characteristically, Sellars set it in Vietnam. Sellars also came up with the idea for Adams' second opera, *The Death of Klinghoffer*, an operatic retelling of the story of the 1985 Palestinian hijacking of the cruise ship Achille Lauro. The libretti for both

BETTY FREEMAN/LEBRECHT COLLECTION

John Adams in action

operas were written by poet Alice Goodman; both were staged by Sellars; and both featured choreography by Mark Morris. There is no doubt that much of their success derived from the strength of that four-way collaboration.

Sellars was also involved in Adams' next opera, *I Was Looking at the Ceiling, and Then I Saw the Sky* (1995): or was it an opera? A musical perhaps, a "story in songs" in which seven young Los Angelenos react to one of that city's more cataclysmic earthquakes. The libretto is by poet June Jordan, who deliberately stripped language back to something akin to doggerel, while Adams' score set 22 discrete musical numbers in a style that embraces Broadway, jazz, pop and blues. Whether this opens up new possibilities for the composer remains to be seen.

Nixon in China

Composed 1982–87.
First performed October 22, 1987.
Libretto by Alice Goodman.

Synopsis

Act I

In February 1972, President Nixon, accompanied by his wife and Henry Kissinger, lands in Peking. His plane, the Spirit of '76, is met by Chou-en-lai. Nixon meets Chairman Mao, but finds his ideas obscure. Later that evening, a banquet produces a rapprochement between the Chinese leader and the American president.

Act II

Pat Nixon is taken on a sightseeing tour. On her return, she joins her husband and Chairman and Madame Mao at a performance of the revolutionary ballet *The Red Detachment of Women*, in which Kissinger somehow becomes involved. Madame Mao denounces counter-revolutionaries.

Act III

It is the Americans' last night in Peking. Each of the opera's main characters considers the events they have witnessed, and what they mean. The last word falls to Chou, who wonders, "How much of what we did was good?"

The critic from the *New York Times*, reviewing *Nixon*, remarked "Mr Adams has done for the arpeggio what McDonald's did for the hamburger". It's a good line, but ignores the opera's real achievements in finding striking orchestral colours to dramatize what might easily have been simply garish. Sections of *Nixon* display the same sort of highly kinetic repetitive rhythms as you'll hear in Philip Glass, but it shows the dramatic potential of a style that combines Minimalist procedures with more dramatic forms of writing. There is humour in Adams' score, as there is in the libretto, but there is also a real poignancy, as in President

Nixon's Act I aria "News has a kind of mystery", which expresses an innocent wonderment at the enormity of the events in which he is participating. It is typical of Adams' subtle delineation of his characters that here "mystery" rhymes (several lines later) with "history", as Tricky Dicky muses "Though we spoke quietly, the eyes and ears of history caught every gesture". Undoubtedly the Nixons have their doltish moments (this opera is by no means a whitewash), but they are not mere caricatures.

Adams shows a virtuoso's command of stylistic allusion, partly as a means to fuel his melodic imagination, but also to serve a dramatic purpose. For example, Madame Mao's entrance aria, "I am the wife of Mao Tse-Tung", brings to mind Mozart's stratospheric writing for the Queen of the Night in *Die Zauberflöte*. Like Mozart's Queen, Mao is an enigma, at once a supernatural being and a creature of flesh and blood, and the allusion (never quite a specific reference) concisely encapsulates her dual nature. If occasionally Adams' word-setting is undistinguished, it always allows the words to be heard, an achievement many European composers might learn something from.

Sylvan, Maddalena, Duykers, Page, Crauey; Orchestra of St Luke's; De Waart.
(Nonesuch 979 177-2; 2 CDs).

Strongly cast, vibrantly played and recorded within weeks of the opera's premiere, this set presents the opera in all its multilayered complexity. Edo De Waart is a long-time champion of Adams' music, and here makes the strongest case for it. The sound is marvellous and the accompanying notes illuminating.

The Death of Klinghoffer

Composed 1991.
First performed March 19, 1991.
Libretto by Alice Goodman.

Synopsis

Prologue

A Chorus of Exiled Palestinians sings of the plight of Palestinians. A Chorus of Exiled Jews reflects on the plight of Jews.

Act I

On board the Achille Lauro. The Captain describes the ship's hijacking by a group of four Palestinians. Passengers, crew and hijackers one by one give their version of events. The Captain is guarded by Mamoud. The two discuss their situation.

Act II

The liner waits for permission to enter the port of Tarius. Wheelchair-bound Leon Klinghoffer is forced to remain separate from the other passengers. The hijackers argue and Klinghoffer is shot (offstage). Klinghoffer is thrown overboard; his body sings an aria. The ship returns to Egypt, where the hijackers disembark. The Captain tells Mrs Klinghoffer that her husband is dead. Marilyn Klinghoffer sings a long aria, ending "They should have killed me. I wanted to die."

What drew Adams to the idea of *Klinghoffer* was "the Sophoclean imponderability" of the events the opera describes. The composer concedes that, despite efforts to remain even-handed, the opera "gives more time and space to the Palestinian cause than it does to the Israeli cause . . . The only thing I can say is that, especially in the States, the Jewish position was well understood, whereas the Palestinian position is constantly subverted."

Nevertheless *Klinghoffer* is a subtle passion play, not a political tract. There is little action. Instead the characters reveal their thoughts and feelings in a succession of arias and choruses that Peter Sellars likens to Bach's *St John Passion*. There is little that could be called characterization, rather a confrontation with entrenched ideas – those of the audience as much as the protagonists'. Like *Nixon*, the opera enjoyed something of a *succés de scandale* when it first appeared, but now seems to have been placed on the shelf. If it's true that there's nothing as old as yesterday's newspaper, perhaps both operas will have to wait for their true audience until such time as they no longer attract headlines like "Front Page to Opera Stage".

Sylvan, Maddalena, Hammons, Perry, Nadler; London Opera Chorus; Orchestra of the Opéra de Lyon; Nagano.
(Nonesuch 7559 79281-2; 2 CDs).

More even than *Nixon*, *Klinghoffer* was conceived as theatre, with Mark Morris's choreography a defining presence. On disc, then, quite a lot goes missing, but Nagano has a fine cast (virtually Adams' house company) and an orchestra with which he has had a long and fruitful collaboration. His direction is tight and searching, and the crisp recording allows you to follow Goodman's libretto word by word.

DIRECTORY OF SINGERS

Below is a tally of the major singers who appear frequently in our listings of recommended CDs, plus stars such as Caruso and Ponselle who made discs in an era when technology permitted the recording only of brief excerpts. We've indicated the areas in which they are strongest and listed those roles for which they are best known in the theatre as well as on record (if no opera title appears after a role, it's because it's a title role). Most of the entries conclude with a recommended recital or excerpts disc; if none is given, it's because none was widely available at the time of going to press.

Theo Adam

1926–

German bass-baritone. Associated throughout his long career with Wagner's operas and, in particular, with the role of Wotan, which he recorded for Karl Böhm at Bayreuth, Adam's large and steely voice was not especially beautiful, but he used it with great intelligence and imagination. Also excellent in Strauss and Mozart, as well as in some contemporary works – notably by Berio, for whom he created Prospero in *Un re in ascolto*.

Roberto Alagna

1963–

Italian-French tenor. Proclaimed "The Fourth Tenor" by those who have been waiting for a successor to the big three. His lyrical voice has matured quickly since he moved from singing cabaret to opera in the late 1980s, and he has progressed no less rapidly through the late bel canto repertoire (eg Nemorino in *L'elisir d'amore*, which he has recorded), via the lighter of Puccini's roles to the heavy Verdi of *Don Carlos* – which he has recorded for EMI. It is questionable whether he should be placing his voice under such strain at such a young age, and the odds are against his keeping up the intense workload. Excellent as Gounod's Roméo and Rodolfo (*La Bohème*). Married to Angela Gheorghiu.

● **Popular Tenor Arias** (EMI CDC 5554772). This flatteringly recorded recital disc has much to offer, not least a splendid performance of "Asile héreditaire" from Rossini's *Guillaume Tell*.

Thomas Allen

1944–

The leading British baritone of the 1980s, Allen has made a speciality of Mozart, in which he has few peers – especially as the Don, to whose character he brings devilish charm and sensuality. He is also remarkable as Tchaikovsky's Onegin, and Janáček's Forester (*Cunning Little Vixen*), both of which he has recorded, but he is an asset wherever intelligent singing acting is required. Also a noted song recitalist.

Pasquale Amato

1878–1942

Italian baritone. One of the legends of the opera house, he possessed a large and ringing voice that had few peers in the Italian repertoire. His attention to textual precision and dramatic detail seem almost pedantic by today's standards, but Puccini was intoxicated by the very sound of his singing, and engaged him to create Jack Rance for the first performance of *La fanciulla del West*. A number of his 78s have been released on CD by Nimbus and Pearl.

● **Pasquale Amato** (Pearl Gemm CD9104). A fine selection of Amato's greatest recordings, including music by Verdi and Puccini.

June Anderson
1950–

American soprano. Anderson is one of the most impressive of the post-Sutherland coloratura sopranos, exceptional in Donizetti. Like Sutherland, she brings engaging warmth to music that can easily sound brittle and facile, and she can open the tone even in the highest registers. Her almost faultless pitch and light vibrato are further bonuses, and it is a shame that her few recordings are so weakly cast. However, for those with a taste for coloratura, her work is always more than worth a listen.

◑ **June Anderson** (Decca 436 377–2DH).
A stupendous recital of arias from various Rossini operas, including *Semiramide*, *Otello* and *Guillaume Tell*.

Giacomo Aragall
1939–

Spanish tenor. Owing to terrible nerves, Aragall has never captured the public imagination as have his two better known Spanish-born colleagues. His naturally light and beautiful voice, famously heard in Bellini (notably *I Capuletti e i Montecchi*), Donizetti and early Verdi, was placed under great strain by his move into heavier, late nineteenth-century repertoire and, with the exception of his performance for Naxos of Turiddù (*Cavalleria rusticana*), he has made few memorable recordings since the late 1980s.

Vladimir Atlantov
1939–

Russian tenor. One of the most exciting singers of his generation, Atlantov has a dark and heroic tenor that is one of the few to present Domingo with any rival as Verdi's Otello – although it is a role he has yet to record. Otherwise, he is best heard in Russian repertoire, especially as Tchaikovsky's Hermann (*Queen of Spades*), which he has recorded twice. His enormously impressive sense of vocal theatre is unique in contemporary Russian opera, and his work on record is reliably consistent.

Arleen Augér
1939–92

American soprano. Greatly loved lyric soprano, adored in Vienna where she shared the lighter repertoire with Gundula Janowitz. She made her debut in 1967 as the Queen of the Night, and was one of the Met's primary Mozart singers from 1978. Also popular at Bayreuth, although it is for her performances of Mozart and Strauss that she will be remembered. Sadly under-recorded, she nonetheless made a memorable contribution to Böhm's recording of Strauss's *Capriccio* and sang a beautiful Carolina on Barenboim's recording of Cimarosa's *Il matrimonio segreto*.

◑ **Arleen Augér** (Decca 440 414-2DM).
A delightful recital disc, including wonderfully sung excerpts from Mozart (*Le nozze di Figaro* and *Don Giovanni*) and Haydn.

Janet Baker
1933–

British mezzo-soprano. A tremendously popular and influential singer, commonly rated the greatest British mezzo of the century. Her dark, powerful and immediately recognizable voice was heard in a huge variety of music, from Purcell and Handel, via Donizetti and Berlioz, to Britten and Walton. For Britten she created Kate Julian in *Owen Wingrave*, and for the latter the mezzo revision of Cressida in *Troilus and Cressida*. A fine singing actress, she surprised many by retiring from the stage at the height of her powers in 1982.

Agnes Baltsa
1944–

Greek mezzo. The old cliché "a voice like a steam-whistle" might be affectionately applied to Baltsa, whose mezzo is among the most arresting of the postwar generation. A stupendously theatrical artist, she brings a sense of barely repressed hysteria to Verdi's heroines, famously the Princess Eboli (in Verdi's *Don Carlos*), which she recorded for EMI. But she is able to refine her voice for Rossini and Mozart, and has made a no less striking impression in Strauss's lyric roles.

⦿ **Agnes Baltsa** (Deutsche Grammophon 431 101-2).
An excellent-value highlights album taken from her complete recordings, including excerpts from *Carmen*, *Tannhäuser* and *Der Rosenkavalier*.

Cecilia Bartoli
1966–

Italian mezzo-soprano. Next to Angela Gheorghiu, she is probably the most naturally gifted, least self-conscious female singer of her generation. Her flawless technique, sonorous tone and theatrical personality have been particularly successful in Mozart and Rossini. However, her intensive workload has alarmed some observers, and if she does not begin to pace herself she may well cause irreparable damage to her voice.

● **Cecilia Bartoli Sings Rossini Arias** (Decca 425 430-2).
Some fabulous performances of a selection of Rossini's finest writing for the mezzo voice, including a riotous account of "Una voce poco fà" from Rossini's *Il Barbiere di Siviglia*.

Ettore Bastianini
1922–67

Italian baritone. Initially a bass, Bastianini turned his dark and velvety voice up a register in 1952 when he learned how to use his head voice to thrilling advantage; but for all the flair of his high notes, it was the simple warmth and grandeur of his singing that made him so popular. Outstanding in Verdi and

Rossini, Bastianini remained true to the Italian repertoire, only once recording anything by a non-Italian composer – Johann Strauss's *Die Fledermaus*. He died from cancer aged only forty-five.

● **Great Voices – Ettore Bastianini** (Memories HR4400/1).

A splendid collection of live excerpts from performances in the 1950s and 1960s, capturing the great man at his indulgent best.

Kathleen Battle

1948–

American soprano. Battle is an old-fashioned coloratura soprano, with a light and delicate projection, just as she has a reputation as an old-fashioned primadonna (the New York Met had a notorious run-in with her in 1992). Her bell-like tone is best heard in Mozart and coloratura roles such as Zerbinetta (in *Ariadne auf Naxos*) and Adina (in *L'elisir d'amore*), both of which she has recorded.

● **Kathleen Battle Sings French Operatic Arias** (Deutsche Grammophon DG 447 114-2).

The American diva in a fireworks display of French coloratura highlights.

Hildegard Behrens

1937–

German soprano. One of the few postwar dramatic sopranos capable of singing Wagner to the standards set by Flagstad and Nilsson. Her voice is by no means huge (certainly not when compared to her predecessors) but it has a sharp, piercing quality that helps it break through even the heaviest orchestrations. Consequently, she is no less valuable as Strauss's Salome, Elektra and Dyer's Wife (*Die Frau ohne Schatten*), all of which she has recorded.

Gabriela Beňačková

1944–

Czech soprano. She was a late starter in the opera house, not making her debut until 1970, and for the first ten years of her career she remained almost exclusively in Prague, where she was the reigning dramatic soprano. Since 1980 she has sung all over the world, specializing in the music of her compatriots Smetana and Janáček. She has excelled as Mařenka (*The Bartered Bride*), Libuše, the Vixen (*The Cunning Little Vixen*) and Jenůfa – all of which she has recorded. A sweet, warm and, when necessary, powerful voice with considerable theatrical impact.

Cathy Berberian

1925–83

American mezzo-soprano. Worked for many years in Italy, where her remarkable range of vocal colour and expression made her much sought after by avant-garde composers – especially Luciano Berio, to whom she was married between 1950 and 1966. She has sung comparatively little opera, although she has recorded Monteverdi's *Poppea* and *Orfeo*.

● **Magnificathy – the Many Voices of Cathy Berberian** (Wergo WER60054-50).

A wild recital of everything from Monteverdi and Debussy to Cage, Gershwin and Lennon & McCartney.

Teresa Berganza

1935–

Spanish mezzo-soprano. A technical wizard, she brought coloratura discipline to a rich and sensuous voice that was as distinctive in Mozart as in Rossini, in which she excelled – recording Rosina (*Barber of Seville*) twice. She was particularly celebrated for her performances of Carmen, in which, while not the most seductive of heroines, she was vocally peerless.

◉ **Great Voices – Teresa Berganza** (Deutsche Grammophon DG 431 102-2).

A choice selection of highlights taken from her catalogue. Excellent value, this single CD includes performances of music by Bizet, Rossini and de Falla.

Carlo Bergonzi

1924–

Italian tenor. One of the most beautiful voices of the century, Bergonzi began his career as a baritone in 1948, and did not move up to the tenor repertoire until 1951, when he swiftly emerged as the leading Verdi stylist of his generation. He used his large and powerful voice with remarkable discretion and taste, and although he lacked ringing high notes, he was nonetheless an exciting artist. He excelled in Verdi but he was also superb as Nemorino (*L'elisir d'amore*), Rodolfo (*La Bohème*) and Pinkerton (*Madama Butterfly*). His voice began to tire around the early 1970s, but he continued into the early 1990s.

◑ **Carlo Bergonzi** (Decca 421 328-2DA).

His earliest Decca recording and, for many, still the most impressive *spinto* tenor recital ever produced. Notable for a hair-raising performance of Alvaro's Act III aria from Verdi's *La forza del destino*.

Walter Berry

1929–

Austrian bass-baritone. Vienna's leading baritone of the 1960s, when he monopolized the high dramatic repertoire, including Ochs (*Rosenkavalier*), Barak (*Die Frau ohne Schatten*) and Wozzeck. He also sang a great deal of Mozart, for which his extremely large voice was not ideal, but from 1966 he began to devote more and more time to Wagner, excelling as Telramund, Wotan and Alberich. Less memorable in the Italian repertory, and unconvincing as Escamillo (*Carmen*), he was, nonetheless, always impressive.

Jussi Björling

1911–60

Swedish tenor. Considered by many to be the greatest lyric tenor of the century, Björling showed startling ability at a very young age, making records while still a teenager, and he made his professional debut aged only nineteen. He sang at the Stockholm Opera until 1938, when he began to devote more time to work in London and New York. Famously lazy, and alcoholic, he hated rehearsals and preferred to sing everything in his mother tongue. He was also prone to making every role sound exactly the same, but the sound was extraordinary, and as Roméo, Faust and anything else that demanded fluid, high-placed singing he was unrivalled.

NIMBUS

Jussi Björling in his prime

◑ **Jussi Björling** (Decca 421 316-2).

A selection of highlights recorded shortly before his death. The voice is in top form and the stereo is highly flattering. A stunning performance of *La fanciulla*'s "Ch'ella mi creda".

◑ **Björling – The First Ten Years** (Nimbus NI 7835).

A remarkable disc of recordings made by the tenor during his late teens and twenties. Nimbus also produce a fine anthology of Björling from 1936 to 1940, but it doesn't quite hit the heights of this one.

Inge Borkh

1921–

Swiss soprano. Greatly underrated and under-recorded, Borkh was one of the leading dramatic sopranos of the 1950s and 1960s. After studying as an actress, she made her debut as a singer in 1941, and she remained in Switzerland until 1951, when a sensational performance in Menotti's *The Consul* led to engagements all over the world. Although never recorded, she was the leading Lady Macbeth next to Callas, but it was as Strauss's demented heroines Salome and Elektra that she will be remembered – especially the latter, which she recorded to stunning effect. She was also a fine Dyer's Wife (*Die Frau ohne Schatten*, another of her recorded repertoire) and a powerful Wagnerian.

◑ **Scenes from Elektra and Salome** (RCA GD60874).

Recorded with Fritz Reiner in the 1950s when her voice was lighter than when she came to record Elektra for Böhm – nonetheless, the atmosphere is palpable.

James Bowman

1941–

English counter-tenor. He made his opera debut in 1967, singing Britten's Oberon at Aldeburgh with the English Opera Group. Since then he has proved himself one of England's most versatile singers. Hugely admired by Britten (who had him create Apollo in *Death in Venice*), his bright, ethereal voice is superb as a Monteverdi and Handel "soprano", in operas such as *Orfeo*, *Poppea*, *Tamerlano*, *Xerxes* and *Giulio Cesare*.

◉ **Handel Heroic Arias** (Hyperion HYPE CDA66483).

Thrillingly sung performances of music from *Rinaldo*, *Giulio Cesare*, *Xerxes* and *Ariodante*.

Renato Bruson

1936–

Italian baritone. An unduly neglected singer of great power and charm, Bruson was for a long time overshadowed by talents such as Bastianini and Cappuccilli, and only since the late 1980s has he come into his own. Initially he was known for bel canto roles, but he has moved on to specialize in Verdi, excelling as Macbeth, Rigoletto and Falstaff (which he recorded with Giulini). Unfortunately, he has been cast, on record at least, with less than first-rank colleagues, and his finest work (eg his *Rigoletto* for Sinopoli) consequently suffers.

Grace Bumbry

1937–

American mezzo-soprano. A student of Lotte Lehmann's, Bumbry was quickly adopted by opera companies attracted to the warmth and resonance of her voice and in 1961 she became the first black soprano to sing at Bayreuth (as Venus in *Tannhäuser*). She shot through the 1960s as one of the hottest stars and remained at the top of her profession as she began to tackle soprano roles such as Salome and Tosca. However, she was at her best in the mezzo roles of Amneris (*Aida*), Eboli (*Don Carlo*) and, most famously, Carmen – all of which she recorded with great success. A vibrant, likable singer, she recently recorded Baba the Turk on Nagano's excellent *The Rake's Progress*.

● **Grace Bumbry – Famous Opera Arias** (Orfeo CO81841A).

Magnificent live recordings of Bumbry at full throttle, in music by Verdi, Massenet, Gounod and Ponchielli.

Montserrat Caballé

1933–

Spanish soprano. A much-loved artist, Caballé's formidable physical frame did nothing to prevent her from becoming one of the heroines of the bel canto revival. Blessed with a gorgeously velvety coloratura, she presented the antithesis of Callas's fire and brimstone vocalism. Indeed, she was criticized for allowing the sound of her voice to dominate the character and meaning of the music. However, at her best (as Lucrezia Borgia and most of the Bellini leads) she was breathtaking. Less successfully, she also sang Strauss's Salome and Marschallin (*Rosenkavalier*), as well as Puccini's Manon and Tosca.

◑ **Great Voices – Montserrat Caballé** (Deutsche Grammophon 431 103-2GB).

The great diva in music for which her voice was perfect. Includes monumental performances from Gounod's *Faust*, and *Roméo et Juliette*.

Maria Callas

1923–77

American-Greek soprano, generally considered the greatest singing actress of the century. Made her debut as Tosca at seventeen, and first sang at Verona in 1947. From then on she sang everything from Isolde and Brünnhilde to Turandot and Elvira (*I puritani*). This bizarre variety of repertoire doubtless contributed to her early decline, but she never possessed a classically beautiful voice. Indeed, for all its power and flexibility it was steely and frequently brittle, and most of her recordings feature cringing high notes and excessive vibrato. However, she brought a fearsome dramatic intensity and immediacy to just about everything she sang, and no other soprano made opera so theatrical an experience. Stunning in the bel canto roles of Bellini and Donizetti, and peerless as Tosca.

◑ **La Divina** (EMI CDC 754702-2).

There are dozens of highlights discs on the market, including many poor-quality live collections, but this gives the best idea of her voice at its most youthful.

◑ **Callas Sings Verdi Arias, Volume I** (EMI CDC7 47730-2).

A selection of highlights from her many Verdi recordings for EMI with Serafin, Votto and Karajan.

Piero Cappuccilli

1929–

Italian baritone. Lacking the distinctive vocal character of Bastianini, Cappuccilli more than compensated through his commitment, which can be felt through just about everything he recorded – a catalogue that embraces most of Verdi's major baritone roles. Thanks to his considerable range, he made a superb Iago, but although there are live, pirate recordings, he never sung the role in the studio.

José Carreras

1946–

Spanish tenor. Born with an extraordinary natural talent (there is a freakish recording of him as a child singing "La donna è mobile"), he was almost certainly the most gifted lyrico-spinto tenor since Bergonzi, and early live recordings attest to an exceptionally beautiful, rich and secure voice. However, by 1980 his indulgence in heavier roles had damaged his voice, and after he conquered leukemia he re-emerged in the late 1980s with a voice that was but a shadow of its former glory. Though his profile attained a new height with the "Three Tenors" circus, his priceless recordings are the early ones, most notably as Edgardo (*Lucia di Lammermoor*) and Don Carlos.

◑ **Verdi Arias and Duets** (Gala GL100.522).

A collection of 1972–75 live excerpts from *I Lombardi*, *Rigoletto*, *Traviata* and *Un ballo*, amply proving that Carreras was one of the very greatest tenors there has ever been.

◑ **Carreras Sings Opera and Operetta Arias** (EMI CDM7 63111-2).

A youthful selection of arias and songs which, though less impressive than the Gala set, will prove much easier to find.

Enrico Caruso

1873–1921

Italian tenor, universally considered the greatest tenor of the twentieth century. It is said that "Caruso made the gramophone, and the gramophone made Caruso", for he was the first tenor to regularly make records. As a young man he had struggled to master his enormous voice, and he found high notes a strain. After study, however, he developed into the ultimate *tenore di forza*, able to sing just about everything from Nemorino to Alvaro and Andrea Chénier. He created roles for Catalani, Giordano, Mascagni and, most famously, Puccini. As he got older his voice darkened so that he could record excerpts from *Otello* (a role he never sang on stage) as well as *La Juive* (his last role). RCA

NIMBUS

Caruso bangs the drum for Pagliacci

have released all his recordings in a complete set of ten CDs.

◗ **Enrico Caruso 1904–20 & 1905–20** (Nimbus NI7803 & N17866).

Not all Caruso's recordings did him justice, but Nimbus have collected some of the very best on these two CDs, from his earliest sessions to his last in 1921. The former contains an unforgettably perfect 1904 recording of "Una furtiva lagrima"; the latter a stupendous account of the Act II aria from *Forza del destino*.

◗ **Enrico Caruso in Ensemble** (Nimbus NI7834).

A stunning collection of highlights from *La forza del destino*, *Madama Butterfly* and *Lucia di Lammermoor* with Scotti, Sembrich and Farrar.

Fyodor Chaliapin

1873–1938

Russian bass. Generally thought to be the greatest Russian bass of the century. His voice was extraordinarily beautiful, uniquely dark, and carried phenomenal authority and presence. He was widely considered among the most intense singing actors of all time and was admired by everyone from Saint-Saëns and Mahler to Rachmaninov and Massenet (both of whom created roles specially for him). He was able to bring every one of his characters to life, and was famously impressive as Boris Godunov, Susanin (*Prince Igor*), the Fausts of Gounod and Boito, and Massenet's Don Quichotte, in which role he was captured on film.

◗ **Fyodor Chaliapin** (Nimbus NI7823/4).

Sensational singing, including excerpts from *Boris Godunov* and Massenet's *Don Quichotte*.

Boris Christoff

1914–

Bulgarian bass. A singer of extraordinary power and commitment, his was the largest, most resonant bass of the 1950s, a decade he dominated as Gounod and Boito's devils, and in the Russian repertoire – especially *Boris Godunov*, which he recorded to inimitable effect. A lyrical bass, he was also able to sing the Wagner repertoire (although the tone was almost too Russian), as well as most of the Verdi bass roles.

◗ **The Early Recordings** (EMI CDH7 61009-2).

These mono recordings capture not just the thundering voice, but the singer's enormous personality. Includes an unrivalled performance of Boris's death scene.

Franco Corelli

1921–

Italian tenor. One of the loudest and most exciting singers of the twentieth century – and almost certainly the most intoxicatingly vulgar. Possessed of a naturally dark bari-tenor, by the late 1950s his technique was so secure that he was able to partner Callas in the tremendously difficult, high-lying bel canto roles of Pollione (*Norma*), Poliuto and Raoul (*Les Huguenots*). However, he was most popular in the high dramatic tenor roles of Manrico (*Il trovatore*), Andrea Chénier and Calaf (*Turandot*). His voice began to fail him during the late 1960s and by the early 1970s he had all but retired.

◗ **Live Opera Excerpts** (Memories HR4204–05; 2 CDs).

A retrospective of his best years, this two-disc set contains some electrifying singing – the excerpts from *Poliuto* and *Les Huguenots* are like nothing else on earth.

◗ **Franco Corelli** (EMI CDM 7692362).

A blinding recital, made in 1961 with an unnamed orchestra, of music by Giordano, Puccini, Verdi and Donizetti. Includes a soulful account of Raoul's Act I aria from *Les Huguenots* and a thrilling performance of "A te, o cara" from *I puritani*.

Fiorenza Cossotto

1935–

Italian mezzo-soprano. The heir to Simoniato's throne, Cossotto made her debut at La Scala in 1957, creating for Poulenc the role of Sister Mathilde in his *Dialogues des Carmélites*, but it was clear from the outset that her dark and steely mezzo was created for the high dramatic bel canto and Verdi repertoire. Although prone to forcing, she was a tremendously exciting singing actress, able to bring genuine power to the low-written roles of Eboli (*Don Carlos*) and Amneris (*Aida*).

Ileana Cotrubas

1939–

Romanian soprano. At her best, Cotrubas was one of the most touching lyric sopranos of the 1970s and 1980s. Her wide repertory included Mozart (Susanna in *Figaro*), Debussy and Tchaikovsky (especially as Tatyana in *Onegin*), but it was as Verdi's lyric heroines Gilda and Violetta that most will remember her. She was much better on stage than in the studio, and few of her recordings really do justice to her creamy, evenly placed soprano.

Régine Crespin

1927–

French soprano. One of the most versatile sopranos of the 1960s, Crespin was equally convincing in French, Italian and German repertory and she made a valuable contribution to postwar singing at Bayreuth, Covent Garden and the New York Met. A riveting Marschallin (*Der Rosenkavalier*) and a hypnotic Sieglinde (*Die Walküre*), she recorded both roles with Solti, triumphing in the latter. As she got older so her voice darkened and she began to sing mezzo roles from 1975, although less successfully. She created the role of the Prioress in Poulenc's *Dialogues des Carmélites*, which she also recorded.

◑ **Régine Crespin** (Decca 440 416-2DM).

A fine collection of opera and operetta, including Berlioz, Offenbach and Gounod, sung with inimitable charm and beauty.

Suzanne Danco

1911–

French soprano. One of the most distinctive French voices of the century, Danco's soprano has a curiously overstated quality that made it perfect for Mozart and Debussy, although she was no less at home singing works as different as Berg's Marie (*Wozzeck*) and Britten's Ellen Orford. Traditionally associated with Ravel's music, much of which she recorded, she was also an excellent song singer.

Lisa della Casa

1919–

Swiss soprano. One of the century's greatest lyric sopranos, della Casa was tutored in the Austrian tradition, central to which were prominent portamento and a dominant head voice. She became famous for her performances of Mozart and Strauss – it is as Strauss's Arabella that she will be primarily remembered. An extraordinary singer, with a beautifully spun and effortless line.

⊙ **Lisa della Casa Sings Strauss** (Testament SBT 1036).

A marvellous release, featuring substantial excerpts from *Ariadne auf Naxos*, together with previously unreleased performances of Strauss songs.

Mario del Monaco

1915–81

Italian tenor. Commonly thought to be the loudest tenor in history, del Monaco boasted extraordinary stamina and power, which made him hugely popular in the verismo repertoire, where his thunderous vulgarity was just about ideal. Self-taught (mainly from listening to 78s), he became synonymous with three roles: Andrea Chénier, Canio from *Pagliacci* and Verdi's Otello, and he recorded them all – the latter two twice. As one of Decca's house singers of the 1950s and 1960s he recorded a huge amount of repertoire; his finest moment came when he recorded *La Gioconda*, opposite his Decca partner Tebaldi. A stupendously entertaining and committed singer, he was much more successful on the stage than in the studio, and is best heard on live recordings.

⊙ **The HMV Milan Recordings** (Testament SBT 1039).

A fascinating disc, containing some of his earliest recordings from the 1940s, when he produced a much less thunderous sound, as well as later, more typical performances from the 1950s.

Victoria de los Angeles

1923–

Spanish soprano. Her beautiful voice was especially well suited to French and Italian repertoire, and on record she is most famous for her performances of Rosina (*Barber of Seville*) and Mimi (*La Bohème*), the latter sung opposite Björling's Rodolfo. Her outstanding musicianship, affecting stage presence and warm personality continue to bring her the affection of thousands who are, perhaps, a little deaf to her waning technique.

◑ **French and Italian Opera Arias** (EMI CDH7 63495-2).

Some exquisite, marvellously intense singing of music from *Bohème*, Verdi's *Otello* and Catalani's *La Wally*. A perfect introduction to her unique voice.

Helge Dernesch

1937–

Austrian soprano. One of the few singers of the 1970s and 1980s able to stand comparison with Birgit Nilsson and Astrid Varnay in the heavy German repertory. A very powerful singer, her voice lacked Nilsson's sheen, just as her artistry missed Varnay's commitment, but she made a notable Leonore (*Fidelio*), Salome, Brünnhilde, Sieglinde (*Die Walküre*) and Isolde, all of which she recorded with Karajan. Her Salome and Isolde were especially admired, and there are few more electric performances of the operas on record.

Placido Domingo

1941–

Spanish tenor. The most versatile and most recorded tenor in history. He has mastered over one hundred roles, most of which he has recorded (sometimes more than once) – although his voice is unsuited to much of this repertoire. In his youth, before his voice darkened into a *tenore di forza*, his lyrical voice was extraordinarily impressive; as the tone broadened his interpretations gained interpretive depth, and he made unforgettable performances, and made priceless recordings, as Don Carlos, Alvaro (*La forza del destino*) and Manrico (*Il trovatore*). A magnificent actor, he has reigned supreme for twenty years as Verdi's Otello, and since the 1980s he has devoted more and more time to Wagner. He is said to be planning Tristan for 1999. He also conducts, and is the director of the Los Angeles Opera.

◑ **The Placido Domingo Album** (RCA GD 60866; 2 CDs).
Arias from Bizet, Donizetti, Leoncavallo and numerous others in this fine collection; the second CD is entirely given over to Verdi arias, showing Domingo at his best.

● **Roman Heroes** (EMI CDC7 54053-2).
A studio recorded selection of French and Italian arias, including music by Bellini, Verdi and Berlioz.

Geraldine Farrar
1882–1967
American soprano. A student of Lilli Lehmann's, Geraldine Farrar was one of the early twentieth-century's most brilliant stars, and was idolized by her American public (who became known as "Gerryflappers") for her striking theatrical presence and the effortless beauty of her voice. She created the Goosegirl (*Königskinder*) for Humperdinck and Angelica for Puccini, although she was most famous as Massenet's Manon. She had a famously torrid affair with Toscanini, who once shouted at her from the pit – "The only stars are in heaven". She retired in 1922, aged just forty.

◑ **Geraldine Farrar** (Nimbus NI 7857).
An excellently transferred cross-section of the repertoire for which she was famous, including extensive excerpts from *Madama Butterfly*.

Brigitte Fassbaender
1939–
German mezzo-soprano. She made her debut when only twenty-two, and swiftly emerged as Christa Ludwig's successor in roles such as Brangäne (*Tristan*), Cherubino (*Nozze di Figaro*) and Octavian (*Rosenkavalier*). Her full and expressive voice is also well suited to flamboyant characters such as Carmen, although it is in German repertoire that she is most at home. A thoughtful musician, she is also a superlative Lieder singer.

● **Siebentodsünden** (Harmonia Mundi HMC90 1420).
Fassbaender at her best in a performance of Weill's *Seven Deadly Sins*.

Kathleen Ferrier
1912–53
British contralto. Generally thought to have been the greatest contralto of the century. She did not make her operatic debut until 1944 when, aged thirty-two, she sang Carmen in a provincial concert performance. She began singing at Glyndebourne two years later, creating Lucretia for Britten. She did not move to Covent Garden until 1953, but cancer limited her to just two performances as Gluck's Orfeo. She died shortly after. Her voice was almost freakishly dark, and some find it unpleasantly masculine, but her strong personality was communicated through everything she did, and her few recorded performances have a rare sincerity.

◑ **Ferrier in Song** (London 430 061-2LM).
Part of Decca's marvellous Ferrier Edition. An unforgettable selection of English songs, including works by Britten and Vaughan Williams.

◑ **Ferrier Sings Opera and Songs** (EMI CDH7 61003-2).
Ferrier singing excerpts from operas by Purcell, Handel and Gluck.

Dietrich Fischer-Dieskau
1925–
German baritone. The most recorded baritone of the century, Fischer-Dieskau dominated both the opera house and concert platform for over thirty years. He was much admired as a young man by Furtwängler, who engaged him for his recording of *Tristan und Isölde*. His huge repertory contained works by composers for whom his voice was simply not suited – notably Romantic Italian opera – but in Mozart, Wagner and, especially, Strauss he was magnificent. Also a powerful Wozzeck and Faust (Busoni) and sensational as Reimann's Lear (which he created for the composer). His voice is highly distinctive, and his diction is a model of theatrical declamation – a quality perhaps best demonstrated in his celebrated recordings of Schubert's songs.

⦿ **Opera Arias** (Deutsche Grammophon DG 431 105-2).
Excellent value, with splendid performances of Mozart and Wagner.

Kirsten Flagstad
1895–1962
Norwegian soprano. The most powerful Wagnerian soprano of the twentieth century. She began life singing essentially light repertoire, including operetta, at the Stockholm Opera and was about to retire when Bayreuth engaged her in 1934. She sang Gutrune and Sieglinde, whereupon it became obvious that she possessed one of the most sensuous, radiant and arresting voices that had ever been brought to Wagner's music. Sang in Wagner extensively at the Met and Covent Garden, although she was also a notable Leonore in *Fidelio*

(a role she recorded at Salzburg with Furtwängler). She retired from the stage in 1952, although she continued to record. One of the most impressive voices ever recorded.

◑ **Kirsten Flagstad** (Nimbus NI 7847).
Fine recordings of Flagstad in her prime, with a superb remastered 78 of her singing the "Liebestod" from *Tristan*.

● **Kirsten Flagstad, Complete Recordings Vol. I** (Simax PSC 1821-1; 2 CDs).
The Simax edition of Flagstad's studio and broadcast excerpts, which currently runs to five volumes, is a mammoth achievement and all the instalments are indispensible listening.

The first volume gives the most complete impression of her voice at its best, presenting her in songs by Schubert, Brahms and Strauss and opera by Beethoven, Weber and Wagner.

Mirella Freni
1935–
Italian soprano. During the early years of her career she became associated with the light, semi-coloratura repertoire, typified by Gounod's Juliette (which she sang at the Met opposite Corelli's Roméo, and later recorded), but as her voice ripened, she grew into Butterfly, Desdemona (*Otello*) and Elizabeth (*Don Carlos*), all of which she recorded to tremendous effect. One of the most popular lyric sopranos of recent years, she has recorded much of the late Romantic Italian and verismo repertoire with Luciano Pavarotti for Decca – particularly celebrated is their performance, with Karajan, of *La Bohème*.

● **Verismo Arias** (Decca 433 316-2).
A splendid studio recital of highlights from Puccini and others.

Gottlob Frick
1906–
German bass. Frick was the owner of a veritable hearse of a voice. It was considered by many to be the darkest, most weighty voice ever brought to Wagner's music. He could modify his enormous voice for Mozart (Sarastro in *Zauberflöte*), Weber (Caspar in *Freischütz*) and Verdi (Philip in *Don Carlos*), but it was his performances as Hunding, Hagen (the *Ring*) and, most famously, Gurnemanz (*Parsifal*) that have secured his immortality.

Mary Garden
1874–1967
Scottish soprano. Garden was a lyric soprano with a broad Scottish accent that frequently carried into her performances – most famously during the first performance of Debussy's *Pelléas et Mélisande*. She also sang Charpentier's Louise during the first production and later created roles for Massenet, notably Chérubin. As Debussy was quick to notice, Garden identified almost obsessively with her characters, and although her voice was no more than averagely pretty, her intelligence and variety of vocal colour enabled her to make much more of her talents.

● **Opera Arias** (Romophone 81008-2).
A good cross-section of early and late recordings, including excerpts from *Pelléas et Mélisande*.

Nicolai Gedda
1925–
Swedish tenor. The lyric tenor par excellence, Gedda was fluent in just about every language for which an opera had been written, and his effortlessly produced voice allowed him to tackle a bewildering variety of repertoire – although, like many others, some of this repertoire (eg Puccini) did not reveal him at his best. However, at his peak (during the 1950s) he made a number of unforgettable records, shining as Don Ottavio (*Don Giovanni*), Gounod's Faust and Lensky (*Eugene Onegin*). The complete Mozart tenor (he was EMI's house artist), he used what was essentially quite a small voice with tremendous intelligence.

Angela Gheorghiu
1963–
Romanian soprano. Her glorious, unforgettably beautiful voice has immense potential, and she has wisely kept herself to a fairly narrow path to date, recording Violetta (*Traviata*) for Decca, Micaëla (*Carmen*) for Teldec and an album of duets with her husband Roberto Alagna. There are similarities between her projection of tone and Callas's, and she is a similarly gifted actress, but the voice, while less theatrical, is considerably sweeter.

● **Angela Gheorghiu** (Decca 452 417-2).
A superb collection of French and Italian lyric and coloratura arias that more than proves the rarity of Gheorghiu's voice.

Nicolai Ghiaurov
1929–
Bulgarian bass. Spent his early years in Sofia and Moscow, where he developed a powerful, traditional technique that gave him a huge range and somewhat metallic quality to his voice. From the late 1950s he was in enormous demand in a variety of music, mostly French, Italian and Russian. He became synonymous with Boris Godunov, Philip (*Don Carlos*) and Boito's Mefistofele.

Beniamino Gigli
1890–1957
Italian tenor. Caruso's successor at the Met in New York, Gigli possessed a much lighter but equally sweet voice, and he became almost as popular, making over a dozen movies and recording nearly as many complete operas. Particularly associated with roles demanding a pure, effortless cantilena, such as Rodolfo and Nemorino, he pushed his

voice into the heavier, darker repertoire – not always to his or the music's advantage. His performances as Chénier and Tonio (*Pagliacci*) were legendary long before he recorded them both. A tremendously likable singer, his old-fashioned technique enabled him to keep singing into his sixties, when he undertook a series of concert tours. Became known as "Gi-hi-li" because of his penchant for sobbing his aspirates.

◑ **Beniamino Gigli** (Nimbus NI7807 & 7817).
Two excellent, wide-ranging selections: the first is from 1918–24 and the second from 1925–40.

Tito Gobbi

1913–1984

Italian baritone. If Callas was the greatest singing actress of the century, then Gobbi was the greatest singing actor. To a repertoire that embraced more than a hundred roles, he brought extraordinary dramatic sensibilities, making even paper-thin creations burst into life. A legend as Verdi's Rigoletto and Iago, he was nonetheless most famous for his many portrayals of Puccini's Scarpia (*Tosca*), a role he recorded twice opposite Callas. His voice lacked body and texture, with an uncertain vibrato and an inconsistent pitch, but he used it with great sincerity and acuity.

◑ **Tito Gobbi – Opera Aria Recital** (EMI CDM7 63109-2).
A selection of music from his most famous recordings, including excerpts from *Chénier*, *Otello* and *Le nozze di Figaro*.

Rita Gorr

1926–

Belgian mezzo-soprano. She made her debut as Fricka in *Das Rheingold* and went on to triumph in the Wagner repertory at Bayreuth and in Verdi across the globe, excelling as Eboli in *Don Carlos*, Amneris in *Aida* and Charlotte in *Werther*. However, it is as Saint-Saäns's Dalila (which she recorded opposite Vickers's Samson) that she is most fondly remembered.

Edita Gruberová

1946–

Czech soprano. One of the greatest coloratura sopranos since the war, Gruberová excelled in the most taxing bel canto repertoire and was one of the few singers of the 1970s and 1980s able to make Strauss's Zerbinetta (*Ariadne auf Naxos*) sound easy. Very popular in Germany, she was less well liked in Italy, where her approach was considered calculated and icy. Stunning as the Queen of the Night (*Die Zauberflöte*), Constanze (*Die Entführung*), Lucia di Lammermoor, Gilda (*Rigoletto*) and Zerbinetta. Apart from her barn-storming recording of *Ariadne auf Naxos* for Masur, her talents have been poorly reflected by her work on record.

● **Queen of Coloratura** (Teldec 4509 93691-2).
Excerpts from her Teldec catalogue, including firecracker performances of music by Mozart, Donizetti, Verdi and Johann Strauss the Younger.

Elizabeth Grümmer

1911–86

German soprano. Originally an actress, she did not make her debut as a singer until she was nearly thirty. Fusing her dramatic skills to a voice of ringing purity, she became an ideal Mozart soprano, and her performances and few recordings (notably of *Don Giovanni*) have become the stuff of opera legend. Also, later on, she became a fine Wagner and Strauss singer, becoming enduringly associated with the role of the Marschallin in *Der Rosenkavalier*.

Hilde Gueden

1915–88

Austrian soprano. A near contemporary of Grümmer's, Gueden developed a similar, though lighter voice, cultivating a distinctive Viennese ring and swoop. Strauss found her particularly captivating, and suggested her as Sophie (*Rosenkavalier*) – in which role she proved ideal, but she also sang the fiendish coloratura of Zerbinetta (*Ariadne auf Naxos*), and made a reputation for herself as a versatile artist able to cross into the Italian repertory. However, her recordings, especially those for Decca, suggest that she was really more at home in Austro-German music.

Thomas Hampson

1950–

American baritone. The heir to Lawrence Tibbett, and similarly skilled in Verdi's music, although, as yet, he has recorded surprisingly little of it. His honeyed and resonant voice, allied to a sometimes overstated theatrical presence, has brought him much fame in a huge variety of music, from Mozart and Wagner, by way of Léhar, to Delius and Puccini.

● **Hampson and Hadley – Opera Duets** (Teldec 9031 73283-2).
Thomas Hampson and Jerry Hadley ("Tom and Jerry") in a series of classic Italian romantic duets.

Barbara Hendricks

1948–

American soprano. One of the most distinctive and effortlessly beautiful soprano voices of recent years. Woefully underexploited by record companies, she has nonetheless excelled in a wide variety of languages and repertoire, from the eighteenth to the twentieth centuries. Her ringing tone and tasteful use of portamento are particularly memorable in Mozart, Gluck and Strauss. Also a striking actress, but she is making fewer and fewer appearances on the stage, preferring the concert hall.

Operetta Arias (EMI CDC7 54626-2).
A beautifully sung selection of music by Lehár, Offenbach and Johann Strauss the Younger.

Wolfgang Holzmair

1952–
German baritone. A protégé of the great Dietrich Fischer-Dieskau, Holzmair began to work extensively in Europe's major opera houses in the 1980s and achieved great success in Mozart's operas, notably as Don Giovanni. His repertoire is wide and he has given memorable performances on record of everything from Mozart to Strauss and Busoni.

Marilyn Horne

1934–
American mezzo-soprano. A legend in her own time, Horne was almost certainly the greatest coloratura mezzo of the century and in the bel canto repertoire her dark, powerful voice, three-octave range and fearsome technique were particularly remarkable. Although she also sang Wagner and Puccini, she is best remembered for her performances of Handel and Rossini, especially as the Italian Girl in Algiers and Semiramide.

Marilyn Horne sings Rossini, Bellini and Donizetti (Decca 421 891-2).
A classic disc of high-octane vocalism recorded in 1964 when she was at the height of her remarkable powers.

Hans Hotter

1909–
German bass-baritone. Hotter's exceptionally powerful voice was first heard in 1929 in the role of the Speaker in *Zauberflöte* – a role he continues to perform into his late eighties – but throughout the 1930s and 1940s he came to dominate the Wagner repertoire in Germany, excelling as Wotan and Sachs. Celebrated for nearly fifty years as one of the century's greatest Wagner voices, his sure technique and intelligence enabled him to sing well into his seventies. He was also much admired by Richard Strauss, who created roles for him in *Friedenstag* and *Capriccio*.

Maria Ivogün

1891–1987
Hungarian soprano. Highly respected in Germany, Ivogün made comparatively few recordings, but she was nonetheless much sought after during the 1920s and 1930s as one of the most talented coloratura sopranos of her generation. Strauss considered her Zerbinetta "without equal", and Beecham admired her as the Queen of the Night. She was married to the great tenor Karl Erb – with whom she sang in the first performance of Pfitzner's *Palestrina* – and she later had much success as a teacher. Elizabeth Schwarzkopf and Rita Streich were among her pupils.

Maria Ivogün (Nimbus NI 7832).
A generous selection of well-transferred highlights from her recorded legacy, including music by Mozart, Handel, Nicolai and Verdi.

Gundula Janowitz

1937–
German soprano. "Discovered" by Karajan, Janowitz was the leading lyric soprano at the Vienna Statsoper during the 1960s, one of its golden decades, when she reigned supreme in the music of Mozart and Strauss. The purity of tone, allied to an inflexible stylistic approach, can make what she is singing seem less important than the manner in which she is singing it. At her best she has one of the beautiful voices on record.

A Portrait of Gundula Janowitz (Deutsche Grammophon 447 352-2GDB2).
Extensive excerpts from operas by Weber and Wagner.

Maria Jeritza

1887–1982
Czech soprano. The most famous and highly paid German-speaking soprano of the interwar period, Jeritza was blessed with a thrilling, evenly projected voice and a great sense of theatre – Puccini praised her for singing Tosca's "Vissi d'arte" lying prostrate. She created Marietta (*Die tote Stadt*) for Korngold, and Ariadne and the Empress (*Die Frau ohne Schatten*) for Strauss and made a number of stunning records. Famously temperamental, she was the passionate rival of Lotte Lehmann.

Maria Jeritza (Preiser 89079).
A stunning collection of some of her rarer recordings, including music by Puccini.

Siegfried Jerusalem

1940–
German tenor. Rated by many as the only true *Heldentenor* of the 1980s and 1990s, he has sung Siegfried on three of the last four recorded *Ring* cycles, and he has recorded every other major Wagner tenor role, most recently Tristan with Barenboim. His voice is by no means huge, but it is powerful and free of strain, with a dark lower range and a thrilling top. He has also made impressive non-Wagnerian appearances as Florestan (*Fidelio*) and Lionel (*Martha*). As the years have passed, his acting has improved immensely, and his voice has darkened admirably.

Raoul Jobin

1906–1974
French-Canadian tenor. One of the greatest French tenors of the century, Jobin made a number of exceptional recordings of most of the central French repertoire, mainly for EMI. His voice is light but it benefits from a slight coarseness that gives his excellent diction and enormous range much greater character. A superb Hoffmann (*Tales*

of Hoffmann) and a memorable Don José (*Carmen*), both of which he recorded for EMI.

Gwyneth Jones
1936–
Welsh soprano. She made her debut as a mezzo-soprano – as Gluck's Orfeo – but soon began singing Wagner soprano roles, using her enormous, tireless voice to great effect as Brünnhilde – which she recorded on the famous Chéreau/Boulez centenary *Ring*. By 1976, however, her voice had lost much of the firmness and discipline that distinguished her performances during the late 1960s, and the vibrato had widened uncontrollably. In her prime – which includes a superb *Fidelio* for Böhm – she was one of the great heroic sopranos.

Sena Jurinac
1921–
Bosnian soprano. Jurinac was one of the most popular Mozart and Strauss sopranos of the postwar era and was especially admired as Octavian (*Rosenkavalier*), which she recorded for Decca under Erich Kleiber. While her silvery Viennese voice was obviously suited to lengthy cantilenas, she also enjoyed much success singing the lighter Wagner roles, as well as Verdi's Desdemona (*Otello*) and Beethoven's Leonore (*Fidelo*).

◑ **Sena Jurinac – Opera and Song Recital** (EMI CDH7 63199-2).
A collection of mono recordings, including Mozart, Smetana, Tchaikovsky and a live recording of Strauss's *Four Last Songs* conducted by Fritz Busch.

James King
1925–
American tenor. Began life as a baritone and turned to tenor roles in 1961, when he swiftly emerged as one of the greatest *Heldentenors* of the century. King was criticized for unrelieved volume and rigid phrasing, but neither detracted from the thrill of his tremendously virile voice, which was best heard in the heavier German repertory. He recorded Siegmund twice – for Solti and later Böhm – and made a fine Bacchus (*Ariadne*) and a sensational Emperor (*Die Frau ohne Schatten*). Also successful as Florestan (*Fidelio*), again for Böhm.

René Kollo
1937–
German tenor. He was the leading Wagner tenor at Bayreuth for over twenty years and is generally considered the heir to Windgassen's throne. Kollo's was an especially light voice and, although he possessed the necessary stamina, his projection lacked weight and he was unable to cut through Wagner's heavy orchestrations. He has recorded every mature Wagner role, as well as a wide cross-section of mainstream German repertory, including operas by Strauss, Beethoven and Weber – but his finest moment came in 1975 when he made a highly successful recording of Korngold's *Die tote Stadt*.

Alfredo Kraus
1927–
Spanish tenor. Kraus is still singing, upholding the tradition of the *tenor di grazia*, a dying breed of high tenor able to spin a supple legato as well as reach the high Cs and Ds. Although he has excelled in Mozart as well as Massenet (he has made excellent recordings of both) it is in the bel canto repertoire that his beautiful, remarkably secure voice excels. Its fluency and his good taste do sometimes decline into blandness but, at his best, he is one of the finest singers of his generation.

◑ **Live Performances** (Memories HR 4233/3; 2 CDs).
There are too few Kraus recitals in the catalogue, but this is the best of those currently available.

◑ **Alfredo Kraus** (EMI CDM7 63104-2).
An excellent disc of highlights taken from Kraus's EMI catalogue, including music from *I puritani*, *La traviata*, *Roméo et Juliette* and *Werther*.

Philip Langridge
1939–
English tenor. The most versatile English tenor since the war, Langridge is an exceptionally intelligent singer who has brought real perception to everything from Handel and Mozart to Britten and Schoenberg. Multilingual, he has also triumphed as Berlioz's Aeneas and Janáček's Laca (*Jenůfa*). He has recorded a huge number of operas, including many twentieth-century works. Excellent in Monteverdi, Gay, Purcell, Mozart, Britten, Janáček, Schoenberg, Shostakovich and Stravinsky. Also recorded Birtwistle's *Punch and Judy*.

Giacomo Lauri-Volpi
1892–1979
Italian tenor. One of the great characters of twentieth-century opera. In a typically flamboyant, self-confident gesture he made his debut under the pseudonym Rubini (Rubini was the most famous tenor of the nineteenth century), and quickly won admirers for the electric thrill of his high-octane tenor. A huge range (up to an easy C sharp), a tremendous technique (which enabled him to carry on singing well into his seventies) and a wide expressive range made him very popular in Italy, not least with Puccini (whom, Lauri-Volpi claimed, wanted him to sing Calaf in the first *Turandot*). He passed on much advice to the young Franco Corelli, who was, in many respects, his natural successor in the heroic Italian repertory.

◑ **Giacomo Lauri-Volpi** (Nimbus NI7845).
A selection of his favourite arias, including a teeth-juddering account of "A te o cara" from *I puritani*.

Richard Leech
1957–
American tenor. One of the young hopes for tenor singing in the wake of the big three. His voice is of average weight, but the top is free of strain and, most importantly, the texture of the voice is warm and slightly Mediterranean, reminiscent of the young Carreras. He has made intelligent choices and, to date, has sung nothing heavier than Rodolfo (*Bohème*), of which he has made a fine recording. Even if the majority of recordings in which he has starred have not set the world on fire, his performances as Gounod's Faust, the Italian Singer (*Rosenkavalier*) and Riccardo (*Un ballo in maschera*) are all worth hearing.

Lotte Lehmann
1888–1976
German soprano. One of the great interpreters of modern opera. She created the Composer (*Ariadne auf Naxos*), the Dyer's Wife (*Die Frau ohne Schatten*) and Christine (*Intermezzo*) for Strauss, and was highly admired both by Furtwängler and by Toscanini, who considered her the greatest Leonore (*Fidelio*) of his lifetime. She was one of the few sopranos to sing all three of the leading roles in *Der Rosenkavalier*, which she recorded as the Marschallin, but her ample tone and large range of expression made her ideal in just about all the major German nineteenth- and early twentieth-century repertoire. Later became a noted producer.

◑ **Der Rosenkavalier** (EMI CHS 7 64487-2; 2 CDs).
A legendary (abridged) recording of Lehmann in her greatest role, the Marschallin, with the equally wonderful Elizabeth Schumann as Octavian and Richard Mayr as Ochs.

◑ **Lotte Lehmann, Volume I** (Pearl GEMMCD 9409).
Lehmann singing extensive excerpts from Puccini operas, as well as operetta.

Sergei Leiferkus
1946–
Russian baritone. One of the first Leningrad soloists to make a career in the west, he quickly established himself during the 1980s through engagements at Wexford, ENO and Covent Garden, where he sang Iago opposite Domingo's Otello. He has since sung all over the world, in a wide variety of repertoire, including Scarpia (*Tosca*) and Escamillo (*Carmen*), but he is generally celebrated for his performances of mainstream Russian roles, notably Onegin and Igor. His baritone is quite light, but he brings unrivalled clarity to his diction and, most importantly, he is a superb actor, famously so as Iago.

Max Lorenz
1901–75
German tenor. One of the most viscerally impressive tenors of the century. He started late, making his debut in 1928, but it was clear from the outset that he was a born *Heldentenor*. He created a number of roles, including Jozef K in Einem's *Der Prozess*, in which his declamatory power was particularly effective, and sang many of the weightier Italian roles, including Otello. But he is best remembered for his performances of Bacchus (*Ariadne auf Naxos*), of which there is a complete recording from 1944, conducted by Böhm, and Tristan, of which there are various pirated highlights available.

Christa Ludwig
1924–
German mezzo-soprano. A student of Zinka Milanov in New York, Ludwig was the world's leading German mezzo between 1955 and 1975, and she was as popular at the Met (where she sang from 1959) as in Bayreuth, Salzburg and Vienna (where she triumphed as Octavian and Carmen). Her voice was unusually ripe and full-bodied, and she used it with unfailing intelligence and theatricality. Superb as Hänsel, remarkable as Brangäne (*Tristan*), miraculous as Adalgisa (*Norma*) – but just about everything with her name on it is worth a listen.

◑ **Das Lied von der Erde** (EMI CDC 747231-2).
This performance of Mahler's valedictory masterpiece is one of Ludwig's greatest performances, conducted by Klemperer with Fritz Wunderlich in ringing form.

Giovanni Martinelli
1885–1969
Italian tenor. The chief *tenore di forza* at the Met between the wars, and Caruso's successor in the verismo repertoire, Martinelli was a tremendously popular singer. He was prone to enjoy himself a little too much, but his extraordinary breath control, pure legato and ringing high notes ensured that, in his prime, he was just about the world's most exciting tenor. Much admired by Puccini, who engaged him to sing the Italian premiere of *Fanciulla del West*, he continued to sing into his seventies (though by the late 1930s his voice had begun to fail) and made his final appearance as the Emperor (*Turandot*) just two years before his death.

◑ **Giovanni Martinelli – Opera Recital** (Nimbus NI 7804).
A thrilling collection showing the tenor at his very best, with excerpts from *Andrea Chénier*, *Pagliacci* and *La forza del destino*.

Eva Marton
1943–
Hungarian soprano. Although she is unquestionably one of the most powerful dramatic sopranos of the present age, Marton's voice had been in and almost out of its prime before record companies came to take advantage of her talents. A star at Bayreuth and New York during the 1970s, she was widely seen as Birgit Nilsson's successor as

Brünnhilde, Elektra and Turandot. During the 1980s she scored tremendous successes on record singing Korngold's Violanta and Bartok's Judith (*Bluebeard's Castle*), but her vibrato was by then beginning to widen painfully and her tone was becoming hard.

Edith Mathis

1938–

Swiss soprano. Made her debut aged eighteen, as the Second Boy in *Zauberflöte*, and swiftly became, for many, della Casa's successor in the Austro-German lyric repertoire. Outstanding in Mozart and Strauss, she made superb contributions to Böhm's Mozart cycle on Deutsche Grammophon, excelling in *Le nozze di Figaro*, *Idomeneo*, *Tito* and *Don Giovanni*. Her finest moment on record, however, was her live recording of Strauss's *Rosenkavalier*, again with Böhm.

Victor Maurel

1848–1923

French baritone. Arguably the most influential baritone of the late nineteenth century, Maurel was the inspiration behind Verdi's Iago (*Otello*) and Falstaff, both of which he premiered for the composer, as well as the revised version of *Simon Boccanegra* in 1881. He also inspired Leoncavallo to write Tonio's Prologue in *I Pagliacci*. His talent as an actor made him such a presence on stage that Verdi once said that even if he whispered the part, Maurel would be the best Iago there was. His voice covered a huge expressive range and although it could not be said to be beautiful, it is utterly absorbing.

The Harold Wayne Collection, Volume 9 (Symposium, SYMCD1101).

A remarkable collection of rare 78s, including excerpts from *Otello*, *Samson et Dalila*, *Tristan und Isolde* and *Die Walküre*.

John McCormack

1884–1945

Irish tenor. McCormack established himself at the Met as one of the leading lyric tenors of the first quarter of the century. However, his acting was (by his own admission) extremely poor and he retired from opera in 1923, devoting the rest of his life to recitals and, in particular, the performance of sentimental ballads, a crime for which many opera fans never forgave him. His voice was one of the most beautiful ever recorded – the tone was uniquely sweet and the ease of projection, the breath control and the fluency of the line were miraculous. Celebrated as Don Ottavio (*Don Giovanni*), Rodolfo (*La Bohème*) and the Duke of Mantua (*Rigoletto*).

Great Voices of the Century – John McCormack (Memoir Records MMOI CDMOIR418).

A selection of arias (by Donizetti, Handel, Mozart etc) and Irish folk songs.

James McCracken

1926–88

American tenor. The first American ever to sing Otello at the Met, McCracken possessed a large and distinctive voice that, while never beautiful, was highly exciting. He was a long time in finding recognition, and he was in his forties before record companies began to sit up and take notice. His ham theatrics are not to everyone's taste, especially on record, but he was undeniably effective on stage. He recorded Don José (*Carmen*) for Bernstein and Otello for Barbirolli.

Sylvia McNair

1956–

American soprano. One of the most beautiful voices of the current generation, McNair made her name working for John Eliot Gardiner on various of his period-performance recordings, notably of Mozart's C minor Mass. She sang little opera until she signed to Philips, who engaged her to record a variety of repertoire from Gluck to Gilbert and Sullivan. The transition to opera appears to be taking rather longer than many predicted, and her potential remains unfulfilled. Has also recorded for Sony, chiefly on Abbado's recording of *Il viaggio a Rheims*.

Waltraud Meier

1956–

German mezzo. The most impressive Wagner mezzo of her generation, she possesses a large and extremely beautiful voice, which she uses with fierce dramatic intensity. A thrilling stage presence, she has become a regular at Bayreuth, where she has tackled all the major roles. She has recorded the role of Kundry (*Parsifal*) three times and made a striking impression as Sieglinde on the Haitink EMI *Ring*, even though the production, as a whole, was a disappointment.

Nellie Melba

1861–1931

Australian soprano. Dame Nellie made her London debut in 1888, and sang there nearly every year, including many farewells, until just two years before her final retirement in 1928. She created no important roles, but the beauty of her voice and the warmth of her personality made her an institution. She is best remembered for her Mimi (*Bohème*) and Marguerite (*Faust*) – both of which she sang at her last farewell, at Covent Garden in 1926 (of which there is a recording) – but she sang a wide range of lyric and coloratura repertoire, using her pure and vibrato-less voice, with its reach to a high F, with unfailing charm and imagination.

Dame Nellie Melba (Romophone 81011-2).

Melba sings music by Mozart, Thomas, Gounod and Puccini. Beware the age of the voice and the primitive technology which, in both cases here, are worse than on most historical recordings.

Lauritz Melchior

1890–1973

Danish tenor. The most famous Wagner *Heldentenor* of the twentieth century, Melchior was a huge man with an inexplicably massive voice, who was able to keep going at full throttle for hours on end. Originally a baritone, his voice had an extraordinarily ominous, dark-hued quality, which, together with a quick and shallow vibrato and ringing top notes, made his voice instantly recognizable. Lazy with diction and prone to ignore both the conductor and the score, he was a law unto himself, but so amazing was his voice that not even at Bayreuth did audiences or staff really care. Although he continued singing into his seventies, he never recorded a complete Wagner role in the studio. He can, nonetheless, be heard on a number of 78s and dozens of live recordings.

◑ **Lauritz Melchior** (Nimbus NI7816).

A generous helping of Wagner, with one or two oddities thrown in, including music by Leoncavallo and Meyerbeer.

Robert Merrill

1917–

American baritone. Just about the most gifted American-born male singer of all time. There was almost nothing beyond him, but he was particularly associated with Rossini and Verdi. He was also a gifted actor, and made a number of films, but it was the flexibility and roaring brilliance of his huge baritone that made him such a popular singer. He recorded extensively and, with the exception of a *Die Fledermaus*, everything he did was Italian.

◑ **Robert Merrill in Opera and Song** (VAI VAI69116).

A selection of favourite operatic numbers, sung with glorious abandon.

Zinka Milanov

1906–89

Croatian soprano. Considered by many to be the greatest Verdi soprano of the century, Milanov had power, warmth and subtlety (including a famously agile mezza-voce pianissimo), and she took an obvious satisfaction in the simple beauty of her ringing, golden tone. She made her debut in 1927 and continued with unfailing success into the late 1950s. Her wide repertory included Donna Anna (*Don Giovanni*), Tosca and Turandot, but it was as Verdi's Leonoras (*La forza del destino* and *Il trovatore*) that she excelled.

Sherrill Milnes

1935–

American baritone. By no means the most subtle singer of his generation, Milnes thrilled the pants off audiences with the sheer dramatic intensity of his singing. Incredible high notes and alarming breath control make for amazing vocal theatre, even if he has a generalized approach to acting. He has recorded most of Verdi's principal baritone roles, with varying success, but he is probably at his best as Jack Rance in Puccini's *Fanciulla del West*.

◑ **Opera Arias** (Decca 443 929-2).

A selection from some of Milnes' most impressive performances, including some of his better Verdi recordings.

Anna Moffo

1932–

American soprano. One of the most talented lyric coloratura sopranos of the 1960s, Moffo made a number of outstanding recordings for RCA, not least as Lucia di Lammermoor opposite Bergonzi's Edgardo. But she was tempted away from her natural repertoire and by the early 1970s, when she recorded a lamentable Carmen, her voice was almost wrecked. Nonetheless, in her prime she was one of the most impressive singers of her day.

◑ **Anna Moffo Recital** (Eurodisc GD69113).

A varied recital of opera and operetta, including music by Donizetti, Puccini and Gounod. Badly recorded, but at present there is no alternative.

Birgit Nilsson

1918–

Swedish soprano. Just about the most impressive dramatic soprano of the century, Nilsson electrified audiences throughout the 1950s and 1960s with her performances of Wagner's warhorses, most famously Isolde and Brünnhilde. She was also astonishing as Turandot and Minnie (*Fanciulla del West*), and vocally powerful as both Elektra and Salome, though neither role suited the colossal dimensions of her soprano. Her voice was awesomely vast, but beneath the steel there was a real warmth that distinguished just about everything she ever recorded.

⦿ **Birgit Nilsson – A Portrait** (Deutsche Grammophon 431 107-2).

A budget issue of Mozart and Wagner highlights, plus a sensational concert performance of the final scene from *Salome* at the Met, conducted by Böhm.

Jessye Norman

1945–

American soprano. Like Birgit Nilsson, Norman is celebrated for the incredible scale of her singing, although her soprano is more traditionally beautiful, lacking the metal that makes Nilsson perhaps the more exciting artist. The remarkable warmth and colour of her voice and the intelligence with which she uses it set her apart, and although she tends to concentrate on concert music, she has recorded a number of operatic roles, most successfully Strauss's Ariadne. The sheer size of her voice makes choosing repertoire a problem (even as

Salome she is overpowering), but she is now devoting more of her time to Wagner, having recorded Sieglinde and Kundry for Levine. Perhaps one day soon she will record Isolde.

Jessye Norman – Song Recital (Philips 422 048-2).
A selection of the great soprano's more intimate repertoire (Handel, Schubert, Schumann), captured live in concert.

Jessye Norman (EMI CDM5 655576-2).
The great diva singing music by Offenbach, Berlioz and Wagner.

PHILIPS/DAVID SEIDNER

Jessye Norman

Leo Nucci

1942 –

Italian baritone. One of the few Italian-born baritones of recent years to successfully tackle Verdi's operas, Nucci has an urgent, sinewy voice, with a thrilling upper register that makes him particularly ideal as Rigoletto and Macbeth. He has sung most of the main Verdi roles and has shown himself to be a marvellous Iago on stage, although his concert recording of the role, with Solti, was a disappointment. In recent years, his vibrato has begun to widen noticeably, and the strain of a huge workload has begun to tell.

Elena Obraztsova

1939–

Russian mezzo-soprano. A tremendous all-round dramatic soprano, although she is especially impressive singing Verdi and verismo. Despite having triumphed all over the world as Marfa (*Khovanshchina*) and the Countess (*Queen of Spades*), she has recorded neither; she remains known outside Russia (where she is idolized) mainly for her few recordings, among which her performance as the Princess on Levine's *Adriana Lecouvreur* is outstanding. A singer of great power, with a voice of exceptional clarity, she is one of the greatest talents of recent years.

Adelina Patti

1843–1919

Italian soprano. One of the legends of opera, Patti was a child prodigy, making her debut aged seven, and had already toured the world by the time she was nineteen. She was a favourite of Rossini's – and sang at his funeral – and won the hearts of just about everyone she met, from Verdi to George Bernard Shaw. She used her light voice with unerring charm and elegance, and was the highest paid opera singer of all time (earning the equivalent of $50,000 a night in 1882) – and opera's most demanding diva. Her recordings were made after her retirement, and they do not do her justice, but they are fascinating listening nonetheless.

Adelina Patti (Pearl GEMMCD 9312).
A fascinating recital of music by Mozart, Gounod and others.

Luciano Pavarotti

1936–

Italian tenor. The most famous and best-selling opera singer of the century. By the mid-1960s he was in complete control of what was one of the most perfect lyric tenor voices of all time. The thrilling tone and bizarrely secure high notes, which made high Cs and Ds sound almost easy (famously in his classic recordings of *La fille du regiment* and *I puritani*), amazed audiences, many of whom had never heard the bel canto repertoire sung in the original keys with such ease and confidence. Inevitably, he was lured away from his natural repertoire (Bellini, Donizetti, etc) by offers to sing the weightier verismo operas, and this slowly had a deleterious effect on his voice. At his best, in the 1970s, he was peerless. Also known for his "bit of fun" as one of the "Three Tenors", a venture that has added considerably to his vast wealth and fame.

Donizetti Arias (Decca 417 638-2DH).
Pavarotti at his lyrical best. Remarkable singing.

King of the High Cs (Decca 433 437-2DA).
A specially recorded operatic recital from the early 1970s with the big man in amazing form, including stunning per-

formances of "Salut d'amore" from Gounod's *Faust* (a role he has sung neither on stage nor on record) and a thunderous "Di quella pira" from *Il trovatore*.

Peter Pears

1910–86

English tenor. England's leading lyric tenor between 1945 and 1960, Pears will be forever associated with the music of Benjamin Britten, for whom he created roles in most of his greatest operas, including *Peter Grimes, Albert Herring*, *The Rape of Lucretia* and *Death in Venice*. Also a noted song recitalist (again premiering an enormous amount by Britten). His voice was small and a little nasal, but he used it with great skill and imagination, and all his performances were well thought-out.

◑ **Britten – Opera Excerpts and Folksongs** (EMI CMS7 64727-2).

A marvellous recital, with Britten conducting Pears in music from *The Rape of Lucretia* and *Peter Grimes*.

Jan Peerce

1904–84

American tenor. He began life as a violinist, and did not turn to singing until the mid-1930s. He made his debut in 1938 – aged thirty-four – and was soon in considerable demand, especially as the Duke of Mantua (*Rigoletto*), Cavaradossi (*Tosca*) and Rodolfo (*Bohème*). He was much admired by Toscanini, who engaged him to record *Rigoletto* (Act III), *Bohème*, *Traviata* and *Un ballo un maschera*. His voice was amazingly virile, with a husky quality that made it appear much heavier than it was, and although high notes never came easy, his technique allowed him to phrase and shape the melodic line like few others.

◑ **Jan Peerce in Opera and Song** (Video Artists International VAI68117).

A selection of classic arias recorded during the tenor's maturity.

Ezio Pinza

1892–1957

Italian bass. In many respects the finest lyric bass of the century, and one of the most popular singers in history, Pinza had a voice of incomparable sweetness and he dominated the New York Met between 1926 and 1948, when he was generally considered opera's greatest sex symbol. From 1948 he devoted himself to the better-paid world of musicals and films (notably a highly successful *South Pacific*). His large and flexible voice was most suited to the roles of Don Giovanni, Philip (*Don Carlos*) and Boris Godunov – just three of his ninety-five roles.

◑ **Ezio Pinza – Recital** (RCA 0902661245-2).

A cross-section of repertoire, embracing popular and neopolitan songs, Mozart, Verdi and Puccini.

Pol Plançon

1851–1914

French bass. The most influential French bass of the late nineteenth century. He created many roles, a number for Massenet (such as Gormas in *Le Cid*), but he was most commonly remembered for his Méphistophélès (Gounod's *Faust*) and his Escamillo (*Carmen*). Although he was capable of elegance, his voice was basically a basso profondo, notable for its clarity of declamation and diction.

◑ **Complete Victor Recordings** (Romophone 82001-2).

A single disc of the great singer's recordings for Victor, in music by Bellini, Gounod, Meyerbeer, Verdi and Massenet.

Rosa Ponselle

1897–1981

American soprano. Generally thought to be the greatest soprano of the twentieth century – an opinion seconded by her most famous pupil, Maria Callas. She was discovered by Caruso, who sang alongside her at her debut as Leonora (*La forza del destino*) in 1918, when she was just twenty-one. Although they never recorded together, they were enormously popular at the Met, where they were frequent partners. She continued at the Met until 1937, whereupon she retired from the stage at the height of her powers, though she made sporadic trips into the studio up until 1954. Serafin called her a "miracle", and the critic Huneker described her voice as "vocal gold". She could sing just about anything, but she restricted herself to just twenty-six roles, and made not a single bad 78, just as she never gave a bad performance.

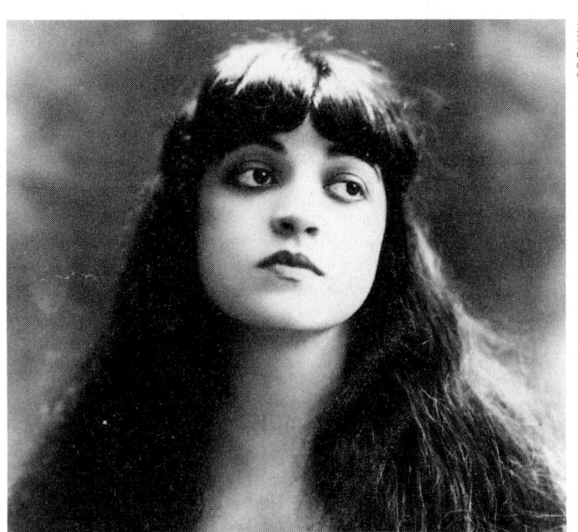

NIMBUS

Rosa Ponselle – the greatest of them all?

◑ Rosa Ponselle Volumes 1, 2 & 3 (Nimbus NI 7805, 7846 & 7878).

Three CDs packed with well-remastered classic performances of excerpts from *La forza del destino*, *Norma*, *Bohème*, *Butterfly*, *Aida*, *Tosca* and plenty more arias – plus a few songs on volume 3. Incredible.

Lucia Popp

1939–94

Czech soprano. A much loved, highly versatile singer, she made her debut as Mozart's Queen of the Night (*Die Zauberflöte*) and remained throughout her career devoted to Mozart, many of whose operas she recorded. Also sang Wagner, Strauss, Puccini and Janáček with notable success; she was still at the height of her powers when she died suddenly.

Hermann Prey

1929–

German baritone. Prey has had one of the longest careers of the postwar years: he made his debut in 1952 and he can still be heard in recital, although he no longer appears in the opera house. His voice is unexceptional in itself, but he sings opera with the same thoughtful phrasing and word-shaping that he brings to song recitals. A brilliant comic actor, he made a particularly fine Beckmesser (*Meistersinger*), and although he was never able to rival the likes of Wächter, he is one of the most consistent singers of his period.

Leontyne Price

1927–

American soprano. Callas is generally regarded as the greatest singing actress of the 1950s and 1960s, but Leontyne Price was the greater singer. There has never been a more beguiling soprano – her expressive range was unparalleled (she could hit high Cs and Ds pianissimo), her projection was perfect, with astonishing breath control, and her musicianship was faultless. She made her New York Met debut at the same time as Corelli (1961) and together they dominated the theatre throughout the 1960s. Amazing as both of Verdi's Leonoras, she was no less exceptional as Amelia (*Un ballo in maschera*), Aida and Carmen, all of which she recorded. She also created the role of Cleopatra for Barber. To celebrate her seventieth birthday, RCA have released a plush set of eleven CDs at mid-price, with a book of biography and interviews.

● Price Sings Barber (RCA 09026 61983-2).

The first performance of the *Hermit Songs* and a fine selection from *Antony and Cleopatra*.

◑ Leontyne Price (Decca 440 402-2DM).

The legendary voice at its most sumptuous in excerpts taken from her Decca catalogue, including music from *Tosca*, *Don Giovanni* and *Ariadne auf Naxos*.

Ruggero Raimondi

1941–

Italian bass. The pre-eminent Verdi bass of the 1970s and 1980s, Raimondi specialized in Attila and Philip (*Don Carlos*), both of which he recorded with great success. His flair for theatre also made him hugely popular as Don Giovanni (in which role he made a successful film) and Boris Godunov. His voice is large, sometimes too large, but in roles that benefit from grand gestures he is magnificent.

Samuel Ramey

1942–

American bass. A late starter, Ramey did not make his debut until he was thirty, but within a remarkably brief span he was in huge demand right across America, thanks primarily to the massive resonance of his basso cantate. He has excelled as the Devil, in works by Gounod, Boito and Stravinsky (*The Rake's Progress*), and he makes a remarkably menacing Don Giovanni and Bluebeard, but in his youth it was for the lyric bel canto repertoire that his voice was justly celebrated.

● Rossini Arias (Teldec 9031-73242-2)

A thrillingly sung recital of Rossini hits, including excerpts from *Il viaggio a Reims*, *Cenerentola* and *Semiramide*.

Katia Ricciarelli

1946–

Italian soprano. In her prime, during the 1970s, Ricciarelli was widely considered the finest Italian lyric soprano after Freni, and she excelled as a Verdi stylist, giving famous performances as Desdemona (which she recorded, on film and tape, opposite Domingo's Otello) and Elizabeth de Valois (*Don Carlos*). Her repertoire also encompassed a lot of Rossini, Bellini and Donizetti, although her voice was perhaps a little too large. She became closely associated with José Carreras, with whom she made a number of records.

● Katia Ricciarelli in Recital (Ermitage ERM151).

A rare but striking collection of live performances, including music from *Anna Bolena*, *La forza del destino*, *Tosca* and *Butterfly*.

Titta Ruffo

1877–1953

Italian baritone. Known as the "The Lion", Ruffo was the third of Serafin's "miracles" (with Ponselle and Caruso) and has perhaps the most extraordinary Italian baritone ever recorded. Unbelievably massive, his voice had a resonance and plushness that made him the Caruso of baritones. His one recording with Caruso, of "Si per ciel" from *Otello*, is extraordinarily rich, and it gives a very good idea of just how powerful his voice was. Some found his manner aggressive, and the quick vibrato, ringing tone and declamatory bravura must have been shocking for those better used to the lyrical conventions of the time. He sang most of the Italian Romantic repertory.

◑ **Titta Ruffo – Opera Recital** (Nimbus NI7810).
Awesome singing from "The Lion", including the legendary duet with Caruso.

Leonie Rysanek
1926–
Austrian soprano. Rysanek sang most of the Wagner repertoire and between 1951 and 1982 became a stalwart at Bayreuth, where she excelled as Senta (*Fliegende Holländer*), Sieglinde (*Walküre*; recorded with Böhm) and Kundry (*Parsifal*). She was also a tremendous Strauss soprano, making a splendid recording of the Empress (*Die Frau ohne Schatten*) for Decca, and there are a number of live recordings of her singing Salome and Elektra. Her repertoire included a number of Italian operas, not least *Otello*, which she recorded memorably opposite Vickers for Serafin. She later turned to mezzo roles such as Klytemnestra (*Elektra*) and Hérodias (*Salome*) with no less complete success.

◑ **Leonie Rysanek – Operatic Recital** (EMI CDH5 65201-2).
Taken from her complete recordings, this thrilling disc includes excerpts from the *Dutchman*, *Arabella*, *Rosenkavalier* and *La forza del destino*.

Matti Salminen
1945–
Finnish bass. Made his debut aged only 21, by which time his tremendously resonant voice had fully matured. He was captivated by Wagner's music, but it was to be ten years before he was invited to Bayreuth, where he divided audiences and critics, many of whom thought his voice simply too huge. Nonetheless, he's a thrilling Wagner bass who was wasted on the Janowski *Ring*. Also a likable Osmin (*Die Entführung*) and Sarastro (*Zauberflöte*), although his voice can dwarf his partners in ensemble.

Tito Schipa
1888–1965
Italian tenor. One of the most perfect lyric tenor voices ever recorded. Although he lacked high notes, Schipa developed an almost perfect technique, which allowed him to shade his voice with unparalleled sensitivity. His tone was light but warm, and he was able to produce the most extraordinary legato. Particularly famous for his mezzo-voce and delicate pianissimo. A legend as Elvino (*La Sonnambula*), Ernesto (*Don Pasquale*, which he recorded complete) and the Duke of Mantua (*Rigoletto*), but also sang some heavier repertoire, including *Werther*. Created Ruggero for Puccini in *La Rondine*. He wisely restricted his repertoire, which enabled him to carry on singing into his seventies.

◑ **Tito Schipa – Opera Recital** (Nimbus NI 7813).
Beautiful singing from the master melody spinner, including music by Puccini, Massenet, Bellini and Donizetti.

Rudolph Schock
1915–86
German tenor. The leading German tenor of the 1940s and 1950s. Possessed an open-throated voice of great penetration and power. He did not have the weight to tackle the *Ring* or Tristan, but he made an unforgettable Lohengrin and a glorious Walther von Stolzing. Also famous for singing Strauss (famously Bacchus in *Ariadne auf Naxos*) and, like Wunderlich after him, operetta.

Paul Schöffler
1897–1877
German baritone. A natural lyric baritone, he was initially something of an all-purpose voice, singing a wide variety of Italian and German roles, but as his voice darkened he became a Wagner specialist, triumphing as Hans Sachs (*Die Meistersinger*). He was also a noted champion of contemporary composers and gave two of the greatest performances of his life when he created the role of Jupiter in Strauss's *Die Liebe der Danae* and – most remarkably – the title role in von Einem's *Dantons Tod*. Both performances are on disc. Also a fine – if Teutonic – Iago.

Peter Schreier
1935–
German tenor. The most respected German lyric tenor of the postwar era. He made his debut in 1957 and became widely known through his work at Dresden Opera between 1959 and 1963. He then moved to Vienna where he became one of Karl Böhm's favourite singers, making many recordings with him for Deutsche Grammophon. Although his voice was by no means beautiful, he used it with great thought and each of his recorded performances is notable for the wit of his characterizations. Starred on most of Böhm's Mozart recordings and was chosen by Carlos Kleiber to sing Max on his recording of *Der Freischütz*. Also excelled in the lyrical Wagner roles, such as Loge (*Das Rheingold*), Mime (*Siegfried*) and David (*Die Meistersinger*).

Elizabeth Schwarzkopf
1915–
German soprano. Schwarzkopf is considered by many to have been the greatest German lyric soprano of the century and one of the finest Mozart singers of all time. She began as a coloratura, singing a huge variety of French, Italian and German repertoire, but under the guidance of her husband, EMI producer Walter Legge, she concentrated on Mozart and Strauss, many of whose operas she recorded for EMI. Although the basic voice was indescribably beautiful, she developed a

very self-conscious style and as the years passed her performances became more and more artificial. Nonetheless, she was always one of postwar opera's most searching singers. Created the role of Anne Truelove in *The Rake's Progress* for Stravinsky.

◑ **Romantic Opera Arias** (EMI CDM 769501-2).
A fine recording, showing her voice at its most sumptuous; includes arias from *Der Freischütz* and *Eugene Onegin*.

Graziella Sciutti

1927–

Italian soprano. The leading soubrette of the immediate postwar period, Sciutti specialized in light comic roles such as Susanna (*Nozze di Figaro*) and Norina (*Don Pasquale*) – both of which she recorded. She worked with most of the great conductors of the day, including Bruno Walther and, famously, Guido Cantelli, for whom she sang Despina in the legendary Milan production of *Così fan tutte* in 1956. Wonderfully vivacious, with a bell-like voice, she made few records, but each is a collectors' item. Also a noted producer.

◑ **Graziella Sciutti – Opera Arias** (Philips 442 750-2).
A splendid collection of arias and songs by, among others, Mozart, Bellini, Donizetti and Rossini.

Renata Scotto

1933–

Italian soprano. Made her debut when only twenty, and quickly made her name as one of the brightest young stars in Maria Callas's trail – indeed, she first came to international fame when she stepped in for Callas as Amina in *La Sonnambula* in 1957. She went on to sing a similar repertoire, triumphing as Norma and Lucia di Lammermoor. However, she took on too much work and tackled roles for which her exquisitely beautiful and ringing voice were unsuited, notably Butterfly and Gioconda. In her prime she was a remarkable Verdi soprano, and gave many memorable performances during the early 1970s opposite the young Carreras.

◑ **Renata Scotto: Aria and Song Recital** (Etcetera KTC 2002).
A beautifully sung recital of songs by Scarlatti, Liszt, Verdi and others.

Cesare Siepi

1920–

Italian bass. One of the best-loved basses of the 1950s and 1960s, particularly in New York, where he was the leading Italian bass between 1950 and 1973. Much admired by Furtwängler, with whom he recorded Don Giovanni, and Erich Kleiber, with whom he recorded the role of Almaviva in Mozart's *Figaro*. He enjoyed a remarkably long career, singing a large cross-section of repertoire, from bel canto to contemporary music. An extraordinary Mefistofele in Boito's opera, which he recorded with Tebaldi and del Monaco for Decca.

◑ **Cesare Siepi** (Decca 440 418-2DM)
A brilliant selection of music from Siepi's complete recordings, including excerpts from *Don Giovanni, Don Carlo, Nabucco* and *Les Huguenots*.

Anja Silja

1940–

German soprano. There have been few more exciting singers in the past half-century, and each of her few recordings would warrant inclusion in any recording hall of fame. Probably the greatest Senta of the century (*Fliegende Holländer*), she was also without comparison as Berg's Lulu and Marie (*Wozzeck*). She was very close to Wieland Wagner, with whom she created many new productions, and later married the conductor Christoph von Dohnányi. She continues to sing, notably as Janáček's Elena Makropulos.

Beverly Sills

1929–

American soprano. The leading American coloratura soprano after Anna Moffo and the one real rival to Joan Sutherland's rule as the leading bel canto stylist. Her voice was less distinctive than Sutherland's, and she was less fortunate in her partners – especially on record – but she nonetheless made a number of excellent recordings, many of operas by Donizetti. She was also one of the few sopranos to sing all three soprano leads in Offenbach's *Tales of Hoffmann*. She retired in 1979 to run New York City Opera.

Giulietta Simoniato

1910–

Italian mezzo-soprano. The most impressive Italian mezzo of the 1940s and 1950s, she possessed a unbelievably powerful and ripe voice, which she wielded with a technique of such security that she was able to sing Verdi's dramatic roles as well as Rossini's coloratura showpieces. Also one of the leading verismo mezzos.

Léopold Simoneau

1918–

Canadian tenor. The most beautiful French tenor voice after Georges Thill, and one of the greatest singers of all time. Blessed with an extraordinarily perfect instrument, he used it with great refinement – famously as Nadir (*Le Pêcheurs de perles*), Tamino (*Zauberflöte*) and Don Ottavio (*Don Giovanni*). The sweet tone, graceful portamento and even projection made his one of the most recognizable voices in operatic history. Although he recorded five of his leading Mozart roles, he did not record any of the Italian bel canto repertoire for which his voice was so perfectly trained.

Elizabeth Söderström

1927–

Swedish soprano. Although she made her debut in 1947, she did not leave the Stockholm Royal Opera until 1957, when she began her long association with Glyndebourne. She debuted at the Met two years later, and from 1960 she was one of the world's most popular artists. A penetrating actress, she brought unforgettable detail to her portrayals of Susanna (*Figaro*), the Countess in both *Figaro* and *Rosenkavalier*, Tatyana (*Eugene Onegin*), Octavian (*Rosenkavalier*) and, most impressively on record, Jenůfa, Elena Makropoulos and Mélisande (*Pelléas et Mélisande*).

Mariano Stabile

1885–1968

Italian baritone. Stabile was the most popular and admired opera buffa singer of the first quarter of the century. Hugely admired by Toscanini, who considered him one of the greatest Falstaffs, he was a typical example of a singer compensating for a basically ordinary voice through the skill and imagination of his characterizations. An outstanding singing actor.

Teresa Stratas

1938–

Canadian soprano. A versatile, long-serving dramatic soprano of considerable personality and intelligence, Stratas made her debut in 1959 (as Mimi in *La Bohème*) and quickly revealed a declamatory incisiveness and power that made her ideal as Violetta (*La traviata*), Salome and Lulu. She has recorded all three, but only the last of them in the studio. She has also recorded *Così fan tutte*, *The Merry Widow* and *The Bartered Bride*. Most recently she made a striking contribution to the DG video production (the only recording) of Corigliano's *Ghosts of Versailles*.

Ludwig Suthaus

1906–71

German tenor. One of the leading Wagner *Heldentenors* of the immediate postwar era. His voice was large, if a little blunt, and he sometimes found the exertions of Tristan and Siegfried a bit too much (though he was Tristan on Furtwängler's legendary *Tristan und Isolde*). He was at his best as Siegmund, which demanded shorter bursts of high-intensity singing, but he was also celebrated as Florestan (*Fidelio*), Verdi's Otello and Bacchus (*Ariadne auf Naxos*).

Joan Sutherland

1926–

Australian soprano. Gifted with an extraordinarily beautiful coloratura soprano, Sutherland was dubbed "La Stupenda" by the stunned Milanese press, and the label stuck for the rest of her career. Her voice was uncommonly large, and her incredible range and acrobatic skill (including an unprecedented trill) made her the reigning singer of Bellini's and Donizetti's heroines. Her large physique highlighted her poor acting, and she was criticized for her poor diction, but no one ever went to hear Sutherland sing in order to listen to the words. Her preferred roles, all of which she recorded, were Elvira (*I puritani*), Norma, Gilda (*Rigoletto*), Lucia di Lammermoor, Maria Stuarda, Marie (*La fille du regiment*) and, perhaps most perfectly, Violetta (*La Traviata*). She was married to the pianist Richard Bonynge, who later became her preferred conductor. Retired in 1990.

◑ **Joan Sutherland** (Decca 440 404-2DM).

Her finest bel canto recordings. A staggeringly impressive recital.

◑ **Joan Sutherland – The Art of the Prima Donna** (Decca 425 493-2DM2).

Another recital of bel canto singing at its very best.

Giuseppe Taddei

1916–

Italian baritone. Considered to be one of the greatest Verdi baritones of the century, Taddei nonetheless made his debut in 1936 in Lohengrin, and he sang a large and generally unsuitable repertoire before settling down to the small number of composers for which he is now remembered: Mozart, Rossini, Donizetti and Verdi. Aside from the odd excursion as Hans Sachs (*Meistersinger*), his chief roles were both Figaros, Dulcamara (*L'elisir d'amore*), Macbeth, Rigoletto and, most impressively, Falstaff, which he recorded twice. A much-loved, long-serving artist, who continued to sing well into his seventies.

◑ **Giuseppe Taddei Sings Arias and Neapolitan Songs** (Preiser 90020)

Wonderful performances of music by Bellini, Donizetti, Cilea, Tosti and De Curtis.

Ferruccio Tagliavini

1913–95

Italian tenor. Tagliavini was the leading successor to Tito Schipa as a lyric tenor, and he triumphed in just about exactly the same repertoire. Unlike Schipa, however, Tagliavini was tempted to take on heavier roles that were beyond his smooth and light voice, and he was well past his best by the late 1950s, when he embarked on a final two-year stint at the Met prior to his retirement in 1965. As a young man, he was outstanding in the bel canto repertoire, and made one of the greatest recordings of all time as Elvino in *La Sonnambula*. He made a large number of recordings for Cetra, famously in a performance of *L'amico Fritz* conducted by Mascagni.

◑ **Ferruccio Tagliavini – Early Operatic Recordings** (Century CRC2164).

A beautiful recital of some of his finest recordings.

Francesco Tamagno

1850–1905

Italian tenor. One of the most exciting and one of the loudest tenors of the nineteenth century, Tamagno was hugely popular some years before Verdi invited him to create the role of Gabriele Adorno in the revised *Simon Boccanegra* in 1881. He was then asked to create the title role of Otello, and a number less important roles for the likes of Leoncavallo and Ponchielli. Widely considered the greatest tenor of his day, he wielded his large and ringing voice (like "the striking of an anvil", according to Verdi) with shameless vulgarity. His huge repertoire included Poliuto, Don Carlos, Arnold (*Guillaume Tell*) and Edgardo (*Lucia di Lammermoor*). He retired in 1904, made a number of recordings of excerpts from *Otello* and died leaving his large and valuable collection of butterflies to the composer Edgard Varèse.

NIMBUS

Francesco Tamagno – the first Otello

◗ **Complete Recordings** (Opal CD9846).
Imperious singing, with highlights from *Otello* and Rossini.

Richard Tauber

1891–1948

Austrian tenor. An idolized singer, famous in opera circles for his Mozart and everywhere else for his performances of popular songs and operetta. His voice was large and capable of tremendous bravura, but he devoted himself for most of his life to lyric repertoire. He sang most things in his own peculiarly Austrian manner, sliding and swooping through everything as if it had been composed by Lehár – for whom he created many roles. He made many films (including the famous *Blossom Time*), composed his own operetta (*Old Chelsea*) and conducted. Sadly, he never recorded anything complete in the studio, although there are a number of live recordings.

◗ **Richard Tauber in Opera** (Nimbus NI7830).
A cross-section of his finest work, including unforgettable excerpts from Korngold's *Die tote Stadt*.

Renata Tebaldi

1922–

Italian soprano. Tebaldi was promoted as Callas's rival throughout the 1950s, and though Callas won the greater publicity, Tebaldi was more widely admired by the opera cognoscenti. She possessed a voice of luxurious beauty, and Toscanini quickly acknowledged her talent when he engaged her to sing at the re-opening of La Scala after the war. She dominated the Met in the dramatic repertoire between 1955 and 1973 and also prevailed in Chicago (usurping Callas) between 1956 and 1969. Heard at her best in Puccini – notably as Butterfly, Mimi (*La Bohème*), Minnie (*La fanciulla del West*), the three Trittico leads and Liù (*Turandot*) – and verismo, chiefly Maddalena (*Andrea Chénier*) and Santuzza (*Cavalleria rusticana*). Also memorable as Gioconda.

◗ **Renata Tebaldi** (Decca 440 408-2).
A beautiful selection from *La Bohème*, *Butterfly*, *Otello* and others.

Kiri Te Kanawa

1944–

New Zealand soprano. Since singing at the wedding of Prince Charles, Te Kanawa has become a household name, but she had already been an opera megastar for nearly two decades by then, and was widely considered one of the world's greatest Mozart sopranos. Her fluent, highly cultured voice can sound a little bland, and she brings the same sweetness to Desdemona (*Otello*) as to the Marschallin (*Rosenkavalier*). Nonetheless, one of the greatest voices of the last forty years.

◗ **Kiri – Portrait** (Decca 417 645-2DH).
A perfect recital of Te Kanawa in a sampler of her favourite repertoire, including Puccini, Bizet, Mozart and Handel.

Bryn Terfel

1965–

Welsh baritone. Currently the world's most popular baritone, and generally regarded as one of the finest Mozart singers of his generation – he has recorded Figaro and both Massetto and Don Giovanni in *Don Giovanni*. Also considered one of the great hopes for Wagnerian singing. Despite having recorded comparatively little opera, he has recorded the role of Jokanaan in Strauss's *Salome* twice. A powerful stage presence adds greatly to the appeal of his warm, open-throated voice.

● **Bryn Terfel – Opera Arias** (Deutsche Grammophon 445 866-2).

A magnificently sung, beautifully played recital from the New York Met, with music by Mozart, Gounod, Verdi, Wagner, Borodin and others.

Luisa Tetrazzini

1871–1940

Italian soprano. The most famous coloratura soprano of the turn of the century, Tetrazzini was one of America's most popular singers, and certainly one of the highest paid of all time, earning $3000 per night in 1900. She was said to have earned over $5 million by the 1930s, but died in poverty. Although famous for her acting inability – she was known to sit on a chair to sing her music and then leave – she was gifted with a voice of great beauty and delicacy, and most of her 78s confirm her as a stratospheric talent. Greatly admired by Caruso, with whom she made a number of records.

◑ **Luisa Tetrazzini – Opera and Song Recital** (Nimbus NI7808).

Some of the greatest coloratura singing on record.

Georges Thill

1897–1984

French tenor. One of the most gifted singers in French history, he was blessed with a light but exuberant lyric tenor, which he used like a man drunk with happiness. He even made tragedy sound like good fun, and especially in Charpentier's *Louise* (which he recorded on tape and film) he revealed a stupendous combination of Italianate verve and Gallic charm.

Jess Thomas

1927–

American tenor. One of the many American *Heldentenors* to emerge during the 1950s, Thomas was as popular at the Met – where he created Caesar in Barber's *Antony and Cleopatra* – as at Bayreuth, where he shone throughout the 1960s as Lohengrin, Tristan, Walther (*Meistersinger*) and Parsifal. Under-recorded, he nonetheless made sensational recordings as Lohengrin, Parisfal and the Emperor in Strauss's *Die Frau ohne Schatten*. His voice was large, evenly produced and, rarely among *Heldentenors*, extremely beautiful.

John Tomlinson

1946–

English bass. He made his debut in 1971 as the Second Priest in *Die Zauberflöte*. A star of Kent Opera, he sang a huge range of repertoire before making his way to Bayreuth in 1988, since when he has become one of the world's leading Wagner basses. Excellent as Hunding and Hagen in the *Ring*, Hans Sachs (*Meistersinger*) and Titurel (*Parsifal*), and truly outstanding as Wotan. His recent recording of Bartok's *Bluebeard's Castle* added to an already remarkably diverse catalogue.

José van Dam

1940–

Belgian baritone. His beautiful voice and elegant stage presence have brought him rare popularity in France. His enormous repertoire embraces everything from Mozart to Messiaen (for whom he created St François) and he has recorded a huge number of operas. Excels in French repertoire, especially Gounod, Offenbach and Debussy. Also a fine Verdi stylist, although the almost diffident elegance of his voice makes him better in less sensationalist opera. Still going strong.

Julia Varady

1941–

Romanian soprano. Although she has been overshadowed by her husband, Dietrich Fischer-Dieskau, Varady has displayed remarkable talents in Mozart, Verdi and Strauss, and she continues to use her ample, intoxicating voice to great effect – most recently as the Empress in Solti's already legendary recording of *Die Frau ohne Schatten*. Also much admired as Tatyana (*Eugene Onegin*), Arabella, Donna Elvira (*Don Giovanni*) and Santuzza (*Cavalleria rusticana*).

Astrid Varnay

1918–

Swedish soprano. The only real rival to Birgit Nilsson's dominion of the Wagner repertory at Bayreuth, Varnay had a voice that was less beautiful and much less reliable than Nilsson's, but it was no less powerful, and she used it with unerring dramatic skill. Inexplicably under-recorded, she can only really be heard at her best on live recordings, notably as Brünnhilde, Isolde, Elektra and, her calling card, Salome. A thrilling performer and a great influence as a teacher, notably of Anja Silja.

Jon Vickers

1926–

Canadian tenor. A remarkable talent, Vickers enjoyed a long and popular career as one of the century's most heroic *Heldentenors*. His voice was thrilling but never strained, and had a baritonal warmth that compensated for the uncertain high notes. This highly individual timbre was backed up by an equally distinctive theatrical sense, and his acting skills are the stuff of legend. Fortunately, he made a film as Otello, a role he recorded to tremendous effect twice – once for Serafin, once for Karajan. Also recorded Florestan (*Fidelio*) twice, as well as a magisterial Tristan, Siegmund (*Walküre*) and Aeneas (*Les Troyens*).

◑ **Italian Opera Arias** (VAI 1016).

Thunderous performances from one of the most exciting singers of the century.

Ramón Vinay

1912–96

Chilean tenor. Began life as a baritone, and although he soon moved up to the tenor register his voice retained a baritonal timbre throughout his long career. He also sang bass roles, but such was the incredible power of his voice that he was able to play only a small number of characters, chiefly Tristan, Siegmund, Siegfried, Samson and, most importantly, Otello – a role in which he has never been equalled. The awesome splendour of the voice, allied to a fearsome theatrical intensity, made him one of the very few things over which Toscanini and Furtwängler agreed. He recorded Otello with the former in 1947, and with the latter four years later at Salzburg. He reverted back to baritone roles in 1962, but left only two studio recordings, the Toscanini *Otello*, and a magnificent Telramund (*Lohengrin*) for Sawallisch. He can also be heard on a number of live recordings – notably the Krauss *Ring*.

Galina Vishnevskaya

1926–

Russian soprano. The most famous and respected Russian soprano since the war, Vishnevskaya had a distinctive and tremendously powerful voice that was heard in a massive range of repertoire – although her operatic recording catalogue contains just the one deviation (Tosca) from the standard Russian fare. Her voice was ideal as Lisa (*Queen of Spades*) and Katerina Izmailova (*Lady Macbeth of Mtsensk*). She is married to the cellist and conductor Rostropovich, with whom she recorded an electric performance of Tatyana (*Eugene Onegin*).

Eberhard Wächter

1929–92

Austrian baritone. If ever a voice merited the description "honeyed", it was Wächter's. Particularly celebrated for his performances of Mozart, Strauss and Wagner, he was magnificent as Don Giovanni, Jokanaan (*Salome*) and just about every one of Wagner's leading baritone roles. One of the most luxurious voices of the 1960s, he was internationally admired, not least by von Einem, although he was less popular in Vienna during the late 1980s, when he became the most controversial postwar Intendant of the State Opera, thanks to his libertarian views on repertoire and ticket-pricing.

Bernd Weikl

1942–

Austrian baritone. Enormously diverse singer, with a vast recorded catalogue embracing everything from Donizetti, Leoncavallo and Mascagni to Mozart, Wagner, Strauss and Tchaikovsky. Weikl's voice lacks the beauty of, for example, Wächter's, but he uses it with incisive theatricality and, more than most, he is best experienced live.

Wolfgang Windgassen

1914–74

German tenor. Although his voice was light compared to Vinay's or King's, Windgassen was the leading Wagner *Heldentenor* of the the 1950s and 1960s. He made his debut in 1941 in the famously taxing Verdi role of Alvaro (*La forza del destino*) and quickly progressed towards the equally arduous Wagner repertory, making his debut at Bayreuth in 1951 in the title role of the first postwar production, *Parsifal*. He prevailed at Bayreuth until 1970, by which time he had recorded all the major Wagner roles except Siegmund. His extensive repertory included Florestan (*Fidelio*) and Eisenstein (*Die Fledermaus*) – the only non-Wagner roles he recorded.

Fritz Wunderlich

1930–66

German tenor. Wunderlich had it all: a perfectly produced, warm but thrilling tenor voice, with a slightly Austrian elan, and although he sang little Wagner during his short life, performances during his final year suggested that he might well have become one of the greatest *Heldentenors* of the century. He was adored by Karl Böhm, with whom he made three of his five recorded operatic performances, and of these his readings of Mozart's Tamino (*Zauberflöte*) and Belmonte (*Entführung*) are peerless. His tragically early death, aged only thirty-three, was caused by falling down stairs.

◑ **Great Voices – Fritz Wunderlich** (Deutsche Grammophon 431 110-2GB).

A selection from his DG catalogue, including excerpts from his priceless Mozart recordings. Some of these selections can also be heard on a now deleted (but still available in some shops) five-disc set that contained a wealth of songs and opera/operetta highlights.

Giovanni Zenatello

1876–1949

Italian tenor. Although he created the role of Pinkerton (*Madama Butterfly*) for Puccini, Zenatello is best remembered for his searing performances of Otello, a role he made his own after Tamagno's death. There are a number of rare live recordings, notably from Covent Garden, which give a better idea of his massively exciting voice than do his studio-made 78s, but almost everything with his name on it is worth a listen. He inaugurated the Verona Arena in 1913 and later became its manager, when he arranged Callas's now legendary debut performances as Gioconda in 1947.

◑ **Complete Recordings, Volume One** (Pearl GEMMCD 9073).

A selection of some of the singer's finest recordings, heavily weighted in favour of his finest repertoire, notably *Otello*.

DIRECTORY OF CONDUCTORS

Below is a brief rundown of those conductors who feature several times in the recordings reviewed in this book. Each entry concentrates on the conductor's work with opera, indicating areas of speciality – and, in some cases, weaknesses.

Claudio Abbado
1933–
Winner of the Koussevitsky Conducting Competition in 1958, Abbado leapt to early fame in 1971 when, not yet forty, he was appointed music director at La Scala. In 1986 he was appointed to the same position in Vienna (until 1991) and in 1990 he became principal conductor of the Berlin Philharmonic. He has wisely restricted himself to a limited number of operas, and on record has revealed a tremendous flair for Mussorgsky and Verdi.

Hermann Abendroth
1883–1956
Abendroth's complicity with the Nazis has all but written him out of the history books. He was at Lübeck Opera before Furtwängler and succeeded Bruno Walter as conductor of the Leipzig Gewandhaus in 1934, remaining there until the end of the war, after which he conducted in East Germany. Conducted at Bayreuth in 1943–44, when he created a now legendary *Die Meistersinger*. A remarkably imaginative, if brutally autocratic musician.

Gerd Albrecht
1935–
One of the unsung heroes of modern opera, Albrecht was appointed principal conductor at Mainz in 1961 then at Lübeck three years later. Principal conductor of the Deutsche Opera, Berlin, from 1972. Always a champion of the unfamiliar and the new, he has premiered works by Henze, Ligeti and Reimann, and has made a study of German operas written during the Weimar Republic.

Ernest Ansermet
1883–1969
Ansermet worked closely with Stravinsky and Britten, premiering *The Rape of Lucretia* in 1946. He spent most of his life conducting concert works with his Orchestre Suisse Romande, but his performances of operas by Debussy and Ravel were widely admired, not least when he recorded all three during the 1950s.

John Barbirolli
1899–1970
A much-loved musician, Barbirolli was greatly admired in English and German late-Romantic repertory. Conducted at Covent Garden in 1928–33 and 1951–54, including performances of *Otello* with Zenatello and *Turandot* with Martinelli. Despite his sensitive ear for singing he spent most of his life working in concert. Nonetheless, his three opera recordings, of *Dido and Aeneas*, *Otello* and *Madama Butterfly*, continue to be greatly admired.

Daniel Barenboim
1942–
Barenboim began his career as a piano prodigy and has become one of the most impressive conductors of the present generation. Prodigiously gifted as a Wagner conductor (he's a Bayreuth favourite), he has recorded comparatively little opera for someone of his ranking, but since taking over the Berlin Statsoper he has begun to record more and more of the standard repertory, notably *Elektra* and *Wozzeck*.

Thomas Beecham

1879–1961

The greatest, most influential English opera conductor of the first quarter of the century, Beecham did much to revitalize opera in England. He conducted the first English performances of numerous operas, including the first *Salome*, *Elektra* (Strauss) and *A Village Romeo and Juliet* (Delius). He was the dominant presence at Covent Garden between 1910 and 1939, during which time he conducted *Tristan*, of which there is a recording on CD. He conducted little opera during the war and almost none after.

Leonard Bernstein

1918–90

In addition to writing for the stage, Bernstein was also active as an opera conductor for most of his working life. He gave the first American performance of *Peter Grimes* in 1946 and worked with Callas at La Scala in 1954–55. He conducted during the 1960s at the Met and later in Vienna (conducting a famous *Falstaff*, which he recorded) but he held no formal directorial positions. Recorded an eccentric *Carmen*, an unorthodox *Rosenkavalier* and a melodramatic *Tristan*.

Artur Bodansky

1877–1939

A student of Zemlinsky's in Vienna, Bodansky made his conducting debut in 1900 and became Mahler's assistant in 1903. He went on to make a name for himself as a Wagner conductor and, in 1914, he directed the first *Parsifal* in England. He moved to the Met in 1915, where he was one of the chief conductors of the German repertory. He was as famous for cutting Wagner's scores as he was for the additions he made to a huge range of operas, from Mozart to Weber and beyond. A fearsome presence in the opera house, he was one of the most exciting conductors of the century, as can be heard from his astonishing broadcast performance of *Siegfried* with Melchior and Flagstad.

Karl Böhm

1894–1981

One of the most comprehensive conducting talents of the century, Böhm was a prominent influence in German music from 1934, when he was appointed director at Dresden (where he gave many world premieres, including operas by Strauss), and again after the war. Following de-Nazification he was again established as one of Germany's leading conductors, rising ever higher as his rivals slowly died out. In 1954 he was re-appointed director of the Vienna Statsoper (resigning two years later) and by 1970 he was one of the last major links with prewar German musical culture. An unsentimental, frequently ruthless conductor, he was superb in Mozart, Wagner (especially the *Ring* and *Tristan*), Strauss and Berg.

Richard Bonynge

1930–

Originally a pianist, he married Joan Sutherland and became a conductor. He is regarded as a specialist in bel canto, in which field he has recorded just about everything worth hearing. He was prone to allow his singers unreasonable liberties in matters of rhythm and pulse – especially his wife – but as he rarely worked with any but the very greatest singers, including Corelli and Pavarotti, he was able to get away with it.

Pierre Boulez

1925–

By general consent the last great conductor-composer. He began conducting opera in 1948, although his attitude to the genre has always been decidedly rocky (he once declared that all opera houses should be blown up, and that nothing by Verdi or Puccini was worth hearing). He has never composed an opera himself, but he did conduct the first performance of the completion of Berg's *Lulu* in 1963, which he has since recorded along with *Wozzeck*, and he has made distinguished recordings of Debussy's *Pelléas et Mélisande* and Schoenberg's *Moses und Aron*. He conducted the centenary Bayreuth *Ring* in 1976.

Fritz Busch

1890–1951

One of the most influential conductors of the early part of this century, Busch was appointed director of the Stuttgart Opera in 1918, where he did much to broaden the repertoire, championing Hindemith, Strauss, Weill and Busoni (he conducted the first *Doktor Faust* in 1925). His reputation on record rests on a series of live Mozart performances from Glyndebourne, made after he was forced to leave Germany in 1933. Widely considered the best vocal accompanist prior to the young Karajan.

Riccardo Chailly

1953–

Currently principal conductor of the Concertgebouw Orchestra in Amsterdam, Chailly has only directed an opera company once, in Bologna between 1986 and 1989, and he has made few opera recordings. None of them stands out amidst the competition, despite their stellar casts.

William Christie

1944–

One of the leading period-performance conductors, Christie was the first American professor appointed at the Paris Conservatoire – in which city he founded his group Les Arts Florissants in 1978. He has made many superb recordings of Baroque opera with them, including works by Charpentier, Campra, Rameau and Lully.

Myung-Whun Chung

1953–

Brother of violinist Kung-Wha Chung, Myung-Whun Chung did not make his debut as an opera conductor until 1986 but his development was so rapid that just three years later he was appointed the first director of the Opéra Bastille in Paris. He has since been replaced, but has conducted some stunning performances. On record his foremost achievement is a sensational reading of Verdi's *Otello*.

André Cluytens

1905–67

A fascinating, old-fashioned conductor, the Belgian-born Cluytens was one of the best-loved directors of the Paris Opéra-Comique (from 1947), and was the first Francophone conductor to work at Bayreuth (from 1955). He made a number of splendid recordings, famously of *Boris Godunov* (Mussorgsky), *Carmen* (Bizet), *Faust* (Gounod), *Les contes d'Hoffmann* (Offenbach) and *Les Pêcheurs de perles* (Bizet). A master of instrumental timbre, he was prone to let his singers do whatever felt right at the time.

Colin Davis

1927–

Davis was director of Covent Garden for fifteen years from 1971, during which time he became known for his performances of Mozart, Berlioz, Verdi and Wagner. In 1977 he became the first Englishman to conduct at Bayreuth. Also a noted champion of Tippett, whose *The Midsummer Marriage* and *Knot Garden* he recorded. He has recorded a lot of Mozart and Verdi, with varying degrees of success, but he has been consistently successful in his performances of Berlioz's music, conducting fine performances of all the operas.

Christoph von Dohnányi

1929–

The grandson of the composer and pianist Ernö von Dohnányi, Christoph has never quite fulfilled his obvious potential as an opera conductor. Studied with Bernstein and then was engaged at Lübeck (like Abendroth and Furtwängler before him). Later moved around various houses, notably Frankfurt and Hamburg. Premiered many new works, including Henze's *Bassarids* and *Der junge Lord*, and has made a name for himself conducting Berg's operas, both of which he has recorded with his wife Anja Silja.

Charles Dutoit

1936–

Originally a viola player, Dutoit did not make an impact as a conductor until he was nearly thirty when, in 1964, he was appointed chief conductor of the Zurich Radio Orchestra. Two years later he moved to Berne and began conducting ballet at the Vienna State Opera, but he was not considered an opera conductor, and since taking over the Montréal Symphony Orchestra in 1977 he has conducted only concert performances of operas, notably for Decca. He has had mixed success with French repertoire, including operas by Ravel and Debussy, and has begun a complete Berlioz cycle for Decca.

Alberto Erede

1908–

One of the century's finest trainers of singers, Erede was a house conductor for Decca during the 1950s, when he was commonly paired with del Monaco and Tebaldi, famously for *Turandot* and *I Pagliacci*. Recorded a fine *Roméo et Juliette* (Gounod) with Jobin. Also capable of tremendously vulgar work, as in his famously ghastly *Rigoletto* with del Monaco and Gueden. Although he has never directed a major company, he was popular at the Met and a big hit throughout Germany.

Ferenc Fricsay

1914–63

Having studied alongside Solti with Kodály and Bartók, Fricsay was launched on his international career after standing in for Klemperer to conduct the world premiere of von Einem's *Dantons Tod* at Salzburg in 1947. He never ran an opera company, but recorded a number of complete operas, including several by Mozart.

Wilhelm Furtwängler

1886–1954

The most influential conductor of the twentieth century, Furtwängler was held up as the antithesis of Toscanini's precision and literalism. That's over-simplifying things, but his enquiring mind and volatility gave his performances great immediacy and tension. After a series of provincial appointments, he became a fulcrum of musical life in Berlin, Vienna and Bayreuth. He fell foul of postwar opinion for remaining in Germany during the war, after which, although he was past his best, he made a number of live and studio recordings. His *Tristan und Isolde*, his two recordings of the *Ring*, and his Salzburg recordings of operas by Mozart and Verdi (*Otello*) are remarkable.

Lamberto Gardelli

1915–

Gardelli studied with Serafin, making his debut in 1944 conducting *Traviata*. He has conducted all over the world, and was popular in New York, but he never ran an opera house and spent most of his time guest conducting. Although he made a number of recordings, most are badly cast. However, during a brief fling with Decca in the early 1960s he conducted a splendid version of Puccini's *Il Trittico* and a fine French-language account of Rossini's *Guillaume Tell*.

John Eliot Gardiner

1943–

Although famed for his disciplined conducting of his own period-performance Monteverdi Choir and Orchestra, Gardiner spent most of the 1980s working in France, and was director of the Opéra between 1983 and 1988. He has produced excellent accounts of Mozart's five central works, as well as a splendid series of Gluck recordings. Is likely to move into heavier repertoire now that he is spending less and less of his time working with period-performance orchestras.

Gianandrea Gavazzeni

1909–96

One of the last of the Italian school epitomized by Toscanini and Serafin, Gavazzeni devoted most of his time up until 1940 to composition, but during the 1940s and 1950s he became one of Italy's most important conductors. In 1965 he was appointed director of La Scala for three short but productive years. He made few recordings but most of them are indispensable. Conducted the finest, most exciting *La Gioconda* on disc and a powerful *Chénier* – both with del Monaco – as well as a delightful account of *L'amico Fritz* with the youthful Pavarotti and Freni.

Valery Gergiev

1953–

Gergiev has become one of the most popular opera conductors of recent years and since he and the Kirov signed to Philips he has overseen nearly a dozen superb ballet and opera recordings. He has been with the Kirov (who are based at the Mariinsky Theatre in St Petersburg) since 1978, when he made his debut conducting a now legendary production of Prokofiev's *War and Peace* (which he has since recorded); he has been the principal conductor since 1988. His recordings include the award-winning Kirov production of *The Fiery Angel* (Prokofiev), *Sadko* (Rimsky-Korsakov), and *Boris Godunov* and *Khovanshchina* (Mussorgsky). A thrilling conductor, his performances can be over-aggressive, but the effects are more often than not unforgettable.

Carlo Maria Giulini

1914–

Giulini was one of EMI's house conductors during its 1950s heyday, when Callas and di Stefano were the biggest names in opera. Of his many recordings made at the time, his *Don Giovanni* (Mozart) is widely considered one of the recordings of the decade. Was chief conductor at La Scala between 1953 and 1956, working closely with Visconti, Zeffirelli and Callas. With the last of these he recorded a legendary live performance of Visconti's production of *La traviata* in 1955. He also recorded fine accounts of *Le nozze di Figaro* and Rossini's *L'Italiana in Algeri* before retiring from opera in 1968. He did not return to the theatre until 1982 when he conducted a now legendary production of Verdi's *Falstaff* in Los Angeles, of which he made a recording for Deutsche Grammophon.

Vittorio Gui

1885–1975

Gui made his debut in 1907 but did not make much headway until 1923, when Toscanini invited him to conduct at La Scala. In 1933 he helped found the Florence Maggio Musicale, where he conducted a huge range of music, building a solid reputation for imaginative readings of the standard repertory. Also revived many long-forgotten works, but his fame rested with his performances of Mozart and Rossini, especially *L'Italiana in Algeri*.

Bernard Haitink

1929–

Originally a violinist with the Concertgebouw Orchestra, Haitink began conducting during the late 1950s, having made his debut in Amsterdam after the scheduled conductor failed to show. He did not make his opera debut until 1963, when he conducted Wagner's *Dutchman*. Nearly ten years passed before he began working at Glyndebourne where, from 1977, he was music director. Ten years on he was appointed director at Covent Garden, where he remains to this day. A powerful but inconsistent opera conductor, Haitink's work has always been much more successful in the theatre than in the studio. His recent recording of *Bluebeard's Castle* was made live, and the differences are clear.

Nikolaus Harnoncourt

1929–

A specialist early-music conductor for many years, Harnoncourt began to turn to more mainstream pastures throughout the 1980s and early 1990s, recording operas by Mozart (notably *Die Entführung aus dem serail*) and Johann Strauss (*Fledermaus* and *Zigeunerbaron*). He has recently begun conducting central Romantic repertoire, chiefly Beethoven's *Fidelio* (with some success) and Weber's *Der Freischütz* (with none), but as an opera conductor he has not really produced anything to compare with his Monteverdi recordings of the 1960s and 1970s.

Désiré Inghelbrecht

1880–1965

Inghelbrecht was assistant at the Paris Opéra-Comique in 1924 and its director from 1932. He moved in 1945 to Paris Opéra, where he was idolized. His only two opera recordings are both of Debussy's *Pelléas et Mélisande*, readings that benefited from his conversations and study with the composer.

René Jacobs

1946–

Originally a counter-tenor, Jacobs turned to conducting in 1977 when he began reviving unexplored Renaissance and Baroque repertoire, producing new performing editions of scores with his own group, the Concerto Vocale. He has conducted all over the world and made more than a hundred recordings, most of them for Harmonia Mundi. He has recorded all Monteverdi's operas as well as works by Cavalli, Gluck, Cesti and Handel. He is artistic director of opera at the Innsbruck Festival and teaches Baroque vocal style at the Scholas Cantorum Basiliensis in Basel.

Eugen Jochum

1902–87

Jochum spent many years touring provincial theatres for short stays as répétiteur and conductor, never settling anywhere for more than a couple of years. Worked at Bayreuth in 1953 (conducting a blistering *Tristan*) and 1954 (producing a thrilling *Tannhäuser* of which there is a recording). His recordings are uneven, but his performances of *Die Entführung aus dem Serail* is notable for its wit, and the singing of Fritz Wunderlich.

Herbert von Karajan

1906–89

One of the most remarkable conductors of the century, Karajan was the epitome of the conductor as dictator, a control freak and probably the most powerful musician on earth after Furtwängler's death in 1954. He was no less gifted as a businessman and he died leaving nearly £200 million to his wife and family. His repertoire embraced just about the whole history of opera, and he was one of the few non-Italians to triumph in the Romantic Italian repertory, especially Verdi, of whose *Il trovatore*, *Aida* and *Don Carlo* he made staggeringly impressive recordings. Famed also for his Wagner, of whose operas he recorded everything except *Tannhäuser.* During the 1960s and early 1970s he reached a peak of inspiration, but later his obsession with homogeneity of sound and sonic opulence made many of his performances empty and showy. Considered by many singers to have been the century's greatest operatic accompanist.

Joseph Keilberth

1908–68

A hugely talented and unjustly neglected conductor, Keilberth succeeded Karl Böhm as director of Dresden Opera in 1945 and began a particularly memorable period as director of Munich Opera between 1959 and his death, during which time he made most of his recordings. Of these, his live 1963 *Arabella* is one of the finest performances of a Strauss opera ever recorded. A remarkable conductor of Wagner, he died conducting *Tristan und Isolde*.

Rudolf Kempe

1910–76

Kempe worked all over Germany before taking over Dresden from Keilberth, after which he was propelled onto the international stage, working with great success at the Met, Bayreuth (where he conducted a new *Ring* in 1960) and Covent Garden. Like Keilberth, he was superb in the standard German repertory, but also excellent in Verdi and Puccini. He recorded only three composers' music, Weber (*Der Freischütz*), Wagner (*Lohengrin* and *Die Meistersinger*) and Strauss (*Rosenkavalier* and *Ariadne auf Naxos*).

Erich Kleiber

1890–1956

A hugely admired and extremely influential conductor, Kleiber devoted most of his life to opera, conducting at Darmstadt from 1912, then at Mannheim and Berlin, where he was appointed Music Director of the Statsoper in 1923, remaining for eleven years. This brilliant period saw many premieres, including that of Berg's *Wozzeck.* Resigned in 1934 and left Germany for Argentina. Did not return until 1950. Four years later he was re-instated as director in Berlin, but then resigned once more over political interference. He did much to develop Covent Garden's repertoire and playing standards. He made just two studio recordings, of Mozart's *Figaro* and Strauss's *Rosenkavalier*; both are remarkable.

Carlos Kleiber

1930–

Son of Erich Kleiber, Carlos made his debut in 1952. Gave up music to study chemistry but returned two years later, this time as a répétiteur in Munich. Conducted across Germany from 1956, then made his debut in Vienna in 1973 and at Bayreuth the following year. A remarkable imagination and a flair for the unusual have distinguished almost all his work and, like his father, he is a perfectionist, demanding extensive rehearsal time. An eccentric, unpredictable musician, he is one of the few conductors of recent years to convey a genuine sense of creative exploration in his work. Sadly, he appears to have retired. His opera recordings – of *La Traviata*, *Die Fledermaus*, *Der Freischütz* and *Tristan und Isolde* – are all exhilarating, though their casting never lives up to the conducting.

Otto Klemperer

1885–1973

One of the most remarkable characters in the history of twentieth-century opera. A student of Pfitzner's, Klemperer became a noted champion of new work during his directorship of the Krolloper in Berlin during the 1930s. Premiered many works, including operas by Weill and Hindemith. Forced to leave Germany in 1933, he settled in the USA then moved to Budapest in 1947 to direct the Opera. After three years he left and devoted himself to concert work. Made a partial return to opera in 1961, making his Covent Garden debut conducting and producing Beethoven's *Fidelio*. Later produced and conducted Mozart's *Die Zauberflöte* and Wagner's *Lohengrin*. Made few opera recordings, but outstanding are his *Fidelio* and *Der fliegende Holländer*. A legendarily tough man, he brought extraordinary gravity to his performances and de-sentimentalized almost everything he conducted.

Hans Knappertsbusch
1888–1965
After working as an assistant to Richter and Siegfried Wagner at Bayreuth, Knappertsbusch became one of the most important Wagner conductors of the century, almost turning *Parsifal* into his personal property after the war, when from 1951 (the year he re-opened the Bayreuth festival) until his death he was the dominant force in Wagner's theatre. An aristocratic, taciturn man, he despised rehearsals, believing in the primacy of the moment – and, as his various recordings of *Parsifal* testify, he was able to create an extraordinary sense of re-birth with each new performance. He recorded only two works – *Die Meistersinger* and *Fidelio* – in the studio, but at least three live accounts of *Parsifal* are available, as is a complete *Ring* from Bayreuth.

Clemens Krauss
1893–1954
Krauss was the antithesis of Klemperer and Knappertsbusch. Hugely talented as a musician, he was a famously scheming man, and a social climber of the highest order. However, he was one of the finest conductors of any generation. Stylish and graceful, he brought lightness and charm to everything he conducted. Director of the Opera in Vienna from 1929, Berlin from 1935 and Munich from 1937 until the end of the war. He became close friends with Richard Strauss and premiered *Arabella*, *Friedenstag*, *Der liebe der Danae* and *Capriccio*, the libretto for which he wrote with the composer. Made few complete recordings, but his performances of *Die Fledermaus*, *Der fliegende Holländer* and the *Ring* (live) are indispensable.

Joseph Krips
1902–74
Krips studied with Weingartner and made a huge impact as music director at the Vienna Statsoper from 1933 until his dismissal by the Nazis in 1938. Returned at the end of the war and conducted the first opera performances, later rebuilding the company at the Statsoper to almost prewar standards. Went on to perform extensively at Salzburg, where he helped to re-establish the festival, and brought similar rejuvenation to Covent Garden. Cherished for his old-fashioned performances of Mozart's operas, notably *Don Giovanni*, which he recorded for Decca. Stylish and cultivated, he was a brilliant vocal accompanist and knew exactly how to get the best from his singers.

Erich Leinsdorf
1912–95
Leinsdorf was an assistant to Bruno Walter and Toscanini at Salzburg between 1934 and 1937, after which he moved to New York, where he made his debut, conducting *Die Walküre* at the Met. So impressed were the management that, in spite of his youth, he was appointed Bodansky's successor as the principal conductor of the German repertory just months later. Conducted at the Met throughout the 1950s, 1960s and 1970s, producing white-hot performances of Wagner, Verdi and Puccini. He recorded extensively for RCA, conducting thrilling performances of Verdi's *Un ballo in maschera*, Puccini's *Madama Butterfly* and Korngold's *Die tote Stadt*. Also broadcast extensively from the Met – including a blistering *Tristan und Isolde* with Melchior and Flagstad in 1941.

James Levine
1943–
Conductor and music director of the New York Met, where he has reigned for a quarter of a century. He has conducted overseas, famously at Bayreuth, where he is much liked by the director Wolfgang Wagner, but it is for his work at the Met that he is most famous. Although he is prone to sentimentality, he is also capable of tremendous theatrical intensity, and he is known as a conductor who brings out the best in his singers. He has recorded most of Wagner's major works and many of Verdi's mature operas, but he has achieved his greatest successes with Tchaikovsky's *Eugene Onegin*, Giordano's *Andrea Chénier* and Cilea's *Adriana Lecouvreur*.

Lorin Maazel
1930–
Maazel was trained as a violinist but turned to the podium full-time in 1960, when he was invited to Bayreuth. He conducted at the Met from 1962 and was appointed the artistic director of the Berlin Deutsche Oper in 1965, where he remained until 1971. Became director of the Vienna Statsoper in 1982, but resigned just two years later. In spite of his obvious abilities, his opera recordings are, for the most part, unremarkable. Exceptions include his performances of Puccini's *Tosca* and *Il trittico*, and Ravel's two operas.

Charles Mackerras
1925–
Australian-born Mackerras studied with the conductor Vaclav Talich in Prague, where he

developed his profound passion and sympathy for the music of Janáček. He made his debut in 1948, in London, conducting Johann Strauss's *Die Fledermaus*, and spent many years working as a guest conductor until 1966, when he was appointed music director at Hamburg Opera. Thereafter he was in great demand, conducting a huge variety of music, chiefly Janáček, Mozart, and Gilbert and Sullivan. He is in the process of recording all Mozart's important operas for the American label Telarc.

Zubin Mehta
1936–

Mehta made his opera debut in Montréal in 1964 conducting *Tosca*, a work he has since recorded twice. He worked at the Met between 1965 and 1971, and at Covent Garden from 1977, and he revealed an acute theatrical flair, as can be heard on his fine recordings of *Il trovatore* and *Turandot*. He became more widely known for his work with the "Three Tenors", and has recently taken over Munich Opera, his first ever theatre appointment. Looks set to devote a great deal of time and money to Wagner.

Giuseppe Molinari-Pradelli
1911–

A solid craftsman, Molinari-Pradelli conducted in provincial theatres before graduating to Milan in 1946; thereafter he made regular appearances around the globe. Favoured by EMI, for whom he recorded a variety of repertoire. Famously, he was the conductor of *Turandot* with Nilsson and Corelli, as well as a host of other interesting, mainstream work, and he excelled in Romantic dramas, especially those in which discipline was a prerequisite. He made few studio recordings, but there are many live recordings, mainly of Verdi and verismo operas.

Riccardo Muti
1941–

Muti studied in Milan with Votto and made his debut in 1970. He was rapidly propelled into the international limelight, conducting at Salzburg in 1971 and Covent Garden in 1977. Appointed music director of La Scala in 1986, he has revived numerous long forgotten operas, including Cherubini's *Lodoïska*, and he was the first conductor to perform the uncut *Guillaume Tell*. He has recorded memorable performances of Verdi's *Nabucco* and *Macbeth*, but he is at his best in the theatre.

Kent Nagano
1951–

After studying with Boulez and Bernstein, Nagano shot to celebrity in 1989 when he was appointed music director of the Opéra de Lyon. One year later he was also made associate principal guest conductor of the London Symphony Orchestra. Nagano conducted the world premiere of John Adams' *The Death of Klinghoffer* in 1991 and made his debut at the Met in 1994 conducting Poulenc's *Dialogues des Carmélites*. Almost every one of his opera recordings has been a major success: in addition to his recordings of the Adams and Poulenc pieces, his accounts of Prokofiev's *Love for Three Oranges*, Busoni's *Turandot* and *Arlecchino*, Floyd's *Susannah* (a Grammy winner), Puccini's *La Bohème* and Stravinsky's *Rake's Progress* are first-rate.

Trevor Pinnock
1946–

One of Britain's most cosmopolitan conductors, Pinnock has established himself with his English Concert, a period-performance group of great style and energy with whom he has made fine recordings of Purcell's *Dido and Aeneas* and *King Arthur*. Also a noted conductor of Handel's operas although, as yet, not on record.

Michel Plasson
1933–

Plasson has made a name for himself through remaining true to a single opera house, in Toulouse, for nearly thirty years. He has turned the orchestra and chorus into one of Europe's finest and, upholding the traditions cultivated by Cluytens, he has done much to bring about a return to regional style – so each of his recordings has a distinctive flavour. He has excelled as a conductor of Offenbach (*Orpheus, Hélène* and *Périchole*) as well as Gounod and Massenet. Although his performances lack fire he is a sensitive musician and this will stand him in good stead as he begins to work more frequently with Roberto Alagna. Their first collaboration is Gounod's *Faust*.

Georges Prêtre
1924–

A student of Cluytens, Prêtre shared much of his teacher's flair for colour and cultivated an idiosyncratic style during his work in the theatres of Lille, Toulouse and Lyon. Gravitated to the Opéra-Comique in 1956, where he conducted the first performance of Poulenc's *La voix humaine* (which he later recorded). He moved to the Opéra in 1959 and became its music director in 1970. Though most at home in French repertoire, he was chosen by EMI to conduct Callas's second *Tosca* in 1964, and he triumphed with his uncommonly muscular reading of *Lucia di Lammermoor* for RCA, with Moffo and Bergonzi.

Fernando Previtali
1907–85

One of the dark horses of Italian opera, Previtali never achieved international recognition, but he was admired at La Scala and made a number of interesting recordings. Most of these were for Cetra, not the world's best-distributed label, so he remains a distant presence as far as recorded opera is concerned.

Simon Rattle

1955–

In 1974, while still a student, Rattle conducted a performance of *L'Enfant et les sortilèges* in London and just three years later he made his operatic debut at Glyndebourne, conducting Janáček's *Cunning Little Vixen*. He has since conducted at Glyndebourne on and off ever since, as well as at English National Opera and Los Angeles Opera. He has recorded just two major operas, Janáček's *Vixen* and Gershwin's *Porgy and Bess*, the latter with notable success. Now that he has left the City of Birmingham Symphony Orchestra he is likely to spread his wings much further.

Mstislav Rostropovich

1927–

Rostropovich was widely considered the world's greatest cellist before he began conducting during the 1970s. He has worked mainly in the concert hall, but his keen sense of theatre and highly strung personality are ideal for the opera house, although he is by no means a natural vocal coach. On record he has had great success conducting Tchaikovsky's *Eugene Onegin*, Mussorgsky's *Boris Godunov* and, most impressively, his friend Prokofiev's *War and Peace*. Also a noted champion of Schnittke's – he conducted, and played in, the world premiere of *Life with an Idiot*. Married to the soprano Galina Vishnevskaya.

Victor de Sabata

1892–1967

A legend during his lifetime, de Sabata was known as "Count Dracula" for his fearsome, skeletal appearance, but he was also one of the most respected conductors of the century. Turning to conducting after success as a composer proved elusive, he became principal conductor at Monte Carlo Opera in 1918, and gave the first performance of Ravel's *Les enfants et les sortilèges* in 1925. Conducted at La Scala from 1930, becoming its director in 1953. Also at Bayreuth from 1939, where he *Tristan* was highly praised. A breathtakingly exciting conductor, he only made two opera recordings – of *Macbeth* (Verdi) and *Tosca* (Puccini) – but they continue to dominate the catalogue.

Wolfgang Sawallisch

1923–

Starting as a répétiteur in 1947 at Augsburg, Sawallisch later became the music director there, where he remained until 1952. Took over at Karajan's old haunt in Aachen, where he was "discovered" by EMI's Walter Legge, who used him for a variety of now classic recordings, famously those involving Legge's wife Elizabeth Schwarzkopf. Of these, his performances of *Arabella* and *Capriccio* are highly regarded. A powerful presence at Bayreuth from 1957, where he conducted new productions of *Tristan*, *Der fliegende Holländer* and *Tannhäuser*. His recordings of *Lohengrin* and *Der fliegende Holländer* are legendary.

Thomas Schippers

1930–77

Schippers made his debut in 1948 and conducted the premiere of Copland's *Tender Land* in 1954; he went on to premiere a number of works by Menotti and Barber, including, most famously, Barber's *Antony and Cleopatra*, which inaugurated the first night of the new Metropolitan Opera theatre in New York. Worked at Bayreuth from 1964 and made a number of recordings for EMI and Decca, most famously the 1964 *Il trovatore* with Franco Corelli. His early death was a great loss to opera.

Tullio Serafin

1878–1968

One of the greatest conductors of the twentieth century, and one of the finest voice trainers of all time, Serafin discovered more great singers than almost any other conductor, among them Callas, Bergonzi and Gobbi. In 1898 he was Toscanini's répétiteur in Milan and did not begin conducting full-time until 1903. He remained active for the following 65 years, conducting many Italian premieres, including Berg's *Wozzeck* in 1942. Moved to the Met in 1924 and gave dozens of American premieres, many by American composers. A genius conducting Verdi and Puccini (a good friend of his), he was the embodiment of the Italian nineteenth-century repertoire traditions – Gobbi called him "the most complete man of the theatre of our time". A remarkable artist, whose work is captured at its best on recordings of *La Bohème*, *Madama Butterfly*, *Il trovatore*, *Norma* and *Otello*.

Giuseppe Sinopoli

1946–

A self-consciously controversial conductor, whose interpretations are marked by sometimes wilful tempi and bizarre phrasing, Sinopoli has recorded a great deal of music, mostly standard works by Verdi, Puccini and Wagner. Although he has benefited from heavyweight casting, little of his work can withstand the competition – his popularity at Bayreuth attests to a talent as yet untapped in the studio.

Georg Solti

1912–

Born in Hungary, Solti studied with Bartók and Kodály in Budapest as a piano virtuoso and composer; in 1936 he moved to Salzburg where, with Leinsdorf, he was an assistant to Toscanini. He made his debut in 1938, conducting Mozart's *Figaro*, and later moved to Munich where, from 1946 to 1952, he was the director of the Opera. In 1949 he conducted the "Tetzet" from Strauss's *Rosenkavalier* at the composer's funeral. He conducted at Covent Garden from 1959 and became its director in 1961. During the following decade he revitalized the house and gained a reputation for unflagging standards. A superb technician and an often thrilling conductor, he has recorded a huge number of operas, although he has missed the target as many times as he has hit it. Successes include memorable performances of Strauss's *Arabella*, *Salome* and *Die Frau ohne Schatten*, Verdi's *Un ballo in maschera* and *Don Carlo*, and, perhaps most famously, the first ever studio *Ring* cycle. His aggressive manner is less well suited to classical repertoire, although he has recorded all Mozart's major operas, in some cases more than once.

Arturo Toscanini

1867–1957

The most famous conductor of the century, Toscanini made a huge impact in Italy, revising operatic practice and premiering dozens of new operas, including Puccini's *La Bohème*, *La fanciulla del West* and *Turandot*. He later moved to America where he became the first conductor to make use of the radio, gramophone and television technologies. A thrilling conductor, his martial approach to music breathed new life into a huge amount of dusty repertoire. He made remarkable recordings of Verdi's *Otello*, *Traviata* and, most wonderfully, *Falstaff*. For more on Toscanini, see p.328.

Antonino Votto

1896–1985

An unfairly neglected conductor of the old school, Votto was a répétiteur for Toscanini between 1924 and 1929 but was soon in great demand as a conductor. During the 1950s he was Callas's favourite conductor and during his conductorship at La Scala (1948–70) they gave many memorable performances – not least a sensational *Andrea Chénier* in 1955 with del Monaco in the title role. In the studio, his performances of *Un ballo in maschera*, *La Bohème*, *La Sonnambula* and *La Gioconda* – all with Callas – are certain to last, and it is a shame that he recorded little else. Look out for live recordings.

DIRECTORY OF OPERA HOUSES AND FESTIVALS

Opera costs a lot of money to produce, so unless you live close to one of the wealthiest houses, like La Scala, Covent Garden or the Met, you're going to have to travel if you want to see a good spread of productions. This section provides essential information on the main opera houses and festivals in Europe, North America, Australia and New Zealand, with details on how to book tickets, how much they cost, and the reputations and specialities of the venues.

With the ever-increasing tendency towards co-production and the buying in of existing productions, you can easily go halfway round the world only to be faced with a production from your home theatre. This is where getting detailed information is essential, and it can be the most frustrating part of getting to see any performance in a foreign country. Companies vary widely in the information they are prepared to issue in advance: some publish the whole schedule before the beginning of the season, others issue details barely a month before performances. Similarly, at some houses you can book from the beginning of the season for any date, while others may put seats on sale only a week in advance of the performance. Wherever possible, we've indicated the booking periods.

Your first point of reference should be one of the specialist opera magazines, such as *Opera*, *Opera Now* in the UK, *Opera News* in the USA, *Das Opernglas* in Germany, and so on. These publish schedules for the cover month and often beyond, but are never comprehensive, so you will probably need to double-check with the theatre you're interested in.

Where the box office has a separate phone number for information, we've given it; otherwise, just call the main number, or write. Be warned, though, that some places, particularly in Italy, will ask for money before sending their season's brochure.

Repertoire, seasons and box offices

In general terms, operas are presented either in **repertoire** or in **stagione** systems. The repertoire system, most common in the German-speaking world, means each theatre draws on a stock of productions in what can seem a random manner. The advantage of this is that in somewhere like Vienna, for example, you can see a different opera each night of the week; the disadvantage is that the system relies on a company's resident ensemble being familiar with a wide range of operas, so performances can lapse into the wearily routine. The *stagione* system, more common in the UK and US, has full runs of each opera, either in isolation or overlapping with the next in the schedule; thus a particular theatre may only offer a single work each month, or as many as three different works in a week.

Most **seasons** run from September or October to June or July; divergences from this are indicated in the listings below. In continental Europe, there are usually performances on Sundays (often a matinee), but not on Mondays (except in the biggest cities); in the UK, North America and Australasia performances are generally given from Monday or Tuesday to Saturday. The majority of theatres operate subscription schemes (details of which are not included here), which inevitably restrict availability of tickets to some extent, though most have a number of performances open purely to box-office sales – *Freiverkauf* in German, *fuori abbonamento* in Italian, *vente libre* in French.

In addition to the main **box office**, every theatre will also have a ticket office open on the evening of the performance; this is sometimes in the same location as the general box office, but more often is a special window in the theatre foyer. In the evening you can rarely book for any performance other than the one that's about to start.

Telephone booking hours usually coincide with the general box office hours. **Postal bookings** should be sent to the address following the company's name, unless another address is given under box office details. Each place has its own regulations (the Italian ones are often particularly strict), but as a rule postal applications are accepted as soon the performance information is published; unless indicated otherwise, the time-spans for ticket sales given in this directory apply to personal and telephone bookings. You should send your request specifying preferred seating areas and perhaps a couple of alternative dates, and give all possible avenues of response (address, phone and fax, etc). Surprisingly, credit cards are rarely accepted at many European theatres (particularly those in Germany); money orders and Eurocheques are the preferred means of advance payment, though many theatres will hold tickets until the day of the performance.

One final tip – for the biggest opera houses you may well find that the **tourist office** for the country in which the house is located will be able to arrange package deals that include tickets. For example, the German tourist office in London was able to supply tickets for Bayreuth in 1996. Some specialist travel agents can also arrange such deals – a good company to try in the UK is *Liaisons Abroad*, 1 Fulham High St, London SW6 3HJ (☎0171/371 8227; Web Site at www.operatravel.com).

How this directory is organized

The entries in this directory are listed by country (in alphabetical order) and are laid out as follows: city; name of company or theatre; location; brief description of the company; ticket prices and conditions; box office address (if different from that of the theatre), opening hours, phone numbers for bookings and information, fax number; and address for postal applications if different from box office address.

Opera houses are increasingly getting wired up to the Internet, and we've given the details of each house's **Web Site** wherever they were available. At the moment the content of these sites varies from general background on the company to the full season's schedules, but it won't be long before all the major houses will be set up to take ticket booking via the Net. Of the numerous music-related Web sites currently in operation, the most useful for opera fans are the **Opera Schedule Server**, a searchable database of worldwide opera performances over the next two years (its address is http://www.fsz.bme.hu/opera/main.html), and the user-friendly **Operabase** (http://operabase.com).

Ticket prices shown are the lowest and highest in the company's usual range; bear in mind that in continental Europe first-night prices are often anything from ten to one hundred percent higher than the normal rate. Concessions for students, over-65s and the unemployed are widely available, though sometimes only at the last minute; the complexity of the concessionary systems makes it impossible to give details here, so if you fall into one of these categories you're best advised to ask at the box office.

AUSTRALIA

Adelaide

State Opera of South Australia, Adelaide Festival Theatre, King William Street, South Australia.

Five performances of each of three popular operas are staged April–Nov. The Paris Chatelet's *Ring* cycle is promised in 1998 – this will be the work's German-language premiere in the southern hemisphere.

Tickets $38–75, on sale from eight weeks before the first opera.

Box Office GPO Box 1515, Adelaide, South Australia 5001. Mon–Fri 9am–8pm, Sat 9am–5pm; ☎08/131 246 (BASS); information ☎08/212 6644; fax 08/231 7646.

Brisbane

Lyric Opera of Queensland, Lyric Theatre, Queensland Performing Arts Complex, Queensland.

Three operas staged in short runs May–Oct.

Tickets $20–75.

Box Office PO Box 3567, South Brisbane, Queensland 4101. Mon–Sat 9am–9pm; ☎07/846 4646; fax 07/844 7790.

Melbourne

Victoria State Theatre, Victorian Arts Centre, 100 St Kilda Road, Melbourne, Victoria.

A season of five or six operas (a healthily varied repertoire) runs in two blocks, July–Aug and Nov–Dec, featuring some fifty performances in all. From mid-March to mid-May the Australian Opera moves in with productions from Sydney.

Tickets $20–95, on sale from June for entire season.

Box Office Mon–Sat 9am–9pm; ☎03/9685 3777 (or 11500 for local calls); information ☎03/9685 3701 or 3703; fax 03/9686 1441.

Sydney

The Australian Opera, Sydney Opera House, Bennelong Point, Sydney, New South Wales.

The only Australian company to offer a full Jan–Oct season, occupying the world-famous, but cramped, harbourside opera house. The Summer Season, with roughly ten performances of each of half a dozen works, runs Jan–early March; the company then takes five or six productions to Melbourne until mid-May, before returning to Sydney for the Winter Season (June–Oct), which offers as many as ten different works. In 1996 the company celebrates its fortieth anniversary with the launch of OzOpera, a national touring company. For details call the number below.

Tickets $35–128, on sale from Dec for whole of following year.

Box Office daily 9am–5pm; ☎02/699 1099 or 315 1088; fax 02/310 4917. Postal applications to: The Opera Centre, PO Box 291, Strawberry Hills, NSW 2012.

Web site http://www.ausopera.org.au/

AUSTRIA

Bregenz Festival (July–August)

Festspielhaus, Platz der Wiener Symphoniker. Only launched in 1979, this month-long festival has quickly established itself as one of the most innovative in Europe, largely for its spectacular open-air productions presented on a floating stage moored to the shore of Lake Konstanz. There is also an indoor theatre (outdoor performances move indoors if the weather is too severe), and each festival usually comprises just two or three works, with one of them outdoors. The casts invariably include well-known names and the orchestra is the Vienna Symphony (rival to the Philharmonic), which also gives concerts (as do visiting orchestras). Conveniently timed (and situated) to be combined with the Salzburg and Munich festivals.

Tickets AS300–1250.

Box Office ☎05574/4920 223; fax 05574/4920 228; postal applications to Postfach 311, 6901 Bregenz.

Graz

Bühnen Graz Steiermark, Kaiser-Josef-Platz 10, 8010 Graz.

This distinguished regional house offers some twelve to fifteen operas a season, with a well-spread schedule ensuring a fair mix of interesting repertoire at any one time.

Tickets AS35–480, with 200 standing places at AS25–35.

Box Office Mon–Fri 8am–8pm, Sat 8am–1pm (8am–6pm on first Sat of month); ☎0316/8000.

Innsbruck

Tiroler Landestheater, Rennweg 2, 6020 Innsbruck.

Six operas a season, usually including rare and new works. The company boasts an excellent orchestra, but the theatre (built in 1969) is rather cold in atmosphere.

Tickets AS50–415, on sale from eight days before the beginning of the month of the performance.

Box Office Mon–Sat 8.30am–8.30pm, Sun 6.30–8.30pm; ☎0512/5207 44; fax 0512/5207 4333.

Klagenfurt

Stadttheater, Theaterplatz 4, 9020 Klagenfurt.

A small, regional, all-purpose theatre, giving some sixty performances a year of four operatic works, among other theatre and operetta.

Tickets AS130–505, plus standing for AS45.

Box Office Tues–Sat 9am–noon & 4–6pm, or until start of performance; ☎0463/54 0 64; information ☎0463/55 2 66 30; fax 0463/50 46 63.

Linz

Linzer Landestheater, Promenade 39, 4020 Linz.

Provincial house in a city whose association with Bruckner means that more attention is paid to orchestral than to operatic repertoire; seven or eight operas are staged a season, along with several musicals.

Tickets AS30–480, on sale from three weeks before the performance.

Box Office Mon–Fri 10am–6pm, Sat 10am–12.30pm; ☎0732/7611 100; fax 0732/7611 308.

Salzburg

Salzburger Landestheater, Schwarzstrasse 22, 5020 Salzburg.

With only four operas a season, the resident Salzburg company can't really compete with the city's much higher-profile Easter and summer festivals, though it does sometimes challenge by duplicating repertoire in the same season.

Tickets AS65–590, on sale fourteen days in advance.

Box Office Tues–Fri 10am–1pm & 5.30–7pm, Sat 5–6.30pm; ☎0662 871 512; fax 0662 871 13.

Salzburg Festival (July–Aug)

The most venerable of all operatic festivals (though with plenty of other music and theatre), Salzburg is now settling down after the inevitable artistic change of direction following the death of its former director, Herbert von Karajan. His successor, Gérard Mortier, has brought in more modern opera and the most daring producers, yet the festival remains essentially the preserve of well-heeled musical society – the ticket prices are exorbitant. Opera performances take place in three auditoria, the Grosses Festspielhaus (with the widest stage in the world), the Kleines Festspielhaus (which includes sixty standing places) and the Felsenreitschule, and feature all the greatest conductors and singers. The Salzburg Easter Festival, under the artistic direction of Claudio Abbado, also stages opera, accompanied by the Berlin Philharmonic. Venues and box office address are the same as for the main festival.

Tickets AS300–4200 (half that for concerts).

Box Office Grosses Festspielhaus, Hofstallgasse 1, ☎0662/84 45 01; fax 0662/84 66 82. Personal booking April–June Mon–Fri 9.30am–3pm; July 1–23 Mon–Sat 9.30am–5pm; July 23–Aug daily 9.30am–5pm. Postal booking begins in the late autumn, closes in early January and tickets are confirmed by invoice by late March; the address is: Ticket Office of the Salzburg Festival, Postfach 140, A-5010 Salzburg. A limited number of subscription tickets are available each March for under-26s (2–5 performances at AS200 each); for information write to Direktion der Salzburger Festspiele, att. Alexander von Donat, Hofstallgasse 1, A-5020 Salzburg.

Vienna

Wiener Staatsoper, Opernring 2, 1010 Vienna.

Staging roughly forty operas a season and resolutely sticking to the repertoire system, this is one of Europe's top houses, heavy with tradition and boasting the best international singers – plus the Vienna Philharmonic in the pit. With its 567 standing places, it is also one of the most accessible.

Tickets AS50–2300, on sale a month in advance (postal bookings must be received at least three weeks in advance); standing places AS20–30 from an hour before curtain-up (queue early for top singers/repertoire).

Box Office Bestellbüro, Hanuschgasse 3, 1010 Vienna (plus agencies in Vienna). Mon–Fri

8am–6pm, Sat & Sun 9am–noon; ☎0222/514 44 2960 or 0222/514 44 2959; credit card bookings ☎0222/513 1513.

TICKETS AS50–2300.

WEB SITE http://www.austria-info.at/kultur/ws-wv/index.html

Wiener Volksoper, Währinger Strasse 78, 1010 Vienna.

Under the same management as the Staatsoper, the Volksoper specializes in operetta, but is branching out into such areas as Janáček, Shostakovich and late Romantics.

TICKETS AS50–850, plus standing for AS15–20.

BOX OFFICE & WEB SITE Same as Staatsoper.

BELGIUM

ANTWERP

De Vlaamse Opera [Flanders Opera], Frankrijklei 3, 2008 Antwerpen.

The Flanders Opera, which divides its performances between Antwerp and Gent, was founded in the late 1980s but has rapidly risen to become one of the most adventurous companies in northern Europe, even overshadowing Brussels. It is renowned for its modern production styles (particularly in Puccini) and devotion to Baroque and contemporary opera. Eight operas (one in concert) are performed Sept–July in short self-contained runs, opening in one theatre before moving to the other.

TICKETS BF250–2100.

BOX OFFICE Tues–Sat 11am–5.45pm; ☎03/233 668.

BRUSSELS

La Monnaie/De Munt, rue Léopold 4, 1000 Bruxelles.

During the 1980s this was one of Europe's leading companies, renowned for adventurous repertoire and production style (especially of Wagner), but it has lost its edge since the departure of Gérard Mortier for the Salzburg Festival. Some ten operas are staged each season from September to June, in self-contained runs.

TICKETS BF300–3000, on sale by post or fax two to four weeks in advance, to personal callers four weeks in advance.

BOX OFFICE Rue de la Reine, 1000 Bruxelles. Tues–Sat 11am–6pm; ☎02/218 1211; fax 02/218 2991.

WEB SITE http://www.demunt.be/demunt/

GENT

De Vlaamse Opera, Opera House, Schouwburgstraat 3, 9000 Gent.

See Antwerp for details of repertoire.

TICKETS BF150–2100.

BOX OFFICE Mon–Sat 11am–5.45pm; ☎09/225 24 25.

LIÈGE

Opéra Royal de Wallonie, Théâtre Royal de Liège, 1 rue des Dominicains, 4000 Liège.

An interesting mix of repertoire (10–12 works a season) in this "operatic centre for the Belgian French community".

TICKETS BF350–2000, on sale from Sept for the whole season.

BOX OFFICE Mon–Sat 11am–1pm & 2–6pm or until first interval; ☎041/23 67 65. Credit cards are accepted, otherwise reserved tickets must be paid for within eight days.

CANADA

MONTRÉAL

Opéra, Théâtre Maisonneuve.

The main company in French-speaking Canada, founded in 1980. Five or six performances each of seven productions are staged each year, plus the occasional new work. French and English surtitles for all performances.

TICKETS C$20–80.

BOX OFFICE 260 Blvd de Maisonneuve Ouest, Montréal, H2X 1Y9. Mon–Fri 9am–5pm; ☎514/985 2258; information ☎514/985-2222; fax 514/985-2219.

WEB SITE http://www.stria.ca/opera-mtl/

TORONTO

Canadian Opera Company, O'Keefe Centre, 1 Front Street East & Elgin Theatre, 189 Yonge Street.

This company is gaining a good international reputation and stages six operas between Sept–April, in one of two theatres.

TICKETS C$27–85 plus day seats for $21 for some performances.

BOX OFFICES at each theatre Mon–Sat 11am–8pm, Sun 11am–2pm; bookings ☎416/872-2262.

VANCOUVER

Queen Elizabeth Theatre, 845 Cambie Street.

Short runs of five operas, mainly from the core repertoire, are presented between mid-October and mid-April, mostly with local artists. Surtitles are used for all performances, including those in English.

TICKETS C$32–90, on sale from Sept 1.

BOX OFFICE Mon–Fri 9am–5pm; ☎604/683-0222; fax 604/682-3981.

WEB SITE http://www2.portal.ca/~vanopera/

CZECH REPUBLIC

Brno

Janáček Theatre, Dvorákova 11, 657 70 Brno.

The opera company in Janáček's home town inevitably features his works heavily, but the range is wide, with a full season in repertoire form.

Tickets CK150–800.

Box office Mon–Fri 12.30–5.30pm, Sat 9am–noon; ☎05/42 32 12 85.

Prague

Národní Divadlo [National Theatre], Národní 2.

The Czech Republic's leading company has been struggling to keep its artists and standards in the face of western competition, but manages to stage a full season of up to sixty works drawn from its repertoire, with Dvořák, Smetana and Janáček to the fore.

Tickets CK200–900, on sale a month in advance to individuals, longer to groups.

Box Office Mon–Sat 10am–6pm, Sun 10am–12.30pm & 3–6pm; ☎02/24 91 42 04; information ☎02/24 91 34 37; fax 02/24 91 15 30. Postal bookings to: Ostrovní 1, PO Box 865, 11230 Praha 1.

Státní Opera [State Opera], Legerova 75.

The Prague State Opera (formerly the Smetana Theatre and then the German Theatre) maintains a similar repertoire to its rival, the National Theatre, though with fewer international pretensions.

Tickets CK100–700 on sale three to four weeks in advance.

Box Office Wilsonova 4, Praha 1; Mon–Fri 10am–5.30pm, Sat & Sun 10am–noon & 1–5.30pm; ☎02/26 53 53.

Stavovské Divadlo [Estates Theatre], Ovocny trh 1.

Under the aegis of the National Theatre, this small eighteenth-century theatre, the venue for the premieres of *Don Giovanni* and *La clemenza di Tito*, still stages primarily Mozart.

Tickets and Box Office details as for Národní Divadlo.

DENMARK

Copenhagen

Royal Danish Opera, Det kongelige Teater, Kgs. Nytorv, 1017 København.

The Royal Danish Opera has for long relied on the considerable talents of the country's native singers, but now, under the artistic directorship of Elaine Padmore (formerly of Wexford), it is beginning to draw in international artists. The company offers a full *stagione* season of a wide range of works.

Tickets DK65–450; whole season can be booked from late summer by post or fax from abroad.

Box Office daily 1–7pm; ☎033/69 69 69; information ☎033/14 10 02; fax 033/69 69 30. Postal applications to: Postbox 2185, DK-1017 København K.

FINLAND

Helsinki

Finnish National Opera, Helsinginkatu 58, 00250 Helsinki.

Now in a new home, this adventurous company has a strong tradition of commitment to new operas by Finnish composers, particularly Aulis Sallinen, but its general repertoire is satisfyingly broad.

Tickets FIM50–250, on sale from two months in advance.

Box Office Mon–Fri 9am–6pm (or curtain up), Sat 3–6pm; ☎00/4030 2211; fax 00/4030 2305.

Web site http://www.kolumbus.fi/opera/english.html

Savonlinna Opera Festival (July–Aug)

After Verona, this is one of the most evocative open-air opera festivals, with fully staged performances in the courtyard of a medieval castle on a lake amid the Finnish forests (Verdi's *Macbeth* is a favourite here). Usually three productions of its own are staged, together with operas from visiting companies.

Tickets FIM150–450.

Box Office Olavinkatu 35, FIN-57130 Savonlinna; Mon–Fri 9am–4pm; ☎057/57 67 50; fax 057/21 866. Tickets also available from agencies in Helsinki and from *Finnair* offices abroad.

FRANCE

Many towns and cities in France share production costs, so the same staging can easily crop up in several places during a season.

Aix-en-Provence Festival (early July to early Aug)

Open-air operas, with a notable contribution from British and American artists, are staged in the courtyard of the former Archbishop's Palace in this beautiful Provencal town, with concerts in a variety of other venues in the area.

Tickets On sale from May.

Box Office Festival d'Aix-en-Provence, Palais de l'Ancien Archevêché, 13100 Aix-en-Provence; ☎0442 23 37 81.

Bordeaux

Grand Théâtre, place de la Comédie, 33074 Bordeaux.

Half a dozen operas feature annually, with a handful of performances of each, though they are in danger of becoming outnumbered by performances of French operetta. Big-name singers are occasionally brought in for prestigious productions, though most of the works are cast with local singers.

Tickets F29–190, on sale by post from a month in advance of the opening (any requests sent too early are reputedly destroyed), in person from the Saturday preceding the first night.

Box Office Tues–Fri 9am–4pm, Sat 11am–4pm; ☎0556 48 58 59.

Colmar

Théâtre Municipal, rue des Unterlinden, 68000 Colmar.

Regular visits by the Strasbourg Opéra du Rhin (see below).

Tickets F30–150, five days in advance.

Box Office Mon–Fri 10am–noon & 4–6.30pm.

Lille

L'Opéra de Lille, 2 rue des bons enfants à Lille, 59800 Lille.

Mounts foor to six productions per season, and also hosts visits by L'Atelier Lyrique of Tourcoing (see below).

Tickets F50–280, on sale from early Oct for the whole season.

Box Office rue Léon Trulin; Mon–Sat 1–6.30pm; ☎0320 55 48 61.

Lyon

Opéra, 1 place de la Comédie, 69001 Lyon.

In its newly rebuilt theatre, Lyon Opéra, first under the musical direction of John Eliot Gardiner and now under Kent Nagano, has been at the forefront of French operatic life for the best part of a decade, putting Paris to shame. Nine or ten operas are staged a season, often including a couple of new works.

Tickets F80–360, on sale early Sept for Oct–Dec, early Dec for Jan–April, early April for May–June.

Box Office Mon–Sat 11am–7pm; ☎0489 41 29 82; fax 0472 00 45 01.

Marseille

Opéra, rue Beauvau, 13001 Marseille.

Marseille stages ten to twelve operas a season, often of rare and interesting repertoire, in blocks of half a dozen performances spread over a two-week period. Very affordable prices.

Tickets F40–150, on sale fifteen days in advance in person or a month by post.

Box Office Tues–Sat 10am–12.30pm & 3–6pm; ☎0491 55 21 22 or 0491 55 21 23.

Web site http:www.planete.net/~gpapain/

Monaco

Opéra de Monte-Carlo, Casino, place du Casino, MC 98007, Monaco.

Brief runs of four operas, Jan–March, in this resolutely snooty house.

Tickets F130–680 (more when star singers are engaged), on sale from mid-Nov; supplement payable for overseas bookings; evening dress obligatory for first nights, jackets and tie for others.

Box Office Atrium du Casino, place du Casino; Tues–Sun 10am–12.30pm & 2–5pm; ☎0492 16 22 99. Postal applications to: Service Location, Opéra de Monte-Carlo, BP 139, MC 98007, Monaco.

Montpellier

Opéra, 11 boulevard Victor Hugo, 34000 Montpellier.

Short runs of about a dozen operas, with a tradition of Berlioz.

Tickets F60–250, on sale two months in advance.

Box Office Mon 2–6pm, Tues–Sat noon–6pm; ☎0467 60 19 99; information ☎0467 60 19 80.

Mulhouse

Théâtre Municipal, rue de la Sinne, 68100 Mulhouse.

Regular visits by the Strasbourg Opéra du Rhin (see below).

Tickets F50–170, three days in advance in person, fifteen days by post.

Box Office Mon–Sat 10am–noon & 4.30–6.30pm; ☎0389 45 20 04.

Nancy

Opéra de Nancy et de Lorraine, 1 rue Sainte Catherine, 54000 Nancy.

Half a dozen performances each of five operas, staged Sept–June.

Tickets F35–265, on sale six weeks in advance.

Box Office Tues–Sat 1–7pm; ☎0383 85 30 60; information ☎0383 85 30 63; fax 0383 85 30 66.

Nantes

Opéra, 1 rue Moliére, 66009 Nantes.

Three or four performances each of some eight operas, staged in a season running Oct–June.

Tickets F35–250, on sale two weeks in advance; no postal bookings accepted from abroad.

Box Office Tues–Fri 12.30–6pm, Sat 9.30am–5pm; ☎0240 69 77 18; information ☎0240 41 90 60.

NICE

Opéra, 4–6 rue Saint-François-de-Paule, 06000 Nice.

Nine operas are staged annually, with an adventurous range of repertoire: Wagner's *Ring* and Berlioz's *Trojans* have appeared in recent years.

TICKETS F50–500.

BOX OFFICE Mon–Sat 10am–6pm; ☎0493 85 67 31; information ☎0493 62 39 62; fax 0493 62 69 26.

PARIS

Opéra-Comique, place Boieldieu, 75002 Paris.

Historically the venue for lighter operatic repertoire and works that were regarded as unsuitable for the Opéra – for example, *Carmen*, because it had spoken dialogue. Five to seven operas are staged annually (Oct–July), together with operettas and other productions.

TICKETS F50–480.

BOX OFFICE 5 rue Favart, 75002 Paris; Mon–Sat 11am–7pm; ☎0142 44 45 46; information ☎0142 44 45 45; fax 0148 26 05 93.

Opéra National de Paris, place de la Bastille, 75004 Paris.

The Paris Opéra has been troubled ever since it left the venerable Palais Garnier for the spanking modern Bastille, which has yet to prove itself as a venue – some opera productions are now being put on in the Garnier again. The repertoire (15 operas Sept–July) is becoming more adventurous, however; performances feature surtitles in both French and English (not visible from some rear seats).

TICKETS F60–760, on sale in person fourteen days in advance, postal bookings up to two months in advance of first night.

BOX OFFICE Personal bookings at place de la Bastille or the Palais Garnier; Mon–Sat 11am–6.30pm; ☎0144 73 13 00; information ☎0144 73 13 99. Postal bookings to Relations avec le Public, Opéra National de Paris, 120 rue de Lyon, 75576 Paris Cedex 12.

Théâtre Musical de Paris-Châtelet, place du Châtelet, 75001 Paris.

Run by the city of Paris, this is proving a significant rival to the "national" opera at the Bastille, staging half a dozen major productions per season, with international casts and directors (and often borrowing London's Philharmonia Orchestra for its pit). Other musical events and concert performances of operas fill the rest of the season.

TICKETS F100–450, on sale by post from July prior to season until three weeks before performance, by phone four weeks to seven days in advance of performance, in person two weeks in advance of performance.

BOX OFFICE Daily 11am–7pm; ☎0140 28 28 40. Postal bookings to: Service des Relations du Public, le Châtelet, 2 rue Edouard Colonne, 75001 Paris.

ROUEN

Opéra de Normandie, Théâtre des Arts, rue du General Leclerc, 76000 Rouen.

Five performances each of some eight to ten operas per season (Oct–June), with a good range of repertoire, including the occasional Wagner.

TICKETS F42–225, on sale from September.

BOX OFFICE Mon–Sat 11am–6pm; ☎0235 98 50 98; information ☎0235 71 41 36; fax 0235 15 33 49.

STRASBOURG

Opéra du Rhin, 19 place Broglie, 67000 Strasbourg.

The leading company in northeast France, staging eight works annually, with occasional performances by visitors and concert performances. The company tours regularly to Colmar and Mulhouse.

TICKETS F30–300, on sale from mid-Sept.

BOX OFFICE Mon–Fri 11am–6pm, Sat 11am–4pm; ☎0388 75 48 23; information ☎0388 75 48 00; fax 0388 24 09 34; postal bookings must be received at least thirty days in advance.

TOULOUSE

Théâtre du Capitole, place du Capitole, 31000 Toulouse.

Short runs of half a dozen varied operas each season, some in concert. The Toulouse Capitole orchestra, under Michel Plasson, is one of France's best.

TICKETS F120–400, on sale from early Oct for whole season, by phone up to six days in advance.

BOX OFFICE Tues–Sat 9am–12.30pm & 2.30–6pm; ☎0561 22 80 22; fax 0561 22 24 34; postal applications to: Service Locations, BP 129, 31014 Toulouse.

TOURCOING

L'Atelier Lyrique, Théâtre Municipal, 1 place Leverrier.

An adventurous small company serving the Pas de Calais region of northern France and neighbouring Belgium, staging short runs of five or six operas Dec–May.

TICKETS F120–190.

BOX OFFICE Mon–Fri 4.30–7pm, Sat 2–6.30pm; ☎0320 70 66 66 (Mon–Fri 2–6pm only). Postal applications to: Service Location, 82 boulevard Gambetta, 59200 Tourcoing.

GERMANY

No country in the world has such a dense network of opera companies as Germany: at least a hundred theatres still stage opera regularly, though many are curtailing activities following reunification and nationwide cuts in arts funding, some going for money-making operettas and musicals at the expense of opera. The main houses are in Berlin, Hamburg, Cologne, Frankfurt and Munich, though many of the smaller companies offer more adventurous repertoire, if not quite the same standards.

AACHEN

Stadttheater, Theaterplatz, 52062 Aachen.

A typical small, provincial German company, staging opera (five per season, including rarities), drama and dance.

TICKETS DM19–51.

BOX OFFICE Mon–Sat 9am–1pm & 5–7pm; ☎0241/4784 244; fax 0241/4784 201.

AUGSBURG

Städtische Bühnen, Stadttheater am Kennedyplatz, 86152 Augsburg.

Ten operas staged per season, with a good range of ambitious repertoire.

TICKETS DM13–43, on sale five days in advance.

BOX OFFICE Mon–Sat 10am–1pm & 5–6pm; ☎0821/36604.

BAYREUTH FESTIVAL (late July to end of Aug).

Bayreuth is a place of pilgrimage for Wagnerians, and deliberately fosters an air of single-minded devotion. Founded by Wagner in 1876 to stage the *Ring* cycle, the festival theatre has staged nothing except his ten mature works, except during a period at the end of World War II. Once it had purged itself of its Nazi associations, the festival led the way in freeing operatic production from the bounds of naturalism, though the composer's grandson, Wolfgang Wagner, still foists his own dull productions on audiences that have now grown accustomed to the likes of Kupfer and Chéreau. The backbone is inevitably the *Ring*, which tends to run for five years in every six, with a new production of one of the other operas usually replenishing the repertoire each season, playing alongside two or three revived productions. Tickets are notoriously difficult to obtain, with a waiting list that extends to about seven years, but German Tourist Board offices abroad sometimes receive a limited allocation, to be sold as part of package holidays in the town.

TICKETS DM30–300, on sale from mid-Oct of previous year.

BOX OFFICE Daily 10am–noon during festival; information Mon–Fri 11am–noon, ☎0921/2 02 21; postal applications to: Postbox 10 02 62, D-95402 Bayreuth.

BERLIN

Deutsche Oper, Bismarckstrasse 35, 10585 Berlin.

Standards have slipped slightly since reunification and the revitalization of the rival Staatsoper, but the Deutsche Oper, founded after the war as the leading house in West Berlin, maintains a wide repertoire (30–35 operas a season) and a distinctive monolithic production style masterminded by Götz Friedrich. The house is still particularly strong in Wagner, though often conducted by lacklustre music director Raphael Frühbeck de Burgos; seats are relatively cheap for such an international house.

TICKETS DM13–135, on sale from Sunday four weeks in advance.

BOX OFFICE Mon–Sat 11am–7pm, Sun 10am–2pm; ☎030/34 381; information ☎030/3410 249; fax 030/3438 455; postal applications to: Kartenbüro der Deutsche Oper Berlin, Richard-Wagner-Strasse 10, 10585 Berlin.

Komische Oper, Behrenstrasse 55–57, 10117 Berlin.

This company has been at the forefront of innovative opera production since the war, first under the direction of Walter Felsenstein, more recently under Harry Kupfer. It has had a shaky transition to post-reunification ways, but maintains its repertoire system, tradition-breaking production style and genuine ensemble feel to performances under music director Yakov Kreizberg. All works are sung in German.

TICKETS DM10–75.

BOX OFFICE Mon–Sat 11am–5.30pm; ☎030/20 260 360; fax 030/20 260 260.

WEB SITE http://www.icf.de/ko/

Berlin Staatsoper, Unter den Linden 5–7, 10109 Berlin.

The original German national opera, then the national house of the DDR, the Staatsoper is one of the success stories of reunification, setting standards for the Deutsche Oper to follow. It stages a full repertoire season, has a superb orchestra and the music director is the highly esteemed Daniel Barenboim.

TICKETS DM10–100.

BOX OFFICE Mon–Sat noon–6pm, Sun 2–6pm; ☎030/204 43 15; fax 030/20 345 483.

BIELEFELD

Stadttheater, Niederwall 27, 33602 Bielefeld.

Remarkably adventurous small company, largely responsible for reviving early twentieth-century late-Romantic operas by the likes of Korngold; stages five operas Aug–June.

TICKETS DM20–45, on sale four weeks in advance; tickets sent on receipt of cheque and sae.

Box Office Brunnenstrasse 3–9; Mon–Fri 9am–5.30pm, Sat 9am–1pm; ☎0521/17 70 77; information ☎0521/51 24 98; postal applications to: Box 10 03 53, 33503 Bielefeld.

Bonn

Oper der Stadt, Am Boeselagerhof 1, 53111 Bonn.

An unusual mixture of the ordinary and the extraordinary characterizes the repertoire of this house, which stages twelve operas per season, often in very long runs, and has attracted artists of the level of Domingo.

Tickets DM19–65, on sale four weeks in advance; postal and phone bookings must be paid for within five days.

Box Office Opernkasse, Mulheimer Platz 1, 53111 Bonn; Mon–Fri 9am–1pm & 2–6pm, Sat 9am–noon; ☎0228/7736 667.

Web site http://www.rhrz.uni-bonn.de/operbonn/info

Braunschweig

Staatstheater, Am Theater, 38100 Braunschweig.

Eight operas per season, including the occasional rarity; recently retired mezzo-soprano Brigitte Fassbaender is the new director of productions.

Tickets DM18–46, on sale four weeks in advance.

Box Office Mon–Fri 10am–1pm & 4–7pm, Sat 10am–1pm; ☎0531/484 2800; fax 0531/484 2727.

Bremen

Bremer Theater, Goetheplatz, 28010 Bremen.

Eight operas a season, with plenty of interest in addition to the standard Mozart/Puccini favourites.

Tickets DM15–65, on sale three weeks in advance; postal bookings must be paid for at least three days before the performance.

Box Office Mon–Fri 1–6pm, Sat 11am–2pm; ☎0421/36 533 33; fax 0421/36 533 04; postal applications to: Postfach 10 10 46, 28010 Bremen.

Bremerhaven

Stadttheater, Theodor-Heuss-Platz, 27519 Bremerhaven.

Eight productions per season, with a varied repertoire neatly complementing neighbouring Bremen.

Tickets DM13–34, on sale two weeks in advance.

Box Office Tues–Fri 10am–1pm & 5–7pm, Sat 10am–1pm; ☎0471/490 01; postal applications to: Postfach 12 05 41, 27519 Bremerhaven.

Coburg

Landestheater, Schlossplatz 6, 96450 Coburg.

Six operas per season, with a wide-ranging repertoire.

Tickets DM15–25, on sale 21 days in advance.

Box Office Tues–Fri 10am–1pm, Sat & Sun 10am–noon; ☎09561/927 42; fax 09561/994 47.

Darmstadt

Staatstheater Darmstadt, Marienplatz 2, 64283 Darmstadt.

Ten operas per season in this comfortable, intimate modern building. Imaginative repertoire, often including new works – as you would expect in the town that nurtured the European postwar musical avant-garde.

Tickets DM15–50, on sale four weeks in advance by post, two weeks in advance by phone or in person.

Box Office Tues–Fri 9.30am–6pm, Sat 10am–1pm, Sun 11am–1pm; ☎06151/28 112 11.

Dortmund

Theater, Kuhstrasse 12, 44137 Dortmund.

One of the leading Ruhr companies, staging ten to twelve operas per season, with the emphasis on the German heavyweights.

Tickets DM15–54, on sale four weeks in advance.

Box Office Tues–Fri 10am–1pm & 4.30–6.30pm, Sat 10am–1pm; ☎0231/502 55 47.

Dresden

Sächsische Staatsoper (Semperoper), Theaterplatz 2, 01067 Dresden.

One of Germany's great historic houses (the magnificent building was only re-opened in 1985 after wartime bombing), which saw premieres of Wagner and Strauss and is still one of the best places to hear both. The pit orchestra is the Dresden Staatskapelle and music director is Giuseppe Sinopoli; tickets are in notoriously short supply.

Tickets DM10–85, on sale four weeks in advance.

Box Office Schinkelwache, Theaterplatz Mon–Fri 10am–noon & 1–5pm, Sat 10am–1pm; ☎0351/49 11 716; fax 0351/49 11 700; postal applications to: Besucherdienst der Sächsische Staatsoper Dresden, Postfach 12 09 08, 01008 Dresden.

Duisberg

Theater der Stadt, Neckarstrasse 1, 47051 Duisberg.

One of the two homes of the Deutsche Oper am Rhein, which offers a full schedule of performances in Duisberg and Düsseldorf, with a generous thirty operas per season in stagione, most appearing in both houses, but with Dusseldorf getting the majority of performances.

Tickets DM12–49, on sale from 20th of month prior to performance.

Box Office Mon–Fri 10am–1pm & 2–4pm; ☎0203/30 09 100; fax 0203/30 09 200.

Düsseldorf

Opernhaus, Heinrich-Heine-Allee 16a, 40213 Düsseldorf.

See Duisberg.

Tickets DM17–80, on sale four weeks in advance.

Box Office Mon–Sat 10am–6pm; ☎0211/89 08 211; fax 0211/89 083 65.

Essen

Aalto-theater, Rolandstrasse 10, 45128 Essen.

One of the most adventurous of the numerous Ruhr companies, staging twenty operas per season; the opera house, designed by Finnish architect Alvar Aalto in 1950, is one of the most remarkable on the continent.

Tickets DM19–71, on sale three months in advance, remaining tickets sold for DM15 from twenty minutes before curtain-up.

Box Office Tues–Fri 10am–7.30pm, Sat 1.30–7.30pm; ☎0201/81 22 200; information ☎0201/81 22 600; fax 0201/81 22 201.

Frankfurt

Oper, Untermainanlage 11, 60311 Frankfurt am Main.

Once at the forefront of operatic production, Frankfurt has been plagued with administrative and financial problems recently, as well as the burning down of its theatre soon after its refurbishment in the late 1980s. It is now running something close to full capacity again under music director Sylvain Cambreling, with twelve to fifteen operas per season – 1994–5 included six *Ring* cycles, for example.

Tickets DM10–122, on sale from the 10th of the month for the following month.

Box Office Willy-Brandt Platz; Mon–Fri 10am–6pm, Sat 10am–2pm; ☎069/212 37 999; fax 069/212 37 222.

Gelsenkirchen

Musiktheater im Revier, Kennedyplatz, 45881 Gelsenkirchen.

Modern theatre giving nine operas per season, usually including Strauss and/or Wagner.

Tickets DM10–44, on sale from four months in advance. Eurocheque or money order required for postal booking.

Box Office Tues–Fri 10am–2pm & 4.30–6.30pm, Sat 10am–2pm; ☎0209/40 97 200; fax 0209/40 97 250.

Gera

Bühnen der Stadt, Küchengartenallee 2, 07548 Gera.

Former East German house, staging nine operas per season – from Mozart to Wagner – at bargain rates.

Tickets DM10–21, on sale from two weeks before beginning of month of performance.

Box Office Mon–Fri noon–5pm for that day's tickets only; advance booking 3–5pm or in Schlosstrasse office Mon–Fri 10am–7pm; ☎0365/24010 or 69 41 05.

Giessen

Stadttheater, Berliner Platz, 35390 Giessen.

Quirky mixture of seven operas per season: recent mix featured Mozart, Sullivan and Milhaud.

Tickets DM8–45, on sale a month in advance, fourteen days for phone bookings.

Box Office Johannesstrasse 1 (behind theatre); Tues–Fri 10am–1pm & 4–6pm, Sat 10am–1pm; ☎0641/79 57 60.

Görlitz

Musiktheater der Stadt, Demianiplatz 2, 02826 Görlitz.

Six operas/operettas per season, with the odd interesting rarity (eg Krása, Marschner).

Tickets DM10–20, on sale three or four weeks in advance.

Box Office Tues–Fri 9am–12.30pm & 2–5.30pm; ☎03581/67 12 85; fax 03581/67 12 98.

Halle

Opernhaus, Universitätsring 24, 06108 Halle.

This company struggles to compete with the standards of neighbouring giants Leipzig and Dresden, but makes real efforts when it comes to repertoire, highlighting the work of the city's most famous son, Handel, and finding room for other non-standard work as well. About a dozen works staged in repertoire system, with operettas and musicals taking a generous slice of the season, as is often the case in eastern Germany.

Tickets DM5–33, on sale from start of month prior to performance.

Box Office In theatre box office Tues–Fri 10am–1.30pm & 2–5.30pm; ☎0345/51 10 355. Second box office at Leipzigerstrasse 82; Mon–Fri 10am–6pm, Sat 10am–1pm; ☎0345/202 64 58.

Hamburg

Staatsoper, Grosse Theaterstrasse 34, 20354 Hamburg.

One of Germany's most distinguished companies, with a strong tradition of presenting Strauss, Wagner and new works; Mahler began his career here, and the present music director is Gerd Albrecht. Thirty works in repertory each season.

Tickets DM10–215, on sale a month before performance.

Box Office Mon–Fri 10am–2pm & 4–6.30pm, Sat 10am–2pm; ☎040/35 17 21; fax 040/35 68 454.

Hannover
Niedersächsische Staatsoper, Opernplatz 1, 30159 Hannover.

An old-fashioned repertoire house – German and Italian classics comprise a solid backbone of the season's thirty operas and operettas, with a sprinkling of novelties. Some Italian works are sung in German.

Tickets DM18–67, on sale from fourteen days in advance.

Box Office Mon–Fri 11am–5.30pm, Sat 11am–1pm; ☎0511/3 68 17 11.

Heidelberg
Theater der Stadt, Theaterstrasse 6, 69117 Heidelberg.

Up to ten operas per season, ranging from Purcell to Hindemith.

Tickets DM22–62, on sale about a month before performance.

Box Office Theaterstrasse 4; Tues–Fri 10am–1pm & 4–6.30pm (4–8pm on Thurs), Sat 10am–1pm; ☎06221/58 35 20.

Hildesheim
Stadttheater, Theaterstrasse 6, 31141 Hildesheim.

Undemanding repertoire of four or five operas per season, often outnumbered by operettas and musicals.

Tickets DM13–35, on sale fourteen days in advance (must be paid for at least one day in advance).

Box Office Mon–Fri 10am–4pm, Sat & Sun 11am–1pm; ☎05121/3 31 64; information ☎05121/16 93 90.

Kaiserslautern
Pfalztheater, Fruchthallstrasse 24–26, 67655 Kaiserslautern.

Seven or eight operas per season, with some non-mainstream repertoire (eg Zemlinsky).

Tickets DM15–40, on sale a month before performance.

Box Office Mon–Sat 10am–4pm; ☎0631/80 022 08; fax 0631/80 022 35.

Karlsruhe
Badisches Staatstheater, Baumeisterstrasse 11, 76137 Karlsruhe.

This theatre and Stuttgart's are the main houses of Baden-Württemburg and each of them stages fourteen operas per season, ranging from Mozart to Wagner.

Tickets DM10–43, on sale from Saturday for following week to personal callers and by phone; postal bookings taken any time up to Saturday before week of performance – payment must be sent in advance.

Box Office Mon–Fri 10am–1pm & 4–6.30pm, Sat 10am–2pm; ☎0721/602 02; fax 0721/37 32 32; postal applications to: Postfach 1449, 76003 Karlsruhe.

Kiel
Opernhaus, Rathausplatz 4, 24103 Kiel.

Ever adventurous small company, particularly noted for rescuscitating forgotten late-Romantic works by the likes of Korngold and Delius. Some twelve operas per season.

Tickets DM5–48, on sale three weeks in advance.

Box Office Tues–Fri 11am–1pm & 4.30–7pm, Sun 11am–1pm; ☎0431/921 00; fax 0431/901 28 38; postal applications to Postfach 16 60, 24015 Kiel.

Koblenz
Theater der Stadt, Deinhardplatz, 56068 Koblenz.

Very minor house, with just four unexciting operas per season.

Tickets DM12–58, on sale two to three weeks in advance.

Box Office Rathaus, Jesuitenplatz 2; Tues–Fri 11am–1pm & 2–4pm, Sat 11am–1pm; ☎0261/1 29 28 04; fax 0261/1 29 28 00.

Köln [Cologne]
Oper der Stadt, Opernhaus, Offenbachplatz, 50505 Köln.

A committed, distinguished company with a good reputation for innovation and variety, staging twenty-one operas per season in a modern theatre.

Tickets DM20–106, on sale from 5th of month before performance; no phone bookings in three days before performance; credit cards accepted.

Box Office Mon–Fri 11am–2pm & 4–6pm, Sat 11am–2pm; ☎0221/221 8400; fax 0221/221 8249.

Web site http://www.rrz.uni-koeln.de/koeln/oper/index.html.

Krefeld
Stadttheater, Theaterplatz 3, 4150 Krefeld 1.

One of the two north German homes of the Vereinigte Städtische Bühnen Krefeld und Mönchengladbach, a company that performs a wide range of repertoire, with six to ten operas per season.

Tickets DM15–35, on sale three weeks in advance.

Box Office Mon–Fri 10am–1pm & 5–7pm, Sat 10am–1pm; ☎02151/2 39 02.

Leipzig
Opernhaus, Augustusplatz 12, 04109 Leipzig.

A house that's particularly strong in twentieth-century repertoire, featuring an annual festival of such music each spring, though financial pressure has recently curtailed some plans. Some 25 to 30 operas are given each season in the repertoire system. The pit orchestra is the Leipzig Gewandhaus Orchestra.

Tickets DM8–45 (for selected performances all seats DM15), on sale two months in advance.

Box Office Mon–Fri 10am–6pm, Sat 10am–1pm; ☎0341/29 10 36; fax 0341/12 61 30 0; postal applications to: Besucherdienst, Postfach 346, 04003 Leipzig.

Lübeck

Bühnen der Hansestadt

With the theatre currently being rebuilt, operas – mostly in concert – are generally staged in other venues; the season's six operas usually have something interesting among them.

Tickets DM20–50.

Box Office Dr-Julius-Leber-Strasse 23, 23552 Lübeck; Tues–Fri 10am–1pm & 4–6pm, Sat 10am–1pm; ☎0451/7 45 52; fax 0451/122 42 77.

Mainz

Staatstheater, Gutenbergplatz 7, 55116 Mainz.

Mainz maintains an interesting repertoire of eight to ten operas per season, with a tradition of staging Britten; can easily be combined with a trip to Wiesbaden across the Rhine.

Tickets DM15–45, on sale about a month before performance.

Box Office Tues–Fri 10am–1pm & 5–7pm, Sat 10am–2pm; ☎06131/28 512 00; fax 06131/28 513 33.

Mannheim

Nationaltheater, Collinistrasse 26, 68151 Mannheim.

This historic company has the names of Weingartner and Furtwängler on its roll-call of past directors, though the present medium-sized theatre dates from the 1950s. Stages twenty-four operas per season with wide-ranging repertoire. The season is punctuated by special performances by guest star singers and conductors, though chances of getting seats for those are slim.

Tickets DM18–66, on sale three weeks before performance.

Box Office Mon–Sat 11am–1pm, Tues–Fri also 2–6pm; ☎0621/248 44; information ☎0621/248 218.

Meiningen

Südthüringisches Staatstheater, Bernhardstrasse 5, 98617 Meiningen.

An adventurous little house in a town with a distinguished musical past (Brahms used to conduct the court orchestra), featuring Wagner and modern works as well as more traditional Weber and Mozart.

Tickets DM10–25, on sale two weeks before the beginning of the month of performance.

Box Office Tues–Fri 10am–12.30pm & 3.30–6pm, Sat 10am–noon; ☎03693/4 512 22; fax 03693/28 10.

Mönchengladbach

Stadthalle Rheydt, Odenkirchener Strasse 78, 4050 Mönchengladbach 2.

See Krefeld.

Tickets DM15–30, on sale four weeks in advance.

Box Office Mon–Fri 10am–1pm & 5–7pm, Sat 10am–1pm, Sun 11am–1pm; ☎02166/4 43 05.

München [Munich]

Bayrische Staatsoper, Nationaltheater, Max-Joseph-Platz 2, 80075 München.

Germany's leading house, famous for Strauss and Wagner and led by many of the top conductors over the years – Zubin Mehta is the latest incumbent. Offering 30–35 operas in repertoire between September and July, the company is now run by Peter Jonas (former head of ENO in London), who is revitalizing production styles and raising a few hackles, particularly with British/US imports (Alden, Jones, Hytner, etc); the last month of the season becomes the Munich Festival (see below).

Tickets DM9–190, on sale one month in advance to personal callers (phone booking begins one day later); postal requests processed eight weeks before performance, but accepted from publication of programme in late spring.

Box Office Maximilianstrasse 11, 80539 München; Mon–Fri 10am–1pm & 2–6pm, Sat 10am–1pm; ☎089/21 85 19 20; recorded information (in German) ☎089/21 85 19 19.

Web site http://www.commed.de/staatsoper/home.html

Staatstheater, Gärtnerplatz 3, 80469 München.

Munich's second house concentrates on the lighter side of opera – the equivalent of Paris's Opéra-Comique. A full repertoire system is in operation, offering up to thirty productions (including operettas) per season.

Tickets DM20–85 (plus standing at DM10–12), a month in advance.

Box Office Mon–Fri 10am–6pm, Sat 10am–1pm; ☎089/201 67 67; fax 089/20 24 12 37; postal applications to: PO Box 14 05 69, 80455 München. Tickets also available from the Nationaltheater box office.

Munich Festival

In effect, this is the last month of the Bayrische Staatsoper's season, in which the best of the year's productions are mixed with one or two new presentations. Tickets can be hard to come by and are hiked up above the general season rates (DM 13–312). Postal bookings from early autumn, when the programme is published; phone and personal bookings from early May.

Münster

Städtische Bühnen, Neubrückstrasse 63, 48143 Münster.

An adventurous small company, dedicated to the staging of new operas and twentieth-century classics.

Tickets DM8–39, on sale three weeks in advance.

Box Office Tues–Fri 9am–1.30pm & 3.30–7pm, Sat 9am–1.30pm, Sun 11am–12.30pm; ☎0251/59 09 100; fax 0251/59 09 202.

Neustrelitz

Landestheater Mecklenburg, Friedrich-Ludwig-Jahn-Strasse, 17235 Neustrelitz.

One of several ex-East German companies now fighting for the continuation of its subsidies. Neustrelitz is a populist and unadventurous company that stages barely twenty performances per season of just three operas, alongside numerous operettas and musicals (though prices are at least egalitarian).

Tickets DM18–22.

Box Office Mon–Fri 10am–12.30pm & 2.30–5.30pm, Sat 10am–1pm; ☎03981/20 64 00.

Nordhausen

Theater, Käthe-Kollwitz-Strasse 15, 99734 Nordhausen.

Another none-too-adventurous ex-Eastern company, but with a reasonal number of operas staged each season.

Tickets DM10–18, on sale from 20th of preceding month for the whole month's performances.

Box Office Tues–Fri 10am–7pm, Sat 4–7pm; ☎03631/34 52; fax 03631/30 05.

Nürnberg [Nuremberg]

Opernhaus, Richard-Wagner-Platz, 90443 Nürnberg.

Twelve operas are staged each season, featuring a good range of repertoire, from Mozart to the very latest work.

Tickets DM11–65, on sale about a month before performance.

Box Office Mon–Fri 9am–1pm & 4–6pm, Sat 8.30am–1pm; ☎0911/2 31 38 08; fax 0911/2 31 35 66.

Oldenburg

Staatstheater, Theaterwall 18, 26019 Oldenburg.

An ambitious company considering the size of its home town, with a good mix of some eight operas per season (Berlioz to Berg); Mozart and Puccini don't feature as heavily here as they do in most other houses.

Tickets DM13–42 (DM8 for standing), on sale for each month's performances from the first working day of the previous month.

Box Office Mon–Fri 10am–1pm & 3–5pm, Sat 10am–1pm; ☎0441/2 57 80.

Osnabrück

Städtische Bühnen, Domhof 10–11, 49074 Osnabrück.

Theatre closed from mid-April 1995 until July 1997 (performances in Stadthalle and Kuppeltheater); eight operas/operettas per season.

Tickets DM17–37, on sale a month in advance; reservations must be paid for at least ten days before performance.

Box Office Tues–Fri 10am–5.30pm, Sat 10am–1pm; ☎0541/3 23 33 14; fax 0541/3 23 32 97.

Pforzheim

Stadttheater, Am Waisenhausplatz 5, 75172 Pforzheim.

Modest provincial company, with five or six unremarkable operas/operettas per season, staged in a small modern theatre.

Tickets DM17–37 (DM7 standing), on sale three weeks in advance.

Box Office Tues–Sat 10am–1pm & 5–7pm; ☎07231/39 24 40.

Regensburg

Städtische Bühnen, Bismarckplatz 7, 93047 Regensberg.

Provincial company with enlightened programming of new works and rarities among the six or seven operas presented per season.

Tickets DM9–50, on sale a week in advance.

Box Office Mon–Fri 10am–1pm & 5–7pm, Sat 10am–noon; ☎0941/5 07 14 28.

Saarbrücken

Saarländisches Staatstheater, Schillerplatz 1, 66111 Saarbrücken.

Seven operas each season, often including Wagner; some productions visit neighbouring Luxembourg.

Tickets D15–45, on sale about a month before performance.

Box Office Mon–Sat 10am–1pm & 4–7pm; ☎0681/3 22 04; fax 0681/30 92 316; postal applications to: Theaterkasse, Postfach 10 27 35, 66027 Saarbrücken.

STUTTGART

Württemburgisches Staatstheater, Oberer Schlossgarten 6, 70173 Stuttgart.

One of Germany's leading houses, staging 20–25 operas per season in a good mix of repertoire (several of Philip Glass's operas were first seen here) and bringing in a fair range of international singers.

TICKETS DM15–80, on sale to personal callers from Saturday for performances in second week; phone bookings accepted for performances in the following week only: postal applications accepted from time of programme publication

BOX OFFICE Mon–Fri 10am–6pm, Sat 9am–1pm; ☎0711/22 17 95; postal applications to: Postfach 10 43 45, 70038 Stuttgart, enclosing blank cheque.

ULM

Ulmer Theater, Olgastrasse 73, 89073 Ulm (Donau).

A challenging range of repertoire, from Mozart to Korngold and Berg (Karajan was music director here before the war). Seven or eight operas per season, plus musicals and plays.

TICKETS DM16–40, on sale from three weeks in advance.

BOX OFFICE Tues–Sat 10–11.30am, Tues–Fri 6–7pm, Sun 11am–1pm; ☎0731/1 61 44 44; fax 0731/1 61 16 19.

WIESBADEN

Hessisches Staatstheater, Christian-Zais-Strasse 3–5, 65189 Wiesbaden.

Rival to Mainz across the Rhine, staging as many as twenty operas per season.

TICKETS DM9–55, on sale from publication of each monthly calendar (about two weeks before beginning of each month).

BOX OFFICE Tues–Fri 11am–2pm & 4–6pm, Sat & Sun 11am–12.30pm; ☎0611/1 323 25; fax 0611/1 323 67. Tickets also available at Mainz box office – see above.

IRELAND

DUBLIN

Grand Opera Society, Gaiety Theatre, South King Street, Dublin 2. DGOS stages just four operas a year, two in early Dec and two at Easter, each performed four or five times.

TICKETS IR£6–39, on sale six to eight weeks in advance.

BOX OFFICE Mon–Sat 11am–7pm; ☎01/677 1717; information ☎01/453 5519.

WEXFORD FESTIVAL OPERA (mid-Oct to early Nov)

Theatre Royal, Wexford, Co. Wexford.

This small seaside town, about fifty miles south of Dublin, has been at the forefront of the operatic festival scene for over forty years, specializing in the revival of rare and unjustly neglected works. Three operas are performed eight or nine times each, together with related operatic and other musical events, with many international and, in particular, young artists.

TICKETS IR£36–48, on sale from early June.

BOX OFFICE June 1 to end of festival Mon–Fri 11am–5pm; ☎053/22144; fax 053/47438.

ISRAEL

TEL AVIV

New Israeli Opera, Tel Aviv Performing Arts Center, 28 Leonardo da Vinci St.

Ten performances each of eight or nine operas (Oct–July).

TICKETS SH84–168, on sale a month in advance.

BOX OFFICE 19 Shaun Hamelech Avenue; Mon–Thurs & Sun 9.30am–8.30pm, Fri 9.30am–1pm, Sat open from two hours before performance; ☎03/692 7777; fax 03/692 7733.

ITALY

BOLOGNA

Teatro Comunale, largo Respighi 1, 40126 Bologna.

One of the high-profile Italian houses, with decent runs of some half-dozen productions a season (Nov–June), often featuring leading conductors, producers and singers, in repertoire ranging from Handel to Berg, via Donizetti and Wagner.

TICKETS L15,000–99,000, on sale up to six weeks before opening night. A limited number of seats may be available for postal booking, which must be paid for immediately by telegraphed money order on confirmation of reservation (no phone bookings accepted from abroad). Applications postmarked more than ten days before booking opens are not accepted.

BOX OFFICE Mon–Fri 3.30–7pm, Sat 9.30am–12.30pm & 3.30–7pm; ☎051/529 999.

WEB SITE http://www.nettuno.it/bo/teatro_comunale/

CATANIA

Teatro Bellini, via Perrotta 12, 95131 Catania.

Hardly surprisingly, the works of Bellini feature prominently in his home town (there is a Bellini festival Sept–Oct), though the eight operas staged in short runs each season (Nov–June) are refreshingly varied.

TICKETS L18,000–100,000, on sale from beginning of October for whole season; postal and phone bookings must be paid for by money order on confirmation of reservation – no other method of payment is accepted.

BOX OFFICE Mon–Sat 10am–noon & 5–8pm; ☎095/715 0921; information ☎095/325 365; fax 095/321 830.

FERRARA

Teatro Comunale, corso Martiri della Libertà 15.

Largely a receiving house, bringing in roughly four productions per season from visiting Italian companies or abroad.

TICKETS L10,000–200,000, usually available from a week before the performance.

BOX OFFICE corso Giovecca 12, 44100 Ferrara; Mon–Sat 10.30am–12.30pm & 5–8pm; ☎0532/202 675; fax 0532/249 391.

FIRENZE [FLORENCE]

Teatro Comunale, corso Italia 16, 50123 Firenze.

A brief autumn season of four or five operas is all that Florence offers operatically outside the Maggio Musicale festival (under whose auspices they are often staged), though artists of the stature of Zubin Mehta and Semyon Bychkov are regulars, as is director Jonathan Miller.

TICKETS L30,000–180,000, on sale by post from mid-July and by phone from early Sept.

BOX OFFICE At corso Italia 16 Tues–Sat 9am–1pm and at via Faenza 139r Mon 3.30–7.30pm, Tues–Sun 10am–7.30pm; ☎055/211 158; postal applications to: Biglietteria Teatro Comunale, via Solferino 15, 50123 Firenze.

MAGGIO MUSICALE FIORENTINO (May to early July).

Florence's spring festival goes some way to make up for the scarcity of opera the rest of the year in the city where, after all, the genre was invented. A handful of operas, often rarities, are staged or given in concert with big-name conductors, singers and producers; plus other orchestral concerts, recitals, ballets, etc.

TICKETS L40,000–110,000, on sale from early April for those outside the region, from early May for others.

BOX OFFICE During festival at Teatro Comunale, corso Italia 16, Tues–Sat 1–7.30pm, and at via Faenza 139r, daily 10am–7.30pm; ☎055/211 158.

GENOVA [GENOA]

Teatro Carlo Felice, Passo al Teatro 4, 16121 Genova.

Genova's opera house has recently been completely renovated and offers a full season of nine or ten operas, predominantly Italian in focus and featuring leading native singers and conductors.

TICKETS L30,000–115,000, on sale from mid-Nov; only postal and fax bookings accepted from abroad; credit cards accepted.

BOX OFFICE Galleria Cardinal Siri 6, 16121 Genova; Tues–Sat 10.30am–1pm & 3–7pm; ☎010/591.697; fax 010/538.1233; to join mailing list, write to Public Relations Service, Ufficio Promozione, Passo al Teatro 4, enclosing L20,000.

MACERATA OPERA FESTIVAL (mid-July to mid-August).

Teatro di Traditione, via Santa Maria della Porta 65.

This small town in the Marche (nearest main city is Ancona) stages three or four operas during its festival, mainly familiar Italian works. Distinguished visiting singers and conductors (eg Carreras) join a variety of local and guest orchestras.

TICKETS L15,000–150,000, on sale by phone or post as soon as the brochure is available (usually May), and from June 1 for booking in person.

BOX OFFICE From 1 June at Piazza Mazzini 10, 62100 Macerata; Mon–Sat 9.30am–1pm & 4–8pm; ☎0733/230 735; fax 0733/261 499.

MILAN

Teatro alla Scala, via Filodrammatico 2, 20121 Milano.

The country's leading house, now under the musical direction of Riccardo Muti, is one of the very few Italian theatres to boast anything close to an international repertoire, with Wagner and Strauss appearing prominently as well as the inevitable Verdi. Demand for tickets is huge, even for the standing places sold thirty minutes before the performance from the Piazza Scala ticket office – you might have to queue all day. Ten to twelve operas are staged in runs of varying length from December to July, sometimes with a couple of pre-season productions in the autumn. Note that the fearsomely authoritarian regulations stipulate "gentlemen spectators are required to attend performances in jacket and tie".

TICKETS L20,000–270,000 (plus standing places at L10,000), on sale two or three weeks in advance; phone booking allowed only from outside region and must be confirmed in writing within 48 hours; a maximum of two tickets per person can be reserved by post or fax, enclosing photocopy of front and back of your credit card (20 percent booking charge).

BOX OFFICE Mon–Sat noon–7pm; ☎02/861781; fax 02/861778; automated service for credit-card bookings ☎02/860787.

WEB SITE http://lascala.milano.it/

NAPLES

Teatro di San Carlo, via San Carlo 98/F, 7972412 Napoli.

Six to eight operas, mostly Italian, are staged each season in this historic house, which is now rather down on its luck, though it does occasionally draw in Pavarotti and his ilk. The music director is Salvatore Accardo.

TICKETS L25,000–180,000.

BOX OFFICE Tues–Sun 10am–1pm & 4.30–6.30pm; ☎081/797 2331.

PESARO ROSSINI FESTIVAL (July–Aug).

Founded in 1980 in Rossini's home town, this festival presents productions of three or four Rossini operas, which often take advantage of the research and new editions produced by the local Rossini Foundation. Performances take place in the Teatro Rossini and Palafestival building, and feature leading Rossini singers and conductors.

TICKETS L25,000–180,000, on sale from April to personal callers, from June for phone bookings.

BOX OFFICE Teatro Rossini, Piazza Lazzarini, 61100 Pesaro; ☎0721/33 184; information ☎0721/30 161; fax 0721/30 979.

ROME

Teatro dell'Opera, via Firenze 72, 00184 Roma.

The Rome opera has been beset by financial scandals and resignations for years, but is now beginning to pull itself out of its artistic rut at least, partly through a new series of co-productions with Covent Garden. It is currently staging a scant forty performances per season (Jan–June) of six or seven operas, though they are no longer exclusively Italian.

TICKETS L20,000–140,000, on sale from mid-Dec; credit cards accepted or cheque in Italian lire.

BOX OFFICE Piazza Beniamino Gigli 1, Tues–Sat 9am–8pm; ☎06/481 7003; fax 06/488 1755.

SPOLETO

Festival dei Due Mondi (late June to mid-July).

Three opera productions are staged among other artistic events in the Festival of Two Worlds, founded in 1958 by Gian Carlo Menotti to specialize in contemporary works and bel canto operas. Several venues are used, but the principal one is the Teatro Nuovo.

TICKETS L15,000–250,000; enclose cheque or banker's draft for ticket prices plus 15 percent surcharge.

BOX OFFICE Piazza del Duomo 9; Mon–Sat 10am–1pm & 4–7pm; postal applications to: Biglietteria Festival dei Due Mondi, Teatro Nuovo, 06049 Spoleto (Perugia).

TURIN

Teatro Regio, piazza Castello 215, 10124 Torino.

Easily combined with a trip to La Scala in Milan, Turin offers an identity and high standard of its own, with some eight operas a season, sometimes including co-productions with Opéra de Lyon, and exhibiting notable strengths in Britten and other twentieth-century repertoire. Puccini's *La Bohéme* was first performed here in February 1896.

TICKETS L35,000–200,000; postal bookings accepted up to twenty days before performance, after which only phone and personal bookings are taken.

BOX OFFICE Tues–Sun 1–6.30pm; ☎011/8815 241; information ☎011/8815 209; fax 011/8815 214.

VENEZIA [VENICE]

La Fenice, Campo San Fantin 1965, 30124 Venezia.

Destroyed by fire in January 1996, La Fenice was one of Italy's historic houses – Verdi's *La Traviata* flopped here at its premiere in 1853, and Britten's *Turn of the Screw* and Stravinsky's *Rake's Progess* also opened here. Rebuilding is due to commence in 1997, on a two-year schedule. In the interim, some eight operas are staged in short, self-contained runs (Oct–July) in the Palafenice, a gigantic tent by the main car park on the Tronchetto island.

TICKETS L30,000–200,000, on sale from a week before each production opens.

BOX OFFICE Mon–Sat 9.30am–12.30pm & 4–6pm; ☎041/521 0161.

VERONA

Teatro Filarmonico, via dei Mutilati 4K, 37121 Verona.

A short season (Jan–May) complements the summer open-air festival (see below), with three or four works performed.

TICKETS L20,000–60,000, on sale as soon as programme is published.

BOX OFFICE Mon–Fri 8.40am–12.20pm & 3–5.50pm, Sat 8.40am–12.20pm; ☎045/800 5151; information ☎045/590 109; fax 045/801 3287. Tickets also available at the Arena box office (see below).

VERONA ARENA FESTIVAL (July–Sept).

Staged in the vast Roman amphitheatre of Verona, this is the grandfather of all open-air opera festivals and one of the most egalitarian. Five or six operas – dominated by the grandest Italian repertoire, from *Aida* (performed every year) to *Turandot* – are given almost nightly performances, with no-expense-spared production values. Selected performances feature some of opera's biggest names.

TICKETS L40,000–265,000, plus 15 percent surcharge if bought more than 24 hours in advance; tickets can be booked through Web Site.

BOX OFFICE Via Dietro Anfiteatro 6B; Mon–Fri 8.40am–12.20pm & 3–5.50pm, Sat 8.40am–12.20pm; on performance dates, Tues–Sun 10am–12.20pm & 3.30–9.30pm; ☎045/800 5151; information ☎045/590 109; fax 045/801 3287.

WEB SITE http://www.cosi.it/verona/verona_home.html

LUXEMBOURG

LUXEMBOURG

Théâtre Municipal, Rond-Point R. Schumann, L-2525 Luxembourg. This receiving house brings in half a dozen productions for three nights each from elsewhere in Europe, including neighbouring Saarbrücken in Germany (Oct–June). As a result, the repertoire is satisfyingly broad.

TICKETS LF600–950, on sale from early Sept.

BOX OFFICE Mon–Fri 3–6.30pm; ☎47 08 95.

NETHERLANDS

AMSTERDAM

De Nederlands Opera, Waterlooplein 22, 1011 PG Amsterdam.

Amsterdam maintains a fascinatingly varied repertoire, with a sprinkling of new works, including by native composers such as Peter Schat and Louis Andriessen, and revivals of rarer older ones. One opera per month Sept–June in stagione.

TICKETS Dfl27.50–95, on sale from a month before first night; tickets reserved by phone must be collected within seven days.

BOX OFFICE Mon–Sat 10am–7.30pm, Sun 11.30am–3pm; ☎20/625 5455.

MAASTRICHT

Opera Zuid, Postbus 104, 6200 AC Maastricht.

Opera Zuid is a purely touring company, concentrating on the southern Netherlands and usually taking two or three ambitious productions on the road each season (several of them borrowed from or co-produced with British companies). Main venues are as follows.

Maastricht, Theater aan het Vrijthof; ☎043/321 0380.

Rotterdam, Rotterdamse Schouwburg; ☎010/411 8110.

Eindhoven, Stadsschouwburg; ☎040/211 1122.

Utrecht, Stadsschouwburg; ☎030/230 3023.

The company also visits half a dozen other theatres, an itinerary that varies for each tour – details of the tour are available on ☎043/321 0166, or fax 043/325 7655.

TICKETS Dfl45–55.

NEW ZEALAND

WELLINGTON

City Opera, State Insurance Opera House.

Limited season of three operas (April–Oct) with tickets in upper-price areas distributed on the rather unpleasant basis of ability to pay vast sums of charitable donations.

TICKETS NZ$10–80, plus $6 booking fee for postal and phone bookings.

BOX OFFICE ☎04/385-0832; postal applications to: Freepost 3091, PO Box 6334, Wellington.

NORWAY

OSLO

Norwegian National Opera, Storgaten 23, 0184 Oslo.

Having recently built up its first *Ring* cycle, the NNO is growing stronger by the year. It stages eleven or twelve operas per season (Aug–June), mixing popular Puccini and Mozart with Wagner and rarer Verdi.

Tickets NK140–340.

Box Office Mon–Sat 10am–6pm; ☎22 42 77 00; fax 22 42 78 77.

Web site http://wit.no/wit/DNO.index.html

POLAND

Warszawa [Warsaw]

Teatr Wielki w Warszawie-Opera Narodowa [The Great Theatre of Warsaw, National Opera], Plac Teatralny 1, 00-950 Warszawa.

The Warsaw National Opera runs a full season (Sept–June), mixing native operas and operettas with international repertoire.

Tickets Zloty 4–30, on sale when bi-monthly calendar appears, usually two weeks before period concerned.

Box Office Mon–Sat 9am–7pm, Sun 10am–2pm & 5–7pm; ☎022/26 50 19; fax 022/26 02 68.

PORTUGAL

Lisbon

Teatro Naçional de São Carlos, Rua Serpa Pinto 9, 1200 Lisboa.

Seven operas staged each season (Sept–June); several of the productions are brought in from abroad, complete with full cast, and there's only about thirty performances overall.

Tickets Esc2500–48,000, on sale from fifteen days before beginning of season; fax and postal reservations are taken up to 48 hours in advance.

Box Office Mon–Sat 1–7pm; ☎01/346 59 14; information ☎01/346 84 08; fax 01/347 17 38.

SPAIN

Madrid

Teatro de la Zarzuela, Jovellanos, 4 28014 Madrid.

Madrid's opera house proper, which hasn't been used for its intended purpose for 75 years, is due to re-open at the end of 1997, but its restoration has been so protracted a business that it would be rash to predict that it will open as planned. In the meantime, the Zarzuela house stages a limited operatic season of six or seven works (Jan–July), in between other events, with a mix of established singers from abroad and younger native talent.

Tickets Pta1000–8000.

Box Office Mon–Sat 10am–6pm; ☎91/429 82 25; fax 91/429 71 57.

SWEDEN

Drottningholm Opera Festival (late May–early Sept).

The eighteenth-century court theatre of King Gustavus III (subject of Verdi's *Un ballo in maschera*) – an hour by bus or boat west of Stockholm – provides a beautiful setting for the revival of operas from the period, centred on the works of Haydn, Handel, Gluck and Mozart. Three productions are usually staged each summer, using period instruments and production styles, and featuring leading specialists in the field.

Tickets SEK95–450, on sale from late March.

Box Office Drottningsholms Teatermuseum, Föreställningar, Box 27050, 10251 Stockholm; ☎08/660 82 25 or 660 82 81; fax 08/665 1473; tickets also available from 2500 computerized BiljettDirekt outlets, mainly located in newsagents and post offices – call ☎077/170 70 70 to find the nearest outlet.

Stockholm

Royal Opera, Gustav Adolfs Torg.

Scandinavia's oldest company presents a full, highly imaginative repertoire of some twenty operas (some in the studio theatre) Sept–June.

Tickets SEK25–280, on sale four weeks in advance.

Box Office Mon–Fri 11am–6pm, Sat 11am–3pm; ☎08/24 82 40; information ☎08/20 35 15; postal applications to: Box 16094, S-103 22 Stockholm. Tickets also available from ATG agncies all over Sweden.

Web site http://www.dataphone.se/~gberkson/operan/

SWITZERLAND

Basel

Theater Basel, Theaterplatz, 4010 Basel.

An adventurous company, with the emphasis on new works, staging six to eight operas per season.

Tickets SF18–97, on sale fourteen days in advance in person or by phone, three months to fourteen days in advance by post (only top two price categories sold by post).

Box Office Mon–Sat 10am–1pm & 3.30–6.45pm; ☎061/295 1133; fax 061/295 1410.

Bern

Stadttheater, Theaterplatz, 3000 Bern 7.

Seven or eight operas per season, with relatively adventurous repertoire but with a more provincial feel to performances and production values than you'd expect from the capital.

Tickets SF10–80, on sale from two weeks in advance in person; postal and phone bookings accepted two months in advance (except for cheapest seats); credit cards accepted for postal and phone bookings from eight days in advance.

Box Office Kornhausplatz 18, 3000 Bern 7; Mon–Sat 10am–6.30pm, Sun 10am–12.30pm; ☎031/311 07 77.

Geneva

Grand Théâtre, 11 bd du Théâtre, 1211 Genève 11.

The rival to Zürich as Switzerland's leading house and arguably the most consistent in the French-speaking world, relying particularly on imported talent from Britain and America. Eight operas per season, roughly one per month Oct–June.

Tickets SF15–100, on sale seven days before opening of each production.

Box Office Bureau de location du Grand Théâtre, place Neuve, Genève; Mon–Fri 10am–7pm, Sat 10am–5pm; ☎022/311 2311.

Lucerne

Stadttheater, Theaterstrasse 2, 6002 Luzern.

A lively, small-town company with a repertoire ranging from Mozart to smaller-scale Strauss; seven operas, musicals and operettas per season.

Tickets SF10–80, on sale from a week in advance.

Box Office Mon–Sat 9am–12.15pm & 4–6.30pm, Sun 10am–noon; ☎041/236 618; fax 041/233 367.

St Gallen

Stadttheater, St Gallen, Museumstrasse 24, CH-9004 St Gallen.

Six operas per season, with ambitious repertoire but a small-town feel to performances.

Tickets SF24–63 on sale from a month in advance.

Box Office Mon–Sat 10am–12.30pm & 4–6pm, Sun 10am–noon; ☎071/260 606.

Zürich

Opernhaus, Theaterplatz, 8008 Zürich.

One of Europe's great underrated houses, Zürich stages a full programme of some thirty operas per season in stagione, attracting big-name performers and an adventurous roster of repertoire and directors; it boasts a fine orchestra. Tickets are notably expensive (as are most things Swiss), though some Volksvorstellung ("people's performances") are much cheaper.

Tickets SF20–124, on sale from a month in advance; postal bookings accepted for open-sale (*Freiverkauf*) performances only.

Box Office In foyer of next-door Bernhardtheater; Mon–Sat 10am–6.30pm (or curtain-up); ☎01/262 0909; postal applications to: Falkenstrasse 1, CH-8008 Zurich.

UNITED KINGDOM

The Royal Opera House and the upper-bracket Glyndebourne Festival are the best-known opera institutions in the UK, but equally important to the life of the genre are the country's touring companies, which present the majority of their shows away from their home base. Where feasible we've indicated the theatres these companies visit, but in some cases the itineraries are so variable that it's best to contact the company HQ for details.

Belfast

Opera Northern Ireland, Grand Opera House, Great Victoria St, Belfast BT2 7HR.

Limited runs of a handful of popular operas are given in autumn and spring.

Tickets £5–30, on sale two months in advance.

Box Office 17 Wellington Place, Belfast BT1 6GB; Mon–Sat 10am-6pm; ☎01232/241 919; fax 01232/329 606.

Cardiff

Welsh National Opera, New Theatre, Park Place, Cardiff CF1 3LN.

Founded in 1946, WNO is the oldest of the full-time regional companies. In its early days it was instrumental in reviving Verdi's early operas (the Welsh choral tradition to the fore), and in the 1970s and 1980s led the way in introducing the modernist production schools of Eastern Europe to Britain. Under music director Carlo Rizzi, the company is returning to its roots with renewed strength in Italian repertoire. Although it lurches from one funding crisis to the next (as do all Britain's companies), it still manages to maintain a rich repertoire of some seven or eight operas per season, mounted in three phases (autumn, winter and spring), each beginning with a few weeks in Cardiff before going on tour. If all goes to plan, it should have a new dockside opera house in time for the millennium.

Tickets New Theatre tickets £8–45.

Box Office Mon–Sat 10am–8pm; ☎01222/394844.

Welsh National Opera tours regularly to the following venues, as well as making brief visits to London.

Birmingham, Hippodrome, Hurst Street, Birmingham B5 4TB; ☎0121/622 7486.

Bristol, Hippodrome, St Augustine's Parade, Bristol BS1 4UZ; ☎0117/922 9944.

Liverpool, Empire Theatre, Lime Street, Liverpool L1 1JE; ☎0151/709 1555.

Llandudno, North Wales Theatre, Promenade, Llandudno LL30 1BB; ☎01492/872000.

Oxford, Apollo Theatre, George St, Oxford OX1 2AG; ☎01865/244 544.

Southampton, Mayflower Theatre, Commercial Rd, Southampton SO15 1GE; ☎01703/229771.

Swansea, Grand Theatre, Singleton St, Swansea SA1 3QJ; ☎01792/475715.

EDINBURGH FESTIVAL (mid-Aug to early Sept).

As part of the world's largest arts festival, Edinburgh acts as a showcase for visiting operatic productions from around the world, though with a consistent input from Scottish Opera. The number of performances varies from year to year – 1995, for example, had two from Scottish Opera and four (of two operas) from the Kirov, plus an American company with a new John Adams work. Acoustically, the recently rebuilt Edinburgh Festival Theatre provides one of the finest operatic venues in the country, a marked contrast with the city's main concert venue, the Usher Hall, where all the visiting orchestras play.

TICKETS £5–45, on sale by fax and post from mid-April, in person from late April.

BOX OFFICE 21 Market Street, Edinburgh EH1 1BW; April–June Mon–Fri 10am–4.30pm, July Mon–Fri 10am–6pm, Sat noon–3pm, Aug–Sept Mon–Sat 9am–7pm, Sun 10am–5pm; ☎0131/225 5756; fax 0131/226 7669.

GARSINGTON OPERA FESTIVAL (June–July).

Garsington Manor, Garsington, Oxford OX44 9DH.

Performances are given in the open air (with fierce under-seat heating) on the terrace of a beautiful manor house associated with the Bloomsbury set. The festival is improving in standard each year, now drawing leading producers and conductors. Three operas per season and, in keeping with itsGlyndebourne-like image, there are 85-minute dinner intervals and an expectation of formal evening wear, but the audience seems even snootier than at Glyndebourne.

TICKETS £60–85, including "a suggested but non-obligatory donation of £40" for development projects.

BOX OFFICE Postal bookings only; information ☎01865/361 636.

GLASGOW

Scottish Opera, Theatre Royal, 282 Hope St, Glasgow G2 3QA.

Scottish Opera is the poor relation of the other British national companies. It has had to go part-time to stave off insolvency triggered by the splitting of arts funding between the British provinces – the Scottish Arts Council will no longer fund SO's touring to northern England, formerly part of its heartland. Artistically it has been on an all-time high under music director Richard Armstrong, but it remains to be seen how it will maintain the status of a national company working for only nine months a year and with a more limited repertoire. The season is in three phases, beginning in Glasgow, then touring to a selection of venues.

TICKETS Glasgow £3.50–44.

BOX OFFICE ☎0141/332 9000.

Scottish Opera includes the following venues in its tours.

Aberdeen, His Majesty's Theatre, Rosemount Viaduct, Aberdeen AB9 1GL; ☎01224/641 122.

Edinburgh, Festival Theatre, 13–29 Nicolson St, Edinburgh EH8 9FT; ☎0131/529 6000.

WEB SITE http://www.arts.gla.ac.uk/scotop.html

GLYNDEBOURNE FESTIVAL OPERA (late May to mid-Aug).

Lewes, East Sussex BN8 5UU.

The new, larger theatre (seating 1200) has opened this most exclusive of operatic ventures to a slightly wider audience. It may still be crawling with overdressed snobs and the top prices may exceed £100, but acoustics are fine from all parts of this beautiful auditorium, so sitting at the back in the cheapest seats is no hardship. Six operas are staged, with the perennial Mozarts and Strauss interspersed with more adventurous fare from rare Rossini to new commissions. Under the overall direction of British high-flyer Graham Vick, the productions are often less stuffy than the audience would like. The emphasis is on younger singers, but mainly those already established on the international circuit; the pit orchestra is the London Philharmonic and the music director Andrew Davis. Bring a picnic to enjoy in the 85-minute dinner interval, when, weather permitting, you can sit and watch the sun go down over the beautiful South Downs from the landscaped gardens. It is possible to get the cheapest tickets for most productions as soon as public booking opens, but most go to those who have priority booking status.

TICKETS £15–105, on sale from late April, plus standing tickets for £10 (priority given to students).

BOX OFFICE Mon–Fri 10am–8pm, Sat 10am–5pm; ☎01273/813813.

Glyndebourne Touring Opera

The touring arm of the Festival Opera hits the road from early Oct to early Dec with three productions, either from the festival or, increasingly, of its own creation. Soloists are often understudies or chorus members from the summer season, but more familiar names are appearing. After two weeks at Glyndebourne, the company usually spends a week each in a selection of the following venues.

Manchester, Palace Theatre, Oxford St, Manchester M1 6FT; ☎0161/242 2503.

Norwich, Theatre Royal, Theatre St, Norwich NR2 1RL; ☎01603/630 000.

Oxford, Apollo Theatre, George St, Oxford OX1 2AG; ☎01865/244544.

Plymouth, Theatre Royal, Royal Parade, Plymouth PL1 2TR; ☎01752/267222.

Southampton, Mayflower Theatre, Commercial Rd, Southampton SO15 1GE; ☎01703/229771.

Woking, New Victoria Theatre, Woking GU21 1QC; ☎01483/761144.

Tickets £10–45 at Glyndebourne, £5–45 elsewhere, on sale as soon as programme is announced in the summer.

Leeds

Opera North, Grand Theatre, New Briggate, Leeds LS1 6NZ.

Originally an offshoot of ENO, Opera North has now risen to become perhaps the most exciting of the regional companies, extending the bounds of the repertoire (from early Verdi to neglected Schreker, Gerhard and Walton) and breathing new life into the classics. Nine operas are divided equally between three seasons (autumn, winter and spring), with some fifty performances in Leeds and the rest on tour.

Tickets £7–36.

Box Office Mon–Sat 10am–7.30pm; ☎0113/245 9351; fax 0113/246 5906.

Opera North includes the following venues in its tours.

Hull, New Theatre, Kingston Square, Hull HU1 3HF; ☎01482/226655.

Manchester, Palace Theatre, Oxford St, Manchester M1 6FT; ☎0161/242 2503.

Newcastle, Theatre Royal, Grey St NE1 6BR; ☎0191/232 2061.

Norwich, Theatre Royal, Theatre St, Norwich NR2 1RL; ☎01603/630 000.

Nottingham, Theatre Royal, Theatre Square, Nottingham NG1 5ND; ☎0115/948 2626.

Sunderland, Empire Theatre, High Street West, Sunderland SR1 3EX; ☎0191/514 2517, fax 0191/510 2150.

London

English National Opera, London Coliseum, St Martin's Lane, London WC2.

A powerhouse of innovative opera during the 1980s, the ENO has declined in prestige since the departure of the Mark Elder/David Pountney/Peter Jonas triumvirate, who left a very distinctive mark on production style and repertoire. There are signs of the new regime regaining the company's old adventurousness, though lowering attendances have led to frustratingly short runs of more offbeat repertoire and long runs of crowd-pullers. The move of conductor Paul Daniel from Opera North in the autumn of 1997 is an enticing prospect. All operas are sung in English, but the size of the theatre (the largest in London at just over 2000 seats) works against audibility. Some eighteen to twenty works are staged each season (Sept–June), with visiting ballet companies occupying the theatre during the summer and often at Christmas.

Tickets £9–48. For booking purposes, the season is divided into three overlapping periods, roughly autumn, winter and spring, with booking opening about six weeks before the first performance in each period. Seats in the balcony at £5 and in the dress circle (Mon–Fri only) at £25 are available from 10am on the day; half-price tickets may be available from 2.30pm on the day from the West End theatre ticket booth in Leicester Square.

Box Office Mon–Sat 10am–8pm; ☎0171/632 8300 (24 hours for credit cards); fax 0171/379 1264 (can be used for credit card bookings).

Royal Opera, Bow Street, London WC2.

The Royal Opera has picked itself up in recent years to rival ENO in terms of adventurousness and standards of performance, though there are still some ancient cardboard stagings in its schedules and the choice of singers is sometimes questionable. As the only company in Britain that can afford (at the opera-goer's expense) to bring in the superstars, it maintains its place among the world's most prestigious companies. The theatre is a frustrating, nineteenth-century horseshoe shape, with far too many seats facing each other rather than the stage. Seat pricing is always its most controversial aspect: the best bargain, if you can get them, are the Upper Slips, with a very restricted view of the stage and minimal comfort but, at £4–7, offering cheap access. The Royal Opera stages about twenty operas per season (Sept–July), with an annual Verdi Festival, leading up to the composer's centenary in 2001, currently extending it through the summer. The theatre closes at the end of the 1996–97 season for two years of rebuilding; during that period various other London venues will be used, such as the Barbican Centre and the Royal Albert Hall.

TICKETS £4–268, on sale in five bi-monthly periods, usually one month before first performance in that period; 65 seats kept for sale on the day.

BOX OFFICE 48 Floral St, London WC2E 7QA; Mon–Sat 10am–8pm; ☎0171/304 4000; information ☎0171/212 9234; fax 0171/497 1256.

South Bank Centre

London's concert-hall complex occasionally hosts productions of opera, ranging from concert performances of often obscure works by Chelsea Opera Group (3–4 a season) to fully staged productions by the cutting-edge Opera Factory (usually one production in Sept, which may then tour).

OPERA FACTORY WEB SITE: http://www.poptel.org.uk/opera/; otherwise information from SBC on ☎0171/921 0600.

Spitalfields Market Opera, 4–5 Lamb St, London E1 6EA.

This new venture, opened in the summer of 1995, is a purpose-built chamber opera venue (seating 500) in an old fruit market close to Liverpool Street Station. The intention is to provide a mixture of home-grown productions and visiting companies from Britain and around the world, as well as to entertain City workers with lunchtime shows.

TICKETS £2–7.50.

BOX OFFICE ☎0171/247 2558.

English Touring Opera

Two seasons of two works at a time begin at Richmond Theatre in London (while rebuilding is in progress at Sadler's Wells theatre) then tour some fifteen British theatres over three-month periods in autumn and spring. Performers are young singers at the outset of their career, but standards in performance and production are high, even if the repertoire is undemanding.

TICKETS £5–25.

BOX OFFICE ☎0171/713 6000.

UNITED STATES OF AMERICA

Opera in the USA is growing in popularity, despite threats to the already minimal national arts funding. There is an enthusiasm for the genre rarely found in Europe, marked by the frequency with which new operas reach the stage, and by a tendency to applaud everything from the curtain-up to the last aria. However, at the moment only New York has the wealth of repertoire and length of season found in most European cities, and the predominance of vast, impersonal theatres makes surtitles a necessity even for English-language performances. One last problem is created by the very success of opera in the USA: the prevalence of subscription packages means that single tickets can be difficult to find for the more prestigious houses.

ASPEN MUSIC FESTIVAL (late June to mid-Aug).

Two to three operas, staged in the Wheeler Opera House, are at the core of this general music festival held in Colorado's high-class mountain resort.

TICKETS $17–38, on sale by phone from mid-May, by post as soon as programme is announced.

BOX OFFICE During festival in the Gondola Building, Durant Avenue; Mon–Sat 9am–4.30pm, Sun 9am–2.30pm; ☎303/925-9042; postal applications to: Ticket Sales, Box AA, Aspen, CO 81612-7428.

CHICAGO

Lyric Opera, Civic Opera House, 20 North Wacker Drive, Chicago, IL 60673-0199.

Eight operas staged from mid-Sept to mid-Feb, with many leading singers. New works have been commissioned as part of a "Toward the 21st Century" initiative, which will also include works by Janáček and Berio.

TICKETS $21–102, on sale from Sept 12; postal bookings accepted approximately one month earlier.

BOX OFFICE Mon–Sat 10am–7pm; ☎312/332-2244 (ext 500); postal applications to: Box 70199 at Civic Opera House.

GLIMMERGLASS OPERA FESTIVAL (July–Aug).

Cooperstown, New York State.

Generous runs of four works (from Handel to Britten) are given in the barn-like Alice Busch Opera Theatre, set in a beautifully rural setting in upstate New York.

TICKETS $20–60.

BOX OFFICE From May 1 at 18 Chestnut St, Cooperstown, NY 13326; Mon–Sat 9am–6pm; ☎607/547 2255; fax 607/547 1257.

HOUSTON

Grand Opera, Brown Theater, Wortham Center, 510 Preston, Houston, TX 77002-1594.

Pioneering American company, with a particular devotion to new works (premieres of Tippett, for example) and American works from the likes of Carlisle Floyd and Virgil Thomson.

TICKETS $20–120, on sale one month before beginning of season (Oct–May).

Box Office Houston Ticket Center, Wortham Center, 550 Prairie, or lower level Jones Hall, 615 Louisiana; both Mon–Fri 9am–6pm, Sat 10am–5pm; ☎713/546-0246; fax 713/228-4355; information ☎1-800/346-HGOA.

Web Site http://www.hgo.com/

Los Angeles

Music Center Opera, 135 North Grand Ave, Los Angeles, CA 90012.

A high-powered company offering eight operas in two short seasons (Sept–Nov & Feb–June), with top-line casts and productions, many shared or borrowed).

Tickets $21–115, on sale from mid-Aug for both seasons.

Box Office Mon–Sat 10am–6pm; ☎213/972-7211; fax 213/972-7670; postal applications to: PO Box 2237, Los Angeles, CA 90051.

Miami

Florida Grand Opera, Dade County Auditorium, 2901 West Flagler St, Miami, and Broward Center for the Performing Arts, 201 SW 5th Ave, Fort Lauderdale.

A new company created out of the former Miami Grand Opera and Fort Lauderdale Opera Guild, with performances divided between Dade and Broward; the repertoire is fairly traditional (hardly surprising given Miami's age profile), but attracts a few star names, and the music director is James Judd.

Box Offices Arturo di Filippi Educational Center, 1200 Coral Way, Miami, FL 33145-2980; ☎305/854-7890; fax 305/856-1042. Josephine S Leiser Opera Center, 221 SW 3rd Ave, Ft Lauderdale, FL 33312; Mon–Fri 9am–5pm; ☎1-800/741-1010

New York

New York City Opera, New York State Theatre, Lincoln Center, New York, NY 10023.

New York's second house, putting on a split season (Sept–Nov & March–April) of about one hundred performances of about fifteen works, with further performances on tour.

Tickets $10-78, on sale by post from June and in person from Aug.

Box Office Mon–Fri 10am–8pm, Sat & Sun 11am–7pm; ☎212/870 5570.

Web Site http://www.interport.net/nycopera/

New York Metropolitan Opera, Lincoln Center, New York, NY 10023.

America's leading house, and the only one to offer a full season in the European sense. With Saturday matinees (broadcast weekly in the US and Europe), the company offers up to eight performances each week Oct–April, bringing in world-class singers, conductors and directors, though the production style tends to be conservative. All performances are now subtitled with individual "Met Titles" installed in the seat-backs. The music director is James Levine.

Tickets $16–137 (plus $4.50 handling fee for phone bookings), on sale from approximately six weeks in advance; standing tickets $11–15, on sale from 10am on Sat for performances in the week starting the following Sat.

Box Office Mon–Fri 10am–8pm, plus Sun noon–6pm from mid-Sept to end of season; ☎212/362 6000.

Web Site http://www.metopera.org/home.html

Saint Louis

Opera Theatre of Saint Louis, Loretto-Hilton Center, 130 Edgar Rd, St Louis, MO 63119-7910.

A short season (late May–June), mixing popular classics and new operas, all sung in English.

Tickets $20–100, on sale from early April.

Box Office Mon–Fri 10am–4pm; ☎314/961-0644; fax 314/961-0612; postal applications to: PO Box 191910 at Loretto-Hilton Center.

San Diego

Civic Theatre, 1200 Third Ave, San Diego, CA 92101.

Five operas are presented in short runs Jan–May, with a few internationally known names bolstering the local talent.

Tickets $20–90, on sale from Dec.

Box Office 202 C Street; Mon–Fri 8.30am–4.30pm; ☎619/236-6510; fax 619/231-6915; postal applications to: PO Box 988, San Diego, CA 92112-0988.

Web Site http://www.sdopera.com/

San Francisco

War Memorial Opera House, 301 Van Ness Ave, San Francisco, CA 94102.

The fall season (Sept–Dec) offers nine works with top singers, though production styles tend to be grandiose and old-fashioned. A more informal series of performances occurs in the late spring season (usually May–June), often featuring a string of visiting companies. The monolithic theatre is so vast that the affordable seats seem miles from the stage – bring powerful opera-glasses. Surtitles are in use throughout. The theatre should re-open in late 1997 after repair of earthquake damage; performances in the interim take place in the Bill Graham Civic Auditorium and the Orpheum Theater.

Tickets $15–135, on sale from late Aug for fall season, from early April for spring season.

Box Office 199 Grove St; Mon–Sat 10am–6pm; ☎415/864-3330; fax 415/626-1729.

Web Site http://www.sfopera.com/

Santa Fe Festival (late June to late Aug).

Opera Theater, Santa Fe, New Mexico.

One of America's major operatic festivals, with a semi-open-air theatre (there are plans to extend the roof over the entire audience) in a spectacular desert setting, seven miles outside Santa Fe. Five operas are staged, ranging from popular classics to new works, and with a fair sprinkling of known names among the casts.

Tickets $20–110, plus 150 standing tickets at $6–8 available on the day, half from 10am, half from 7.45pm (all performances start at 9pm); personal sales from early May; postal booking from early April.

Box Office Opera Theater and at Eldorado Hotel, 309 West San Francisco, and Galisteo Ticket Center, Galisteo/Water streets – both in Sante Fe itself; Mon–Sat 10am–4pm; ☎505/986-5900; fax 505/986-5966 ($2 handling fee for faxed ticket orders); postal applications to: PO Box 2408, Santa Fe, New Mexico 87504-2408.

Seattle

Seattle Center Opera House, 321 Mercer St.

Five operas are staged July–May, often dual-cast ("gold" and "silver", depending on the renown of the singers). The company is famous for its Wagner, with a *Ring* cycle brought out every few years.

Tickets $30–100, on sale from eight weeks before opening of each production.

Box Office 1020 John St; Mon–Sat 9am–5pm; ☎206/389-7676; fax 206/389-7689; postal applications to: PO Box 9248, Seattle, WA98109.

Spoleto Festival USA (early June).

Charleston, South Carolina.

A two-week-long festival, with just a couple of operas, usually interesting (Strauss and Henze in 1995), at the Gaillard Municipal Auditorium and Dock Street Theatre, among other music and arts events.

Tickets $10–75, on sale from mid-Jan.

Box Office Gaillard Auditorium, 77 Calhoun St; Mon–Sat 10am–6pm; ☎803/720-1116; fax 803/720-1121.

Matthew Rye

GLOSSARY

Accelerando
Gradually increasing in speed.

Accent
A stress on a particular note or beat, highlighting its place within a musical phrase.

Adagio
Slow and drawn-out tempo.

Allegro
Fast and lively tempo. Frequently applied at the end of a scene and/or act.

Alto
1. The highest of the male voices.
2. The lowest of the female voices.
3. Prefix used to denote an instrument that is lower in pitch and darker in tone than a treble instrument – eg alto saxophone, alto flute.

Andante
Moderate tempo. Slightly faster than Adagio – literally "walking pace".

Aria
Italian for "air". A term used since the time of Alessandro Scarlatti to describe an independent solo vocal piece within an opera, frequently created to display the artist's vocal facility.

Arietta
An abbreviated and simpler form of aria.

Arioso
Literally "like an aria": an arioso is traditionally a brief, melodic conversational passage in strict time (see "Recitative") .

Arpeggio
A chord performed as a broken run of notes.

Atonal
Music that is not in any key. With atonal music the traditional harmonic language no longer applies and the twelve notes of the octave function independently of any key centre. Atonality is associated above all with Schoenberg, Berg and Webern.

Ballet
Dance form in which a story is told through the unification of music and dance. Originated in the French court of the sixteenth century. Used by Lully as an interlude in his operas, then evolved into the hybrid opera-ballet. During the nineteenth century ballets became a central feature of Grand Opéra, and the genre soon branched off into its own independent art form. Dominated by the French until Tchaikovsky's emergence during the 1870s.

Baritone
The male voice between tenor and bass.

There are a number of specific baritone categories:

Bariton, a generic term for a French-style baritone, eg Escamillo (*Carmen*).

Basse-taille, a light lyric baritone traditionally heard in Baroque and Classical French opera, eg Lully and Rameau.

Heldenbariton, the most powerful of the baritone voices, used in Wagner and Strauss, eg Wotan (*Der Ring*) and Orestes (*Elektra*).

Spielbariton, a dark comic voice called for by German comic opera, eg Don Giovanni.

Baroque
Music composed between 1600 and 1750, spanning the period from Monteverdi to Handel. The period before Classical.

Bass

1. The lowest part of a chord or piece of music.
2. The lowest of the male voices.

There are a number of specific bass voice categories:

> **Basse-bouffe/basso-buffo**, a rich, comic voice used in French light opera and operetta, eg Jupiter (*Orpheus in the Underworld*), and an Italian comic character voice common in Italian and German opera, eg Osmin in Mozart's *Die Entführung* and Donizetti's Don Bartolo (*L'elisir d'amore*).
>
> **Basso cantante**, a light lyric bass, frequently a character voice, eg Padre Guardino (*La forza del destino*).
>
> **Bass-contre**, a middle-weight bass-baritone common in early French opera, especially Rameau.
>
> **Basso profondo**, a dark Italian heroic bass employed extensively by Verdi, eg Ramfis in *Aida*.

Bel canto
Literally "beautiful song". A late eighteenth-/early nineteenth-century school of singing, characterized by a concentration on beauty of tone and virtuosic agility. Rossini, Bellini and Donizetti are the main bel canto composers.

Bitonal
Music that uses two keys at the same time. Used by Strauss and Stravinsky.

Buffa/buffo
Italian for "comic"; eg opera buffa.

Cabaletta
An heroic but brief showpiece (frequently coming after an aria) built upon a rapid, unchanging rhythm. The most famous example is Manrico's "Di quella pira" from Verdi's *Il Trovatore*.

Cadence
The closing sequence of a musical phrase or composition. The "perfect cadence" gives a sense of completion; the "imperfect cadence" leaves the music hanging in mid-air.

Cadenza
In opera, a solo passage designed to show off a singer's technical abilities, generally occurring at the end of an aria, above the penultimate chord of a cadence. Traditionally based upon themes from the main body of music, and traditionally improvised by the artist, though by the middle of the nineteenth century it was common for composers to write their own.

Cantabile
A "singing" style. An exaggerated form of legato.

Cantilena
An extremely long and fluid type of melody.

Canzona
A verse form originating in fourteenth-century folk traditions. The term became widely applied to any song with a folk-like character.

Castrato
A male singer, castrated as a child, with a soprano or contralto voice of exceptional power and beauty. Very popular during the seventeenth and eighteenth centuries (see p.16). The last castrati died in the early part of the twentieth century.

Cavatina
An eighteenth-century term used to describe a lyrical operatic song or aria in a single section, thus distinguishing it from a traditional aria in which there was a "da capo" section.

Chest voice
The standard vocal register used by all but falsetto and coloratura singers. Most conventionally written operatic music is now sung using the chest voice, although for high notes the head voice is used to introduce a brighter, more ringing quality.

Chord
Any simultaneous combination of notes.

Chromaticism
Use of notes not belonging to the diatonic scale – ie using sharps, flats and naturals alien to the established key. The chromatic scale comprises twelve ascending or descending semi-tones. Chromaticism played a major part in middle and late Romantic music – Wagner in particular.

Classical
Now a generic term for all western art music. Specifically, however, it refers to the post-Baroque period roughly between 1750 and 1830. Pre-eminent Classical composers were Haydn, Mozart and Beethoven.

Coloratura
Soprano voice capable of great range, agility and delicacy. Famous coloratura roles include *The Magic Flute*'s Queen of the Night, many of the bel canto heroines and many of the *opéra-lyrique* female roles – notably those by Gounod and Thomas.

Commedia dell'arte
A dramatic genre of unknown origin that evolved in sixteenth-century Italy and had a profound influence on the development of opera. It was essentially a form of improvised comedy, based upon a scenario rather than pre-written dialogue, and made use of generic characters such as Arlecchino (Harlequin) and Pulchinello (the original Mr Punch).

Contralto
The lowest of the female voices – the same as an alto, but alto is associated with sacred and choral music, whereas contralto is purely operatic.

Contrapuntal
Adjective derived from "counterpoint".

Counterpoint
The placing of two or more musical parts against each other.

Counter-tenor
The highest male voice (also known as alto).

Da Capo
Means "repeat from the beginning".

Deus ex machina
"God from the machine": a device used in Greek and Renaissance drama and in sixteenth- and seventeenth-century opera to bring about a happy ending, through the intervention of a god or allegorical figure. The conclusion of Monteverdi's *Orfeo* is a prime example.

Diatonic
Music using the major and minor scales: music constructed exclusively of the notes defined by the key.

Dissonance
A combination of notes that jars the ear.

Dodecaphonic music
See "serial music".

Dramma giocoso
Comic operatic style developed by Goldoni, in which serious and comic characters share the stage. The most famous example is Mozart's *Don Giovanni*.

Dynamics
The qualities and degrees of softness and loudness.

Entr'acte
Musical interlude – like an intermezzo – dividing the acts of an opera.

Expressionism
As in the visual arts, a term used to describe works in which the artist's state of mind is the primary concern; similarly applied above all to German music of the early twentieth century, as composed by Strauss, Schreker, Berg and Schoenberg.

Falsetto
Italian for "false" or "altered". A voice employed by male singers to reach extremely high, female registers. Usually used as a special effect, as in Falstaff's imitation of Mistress Ford in Verdi's opera. Comes closest in tone to the counter-tenor, which is essentially a highly cultivated and disciplined form of falsetto singing.

Fioritura
Vocal embellishment.

Fugue
A highly complicated contrapuntal form in which two or more voices are built around a single theme. Their entries are in direct imitation of the theme's opening but each voice is developed independently, so that ultimately the two or more voices are complete melodies in themselves. An operatic device that allows several characters to express themselves simultaneously. Common throughout the whole history of opera, although the most famous examples come in the second act of Wagner's *Die Meistersinger* and the finale of Verdi's *Falstaff*.

Gesamtkunstwerk
Literally "total work of art". Wagner's term for his dramatic ideal in which music, drama, painting and poetry would unite to create a new art form.

Grand Opéra
An enormously popular form of opera, prominent in Paris during the mid-nineteenth century, in which the production values were as important, if not more so, than the music. Pioneered by the librettist Scribe, the composer Meyerbeer and the designer Daguerre, the formula was simple: the principal requirements were five acts, a strong sense of local colour, a huge troupe of performers, a central love interest, weighty choruses, lengthy ballets, opulent duets, extended confrontations (frequently between opposing families) and a cataclysmic, preferable disastrous, conclusion – such as the sinking of a ship, or the eruption of a volcano. Shorn of its acute accent, the term is now applied to almost any large-scale opera (eg Verdi's *Don Carlos*).

Habañera
A slow Cuban dance in duple time. Used by Bizet in *Carmen*.

Harmony
The simultaneous grouping of notes to form a musically significant whole; the basic unit of harmony is the chord. Harmony can colour any single melodic line in innumerable different ways and a composer's harmonic language is one of his or her most immediately identifiable characteristics.

Head voice
A vocal technique whereby the sung tone is raised from the chest (where it is normally produced) into the head, where the skull causes the tone to ring out. Especially used by tenors for very high notes or by those who wish to conserve their energy.

Heldentenor
German for "heroic tenor". A term used to describe the loudest and strongest tenor voice, especially necessary for performances of Wagner and Strauss.

Impressionism
Term taken from painting, to describe music in which evocation of tone and atmosphere are the dominant considerations; typified by Debussy and his followers.

Instrumentation
The scoring of music for individual instruments within a complete score. Not the same as orchestration, which refers to a composer's skill in writing for groups of instruments.

Intermedi
Musical interludes performed between the acts of a play in late sixteenth- and early seventeenth-century Italy, involving dance, song and often spectacular scenic effects. The very first operas evolved from *intermedi*, which were also the forerunners of the intermezzo (see below).

Intermezzo
1. Originally a short comic diversion played between the acts of a play, but later developed as a separate operatic entertainment in which there were two or, at most, three characters, who played out a simple, invariably domestic scenario – eg Pergolesi's *La serva padrona*.
2. A brief instrumental or orchestral diversion performed during an opera's scene changes, to denote the passing of time. The intermezzo in Mascagni's *Cavalleria rusticana* is perhaps the best known.

Interval
The distance between two notes. Intervals are expressed numerically – thirds, fourths etc (though "octave" is used rather than "eighth"). Composers' preferred intervals are highly recognizable aspects of style.

Key
The basis of tonal music. The keynote is the foundation of the key, which classifies the notes lying at specified intervals from that keynote – thus the key of C major specifies the notes of the major scale, whereas C minor specifies the notes of the minor scale, which has different intervals from the major. As there are twelve notes in the chromatic scale, it follows that there are twenty-four keys. Each key has a certain number of flats and sharps, signified by the key signature. Notes other than those belonging to a work's key are referred to as "accidentals". Accidentals are the basis of chromaticism.

Largo
Slow and broad tempo.

Legato
Instruction to sing or play smoothly.

Leitmotif
Literally "leading motif". First used with reference to Weber, to describe a short, constantly recurring musical phrase that relates to a character, emotion or object. Associated above all with Wagner, who turned the leitmotif into a means of blending numerous associations and making structural connections across vast spans of time.

Libretto
The text of an opera; literally "little book".

Mezza voce
"Half voice". A direction to sing quietly, without changing the basic colour of the voice. Not the same as falsetto.

Mezzo-soprano
The lowest of the soprano voices. One above contralto.

Minimalism
First used in connection with American composers such as Philip Glass, John Adams and Steve Reich, who rejected the complexities of the European avant-garde in favour of music which was constructed from repeating cycles or additions of small phrases. Now used also for European composers such as John Tavener, whose music has affinities with the religious music of the pre-Renaissance period.

Motif (or motiv or motive)
A brief but recognizable musical idea, usually melodic but sometimes rhythmic.

Note-row
The foundation of serialism; the order in which a composer chooses to arrange the composition's basic twelve notes, none of which can be repeated until the other eleven have been deployed. See "serialism".

Number
A self-contained unit, such as an aria, duet, trio or chorus; a "numbers opera" is an opera constructed from a chain of such units, and most opera up to the mid-nineteenth century conforms to this form.

Obbligato
An instrumental solo played above or beneath as an accompaniment to the sung line. Verdi's obbligati are particularly beautiful.

Octave
The interval that divides two notes of the same written pitch – eg C to C'.

Opera buffa
Italian comic opera of the eighteenth and nineteenth centuries.

Opéra comique
French for "comic opera", but the term describes a French opera that includes text to be spoken, not sung or declaimed through recitative. The Paris Opéra allowed no spoken dialogue, whereas the Paris Opéra-Comique made it a necessity. Opéra comiques were rarely comic, although most contained comic characters for light relief. The most famous example is Bizet's *Carmen*.

Opéra lyrique
A form of opera popular in France during the second half of the nineteenth century. The defining qualities were a sentimental premise, a core love interest, long and sweet melodies and a penchant for light coloratura. Typified by Gounod's *Faust* and Thomas's *Mignon*.

Opera semiseria
An opera seria with the addition of comic or sentimental episodes. The most famous example is Cimarosa's *Il matrimonio segreto*.

Opera seria
Serious or tragic opera of the eighteenth and nineteenth centuries. Established and mastered by Metastasio.

Operetta
A light, romantic, often comic song-based work of music theatre, popular between the 1860s and the 1930s. Mastered by Offenbach, Johann Strauss the Younger and Lehár.

Orchestration
The art of writing for an orchestra, demanding an understanding of the qualities of each instrumental section, and an ability to manage and combine them.

Ornaments (or embellishments)
Notes added to the printed score in performance by a singer. Up to the late eighteenth century, composers indicated where such additions were required; by the start of the nineteenth century this improvisatory element had been virtually quashed.

Ostinato
A melodic figure that is repeated throughout the course of an opera, applied through the use of a ground bass. Used extensively during the seventeenth century for laments, eg Purcell's "When I am laid in earth" (*Dido and Aeneas*).

Overture
An orchestral introduction to an opera.

Polytonality
The use of two or more keys at the same time.

Prelude
An orchestral introduction to a scene or act. There is no absolute distinction between a prelude and an overture, although preludes are generally shorter and, more often than not, run directly into the opera, whereas a pause usually punctuates the end of an overture.

Recitative
Semi-sung dialogue and narrative in opera. In its rhythmic freedom it is closer to dramatic speech than to song. Unlike arioso, there is no written melody, only a guide to the harmonic foundation, which the singer follows at his or her discretion.

Répétiteur
Musician in an opera company who rehearses and coaches the cast at the piano prior to full orchestral rehearsals with the conductor.

Rescue opera
The name given to an opera in which the scenario revolves around the rescue of a heroine and/or hero from impending peril, whether prison or death. Especially popular around the time of the French Revolution, which produced many (frequently fictional) tales of rescue and derring-do. The most famous examples are by Cherubini (*Lodoïska*) and Beethoven (*Fidelio*).

Rubato
A subtle flexibility of pace that subtly alters the shape of a phrase but does not affect its pulse, tempo or structure. A necessity in bel canto, especially Bellini. Summarized by Liszt as being like the collective motion of the leaves of a tree.

Serialism
Also known as "twelve-tone" or "dodecaphonic" music, serialism was developed by Schoenberg as a replacement for traditional harmonic and tonal languages. A serial composition is based upon a twelve-note theme (the "tone-row" or "note-row"), which can then be used in different ways: forwards, backwards, upside down and backwards, or superimposed to create chords. Its most extreme form, in which predetermined rules govern every aspect of the piece, including volume and speed, is known as total serialism.

Singspiel
German genre – in essence a comic opera with spoken dialogue instead of recitative. Famous examples are *The Magic Flute* and *Der Freischütz*.

Soprano
The highest female voice.

There are a number of specific soprano categories:

> **Coloratura soprano**, the most agile and acrobatic of all voices, eg Mozart's Queen of the Night (*Die Zauberflöte*).

Dramatischer sopran, the most powerful of the German female voices, eg Wagner's Isolde (*Tristan und Isolde*) and Strauss's Elektra.

Soprano léger, a light, frequently comic soprano, eg Mozart's Despina (*Così fan tutte*).

Soprano lyrico spinto, an Italian medium-weight soprano capable of great dramatic power as well as delicate sweetness, eg Puccini's Madama Butterfly.

Soprano lyrique, a smooth, unusually agile French romantic voice, eg Delibes's Lakmé.

Soubrette
In eighteenth-century opera, a serving-girl caricature who uses her cunning and wit to sort out problems, eg Mozart's Despina (*Così fan tutte*). Later used to describe the light and fluttery voice type, such as Marzelline (*Fidelio*) and Adèle (*Fledermaus*).

Spinto
Italian for "pushed". The term is used to describe a lyrical voice (*lyrico spinto*) able to tackle heroic music. Can be applied to a soprano, but the term is generally applied to tenors.

Sprechgesang
Literally "speechsong", a singing style midway between song and speech. Invented by Schoenberg (although it was anticipated by Wagner), the technique requires the singer to approximate the pitch of the note and deliver it with the right amount of colour. The best known and finest example of its use in opera is Berg's *Wozzeck*.

Sprechstimme
The term applied to a voice notated in *Sprechgesang*.

Staccato
The opposite of legato. A direction for a note to be played or sung shorter than it is marked, detaching it from the note that follows. The best known operatic example is Riccardo's "Laughing Scherzo" in Verdi's *Un ballo in maschera*.

Strophic
A term used to describe a song or aria in which the same music is used for each verse, eg "Nessun Dorma".

Syncopation
Emphasis on the off-beat; characteristic of jazz and much used in early twentieth-century operas, especially by Krenek and Weill.

Tempo
The pace of a work.

Tenor
The second highest male voice.

There are a number of specific voice categories:

Heldentenor (see p.652).

Spieltenor, a light German, frequently comic voice, eg Pedrillo (*Die Entführung aus dem Serail*) and David (*Die Meistersinger*).

Ténor, a generic term for the nineteenth-century French tenor voice, eg Bizet's Don José (*Carmen*).

Ténor-bouffe, a light comic voice, eg Offenbach's Paris (*La belle Hélène*).

Tenore di forza, a heroic voice, demanding uncommon power and stamina, eg Verdi's Otello.

Tenore di grazia, a lyric romantic voice, calling for agility and pure legato, eg Donizetti's Nemorino (*L'elisir d'amore*).

Tenore spinto, a lyric Italian voice required to push to short bursts of dramatic intensity, eg Puccini's Rodolfo (*La Bohème*).

Tenor Trial, the lightest of character voices, eg Ravel's Torquemada (*L'heure espagnol*). So named after the eighteenth-century tenor Antoine Trial.

Tessitura
The natural range of a voice, or the range within which lie most of the notes of a role.

Through-composed
A term used to describe an opera in which each episode flows evenly and naturally into the next.

Timbre
The quality of a sound – literally its "stamp". Also known as "tone colour", it's the timbre that distinguishes voices and instruments from one another – it's what makes the difference between a middle C played by a flute and a middle C played by an oboe.

Time signature
The numbers at the beginning of a composition, movement or section (or, indeed, midway through a phrase in some twentieth-century scores) that indicate the number and kind of beats in a bar – 4/4, 3/4, 9/16 etc.

Tonality
Adherence to a single key.

Tragédie lyrique
The common term for French serious opera of the seventeenth and eighteenth centuries; principal exponents were Lully and Rameau.

Travesti
Italian for "disguised". Refers to a singer (generally a soprano) who performs as someone of the opposite

sex (generally a boy), eg Cherubino (*Le nozze di Figaro*) and Octavian (*Der Rosenkavalier*).

Twelve-tone
See "serialism".

Verismo
"Realism" in Italian. A short-lived, but enormously popular form of opera that dominated Italian music during the last decade of the nineteenth century. Exemplified by Leoncavallo's *Pagliacci* and Mascagni's *Cavalleria rusticana*, verismo operas were generally one-act works of intense action and high-voltage emotion, conveyed through music that relied heavily upon shock tactics.

Vibrato
Rapid but small vibrations in pitch – most often used in reference to string players, singers and wind players. Up to the twentieth century it was used sparingly, as an expressive colouring, but it has now become a fundamental part of vocal technique, sometimes leading to ugly and painful noises. Can take some getting used to, although the very best singers rarely abuse it.

Vorspiel
German for Prelude.

Waltz
A dance in triple time. Especially popular throughout the nineteenth century in Austria – most famously through the music of the Strauss family.

Zeitoper
"Topical Opera", a populist genre associated with 1920s Germany, especially the work of Krenek and Weill.

INDEX

Opera titles are listed in *italic*; composers who have their own sections in this guide are in **bold**. For opera titles, the definite or indefinite article has been omitted wherever it is the first word of the title – thus *La Traviata* is to be found under T for *Traviata*. Compound surnames such as di Stefano and del Monaco have been alphabetized by the upper-case name – thus Victor de Sabata is to be found under S, Anne Sofie von Otter under O, and so forth.

A

B

C

D

G

H

I

J

K

L

M

N

O

P

Q

R

S

T

X

Y

Z

IF KNOWLEDGE IS POWER, THIS ROUGH GUIDE IS A POCKET-SIZED BATTERING RAM

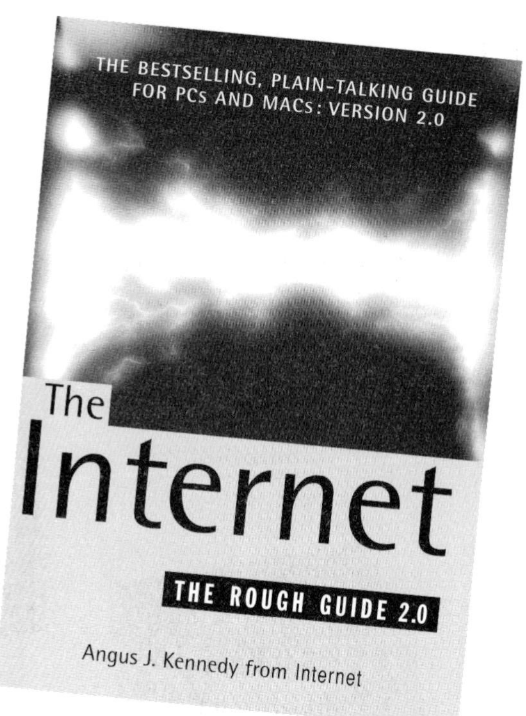

Written in plain English, with no hint of jargon, the Rough Guide to the Internet will make you an Internet guru in the shortest possible time. It cuts through the hype and makes all others look like nerdy textbooks

ROUGH GUIDES ON THE WEB

Visit our website www.roughguides.com for news about the latest books, online travel guides and updates, and the full text of our Rough Guide to Rock.

AT ALL BOOKSTORES • DISTRIBUTED BY PENGUIN